Business

SIXTH CANADIAN EDITION

RICKY W. GRIFFIN Texas A&M University

RONALD J. EBERT University of Missouri–Columbia

FREDERICK A. STARKE University of Manitoba

With Chapter 4 and the Entrepreneurship and New Ventures boxes written by

MONICA DIOCHON St. Francis Xavier University

Toronto

Library and Archives Canada Cataloguing in Publication

Griffin, Ricky W.
Business / Ricky W. Griffin, Ronald J. Ebert, Frederick A. Starke. — 6th Canadian ed.

Includes bibliographical references and index.
ISBN-13: 978-0-13-173429-6
ISBN-10: 0-13-173429-6

1. Industrial management. 2. Business enterprises. 3. Industrial management—Canada. 4. Business enterprises—Canada. I. Ebert, Ronald J. II. Starke, Frederick A., 1942– III. Title.

HD31.G75 2007 658 C2007-900989-1

ISBN-13: 978-0-13-173429-6
ISBN-10: 0-13-173429-6

Editor-in-Chief: Gary Bennett
Acquisitions Editor: Karen Elliott
Marketing Manager: Eileen Lasswell
Developmental Editor: Michelle Harrington
Production Editor: Cheryl Jackson
Copy Editor: Catharine Haggert
Proofreader: Claudia Forgas
Production Coordinator: Andrea Falkenberg
Composition: Jansom
Photo and Permissions Research: Natalie Barrington
Art Director: Julia Hall
Cover and Interior Design: Anthony Leung
Cover Image: Masterfile Corporation

1 2 3 4 5 11 10 09 08 07

Printed and bound in the United States.

To Ann, Eric, and Grant

OVERVIEW

CONTENTS

APPENDICES

PREFACE

Welcome to the sixth Canadian edition of *Business*! In this edition, we continue to emphasize our principle of *"Doing the Basics Best."* Cutting-edge firsts, up-to-date issues that shape today's business world, and creative pedagogy help students build a solid foundation of business knowledge. This new, sixth edition continues with the strengths that made the first five editions so successful—comprehensiveness, accuracy, currency, and readability.

Changes in the Sixth Canadian Edition

Business incorporates the rapid changes taking place as well as many of the changes suggested by instructors and students involved in Introductory Business. The key changes are:

- The chapter on business ethics and social responsibility (Chapter 3, Conducting Business Ethically and Responsibly) now occupies an earlier spot in the text so that students will have an increased consciousness of the importance of this area as they read subsequent chapters in the text.
- Chapter 4 (Understanding Entrepreneurship, Small Business, and New Venture Creation) has been significantly revised to include a larger focus on how new businesses are started.
- More than 95% of the opening cases, boxed inserts, and end-of-chapter cases are either new or updated.
- Many new examples of business practice have been included in each of the chapters. For example, new material on income trusts and hedge funds has been added to Chapter 19. Some of these examples are brief and some are more detailed, but they all increase students' understanding of important business issues.
- Each chapter contains two new boxed inserts. The first of these, "Entrepreneurship and New Ventures," provides real-life examples of Canadian entrepreneurs who saw an opportunity to provide a new product or service in the marketplace and the activities they carried out in order to be successful. The second series, entitled "Business Accountability," focuses student attention on business behaviour that is of significant public concern. Each insert describes an accountability issue that is currently confronting a real Canadian or international company and the steps that are being taken to make business managers more accountable for their actions.
- New CBC *Venture* video cases are included at the end of each major section of the text.
- A new feature called "Planning for Your Career" has been introduced at the end of each major section of the text. This feature contains career-planning activities that help students tie the content of each major section of the text to their career-planning efforts. For example, the focus of this feature at the end of the marketing section of the text is on how students can present themselves as business professionals to prospective employers.
- Another new feature, "Managing Your Personal Finances," is contained in Appendix B at the end of the text. This feature has been overwhelmingly requested by students and instructors and presents a down-to-earth, hands-on approach that will help students manage their personal

finances. The practical information found in this feature includes a worksheet for determining net worth, insightful examples demonstrating the time value of money, a method for determining how much to invest now in order to build a future nest egg of a certain size, suggestions on how to manage credit card debt, guidelines for purchasing a house, and a personalized worksheet for setting financial goals. The information contained in this feature will be immensely useful to students.

- The business law material is found in Appendix A and the material on insurance from the fifth edition has been moved to the CD-ROM that comes with the text.
- Yet another new feature is the inclusion of five supplementary cases in Appendix C at the end of the text. These cases are more detailed than those found at the end of each chapter, and allow students to consider more extensive information as they do their analysis and make recommendations about how to resolve the issue presented in the case.
- The "Crafting Your Business Plan" exercises (which were found at the end of each chapter in the fifth edition) are now included on a CD-ROM that comes with the text. This exercise gives students the opportunity to apply text material to the task of developing a business plan, using the Business Plan Pro software. The new version of this software allows users to create plans with greater ease and speed.

Major Themes

Five major themes are evident throughout this new edition. It is important that students understand these themes since their careers in business will be significantly affected by them.

- **The theme of change.** The dramatic changes that have been occurring during the past decade continue apace. The development of new business processes, new products, and new services all make the study of change in business exciting and necessary. In nearly every aspect of business today there are totally new ways of doing things. These new ways are replacing traditional business practices, usually with surprising speed and often with better competitive results. Given these developments, we as authors felt that our goal had to be to communicate the theme of change by describing how real-world business firms cope with organizational change and conflict. Thus, we have tried to capture the flavour and convey the excitement of the "new economy" in all of its rapidly evolving practices.
- **The growth of international business.** The globalization of the economy is one of the dominant challenges of the twenty-first century. To keep students aware of this challenge, we've included many examples and cases that describe the experiences of Canadian companies in the global marketplace. We also describe how global companies have impacted the domestic Canadian market. In addition to these examples throughout the text, we devote an entire chapter to international business (Chapter 5, Understanding International Business).
- **The role of ethics and social responsibility.** Business ethics and social responsibility are generating a sharply increased level of discussion and debate as a result of the highly publicized criminal trials of top managers at companies like Enron, WorldCom, and others. We devote an entire chapter to the discussion of ethical and social responsibility issues (Chapter 3, Conducting Business Ethically and Responsibly) because these issues are so important to modern business. Ethical issues are also raised in nearly every chapter of the text.

- **The significance of small business.** Since many students will not work for major corporations, we have provided coverage of both large and small companies throughout the text. In various chapters, the implications of various ideas for small business are discussed. As well, a major section in Chapter 4 (Understanding Entrepreneurship, Small Business, and New Venture Creation) is devoted to small business and new business start-ups.
- **The importance of information and communication technology.** In our information-based society, the people and organizations that learn how to obtain and use information will be the ones that succeed. The explosive growth and change in these systems is recognized as we devote an entire chapter to the management of information (Chapter 13, Managing Information Systems and Communication Technology).
- **The quality imperative.** Quality and productivity became the key to competitive success for many companies in the global marketplace during the 1990s. These topics continue to dominate the thinking of managers in the twenty-first century, and we devote a full chapter to their coverage (Chapter 12, Increasing Productivity and Quality).

Major Features of the Text

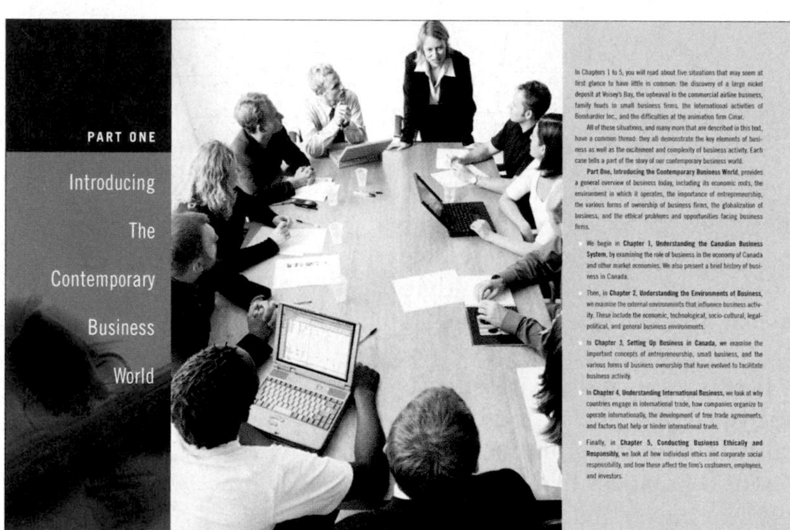
PART ONE

Introducing The Contemporary Business World

In Chapters 1 to 5, you will read about five situations that may seem at first glance to have little in common: the discovery of a large nickel deposit at Voisey's Bay, the upheaval in the commercial airline business, family feuds in small business firms, the international activities of Bombardier Inc., and the difficulties at the animation firm Cinar.

All of these situations, and many more that are described in this text, have a common thread: they all demonstrate the key elements of business as well as the excitement and complexity of business activity. Each case tells a part of the story of our contemporary business world.

Part One, Introducing the Contemporary Business World, provides a general overview of business today, including its economic roots, the environment in which it operates, the importance of entrepreneurship, the various forms of ownership of business firms, the globalization of business, and the ethical problems and opportunities facing business firms.

- We begin in **Chapter 1, Understanding the Canadian Business System**, by examining the role of business in the economy of Canada and other market economies. We also present a brief history of business in Canada.
- Then, in **Chapter 2, Understanding the Environments of Business**, we examine the external environments that influence business activity. These include the economic, technological, socio-cultural, legal-political, and general business environments.
- In **Chapter 3, Setting Up Business in Canada**, we examine the important concepts of entrepreneurship, small business, and the various forms of business ownership that have evolved to facilitate business activity.
- In **Chapter 4, Understanding International Business**, we look at why countries engage in international trade, how companies organize to operate internationally, the development of free trade agreements, and factors that help or hinder international trade.
- Finally, in **Chapter 5, Conducting Business Ethically and Responsibly**, we look at how individual ethics and corporate social responsibility, and how these affect the firm's customers, employees, and investors.

CHAPTER 6

Managing The Business Enterprise

After reading this chapter, you should be able to:

1. Explain the importance of setting *goals* and formulating *strategies* as the starting points of effective management.
2. Describe the four activities that constitute the *management process*.
3. Identify *types of managers* by level and area.
4. Describe the five basic *management skills*.
5. Describe the development and explain the importance of *corporate culture*.

What to Do After Seagram?

In May 2003, Edgar Bronfman, Jr., and his father Edgar Bronfman, Sr., both resigned from the board of Paris-based Vivendi Universal. They had been given positions on the board when Vivendi purchased Seagram, the legendary Canadian liquor company, in 2000. After their resignation, the Bronfmans announced that they wanted to buy back Vivendi's entertainment business, which includes Universal Studios and Polygram. This is just the latest chapter in a long and complicated story of a famous Canadian family.

The Seagram Company was started in the 1920s by Sam Bronfman, who sold liquor by mail order. His son, Edgar Bronfman, Sr., became CEO in 1957, and for the next 40 years the company focused on the production of wine and distilled spirits. In the process, it became a household name in Canada. In the mid-1990s, the company (now led by third-generation family member Edgar Bronfman, Jr.) made some dramatic strategic moves that turned the company away from its traditional products and moved it toward the high-risk entertainment business. For example, Edgar Jr. bought MCA Inc. (now Universal) for $5.7 billion and Polygram NV for $10.6 billion. These moves caused some people to recall Sam Bronfman's concern that third-generation family members often dissipate the family fortune. Edgar Jr. was keenly aware of the criticism that was being directed his way, and he was determined not to fulfill his grandfather's prophecy.

In mid-2000, he sold Seagram to Vivendi SA, a French conglomerate, for approximately $33 billion in stock. The CEO of Vivendi was Jean-Marie Messier, who had a grandiose vision that his company would become a French media and telecom powerhouse that was capable of competing head-to-head with U.S. media giants. Messier concluded that Vivendi (which started as a water utility) needed to acquire a Hollywood studio to provide things like movies and music to fulfill his vision. The only company that had what Messier wanted, and was priced low enough, was Seagram, so Messier bought it.

As part of the deal, Edgar Jr. was appointed a vice-chairman of the merged companies, with responsibilities for music and internet activities. From a financial perspective the deal looked good because Seagram was paid the equivalent of approximately $75 for each of its shares, even though the shares were trading at less than $50 on the stock exchange. The Seagram family fortune actually increased as a result of the deal, and it seemed that Edgar Jr. had avoided his grandfather's concern that the third generation would fritter away the family fortune.

But the deal soon started looking bad for Seagram. Critics had been saying all along that Messier's acquisition strategy was misguided and unworkable, and time proved the critics right. By the end of 2001, Vivendi was in deep financial trouble, and its stock price had declined to $50 per share (from a high of more than $130 per share in early 2000). In 2002, Messier was ousted from Vivendi after board members became convinced that the company was headed for disaster.

By this time, the Seagram fortune had declined markedly because the family had taken Vivendi stock instead of cash when Vivendi originally purchased Seagram. When the merger with Vivendi was first announced, the Seagram family fortune was worth nearly U.S.$7 billion, but by 2003, the value of Seagram's investment in Vivendi was less than U.S.$1 billion. People started thinking that Sam Bronfman was right after all.

The latest rumours about Edgar Bronfman, Jr. include speculation that he wants to get back into the entertainment business to repair his image among his family members and to avoid fulfilling his grandfather's prediction. But he also seems to have a genuine interest in being actively involved in the day-to-day management of an entertainment company. ♦

The text contains the following features to stimulate student interest in, and understanding of, the material that is presented about business.

Part Opener

At the beginning of each of the five parts of the book is a brief outline introducing the material that will be discussed in that part. These outlines give students a glimpse of the "big picture" as they start reading about a new area of the business world.

Chapter Materials

Each chapter contains several features that are designed to increase student interest in, and understanding of, the material being presented. These features are as follows:

Chapter learning objectives. A list of numbered learning objectives is presented at the beginning of each chapter. These objectives—which guide students in determining what is important in each chapter—are also referenced in the margins opposite the relevant content in the chapter.

Chapter opening case. Each chapter begins with a description of a situation that is faced by a real Canadian or international company. The subject matter of the opening case is relevant to the material presented in the chapter, and therefore helps students bridge the gap between theory and practice.

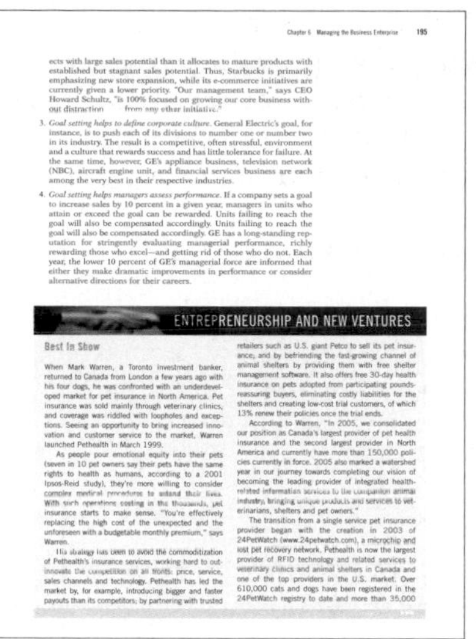
ENTREPRENEURSHIP AND NEW VENTURES

Best In Show

BUSINESS ACCOUNTABILITY

Controversy in the Liquor Business

Boxed inserts. Each chapter contains two boxed inserts: "Business Accountability" and "Entrepreneurship and New Ventures." As noted above, the *Business Accountability* boxes raise student consciousness about business responsibility to its constituents. The *Entrepreneurship and New Ventures* boxes tell interesting stories of how Canadian entrepreneurs identified a need for a new product or service, and how they set up a company to effectively satisfy that need.

End-of-Chapter Materials

Several important pedagogical features are found at the end of each chapter. These are designed to help students better understand the contents of the chapter.

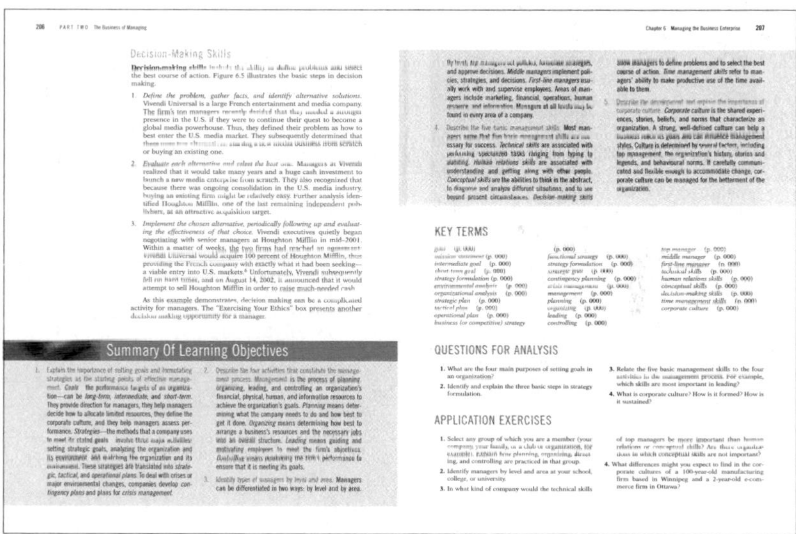
Decision-Making Skills

Summary Of Learning Objectives

KEY TERMS

QUESTIONS FOR ANALYSIS

APPLICATION EXERCISES

Summary of learning objectives. The material in each chapter is concisely summarized, using the learning objectives as the organizing scheme. This helps students understand the main points that were presented in the chapter.

Key terms. In each chapter, the key terms that students should know are highlighted in the text, defined in the margin, and listed alphabetically at the end of the chapter (with page references).

Questions and exercises. There are two types of questions here: *analysis questions* (which require students to think beyond simple factual recall and apply the concepts they have read about), and *application exercises* (which require students to visit local businesses or to interview managers and gather additional information that will help them understand how business firms operate).

Building your business skills. This feature involves in-depth exercises that allow students to examine some specific aspect of business in detail. The exercise may ask students to work individually or in a group to gather data about an interesting business issue, and then develop a written report or a class presentation based on the information that was gathered. Each exercise begins with a list of goals, a description of the situation, a step-by-step methodology for proceeding, and follow-up questions to help students focus their responses to the challenge.

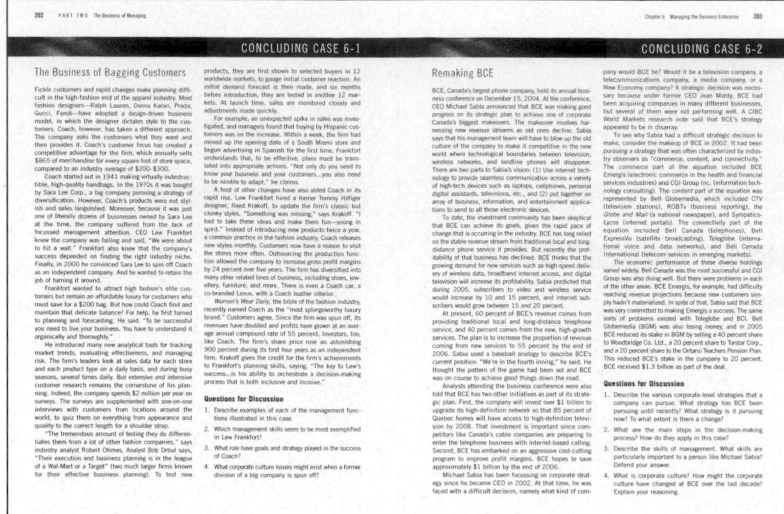

Exercising your ethics. In this feature, students are presented with a description of a situation that leads to an ethical dilemma, and are then asked several questions that focus on how to approach and resolve the ethical challenge.

Concluding cases. Each chapter concludes with two case studies that focus on real Canadian or international companies. These cases are designed to help students apply the chapter material to a real company that is currently in the news. At the end of each case, several questions guide students in their analysis.

End-of-Part Material

CBC video cases. At the end of each of the five major parts of the text, two CBC video cases are presented. The instructor can show the *Venture* episode in class and then either conduct a class discussion using the questions at the end of the written case as a guide, or ask students to complete a written assignment which requires answering the questions at the end of the case. This approach to teaching adds a major new dynamic to classes because students will be able to relate text material to actual Canadian business situations. The cases are also available on the Companion Website for *Business*, Sixth Canadian Edition.

Planning for your career. This new feature helps students relate their career-planning activities to the chapters in each major section of the text. This very practical feature requires students to think about some very specific things they will need to do to be effective in career planning.

Supplementary Materials

PRENTICE HALL mybusinesslab

MyBusinessLab is an online grading, assessment, and study tool for faculty and students. It engages students and helps them focus on what they need to study. It can help students get a better grade because they are learning in an interactive and focused environment.

MyBusinessLab delivers all classroom resources for instructors and students in one place. All resources are organized by Learning Objective so that lectures and studying can be customized more conveniently than ever before. Resources include:

- **Diagnostic tests** for student review. This quizzing can be monitored by professors. Results reveal which learning objectives students are struggling with so professors can customize their review and assessment.
- **Personalized Study Plan** based on each student's results in the diagnostic test offers students remediation (by learning objective) to help them focus on the concepts they find most challenging.

- **Case-Based Adaptive Questions.** Scenario-based questioning (by learning objective) gives students a chance to apply what they have learned and practise their critical thinking skills. There is one case per chapter (approximately one page long). Students answer the case questions and their answer determines the next question they see. Depending on their answers, they could answer anywhere from 10–55 questions per case due to the adaptive nature of the cases.
- **Links** to the Griffin/Ebert/Starke *Business*, Sixth Canadian Edition, **eText**.
- **Business News Cases.** Business concepts come to life for your students. Online Canadian news articles are linked to three mini cases with questions for your students to answer. These will be updated twice a year to ensure relevance and currency. The Business News cases will be linked to specific chapters within *Business*, Sixth Canadian Edition. Solutions will be made available to faculty.
- Ability to mark homework, quizzes, and tests automatically and have them automatically populate in your grade book.
- **Glossary Flashcards.** Quick and fun study of business terms.
- **Additional quizzing** for review. Pretest and Post Test.

For Instructors

Instructor's Resource Centre. Instructor resources are password protected and available for download via **www.pearsoned.ca**. For your convenience, these resources are also available on the Instructor's Resource CD-ROM.

MyTest (ISBN-13: 978-0-13-179198-5). MyTest from Pearson Canada is a powerful assessment generation program that helps instructors easily create and print quizzes, tests, and exams, as well as homework or practice handouts. Questions and tests can all be authored online, allowing instructors ultimate flexibility and the ability to efficiently manage assessments at any time, from anywhere.

Pearson TestGen (ISBN-13: 978-0-13-179202-9). *Pearson TestGen* is a special computerized test item file that enables instructors to view and edit the existing questions, add questions, generate tests, and print the tests in a variety of formats. Powerful search and sort functions make it easy to locate questions and arrange them in any order desired. TestGen also enables instructors to administer tests on a local area network, have the tests graded electronically, and have the results prepared in electronic or printed reports. The Pearson TestGen is compatible with IBM or Macintosh systems.

Instructor's Resource Manual (ISBN-13: 978-0-13-179199-2). The *Instructor's Resource Manual* contains chapter outlines, teaching tips, and suggestions on how to use the text effectively. It includes material for classroom use, such as careers in business and additional cases. The manual also provides answers to the end-of-chapter questions and cases (including Building Your Business Skills, Exercising Your Ethics, and the CBC Video Cases).

PowerPoint® Presentations (ISBN-13: 978-0-13-1791200-5). *PowerPoint Presentations,* which are also available for downloading from the Companion Website, offer an average of about 40 PowerPoint slides per chapter, outlining the key points in the text. The slides include lecture notes that provide page references to the text, summaries, and suggestions for student activities or related questions from the text.

CBC Video Library (VHS: ISBN-13: 978-0-13-244002-8. DVD: ISBN-13: 978-0-13-244001-1). The CBC Video Library for *Business*, Sixth Canadian Edition, includes 10 segments from the CBC program *Venture* that accompany the video cases found at the end of each part in the text. These cases focus on Canadian companies and discuss business issues from a Canadian point of view. The cases are also available on the Companion Website, and answers are discussed in the Instructor's Resource Manual. (Please contact your Pearson Education Canada sales representative for details.)

Videos. Twenty custom videos help students see how real-life businesses and the people who run them apply fundamental business principles on a daily basis. Ask your Pearson Education Canada sales representative for details!

Pearson Custom Publishing (www.prenhall.com/custombusiness). Pearson Custom Publishing can provide you and your students with texts, cases, and articles to enhance your course. Choose material from Darden, Ivey, Harvard Business School Publishing, NACRA, and Thunderbird to create your own custom casebook. Contact your Pearson Education Canada sales representative for details.

Online Learning Solutions. Pearson Education Canada supports instructors interested in using online course management systems. We provide text-related content in WebCT, Blackboard, and Course Compass. To find out more about creating an online course using Pearson content in one of these platforms, contact your Pearson Education Canada sales representative.

New! Instructor's ASSET. Pearson Education Canada is proud to introduce Instructor's ASSET, the Academic Support and Service for Educational Technologies. ASSET is the first integrated Canadian service program committed to meeting the customization, training, and support needs for your course. Ask your Pearson Education Canada sales representative for details!

Your Pearson Education Canada Sales Representative. Your Pearson sales rep is always available to ensure you have everything you need to teach a winning course. Armed with experience, training, and product knowledge, your Pearson rep will support your assessment and adoption of any of the products, services, and technology outlined here to ensure our offerings are tailored to suit your individual needs and the needs of your students. Whether it's getting instructions on TestGen software or specific content files for your new online course, your Pearson sales representative is there to help. (Also available for your students. Ask your Pearson sales rep for details!)

For Students

Student CD-ROM. Designed to complement the content of the text, the Companion CD-ROM features loads of useful information to help and encourage students: the CBC videos and their cases, a glossary organized by chapter, Crafting your Business Plan exercises, and additional material on insurance.

Crafting Your Business Plan. Chapter-ending exercises apply text material to the task of developing a business plan using Business Plan Pro software. The new version of this software allows users to create plans with greater ease and speed. The education version of the best-selling Business Plan Pro software can be packaged with the text for an extra charge in a value pack.

Business PlanPro Software. Business PlanPro (BPP) provides students with a step-by-step approach to creating a comprehensive business plan. The software is designed to stimulate student thinking about the many tasks and decisions that go into planning and running a business. Preformatted report templates, charts, and tables handle the mechanics so that students can focus on the thinking. Planners can also publish to a protected internet site, where readers can access all or part of posted plans. Available for a small extra charge in a value-package. Ask your Pearson sales representative for details!

Companion Website. The Companion Website provides an audio glossary to help students with pronunciation of terms and "flashcards" to help students review key terms and concepts. The PowerPoint® Presentations are available for downloading by both students and instructors. The Instructor's Resource Manual is also available for downloading in a protected area for instructors. Visit the site at **www.pearsoned.ca/griffin**.

Acknowledgments

We owe special thanks to Catharine Haggert, for her excellent copy editing; Claudia Forgas, for her careful proofreading; Cheryl Jackson, Production Editor, for her efficient management of this project; and Natalie Barrington for her fine photo research. Thanks are also due to Steve O'Hearn, Publisher; Gary Bennett, Editor-in-Chief; Karen Elliott, Acquisitions Editor; Michelle Harrington and Pamela Voves, Developmental Editors; Eileen Lasswell, Marketing Manager, Business and Economics; and all the members of the Pearson Education Canada sales team.

We appreciate the insights and suggestions of the following individuals who provided feedback on the fifth edition or reviewed the manuscript for the new edition:

Sofy Carayannopoulos, Wilfrid Laurier University
Alex Faseruk, Memorial University of Newfoundland
Suzanne Iskander, Humber College Institute of Technology & Advanced Learning
Bob Sproule, University of Waterloo
Patricia Stoll, Seneca College of Applied Arts and Technology
William Thurber, Brock University
Heather Johnston, Brandon University
Cindy Stewart, University of British Columbia
Lesley J. Moffitt, Assiniboine Community College
Dwight Heinrichs, University of Regina

Frederick A. Starke
2007

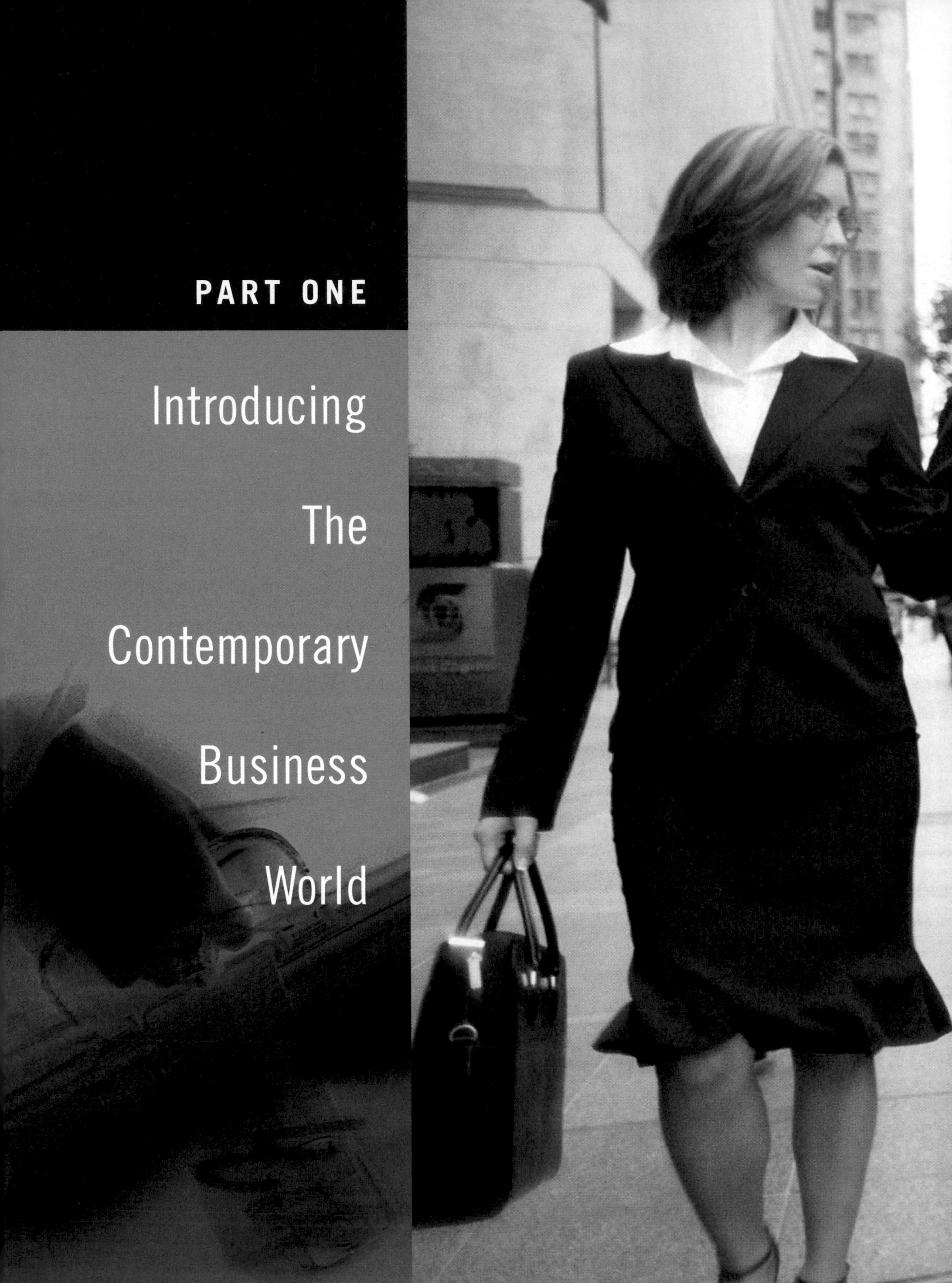

PART ONE

Introducing The Contemporary Business World

In the Opening Cases in Chapters 1 to 5, you will read about five situations that may seem to have little in common at first glance: Canadian megaprojects that focus on the extraction of oil and nickel, the importance of productivity for our standard of living, the unethical behaviour of some business managers, entrepreneurs starting new businesses, and the exporting of Canadian goods and services to other countries. All of these situations, and many more that are described in this text, have a common thread—they all demonstrate the key elements of business as well as the excitement and complexity of business activity. Each case tells a part of the story of our contemporary business world.

Part One, Introducing the Contemporary Business World, provides a general overview of business today, including its economic roots, the environment in which it operates, the importance of entrepreneurship, the various forms of ownership of business firms, the globalization of business, and the ethical problems and opportunities facing business firms.

- We begin in **Chapter 1, Understanding the Canadian Business System**, by examining the role of business in the economy of Canada and other market economies. We also present a brief history of business in Canada.
- Then, in **Chapter 2, Understanding the Environments of Business**, we examine the external environments that influence business activity. These include the economic, technological, socio-cultural, legal-political, and general business environments.
- Next, in **Chapter 3, Conducting Business Ethically and Responsibly**, we look at individual ethics and corporate social responsibility, and how these affect the firm's customers, employees, and investors.
- In **Chapter 4, Understanding Entrepreneurship, Small Business, and New Venture Creation**, we examine the important concepts of entrepreneurship, small business, and the various forms of business ownership that have evolved to facilitate business activity.
- Finally, in **Chapter 5, Understanding International Business**, we look at why countries engage in international trade, how companies organize to operate internationally, the development of free trade agreements, and factors that help or hinder international trade.

CHAPTER 1

Understanding the Canadian Business System

After reading this chapter, you should be able to:

1. Define the nature of Canadian *business* and identify its main goals.
2. Describe different types of global *economic systems* according to the means by which they control the *factors of production* through *input* and *output markets*.
3. Show how *demand* and *supply* affect resource distribution in Canada.
4. Identify the elements of *private enterprise* and explain the various *degrees of competition* in the Canadian economic system.
5. Trace the *history of business* in Canada.

In the world of business, Canada is famous for its rich supply of natural resources such as oil, gas, gold, nickel, and copper. Extracting and selling these resources has long been an important activity for Canadian business firms. Two major projects currently underway in Canada's north—the Alberta Tar Sands and Voisey's Bay—illustrate the rewards and risks associated with such business activity. Both of these cases show that the process can be long and complex, particularly for megaprojects.

THE ALBERTA TAR SANDS

People have known about the sticky bitumen of northern Alberta for many years. Attempts were made to drill conventional oil wells there nearly 100 years ago, but they were unsuccessful. In 1967 the Great Canadian Oil Sands Project began the modern era in tar sands development. But ups and downs in oil prices in the 1970s and 1980s led many businesspeople to believe the tar sands were not economically viable. More recently, with the strong surge in oil prices and talk of future oil shortages, the rate of development of the tar sands has increased dramatically.

It is estimated that there are 2.5 *trillion* barrels of oil trapped in the tar sands around Fort McMurray, Alberta. That far exceeds the reserves of even Saudi Arabia. Over the last 30 years, various companies have spent about $34 billion dollars to develop this area. Over the next 10 years another $87 billion is likely to be spent. By then, production will reach about two million barrels of oil each day. This is comparable to the major oil producers in the Middle East. All of this activity is making the rest of the world sit up and take notice of Canada's potential.

Several companies are important players in the development of the tar sands, including Suncor Energy Inc., Canadian Natural Resources Ltd., Petro-Canada, and Syncrude Canada Ltd. The megaprojects currently underway at these companies have generated a huge demand for both people and raw materials. One project at Suncor alone required 21 million construction hours, 3 million engineering hours, and 150 000 cubic metres of concrete. At its peak, the Syncrude upgrader project employed 6000 workers. By 2010, nearly 30 000 tradespeople will be needed in the area, and this number does not include those who will actually be needed to work in the mines. Approximately 80 000 people will find work in this area by 2014, and another 240 000 jobs will appear elsewhere as a result of the mining activity in the tar sands.

The plans being made by Canadian Natural Resources Ltd. are typical. It will spend $25 billion on tar sands development by 2017. This is in addition to the $11 billion the company has already spent. Although the company only started operations in 1989, it has now become the #2 oil and gas producer in Canada. If events unfold as planned, the company will be producing approximately one million barrels of oil a day.

VOISEY'S BAY

After years of delay, the nickel mining project at Voisey's Bay in Labrador is finally going ahead. The story began in 1993, when two diamond prospectors stumbled upon one of the world's richest nickel finds in the rolling hills of northeast Labrador. In 1996, Inco bought controlling interest in the site for $4.3 billion so it could maintain its dominance in world nickel markets. But in 1997, Inco announced that it would have to delay development of the site because of a time-consuming and expensive environmental review process. To complicate matters, the government of Newfoundland was demanding that Inco build a smelter in the province, and the Innu Nation was asking for a 3 percent smelter royalty.

Over the next eight years, many further delays took place as Inco tried to negotiate a deal that was acceptable to the government of Newfoundland. After many false starts, an agreement was finally reached in 2002. The agreement included the provision that the mine would become operational in 2006 and that a smelter would be built in Argentia in 2011. In 2004 alone, Inco poured nearly $250 million dollars into the project.

The project is not without risk to Inco because it plans to use an unproven technology at Argentia that relies on chemicals instead of heat to produce nickel from concentrate. To explore this new process, Inco has built a test facility in a 1:10 000 scale model. By 2008, Inco must tell the province whether it will use the new technology or the conventional one. Whatever decision is made on the processing technology, once the mine is operational, each year it will produce 110 million pounds of nickel concentrate, 70 million pounds of copper concentrate, and will add about $300 million to Inco's cash flow. In 2005, the project at Voisey's Bay provided employment for about 1000 people, but that will drop to about 400 once regular operations begin. The Argentia smelter will also employ about 400 people. About one-third of the workers at Voisey's Bay are Aboriginal.

Industry observers agree that Inco paid too much for Voisey's Bay and that it took far too long to develop the site. But with nickel prices at 16-year highs and customers demand for the product at high levels as well, Inco is poised to reap considerable rewards from the project. ◆

THE CONCEPT OF BUSINESS AND PROFIT

business An organization that seeks to earn profits by providing goods and services.

profit What remains (if anything) after a business's expenses are subtracted from its sales revenues.

The stories of Inco's involvement with the nickel discovery at Voisey's Bay and the development of the Alberta tar sands are classic Canadian business stories. But what do you think of when you hear the word *business*? Does it conjure up images of large and successful corporations like Inco and Wal-Mart? Or do you think of less successful companies like Jetsgo or Enron? Perhaps you think of smaller companies like your local supermarket or favourite restaurant. Actually, each of these firms is a **business**—an organization that produces or sells goods or services in an effort to make a profit. **Profit** is what remains after a business's expenses have been subtracted from its revenues. Profits reward the owners of businesses for taking the risks involved in investing their time and money. These amounts can be very

"Your Honor, my client pleads guilty to an overzealous but well-intentioned pursuit of the profit motive."

large if the business is managed well. Among the most profitable companies in 2005 were the Royal Bank of Canada ($3.3 billion), Manulife Financial ($3.2 billion), and Imperial Oil Ltd. ($2.6 billion).[1]

In Canada's economic system, businesses exist to earn profits for owners who are free to set them up. But consumers also have freedom of choice. In choosing how to pursue profits, businesses must take into account what consumers want or need. No matter how efficient a business is, it won't survive if there is no demand for its goods or services. Neither a snow-blower shop in Victoria nor a beach-umbrella store in Rankin Inlet is likely to do very well.

1 Define the nature of Canadian *business* and identify its main goals.

But if enterprising business people can identify either unmet consumer needs or better ways of satisfying consumer needs, they can be successful. In other words, someone who can spot a promising opportunity and then develop a good plan for capitalizing on it can succeed. The opportunity always involves goods or services that consumers want or need—especially if no one else is supplying them or if existing businesses are doing so inefficiently or incompletely.

Businesses produce most of the goods and services we consume and employ the majority of working people. They create most new innovations and provide opportunities for other businesses, which serve as their suppliers. A healthy business climate also contributes directly to our quality of life and standard of living. New forms of technology, service businesses, and international opportunities promise to keep production, consumption, and employment growing indefinitely. Business profits enhance the personal incomes of millions of owners and stockholders, and business taxes help to support governments at all levels. Many businesses support charities and provide community leadership.

In this chapter, we begin your introduction to Canadian business by looking at its role in our economy and society. Because a variety of economic systems are found around the world, we will first consider how the dominant ones operate. Once you have some understanding of different systems, you can better appreciate the workings of our own system. As you will see, the effect of economic forces on Canadian businesses and the effect of Canadian businesses on our economy produce dynamic and sometimes volatile results. We conclude the chapter by briefly tracing the history of Canadian business.

ECONOMIC SYSTEMS AROUND THE WORLD

2 Describe different types of global *economic systems* according to the means by which they control the *factors of production* through *input* and *output markets*.

A Canadian business is different in many ways from one in China. And both are different from businesses in Japan, France, or Peru. A major determinant of how organizations operate is the kind of economic system that characterizes the country in which they do business. An **economic system** allocates a nation's resources among its citizens. Economic systems differ in terms of who owns and controls these resources, known as the "factors of production" (see Figure 1.1).

economic system The way in which a nation allocates its resources among its citizens.

Factors of Production

The key difference between economic systems is the way in which they manage the **factors of production**—the basic resources that a country's businesses use to produce goods and services. Traditionally, economists have focused on four factors of production: *labour, capital, entrepreneurs*, and *natural resources*. *Information resources* are now often included as well.[2]

factors of production The resources used to produce goods and services: labour, capital, entrepreneurs, and natural resources.

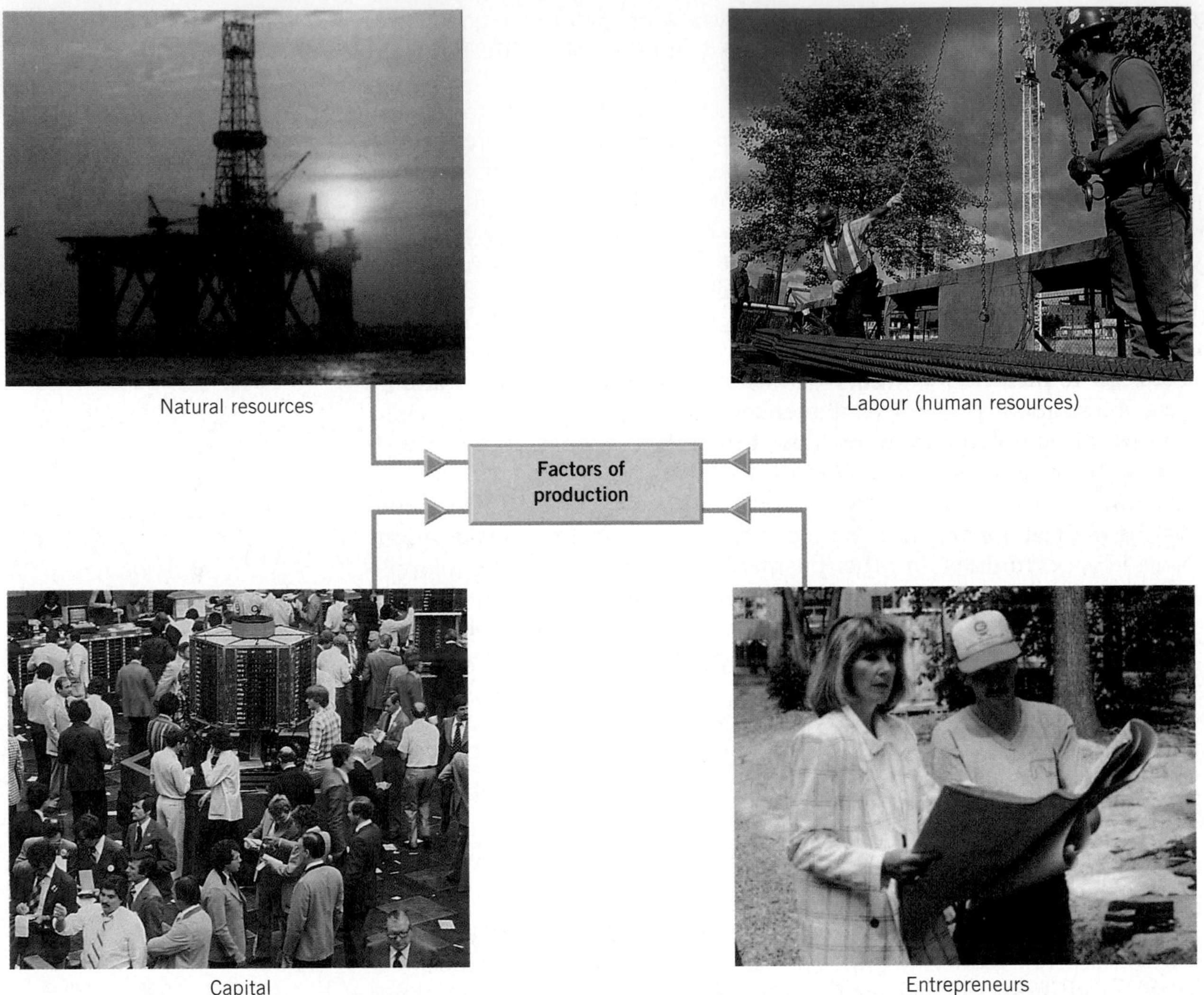

Figure 1.1 Factors of production are the basic resources a business uses to create goods and services. The four basic factors are natural resources, labour, capital, and entrepreneurs.

Labour

labour The mental and physical training and talents of people; sometimes called human resources.

The people who work for a company represent the first factor of production, **labour**. Sometimes called *human resources*, labour is the mental and physical capabilities of people. Carrying out the business of such a huge company as Imperial Oil, for example, requires a labour force with a wide variety of skills ranging from managers to geologists to truck drivers. Employees who are well trained and knowledgeable can be a real competitive advantage for a company.

Capital

capital The funds needed to operate an enterprise.

Obtaining and using labour and other resources requires **capital**—the financial resources needed to operate an enterprise. You need capital to start a new business and then to keep it running and growing. Inco needs millions of dollars in cash (and millions more in equipment and other assets) to run its operations. A major source of capital for small businesses is personal investment by owners. Investments can come from individual entrepreneurs, from partners who start businesses together, or from investors who buy stock. Revenue from the sale of products is a key and ongoing source of capital once a business has opened its doors.[3]

Entrepreneurs

The people who accept the opportunities and risks involved in creating and operating businesses are entrepreneurs. Jimmy Pattison and Izzy Asper (who died in 2003) are well-known Canadian **entrepreneurs**. AOL was started by James Kimsey, who had the technical skills to understand how the internet works, the conceptual skills to see its huge future potential, and the risk-taking acumen to bet his own career and capital on the idea of AOL.

entrepreneur An individual who organizes and manages labour, capital, and natural resources to produce goods and services to earn a profit, but who also runs the risk of failure.

Natural Resources

Land, water, mineral deposits, and trees are examples of **natural resources**. Newer perspectives, however, tend to broaden the idea of "natural resources" to include all physical resources. For example, Imperial Oil makes use of a wide variety of natural resources. It obviously has vast quantities of crude oil to process each year. But Imperial Oil also needs the land where the oil is located, as well as land for its refineries and pipelines.

natural resources Items used in the production of goods and services in their natural state, including land, water, mineral deposits, and trees.

Information Resources

While the production of tangible goods once dominated most economic systems, today **information resources** play a major role. Businesses themselves rely heavily on market forecasts, the specialized expertise and knowledge of people, and various forms of economic data for much of their work. Much of what they do results in either the creation of new information or the repackaging of existing information for new users and different audiences. America Online, for example, does not produce tangible products. Instead, it provides numerous online services for its millions of subscribers in exchange for monthly access fees. AOL is in the information business.

information resources Information such as market forecasts, economic data, and specialized knowledge of employees that is useful to a business and that helps it achieve its goals.

Types of Economic Systems

Different types of economic systems manage the factors of production in different ways. In some systems, ownership is private; in others, the government owns the factors of production. Economic systems also differ in the way that decisions are made about production and allocation. A **command economy**, for example, relies on a centralized government to control all or most factors of production and to make all or most production and allocation decisions. In **market economies**, individuals—producers and consumers—control production and allocation decisions through supply and demand. We will describe each of these economic types and then discuss the reality of the *mixed market economy*.

command economy An economic system in which government controls all or most factors of production and makes all or most production decisions.

market economy An economic system in which individuals control all or most factors of production and make all or most production decisions.

Command Economies

The two most basic forms of command economies are communism and socialism. As originally proposed by the nineteenth-century German economist Karl Marx, **communism** is a system in which the government owns and operates all sources of production. Marx envisioned a society in which individuals would ultimately contribute according to their abilities and receive economic benefits according to their needs. He also expected government ownership of production factors to be only temporary. Once society had matured, government would "wither away" and the workers would gain direct ownership. But as the Business Accountability box demonstrates, things have not worked out the way Marx predicted, and most countries have now abandoned communism in favour of a more market-based economy.

communism A type of command economy in which the government owns and operates all industries.

In a less extensive command economic system called **socialism**, the government owns and operates only selected major industries. Smaller businesses such as clothing stores and restaurants may be privately owned.

socialism A kind of command economy in which the government owns and operates the main industries, while individuals own and operate less crucial industries.

BUSINESS ACCOUNTABILITY

Whatever Happened to Communism?

In 2005, GlobeScan conducted a poll of over 20 000 people in 20 different countries and asked them whether they agreed with the following statement: "The free market economy is the best system." Where do you think the highest support for capitalism was found? Not in the United States or Canada or Germany or Italy or Japan, but in *China*, where 74 percent of people polled agreed with the statement. This is a surprising finding, given the Chinese government's strong support of the communist economic ideology. Other countries with high agreement scores were the United States (71 percent), India (70 percent), and South Korea (66 percent). Countries with surprisingly low scores were Argentina (42 percent), Brazil (57 percent), and Mexico (61 percent). These low scores are likely the result of rushing free market reforms amid much corruption in Latin American countries.

It is surprising how rapidly free market systems have become popular. Until the 1980s, the former Soviet Union, most Eastern European countries, China, North Korea, Vietnam, Albania, and Cuba all embraced communist economic systems. During the early 1990s, however, one country after another renounced communism as both an economic and a political system. Today, Cuba, North Korea, Vietnam, and the People's Republic of China are among the few nations that claim to have a communist system. But while these countries may claim to be communist, the reality is quite different. They have all been swept up in the worldwide movement toward free market systems (some more than others).

Cuba's movement toward free markets has been underway for about a decade. Even though free-market activities are technically illegal, they have been increasing since the mid-1990s. Now, special shops that once were reserved for diplomats sell goods to Cubans from all walks of life. These stores are surrounded by paid bicycle-parking lots, car washes, and stalls selling homegrown produce and homemade handicrafts. This "street-corner commerce" reflects a rapid growth in private enterprise as a solution to problems that Cuba's centralized economy was never able to solve.

Dramatic and highly publicized changes are taking place in China, which has suddenly burst upon the world scene as an awakening economic giant. It seems hard to believe now, but before 1979 people who sold watches on street corners in China were sentenced to years of hard labour. In 1999, China's constitution was amended to elevate private enterprise to a place alongside the state sector in China's official economic ideology. Since that time, the private sector has become incredibly productive, and China is the world's fastest growing economy. For example, it is estimated that China produces 60 percent of all the toys in the world. China's reputation for being a low-cost producer of goods is legendary. It is also a vast and rapidly growing market for many of the products that Canadian firms produce—chemicals, ores, cereals, and wood products. Over the longer term, it will be difficult for the Chinese government to maintain a communist economic and political ideology while the people of China eagerly embrace the free market system.

In terms of movement away from the communist ideology, perhaps the most striking changes are those occurring in North Korea. Until very recently, North Korea was an extreme example of the communist economic system, and the country was so isolated from world commerce that it was known as the "Hermit Kingdom." Now, large numbers of "sidewalk entrepreneurs" sell items like food and drinks in public places in North Korea, where just a few years ago they would have been imprisoned for "profiteering." In the Yanggakdo Hotel, visitors can play slot machines or roulette at the Casino Pyongyang.

As recently as the late 1990s, the official government position was that merchants were a class of people who should be eradicated because they bought products at low prices and sold them to consumers at high prices (and, it was argued, they used deceit and fraud in the process). Now, the communist party newspaper quotes North Korean dictator Kim Jong Il as saying that he favours profits under socialist economic management. These changes in the government's position have attracted the attention of foreign companies who are becoming more interested in investing in North Korea. In 2005, for example, the London-based Anglo-Sino Capital Partners formed the Chosun Development & Investment Fund and planned to raise $50 million for investment in North Korea. North Korea still has a long way to go toward a free market system, but the movement has started. These changes in so many different countries reflect consumer beliefs that market-based economies are more responsive and accountable to consumer needs.

Although workers in socialist countries are usually allowed to choose their occupations or professions, a large proportion generally works for the government. Many government-operated enterprises are inefficient, since management positions are frequently filled based on political considerations rather than on ability. Extensive public welfare systems have also resulted in very high taxes. Because of these factors, socialism is generally declining in popularity.[4]

Market Economies

A **market** is a mechanism for exchange between the buyers and sellers of a particular good or service. To understand how a *market economy* works, consider what happens when a customer goes to a fruit stand to buy apples. Let's say that while one vendor is selling apples for $1 per kilogram, another is charging $1.50. Both vendors are free to charge what they want, and customers are free to buy what they choose. If both vendors' apples are of the same quality, the customer will buy the cheaper ones. But if the $1.50 apples are fresher, the customer may buy them instead. In short, both buyers and sellers enjoy freedom of choice.

market A mechanism for exchange between the buyers and sellers of a particular good or service.

The internet is a technologically sophisticated market that brings buyers and sellers together through ecommerce. When people talk about ecommerce, they usually think of business-to-consumer (B2C) transactions such as buying books over the internet for personal use. But business-to-business (B2B) transactions are also very important.

B2B involves businesses joining together to create ecommerce companies that make them more efficient when they purchase the goods and services they need. B2B transactions actually far exceed B2C transactions in dollar value. Worldwide, B2B transactions exceed $200 billion.

Thirty of the world's large commercial airlines, including Air Canada, have joined forces to purchase fuel, equipment, aircraft parts, and maintenance through an ecommerce site called Aeroxchange Ltd. In total, the airlines purchase about U.S.$50 billion on the site. Air Canada expects to save $11 million–$14 million on the items it buys through the exchange. The exchange also lowers transaction, processing, and inventory costs for the airlines.

Input and Output Markets. Figure 1.2 provides a useful and more complete model for better understanding how the factors of production work in a pure market economy. According to this view, businesses and households interact in two different market relationships.[5] In the **input market**, firms buy resources from households, which are thus resource suppliers. In the **output market**, firms supply goods and services in response to demand on the part of households. (We will provide a more detailed discussion of supply and demand later in this chapter.)

input market Firms buy resources that they need in the production of goods and services.

output market Firms supply goods and services in response to demand on the part of consumers.

As you can see in Figure 1.2, the activities of these two markets create a circular flow. Ford Motor Co., for example, relies on various kinds of inputs. It buys labour directly from households, which may also supply capital from accumulated savings in the form of stock purchases. Consumer buying patterns provide information that helps Ford decide which models to produce and which to discontinue. In turn, Ford uses these inputs in various ways and becomes a supplier to households when it designs and produces various kinds of automobiles, trucks, and sports utility vehicles and offers them for sale to consumers.

Capitalism. Individuals, meanwhile, are free to work for Ford or an alternative employer and to invest in Ford stock or alternative forms of saving or consumption. Similarly, Ford can create whatever vehicles it chooses and

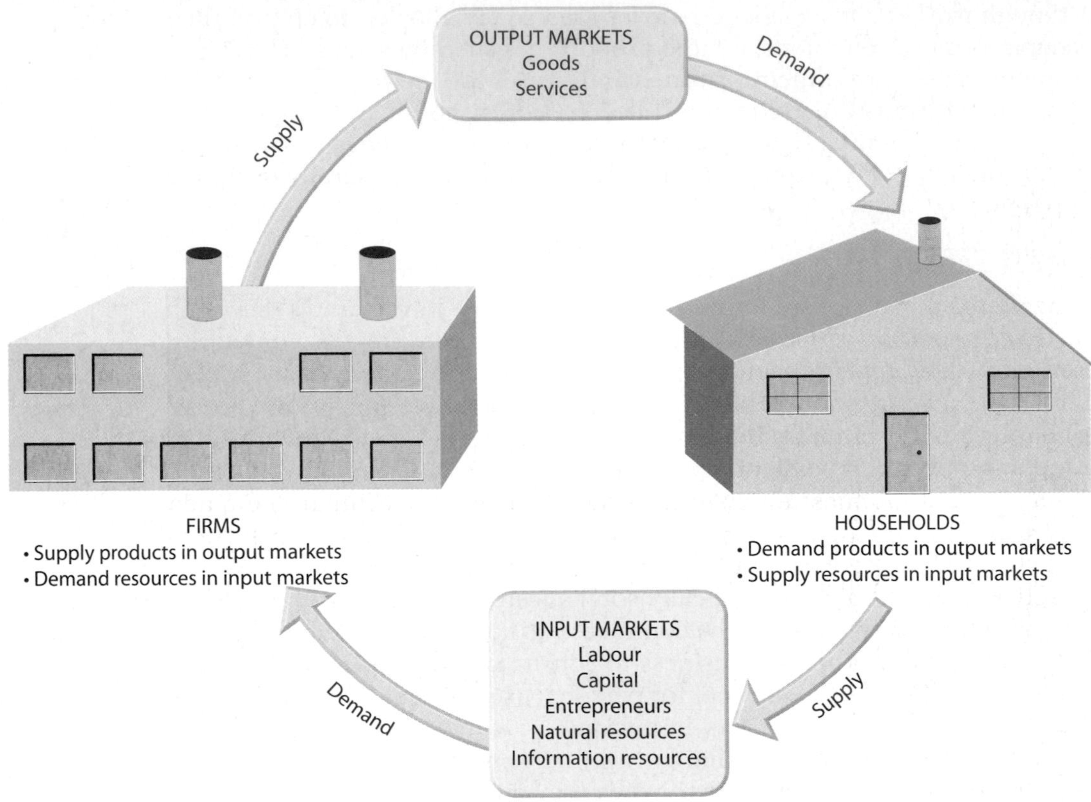

Figure 1.2 Circular flow in a market economy.

price them at whatever value it chooses. But consumers are then free to buy their next car from Ford or Toyota or BMW. This process contrasts markedly with that of a command economy, in which individuals may be told where they can and cannot work, companies are told what they can and cannot manufacture, and consumers may have little or no choice as to what they purchase or how much they pay for items. The political basis of market processes is called **capitalism**, which sanctions the private ownership of the factors of production and encourages entrepreneurship by offering

capitalism An economic system in which markets decide what, when, and for whom to produce.

According to the model of circular flow in a market economy, shoppers at a Wal-Mart de Mexico play the same role in the output market as consumers everywhere. They demand goods supplied by a retail firm. Likewise, you can think of the employees who work for companies from which Wal-Mart buys its products as households that supply the input market with labour, time, and skills.

profits as an incentive. The economic basis of market processes is the operation of demand and supply, which we discuss later in the chapter.

Mixed Market Economies

In their pure forms, command and market economies are often viewed as two extremes or opposites. In reality, however, most countries rely on some form of **mixed market economy**—a system featuring characteristics of both command and market economies. For example, most countries of the former Eastern bloc have now adopted market mechanisms through a process called **privatization**—the process of converting government enterprises into privately owned companies. In recent years this practice has also begun to spread to many other countries as well. For example, the postal system in most countries is government-owned and -managed, regardless of whether the country has a command or market economy. The Netherlands, however, recently began the process of privatizing its TNT Post Group N.V., already among the world's most efficient post office operations. Similarly, Canada has recently privatized its air traffic control system. In each case, the new enterprise reduced its payroll, boosted efficiency and productivity, and quickly became profitable.[6]

mixed market economy An economic system with elements of both a command economy and a market economy; in practice, typical of most nations' economies.

privatization The transfer of activities from the government to the public sector.

Another trend is **deregulation**—the reduction in the number of laws affecting business activity and in the powers of government enforcement agencies. In most cases, deregulation frees companies to do what they want without government intervention, thereby simplifying the task of management. Deregulation is evident in many industries, including airlines, pipelines, banking, trucking, and communication.

deregulation A reduction in the number of laws affecting business activity.

INTERACTIONS BETWEEN BUSINESS AND GOVERNMENT

In Canada's mixed economic system, there are many important interactions between business and government. We first look at how government influences business, and then examine the way that business influences government.

How Government Influences Business

Government plays several different roles in the Canadian economy, and each of these roles influences business activity in some way. The roles government plays follow.

Government as Customer

Government buys thousands of different products and services from business firms, including office supplies, office buildings, computers, battleships, helicopters, highways, water treatment plants, and management and engineering consulting services. The government is also the largest purchaser of advertising in Canada. Many businesses depend on government purchasing, if not for their survival, at least for a certain level of prosperity. Government expenditures on goods and services amount to billions of dollars each year.

Government as Competitor

Government also competes with business through Crown corporations, which are accountable to a minister of parliament for their conduct.

Crown corporations exist at both the provincial and federal level, and account for a significant and wide variety of economic activity in Canada (see Table 1.1).

Government as Regulator

Canadian Radio-television and Telecommunications Commission (CRTC) A federal regulatory agency that issues and renews broadcast licences.

Canadian Transport Commission (CTC) A federal regulatory agency that makes decisions about route and rate applications for commercial air and railway companies.

Canadian Wheat Board A federal regulatory agency that regulates the prices of wheat.

Federal and provincial governments in Canada regulate many aspects of business activity. Government regulates business through many administrative boards, tribunals, or commissions. At the federal level, examples include the **Canadian Radio-television and Telecommunications Commission (CRTC)**, which issues and renews broadcast licences, the **Canadian Transport Commission (CTC)**, which makes decisions about route and rate applications for commercial air and railway companies, and the **Canadian Wheat Board**, which regulates the prices of wheat. Provincial boards and commissions also regulate business through their decisions. Sometimes business people feel that government is unfair in the way it performs its role as regulator. Concluding Case 1-2 gives an example of one such situation.

There are several important reasons for regulating business activity. These include protecting competition, protecting consumers, achieving social goals, and protecting the environment.

Protecting Competition. One of the reasons that government regulates business is to ensure that healthy competition exists among business firms, because competition is crucial to a market economy. Without restrictions, a large company with vast resources could drive smaller firms out of the market. Competition policy tries to eliminate restrictive trade practices and thereby stimulate maximum production, distribution, and employment.

The guidelines for Canada's competition policy are contained in The Competition Act, which prohibits a variety of practices (see Table 1.2). Section 38, for example, prohibits something called *resale price maintenance*. In 2005, Labatt Brewing Co. pleaded guilty to resale price maintenance and was fined $250 000 after its sales representatives gave money to store operators who agreed to not lower prices on some brands of beer. This activity meant that customers had to pay higher prices for beer. A Labatt competitor, Sleeman Breweries, was also fined for resale price maintenance in 2002.[7]

Hazardous Products Act Regulates banned products and products that can be sold but must be labelled hazardous.

Protecting Consumers. The federal government has initiated many programs that protect consumers. Consumer and Corporate Affairs Canada administers many of these. Important legislation includes the **Hazardous Products Act** (which requires poisonous, flammable, explosive, or corrosive products to be

Table 1.1 The Top 10 Crown Corporations in Canada, 2005

Company	Annual Revenues (in billions of $)
1. Hydro-Quebec	$ 10.8
2. Canada Post Corp.	6.6
3. Ontario Lottery and Gaming Corp.	5.8
4. Ontario Power Generation Inc.	5.7
5. Canada Mortgage and Housing Corp.	5.2
6. Caisse de dépôt et placement du Québec	4.7
7. Canadian Wheat Board	3.7
8. Insurance Corp. of British Columbia	3.7
9. British Columbia Hydro and Power Authority	3.7
10. Liquor Control Board of Ontario	3.5

Table 1.2 The Competition Act

Section 32	Prohibits conspiracies and combinations formed for the purpose of unduly lessening competition in the production, transportation, or storage of goods. Persons convicted may be imprisoned for up to five years or fined up to $1 million or both.
Section 33	Prohibits mergers and monopolies that substantially lessen competition. Individuals who assist in the formation of such a monopoly or merger may be imprisoned for up to two years.
Section 34	Prohibits illegal trade practices. A company may not, for example, cut prices in one region of Canada while selling at a higher price everywhere else if this substantially lessens competition. A company may not sell at "unreasonably low prices" if this substantially lessens competition. (This section does not prohibit credit unions from returning surpluses to their members.)
Section 35	Prohibits giving allowances and rebates to buyers to cover their advertising expenses, unless these allowances are made available proportionally to other purchasers who are in competition with the buyer given the rebate.
Section 36	Prohibits misleading advertising including (1) false statements about the performance of a product, (2) misleading guarantees, (3) pyramid selling, (4) charging the higher price when two prices are marked on an item, and (5) referral selling.
Section 37	Prohibits bait-and-switch selling. No person can advertise a product at a bargain price if there is no supply of the product available to the consumer. (This tactic baits prospects into the store, where salespeople switch them to higher-priced goods.) This section also controls the use of contests to sell goods, and prohibits the sale of goods at a price higher than the advertised one.
Section 38	Prohibits resale price maintenance. No person who produces or supplies a product can attempt to influence upward, or discourage reduction of, the price of the good in question. It is also illegal for the producer to refuse to supply a product to a reseller simply because the producer believes the reseller will cut the price.

appropriately labelled), the **Tobacco Act** (which prohibits cigarette advertising on billboards and in stores), the **Weights and Measures Act** (which sets standards of accuracy for weighing and measuring devices), the **Textile Labelling Act** (which regulates the labelling, sale, importation, and advertising of consumer textile articles), and the **Food and Drug Act** (which prohibits the sale of food that contains any poisonous or harmful substances). Consumers are also protected by municipal bylaws such as the "no-smoking" bylaws that are so controversial in some Canadian cities.

Tobacco Act Prohibits cigarette advertising on billboards and in retail stores, and assigns financial penalties to violators.

Weights and Measures Act Sets standards of accuracy for weighing and measuring devices.

Textile Labelling Act Regulates the labelling, sale, importation, and advertising of consumer textile articles.

Food and Drug Act Prohibits the sale of food unfit for human consumption and regulates food advertising.

Achieving Social Goals. Social goals promote the well-being of our society. Social goals include universal access to health care, safe workplaces, employment insurance, and decent pensions. All of these goals require the interaction of business firms and government.

Protecting the Environment. Key government legislation designed to protect the environment includes the **Canada Water Act** (which controls water quality in fresh and marine waters), the **Fisheries Act** (which controls the discharge of any harmful substance into water), and the **Environmental Contaminants Act** (which establishes regulations for airborne substances that are a danger to human health or the environment).

Canada Water Act Controls water quality in fresh and marine waters of Canada.

Fisheries Act Regulates the discharge of harmful substances into water.

Environmental Contaminants Act Establishes regulations for airborne substances that are a danger to human health or to the environment.

Government as Taxation Agent

Taxes are imposed and collected by federal, provincial, and local governments. **Revenue taxes** (e.g., income taxes) are levied by governments primarily to provide revenue to fund various services and programs. **Progressive revenue taxes** are levied at a higher rate on higher-income taxpayers and at a lower rate on lower-income taxpayers. **Regressive revenue taxes** (e.g., sales tax) are levied at the same rate regardless of a person's income. They cause poorer people to pay a higher percentage of their

revenue taxes Taxes whose main purpose is to fund government services and programs.

progressive revenue taxes Taxes levied at a higher rate on higher-income taxpayers and at a lower rate on lower-income taxpayers.

regressive revenue taxes Taxes that cause poorer people to pay a higher percentage of income than richer people pay.

restrictive taxes Taxes levied to control certain activities that legislators believe should be controlled.

income for these taxes than rich people pay. **Restrictive taxes** (e.g., taxes on alcohol, tobacco, and gasoline) are levied partially for the revenue they provide, but also because legislative bodies believe that the products in question should be controlled.

Government as Provider of Incentives

Federal, provincial, and municipal governments offer incentive programs that help stimulate economic development. In Quebec, for example, Hyundai Motors received \$6.4 million to build a production facility and an additional \$682 000 to train workers. Both Toyota and Hyundai have received millions of dollars in incentives from government in the form of training incentives, interest-free loans, and the suspension of customs duties.[8]

Governments also offer incentives through the many services they provide to business firms through government organizations. These include the Export Development Corporation (which assists Canadian exporters by offering export insurance against nonpayment by foreign buyers and long-term loans to foreign buyers of Canadian products), Energy, Mines and Resources Canada (which provides geological maps of Canada's potential mineral-producing areas), and Statistics Canada (which provides data and analysis on almost every aspect of Canadian society).

There are many other government incentive programs, including municipal tax rebates for companies that locate in certain areas, design assistance programs, and remission of tariffs on certain advanced technology production equipment. Government incentive programs may or may not have the desired effect of stimulating the economy. They may also cause difficulties with our trading partners.

Government as Provider of Essential Services

The federal, provincial, and municipal governments facilitate business activity through the wide variety of services they supply. The federal government provides highways, the postal service, the minting of money, the armed forces, and statistical data on which to base business decisions. It also tries to maintain stability through fiscal and monetary policy. Provincial and municipal governments provide streets, sewage and sanitation systems, police and fire departments, utilities, hospitals, and education. All of these activities create the kind of stability that encourages business activity.

How Business Influences Government

lobbyist A person hired by a company or an industry to represent its interests to government officials.

While government activity influences what businesses do, businesses also influence the government through lobbyists, trade associations, and advertising (see Figure 1.3). A **lobbyist** is a person hired by a company or industry to represent its interests to government officials. The Association of Consulting Engineers of Canada, for example, regularly lobbies the federal and provincial governments to make use of the skills possessed by private sector consulting engineers on projects like city water systems. Some business lobbyists have training in the particular industry, public relations experience, or a legal background. A few have served as legislators or government regulators.

The Lobbyists Registration Act came into effect in 1989. Lobbyists must register with the Registrar of Lobbyists so that it is clear which individuals are being paid for their lobbying activity. For many lobbying efforts, there are opposing points of view. The Canadian Cancer Society and the Tobacco Institute present very different points of view on cigarette smoking and cigarette advertising.

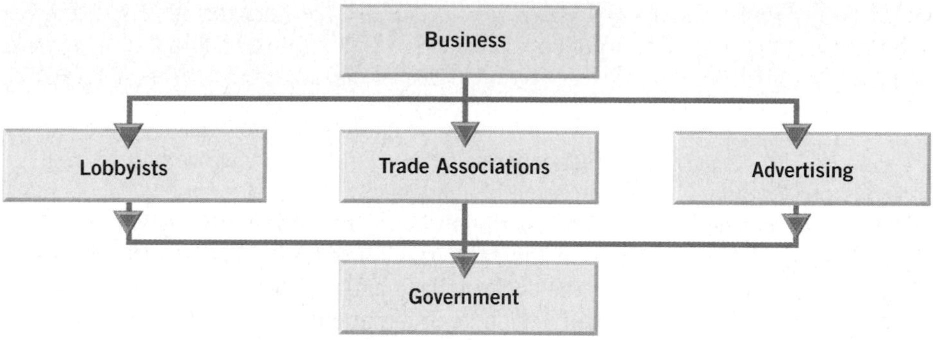

Business

Lobbyists | Trade Associations | Advertising

Government

Figure 1.3 Business influences the government in a variety of ways.

Employees and owners of small businesses that cannot afford lobbyists often join **trade associations**, which may act as an industry lobby to influence legislation. They also conduct training programs relevant to the particular industry, and they arrange trade shows at which members display their products or services to potential customers. Most publish newsletters featuring articles on new products, new companies, changes in ownership, and changes in laws affecting the industry.

trade association An organization dedicated to promoting the interests and assisting the members of a particular industry.

Corporations can influence legislation indirectly by influencing voters. A company can, for example, launch an advertising campaign designed to get people to write their MPs, MPPs, or MLAs demanding passage—or rejection—of a particular bill that is before parliament or the provincial legislature.

THE CANADIAN MARKET ECONOMY

Understanding the complex nature of the Canadian economic system is essential to understanding Canadian businesses. In the next few pages, we will examine the workings of our market economy in more detail. Specifically, we look at demand and supply in a market economy, private enterprise, and degrees of competition.

3 Show how *demand* and *supply* affect resource distribution in Canada.

Demand and Supply in a Market Economy

In economic terms, a market is not a specific place, like a supermarket, but an exchange process between buyers and sellers. A market economy consists of many different markets. We have already described input and output markets, but we need to remember that the inputs used by business and the products created by business have their own markets. In each of these markets, businesses decide what inputs to buy, what to make and in what quantities, and what prices to charge. Likewise, customers decide what to buy and how much they want to pay. Literally billions of such exchanges take place every day between businesses and individuals; between businesses; and among individuals, businesses, and governments. Moreover, exchanges conducted in one area often affect exchanges elsewhere.

The Laws of Demand and Supply

On all economic levels, decisions about what to buy and what to sell are determined primarily by the forces of demand and supply.[9] **Demand** is the willingness and ability of buyers to purchase a product (a good) or a service.

demand The willingness and ability of buyers to purchase a product or service.

ENTREPRENEURSHIP AND NEW VENTURES

Pulse of a Nation

At 33 years of age, Murad Al-Katib has put Canada—and its lentils—on the international map. As president and CEO of Saskcan Pulse Trading of Regina, Al-Katib has, in three years, taken his company from a home-based venture to an award-winning agribusiness that processes and exports pulse—lentils, chick peas, and peas—to more than 60 countries.

Observing the growth in the export of lentils to Turkey, Al-Katib saw the opportunity for value-added processing. "I didn't want to see the lentil story end up like the mustard story," he said, where Saskatchewan supplies the raw material for almost all of the many prepared mustards made in France. "I identified potential partners there [in Turkey], including one of the world's largest buyers of red lentils [Arbel] and convinced them that we should do the processing in Saskatchewan. That's how Saskcan was born." The company has attracted millions of dollars in investment, largely due to Arbel's proprietary technology for splitting and oiling the red lentils and their expertise in setting up and operating the processing plant. Indeed, the facility has added about 40 percent to the market value of the crops.

Several factors have contributed to the boom in lentil crops over the past several years: international demand; a desire to produce a commodity that is less volatile in price than wheat; the drive to avoid a price-fixing, central marketing agency such as the Saskatchewan Wheat Board; and the need to rotate traditional crops with ones that restore nitrogen levels to the soil, which lentil plants do.

Product quality is important at Saskcan. "At first, we were a bit of a mystery to clients who wondered if, in Canada, we could produce a red split lentil that lived up to Turkish and Indian quality standards," Al-Katib recalls. "But the quality of our first shipment of red split lentils was likely among the best in the world. From then on, our business just continued to grow." As Al-Katib explains, "January 2003 was our first load of red split lentils. To go from that to being the second-largest exporter in the world...yeah, we've had to overcome some challenges."

Transportation is one of those challenges, particularly in the face of soaring fuel costs. All the lentils must be containerized and shipped by rail from a landlocked region to international ports. "We are so far from world markets that transit time can take several weeks. Our competitors can deliver faster, so we have to be very competitive with our pricing," explains Al-Katib. The transportation costs alone make up about 20 percent of the market cost of Canadian lentils, as compared to about seven percent for rival Turkish lentils. "We've designed an automated system that makes us very efficient at processing, and that has been a big help," he says.

Another challenge is dealing with customers from 33 different countries, with many distinct cultures and languages. For example, in the Middle East, bright, shiny red lentils are considered the most valuable, while in Europe, a dull finish is more popular. That means some of Saskcan's product is highly polished with oil, while other batches are untouched.

From a relatively minor specialty crop five years ago, Canada's lentil production has grown to more than 900 000 tonnes annually, of which 98 percent is produced in Saskatchewan. "This has become a $1-billion industry in Canada," says Al-Katib, and Saskcan has grown along with it. The company is the largest processor and exporter of red lentils in the western hemisphere, and the second-largest exporter of red lentils in the world. For Saskcan's business model to continue working, however, the venture must constantly race to remain the world's lowest-cost producer of lentils.

Despite unpredictable growing conditions and the strong Canadian dollar, Al-Katib is optimistic that given the continuing shift from green to red lentils, crops which command a premium price on international markets, ongoing investment in the development of new seeds and refined varieties will foster Saskcan's growth.

supply The willingness and ability of producers to offer a good or service for sale.

law of demand The principle that buyers will purchase (demand) more of a product as price drops.

law of supply The principle that producers will offer (supply) more of a product as price rises.

Supply is the willingness and ability of producers to offer a good or service for sale. Generally speaking, demand and supply follow basic "laws":

- The **law of demand**: Buyers will purchase (demand) more of a product as its price drops and less of a product as its price increases.
- The **law of supply**: Producers will offer (supply) more of a product for sale as its price rises and less as its price drops.

The Demand and Supply Schedule

To appreciate these laws in action, consider the market for pizza in your town. If everyone in town is willing to pay $25 for a pizza (a high price), the town's only pizzeria will produce a large supply. If everyone is willing to pay only $5 (a low price), however, the restaurant will make fewer pizzas. Through careful analysis, we can determine how many pizzas will be sold at different prices. These results, called a **demand and supply schedule**, are obtained from marketing research and other systematic studies of the market. Properly applied, they help managers better understand the relationships among different levels of demand and supply at different price levels.

demand and supply schedule Assessment of the relationships between different levels of demand and supply at different price levels.

Demand and Supply Curves

The demand and supply schedule, for example, can be used to construct demand and supply curves for pizza in your town. A **demand curve** shows how many products—in this case, pizzas—will be demanded (bought) at different prices. A **supply curve** shows how many pizzas will be supplied (cooked) at different prices.

demand curve Graph showing how many units of a product will be demanded (bought) at different prices.

supply curve Graph showing how many units of a product will be supplied (offered for sale) at different prices.

Figure 1.4 shows hypothetical demand and supply curves for pizzas. As you can see, demand increases as price decreases; supply increases as price increases. When the demand and supply curves are plotted on the same graph, the point at which they intersect is the **market price** or **equilibrium price**—the price at which the quantity of goods demanded and the quantity of goods supplied are equal. Note in Figure 1.4 that the equilibrium price for pizzas in our example is $10. At this point, the quantity of pizzas demanded and the quantity of pizzas supplied are the same: 1000 pizzas per week.

market price (or equilibrium price) Profit-maximizing price at which the quantity of goods demanded and the quantity of goods supplied are equal.

Surpluses and Shortages

But what if the restaurant chooses to make some other number of pizzas? For example, what would happen if the owner tried to increase profits by making more pizzas to sell? Or what if the owner wanted to reduce overhead, cut back on store hours, and reduce the number of pizzas offered for sale? In either case, the result would be an inefficient use of resources—and perhaps lower profits. For example, if the restaurant supplies 1200 pizzas and tries to sell them for $10 each, 200 pizzas will not be purchased. The demand schedule clearly shows that only 1000 pizzas will be demanded at this price. The pizza maker will have a **surplus**—a situation in which the quantity supplied exceeds the quantity demanded. The restaurant will thus lose the money it spent making those extra 200 pizzas.

surplus Situation in which quantity supplied exceeds quantity demanded.

Conversely, if the pizzeria supplies only 800 pizzas, a **shortage** will result: the quantity demanded will be greater than the quantity supplied. The pizzeria will "lose" the extra money that it could have made by producing 200 more pizzas. Even though consumers may pay more for pizzas because of the shortage, the restaurant will still earn lower profits than it would have if it had made 1000 pizzas. In addition, it will risk angering customers who cannot buy pizzas. To optimize profits, therefore, all businesses must constantly seek the right combination of the price charged and the quantity supplied. This "right combination" is found at the equilibrium point.

shortage Situation in which quantity demanded exceeds quantity supplied.

When there are shortages of commodities, the price of the commodity rises and there may be an increase in criminal behaviour. For example, as the price of stainless steel and aluminum rose during the last few years, thieves began stealing items such as beer kegs, railway baggage carts, railroad tracks, light poles, and guard rails along highways. These items were then sold to scrap yards for cash.[10]

Ginseng—a plant known for its healing properties—demonstrates the ideas about shortages and surpluses. In 1982, less than 25 metric tonnes of ginseng were grown in Canada, and growers received about $187 per kilogram for it. There was essentially a shortage of ginseng. Many new growers therefore got into the market because they saw a chance to make money supplying ginseng. With more growers, production increased rapidly, and by 1999, 2200 metric tonnes were being produced. But by then, growers were getting only about $33 per kilogram. By 2001, there was a surplus of ginseng.[11]

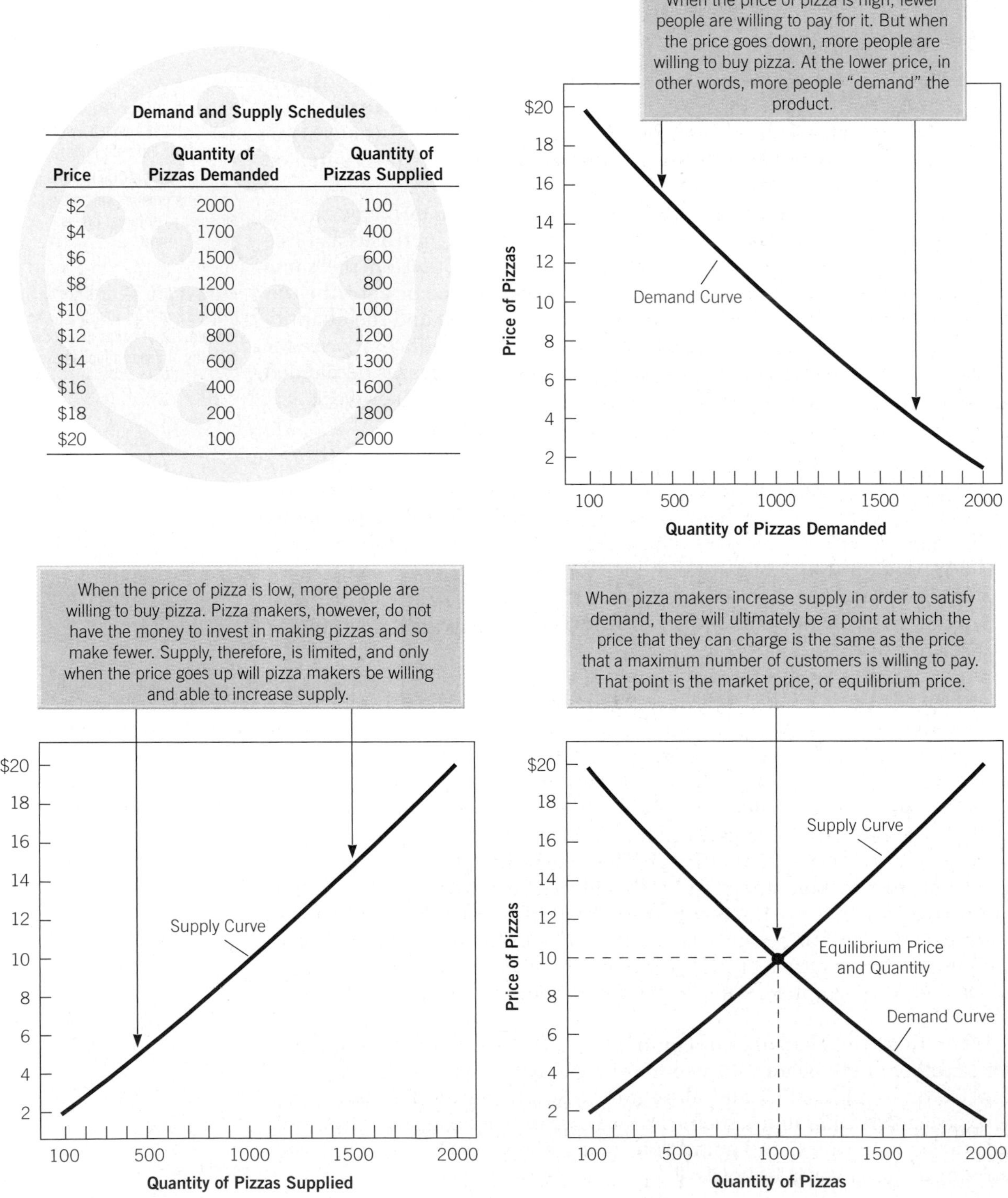

Demand and Supply Schedules

Price	Quantity of Pizzas Demanded	Quantity of Pizzas Supplied
$2	2000	100
$4	1700	400
$6	1500	600
$8	1200	800
$10	1000	1000
$12	800	1200
$14	600	1300
$16	400	1600
$18	200	1800
$20	100	2000

Figure 1.4 Demand and supply.

Applied Materials specializes in the high-tech equipment used to make flat panel TV screens. You can buy a 40-inch TV with a plasma-display screen for $4000. That's down about 45 percent in just two years because flat screen TVs have caught on and demand has grown dramatically. The latest thing is the liquid crystal display (LCD) panel, but because it's still new, a 40-inch LCD TV costs more than twice as much as a flat screen TV.

Private Enterprise and Competition in a Market Economy

Market economies rely on a **private enterprise** system—one that allows individuals to pursue their own interests with minimal government restriction. In turn, private enterprise requires the presence of four elements: private property rights, freedom of choice, profits, and competition.

private enterprise An economic system characterized by private property rights, freedom of choice, profits, and competition.

- *Private property rights*. Ownership of the resources used to create wealth is in the hands of individuals.[12]
- *Freedom of choice*. You can sell your labour to any employer you choose. You can also choose which products to buy, and producers can usually choose whom to hire and what to produce.
- *Profits*. The lure of profits (and freedom) leads some people to abandon the security of working for someone else and to assume the risks of entrepreneurship. Anticipated profits also influence individuals' choices of which goods or services to produce.
- *Competition*. If profits motivate individuals to start businesses, **competition** motivates them to operate those businesses efficiently. Competition occurs when two or more businesses vie for the same resources or customers. To gain an advantage over competitors, a business must produce its goods or services efficiently and be able to sell at a reasonable profit. To achieve these goals, it must convince customers that its products are either better or less expensive than those of its competitors. Competition, therefore, forces all businesses to make products better or cheaper. A company that produces inferior, expensive products is likely to fail. We discuss competition more fully in the next section.

Identify the elements of *private enterprise* and explain the various *degrees of competition* in the Canadian economic system.

competition The vying among businesses in a particular market or industry to best satisfy consumer demands and earn profits.

Degrees of Competition

Even in a free enterprise system, not all industries are equally competitive. Economists have identified four degrees of competition in a private enterprise system: *perfect competition, monopolistic competition, oligopoly,* and *monopoly*. Table 1.3 summarizes the features of these four degrees of competition.

Table 1.3 Degrees of Competition

Characteristic	Perfect Competition	Monopolistic Competition	Oligopoly	Monopoly
Example	Local farmer	Stationery store	Steel industry	Public utility
Number of competitors	Many	Many, but fewer than in perfect competition	Few	None
Ease of entry into industry	Relatively easy	Fairly easy	Difficult	Regulated by government
Similarity of goods or services offered by competing firms	Identical	Similar	Can be similar or different	No directly competing goods or services
Level of control over price by individual firms	None	Some	Some	Considerable

perfect competition A market or industry characterized by a very large number of small firms producing an identical product so that none of the firms has any ability to influence price.

Perfect Competition. For **perfect competition** to exist, two conditions must prevail: (1) all firms in an industry must be small and (2) the number of firms in the industry must be large. Under these conditions, no single firm is powerful enough to influence the price of its product. Prices are therefore determined by such market forces as supply and demand. In addition, these two conditions also reflect four principles:

1. The products of each firm are so similar that buyers view them as identical to those of other firms.
2. Both buyers and sellers know the prices that others are paying and receiving in the marketplace.
3. Because each firm is small, it is easy for firms to enter or leave the market.
4. Going prices are set exclusively by supply and demand and accepted by both sellers and buyers.

Canadian agriculture is a good example of perfect competition. The wheat produced on one farm is the same as that from another. Both producers and buyers are aware of prevailing market prices. It is relatively easy to start producing wheat and relatively easy to stop when it's no longer profitable.

monopolistic competition A market or industry characterized by a large number of firms supplying products that are similar but distinctive enough from one another to give firms some ability to influence price.

Monopolistic Competition. Fewer sellers are involved in **monopolistic competition** than in perfect competition, but because there are still many buyers, sellers try to make products at least *seem* to differ from those of competitors. Differentiating strategies include brand names (Tide and Cheer), design or styling (Polo and Tommy Hilfiger jeans), and advertising (Coke and Pepsi). For example, in an effort to attract health-conscious consumers, the Kraft Foods division of Philip Morris promotes such differentiated products as low-fat Cool Whip, low-calorie Jell-O, and sugar-free Kool-Aid.

Monopolistically competitive businesses may be large or small, but they can still enter or leave the market easily. For example, many small clothing stores compete successfully with large apparel retailers such as Liz Claiborne and Limited Brands. bebe Stores is a good case in point. The small clothing chain controls its own manufacturing facilities and can respond just as quickly as firms like Gap Inc. to changes in fashion tastes.[13] Many single-store clothing businesses in college towns compete by developing their own T-shirt and cap designs with copyrighted slogans and logos.

Product differentiation also gives sellers some control over prices. For instance, even though Sears shirts may have similar styling and other features, Ralph Lauren Polo shirts can be priced with little regard for lower Sears prices. But there are limits. Although Polo might be able to sell shirts for, say, $20 more than a comparable Sears shirt, it could not sell as many shirts if they were priced at $200 more.

Oligopoly. When an industry has only a handful of sellers, an **oligopoly** exists. As a general rule, these sellers are quite large. It is difficult for new competitors to enter the industry because large capital investment is needed. Thus oligopolistic industries like the automobile, airline, and steel industries tend to stay that way.[14] For example, only two companies make large commercial aircraft: Boeing (a U.S. company) and Airbus (a European consortium). Furthermore, as the trend toward globalization continues, most experts believe that, as one forecaster puts it, "global oligopolies are as inevitable as the sunrise."[15]

oligopoly A market or industry characterized by a small number of very large firms that have the power to influence the price of their product and/or resources.

Oligopolists have more control over their strategies than monopolistically competitive firms, but the actions of one firm can significantly affect the sales of every other firm in the industry. For example, when one firm cuts prices or offers incentives to increase sales, the others usually protect sales by doing the same. Likewise, when one firm raises prices, others generally follow suit. Therefore, the prices of comparable products are usually similar. When an airline announces new fare discounts, others adopt the same strategy almost immediately. Just as quickly, when discounts end for one airline, they usually end for everyone else.

Monopoly. When an industry or market has only one producer, a **monopoly** exists. Being the only supplier gives a firm complete control over the price of its product. Its only constraint is how much consumer demand will fall as its price rises. Until 1992, the long-distance telephone business was a monopoly in Canada, and cable TV, which has had a local monopoly for years, will lose it when telephone companies and satellite broadcasters are allowed into the cable business.[16]

monopoly A market or industry with only one producer, who can set the price of its product and/or resources.

In Canada, laws such as the Competition Act forbid many monopolies, and the prices charged by so-called "natural monopolies" are closely watched by provincial utilities boards. **Natural monopolies** are found in industries in which one company can most efficiently supply all the product or service that is needed. For example, the argument is typically made that a single provincial electric company can supply all the power (product) needed in an area. The argument is made that duplicate facilities—such as two nuclear power plants, two sets of power lines, and so forth—would be wasteful. The assumption that certain activities qualify as natural monopolies is increasingly being challenged, however. For example, the Royal Mail Group's 350-year monopoly of the British postal service ended in 2006 and rival companies are now allowed to compete with Royal Mail.[17]

natural monopoly A market or industry in which having only one producer is most efficient because it can meet all of consumers' demand for the product.

A BRIEF HISTORY OF BUSINESS IN CANADA

A look at the history of business in Canada shows a steady development from sole proprietorships to the complex corporate structures of today. In this section, we will trace the broad outlines of the development of business

Consumers often buy products under conditions of monopolistic competition. For example, there are few differences between various brands of toothpaste, cold tablets, detergents, canned goods, and soft drinks.

5 Trace the *history of business* in Canada.

in Canada. Table 1.4 highlights some of the specific events in Canadian business history.[18]

The Early Years

Business activity and profit from commercial fishing were the motivation for the first European involvement in Canada. In the late 1400s, ships financed by English entrepreneurs came to the coast of Newfoundland to fish for profit. By the late 1500s, the Newfoundland coast was being visited by hundreds of fishing vessels each year.

Beginning in the 1500s, French and British adventurers began trading with the native peoples. Items such as cooking utensils and knives were exchanged for beaver and other furs. One trading syndicate made over 1000 percent profit on beaver skins sold to a Paris furrier. Trading was aggressive and, over time, the price of furs rose as more and more Europeans bid for them. Originally the fur trade was restricted to eastern Canada, but by the late 1600s, coureurs de bois were travelling far to the west in search of new sources of furs.

European settlers who arrived in Canada in the sixteenth and seventeenth centuries initially had to farm or starve. Gradually, however, they began to produce more than they needed for their own survival. The governments of the countries from which the settlers came (notably England and France) were strong supporters of the mercantilist philosophy. Under mercantilism, colonists were expected to export raw materials like beaver pelts and lumber at low prices to the mother country. These raw materials were then used to produce finished goods such as fur coats, which were sold at high prices to settlers in Canada. Attempts to develop industry in Canada were thwarted by England and France, who enjoyed large profits from mercantilism. As a result, Canadian manufacturing was slow to develop.

Table 1.4 Some Important Dates in Canadian Business History

Date	Event
1490	English fishermen active off the coast of Newfoundland
1534	Account of first trading with native peoples written by Jacques Cartier
1670	Hudson's Bay Company founded
1730–40	Hat-making industry arises in Quebec and is stifled by French home officials
1779	North West Company forms
1785	Molson brewery opens
1805	First Canadian paper mill built at St. Andrew's, Quebec
1809	First steamboat (the *Accommodation*) put into service on the St. Lawrence River by John Molson
1817	Bank of Montreal chartered
1821	Hudson's Bay Company and North West Company merge
1830–50	Era of canal building
1850–60	First era of railroad building
1855	John Redpath opens first Canadian sugar refinery in Montreal
1857–58	First oil well in Canada drilled near Sarnia, Ontario
1861	Toronto Stock Exchange opens
1869	Eaton's opens for business in Toronto
1880–90	First western land boom
1885	Last spike driven to complete the Canadian Pacific Railroad
1896	First large pulp and paper mill in Canada opened at Sault Ste. Marie, Ontario
1897–99	Klondike gold rush
1917–22	Creation of Canadian National Railways
1926	U.S. replaces Great Britain as Canada's largest trading partner
1927	Armand Bombardier sells first "auto-neige" (forerunner of the snowmobile)
1929	Great stock market crash
1929–33	Great Depression
1930	Canadian Airways Limited formed
1932	Canadian Radio Broadcasting Corporation formed (it became the CBC in 1936)
1935	Bank of Canada begins operations
1937	Canadian Breweries Limited is formed
1947–51	Early computer built at the University of Toronto
1947	Leduc Number 1 oil well drilled in Alberta
1949	A.V. Roe (Avro) makes Canada's first commercial jetliner
1965	Auto Pact signed with the U.S.
1969	Canada becomes world's largest potash producer
1989	Free trade agreement with U.S. comes into effect
1993	North American Free Trade Agreement comes into effect
1995–99	Rapid increase in stock prices
2000	Prices of most stocks decline sharply
2003–04	Canadian internet pharmacies begin selling prescription drugs to U.S. citizens
2006	Softwood lumber dispute with U.S. settled

The Factory System and the Industrial Revolution

British manufacturing took a great leap forward around 1750 with the coming of the **Industrial Revolution**. A new level of production was made possible by advances in technology and by the development of the **factory system**. Instead of hundreds of workers turning out items one at a time in their cottages, the factory system brought together in one place all of the materials and workers required to produce items in large quantities, along with newly created machines capable of **mass production**.

Industrial Revolution A major change in goods production that began in England in the mid-eighteenth century and was characterized by a shift to the factory system, mass production, and specialization of labour.

factory system A process in which all the machinery, materials, and workers required to produce a good in large quantities are brought together in one place.

mass production The manufacture of products of uniform quality in large quantities.

specialization The breaking down of complex operations into simple tasks that are easily learned and performed.

Mass production offered savings in several areas. It avoided unnecessary duplication of equipment. It allowed firms to purchase raw materials at better prices by buying large lots. And most important, it encouraged **specialization** of labour. No longer did production require highly skilled craftspeople who could do all the different tasks required to make an item. A series of semiskilled workers, each trained to perform only one task and supported by specialized machines and tools, greatly increased output.

In spite of British laws against the export of technology and against manufacturing in North America, Canadian manufacturing existed almost from the beginning of European settlement. Modest manufacturing operations were evident in sawmills, breweries, gristmills for grinding grain, tanneries, woollen mills, shoemakers' shops, and tailors' shops. These operations were so successful that by 1800, exports of manufactured goods were more important than exports of fur.

With the advent of steam power in the early 1800s, manufacturing activity began to increase rapidly. By 1850, more than 30 factories—employing more than 2000 people—lined the Lachine Canal in Montreal alone. Exports of timber to England in 1850 were 70 times greater than what they had been in 1800. The demand for reliable transportation was the impetus for canal building in the mid-1800s and then the railroad-building boom in the mid- and late-1800s.

The Entrepreneurial Era

One of the most significant features of the last half of the nineteenth century was the emergence of entrepreneurs willing to take risks in the hope of earning huge profits. Adam Smith in his book *The Wealth of Nations* argued that the government should not interfere in the economy, but should let businesses function without regulation or restriction. The Canadian government often adopted this laissez-faire attitude. As a result, some individuals became immensely wealthy through their aggressive business dealings. Some railway, bank, and insurance executives made over $25 000 per year in the late 1800s, and their purchasing power was immense. Entrepreneurs such as Joseph Flavelle, Henry Pellatt, and John MacDonald lived in ostentatious mansions or castles.

The size and economic power of some firms meant that other businesses had difficulty competing against them. At the same time, some business executives decided that it was more profitable to collude than to compete. They decided among themselves to fix prices and divide up markets. Hurt by these actions, Canadian consumers called for more regulation of business. In 1889, the first anti-combines legislation was passed in Canada, and legislation regulating business has increased ever since.

The Production Era

The concepts of specialization and mass production that originated in the Industrial Revolution were more fully refined as Canada entered the twentieth century. The Scientific Management Movement focused management's attention on production. Increased efficiency via the "one best way" to accomplish tasks became the major management goal.

production era The period during the early twentieth century when businesses focused almost exclusively on improving productivity and manufacturing methods.

Henry Ford's introduction of the moving assembly line in the United States in 1913 ushered in the **production era**. During the production era, less attention was paid to selling and marketing than to technical efficiency when producing goods. By using fixed workstations, increasing task specialization, and moving the work to the worker, the assembly line increased productivity and lowered prices, making all kinds of products affordable for the average person. It also increased the available labour pool because many people could be trained to carry out assembly line tasks. Formerly, the labour pool was limited because relatively few people had the high skill levels of craftspeople.

During the production era, large businesses began selling stock—making shareholders the owners—and relying on professional managers. The growth of corporations and improved production output resulting from assembly lines came at the expense of worker freedom. The dominance of big firms made it harder for individuals to go into business for themselves. Company towns run by the railroads, mining corporations, and forest products firms gave individuals little freedom of choice over whom to work for and what to buy. To restore some balance within the overall system, both government and labour had to develop and grow. Thus, this period saw the rise of labour unions and collective bargaining. We will look at this development in more detail in Chapter 9. The Great Depression of the 1930s and the Second World War caused the federal government to intervene in the economic system on a previously unimaginable scale.

Today, business, government, and labour are frequently referred to by economists and politicians as the three *countervailing powers* in our society. All are big. All are strong. Yet, none totally dominates the others.

The Sales and Marketing Eras

By the 1930s, business's focus on production had resulted in spectacular increases in the amount of goods and services for sale. As a result, buyers had more choices and producers faced greater competition in selling their wares. Thus began the so-called **sales era**. According to the ideas of this time, a business's profits and success depended on hiring the right salespeople, advertising heavily, and making sure products were readily available. Business firms were essentially production- and sales-oriented, and they produced what they thought customers wanted, or simply what the company was good at producing. This approach is still used by firms that find themselves with surplus goods that they want to sell (e.g., used-car dealerships).

sales era The period during the 1930s and 1940s when businesses focussed on sales forces, advertising, and keeping products readily available.

Following the Second World War, pent-up demand for consumer goods kept the economy rolling. While brief recessions did occur periodically, the 1950s and 1960s were prosperous times. Production increased, technology advanced, and the standard of living rose. During the **marketing era**, business adopted a new philosophy of how to do business—use market research to determine what customers want, and then make it for them. Firms like Procter & Gamble and Molson were very effective during the marketing era, and continue to be profitable today. Each offers an array of products within a particular field (toothpaste or beer, for example) and gives customers a chance to pick what best suits their needs.

marketing era The period during the 1950s and 1960s when businesses began to identify and meet consumer wants to make a profit.

The Finance Era

In the 1980s, emphasis shifted to finance. In the **finance era** there was a sharp increase in mergers and in the buying and selling of business enterprises. Some people now call it the "decade of greed." As we will see in the next chapter, during the finance era there were many hostile takeovers and a great deal of financial manipulation of corporate assets by so-called corporate raiders. Critics charged that these raiders were simply enriching themselves and weren't creating anything of tangible value by their activity. They also charged that raiders were distracting business managers from their main goals of running the business. The raiders responded that they were making organizations more efficient by streamlining, merging, and reorganizing them.

finance era The period during the 1980s when there were many mergers and much buying and selling of business enterprises.

The Global Era

The last few years have seen the continuation of technological advances in production, computer technology, information systems, and communication capabilities. They have also seen the emergence of a truly global economy. Canadians drive cars made in Japan, wear sweaters made in Italy, drink beer brewed in Mexico, and listen to stereos made in Taiwan. But we're not alone in this. People around the world buy products and services from foreign companies.

While it is true that many Canadian businesses have been hurt by foreign imports, numerous others have profited by exploring new foreign markets themselves. And domestic competition has forced many businesses to

China opened its economy to foreign investors in the 1980s and joined the World Trade Organization in 2001. Now the Chinese buy as many cars as the Germans and more photographic film than the Japanese. They also buy more cellphones than anyone anywhere, and the opening of the Chinese market has created a windfall for makers of wireless handsets, including Motorola (U.S.), Siemens (Germany), Samsung (South Korea), and Nokia (Finland).

work harder than ever to cut costs, increase efficiency, and improve product and service quality. We will explore a variety of important trends, opportunities, and challenges of the global era throughout this book.

Most of these software developers are among the 65 000 engineers that the Indian State of Andhra Pradesh graduates every year—up from 7500 just 10 years ago. Microsoft operates an R&D centre in the capital city of Hyderabad, where Oracle, Computer Associates, and IBM also have facilities. The city is prospering as a hub not only for software programming, but for telephone call centres and pharmaceuticals as well.

The Internet Era

The turn of the century has been accompanied by what many experts are calling the internet era of business. Internet usage in North America grew from about 100 users per 1000 people in 1995 to over 750 users per 1000 people in 2005. The growth rate in Western Europe and the Asia-Pacific region, however, is expected to be even faster. The growth of the internet affects business in at least three different ways:

1. The internet will give a dramatic boost to trade in all sectors of the economy, especially services. If the internet makes it easier for all trade to grow, this is particularly true for trade in services on an international scale.
2. The internet will level the playing field, at least to some extent, between larger and smaller enterprises, regardless of what products or services they sell. In the past, a substantial investment was typically needed to enter some industries and to enter foreign markets. Now, however, a small business based in central Alberta, southern Italy, eastern Malaysia, or northern Brazil can set up a website and compete quite effectively with much larger businesses located around the world.
3. The internet holds considerable potential as an effective and efficient networking mechanism among businesses. Business-to-business (B2B) networks can link firms with all of their suppliers, business customers, and strategic partners in ways that make it faster and easier for them to do business together.

Summary of Learning Objectives

1. **Define the nature of Canadian *business* and identify its main goals.** *Businesses* are organizations that produce or sell goods or services to make a profit. *Profits* are the difference between a business' revenues and expenses. The prospect of earning profits encourages individuals and organizations to open and expand businesses. The benefits of business activities also extend to wages paid to workers and to taxes that support government functions.

2. **Describe different types of global *economic systems* according to the means by which they control the *factors of production* through *input* and *output markets*.** An *economic system* is a nation's system for allocating its resources among its citizens. Economic systems differ in terms of who owns or controls the basic *factors of production*: labour, capital, entrepreneurs, natural resources, and, more recently, information resources. In *command economies*, the government controls all or most of these factors. In *market economies*, which are based on the principles of capitalism, individuals and businesses control the factors of production and exchange them through *input and output markets*. Most countries today have *mixed market economies* that are dominated by one of these systems but include elements of the other. The process of *privatization* is an important means by which many of the world's planned economies are moving toward mixed market systems.

3. **Show how *demand* and *supply* affect resource distribution in Canada.** The Canadian economy is strongly influenced by markets, demand, and supply. *Demand* is the willingness and ability of buyers to purchase a good or service. *Supply* is the willingness and ability of producers to offer goods or services for sale. Demand and supply work together to set a *market* or *equilibrium price*—the price at which the quantity of goods demanded and the quantity of goods supplied are equal.

4. **Identify the elements of *private enterprise* and explain the various *degrees of competition* in the Canadian economic system.** The Canadian economy is founded on the principles of *private enterprise: private property rights, freedom of choice, profits*, and *competition*. Degrees of competition vary because not all industries are equally competitive. Under conditions of *perfect competition*, numerous small firms compete in a market governed entirely by demand and supply. An *oligopoly* involves a handful of sellers only. A *monopoly* involves only one seller.

5. **Trace the *history of business* in Canada.** Modern business structures reflect a pattern of development over centuries. Throughout much of the colonial period, sole proprietors supplied raw materials to English manufacturers. The rise of the factory system during the Industrial Revolution brought with it mass production and specialization of labour. During the entrepreneurial era in the nineteenth century, large corporations—and monopolies—emerged. During the production era of the early twentieth century, companies grew by emphasizing output and production. During the sales and marketing eras of the 1950s and 1960s, business began focussing on sales staff, advertising, and the need to produce what consumers wanted. In the 1980s there was increased buying and selling of businesses, and in the 1990s a significant global economy emerged. Many Canadian companies have profited from exporting their goods to foreign markets. The most recent development is the use of the internet to boost business. To some extent, the internet should level the playing field between large and small companies.

KEY TERMS

business, 6
Canada Water Act, 15
Canadian Radio-television and Telecommunications Commission (CRTC), 14
Canadian Transport Commission (CTC), 14
Canadian Wheat Board, 14
capital, 8
capitalism, 12
command economy, 9
communism, 9
competition, 21
demand, 17
demand and supply schedule, 19
demand curve, 19
deregulation, 13
economic system, 7
entrepreneur, 9
Environmental Contaminants Act, 15
factors of production, 7
factory system, 25
finance era, 27
Fisheries Act, 15
Food and Drug Act, 15
Hazardous Products Act, 14
Industrial Revolution, 25
information resources, 9
input market, 11
labour (or human resources), 8
law of demand, 18
law of supply, 18
lobbyist, 16
market, 11
market economy, 9
market price (or equilibrium price), 19
marketing era, 27
mass production, 25
mixed market economy, 13
monopolistic competition, 22
monopoly, 23
natural monopoly, 23
natural resources, 9
oligopoly, 23
output market, 11
perfect competition, 22
private enterprise, 21
privatization, 13
production era, 26
profit, 6
progressive revenue taxes, 15
regressive revenue taxes, 15
restrictive taxes, 16
revenue taxes, 15
sales era, 27
shortage, 19
socialism, 9
specialization, 25
supply, 18
supply curve, 19
surplus, 19
Textile Labelling Act, 15
Tobacco Act, 15
trade association, 17
Weights and Measures Act, 15

QUESTIONS FOR ANALYSIS

1. Is one factor of production more important than the others? If so, which one? Why?
2. On various occasions, government provides financial incentives to business firms. For example, the Canadian government provided expert assistance to Bombardier Inc. with its Technology Transfer Program. Is this consistent with a basically free market system? Explain how this might distort the system.
3. In recent years, many countries have moved from planned economies to market economies. Why do you think this has occurred? Can you envision a situation that would cause a resurgence of planned economies?
4. Find an example where a surplus of a product led to decreased prices. Then find an example where a shortage led to increased prices. What eventually happened in each case? Why? Is what happened consistent with what economics predicts? Why?
5. Familiarize yourself with a product or service that is sold under conditions of perfect competition. Explain why it is an example of perfect competition and identify the factors that make it so. Then do the same for a product in each of the other three competitive situations described in the chapter.
6. Analyze how the factors of production work together for a product or service of your choice.
7. Government plays a variety of roles in the Canadian mixed economy. Consider each of the roles discussed in the text and state the criteria you would use to decide whether government involvement in each role is excessive, insufficient, or about right.

APPLICATION EXERCISES

1. Choose a locally owned business. Interview the owner to find out how the business uses the factors of production and have the owner describe the means of acquiring them.
2. Visit a local shopping mall or shopping area. List each store that you see and determine what degree of competition it faces in its immediate environment. For example, if there is only one store in the mall that sells shoes, that store represents a monopoly. Note those businesses with direct competitors (two jewellery stores) and show how they compete with one another.
3. Go to the library or log onto the internet and research 10 different industries. Classify each according to degree of competition.

BUILDING YOUR BUSINESS SKILLS

Analyzing the Price of Doing Ebusiness

Goal

To encourage students to understand how the competitive environment affects a product's price.

The Situation

Assume that you own a local business that provides internet access to individuals and businesses (this kind of business is called an ISP, or internet service provider). Yours is one of four such businesses in the local market. Each of the four companies charges the same price: $20 per month for unlimited dial-up service. Your business also provides users with email service; two of your competitors also offer email service. One of these same two competitors, plus the third, also provides the individual user with a free, basic personal webpage. One competitor just dropped its price to $14 per month, and the other two have announced their intentions to follow suit. Your break-even price is $10 per customer; that is, you must charge $10 for your service package to cover your costs (but not earn any profit). You are concerned about getting into a price war that may destroy your business.

Method

Divide into groups of four or five people. Each group is to develop a general strategy for handling competitors' price changes. In your discussion, take the following factors into account:

- how the demand for your product is affected by price changes
- the number of competitors selling the same or a similar product
- the methods—other than price—you can use to attract new customers and/or retain current customers

Analysis

Develop specific pricing strategies based on each of the following situations:

- Within a month after dropping the price to $14, one of your competitors raises its price back to $18.
- Two of your competitors drop their prices further—to $12 per month. As a result, your business falls off by 25 percent.
- One of your competitors that has provided customers with a free webpage has indicated that it will start charging an extra $4 per month for this optional service.
- Two of your competitors have announced that they will charge individual users $12 per month, but will charge businesses a higher price (not yet announced).
- All four providers (including you) are charging $11 per month. One goes out of business, and you know that another is in poor financial health.

Follow-Up Questions

1. Discuss the role that various inducements other than price might play in affecting demand and supply in the market for internet service.
2. Is it always in a company's best interest to feature the lowest prices?
3. Eventually, what form of competition is likely to characterize the market for internet service?

EXERCISING YOUR ETHICS

Prescribing a Dose of Competitive Medicine

The Purpose of the Assignment

Demand and supply are key elements of the Canadian economic system. So, too, is competition. This exercise will challenge you to better understand the ethical dimensions of a system that relies on demand, supply, and competition.

The Situation

You are a business person in a small town, where you run one of two local pharmacies. The population and economic base are fairly stable. Each pharmacy controls about 50 percent of the market. Each is reasonably profitable, generating solid if unspectacular revenues.

The Dilemma

The owner of the other pharmacy has just approached you. He has indicated an interest either in buying your pharmacy or in selling his to you. He argues that neither of you can substantially increase your profits and complains that if one pharmacy raises its prices, customers will simply go to the other one. He tells you outright that if you sell to him, he plans to raise prices by 10 percent. He believes that the local market will have to accept the increase for two reasons: (1) The town is too small to attract national competitors, and (2) local customers aren't likely to go elsewhere to shop because the nearest town with a pharmacy is 60 kilometres away.

Questions for Discussion

1. What are the roles of supply, demand, and competition in this scenario?
2. What are the underlying ethical issues?
3. What would you do if you were actually faced with this situation?

CONCLUDING CASE 1-1

Supply and Demand: Some Practical Lessons

The prices of many different commodities are influenced by the supply of, and demand for, these commodities. Variations in demand and supply have implications for both businesses and for consumers, as the following stories about oil, palladium, and coffee demonstrate.

Oil

The sign in front of one gas station summed it up nicely: The prices listed for the three grades of gasoline were "An arm," "A leg," and "Your firstborn." While the sign no doubt led to a few smiles from motorists, its sentiments were far from a laughing matter. Indeed, in early 2006, retail gasoline prices in Canada and the United States were very high, exceeding \$2.30 per gallon in the U.S. and \$0.95 per litre in Canada.

Gasoline prices have fluctuated many times in the past. For example, an Arab embargo on petroleum in 1971 led to a major price jump. But the higher prices spurred new exploration, and as new oil fields came online and supplies increased, prices eventually dropped again. Subsequent supply disruptions due to political problems in Venezuela, Nigeria, and Iraq have also caused short-term price jumps, after which the price again dropped.

But people who are knowledgeable about oil say that from now on the price of oil is likely to go in only one direction—up. Why? Because the supply of easily recoverable oil is limited, and demand continues to increase because of the surging global economy, particularly in China and India. What's worse, the global supply of oil will soon peak and then slowly begin to decline. While no one can pinpoint exactly when the decline will start, virtually all the experts agree that it will happen well before 2050. Canada's prominence in energy production will increase as the output from the tar sands steadily increases during this same period of time (see the Opening Case).

What happens then? Although there will be gradual reductions in supply, oil and gas will remain available for at least another century—but at prices that will make those of today seem like a bargain. Firms that can produce alternative sources of energy will spring up, and those who find viable answers will prosper.

▶▶▶

Palladium

Most people have never heard of palladium, a greyish metal produced primarily in Russia and South Africa. In the 1990s, when automakers adopted tighter pollution emission standards, they switched from platinum to palladium because palladium does a better job of cleaning auto emissions, and because at that time palladium was much cheaper than platinum. The automobile manufacturers knew that switching to palladium would cause demand to exceed world production, which was then about 5 million ounces per year. They also knew that this increased demand would cause the price of palladium to rise, but they were not prepared for the price rise that actually occurred when Russian exports of palladium suddenly ceased in 1997. The official explanation was a bureaucratic problem, and when supplies resumed, the price dropped again to about $200 per ounce.

In 1998, the same thing happened, but this time the price went up to over $400 per ounce. When supplies resumed, the price dropped back to only $300 per ounce. Now the auto manufacturers were becoming very concerned, and they began trying to figure out how to use less palladium and still meet the tighter pollution standards. By 2000, when the price of palladium had risen to over $1000 per ounce, automakers took the unprecedented step of stipulating the maximum amount of palladium that would be allowed in engineers' car designs.

In 2002, Ford Motor Company took a $1 billion write-off on the value of the palladium it had stockpiled for use in its automobile catalytic converters. Ford originally stockpiled this raw material because it thought it would need increasing amounts of palladium, and because it was concerned that palladium was going to be high-priced and hard to get. At the same time, however, Ford's engineers were succeeding in figuring out ways to reduce the amount of palladium they needed. So, Ford's purchasing agents were buying lots of palladium at high prices (fearing the price would go even higher) while Ford's engineers were figuring out ways to reduce the company's need for the metal.

By 2001, the price of palladium had again dropped to about $400 dollars per ounce. This happened because demand dropped (other automakers had also discovered ways to get by with less palladium) and supplies increased (because the extremely high prices of palladium in 1999–2000 had caused more producers to get into the business of supplying the market).

Coffee

This is another commodity whose price soared in 2005. Between October 2004 and February 2005, for example, the price of high quality Arabica coffee beans (the type used by specialty coffee stores like Starbucks) increased by 79 percent. High demand from consumers, coupled with falling supplies caused the price increase. The increased cost of this popular commodity is quickly passed on to consumers.

Like oil, coffee is a commodity that has experienced many ups and downs over the years. The current high-price situation is a dramatic change from 2001, when coffee prices hit a 30-year low because of an oversupply of coffee beans. The low prices in 2001 were, in turn, caused by the high coffee prices in 1994 and 1995, which motivated farmers to plant a lot of acres of coffee beans in an attempt to cash in on the high prices. Since it takes 3–4 years for a coffee tree to mature, a lot of coffee beans started hitting the market in 1998 and 1999, and that increased the supply and drove prices down. But by 2001 the low prices had discouraged growers from planting more coffee trees, and that caused production to fall, leading to the current drop in supply. This up-and-down cycle is hard to break.

Questions for Discussion

1. What are the basic factors of production in the petroleum industry?
2. Describe the concepts of input and output markets as they apply to the petroleum industry.
3. Explain how the concepts of demand and supply combine to determine market prices for diverse commodities like palladium, oil, and coffee.
4. Does the global energy situation increase or decrease your confidence in a capitalistic system based on private enterprise?
5. Did automakers respond to increases in the price of palladium in the way predicted by economic theory? Explain.
6. Not everyone agrees that there is an impending oil crisis. Develop arguments that we are not likely to run out of oil any time soon.

CONCLUDING CASE 1-2

Business, Government, and Liquor

The liquor business is no stranger to controversy. In addition to the moral and health issues with regard to the use of alcohol, there are also complex issues of who should control the sale of liquor, and how closely regulated the industry should be.

For many years, all provincial governments held a monopoly on the sale of liquor. But with the worldwide move to privatization that began in the 1990s, various provinces began looking at the possibility of privatizing liquor sales. In 2005, a government-appointed panel in Ontario called for the privatization of the Liquor Control Board of Ontario (LCBO). But the Ontario finance minister rejected the idea, apparently because the Crown Corporation is popular with consumers, and because liquor suppliers like dealing with just one big buyer instead of many smaller ones. The LCBO's unionized employees were also very vocal in their opposition to privatization.

Critics of the LCBO say that it should be privatized because it is inefficient and it doesn't make any profit. Supporters, on the other hand, argue that it *is* profitable. Which claim is more reasonable? Consider these numbers: In its 2003–2004 financial statement, the LCBO reported a gross margin on sales of 47.6 percent (most food retailers, by comparison achieve 2–3 percent). The LCBO achieved this high return by counting the provincial liquor tax it collected as profit. Critics point out that if this tax is subtracted from the LCBO's net income, there is no profit at all. The critics say this tax revenue *should* be subtracted, since private sector firms are not be able to claim government taxes they collect as profit.

The Ontario dispute is just one example of the long-running debate about privatization. In Alberta, for example, the province announced in 1993 that it was getting out of the liquor business and that it would allow private sector operators to begin selling liquor. It was doing so because it said it would save $65 million annually in salaries and operating costs. Within a year, 500 privately owned liquor stores had opened up. In 2003, a policy research group at the University of Alberta issued a report that analyzed the province of Alberta's 10-year experience with privatized liquor stores. The report reached the following conclusions:

- Liquor prices had increased by about one-third since 1993 (12 percent more than inflation for the period).
- The province had lost $511 million in revenue since liquor stores were privatized.
- The number of liquor stores had more than tripled since privatization.

The report concluded that the benefits of privatization were modest at best.

Also in 2003, the B.C. branch of the Consumers Association of Canada (CAC) compared liquor prices in British Columbia (where the government had a monopoly on liquor sales) with prices in Alberta. It found that B.C. prices were competitive with, or lower, than prices in Alberta. The study also concluded that if British Columbia privatized its liquor sales consumers would pay 10–20 percent more. The B.C. government had, in fact, been looking at the possibility of closing 224 government liquor stores and replacing them with privately owned stores. But the provincial government put the plan on hold so they could do more analysis of the situation. Not surprisingly, the Government and Service Employees Union expressed concerns about what privatization would do to its members' jobs.

Another interesting comparison involves Quebec and Ontario, both of which have provincial monopolies in the sale of liquor. Prices of most liquor products are higher in Quebec than they are in Ontario. Even when a Société des alcools du Québec (SAQ) store in Quebec has a sale, prices may be higher than non-sale items in Ontario. For example, during one period in 2006, a bottle of Australian Wyndham Estate Cabernet Merlot that was on sale at SAQ cost $17, while the regular price in Ontario was just $14.60. Critics of the Quebec government's liquor monopoly argue that SAQ's new "Customer First" slogan is a joke. The government's position was not helped when newspapers reported that several European wine distributors claimed that SAQ had urged them to raise their prices rather than pass on savings to Quebec consumers as a result of the rising value of the Canadian dollar relative to the euro. All of this negative publicity has given supporters of privatization some hope that the government will get out of the liquor business.

The dispute about privatization is not the only issue that has arisen in the liquor industry. There is also debate about which roles the government should play. In the recent past, government has acted as both a regulator and competitor of private sector liquor companies. In the late 1990s, for example, Magnotta Winery Corp. was denied shelf space for its products by the LCBO. Magnotta therefore started selling its wine at its own on-site store at the vineyard. The company wanted to charge $3.95 for a 750-mL bottle, which was lower than the LCBO's price of $5.15. But the LCBO ruled that Magnotta couldn't sell its products for less than the cheapest wine carried in an LCBO store. Magnotta was also involved in several other well-publicized disputes with the LCBO. Finally, in 2000, the

▶▶▶

province of Ontario stripped its government-owned liquor stores of their regulatory status to make competition fairer.

The same sort of dispute was evident in Manitoba, where 6 privately owned wine stores sold over half the wine in Winnipeg, while 22 Manitoba Liquor Control Commission (MLCC) stores sold the rest. A Probe Research poll showed that 90 percent of Winnipeggers didn't want the province to phase out private wine stores. More than half of those polled said that private wine stores forced the MLCC stores to improve their service by providing competition. The private wine sellers in Manitoba also argued that the MLCC was in a conflict of interest because it had the power to regulate its competitors. They filed a lawsuit against the MLCC in 2000, claiming that the MLCC had engaged in various unfair business practices in an attempt to steal customers from the private wine stores. In 2006, it was disclosed that the MLCC had paid $8 million to the wine stores in an out-of-court settlement.

Questions for Discussion

1. What are the different roles that government plays in the Canadian mixed economic system? What are the appropriate roles that the government should play in the liquor business?
2. What roles does government play in, say, retail trade and manufacturing? Should the government's role in the liquor business be different from its role in retail trade or manufacturing?
3. Should the sale of liquor be a government monopoly, or should other provinces do what Alberta did? Defend your answer.
4. Critics argue that government-run monopolies like liquor stores should make a profit. Is this a reasonable claim? Explain.

CHAPTER 2

Understanding the Environments of Business

After reading this chapter, you should be able to:

1. Explain the concepts of *organizational boundaries* and *multiple organizational environments*.
2. Explain the importance of the *economic environment* to business and identify the factors used to evaluate the performance of an economic system.
3. Describe the *technological environment* and its role in business.
4. Describe the *political-legal environment* and its role in business.
5. Describe the *socio-cultural environment* and its role in business.
6. Identify emerging challenges and opportunities in the *business environment*.
7. Understand recent trends in the *redrawing of corporate boundaries*.

Productivity and the Standard of Living

Compared with the United States, Canada's standard of living has been slipping for the last two decades. In 1980, Canada's standard of living was 90 percent of the U.S. level. By 2002, it had slipped to 87 percent, and by 2004 to 84 percent. It is projected to drop to 77 percent by 2010. If our standard of living continues to drop, Canadians will experience a decline in the quality of health care, social programs, and overall quality of life. We also risk losing our finest brains, talent, and companies if we fail to hold our own against the United States.

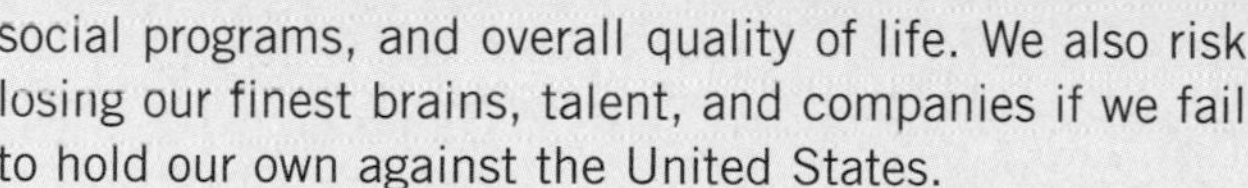

What is causing the standard of living to drop in Canada relative to the United States (and to other countries)? One major factor is Canada's relatively slow *productivity growth rate*. Data developed by the Paris-based Organisation for Economic Co-operation and Development (OECD) show that Canada's labour productivity (that is, GDP per hour worked) did not increase at all in 2004. Most other industrialized countries achieved increases of 1.5–2.5 percent. The same kinds of concerns are expressed in the Conference Board of Canada's annual "Performance and Potential Report" which rates the world's 24 richest economies on various factors, including productivity. In the 2005 Report, Canada ranked only 12th in productivity (down from 3rd place in 2003 and 6th place in 2004). The Conference Board attributed this downward trend to poor productivity growth.

As the number of working-age people decreases over the next several decades, our standard of living will decline further unless the remaining people in the workforce can produce more per person—in other words, productivity must increase. If we are going to compete with the surging economies of India and China in the global market, we must become more productive. If we don't, we will lose export possibilities and the jobs that go with them. That will also contribute to a decline in the Canadian standard of living.

Why is Canadian productivity growing so slowly? Various organizations, including the Ottawa-based Centre for the Study of Living Standards, have identified several different causes:

- Productivity in the information and communications technology sector has dropped off sharply since 2000; prior to that time it was increasing rapidly.
- The prices of commodities like oil and gas have increased dramatically in the last few years, and this has motivated companies to exploit marginal reserves where productivity is low.
- R&D intensity (the ratio of R&D spending to gross GDP) has dropped.
- Exports, as a percent of GDP, dropped from 45.6 percent in 2000 to 38.2 percent in 2004.
- The scale of manufacturing firms in Canada is smaller than in the United States, and small plants are less productive than large ones.
- Worker stress is reducing productivity (66 percent of Canadian CEOs who were polled in 2005 by Ipsos-Reid said that employee stress was the biggest drain on productivity); other factors reducing productivity were poor management practices and lack of effective training programs.
- The decline of the Canadian dollar between 1995 and 2001 meant that manufacturers had little incentive to increase productivity (because they could sell their goods easily in the United States).
- Canadian business firms conduct less research and development (R&D) than companies in many other countries. For example, Canadian R&D as a percentage of GNP was less than half that of Sweden. In a survey of 24 countries, Canada ranked 11th in R&D spending.

What is the solution to the productivity problem? Clearly, we must boost our productivity growth rate if we are to raise our standard of living. The following actions have been suggested:

- Put more money into post-secondary education.
- Develop more partnerships between business and academic institutions.
- Invest in upgrading workforce skills, and increase the availability of vocational, technical, and apprenticeship programs for students who don't attend university.
- Create greater incentives to rejoin the workforce for those on welfare.
- Levy training costs on businesses like some European countries do.
- Stop subsidizing uncompetitive industries like shipbuilding.

- Cut personal and corporate income tax rates.
- Allow more aggressive write-off schedules for capital investments by businesses.

What do Canadians think about the issue of productivity and the standard of living? Surveys that have been conducted during the last few years reveal the following answers to several important questions:

- *"How do you think the average personal income for a Canadian worker compares with that for a U.S. worker?"* (half of the respondents said it was lower, one-fifth said it was higher, and one-fifth said it was the same).
- *"How do you think Canada compares with the United States in terms of quality of life?"* (70 percent said it was higher and 18 percent said it was the same).
- *"How do you think Canada compares with the United States in terms of standard of living?"* (37 percent said it is higher in Canada, 34 percent thought it was the same, and 28 percent said it was lower).
- *"How do you think Canada's level of productivity compares with that of the United States?"* (50 percent felt it was worse, 25 percent felt it was the same, and 20 percent felt it was better).

When asked if they agreed or disagreed with the statement "Increasing productivity is essential to improving our standard of living," 82 percent agreed. When asked if they agreed or disagreed with the statement "If we don't improve our productivity, our quality of life will suffer," 70 percent agreed. ◆

ORGANIZATIONAL BOUNDARIES AND ENVIRONMENTS

external environment Everything outside an organization's boundaries that might affect it.

All businesses, regardless of their size, location, or mission, operate within a larger external environment. This **external environment**—which consists of everything outside an organization's boundaries that might affect it—plays a major role in determining the success or failure of any organization. Managers must therefore have an accurate understanding of the environment facing their company, and then strive to operate and compete within it. While no single firm can control the environment, managers should not simply react to changes; they should also be proactive and at least try to influence their environment.

To better explain the environment of business, we begin by discussing *organizational boundaries*, and then we introduce the concept of *multiple organizational environments*.

Organizational Boundaries

organizational boundary That which separates the organization from its environment.

1 Explain the concepts of *organizational boundaries* and *multiple organizational environments.*

An **organizational boundary** separates the organization from its environment. Boundaries were once relatively easy to identify, but they are becoming increasingly complicated and hard to pin down. Consider the simple case of a small neighbourhood grocery that includes a retail customer area, a storage room, and an owner/manager's office. In many ways, the store's boundary coincides with its physical structure. When you walk through the door, you're crossing the boundary into the business, and when you go back onto the sidewalk, you cross the boundary back into the environment.

But even this simple example isn't as simple as it seems. During the course of the business day, distributors of soft drinks, beer, snack foods, ice, and bread products may enter the store, inventory the products that they distribute, and automatically refill coolers and shelves just as if they were employees. Although these distributors are normally considered part of the environment rather than the organization, during the time that they're inside the store, they are essentially part of the business. Assuming that they're store employees, customers may ask them questions as they restock shelves. The bread distributor may even offer someone a fresh loaf instead of the one that he or she has taken from the shelf.

Now consider the case of a large domestic business (such as GM Canada) that is owned by an even larger international corporation (U.S.-based General Motors). The domestic business has a complex network of relationships with other businesses. GM Canada, for example, deals with companies that supply tires, glass, steel, and engines. But GM Canada also functions within the boundaries of its international parent, which has its own network of business relationships, some overlapping and some distinct from GM Canada's network.

We can also examine similar complexities from the customer's perspective. McDonald's, for example, has a contract with Coca-Cola, stipulating that it will sell only Coke soft-drink products. McDonald's also has partnerships with Wal-Mart and Disney that allow it to open stores inside those firms' facilities. So when you buy a Coca-Cola soft drink from a McDonald's restaurant located inside a Wal-Mart store or Disney theme park, you are essentially affecting, and being affected by, multiple businesses. As you can see, the boundaries of any specific business are becoming increasingly difficult to define and more complicated to manage.

Multiple Organizational Environments

Although we tend to speak of "the external environment" as if it were a single entity, organizations actually have multiple environments. Some of them are relatively general. Prevailing economic conditions, for instance, will affect the performance of almost every business. But other dimensions are much more precise. Our neighbourhood grocery will be influenced not only by an increase in unemployment in the area, but also by the pricing and other marketing policies of its nearest competitor.

Figure 2.1 shows the major dimensions and elements of the external environment as it affects most businesses. As you can see, these include economic conditions, technology, political-legal considerations, social issues, the global environment, issues of ethical and social responsibility, the business environment itself, and numerous other emerging challenges and opportunities. Because this book provides detailed coverage of global and ethical issues in Chapters 3 and 5, respectively, we will introduce them here only as they relate directly to the other areas in this chapter.

THE ECONOMIC ENVIRONMENT

The **economic environment** refers to the conditions of the economic system in which an organization operates.[1] For example, McDonald's Canadian operations are (as of this writing) functioning in an economic environment characterized by moderate growth, moderate unemployment, and low inflation. Moderate unemployment means that most people can afford to eat out, but it also means that McDonald's must pay higher wages to attract employees. Low inflation means that McDonald's pays relatively constant prices for its supplies, but it also means that McDonald's can't really increase the prices it charges consumers.

economic environment Conditions of the economic system in which an organization operates.

2 Explain the importance of the *economic environment* to business and identify the factors used to evaluate the performance of an economic system.

Given the importance of the economic environment, we will closely examine the three key goals of the Canadian economic system: *economic growth*, *economic stability*, and *full employment*. We begin by focussing on the tools we use to measure economic growth, including *aggregate output*, *standard of living*, *gross domestic product*, and *productivity*. We then discuss the main threats to economic stability—namely, *inflation* and *unemployment*. We conclude this section by discussing government attempts to manage the Canadian economy in the interest of meeting national economic goals.

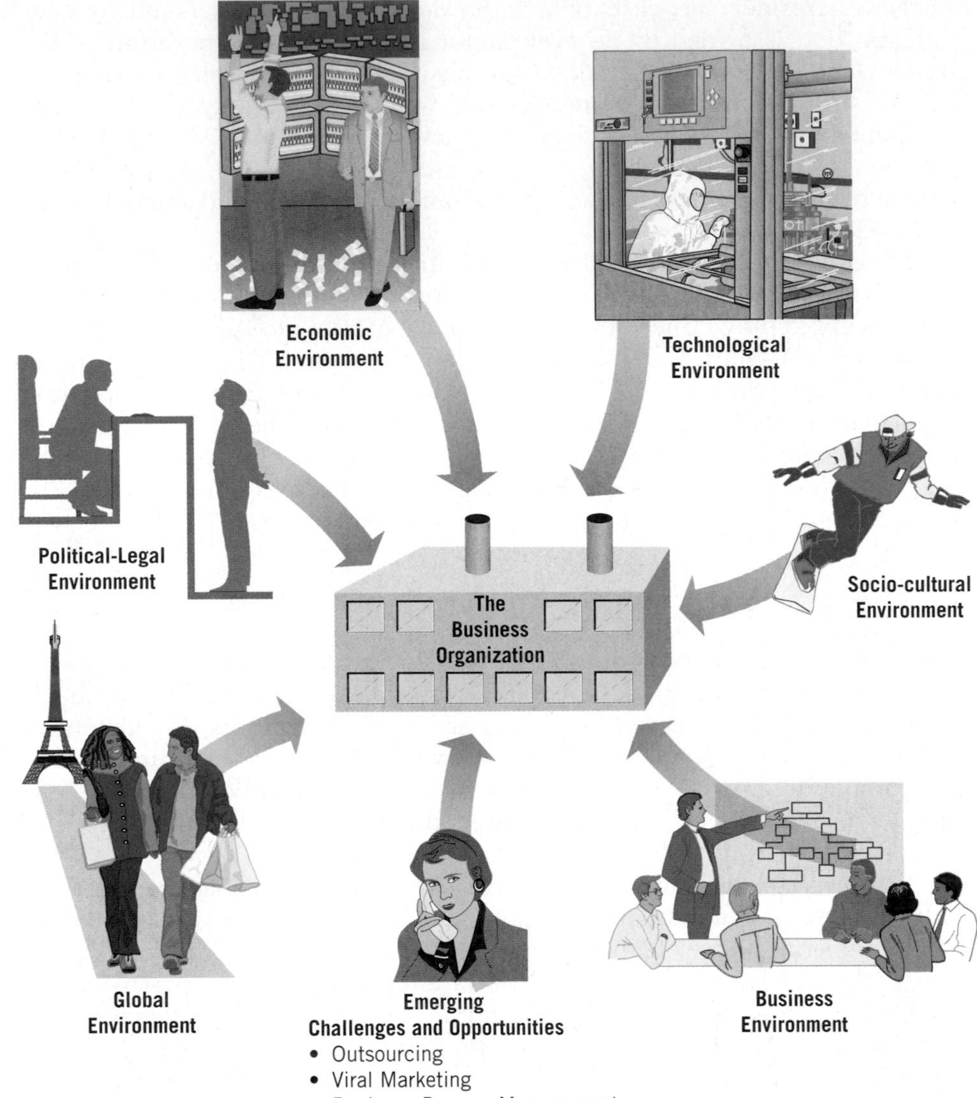

Figure 2.1 Dimensions of the external environment.

Economic Growth

At one time, about half the population of Canada was involved in producing food. Today, less than 2.5 percent of the population works in agriculture. Agricultural efficiency has improved because we devised better ways of producing products and invented better technology for getting the job done. We can therefore say that agricultural production has grown because we have been able to increase total output in the agricultural sector.

The Business Cycle

business cycle Pattern of short-term ups and downs (expansions and contractions) in an economy.

recession Period during which aggregate output, as measured by real GDP, declines.

depression Particularly severe and long-lasting recession.

We can apply the same concepts to a nation's economic system, but the computations are much more complex. A fundamental question, then, is how we know whether or not an economic system is growing. Experts call the pattern of short-term ups and downs in an economy the **business cycle**. It has four recognizable phases: peak, recession, trough, and recovery (see Figure 2.2). A **recession** is a period during which aggregate output declines. If a recession lasts for a prolonged period, it is called a **depression**. Periods

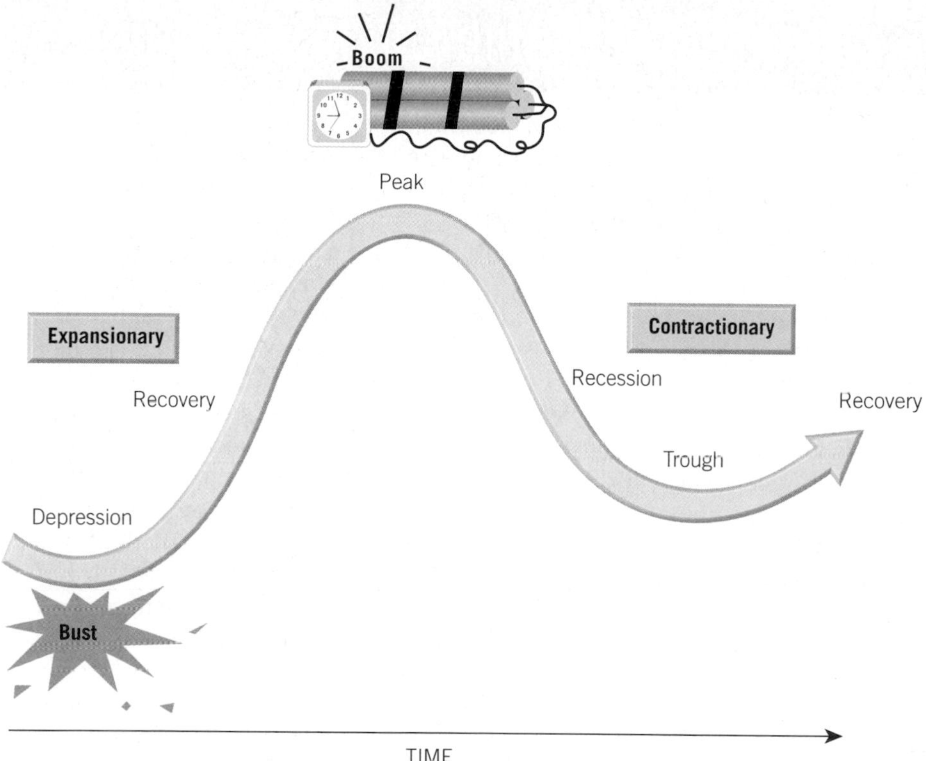

Figure 2.2 The business cycle.

of expansion and contraction can vary from several months to several years. During the latter half of the 1990s, the Canadian economy was continuously expanding, leading some people to believe that the business cycle was a thing of the past. This belief was particularly evident among people who invested in high-tech stocks. They learned a hard lesson when tech stocks crashed in 2000.

Aggregate Output and the Standard of Living

The main measure of growth in the business cycle is **aggregate output**: the total quantity of goods and services produced by an economic system during a given period.[2] To put it simply, an increase in aggregate output is growth (or economic growth).[3] When output grows more quickly than the population, two things usually follow: Output per capita—the quantity of goods and services per person—goes up and the system provides relatively more of the goods and services that people want.[4] And when these two things occur, people living in an economic system benefit from a higher **standard of living**, which refers to the total quantity and quality of goods and services that they can purchase with the currency used in their economic system.

aggregate output Total quantity of goods and services produced by an economic system during a given period.

standard of living Total quantity and quality of goods and services that a country's citizens can purchase with the currency used in their economic system.

Among other things, then, growth makes possible higher standards of living. Thus, to know how much your standard of living is improving, you need to know how much your nation's economic system is growing.

Gross Domestic Product

The term **gross domestic product (GDP)** refers to the total value of all goods and services produced within a given period by a national economy through domestic factors of production. If GDP is going up, the nation is experiencing economic growth. Canada's GDP in 2005 was $1.3 trillion.[5]

gross domestic product (GDP) Total value of all goods and services produced within a given period by a national economy through domestic factors of production.

ENTREPRENEURSHIP AND NEW VENTURES

Want a MacBrioche with That MacEspresso?

McDonald's has become an international icon of the fast-food industry. With 30 000 restaurants in 121 countries, the Golden Arches have become as recognizable to foreign consumers as the shape of a Coca-Cola bottle. Yet in recent years, McDonald's seems to have lost its competitive edge both at home and abroad. In the United States, for example, the company's menu is seen as unhealthy, its stores are outdated, and its customer service skills seem to be slipping. McDonald's no longer leads in technology, with rivals inventing new processing and cooking technologies. The firm's traditional markets, children and young men, are spending less on food while markets McDonald's doesn't target, notably women and older consumers, spend more. Profits have dropped and Starbucks has replaced McDonald's as the food industry success story.

To grow, McDonald's has had to expand aggressively into foreign markets, especially in Europe and Asia. However, consumers in many of those countries do not always like McDonald's "Americanized" look and products. So the burger maker has had to cater to local tastes. That means serving brioche and espresso in France, salmon sandwiches in Scandinavia, and beer in Germany. A Premiere line features more expensive and upscale offerings, such as chicken served on focaccia bread with salsa.

McDonald's is also customizing the look of its stores. In France, the "Mountain" has ski-chalet décor—hardwood floors, televisions, and armchairs. The "Music" features 1950s-style booths with their own CD players. Managers hope that the customers attracted to the more upscale restaurants may also be willing to pay more for premium food. Charlie Bell, McDonald's European president, claims, "Our future business will be selling more than burgers and fries."

So far the new appearance and menu are paying off. U.S. sales continue their downward trend, but French sales increased after the makeover. Ken Clement, a franchisee and former McDonald's vice president, claims the changes are not necessary in the United States. "People are not coming to swoon over the décor," he says. "They are coming in and getting out of here. They don't give a rip what is inside." However, if the French market continues to improve, the innovations may make it to the States, where the risk and the return could be great. The change could alienate McDonald's traditional customers, or it could revitalize the firm and spark a renaissance for the entire fast-food industry.

gross national product (GNP) Total value of all goods and services produced by a national economy within a given period regardless of where the factors of production are located.

Sometimes, economists also use the term **gross national product (GNP)**, which refers to the total value of all goods and services produced by a national economy within a given period regardless of where the factors of production are located. Thus, the profits earned by a Canadian company abroad are included in GNP, but not in GDP. Conversely, profits earned by foreign firms in Canada are included in GDP. Consider the example of a Canadian-owned manufacturing plant in Brazil. The profits earned by the factory are included in Canadian GNP—but not in GDP—because its output is not produced domestically (that is, in Canada). Conversely, those profits are included in Brazil's GDP—but not GNP—because they are produced domestically (that is, in Brazil). Calculations like these quickly become complex because of different factors of production. The labour, for example, will be mostly Brazilian but the capital mostly Canadian. Thus, wages paid to Brazilian workers are part of Brazil's GNP even though profits are not.

GDP and GNP are useful measures of economic growth because they allow us to track an economy's performance over time. An organization called Redefining Progress has proposed a more realistic measure to assess economic activity—the Genuine Progress Indicator (GPI). GPI treats activities that harm the environment or our quality of life as costs and gives them negative values. For example, the Exxon Valdez oil spill in 1986 increased GDP because the activities required to clean up the mess were included in traditional measurements of economic growth. But the oil spill was not a good thing. The new GPI measure shows that while GDP has been increasing for many years, GPI has been falling since the 1970s.[6]

Real Growth Rates. GDP and GNP usually differ slightly, but GDP is the preferred method of calculating national income and output. The *real growth rate of GDP*—the growth rate of GDP *adjusted for inflation and changes in the value of the country's currency*—is what counts. Remember that *growth depends on output increasing at a faster rate than population*. If the growth rate of GDP exceeds the rate of population growth, then our standard of living should be improving.

GDP per Capita. *GDP per capita* means GDP per person. We get this figure by dividing total GDP by the total population of a country. As a measure of economic well-being of the average person, GDP per capita is a better measure than GDP. The United States has the highest GDP per capita of any country ($33 123), followed by Ireland ($30 910), Switzerland ($28 684), and Canada ($28 344).[7]

Real GDP. "Real GDP" means that GDP has been adjusted. To understand why adjustments are necessary, assume that pizza is the only product in an economy. Assume that in 2005, a pizza cost $10, and in 2006 it cost $11. In both years, exactly 1000 pizzas were produced. In 2005, the GDP was $10 000 ($10 × 1000); in 2006, the GDP was $11 000 ($11 × 1000). Has the economy grown? No. Since 1000 pizzas were produced in both years, aggregate output remained the same. The point is that we should not be misled into believing that an economy is doing better than it is. If it is not adjusted, GDP for 2006 is **nominal GDP**, that is, GDP measured in current dollars or with all components valued at current prices.[8]

nominal GDP GDP measured in current dollars or with all components valued at current prices.

Purchasing Power Parity. In our example, current prices would be 2006 prices. On the other hand, we calculate **real GDP** when we calculate GDP to account for *changes in currency values and price changes*. When we make this adjustment, we account for both GDP and **purchasing power parity**—the principle that exchange rates are set so that the prices of similar products in different countries are about the same. Purchasing power parity gives us a much better idea of *what people can actually buy with the financial resources allocated to them by their respective economic systems*. In other words, it gives us a better sense of standards of living around the world.

real GDP GDP calculated to account for changes in currency values and price changes.

purchasing power parity Principle that exchange rates are set so that the prices of similar products in different countries are about the same.

Productivity

A major factor in the growth of an economic system is **productivity**, which is a measure of economic growth that compares how much a system produces with the resources needed to produce it. Let's say, for instance, that it takes 1 Canadian worker and 1 Canadian dollar to make 10 soccer balls in an 8-hour workday. Let's also say that it takes 1.2 Saudi workers and the equivalent of $1.2 (in riyals, the currency of Saudi Arabia) to make 10 soccer balls in the same 8-hour workday. We can say, then, that the Canadian soccer-ball industry is more *productive* than the Saudi soccer-ball industry. The two factors of production in this extremely simple case are labour and capital.

productivity Measure of economic growth that compares how much a system produces with the resources needed to produce it.

Now let's look at productivity from a different perspective. If more products are being produced with fewer factors of production, what happens to the prices of these products? They go down. As a consumer, therefore, you would need less of your currency to purchase the same quantity

Extremely high productivity levels can be attained using automated equipment such as that in this soft drink bottling operation. Productivity is high because relatively few workers are able to produce large quantities of the product.

of these products. In short, your standard of living—at least with regard to these products—has improved. If your entire economic system increases its productivity, then your overall standard of living improves. In fact, *standard of living improves only through increases in productivity*.[9] Real growth in GDP reflects growth in productivity. We examine productivity in more detail in Chapter 12.

There are several factors that can help or hinder the growth of an economic system, but we'll focus on just two of them: *balance of trade* and the *national debt*.

balance of trade The total of a country's exports (sales to other countries) minus its imports (purchases from other countries).

Balance of Trade. The **balance of trade** is the economic value of all the products that a country *exports* minus the economic value of its *imported* products. The principle here is quite simple:

- A *positive* balance of trade results when a country exports (sells to other countries) more than it imports (buys from other countries). A positive balance of trade helps economic growth.
- A *negative* balance of trade results when a country imports more than it exports. A negative balance of trade inhibits economic growth.

A negative balance of trade is commonly called a *trade deficit*. Canada usually has a positive balance of trade. It is therefore a *creditor nation* rather than a *debtor nation*. In 2005, for example, Canada received $66.6 billion more for exports than it spent on imports.[10] By contrast, the United States usually has a negative balance of trade. In 2005, for example, it spent $725 billion more on imports than it received for exports.[11] It is therefore a debtor nation rather than a creditor nation. A trade deficit negatively affects economic growth because the money that flows out of a country can't be used to invest in productive enterprises, either at home or overseas.

national debt The total amount of money that the government owes its creditors.

National Debt. A country's **national debt** is the amount of money that the government owes its creditors. Like a business, the government takes in revenues (primarily in the form of taxes) and has expenses (military spending, social programs, and so forth). For many years, the government of Canada incurred annual **budget deficits**; that is, the government spent more money each year than it took in. These accumulated annual deficits have created a huge national debt—the amount of money that Canada owes its creditors.

budget deficit The result of the government spending more in one year than it takes in during that year.

Until the mid-1990s annual budget deficits and the total national debt were increasing at an alarming rate. From Confederation (1867) to 1981, the *total* accumulated debt was only $85.7 billion, but in the period 1981–94, *annual deficits* were in the $20- to $40-billion range. Since 1994, however, things have changed dramatically. Annual deficits declined rapidly between 1994 and 1996, and in 1997 the first budget surplus in many years occurred. Now, Canada is the only highly industrialized country in the world that continues to have a budget surplus. In 2005, government revenues were $234.9 billion and expenditures were $219.8 billion.[12]

How does the national debt affect economic growth? While taxes are the most obvious way the government raises money, it also sells *bonds*—securities through which it promises to pay buyers certain amounts of money by specified future dates. The government sells bonds to individuals, households, banks, insurance companies, industrial corporations, non-profit organizations, and government agencies, both at home and overseas.[13] These bonds are attractive investments because they are extremely safe: The Canadian government is not going to *default* on them (that is, fail to make payments when due). Even so, they must also offer a decent return on the buyer's investment, and they do this by paying interest at a competitive rate. By selling bonds, therefore, the Canadian government competes with every other potential borrower—individuals, households, businesses, and other organizations—for the available supply of loanable money. The more money the government borrows, the less money is available for the private borrowing and investment that increases productivity.

Economic Stability

We have now learned a great deal about a market economy and the way it allocates resources among its citizens. We know that households, for example, receive capital in return for labour. We know that when households enter consumer markets to purchase goods and services, their decisions (and those of the firms trying to sell them goods and services) are influenced by the laws of demand and supply. We know that the laws of demand and supply result in equilibrium prices when the quantity of goods demanded and the quantity of goods supplied are equal. We know that households enjoy higher standards of living when there is balanced growth in the quantity of goods demanded and the quantity of goods supplied. We know that we can measure growth and productivity in terms of gross domestic product and standard of living in terms of the purchasing power parity of a system's currency: Living standards are stable when purchasing power parity remains stable.[14]

We may thus conclude that a chief goal of an economic system is **stability**: a condition in which the amount of money available in an economic system and the quantity of goods and services produced in it are growing at about the same rate. Now we can focus on certain factors that threaten stability—namely, *inflation, deflation*, and *unemployment*.

stability Condition in an economic system in which the amount of money available and the quantity of goods and services produced are growing at about the same rate.

Inflation

Inflation occurs when there are widespread price increases throughout an economic system. How does it threaten stability? Inflation occurs when the amount of money injected into an economy outstrips the increase in actual output. When this happens, people will have more money to spend, but there will still be the same quantity of products available for them to buy.

inflation Occurrence of widespread price increases throughout an economic system.

As they compete with one another to buy available products, prices go up. Before long, high prices will erase the increase in the amount of money injected into the economy. Purchasing power, therefore, declines.

Obviously, then, inflation can also hurt you as a consumer because your primary concern when deciding whether to purchase a product is often price. In other words, you will probably decide to make a purchase if the value of the product justifies the price that you'll have to pay. Now look at Table 2.1, which reduces a hypothetical purchase decision to three bare essentials:

1. Your household income over a three-year period
2. The price of a hamburger over a three-year period
3. The rates of increase for both over a three-year period

In which year did the cost of a hamburger go up? At first glance, you might say in both YR2 and YR3 (to $4 in YR2 and to $7.50 in YR3). In YR2, your income kept pace: Although a hamburger cost twice as much, you had twice as much money to spend. In effect, the price to you was actually the same. In YR3, however, your income increased by 250 percent while the price of a hamburger increased by 275 percent. In YR3, therefore, you got hit by inflation (how hard, of course, depends on your fondness for hamburgers). This ratio—the comparison of your increased income to the increased price of a hamburger—is all that counts if you want to consider inflation when you're making a buying decision. Inflation, therefore, can be harmful to you as a consumer because *inflation decreases the purchasing power of your money*.

consumer price index (CPI) Measure of the prices of typical products purchased by consumers living in urban areas.

Measuring Inflation: The CPI. Remember that inflation means widespread price increases throughout an economic system. It stands to reason, therefore, that we can measure inflation by measuring price increases. To do this, we can turn to such price indexes as the **consumer price index (CPI)**, which measures changes in the cost of a "basket" of 600 different goods and services that a typical family might buy. What is included in the basket has changed dramatically over the years as new products and services have become available and old ones fall out of favour. For example, the first CPI in 1913 included items like coal, spirit vinegar, and fruit, while in 2005 the index included DVD home theatre systems, MP3 portable players, and plasma televisions.[15] These changes in the CPI reflect changes that have occurred in the pattern of consumer purchases. For example, in 1961, about 53 percent of consumer spending went to necessities like food, housing, and clothing. By 2000, only 40 percent of consumer spending went to necessities.[16] Figure 2.3 shows how inflation has varied over the last 20 years in Canada.

Table 2.1 When Did the Cost of a Hamburger Go Up?

YR1 Income	YR2 Income	YR2 % Increase Over YR1 Base	YR3 Income	YR3 % Increase Over YR1 Base
$5000	$10 000	100	$17 500	250
YR1 Hamburger Price	**YR2 Hamburger Price**	**YR2 % Increase Over YR1 Base**	**YR3 Hamburger Price**	**YR3 % Increase Over YR1 Base**
$2	$4	100	$7.50	275

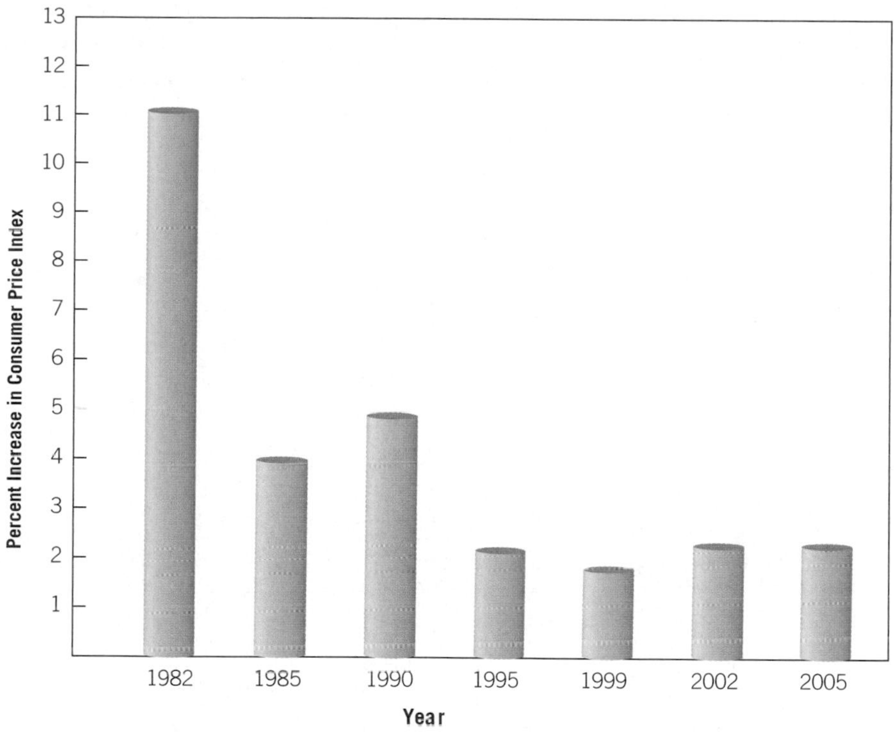

Figure 2.3 During the past decade, the rate of price increases in Canada has been low and quite stable.

Deflation

When **deflation** (generally falling prices) occurs, the Bank of Canada reduces interest rates in an attempt to increase consumer demand. Prices may fall because industrial productivity is increasing and cost savings can be passed on to consumers (this is good), or because consumers have high levels of debt and are therefore unwilling to buy very much (this is bad).

deflation A period of generally falling prices.

Unemployment

Unemployment is the level of joblessness among people actively seeking work. There are various types of unemployment: *frictional unemployment* (people are out of work temporarily while looking for a new job); *seasonal*

unemployment Level of joblessness among people actively seeking work in an economic system.

During the depression of the 1930s, unemployment was very high, with nearly one-quarter of the population unable to find work. Lines of unemployed workers outside soup kitchens were an unfortunate reality during those difficult economic times.

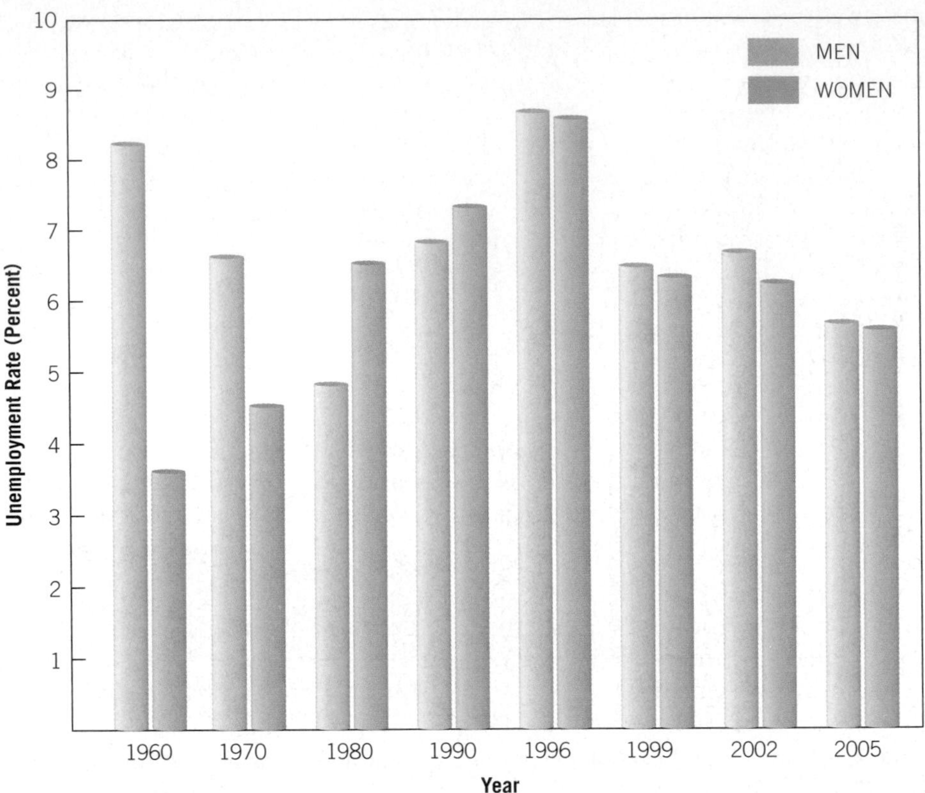

Figure 2.4 Historical unemployment rate.
During the period 1970–96, there was a steady upward trend in unemployment rates, but the rate began to decline in the late 1990s.

unemployment (people are out of work because of the seasonal nature of their jobs); *cyclical unemployment* (people are out of work because of a downturn in the business cycle); and *structural unemployment* (people are unemployed because they lack the skills needed to perform available jobs). Unemployment rates have varied greatly over the years, as Figure 2.4 shows, with the rates for men generally being higher than the rates for women.

When unemployment is low, there is a shortage of labour available for businesses. As these businesses compete with one another for the available supply of labour, they raise the wages that they are willing to pay. Then, because higher labour costs eat into profit margins, businesses raise the prices of their products. Thus, although consumers have more money to inject into the economy, this increase is soon erased by higher prices. Purchasing power declines.

If wage rates get too high, businesses will respond by hiring fewer workers and unemployment will go up. But if that happens, demand may decline because unemployed workers don't purchase as much. Because of reduced sales, companies may further cut back on hiring and unemployment will go even higher. What if the government tries to correct this situation by injecting more money into the economic system—say, by cutting taxes or spending more money? Prices in general may go up because of increased consumer demand, but then inflation sets in, and purchasing power declines.[17]

Managing the Canadian Economy

fiscal policies Policies by means of which governments collect and spend revenues.

The government acts to manage the Canadian economic system through two sets of policies: fiscal and monetary. It manages the collection and spending of its revenues through **fiscal policies**. Tax increases can function as fiscal policies, not only to increase revenues but to manage the economy as well. When there is evidence that the growth rate of the economy is decreasing, tax cuts will normally stimulate renewed economic growth. When the government of Canada cuts taxes that people have to pay, government action is being taken to bring stability to the economic system.

Monetary policies focus on controlling the size of the nation's money supply. Working primarily through the Bank of Canada (the nation's central bank), the government can influence the ability and willingness of banks throughout the country to lend money. It can also influence the supply of money by prompting interest rates to go up or down. The power of the Bank of Canada to make changes in the supply of money is the centrepiece of the Canadian government's monetary policy. The principle is fairly simple:

monetary policies Policies by means of which the government controls the size of the nation's money supply.

- Higher interest rates make money more expensive to borrow and thereby reduce spending by both those who produce goods and services and by those who buy those goods and services. When the Bank of Canada restricts the money supply, we say that it is practising a *tight monetary policy*.
- Lower interest rates make money less expensive to borrow and thereby increase spending by both those who produce goods and services and by the consumers who buy those goods and services. When the Bank of Canada loosens the money supply—and thus stimulates the economy—we say that it is practising an *easy monetary policy*.

In both Canada and the United States, the interest rate was cut several times in late 2001 to help the economy recover from the terrorist attacks in the United States on September 11. But in Canada, we experienced a recovery during 2002, so the Bank of Canada had actually been raising interest rates to head off the possibility of inflation. By mid-2003, however, the Bank of Canada decided to hold interest rates steady to protect the economic recovery. But by 2006, interest rates were again on the rise, and the economy was very strong.

In short, the Bank of Canada can influence the aggregate market for products by influencing the supply of money. Taken together, fiscal policy and monetary policy make up **stabilization policy**: government economic policy whose goal is to smooth out fluctuations in output and unemployment and to stabilize prices.

stabilization policy Government policy, embracing both fiscal and monetary policies, whose goal is to smooth out fluctuations in output and unemployment and to stabilize prices.

THE TECHNOLOGICAL ENVIRONMENT

Technology has a variety of meanings, but as applied to the environment of business, it generally includes all the ways firms create value for their constituents. Technology includes human knowledge, work methods, physical equipment, electronics and telecommunications, and various processing systems that are used to perform business activities. Although technology is applied within the organization, the forms and availability of that technology come from the general environment.

technology All the ways firms create value for their constituents.

Describe the *technological environment* and its role in business. 3

Research and Development (R&D)

Technological improvements and innovation in general are important contributors to the economic development of a country. The innovation process includes **research and development (R&D)**, which provides new ideas for products, services, and processes. (See Chapter 16 for a discussion of the importance of R&D in the marketing of products.) There are two types of

research and development (R&D) Those activities that are necessary to provide new products, services, and processes.

basic (or pure) R&D Improving knowledge in an area without a primary focus on whether any discoveries that might occur are immediately marketable.

applied R&D Focussing specifically on how a technological innovation can be put to use in the making of a product or service that can be sold in the marketplace.

R&D. **Basic (or pure) R&D** involves improving knowledge in an area without a primary focus on whether any discoveries that might occur are immediately marketable. For example, chemists in a laboratory might examine how certain chemical compounds behave. The knowledge gained from this activity might or might not result in a marketable product. **Applied R&D**, on the other hand, means focussing specifically on how a technological innovation can be put to use in the making of a product or service that can be sold in the marketplace.

R&D spending in Canada in 2005 totalled about $13.8 billion.[18] The Canadian private sector accounts for about 54 percent of R&D, the government 9 percent, and universities 35 percent.[19] In the private sector, a large proportion of R&D is carried out by just a few large firms, and just 0.8 percent of firms accounted for 56 percent of the R&D performed.[20] A large proportion of R&D personnel in Canada are concentrated in industries like computer system design, information, communications equipment, and scientific research.[21] Quebec and Ontario accounted for 84 percent of all R&D activities in Canada.[22]

As a proportion of GDP, Canada's level of R&D lags behind that of other countries (see Figure 2.5). This lag exists partly because many Canadian businesses are subsidiaries of large U.S. companies that carry out their R&D in the United States. When we take into account that the GDP of countries like Japan, the United States, and Germany is much larger than the GDP of Canada, it means that R&D spending in Canada (in terms of absolute dollars) is a tiny fraction of what is spent in other countries.

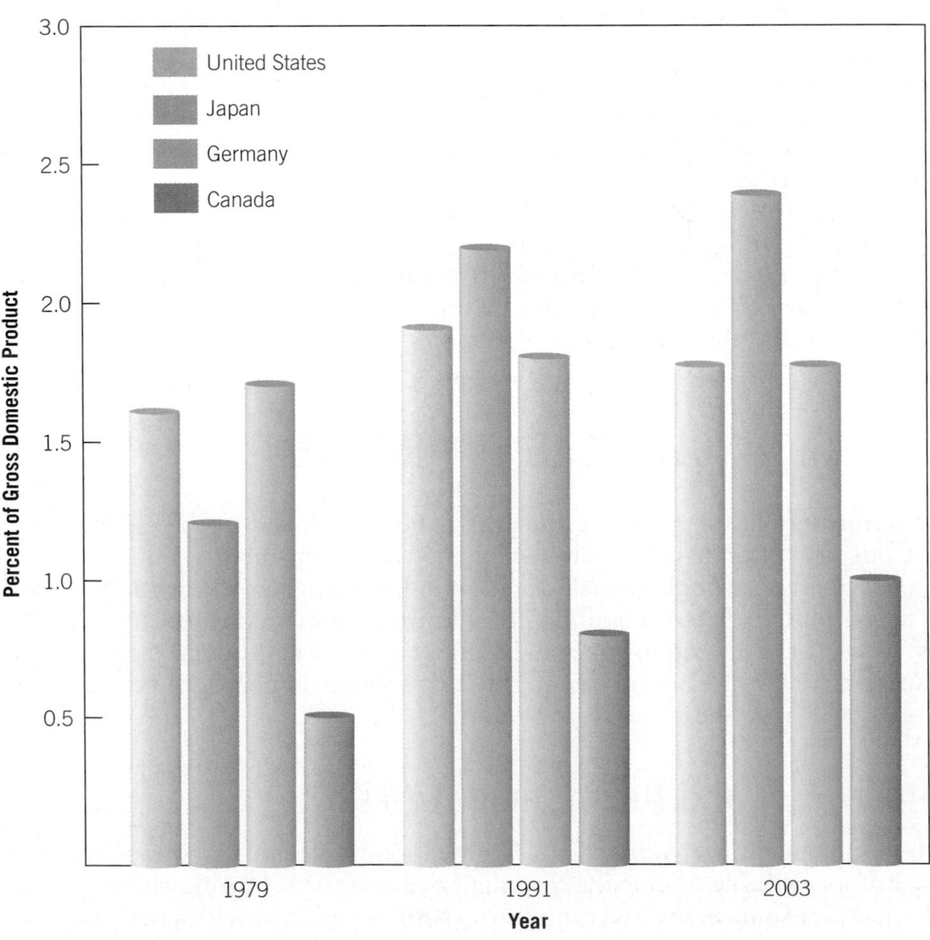

Figure 2.5 R&D expenditures as a proportion of GDP.

Product and Service Technologies

Product and service technologies are the technologies employed for creating products—both physical goods and services—for customers. Although many people associate technology with manufacturing, it is also a significant force in the service sector. Just as an automobile is built as it follows a predetermined pathway along an assembly line, a hamburger at McDonald's is cooked, assembled, and wrapped and bagged as it moves along a predefined path. The rapid advancement of the internet into all areas of business is also a reflection of the technological environment. Indeed, new technologies continue to revolutionize nearly every aspect of business, ranging from the ways that customers and companies interact to where, when, and how employees perform their work.

Companies must constantly be on the lookout for technological breakthroughs that might make their products or services obsolete and thereby threaten their survival. Many of these breakthroughs do not come from direct competitors or even from the industry the company is part of. Microsoft, for example, originally didn't pay much attention to internet technology because it was busy competing with companies like WordPerfect in the word processing and operating software market. When Netscape entered the market with a browser program that threatened to make operating systems unnecessary, Microsoft had to spend a lot of time and money developing its own Internet Explorer browser.[23]

Companies must decide how much emphasis they are going to place on R&D as a competitive tool. **R&D intensity** refers to R&D spending as a percentage of the company's sales revenue. Research has shown that companies with a high R&D intensity are better able to gain market share in global markets.[24] If a company has a strategy to be the technological leader in its industry, it will likely have a high R&D intensity. Alternatively, if its strategy is to be a technology follower, it will likely have a much lower R&D intensity. Being a technological leader is riskier, but can yield very large profits if technological innovations are developed and marketed effectively. Being a technological follower is less risky, but presents fewer opportunities for large profits because very few technological innovations will be evident.

R&D intensity R&D spending as a percentage of a company's sales revenue.

Technology is the basis of competition for some firms, especially when the company's goal is to be the technology leader in their industry. A company, for example, might focus its efforts on being the low-cost producer or always having the most technologically advanced products on the market. But because of the rapid pace of new developments, keeping a leadership position based on technology is increasingly difficult. Another challenge is meeting constant demands to decrease *cycle time*—the time that it takes a firm to accomplish some recurring activity or function from beginning to end. **Technology transfer** refers to the process of getting a new technology out of the lab and into the marketplace where it can generate profits for the company. Efficient technology transfer means an increased likelihood of business success.

technology transfer The process of getting a new technology out of the lab and into the marketplace.

Businesses are more competitive if they can systematically decrease cycle times. Many companies, therefore, now focus on decreasing cycle times in areas ranging from developing products to making deliveries and collecting credit payments. Twenty years ago, it took an automaker about five years from the decision to launch a new product until it was available in dealer showrooms. Now most companies can complete the cycle in less than two years. The speedier process allows them to respond more quickly to changing economic conditions, consumer preferences, and new competitive products while recouping their product-development costs more quickly.

Some firms compete directly on how quickly they can get things done for consumers. In the early days of personal computers, for instance, getting a made-to-order system took six to eight weeks. Today, firms like Dell can usually ship exactly what the customer wants in a matter of days.

Intel exemplifies the challenge and the risks of adopting a strategic dependence on technological leadership. In 1964, before co-founding Intel with Bob Noyce in 1968, Gordon Moore made a prediction about transistors on integrated circuits (the processing components of microcomputers) that eventually became known as Moore's Law: He said that the amount of information stored on a given amount of silicon would double every two years. In effect, this rate would entail a twofold increase in processing power every 24 months—a seemingly impossible pace. Intel, however, has adopted Moore's Law as a performance requirement for each new generation of processor since 1970, up through the Itanium 2.

Intel spent $7.5 billion in 2001 for research and development, and is aggressively searching for ways to cram twice as many transistors into a space that already holds millions. Such a task will require a revolution in technology that, as yet, Intel hasn't found. Without a technological breakthrough, Moore's Law—and Intel's technological leadership position—may not be sustainable. The financial stakes, of course, are high. If Intel can't meet industry-wide goals, it faces threats from new competitors, such as Advanced Micro Devices (AMD), whose microprocessor market share recently grew from 13 percent to 18 percent in just one year.

Process Technologies

Process technologies are used to improve a firm's performance of its internal operations (such as accounting, managing information flows, creating activity reports, and so forth). They also help create better relationships with external constituents, such as suppliers and customers. One recent process technology innovation that is worthy of special mention is **enterprise resource planning (ERP)**, a large-scale information system for organizing and managing a firm's processes across product lines, departments, and geographic locations. Company-wide processes—such as materials management, production planning, order management, and financial reporting—can all be managed by ERP. Figure 2.6 shows some of the areas

enterprise resource planning (ERP) Large-scale information system for organizing and managing a firm's processes across product lines, departments, and geographic locations.

On the surface, low-fat corn and salmon that grow twice as fast would seem to be a good way of improving the food supply. But not everybody is happy about such developments in the modern technological environment. Environmentalists are afraid that genetically modified crops (which they call "Frankenfoods") will sneak into natural populations, outbreed wild species, and threaten biodiversity. Or else they'll cross-pollinate and engineer species that are downright dangerous for human consumption.

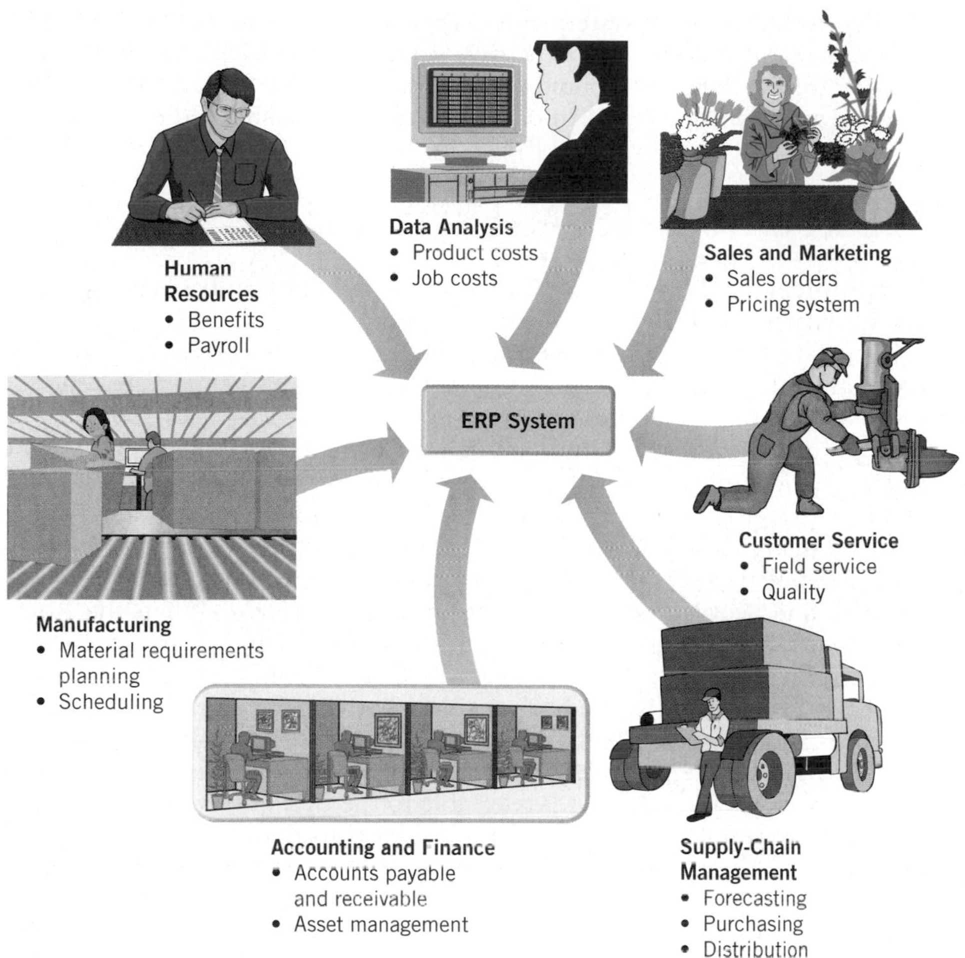

Figure 2.6 ERP applications.

in which ERP can be applied, including some of the common processes performed in each area.[25]

In developing the ERP system, the firm starts by identifying the processes that need critical attention, such as supplier relationships, materials flows, or customer order fulfillment. The resulting system would thus integrate the sales process with production planning and then both of these operations into the financial accounting system. Let's say that a customer in Rome orders a product to be manufactured in Ireland. The ERP-integrated seller can schedule the order shipment via air cargo to Rome, where it can be picked up by a truck at the airport and delivered to the customer's warehouse by a specified date. All of these activities are synchronized in one massive database.

The ERP also stores updated real-time information on activities, reports recent and upcoming transactions, and posts electronic notices that certain action is required if certain schedules are to be met. It coordinates internal operations with activities by outside suppliers and notifies customers of current order status and upcoming deliveries and billings. It can integrate financial flows among the firm, its suppliers, customers, and banks and generate up-to-the-minute financial reports at a moment's notice (reduced from the traditional one-month time span).

One Canadian company that uses ERP is Crestline Coach Ltd., a relatively small company in Saskatoon that builds customized emergency vehicles and replacement parts. When problems developed with Crestline's old software—for example, customers had to wait days for parts—management decided to buy an ERP system called Business One from SAP Canada Inc. This was a scaled-down, less expensive version of the ERP systems that are usually sold to large companies. With the new ERP system, if Crestline receives an order for a replacement part it can usually ship it the same day.[26]

THE POLITICAL-LEGAL ENVIRONMENT

political-legal environment Conditions reflecting the relationship between business and government, usually in the form of government regulation.

4 Describe the *political-legal environment* and its role in business.

The **political-legal environment** reflects the relationship between business and government, usually in the form of government regulation of business. It is important for several reasons. First, the legal system defines in part what an organization can and can't do. Although Canada is a free market economy, it still has major regulation of business activity, as we saw in Chapter 1.

Pro- or anti-business sentiment can further influence business activity. During periods of pro-business sentiment, firms find it easier to compete and have fewer concerns about antitrust issues. On the other hand, during a period of anti-business sentiment, firms may find their competitive activities more restricted. There may, for example, be fewer opportunities for mergers and acquisitions because of antitrust concerns. When the Royal Bank wanted to merge with the Bank of Montreal, the Canadian government blocked the merger on the grounds that it would reduce competition and harm consumers. Nestlé has considered buying Hershey for some time, but the Swiss-owned company worries that the acquisition would be blocked because the two firms, if combined, would dominate the U.S. confectionery market at a level unacceptable to the U.S. government.

Political stability is also an important consideration, especially for international firms. No business wants to set up shop in another country unless trade relationships with that country are relatively well defined and stable. Thus, Canadian firms are more likely to do business with England, Mexico, and the United States than with Haiti and Afghanistan. Similar issues also pertain to assessments of local and provincial governments. A new mayor or provincial leader can affect many organizations, especially small firms that do business in a single location and are thus susceptible to zoning restrictions, property and school taxes, and the like.

Relations between sovereign governments can also affect business activity. When Canada refused to send troops to support the U.S.-led invasion of Iraq, relations between the United States and Canada were very cool for a time. A survey revealed that nearly half the Americans polled said they would consider switching away from Canadian goods in favour of goods from other countries because of Canada's lack of support of the war. This would obviously have a negative effect on Canadian exports if U.S. consumers acted on these opinions.[27]

THE SOCIO-CULTURAL ENVIRONMENT

socio-cultural environment Conditions including the customs, values, attitudes, and demographic characteristics of the society in which an organization functions.

The **socio-cultural environment** includes the customs, values, attitudes, and demographic characteristics of the society in which an organization functions. Socio-cultural processes determine the goods and services as well as the standards of business conduct that a society is likely to value and accept.

5 Describe the *socio-cultural environment* and its role in business.

Customer Preferences and Tastes

Customer preferences and tastes vary both across and within national boundaries. In some countries, consumers are willing and able to pay premium prices for designer clothes with labels such as Armani or Calvin

Klein. But the same clothes have virtually no market in other countries. Product usage also varies between nations. In China, bicycles are primarily seen as a mode of transportation, but in Canada, they are marketed primarily for recreational purposes.

Similarly, consumer preferences can also vary widely within the same country. Customs and product preferences in Quebec, for example, differ from those in other parts of Canada. In the United States, pre-packaged chili is more popular in the southwest states than in the northeast. McDonald's is just one company that is affected by socio-cultural factors. In response to concerns about nutrition and health, McDonald's has added salads to its menus and experimented with other low-fat foods. It was the first fast-food chain to provide customers with information about the ingredients in its products, and it attracted media attention when it announced that it would reduce the fat content in its popular french fries.

Consumer preferences and tastes also change over time. Preferences for colour, style, and so forth change from season to season. In some years, brightly coloured clothes sell best, while in other years people want more subdued colours. Some of these changes are driven by consumers, and some are driven by companies trying to convince consumers to adopt new styles. Soft drinks usually sell better during the hot summer months than in the cold winter months. Drinking whiskey, vodka, and gin and smoking cigarettes are less common today than they were just a few years ago. These and many other related issues regarding businesses and their customers are explored more fully in Part 4 of this book, which deals with the marketing of products and services.

Finally, socio-cultural factors influence the way workers in a society feel about their jobs and organizations. In some cultures, work carries meaningful social significance, with certain employers and job titles being highly desired by workers. But in other cultures, because work is simply a means to an end, people are concerned only with pay and job security. McDonald's has occasionally struggled with its operations in the Middle East because many people there are not interested in working in food-service operations.

Ethical Compliance and Responsible Business Behaviour

An especially critical element of the socio-cultural environment is the practice of ethical conduct and social responsibility. We cover these areas in detail in Chapter 3, but a preview of them is justified here. The central issue revolves around the fact that rapid changes in business relationships, organizational structures, and financial flows pose difficulties in keeping accurate track of a company's financial position. The public—current and potential investors—often gets blurred pictures of a firm's competitive health. The stakeholders of business firms—employees, stockholders, consumers, unions, creditors, and government—are entitled to a fair accounting so they can make enlightened personal and business decisions. Keeping up with today's increasingly fast-paced business activities is putting a strain on the accounting profession's traditional methods for auditing, financial reporting, and time-honoured standards for professional ethics.

The Enron scandal in the United States, for example, involved fast-moving financial transactions among layers of subsidiary firms, which were designed to conceal Enron's shaky financial condition. Enron's accounting reports failed completely to reflect the firm's disastrous financial and managerial condition. In a blatant display of social irresponsibility and unethical behaviour, Enron's public reports concealed many of its partnerships (and obligations) with other companies, thus hiding its true operating condition. This activity netted prison terms for several Enron executives.

Arthur Andersen LLP, the accounting firm that audited Enron's finances, did not catch its client's distorted reports. Perhaps Andersen's desire for future high-revenue consulting services with Enron motivated the auditors to turn a blind eye to questionable practices that eventually showed up during audits of Enron's finances. Andersen's unethical and illegal practices—including obstruction of justice for shredding and doctoring documents related to Enron audits—destroyed the public's trust and Arthur Andersen as a company.

These activities were not limited to U.S. companies. In a report released on July 28, 2003, court-appointed examiner Neal Batson charged that the Canadian Imperial Bank of Commerce, one of Enron's lenders, knew that Enron was concealing billions of dollars in debts. The report further charged that CIBC helped Enron executives manipulate their financial statements. In 2004, CIBC agreed to pay $480 million to settle allegations that it facilitated accounting fraud at Enron. The CEO of CIBC admitted that the company had "stumbled" in the area of trust and reputation.[28]

Appropriate standards of business conduct vary across cultures. In Canada, accepting bribes in return for political favours is unethical. In other countries, however, payments to local politicians are expected in return for favourable responses to such common business transactions as zoning and operating permits. The shape of the market, the ethics of political influence, and the attitudes of its workforce are only a few of the many ways in which culture can affect an organization. We examine these issues in more detail in Chapter 6.

THE BUSINESS ENVIRONMENT

6 Identify emerging challenges and opportunities in the *business environment*.

Business today is faster paced, more complex, and more demanding than ever before. The 2005 KPMG/Ipsos-Reid poll of CEOs found that the three most serious issues facing Canadian businesses are (1) taxation, (2) the value of the Canadian dollar, and (3) the need for an educated/skilled workforce.[29] These three issues are all important elements of the business environment.

The business environment is complex. As businesses aggressively try to differentiate themselves, there has been a trend toward higher quality products, planned obsolescence, and product life cycles measured in weeks or months rather than years. This, in turn, has created customer expectations for instant gratification. Ultimately consumers and business customers want high-quality goods and services—often customized—with lower prices and immediate delivery. Sales offices, service providers, and production facilities are shifting geographically as new markets and resources emerge in other countries. Employees want flexible working hours and opportunities to work at home. Stockholder expectations also add pressure for productivity increases, growth in market share, and larger profits. At the same time, however, a more vocal public demands more honesty, fair competition, and respect for the environment.

The Industry Environment

Each business firm operates in a specific industry, and each industry has different characteristics. The intensity of the competition in an industry has a big influence on how a company operates. To be effective, managers must understand the company's competitive situation, and then develop a competitive strategy to exploit opportunities in the industry.

One of the best known examples of an effective competitive strategy is Wal-Mart's satellite-based distribution system (discussed in Chapter 17). WestJet has a unique management system that helps it minimize aircraft turnaround time and thus keep its costs lower than its competitors. Managers try hard to find a competitive strategy for their firm, because doing so will slow down or stop new competitors from entering the industry.

One of the most popular tools to analyze competitive situations in an industry is Michael Porter's five forces model.[30] The model (see Figure 2.7) helps managers analyze five important sources of competitive pressure, and then decide what their competitive strategy should be. We briefly discuss each of the elements of the model in the following paragraphs.

Rivalry Among Existing Competitors

The amount of rivalry between companies varies across industries. Rivalry can be seen in activities like intense price competition, elaborate advertising campaigns, and an increased emphasis on customer service. For many years, the rivalry among Chartered Accountants, Certified General Accountants, and Certified Management Accountants in Canada was low-key, but it has recently become much more intense. These firms are responding by trying to attain more market power, cutting costs, making pricing deals with clients, and trying to find ways to differentiate themselves from their competitors.

Threat of Potential Entrants

When new competitors enter an industry, they may cause big changes. For example, when Microsoft introduced Encarta, it caused the sale of hard-copy encyclopedias by companies like Encyclopaedia Britannica to drop sharply. If it is easy for new competitors to enter a market, competition will likely be intense and the industry will not be very attractive. Some industries (for example, automobile manufacturing) are very capital-intensive and are therefore difficult to enter, but others (for example, home cleaning or lawn care services) are relatively easy to enter.

Suppliers

The amount of bargaining power suppliers have in relation to buyers helps determine how competitive an industry is. When there are only a few

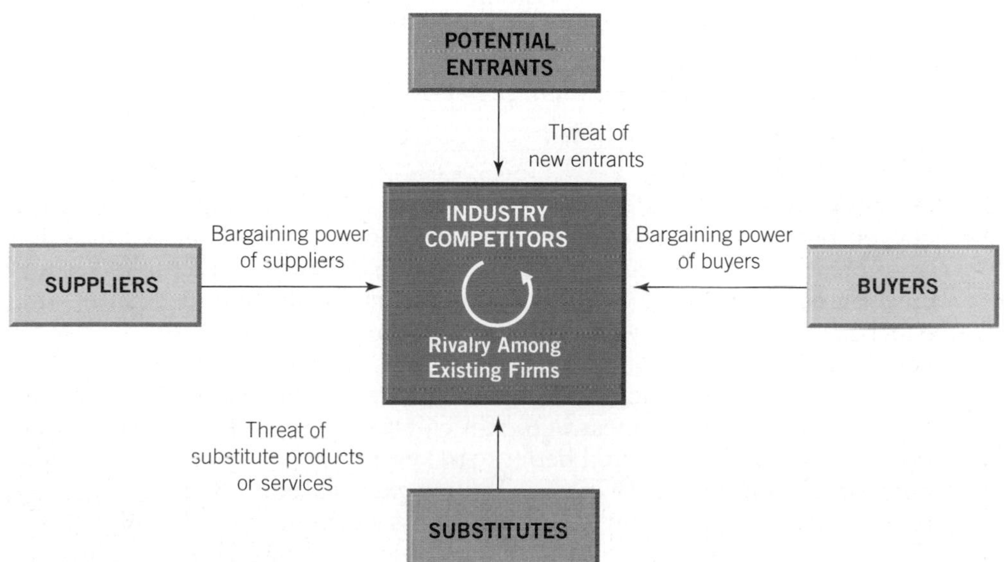

Figure 2.7 Michael Porter's five forces model.

suppliers in an industry, they tend to have great bargaining power. The power of suppliers is influenced by the number of substitute products that are available (i.e., products that perform the same or similar functions). When there are few substitute products, suppliers obviously have more power.

Buyers

When there are only a few buyers and many suppliers, the buyers have a great deal of bargaining power. Retail powerhouse Wal-Mart, for example, is often cited as a buyer that puts tremendous pressure on its suppliers to reduce their prices. Wal-Mart can do this because it buys so much from these suppliers.

Substitutes

If there are many substitute products available, the industry is more competitive. For example, various synthetic fibres can be used as substitutes for cotton.

Managers use Porter's ideas to help them decide the level of competitive intensity in an industry. A good example is the emergence of the internet in the sale of airline tickets. By making it easier for consumers to compare prices, the internet has increased the competitive intensity of the airline industry (and many other industries, for that matter). In the airline industry, the internet increased the bargaining power of ticket buyers.

Emerging Challenges and Opportunities in the Business Environment

core competency Skills and resources with which an organization competes best and creates the most value for owners.

The most successful firms are dealing with challenges and opportunities in today's business environment by focussing on their **core competencies**—the skills and resources with which they compete best and create the most value for owners. They outsource non-core business processes, paying suppliers and distributors to perform them and thereby increasing their reliance on suppliers. These new business models call for unprecedented coordination—not only among internal activities, but also among customers, suppliers, and strategic partners—and they often involve globally dispersed processes and supply chains.

In this section, we'll discuss some of the most publicized steps that companies have taken to respond to challenges and opportunities in the business environment. These developments include *outsourcing, viral marketing,* and *business process management*.

Outsourcing

outsourcing Strategy of paying suppliers and distributors to perform certain business processes or to provide needed materials or services.

Outsourcing is the strategy of paying suppliers and distributors to perform certain business processes or to provide needed materials or services. For example, the cafeteria in a museum may be important to employees and customers, but running it is not the museum's main line of business and expertise. The museum's primary focus is on exhibits that will interest the general public, not on food-service operations. That's why museums usually outsource cafeteria operations to food-service management companies whose main line of business is to run cafeterias. The result is more attention to museum exhibits and better food service for customers. Firms today outsource numerous activities, including payroll, employee training, and research and development. As the Business Accountability box illustrates, concerns about outsourcing have increased as it has become more and more widely used.

BUSINESS ACCOUNTABILITY

Outsourcing: Good or Bad?

Outsourcing is an increasingly popular strategy because it helps firms focus on their core activities and avoid getting sidetracked by secondary activities. The Bank of Montreal (BMO), for example, outsourced its human resource processing services to Exult Inc. Over 100 people who used to work for BMO now work for Exult. They manage payroll and benefits administration, employee records, HR call centre services, and other functions that used to be performed in-house at BMO. The new arrangement will mean a 20 percent reduction in HR costs for BMO. It will also free up BMO managers to concentrate on more "value-added" work.

The Bank of Montreal outsourcing decision involved moving jobs from one company to another within Canada. But a lot of outsourcing involves moving jobs from Canada to a foreign country, and that is why there is so much concern about it. In the short run, it is obvious that Canadian jobs will be lost when outsourcing takes place. But in the longer run, it is possible that outsourcing may be beneficial. How can that be? The reasoning goes something like this: Canadian companies will continue to outsource more manufacturing work to take advantage of low-cost foreign suppliers. This will allow the Canadian companies to reduce their costs and be more effective in highly competitive global markets. This, in turn, will raise Canadian productivity and improve the standard of living in Canada.

The chief economist for the Export Development Corporation (EDC) says that the main reason for the large increases in U.S. productivity between 1998 and 2002 was outsourcing, so Canada may get the same benefit if it outsources increasing amounts of work. On the negative side, it will obviously reduce the number of jobs in Canada, at least in the short run. That, in turn, may reduce demand and cause economic growth to decline. Our balance of trade might also be negatively affected.

In an increasingly global economy, competitive pressures are intense, and these can cause sweeping change in certain industries. In the automobile business, for example, companies like Ford and GM have to compete with highly efficient Japanese companies like Toyota and Honda. Ford and GM must therefore cut costs wherever possible. But they have rather restrictive labour contracts with the United Auto Workers union that prevent them from easily cutting costs in terms of their own employees, so they have hit upon a new strategy: Put pressure on the companies that supply them with auto parts.

The case of Superior Industries International, a California-based company that makes aluminum wheels for Ford and GM, is instructive. Superior got blunt messages from both Ford and General Motors to match the price that Chinese wheel suppliers were charging or they would buy from a company that could match the price. Since 85 percent of Superior's business was with Ford and GM, it had little alternative but to start outsourcing some work to Chinese factories to lower their costs. To do this, Superior got involved in a joint venture with a Chinese company near Shanghai to build aluminum wheels. The operation will start small and increase as years go by. This means that there is no guarantee that North American jobs at Superior will continue in the long run.

Wages in China average about 90 cents per hour compared to $22 per hour in North America. Even after taking into account the large distance between China and North American markets, the cost of Chinese-made radios, cables, brakes, and wheels is still 20 to 40 percent lower than products made in North America. This is causing jobs in the North American auto parts industry to disappear at a rapid rate. What is interesting is that this trend has just started. Since Ford and GM currently buy less than 5 percent of their parts from China, there is room for dramatically increased amounts of outsourcing. The implication for jobs is not positive.

In addition to the loss of *workers'* jobs, there can also be a downside for the *business* as well. At Superior, for example, profit margins have taken a hit as the company has lowered prices to keeps its business with Ford and GM. In earlier years, Superior usually achieved profit margins of 12 percent, but now that has been reduced to 5.5 percent.

There are other problems with outsourcing. A Dun & Bradstreet study found that one-quarter of all outsourcing relationships fail within two years, and one-half within five. In addition, many executives feel that suppliers too often don't understand what they are supposed to do, that they charge too much, and that they provide poor service. Moreover, when disruptions occur in the supply chain, the costs to both parties can be high. For one thing, replacing failed outsourced operations can be very expensive, especially if the firm wants to go back to performing the outsourced activity itself. Another risk in outsourcing is the loss of control over both operations and information.

▶▶▶

In spite of these problems, outsourcing is here to stay because of the increasingly global nature of business, and because competitive pressures to reduce costs are so great. But the "look" of outsourcing may change. Consider the "reverse outsourcing" that occurred when India's Bharti Tele-Ventures Ltd. signed a $400 million outsourcing deal with three European companies—Ericsson (Sweden), Nokia (Finland), and Siemens (Germany). Hundreds of technicians who used to maintain Bharti's wireless network are now employed by these European companies (but the employees work in India, not in Europe). Bharti also outsourced most of its information technology services to IBM. To get the contract, IBM had to beat out several Indian companies that were competing for the contract. As a result of these outsourcing deals, Bharti now has just a few of its own employees. It is using outsourcing to reduce its costs so that it will be the lowest-cost provider of cell-phone minutes in India.

Viral Marketing

viral marketing Strategy of using the internet and word-of-mouth marketing to spread product information.

Combining technology with marketing methods usually results in new ways to attract customers. **Viral marketing**, which uses word of mouth that spreads information like a virus from customer to customer, relies on the vast reaches of the internet to replace face-to-face communications. Messages about new cars, sports events, and numerous other goods and services travel on the internet among potential customers who pass the information on to others. Using various formats—games, contests, chat rooms, and bulletin boards—marketers encourage potential customers to try out products and tell other people about them.[31]

The Organic Trade Association (OTA), which promotes organic foods, created a successful viral marketing program when it partnered with Free Range Graphics, and produced a 5-minute online spoof of the latest Star Wars movie. The film—which is called *Store Wars: The Organic Rebellion*—has characters such as Cuke Skywalker and Darth Tater, and has been passed around the internet by consumers who favour organic foods.[32]

Viral marketing leads to faster consumer awareness and wider reach than traditional media messages, and at a lower cost. The OTA's short film, for example, was seen by 10 million people in its first four months. Viral marketing works because people increasingly rely on the internet for information that they used to get from other media such as newspapers, and because the customer becomes a participant in the process of spreading the word by forwarding information to other internet users.

Business Process Management

Every company performs numerous processes that provide the goods or services, whether for customers or for other departments within the firm. Human resource departments perform interviewing and hiring processes; payroll departments perform the employee-payment process; the purchasing department performs the process of ordering materials; accounting performs the financial reporting process; marketing performs the process of taking orders from customers. A **process**, in short, is any activity that adds value to some input, transforming it into an output for a customer (whether external or internal).[33]

process Any activity that adds value to some input, transforming it into an output for a customer (whether external or internal).

business process management An approach by which firms move away from department-oriented organization and toward process-oriented team structures that cut across old departmental boundaries.

In today's business environment, many firms are moving away from the department-oriented organization (one that is organized around departments grouped according to processes or functions). Firms are moving toward process-oriented team structures that cut across old departmental boundaries. This approach is called **business process management**. Often, companies begin by asking, "What must we do well to stay in business and win new orders?" Next, they identify the major processes that must be performed well to satisfy these general goals. Then they organize resources and skills around those essential processes. By organizing according to processes rather than functional departments, they gain a number of benefits. Decision making is faster and more customer-oriented, materials and operations are coordinated, and products get to customers more rapidly.[34]

REDRAWING CORPORATE BOUNDARIES

Understand recent trends in the *redrawing of corporate boundaries.* 7

Successful companies are responding to challenges in the environment by redrawing traditional organizational boundaries, and by joining together with other companies to develop new goods and services. Some of these relationships are permanent, but others are temporary alliances formed on short notice so that, working together, partners can produce and deliver products with shorter lead times than either firm could manage alone.

Several trends in redrawing corporate boundaries have become evident in recent years. They include *acquisitions and mergers, divestitures and spinoffs, employee-owned corporations, strategic alliances,* and *subsidiary/parent corporations*.

Acquisitions and Mergers

In an **acquisition**, one firm simply buys another firm. For example, America Online bought Time Warner and Air Canada bought Canadian Airlines International. The transaction is similar to buying a car that then becomes your property. In contrast, a **merger** is a consolidation of two firms, and the arrangement is more collaborative. For example, Canadian National Railways merged with the Illinois Central Railroad, Rogers Communication merged with Groupe Videotron Ltd., and Toronto-Dominion Bank merged with Canada Trust. When the companies are in the same industry, as when Agricore and United Grain Growers merged to form Agricore United, it is called a **horizontal merger**. When one of the companies in the merger is a supplier or customer to the other, it is called a **vertical merger**. Finally, when the companies are in unrelated businesses, it is called a **conglomerate merger**.

A merger or acquisition can take place in one of several different ways. In a **friendly takeover**, the acquired company welcomes the acquisition, perhaps because it needs cash or sees other benefits in joining the acquiring firm. But in a **hostile takeover**, the acquiring company buys enough of the other company's stock to take control even though the other company is opposed to the takeover.

A **poison pill** is a defence that management adopts to make a firm less attractive to an actual or potential hostile suitor in a takeover attempt. The objective is to make the "pill" so distasteful that a potential acquirer will not want to swallow it. BCE Inc., for example, adopted a poison pill that allowed its shareholders to buy BCE stock at a 50 percent discount if another company announced its intention to acquire 20 percent or more of BCE's shares.[35]

acquisition One firm buys another firm and absorbs it into its operations.

merger The union of two companies to form a single new business.

horizontal merger A merger of two firms that have previously been direct competitors in the same industry.

vertical merger A merger of two firms that have previously had a buyer-seller relationship.

conglomerate merger A merger of two firms in completely unrelated businesses.

friendly takeover An acquisition in which the management of the acquired company welcomes the firm's buyout by another company.

hostile takeover An acquisition in which the management of the acquired company fights the firm's buyout by another company.

poison pill A defence that management adopts to make a firm less attractive to an actual or potential hostile suitor in a takeover attempt.

Divestitures and Spinoffs

A **divestiture** occurs when a company decides to sell part of its existing business operations to another corporation. For example, Unilever—the maker of Close-Up toothpaste, Dove soap, Vaseline lotion, and Q-tips—at

divestiture Occurs when a company sells part of its existing business operations to anoher company.

one time owned several specialty chemical businesses that made ingredients for its consumer products. The company decided that it had to focus more on the consumer products themselves, so it sold the chemical businesses to ICI, a European chemical company.

In other cases, a company might set up one or more corporate units as new, independent businesses because a business unit might be more valuable as a separate company. This is known as a **spinoff**. For example, PepsiCo spun off Pizza Hut, KFC, and Taco Bell into a new, separate corporation called Tricon Global Restaurants (now called Yum! Brands Inc.). Canadian Pacific spun off Canadian Pacific Railways, CP Ships, PanCanadian Petroleum, and Fording Coal.

spinoff Strategy of setting up one or more corporate units as new, independent corporations.

Employee-Owned Corporations

Corporations are sometimes owned by the employees who work for them. While the individuals who founded them own many smaller corporations, there is a growing trend today for employees to buy significant stakes of larger corporations. The current pattern is for this ownership to take the form of **employee stock ownership plans**, or **ESOPs**.

employee stock ownership plan (ESOP) An arrangement whereby a corporation buys its own stock with loaned funds and holds it in trust for its employees. Employees "earn" the stock based on some condition such as seniority. Employees control the stock's voting rights immediately, even though they may not take physical possession of the stock until specified conditions are met.

A corporation might decide to set up an ESOP to stimulate employee motivation or to fight a hostile takeover attempt. Here's how it works: The company first secures a loan, which it then uses to buy shares of its stock on the open market. Some of the future profits made by the corporation are used to pay off the loan. The stock, meanwhile, is controlled by a bank or other trustee. Employees gradually gain ownership of the stock, usually on the basis of seniority. But even though they might not have physical possession of the stock for a while, they control its voting rights immediately.

A survey of 471 Canadian and U.S. companies conducted by Western Compensation & Benefits Consultants of Vancouver found that three-quarters of the companies that have adopted ESOPs have experienced improvement in both sales and profits. Canadian companies such as Celestica and St. Laurent Paperboard Inc. have found that ESOPs give employees an increased sense of belonging in the company.[36]

Strategic Alliances

strategic alliance An enterprise in which two or more persons or companies temporarily join forces to undertake a particular project.

A **strategic alliance**, or joint venture, involves two or more enterprises co-operating in the research, development, manufacture, or marketing of a product. For example, GM and Suzuki formed a strategic alliance at the Ingersoll, Ontario, plant where Trackers and Grand Vitaras are made. Northern Empire, Stornoway, and Hunter Exploration Group formed a three-way joint venture to explore for diamonds on Melville Island in the Arctic Ocean.[37] Inco Ltd. and LionOre Mining International formed a joint venture to do research on processing technologies for the recovery of base metals from sulphide ores.[38]

Companies form strategic alliances for two main reasons: (1) to help spread the risk of a project, and (2) to get something of value (like technological expertise) from their strategic partner.

Subsidiary and Parent Corporations

subsidiary corporation One that is owned by another corporation.

parent corporation A corporation that owns a subsidiary.

Sometimes corporations own other corporations. A **subsidiary corporation** is one that is owned by another corporation. The corporation that owns the subsidiary is called the **parent corporation**. For example, Unilever is the parent corporation of Lever Brothers, Lipton, and Chesebrough Ponds.

Summary of Learning Objectives

1. **Explain the concepts of *organizational boundaries* and *multiple organizational environments.*** All businesses operate within a larger *external environment.* An *organizational boundary* is that which separates the organization from its environment. Boundaries were once relatively easy to identify; they are becoming harder to pin down. Organizations have multiple environments. Some environments are relatively general, such as prevailing economic conditions. Others are much more precise, such as the pricing policies of competitors. A full picture of a company's organizational environments would include the following elements: economic conditions, technology, political-legal considerations, social issues, the global environment, issues of ethical and social responsibility, the business environment itself, and numerous other emerging challenges and opportunities.

2. **Explain the importance of the *economic environment* to business and identify the factors used to evaluate the performance of an economic system.** The *economic environment* is the economic system in which business firms operate. The health of this environment affects business firms. The three key goals of the Canadian system are economic growth, economic stability, and full employment. *Economic growth* is influenced by the pattern of short-term ups and downs in an economy known as the *business cycle.* The main measure of *growth* in this cycle is *aggregate output.* An increase in aggregate output is growth. *Gross domestic product (GDP)* is the total value of all goods and services produced within a given period by a national economy through domestic factors of production. If GDP is going up, so is aggregate output; if aggregate output is going up, we have economic growth.

   Economic stability means that the amount of money available in an economic system and the quantity of goods and services produced in it are growing at about the same rate. There are three threats to stability: inflation, deflation, and unemployment.

   Unemployment is the level of joblessness among people actively seeking work. If people in different sectors lose their jobs at the same time, overall income and spending drop and businesses cut spending further—including spending on labour—and unemployment goes up further. This kind of unemployment is called *cyclical unemployment.* Meanwhile, producers also start producing less because they can't sell as much. Aggregate output then decreases and we have a *recession.* A prolonged and deep recession is a *depression.*

   The government manages the economy through *fiscal policies* and *monetary policies.* Through the Bank of Canada, the Canadian government can influence the ability and willingness of banks to lend money. It can also influence the supply of money by prompting interest rates to go up or down.

3. **Describe the *technological environment* and its role in business.** *Technology* refers to all the ways by which firms create value for their constituents, including human knowledge, work methods, physical equipment, electronics and telecommunications, and various processing systems. There are two general categories of business-related technologies: *product and service technologies* and *business process technologies.* Product and service technologies create products—both physical goods and services—for customers. Business process technologies are used to improve a firm's performance of internal operations (such as accounting) and to help to create better relationships with external constituents, such as suppliers and customers. *Enterprise resource planning (ERP)* is a large-scale information system for organizing and managing a firm's processes across product lines, departments, and geographic locations.

4. **Describe the *political-legal environment* and its role in business.** The *political-legal environment* reflects the relationship between business and government, usually in the form of government regulation. The legal system defines in part what an organization can and can't do. Various government agencies regulate important areas such as advertising practices, safety and health considerations, and acceptable standards of business conduct. Pro- or anti-business sentiment in government can further influence business activity. During periods of pro-business sentiment, firms find it easier to compete and have fewer concerns about antitrust issues. During periods of anti-business sentiment, firms may find their competitive activities more restricted.

5. **Describe the *socio-cultural environment* and its role in business.** The *socio-cultural environment* includes the customs, values, and demographic characteristics of the society in which an organization functions. Socio-cultural processes determine the goods and services as well as the standards of business conduct that a society values and accepts. Appropriate standards of conduct also vary across cultures. The shape of the market, the ethics of political influence, and the attitudes of its workforce are only a few of the many ways in which culture can affect an organization.

6. **Identify emerging challenges and opportunities in the *business environment*.** Successful companies are responding to challenges in new ways. They are focussing on their core competencies. The innovative ways in which companies respond to emerging challenges and opportunities include *outsourcing*, *viral marketing*, and *business process management*. Outsourcing is the strategy of paying suppliers and distributors to perform certain business processes or to provide needed materials or services. Viral marketing relies on the internet to replace face-to-face communications. Many firms are moving away from the department-oriented organization and toward process-oriented team structures that cut across old departmental boundaries—an approach called business process management.

7. **Understand recent trends in the *redrawing of corporate boundaries*.** An *acquisition* occurs when one firm buys another outright. A *merger* occurs when two firms combine to create a new company. A *divestiture* occurs when a corporation sells a part of its existing business operations or sets it up as a new and independent corporation. When a firm sells part of itself to raise capital, the strategy is known as a *spinoff*. The *employee stock ownership plan* (ESOP) allows employees to own a significant share of the corporation through trusts established on their behalf. In a *strategic alliance*, two or more organizations collaborate on a project for mutual gain.

KEY TERMS

QUESTIONS FOR ANALYSIS

1. It has been argued that inflation is both good and bad. How can this be? Explain. Are government efforts to control inflation well-advised? Explain.
2. What are the benefits and risks of outsourcing? What, if anything, should be done about the problem of Canadian companies outsourcing jobs to foreign countries? Defend your answer.
3. Why is it important for managers to understand the environment in which their businesses operate?
4. Explain how current economic indicators such as inflation and unemployment affect you personally. Explain how they will affect you as a manager.
5. Using a product or service of your choice, explain how the various environments of business impact the sales possibilities of the product or service.
6. What is the current climate regarding the regulation of business? How might it affect you if you were a manager today?
7. At first glance, it might seem as though the goals of economic growth and stability are inconsistent with one another. How can you reconcile this apparent inconsistency?

APPLICATION EXERCISES

1. Select two businesses with which you are familiar. Identify the major elements of their external environments that are most likely to affect them in important and meaningful ways.
2. Using the internet, identify the major suppliers of software for enterprise resource planning. Try to locate information about their primary customers.
3. Interview two business owners or managers. Ask them to describe for you the following things: (a) what business functions, if any, they outsource; (b) whether or not they are focussing more attention on business process management now than in the past; and (c) how the events of September 11, 2001, have affected their work.

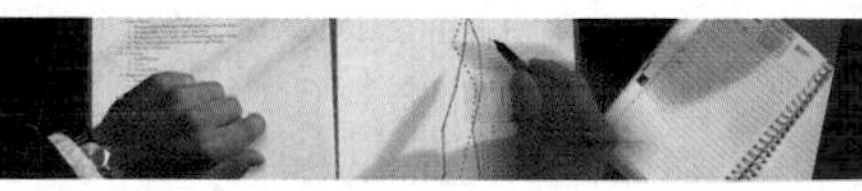

BUILDING YOUR BUSINESS SKILLS

The Letdown from Environmental Upheaval

Goal

To encourage students to understand how local events can affect other businesses in a number of ways.

The Situation

The collapse of Enron affected literally hundreds of other businesses. While attention has been directed primarily at the demise of Arthur Andersen, many other businesses suffered as well. For example, Enron's headquarters was located in a large office building on the edge of Houston's downtown business district. Because of both Enron's rapid growth and the prosperity of its employees, numerous other service providers had set up shop nearby—a shoeshine stand, a coffee shop, a bank branch, a dry cleaner, and two restaurants. When Enron collapsed, the demand for services provided by these small businesses dropped sharply.

Larger businesses were also caught up in the ripple effect. Enron, for example, had bought the rights to name the new home of baseball's Houston Astros Enron Field. The Astros were forced to remove all Enron signage and seek a new sponsor. Continental Airlines dominates the air traffic market out of Houston, and Enron was one of Continental's largest corporate clients. Combined with the events of September 11, 2001, and major staff reductions at Compaq Computer, another big Continental client, the end of business travel by Enron managers cost the airline considerable revenue.

Assignment

Divide up into groups of four or five students. Each group should begin by doing the following:

Step 1

Identify five kinds of small businesses likely to have been affected by Enron's collapse. You can include some of those identified above, but identify at least two others.

Step 2

Identify five kinds of large businesses likely to have been affected by Enron's collapse. Again, you can use some of those identified above, but identify at least two others.

Step 3

As a group, develop answers to each of the following:

1. For each company that you identify, both small and large, describe the specific effects of the Enron collapse on its business.
2. Describe the most logical organizational response of each company to these effects.
3. What kinds of plans, if any, should each organization develop in the event of similar future events?
4. Identify businesses that might have benefited economically from the collapse of Enron.

Alternative Assignment

Select a different high-profile environmental upheaval, such as the U.S. duties that were placed on Canadian softwood lumber being shipped to the United States, and substitute it for Enron. Then proceed with Steps 1–3 above.

Follow-Up Questions

1. What does this exercise demonstrate about the pitfalls of relying too heavily on one business?
2. Could any of these businesses have been better prepared for the Enron collapse?
3. Managers must be on the alert for environmental changes that might negatively affect their business. Is it possible for a manager to spend too much time trying to anticipate future events? Why or why not?

EXERCISING YOUR ETHICS

Assessing the Ethics of Trade-Offs

The Purpose of the Assignment

Managers must often make choices among options that are presented by environmental circumstances. This exercise will help you better appreciate the nature and complexity of the kinds of trade-offs that often result.

The Situation

You are owner and manager of a medium-sized non-unionized manufacturing company located in a town of about 15 000 people. The nearest major city is about 200 kilometres away. With about 500 workers, you are one of the five largest employers in town. A regional recession has caused two of the other largest employers to close down (one went out of business and the other relocated to another area). A new foreign competitor has set up shop in the area, but local unemployment has still risen sharply. All in all, the regional economic climate and the new competitor are hurting your business. Your sales have dropped 20 percent this year, and you forecast another drop next year before things begin to turn around.

The Dilemma

You face two unpleasant choices.

Choice 1: You can tell your employees that you need them to take cuts in pay and benefits. You know that because of the local unemployment rate, you can easily replace anyone who refuses. Unfortunately, you may need your employees to take another cut next year if your forecasts hold true. At the same time, you do have reason to believe that when the economy rebounds (in about two years, according to your forecasts), you can begin restoring pay cuts. Here are the advantages of this choice: You can probably (1) preserve all 500 jobs, (2) maintain your own income, (3) restore pay cuts in the future, and (4) keep the business open indefinitely. And the disadvantages: Pay cuts will (1) pose economic hardships for your employees and (2) create hard feelings and undercut morale.

Choice 2: You can maintain the status quo as far as your employees are concerned, but in that case, you'll be facing two problems: (1) You'll have to cut your own salary. While you can certainly afford to live on less income, doing so would be a blow to your personal finances. (2) If economic conditions get worse and/or last longer than forecast, you may have to close down altogether. The firm has a cash surplus, but because you'll have to dip into these funds to maintain stable wages, they'll soon run out. The advantages of this option: You can (1) avoid economic hardship for your workers and (2) maintain good employee relations. The downside: You will reduce your own standard of living and may eventually cost everyone his or her job.

Questions for Discussion

1. What are the basic ethical issues in this situation?
2. Can you identify any other options?
3. Of the two options posed in the situation as presented, which would you choose? Why?

CONCLUDING CASE 2-1

Corporate Reputations: Mixed Evidence

During the last few years, there has been a great deal of negative publicity about business activity. Because of illegal and unethical behaviour, sky-high executive salaries, or simply poor performance, business has lost a lot of respect lately. But there is another side to the story, and it doesn't get enough attention. That story concerns the large number of corporations that perform well and do good things for the constituents in their external environment. And they do it without a lot of fanfare.

Who are these companies? Each year since 1994, KPMG/Ipsos-Reid has published a list of the most respected corporations in Canada. In 2005, 250 leading Canadian CEOs were asked to assess Canadian corporations on eight performance categories such as long-term investment value, innovation and product/service development, financial performance, corporate social responsibility, corporate governance, human resource management, and customer service. The winner for 2005 was the Royal Bank of Canada (RBC) by a wide margin (RBC also came in first in the 2004 survey). The next four companies (in order) were Research In Motion, EnCana Corp., WestJet Airlines, and the Bank of Nova Scotia.

Some critics say that banks have an undue advantage in surveys like these because they are so rich that they are able to be very involved in philanthropy. Both CEOs and the general public are likely to be impressed by large charitable donations that banks make, and such activity gives banks a lot of free publicity. On the other hand, Canadian consumers are often not very impressed with banks, arguing that they charge too much for services and do not pay high enough interest on money deposited with them.

Respect and reputation are things that can quickly change. For example, in 1999, Nortel Networks ranked first in the survey, but with its recent troubles it ranked only 40th in the 2005 survey. And Bombardier, which ranked first in 2001, dropped to 28th place in 2005. Negative publicity about a company can obviously cause it to drop in the rankings. Canadian Imperial Bank of Commerce dropped from 10th place in 2004 to 18th place in 2005 after it received negative publicity about its role in the Enron debacle.

Surveys about corporate reputations are also conducted in the United States. The Reputation Quotient study is a joint effort of Harris Interactive Inc., a Rochester, New York-based research firm, and the Reputation Institute of New York. A 2005 survey asked nearly 20 000 people to name two companies with the best reputation and two companies with the worst reputation. Respondents evaluated the companies on factors such as emotional appeal, financial performance, social responsibility, and workplace environment. In total, 60 companies were named by those who were surveyed.

The company with the best reputation was Johnson & Johnson, a manufacturer of baby products and pharmaceuticals. The next four companies (in order) were Coca-Cola, Google, United Parcel Service, and 3M. Johnson & Johnson has had considerable success staying at the top of the Reputation Quotient (it has been ranked first every year since 1999). Apparently, consumers have warm feelings about the company because of its baby products.

The worst company was Enron (ranked 60th). Other poorly ranked companies were MCI (formerly WorldCom), Adelphia Communications, and Halliburton. All of these companies have received significant negative publicity in recent years for various misdeeds. The actions of a relatively small number of companies have influenced how people in the United States view business. In the 2005 survey, 71 percent of respondents rated the reputation of American business as either "not good" or "terrible."

It's not just individual companies that can run into difficulty. During the last few years, the reputations of entire industries have declined. For example, consumer impressions of the pharmaceutical and oil industries are negative because of a widely held belief that these industries are overcharging consumers for the products they sell. The tobacco industry has also had problems because consumers think that information about the negative effects of smoking and nicotine was withheld from the public.

When we consider negative information about business firms, we must remember that only a very small proportion of them are actually engaging in illegal or unethical behaviour. A review of the Canadian and U.S. reputation lists—and the criteria that are used to generate them—provides some reassuring testimony on the vitality and values of many businesses. It also shows the manner in which they conduct their operations, and gives us some insights into how companies must perform to gain the kind of stellar reputation necessary to get on the list.

These criteria all have one underlying theme: They reflect in one way or another the extent to which an organization and its managers effectively meet or exceed the needs and expectations of their external constituents. For example, hiring and developing the brightest and most motivated people from the labour market results in high levels of employee talent. Likewise, respecting the needs of shareholders and other investors affects several criteria, including financial soundness, use of corporate assets, and long-term investment value. Says one expert, "We admire companies that cater to their constituents."

Questions for Discussion

1. What is your opinion of the value of the rankings like these? How might the different ways the Canadian and U.S. surveys are conducted influence the results?
2. Do you think the criteria that are used are appropriate? Can you suggest others?
3. Is the ranking something that investors should rely on in buying stock?
4. If you were a top manager and wanted your firm to move up in the rankings, how would you proceed?

CONCLUDING CASE 2-2

Maybe Malthus Was Wrong

Most people have heard of Thomas Malthus, who became famous by proposing that all species have a tendency to reproduce to the point where their food supply runs out. The application of this idea to human population was simple: The world's population would tend to increase until the food supply was no longer sufficient to support everyone. Starvation would then result. But is this correct? Recent population trends are very startling, and call into question the predictions of Malthus.

The fertility rate—the average number of lifetime births per woman—declined in many industrialized European countries in the mid-twentieth century, and has stayed low ever since. In fact, it has stayed below the "replacement rate"—the rate needed to ensure that the population maintains itself. That rate is 2.1 births per woman. Some of the implications of Europe's declining fertility rate are profound. In Russia, for example, the current population of 150 million people will drop to 105 million by 2050 if current trends continue.

While the fertility rate is low in industrialized Europe, in developing countries it has always been high. And, until recently, it was assumed that it would always be high. This would lead, it was feared, to eventual overpopulation of the world and Malthusian famine on a large scale. But something unexpected is happening. Fertility rates in most developing countries, including India, Mexico, and Iran, are declining.

In 2000, the United Nations population division predicted that the fertility rate in developing countries in 2050 would be 2.1 children per woman. But in 2002, it revised its prediction downward to 1.85 children per woman. If this latest prediction turns out to be accurate, the world's population should stabilize at about 9 billion people by 2050. This is a significant change from predictions that were made in 1992, when it was thought that world population would reach 12 billion people by 2050. There are several interesting implications of a stabilizing world population:

- In the future, a smaller proportion of the population in most countries will be children, and a larger proportion will be very old people.
- More and more women will be involved in the worldwide workforce because they are having fewer children, and they are having them later in life.
- The population of Japan will start declining in 2006, so businesses there will have to find ways to increase productivity to cope with the decline in the working population.
- Mexico's fertility rate has dropped precipitously in the last 25 years (from 7.0 to 2.1), and that means that for the first time in its history Mexico has the opportunity to develop a significant middle class of consumers; but this development may also make it difficult for Mexico to compete with other emerging markets for foreign investment.
- Countries where the fertility rate has dropped sharply will benefit from a so-called demographic bonus: Labour costs decline because a greater proportion of the population works when there are fewer children; Thailand and China are just two countries that have benefited this way, and India will soon start benefiting.

Some countries are so concerned about the decline in fertility rates that they have begun offering incentives to convince women to have more babies. In Australia, for example, couples that have a baby can put off a house loan payment for three months. In Singapore, parents are paid a bonus in cash if they have one more child. But these initiatives have had virtually no effect. It seems that the combination of high literacy rates, increasing prosperity, and improvements in women's rights are an irresistible force in reducing fertility rates.

Questions for Discussion

1. Consider each of the issues discussed in the chapter with regard to the economic environment. What will be the impact of declining fertility rates on each of these issues? Be specific.
2. What will be the impact of declining fertility rates on the technological, political-legal, and socio-cultural environments? Be specific.
3. If the fertility rate continues to decline worldwide, what are the implications for individual business firms? Be specific.

CHAPTER 3

Conducting Business Ethically and Responsibly

After reading this chapter, you should be able to:

1. Explain how individuals develop their personal *codes of ethics* and why ethics are important in the workplace.
2. Distinguish *social responsibility* from *ethics*, identify *organizational stakeholders*, and characterize social consciousness today.
3. Show how the concept of social responsibility applies both to environmental issues and to a firm's relationships with customers, employees, and investors.
4. Identify four general *approaches to social responsibility* and describe the four steps a firm must take to implement a *social responsibility program*.
5. Explain how issues of social responsibility and ethics affect small businesses.

The Price of Bad Behaviour

During the last few years, many business executives have been hit with charges that they made undisclosed loans to shareholders, obstructed justice, engaged in insider trading and tipping, manipulated financial statements, and misled clients and investors. Some of these executives—for example, Garth Drabinsky and Myron Gottlieb (Livent Inc.), Bernie Ebbers (WorldCom), Ken Lay (Enron), Conrad Black (Hollinger International), and Jean Brault (Groupaction Marketing)—received a lot of publicity. Three Canadian banks that were involved in the Enron debacle also received bad press.

Garth Drabinsky and Myron Gottlieb. Livent Inc., a live theatre company with theatres in Toronto, Vancouver, Chicago, and New York, was founded by Drabinsky and Gottlieb. In 1998, questions were raised about Livent's finances by new owners who had bought into the company. Shortly thereafter, Drabinsky and Gottlieb were fired. They were eventually charged with defrauding investors and creditors of about $500 million. Progress in the case has been very slow, and the trial is not expected to start until 2007. Drabinsky and Gottlieb have consistently denied any wrongdoing. In a related development, the Institute of Chartered Accountants of Ontario (ICAO) charged four partners of Deloitte & Touche LLP with breaching the Institute's rules of professional conduct regarding Livent. Deloitte also denies any wrongdoing.

Bernie Ebbers. Canadian-born Bernie Ebbers had risen from Alberta milkman and nightclub bouncer to become CEO of WorldCom, one of the largest companies in the United States. It was alleged that Ebbers conspired with subordinates to "cook the books" when a business downturn occurred. These actions wiped out $100 billion of the company's market value, cost 17 000 people their jobs, and lost some investors their life savings. Scott Sullivan, one of Ebbers' subordinates, pled guilty and testified that Ebbers had ordered him to cook the books to hit earnings targets. In March 2005, Ebbers was found guilty on nine charges of securities fraud and filing false documents. He was sentenced to 25 years in prison for his role in the collapse of WorldCom Inc.

Ken Lay. The former CEO of Enron was well-known as a "hands-off" manager, and he claimed that he was unaware of the financial manipulations that had been carried out by some of his subordinates, notably Andrew Fastow, the chief financial officer. These manipulations included moving debt "off the balance sheet" to make it look like Enron was in better financial shape than it was. The jury didn't buy Lay's story that he was the victim of his subordinates' misbehaviour, and in 2006 he was convicted of a variety of charges, including conspiracy and securities fraud. His sentencing hearing was scheduled for September 11, 2006, but he died of a heart attack in July 2006.

Conrad Black. In 2005, David Radler, Conrad Black's longtime business partner, pled guilty to his part in a $32 million fraud at Hollinger International where Black was CEO. Radler was given 29 months in jail and a $250 000 fine. He also agreed to cooperate with a criminal investigation of Conrad Black. Radler's guilty plea was not good news for Conrad Black, who was still awaiting trial on charges that he and three associates illegally diverted $84 million out of investors' pockets and into their own. Black denies any wrongdoing and notes that all his actions were approved by the board of directors of Hollinger. Prosecutors charge that Black used fraud to obtain board and audit committee approval to make payments to himself, and that he made false statements and omitted facts about the payment to shareholders and regulators. Black's trial had not started as of July 2006.

Jean Brault. In 2002, rumours began circulating that the federal Liberal government had paid millions of dollars to the advertising firm Groupaction Marketing to help raise Canada's profile in Quebec after the 1995 sovereignty referendum. The trouble was, no work was ever done. An inquiry resulted in many criminal charges being laid, including six charges of fraud against Jean Brault, who ran Groupaction Marketing. He eventually pled guilty to five of the charges and admitted to paying salaries to Liberal party workers who never did any work. He was sentenced to 30 months in prison.

Canadian Banks. The Royal Bank of Canada (RBC), the Toronto-Dominion (TD) bank, and the Canadian Imperial Bank of Commerce (CIBC) were among many defendants in a $25 billion class action suit filed against financial institutions by individuals who lost money when Enron went under in 2001. In 2005, RBC paid $25 million to settle its liability, and the interim CEO at Enron agreed that RBC played only a minor role in Enron's collapse. Also in 2005, CIBC agreed to pay $2.4 *billion* to get out of the Enron class action lawsuit. That is the biggest payout of any of the financial institutions that were sued (U.S.-based JP Morgan Chase & Co. paid $2.2 billion and Citigroup paid $2 billion). CIBC denied any wrongdoing and said the payment was designed to reduce the uncertainty of future litigation over Enron.

As we consider these cases, we might conclude that the ethical level of business executives has declined in recent years. That's a possibility, but a more likely explanation is that the stock market "bubble" of the late 1990s magnified some already existing human weaknesses, including greed and a tendency to "skate on the edge." Human greed probably hasn't increased in the last few years, but the opportunities to satisfy it have. Another reason is the failure of checks and balances that were supposed to prevent this kind of behaviour. Professionals such as accountants, lawyers, audit committees, government regulators, the press, and securities analysts are supposed to make sure that executives do not do things that are detrimental to shareholders, but critics feel that they often fail to do their job. A third reason is stock options (see Concluding Case 19-2), which may give executives an incentive to behave badly.

The best explanation of unethical executive behaviour is probably a combination of these three reasons. But what does the future hold? Were the excesses of the executives listed above caused by just a "few bad apples," or is the system broken? The view that there are just a "few bad apples" is supported by some statistics. For example, in the United States (where much of the high-profile bad behaviour has occurred), the Securities and Exchange Commission (SEC) investigated 570 companies in 2001. That sounds like a lot, but it's only slightly higher than the number investigated in 1994. Another statistic: only about one company in 100 restates its earnings. This suggests that the system needs only a minor fix-up.

The counter view is that there really has been a decline in the general level of ethical behaviour, and that the headline cases are just symptomatic of a very big problem. If we accept this view, it follows that the current legislation is inadequate to deal with the problem, and the only solution is to develop tough new legislation that will control the tendency of executives to behave in an unethical and illegal fashion. ◆

ETHICS IN THE WORKPLACE

ethics Individual standards or moral values regarding what is right and wrong or good and bad.

ethical behaviour Behaviour that conforms to individual beliefs and social norms about what is right and good.

unethical behaviour Behaviour that individual beliefs and social norms define as wrong and bad.

business ethics Ethical or unethical behaviours by a manager or employee of an organization.

Ethics are beliefs about what is right and wrong or good and bad. An individual's personal values and morals and the social context in which they occur determine whether a particular behaviour is perceived as ethical or unethical. **Ethical behaviour** is behaviour that conforms to individual beliefs and social norms about what is right and good. **Unethical behaviour** is behaviour that individual beliefs and social norms define as wrong and bad. **Business ethics** is a term often used to refer to ethical or unethical behaviour by a manager or employee of an organization.

Individual Ethics

1 Explain how individuals develop their personal *codes of ethics* and why ethics are important in the workplace.

Because ethics are based on both individual beliefs and social concepts, they vary from person to person, from situation to situation, and from culture to culture. Social standards are broad enough to support differences in beliefs. Without violating general standards, therefore, people may develop personal codes of ethics reflecting a wide range of attitudes and beliefs.

Thus ethical and unethical behaviour is determined partly by the individual and partly by culture. For instance, virtually everyone would agree that if you see someone drop a $20 bill in a store, it would be ethical to return it to the owner. But there'll be less agreement if you find $20 and don't know who dropped it. Should you turn it in to the lost-and-found department? Or, since the rightful owner isn't likely to claim it, can you just keep it?

Societies generally adopt formal laws that reflect prevailing ethical standards or social norms. For example, because most people regard theft as unethical, we have laws against such behaviour and ways of punishing those who steal. We try to make unambiguous laws, but interpreting and applying them can still lead to ethical ambiguities. Real-world situations can often be interpreted in different ways, and it isn't always easy to apply statutory standards to real-life behaviour. Samuel Waksal, former CEO of ImClone, was convicted of insider trading for tipping off certain investors, including Martha Stewart and members of his own family, about the impending fall of ImClone stock. Stewart said that she simply ordered her broker to sell the stock if it slipped below $60. But in 2004, she was convicted of lying to investigators and served several months in prison. Meanwhile, Waksal's daughter, who also sold her ImClone stock after getting information from her father, has so far been treated as an "innocent tippee"—someone who got inside information but didn't think that's what it was at the time.[1]

The epidemic of scandals ranging from Enron and Arthur Andersen to Tyco and WorldCom only serves to show how willing people can be to take advantage of potentially ambiguous situations. The Business Accountability box describes another situation where there are conflicting views about what is ethical.

Individual Values and Codes

How should we deal with business behaviour that we regard as unethical—especially when it's legally ambiguous? No doubt we have to start with the individuals in a business—its managers, employees, agents, and other legal representatives. Each of these people's personal code of ethics is determined by a combination of factors. We start to form ethical standards as children in response to our perceptions of the behaviour of parents and other adults. Soon, we enter school, where peers influence us, and as we grow into adulthood, experience shapes our lives and contributes to our ethical beliefs and our behaviour. We also develop values and morals that contribute to ethical standards. If you put financial gain at the top of your priority list, you may develop a code of ethics that supports the pursuit of material comfort. If you set family and friends as a priority, you'll no doubt adopt different standards.

When telecommunications giant WorldCom (now MCI) collapsed amid a record-setting $1 billion bankruptcy in 2003, just about everybody who had anything to do with corporate accounting was arrested. Chief Financial Officer Scott Sullivan pleaded guilty to criminal charges and agreed to testify against his former boss, Canadian-born Bernard Ebbers (pictured here). In 2006, Ebbers was sentenced to 25 years in prison for his role in the collapse.

Because ethics are both personally and culturally defined, differences of opinion can arise as to what is ethical or unethical. For example, many people who would never think of taking a candy bar from a grocery store routinely take home pens and pads of paper from their offices. Other people who view

BUSINESS ACCOUNTABILITY

Crossing the Ethical Line?

In 2005, the CIBC World Markets sued six former employees after they left the company and started a new rival firm, Genuity Capital Markets (a total of 18 people left CIBC for Genuity). While asking for $10 million in damages, CIBC charged that the six people (a) planned their new company while they were still on CIBC's payroll, (b) took confidential information with them when they left CIBC, and (c) attempted to steal both top performers and clients from CIBC for the new company. All of this occurred, it is alleged, while the six executives were being handsomely paid by CIBC.

The defendants in the lawsuit are David Kassie (formerly CEO of CIBC World Markets), Daniel Daviau (formerly an investment banker at CIBC who specialized in the technology and media sectors), Phil Evershed (former head of mergers and acquisitions at CIBC), Earl Rotman (CIBC World Markets vice-chairman), John Esteireiro (head trader at CIBC), and David Morrsion (a top salesman). Evershed, Rotman, and Daviau each received more than $3 million in salary and severance pay from the bank just before they left for Genuity. One of the conditions of their leaving was that they would not try to hire any CIBC employees for 21 months.

In the document it filed with a Toronto court, CIBC provided detailed information from hundreds of pages of emails allegedly showing how the six former employees had frequently discussed the formation of Genuity while they were still employed at CIBC. It was also alleged that these emails listed the names of CIBC employees who were to be recruited for the new company. One other serious allegation has been made by CIBC: that an IT specialist downloaded confidential client information before she left CIBC (the IT specialist claims that she was simply copying disks for her successor, that she didn't give the information to Genuity, and that Genuity is willing to open its computers to support her story).

The founders of Genuity argue that they have done nothing unethical or illegal. One of the key points in their defence is that they didn't break any rules by hiring employees of CIBC to work at Genuity, because these employees had already decided to leave CIBC. Genuity simply provided them with a new place to work.

Some observers think this lawsuit is not so much about Genuity as it is about duty, integrity, honour, and trust. In other words, it's about business ethics. As the leader in the industry, CIBC is not really very concerned about a small new competitor like Genuity being started, but it is concerned about the "slippery" way that it was formed. CIBC also wants to send a message to its remaining employees that CIBC's corporate culture is all about honesty and fair dealing, and that its culture is so important that CIBC will pursue employees (or former employees) who don't act appropriately. The CIBC also wants to hold the six former employees to a certain ethical standard because they were paid very well for the work they did.

Others who have analyzed this interesting situation question the quality of the leadership that was evident at CIBC in the year or so before the employee exodus. They ask, for example, what the board of directors at CIBC was doing when rumours about the start of Genuity were swirling around Bay Street. They also ask what effect the hiring of Kassie's replacement at CIBC had on employees who did not leave (the defendants claim that once Kassie's replacement was announced, that Genuity received many applications from CIBC employees).

It is not clear that this dispute will ever actually be heard in court because both sides have much to lose. CIBC has the financial resources to support an expensive court battle, but if it loses it will not be able to make its point about the importance of ethical behaviour. Genuity, on the other hand, is a new company that needs to establish a reputation of integrity, and a nasty court fight isn't going to do much to help the company achieve that goal.

In the past, lawsuits like this one usually did not result in a full trial, but were settled with a small award (for example, the loser made a contribution to charity). When a full trial does happen, the usual ruling is that individuals have the right to work where they want, but that taking data or enticing a group to leave are not acceptable. Since CIBC alleged that the latter two things occurred, a full trial would be very interesting.

themselves as law-abiding citizens have no qualms about using radar detectors to avoid speeding tickets. In each of the situations, people will choose different sides of the issue and argue that their actions are ethical.

Managerial Ethics

Managerial ethics are the standards of behaviour that guide individual managers in their work.[2] Although your ethics can affect your work in any number of ways, it's helpful to classify them in terms of three broad categories.

managerial ethics Standards of behaviour that guide individual managers in their work.

Behaviour Toward Employees

This category covers such matters as hiring and firing, wages and working conditions, and privacy and respect. Ethical and legal guidelines suggest that hiring and firing decisions should be based solely on ability to perform a job. A manager who discriminates against any ethnic minority in hiring exhibits both unethical and illegal behaviour. But what about the manager who hires a friend or relative when someone else might be more qualified? Such decisions may not be illegal; but they may be objectionable on ethical grounds.

Wages and working conditions, though regulated by law, are also areas for controversy. Consider a manager who pays a worker less than he deserves because the manager knows that the employee can't afford to quit or risk his job by complaining. While some people will see the behaviour as unethical, others will see it as smart business. Cases such as these are hard enough to judge, but consider the behaviour of Enron management toward company employees. It encouraged employees to invest retirement funds in company stock and then, when financial problems began to surface, refused to permit them to sell the stock (even though top officials of the company were allowed to sell their stock). Ultimately, the firm's demise cost thousands of jobs.

Behaviour Toward the Organization

Ethical issues also arise from employee behaviour toward employers, especially in such areas as conflict of interest, confidentiality, and honesty. A conflict of interest occurs when an activity may benefit the individual to the detriment of his or her employer. Most companies have policies that forbid buyers from accepting gifts from suppliers. Businesses in highly competitive industries—software and fashion apparel, for example—have safeguards against designers selling company secrets to competitors. Relatively common problems in the general area of honesty include such behaviour as stealing supplies, padding expense accounts, and using a business phone to make personal long-distance calls. Most employees are honest, but most organizations are nevertheless vigilant. Again, Enron is a good example of employees' unethical behaviour toward an organization. Top managers not only misused corporate assets, but they often committed the company to risky ventures to further personal interests.

Behaviour Toward Other Economic Agents

Ethics also come into play in the relationship between the firm and its so-called primary agents of interest—mainly customers, competitors, stockholders, suppliers, dealers, and unions. In dealing with such agents, there is room for ethical ambiguity in just about every activity—advertising, financial disclosure, ordering and purchasing, bargaining and negotiation, and other business relationships.

For example, businesses in the pharmaceuticals industry are under criticism because of the rising prices of drugs. They argue that high prices cover the costs of research and development programs to develop new drugs. The solution to such problems seems obvious: Find the right balance between reasonable pricing and *price gouging* (which means responding to increased demand with overly steep price increases). But like so many questions involving ethics, there are significant differences of opinion about the proper balance.[3]

Another area of concern is competitive espionage. In 2004, Air Canada sued WestJet for $220 million, claiming that a WestJet executive had electronically snooped on Air Canada's confidential reservation database, which contained important competitive information that would be beneficial to WestJet. WestJet then filed a $30 million counter-suit, claiming that Air Canada had filed its suit in an attempt to destroy WestJet's reputation. It also claimed that Air Canada had "set up" WestJet by allowing one of WestJet's executives to get into the supposedly confidential Air Canada database. WestJet also charged that Air Canada had hired a firm to steal the garbage of a WestJet executive in the hopes of finding important financial information about WestJet.[4] In 2005, a judge denied WestJet's claim. In mid-2006, the Air Canada claim was still in process.

The difficulty of dealing with these problems is compounded by the fact that business practices vary globally. In many countries, bribes are a normal part of doing business. However, in Canada and the United States, bribes are seen as unethical and illegal. For example, in 2006 the Gemological Institute of America (GIA) fired several employees after they had accepted bribes from diamond dealers. In return for the bribes, the GIA employees rated the dealers' diamonds higher than they should have been, and this allowed the dealers to sell them for a much higher price. The GIA also banned two groups of dealers from having their diamonds rated by the GIA.[5]

Assessing Ethical Behaviour

By definition, what distinguishes ethical behaviour from unethical behaviour is often subjective and subject to differences of opinion.[6] So, how does one go about deciding whether a particular action or decision is ethical? A three-step model can be used for applying ethical judgments to situations that may arise during the course of business activities:

1. Gather the relevant factual information.
2. Determine the most appropriate moral values.
3. Make an ethical judgment based on the rightness or wrongness of the proposed activity or policy.

Unfortunately, the process does not always work as smoothly as the three steps suggest. What if the facts are not clear-cut? What if there are no agreed-upon moral values? Nevertheless, a judgment and a decision must be made. Experts point out that, otherwise, trust is impossible; and trust, they add, is indispensable to any business transaction.

To more fully assess the ethics of a particular behaviour, we need a more refined process. Let's consider a common dilemma faced by managers involving their expense accounts. Companies routinely provide managers with accounts to cover work-related expenses when they are travelling on company business and/or entertaining clients for business purposes. Common examples of such expenses include hotel bills, meals, rental cars or taxis, and so forth. Employees, of course, are expected to claim only those expenses that are accurate and work-related. For example, if a manager takes a client to dinner while travelling on business and spends $100, submitting a receipt for that dinner to be reimbursed for $100 is clearly accurate and appropriate. Suppose, however, that the manager then has a

$100 dinner the next night in that same city with a good friend for purely social purposes. Submitting that receipt for full reimbursement would be unethical. A few managers, however, will rationalize that it is acceptable to submit a receipt for dinner with a friend. They will argue, perhaps, that they are underpaid and are simply increasing the income due to them.

Other principles that come into play in a case like this include various ethical norms. Consider four such norms and the issues that they entail:

Utility: Does a particular act optimize what is best for those who are affected by it?
Rights: Does it respect the rights of the individuals involved?
Justice: Is it consistent with what we regard to be fair?
Caring: Is it consistent with people's responsibilities to each other?

Figure 3.1 incorporates the consideration of these ethical norms.

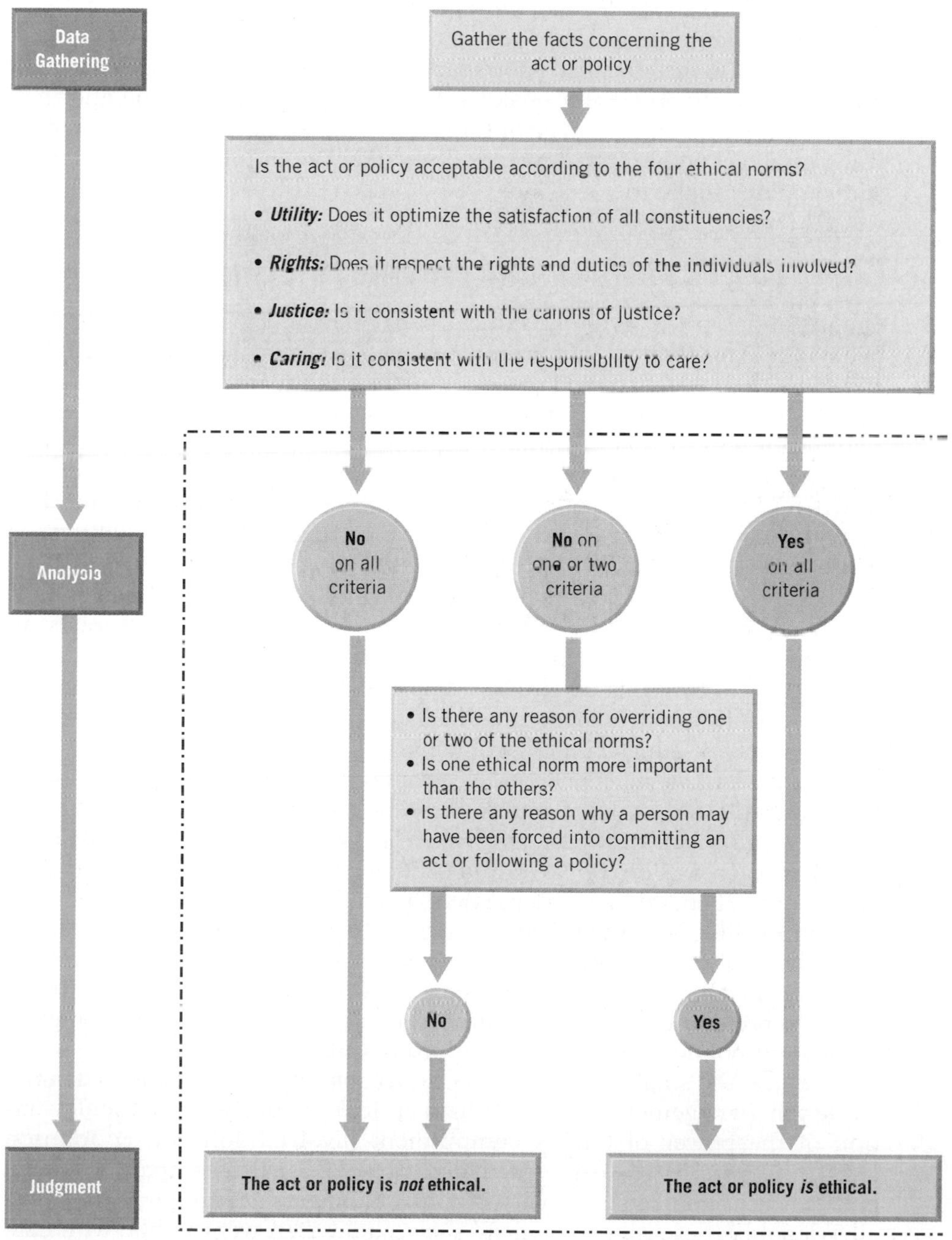

Figure 3.1 Expanded model of ethical judgment making.

Now, let's return to the case of the inflated expense account. While the utility norm would acknowledge that the manager benefits from padding an expense account, others, such as co-workers and owners, do not. Likewise, most experts would agree that it does not respect the rights of others. Moreover, it is clearly unfair and compromises the manager's responsibilities to others. This particular act, then, appears to be clearly unethical.

Figure 3.1, however, also provides mechanisms for considering unique circumstances—those that apply only in certain limited situations. Suppose, for example, that the manager loses the receipt for the legitimate dinner but retains the receipt for the social dinner. Some people will argue that it is acceptable to submit the illegitimate receipt because the manager is only doing so to be reimbursed for what he or she is entitled to. Others, however, will continue to argue that submitting the other receipt is wrong under any circumstances. We won't pretend to arbitrate the case. For our purposes, we will simply make the following point: Changes in the situation can make issues more or less clear-cut.

When judging how ethical a certain behaviour is, one of the simplest "tests" to use is the so-called "newspaper test." This means asking yourself this question: If you were to make a decision on an ethical issue and then read about it on the front page of tomorrow's paper, how would you feel? If you would feel embarrassed, you are very likely violating ethical standards and shouldn't make the decision.

Company Practices and Business Ethics

Organizations try to promote ethical behaviour and discourage unethical behaviour. As unethical and even illegal behaviour by both managers and employees plagues more and more companies, many firms have taken additional steps to encourage ethical behaviour in the workplace. Many, for example, establish codes of conduct and develop clear ethical positions on how the firm and its employees will conduct its business. An increasingly controversial area regarding business ethics and company practices involves the privacy of email and other communications that take place inside an organization.

Technological developments are creating all sorts of brand-new ethical problems—cloning, satellite reconnaissance, and bioengineered foods, to name just a few. For every innovation that promises convenience or safety, there seems to be a related ethical issue. The internet and email, for example, are certainly convenient and efficient, but they present business people with a variety of ethics-related problems.

In one set of age-old concerns, electronic communications merely substitute for traditional forms of communication, such as mail or the telephone. By the same token, however, they make it possible to run all the classic swindles, such as Ponzi or pyramid schemes, with greater efficiency than ever before. Federal law-enforcement personnel routinely surf the web looking for illegal or unethical practices, often finding hundreds of questionable sites in a typical sting. Employers are also using email to test employee loyalty, as in the case of the manager who sent false emails to his workers, pretending to be a recruiter from a competing firm. Any employees who responded were skipped for promotion.

Perhaps the single most effective step a company can take is to demonstrate top management support of high ethical standards. A classic illustration of the power of ethical commitment involved Johnson & Johnson (J&J). In 1982, it was discovered that capsules of the company's Tylenol pain reliever had been laced with cyanide. Managers at J&J quickly recalled all Tylenol bottles still on retailers' shelves and then went public with candid information throughout the crisis. J&J's ethical choices proved to be a crucial factor in its campaign to rescue its product. Both the firm and the brand bounced back much more quickly than anyone thought possible. More recently, when some Belgian schoolchildren became ill after drinking Coke, the company quickly determined what the problem was and Coke's CEO made a public apology. The furor died down almost immediately.[7]

In addition to demonstrating an attitude of honesty and openness, firms can take specific and concrete steps to formalize their commitment to ethical business practices. Two of the most common approaches to formalizing commitment are adopting written codes and instituting ethics programs.

Adopting Written Codes

Many companies have adopted written codes of ethics that formally acknowledge their intent to do business in an ethical manner. Most codes of ethics are designed to perform one or more of the following functions:

- They may increase public confidence in a firm or its industry.
- They may help stem the tide of government regulation—that is, aid in self-regulation.
- They may improve internal operations by providing consistent standards of both ethical and legal conduct.
- They can help managers respond to problems that arise as a result of unethical or illegal behaviour.

Figure 3.2 shows the code of ethics adopted by Mountain Equipment Co-op.

Figure 3.3 illustrates the central role that corporate ethics and values should play in corporate policy. Although strategies and practices can change frequently and objectives can change occasionally, an organization's core principles and values should remain steadfast.

Our Purpose

To support people in achieving the benefit of wilderness-oriented recreation.

Our **purpose** is what we resolve to do.

Our Vision

Mountain Equipment Co-op is an innovative, thriving co-operative that inspires excellence in products and services, passion for wilderness experiences, leadership for a just world, and action for a healthy planet.

Our **vision** is our picture of the future and outlines where we want to go.

Our Mission

Mountain Equipment Co-op provides quality products and services for self-propelled wilderness-oriented recreation, such as hiking and mountaineering, at the lowest reasonable price in an informative, respectful manner. We are a member-owned co-operative striving for social and environmental leadership.

Our **mission** tells us what business we are in, who we serve, and how. It represents the fundamental reason for MEC's existence.

Our Values

We conduct ourselves ethically and with integrity. We show respect for others in our words and actions. We act in the spirit of community and co-operation. We respect and protect our natural environment. We strive for personal growth, continual learning, and adventure.

Our **values** influence our conduct both collectively as an organization, and individually as employees, directors and members of our community. We strive to have our actions reflect these values, demonstrate personal accountability, and be publicly defensible.

Figure 3.2 Mountain Equipment Co-op's statements of purpose, vision, mission, and values make up their code of ethics.

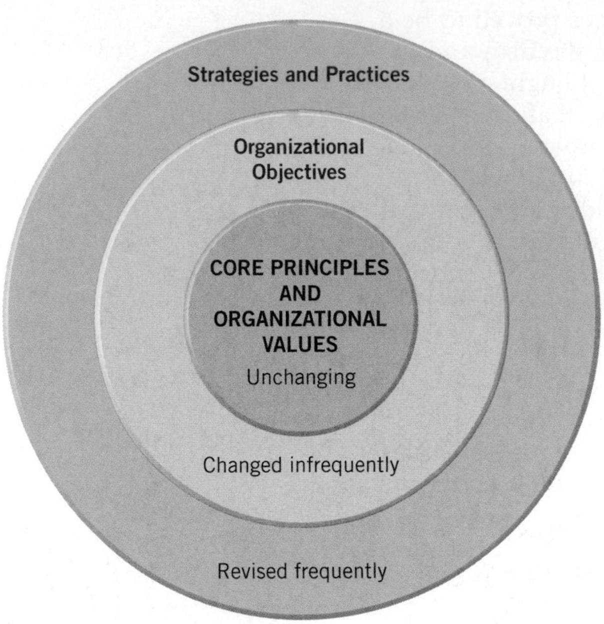

Strategies and Practices

Organizational Objectives

CORE PRINCIPLES AND ORGANIZATIONAL VALUES

Unchanging

Changed infrequently

Revised frequently

Figure 3.3 Core principles and organizational values.

Two-thirds of Canada's largest corporations have codes of ethics (90 percent of large U.S. firms do). More and more regulatory and professional associations in Canada are recommending that corporations adopt codes of ethics. The Canada Deposit Insurance Corp., for example, requires that all deposit-taking institutions have a code of conduct that is periodically reviewed and ratified by the board of directors. The Canadian Competition Bureau, the Canadian Institute of Chartered Accountants, and the Ontario Human Rights Commission are all pushing for the adoption of codes of ethics by corporations.[8] Many Canadian and U.S. firms are adding a position called "Ethics Director" or "Ethics Officer."

Instituting Ethics Programs

Many examples suggest that ethical responses can be learned through experience. For instance, in the Tylenol case, company employees didn't wait for instructions or a company directive for dealing with the problem. They knew that they should get to retailers' shelves and pull the product as quickly as possible. They reported simply "knowing" that this was what the company should do.

But can business ethics be taught, either in the workplace or in schools? Not surprisingly, business schools have become important players in the debate about ethics education. Even though business schools must address the issue of ethics in the workplace, the practical reality is that companies must take the chief responsibility for educating employees. In fact, more and more firms are doing so. Imperial Oil, for example, conducts workshops for employees that emphasize ethical concerns. The purpose of these workshops is to help employees put Imperial Oil's ethics statement into practice.

SOCIAL RESPONSIBILITY

social responsibility A business's collective code of ethical behaviour toward the environment, its customers, its employees, and its investors.

organizational stakeholders Groups, individuals, and organizations that are directly affected by the practices of an organization and that therefore have a stake in its performance.

2 Distinguish *social responsibility* from *ethics*, identify *organizational stakeholders*, and characterize social consciousness today.

Ethics affect individual behaviour in the workplace. **Social responsibility**, however, refers to the way in which a business tries to balance its commitments to certain groups and individuals in its social environment. **Organizational stakeholders** are those groups, individuals, and organizations that are directly affected by the practices of an organization and that therefore have a stake in its performance.[9]

But which of these stakeholders should be given the most attention? One view, often called *managerial capitalism*, is that a company's only social responsibility is to make as much money as possible for its shareholders, as long as it doesn't break any laws. An opposing view is that companies must be responsible to various stakeholders, including *customers*, *employees*, *investors*, *suppliers*, and the *local communities* in which they do business. Some of these stakeholders may be particularly important to the organization and so it will have to pay particular attention to their needs and expectations.

The Stakeholder Model of Responsibility

Most companies that strive to be responsible to their stakeholders concentrate on the five groups shown in Figure 3.4. They may then select other stakeholders that are particularly relevant or important to the organization and try to address their needs and expectations as well.

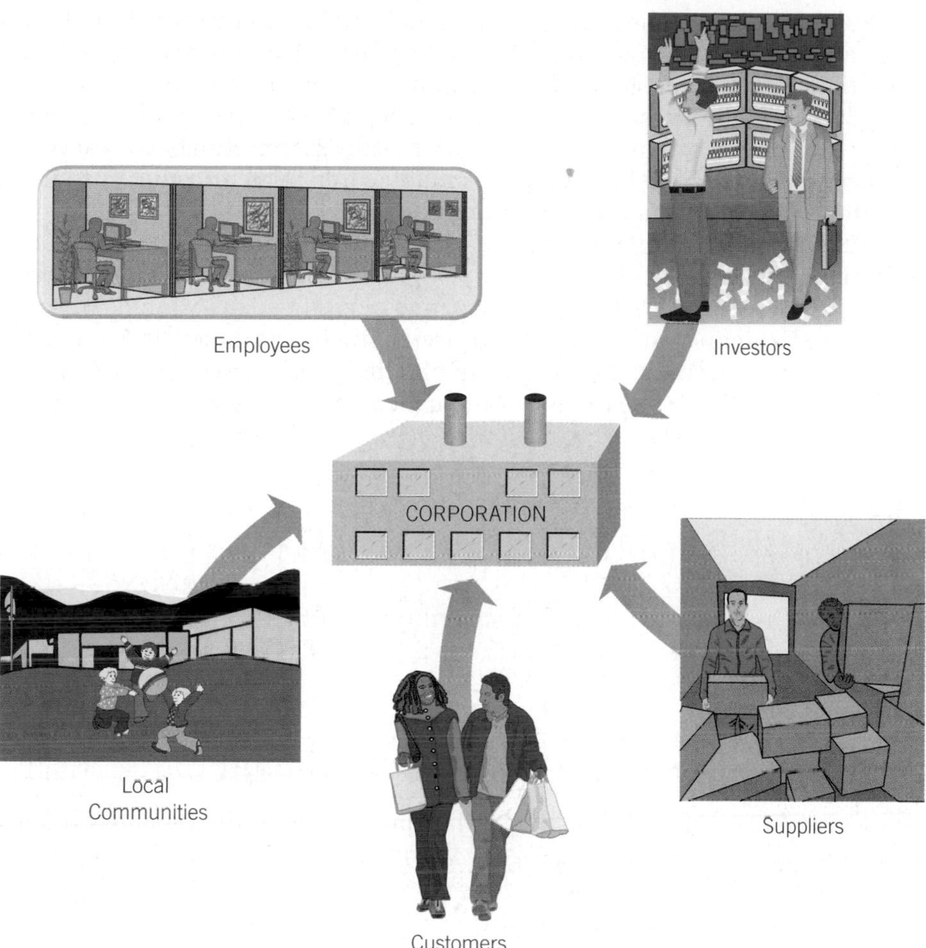

Figure 3.4 Major corporate stakeholders.

Contemporary Social Consciousness

Canadian society and Canadian business have changed dramatically in the last two centuries. Not surprisingly, so have views about social responsibility. The late nineteenth century was characterized by the entrepreneurial spirit and the laissez-faire philosophy. During this era of labour strife and predatory business practices, both individual citizens and the government became concerned about unbridled business activity. This concern was translated into laws regulating basic business practices.

During the Great Depression of the 1930s, many people blamed the failure of businesses and banks and the widespread loss of jobs on a general climate of business greed and lack of restraint. Out of the economic turmoil emerged new laws that described an increased expectation that business should protect and enhance the general welfare of society.

During the social unrest of the 1960s and 1970s, business was often characterized as a negative social force. Eventually, increased activism prompted increased government regulation in a variety of areas. Health warnings, for example, were placed on cigarettes, and stricter environmental protection laws were enacted.

Social consciousness and views toward social responsibility continue to evolve in the twenty-first century. Today's attitudes seem to be moving toward an enlightened view stressing the need for a greater social role for business. An increased awareness of the global economy and heightened campaigning on the part of environmentalists and other activists have combined to make many businesses more sensitive to their social responsibilities.

For example, retailers such as Sears have policies against selling handguns and other weapons, and toy retailer Toys "R" Us refuses to sell toy guns that look too realistic. Firms in numerous other industries have also integrated socially conscious thinking into their production plans and marketing efforts. The production of environmentally safe products, for example, has become a potential boom area, as many companies introduce products designed to be "environmentally friendly."

Electrolux, a Swedish appliance maker, has developed a line of water-efficient washing machines, a solar-powered lawnmower, and, for Brazil, the first refrigerators that are free of ozone-depleting refrigerants. Herman Miller, a Michigan-based office-furniture business, uses recycled materials and focuses on products that are simple in design, durable, and recyclable. Ford has set up an independent brand called Th!nk to develop and market fuel cells.[10]

AREAS OF SOCIAL RESPONSIBILITY

3 Show how the concept of social responsibility applies both to environmental issues and to a firm's relationships with customers, employees, and investors.

In defining its sense of social responsibility, most firms must confront four areas of concern: responsibilities toward the environment, customers, employees, and investors.

Responsibility Toward the Environment

pollution The injection of harmful substances into the environment.

One critical area of social responsibility involves how the business relates to its physical environment. In the following sections, we focus on the nature of the problems in these areas and on some of the current efforts to address them.[11] Controlling **pollution**—the injection of harmful substances into the environment—is a significant challenge for contemporary business. Although noise pollution is attracting increased concern, air pollution, water pollution, and land pollution are the subjects of most anti-pollution efforts by business and governments.[12]

The Kyoto Summit in 1997 was an attempt by various governments to reach agreement on ways to reduce the threat of pollution. Australia is the world's largest greenhouse gas emitter per capita, contributing 7.3 percent of the world's total. The United States (at 6.5 percent) and Canada (at

Why would a Western environmental group team up with a domestic logging company to help local villagers log a forest in a remote area of Indonesia? For one thing, the villagers are very poor. For another, the Nature Conservancy believes that it can enforce sustainable practices if the logger, Sumalindo Lestari Jaya, co-operates. The group also thinks that it can trust Sumalindo because it's already been successful in applying pressure to Western retailers like Home Depot and IKEA, who buy wood and paper from the Indonesian supplier.

ENTREPRENEURSHIP AND NEW VENTURES

Actions Speak Louder Than Words

When it comes to corporate social responsibility (CSR), one notable Canadian trailblazer is Mountain Equipment Co-op (MEC). MEC was formed in 1971 by four students from the University of British Columbia whose vision was to "inspire excellence in products and services, passion for wilderness experiences, leadership for a just world, and action for a healthy planet." The company's actions speak louder than words.

MEC's commitment to the environment is demonstrated in many aspects of its business, including the name of its CSR program: Social and Environmental Responsibility. The program's mandate ensures that environmental and social issues are weighed equally.

As a co-operative, MEC does not issue investment shares. Only MEC members—the customers—are permitted to own shares in the company, which are valued at five dollars apiece. Because MEC does not issue investment shares, maximizing shareholder wealth is not its exclusive focus. While MEC members may not see a direct financial return on their shares, in effect, they pass the returns on to the communities and groups that benefit from MEC's altruistic activities.

Some of MEC's revenue each year is allocated to sustainable community development projects, typically through donations for charitable or educational purposes. The MEC Endowment Fund for the Environment—MEC's own registered charity—was created in 1993. Each year, 0.4 percent of the previous year's sales are injected into MEC's Environment Fund. At first glace, this may not seem like a substantial amount, but that 0.4 percent translates into an average of $750 000 per year in contributions to environmental conservation and wilderness protection projects, research, and education. The endowment fund, which accepts tax deductible donations, is currently valued at $1.2 million and has historically been used to support land acquisition projects.

But to truly practise social and environmental responsibility, MEC recognizes that it must do more than provide money to environmental organizations. Product manufacturers must adhere to a strict set of guidelines established to ensure that the products sold in MEC stores are manufactured in safe and healthy workplaces where human and civil rights are respected.

The co-op is even more scrupulous about MEC-brand products (58 percent of which are manufactured in Canada), which comprise approximately 60 percent of sales. In addition to its own Supply Team Evaluation Process, MEC uses third-party, independent audits to ensure that the suppliers of MEC-brand products avoid child and forced labour and that workers are treated with respect and dignity and are not subjected to harassment, discrimination, or abuse. Workers must be allowed to join unions and bargain collectively, and they must be paid fairly and directly. Safe and healthy work environments must comply with local health and safety laws and regulations. Suppliers of MEC-brand products are also required to implement and maintain systems to minimize negative impacts of manufacturing and packaging on the environment and to ensure that waste is disposed of in an environmentally responsible manner.

For the past five years, MEC has been greening its buildings by making design, materials, and construction decisions based on environmental considerations. To be considered green by MEC's standards, a building must be built and sustained by resources available within its immediate area. And it should enhance (or at least not detract from) its natural environment. MEC building designers scrutinize every building element and make choices based on a number of criteria, including embodied energy and pollution content, energy efficiency, and recycling potential. Some of the more tangible innovations found in MEC's green buildings include the use of geothermal energy heat pumps in Montreal, a demonstration straw-bale wall in Ottawa, and composting toilets in Winnipeg.

When construction on MEC's Winnipeg store was completed in 2002, it became the second retail building in Canada to meet the national C2000 Green Building Standard—second only to MEC's Ottawa location.

6.4 percent) are close behind. Canada is the only one of the three leading emitters that has signed the Protocol. Transalta is the Canadian company with the biggest emission problem, but it has a plan to reduce its greenhouse gas emissions by 15 percent.[13] In 2006, the Conservative government said Canada would not be able to meet the targets for reducing pollution, and that it would continue with the Protocol only if the targets were renegotiated.[14]

Air Pollution

Air pollution results when a combination of factors converge to lower air quality. Large amounts of chemicals, such as the carbon monoxide emitted by automobiles, contribute to air pollution. Smoke and other chemicals emitted by manufacturing plants also help to create air pollution.

Legislation has gone a long way toward controlling air pollution. Under new laws, many companies have had to install special devices to limit the pollutants they expel into the atmosphere. Such clean-up efforts are not without costs, however. The bill to private companies for air pollution control devices runs into billions of dollars.

Figure 3.5 tells a troubling story. The chart shows atmospheric carbon dioxide (CO_2) levels for the period between 1750 and 2000, and it offers three possible scenarios for future levels under different sets of conditions. The three projections—lowest, middle, highest—were developed by the Intergovernmental Panel on Climate Change, which calculated likely changes in the atmosphere during this century if no efforts were made to

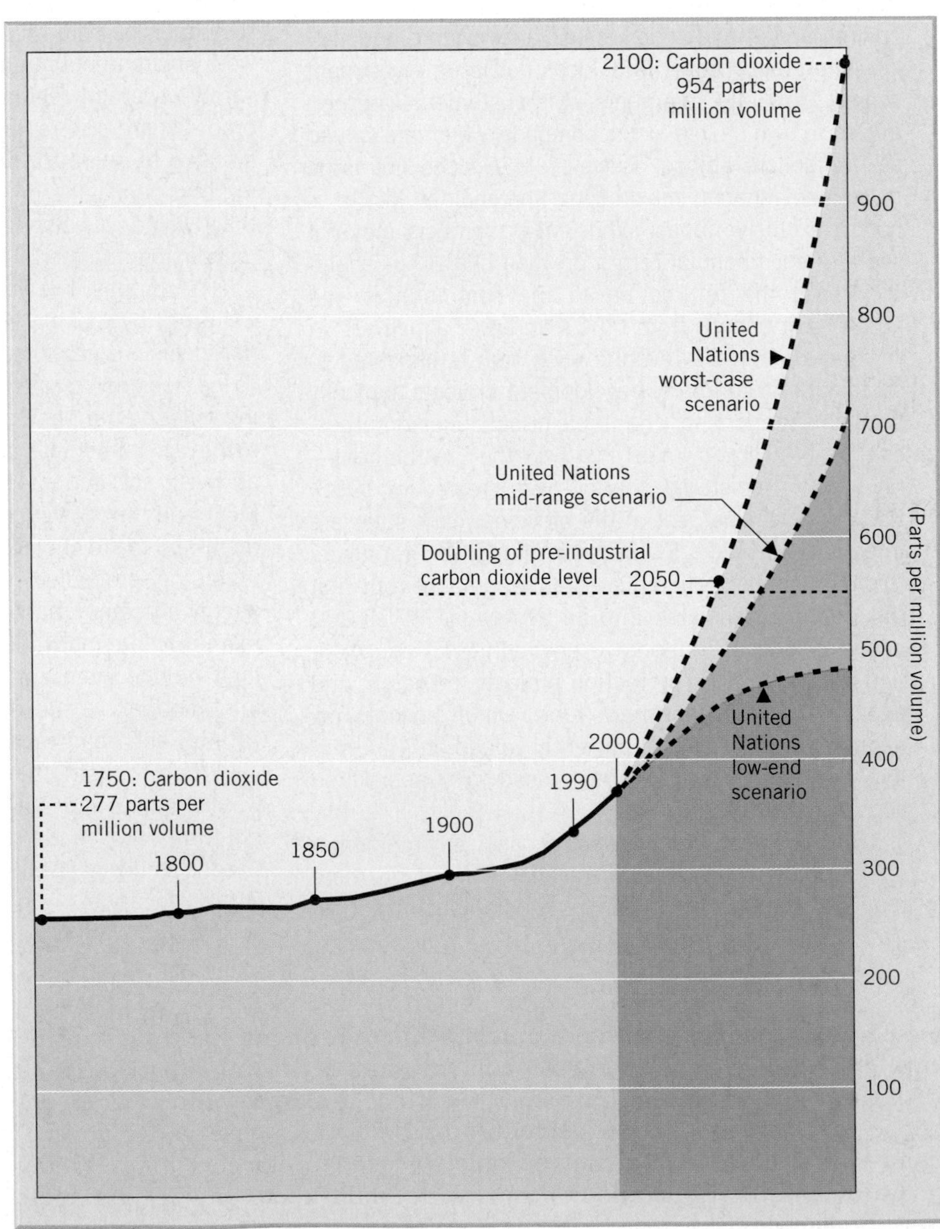

Figure 3.5 CO_2 emissions, past and future.

reduce so-called greenhouse emissions—waste gases that trap heat in the atmosphere. The criteria for estimating changes are population, economic growth, energy supplies, and technologies: The less pressure exerted by these conditions, the less the increase in CO_2 levels. Energy supplies are measured in exajoules—roughly the annual energy consumption of a large metropolitan area like New York or London.

Under the lowest, or best-case, scenario, by 2100 the population would only grow to 6.4 billion people, economic growth would be no more than 1.2 to 2.0 percent a year, and energy supplies would require only 8000 exajoules of conventional oil. However, under the highest, or worst-case, scenario, the population would increase to 11.3 billion people, annual economic growth would be between 3.0 and 3.5 percent, and energy supplies would require as much as 18 400 exajoules of conventional oil.

The resulting changes in climate would be relatively mild, and we would not experience dramatic changes in the weather. We would, however, increase the likelihood of having troublesome weather around the globe: droughts, hurricanes, and so forth. The charges levelled against greenhouse emissions are disputed, but as one researcher puts it, "The only way to prove them for sure is hang around 10, 20, or 30 more years, when the evidence would be overwhelming. But in the meantime, we're conducting a global experiment. And we're all in the test tube."[15]

Water Pollution

For years, businesses and municipalities dumped their waste into rivers, streams, and lakes with little regard for the effects. Thanks to new legislation and increased awareness on the part of businesses, water quality is improving in many areas. Millar Western Pulp Ltd. built Canada's first zero-discharge pulp mill at Meadow Lake, Saskatchewan. There is no discharge pipe to the river, no dioxin-forming chlorine, and next to no residue. Dow Chemical built a plant at Fort Saskatchewan that will not dump any pollutants into the nearby river.[16]

Land Pollution

Two key issues are associated with land pollution. The first issue is how to restore the quality of land damaged and abused in the past. In 1998, 5 million cubic litres of toxic waste escaped from a holding pond at a zinc mine in Spain that was operated by the Canadian firm Boliden Ltd. Thousands of hectares of agricultural land were contaminated.[17] A second issue is how to prevent such problems in the future. Changes in foresting practices, limits on types of mining, and new forms of solid waste disposal are all attempts to address this issue, although such changes are often opposed.

Concern for the environment has influenced the actions of many Canadian firms as they do business abroad. In many cases, there is opposition to a project by the local people because they fear that some sort of pollution will result. For example, Calgary-based TVI Pacific Inc.'s planned open-pit mine and cyanide processing plant in the Philippines led to violent clashes between the company and the Subanon people. Critics of Inco Ltd.'s Goro mine in New Caledonia claimed that it would damage the second-largest barrier reef system in the world. And a group of villagers in Thailand objected to a potash mine that was proposed by Asia Pacific Potash Corp., arguing that the project would increase salt levels in the soil and damage their ability to grow rice.[18]

Toxic Waste Disposal. Toxic wastes are dangerous chemical and/or radioactive by-products of various manufacturing processes. Because toxic waste cannot usually be processed into harmless material or destroyed, it must be stored somewhere. The problem is—where? Few people want a toxic waste storage facility in their town. Toxic waste disposal and clean-up have become increasingly important areas of debate and concern in recent years.

Many business firms are now acting to reduce various forms of pollution. Under the Canadian and Ontario environmental protection acts, liability for a business firm can run as high as $2 million per day. To protect themselves, companies must prove that they showed diligence in avoiding an environmental disaster such as an oil or gasoline spill.[19] The Environmental Choice program, sponsored by the federal government, licenses products that meet environmental standards set by the Canadian Standards Association. Firms whose products meet these standards can put the logo—three doves intertwined to form a maple leaf—on their products.[20]

Recycling. The conversion of waste materials into useful products—recycling—is a relatively new industry that has developed as part of increased consciousness about land pollution. Certain products, such as aluminum beverage cans and glass, can be very efficiently recycled. Others, such as plastics, are more troublesome. Many local communities actively support various recycling programs, including curbside pickup of aluminum, plastics, glass, and pulp paper.

biomass The plant and animal waste that is used to produce energy.

The plant and animal waste used to produce energy is referred to as **biomass**. Waste materials like sawdust, manure, and sludge are increasingly being turned into useful products. Ensyn Corp., for example, converts sawdust into liquid fuel by blasting wood waste with a sand-like substance that is heated. What's left is bio-oil.[21]

Responsibility Toward Customers

Social responsibility toward customers generally falls into one of two categories: providing quality products and pricing those products fairly. As with the environment, firms differ in their level of concern about responsibility to customers. Yet unlike environmental problems, customer problems do not require expensive technological solutions. Most such problems can be avoided if companies obey the laws regarding consumer rights, avoid illegal pricing practices, and behave ethically when advertising their products.

Rights of Consumers

consumerism A social movement that seeks to protect and expand the rights of consumers in their dealings with businesses.

Much of the current interest in business responsibility toward customers can be traced to the rise of consumerism. **Consumerism** is a form of social activism dedicated to protecting the rights of consumers in their dealings with businesses.

Consumers have the following rights:

1. The right to safe products. For example, when you buy a new paint sprayer, it must be safe to use for spraying paint. It must come with instructions on how to use it, and it must have been properly tested by its manufacturer. Dow Corning Corp. halted production of silicone breast implants after questions were raised about the product's safety. When the British government announced a possible link between "mad cow disease" and Creutzfeld-Jakob disease, McDonald's and Burger King suspended the sale of all British beef products. More recently, Canadian beef was banned from the United States when one case of mad cow disease was found in Alberta.
2. The right to be informed about all relevant aspects of a product. Food products must list their ingredients. Clothing must be labelled with information about its proper care. And banks must tell you exactly how

much interest you are paying on a loan. Cereal companies have come under fire recently for some of the claims they have made about the oat bran content of their cereals, as well as its likely effects.

3. The right to be heard. Many companies today have complaints offices. Retailers like Kmart offer a money-back guarantee if consumers aren't satisfied. Procter & Gamble puts a toll-free number on many of its products that consumers can call if they have questions or complaints. When companies refuse to respond to consumer complaints, consumer protection agencies such as the Better Business Bureau and consumer interest groups such as the Airline Passengers Association may intervene.
4. The right to choose what they buy. Central to this right is free and open competition among companies. In times past, "gentlemen's agreements" were often used to avoid competition or to divide up a market so that firms did not have to truly compete against each other. Such practices are illegal today and any attempts by business to block competition can result in fines or other penalties.
5. The right to be educated about purchases. All prescription drugs now come with detailed information regarding dosage, possible side effects, and potential interactions with other medications.
6. The right to courteous service. This right is hard to legislate, but as consumers become increasingly knowledgeable, they're more willing to complain about bad service. Consumer hotlines can also be used to voice service-related issues.

The problems with the diet pill called Pondimin illustrate what can happen to a firm that violates one or more of these consumer rights. Throughout the early 1990s, American Home Products aggressively marketed the drug, which contained fenfluramine. Doctors wrote millions of prescriptions for Pondimin and other medications containing fenfluramine. In 1997, however, a link was discovered between the pills and heart-valve disease. A class-action lawsuit followed, and the firm eventually agreed to pay $3.75 billion to individuals who had used the drug.[22]

Unfair Pricing

Interfering with competition can also mean illegal pricing practices. **Collusion** among companies—getting together to "fix" prices—is against the law. Polar Plastic Ltd. of Montreal pled guilty to conspiring to fix prices of disposable cups, glasses, and cutlery in the U.S. market. Although secret meetings and phone conversations took place between executives of competing companies as they tried to fix prices, the conspiracy was not successful.[23]

collusion An illegal agreement among companies in an industry to "fix" prices for their products.

The U.S. Justice Department is investigating 150 cases of pricing fraud by some of the world's biggest drug companies. The main allegation is that drug companies inflate prices of the drugs they sell to government-paid programs. In 2003 and 2004, several drug companies paid the following penalties: Pfizer ($430 million), Schering-Plough ($345 million), Bayer ($257 million), and GlaxoSmithKline ($88 million). The new charges may mean that up to $1 billion in fines will eventually be levied.[24]

Under some circumstances, firms can also come under attack for price gouging—responding to increased demand with overly steep (and often unwarranted) price increases. For example, when DaimlerChrysler launched its PT Cruiser in 2000, demand for the vehicles was so strong that some dealers sold them only to customers willing to pay thousands of dollars over sticker prices. Some Ford dealers adopted a similar practice when the new Thunderbird was launched in 2002. As we saw in Chapter 1, this illustrates what can happen when there is a shortage of a product.

Of all roadway accidents, 25 percent are distraction-related, and the biggest distractions for motorists are handheld gadgets like cellphones, pagers, and the like. In fulfilling their responsibility to consumers, some companies are conducting tests which yield important data about roadway accidents. Ford Motor Co., for example, has a Virtual Test Track Experiment simulator that determines how often drivers get distracted. Under normal circumstances, an adult driver will miss about 3 percent of the simulated "events" (like an ice patch or a deer on the road) that Ford contrives for a virtual road trip. If they're on the cellphone, they'll miss about 14 percent. Teenagers miss a scary 54 percent of the events.

Ethics in Advertising

In recent years increased attention has been given to ethics in advertising and product information. Because of controversies surrounding the potential misinterpretation of words and phrases such as "light," "reduced calorie," "diet," and "low fat," food producers are now required to use a standardized format for listing ingredients on product packages. There are several key ethical issues in advertising, including truth-in-advertising claims, the advertising of counterfeit brands, the use of stealth advertising, and advertising that is morally objectionable.

Truth in Advertising. Concerns about truth in advertising are becoming more noticeable on the international scene. In July 2005, for example, Chinese government officials investigated Procter & Gamble's claim that its Pantene shampoo made hair "10 times stronger." A few months earlier, P&G paid a $24 000 fine after one consumer complained that SK-II Skin Cream was not the "miracle water" it claimed to be and that it did not make her skin "look 12 years younger in 28 days."[25]

Advertising of Counterfeit Brands. Another issue concerns the advertising and sale of counterfeit brand names. Canadians tourists who visit New York often go to booths on Canal Street, which is famous for the "bargains" that can be had on supposedly name brand items like Cartier, Panerai, Vacheron, Montblanc, and Louis Vuitton. Many of the items being sold are counterfeit, although it can be very hard to tell the difference between these "knockoffs" and the genuine article. A fake Cartier Roadster watch, for example, can be bought on Canal Street for U.S.$45, while a real one costs about U.S.$3400. Naturally, legitimate manufacturers of these high-end products are trying to stamp out this counterfeit trade in their products.[26]

China is the source of many counterfeit products. For example, knockoffs of Suzuki motorcycles hit the market just a few weeks after the genuine product became available. These knockoffs were sold to customers as the real thing, but they had not been subjected to rigorous quality control like real Suzuki motorcycles are. Robert Kwauk, a Beijing lawyer, says that the idea of producing knockoffs is tolerated much more in the Chinese culture than it is in Western culture.[27] North Korea has become one of the leading counterfeiters of name brand cigarettes like Marlboro.[28]

stealth (undercover) advertising Involves companies paying individuals to extol the virtues of their products, without disclosing that they are paid to do so.

Stealth (Undercover) Advertising. **Stealth (or undercover) advertising**—which is a variation of viral marketing that we discussed in Chapter 2—involves companies paying individuals to extol the virtues of their products to other individuals. The ethics of this are questionable when the paid individuals do not reveal that they are being paid by a company, so the recipient of the advertising is not aware that it is advertising. For example, one advertising agency hired models to pose as "tourists." These models asked real tourists to take their picture with a new Sony Ericsson camera cellphone. The models then talked up the advantages of the new product to the unsuspecting real tourists. Commercial Alert, a U.S.-based consumer protection group, wants a government investigation of these undercover marketing tactics.[29]

Morally Objectionable Advertising. A final ethical issue concerns advertising that consumers consider to be morally objectionable. Benetton, for example, aired a series of commercials featuring inmates on death row. The ads, dubbed "We, on Death Row," prompted such an emotional outcry that Sears dropped the Benetton USA clothing line.[30] Other ads receiving criticism include Victoria's Secret models in skimpy underwear, and campaigns by tobacco and alcohol companies that allegedly target young people.

Responsibility Toward Employees

Organizations also need to employ fair and equitable practices with their employees. Later, in Chapter 8, we describe the human resource management activities essential to a smoothly functioning business. These same activities—recruiting, hiring, training, promoting, and compensating—are also the basis for social responsibility toward employees. A company that provides its employees with equal opportunities for rewards and advancement without regard to race, sex, or other irrelevant factors is meeting its social responsibilities. Firms that ignore their responsibility to employees leave themselves open to lawsuits. They also miss the chance to hire better and more highly motivated employees.

Legal and Social Commitments

Some progressive companies go well beyond these legal requirements, hiring and training the so-called hard-core unemployed (people with little education and training and a history of unemployment) and those who have disabilities. The Bank of Montreal, for example, sponsors a community college skills upgrading course for individuals with hearing impairments. The Royal Bank provides managers with discrimination awareness training. Rogers Cablesystems Ltd. provides individuals with mobility restrictions with telephone and customer-service job opportunities.[31] Bell Canada employs more than 1000 people with disabilities (2 percent of its permanent workforce). But, in Canada, over 50 percent of those with physical disabilities are still unemployed.[32]

In addition to their responsibility to employees as resources of the company, firms have a social responsibility to their employees as people. Firms that accept this responsibility ensure that the workplace is safe, both physically and emotionally. They would no more tolerate an abusive manager or one who sexually harasses employees than they would a gas leak.

The safety of workers is an important consideration for all organizations. The required use of hardhats, for example, is designed to protect workers from head injuries.

Business firms also have a responsibility to respect the privacy of their employees. While nearly everyone agrees that companies have the right to exercise some level of control over their employees, there is great controversy about exactly how much is acceptable in areas such as drug testing and computer monitoring. When Canadian National Railways instituted drug testing for train, brake, and yard employees, 12 percent failed. Trucking companies have found that nearly one-third of truckers who have been involved in an accident are on drugs.[33]

Employees are often unaware that they are being monitored by managers who are using new computer technology. Computer software firms even sell programs called "Spy" and "Peek" to facilitate monitoring. This type of monitoring increases employee stress levels because they don't know exactly when the boss is watching them. A lawsuit was brought against Nortel Networks by employees who charged that the firm installed telephone bugs and hidden microphones in one of its plants.[34]

Whistle-Blowers. Respecting employees as people also means respecting their behaviour as ethically responsible individuals. Suppose, for instance, an employee discovers that a business has been engaging in practices that are illegal, unethical, or socially irresponsible. Ideally, this employee should be able to report the problem to higher-level management, confident that managers will stop the questionable practices. Enron's Sherron Watkins reported concerns about the company's accounting practices well before the company's problems were made public, warning top management that Enron would "implode in a wave of accounting scandals." CEO Kenneth Lay commissioned a legal review of the firm's finances but told his investigators not to "second-guess" decisions by Enron's auditor, accounting firm Arthur Andersen.[35]

Too often, people who try to act ethically on the job find themselves in trouble with their employers. If no one in the organization will take action, the employee might elect to drop the matter. Occasionally, however, the individual will inform a regulatory agency or perhaps the media. At this point, he or she becomes a **whistle-blower**—an employee who discovers and tries to put an end to a company's unethical, illegal, or socially irresponsible actions by publicizing them.[36] The 1999 Al Pacino–Russell Crowe movie *The Insider* told the true story of a tobacco-industry whistle-blower named Jeffrey Wigand.

whistle-blower An individual who calls attention to an unethical, illegal, and/or socially irresponsible practice on the part of a business or other organization.

Unfortunately, whistle-blowers are often demoted—and even fired—when they take their accusations public. Jeffrey Wigand was fired. "I went from making $300 000 a year," he reports, "plus stock options, plus, plus, plus—to making $30 000. Yes, there is a price I've paid."[37] Even if they retain their jobs, they may still be treated as outsiders and suffer resentment or hostility from co-workers. Many co-workers see whistle-blowers as people who simply can't be trusted. One recent study suggests that about half of all whistle-blowers eventually get fired, and about half of those who get fired subsequently lose their homes and/or families.[38] New federal legislation to protect whistle-blowers was introduced in Canada in 2003.

When Phillip Adams worked in the computer industry, he discovered a flaw in the chip-making process that, under certain circumstances, could lead to data being randomly deleted or altered. He reported the flaw to manufacturers, but several years later, he found that one company, Toshiba, had ignored the problem and continued to make flawed chips for 12 years. He went on to report the problem and became actively involved in a class-action lawsuit based heavily on his research. Toshiba eventually agreed to a U.S.$2.1 billion settlement. Adams's share was kept confidential, but he did receive a substantial reward for his efforts.[39] Unfortunately, the prospect of large cash rewards has also generated a spate of false or questionable accusations.

Responsibility Toward Investors

It may sound odd to say that a firm can be irresponsible toward investors, since they are the owners of the company. But if managers abuse their firm's financial resources, the ultimate losers are the owners, since they do not receive the earnings, dividends, or capital appreciation due them.

Improper Financial Management

Occasionally, organizations are guilty of financial mismanagement. In other cases, executives have been "guilty" of paying themselves outlandish salaries, spending huge amounts of company money for their own personal comfort, and similar practices. Creditors can do nothing. Even shareholders have few viable options. Trying to force a management changeover is not only difficult, it can drive down the price of the stock, a penalty shareholders are usually unwilling to assign themselves.

Cheque Kiting

Cheque kiting involves writing a cheque from one account, depositing it in a second account, and then immediately spending money from the second account while the money from the first account is still in transit. A cheque from the second account can also be used to replenish the money in the first account, and the process starts all over again. This practice obviously benefits the person doing the cheque kiting, but is irresponsible because it involves using other peoples' money without paying for it.

cheque kiting The illegal practice of writing cheques against money that has not yet arrived at the bank on which the cheque has been written, relying on that money arriving before the cheque clears.

Insider Trading

Another area of illegal and socially irresponsible behaviour by firms toward investors is the practice of insider trading. **Insider trading** occurs when someone uses confidential information to gain from the purchase or sale of stocks. The most famous recent example is, of course, Martha Stewart, who served jail time. More detail about insider trading is provided in the Opening Case for Chapter 19.

insider trading The use of confidential information to gain from the purchase or sale of stock.

Misrepresentation of Finances

Certain behaviours regarding financial representation are also illegal. In maintaining and reporting its financial status, every corporation must conform

"From a purely business viewpoint, taking what doesn't belong to you is usually the cheapest way to go."

to generally accepted accounting principles (GAAP)—see Chapter 14. Sometimes, however, unethical managers project profits far in excess of what they actually expect to earn; others go so far as to hide losses and/or expenses to boost paper profits. When the truth comes out, however, the damage is often substantial.

Various issues involving the misrepresentation of finances were central in the Enron case. One review, for example, called Enron's accounting practices "creative and aggressive." It seems that CFO Andrew Fastow had set up a complex network of partnerships that were often used to hide losses. Enron, for instance, could report all the earnings from a partnership as its own while transferring all or most of the costs and losses to the partnership. Inflated profits would then support increased stock prices.[40]

IMPLEMENTING SOCIAL RESPONSIBILITY PROGRAMS

Thus far, we have discussed social responsibility as if a consensus exists on how firms should behave in most situations. In fact, dramatic differences of opinion exist as to the appropriateness of social responsibility as a business goal. As you might expect, some people oppose any business activity that cuts into profits to investors. Others argue that responsibility must take precedence over profits.

Even people who share a common attitude toward social responsibility by businesses may have different reasons for their beliefs. Some opponents of such activity fear that if businesses become too active in social concerns, they will gain too much control over how those concerns are addressed. They point to the influence many businesses have been able to exert on the government agencies that are supposed to regulate their industries. Other critics of business-sponsored social programs argue that companies lack the expertise needed. They believe that technical experts, not businesses, should decide how best to clean up a polluted river, for example.

Supporters of social responsibility believe that corporations are citizens just like individuals and therefore need to help improve our lives. Others point to the vast resources controlled by businesses and note that since businesses often create many of the problems social programs are designed to alleviate, they should use their resources to help. Still others argue that social responsibility is wise because it pays off for the firm.

The late Max Clarkson, formerly a top-level business executive and director of the Centre for Corporate Social Performance and Ethics at the University of Toronto, said that business firms that had a strong consciousness about ethics and social responsibility outperform firms that do not. After designing and applying a social responsibility rating system for companies, he found that companies that had the highest marks on questions of ethics and social responsibility also had the highest financial performance.[41]

Approaches to Social Responsibility

4 Identify four general *approaches to social responsibility* and describe the four steps a firm must take to implement a *social responsibility program*.

Given these differences of opinion, it is little wonder that corporations have adopted a variety of approaches to social responsibility. As Figure 3.6 illustrates, the four stances an organization can take concerning its obligations to society fall along a continuum ranging from the lowest to the highest degree of socially responsible practices.

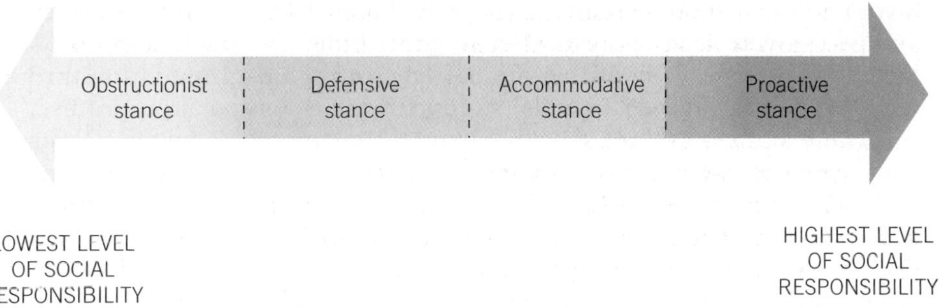

Figure 3.6 Spectrum of approaches to corporate social responsibility.

Obstructionist Stance

The few organizations that take what might be called an **obstructionist stance** to social responsibility usually do as little as possible to solve social or environmental problems. When they cross the ethical or legal line that separates acceptable from unacceptable practices, their typical response is to deny or cover up their actions. Firms that adopt this position have little regard for ethical conduct and will generally go to great lengths to hide wrongdoing.

obstructionist stance A company does as little as possible to solve social or environmental problems.

Defensive Stance

One step removed from the obstructionist stance is the **defensive stance**, whereby the organization will do everything that is required of it legally but nothing more. This approach is most consistent with arguments against corporate social responsibility. Managers who take a defensive stance insist that their job is to generate profits. Such a firm, for example, would install pollution-control equipment dictated by law, but would not install higher-quality equipment even though it might further limit pollution.

defensive stance An organization does only what is legally required and nothing more.

Tobacco companies generally take this position in their marketing efforts. In Canada and the United States, they are legally required to include warnings to smokers on their products and to limit advertising to prescribed media. Domestically, they follow these rules to the letter of the law but use more aggressive marketing methods in countries that have no such rules. In many Asian and African countries, for example, cigarettes are heavily promoted, contain higher levels of tar and nicotine than those sold in Canada and the United States, and carry few or no health warning labels. Firms that take this position are unlikely to cover up wrongdoing, will generally admit to mistakes, and will take appropriate corrective actions.

Accommodative Stance

A firm that adopts an **accommodative stance** meets its legal and ethical requirements, but will also go further in certain cases. Such firms voluntarily agree to participate in social programs, but solicitors must convince them that these programs are worthy of their support. Many organizations respond to requests for donations to community hockey teams, Girl Guides, youth soccer programs, and so forth. The point, however, is that someone has to knock on the door and ask; accommodative organizations do not necessarily or proactively seek avenues for contributing.

accommodative stance A company meets all of its legal and ethical requirements, and in some cases even goes beyond what is required.

Proactive Stance

The highest degree of social responsibility a firm can exhibit is the **proactive stance**. Firms that adopt this approach take to heart the arguments in

proactive stance An organization actively seeks opportunities to be socially responsible.

favour of social responsibility. They view themselves as citizens in a society and proactively seek opportunities to contribute. The most common—and direct—way to implement this stance is by setting up a foundation through which to provide direct financial support for various social programs.

These stances are not sharply distinct; they merely label stages along a continuum of social responsibility. Organizations do not always fit neatly into one category or another. The Ronald McDonald House program has been widely applauded, for example, but McDonald's has also come under fire for allegedly misleading consumers about the nutritional value of its food products. Likewise, while UPS has sincere motives for helping Olympic athletes, the company will also benefit by featuring their photos on its envelopes and otherwise promoting its own benevolence.

Corporate Charitable Donations. Donating money to different "causes" is one way that business firms try to show that they are socially responsible. Many groups that used to receive government funding (but no longer do because of government spending cuts) are increasingly seeking corporate support for their activities. More and more corporations are being asked to donate money to educational institutions, welfare agencies, service clubs, arts and culture groups, and athletic organizations.

A Decima Research survey found that 80 percent of Canadians think that businesses should give some of their profits to social causes.[42] An Environics survey of people in 23 different countries found that two-thirds of them thought that business was not doing enough if it simply abided by the law and provided employment. Instead, these people think that companies should also contribute to the broader goals of society.[43] A third survey, conducted by the Centre for Philanthropy, found that Canadian corporations contributed less than 2 percent of all charitable revenue. Canadians think that this number is closer to 20 percent, and that it should be 30 percent.[44]

Corporations that gave substantial amounts of money to charity in 2005 were the RBC Financial Group ($40 million), BMO Financial Group ($29.5 million), and TELUS Corp. ($11 million). Corporations typically give less than half of 1 percent of their pre-tax profits to charity, but many have demonstrated a willingness to give money and products when disasters strike.

When seven people died in Walkerton, Ontario, as a result of drinking contaminated water, companies such as Petro-Canada, Shoppers Drug Mart, Sobeys, and Zellers contributed products such as bleach and bottled water. And when thousands of people died in the Asian tsunamis of 2004, companies from around the world rushed aid to the stricken areas. They donated drugs, mobile telephones, machinery, medical equipment, water, and free travel for relief workers.[45] Companies generally receive favourable publicity when they make contributions like these, but they can be accused of being opportunistic if they attempt to publicize their donations.[46]

Most large business firms in Canada have clear procedures for dealing with requests from charities and community organizations. The company first determines how much money it will give each year, usually stated as a percentage of profit. It then decides which specific organizations will receive the money and the amount each will receive. The board of directors makes these decisions after it receives a recommendation from a committee that has been set up to consider charitable requests. Companies are increasingly taking a community-based approach to giving; they try to determine how they can achieve value for the community (and the company) with their donations.

Managing Social Responsibility Programs

Making a company truly socially responsible in the full sense of the proactive stance takes an organized and managed program. In particular, managers must take four steps to foster social responsibility, as shown in Figure 3.7.

1. Social responsibility must start at the top and be considered as a factor in strategic planning. Without the support of top management, no program can succeed. Thus, top management must embrace a strong stand on social responsibility and develop a policy statement outlining that commitment.

2. A committee of top managers must develop a plan detailing the level of management support. Some companies set aside percentages of profits for social programs. Levi Strauss, for example, earmarks 2.4 percent of pre-tax earnings for worthy projects. Managers must also set specific priorities. For instance, should the firm train the hard-core unemployed or support the arts?

3. One executive must be put in charge of the firm's agenda. Whether the role is created as a separate job or added to an existing one, the selected individual must monitor the program and ensure that its implementation is consistent with the firm's policy statement and strategic plan.

4. The organization must conduct occasional social audits. **Social audits** are systematic analyses of its success in using funds earmarked for its social responsibility goals.[47] Consider the case of a company whose strategic plan calls for spending $100 000 to train 200 hard-core unemployed people and to place 180 of them in jobs. If at the end of a year, the firm has spent $98 000, trained 210 people, and filled 175 jobs, a social audit will confirm the program's success. But if the program has cost $150 000, trained only 90 people, and placed only 10 of them, the audit will reveal the program's failure. Such failure should prompt a rethinking of the program's implementation and its priorities.

social audit A systematic analysis of how a firm is using funds earmarked for social-responsibility goals and how effective these expenditures have been.

In addition to social audits, Canadian businesses are increasingly publishing sustainability reports. These reports go beyond simply financial

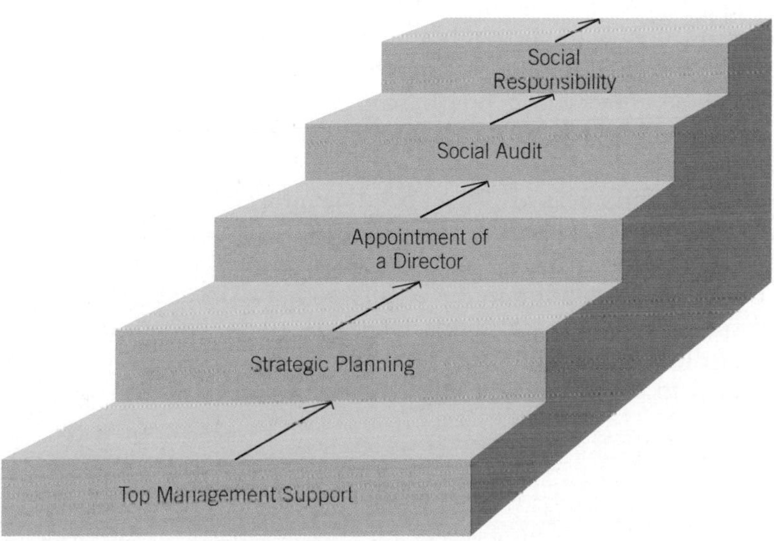

Figure 3.7 Establishing a social responsibility program involves four basic steps.

Ronald McDonald House helps the families of children who are in hospital care. It is supported by McDonald's and is an excellent example of socially responsible behaviour by a business corporation.

reporting and explain how the company is performing on issues such as the environment, employee relations, workplace diversity, and business ethics. A study by Ottawa-based Stratos Inc. found that 70 percent of Canada's largest public companies now report at least some sustainability performance information.[48] Social audits and sustainability reports together constitute **triple bottom line reporting**—measuring the social, environmental, and economic performance of a company.[49]

triple bottom line reporting Measuring the social, environmental, and economic performance of a company.

Social Responsibility and the Small Business

5 Explain how issues of social responsibility and ethics affect small businesses.

Although many of the examples in this chapter illustrate responses to social responsibility and ethical issues by big business, small businesses face many of the same questions. As the owner of a garden supply store, how would you respond to a building inspector's suggestion that a cash payment would expedite your application for a building permit? As the manager of a nightclub, would you call the police, refuse service, or sell liquor to a customer whose ID card looks forged? Or as the owner of a small laboratory, would you actually call the board of health to make sure that it has licensed the company you want to contract with to dispose of the lab's medical waste? Is the small manufacturing firm justified in overcharging a customer by 5 percent whose purchasing agent is lax? Who will really be harmed if a small firm pads its income statement to help get a much-needed bank loan?

Can a small business afford a social agenda? Should it sponsor hockey teams, make donations to the United Way, and buy light bulbs from the Lion's Club? Is joining the Chamber of Commerce and supporting the Better Business Bureau too much or just good business? Clearly, ethics and social responsibility are decisions faced by all managers in all organizations, regardless of rank or size. One key to business success is to decide in advance how to respond to these issues.

Summary of Learning Objectives

1. **Explain how individuals develop their personal *codes of ethics* and why ethics are important in the workplace.** Individual codes of ethics are derived from social standards of right and wrong. Ethical behaviour is behaviour that conforms to generally accepted social norms concerning beneficial and harmful actions. Because ethics affect the behaviour of individuals on behalf of the companies that employ them, many firms are adopting formal statements of ethics. Unethical behaviour can result in loss of business, fines, and even imprisonment.
2. **Distinguish *social responsibility* from *ethics*, identify *organizational stakeholders*, and characterize social consciousness today.** Social responsibility refers to the way a firm attempts to balance its commitments to organizational stakeholders. One way to understand social responsibility is to view it in terms of stakeholders—those groups, individuals, and organizations that are directly affected by the practices of an organization and that therefore have a stake in its performance. Until the second half of the nineteenth century, businesses often paid little attention to stakeholders. Since then, however, both public pressure and government regulation, especially as a result of the Great Depression of the 1930s and the social activism of the 1960s and 1970s, have forced businesses to consider public welfare, at least to some degree. A trend toward increased social consciousness, including a heightened sense of environmental activism, has recently emerged.
3. **Show how the concept of social responsibility applies both to environmental issues and to a firm's relationships with customers, employees, and investors.** Social responsibility toward the environment requires firms to minimize pollution of air, water, and land. Social responsibility toward customers requires firms to provide products of acceptable quality, to price products fairly, and to respect consumers' rights. Social responsibility toward employees requires firms to respect workers both as resources and as people who are more productive when their needs are met. Social responsibility toward investors requires firms to manage their resources and to represent their financial status honestly.
4. **Identify four general *approaches to social responsibility* and describe the four steps a firm must take to implement a *social responsibility program*.** An obstructionist stance on social responsibility is taken by a firm that does as little as possible to address social or environmental problems and that may deny or attempt to cover up problems that may occur. The defensive stance emphasizes compliance with legal minimum requirements. Companies adopting the accommodative stance go beyond minimum activities, if asked. The proactive stance commits a company to actively seek to contribute to social projects. Implementing a social responsibility program entails four steps: (1) drafting a policy statement with the support of top management, (2) developing a detailed plan, (3) appointing a director to implement the plan, and (4) conducting social audits to monitor results.
5. **Explain how issues of social responsibility and ethics affect small businesses.** Managers and employees of small businesses face many of the same ethical questions as their counterparts at larger firms. Small businesses face the same issues of social responsibility and the same need to decide on an approach to social responsibility. The differences are primarily differences of scale.

KEY TERMS

accommodative stance, 93
biomass, 86
business ethics, 72
cheque kiting, 91
collusion, 87
consumerism, 86
defensive stance, 93
ethical behaviour, 72
ethics, 72
insider trading, 91
managerial ethics, 75
obstructionist stance, 93
organizational stakeholders, 80
pollution, 82
proactive stance, 93
social audit, 95
social responsibility, 80
stealth (undercover) advertising, 88
triple bottom line reporting, 96
unethical behaviour, 72
whistle-blower, 90

QUESTIONS FOR ANALYSIS

1. Write a one-paragraph description of an ethical dilemma which you, or someone you know, faced recently. What was the outcome in the situation? Was it consistent with what you thought should have occurred? Why or why not? Analyze the situation using the ideas presented in the chapter. Make particular reference to the ethical norms of utility, rights, justice, and caring in terms of how they impacted the situation. What would each of these suggest about the correct decision? Does this analysis lead you to a different conclusion about the best outcome? Explain.
2. Develop an example of the way in which your personal code of ethics might clash with the operations of a specific company. How might you try to resolve these differences?
3. What kind of wrongdoing would most likely prompt you to be a whistle-blower? What kind of wrongdoing would be least likely? Why?
4. In your opinion, which area of social responsibility is most important? Why? Are there areas other than those noted in the chapter that you consider important?
5. Identify some specific ethical or social responsibility issues that might be faced by small business managers and employees in each of the following areas: environment, customers, employees, and investors.
6. Choose a product or service and explain the social responsibility concerns that are likely to be evident in terms of the environment, customers, employees, and investors.
7. Analyze the forces that are at work from both the company's perspective and the whistle-blower's perspective. Given these forces, what characteristics would a law to protect whistle-blowers have to have to be effective?
8. Pick a product or service that demonstrates the defensive approach to social responsibility. What has been the impact of that stance on the company that is using it? Now pick a product or service for each of the other stances (obstructionist, accommodative, and proactive) and do the same analysis. Why did these companies adopt the particular stance they did?

APPLICATION EXERCISES

1. Develop a list of the major stakeholders of your college or university. As a class, discuss the ways in which you think the school prioritizes these stakeholders. Do you agree or disagree with this prioritization?
2. Using newspapers, magazines, and other business references, identify and describe at least three companies that take a defensive stance to social responsibility, three that take an accommodative stance, and three that take a proactive stance.

BUILDING YOUR BUSINESS SKILLS

To Lie Or Not to Lie: That Is the Question

Goal

To encourage students to apply general concepts of business ethics to specific situations.

Background

Workplace lying, it seems, has become business as usual. According to one survey, one-quarter of working adults said that they had been asked to do something illegal or unethical on the job. Four in 10 did what they were told. Another survey of more than 2000 secretaries showed that many employees face ethical dilemmas in their day-to-day work.

Assignment

Step 1

Working with four other students, discuss ways in which you would respond to the following ethical dilemmas. When there is a difference of opinion among group members, try to determine the specific factors that influence different responses.

- Would you lie about your supervisor's whereabouts to someone on the phone?
- Would you lie about who was responsible for a business decision that cost your company thousands of dollars to protect your own or your supervisor's job?

▶▶▶

- Would you inflate sales and revenue data on official company accounting statements to increase stock value?
- Would you say that you witnessed a signature when you did not if you were acting in the role of a notary?
- Would you keep silent if you knew that the official minutes of a corporate meeting had been changed?
- Would you destroy or remove information that could hurt your company if it fell into the wrong hands?

Step 2

Research the commitment to business ethics at Johnson & Johnson (www.jnj.com/our_company/our_credo/index.htm) and Texas Instruments (www.ti.com/corp/docs/company/citizen/ethics/index.shtml) by visiting their respective websites. As a group, discuss ways in which these statements are likely to affect the specific behaviours mentioned in Step 1.

Step 3

Working with group members, draft a corporate code of ethics that would discourage the specific behaviours mentioned in Step 1. Limit your code to a single typewritten page, but make it sufficiently broad to cover different ethical dilemmas.

Follow-Up Questions

1. What personal, social, and cultural factors do you think contribute to lying in the workplace?
2. Do you agree or disagree with the following statement? "The term *business ethics* is an oxymoron." Support your answer with examples from your own work experience or that of a family member.
3. If you were your company's director of human resources, how would you make your code of ethics a "living document"?
4. If you were faced with any of the ethical dilemmas described in Step 1, how would you handle them? How far would you go to maintain your personal ethical standards?

EXERCISING YOUR ETHICS

Taking a Stance

The Situation

A perpetual debate revolves around the roles and activities of business owners in contributing to the greater social good. Promoting the so-called proactive stance, some people argue that businesses should be socially responsible by seeking opportunities to benefit the society in which they are permitted to conduct their affairs. Others maintain a defensive stance, saying that because businesses exist to make profits for owners, they have no further obligation to society.

The Dilemma

Pair up with one of your classmates. Using a coin toss, each of you should be assigned to one side of this debate. You and your partner should then enter into a dialogue to formulate the three most convincing arguments possible to support each side. Then select the single strongest argument in support of each position. Each team of two partners should then present to the class its strongest arguments for and against social responsibility on the part of business.

Questions for Discussion

1. Which side of the debate is easier to defend? Why?
2. What is your personal opinion about the appropriate stance that a business should take regarding social responsibility?
3. To what extent is the concept of social responsibility relevant to non-business organizations such as universities, government units, health-care organizations, and so forth?

CONCLUDING CASE 3-1

High Seas Dumping

Cruising has become a very popular vacation. More than eight million passengers take an ocean voyage each year, cruising many areas of the world's oceans in search of pristine beaches and clear tropical waters. The Caribbean Sea, the Mediterranean Sea, and the coast of Alaska are among the most popular destinations, while the coasts of Europe and Asia are also growing in popularity. The tourists and the giant ships that carry them are usually welcome for the revenues that they bring, but these ships also bring something much less desirable—pollution.

A modern cruise ship carries an average of 2000 passengers and 1000 crew members. That many people generate a lot of waste. On a typical day, a ship will produce seven tons of solid garbage, which is incinerated and then dumped (15 gallons of highly toxic chemical waste; 30 000 gallons of sewage; 7000 gallons of bilge water containing oil; and 225 000 gallons of "grey" water from sinks and laundries). Cruise ships also pick up ballast water whenever and wherever it's needed and then discharge it later, releasing animals and pollution from other parts of the world. Multiply this problem by more than 167 ships worldwide, cruising 50 weeks per year, and the scope of the environmental damage is staggering.

Environmental groups see the top pollution-related problem as death of marine life, including extinction. Foreign animals bring parasites and diseases, and in some cases, replace native species entirely. Bacteria that are harmless to human beings can kill corals that provide food and habitat for many species. Oil and toxic chemicals are deadly to wildlife even in minute quantities. Turtles swallow plastic bags, thinking they are jellyfish, and starve, while seals and birds drown after becoming entangled in the plastic rings that hold beverage cans.

Other problems include the habitat destruction or disease that affects certain industries. For example, cholera, picked up in ships' ballast water off the coast of Peru, caused a devastating loss to fish and shrimp harvesters in the Gulf of Mexico in the 1990s when infected catches had to be destroyed. Heavy metal poisoning of fish is rising, and concern is on the rise that the poisons are moving up the food chain from microscopic animals, to fish, and ultimately to humans. Phosphorus found in detergents causes an overgrowth of algae, which then consume all the available oxygen in the water, making it incapable of supporting any flora or fauna.

Lack of regulation is the biggest obstacle to solving the problem. By international law, countries may regulate oceans for three miles off their shores. International treaties provide some additional regulation up to 25 miles offshore. Beyond the 25-mile point, however, ships are allowed free rein. Also, each country's laws and enforcement policies vary considerably, and even when laws are strict, enforcement may be limited. One would think that cruise lines would be cognizant of the importance of clean and safe seas for their own economic well-being. Sadly, however, this is often not the case.

Intentional illegal dumping may be growing in scope. Over the last decade, for instance, as enforcement has tightened, 10 cruise lines have collectively paid $48.5 million in fines related to illegal dumping. In the largest settlement to date, Royal Caribbean paid $27 million for making illegal alterations to facilities, falsifying records, lying to the U.S. Coast Guard, and deliberately destroying evidence. The fine may seem high, but it covers 30 different charges and 10 years' of violations and seems small compared to the firm's billions of profits over the past few years. Royal Caribbean's fine was less than what the firm would have paid to dispose of the waste properly over a one-year period. In addition, a lawsuit is pending regarding the firing of a whistle-blower, the firm's former vice president for safety and environment. "This [case] is like the Enron of the seas," says attorney William Amlong, who represents the whistle-blower.

Critics are speaking out against the cruise lines' profiteering from an environment that they are destroying, but they note that the companies won't stop as long as the profits continue. Technology exists to make the waste safe, but industry experts estimate that dumping can save a firm millions of dollars annually. From that perspective, Royal Caribbean and Norwegian are making understandable decisions.

Questions for Discussion

1. What are the major legal issues in this case? What are the major ethical issues?
2. Aside from personal greed, what factors might lead a cruise line to illegally dump waste into the ocean?
3. Which approach to social responsibility do cruise lines appear to be taking?
4. Distinguish between ethical issues and social responsibility issues as they apply to this problem.

CONCLUDING CASE 3-2

Ethical Lapses at Volkswagen

In 2005, a middle manager named Klaus-Joachim Gebauer was fired from Volkswagen (VW) for allegedly embezzling money from the company. A few weeks later, he began making serious allegations about unethical behaviour at VW. Specifically, he claimed that VW had sent several German labour leaders to Brazil so they could tour VW's production facilities in Sao Paulo and meet with local Brazilian union officials. Gebauer (who went along on the trip) alleged that after the business part of the trip was over, the group checked into the Othon Palace and then explored the "nightlife" of Rio. This included visits to prostitutes. Gebauer paid for everything and then submitted phony receipts so that VW would reimburse him for all the expenses the group incurred on the trip. He says he was told by his boss to do this in order to gain worker representatives' support for VW management.

Gebauer claims that this was just one of many trips that VW paid for during the period 1996–2004. Visits were also made to Argentina, India, Portugal, France, Poland, and the Czech Republic. For each of these trips, Gebauer drew up a legitimate-looking business agenda, which he says was a complete fake. German state prosecutors are now looking into the allegations, particularly the ones that VW illegally used company funds to pay for labour leaders to go on pleasure junkets.

There has long been a "cozy" relationship between management and labour in German companies, partly as a result of German laws. For example, approximately half the positions on supervisory boards of German companies are occupied by workers' representatives. In addition, German law requires that companies pay for legitimate business expenses of its labour representatives. Many observers have concluded that the close relationship between labour and management explains Germany's economic success during the past 30 years because Germany was able to avoid much of the labour strife that occurred in so many other countries. But now, critics are pointing to the problems that such a close relationship can cause.

When Gebauer initially made his charges, VW dismissed his claims and pointed out that he had been fired for embezzlement and for seeking kickbacks from possible VW business partners. But as time passed, Gebauer's allegations began to look more credible. By early 2006, prosecutors had identified nine individuals (including some labour representatives) who may have been involved. The prosecutors also said they had uncovered evidence of criminal wrongdoing.

VW now appears to be accepting that something was not right, because it asked KPMG to investigate the abuse of travelling expenses by some employees. The CEO of VW, Bernd Pischetsrieder, said that the auditors found that $740 000 had been paid to an acquaintance of VW's labour leader Klaus Volkert for "services" that were not approved. VW also acknowledged that the necessary control system to catch improper expenses was not in place.

This unpleasant situation is not the only one that VW has been involved in during the last decade. In the 1990s, the company also received bad publicity when its chief purchasing agent, Jose Ignacio Lopez de Arriortua, was charged by the U.S. Justice Department with stealing secret General Motors documents and turning them over to VW (Lopez had previously been the chief purchasing agent for General Motors and had access to GM's plans). GM also filed a civil suit against VW claiming that Lopez stole GM's plans for new cars, parts lists, price lists, and plans for a secret manufacturing plant. It claimed that VW used this information to lower its costs and to gain market share at GM's expense.

VW originally denied the allegations, but then the district attorney of Darmstadt, Germany, discovered confidential GM documents at the home of another former GM executive who had, like Lopez, defected to VW. At stake was the public's perception of VW's ethics—an intangible factor that could affect the company's sales. When a German polling organization asked 1000 Germans what they thought of the Lopez affair, 65 percent believed that there was "something to" the allegations, while only 7 percent felt they were unfounded.

VW eventually agreed to give GM $100 million in cash, and to purchase $1 billion in parts from GM. Lopez also resigned from VW and GM dropped its civil suit.

Questions for Discussion

1. What factors at VW encouraged the behaviour that Mr. Gebauer described?
2. What steps should VW take to ensure that such behaviour is not allowed to occur again?
3. How concerned should a company like VW be with the public's reaction to questionable behaviour by its managers? Defend your answer.
4. Consider the Lopez situation. Does an employee have an ethical responsibility to maintain the confidentiality of information gained on the job with one company when taking a job with a competing company? Explain your reasoning.

CHAPTER 4*

Understanding Entrepreneurship, Small Business, and New Venture Creation

After reading this chapter, you should be able to:

1. Explain the meaning of and interrelationship among the terms *small business*, *new venture creation*, and *entrepreneurship*.
2. Describe the role of small and new businesses in the Canadian economy.
3. Explain the *entrepreneurial process* and describe its three key elements.
4. Describe three alternative strategies for becoming a business owner—*starting*, *buying an existing business*, and *buying a franchise*.
5. Describe four forms of *legal organization* for a business and discuss the advantages and disadvantages of each.
6. Identify four key reasons for success in small businesses and four key reasons for failure.

*This chapter was written by Dr. Monica Diochon, St. Francis Xavier University.

Stepping Up

The year was 1994. Sandra Wilson, a young wife and mother, was downsized out of her airline job. She welcomed the chance to spend more time with her 18-month-old son Robert, and became inspired by his tiny feet. Lovingly she handcrafted a pair of brightly coloured, soft-soled leather shoes for young Robert. Indeed, the shoes seemed to improve his balance as the soft soles allowed him to "feel" the floor while he toddled about.

Wilson began to wonder: If these soft-soled shoes worked so well for Robert, perhaps other mothers would find them a good product for their children's developing feet. Wilson saw this as an opportunity to start her own business. Naming the footwear after her son, "Robeez" was born. After hand-stitching 20 pairs of her footwear, she attended the 1994 Vancouver Gift Show trade exhibition. The response? Overwhelming. The orders flooded in and she signed up 15 retailers ready to sell her product.

Wilson threw herself into production. Her home's basement became Robeez Footwear's early headquarters, and she quickly immersed herself into learning all there was to know about leather, cutting, sewing, design, sales, and distribution. It was the beginning of an incredible growth story.

To keep up with the booming sales, Wilson hired her first sales representative in March 1995 and by May 1997, Robeez was online. The company moved out of Wilson's basement in May 1999 and into its first commercial space. Since then, the company has relocated and expanded into larger premises to accommodate its rapidly expanding operations. In August 2001, sales topped $1.2 million and doubled by the following year. Today, sales of this Burnaby, British Columbia, business exceed the $25 million mark and continue to grow rapidly.

In June 2006, for the fourth year in a row, Robeez achieved a top-20 spot on the prestigious *Profit* 100 ranking of Canada's fastest-growing companies. Not bad for a business that started out in Wilson's basement with three employees. Wilson says Robeez' relaxed supportive culture is vital to its growth. Robeez weaves fun and training into the routine, which breaks the monotony of many of the sewing jobs. Wilson's belief in her company's culture explains why Robeez' European headquarters was started by a Welsh couple with a passion for Robeez' values. Today, the European office leads plans for cross-Atlantic distribution, with over two dozen full-time employees and regional sales representatives. "People ask, 'What the heck are you doing in Wales?'" says Wilson. "Well, that's where the right people are. We felt it was really important to get the people first, then do the business."

Today, Robeez is recognized as the world's leading manufacturer of soft-soled leather footwear for newborns to four-year-olds. The company has 450 employees and sells more than 90 designs of shoes and booties in over 6500 stores in countries throughout North America, Europe, Australia, and parts of Asia. Recommended by experts and the first choice of parents, the hallmark of the meticulously crafted footwear is the skid-resistant soles that promote the healthy development of little feet by encouraging feet to flex and toes to grip. In September 2006, Robeez joined The Stride Rite Corporation's family of well-known footwear brands including Keds, Sperry Top-Sider, Tommy Hilfiger Footwear, Stride Rite, and Saucony. Wilson remains with the company as a consultant, and her ongoing participation will ensure the continuation of the unique Robeez design and brand vision. ◆

THE LINKS AMONG SMALL BUSINESS, NEW VENTURE CREATION, AND ENTREPRENEURSHIP

Every day, approximately 380 businesses are started in Canada.[1] New firms create the most jobs,[2] are noted for their entrepreneurship, and are typically small. But does this mean that most small businesses are entrepreneurial? Not necessarily.

The terms *small business, new venture,* and *entrepreneurship* are closely linked terms, but each idea is distinct. In the following paragraphs we will explain these terms to help you understand these topics and how they are interrelated.

Small Business

1 Explain the meaning of and interrelationship among the terms *small business, new venture creation,* and *entrepreneurship.*

Defining a "small" business can be a bit tricky. Various measures might be used, including the number of people the business employs, the company's sales revenue, the size of the investment required, or the type of ownership structure the business has. Some of the difficulties in defining a small business can be understood by considering the way the Canadian government collects and reports information on small businesses.

Industry Canada is the main federal government agency responsible for small business. In reporting Canadian small business statistics, the government relies on two distinct sources of information, both provided by Statistics Canada: the Business Register (which tracks businesses), and the Labour Force Survey (which tracks individuals). To be included in the register, a business must have at least one paid employee, annual sales revenues of $30 000 or more, or be incorporated (we describe incorporation later in the chapter). A goods-producing business in the register is considered small if it has fewer than 100 employees, while a service-producing business is considered small if it has fewer than 50 employees.

The Labour Force Survey uses information from *individuals* to make estimates of employment and unemployment levels. Individuals are classified as self-employed if they are working owners of a business that is either incorporated or unincorporated, if they work for themselves but do not have a business (some musicians, for example, would fall into this category), or if they work without pay in a family business.[3]

In its publication *Key Small Business Statistics* (www.strategis.gc.ca/epic/internet/insbrp-rppe.nsf/en/rd00760e.html), Industry Canada reports that there are 2.2 million "business establishments" in Canada and about 2.5 million people who are "self-employed."[4] There is no way of identifying how much overlap there is in these two categories, but we do know that an unincorporated business operated by a self-employed person (with no employees) would *not* be counted among the 2.2 million *businesses* in the register. This is an important point because the majority of businesses in Canada have no employees (just the owner), nor are they incorporated.

These facts need to be kept in mind when considering statistics or research that excludes these firms. When either of these indicators is used to find businesses to study, the number of new firms will be underestimated. A study by the Panel Study of Entrepreneurial Dynamics (PSED), conducted by members of the Entrepreneurship Research Consortium (ERC), tracked a sample of Canadian **nascent entrepreneurs**—people who were trying to start a business—over four years. Only 15 percent of those who reported establishing an operating business had incorporated their firm.[5]

nascent entrepreneurs People who are trying to start a business from scratch.

For our purposes, we define a **small business** as an owner-managed business with less than 100 employees. We do so because it enables us to make better use of existing information, and because you are now aware of how definitions can affect our understanding of small businesses.

small business An owner-managed business with less than 100 employees.

The New Venture/Firm

Various criteria can also be used to determine when a new firm comes into existence. Three of the most common are when it was formed, whether it was incorporated,[6] and if it sold goods and/or services. A business is considered to be new if it has become operational within the previous 12 months, if it adopts any of the main organizational forms (proprietorship, partnership, corporation, or co-operative), and if it sells goods or services. Thus, we define a **new venture** (or **new firm**) as a recently formed commercial organization that provides goods and/or services for sale.

new venture/firm A recently formed commercial organization that provides goods and/or services for sale.

Entrepreneurship

Entrepreneurship is the process of identifying an opportunity in the marketplace and accessing the resources needed to capitalize on that opportunity.[7] **Entrepreneurs** are people who recognize and seize opportunities. For example, Ken Woods and John Gagliardi are two entrepreneurs who recognized an opportunity in the marketplace for higher quality beer and formed the Ontario-based Black Oak Brewing Company. They've already developed several award-winning beers such as Black Oak Nut Brown Ale, Pale Ale, and Premium Lager. A website for Toronto beer lovers called The Bar Towel rates these beers very positively.[8]

entrepreneurship The process of identifying an opportunity in the marketplace and accessing the resources needed to capitalize on it.

entrepreneurs People who recognize and seize opportunities.

Small businesses are usually independently owned and influenced by unpredictable market forces. As a result, they often provide an environment to use personal attributes—such as creativity—that have come to be associated with entrepreneurs.[9] But do not assume that only small business owners exhibit entrepreneurial characteristics. Many successful managers in large organizations in both the public and private sectors also exhibit similar characteristics.[10] Entrepreneurship therefore occurs in a wide range of contexts:[11] not just in small or new firms, but also in old firms, in large firms, in firms that grow slowly, in firms that grow rapidly, in non-profit organizations, and in the public sector.

People who exhibit entrepreneurial characteristics and create something new within an existing large firm or organization are called **intrapreneurs**. One large firm renowned for encouraging intrapreneurship is Procter & Gamble. It has earned this reputation by having divisions that focus on creating new products for specific markets.[12] The Swiffer product line is one example. Once the basic Swiffer mop was launched successfully, a whole range of products was added such as the Swiffer WetJet and Swiffer Dusters. A key difference between intrapreneurs and entrepreneurs is that intrapreneurs typically don't have to concern themselves with getting the resources needed to bring the new product to market since their employer provides the resources.

intrapraneurs People who create something new within an existing large firm or organization.

Starting a business from scratch involves dealing with a great deal of uncertainty, ambiguity, and unpredictability. For example, who knows how many customers the business will attract or where the needed financial resources will come from? This means that every new venture founder needs to exercise some of the personal attributes that entrepreneurs are noted for. Therefore, when we explore the entrepreneurial process later in the chapter, we will do so within a new venture context. Before doing so, we will outline the role of small and new businesses in the Canadian economy.

A common type of small business in Canada is the convenience store. It attracts customers from its immediate area through its long hours of operation and the product lines it carries.

THE ROLE OF SMALL AND NEW BUSINESSES IN THE CANADIAN ECONOMY

2 Describe the role of small and new businesses in the Canadian economy.

As we will see in this section, small and new businesses play a key role in the Canadian economy. However, recognition of this role is relatively recent. Prior to the 1980s, large businesses were the focus of attention in terms of economic impact within industrialized nations.

Small Businesses

It may surprise you to learn that close to 98 percent of all businesses in Canada are small (having less than 100 employees). As Figure 4.1 shows, this percentage holds true at the provincial level as well. In terms of distribution, you can see that approximately 58 percent of all business establishments in Canada—whether small or large—are located in Ontario and Quebec. Virtually all the rest are divided up between the western provinces (36 percent) and the Atlantic provinces (6 percent). The Northwest Territories, the Yukon, and Nunavut only represent 0.3 percent of Canada's businesses.

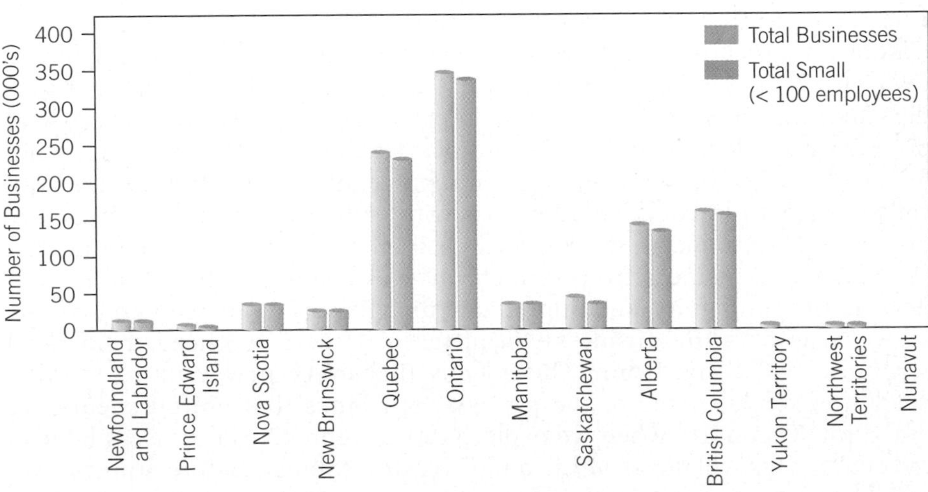

Figure 4.1 Employer businesses by firm size (number of employees) in provinces and territories, June 2005.

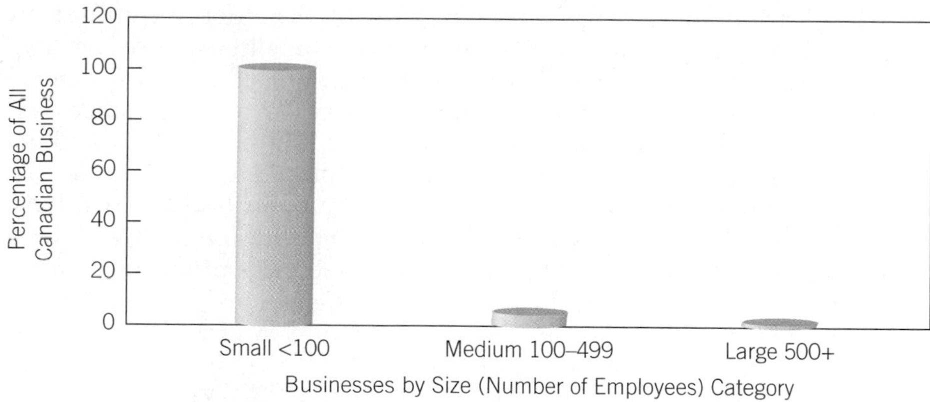

Figure 4.2a Small, medium, and large businesses as a percentage of total businesses.

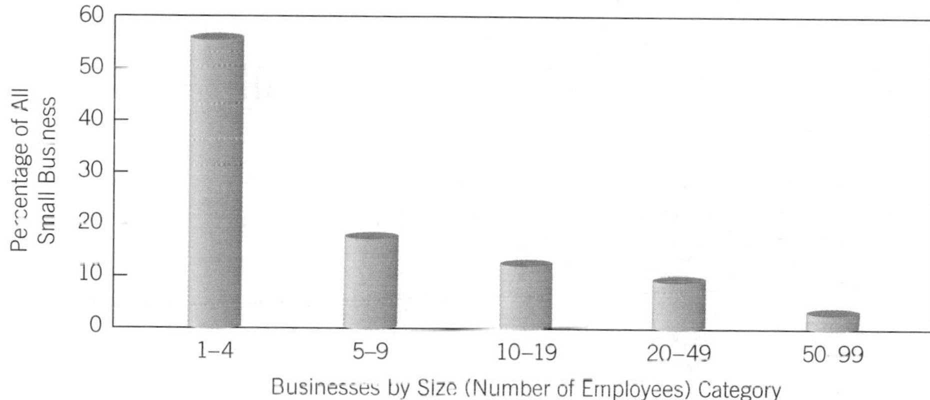

Figure 4.2b Small business size categories as a percentage of all small businesses.

How does the Canadian allocation of small (fewer than 100 employees), medium (100–499 employees), and large businesses (500+ employees) compare to that of the United States? Virtually identical! In Canada, as Figure 4.2a illustrates, 97.6 percent of the 1 048 286 employer businesses (or approximately half of the 2.2 million business establishments[13]) are small, 2.1 percent are medium-sized, and 0.3 percent are large. In the United States, slightly more than 97 percent are small, 2 percent are medium-sized, and 0.3 percent are large. As Figure 4.2b shows, when we further subdivide the Canadian "small" size category, we can see that the majority of small businesses (57 percent) have fewer than five employees.

While the previous figures profile the number of businesses in Canada by size, we now look at how many people work in small- versus medium- and large-sized businesses. According to Statistics Canada, there were 10 317 481 **private sector** employees in 2005. The term private sector generally refers to the part of the economy that is made up of companies and organizations that are not owned or controlled by the government.

private sector The part of the economy that is made up of companies and organizations that are not owned or controlled by the government.

Figure 4.3a shows that close to 49 percent of these employees (5.0 million) worked for small businesses; 16 percent (over 1.6 million) worked for medium-sized enterprises (those with 100 to 499 employees); and 35 percent (3.7 million) for large businesses.[14] These proportions have changed little over the last decade. When the small firm category is further subdivided (fewer than 4 employees, 5 to 19, 20 to 49, and 50 to 99), we see from Figure 4.3b that businesses with between 5 and 19 employees account for the highest percentage of employment.

The distribution of employment by size of firm varies considerably across industries. According to Industry Canada, small businesses account for over two-thirds of employment in four industries:[15] non-institutional health care (90 percent), the construction industry (77 percent), other services (73 percent), and accommodation and food (69 percent). In another five industries at least half of the workforce is employed by small businesses.

We conclude this section by considering the contribution small businesses make to the economy in terms of *gross domestic product (GDP)*. GDP refers to the market value of all final goods and services produced within a country in a given period of time. While GDP figures are not available by firm size, Industry Canada uses an approximation in estimating the percentage of small business's contribution to Canada's GDP. Over the past decade, the annual contribution has been valued at 25 percent[16]—less than the sector's contribution to employment but significant nonetheless.

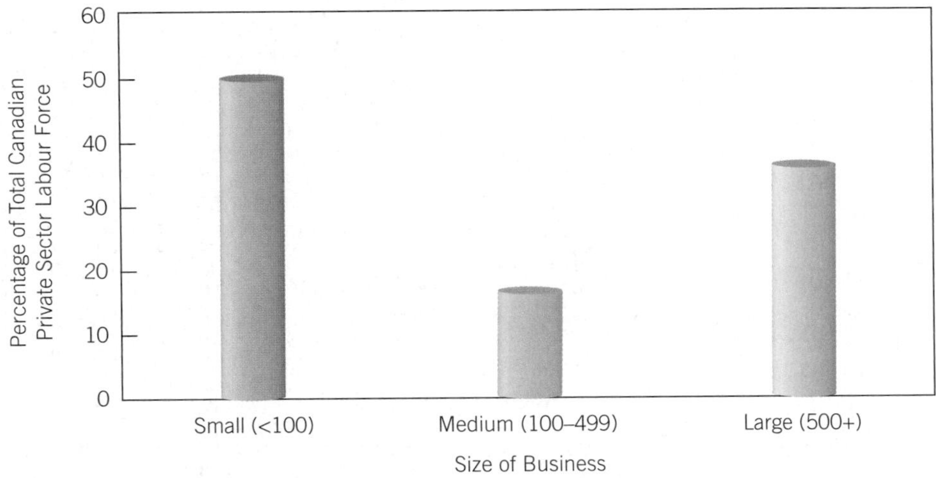

Figure 4.3a Employment in private sector labour force by size of business enterprise.

Note: SEPH data exclude self-employed workers who are not on a payroll and employees in the following industries: agriculture, fishing and trapping, private household services, religious organizations, and military personnel of defence services. The data breaking down employment by size of firm also exclude unclassified industries.

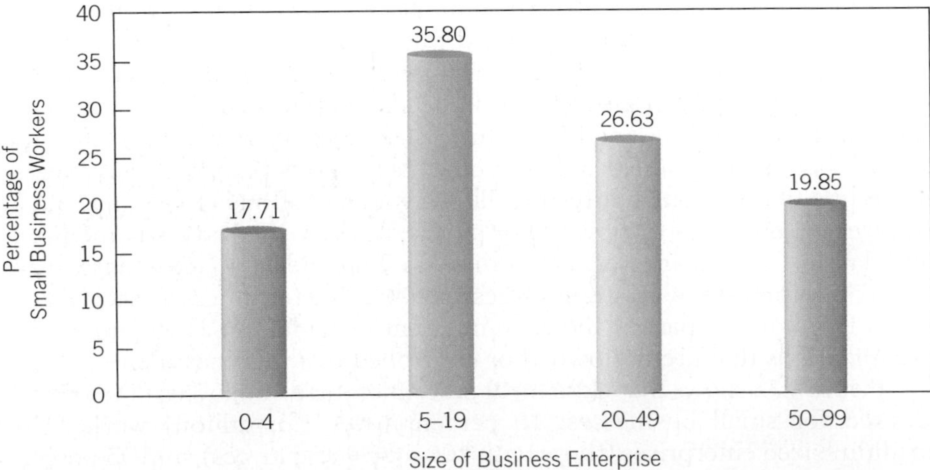

Figure 4.3b Small business employment of private sector labour force by size category.

Note: SEPH data exclude self-employed workers who are not on a payroll and employees in the following industries: agriculture, fishing and trapping, private household services, religious organizations, and military personnel of defence services. The data breaking down employment by size of firm also exclude unclassified industries.

New Ventures

New firms are not only the main source of job creation, they are also responsible for the vast majority of new products and services.[17] According to Statistics Canada, the number of firms in Canada grew 12 percent between 1991 and 2003. Alberta led in growth with 38 percent; British Columbia and Ontario followed with 20 percent and 14 percent, respectively.[18]

Most of the growth in firms occurred in the services-producing sector, with the number of firms in high-knowledge industries such as high-technology and biotechnology nearly doubling (from 32 000 to 62 000 firms). In the goods-producing sector, the number of firms in high-knowledge industries also grew at a much faster pace than in other industries.

Between 1991 and 2003, the number of businesses grew by an average of 9300 each year, with 8800 of these being small- and medium-sized enterprises (SMEs). In terms of who has been responsible for the growth in new firms, it may surprise you to learn that women are playing a far more prominent role than ever before. Kyla Eaglesham, the owner of Madeleines Cherry Pie and Ice Cream Parlour, is typical. After doing a lot of research on the ice cream and dessert industry, she left her job as a flight attendant and opened a dessert café in Toronto's trendy Annex neighbourhood. The store attracts customers who want "a little bit of cottage country in the heart of Toronto."[19]

There are now more than 800 000 women entrepreneurs in Canada, and the number has been increasing by more than 3 percent each year in recent years.[20] Female entrepreneurs are honoured each year at the Canadian Woman Entrepreneur Awards. In 2005, four women were honoured for the businesses they founded. They were Andrea Feunekes (New Brunswick-based Remsoft Inc.), Sherri Stevens (Ontario-based Stevens Resource Group), Sharon McNamara (Nova Scotia-based KilnArt), and Lynda Powless (Ontario-based Turtle Island News).[21]

Research conducted by Industry Canada shows that over the past two decades the number of female entrepreneurs has grown by 208 percent compared with just a 38 percent increase for men.[22] Between 1991 and 2001, self-employment among women increased by 43 percent, as compared with an increase of 21 percent among men. In 2000, majority women-owned SMEs had annual revenues of $72 billion, which is about 8 percent of all revenues from Canada's SMEs; in 2001, majority female-owned businesses employed 974 000 full or contract employees.

Many young entrepreneurs are also involved in creating new ventures in Canada. Consider the following examples:

- Geraldine McManus, who started Ab-Original Wear, buys artwork from Aboriginal artists and then reproduces it on T-shirts, crew-neck shirts, and sweatshirts. The clothing products feature Aboriginal artwork on the front and an inspirational message from a chief or elder on the back. The store also sells crafts made by local Aboriginal artists and miniature log cabins that McManus makes herself from recycled wood.[23]
- The Ben Barry Agency is an Ottawa-based modelling businesses that promotes models who are considered unorthodox—various sizes and ages, different racial backgrounds, and those who have physical disabilities. The models have appeared in government advertising campaigns, and on fashion runways in shopping malls. Barry works with company management to define their clientele and then chooses models who will best reflect the store's typical shoppers.[24]
- Tell Us About Us (TUAU) is a Winnipeg-based company specializing in market research and customer satisfaction programs. Owners Tyler Gompf and Scott Griffith recently signed a seven-figure deal to provide mystery shopper service to Dunkin Donuts, Baskin-Robbins, and Togo's

in the United States and Canada. The mystery shoppers will note any problems at a retail site and TUAU will then measure how quickly the problems are fixed.[25]

In considering the government statistics on new ventures, we must be mindful that they exclude businesses without employees. Conceivably, a business counted as "new" could have been operating for several years before being statistically counted as a new business. How can this happen? Recall, from our earlier discussion, that an unincorporated business operated by a self-employed person (with no employees) would *not* be included in Statistics Canada's Business Register. If such a business operated for several years prior to hiring employees it would only be classified as a new business when the employees were acquired.

We began the discussion of small and new businesses in the Canadian economy by stating that 98 percent of all businesses are small. While individually, one large business easily outperforms the contribution of a countless number of small businesses, collectively, SMEs outperform large businesses in many areas, particularly in terms of their contribution to employment. New businesses, too, lead the way when it comes to innovation and new technology.

THE ENTREPRENEURIAL PROCESS

3 Explain the *entrepreneurial process* and describe its three key elements.

The entrepreneurial process is like a journey (see Figure 4.4). To get to the destination (the start-up of a new venture), the entrepreneur must identify a business opportunity and access the resources needed to capitalize on it. Along the way, social, economic, political, and technological factors in the broader environment will have an influence, but we will focus our attention on understanding the three key process elements—the entrepreneur, the opportunity, and resources—and how they interact. As these key elements interact, they may be mismatched or well-matched. If elements are mismatched (a "misfit"), the journey may be abandoned before the destination is reached. For example, if an entrepreneur identifies an opportunity for a new health service but does not have the relevant background and skills to deliver the service, the business may never get off the ground. Conversely, if the process elements are well-matched (a "fit"), the new business venture will likely become operational. After start-up, the venture's next phase of development will result in one of the following outcomes: growth, stability (staying the same), decline, or demise (ceasing to exist).

The Entrepreneur

Since the entrepreneur is at the heart of the entrepreneurial process, researchers have paid considerable attention to identifying the personal characteristics of entrepreneurs. The profiles provided in Table 4.1 illustrate how wide-ranging these characteristics are.[26] Some are behavioural (for example, high energy level), others are personality traits (for example, independence), and still others are skills (for example, problem solving).

While the idea that people are "born" entrepreneurs is still quite popular, nothing could be further from the truth.[27] In fact, entrepreneurial characteristics have been found to be widely distributed in the population.[28] We also know that personal characteristics often have less impact on a person's actions than the situation a person is in.[29] What is really important is not who the person *is* but what the person *does*.[30] The two main things that entrepreneurs need to do are to identify an opportunity and access resources.

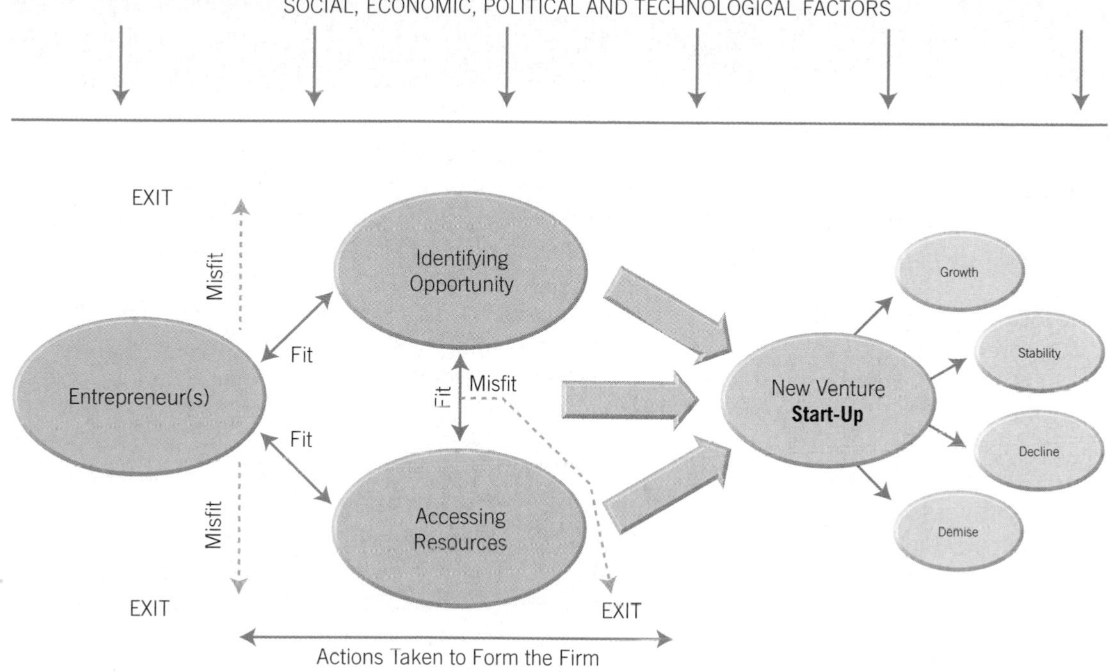

Figure 4.4 The entrepreneurial process in a new venture context.

Identifying Opportunities

Identifying opportunities involves generating ideas for new (or improved) products, processes, or services, screening those ideas so that the one that presents the best opportunity can be developed, and then developing the opportunity.

Table 4.1 Entrepreneurial Characteristics

Kuratko and Hodgetts (2007)	Hornday (1982)	Timmons and Spinelli (2007)
Commitment, Determination, and Perseverance	Self-Confidence	Commitment and Determination
Drive to Achieve	Perseverence, Determination	Leadership
Opportunity Orientation	Drive to Achieve	Opportunity Obsession
Initiative and Responsibility	Energy, Diligence	Tolerance of Risk, Ambiguity, and Uncertainty
Persistent Problem Solving	Resourcefulness	Creativity, Self-Reliance, and Adaptability
Seeking Feedback	Calculated Risk Taking	Motivation to Excel
Internal Locus of Control	Need to Achieve	Courage
Tolerance for Ambiguity	Creativity	Creativity and Innovativeness
Calculated Risk Taking	Initiative	Energy, Health, and Emotional Stability
Integrity and Reliability	Flexibility	Values
Tolerance for Failure	Positive Response to Challenges	Capacity to Inspire
High Energy Level	Independence	Intelligence
Creativity and Innovativeness	Perceptiveness	
Vision	Dynamism, Leadership	
Self-Confidence and Optimism	Positive Attitude	
Independence	Ability to Get Along with People	
Team Building	Responsiveness to Suggestions and Criticism	
	Profit Orientation	
	Perceptiveness	

ENTREPRENEURSHIP AND NEW VENTURES

A Web-Hosting Vision

Vision, they say, is the ability to look at something and see what isn't there. Franc Nemanic's vision was 20/20 back in 1999, when he started eyeing online business opportunities. He noticed that while Canada's big phone companies and cable operators were rushing to offer web access, they weren't doing much to help small businesses build websites to cash in on the internet boom.

Franc's brother John, then the CEO of popular download site Tucows, warned that web hosting is a technically demanding business. But Franc saw that as a plus. If he could sell web-hosting services wholesale rather than retail, he figured, complexity would work in his favour, motivating telcos and internet service providers to private-label his services rather than develop their own web-hosting infrastructure.

Nemanic quit his job, wrote a business plan, and launched Mississauga, Ontario–based Hostopia.com Inc. Fortunately, he had another asset besides vision: big brother John and his business partners at Tucows, brothers Bill and Colin Campbell, had just sold that firm and were happy to be lead investors in Hostopia's U.S.$2.6-million financing. That first year, Hostopia attracted U.S.$109 202 in revenue. And despite the internet bust—which Nemanic, the firm's 37-year-old president, remembers as "nuclear winter"—sales grew to U.S.$14.3 million, a five-year sales growth of 13 000 percent that led to a top spot on the 2005 *Profit* 100.

How did Hostopia survive the meltdown and grow? Nemanic's tactics could fill a textbook on coping with hard times. "You either fight or die," he says. "I never spent a moment not trying to find customers." In September 2000, Nemanic called a staff meeting and explained that Hostopia had to sign up 100 new websites a day by the end of 2001, a fourfold increase that required more and bigger telco clients. "A sense of urgency motivates the whole organization," says Nemanic. "We told them where we were and what we had to accomplish to survive. It made them realize we were all going to sink or swim as a team."

Nemanic kept his team paddling by providing a daily report on Hostopia's progress toward its target. "It was a continuous process of communication." He says even non-sales staff adopted the mission, with administrators and programmers focussing their efforts on helping sales. "As long as you have a customer-centric attitude and you're focussed on helping other people achieve their goals," says Nemanic, "everyone will achieve their goal."

Hopes were rising and so were the numbers when Hostopia signed up TELUS Corp. in 2001, a big deal that ensured Hostopia's survival. Better yet, in August 2001, TELUS Ventures, the phone giant's venture-capital arm, invested U.S.$5 million in the company. Suddenly, Hostopia was cash-flow positive with a marquee customer.

In the summer of 2002, Nemanic moved to Ft. Lauderdale, Florida, to oversee U.S. sales. Today, he says Hostopia owns 40 percent of the U.S. and Canadian market for private-label, small-biz website hosting. But there's still room for growth, because its biggest rivals are telcos that run these services in-house, and they might be persuaded to outsource that business to specialists. Hostopia certainly has an appealing sales pitch: "We cut their operating expenses by 30 to 40 percent," says Nemanic, "and we wipe out their capital expenditures."

Hostopia's three major investors remain active players. Chairman John Nemanic keeps tabs on Hostopia's software development office in Ukraine. Bill Campbell is CEO and CTO, while Colin Campbell is COO. With Franc, they focus on maintaining the company's technological edge, introducing product updates quarterly. Plus, Hostopia is eyeing a public offering in early 2006, Franc says, "provided we build appropriate momentum." That shouldn't be a problem: After growing 60 percent last year, Franc says, Hostopia will probably expand 35 percent more this year, "but we're pushing for a higher number." That's persistence of vision.

Idea Generation

Typically, generating ideas involves abandoning traditional assumptions about how things work and how they ought to be, and seeing what others do not. If the prospective new (or improved) product, process, or service can be profitably produced and is attractive relative to other potential venture ideas, it might present an opportunity.

Where do ideas come from? Most new ventures do not emerge from a deliberate search for viable business ideas. Rather the majority originate from events relating to work or everyday life.[31] In fact, work experience is the most common source of ideas, accounting for 45 to 85 percent of those generated. As an employee, the prospective entrepreneur is familiar with the product or service, and the customers, suppliers, and competitors. He or she is aware of marketplace needs, can relate those needs to personal capabilities, and can determine whether he or she is capable of producing products or services that can fill the void. The next most frequent sources of venture ideas are a personal interest/hobby (16 percent) and a chance happening (11 percent).[32] A chance happening refers to a situation where a venture idea comes about unexpectedly. For example, while on vacation in another country you might try a new snack food that you feel would be in demand if introduced to the Canadian market.

Screening

Entrepreneurs often generate many ideas, and screening them is a key part of the entrepreneurial process. The faster you can weed out the "dead-end" venture ideas, the more time and effort you can devote to the ones that remain. The more of the following characteristics that an idea has, the greater the opportunity it presents.

The Idea Creates or Adds Value for the Customer. A product or service that creates or adds value for the customer is one that solves a significant problem, or meets a significant need in new or different ways. Consider Sally Fox's idea for eliminating the dyeing process in textile operations.[33] By cross-breeding long-fibre white cotton and short-fibre coloured cotton she developed FoxFibre®, an environmentally friendly new cotton fibre that is naturally grown in several colours and is long enough to be spun commercially.

The Idea Provides a Competitive Advantage that Can Be Sustained. A competitive advantage exists when potential customers see the product or service as better than that of competitors. Sustaining a competitive advantage involves maintaining it in the face of competitors' actions or changes in the industry. All other things being equal, the longer markets are in a state of flux, the greater the likelihood of being able to sustain a competitive advantage. The absence of a competitive advantage or developing a competitive advantage that is not sustainable constitute two fatal flaws of many new ventures.[34]

To continue Sally Fox's story, shortly after she sold her first crop she was running a $10 million business with well-known companies like Levi's, L.L. Bean, Land's End, and Esprit as customers. But Fox's journey turned out to be bumpy. She had to relocate twice in response to pressure from powerful cotton growers who were afraid that her coloured varieties would contaminate their own crops. Also, once spinning mills began moving to Southeast Asia and South America, Fox's cotton lost the financial advantage it had over traditional cotton. (In their new locations, spinning mills no longer had to treat and dispose of the toxic waste from the cotton-dyeing process—a cost saving of about $2 per pound.) Because the overseas mills were unwilling or unable to process the relatively small quantities of cotton her farmers produced, she lost her big customers. Fox now concentrates on smaller mills and smaller customers, and she is rebuilding her business and her network of growers.

The Idea Is Marketable and Financially Viable. While it is important to determine whether there are enough customers who are willing to buy the product or service, it is also important to determine whether sales will lead to profits.[35] Estimating the market demand requires an initial understanding of who the customers are, what their needs are, and how the product or service will satisfy their needs better than competitors' products will. It also requires a thorough understanding of the key competitors who can provide similar products, services, or benefits to the target customer. For example, 10 years ago few people thought that manufacturers of cellphones would be competitors of camera manufacturers in providing real-time photos through digital imaging. Customers define the competition in terms of who can best satisfy their needs.

sales forecast An estimate of how much of a product or service will be purchased by prospective customers over a specific period.

After learning about the competition and customers, the entrepreneur must prepare a sales forecast. A **sales forecast** is an estimate of how much of a product or service will be purchased by the prospective customers for a specific period of time—typically one year. Total sales revenue is estimated by multiplying the units expected to be sold by the selling price. The sales forecast forms the foundation for determining the financial viability of the venture and the resources needed to start it.

Determining financial viability involves preparing financial forecasts, which are two- to three-year projections of a venture's future financial position and performance. They typically consist of an estimate of *start-up costs*, *a cash budget*, *an income statement*, and *a balance sheet* (see Chapter 14 for more detail about these financial documents). A cash budget forecasts the cash receipts and cash disbursements of the business; the income statement shows the profit or loss; and the balance sheet shows the assets (what the business owns), the liabilities (what is owed), and the owners' equity (owners' investment, including any profits that the business retains). These projections serve as the basis for decisions regarding whether to proceed with the venture, and if so, the amount and type of financing to be used in financing the new business.

The Idea Has Low Exit Costs. The final consideration is the venture's exit costs. Exit costs are low if a venture can be shut down without a significant loss of time, money, or reputation.[36] If a venture is not expected to make a profit for a number of years, its exit costs are high, since the project cannot be reasonably abandoned in the short term. On the other hand, if the venture is expected to make a profit quickly, its exit costs will be lower, making the idea more attractive.

Developing the Opportunity

As the "dead-end" venture ideas are weeded out, a clear notion of the business concept and an entry strategy for pursuing it needs to be developed. As the process proceeds, the business concept often changes from what was originally envisioned. Some new ventures develop entirely new markets, products, and sources of competitive advantage once the needs of the marketplace and the economies of the business are better understood. So, while a vision of what is to be achieved is important, it is equally important to be responsive to new information and to be on the lookout for opportunities that were not originally anticipated. For example, if customers are not placing orders, as was the case with Sally Fox, it is important to find out why and make the appropriate adjustments.

franchise An arrangement in which a buyer (franchisee) purchases the right to sell the product or service of the seller (franchiser).

New ventures use one or more of three main entry strategies: They introduce a totally new product or service; they introduce a product or service that will compete directly with existing competitive offerings but add a new twist (such as offering the option of customizing the standard product); or they franchise.[37] A **franchise** is an arrangement in which a buyer (franchisee) purchases the right to sell the product or service of the seller (franchiser). We discuss franchising in more detail later in the chapter.

When capital requirements are high, such as when a manufacturing operation is being proposed, there is a need for considerable research and planning. Similarly, if product development or operations are fairly complex, research and analysis will be needed to ensure that the costs associated with effectively coordinating tasks will be minimized. In these circumstances, or when the aim is to attract potential investors, then a comprehensive written business plan will be required. A **business plan** is a document that describes the entrepreneur's proposed business venture; explains why it is an opportunity; and outlines its marketing plan, its operational and financial details, and its managers' skills and abilities.[38] The contents of a business plan are shown in Table 4.2.

business plan A document that describes the entrepreneur's proposed business venture; explains why it is an opportunity; and outlines its marketing plan, its operational and financial details, and its managers' skills and abilities.

If market conditions are changing rapidly, the benefits gained from extensive research and planning diminish quickly. By the time the entrepreneur is ready to start, new competitors may have entered the market, prices may have changed, a location may no longer be available, and so on. Similarly, if the product is highly innovative, market research is of less value since the development of entirely new products involves *creating* needs and wants rather than simply responding to existing needs. Consequently, measuring the capacity of the product or service to fill existing customer needs or wants is less critical.

Table 4.2 A Business Plan

A well-written business plan is formally structured, easy to read, and avoids confusion. By organizing the information into sections, it makes dealing with the information more manageable. The amount of detail and the order of presentation may vary from one venture to another and according to whom the plan is being prepared for (an investor will require more detail than if the plan is being prepared for internal use by the entrepreneur). An outline for a standard business plan is provided below. While formats vary, with some better suited to the type of venture being proposed than others, most contain the following elements.

I.	**Cover Page**: Name of venture and owners, date prepared, contact person, his/her address, telephone and fax numbers, email address, and the name of the organization the plan is being presented to. The easier it is for the reader to contact the entrepreneur, the more likely the contact will occur.
II.	**Executive Summary**: A one- to three-page overview of the total business plan. Written after the other sections are completed, it highlights their significant points, and aims to create enough excitement to motivate the reader to continue.
III.	**Table of Contents**: This element lists major sections with page numbers for both the body and the appendices of the plan.
IV.	**Company Description**: Explains the type of company and tells whether it is a manufacturing, retail, service, or other type of business. It also describes the proposed form of organization: sole proprietorship, partnership, corporation, or co-operative. A typical organization of this section is as follows: name and location; company objectives; nature and primary product or service of the business; current status (start-up, buyout, or expansion) and history if applicable; and legal form of organization.
V.	**Product or Service Description**: Describes the product or service and indicates what is unique about it. This section explains the value that is added for customers—why people will buy the product or service; features of the product or service providing a competitive advantage; legal protection (patents, copyrights, trademarks, if relevant); and dangers of technical or style obsolescence.
VI.	**Marketing**: This section has two key parts, the market analysis and the marketing plan. The market analysis convinces the reader that the entrepreneur understands the market for the product or service and can deal effectively with the competition to achieve sales projections. The marketing plan explains the strategy for achieving sales projections.
VII.	**Operating Plan**: Explains the type of manufacturing or operating system to be used. Describes the facilities, labour, raw materials, and processing requirements.
VIII.	**Management**: Identifies the key players—the management team, active investors, and directors—and cites the experience and competence they possess. This section includes a description of the management team, outside investors and directors and their qualifications, outside resource people, and plans for recruiting and training employees.
IX.	**Financial Plan**: Specifies financial needs and contemplated sources of financing. Presents projected financial statements, including a cash budget, a balance sheet, and an income statement.
X.	**Supporting Details/Appendix**: Provides supplementary materials to the plan such as résumés and other important supporting data.

Contrary to what many people might think, planning does not have to be completed before action is taken. For example, if an electrical contracting business is being proposed in an area where there is a shortage of tradespeople, it would be important to seek out qualified employees prior to conducting other analyses that are needed to complete the business plan. Such early action also helps to build relationships that can be drawn on later. Obviously, some ventures do not lend themselves to early action, particularly those which are capital intensive. Since most entrepreneurs have limited resources, it is important to concentrate on the issues that can be dealt with, *and* that will help determine whether to proceed and how to proceed.[39]

Accessing Resources

bootstrapping Doing more with less.

Typically, entrepreneurs acquire the various resources needed to make the venture a reality by **bootstrapping**, which means "doing more with less." Usually the term refers to financing techniques whereby entrepreneurs make do with as few resources as possible and use other peoples' resources wherever they can. However, bootstrapping can also refer to the acquisition of other types of resources such as people, space, equipment, or materials that are loaned or provided free by customers or suppliers.

Financial Resources

There are two main types of financing—*debt* and *equity* (see Chapter 20 for a detailed discussion of debt and equity). Briefly, *debt financing* refers to money that is borrowed. The borrower is obliged to repay the full amount of the loan in addition to interest charges on the debt. *Equity financing* refers to money that the entrepreneur (or others) invests in a business in return for an ownership interest. Equity investors, as owners, are keenly interested in how any profit will be distributed. Choosing between debt and equity involves trade-offs with regard to potential profitability, financial risk, and control. On the one hand, borrowing money increases the potential for higher rates of return to the entrepreneur when the business is performing well. On the other hand, equity makes it possible to reduce risk by giving up some control.

collateral Assets that a borrower uses to secure a loan or other credit, and that are subject to seizure by the lender if the loan isn't repaid according to the specified repayment terms.

Since a business is at its riskiest point during the start-up phase, equity is usually more appropriate and accessible than debt. However, most new venture founders prefer debt because they are reluctant to give up any control to outsiders. To obtain debt financing the entrepreneur must have an adequate equity investment in the business—typically 20 percent of the business's value—and collateral (or security). **Collateral** refers to items (assets) owned by the business (such as a building and equipment) or by the individual (such as a house or car) that the borrower uses to secure a loan or other credit. These items can be seized by the lender if the loan isn't repaid according to the specified terms. To lenders, equity investment demonstrates the commitment of the entrepreneur, as individuals tend to be more committed to a venture if they have a substantial portion of what they own invested in it.

The most common sources of *debt* financing include:

1. *Financial institutions.* While commercial banks are the main providers of debt financing for established small businesses, it is usually difficult for a new business to borrow from a bank. Banks are risk averse, and loans to new businesses are considered very risky, largely because the business has yet to establish its ability to repay the loan. Typically, if an entrepreneur is able to get bank financing for a new venture it is because the loan is in the form of a personal loan (as opposed to a business loan). The most common way to obtain a personal loan is to mortgage a house or borrow against the cash value of a life insurance policy.

In addition to commercial banks, other sources of debt financing include trust companies, co-operatives, finance companies, equipment companies, credit unions, and government agencies. Since finance companies lend in high-risk situations, their interest rates tend to be high. The federal and provincial governments have a wide range of financial assistance programs for small businesses. Among the various forms of assistance are low-interest loans, loan guarantees, interest-free loans, and wage subsidies.

2. *Suppliers.* Another source of financing is suppliers who provide goods (such as inventory) or services to the entrepreneur with an agreement to bill them later. This is referred to as *trade credit*. Trade credit can be very helpful in getting started, as it means that inventory, for example, can be acquired without paying cash for it which, in turn, frees up money to pay for other start-up costs. This type of financing is short-term; 30 days is the usual payback period. The amount of trade credit available to a new firm depends on the type of business and the supplier's confidence in the firm. Frequently, though, a new business has trouble getting trade credit since its capacity to repay has yet to be demonstrated.

The most common sources of *equity* financing include:

1. **Personal savings.** New venture founders draw heavily on their own finances to start their businesses. Most try to save as much as they can in preparation for start-up.
2. **Love money**. This type of financing includes investments from friends, relatives, and business associates. It is called "love money" because it is often given more on the basis of the family relationship or friendship than on the merit of the business concept.
3. **Private investors.** One popular source of equity capital is informal capital from private investors, also known as *angels*. Usually, these investors are financially well off individuals, many of whom are successful entrepreneurs who wish to recycle their wealth by investing in new businesses. Typically, the investment does not exceed $100 000.
4. **Venture capitalists.** Investments by venture capitalists come from professionally managed pools of investor money (venture capital). Since the risk of receiving little or no return on investment is high, only deals that present an attractive, high-growth business opportunity with a return between 35 and 50 percent are considered. Very few new ventures meet this criterion. Compared to angels, venture capitalists finance fewer firms in Canada.

Besides these conventional sources of financing, the possibilities for bootstrap financing are endless. For example, an entrepreneur might require an advance payment from customers, in full or in part. Equipment can be leased rather than purchased (which reduces the risk of equipment becoming obsolete). Office furniture can be rented, premises can be shared, and the manufacture of products can be subcontracted, thereby avoiding the expense of procuring material, equipment, and facilities. All of these activities free up cash which can then be used for other purposes.

Other Resources

Businesses may be owned by one person, but entrepreneurship is not a solo process. There are various stakeholders who provide resources to the venture including partners, employees, customers, suppliers, professionals, consultants, government agencies, lenders, shareholders, and venture capitalists. Sometimes ownership is shared with one or more of these stakeholders in order to acquire the use of their resources. When ownership is shared, there are decisions to be made about who to share it with, how much each stakeholder will own, at what cost, and under what conditions. The form of legal organization chosen affects whether ownership can be shared and whether resources can be accessed. We discuss this important point later in the chapter.

Deciding whether to share ownership by forming a venture team involves considering whether having a team is desirable or necessary, and whether the aim is to build a company with high growth potential. Whether a team is *necessary* depends upon:

- *The size and scope of the venture:* How many people does the venture require? Is it a one-person operation or does it need contributions from others? Can people be hired to fill the key roles as they are required?
- *Personal competencies:* What are the talents, know-how, skills, track-record, contacts, and resources that the entrepreneur brings to the venture? How do these match up with what the venture needs to succeed? If gaps are identified, the entrepreneur needs to decide what competencies are needed to complement his or hers and when they are needed.

The nature of the team depends upon the match-up between the lead entrepreneur and the opportunity, and how fast and aggressively he or she plans to proceed. Most teams tend to be formed in one of two ways: (a) one person has an idea (or wants to start a business), and then several associates join the team over the first few years of the venture's operation, or (b) an entire team is formed at the outset based on such factors as a shared idea, a friendship, or an experience.

The ideal team consists of people with complementary skills covering the key success areas for the business (for example, marketing, finance, production, etc.). Small founding teams tend to work better than big ones. It is quite common for the initial team to consist of just two people—a craftsperson and a salesperson.

If the entrepreneur does not have his or her sights set on establishing a venture with high growth potential, going solo may be a realistic option. Some new venture founders bring on additional team members only as the business can afford them. Most successful solo businesses are simple types of ventures, such as small retail stores or services.[40] The odds for survival, growth, profitability, and attracting capital are increased by a team approach.[41]

Assessing the "Fit" Between Elements in the Entrepreneurial Process

Assessing the "fit" between the key elements in the entrepreneurial process is an ongoing task, since the shape of the opportunity, and consequently the resources and people needed to capitalize on it, typically changes as it is developed. It is the entrepreneur that stands to gain the most by attending to these "fits" and any changes they may require, although other stakeholders, such as investors, will be considering them as well.

The Entrepreneur–Opportunity Fit

The first assessment of fit is between the entrepreneur and the opportunity. The entrepreneur needs to decide whether the opportunity, as identified, is something he or she *can do* and *wants to do*. A realistic self-assessment is important. Prospective ventures that are of limited personal interest and require skills and abilities that do not fit well with those of the entrepreneur should be quickly eliminated. For example, it does little good to identify an opportunity for an ecotourism business in a wilderness area if the entrepreneur is a sedentary urban dweller.

Once the entrepreneur has chosen the opportunity he or she wants to pursue, the success of the venture depends heavily upon the individual or individuals involved. No matter how good the product or service concept is, as the opportunity changes shape, it may demand skills a single entrepreneur lacks. This may prompt a decision to acquire the needed skills either by forming a team or by getting further training.

The Opportunity–Resources Fit

Assessing the opportunity–resources fit involves determining whether the resources needed to capitalize on the opportunity can be acquired. As the opportunity changes shape, so too will the resource requirements. When challenges or risks arise, the aim is to determine whether they can be resolved, and if so, to deal with them as quickly as possible. For example, if the venture requires a greater financial investment than originally anticipated, this does not necessarily mean that the venture should be abandoned. Other options such as taking on partners or leasing rather than building a facility may be viable. Of course, some ventures may not be viable regardless of the alternatives considered.

The Entrepreneur–Resources Fit

Once the resource requirements of the venture have been determined, the entrepreneur needs to assess whether he or she has the capacity to meet those requirements. For example, an entrepreneur with a stellar reputation for software development will have an easier time attracting employees for a venture specializing in software than someone with no track record. If that same entrepreneur is well connected with people in the industry, he or she will be more likely to gain commitments from customers, and, in turn, investors.

START-UP AND BEYOND

Entrepreneurs must make the right start-up decisions, but they must also pay attention to how the business will be run beyond the start-up phase. In this section, we examine three important topics that are relevant to these issues. First, we describe the three main ways that entrepreneurs start up a small business. Next, we look at the four main organizing options that are available to entrepreneurs. We conclude the chapter with a look at the reasons for success and failure in small business.

Starting Up a Small Business

Most entrepreneurs start up a small business in one of three ways: they start a business from scratch, they buy an existing business, or they buy a franchise. We have already examined the "starting from scratch" alternative in detail in the preceding section, so we focus here on the latter two options.

Buying an Existing Business

About one-third of all new businesses that were started in the past decade were bought from someone else. Many experts recommend buying an existing business because the odds of success are better. An existing business has already proven its ability to attract customers. It has also established relationships with lenders, suppliers, and other stakeholders. Moreover, an existing track record gives potential buyers a much clearer picture of what to expect than any estimate of a new business's prospects.

4 Describe two alternative strategies for becoming a business owner—*buying an existing business* and *buying a franchise.*

But an entrepreneur who buys someone else's business may not be able to avoid certain problems. For example, the business may have a poor reputation, its location may be poor, it may be difficult to determine an appropriate purchase price, and there may be uncertainty about the exact financial shape the business is in.

Taking Over a Family Business. A special case of buying an existing business involves family businesses. Taking over a family business poses both challenges and opportunities. On the positive side, a family business can provide otherwise unobtainable financial and management resources because of the personal sacrifices of family members. Family businesses often have a strong reputation or goodwill that can result in important community and business relationships. As well, employee loyalty is often high, and an interested, unified family management and shareholders group may emerge.

Toronto-based hosiery manufacturer Phantom Industries Inc. is an example of a family-owned business that has been successful through three generations of family members.[42] Another example is Irving Oil Ltd., the giant New Brunswick-based company, which now has fifth-generation members running businesses that are part of its empire.[43]

On the other hand, major problems can arise in family businesses. There may be disagreements over which family members assume control. If the parent sells his or her interest in the business, the price to be paid may be an issue. The expectation of other family members may also be problematic. Some family members may feel that they have a right to a job, promotion, and impressive title simply because they are part of the family.[44] Choosing an appropriate successor and ensuring that he or she receives adequate training and disagreements among family members about the future of the business are two other problem areas. Examples of family businesses that encountered serious problems are Saskatchewan-based Mitchell's Gourmet Foods (internal family feuding about who would control the company), Cuddy International Corp. (disagreements about which of the founder's sons were capable of running the business), and Eatons (inability to adapt to changing market conditions).[45]

Buying a Franchise

If you drive or walk around any Canadian town, you will notice retail outlets with names like McDonald's, Pizza Pizza, Swiss Chalet, Yogen Früz, 7-Eleven, Re/Max, Comfort Inn, Blockbuster Video, Sylvan Learning Centre, and Super Lube. What do all these businesses have in common? They are all franchises, operating under licences issued by parent companies to local entrepreneurs who own and manage them.

Franchising became very visible in the 1950s with fast-food franchisers like McDonald's, but it actually started in the early 1800s. In 1898, General Motors began franchising retail dealerships, and similar systems were created by Rexall (pharmacies) in 1902 and by Howard Johnson (restaurants and motels) in 1926. Franchising continues to increase in importance in the twenty-first century. Depending on how it is defined, franchising now accounts for 43 percent of retail sales in Canada.[46] There are thousands of franchise establishments in Canada, and they generate approximately $30 billion in annual sales revenue.

franchising agreement Stipulates the duties and responsibilities of the franchisee and the franchiser.

A franchise is an arrangement that gives franchisees (buyers) the right to sell the product of the franchiser (the seller). A **franchising agreement** outlines the duties and responsibilities of each party. For example, it stipulates the amount and type of payment that franchisees must make to the franchiser. Franchisees usually make an initial payment for the right to operate a local outlet of the franchise; they also make royalty payments to the franchiser ranging from 2 to 30 percent of the franchisee's annual revenues or profits. The franchisee also pays an advertising fee so that the franchiser can advertise in the franchisee's local area. Franchise fees vary widely, from $30 000 for a Fantastic Sams's hair salon, to $1 million for a Burger King franchise, to hundreds of millions for a professional sports franchise.

The Advantages of Franchising. Both franchisers and franchisees benefit from the franchising way of doing business (see Table 4.3).

Is Franchising for You? Do you think you would be happy being a franchisee? The answer depends on a number of factors, including your willingness to work hard, your ability to find a good franchise to buy, and the financial resources you possess. If you are thinking seriously of going into franchising, you should consider several areas of costs that you will incur:

- the franchise sales price
- expenses that will be incurred before the business opens
- training expenses
- operational expenses for the first six months
- personal financial needs for the first six months
- emergency needs

ORGANIZING OPTIONS (FORMS OF BUSINESS OWNERSHIP)

Describe the four forms of *legal organization* for a business and discuss the advantages and disadvantages of each. 5

Whether they intend to run a small farm, a large factory, an online retail business, a hair salon, or any one of many other types of business, entrepreneurs must decide which form of legal ownership best suits their needs.

Table 4.3 The Benefits of Franchising

For the Franchiser	For the Franchisee
■ The franchiser can attain rapid growth for the chain by signing up many franchisees in many different locations.	■ Franchisees own a small business that has access to big business management skills.
■ Franchisees share in the cost of advertising.	■ The franchisee does not have to build up a business from scratch.
■ The franchiser benefits from the investment money provided by franchisees.	■ Franchisee failure rates are lower than when starting one's own business.
■ Advertising money is spent more efficiently (the franchiser teams up with local franchisees to advertise only in the local area).	■ A well-advertised brand name comes with the franchise and the franchisee's outlet is recognizable because it looks like all other outlets in the chain.
■ The franchiser benefits because franchisees are motivated to work hard for themselves; the more revenue the franchisee generates, the more money the franchiser makes.	■ The franchiser may send the franchisee to a training program run by the franchiser (e.g., the Canadian Institute of Hamburgerology run by McDonald's).
■ The franchiser is freed from all details of a local operation, which are handled by the franchisee.	■ The franchiser may visit the franchisee and provide expert advice on how to run the business.
	■ Economies in buying allow franchisees to get lower prices for the raw materials they must purchase.
	■ Financial assistance is provided by the franchiser in the form of loans; the franchiser may also help the franchisee obtain loans from local sources.
	■ Franchisees are their own bosses and get to keep most of the profit they make.

Four options are available: the sole proprietorship, the partnership, the corporation, and the cooperative.

The Sole Proprietorship

sole proprietorship A business owned and operated by one person.

The **sole proprietorship** is a business owned and operated by one person. Legally, if you set up a business as a sole proprietorship, your business is considered to be an extension of yourself (and not a separate legal entity). Though usually small, a sole proprietorship may be as large as a steel mill or as small as a lemonade stand. While the majority of businesses in Canada are sole proprietorships, this form of ownership accounts for only a small proportion of total business revenues.

Advantages of a Sole Proprietorship

Freedom may be the most important benefit of a sole proprietorship. Sole proprietors answer to no one but themselves since they don't share ownership. A sole proprietorship is also easy to form. If you operate the business under your own name, with no additions, you don't even need to register your business name to start operating as a sole proprietor; you can go into business simply by putting a sign on the door. The simplicity of legal setup procedures makes this form appealing to self-starters and independent spirits, as do low start-up costs.

Another attractive feature is tax benefits. Most businesses suffer losses in their early stages. Since the business and the proprietor are legally one and the same, these losses can be deducted from income the proprietor earns from personal sources other than the business.

Disadvantages of a Sole Proprietorship

unlimited liability Personal liability for all debts of the business.

A major drawback is **unlimited liability**: A sole proprietor is personally liable (responsible) for all debts incurred by the business. If the business fails to generate enough cash, bills must be paid out of the owner's pocket. Another disadvantage is lack of continuity: A sole proprietorship legally dissolves when the owner dies. Finally, a sole proprietorship depends on the resources of one person whose managerial and financial limitations may constrain the business. Sole proprietors often find it hard to borrow money to start up or expand. Many bankers fear that they won't be able to recover loans if the owner becomes disabled.

The Partnership

partnership A form of organization established when two or more individuals agree to combine their financial, managerial, and technical abilities for the purpose of operating a business for profit.

general partners Partners who are actively involved in managing the firm and have unlimited liability.

limited partners Partners who don't participate actively in the business and whose liability is limited to the amount they invested in the partnership.

general partnership A type of partnership where all partners are jointly liable for the obligations of the business.

limited partnership A type of partnership with at least one general partner (who has unlimited liability) and one or more limited partners. The limited partners cannot participate in the day-to-day management of the business or they risk the loss of their limited liability status.

The **partnership**, frequently used by professionals like accountants and lawyers, is established when two or more individuals (partners) agree to combine their financial, managerial, and technical abilities for the purpose of operating a business for profit. Partnerships are often an extension of a business that began as a sole proprietorship. The original owner may want to expand, or the business may have grown too big for a single person to handle.

There are two basic types of partners in a partnership. **General partners** are actively involved in managing the firm and have unlimited liability. **Limited partners** don't participate actively in the business, and their liability is limited to the amount they invested in the partnership. A **general partnership** is the most common type of partnership and is similar in nature to the sole proprietorship in that all the (general) partners are jointly liable for the obligations of the business. The other type of partnership—a **limited partnership**—consists of at least one general partner (who has unlimited liability) and one or more limited partners. The limited partners can not participate in the day-to-day management of the business or they risk the loss of their limited liability status.

Advantages of a Partnership

The most striking advantage of a general partnership is the ability to grow by adding talent and money. Partnerships also have a somewhat easier time borrowing funds than do sole proprietorships because banks and other lending institutions prefer to make loans to enterprises that are not dependent on a single individual. Partnerships can also invite new partners to join by investing money.

Like a sole proprietorship, a partnership is simple to organize, with few legal requirements. Even so, all partnerships must begin with an agreement of some kind. It may be written, oral, or even unspoken. Wise partners, however, insist on a written agreement to avoid trouble later. This agreement should answer such questions as

- How will disagreements be resolved?
- Who invested what sums of money in the partnership?
- Who will receive what share of the partnership's profits?
- Who does what and who reports to whom?
- How will the partnership be dissolved?
- How would leftover assets be distributed among the partners?

The partnership agreement is strictly a private document. No laws require partners to file an agreement with some government agency. Nor are partnerships regarded as legal entities. In the eyes of the law, a partnership is nothing more than two or more persons working together. The partnership's lack of legal standing means that the partners are taxed as individuals.

Disadvantages of a Partnership

As with sole proprietorships, unlimited liability is the greatest drawback of a general partnership. By law, each partner may be held personally liable for all debts incurred in the name of the partnership. And if any partner incurs a debt, even if the other partners know nothing about it, they are all liable if the offending partner cannot pay up. Another problem with partnerships is lack of continuity. When one partner dies or pulls out, a partnership dissolves legally, even if the other partners agree to stay to continue the business.

A related drawback is the difficulty of transferring ownership. No partner may sell out without the other partners' consent. Thus, the life of a partnership may depend on the ability of retiring partners to find someone compatible with the other partners to buy them out. Finally, a partnership provides little or no guidance in resolving conflict between the partners. For example, suppose one partner wants to expand the business rapidly and the other wants it to grow slowly. If under the partnership agreement the two are equal, it may be difficult for them to decide what to do.

A practical illustration of the kinds of problems that can arise in partnerships is described in the Exercising Your Ethics feature found at the end of the chapter.

The Corporation

When you think of corporations you probably think of giant businesses such as Air Canada, Imperial Oil, or Nortel Networks. The very word "corporation" suggests bigness and power. Yet, the tiny corner newsstand has as much right to incorporate as does a giant oil refiner. And the newsstand and oil refiner have the same basic characteristics that all corporations share: legal status as a separate entity, property rights and obligations, and an indefinite lifespan. The Top 10 corporations in Canada are listed in Table 4.4.

A corporation has been defined as "an artificial being, invisible, intangible, and existing only in contemplation of the law."[47] As such, corporations may sue and be sued, buy, hold, and sell property, make and sell products to consumers, and commit crimes and be tried and punished for them. Simply defined, a **corporation** is a business that is a separate legal entity that is liable for its own debts and whose owners' liability is limited to their investment.

corporation A business that is a separate legal entity that is liable for its own debts and whose owners' liability is limited to their investment.

stockholders A share of ownership in a corporation.

Stockholders—investors who buy shares of ownership in the form of stock—are the real owners of the corporation (the different kinds of stockholders are described in Chapter 18). Profits may be distributed to stockholders in the form of dividends, although corporations are not required to pay dividends. Instead, they often reinvest any profits in the business.

board of directors A group of individuals elected by a firm's shareholders and charged with overseeing, and taking legal responsibility for, the firm's actions.

The **board of directors** is the governing body of a corporation. Its basic responsibility is to ensure that the corporation is run in a way that is in the best interests of the shareholders. The board chooses the president and other officers of the business and delegates the power to run the day-to-day activities of the business to those officers. The board sets policy on paying dividends, on financing major spending, and on executive salaries and benefits. Large corporations tend to have large boards with as many as 20 or 30 directors. Smaller corporations, on the other hand, tend to have no more than five directors. The Business Accountability box describes some recent issues that have arisen regarding boards of directors.

inside directors Members of a corporation's board of directors who are also full-time employees of the corporation.

outside directors Members of a corporation's board of directors who are not also employees of the corporation on a day-to-day basis.

Inside directors are employees of the company and have primary responsibility for the corporation. That is, they are also top managers, such as the president and executive vice-president. **Outside directors** are not employees of the corporation in the normal course of its business. Attorneys, accountants, university officials, and executives from other firms are commonly used as outside directors.

Table 4.4 Top 10 Corporations in Canada, 2005 (Ranked by Sales Revenue)

Corporation	Sales Revenue (billions of dollars)
1. General Motors of Canada	$34.9
2. Manulife Financial Corp.	32.0
3. George Weston Ltd.	31.3
4. Royal Bank of Canada	29.4
5. Imperial Oil Ltd.	27.9
6. Magna International Inc.	27.6
7. Power Corp. of Canada	26.6
8. Alcan Inc.	24.6
9. Sun Life Financial Inc.	21.9
10. DaimlerChrysler Canada Inc.	20.8

BUSINESS ACCOUNTABILITY

Getting on Boards

Boards of directors today are under pressure to become actively involved in planning and monitoring corporate activity. At WorldCom, Tyco, and other corporations, the boards were either unaware of the misdeeds taking place around them or, in some cases, actually were party to those activities. At Enron, for example, the board of directors several times voted to waive its policies regarding independence and arms-length transactions, allowing executives to continue their fraud unhampered. When the negligence of these boards was publicly exposed, investors cried out for reform.

Investors want boards to take a more active role in decision making and to provide more oversight. Most corporations, eager to distance themselves from scandal, are considering transformation of their boards of directors. The most effective boards are composed of more outsiders than insiders. This allows the directors to have independence from the powerful CEO. To enhance decision making ability, board members should come from diverse backgrounds and have top-level management experience. Directors should own a substantial amount of the company's stock. Boards should be actively involved in decision making, such as meeting regularly, setting the overall corporate strategy, and having access to confidential information. Boards that do not meet these criteria may be too cozy with corporate executives and thus fail to vigilantly safeguard the interests of shareholders.

Specific questions that should be asked are as follows:

- Are the majority of the board's members independent of the company (i.e., they are not part of the company's management, they don't work for another company that does business with the company, and they do not come from a parent company that controls the company)?
- Are the majority of the compensation committee's members independent (the compensation committee determines executive pay)?
- Are the majority of the nominating committee's members independent (the nominating committee recommends new board members)?
- Does the company have a system for formally evaluating the performance of its board of directors?
- Do the directors and the CEO own stock in the company?
- Do directors have to stand for re-election every year?
- Does the company have a written statement of its corporate governance practices?
- Does the company have only voting common shares and no non-voting shares?

Many high-tech companies are defying these guidelines. For example, the board of Amazon.com has just five members, is chaired by CEO Jeff Bezos, and lacks any real semblance of independence. Pat McGurn, a director at Institutional Shareholder Services, says, "People are coming to view Amazon's problems as the result of poor corporate governance rather than the effect of the economy in general. Unfortunately, the board doesn't seem to see governance as part of the solution."

This problem is not restricted to high-tech companies. In 2003, Gerald Schwartz, CEO of Onex Corporation, named his wife to sit on the board of directors of Onex. Institutional shareholders and corporate governance experts said such a move is contrary to the efforts of most public companies to increase the independence of their directors. One securities lawyer asked how a board member could evaluate a CEO's performance if the CEO is her husband.

Each year the *Report on Business* ranks Canadian corporations in terms of four key areas: board composition, board compensation, shareholder rights, and disclosure. In 2005, the top-ranked companies were SNC-Lavalin Group Inc., Bank of Montreal, Bank of Nova Scotia, and Suncor Energy (in that order). The lowest-ranked companies were Reitmans (Canada) Ltd., Duvernay Oil Corp., and Northern Orion Resources.

chief executive officer The person responsible for the firm's overall performance.

Corporate officers are the top managers hired by the board to run the corporation on a day-to-day basis. The **chief executive officer (CEO)** is responsible for the firm's overall performance. Other corporate officers typically include the president, who is responsible for internal management, and various vice-presidents, who oversee functional areas such as marketing or operations.

Types of Corporations

public corporation A business whose stock is widely held and available for sale to the general public.

There are two types of private sector corporations (corporations can also be found in the municipal, provincial, federal, and nonprofit sectors). The **public corporation** is a business whose shares of stock are widely held and available for sale to the general public. The shares of public corporations like George Weston, Air Canada, and Canadian Pacific are traded on securities exchanges and are widely available to the general public for purchase (see Chapter 19).

private corporation A business whose stock is held by a small group of individuals and is not usually available for sale to the general public.

By contrast, the shares of stock of a **private corporation** are held by only a few shareholders, are not widely available for purchase, and may have restrictions on their sale. For example, Kroeker Farms, a large agribusiness in Manitoba is owned by nine members of one family. Other private corporations are Para Paints of Canada and Bata Shoes. The vast majority of corporations are privately held.

initial public offering (IPO) Selling shares of stock in a company for the first time to the general investing public.

Most new corporations start out as private corporations, because few investors will buy an unknown stock. As the corporation grows and develops a record of success, it may issue shares to the public as a way of raising additional money. This is called its **initial public offering (IPO)**. In 2005, E.D. Smith, a maker of jams and pie fillings, went public with a $110 million IPO, and Tim Hortons announced plans for an IPO in 2006. IPOs were not very attractive to investors during the stock market decline of 2001–2003, but they became more popular as the stock market recovered. In 2001, for example, there were 1924 IPOs worth $26 billion, but in 2004 there were 2752 IPOs worth over $48 billion.[48]

A public corporation can also "go private," which is the reverse of going public. In 2004, Cara Operations Ltd.—the parent company of Harvey's, Swiss Chalet, and Second Cup—went private, and Magna International Inc. announced that would take its three publicly traded auto parts subsidiaries private.[49]

income trust The income trust structure involves corporations distributing all or most of their earnings to investors and thereby reduces the corporation's income tax liability.

During the last few years, many corporations converted to an **income trust** structure which allowed them to avoid paying corporate income tax if they distributed all or most of their earnings to investors. For example, Bell Canada Enterprises could have avoided an $800 million tax bill for 2008 by becoming an income trust. The federal government estimated that it was going to lose billions of dollars of tax revenue because so many corporations were becoming income trusts. In a surprise move in 2006, the government announced that it would begin taxing income trusts more like corporations by 2011. This announcement caused a significant decline in the market value of income trusts and it also means that very few corporations will now convert to an income trust structure.[50]

Formation of the Corporation

The two most widely used methods to form a corporation are federal incorporation under the Canada Business Corporations Act and provincial incorporation under any of the provincial corporations acts. The former is used if the company is going to operate in more than one province; the latter is used if the founders intend to carry on business in only one province. Except for banks and certain insurance and loan companies, any company can be federally incorporated under the Canada Business Corporations Act. To do so, articles of incorporation must be drawn up. These articles include such information as the name of the corporation, the type and number of shares to be issued, the number of directors the corporation will have, and the location of the company's operations. The specific procedures and information required for provincial incorporation vary from province to province.

All corporations must attach the word "Limited" (Ltd./Ltée), "Incorporated" (Inc.), or "Corporation" (Corp.) to the company name to indicate clearly to customers and suppliers that the owners have limited liability for corporate debts. The same sorts of rules apply in other countries. British firms, for example, use PLC for "public limited company" and German companies use AG for "Aktiengesellschaft" (corporation).

Advantages of Incorporation

The biggest advantage of the corporate structure is **limited liability**, which means that the liability of investors is limited to their personal investment in the corporation. In the event of failure, the courts may seize a corporation's assets and sell them to pay debts, but the courts cannot touch the investors' personal possessions. If, for example, you invest $1000 in a corporation that goes bankrupt, you may lose your $1000, but no more. In other words, your liability is limited to $1000.

limited liability The liability of investors is limited to their personal investments in the corporation.

Another advantage of a corporation is continuity. Because it has a legal life independent of its founders and owners, a corporation can, in theory, continue forever. Shares of stock may be sold or passed on to heirs, and most corporations also benefit from the continuity provided by professional management. Finally, corporations have advantages in raising money. By selling **stock**, they expand the number of investors and the amount of available funds. The term stock refers to a share of ownership in a corporation. Continuity and legal status tend to make lenders more willing to grant loans to corporations.

stock A share of ownership in a corporation.

Disadvantages of Incorporation

One of the disadvantages for a new firm in forming a corporation is the cost (approximately $2500). Corporations also need legal help in meeting government regulations because they are far more heavily regulated than are proprietorships or partnerships. Some people say that **double taxation** is another problem with the corporate form of ownership. By this they mean that a corporation must pay corporate income taxes on its profits, and then shareholders must also pay personal income taxes on the **dividends** they receive from the corporation. The dividend a corporation pays is the amount of money, normally a portion of the profits, which is distributed to the shareholders. Since dividends paid by the corporation are not tax deductible for the corporation, this amounts to double taxation. Others point out that shareholders get a "dividend tax credit," which largely offsets the effect of double taxation.

double taxation A corporation must pay income taxes on its profits, and then shareholders must also pay personal income taxes on the dividends they receive from the corporation.

dividends The amount of money, normally a portion of the profits, which is distributed to the shareholders.

The Co-operative

A **co-operative** is an incorporated form of business that is organized, owned, and democratically controlled by the people who use its products and services, and whose earnings are distributed on the basis of their use of the co-operative rather than their level of investment. As such, it is formed to benefit its owners in the form of reduced prices and/or the distribution of surpluses at year-end. The process works like this: suppose some farmers believe they can get cheaper fertilizer prices if they form their own company and purchase in large volumes. They might then form a co-operative, which

co-operative An incorporated form of business that is organized, owned, and democratically controlled by the people who use its products and services, and whose earnings are distributed on the basis of use of the co-operative rather than level of investment.

can be either federally or provincially chartered. Prices are generally lower to buyers and, at the end of the fiscal year, any surpluses are distributed to members on the basis of how much they purchased. If Farmer Jones bought 5 percent of all co-op sales, he would receive 5 percent of the surplus.

The co-operative's start-up capital usually comes from shares purchased by the co-operative's members. Sometimes all it takes to qualify for membership in a co-operative is the purchase of one share with a fixed (and often nominal) value. Federal co-operatives, however, can raise capital by issuing investment shares to members or non-members. Co-operatives, like investor-owned corporations, have directors and appointed officers.

Voting rights are different from those in a corporation. In a co-operative, each member is entitled to one vote, regardless of how many shares he or she owns.

Types of Co-operatives

There are hundreds of different co-operatives, but they generally function in one of six main areas of business:

- *Consumer co-operatives.* These organizations sell goods to both members and the general public (e.g., co-op gasoline stations, agricultural implement dealers).
- *Financial co-operatives.* These organizations operate much like banks, accepting deposits from members, giving loans, and providing chequing services (e.g., credit unions).
- *Insurance co-operatives.* These organizations provide many types of insurance coverage, such as life, fire, and liability (for example, the Co-operative Hail Insurance Company of Manitoba).
- *Marketing co-operatives.* These organizations sell the produce of their farm members and purchase inputs for the production process (e.g., seed and fertilizer). Some, like Federated Co-operatives, also purchase and market finished products.
- *Service co-operatives.* These organizations provide members with services, such as recreation.
- *Housing co-operatives.* These organizations provide housing for members, who purchase a share in the co-operative, which holds the title to the housing complex.

In terms of numbers, co-operatives are the least important form of ownership. However, they are of significance to society and to their members since they may provide services that are not readily available, or that cost more than the members would otherwise be willing to pay. Table 4.5 compares the various forms of business ownership using different characteristics.

Advantages of a Co-operative

Co-operatives have many of the same advantages of investor-owned corporations such as limited liability of owners and continuity. A key benefit of a co-operative relates to its structure. As noted above, each member has only one vote in the affairs of the co-operative, regardless of how many shares he or she holds. This system prevents voting and financial control of the business by a few wealthy individuals. This is particularly attractive to members who are less wealthy than other members of the co-operative.

Table 4.5 A Comparison of Four Forms of Business Ownership

Characteristic	Sole Proprietorship	Partnership	Corporation	Co-operative
Protection against liability for bad debts	low	low	high	high
Ease of formation	high	high	medium	medium
Permanence	low	low	high	high
Ease of ownership transfer	low	low	high	high
Ease of raising money	low	medium	high	high
Freedom from regulation	high	high	low	medium
Tax advantages	high	high	low	high

Whereas investor-owned corporations are typically exposed to double taxation because dividends to shareholders are distributed out of after-tax corporate income, co-operatives are allowed to deduct patronage refunds to members out of before-tax income. Thus, income may only be taxed at the individual member level rather than at both the co-operative and member level. In other words, a co-operative does not pay tax on income that it distributes as patronage dividends.[51]

Disadvantages of a Co-operative

One of the main disadvantages of co-operatives relates to attracting equity investment. Since the benefits from being a member of a co-operative arise through the level of use of the co-operative rather than the level of equity invested, members do not have an incentive to invest in equity capital of the co-operative. Another drawback is that democratic voting arrangements and dividends based purely on patronage turn off some entrepreneurs from forming or joining a co-operative.

SUCCESS AND FAILURE IN SMALL BUSINESS

6 Identify four key reasons for success in small businesses and four key reasons for failure.

Why do some ventures succeed while others fail? This question is difficult to answer since most of what we know is based on businesses that may under- or over-represent firms that succeed or fail. As outlined earlier, when the focus is on businesses with employees, as is the case with a great deal of research, businesses run by the self-employed (with no employees) are ignored. Much of what we know about business "failure" is based upon all firms that simply stopped operating, even though a business can cease operations for a variety of reasons other than failure, such as retirement or a decision by the entrepreneur to move on to something else.[52] Keeping these considerations in mind, we now outline the factors that have typically been associated with success and failure.

A 2005 study conducted by CIBC World Markets found that small businesses with above-average revenue growth were run by owners who had more education, used professional advisors, adopted the corporate form of ownership, did outsourcing work for other companies, had a high level of internet connectivity, and used the internet to sell outside of Canada.[53]

Reasons for Success

Beyond the specific findings like the CIBC study, four general factors typically explain the success of small business owners:

1. *Hard work, drive, and dedication.* Small business owners must be committed to succeeding and be willing to put in the time and effort to make it happen. Long hours and few vacations generally characterize the first few years of new business ownership.
2. *Market demand for the product or service.* Careful analysis of market conditions can help small business people assess the probable reception of their products. If the area around a college has only one pizza parlour, a new pizzeria is more likely to succeed than if there are already 10 in operation.
3. *Managerial competence.* Successful small business people have a solid understanding of how to manage a business. They may acquire competence through training (taking courses), experience, or by using the expertise of others. Few, however, succeed alone or straight out of university or college. Most spend time in successful companies or partner with others to bring expertise to a new business.
4. *Luck.* Luck also plays a role in the success of some firms. For example, after one entrepreneur started an environmental clean-up firm, he struggled to keep his business afloat. Then the government committed a large sum of money for toxic waste clean-up. He was able to get several large contracts, and his business is now thriving.

Reasons for Failure

Small businesses collapse for a number of reasons (see Table 4.6). Entrepreneurs may have no control over some of these factors (for example, weather, fraud, accidents), but they can influence most items on the list. Four general factors are particularly important:

1. *Managerial incompetence or inexperience.* Some entrepreneurs put their faith in common sense, overestimate their own managerial skills, or believe that hard work alone ensures success. If managers don't know how to make basic business decisions or don't understand basic management principles, they aren't likely to succeed in the long run.
2. *Neglect.* Some entrepreneurs try to launch ventures in their spare time, and others devote only limited time to new businesses. But starting a small business demands an overwhelming time commitment. If you aren't willing to put in the time and effort that a business requires, you aren't likely to survive.
3. *Weak control systems.* Effective control systems keep a business on track and alert managers to potential trouble. If your control systems don't signal impending problems, you may be in serious trouble before you spot more obvious difficulties.
4. *Insufficient capital.* Some entrepreneurs are overly optimistic about how soon they'll start earning profits. In most cases, it takes months or even years. Amazon.com didn't earn a profit for 10 years but obviously still required capital to pay employees and to cover other expenses. Experts say you need enough capital to operate at least six months without earning a profit; some recommend enough to last a year.[54]

Table 4.6 Causes of Small Business Failure

Poor management skills
- poor delegation and organizational ability
- lack of depth in management team
- entrepreneurial incompetence, such as a poor understanding of finances and business markets
- lack of experience

Inadequate marketing capabilities
- difficulty in marketing product
- market too small, nonexistent, or declines
- too much competition
- problems with distribution systems

Inadequate financial capabilities
- weak skills in accounting and finance
- lack of budgetary control
- inadequate costing systems
- incorrect valuation of assets
- unable to obtain financial backing

Inadequate production capabilities
- poorly designed production systems
- old and inefficient production facilities and equipment
- inadequate control over quality
- problems with inventory control

Personal reasons
- lost interest in business
- accident, illness
- death
- family problems

Disasters
- fire
- weather
- strikes
- fraud by entrepreneur or others

Other
- mishandling of large project
- excessive standard of living
- lack of time to devote to business
- difficulties with associates or partners
- government policies change

Summary of Learning Objectives

1. **Explain the meaning of and interrelationship among the terms *small business*, *new venture creation*, and *entrepreneurship*.** A small business has less than 100 employees. A new firm is one that has become operational within the previous 12 months, has adopted any of four main organizational forms—*sole proprietorship*, *partnership*, *corporation*, or *co-operative*—and sells goods or services. Entrepreneurship is the *process* of identifying an opportunity in the marketplace and accessing the resources needed to capitalize on it. In relation to small and/or new businesses, entrepreneurship is the process by which a small business or a new business is created.
2. **Describe the role of small and new businesses in the Canadian economy.** While 98 percent of employer businesses in Canada are small (they have less than 100 employees), 49 percent of the total private sector labour force works for small businesses. The distribution of employment by size of firm varies across industries. The small business sector's capacity for entrepreneurship and innovation accounts for much of the job creation this sector contributes to the economy, with start-ups accounting for most of the growth. On average, the number of businesses increased by 9300 each year during the 1991–2003 period, with most of the growth occurring in the services-producing sector. As the number of businesses has increased, so too has the number of women-led firms.
3. **Explain the *entrepreneurial process* and describe its three key elements.** The entrepreneurial process occurs within a social, political, and economic context and consists of three key elements: the entrepreneur, the opportunity, and resources. The *entrepreneur* is the driving force in identifying an opportunity and accessing the resources to capitalize on it. Opportunities don't simply materialize, entrepreneurs create them. *Opportunity* identification involves generating ideas, screening them to determine their potential, and developing the ones that remain. Entrepreneurs typically access the various *resources* needed by *bootstrapping*—doing more with less. These resources are both financial and non-financial. Two types of financing—*debt* and *equity*—can be accessed from a range of sources.
4. **Describe two alternative strategies for becoming a business owner—*buying an existing business* and *buying a franchise*.** It is necessary to work through the entrepreneurial process when *starting a business from scratch*. Whether start-up efforts will result in a new business often depends upon how well matched the entrepreneur's skills and abilities are with the opportunity and the resources required, as well as how well matched the opportunity and resources are. Of the ventures that are brought to fruition, some will grow, while others will decline, die, or remain stable. Generally, when someone buys an existing business, the odds of success are better. An existing business has already proven its ability to attract customers. It has also established relationships with lenders, suppliers, and other stakeholders. Moreover, an existing track record gives potential buyers a much clearer picture of what to expect than any estimate of a new business's prospects. On the other hand, there may be uncertainty about the exact financial shape the business is in, the business may have a poor reputation, the location may be poor, or it may be difficult to determine an appropriate purchase price. A special case of buying an existing business involves family businesses, which pose both opportunities and challenges. In buying a *franchise* the buyer (franchisee) purchases the right to sell the product or service of the seller (franchiser) according to the terms of the franchising agreement. In return the franchiser provides assistance with the business's start-up as well as with ongoing operations once the business opens its doors.
5. **Describe four forms of *legal organization* for a business and discuss the advantages and disadvantages of each.** A *sole proprietorship* is a business owned and operated by one person. Answering only to themselves, sole proprietors enjoy considerable freedom in running the business. The ease of setting up a sole proprietorship makes it appealing to self-starters, as do the low start-up costs and the tax benefits. A major drawback is unlimited liability. A sole proprietor is personally liable for all debts incurred by the business. Another disadvantage is lack of continuity: A sole proprietorship dissolves when the owner dies. Finally, a sole proprietorship depends on the resources of a single individual.

   A *general partnership* is similar to a sole proprietorship in that all partners have unlimited liability for the obligations of the business. The biggest advantage is its ability to grow by adding new talent and money. Because banks prefer to make loans to enterprises that are not dependent on single individuals, it's easier for partnerships to borrow money. They can also invite new partners to join by investing. Although a partnership is easy to form and has few legal requirements, all partnerships should have a partnership agreement. Partners are taxed as individuals, and unlimited liability is a drawback. Each partner may be liable for all partnership debts. Partnerships may lack continuity, and transferring ownership may be hard. No partner may sell out without the consent of the others.

All *corporations* share certain characteristics: They are separate legal entities, they have property rights and obligations, and they have indefinite lifespans. They may sue and be sued; buy, hold, and sell property; make and sell products; and be tried and punished for crimes committed. The biggest advantage of incorporation is limited liability: Investor liability is limited to one's personal investments in the corporation. If the business fails, the courts may sell a corporation's assets but cannot touch the personal possessions of investors. Another advantage is continuity—a corporation can continue forever. Shares can be sold or passed on to heirs, and most corporations benefit from the continuity of professional management. Finally, corporations have advantages in raising money. By selling stock, they expand the number of investors and the amount of available funds. Legal protections tend to make lenders more willing to grant loans.

Start-up costs and complexity are among the disadvantages of incorporating. Corporations are heavily regulated and must meet complex legal requirements in the provinces in which they're chartered. A potential drawback to incorporation is *double taxation.* A corporation pays income taxes on company profits, and its stockholders pay taxes on income returned by their investments. Thus, corporate profits are taxed twice—at the corporate and at ownership levels (but the dividend tax credit given to owners may offset the effects of double taxation). Of the two types of private-sector corporations—public and privately held—the vast majority are privately held. In forming a corporation, a business will incorporate federally if it is going to operate in more than one province and provincially if it is going to operate in only one province.

A *co-operative* is an organization that is formed to benefit its owners in the form of reduced prices and/or the distribution of surpluses at year-end. It is an incorporated business that is organized, owned, and democratically controlled by the people who use its products and services. The distribution of its earnings (or surpluses) is based upon the use of the co-operative rather than the level of investment. In addition to the two main advantages co-operatives share with corporations—limited liability and continuity—they also have two benefits that corporations don't have. Since all members have one vote, this democratic control ensures a few people cannot dominate the decision making. Additionally, co-operatives aren't subject to double taxation since surpluses are distributed to members from pre-tax profits. Co-operatives are not without disadvantages. The main drawback is that co-operatives often have difficulty raising equity, since members gain financial benefit according to their use of the co-operative, not according to the amount they have invested. While there are hundreds of different co-operatives, they usually function in one of six areas of business: consumer co-operatives, financial co-operatives, insurance co-operatives, marketing co-operatives, service co-operatives, or housing co-operatives.

C. **Identify four key reasons for success in small businesses and four key reasons for failure.** Four basic factors explain most small-business success: (1) hard work, drive, and dedication; (2) market demand for the product or service; (3) managerial competence; and (4) luck. Four factors contribute to small-business failure: (1) managerial incompetence or inexperience; (2) neglect; (3) weak control systems; and (4) insufficient capital.

KEY TERMS

board of directors, 124
bootstrapping, 116
business plan, 115
chief executive officer, 126
collateral, 116
co-operative, 127
corporation, 124
dividends, 127
double taxation, 127
entrepreneurs, 105
entrepreneurship, 105
franchise, 114
franchising agreement, 120
general partners, 122
general partnership, 122
income trust, 126
initial public offering (IPO), 126
inside directors, 124
intrapreneurs, 105
limited liability, 127
limited partners, 122
limited partnership, 122
nascent entrepreneurs, 104
new venture/firm, 105
outside directors, 105
partnership, 122
private sector, 107
private corporation, 126
public corporation, 126
sales forecast, 114
small business, 105
sole proprietorship, 122
stock, 127
stockholders, 124
unlimited liability, 122

QUESTIONS FOR ANALYSIS

1. What are some of the problems that are encountered when we try to define the term "small business"?
2. Why are new ventures the main source of job creation and new product/service ideas?
3. Do you think that you would be a successful entrepreneur? Why or why not?
4. Consider a new product or service that has recently become available for purchase by consumers. To what extent did this product or service possess the "screening" characteristics that are described in the chapter (adding value, providing competitive advantage, etc.)?
5. Using the product or service you described in Question 4, analyze the extent to which there is a good "fit" between the various elements in the entrepreneurial process.
6. Why might a corporation choose to remain private? Why might it choose to "go public"?

APPLICATION EXERCISES

1. Identify three trends—whether in fashion, lifestyle, or something else—and generate three ideas for capitalizing on each one of them.
2. Find a newspaper or magazine article that describes someone who is an entrepreneur. Use the information provided to explain what makes this person an entrepreneur.
3. Spend some time watching what people do and how they do it, and then (a) identify two ways to make what they do easier, and (b) describe two problems you observed and identify strategies for resolving those problems.
4. Interview the owner/manager of a sole proprietorship or general partnership. What characteristics of that business form led the owner to choose it? Does the owner ever contemplate changing the form of ownership of the business? Why or why not?

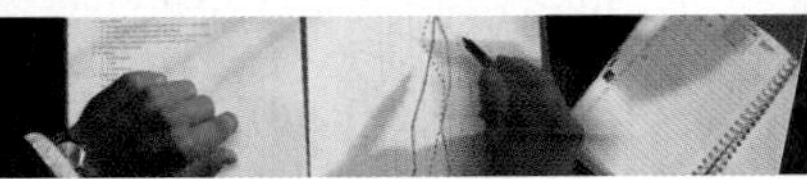

BUILDING YOUR BUSINESS SKILLS

Working the Internet

Goal

To encourage students to define opportunities and problems for small companies doing business on the internet.

The Situation

Suppose you and two partners own a gift basket store, specializing in special-occasion baskets for individual and corporate clients. Your business is doing well in your community, but you believe there may be opportunity for growth through a virtual storefront on the internet.

Assignment

Step 1

Join with two other students and assume the role of business partners. Start by researching internet businesses. Look at books and articles at the library and contact the following websites for help:

- Canada Business—Services for Entrepreneurs: www.cbsc.org
- U.S. Small Business Administration: www.sba.gov
- IBM Small Business Center: www.businesscenter.ibm.com
- Apple Small Business Home Page: www.apple.com/business/

These sites may lead you to other sites, so keep an open mind.

Step 2

Based on your research, determine the importance of the following small business issues:

- an analysis of changing company finances as a result of expansion to the internet
- an analysis of your new competitive marketplace (the world) and how it affects your current marketing approach, which focusses on your local community
- identification of sources of management advice as the expansion proceeds
- the role of technology consultants in launching and maintaining the website
- customer service policies in your virtual environment

Follow-Up Questions

1. Do you think your business would be successful on the internet? Why or why not?
2. Based on your analysis, how will internet expansion affect your current business practices? What specific changes are you likely to make?
3. Do you think that operating a virtual storefront will be harder or easier than doing business in your local community? Explain your answer.

EXERCISING YOUR ETHICS

Breaking Up Is Hard to Do

The Situation

Connie and Mark began a 25-year friendship after finishing college and discovering their mutual interest in owning a business. Established as a general partnership, their home-furnishings centre is a successful business sustained for 20 years by a share-and-share-alike relationship. Start-up cash, daily responsibilities, and profits have all been shared equally. The partners both work four days each week except when busy seasons require both of them to be in the store. Shared goals and compatible personalities have led to a solid give-and-take relationship that helps them overcome business problems while maintaining a happy interpersonal relationship.

The division of work is a natural match and successful combination because of the partners' different but complementary interests. Mark buys the merchandise and maintains up-to-date contacts with suppliers; he also handles personnel matters (hiring and training employees). Connie manages the inventory, buys shipping supplies, keeps the books, and manages the finances. Mark does more selling, with Connie helping out only during busy seasons. Both partners share in decisions about advertising and promotions.

The Dilemma

Things began changing two years ago, when Connie became less interested in the business and got more involved in other activities. While Mark's enthusiasm remained high, Connie's time was increasingly consumed by travel, recreation, and community-service activities. At first, she reduced her work commitment from four to three days a week. Then she indicated that she wanted to cut back further, to just two days. "In that case," Mark replied, "we'll have to make some changes."

Mark insisted that profit sharing be adjusted to reflect his larger role in running the business. He proposed that Connie's monthly salary be cut in half (from $4000 to $2000). Connie agreed. He recommended that the $2000 savings be shifted to his salary because of his increased workload, but this time Connie balked, arguing that Mark's current $4000 salary already compensated him for his contributions. She proposed to split the difference, with Mark getting a $1000 increase and the other $1000 going into the firm's cash account. Mark said no and insisted on a full $2000 raise. To avoid a complete falling out, Connie finally gave in, even though she thought it unfair for Mark's salary to jump from $4000 per month to $6000. At that point, she made a promise to herself: "To even things out, I'll find a way to get $2000 worth of inventory for personal use each month."

Questions for Discussion

1. Identify the ethical issues, if any, regarding Mark's and Connie's respective positions on Mark's proposed $2000 salary increase.
2. What kind of salary adjustments do you think would be fair in this situation? Explain why.
3. There is, of course, another way for Mark and Connie to solve their differences: Because the terms of participation have changed, it might make sense to dissolve the existing partnership. What do you recommend in this regard?

CONCLUDING CASE 4-1

The Big Cheese

People familiar with the business landscape in Vermont point with justifiable pride to Ben Cohen and Jerry Greenfield, founders of Ben and Jerry's Homemade Holdings Inc., as the state's foremost entrepreneurs. But the ice cream boys are getting some competition these days from another pair of entrepreneurs who are making a popular line of cheese products the cream of local business.

The story starts in 1919, when 94 Vermont dairy farmers banded together to create a co-operative to make and market cheese. The initial membership fee was $5.00 per cow and a cord of wood to fuel the boiler. Cabot Creamery (www.cabotcheese.com) is now a multi-million-dollar dairy-products company with a membership of 1500 farm families. Its cheeses have won numerous awards, including Best Cheddar in the World at the World Cheese Championship in Green Bay, Wisconsin.

Cabot has always built its brand on quality. Whereas many companies use enzymes to speed up the cheese-making process, Cabot uses only natural methods. Naturally processing high-quality cheese means that a 640-pound block of cheddar might have to sit in a warehouse for a year before it gets its rich, full-bodied flavour.

At any time, therefore, Cabot might have 25 million pounds of cheese in the warehouse. And because costs are pegged to the price of milk when the cheese is first manufactured, profit margins are hard to predict. Managers have to forecast both the price of milk and the demand for cheese as much as a year in advance. Furthermore, the price of milk fluctuates just as much as the price of crude oil. "There's a pretty good temptation to play around with enzymes," admits Cabot CEO Richard Stammer. "If you can put out an extra-sharp cheddar in 5 months instead of 12, you're less likely to get stung by a spread in the price of milk."

In the early 1990s, Cabot was in danger of going under. Even with revenues of $35 million a year, annual profits were less than $1 million. Members were getting restless, and there was talk of abandoning Cabot and launching a new co-operative. But because a new venture would have been a big risk, members decided on another approach: In 1992, Cabot agreed to be taken over by Agri-Mark Inc., a dairy co-op based in Methuen, Massachusetts. Agri-Mark (www.agrimark.net) was the fourteenth largest dairy co-op in the United States and wanted to expand. Given the obvious fit between a dairy co-op and a cheese maker, the move seemed like a good one.

After Agri-Mark took control of Cabot in 1992, parent-company president Paul Johnston decided to install a new CEO. He didn't have to look far. His choice was Richard Stammer, Agri-Mark's chief economist. While Johnston was working his way up the ladder at an Agri-Mark milk-producing plant, Stammer had been an economics professor at Rutgers, where he had developed a strong understanding of the dynamics of prices in agricultural markets.

Johnston and Stammer couldn't have been more different, but they worked well together. Johnston is a demanding boss known for his bluntness and, occasionally, lack of tact. Stammer is reserved, polite, and gracious. But the two executives have managed to set aside their differences and focus on a common goal: running an efficient business that earns profits for its owners.

Among the first things they did was improve forecasting methods. The process is never perfect, but Cabot now does a much better job of predicting demand and prices for milk and cheese. They also set about to make Cabot a national brand by concentrating more heavily on product marketing. So far, the plan seems to be paying off: Profits have topped $8 million on annual revenues of $175 million.

Questions for Discussion

1. Why do you think Cabot is organized as a co-operative?
2. What role has entrepreneurship played in the history and success of Cabot?
3. Under what circumstances might it make sense for Cabot to reorganize as a corporation?
4. What issues of taxation and legal liability might be especially pertinent for Cabot and Agri-Mark?

CONCLUDING CASE 4-2

Getting in on the Ground Floor

Larry Gibson, 51, oversees a business empire that employs 80 people full time, (plus 110 under contract) and is projected to have sales of $30 million this year. But things didn't start out that way. Gibson got into the flooring business after finding university too slow for his liking. After working as a flooring installer in Halifax, he went west in the late 1970s and worked in Calgary and in the Arctic, honing his commercial estimating skills before returning to Nova Scotia in 1983.

After five years of managing Eaton's flooring business in Halifax, he got word that his division was closing in May, 1988. At the time Eaton's still had contracts and warranties outstanding. "So they came to me and said, 'Will you take these contracts on and go out on your own?'" Using personal savings, he and his wife Patricia bought a dilapidated Halifax building from which to launch a floor-covering business and took over the chain's local flooring accounts, setting up shop under the Install-A-Flor name.

The weekend before opening the doors in July 1988, Patricia started to cry, wondering if they were doing the right thing. Reassurance was not long in coming. Gibson's phone rang at 8:30 opening day, and on the line—unaware that Gibson's phone was resting on a sawhorse, since his office wasn't furnished yet—was Atlantic property developer Armour Construction. Gibson's earlier bid to install flooring in a 185-unit complex had been accepted. The deal was worth $440 000 over 15 months.

He says that first sale taught him that "if you believe you can do something, then put your mind and heart to it. There's always an element of surprise and the unforeseen, and it can be good or it can be bad. In my case, it was good and lucky." Indeed, Larry Gibson is known for his commitment to hard work, providing the best possible service, and delivering a quality product at a competitive price. He credits the nuns at the convent school in Herring Cove for instilling discipline in him and says the unexpected death of his father when he was 10 helped give him drive.

Mr. Gibson said the first few years of heads-down, all-out work took its toll on his health. "I was gritting my teeth at night and my stomach had a big knot in it, basically, because we started with nothing and always worried about turning that dollar and getting financial institutions and suppliers to believe in me," he recalled. "It was always tight."

Mr. Gibson credits his wife, who handles the business's finances and administration, with helping him through the early days. "I'd go home, we'd sit at the table—most people have salt shakers; we had a calculator. We would do quantity measures on plans and I would bid, bid, bid." That effort resulted in a 633 percent growth over the company's first five years. "When we first started, it was difficult to convince suppliers to sell us their products," recalls Patricia, "because selling to a newcomer is sometimes a bit of a risk. But Larry and I have a policy of 'Never take no for an answer. There's always another way.' We stuck with it and gained people's confidence."

Today, the business includes seven Floors Plus retail stores in Nova Scotia and New Brunswick, as well as specialty and contract divisions that operate internationally and have specialties such as clean room technology—on-site thermal welding and moulding of plastics—that is used in medical operating theatres and food-processing facilities. "Right now we're doing a school in Bermuda," said Mr. Gibson, adding that the business has opened offices in China and Ontario.

Contracting represents 40 percent of the company's business, with retail accounting for another 40 percent and the growing wholesale business, named Dantra (after his two children Daniel and Tracy, who both work in the family firm), representing 20 percent.

"We have a lack of supply here of specialty products," Mr. Gibson said in explaining the company's diversification. "Nobody's going to come in here and say, 'Listen, I want you to do clean rooms.' You've got to search this stuff out and find a market for it. It's not just about money, it's about service, being a leader and having knowledge about the market."

Market knowledge is market power, and Mr. Gibson has gained that by going all over the world in search of new business opportunities. "We know from traveling the styles that are coming," he said, noting that he is largely in the business of selling fashion. "The (Atlantic) area is a couple of years behind Toronto, New York, and even European or Asian markets. So we know we've got time to react if we react quickly."

Questions for Discussion

1. According to Statistics Canada's Business Register, would Install-a-Flor be considered a small business? Why or why not?
2. Assess the fit between Larry Gibson and the opportunity when Install-a-Flor was started. What personal characteristics contributed most to his success?
3. To what extent did Larry Gibson use bootstrapping in getting his business started? Explain.
4. Assess Larry Gibson's capacity for identifying opportunities according to the characteristics outlined in the opportunity screening section of the chapter.
5. What benefits or drawbacks are evident in this family business?
6. Would you recommend that Install-a-Flor go public?
7. Clearly, Install-a-Flor is no longer a new business. But is it entrepreneurial?

CHAPTER 5

Understanding International Business

After reading this chapter, you should be able to:

1. Describe the rise of international business and identify the *major world marketplaces.*
2. Explain how different forms of *competitive advantage, import-export balances, exchange rates,* and *foreign competition* determine the ways in which countries and businesses respond to the international environment.
3. Discuss the factors involved in deciding to do business internationally and in selecting the appropriate *levels of international involvement* and *international organizational structure.*
4. Describe some of the ways in which *social, cultural, economic, legal,* and *political differences* act as barriers to international trade.
5. Explain how *free trade agreements* assist world trade.

Canadian Exporters: Opportunities and Problems

Approximately 40 percent of all goods and services that are produced in Canada are exported. This means that Canada is the most export-focussed industrialized country in the world. Exporting is done by both large and small firms, and by goods-producing and service-producing firms. Consider just a few examples:

- McCain Foods is a formidable presence in Europe, where it holds a 75 percent share of the market for "oven fries" in Germany. It also dominates the frozen french fry market in France and England.
- Abitibi-Price sells newsprint and other forest products around the world
- Seagull Pewter & Silversmiths Ltd., Magic Pantry Foods, and Lovat Tunnel Equipment have all won Canada Export Awards.
- Sabian Cymbals sells 90 percent of its products to 80 different countries.
- Electrovert Ltd. does 95 percent of its business outside Canada.
- Tesma International (which is controlled by Magna International) opened a factory in China in 2004 to produce engine-belt tensioners for Volkswagen AG.

The rapid growth in the world economy has created substantial export opportunities for Canadian firms, but Canadian managers must understand foreign cultures if they are to be successful exporters. Recent developments in China and South Africa illustrate both these aspects of exporting.

China's GDP has been growing at by an average of 8 percent annually for the last decade; this is more than double the growth rate achieved in Canada or the United States. China was world's sixth biggest economy in 2004 and its share of global output is expected to double by 2020. China is now responsible for more than 30 percent of *total* global manufacturing output. It consumes about half of all cement used in the world, more than one-third of all steel, and nearly one-third of all coal.

This dramatic growth in China's GDP means big export opportunities for Canadian companies producing oil, lumber, nickel, coal, zinc, cement, and seafood. Some of these opportunities have already been realized. During the last decade, for example, Canadian exports of fish to China have increased by nearly 2000 percent, chemicals and nickel over 1200 percent, and auto parts and wood pulp over 500 percent.

Services are also being successfully exported to China. Manulife Financial Corp., which has made a major commitment to sell insurance in China, entered the Chinese market in 1996 through a joint venture with Sinochem, a state-owned trading company. Manulife trains raw recruits by emphasizing training and team building so that its sales agents can provide good service to customers. The venture now has 8 percent of the Chinese market and Manulife is the second-ranking foreign insurance firm in China.

Canadian managers must be sensitive to foreign cultures when exporting. Jonathan Fischer, the president of Georgetown, Ontario-based Mold Masters Ltd., discovered this when he went to Shanghai to visit some of his firm's customers. At one meeting he attended, he was dismayed to hear Chinese buyers yelling at his salespeople. When he asked his Chinese managers what was going on, they explained that the buyers were simply demanding lower prices and faster delivery times, and that the shouting was typical of negotiations in China. Fischer learned that the Chinese negotiating style is tough, focusses on price, appears theatrical, and emphasizes hierarchy, but it also requires giving the other side the opportunity to "save face" somewhere in the negotiations. In these negotiations, Western managers have to avoid losing their temper. They must also patiently hold their ground and be prepared to give up something to the other side for the important face saving aspect of negotiations.

The benefits of cultural sensitivity are illustrated by the experience of McCain Foods Ltd., which entered the South African market in 2000. It was initially successful at selling french fries and frozen vegetables to white South Africans, but unsuccessful at selling these products to black South Africans. The company discovered that blacks didn't eat frozen food because they were unfamiliar with it, and because most lived in areas that did not have the electricity needed to run freezers (and they couldn't afford freezers anyway). But there is a growing middle class in South Africa, so McCain began trying to reach this group by providing single-serving packages of frozen vegetables that could be consumed in one meal. This eliminated the need for a freezer.

McCain also adopted a much more unusual strategy. It discovered that funerals are significant events in the South African culture, and that the cost of hosting the traditional funeral lunch is very expensive for the family of the deceased. So the company offered to help grieving families by matching the family's purchases of frozen foods on a one-for-one basis. The families were grateful for the support and were happy to have the McCain name prominently displayed at their funerals. When these individuals go shopping in the future, they will immediately recognize the McCain brand. By 2004, McCain held 70 percent of the market for frozen vegetables and 90 percent of the market for potato products in South Africa.

Cultural sensitivity is only one of the issues that Canadian exporters must deal with. Consider the problems encountered by Kantain Products Ltd. of Kitchener, Ontario. The company makes chemical tank liners and is doing well in Canada because of the environmental movement. Glen Lippert, the president of Kantain, decided that his product was good enough to sell in the United States, but when he tried to buy liability insurance for his anticipated activities in the United States, he discovered that the premiums would be at least $50 000 per year. This amount far outweighed the amount of potential profit he thought he could make initially, so he abandoned his plan to sell in the U.S.

Many Canadian firms that have actually entered the U.S. market have been given a rough ride. This is particularly true in the retail store business, where companies like Shoppers Drug Mart, Canadian Tire Corp., Future Shop Ltd., Dylex, and Mark's Work Wearhouse all suffered major defeats. In 2004, Jean Coutu Group purchased 1549 Eckerd pharmacies in the United States, making Coutu the fourth-largest U.S. chain drug retailer. To date, financial returns have not been as good as the company had hoped. ◆

THE RISE OF INTERNATIONAL BUSINESS

globalization The integration of markets globally.

imports Products that are made or grown abroad and sold in Canada.

exports Products made or grown in Canada that are sold abroad.

The total volume of world trade today is immense—around $8 trillion each year. As more and more firms engage in international business, the world economy is fast becoming a single interdependent system—a process called **globalization**. Even so, we often take for granted the diversity of goods and services available today as a result of international trade. Your television set, your shoes, and even the roast lamb on your dinner table may all be **imports**—that is, products made or grown abroad but sold in Canada. At the same time, the success of many Canadian firms depends in large part on **exports**—products made or grown domestically and shipped for sale abroad.

The Contemporary Global Economy

International business is nothing new. Trade between nations can actually be traced back as far as 2000 BCE, when North African tribes took dates and clothing to Assyria and Babylonia in the Middle East and traded them for olive oil and spices. Christopher Columbus's voyages of discovery were motivated by the search for new trade routes. Still, there is a tendency for people to forget that international business has been around for a long time. An understanding of historical forces can significantly improve our understanding of the contemporary global economy—how it works, why it works, and what trends will likely shape its future.[1]

MIT professor Paul Krugman argues that what we now regard as an extremely active "global economy" is not as big a change as you might imagine. He points out that imports now represent only a slightly higher proportion of GDP than they did 100 years ago, and that capital mobility (the movement of money from country to country) is about the same as it was in 1914. At that time, moreover, England's trade surplus—4 percent of GDP—was the same as the surplus enjoyed by Japan during the peak decade of the 1980s.

On the other hand, it is also true that international trade is becoming increasingly central to the fortunes of most nations of the world, as well as to their largest businesses. Whereas in the past many nations followed strict policies to protect domestic business, today more and more countries are aggressively encouraging international trade. They are more freely opening their borders to foreign businesses, offering incentives for their own domestic businesses to expand internationally, and making it easier for foreign firms to partner with local firms through various alliances. Similarly, as more and more industries and markets become global, firms that compete in them are also becoming global.

Several forces have combined to spark and sustain globalization. For one thing, governments and businesses have simply become more aware of the benefits of globalization to their countries and shareholders. For another, new technologies make international travel, communication, and commerce increasingly easier, faster, and cheaper than ever before. Overseas phone calls and seaborne shipping costs per tonne have both declined over the last several decades. Likewise, transatlantic travel once required several days aboard a ship. Today, travellers can easily fly between major cities in North America and Europe in less than a day. Finally, there are competitive pressures: Sometimes, a firm simply must enter foreign markets just to keep up with its competitors.

The Major World Marketplaces

The contemporary world economy revolves around three major marketplaces: North America, Europe, and Asia Pacific. These three geographic regions are home to most of the world's largest economies, biggest multinational corporations, most influential financial markets, and highest-income consumers.

The World Bank, an agency of the United Nations, uses **per capita income**—the average income per person—as a measure to divide countries into one of four groups:[2]

per capita income The average income per person of a country.

Describe the rise of international business and identify the *major world marketplaces*. 1

- *High-income countries* are those with per capita income greater than U.S.$10 065. These include Canada, the United States, most countries in Europe, Australia, New Zealand, Japan, South Korea, Kuwait, the United Arab Emirates, Israel, Singapore, and Taiwan. Hong Kong, while technically no longer an independent nation, also falls into this category.
- *Upper-middle-income countries* are those with per capita income between U.S.$3255 and U.S.$10 065. This group includes, among others, the Czech Republic, Greece, Hungary, Poland, most countries comprising the former Soviet Bloc, Turkey, Mexico, Argentina, and South Africa.
- *Low middle-income countries* are those with per capita income between U.S.$825 and U.S.$3255. Among the countries in this group are Colombia, Guatemala, Samoa, and Thailand. Some of these, including China and India, have huge populations and are seen as potentially attractive markets for international business.
- *Low-income countries* (often called developing countries) are those with annual per-capita income of less than U.S.$825. Due to low literacy rates, weak infrastructures, unstable governments, and related problems, these countries are less attractive to international business. For example, the East African nation of Somalia is plagued by drought, civil war, and starvation, and plays virtually no role in the world economy.

North America

The United States dominates the North American business region. It is the single largest marketplace and enjoys the most stable economy in the world. Canada also plays a major role in the international economy. Moreover, the United States and Canada are each other's largest trading

Despite the technology boom that has made its economy one of the fastest-growing in the world, India remains a low income country. More than 330 million people—nearly 40 percent of the population—live in poverty. Because two-thirds of the population still depends on agriculture, the prosperity generated by the manufacture of auto components and the provision of information-technology services has had little effect on the fortunes of vast numbers of people.

partner. Many U.S. firms, such as General Motors and Procter & Gamble, have maintained successful Canadian operations for years, and many Canadian firms, such as Bombardier, Nortel Networks, and Alcan Aluminum, are also major international competitors.

Mexico has also become a major manufacturing centre, especially along the southern U.S. border, where cheap labour and low transportation costs have encouraged many firms, from the United States and other countries, to build manufacturing plants. The auto industry has been especially active. For example, DaimlerChrysler, General Motors, Volkswagen, Nissan, and Ford have large assembly plants in this region. Moreover, several of their major suppliers have also built facilities in the area. From 1993 to 2001, exports of automobiles and automobile parts from Mexico increased from $7.2 billion to a stunning $23.6 billion, and the auto industry in Mexico now employs over 400 000 workers.[3]

Europe

Europe has often been regarded as two regions—Western Europe and Eastern Europe. Western Europe, dominated by Germany, the United Kingdom, France, and Italy, has long been a mature but fragmented marketplace. But the transformation of the European Union (EU) in 1992 into a unified marketplace has further increased the region's importance. Major international firms such as Unilever, Renault, Royal Dutch/Shell, Michelin, Siemens, and Nestlé are all headquartered in Western Europe.

Ecommerce and technology have also become increasingly important in this region.[4] There has been a surge in internet start-ups in southeast England, the Netherlands, and the Scandinavian countries, and Ireland is now the world's number-two exporter of software (after the United States).[5] Strasbourg, France, is a major centre for biotech start-ups. Barcelona, Spain, has many flourishing software and internet companies, and the Frankfurt region of Germany is dotted with both software and biotech start-ups.[6]

Eastern Europe, once primarily communist, has also gained in importance, both as a marketplace and as a producer. For example, such multinational corporations as Daewoo, Nestlé, General Motors, and ABB Asea Brown Boveri have all set up operations in Poland. Similarly, Ford, General Motors, Suzuki, and Volkswagen have all built new factories in Hungary. On the other hand, government instability has hampered economic development in Russia, Bulgaria, Albania, Romania, and other countries in this region.

Asia-Pacific

Asia-Pacific consists of Japan, China, Thailand, Malaysia, Singapore, Indonesia, South Korea, Taiwan, the Philippines, Australia, and New Zealand. Some experts still identify Hong Kong as a separate part of the region, although the former city-state is now actually part of China. Vietnam is sometimes included as part of the region. Fuelled by strong entries in the automobile, electronics, and banking industries, the economies of these countries grew rapidly in the 1970s and 1980s. Unfortunately, a currency crisis in the late 1990s generally slowed growth in virtually every country of the region.

The currency crisis aside, however, Asia-Pacific is an important force in the world economy and a major source of competition for North American firms. Led by firms such as Toyota, Toshiba, and Nippon Steel, Japan dominates the region. In addition, South Korea (with such firms as Samsung and Hyundai), Taiwan (owner of Chinese Petroleum and manufacturing home of many foreign firms), and Hong Kong (a major financial centre) are also successful players in the international economy. China, the most densely populated country in the world, continues to emerge as an important market in its own right. In fact, most indicators suggest that the Chinese economy is now the world's third largest, behind the United States and Japan.

As in North America and Western Europe, technology promises to play an increasingly important role in this region. In Asia, however, the emergence of technology firms has been hampered by a poorly developed electronic infrastructure, slower adoption of computers and information technology, a higher percentage of lower-income consumers, and the aforementioned currency crisis. Thus, while the future looks promising, technology companies in this region are facing several obstacles as they work to keep pace with competitors based elsewhere.[7]

Figure 5.1 shows a map of the Association of Southeast Asian Nations (ASEAN) countries of Asia-Pacific. ASEAN (pronounced OZZIE-on) was founded in 1967 as an organization for economic, political, social, and cultural co-operation. In 1995, Vietnam became the group's first communist member. Today, the ASEAN group has a population of over 500 million and a GNP of approximately $800 billion.[8]

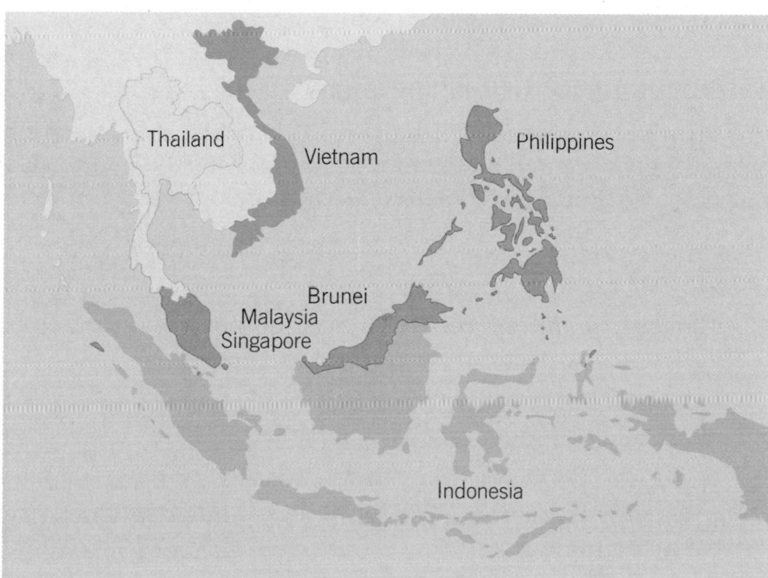

Figure 5.1 The nations of ASEAN.

Forms of Competitive Advantage

2 Explain how different forms of *competitive advantage, import-export balances, exchange rates,* and *foreign competition* determine the ways in which countries and businesses respond to the international environment.

Why are there such high levels of importing, exporting, and other forms of international business activity? Because no country can produce all the goods and services that its people need. Thus, countries tend to export products that they can produce better or less expensively than other countries, using the proceeds to import products that they cannot produce as effectively.

Of course, this principle does not fully explain why various nations export and import what they do. Such decisions hinge partly on the kind of advantages a particular country may enjoy regarding its abilities to create and/or sell various products and resources.[9] Traditionally, economists focussed on *absolute* and *comparative advantage* to explain international trade. But because this approach focusses narrowly on such factors as natural resources and labour costs, a perspective has emerged that focusses on the more complex idea of *national competitive advantage*.

Absolute Advantage

absolute advantage A nation's ability to produce something more cheaply or better than any other country.

An **absolute advantage** exists when a country can produce something more cheaply and/or of higher quality than any other country. Saudi oil, Brazilian coffee beans, and Canadian timber approximate absolute advantage, but examples of true absolute advantage are rare. In reality, "absolute" advantages are always relative. For example, most experts say that the vineyards of France produce the finest wines in the world. But the burgeoning wine business in California and Ontario attests to the fact that producers there can also produce very good values in wine—wines that are perhaps almost as good as French wines and that also are available in more varieties and at lower prices.

Comparative Advantage

comparative advantage A nation's ability to produce some products more cheaply or better than it can others.

A country has a **comparative advantage** in goods that it can produce more efficiently or better than other goods. For example, if businesses in a given country can make computers more efficiently than they can make automobiles, that nation's firms have a comparative advantage in computer manufacture. Canada has a comparative advantage in farming (because of fertile land and a temperate climate), while South Korea has a comparative advantage in electronics manufacturing (because of efficient operations and cheap labour). As a result, Canadian firms export grain to South Korea and import VCRs and stereos from South Korea.

National Competitive Advantage

national competitive advantage A country will be inclined to engage in international trade when factor conditions, demand conditions, related and supporting industries, and strategies/structures/rivalries are favourable.

In recent years, a theory of national competitive advantage has become a more widely accepted model of why nations engage in international trade.[10] Basically, **national competitive advantage** derives from four conditions:

1. *Factor conditions* are the factors of production that we identified in Chapter 1.
2. *Demand conditions* reflect a large domestic consumer base that promotes strong demand for innovative products.
3. *Related and supporting industries* include strong local or regional suppliers and/or industrial customers.
4. *Strategies, structures, and rivalries* refer to firms and industries that stress cost reduction, product quality, higher productivity, and innovative new products.

Figure 5.2 shows why these four attributes are referred to as a national diamond. The interaction of the four elements determines the environment in which a nation's firms compete. When all of these conditions exist, a nation will naturally be inclined to engage in international business. Japan, for instance, has strong domestic demand for automobiles. Its automobile producers have well-oiled supplier networks, and domestic firms have competed intensely with each other for decades. This set of circumstances explains why Japanese automobile companies such as Toyota, Honda, Nissan, and Mazda are generally successful in foreign markets.

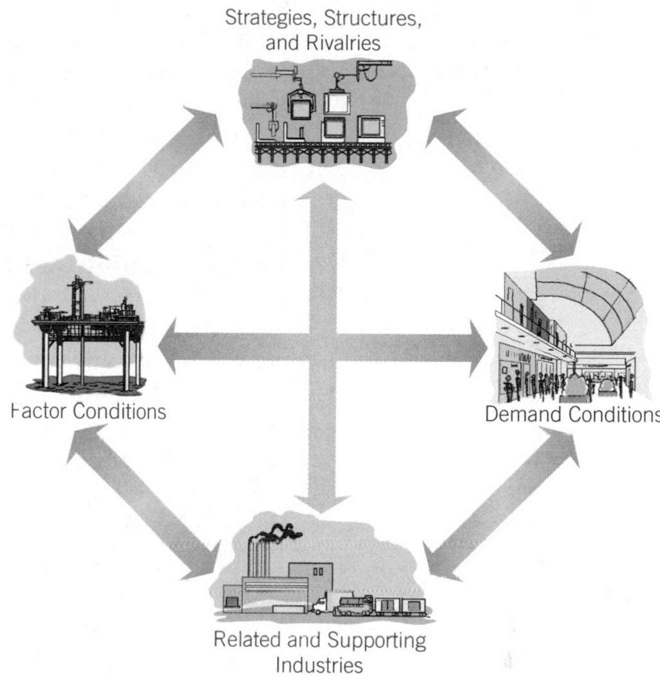

Figure 5.2 Attributes of national competitive advantage.

International competitiveness refers to the ability of a country to generate more wealth than its competitors in world markets. Each year, the World Economic Forum publishes a global competitiveness ranking. The ranking is based on both hard economic data and on a poll of business leaders in many countries. In 2006, the top three countries on the list were Switzerland, Finland, and Sweden. The United States ranked sixth and Canada sixteenth. Canada's high taxes, regulated industries, and overly conservative capital market institutions were listed as the reasons for Canada's lower rating.[11]

international competitiveness The ability of a country to generate more wealth than its competitors in world markets.

Import–Export Balances

Although international trade involves many advantages, trading with other nations can pose problems if a country's imports and exports do not strike an acceptable balance. In deciding whether an overall balance exists, economists use two measures: *balance of trade* and *balance of payments*.

Balance of Trade

A nation's **balance of trade** is the difference in value between its total exports and its total imports. A country that exports more than it imports

balance of trade The difference in value between a country's total exports and its total imports.

If local boosters have their way, the success of the *The Lord of the Rings*—whose fictional *Middle Earth* is really New Zealand's South Island—will turn the dramatic scenery of New Zealand into an advantage in competing for global business. The national film promotion board appeals to foreign producers by stressing the country's variety of unspoiled landscapes (and largely non-union workforce), and *Rings*-related tourism has already become a thriving business. On the web, Tourism New Zealand invites you to "Experience the Home of Middle Earth," and Air New Zealand bills itself as the "Airline to Middle Earth."

trade surplus Occurs when a country exports more than it imports.

trade deficit Occurs when a country imports more than it exports.

has a favourable balance of trade, or **trade surplus**. A country that imports more than it exports has an unfavourable balance of trade, or **trade deficit**. Canada has enjoyed a favourable balance of merchandise trade for many years (see Figure 5.3). The United States is by far the largest trading partner Canada has, and our overall trade balance is favourable only because we export so much more to the United States than we import from them. Canada's trade balance with almost all of its other trading partners is unfavourable (see Table 5.1). As you can see, we import more from the European Union and Japan than we export to those countries; we import far more than we export from all other countries as well.

A study by the World Trade Organization (WTO) found that Canada's economic dependence on the United States is growing, and that this trend leaves Canada vulnerable. The United States accounts for about 85 percent of Canada's merchandise exports and two-thirds of its imports. What's worse, only 50 companies operating in Canada account for nearly half of all merchandise exports, and these companies are often U.S.-owned. Although Canada is an exporting powerhouse, our exports are too focussed on the United States. Canada has too many of its eggs in one basket.[12]

Balance of Payments

balance of payments The difference between money flowing in to and out of a country as a result of trade and other transactions.

The **balance of payments** refers to the flow of money in to or out of a country. The money a nation pays for imports and receives for exports—that is, its balance of trade—comprises much of its balance of payments. Other financial exchanges are also factors. For example, money spent by tourists, money spent on foreign-aid programs, and money spent and received in the buying and selling of currency on international money markets all affect the balance of payments.

An unfavourable balance means that more money is flowing out than in. For Canada to have a favourable balance of payments for a given year, the total of (a) our exports, (b) foreign tourist spending in this country, (c) foreign investments here, and (d) earnings from overseas investments must be

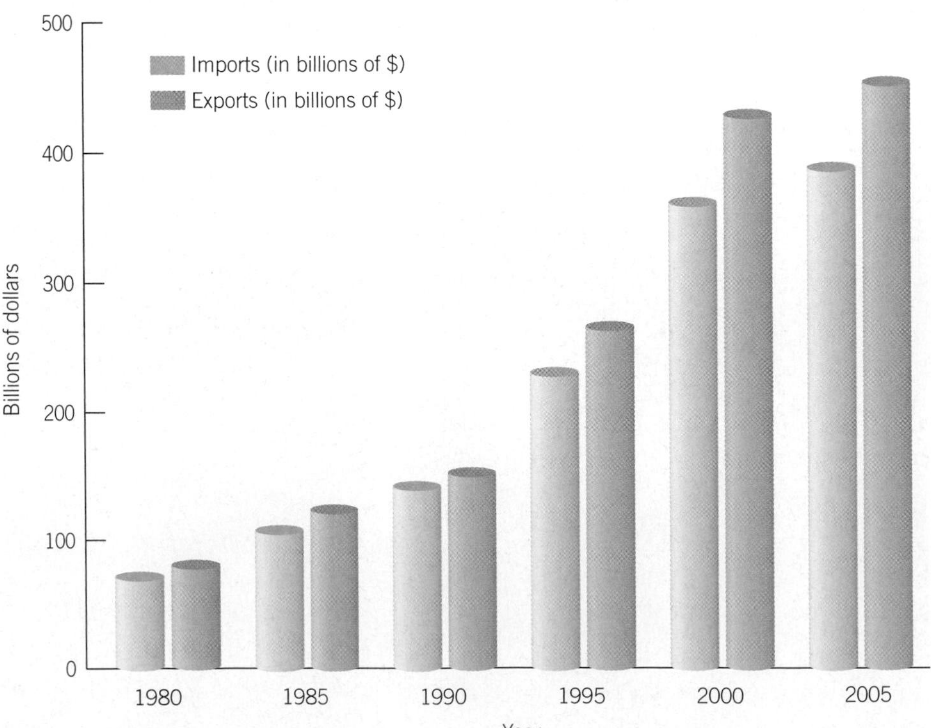

Figure 5.3 Canadian imports and exports of merchandise.

Table 5.1 Canadian Exports to and Imports from Selected Countries, 2005

Country	Exports to (in billions of $)	Imports from (in billions of $)
United States	$369.2	$258.4
European Union	28.9	38.3
Japan	10.4	11.1
All others	44.9	78.9

greater than the total of (a) our imports, (b) Canadian tourist spending overseas, (c) our foreign aid grants, (d) our military spending abroad, (e) the investments made by Canadian firms abroad, and (f) the earnings of foreigners from their investments in Canada. (See Figure 5.4.) Canada has had an unfavourable balance of payments for many years. In 2005, for example, $112 billion more money flowed out of Canada than flowed in.[13]

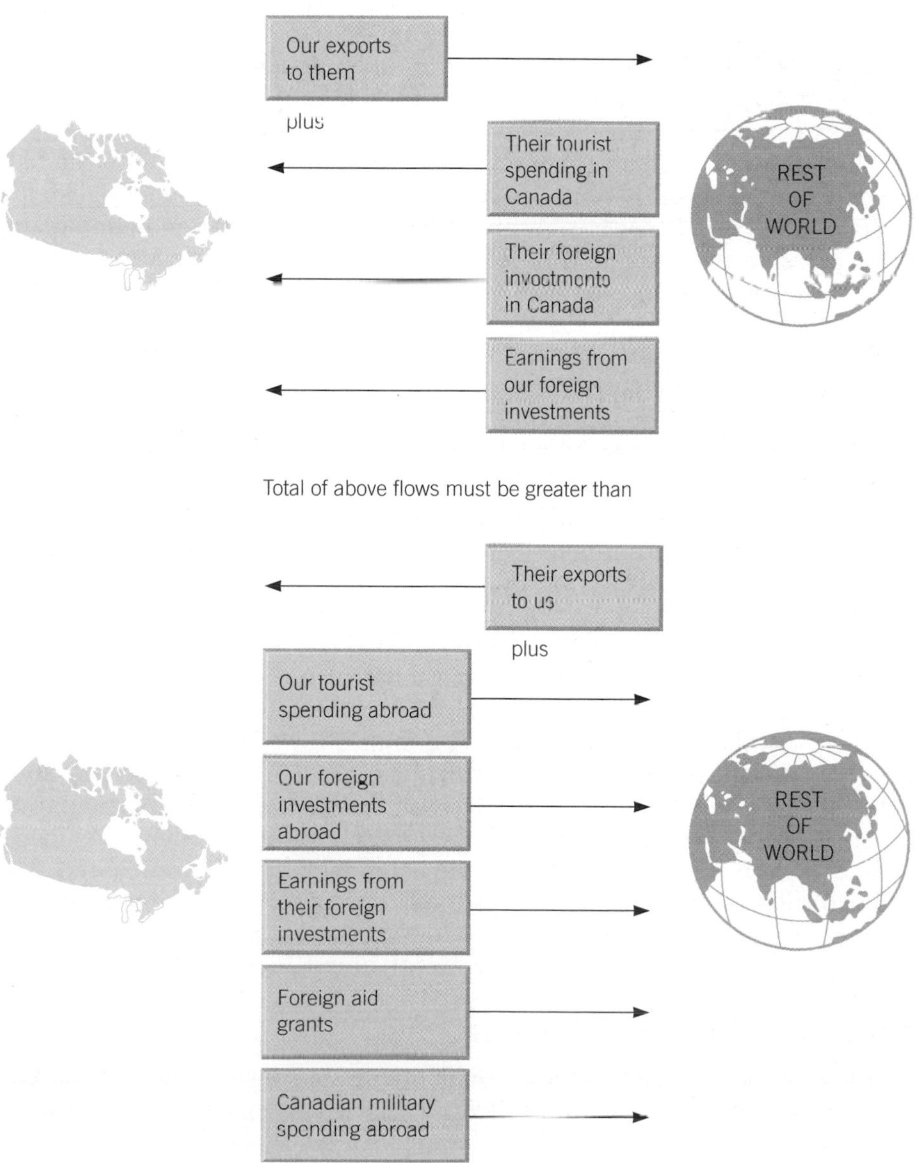

Figure 5.4 Requirements for Canada to have a favourable balance of payments. (The arrows indicate the direction of the flow.)

Exchange Rates

exchange rate The ratio of one currency to another.

The balance of imports and exports between two countries is affected by the rate of exchange between their currencies. An **exchange rate** is the rate at which the currency of one nation can be exchanged for that of another.[14] In August 2003, the exchange rate between Canadian dollars and British pounds was 1 to 2.26. This means that it costs $2.26 in Canadian dollars to "buy" one British pound; alternatively, it costs only 0.44 of a British pound to "buy" one Canadian dollar. This exchange rate means that 0.44 of a British pound and one Canadian dollar should have exactly the same purchasing power.

At the end of the Second World War, the major nations of the world agreed to establish fixed exchange rates. Under *fixed exchange rates*, the value of any country's currency relative to that of another country remains constant. Today, however, *floating exchange rates* are the norm, and the value of one country's currency relative to that of another country varies with market conditions. For example, when many English citizens want to spend pounds to buy Canadian dollars (or goods), the value of the dollar relative to the pound increases, or becomes "stronger"; *demand* for the Canadian dollar is high. In other words, a currency is said to be "strong" when demand for it is high. It is also "strong" when there is high demand for the goods manufactured at the expense of that currency. Thus, the value of the dollar rises with the demand for Canadian goods. In reality, exchange rates typically fluctuate by very small amounts on a daily basis. More significant variations usually occur over greater spans of time.

Fluctuation in exchange rates can have an important impact on the balance of trade. Suppose, for example, that you wanted to buy some English tea for 10 British pounds per box. At an exchange rate of 2.26 Canadian dollars to the British pound, a box will cost you $22.60 (10 pounds × 2.26 = 22.60). But what if the pound is weaker? At an exchange rate of, say, 1.5 dollars to the pound, the same box of tea would cost you only $15.00 (10 pounds × 1.5 = $15.00).

Changes in the exchange rate, of course, would affect more than just the price of tea. If the Canadian dollar becomes stronger in relation to the British pound, the prices of all Canadian-made products would rise in England and the prices of all English-made products would fall in Canada. As a result, the English would buy fewer Canadian-made products, and Canadians would be prompted to spend more on English-made products. The result could conceivably be a Canadian trade deficit with England. The recent increase in the value of the Canadian dollar has Canadian exporters very concerned (see the Opening Case for Chapter 18 on p. 589).

euro A common currency shared among most of the members of the European Union (excluding Denmark, Sweden, and the United Kingdom).

One of the most significant developments in foreign exchange has been the introduction of the **euro**—a common currency among most of the members of the European Union (Denmark, Sweden, and the United Kingdom do not participate). The euro was officially introduced in 2002 and will, for a while, circulate along with currencies of the participating nations. But those currencies will be phased out, and they are to be replaced by the euro as the only accepted currency. The EU anticipates that the euro will become as important as the dollar and the yen in international commerce. Though of course subject to fluctuation, the euro has risen in value against the U.S. dollar and was worth about U.S.$1.20 in 2006.

Exchange Rates and Competition

Companies that conduct international operations must watch exchange-rate fluctuations closely because these changes affect overseas demand for their products and can be a major factor in international competition. In general, when the value of a country's domestic currency rises—becomes "stronger"—companies based there find it harder to export products to foreign markets and easier for foreign companies to enter local markets. It also makes it more cost-efficient for domestic companies to move production operations to lower-cost sites in foreign countries. When the value of a country's currency declines—becomes "weaker"—just the opposite patterns occur. Thus, as the value of a country's currency falls, its balance of trade should improve because domestic companies should experience a boost in exports. There should also be a corresponding decrease in the incentives for foreign companies to ship products into the domestic market.

A good case in point is the recent fluctuation of the Canadian dollar relative to the U.S. dollar. In 1990, the Canadian dollar was worth about U.S.91 cents; this was high enough to motivate Canadian consumers to shop for bargains in the United States. But during the 1990s, the Canadian dollar weakened dramatically, and by 2002 had dropped to only U.S.63 cents. At that price, it was cheaper for U.S. consumers to drive across the border to shop in Canada. Table 5.2 illustrates the effects of this trend. For example, in 2002 the same hamburger that cost U.S.$2.39 in Niagara Falls, New York, sold for only U.S.$2.18 just across the border in Ontario. Likewise, a café latte in Seattle cost U.S.$2.70 but in Vancouver only U.S.$2.29. As one Vancouver store owner put it, "There has been an exact switch. Five years ago (in 1997), we would go down to Seattle to get good deals. Now (in 2002) the Americans come here for shopping."[15]

But the situation is changing again. In 2004, the value of the Canadian dollar started increasing, and by mid-2006 it was worth U.S.90 cents. If this trend continues, Canadians will once again be driving to the United States to get bargains just like they used to in the early 1990s.

INTERNATIONAL BUSINESS MANAGEMENT

3 Discuss the factors involved in deciding to do business internationally and in selecting the appropriate *levels of international involvement* and *international organizational structure.*

Wherever a firm is located, its success depends largely on how well it is managed. International business is so challenging because the basic functions of management—planning, organizing, directing, and controlling—are much more difficult to carry out when a business operates in several markets scattered around the globe. (We discuss these functions of management in detail in Chapter 6.)

Managing, of course, means making decisions. In this section, we examine the three most basic decisions that a company's management must make when faced with the prospect of globalization. The first decision is whether to "go international" at all. Once that decision has been made, managers must decide on the company's level of international involvement and on the organizational structure that will best meet its global needs.

Table 5.2 Canadian Versus U.S. Prices

	Niagara Falls NY	Niagara Falls ON
Saturday stay at Days Inn, with Jacuzzi	$260.00	$165.00
Whopper with cheese at Burger King	$2.39	$2.18
	Seattle	**Vancouver**
Lauryn Hill CD	$17.99	$12.60
Nintendo 64 game system	$130.00	$119.00
Grande latte at Starbucks	$2.70	$2.29
Levi's 501 jeans at Original Levi's Store	$50.00	$45.00

"Going International"

The world economy is becoming globalized, and more and more firms are conducting international operations. As Figure 5.5 shows, several factors enter into the decision to go international. One overriding factor is the business climate of other nations. Even experienced firms have encountered cultural, legal, and economic roadblocks. (These problems are discussed in more detail later in this chapter.) In considering international expansion, a company should also consider at least two other questions: Is there a demand for its products abroad? If so, must those products be adapted for international consumption?

Gauging International Demand

In considering international expansion, a company should also consider at least two other questions:

1. Is there a demand for my products abroad?
2. If so, must I adapt those products for international consumption?

Products that are successful in one country may be useless in another. Snowmobiles are popular for transportation and recreation in Canada, and they have actually revolutionized reindeer herding in Lapland, but there's no demand for them in Central America. Although this is an extreme example, the point is basic: Foreign demand for a company's product may be greater than, the same as, or weaker than domestic demand. Even when there is demand, advertising may still need to be adjusted. For instance, in Canada bicycles and small motorcycles are mainly used for recreation, but in many parts of Asia they are seen as transportation. Market research and/or the prior market entry of competitors may indicate whether there's an international demand for a firm's products.

Some products—like U.S. movies and video games—are popular all over the world. U.S. movies like *Harry Potter* and *Spider-Man* earn signifi-

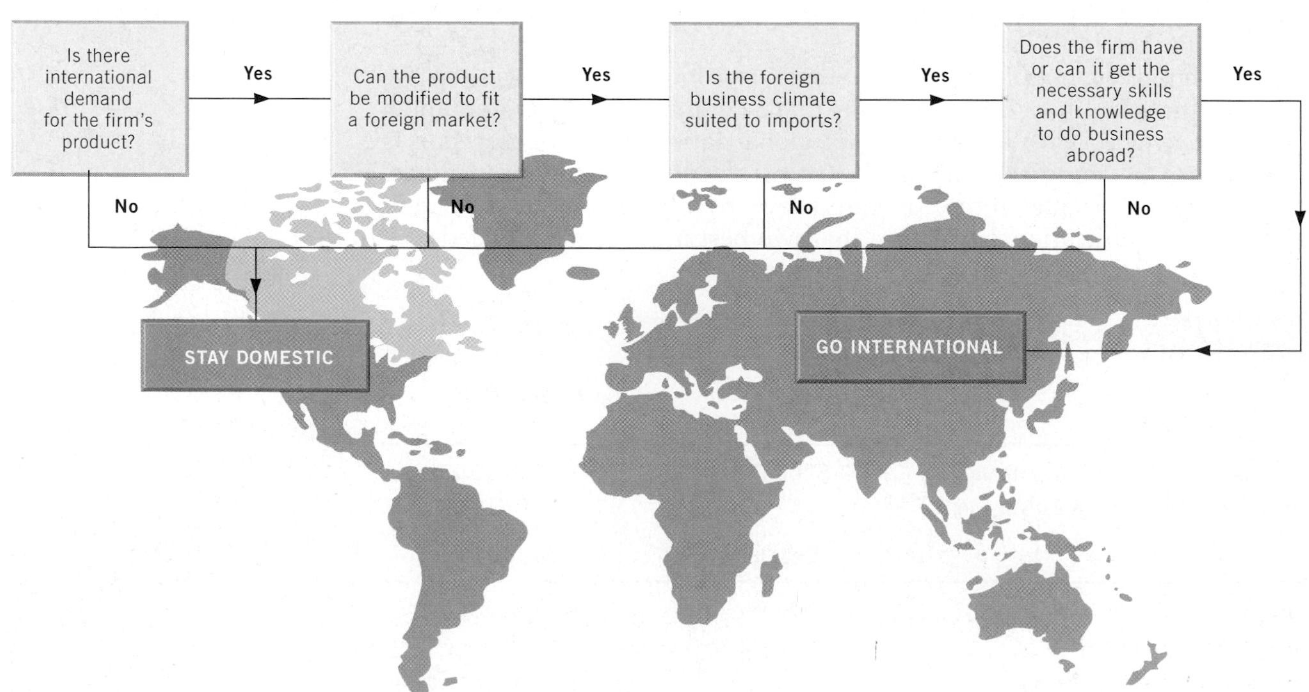

Figure 5.5 The decision to go international.

cant revenues in the United States, but generate even more revenues overseas. Super Mario Brothers is advertised on billboards in Bangkok, Thailand, and Bart Simpson piñatas are sold at Mexico City bazaars.

Adapting to Customer Needs

If there is international demand for its product, a firm must consider whether and how to adapt that product to meet the special demands and expectations of foreign customers. Movies, for example, have to be dubbed into foreign languages. Likewise, McDonald's restaurants sell wine in France, beer in Germany, and meatless sandwiches in India to accommodate local tastes and preferences. Ford products must have their steering wheels mounted on the right if they are to be sold in England and Japan. When Toyota launches upscale cars at home, it retains the Toyota nameplate; but those same cars are sold under the Lexus nameplate in Canada because the firm has concluded that Canadian consumers there will not pay a premium price for a "Toyota."

Levels of Involvement in International Business

After a firm decides to go international, it must decide on the level of its international involvement. Several different levels of involvement are possible. At the most basic level, a firm may act as an *exporter* or *importer*, organize as an *international firm*, or operate as a *multinational firm*. Most of the world's largest industrial firms are multinationals.

Exporters and Importers

An **exporter** is a firm that makes products in one country and then distributes and sells them in other countries. An **importer** buys products in foreign markets and then imports them for resale in its home country. Exporters and importers tend to conduct most of their business in their home nations, but some companies export a large proportion of what they produce. Importing and exporting represent the lowest level of involvement in international operations, but they are excellent ways to learn the fine points of global business.

exporter A firm that makes products in one country and then distributes and sells them in others.

importer A firm that buys products in foreign markets and then imports them for resale in its home country.

Almost 40 percent of all goods and services produced in Canada are exported, and Canada ranks first among the G8 countries in the proportion of its production that is exported.[16] Canada's exports to the world rose from $275 billion in 1996 to $411 billion in 2004.[17]

Small firms also export products and services. Lingo Media Inc. is the largest supplier of English-language textbooks in China's primary school system.[18] The Entrepreneurship and New Ventures box describes another company that became an exporter of an unlikely product.

International Firms

As firms gain experience and success as exporters and importers, they may move to the next level of involvement. An **international firm** conducts a significant portion of its business abroad. International firms also maintain manufacturing facilities overseas. Wal-Mart, for instance, is an international firm. Most of the retailer's stores are still in the United States, but the company is rapidly expanding into Canada and other markets.

international firm A company that conducts a significant portion of its business abroad and maintains manufacturing facilities overseas.

Although an international firm may be large and influential in the global economy, it remains basically a domestic firm with international operations: Its central concern is its own domestic market. Despite its obvious presence (and impact) in Canada, Wal-Mart still earns 90 percent of its revenues from U.S. sales.

ENTREPRENEURSHIP AND NEW VENTURES

Rolling in the Worldwide Dough

Is any business more confined to a local market than a bakery? Breads and pastries get stale quickly, and even the largest operations, such as those that make buns for McDonald's, only move products over short distances. But a baker in Paris has refused to accept geographic limitations and is now selling his famous bread in global markets.

When Lionel Poilane took over the family business about 30 years ago, he was determined to return breadmaking to its roots. As a result of studying the craft of breadmaking, Polaine built clay ovens based on sixteenth-century plans and technology. Then he trained his breadmakers in ancient techniques and soon began selling old-style dark bread known for a thick, chewy, fire-tinged flavour. It quickly became a favourite in Parisian bistros, and demand soared.

To help meet demand, Poilane built two more bakeries in Paris, and today he sells 15 000 loaves of bread a day—about 2.5 percent of all the bread sold in Paris. Polaine has opened a bakery in London, but his efforts to expand to Japan were stymied because local ordinances prohibited wood-burning ovens, and Polaine refused to compromise. During this negotiation process, however, he realized that he didn't really *want* to build new bakeries all over the world. "I'm not eager to have a business card that says 'Paris, London, New York' on it," he explains.

Instead, he turned to modern technology to expand his old-fashioned business. The key was the big FedEx hub at Roissy-Charles-de-Gaulle airport near Polaine's largest Paris bakery. After launching a website with minimal marketing support, Polaine started taking international orders. New orders are packaged as the bread cools and then picked up by FedEx. At about 4 pounds, the basic loaf travels well, and a quick warm-up in the customer's oven gives it the same taste it had when it came out of Polaine's oven. Today, a loaf of bread baked in Paris in the morning can easily be reheated for tomorrow night's dinner in more than 20 countries.

Multinational Firms

multinational firm Controls assets, factories, mines, sales offices, and affiliates in two or more foreign countries.

Most **multinational firms** do not ordinarily think of themselves as having domestic and international divisions. Instead, planning and decision making are geared to international markets.[19] The locations of headquarters are almost irrelevant. Royal Dutch/Shell, Nestlé, IBM, and Ford are well-known multinationals.

The economic importance of multinational firms should not be underestimated. Consider, for example, the economic impact of the 500 largest multinational corporations. In 2003, these 500 firms generated $15 trillion in revenues and $382 billion in owner profits. They employed over 51 million people, bought supplies, materials, parts, equipment, and materials from thousands of other firms, and paid billions of dollars in taxes. Moreover, their activities and products have affected the lives of hundreds of millions of consumers, competitors, and investors (sometimes in a not very positive way).[20]

On various occasions, organized protests have been mounted against the activities of multinational corporations. For example, when the Ecuadorean government renewed its commitment to extract oil from the Amazon River basin in 2004, a protest movement began among people in a region called Sarayacu. They battled with both the Ecuadorean government and the Argentine oil company, which was given a 2000 square kilometre concession to explore for oil on Sarayacu land. The protest included lodging a legal complaint against the government, demonstrations, letter writing, sabotage, theft of oil company equipment, and detention of oil company workers. Attempts to resolve problems like these include the development of the Equator Principles, which are a set of guidelines designed to deal with the impact of corporate activity on indigenous people.[21]

International Organizational Structures

Different levels of involvement in international business require different kinds of organizational structure. For example, a structure that would help coordinate an exporter's activities would be inadequate for the activities of a multinational firm. In this section, we briefly consider the spectrum of international organizational strategies, including *independent agents, licensing arrangements, branch offices, strategic alliances,* and *direct investment*.

Independent Agents

An **independent agent** is a foreign individual or organization that agrees to represent an exporter's interests in foreign markets. Independent agents often act as sales representatives: They sell the exporter's products, collect payment, and ensure that customers are satisfied. Independent agents often represent several firms at once and usually do not specialize in a particular product or market. Levi Strauss uses agents to market clothing products in many small countries in Africa, Asia, and South America.

independent agent A foreign individual, or organization, who agrees to represent an exporter's interests in foreign markets.

Licensing Arrangements

Canadian companies seeking more substantial involvement in international business may opt for **licensing arrangements**. Firms give individuals or companies in a foreign country the exclusive right to manufacture or market their products in that market. In return, the exporter typically receives a fee plus ongoing payments called royalties.[22] Royalties are usually calculated as a percentage of the licence holder's sales. For example, Can-Eng Manufacturing, Canada's largest supplier of industrial furnaces, exports its furnaces under licensing arrangements with businesses in Japan, Brazil, Germany, Korea, Taiwan, and Mexico.

licensing arrangement An arrangement by an owner of a process or product to allow another business to produce, distribute, or market it for a fee or royalty.

Franchising is a special form of licensing that is also growing in popularity.[23] McDonald's and Pizza Hut franchise around the world. Similarly, Accor SA, a French hotel chain, franchises its Ibis, Sofitel, and Novotel hotels. Allied Domecq PLC, a British firm, owns and franchises Baskin-Robbins and Dunkin' Donuts stores in dozens of countries.

Branch Offices

Instead of developing relationships with foreign companies or independent agents, a firm may simply send some of its own managers to overseas **branch offices**, where it has more direct control than it does over agents or licence holders. Branch offices also give a company a more visible public presence in foreign countries. Potential customers tend to feel more secure when a business has branch offices in their country.

branch office A location that an exporting firm establishes in a foreign country in order to sell its products more effectively.

Strategic Alliances

The concept of a **strategic alliance** was introduced in Chapter 2. In international business, it means that a company finds a partner in a foreign country where it would like to conduct business. Each party agrees to invest resources and capital in a new business or else to co-operate in some way for mutual benefit. This new business—the alliance—is then owned by the partners, who divide its profits. For example, Canadian publisher Lingo Media Inc. is involved in a strategic alliance with the state-owned People's Education Press, the market leader in providing textbooks to Chinese schools.[24]

strategic alliance An enterprise in which two or more persons or companies temporarily join forces to undertake a particular project.

The number of strategic alliances among major companies has increased significantly over the last decade and is likely to grow even more. In many countries, including Mexico, India, and China, laws make alliances virtually the only way to do international business within their borders.

Mexico, for example, requires all foreign firms investing there to have local partners. Similarly, Disney's new theme park near Hong Kong is a joint venture with local partners. Vancouver-based Westport Innovations, which makes natural gas engines, is now selling its products to China through a strategic alliance with Cummins Inc., a U.S.-based company that is selling buses powered by clean air technology to the city of Beijing.[25]

In addition to easing the way into new markets, strategic alliances give firms greater control over their foreign activities than independent agents and licensing arrangements. (At the same time, of course, all partners in an alliance retain some say in its decisions.) Perhaps most important, alliances allow firms to benefit from the knowledge and expertise of their foreign partners. Microsoft, for example, relies heavily on strategic alliances as it expands into new international markets. This approach has successfully enabled the firm to learn the intricacies of doing business in China and India, two very large emerging markets that are difficult to crack.

Foreign Direct Investment

foreign direct investment (FDI) Buying or establishing tangible assets in another country.

Foreign direct investment (FDI) means buying or establishing tangible assets in another country.[26] Dell Computer, for example, built a new assembly plant in Europe, and Volkswagen built a new factory in Brazil. As we've seen, many Canadian firms export goods and services to foreign countries, and they also set up manufacturing operations in other countries. But a debate has been going on for many years in Canada about how FDI in Canada affects Canadians. The *Foreign Investment Review Agency* (FIRA), which was established in 1973, was designed to ensure that FDI benefited Canadians. After FIRA was established, the proportion of various industries controlled by foreign firms declined from a high of 38 percent in the early 1970s to a low of 21 percent in 1985.[27]

Investment Canada Replaced FIRA in 1985; designed primarily to attract and facilitate foreign investment in Canada.

In 1985, FIRA's title was changed to **Investment Canada**, and its mandate was changed to focus on attracting foreign investment to Canada. Since the late 1980s, foreign ownership of Canadian industry has again been on the rise, and now stands at 30 percent.[28] Foreign ownership may actually be higher than it appears, since many firms that appear to be Canadian are actually multinational companies. For example, before it was bought by Paris-based Vivendi, Seagram had been run from New York City, and Nortel Networks runs all of its business divisions from Dallas, Texas. Canadian business leaders have sounded the warning that Canadian firms are vulnerable to takeovers by foreign companies.[29] This concern is a bit ironic, since business leaders have generally been the ones most in favour of free trade. Table 5.3 lists the top 10 foreign-owned companies in Canada.

BARRIERS TO INTERNATIONAL TRADE

4 Describe some of the ways in which *social, cultural, economic, legal,* and *political differences* act as barriers to international trade.

Whether a business is selling to just a few foreign markets or is a true multinational, a number of differences between countries will affect its international operations. Success in foreign markets will largely depend on the way the business responds to social, economic, legal, and political barriers to international trade.

Social and Cultural Differences

Any firm involved in international business needs to understand something about the society and culture of the countries in which it plans to operate. Unless a firm understands these cultural differences—either by itself or by

Table 5.3 The Top 10 Foreign-Controlled Companies in Canada, 2006

Company	Annual Revenues (in billions of $)
1. General Motors of Canada	$34.9
2. Imperial Oil Ltd.	27.7
3. DaimlerChrysler Canada	20.8
4. Shell Canada Ltd.	14.1
5. Ford Motor Co. of Canada Ltd.	13.8
6. Wal-Mart Canada Corp.	13.5
7. Honda Canada Inc.	13.0
8. Ultramar Ltd.	9.5
9. Costco Wholesale Canada	8.1
10. McKesson Canada Corp.	7.1

acquiring a partner that does—it will probably not be successful in its international business activities.

Some differences are relatively obvious. Language barriers can cause inappropriate naming of products. In addition, the physical stature of people in different countries can make a difference. For example, the Japanese and French are slimmer and shorter on average than Canadians, an important consideration for firms that intend to sell clothes in these markets.

Differences in the average age of the local population can also have ramifications for product development and marketing. Countries with growing populations tend to have a high percentage of young people. Thus, electronics and fashionable clothing would likely do well. Countries with stable or declining populations tend to have more old people. Generic pharmaceuticals might be more successful in such markets.

In addition to such obvious differences, a wide range of subtle value differences can have an important impact on international business. For example, many Europeans shop daily. To Canadians used to weekly trips to the supermarket, the European pattern may seem like a waste of time. But for Europeans, shopping is not just "buying food." It is also meeting friends, exchanging political views, gossiping, and socializing.

Even more subtle behavioural differences that can influence business activity exist. For example, crossing your legs in a business meeting in Saudi Arabia is inappropriate, because showing the sole of your foot is viewed as an insult to the other people in the room. In Portugal, it is considered rude to discuss business during dinner, and in Taiwan, tapping your fingers on the table is a sign of appreciation for a meal. Knowledge of local dos and don'ts is important in international business activity.

Tunisian-born French entrepreneur Tawfik Mathlouthi doesn't like U.S. policy in the Middle East, but he does like the American way of doing business. He created Mecca-Cola for Muslims who like Coke but want to protest U.S. foreign policy by boycotting American products. With a core market of Muslims in France, Mecca-Cola is now sold elsewhere in Europe, and Coke (which has taken no legal action regarding the look-alike label) admits that Mecca-Cola and similar products have hurt its international business, mostly in such countries as Egypt and Morocco.

Economic Differences

Although cultural differences are often subtle, economic differences can be fairly pronounced. In dealing with economies like those of France and Sweden, for example, firms must be aware of when—and to what extent—the government is involved in a given industry. The French government, for example, is heavily involved in all aspects of airplane design and manufacturing.

BUSINESS ACCOUNTABILITY

How to Wake Up a Zombie

There is a longstanding tradition in Japan whereby the government often props up failing businesses through low-cost or no-cost loans. The fear has been that if businesses fail people will lose their jobs and the highly integrated Japanese industrial system will suffer. These businesses, some of which have been bailed out literally dozens of times, are called "Zombie" firms. The major downside of this practice, though, is that it reduces accountability. Managers haven't always had to worry about profits or efficiency, because they knew the government would bail them out. "This kind of intervention can work in the short term. But from a long term point of view, it has terrible implications: Investors understand that the market is artificial, and accordingly they pull back," states analyst Jean-Marie Eveillard.

In recent years, more Japanese firms are accepting responsibility for their own survival. Cosmetics maker Shiseido held too much inventory and had overly high expenses, leading to a $550 million loss over two years. But rather than call for a government bailout, Shiseido executives focussed on making fundamental improvements. Better technology allowed them to control and forecast inventory more effectively. They cut costs throughout the corporation and curtailed their product line. After Shiseido returned to profitability, chief logistics officer Seiji Nishimori boasted, "We're showing other Japanese companies that it's possible to reverse a slide."

Canon, the world's leading maker of copiers and laser printers, has also taken a disciplined approach to performance improvement. CEO Fujio Mitarai replaced every manufacturing line at the firm's 29 Japanese factories with small, self-directed teams of a half dozen workers who do the work previously done by 30 labourers. The teams discovered more efficient inventory management techniques, and Canon was able to close 20 of its 34 parts warehouses. "Manufacturing is where most of the costs lie," Mitarai claims. Canon earnings improved by 53 percent, enabling Mitarai to conclude, "We're much more profitable today because of these changes."

The success of notable high performers such as multinational Toyota has caused Japanese firms to realize the benefit of global cost competitiveness. High-tech companies are abandoning manufacturing and switching attention to research and development to counteract an influx of inexpensive electronics from China, Taiwan, and Korea. For example, NEC has moved out of the unprofitable semiconductor chip-making business and has focussed on more lucrative cellphones and software. Sharp, too, has given up on low-margin PC monitors and refocussed its operations on innovative products such as liquid crystal displays for PDAs. Sony is working on revolutionary new computer chips while reducing its investment in consumer electronics.

All three companies say they now listen to their consumers more closely. "We were proud of our great technology, and [we] just pumped out products without thinking of our customers' needs," says NEC director Kaoru Tosaka. "Now, we're emphasizing efficiency, profits, and clients."

The zombies need to hear the lessons that these stellar firms have learned. Watch inventory. Cut costs where possible. Use information technology more effectively. Simplify product lines. Experiment with new ways of organizing. Shut down money-losing businesses. Choose areas where the firm can add value. Listen to customer feedback. If the zombies adopt these suggestions, the Japanese—and the rest of the world—would surely benefit.

Similarly, a foreign firm doing business in a command economy must understand the unfamiliar relationship of government to business, including a host of idiosyncratic practices. General Motors, which entered a $100 million joint venture to build pickup trucks in China, found itself faced with an economic system that favoured state-owned companies over foreign investors. So, while its Chinese suppliers passed on inflation-based price increases for steel and energy, GM could not in turn pass increases on to Chinese consumers. With subsidized state-owned automakers charging considerably less per truck, GM had no choice but to hold its own prices—and lose money on each sale.

Legal and Political Differences

Closely linked to the structure of the economic systems in different countries are the legal and political issues that confront businesses as they try to expand internationally. These issues include *tariffs and quotas, local-content laws,* and *business-practice laws*. An awareness of differences in these areas can be crucial to a business's success.

Quotas, Tariffs, and Subsidies

Even free-market economies often use some form of quota and/or tariff that affects the prices and quantities of foreign-made products in those nations. A **quota** restricts the total number of certain products that can be imported into a country. It indirectly raises the prices of those imports by reducing their supply. The ultimate form of quota is an **embargo**: a government order forbidding exportation and/or importation of a particular product—or even all products—of a particular country. For example, many countries control bacteria and disease by banning certain plants and agricultural products.

quota A restriction by one nation on the total number of products of a certain type that can be imported from another nation.

embargo A government order forbidding exportation and/or importation of a particular product.

A **tariff** is a tax charged on imported products. Tariffs raise the price of imports to consumers who must pay not only for the products but also for the tariff. A *revenue tariff* is imposed strictly to raise money for the government. But most tariffs in effect today are *protectionist tariffs* meant to discourage the importation of a particular product. In 2004, for example, the Canadian government placed a 34.6 percent tariff on barbecues made in China after complaints were received that Chinese companies were unfairly subsidizing the production of barbecues.[30]

tariff A tax levied on imported products.

Governments impose quotas and tariffs for a variety of reasons. For example, the U.S. government restricts the number of Japanese automobiles that can be imported into that country. Italy imposes high tariffs on imported electronic goods. Consequently, Sony Walkmans cost almost $150, and CD players are prohibitively expensive there. Canada also imposes tariffs on many imported goods.

In 2002, the U.S. Commerce Department imposed a 29 percent tariff on softwood lumber exported from Canada to the United States (84 percent of

The long-standing softwood lumber dispute between the United States and Canada has hurt Canadian companies in the forestry industry. The dispute was settled in 2006, but much unhappiness is evident, and critics have charged that the Conservative government caved in to American pressure.

Canadian lumber is exported to the United States). Ottawa immediately appealed the decision under the provisions of both the North American Free Trade Agreement (NAFTA) and the World Trade Organization (WTO). During 2002 and 2003, both the WTO and NAFTA ruled against the United States on various points in the appeal and said that duties on Canadian lumber must be cut drastically. In spite of these rulings, the United States continued to impose the duties. Since the duties were first imposed, the Canadian lumber industry has paid over $5 billion in duties to the United States.[31] A tentative resolution was reached in July 2006, when the United States agreed to pay back 78 percent of the duties imposed on Canadian lumber, on the condition that Canada agree that its share of the U.S. lumber market would be capped at 34 percent.[32] Several Canadian lumber companies said that they weren't happy with that, but an agreement was eventually reached that went into effect in October 2006.[33]

subsidy A government payment to help domestic business compete with foreign firms.

A **subsidy** is a government payment to help a domestic business compete with foreign firms. Many European governments subsidize farmers to help them compete with U.S. grain imports. The U.S. government has for many years paid large subsidies to U.S. cotton farmers. In 2005, U.S. farmers were paid a total of $23 billion by their government.[34]

When the government of a country pays subsidies to one of its domestic industries, it can have a negative effect on other producers in other countries. The European Union, for example, pays subsidies to encourage sugar cultivation in unlikely places like Sweden and Finland. This has created a surplus of sugar on the world market, reducing prices and contributing to poverty-level income for sugar producers in some developing countries in the tropics.[35] The WTO has ruled that these subsidies are unreasonable, but the EU is appealing. In 2005, the WTO ruled that the U.S. government's subsidies to its cotton growers broke trade rules, depressed world cotton prices, and hurt Brazilian cotton producers.[36] These subsidies also hurt small cotton farmers in Africa.[37] Canada's supply management system, which restricts imports and guarantees markets for producers of chickens, turkeys, eggs, and milk, could also come under fire since the WTO views the system as an unfair subsidy to producers.[38]

protectionism Protecting domestic business at the expense of free market competition.

Protectionism—the practice of protecting domestic business at the expense of free market competition—has both advocates and critics. Supporters argue that tariffs and quotas protect domestic firms and jobs. In particular, they protect new industries until they are truly able to compete internationally. Some claim that, since other nations have such measures, so must we. Still others justify protectionism in the name of national security. They argue that a nation must be able to produce goods needed for its survival in the event of war and that advanced technology should not be sold to potential enemies.

But opponents of protectionism are equally vocal. They note that protectionism reduces competition and drives up prices to consumers. They cite it as a cause of friction between nations. They maintain that, while jobs in some industries would be lost if protectionism ceased, jobs in other industries would expand if all countries abolished tariffs and quotas.

Protectionism sometimes takes on almost comic proportions. Neither European countries nor the United States grow bananas, but both European and U.S. firms buy and sell bananas in foreign markets. Problems arose when the EU put a quota on bananas imported from Latin America—a market dominated by two U.S. firms, Chiquita and Dole—to help firms based in current and former European colonies in the Caribbean. To retaliate, the United States imposed a 100 percent tariff on certain luxury products imported from Europe, including Louis Vuitton handbags, Scottish cashmere sweaters, and Parma ham.[39]

Local-Content Laws

A country can affect how a foreign firm does business there by enacting **local-content laws**, which require that products sold in a particular country be at least partly made in that country. These laws typically mean that firms seeking to do business in a country must either invest directly in that country or have a joint-venture partner from that country. In this way, some of the profits from doing business in a foreign country are shared with the people who live there.

local-content laws Laws requiring that products sold in a particular country be at least partly made in that country.

Many countries have local-content laws. In a fairly extreme case, Venezuela forbids the import of any product if a like product is made in Venezuela. In 2005, Venezuela's president said he would cancel all mining licences and stop issuing new ones to foreign companies. This move was designed to protect the many small, local miners operating in Venezuela. Oil and gas licences held by foreign companies had already been cancelled. These actions have made foreign companies much more reluctant to invest in Venezuela.[40]

Local-content laws may even exist within a country; when they do, they act just like trade barriers. In Canada, for example, a low bid on a bridge in British Columbia was rejected because the company that made the bid was from Alberta. The job was given to a B.C. company. A New Brunswick window manufacturer lost a contract in Nova Scotia despite having made the lowest bid; the job went to a Nova Scotia company. Recognizing that these interprovincial barriers are not helping Canada's international competitiveness, the federal government has committed itself to removing such barriers.

The Agreement on Internal Trade (AIT) requires all 10 Canadian provinces to remove barriers to agricultural trade. But when Quebec—which has a strong dairy lobby—prohibited margarine coloured to look like butter, it was in violation of the agreement.[41] Unilever Canada Ltd. has challenged the legality of the ban on coloured margarine in court.[42] In another case, Prince Edward Island ignored a dispute panel ruling that stated P.E.I.'s milk import restrictions violated the AIT.[43] A third case involves the question of who is allowed to audit the financial statements of public companies. At present, only Chartered Accountants (CAs) are allowed to do this in Quebec. This rule is being challenged by the Certified General Accountants (CGAs), who have auditing rights in most other provinces.[44] If provincial governments do not honour their obligations, the AIT will become meaningless.

Business-Practice Laws

Many businesses entering new markets encounter problems in complying with stringent regulations and bureaucratic obstacles. Such practices are affected by the **business-practice laws** that host countries use to govern business practices within their jurisdictions. As part of its entry strategy in Germany, Wal-Mart has had to buy existing retailers rather than open brand-new stores. Why? Because the German government is not currently issuing new licences to sell food products. Wal-Mart also had to stop refunding price differences on items sold for less by other stores because the practice is illegal in Germany. Finally, Wal-Mart must comply with business-hour restrictions: Stores can't open before 7 a.m., must close by 8 p.m. on weeknights and 4 p.m. on Saturday, and must remain closed on Sunday.

business-practice laws Laws or regulations governing business practices in given countries.

Sometimes, what is legal (and even accepted) business practice in one country is illegal in another. The most prominent example is paying bribes to government officials to get business. Transparency International (TI), an organization devoted to stamping out global corruption, says that bribery is most devastating and common in developing countries because government officials in those countries are poorly paid. TI publishes a "Corruption Perceptions Index" that ranks countries based on the amount of abuse by public officials for their own private gain. The 2005 index showed that the least corrupt countries are Iceland, Finland, New Zealand, and Denmark. The most corrupt countries are Turkmenistan, Bangladesh, and Chad.[45]

Calgary-based Niko Resources experienced first-hand some of the difficulties of doing business in a corrupt country. When it tried to develop two natural gas fields in Bangladesh, the company discovered that it was common for companies to give "gifts" to members of the media so that they would report favourably on company activities. After Niko refused to make any payments (and after two unfortunate accidents in Niko's gas fields), the media began portraying Niko as an irresponsible company. Then, feuding politicians seized the opportunity to use Niko as a scapegoat during a political campaign. Niko's reputation is Bangladesh has suffered greatly, and the government has demanded $12 million for environmental damage.[46]

cartel Any association of producers whose purpose is to control the supply and price of a given product.

Cartels and Dumping. A **cartel** is an association of producers whose purpose is to control the supply and price of a commodity. The most famous cartel is the Organization of Petroleum Exporting Countries (OPEC). It has given oil-producing countries considerable power in the last 25 years. In 1994, the major aluminum producing countries, including Canada, worked out a deal to curb world aluminum production in an attempt to raise prices.[47] The diamond and shipping cartels have also been successful in keeping the prices they charge artificially high.[48] In 2000, the world's coffee-producing countries formed an OPEC-style cartel to control the price of coffee. They immediately raised coffee prices by 37 percent, which increased the price of a cup of coffee by about 15 cents. Surprisingly, most coffee buyers were sympathetic to the cartel, since coffee prices had been at their lowest level in seven years and coffee farmers in developing countries were struggling.[49]

dumping Selling a product for less abroad than in the producing nation; illegal in Canada.

Many countries forbid **dumping**—selling a product abroad for less than the comparable price charged at home. Anti-dumping legislation typically views dumping as occurring if products are being sold at prices less than fair value, or if the result unfairly harms domestic industry. In 1992, Canada imposed anti-dumping duties on bicycles made in China, but in 2004 the duties were dropped because Chinese companies provided evidence that they could indeed make bicycles as cheaply as they said they could.[50]

Overcoming Barriers to Trade

5 Explain how *free trade agreements* assist world trade.

Despite the barriers to trade described so far, international trade is flourishing. This is because both organizations and free trade treaties exist to promote international trade. The most significant of these are the General Agreement on Tariffs and Trade (GATT), the World Trade Organization (WTO), the European Union (EU), and the North American Free Trade Agreement (NAFTA).

General Agreement on Tariffs and Trade

General Agreement on Tariffs and Trade (GATT) International trade agreement to encourage the multilateral reduction or elimination or trade barriers.

The **General Agreement on Tariffs and Trade (GATT)**, which was often humorously referred to as the General Agreement to Talk and Talk, was signed after the Second World War. Its purpose was to reduce or eliminate trade barriers, such as tariffs and quotas. It did so by encouraging nations to protect domestic industries within agreed-upon limits and to engage in multilateral negotiations. While 92 countries signed GATT, not all complied with its rules. The United States was one of the worst offenders. A revision of GATT went into effect in 1994, but many issues remained unresolved—for example, the opening of foreign markets to most financial services.

Fisherman Ratish Karthikeyan can sometimes double the revenue from a day's take by phoning around to compare prices at markets within reach of his boat. India is a thriving export market for cellphones. About half of India's 600 000 rural communities aren't even wired for fixed-line phone service. The number of mobile-phone users in India should jump from 3 million to 30 million in the next few years.

World Trade Organization

World Trade Organization (WTO) Organization through which member nations negotiate trading agreements and resolve disputes about trade policies and practices.

On January 1, 1995, the **World Trade Organization (WTO)** came into existence as the successor to GATT. The 140 member countries are required to open markets to international trade, and the WTO is empowered to pursue three goals:

1. Promote trade by encouraging members to adopt fair trade practices
2. Reduce trade barriers by promoting multilateral negotiations
3. Establish fair procedures for resolving disputes among members

The WTO is overseeing a one-third reduction in import duties on thousands of products that are traded between countries. Canada, the United States, and the European Union are founding members of the WTO.[51] Unlike GATT, the WTO's decisions are binding, and many people feared that it would make sweeping decisions and boss countries around. But the WTO is off to a slow start. It has not been very successful in toppling global barriers to trade in three critical areas—world financial services, telecommunications, and maritime markets—because political leaders from various countries are fearful of the consequences of freer trade.[52] But the WTO did rule in 1999 that Canada had to scrap the Auto Pact because it was essentially an export subsidy program, which is prohibited.[53] It also ruled in 2003 that the United States acted illegally when it placed import duties on steel from the European Union, but exempted Canadian steel from the import duties (because of NAFTA).[54]

One of the most controversial issues confronting the WTO is agricultural subsidies. Governments in industrialized countries often pay subsidies to their own farmers to grow certain crops, but these subsidies distort international markets for agricultural commodities and hurt growers in poor countries, particularly in Africa.

On several occasions when the WTO has held talks on trade liberalization, protestors have disrupted the meetings. WTO meetings in Seattle, Prague, and Montreal were disrupted by protestors who resent the power of the WTO and who are concerned about what world trade is doing to both the environment and the developing countries that are not sharing in its benefits.[55] Protestors included labour unions (who regard Third World imports as unfair), environmentalists (who are concerned about business activity harming the environment), social activists (who are concerned about poor working conditions in developing countries), and farmers (who are concerned about the effect of free trade on grain prices).

The European Union (EU)

European Union (EU) Agreement among major Western European nations to eliminate or make uniform most trade barriers affecting group members.

Originally called the Common Market, the **European Union (EU)** initially included only the principal Western European nations like Italy, Germany, France, and the United Kingdom. But by 2006, 25 countries belonged to the EU, including eight former communist countries and two Mediterranean islands, which joined in 2004. Several other countries are also in the process of applying for membership, including Romania, Bulgaria, Turkey, Macedonia, and Croatia. The EU has eliminated most quotas and set uniform tariff levels on products imported and exported within their group. The EU is the largest free marketplace in the world, and produces nearly one-quarter of global wealth.[56]

North American Free Trade Agreement

North American Free Trade Agreement (NAFTA) Agreement to gradually eliminate tariffs and other trade barriers among the United States, Canada, and Mexico.

The **North American Free Trade Agreement (NAFTA)** came into effect in 1994. It removes tariffs and other trade barriers among Canada, the United States, and Mexico. An earlier agreement, the Canada–U.S. Free Trade Agreement (FTA), took effect in 1989. Its goal was to achieve freer trade between Canada and the United States. Surveys conducted prior to the introduction of the FTA showed that the majority of Canadians were opposed to free trade. They feared that (1) jobs would be lost to other countries, (2) Canada would be flooded with products manufactured in lower-wage countries such as Mexico, (3) Canada would lose the right to control its own environmental standards, (4) the United States might take our natural resources, and (5) Canadian cultural sovereignty would be lost.

Supporters of free trade, by contrast, argued that (1) access to U.S. markets would be guaranteed by free trade, and this would protect Canadian employment, (2) Canadian exports would increase because of free trade, (3) the environment was not covered in free trade agreements, (4) there was nothing in the free trade agreement that threatened Canada's control over its energy resources, and (5) the free trade agreement was about trade and tariffs, not cultural sovereignty.

What has actually happened since NAFTA took effect? In 2004, a group of economists at the Canadian Economics Association concluded that free trade has not been as good for Canada as predicted by its supporters, nor as bad for Canada as predicted by its detractors.[57] Several specific effects are noticeable:

- NAFTA has created a much more active North American market.
- Direct foreign investment has increased in Canada.
- U.S. imports from (and exports to) Mexico have increased.
- Canada has become an exporting powerhouse.
- Trade between the United States and Canada has risen sharply, and Canada enjoys a large trade surplus with the United States.
- Before free trade, Canadian exports accounted for about one-quarter of GDP, but now exports account for 40 percent. In the manufacturing sector, 60 percent of output is now exported. Canada is the most trade-intensive country in the G8 group. One job in three is now devoted to producing goods and services for export.[58]

Other Free Trade Agreements in the Americas

NAFTA is the most publicized trade agreement in the Americas, but there has been a flurry of activity among other countries as well. On January 1, 1995, a free trade agreement known as Mercosur went into effect between Argentina, Brazil, Uruguay, and Paraguay. By 2005, tariffs were eliminated on 80 percent of the goods traded between those four countries. Brazil has proposed enlarging Mercosur into a South American Free Trade Area (SAFTA), which might eventually negotiate with NAFTA to form an Americas Free Trade Area (AFTA).

There are several other free trade areas in existence in the Americas as well: the Andean Pact (Bolivia, Ecuador, Colombia, Peru, and Venezuela), the Central American Common Market (Costa Rica, El Salvador, Guatemala, Honduras, and Nicaragua), the G-3 group (Colombia, Mexico, and Venezuela), and the Caribbean Common Market (many of the island nations of the Caribbean).[59] The population of the various free trade areas of the Americas totals nearly 900 million. The economies of many of these nations are growing rapidly, and they will become increasingly important to Canada during the next decade.

Free Trade Agreements Elsewhere

Free trade agreements are not restricted to the Americas. A high level of activity is evident around the world as groups of nations band together to form regional trade associations for their own benefit. Some examples:

- the ASEAN Free Trade Area (Brunei, Indonesia, Malaysia, the Philippines, Singapore, Thailand, and Vietnam)
- the Asia-Pacific Economic Cooperation (many nations of the Pacific Rim, as well as the United States, Canada, and Mexico)
- the Economic Community of Central African States (many nations in equatorial Africa)
- the Gulf Cooperation Council (Bahrain, Kuwait, Oman, Qatar, Saudi Arabia, and United Arab Emirates).

Summary of Learning Objectives

1. **Describe the rise of international business and identify the *major world marketplaces*.** More and more business firms are engaged in international business. The term *globalization* refers to the process by which the world economy is fast becoming a single interdependent entity. The global economy is characterized by a rapid growth in the exchange of information and trade in services. The three major marketplaces for international business are *North America* (the United States, Canada, and Mexico), *Western Europe* (which is dominated by Germany, the United Kingdom, France, and Italy), and *Asia-Pacific* (where the dominant country, Japan, is surrounded by such rapidly advancing nations as South Korea, Taiwan, Hong Kong, and China).
2. **Explain how different forms of *competitive advantage*, *import-export balances*, *exchange rates*, and *foreign competition* determine the ways in which countries and businesses respond to the international environment.** With an absolute advantage, a country engages in international trade because it can produce a good or service more efficiently than any other nation. But more often countries trade because they enjoy comparative advantages, that is, they can produce some items more efficiently than they can produce other items. A country that exports more than it imports has a favourable balance of trade, while a country that imports more than it exports has an unfavourable balance of trade. If the exchange rate decreases (the value of the Canadian dollar falls),

our exports become less expensive for other countries so they will buy more of what we produce. The reverse happens if the value of the Canadian dollar increases. Changes in the exchange rate therefore have a strong impact on our international competitiveness.

3. **Discuss the factors involved in deciding to do business internationally and in selecting the appropriate *levels of international involvement* and *international organizational structure.*** In deciding whether to do business internationally, a firm must determine whether a market for its product exists abroad, and if so, whether the firm has the skills and knowledge to manage such a business. It must also assess the business climates of other nations to ensure that they are conducive to international operations. A firm must also decide on its level of international involvement. It can choose to be an *exporter* or *importer*, to organize as an *international firm*, or to operate as a *multinational firm*. The choice will influence the organizational structure of its international operations, specifically, its use of *independent agents*, *licensing arrangements*, *branch offices*, *strategic alliances*, and *direct investment*.

4. **Describe some of the ways in which *social, cultural, economic, legal,* and *political differences* act as barriers to international trade.** *Social* and *cultural differences* that can serve as barriers to trade include language, social values, and traditional buying patterns. Differences in economic systems may force businesses to establish close relationships with foreign governments before they are permitted to do business abroad. *Quotas, tariffs, subsidies,* and *local-content laws* offer protection to local industries. Differences in *business-practice laws* can make standard business practices in one nation illegal in another.

5. **Explain how *free trade agreements* assist world trade.** Several *trade agreements* have attempted to eliminate restrictions on free trade internationally. The *General Agreement on Tariffs and Trade* (GATT) was instituted to eliminate tariffs and other trade barriers among participating nations. The *European Union* (EU) has eliminated virtually all trade barriers among the 25 member nations. The *North American Free Trade Agreement* (NAFTA) eliminates many of the barriers to free trade that exist among the United States, Canada, and Mexico.

KEY TERMS

absolute advantage, 144
balance of payments, 146
balance of trade, 145
branch office, 153
business-practice laws, 159
cartel, 160
comparative advantage, 144
dumping, 160
embargo, 157
euro, 148
European Union (EU), 162
exchange rate, 148
exports, 140
exporter, 151
foreign direct investment (FDI), 154
General Agreement on Tariffs and Trade (GATT), 160
globalization, 140
imports, 140
importer, 151
independent agent, 153
international competitiveness, 145
international firm, 151
Investment Canada, 154
licensing arrangement, 153
local-content laws, 159
multinational firm, 152
national competitive advantage, 144
North American Free Trade Agreement (NAFTA), 162
per capita income, 141
protectionism, 158
quota, 157
strategic alliance, 153
subsidy, 158
tariff, 157
trade deficit, 146
trade surplus, 146
World Trade Organization (WTO), 161

QUESTIONS FOR ANALYSIS

1. How does the economic system of a country affect foreign firms interested in doing business there?
2. Make a list of all the major items in your bedroom. Identify the country in which each item was made. Give possible reasons why that nation might have a comparative advantage in producing this good.
3. Assume that you are the manager of a small firm seeking to enter the international arena. What information would you need about the market that you're thinking of entering?
4. Do you think that a firm that is operating internationally is better advised to adopt a single standard

of ethical conduct or to adapt to local conditions? Under what kinds of conditions might each approach be preferable?

5. What aspects of the culture in your province or region would be of interest to a foreign firm thinking about locating there?
6. Do you support protectionist tariffs for Canada? If so, in what instances and for what reasons? If not, why not?
7. Is NAFTA good for Canada? Give supporting reasons for your answer.
8. Explain how it is possible for a country to have a positive balance of trade and a negative balance of payments.

APPLICATION EXERCISES

1. Interview the manager of a local firm that does at least some business internationally. Identify reasons why the company decided to "go international," as well as the level of the firm's international involvement and the organizational structure it uses for its international operations.
2. Select a product familiar to you. Using library references, learn something about the culture of India and identify the problems that might arise in trying to market this product to India's citizens.

BUILDING YOUR BUSINESS SKILLS

Putting Yourself in Your Place

Goal

To encourage students to apply global business strategies to a small-business situation.

Background

Some people might say that Yolanda Lang is a bit too confident. Others might say that she needs confidence—and more—to succeed in the business she's chosen. But one thing is certain: Lang is determined to grow INDE, her handbag design company, into a global enterprise. At only 28 years of age, she has time on her side—if she makes the right business moves now.

These days, Lang spends most of her time in Milan, Italy. Backed by $50 000 of her parents' personal savings, she is trying to compete with Gucci, Fendi, and other high-end handbag makers. Her target market is women willing to spend $200 on a purse. Ironically, Lang was forced to set up shop in Italy because of the snobbishness of these customers, who buy high-end bags only if they're European-made. "Strangely enough," she muses, "I need to be in Europe to sell in North America."

To succeed, she must first find ways to keep production costs down—a tough task for a woman in a male-dominated business culture. Her fluent Italian is an advantage, but she's often forced to turn down inappropriate dinner invitations. She also has to figure out how to get her 22-bag collection into stores worldwide. Retailers are showing her bags in Italy and Japan, but she's had little luck in the United States. "I intend to be a global company," says Lang. The question is how to succeed first as a small business.

Assignment

Step 1

Join together with three or four other students to discuss the steps that Lang has taken so far to break into the U.S. retail market. These steps include

- buying a mailing list of 5000 shoppers from high-end department store Neiman Marcus and selling directly to these customers
- linking with a manufacturer's representative to sell her line in major U.S. cities while she herself concentrates on Europe

Step 2

Based on what you learned in this chapter, suggest other strategies that might help Lang grow her business. Working with group members, consider whether the following options would help or hurt Lang's business. Explain why a strategy is likely to work or likely to fail.

- Lang could relocate to the United States and sell abroad through an independent agent.
- Lang could relocate to the United States and set up a branch office in Italy.
- Lang could find a partner in Italy and form a strategic alliance that would allow her to build her business on both continents.

Step 3

Working alone, create a written marketing plan for INDE. What steps would you recommend that Lang take to reach her goal of becoming a global company? Compare your written response with those of other group members.

Follow-Up Questions

1. What are the most promising steps that Lang can take to grow her business? What are the least promising?
2. Lang thinks that her trouble breaking into the U.S. retail market stems from the fact that her company is unknown. How would this circumstance affect the strategies suggested in Steps 1 and 2?
3. When Lang deals with Italian manufacturers, she is a young, attractive woman in a man's world. Often, she must convince men that her purpose is business and nothing else. How should Lang handle personal invitations that get in the way of business? How can she say no while still maintaining business relationships? Why is it often difficult for women to do business in male-dominated cultures?
4. The American consulate has given Lang little business help because her products are made in Italy. Do you think the consulate's treatment of an American business person is fair or unfair? Explain your answer.
5. Do you think Lang's relocation to Italy will pay off? Why or why not?
6. With Lang's goals of creating a global company, can INDE continue to be a one-person operation?

EXERCISING YOUR ETHICS

Paying Heed to Foreign Practices

The Purpose of the Assignment

Managers conducting business in other countries must often contend with differences in legal systems, customs, values, attitudes, and business practices. This exercise will help you better understand how such differences can affect the success of managers and companies trying to conduct business in foreign markets.

The Situation

Assume that you're an up-and-coming manager in a regional Canadian distribution company. Firms in your industry are just beginning to enter foreign markets, and you've been assigned to head up your company's new operations in a Latin American country. Because two of your competitors are also trying to enter this same market, your boss wants you to move as quickly as possible. You also sense that your success in this assignment will likely determine your future with the company.

You have just completed meetings with local government officials, and you're pessimistic about your ability to get things moving quickly. You've learned, for example, that it will take 10 months to get a building permit for a needed facility. Moreover, once the building is up, it will take another six months to get utilities. Finally, the phone company says that it may take up to two years to install the phone lines that you need for high-speed internet access.

The Dilemma

Various officials have indicated that time frames could be considerably shortened if you were willing to pay special "expediting" fees. You realize, of course, that these "fees" are bribes, and you're well aware that the practice of paying such "fees" is both unethical and illegal in Canada. In this foreign country, however, it's not illegal and not even considered unethical. Moreover, if you don't pay and one of your competitors does, you'll be at a major competitive disadvantage. In any case, your boss isn't likely to understand the long lead times necessary to get the operation running. Fortunately, you have access to a source of funds that you could spend without the knowledge of anyone in the home office.

Questions for Discussion

1. What are the key ethical issues in this situation?
2. What do you think most managers would do in this situation?
3. What would you do?

CONCLUDING CASE 5-1

Where Does Management Stand on Beer Breaks?

Is there anything left to be said about the retailer that has become the most profitable corporation on earth? Wal-Mart is gigantic, by any measure. It has 1.3 million workers in 4688 stores worldwide, that are visited by more than 100 million customers every *week*. Annual sales exceed $250 billion, and Wal-Mart is the first non-manufacturing firm ever to occupy the #1 position on the Fortune 500 list. But Wal-Mart has set its sights on aggressive expansion into markets of specialty retailers such as Toys "R" Us and Best Buy, and it continues to introduce new products into existing stores. But even with all this domestic activity, Wal-Mart still finds expansion into international markets its most appealing option.

Wal-Mart's international expansion began in 1991, when a Sam's Club opened near Mexico City. Today, the firm's International Division operates 1100 overseas outlets, with stores in Argentina, Brazil, Canada, China, Germany, Korea, Mexico, Puerto Rico, and the United Kingdom. Interestingly, in each of these markets, acquisitions have played as important a role as expansion from within. In Canada, for example, Wal-Mart entered the market by buying up 122 Woolco stores. German operations began with the acquisition of 21 Wertkauf hypermarkets and 74 Interspar stores. Most ambitious to date, however, have been the company's activities in Britain, where it bought 230 ASDA stores in 1999. The process for integrating acquired stores into Wal-Mart operations involves changing names, renovating facilities, bringing in U.S. store managers, and altering product mixes.

Wal-Mart is still learning how to deal effectively with international differences in culture and business practices. An initial problem was the relatively small size of the acquired stores, most of which had only one-third the floor space of a typical Wal-Mart. Wal-Mart's "one-stop" strategy depends, in part, on size—having everything under one roof—but European customers don't like the impersonal feel of very large stores. In addition, because they typically shop more frequently than Americans and buy less at each visit, they see no reason to be pushing large carts around. Thus the dilemma for Wal-Mart management: Although smaller carts would allow it to cram more products into limited store space, small carts don't encourage large purchases. Finally, Europeans don't care for greeters. "Germans are skeptical," explains an analyst at Deutsche Bank. "They don't want to be paying the salary of that guy at the door."

Regulation creates yet another set of hurdles. In England and Germany, 24-hour stores are banned. A German court upheld employees' rights to wear earrings and sport facial hair, and when the company tried to forbid English employees from drinking beer during lunch breaks, English labour unions threatened to go to court. European laws are also quite strict about the sale of "loss leaders"—popular products that are sold below cost to bring customers into stores. Negotiations with suppliers are also heavily regulated. In Mexico, Wal-Mart ran afoul of local authorities when it demanded deep discounts from many suppliers.

Wal-Mart's entry into a new market "is a nightmare for a lot of retailers," says retail consultant Michael P. Godliman. To fight back, local retailers have imitated Wal-Mart's strategy—namely, by cutting costs and increasing variety—and many have also added products and services geared to local tastes. Soriana supermarkets of Mexico, for example, wages war with in-store mariachi concerts. "Wal-Mart is formidable, but we aren't afraid of the challenge," says Soriana CEO Ricardo Martín. Hoping to forestall Wal-Mart's entry into France, the second-largest retail market in Europe, domestic retailer Carrefour has added amenities such as travel agents and shoe fitters and banned fluorescent lighting. More importantly, a recently announced merger with France's number-two retailer, Promodes, boosts Carrefour's market power. Carrefour, testifies one French retail executive, is "just relentless. The toughest competitor I've ever seen anywhere." Other European retailers, such as Dutch grocer Ahold, are also considering pre-emptive mergers.

Wal-Mart's results from international operations have not been as good as those achieved in the United States. Sales are increasing, but at a slower rate than in previous years. Gross margins on international sales were 4.1 percent, compared to 7.1 percent for U.S. stores. But the company is flush with the profits from its thousands of domestic stores and does not intend to be deterred. The international retailing industry will undoubtedly consolidate until just a few very large, cross-border retailers remain. Wal-Mart will obviously be one of them.

Questions for Discussion

1. What are some of the advantages that Wal-Mart hopes to gain by globalization? What are some of the challenges that it faces in its efforts to globalize?
2. What methods has Wal-Mart used to globalize? Are they the most appropriate methods for the firm? Why or why not?
3. In an effort to reduce trade barriers, nations are entering into more international agreements. In your opinion, will this trend help or hurt Wal-Mart?

CONCLUDING CASE 5-2

International Challenges in the Clothing Industry

On January 1, 2005, import quotas in Canada were lifted for members of the World Trade Organization. Prior to that time, the amount of textiles and apparel that could be imported into Canada from countries like China and India was limited to protect domestic Canadian industries. The Canadian government unveiled a $600 million aid package to help Canadian companies cope with the expected increase in cheap imports, but many in the industry didn't think this would help much. A mere seven months after the import quotas were lifted, the Canadian apparel industry had lost about 20 percent of its workforce. Many of these jobs were shifted to low-wage countries as companies tried to reduce their costs to compete with Chinese imports.

The town of Huntingdon, Quebec (population 2600), discovered first-hand what the new trade rules meant even before they were implemented. In December 2004, townspeople learned that Huntingdon Mills was bankrupt and that 215 jobs would be lost, and that Cleyn & Tinker would soon shut down, costing 600 workers their jobs. The closing of the two textile mills meant a 25 percent decline in the town's tax revenue, and increased the unemployment rate (already at 20 percent). Workers don't put all the blame on China. They feel that the Canadian government is accountable because it gave undue import preferences to Caribbean and other poor countries, and that it didn't do enough to keep the Canadian dollar from rising and making Canada's textile exports more expensive.

Two successful apparel companies in Quebec—Peerless Clothing Inc. and Gildan Activewear—are also trying to determine what the dropping of import quotas will mean for them. Peerless operates the largest men's tailored clothing factory in North America, producing 30 000 suits and 40 000 pairs of trousers each week. Annual sales exceed $300 million, and Peerless has captured 20 percent of the U.S. men's suit market. A U.S. retailer who orders a suit on a Monday knows it will show up the next *day* at Peerless's St. Albans, Vermont, shipping centre, ready to be sent anywhere in the United States. Part of Peerless's success is attributed to owner Alvin Segal's invention of the "engineered suit," where a high-quality suit is made using assembly line efficiencies. The company has also benefited from the Canada–U.S. free trade agreement; Segal landed contracts with major U.S. retailers and with labels like Ralph Lauren and Calvin Klein.

Gildan Activewear has become a global T-shirt powerhouse by focussing on being the highest-quality, lowest-cost provider of "blank" 100 percent cotton T-shirts, which are sold to wholesalers and then imprinted with logos and designs. Using this strategy, Gildan has achieved annual sales of $600 million and has captured 29 percent of the U.S. imprinted T-shirt market. Its goal is 40 percent of the U.S. market. Unlike Peerless, Gildan aggressively uses offshore manufacturing facilities, mostly in the Caribbean where labour costs are low.

Both Peerless and Gildan have to keep an eye on future imports from China. The vice-chairman of Peerless says that since Peerless imports most of its textiles from abroad, the elimination of the 16 percent tariff on yarn that Peerless imports will enable it to enjoy a significant reduction in costs, allowing it to be price-competitive. Gildan's executive vice-president said his company will be able to meet the threat from China because of Gildan's economies of scale, its state-of-the-art factories, and its already low labour costs.

The government aid package is designed to help both the capital-intensive textile industry and the labour-intensive apparel industry, but the interests of these two industries often do not coincide. The apparel industry pays relatively low wages, buys the lowest-cost fabric it can find, and is able to shift production to wherever it makes the most economic sense. By contrast, the textile industry pays higher wages and invests in new technology to remain competitive in its Canadian base. The irony is that the new regulations will allow Canadian apparel makers to import yarn duty-free. That means that they can use textiles that are not made in Canada, thus hurting Canadian textile mills.

Questions for Discussion

1. Explain how exchange rates and the value of the Canadian dollar have affected the garment industry. Should the Canadian government try to influence the value of the Canadian dollar? Defend your answer.
2. Describe the key arguments made by supporters of protectionism. To what extent are these arguments relevant for the current situation in the garment industry? Describe the key arguments made by those who support free trade. To what extent are these relevant for the current situation in the garment industry?
3. To what extent should the Canadian government intervene and protect industries like the garment industry? Defend your answer.
4. *"There should be no tariffs at all on products moving between any countries. Only then will the world's economic system be operating at full efficiency."* Do you agree or disagree with this statement? Explain.

PLANNING FOR YOUR CAREER

Knowing What You Want

What kind of job do you want when you finish school? A glamorous position with a global firm that routinely flies you from New York to London, Tokyo, and Rio? To start your own business and perhaps become the next Bill Gates? Or maybe just the "perfect job"—the one that will fulfill all your needs while providing adequate security and satisfying rewards? In a perfect world, of course, you can take your pick. But in the world we live in, of course, none of these options is likely to be available—at least not right away and not without any hitches.

Even global giants such as Nestlé and Toyota assign entry-level managers to domestic tasks. New businesses are also difficult to start with no experience, capital, or business plan. Many people change jobs at least a few times until they find one they truly want. So, what can you do *now* to better prepare for a future career? This exercise gives you an opportunity to take a closer look at yourself to get a better idea of where you might be headed.

Assignment

Start by reading Chapter 1 in *Beginning Your Career Search*, 3rd ed., by James S. O'Rourke IV. Use this chapter as a frame of reference in doing the following activities:

1. Develop a list of your major personal strengths. Examples might include such things as (1) excellent communications skills, (2) strong math background, (3) fluency in multiple languages, and so forth.
2. Develop a list of your major personal weaknesses, such as (1) fear of speaking in front of a group, (2) limited knowledge of foreign cultures, (3) weak science background, and so forth.
3. Develop a list of the qualities or characteristics that you think best reflect who and what you are. Are you (1) a risk taker, (2) a person who prefers to work alone, (3) a person who prefers to follow others, and so forth? (Note that none of these qualities is necessarily good or bad.)
4. Develop a list of what are most likely to be important to you in a career, at least initially. Examples might be (1) a job that will provide strong training and development opportunities, (2) a job in a certain geographic area, (3) a job with a certain kind of company, and so forth.
5. Develop a list of what you hope to avoid in your career, if possible, such as (1) stress and long hours, (2) a lot of travel, (3) working with overly aggressive and competitive people, and so forth.

Now, draft an action plan that you can follow—some guidelines that might help you to better prepare for a job or career in relation to each of your five lists. Your plan should address ways to capitalize on your strengths, overcome your weaknesses, fit a job to your personal characteristics, meet many of your preferences, and avoid most of what you dislike. For instance, if you have a fear of speaking in front of a group, you might plan to take a public speaking course. If you are a risk taker, you might begin by exploring career options that include some opportunity to take risks (such as working in a new venture or start-up operation) as opposed to options that involve less risk (such as working for a national retail chain that has a variety of standard operating procedures).

Remember, of course, that this action plan is simply a draft. Even if you try to apply it to your educational choices, you'll need to revise and update it constantly. Jobs will change, the world will change, and you will change. But that's part of the fun of thinking about your future, isn't it? After all, it's a blank screen for you to write on, to edit, to erase, and then to write on some more.

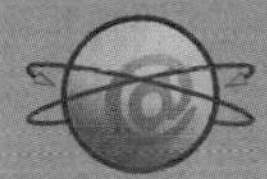

Visit the Companion Website at **www.pearsoned.ca/griffin** to view the CBC video segments that accompany the following cases.

CBC CBC VIDEO CASE I-1

Wormboy

Tom Szaky is a young Canadian who is betting big bucks on his ability to sell worm poop. The son of two doctors, Tom was on track to get a degree from prestigious Princeton in the United States. But one day he discovered a friend's worm composter, and when he found out that the worms ate garbage, he got an idea for a business. He quit Princeton and started Terra Cycle, a company which makes plant food from worm droppings. Now he is trying to make a fortune off worms.

Terra Cycle's office is in a basement, but the plant food is made in a factory containing 250 000 worms. The worm droppings are mixed with water, pumped into used bottles, and shipped to customers in used boxes. Szaky says he won't harm the environment in his quest to make money. This is eco-capitalism at its finest, because Tom Szaky is turning garbage into gold.

Several of Szaky's friends are working in his company with him. Robin, the vice-president of sales, wants to get Terra Cycle into big box stores like Home Depot and Wal-Mart, but he's also going after smaller chains as well. Robin doesn't have experience with big box stores, and investors want someone experienced to be head of sales. But Szaky finds that it is hard to fire a friend. Another friend, Alex, is a high school buddy who also quit Princeton. He runs Terra Cycle's lawn program. His first big contract was repairing a lawn at Princeton. Alex does a good job of bringing back Princeton's grass, but he hasn't done much to get other sales. So Szaky puts pressure on Alex to get more customers.

In this business, Szaky needs all the help he can get, so he has talked several students into volunteering to work for him. In return for their work, they get business experience and stock options. Szaky bought a run-down mansion and turned it into the staff dorm for the volunteers. He furnished the house with some castoff items that he got from friends at Princeton.

Szaky has several problems he must solve. First, he is spending about $50 000 a month for things like salaries, rent, and food for the worms. So far, he has raised over a million dollars, but he has already spent most of that. Not much money is coming in from sales because Terra Cycle is sold only in a few stores. Second, some of his workers are doing sloppy work. For example, there were errors in a business plan that was given to potential investors, and this did not increase their confidence in the company. Perhaps counting on student volunteers was a mistake.

Third, sales must be increased. Szaky therefore goes on the road to pitch his product—called Plant Jelly—to various companies. One of them is QVC, a home shopping channel that reaches 86 million homes in the United States. He will get 15 minutes of air time to pitch the product. Terra Cycle's chief scientist thinks Szaky is moving too fast because Plant Jelly hasn't really been tested for effectiveness. But Szaky has a gut feeling the product will work, so he goes ahead. (Some time later, Szaky gets test results showing that Plant Jelly does indeed work.)

On his trip, Szaky meets with seven different retailers, but now some time has passed and he still hasn't heard anything positive from any of them. He is wondering whether eco-capitalism can sell in a big box world. But he believes in his product, so he plans another risky move: He wants to turn a warehouse into a factory that will be able to produce a lot of Plant Jelly if he gets a big box order. It will cost $300 000 to renovate the warehouse, but he doesn't have any money to do the work.

Szaky realizes that he is going to have to start selling reality instead of just potential. In a meeting with venture capitalists, he asks for $4.5 million. He argues that his product has high margins because it is made from garbage. But the venture capitalists are reluctant, partly because of Szaky's age (22).

Finally Szaky gets a call from Wal-Mart and learns that Robin has succeeded in getting a $300 000 order for the spring. Now the company must actually make all that plant food. To do that, the new factory must somehow be financed and set up in very short order. Szaky also has to try to win over another big investor. It's a good thing he works well under pressure. Maybe quitting Princeton wasn't such a bad idea after all.

Questions for Discussion

1. Explain the difference between *entrepreneurship*, *small business*, and *new venture creation* as it applies to Szaky's activities.
2. Use Figure 4.4 on p. 111 to explain Szaky's activities so far.
3. What is *bootstrapping*? How is this idea relevant to Szaky?
4. What kind of financing is Szaky using for his business?
5. What form of business ownership would be most appropriate for Szaky's business?

Source: "Worm Boy," *Venture*, February 6, 2005.

CBC CBC VIDEO CASE I-2

Corporate Espionage

Spying, intrigue, and shredded documents are activities we normally associate with countries spying on one another. But these activities are also evident in the business world. And make no mistake about it, Canada is just as likely a place for shenanigans as the United States. Norman Inkster, who helps companies fight off corporate spies, says that business firms engage in corporate espionage much more often than we ever hear about. And, he says, "getting a leg up" can be "low down and dirty." Consider the case of Air Canada versus WestJet.

It all started when a WestJet executive got a password that allowed him to access an Air Canada website that was supposed to be confidential and available only to Air Canada employees. This website gave the WestJet executive access to Air Canada's "load factor" on each one of its routes. This was critical information that allowed WestJet to identify Air Canada's strong and weak flights and then to develop a competitive strategy based on that information.

Air Canada learned that someone at WestJet was accessing their website only after someone tipped them off. In an attempt to find out just what WestJet knew, Air Canada hired private investigators to steal the WestJet executive's garbage. The garbage contained a lot of shredded paper, which was sent to Church Street Technology, a company that has developed a system for reassembling shredded pages. Owner Cody Ford first sorts the strips of shredded paper, then tapes them to a blank sheet of paper and scans them. A specialized computer program then reassembles the original document. Ford says that he can easily reassemble shredded documents.

While this was going on, WestJet was not idle. When the WestJet executive's garbage was stolen, a neighbour noticed and phoned the police. They informed the executive, so he took pictures of the investigators the next time they came for his garbage. The pictures appeared in the *Globe and Mail.*

Once Air Canada had determined what WestJet knew, and once WestJet knew that Air Canada had stolen one of their executive's garbage, the rivalry between the two companies moved from the boardroom to the courtroom, and the companies sued each other over allegations of corporate espionage. Air Canada filed a $220 million lawsuit against WestJet, accusing it of using the website information to schedule competing flights. WestJet counter-sued Air Canada, accusing it of trespassing and stealing private property.

The lawsuit was settled in 2006. WestJet apologized to Air Canada and said that its conduct was both unethical and unacceptable, and that WestJet accepted full responsibility for its misconduct. WestJet agreed to pay $5 million to Air Canada for the expenses Air Canada incurred while investigating the unauthorized accessing of its website. WestJet also agreed to contribute $10 million to children's charities. Clive Beddoe, CEO of WestJet, also apologized to WestJet shareholders and said this shouldn't have happened. WestJet's lawsuit against Air Canada was dismissed.

Questions for Discussion

1. Do you think that WestJet behaved in an unethical fashion? Why or why not? Do you think that Air Canada behaved in an unethical fashion? Why or why not?
2. Analyze this problem using the model in Figure 3.1 on p. 77. Work through the model step-by-step and explain your conclusions at each step in the process. What conclusions do you reach at the end of the process about the behaviour of WestJet and Air Canada?
3. Suppose that you are confronted with a situation where you strongly believe that another person acted in an unethical fashion, but that person totally disagreed with you. How would you go about convincing that person that their behaviour was unethical?
4. *"The WestJet executive who gained access to Air Canada's website did not behave in an unethical fashion. He simply used the information he was given to gather information from Air Canada's website. He then analyzed Air Canada's business activity and developed a strategy for WestJet that took advantage of that knowledge. This is simply an example of a person using information to his advantage."* Do you agree or disagree with this statement? Explain.

Sources: "Under the Radar," *Venture*, October 31, 2004; www.cbc.ca/canada/calgary/story/2006/05/29/ca-westjet-settlement-20060529.html.

PART TWO

The Business of Managing

Corporate strategy, organizational structure, workforce diversity, labour–management relations, and employee motivation and satisfaction are five issues you will read about in the opening cases of Chapters 6 to 10. These and many other issues must be dealt with if companies hope to grow and prosper. Managers in all business firms—indeed, in any kind of organization—must carry out the basic management functions of planning, organizing, leading, and controlling. These important functions are the focus of this section of the text.

Part Two, The Business of Managing, provides an overview of business management today. It includes a look at the importance of managers in business firms, how businesses are structured to achieve their goals, the management of the firm's human resources, labour–management relations, and the importance of motivating and leading employees.

- We begin in **Chapter 6, Managing the Business Enterprise**, by describing how managers set goals and choose corporate strategies. The basic functions of management—planning, organizing, leading, and controlling—are examined, as are the different types and levels of managers that are found in business firms, and the corporate culture that is created in each firm.
- In **Chapter 7, Organizing the Business Enterprise**, we look at the basic organizational structures that companies have adopted, and the different kinds of authority that managers can have. The impact of the informal organization is also analyzed.
- In **Chapter 8, Managing Human Resources**, we explore the activities that are necessary to effectively manage employees, including assessing employee needs, training, promoting, and compensating employees.
- In **Chapter 9, Understanding Labour–Management Relations**, we look at the development of the union movement in Canada, why and how workers organize, and how government legislation has affected workers' rights to organize into unions.
- Finally, in **Chapter 10, Motivating and Leading Employees**, we examine the reasons why firms should establish good relationships with their employees, and how managers' attempts to maintain productivity can affect their relations with employees.

CHAPTER 6

Managing the Business Enterprise

After reading this chapter, you should be able to:

1. Explain the importance of setting *goals* and formulating *strategies* as the starting points of effective management.
2. Describe the four activities that constitute the *management process*.
3. Identify *types of managers* by level and area.
4. Describe the five basic *management skills*.
5. Describe the development and explain the importance of *corporate culture*.

Looking for Redemption?

Edgar Bronfman Jr. is the chairman of Warner Music Group, which includes record labels such as Warner Bros., Atlantic, Electra, and the Christian music producer Word Records. He is the son of Edgar Bronfman Sr., who was CEO of the Seagram Company. Seagram was started in the 1920s by Sam Bronfman, who sold liquor by mail order. Sam's son, Edgar Bronfman Sr. became CEO in 1957, and for the next 40 years the company focussed on the production of wine and distilled spirits. In the process, it became a household name in Canada.

In the mid-1990s, Edgar Bronfman Jr. took over leadership of Seagram from his father and made some dramatic strategic moves that turned the company away from its traditional products and moved it toward the high-risk entertainment business. For example, the company bought MCA Inc. (now Universal) and Polygram NV. These moves caused some people to recall founder Sam Bronfman's observation that third-generation family members often dissipate the family fortune. Edgar Jr. was well aware of this criticism, and he was determined not to fulfill his grandfather's prophecy.

Things seemed to go well for a time under Edgar Jr.'s leadership. In 2000, he sold Seagram to the French conglomerate Vivendi SA for $33 billion in Vivendi stock. This looked like a good deal because Seagram was paid the equivalent of $75 for each of its shares, even though Seagram's shares were trading at less than $50 at the time. But things soon turned sour. By the end of 2001, Vivendi was in deep financial trouble, and its stock price had declined from $130 to $50 per share. The Seagram fortune declined along with Vivendi's decline because Bronfman had taken Vivendi stock instead of cash when he sold Seagram. When the merger with Vivendi was originally announced, the Seagram family fortune was worth about U.S.$7 billion, but by 2003, it had declined to less than U.S.$1 billion. People started thinking Sam Bronfman was right after all.

In spite of these setbacks, Edgar Bronfman Jr. was determined to get back on the winning track. In 2003, he was unsuccessful in his attempt to buy Vivendi's film and TV assets, but in 2004 he and several partners were successful in purchasing Warner Music Group. Bronfman has adopted a corporate strategy based on the assumption that consumers will increasingly bypass traditional music stores and instead buy online digital music. He wants Warner Music Group to be a major player in emerging markets such as ringtones and ringbacks (where cellphones are programmed to play different tunes depending on who is calling the cellphone). He also thinks that music will be distributed through many more distribution channels than has historically been the case. He predicts that by 2009 about one-quarter of music revenue will come from digital music.

To pursue this strategy, Bronfman has borrowed a lot of money. So far, he is using some of this borrowed money to reward his shareholder partners. The partners have already taken more than $1 billion out of the firm. Standard & Poor's Corp., a bond rating firm, criticized this distribution, saying that it put the company's balance sheet at risk. For the 10 months ending September 30, 2004, Warner Music lost $136 million. Industry observers feel that Bronfman is counting far too much on future revenue, particularly since the music industry's attempts to defeat online piracy have not been very successful.

It is too early to tell if Bronfman's strategy is going to work. If it does, he will be seen as a top manager who had the vision and insight to position Warner Music Group so that it could capitalize on a major trend. If the strategy doesn't work, critics will keep saying that old Sam Bronfman was right. ◆

WHO ARE MANAGERS?

All corporations depend on effective management. Regardless of the type of business they work in, managers like Edgar Bronfman perform many of the same functions, are responsible for many of the same tasks, and have many of the same responsibilities. The work of all managers involves developing strategic and tactical plans. They must also analyze their competitive environments and plan, organize, direct, and control day-to-day operations.

Although our focus is on managers in *business* settings, remember that the principles of management apply to all kinds of organizations. Managers work in charities, churches, social organizations, educational institutions, and government agencies. The prime minister of Canada, the president of the University of Toronto, the executive director of the United Way, the dean of your business school, and the chief administrator of your local hospital are all managers. Remember, too, that managers bring to small organizations many of the same kinds of skills—the ability to make decisions and respond to a variety of challenges—that they bring to large ones. Regardless of the nature and size of an organization, managers are among its most important resources.

SETTING GOALS AND FORMULATING STRATEGY

goals Objectives that a business hopes and plans to achieve.

1 Explain the importance of setting *goals* and formulating *strategies* as the starting points of effective management.

The starting point in effective management is setting **goals**, objectives that a business hopes (and plans) to achieve. Every business needs goals, and we begin by discussing the basic aspects of organizational goal setting. However, deciding what it *intends* to do is only step one for an organization. A company's managers must also make decisions about *actions* that will and will not achieve its goals. From this perspective, *strategy* is the broad program that underlies those decisions; the basic steps in formulating strategy are discussed later in the chapter.

Setting Goals

Goals are performance targets, the means by which organizations and their managers measure success or failure at every level. In this section, we identify the main purposes for which organizations establish goals, classify the basic levels of business goals, and describe the process by which goals are commonly set.

The Purposes of Goal Setting

An organization functions systematically because it sets goals and plans accordingly. Indeed, an organization functions as such because it commits its resources on all levels to achieving its goals. Specifically, we can identify four main purposes in organizational goal setting:

1. *Goal setting provides direction, guidance, and motivation for all managers.* If managers know precisely where the company is headed, there is less potential for error in the different units of the company. Starbucks, for example, has a goal of increasing capital spending by 15 percent, with all additional expenditures devoted to opening new stores. This goal clearly informs everyone in the firm that expansion into new territories is a high priority for the firm.

2. *Goal setting helps firms allocate resources.* Areas that are expected to grow will get first priority. The company allocates more resources to new projects with large sales potential than it allocates to mature prod-

ucts with established but stagnant sales potential. Thus, Starbucks is primarily emphasizing new store expansion, while its ecommerce initiatives are currently given a lower priority. "Our management team," says CEO Howard Schultz, "is 100 percent focused on growing our core business without distraction...from any other initiative."

3. *Goal setting helps to define corporate culture.* General Electric's goal, for instance, is to push each of its divisions to number one or number two in its industry. The result is a competitive, often stressful, environment and a culture that rewards success and has little tolerance for failure. At the same time, however, GE's appliance business, television network (NBC), aircraft engine unit, and financial services business are each among the very best in their respective industries.
4. *Goal setting helps managers assess performance.* If a company sets a goal to increase sales by 10 percent in a given year, managers in units who attain or exceed the goal can be rewarded. Units failing to reach the goal will also be compensated accordingly. GE has a long-standing reputation for stringently evaluating managerial performance, richly rewarding those who excel—and getting rid of those who do not. Each year, the lower 10 percent of GE's managerial force are informed that either they make dramatic improvements in performance or consider alternative directions for their careers.

Kinds of Goals

Naturally, goals differ from company to company, depending on the firm's purpose and mission. Every enterprise, of course, has a *purpose*—a reason for being. Businesses seek profit, universities work to discover and transmit new knowledge, and government agencies exist to provide service to the public. Most enterprises also have a **mission statement**—a statement of how it will achieve its purpose. Bell Canada's mission, for example, is to be a world leader in helping communicate and manage information. DaimlerChrysler's mission statement emphasizes "delighted customers." Atco Ltd.'s mission is to provide products and services to the energy and resource industries, and to invest principally in energy-related assets in North America. The mission of Investor's Group is to satisfy clients who need general and comprehensive financial planning. Mission statements

mission statement An organization's statement of how it will achieve its purpose in the environment in which it conducts its business.

National leaders are managers, too, and those at the highest levels, like Russian President Vladimir Putin (centre), set goals for overall economic growth. When Economic Minister German Gref (left) announced an anticipated growth rate of 5.2 percent for the coming year, Putin publicly admonished his entire cabinet for setting their economic sights too low. Applauding his boss's policy (and responding to his management style), Gref quickly revised his estimate to a rosier 6.4 percent, citing the likelihood that oil prices would be higher than he had originally thought.

should also include some statement about the company's core values and its commitment to ethical behaviour.

Two business firms can have the same purpose—for example, to sell watches at a profit—yet they have very different missions. Timex sells low-cost, reliable watches in outlets ranging from department stores to corner drugstores. Rolex, on the other hand, sells high-quality, high-priced fashion watches through selected jewellery stores.

Regardless of a company's purpose and mission, every firm needs long-term, intermediate, and short-term goals:

long-term goals Goals set for extended periods of time, typically five years or more into the future.

- **Long-term goals** relate to extended periods of time—typically five years or more into the future. MasterCard, for example, might set a long-term goal of doubling the number of participating merchants during the next 10 years. Similarly, Sony might adopt a long-term goal to increase its share of the digital SLR market by 10 percent during the next five years.

intermediate goals Goals set for a period of one to five years.

- **Intermediate goals** are set for a period of one to five years into the future. Companies usually have intermediate goals in several areas. For example, the marketing department's goal might be to increase sales by 3 percent in two years. The production department might want to decrease expenses by 6 percent in four years. Human resources might seek to cut turnover by 10 percent in two years. Finance might aim for a 3 percent increase in return on investment in three years.

short-term goals Goals set for the very near future, typically less than one year.

- Like intermediate goals, **short-term goals**—which are set for one year or less—are developed for several different areas. Increasing sales by 2 percent this year, cutting costs by 1 percent next quarter, and reducing turnover by 4 percent over the next six months are all short-term goals.

Formulating Strategy

strategy formulation Creation of a broad program for defining and meeting an organization's goals.

Planning is concerned with the nuts and bolts of setting goals, choosing tactics, and establishing schedules. In contrast, strategy tends to have a wider scope. It is by definition a "broad program" that describes an organization's intentions. A business strategy outlines how it intends to meet its goals, and includes the organization's responsiveness to new challenges and new needs. **Strategy formulation** involves three basic steps, as shown in Figure 6.1.

Setting Strategic Goals

strategic goals Long-term goals derived directly from a firm's mission statement.

Strategic goals are long-term goals derived directly from the firm's mission statement. For example, Bernd Pischetsrieder, CEO of Volkswagen, has clear strategic goals for the European automaker. When he took over, Volkswagen was only marginally profitable, was regarded as an also-ran in

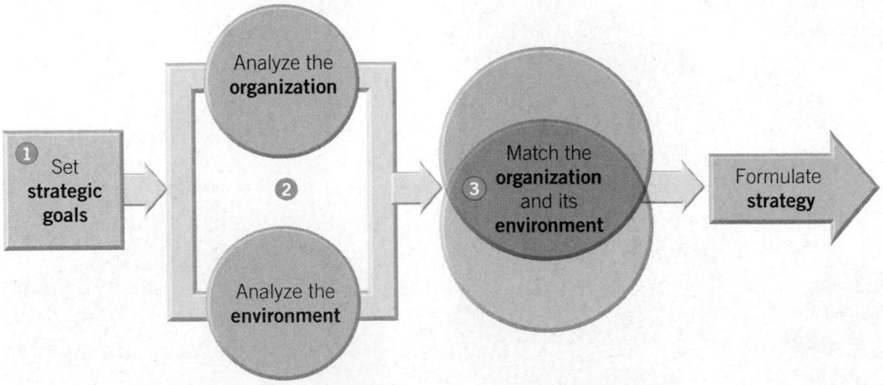

1 Set strategic goals
2
Analyze the organization
Analyze the environment
3 Match the organization and its environment
Formulate strategy

Figure 6.1 Strategy formulation.

the industry, and was thinking of pulling out of the U.S. market because its sales were so poor. Over the next few years, however, Pischetsrieder totally revamped the firm and now it is making big profits. Volkswagen is now a much more formidable force in the global automobile industry.[1]

SWOT Analysis. After strategic goals have been established, organizations usually go through a process called a **SWOT analysis** as they continue to formulate their strategy. This process involves assessing organizational *S*trengths and *W*eaknesses (the *S* and the *W*) and environmental *O*pportunities and *T*hreats (the *O* and the *T*). Note that strengths and weaknesses are internal to the company, while opportunities and threats are external. In formulating strategy, companies attempt to capitalize on organizational strengths and take advantage of environmental opportunities. During this same process, they seek ways to overcome organizational weaknesses and cope with environmental threats.[2]

SWOT analysis Identification and analysis of organizational strengths and weaknesses and environmental opportunities and threats as part of strategy formulation.

Analyzing the Organization and Its Environment

The term **environmental analysis** means scanning the environment for threats and opportunities. Changing consumer tastes and hostile takeover offers are *threats*, as are new government regulations. Even more important threats come from new products and new competitors. *Opportunities*, meanwhile, are areas in which the firm can potentially expand, grow, or take advantage of existing strengths.

environmental analysis The process of scanning the environment for threats and opportunities.

Consider, for example, the case of British entrepreneur Richard Branson and his company, Virgin Group Ltd. Branson started the firm in 1968, when he was 17, naming it in acknowledgment of his own lack of experience in the business world. Over the years, he has built Virgin into one of the world's best-known brands, comprising a conglomeration of over 200 entertainment, media, and travel companies worldwide. Among the best known of his enterprises are Virgin Atlantic (an international airline), Virgin Megastores (retailing), and V2 Music (record labels). Branson sees potential threats from other competitors such as British Airways and KLM for Virgin Atlantic, Tower Records for retailing, and the EMI Group for recorded music.

But he also sees significant opportunities because of his firm's strong brand name (especially in Europe). Indeed, one of his most recent ventures is a new ecommerce firm. The business is called Virgin Mobile and operates like a cellular telephone company. But in addition to providing conventional cellular service, the Virgin telephone permits the user to press a red button to go directly to a Virgin operator who can sell products, make airline and hotel reservations, and provide numerous other services. A companion website complements the cellular service and its related programs. Virgin Mobile signed up more than one million new customers during its first year of operation and is one of the market leaders in Great Britain.[3]

In addition to performing environmental analysis, which is analysis of *external* factors, managers must examine *internal* factors. The purpose of **organizational analysis** is to better understand a company's strengths and weaknesses. Strengths might include surplus cash, a dedicated workforce, an ample supply of managerial talent, technical expertise, or weak competition. The absence of any of these strengths could represent an important weakness.

organizational analysis The process of analyzing a firm's strengths and weaknesses.

Branson, for example, started up Virgin Mobile in part because he saw so many of his current operations as old-line, traditional businesses that might be at future risk from new forms of business and competition. One strength he has employed has been the widespread name recognition that his businesses enjoy. Another strength relates to finances. Branson sold 49 percent of Virgin Atlantic to Singapore Airlines for almost $1 billion in cash, retaining ownership control but raising all of the funds he needed to launch his new venture. On the other hand, he also admits that neither he nor most of his senior managers have much experience in or knowledge about ecommerce, which may be a significant weakness.

Matching the Organization and Its Environment

The final step in strategy formulation is matching environmental threats and opportunities with corporate strengths and weaknesses. The matching process is the heart of strategy formulation: More than any other facet of strategy, matching companies with their environments lays the foundation for successfully planning and conducting business.

ENTREPRENEURSHIP AND NEW VENTURES

Best in Show

When Mark Warren, a Toronto investment banker, returned to Canada from London a few years ago with his four dogs, he was confronted with an underdeveloped market for pet insurance in North America. Pet insurance was sold mainly through veterinary clinics, and coverage was riddled with loopholes and exceptions. Seeing an opportunity to bring increased innovation and customer service to the market, Warren launched Pethealth in March 1999.

As people pour emotional equity into their pets (seven in 10 pet owners say their pets have the same rights to health as humans, according to a 2001 Ipsos-Reid study), they're more willing to consider complex medical procedures to extend their lives. With such operations costing in the thousands, pet insurance starts to make sense. "You're effectively replacing the high cost of the unexpected and the unforeseen with a budgetable monthly premium," says Warren.

His strategy has been to avoid the commoditization of Pethealth's insurance services, working hard to out-innovate the competition on all fronts: price, service, sales channels, and technology. Pethealth has led the market by, for example, introducing bigger and faster payouts than its competitors; by partnering with trusted retailers such as U.S. giant Petco to sell its pet insurance; and by befriending the fast-growing channel of animal shelters by providing them with free shelter management software. It also offers free 30-day health insurance on pets adopted from participating pounds—reassuring buyers, eliminating costly liabilities for the shelters, and creating low-cost trial customers, of which a significant percentage renew their policies once the trial ends.

According to Warren, "In 2005, we consolidated our position as Canada's largest provider of pet health insurance and are now the second largest provider in North America. 2005 also marked a watershed year in our journey towards completing our vision of becoming the leading provider of integrated health-related information services to the companion animal industry, bringing unique products and services to veterinarians, shelters, and pet owners."

The transition from a single-service pet insurance provider began with the creation in 2003 of 24PetWatch (www.24petwatch.com), a microchip and lost pet recovery network. Pethealth is now the largest provider of RFID (radio frequency identification) technology and related services to veterinary clinics and animal shelters in Canada, and one of the top providers in the U.S. market.

In 2005, Pethealth rolled out additional innovative new services, 24PetMedInfo and 24PetMedAlert, that offer pet owners the ability to both track their pets' medical records online and also to allow emergency veterinary personnel to access the information in a lost pet emergency. 2005 also marked the launch of the Company's suite of .NET-based software solutions for veterinary clinics and animal welfare organizations throughout North America.

PetPoint™ (www.petpoint.com) is the first web-hosted management software program for animal welfare organizations in North America. In addition to providing a more efficient platform for shelters to manage their day-to-day operations, PetPoint also allows shelters to easily provide Pethealth's ShelterCare insurance and 24PetWatch microchip programs electronically at the point of adoption. PetPoint is now the leading management software solution to animal welfare organizations in North America.

EVE™ (www.eveforclinics.com), is the first web-based claims adjudication software for veterinary clinics. This program, the first of its kind in the pet insurance industry in North America, allows claims to be processed online at the veterinary clinic, thus enhancing the clinic/client relationship.

Over the long term, this process may also determine whether a firm typically takes risks or behaves more conservatively. Either strategy can be successful. Blue Bell, for example, is one of the most profitable ice-cream makers in the world, even though it sells its products in only about a dozen U.S. states. Based in Brenham, Texas, Blue Bell controls more than 50 percent of the market in each state where it does business. The firm has resisted the temptation to expand too quickly. Its success is based on product freshness and frequent deliveries—strengths that may suffer if the company grows too large.

A Hierarchy of Plans

Plans can be viewed on three levels: strategic, tactical, and operational. Managerial responsibilities are defined at each level. The levels constitute a hierarchy because implementing plans is practical only when there is a logical flow from one level to the next.

- **Strategic plans** reflect decisions about resource allocations, company priorities, and the steps needed to meet strategic goals. They are usually set by the board of directors and top management. General Electric's decision that viable products must be number one or number two within their respective categories is a matter of strategic planning.
- **Tactical plans** are shorter-range plans concerned with implementing specific aspects of the company's strategic plans. They typically involve upper and middle management. Coca-Cola's decision to increase sales in Europe by building European bottling facilities is an example of tactical planning.
- **Operational plans**, which are developed by middle- and lower-level managers, set short-term targets for daily, weekly, or monthly performance. McDonald's, for example, establishes operational plans when it explains precisely how Big Macs are to be cooked, warmed, and served.

strategic plans Plans that reflect decisions about resource allocations, company priorities, and steps needed to meet strategic goals.

tactical plans Generally, short-range plans concerned with implementing specific aspects of a company's strategic plans.

operational plans Plans setting short-term targets for daily, weekly, or monthly performance.

corporate-level strategy Identifies the various businesses that a company will be in, and how these businesses will relate to each other.

business-level (competitive) strategy Identifies the ways a business will compete in its chosen line of products or services.

functional strategies Identify the basic courses of action that each department in the firm will pursue so that it contributes to the attainment of the business's overall goals.

Levels of Strategies

There are three levels of strategy in a business firm (see Figure 6.2). A **corporate-level strategy** identifies the various businesses that a company will be in, and how these businesses will relate to each other. A **business-level (competitive) strategy** identifies the ways a business will compete in its chosen line of products or services. **Functional strategies** identify the

In the wake of a disastrous industry-wide slump in 2001, Cisco Systems, a giant maker of communications equipment, was forced to radically revise its strategic plans. Where engineers once pursued their own pet projects, engineering is now centralized under a group of top managers. Where individual units once chose their own suppliers, a committee now oversees all partnerships. Where the product line once consisted solely of networking apparatus, the company has branched out into a variety of new high-tech markets.

basic courses of action that each department in the firm will pursue so that it contributes to the attainment of the business's overall goals. Each of these strategies is discussed below.

Corporate-Level Strategies

There are several different corporate-level strategies that a company might pursue, including concentration, growth, integration, diversification, and investment reduction.

concentration strategy Involves focussing the company on one product or product line.

Concentration. A **concentration strategy** involves focussing the company on one product or product line. Organizations that have successfully pursued a concentration strategy include McDonald's and Canadian National Railway. The main advantage of a concentration strategy is that the company can focus its strengths on the one business it knows well. The main disadvantage is the risk inherent in putting all of one's eggs in one basket.

market penetration Boosting sales of present products by more aggressive selling in the firm's current markets.

product development Developing improved products for current markets.

geographic expansion Expanding operations in new geographic areas or countries.

Growth. Companies have several growth strategies available to them, all of which focus on *internal* activities that will result in growth. These strategies include **market penetration** (boosting sales of present products by more aggressive selling in the firm's current markets), **product development** (developing improved products for current markets), and **geographic expansion** (expanding operations in new geographic areas or countries). CanJet, for example, is using a geographic expansion strategy, since it started by offering service in Eastern Canada but has now added flights to cities in Western Canada.[4]

horizontal integration Acquiring control of competitors in the same or similar markets with the same or similar products.

vertical integration Owning or controlling the inputs to the firm's processes and/or the channels through which the products or services are distributed.

diversification Expanding into related or unrelated products or market segments.

Integration. There are two basic integration strategies, both of which focus on *external* activities that will result in growth. **Horizontal integration** means acquiring control of competitors in the same or similar markets with the same or similar products. For example, Hudson's Bay Company purchased Kmart and Zellers. **Vertical integration** means owning or controlling the inputs to the firm's processes and/or the channels through which the products or services are distributed. Thus, major oil companies like Shell not only drill and produce their own oil, but refine the oil into different products and then sell those products through company-controlled outlets across Canada. Another example of vertical integration is Irving Forest Products' purchase of Royale Tissue from Procter & Gamble.

Figure 6.2 Hierarchy of strategy.

Diversification. **Diversification** means expanding into related or unrelated products or market segments. Diversification helps the firm avoid the problem of having all of its eggs in one basket by spreading risk among several products or markets. *Related diversification* means adding new, but related, products or services to an existing business. For example, CN diversified into trucking, an activity that is clearly related to railway operations. Maple Leaf Gardens Ltd., which already owned the Toronto Maple Leafs, also acquired the Toronto Raptors basketball team. *Conglomerate diversification* means diversifying into products or markets that are not related to the firm's present businesses. For example, Brascan Ltd. owns companies in the mining, real estate, electric power generation, and financial services businesses. Conglomerate diversification is not nearly as popular as it was a few years ago.

Investment Reduction. **Investment reduction** means reducing the company's investment in one or more of its lines of business. One investment-reduction strategy is *retrenchment*, which means the reduction of activity or operations. For example, Federal Industries formerly was a conglomerate with interests in trucking, railways, metals, and other product lines, but it retrenched and now focusses on a more limited set of customers and products. *Divestment* is another investment-reduction strategy; it involves selling or liquidating one or more of a firm's businesses. For example, BCE sold its Yellow Pages and White Pages for $4 billion.

investment reduction Reducing the company's investment in one or more of its lines of business.

Business-Level (Competitive) Strategies

Whatever corporate-level strategy a firm decides on, it must also have a competitive strategy. A competitive strategy is a plan to establish a profitable and sustainable competitive position against the forces that determine industry competition.[5] Michael Porter identifies three competitive strategies: cost leadership, differentiation, and focus.

Cost Leadership. **Cost leadership** means becoming the low cost leader in an industry. Wal-Mart is an industry cost leader. Its distribution costs are minimized through a satellite-based warehousing system, its store-location costs are minimized by placing stores on low-cost land, and the stores themselves are very plain. Montreal-based Gildan Activewear is dedicated to achieving the lowest possible costs in producing its T-shirts. The company has captured 29 percent of the U.S. imprinted T-shirt market with this strategy.[6]

cost leadership Becoming the low cost leader in an industry.

Differentiation. In a **differentiation strategy**, a firm seeks to be unique in its industry along some dimension that is valued by buyers. For example, Caterpillar Tractor emphasizes durability, Volvo stresses safety, Apple Computer stresses user-friendly products, and Mercedes-Benz emphasizes quality.

differentiation strategy A firm seeks to be unique in its industry along some dimension that is valued by buyers.

Focus. A **focus strategy** means selecting a market segment and serving the customers in that market niche better than competitors. Before it was acquired by Nexfor, Fraser Inc. focussed on producing high-quality, durable, lightweight paper that is used in bibles. While it still has a good reputation in the production of bible paper, Nexfor Fraser Papers is more diversified now and produces papers for a variety of uses, including dog food bags and doughnut boxes.

focus strategy Selecting a market segment and serving the customers in that market niche better than competitors.

Functional Strategies

Each business's choice of competitive strategy (cost leadership, differentiation, or focus) is translated into supporting functional strategies for each of its departments to pursue. A functional strategy is the basic course of action that each department follows so that the business accomplishes its overall goals. To implement its cost-leadership strategy, for example, Wal-Mart's distribution department pursued a functional strategy of satellite-based warehousing that ultimately drove distribution costs down to a minimum.

CONTINGENCY PLANNING AND CRISIS MANAGEMENT

Because business environments are often difficult to predict, and because the unexpected can create major problems, most managers recognize that even the best-laid plans sometimes become impractical. For instance, when

Walt Disney Co. announced plans to launch a cruise line replete with familiar Disney characters and themes, managers also began aggressively developing and marketing packages linking three- and four-day cruises with visits to Disney World in Florida. The first sailing was scheduled for early 1998, and the company began to book reservations a year in advance. However, the shipyard constructing Disney's first ship (the *Disney Magic*) notified the company in October 1997 that it was behind schedule and that the ship would be delivered several weeks late. When similar problems befall other cruise lines, they can offer to rebook passengers on alternative itineraries. But because Disney had no other ship, it had no choice but to refund the money it had collected as prebooking deposits for its first 15 cruises.

The 20 000 displaced customers were offered substantial discounts if they rebooked on a later cruise. Many of them, however, could not rearrange their schedules and requested full refunds. Moreover, quite a few blamed Disney, and a few expressed outrage at what they perceived to be poor planning by the entertainment giant. Fortunately, *Disney Magic* was eventually launched and has now become both very popular and very profitable.[7]

Because managers know that such things can happen, they often develop alternative plans in case things go awry. Two common methods of dealing with the unknown and unforeseen are *contingency planning* and *crisis management*.

Contingency Planning

contingency planning Identifying aspects of a business or its environment that might entail changes in strategy.

Contingency planning takes into account the need to find solutions for specific aspects of a problem. By its very nature, a contingency plan is a hedge against changes that might occur. **Contingency planning**, then, is planning for change: It attempts to identify in advance important aspects of a business or its market that might change. It also identifies the ways in which a company will respond to changes. Today, many companies use computer programs for contingency planning.

Suppose, for example, that a company develops a plan to create a new business. It expects sales to increase at an annual rate of 10 percent for the next five years and develops a marketing strategy for maintaining that level. But suppose that sales have increased by only 5 percent by the end of the first year. Does the company abandon the business, invest more in advertising, or wait to see what happens in the second year? Any of these alter-

Commercial airlines have contingency plans to deal with problems like major snowstorms. These contingency plans involve making sure that planes are not stranded at airports that are experiencing snow delays.

natives is possible. However, things will go more smoothly if managers have decided in advance what to do in the event of lower sales. Contingency planning can help them do exactly that.

Disney learned from its mistake with its first ship, and when the second ship (the *Disney Wonder*) was launched a year later, managers did several things differently. First, they allowed for an extra two weeks between when the ship was supposed to be ready for sailing and its first scheduled cruise. They also held open a few cabins on *Disney Magic* as a backup for any especially disgruntled customers who might need to be accommodated due to unexpected delays launching *Disney Wonder*.

Crisis Management

Crisis management involves an organization's methods for dealing with emergencies that require an immediate response. The terrorist attack on the World Trade Center on September 11, 2001, was an extreme example of the need for crisis management. In the attack, all business firms in the World Trade Center lost the place where they conducted business, and some firms also lost hundreds of their employees.

crisis management An organization's methods for dealing with emergencies.

When Italian food giant Parmalat Finanziaria S.p.A. couldn't account for $11.7 billion in funds, its Canadian division, headed by CEO Marc Caira, faced a major crisis. Caira responded by auditing the Canadian operation's accounting practices to make sure his division wasn't part of the problem. After he had determined it wasn't, he then took a variety of actions to reassure customers, employees, and investors that everything was fine in the Canadian division. He did this by continuously communicating with the company's key constituents. Caira's actions worked. The year after the Parmalat scandal broke in Italy, the Canadian division recorded its highest sales and profits ever.[8]

McDonald's faced a different kind of crisis—slowly declining sales. Top management decided on some major strategy changes, including a de-emphasis on growth and more emphasis on healthy food offerings, improved service, and more attention to customer needs. The change was successful. The company now serves 2 million more customers each day than it did in 2003, and its stock price is up 148 percent since 2003.[9]

To prepare for emergencies, many organizations develop crisis plans. In recent years, a new technology called *disruption management* (DM) has emerged. It stresses internal self-reliance in planning for and preparing response to disruptions in an organization's external environment. Consider a shutdown caused by a snowstorm at Toronto's Pearson International Airport. An airline's least costly solution would be to simply cancel all incoming flights immediately. This approach cuts the airline's operating costs, but it is a terrible option for passengers who can't get where they're going. A DM approach would consider alternatives such as rescheduling flights into neighbouring airports and providing ground transportation into Toronto. A DM model would quickly simulate the costs and benefits of these and other options to help managers make an effective decision.

Describe the four activities that constitute the *management process*. 2

THE MANAGEMENT PROCESS

Management is the process of planning, organizing, leading, and controlling an enterprise's financial, physical, human, and information resources to achieve the organization's goals of supplying various products and services. Thus, the CEO of Walt Disney Productions is a manager because he regularly carries out these four functions as films are being made. Actors

management The process of planning, organizing, leading, and controlling a business's financial, physical, human, and information resources in order to achieve its goals.

such as Julia Roberts or Tom Cruise, while they may be the stars of the movies, are not managers because they don't carry out the four functions of management. The Business Accountability box explains the dynamic nature of managerial jobs.

The planning, organizing, leading, and controlling aspects of a manager's job are interrelated. While these activities generally follow one another in a logical sequence, sometimes they are performed simultaneously or in a different sequence altogether. In fact, a manager is likely to be engaged in all these activities during the course of a business day.

BUSINESS ACCOUNTABILITY

What Do Managers Actually Do?

Henry Mintzberg of McGill University conducted a detailed study of the work of five chief executive officers and found the following:

1. Managers work at an unrelenting pace.
2. Managerial activities are characterized by brevity, variety, and fragmentation.
3. Managers have a preference for "live" action, and emphasize work activities that are current, specific, and well-defined.
4. Managers are attracted to the verbal media.

Mintzberg believes that a manager's job can be described as 10 roles (in three categories) that must be performed. The manager's formal authority and status give rise to three *interpersonal roles*: (1) *figurehead* (duties of a ceremonial nature, such as attending a subordinate's wedding); (2) *leader* (being responsible for the work of the unit); and (3) *liaison* (making contact outside the vertical chain of command). These interpersonal roles give rise to three *informational roles*: (1) *monitor* (scanning the environment for relevant information); (2) *disseminator* (passing information to subordinates); and (3) *spokesperson* (sending information to people outside the unit).

The interpersonal and informational roles allow the manager to carry out four *decision-making roles*: (1) *entrepreneur* (improving the performance of the unit); (2) *disturbance handler* (responding to high-pressure disturbances, such as a strike at a supplier); (3) *resource allocator* (deciding who will get what in the unit); and (4) *negotiator* (working out agreements on a wide variety of issues, such as the amount of authority an individual will be given).

Managers in a 2005 study conducted by Toronto's Pace Productivity felt that they should have spent about half their time on activities such as managing staff, providing direction, and coaching, but that they actually were able to spend only 18 percent of their time on "people management." Managers also thought that they should have spent about 6 percent of their time on administrative tasks, but they actually spent 25 percent of their time on those activities. The time managers thought they should spend on planning was about the same as what they actually spent. Consistent with Mintzberg's original findings, the Pace data also showed that managers' lives are very hectic, and their focus shifts rapidly from activity to activity. For example, for the average manager, 43 different activities lasted an average of just 16 minutes each.

Insight into what managers actually do can also be gained by looking at the so-called *functions* of management (planning, organizing, leading, and controlling). Consider the work of Marina Pyo, who is publisher, School Division, at Pearson Education Canada, a publisher of textbooks for elementary and secondary schools, colleges, and universities. Her job is to manage the activities that are necessary to develop resources in math and science for the Canadian elementary school market. Her work is at times intense, fragmented, rewarding, frustrating, and fast-paced. In short, she is a typical manager.

Pyo carries out the *planning* function when she drafts a plan for a new book. She is *organizing* when she develops a new organization chart to facilitate goal achievement. She is *leading* when she meets with a subordinate to discuss that person's career plans. And she is *controlling* when she checks sales prospects for a book before ordering a reprint.

Some of Pyo's activities do not easily fit into this "functions of management" model. For example, it is not clear which function she is performing when she negotiates the size of a reprint run with the manager of the sales division, or when she talks briefly with the president of her division about recent events in Pyo's area of responsibility.

Planning

Determining what the organization needs to do and how best to get it done requires planning. **Planning** has three main components. As we have seen, it begins when managers determine the firm's goals. Next, they develop a comprehensive strategy for achieving those goals. After a strategy is developed, they design tactical and operational plans for implementing the strategy.

planning That portion of a manager's job concerned with determining what the business needs to do and the best way to achieve it.

The planning process has five basic steps. In *step 1*, goals are established for the organization. A commercial airline, for example, may set a goal to fill every seat on every flight. In *step 2*, managers identify whether a gap exists between the company's desire and actual position. For example, a year-end financial analysis will reveal whether a company met its profitability objectives. In *step 3*, managers develop plans to achieve the desired objectives. Objectives indicate *what* results are desired, while plans indicate *how* these objectives are to be achieved. In *step 4*, the plans that have been decided upon are implemented. This is the point in the planning process where thinking is converted into action. In *step 5*, the effectiveness of the plan is assessed. This requires comparing actual results with planned performance.

When Yahoo! was created, for example, the company's top managers set a strategic goal of becoming a top firm in the then-emerging market for internet search engines. But then came the hard part—figuring out how to do it. They started by assessing the ways in which people actually use the web. They also studied ways in which they would probably use it in the future, analyzed the successful strategies of other growing firms, and assessed the ways in which big companies were using the internet. They concluded that people wanted an easy-to-understand web interface. They also wanted to be able to satisfy a wide array of needs, preferences, and priorities by going to as few sites as possible to find what they were looking for.

One key component of Yahoo!'s strategy, therefore, was to foster partnerships and relationships with other companies so that potential web surfers could draw upon several sources through a single portal—which would, of course, be Yahoo! Thus, the goal of partnering emerged as one set of tactical plans for moving forward. Yahoo! managers then began fashioning alliances with such diverse partners as Reuters, Standard & Poor's, and the Associated Press (for news coverage), RE/MAX (for real estate information), and a wide array of information providers specializing in sports, weather, entertainment, shopping, travel, and so forth.

Organizing

The portion of a manager's job that is concerned with mobilizing the necessary resources to complete a particular task is known as **organizing** (we examine this topic further in Chapter 7). The importance of the organizing function of management can be seen by considering what happened at Hewlett-Packard, which lost some of its lustre a few years ago. One of the major reasons for its slide could be traced back to what had once been a major strength. Specifically, HP had long prided itself on being little more than a corporate confederation of individual businesses. Sometimes these businesses even ended up competing against themselves. This approach had been beneficial for much of the firm's history: It was easier for each business to make its own decisions quickly and efficiently, and the competition kept each unit on its toes. By 1998, however, problems started to become apparent, and no one could quite figure out what was going on.

organizing That portion of a manager's job concerned with mobilizing the necessary resources to complete a particular task.

Enter Ann Livermore, then head of the firm's software and services business. Livermore realized that it was the structure that had served so well in the past that was now holding the firm back. Specifically, to regain its competitive edge HP needed an integrated, organization-wide internet strategy. Unfortunately, the company's highly decentralized organization made that impossible. Livermore led the charge to create one organization to drive a single internet plan. "I felt we could be the most powerful company in the industry," she says, "if we could get our hardware, software, and services aligned." In fact, a reorganized HP has bounced back and is quickly regaining its competitive strength.[10]

Leading

leading That portion of a manager's job concerned with guiding and motivating employees to meet the firm's objectives.

The activities involving interactions between managers and their subordinates to meet the firm's objectives are known as **leading** (or directing). By definition, managers have the power to give orders and demand results. Leading, however, goes beyond merely giving orders. Leaders attempt to guide and motivate employees to work in the best interests of the organization. At discount airline WestJet, for example, CEO Clive Beddoe has been very successful in motivating employees to go above and beyond normal work practices to ensure the company's (and their own) financial success. We discuss leadership more fully in Chapter 10.

Controlling

controlling That portion of a manager's job concerned with monitoring the firm's performance and, if necessary, acting to bring it in line with the firm's goals.

Controlling is the process of monitoring a firm's performance to make sure that the firm is meeting its goals.

Figure 6.3 illustrates the control process that begins when management establishes standards, often for financial performance. If, for example, a company wants to increase sales by 20 percent over the next 10 years, then an appropriate standard might be an increase of about 2 percent a year. Managers then measure actual performance against standards. If the two amounts agree, the organization continues along its present course. If they vary significantly, however, one or the other needs adjustment. If sales have increased 2.1 percent by the end of the first year, things are probably fine. If sales have dropped 1 percent, some revision in plans may be needed. Perhaps the original goal should be lowered or more money should be spent on advertising.

Japanese organizations don't usually like radical restructuring, but when Senichi Hoshino took over the hapless Hanshin Tigers, he axed 24 of the team's 70 players and replaced them with free agents. He required everyone on the roster to compete for a position, tracked performance daily, and made individual coaches directly responsible for seeing that players executed certain skills. Soon after that, the Tigers won the pennant—a particularly important achievement, because superstition says that when the Tigers win, Japan will soon enjoy a period of prolonged prosperity.

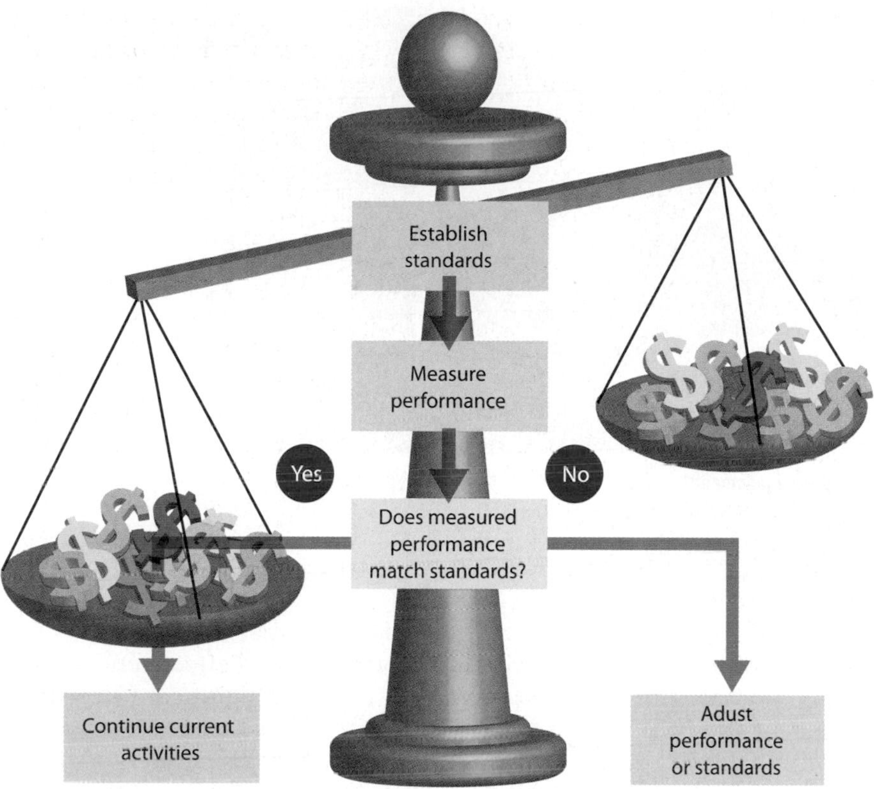

Figure 6.3 The control process.

Control can also show where performance is running better than expected and, thus, can serve as a basis for providing rewards or reducing costs. For example, when Ford introduced its Explorer SportsTrac (an SUV with a pickup bed), initial sales were so strong that the firm was able to delay a major advertising campaign for three months because it was selling all the vehicles it could make anyway.

TYPES OF MANAGERS

Identify *types of managers* by level and area. 3

Although all managers plan, organize, lead, and control, not all managers have the same degree of responsibility for each activity. Moreover, managers differ in the specific application of these activities. Thus we can divide managers by their *level* of responsibility or by their *area* of responsibility.

Levels of Management

The three basic levels of management are top, middle, and first-line management. In most firms there are more middle managers than top managers and more first-line managers than middle managers. Moreover, as the categories imply, the power of managers and the complexity of their duties increase as we move up the pyramid.

Top Managers

top managers Those managers responsible for a firm's overall performance and effectiveness and for developing long-range plans for the company.

The small number of executives who guide the fortunes of most companies are **top managers**. Common titles for top managers include president, vice-president, treasurer, chief executive officer (CEO), and chief financial

First-line management

Middle management

Top management

Organizations have three basic levels of management.

officer (CFO). Top managers are responsible to the board of directors and shareholders of the firm for its overall performance and effectiveness. They set general policies, formulate strategies, oversee all significant decisions, and represent the company in its dealings with other businesses and government.[11] Each year, KPMG/Ipsos-Reid surveys business leaders and asks them to pick the most respected CEO in Canada. Gwyn Morgan, retired CEO of EnCana, won the award for 2005.[12]

Middle Managers

middle managers Those managers responsible for implementing the decisions made by top managers.

Although below the ranks of the top executives, **middle managers** occupy positions of considerable autonomy and importance. Titles such as plant manager, operations manager, and division manager are typical of middle-management jobs. In general, middle managers are responsible for implementing the strategies, policies, and decisions of the top managers. For example, if top management decides to bring out a new product in 12 months or to cut costs by 5 percent, middle management will have to decide to increase the pace of new product development or to reduce the plant's workforce. With companies increasingly seeking ways to cut costs, the job of middle manager has lately become precarious in many large companies.

First-Line Managers

first-line managers Those managers responsible for supervising the work of employees.

Those who hold titles such as supervisor, office manager, and group leader are **first-line managers**. Although they spend most of their time working with and supervising the employees who report to them, first-line managers' activities are not limited to that arena. At a building site, for example, the project manager not only ensures that workers are carrying out construction as specified by the architect, but also interacts extensively with materials suppliers, community officials, and middle and top managers at the home office. The manager of a Canadian Tire store and the flight-services manager for a specific Air Canada flight would also be considered first-line managers.

Areas of Management

Within any large company, the top, middle, and first-line managers work in a variety of areas, including marketing, finance, operations, human resources, and information.

Marketing Managers

Marketing includes the development, pricing, promotion, and distribution of a product or service. *Marketing managers* are responsible for getting products and services to buyers. Marketing is especially important for firms dealing in consumer products, such as Procter & Gamble, Coca-Cola, and Roots. These firms often have large numbers of marketing managers at various levels. For example, a large firm will probably have a vice-president for marketing (top manager), regional marketing managers (middle managers), and several district sales managers (first-line managers). A marketing person often rises to the top of this type of corporation. In contrast, firms that produce industrial products such as machinery and janitorial supplies tend to put less emphasis on marketing and to have fewer marketing managers. However, these firms do not ignore marketing altogether. In recent years, law firms and universities have also come to recognize the value and importance of marketing. We look at marketing in detail in Chapters 15 to 17.

Financial Managers

Management of a firm's finances, including its investments and accounting functions, is extremely important to its survival. Nearly every company has *financial managers* to plan and oversee its financial resources. Levels of financial management may include a vice-president for finance (top), division controller (middle), and accounting supervisor (first-line). For large financial institutions, effective financial management is the company's reason for being. No organization, however, can afford to ignore the need for management in this area. Chapters 18 to 20 cover financial management in detail.

Operations Managers

A firm's operations are the systems by which it creates goods and services. *Operations managers* are responsible for production control, inventory control, and quality control, among other duties. Manufacturing companies like Steelcase, Bristol Aerospace, and Sony need operations managers at many levels. Such firms typically have a vice-president for operations (top), plant managers (middle), and foremen or supervisors (first-line). In recent years, sound operations management practices have also become increasingly important to service organizations, hospitals, universities, and the government. Operations management is the subject of Chapters 11 and 12.

Human Resource Managers

Every enterprise uses human resources. Most companies have *human resource managers* to provide assistance to other managers when they are hiring employees, training them, evaluating their performances, and determining their compensation level. In many companies, human resource managers are involved in negotiations with labour unions. Large firms may have several human resource departments, each dealing with specialized activities. Imperial Oil, for example, has separate departments to deal with recruiting and hiring, wage and salary levels, and labour relations. Smaller firms may have a single department, while very small organizations may have a single person responsible for all human resource activities. Chapters 8 to 10 address issues involved in human resource management.

Information Managers

A new type of managerial position appearing in many organizations is that of *information manager*. These managers are responsible for designing and implementing various systems to gather, process, and disseminate information. Dramatic increases in both the amount of information available to managers and the ability to manage it have led to the emergence of this important function. While relatively few in number now, the ranks of information managers are increasing at all levels. Federal Express, for example, has a chief information officer. Middle managers engaged in information management help design information systems for divisions or plants. Computer systems managers within smaller businesses or operations are first-line managers. Information management is discussed in Chapter 13.

Other Managers

Some firms have more specialized managers. Chemical companies such as CIL have research and development managers, for example, whereas companies such as Petro-Canada and Apple have public relations managers. The range of possibilities is endless; the areas of management are limited only by the needs and imagination of the firm.

BASIC MANAGEMENT SKILLS

4 Describe the five basic *management skills.*

While the range of managerial positions is almost limitless, the success that people enjoy in those positions is often limited by their skills and abilities. Effective managers must possess several skills: *technical, human relations, conceptual, decision-making,* and *time management skills*.

Technical Skills

technical skills Skills associated with performing specialized tasks within a firm.

human relations skills Skills in understanding and getting along with people.

Skills associated with performing specialized tasks within a company are called **technical skills**. A secretary's ability to type, an animator's ability to draw a cartoon, and an accountant's ability to audit a company's records are all technical skills. People develop their technical skills through education and experience. The secretary, for example, probably took a keyboarding course and has had many hours of practice both on and off the job. The animator may have had training in an art school and probably learned a great deal from experienced animators on the job. The accountant earned a university degree and, possibly, professional certification.

As Figure 6.4 shows, technical skills are especially important for first-line managers. Most first-line managers spend considerable time helping employees solve work-related problems, monitoring their performance, and training them in more efficient work procedures. Such managers need a basic understanding of the jobs they supervise.

As a manager moves up the corporate ladder, however, technical skills become less and less important. Top managers, for example, often need only a cursory familiarity with the mechanics of basic tasks performed within the company. Michael Eisner, for example, freely admits that he can't draw Mickey Mouse or build a ride for Disney World.

Meg Whitman, the CEO of eBay, understands the importance of human relations in a business whose model is helping sellers find buyers and buyers find sellers. At conventions where 10 000 of eBay's 28 million customers gather to communicate without the medium of cyberspace, Whitman autographs (collectible) eBay trading cards of herself and depends on ordinary users to tell her what works and what doesn't work at the online auction company.

Human Relations Skills

Effective managers must have good **human relations skills**—the skills that enable them to understand and get along with other people. A manager with poor human relations skills will have trouble getting along with subordinates, which will, in turn, cause valuable employees to quit or transfer, and contribute to poor morale. When Development Dimensions International (DDI) asked 944 human resource professionals to state the reasons why newly promoted managers fail, 53 percent said it was because of poor people skills.[13]

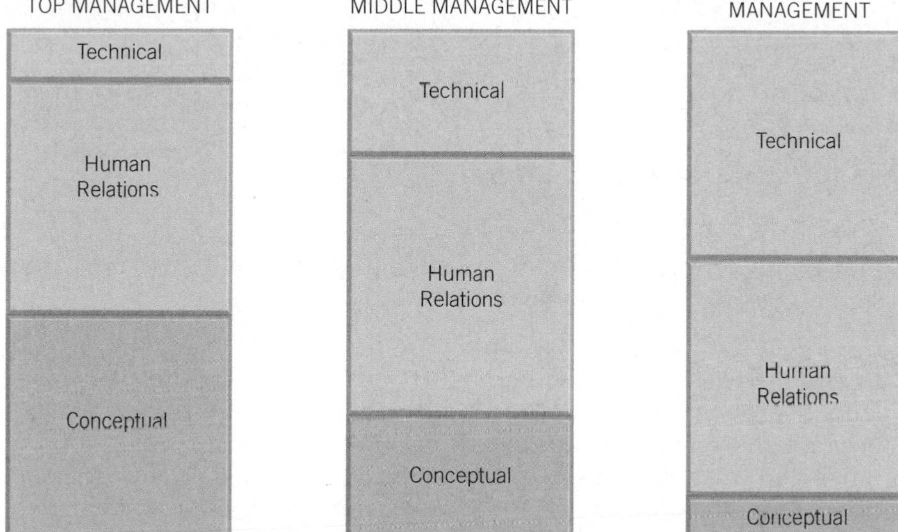

Figure 6.4 Different levels in an organization require different combinations of managerial skills.

While human relations skills are important at all levels, they are probably most important for middle managers, who must often act as bridges between top managers, first-line managers, and managers from other areas of the organization. Managers should possess good communication skills. Many managers have found that being able to understand others—and to get them to understand—can go far toward maintaining good relations in an organization.

Conceptual Skills

Conceptual skills refer to a person's ability to think in the abstract, to diagnose and analyze different situations, and to see beyond the present situation. Conceptual skills help managers recognize new market opportunities (and threats). They can also help managers analyze the probable outcomes of their decisions. The need for conceptual skills differs at various management levels: Top managers depend most on conceptual skills, first-line managers least. Although the purposes and everyday needs of various jobs differ, conceptual skills are needed in almost any job-related activity.

conceptual skills Abilities to think in the abstract, diagnose and analyze different situations, and see beyond the present situation.

In many ways, conceptual skills may be the most important ingredient in the success of executives in ecommerce businesses. For example, the ability to foresee how a particular business application will be affected by or can be translated to the internet is clearly conceptual in nature.

Decision-Making Skills

Decision-making skills include the ability to define problems and select the best course of action. Figure 6.5 illustrates the basic steps in decision making.

decision-making skills Skills in defining problems and selecting the best courses of action.

1. *Define the problem, gather facts, and identify alternative solutions.* Vivendi Universal is a large French entertainment and media company. The firm's top managers recently decided that they needed a stronger presence in the United States if they were to continue their quest to become a global media powerhouse. Thus, they defined their problem as how to best enter the U.S. media market. They subsequently determined

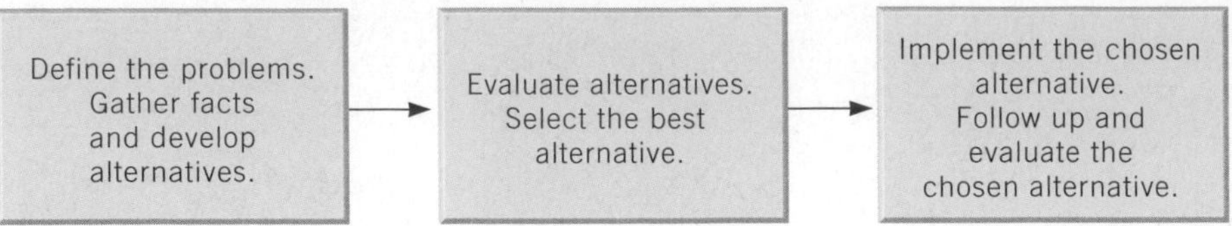

Figure 6.5 The decision-making process.

that there were two alternatives: starting a new media business from scratch or buying an existing one.

2. *Evaluate each alternative and select the best one.* Managers at Vivendi realized that it would take many years and a huge cash investment to launch a new media enterprise from scratch. They also recognized that because there was ongoing consolidation in the U.S. media industry, buying an existing firm might be relatively easy. Further analysis identified Houghton Mifflin, one of the last remaining independent publishers, as an attractive acquisition target.

3. *Implement the chosen alternative, periodically following up and evaluating the effectiveness of that choice.* Vivendi executives quietly began negotiating with senior managers at Houghton Mifflin in mid-2001. Within a matter of weeks, the two firms had reached an agreement: Vivendi Universal would acquire 100 percent of Houghton Mifflin, thus providing the French company with exactly what it had been seeking—a viable entry into U.S. markets.[14] Unfortunately, Vivendi subsequently fell on hard times, and on August 14, 2002, it announced that it would attempt to sell Houghton Mifflin to raise much-needed cash.

As this example demonstrates, decision making can be a complicated activity for managers. The Exercising Your Ethics box at the end of the chapter presents another decision-making opportunity for a manager.

Time Management Skills

time management skills Skills associated with the productive use of time.

Time management skills refer to the productive use that managers make of their time. In 2005, for example, Talisman Energy CEO James Buckee was paid a total of $23.3 million (including bonuses and options).[15] Assuming that he worked 50 hours a week and took two weeks vacation, Burton earned about $9200 per hour, or about $153 per minute. Any time that Buckee wastes represents a large cost to Talisman Energy and its stockholders.

To manage time effectively, managers must address four leading causes of wasted time:

- *Paperwork.* Some managers spend too much time deciding what to do with letters and reports. Most documents of this sort are routine and can be handled quickly. Managers must learn to recognize those documents that require more attention.

- *The telephone.* Experts estimate that managers are interrupted by the telephone every five minutes. To manage time more effectively, they suggest having a secretary screen all calls and setting aside a certain block of time each day to return the important ones.

- *Meetings.* Many managers spend as much as four hours per day in meetings. To help keep this time productive, the person handling the meeting should specify a clear agenda, start on time, keep everyone focussed on the agenda, and end on time.

- *Email.* More and more managers are also relying heavily on email and other forms of electronic communication. Like memos and telephone calls, many email messages are not particularly important; some are even trivial. As a result, time is wasted when managers have to sort through a variety of electronic folders, in-baskets, and archives. As the average number of electronic messages grows, the potential time wasted also increases.

Management Skills for the Twenty-First Century

Managers face some major challenges in the twenty-first century. We will touch on two of the most significant challenges: *global management* and *technology*.

Global Management Skills

Tomorrow's managers must equip themselves with the special tools, techniques, and skills necessary to compete in a global environment. They will need to understand foreign markets, cultural differences, and the motives and practices of foreign rivals.

On a more practical level, businesses will need managers who are capable of understanding international operations. In the past, most Canadian businesses hired local managers to run their operations in the various countries in which they operated. More recently, however, the trend has been to transfer Canadian managers to foreign locations. This practice helps firms better transfer their corporate cultures to foreign operations. In addition, foreign assignments help managers become better prepared for international competition as they advance within the organization.[16]

MTV needed someone to run its operation in China who understood both conservative Chinese television regulators and China's young urban elite. The company chose Li Yifei, a former UN intern, public relations consultant, and tai chi champion. Li has already brought the Chinese equivalent of the MTV awards to state-owned television, and the show had 150 million viewers.

Management and Technology Skills

Another significant issue facing tomorrow's manager is technology, especially as it relates to communication. Managers have always had to deal with information. In today's world, however, the amount of information has reached staggering proportions. New forms of technology have added to a manager's ability to process information while simultaneously making it even more important to organize and interpret an ever-increasing amount of input.

Technology has also begun to change the way the interaction of managers shapes corporate structures. Computer networking, for example, exists because it is no longer too expensive to put a computer on virtually every desk in the company. In turn, this elaborate network controls the flow of the firm's lifeblood—information. Information no longer flows strictly up and down through hierarchies. It now flows to everyone at once. As a result, decisions are made more quickly—and more people are directly involved. With email, teleconferencing, and other forms of communication, neither time nor distance—nor such corporate "boundaries" as departments and divisions—can prevent people from working more closely together. More than ever, bureaucracies are breaking down, while planning, decision making, and other activities are beginning to benefit from group building and teamwork.

MANAGEMENT AND THE CORPORATE CULTURE

5 Describe the development and explain the importance of *corporate culture.*

corporate culture The shared experiences, stories, beliefs, norms, and ethical stance that characterize a firm.

Every organization—big or small, more successful or less successful—has an unmistakable "feel" to it. Just as every individual has a unique personality, every company has a unique identity, called **corporate culture**—the shared experiences, stories, beliefs, norms, and ethical stance that characterize an organization. This culture helps define the work and business climate that exists in an organization.

A 2005 survey of executives at 107 Canadian companies revealed the following views among managers:

- The three companies with the most admired corporate cultures were WestJet Airlines, Tim Hortons, and Royal Bank of Canada.
- Over 80 percent of the executives surveyed said that corporate culture had an impact on financial performance.
- Nearly two-thirds of those surveyed said their company did not monitor its corporate culture.
- Nearly three-quarters of those surveyed said their firm's corporate culture was not what they wanted it to be.[17]

A strong corporate culture directs employees' efforts and helps everyone work toward the same goals. Some cultures, for example, stress financial success to the extreme, while others focus more on quality of life. A strong corporate culture also helps newcomers learn accepted behaviours. If financial success is the key to a culture, newcomers quickly learn that they are expected to work long, hard hours and that the "winner" is the one who brings in the most revenue. But if quality of life is more fundamental, newcomers learn that it's more acceptable to spend less time at work and that balancing work and non-work is encouraged. The survey mentioned above found that only 36 percent of executives felt that the corporate culture of their company was strong.

The following examples illustrate how culture differs across firms:

- Magna International, a large Canadian producer of auto parts, is a firm with a strong culture. Its founder, Frank Stronach, is well known for his views about employees, working conditions, daycare centres, unions, the free enterprise system, and profit distribution.[18]
- Four Seasons Hotels and Resorts has a different, but equally strong, culture. Managers are judged by deeds, not words, and act as role models; employees take their cues from the managers.[19]
- At Toyota's Cambridge, Ontario, plant the corporate culture stresses values, principles, and trust. The culture is one of continuous improvement.[20]
- At WestJet Airlines the corporate culture emphasizes profit maximization. Most of the employees own shares in the company, and all of them get to keep some of the profits. This is a powerful incentive for them to work productively.[21]

Forces Shaping Corporate Culture

A number of forces shape corporate cultures. First, the values held by top management help set the tone of the organization and influence its business goals and strategies. Frank Stronach (Magna International), Timothy

Eaton (Eaton's), Max Ward (Wardair), Larry Clark (Spar Aerospace), and Jean de Grandpre (BCE) are just a few of the leaders who have had a profound impact on the culture of their respective organizations. Even a large, longtime firm like Ford still bears the traces of founder Henry Ford.

Mainframe Entertainment of Vancouver has one of the lowest turnover rates in the animation business. Its culture emphasizes giving young artists and designers opportunities to acquire new skills and develop leadership potential—opportunities not available in the bigger Los Angeles studios.

The firm's history also helps shape its culture. The championship banners that line the arena where the Montreal Canadiens play signify that they are winners. Maintaining a corporate culture draws on many dimensions of business life. Shared experiences resulting from norms sustain culture. Thus, working long hours on a special project becomes a shared experience for many employees. They remember it, talk about it among themselves, and wear it as a badge of their contribution to the company.

Stories and legends are also important. Walt Disney has been dead for many years now, but his spirit lives on in the businesses he left behind. Quotations from Disney are affixed to portraits of him throughout the company's studios. And Disney's emphasis on family is still visible in corporate benefits such as paying for spouses to accompany employees on extended business trips. In fact, employees are often called "the Disney family."

Finally, strong behavioural norms help define and sustain corporate cultures. For example, a strong part of the culture at Hewlett-Packard Canada is that everyone wears a name tag and that everyone is called by his or her first name. And at Sony Corporation every employee wears a corporate smock.

Communicating the Culture and Managing Change

Corporate culture influences management philosophy, style, and behaviour. Managers, therefore, must carefully consider the kind of culture they want for their organization, then work to nourish that culture by communicating with everyone who works there. Wal-Mart, for example, is acutely conscious of the need to spread the message of its culture as it opens new stores in new areas. One of the company's methods is to regularly assign veteran managers to lead employees in new territories. At Continental Airlines, Gordon Bethune delivers weekly messages to all employees to update them on what's going on in the firm; the employees can either listen to Bethune's message on a closed-circuit broadcast or else call a toll-free telephone number and hear a recorded version at their own convenience.

Communicating the Culture

To use its culture to a firm's advantage, managers must accomplish several tasks, all of which hinge on effective communication. First, managers themselves must have a clear understanding of the culture. Second, they must transmit the culture to others in the organization. Communication is thus one aim in training and orienting newcomers. A clear and meaningful statement of the organization's mission is also a valuable communication tool. Finally, managers can maintain the culture by rewarding and promoting those who understand it and work toward maintaining it.

Managing Change

Organizations must sometimes change their cultures. Ontario Hydro, for example, had an "engineering" culture for many years. This meant that everything was planned and analyzed down to the last detail before any action was taken. But Ontario Hydro's culture has changed to a more consumer-oriented, risk-taking culture as it tries to cope with large debt and changes in its markets. The RCMP is also much different now than it was in the days when military tradition dominated the organization. It completed a "visioning process" that resulted in a new mission statement, a new set of core values, and a commitment to the communities in which it works.[22]

Until recently, CIBC has had an aggressive, deal-making culture that caused it to go head-to-head with large Wall Street companies in the United States. But after several major failures in the United States, CIBC's culture has become much more conservative. It is so conservative that it is alone among big Canadian banks in not having a foreign growth strategy. Outgoing president John Hunkin said that he was pleased that people now think that CIBC is the most conservative bank in Canada.[23]

When cultural change is required, the process usually goes through three stages:

1. At the highest level, analysis of the company's environment highlights extensive change as the most effective response to its problems. Conflict and resistance typically characterize this period.
2. Top management begins to formulate a vision of a new company. Whatever that vision is, it must include renewed focus on the activities of competitors and the needs of customers.
3. The firm sets up new systems for appraising and compensating employees that enforce its new values. The purpose is to give the new culture solid shape from within the firm.

Sometimes this three-stage process is never completed. Consider what happened at Nortel Networks, which hired a new president and a new chief technology officer in 2005 in an attempt to resolve some of the company's problems. Both of these individuals had worked at Cisco Systems Inc., and it was thought that they would be a great addition to a troubled company like Nortel. But Cisco has a hard-driving sales culture, while Nortel's culture is much less intense. Within three months, both new managers resigned from Nortel. CEO Bill Owens said their departure was due to different management styles and a different vision for the future of the company. In short, there was a culture clash that caused the new hires to leave the company, and the culture they envisioned will not be implemented at Nortel.[24]

Summary of Learning Objectives

1. **Explain the importance of setting *goals* and formulating *strategies* as the starting points of effective management.** *Goals*—the performance targets of an organization—can be *long-term, intermediate,* and *short-term.* They provide direction for managers, they help managers decide how to allocate limited resources, they define the corporate culture, and they help managers assess performance. *Strategies*—the methods that a company uses to meet its stated goals—involve three major activities: setting strategic goals, analyzing the organization and its environment, and matching the organization and its environment. These strategies are translated into *strategic, tactical,* and *operational plans.* To deal with crises or major environmental changes, companies develop *contingency plans* and plans for *crisis management.*

2. **Describe the four activities that constitute the *management process*.** *Management* is the process of planning, organizing, leading, and controlling an organization's financial, physical, human, and information resources to achieve the organization's goals. *Planning* means determining what the company needs to do and how best to get it done. *Organizing* means determining how best to arrange a business's resources and the necessary jobs into an overall structure. *Leading* means guiding and motivating employees to meet the firm's objectives. *Controlling* means monitoring the firm's performance to ensure that it is meeting its goals.
3. **Identify *types of managers* by level and area.** Managers can be differentiated in two ways: by level and by area. By level, *top managers* set policies, formulate strategies, and approve decisions. *Middle managers* implement policies, strategies, and decisions. *First-line managers* usually work with and supervise employees. Management areas include marketing, financial, operations, human resources, and information. Managers at all levels may be found in every area of a company.
4. **Describe the five basic *management skills*.** Most managers agree that five basic management skills are necessary for success. *Technical skills* are associated with performing specialized tasks ranging from typing to auditing. *Human relations skills* are associated with understanding and getting along with other people. *Conceptual skills* are the abilities to think in the abstract, to diagnose and analyze different situations, and to see beyond present circumstances. *Decision-making skills* allow managers to define problems and to select the best course of action. *Time management skills* refer to managers' ability to make productive use of the time available to them.
5. **Describe the development and explain the importance of *corporate culture*.** *Corporate culture* is the shared experiences, stories, beliefs, norms, and ethical stance that characterize an organization. A strong, well-defined culture can help a business reach its goals and can influence management styles. Culture is determined by several factors, including top management, the organization's history, stories and legends, and behavioural norms. If carefully communicated and flexible enough to accommodate change, corporate culture can be managed for the betterment of the organization.

KEY TERMS

business-level (competitive) strategy, 181
concentration strategy, 182
conceptual skills, 193
contingency planning, 184
controlling, 188
corporate culture, 196
corporate-level strategy, 181
cost leadership, 183
crisis management, 185
decision-making skills, 193
differentiation strategy, 183
diversification, 182
environmental analysis, 179
first-line managers, 190
focus strategy, 183
functional strategies, 181
geographic expansion, 182
goals, 176
horizontal integration, 182
human relations skills, 192
intermediate goals, 178
investment reduction, 183
leading, 188
long-term goals, 178
management, 185
market penetration, 182
middle managers, 190
mission statement, 177
operational plans, 181
organizational analysis, 179
organizing, 187
planning, 187
product development, 182
short-term goals, 178
strategic goals, 178
strategic plans, 181
strategy formulation, 178
SWOT analysis, 179
tactical plans, 181
technical skills, 192
time management skills, 194
top managers, 189
vertical integration, 182

QUESTIONS FOR ANALYSIS

1. How are the five basic management *skills* related to the four *functions* of management?
2. What is the relationship between Mintzberg's *roles* of management and the more traditional *functions* of management? Use examples to clarify your answer.
3. Select any group of which you are a member (your company, your family, or a club or organization, for example). Explain how planning, organizing, directing, and controlling are practised in that group.
4. Identify managers by level and area at your school, college, or university.
5. In what kind of company would the technical skills of top managers be more important than human relations or conceptual skills? Are there organizations in which conceptual skills are not important?
6. What differences might you expect to find in the corporate cultures of a 100-year-old manufacturing firm based in Winnipeg and a 2-year-old ecommerce firm in Ottawa?
7. Perform a SWOT analysis for the school you are currently attending.
8. Consider the various corporate-level strategies discussed in the text (concentration, growth, integration, diversification, investment reduction). What is the relationship between these various strategies? Are they mutually exclusive? Are they complementary? Explain.

APPLICATION EXERCISES

1. Interview a manager at any level of a local company. Identify that manager's job according to level and area. Show how planning, organizing, directing, and controlling are part of this person's job. Inquire about the manager's education and work experience. Which management skills are most important for this manager's job?
2. Compare and contrast the corporate cultures of two companies that do business in most communities. Be sure to choose two companies in the same industry—for example, a Bay department store and a Wal-Mart discount store.

BUILDING YOUR BUSINESS SKILLS

Speaking with Power

Goal

To encourage students to appreciate effective speaking as a critical human relations skill.

Background

A manager's ability to understand and get along with supervisors, peers, and subordinates is a critical human relations skill. At the heart of this skill, says Harvard University professor of education Sarah McGinty, is the ability to speak with power and control. McGinty defines "powerful speech" in terms of the following characteristics:

- the ability to speak at length and in complete sentences
- the ability to set a conversational agenda
- the ability to deter interruption
- the ability to argue openly and to express strong opinions about ideas, not people
- the ability to make statements that offer solutions rather than pose questions
- the ability to express humour

Taken together, says McGinty, "all this creates a sense of confidence in listeners."

Assignment

Step 1

Working alone, compare your own personal speaking style with McGinty's description of powerful speech by taping yourself as you speak during a meeting with classmates or during a phone conversation. (Tape both sides of the conversation only if the person to whom you are speaking gives permission.) Listen for the following problems:

- unfinished sentences
- an absence of solutions
- too many disclaimers ("I'm not sure I have enough information to say this, but...")
- the habit of seeking support from others instead of making definitive statements of personal conviction (saying, "As Emily stated in her report, I recommend consolidating the medical and fitness

▸▸▸

functions," instead of "I recommend consolidating the medical and fitness functions")

- language fillers (saying, "you know," "like," and "um" when you are unsure of your facts or uneasy about expressing your opinion)

Step 2

Join with three or four other classmates to evaluate each other's speaking styles. Finally,

- Have a 10-minute group discussion on the importance of human relations skills in business.
- Listen to other group members, and take notes on the "power" content of what you hear.
- Offer constructive criticism by focussing on what speakers say rather than on personal characteristics (say, "Bob, you sympathized with Paul's position, but I still don't know what you think," instead of, "Bob, you sounded like a weakling").

Follow-Up Questions

1. How do you think the power content of speech affects a manager's ability to communicate? Evaluate some of the ways in which effects may differ among supervisors, peers, and subordinates.
2. How do you evaluate yourself and group members in terms of powerful and powerless speech? List the strengths and weaknesses of the group.
3. Do you agree or disagree with McGinty that business success depends on gaining insight into your own language habits? Explain your answer.
4. In our age of computers and email, why do you think personal presentation continues to be important in management?
5. McGinty believes that power language differs from company to company and that it is linked to the corporate culture. Do you agree, or do you believe that people express themselves in similar ways no matter where they are?

EXERCISING YOUR ETHICS

Making Room for Alternative Actions

The Situation

Assume that you are the manager of a large hotel adjacent to a medical centre in a major city. The medical centre itself consists of 10 major hospitals and research institutes. Two of the hospitals are affiliated with large universities and two with churches. Three are public and three are private. The centre has an international reputation and attracts patients from around the world.

Because so many patients and their families travel great distances to visit the medical centre and often stay for days or weeks, there are also eight large hotels in the area, including three new ones. The hotel that you manage is one of the older ones and, frankly, is looking a bit shabby. Corporate headquarters has told you that the hotel will either be closed or undergo a major remodelling in about two years. In the meantime, you are expected to wring every last cent of profit out of the hotel.

The Dilemma

A storm has just struck the area and brought with it major flooding and power outages. Three of the medical centre hospitals have been shut down indefinitely, as have six of the nearby hotels. Fortunately, your hotel sustained only minor damage and is fully functional. You have just called a meeting with your two assistant managers to discuss what actions, if any, you should take.

One assistant manager has urged you to cut room rates immediately for humanitarian reasons. This manager also wants you to open the hotel kitchens 24 hours a day to prepare free food for rescue workers and meals to donate to the hospitals, whose own food service operations have been disrupted. The other assistant manager, meanwhile, has urged just the opposite approach: raise room rates by at least 20 percent and sell food to rescue workers and hospitals at a premium price. Of course, you can also choose to follow the advice of neither and continue doing business as usual.

Questions for Discussion

1. What are the ethical issues in this situation?
2. What do you think most managers would do in this situation?
3. What would you do?
4. Once you have made your decision, how would you implement it, given the short time frame that is available?
5. How would you measure the success of your decision?

CONCLUDING CASE 6-1

The Business of Bagging Customers

Fickle customers and rapid changes make planning difficult in the high-fashion end of the apparel industry. Most fashion designers—Ralph Lauren, Donna Karan, Prada, Gucci, Fendi—have adopted a design-driven business model, in which the designer dictates style to the customers. Coach, however, has taken a different approach. The company asks the customers what they want and then provides it. Coach's customer focus has created a competitive advantage for the firm, which annually sells $865 of merchandise for every square foot of store space, compared to an industry average of $200–$300.

Coach started out in 1941 making virtually indestructible, high-quality handbags. In the 1970s it was bought by Sara Lee Corp., a big company pursuing a strategy of diversification. However, Coach's products were not stylish and sales languished. Moreover, because it was just one of literally dozens of businesses owned by Sara Lee at the time, the company suffered from the lack of focussed management attention. CEO Lew Frankfort knew the company was failing and said, "We were about to hit a wall." Frankfort also knew that the company's success depended on finding the right industry niche. Finally, in 2000 he convinced Sara Lee to spin off Coach as an independent company. And he wanted to retain the job of turning it around.

Frankfort wanted to attract high fashion's elite customers but remain an affordable luxury for customers who must save for a $200 bag. But how could Coach find and maintain that delicate balance? For help, he first turned to planning and forecasting. He said, "To be successful you need to live your business. You have to understand it organically and thoroughly."

He introduced many new analytical tools for tracking market trends, evaluating effectiveness, and managing risk. The firm's leaders look at sales data for each store and each product type on a daily basis, and during busy seasons, several times daily. But extensive and intensive customer research remains the cornerstone of his planning. Indeed, the company spends $2 million per year on surveys. The surveys are supplemented with one-on-one interviews with customers from locations around the world, to quiz them on everything from appearance and quality to the correct length for a shoulder strap.

"The tremendous amount of testing they do differentiates them from a lot of other fashion companies," says industry analyst Robert Ohmes. Analyst Bob Drbul says, "Their execution and business planning is in the league of a Wal-Mart or a Target" (two much larger firms known for their effective business planning). To test new products, they are first shown to selected buyers in 12 worldwide markets, to gauge initial customer reaction. An initial demand forecast is then made, and six months before introduction, they are tested in another 12 markets. At launch time, sales are monitored closely and adjustments made quickly.

For example, an unexpected spike in sales was investigated, and managers found that buying by Hispanic customers was on the increase. Within a week, the firm had moved up the opening date of a South Miami store and begun advertising in Spanish for the first time. Frankfort understands that, to be effective, plans must be translated into appropriate actions. "Not only do you need to know your business and your customers...you also need to be nimble to adapt," he claims.

A host of other changes have also aided Coach in its rapid rise. Lew Frankfort hired a former Tommy Hilfiger designer, Reed Krakoff, to update the firm's classic but clunky styles. "Something was missing," says Krakoff. "I had to take these ideas and make them fun—young in spirit." Instead of introducing new products twice a year, a common practice in the fashion industry, Coach releases new styles monthly. Customers now have a reason to visit the stores more often. Outsourcing the production function allowed the company to increase gross profit margins by 24 percent over five years. The firm has diversified into many other related lines of business, including shoes, jewellery, furniture, and more. There is even a Coach car, a co-branded Lexus, with a Coach leather interior.

Women's Wear Daily, the bible of the fashion industry, recently named Coach as the "most splurgeworthy luxury brand." Customers agree. Since the firm was spun off, its revenues have doubled and profits have grown at an average annual compound rate of 55 percent. Investors, too, like Coach. The firm's share price rose an astonishing 900 percent during its first four years as an independent firm. Krakoff gives the credit for the firm's achievements to Frankfort's planning skills, saying, "The key to Lew's success...is his ability to orchestrate a decision-making process that is both inclusive and incisive."

Questions for Discussion

1. Describe examples of each of the management functions illustrated in this case.
2. Which management skills seem to be most exemplified in Lew Frankfort?
3. What role have goals and strategy played in the success of Coach?
4. What corporate culture issues might exist when a former division of a big company is spun off?

CONCLUDING CASE 6-2

Remaking BCE

BCE, Canada's largest phone company, held its annual business conference on December 15, 2004. At the conference, CEO Michael Sabia announced that BCE was making good progress on its strategic plan to achieve one of corporate Canada's biggest makeovers. The makeover involves harnessing new revenue streams as old ones decline. Sabia says that his management team will have to blow up the old culture of the company to make it competitive in the new world where technological boundaries between television, wireless networks, and landline phones will disappear. There are two parts to Sabia's vision: (1) Use internet technology to provide seamless communication across a variety of high-tech devices such as laptops, cellphones, personal digital assistants, televisions, etc., and (2) put together an array of business, information, and entertainment applications to send to all those electronic devices.

To date, the investment community has been skeptical that BCE can achieve its goals, given the rapid pace of change that is occurring in the industry. BCE has long relied on the stable revenue stream from traditional local and long-distance phone service it provides. But recently the profitability of that business has declined. BCE thinks that the growing demand for new services such as high-speed delivery of wireless data, broadband internet access, and digital television will increase its profitability. Sabia predicted that during 2005, subscribers to video and wireless service would increase by 10 and 15 percent, and internet subscribers would grow between 15 and 20 percent.

At present, 60 percent of BCE's revenue comes from providing traditional local and long-distance telephone service, and 40 percent comes from the new, high-growth services. The plan is to increase the proportion of revenue coming from new services to 55 percent by the end of 2006. Sabia used a baseball analogy to describe BCE's current position: "We're in the fourth inning," he said. He thought the pattern of the game had been set and BCE was on course to achieve good things down the road.

Analysts attending the business conference were also told that BCE has two other initiatives as part of its strategic plan. First, the company will invest over $1 billion to upgrade its high-definition network so that 85 percent of Quebec homes will have access to high-definition television by 2008. That investment is important since competitors like Canada's cable companies are preparing to enter the telephone business with Internet-based calling. Second, BCE has embarked on an aggressive cost cutting program to improve profit margins. BCE hopes to save approximately $1 billion by the end of 2006.

Michael Sabia has been focussing on corporate strategy since he became CEO in 2002. At that time, he was faced with a difficult decision, namely what kind of company would BCE be? Would it be a television company, a telecommunications company, a media company, or a New Economy company? A strategic decision was necessary because under former CEO Jean Monty, BCE had been acquiring companies in many different businesses, but several of them were not performing well. A CIBC World Markets research note said that BCE's strategy appeared to be in disarray.

To see why Sabia had a difficult strategic decision to make, consider the makeup of BCE in 2002. It had been pursuing a strategy that was often characterized by industry observers as "commerce, content, and connectivity." The *commerce* part of the equation included BCE Emergis (electronic commerce in the health and financial services industries) and CGI Group Inc. (information technology consulting). The *content* part of the equation was represented by Bell Globemedia, which included CTV (television stations), ROBTv (business reporting), the *Globe and Mail* (a national newspaper), and Sympatico-Lycos (internet portals). The connectivity part of the equation included Bell Canada (telephones), Bell ExpressVu (satellite broadcasting), Teleglobe (international voice and data networks), and Bell Canada International (telecom services in emerging markets).

The economic performance of these diverse holdings varied widely. Bell Canada was the most successful and CGI Group was also doing well. But there were problems in each of the other areas. BCE Emergis, for example, had difficulty reaching revenue projections because new customers simply hadn't materialized. In spite of that, Sabia said that BCE was very committed to making Emergis a success. The same sorts of problems existed with Teleglobe and BCI. Bell Globemedia (BGM) was also losing money, and in 2005 BCE reduced its stake in BGM by selling a 40 percent share to Woodbridge Co. Ltd., a 20 percent share to Torstar Corp., and a 20 percent share to the Ontario Teachers Pension Plan. This reduced BCE's stake in the company to 20 percent. BCE received $1.3 billion as part of the deal.

Questions for Discussion

1. Describe the various corporate-level strategies that a company can pursue. What strategy has BCE been pursuing until recently? What strategy is it pursuing now? To what extent is there a change?
2. What are the main steps in the decision-making process? How do they apply in this case?
3. Describe the skills of management. What skills are particularly important to a person like Michael Sabia? Defend your answer.
4. What is corporate culture? How might the corporate culture have changed at BCE over the last decade? Explain your reasoning.

CHAPTER 7

Organizing the Business Enterprise

After reading this chapter, you should be able to:

1. Discuss the elements that influence a firm's *organizational structure*.
2. Explain how *specialization* and *departmentalization* are the building blocks of organizational structure.
3. Distinguish between *responsibility* and *authority* and explain the differences in decision making in *centralized* and *decentralized organizations*.
4. Explain the differences between *functional*, *divisional*, *project*, and *international organizational structures*, and describe the most popular new forms of organizational design.
5. Describe the *informal organization* and discuss *intrapreneuring*.

Frantic Films Is Getting More Organized

Frantic Films is a Winnipeg-based film and TV production company. Founded in 1997, the company has grown rapidly and now has more than 100 employees in four different locations. Shortly after its founding, it was named one of Canada's Hottest 50 Start-Ups by *Profit Magazine*. By 2004, it ranked #23 on the list of Canada's fastest-growing companies, and in 2005 it ranked #5 on the list of Manitoba's fastest-growing companies. In addition to being a fast-growing company, Frantic has also received numerous awards. A partial list includes the following:

- National Research Council recognition as a Canadian innovation leader
- Lions Gate Innovative Producers Award
- New Media Visionary Award nomination
- Blizzard Award (for the documentary series "Quest for the Bay")
- Finalist in the Ernst & Young Entrepreneur Of The Year award competition (multiple years)

Frantic Films is a private corporation that is owned and managed by three principal shareholders—Jamie Brown (chief executive officer), Chris Bond (president), and Ken Zorniak (chief operating officer). With its rapid growth, the company's organization chart has been revised several times, but its three original divisions—Visual Effects, Live Action, and TV Commercials—continue to be very important (see Figure 7.1).

The *visual effects* division (Frantic Films VFX Services Inc.) produces visual effects for TV and movies. Using visual effects software packages such as Maya, Houdini, Digital Fusion, and 3Dstudio Max, the division has established a reputation as one of the top visual effects providers in North America. The majority of the employees at Frantic are in this division. Its output includes visual effects for films like *Superman Returns*, *Stay*, *X-Men 3*, *The Italian Job*, *Catwoman*, *The Core*, and *Swordfish*. The division uses a matrix structure to complete film projects. This means that a project team, made up of specialists in areas like 3D animation, 2D animation, compositing, and hardware/software support, is put together. When the project is completed, the team disbands and its members are assigned to other projects. These teams are typically given specific goals that must be achieved, and then the team members use their technical expertise to decide how they can best achieve the goal.

The *TV commercial* division (Frantic Films Commercial Projects Inc.) produces television commercials for local Winnipeg companies, as well as for national and international clients. It also provides visual effects for commercials produced by other companies. The writers, producers, designers, compositors, animators, and editors have created award-winning spots for local, national, and international companies as diverse as the Royal Winnipeg Ballet, the Disney Channel, and Procter & Gamble Canada.

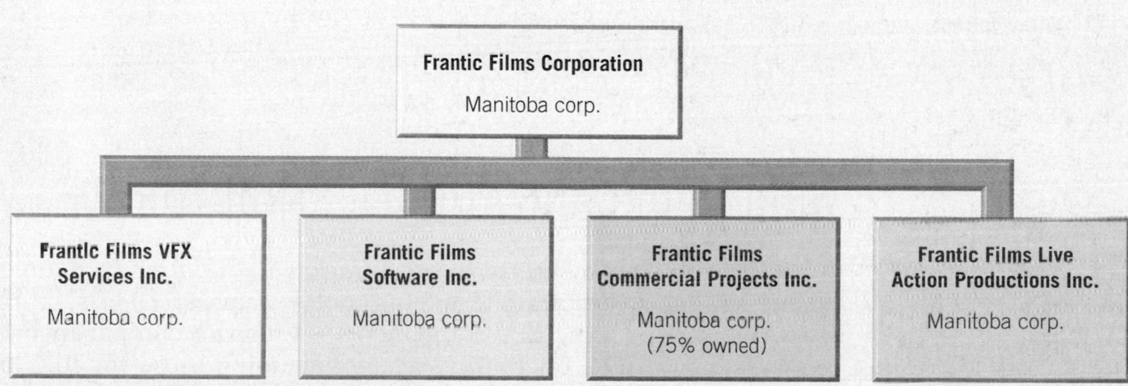

Figure 7.1 Organization chart for Frantic Films.

The *live action* division (Frantic Films Live Action Productions Inc.) produces and owns programs that have been broadcast around the world in over 40 countries. The division first develops the ideas for a program, then promotes the idea to broadcasters and financiers. If there is a strong interest, a budget is provided and the division produces the program. Frantic has produced documentary programs such as *Pioneer Quest* (one of the highest rated documentary series ever broadcast on a Canadian specialty channel), lifestyle series, (*'Til Debt Do Us Part*), television movies (*Zeyda* and the *Hitman*), and feature films (*Lucid*). Once a program is completed, rights are transferred to the releasing company and the individual, single-purpose production companies created for each show are wound up.

Recently, a software division has been created (Frantic Films Software Inc.). It employs seven individuals with specialized expertise, some of whom are computer science grads. When software division employees discovered that off-the-shelf software did not meet their needs, they began creating their own new stand-alone software to enhance certain visual effects like virtual water and smoke. This software was used to create the fluid-based character Tar Monster in the movie *Scooby-Doo II*.

Each of the divisions at Frantic Films operates fairly independently, but the company is still small enough that individuals from one division sometimes get involved in decisions in other divisions. For example, since the company does not have a marketing vice-president, marketing decisions are often made jointly by Brown, Bond, and Zorniak for each of the divisions. This means that Frantic Films does not have a "pure" functional or divisional structure.

When the company was first formed, the authority structure of the company was quite centralized because the principal shareholders had both the expertise to make decisions and the motivation to do so. But Brown thinks it is important to increase the involvement of lower-level workers in decisions, so he is trying to delegate more authority to them. Some progress has been made in this area. For example, managers in some of the divisions were recently given the authority to spend up to $5000 without having to get the approval of top management. This change was made because the top managers found that they were spending too much time discussing whether to approve requests for relatively small amounts of money. So, they essentially delegated more authority to division managers by giving them the discretion to spend up to $5000. Brown also encourages employees to make recommendations on various issues to top management. He recognizes that giving employees more discretion can sometimes lead to less-than-optimal decisions, but he also wants to give people more experience in making decisions that affect the company.

Like all rapidly growing companies, Frantic Films has experienced certain "growing pains" with regard to its organizational structure. For example, offices were set up in California and British Columbia to get more visual effects business in those local areas, but until recently, there have not been dedicated sales people responsible for generating work there. While employees in those offices have been fully employed, they are more costly. The original idea was to have them obtain work that could be sent to the lower-cost Winnipeg office, but more work is being done by a growing workforce in the satellite offices. Top management is now in the process of determining the changes that are needed to make the organization's structure more effective.

The other structural problem concerns the division of duties between Brown, Bond, and Zorniak. When the company first formed, all three principals were involved in decision making for all the divisions. But as the company has grown, each individual has gradually become more focussed. For example, Brown has primary responsibility for the live action division, while Zorniak and Bond have primary responsibility for the visual effects division. There have been some discussions among the three principals about having one person be responsible for all three divisions so that work can be better coordinated, but so far they have not been able to agree on a course of action. ◆

WHAT IS ORGANIZATIONAL STRUCTURE?

1 Discuss the elements that influence a firm's *organizational structure.*

What do we mean by the term *organizational structure*? In many ways, a business is like an automobile. All automobiles have an engine, four wheels, fenders and other structural components, an interior compartment for passengers, and various operating systems including those for fuel, braking, and climate control. Each component has a distinct purpose but must also work in harmony with the others. Automobiles made by competing firms all have the same basic components, although the way they look and fit together may vary.

Similarly, all businesses have common structural and operating components, each of which has a specific purpose. Each component must fulfill its own purpose while simultaneously fitting in with the others. And, just like automobiles made by different companies, how these components look and fit together varies from company to company. Thus, **organizational structure** is the specification of the jobs to be done within a business and how those jobs relate to one another.

organizational structure The specification of the jobs to be done within a business and how those jobs relate to one another.

Every institution—be it a for-profit company like Frantic Films, a not-for-profit organization like the University of Saskatchewan, or a government agency like the Canadian Wheat Board—must develop the most appropriate structure for its own unique situation. What works for Air Canada will not work for Canada Revenue. Likewise, the structure of the Red Cross will not work for the University of Toronto.

Determinants of Organizational Structure

How is an organization's structure determined? Does it happen by chance or is there some logic that managers use to create structure? Does it develop by some combination of circumstance and strategy? Ideally, managers carefully assess a variety of important factors as they plan for and then create a structure that will allow their organization to function efficiently.

Many elements work together to determine an organization's structure. Chief among these are the organization's *purpose, mission,* and *strategy*. A dynamic and rapidly growing enterprise, for example, achieved that position because of its purpose and successful strategies for achieving it. Such a firm will need a structure that contributes to flexibility and growth. A stable organization with only modest growth will function best with a different structure.

Size, technology, and changes in environmental circumstances also affect structure. A large manufacturer operating in a strongly competitive environment requires a different structure than a local barbershop or video store. Moreover, even after a structure has been created, it is rarely free from tinkering—or even outright re-creation. Indeed, most organizations change their structures almost continually.

Since it was first incorporated in 1903, for example, Ford Motor Co. has undergone literally dozens of major structural changes, hundreds of moderate changes, and thousands of minor changes. In the last decade alone, Ford has initiated several major structural changes. In 1994, the firm announced a major restructuring plan called *Ford 2000*, which was intended to integrate all of Ford's vast international operations into a single, unified structure by 2000. By 1998, however, midway through implementation of the plan, top Ford executives announced major modifications, indicating that (1) additional changes would be made, (2) some previously planned changes would not be made, and (3) some recently realigned operations would be changed again. In 1999, managers announced another sweeping set of changes intended to eliminate corporate bureaucracy, speed decision making, and improve communication and working relationships among people at different levels of the organization.[1] In 2001, still more changes were announced that were intended to boost the firm's flagging bottom line and stem a decline in product quality.[2]

The Chain of Command

Most businesses prepare **organization charts** that illustrate the company's structure and show employees where they fit into the firm's operations. Figure 7.2 shows the organization chart for a hypothetical company. Each

organization chart A physical depiction of the company's structure showing employee titles and their relationship to one another.

chain of command Reporting relationships within a business; the flow of decision-making power in a firm.

box represents a job within the company. The solid lines that connect the boxes define the chain of command, or the reporting relationships within the company. For example, the plant manager reports directly to the vice-president for production who, in turn, reports to the president. When the **chain of command** is not clear, many different kinds of problems can result.

THE BUILDING BLOCKS OF ORGANIZATIONAL STRUCTURE

2 Explain how *specialization* and *departmentalization* are the building blocks of organizational structure.

The first step in developing the structure of any business, large or small, is twofold:

- *Specialization*: determining who will do what
- *Departmentalization*: determining how people performing certain tasks can best be grouped together

These two tasks are the basic building blocks of all business organization.

Specialization

job specialization The process of identifying the specific jobs that need to be done and designating the people who will perform them.

The process of identifying the specific jobs that need to be done and designating the people who will perform them leads to **job specialization**. In a sense, all organizations have only one major "job"—for example, making a profit by manufacturing and selling men's and boys' shirts. But this job, of

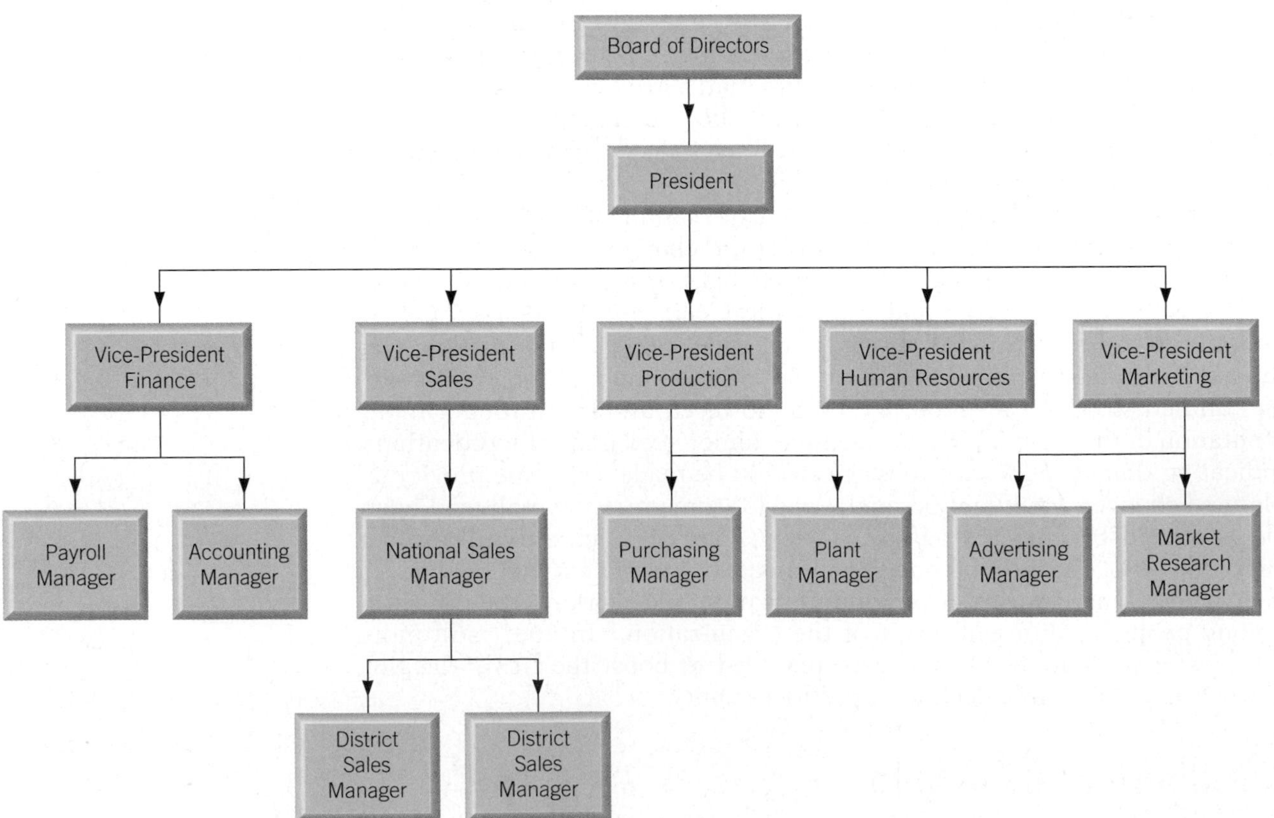

Figure 7.2 An organization chart shows key positions in the organization and interrelationships among them. An actual organization chart would, of course, be far more complex and include individuals at many more levels. Indeed, because of their size, larger firms cannot easily draw a diagram with everyone on it.

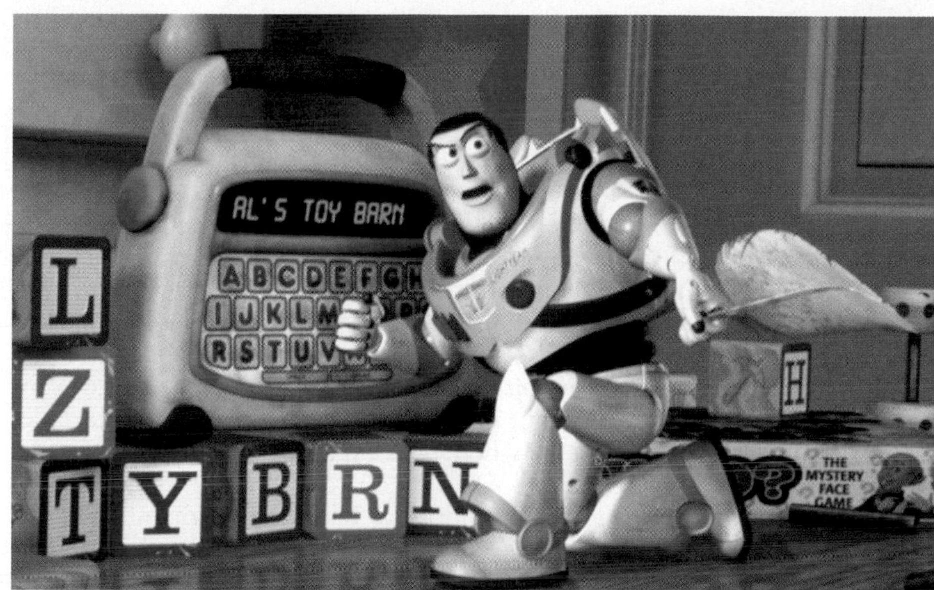

Organizational and industry-wide growth don't always result in greater job specialization. Animated feature films like *Toy Story 2* are now created by small teams of people who use point-and-click techniques to perform just about every job required by a project. The *Toy Story* movies, as well as *Finding Nemo* and *The Incredibles*, were made by Pixar Animation Studios, which works solely with computer-created animation. According to many experts, Pixar may soon take over industry leadership from Disney.

course, is broken into smaller components. In turn, each component is assigned to an individual. Consider the manufacture of men's shirts. Because several steps are required to produce a shirt, each job is broken down into its component parts—that is, into a set of tasks to be completed by a series of individuals or machines. One person, for example, cuts material for the shirt body, another cuts material for the sleeves, and a third cuts material for the collar. Components are then shipped to a sewing room, where a fourth person assembles the shirt. In the final stage, a fifth person sews on the buttons.[3]

Specialization and Growth

In a very small organization, the owner may perform every job. As the firm grows, however, so does the need to specialize jobs so that others can perform them. To see how specialization can evolve in an organization, consider the case of Mrs. Fields Cookies. When Debbi Fields opened her first store, she did everything herself: bought the equipment, negotiated the lease, baked the cookies, operated the store, and kept the records. As the business grew, however, Fields found that her job was becoming too much for one person. She first hired a bookkeeper to handle her financial records. She then hired an in-store manager and a cookie baker. She herself concentrated on advertising and promotions. Her second store required another set of employees—another manager, another baker, and some salespeople. While Fields focussed her attention on other expansion opportunities, she turned promotions over to a professional advertising director. Thus the job that she once did all by herself was increasingly broken down into components and assigned to different individuals.

Job specialization is a natural part of organizational growth. It is neither a new idea nor limited to factory work. In the ancient art of winemaking, for example, a high degree of specialization has existed for centuries. The activities necessary to make wine—picking and crushing grapes, fermenting the juice, aging and clarifying the wine, and selling it through specialized intermediaries—are performed by individuals who can draw on the knowledge and experience of their predecessors.

Job specialization has certain advantages: Individual jobs can be performed more efficiently, the jobs are easier to learn, and it is easier to replace people who leave the organization. On the other hand, if job specialization is carried too far and jobs become too narrowly defined, people get bored, derive less satisfaction from their jobs, and often lose sight of how their contributions fit into the overall organization.

Departmentalization

departmentalization The process of grouping jobs into logical units.

profit centre A separate company unit responsible for its own costs and profits.

After jobs are specialized, they must be grouped into logical units. This process is called **departmentalization**. Departmentalized companies benefit from the division of activities. Control and coordination are narrowed and made easier, and top managers can see more easily how various units are performing. Departmentalization allows the firm to treat a department as a **profit centre**—a separate unit responsible for its own costs and profits. Thus, by assessing profits from sales in a particular area—for example, men's clothing—Sears can decide whether to expand or curtail promotions in that area.

Managers do not group jobs randomly. They group them logically, according to some common thread or purpose. In general, departmentalization may occur along *functional, customer, product, geographic,* or *process* lines (or any combination of these).

Functional Departmentalization

functional departmentalization Departmentalization according to functions or activities.

Many service and manufacturing companies develop departments according to a group's functions or activities—a form of organization known as **functional departmentalization**. Such firms typically have production, marketing and sales, human resource, and accounting and finance departments. Departments may be further subdivided. For example, the marketing department might be divided geographically or into separate staffs for market research and advertising.

Customer Departmentalization

customer departmentalization Departmentalization according to the types of customers likely to buy a given product.

Stores like HMV are divided into departments—a classical music department, an R&B department, a pop department, and so on. Each department targets a specific customer category (people who want to buy different genres of music). **Customer departmentalization** makes shopping easier by providing identifiable store segments. Thus, a customer shopping for Shania Twain's latest CD can bypass World Music and head straight for Country. Stores can also group products in locations designated for deliveries, special sales, and other service-oriented purposes. In general, when it is departmentalized the store is more efficient and customers get better service—in part because salespeople tend to specialize and gain expertise in their departments.[4]

Product Departmentalization

product departmentalization Departmentalization according to the products being created or sold.

Both manufacturers and service providers often opt for **product departmentalization**—dividing an organization according to the specific product or service being created. A bank, for example, may handle consumer loans in one department and commercial loans in another. On a larger scale, 3M Corp., which makes both consumer and industrial products, operates different divisions for Post-it brand tape flags, Scotch-Brite scrub sponges, and the Sarns 9000 perfusion system for open-heart surgery.

Geographic Departmentalization

geographic departmentalization Departmentalization according to the area of the country or world supplied.

Some firms may be divided according to the area of the country—or even the world—they serve. This is known as **geographic departmentalization**. The Personal Services division of Montreal Trust, for example, is organized

Many department stores are departmentalized by product. Concentrating different products in different areas of the store makes shopping easier for customers.

around four regions—Atlantic, Quebec, Central, and BC/Western. Levi Strauss has one division for the United States, one for Europe, and one for the Asia-Pacific region.

The Business Accountability box describes some difficulties that companies can encounter when they try to choose between product and geographic departmentalization.

Process Departmentalization

process departmentalization Departmentalization according to the production process used to create a good or service.

Other manufacturers favour **process departmentalization**, in which the organization is divided according to production processes. This principle, for example, is logical for the pickle maker Vlasic, which has separate departments to transform cucumbers into fresh-packed pickles, pickles cured in brine, and relishes. Cucumbers destined to become fresh-packed pickles must be packed into jars immediately, covered with a solution of water and vinegar, and prepared for sale. Those slated for brined pickles must be aged in brine solution before packing. Relish cucumbers must be minced and combined with a host of other ingredients. Each process requires different equipment and worker skills.

Because different forms of departmentalization have different advantages, larger companies tend to adopt different types of departmentalization for various levels. For example, the company illustrated in Figure 7.3 uses functional departmentalization at the top level. At the middle level, production is divided along geographic lines. At a lower level, departmentalization is based on product groups.

ESTABLISHING THE DECISION-MAKING HIERARCHY

After jobs have been appropriately specialized and grouped into manageable departments, the next step in organizing is to establish the decision-making hierarchy. That is, managers must explicitly define *reporting relationships* among positions so that everyone will know who has responsibility for various decisions and operations. The goal is to figure out how to structure and stabilize the organizational framework so that everyone works together to achieve common goals.

BUSINESS ACCOUNTABILITY

Product Versus Geographical Departmentalization: What's the Right Choice?

Geographic departmentalization ensures quick, responsive reaction to the needs of the company's customers in certain geographic areas. On the other hand, it may also lead to duplicate production and other facilities, and compartmentalization of knowledge in those same geographic areas. So, it's not easy to decide whether to organize geographically or around products.

Organizing geographically grew in popularity as globalization occurred and firms expanded across national borders. Years ago, when relatively limited communications made it difficult to take the pulse of consumer needs or monitor operations abroad, it made sense to let local managers in foreign countries run their regional or country businesses as more or less autonomous companies. However, two trends are making this structure less popular today. First, information technology is reducing the impediments to cross-border communication. Second, global competition is so intense that firms can't afford to miss an opportunity to quickly transfer product improvements from one region to another.

Many firms are therefore switching from geographic to product departmentalization. For example, food company Heinz abandoned geographical departmentalization and is now organized by products. Managers in the United States work with those in Europe, Asia, and other regions to apply the best ideas from one region to all the others.

The Canadian Imperial Bank of Commerce (CIBC) also reorganized to break down the walls between the conservative and traditional retail/commercial banking side, and the more volatile investment banking side. The company is now organized around product lines.

Exide Corp., the world's largest producer of automotive and industrial batteries, has also shifted from geographical to product departmentalization. Previously, Exide's structure consisted of about 10 "country organizations." The head of each country organization had considerable latitude to make decisions that were best for that person's country. It also meant that each country manager focussed on products that were marketable in that country. Under the new product system, global business units have been formed to oversee the company's various product lines such as car and industrial batteries. But the change has not been without problems. For example, when Exide made an acquisition, some top executives got upset when their unit was made subordinate to the newly acquired unit. It wasn't long before Exide was tinkering with its organization chart again.

Either approach—products or geography—can cause problems if taken to an extreme. If a company organizes by products, it can standardize manufacturing, introduce new products around the world faster, and eliminate overlapping activities. But if too much emphasis is placed on product and not enough on geography, a company is likely to find that local decision making is slowed, pricing flexibility is reduced, and products are not tailored to meet the needs of a specific country's customers.

Ford Motor Co. experienced exactly these problems when it decided to move toward the product model. The reorganization saved the company $5 billion in its first few years of operation, but Ford's market share declined during the same period. This is what we would expect to happen when too much emphasis is placed on product departmentalization. Ford responded to this drop in market share by giving executives in various regions more authority to decide what types of vehicles were best for their local market. In other words, it moved back a bit toward the geographical model.

Procter & Gamble also encountered problems after it replaced country organizations with global business units in an attempt to globalize P&G brands like Tide, Pampers, and Crest. The reorganization caused great upheaval within the company as thousands of employees shifted into new jobs. As many as half of all company executives took on new roles. The CEO who ordered the change left the company just 17 months into his job.

A major question that must be asked about any organization is this: *Who makes which decisions?* The answer almost never focusses on an individual or even on a small group. The more accurate answer usually refers to the decision-making hierarchy. The development of this hierarchy generally results from a three-step process:

1. *Assigning tasks*: determining who can make decisions and specifying how they should be made

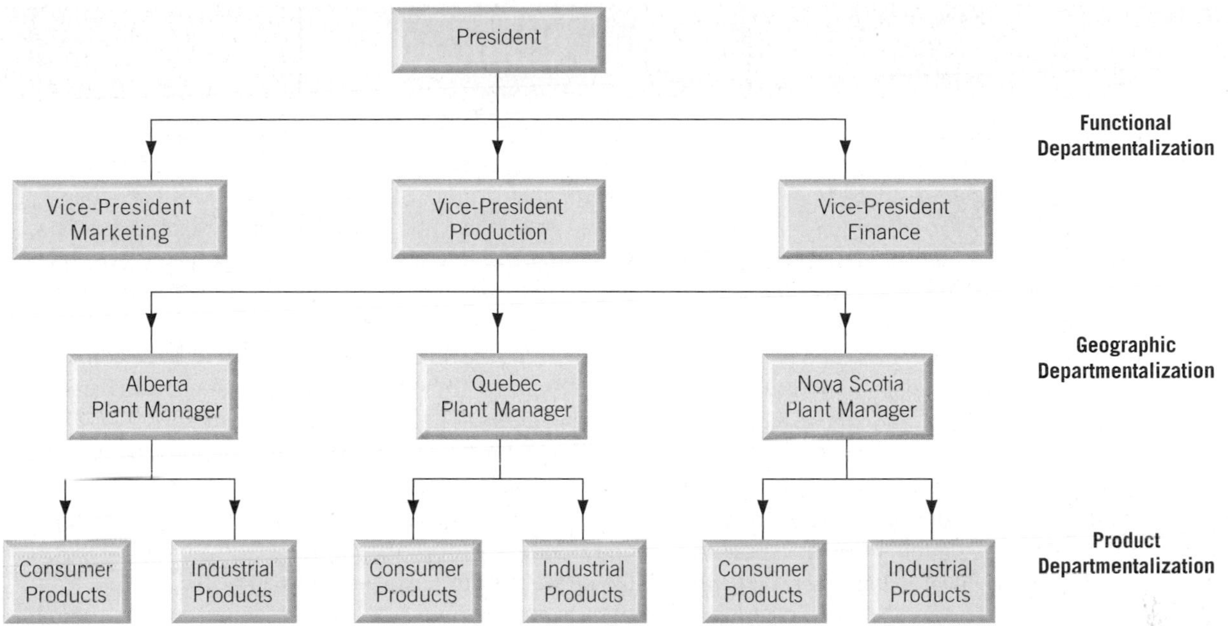

Figure 7.3 Most organizations use multiple bases of departmentalization. This organization, for example, is using functional, geographic, and product departmentalization.

2. *Performing tasks*: implementing decisions that have been made
3. *Distributing authority*: determining whether the organization is to be centralized or decentralized

To see this process in action, consider what has been happening at McDonald's, where executives have been systematically changing the firm's decision-making hierarchy. McDonald's has always been—and continues to be—highly centralized. But executives recently restructured both the company's decision-making processes and its operations. For instance, they reduced staff at corporate headquarters in Illinois, and established five regional offices throughout the United States. Now, many decisions are made at the regional level. They also clamped a lid on domestic growth and increased international expansion. In addition, they purchased stakes in three new restaurant chains with an eye on expansion: Donatos Pizza; Chipotle Mexican Grill; and Aroma, a British coffee chain. Four new managers have been installed, one to head up international operations and the others to oversee the three new restaurant partner groups. All four of these executives reported directly to the CEO.[5]

Assigning Tasks

The question of who is supposed to do what and who is entitled to do what in an organization is complex. In any company with more than one person, individuals must work out agreements about responsibilities and authority. **Responsibility** is the duty to perform an assigned task. **Authority** is the power to make the decisions necessary to complete the task.

Distinguish between *responsibility* and *authority* and explain the differences in decision making in *centralized* and *decentralized organizations.* 3

For example, imagine a mid-level buyer for The Bay who encounters an unexpected opportunity to make a large purchase at an extremely good price. Let's assume that an immediate decision is absolutely necessary—but that this decision is one that this buyer has no authority to make without confirmation from above. The company's policies on delegation and authority are inconsistent, since the buyer is responsible for purchasing the clothes that will be sold in the upcoming season but lacks the authority to make the needed purchases.

responsibility The duty to perform an assigned task.

authority The power to make the decisions necessary to complete a task.

ENTREPRENEURSHIP AND NEW VENTURES

The Techie Trio

When the three young owners of Triotech Amusement Inc. (Frederic Lachance, 35, David Lachance, 27, and Ernest Yale, 34) took their video game prototype to a trade show in Atlanta in 1999, it was their "make it or break it" chance. On the last day of the show, they made a sale, and from that first success have gone on to build a business that now has sales of close to $8 million.

Brothers David and Frederic Lachance were operating an internet café in Joliette, Quebec, in 1998 when they started providing "cabins" where people could play games over a network. This led to the idea of creating and selling closed cabins for game playing. With the help of software developer Ernest Yale they came up with their first product, Cyberpod. The three invested everything they had in the machine, and rented a truck and drove it to the Atlanta tradeshow where it was sold to an American distributor. "That's how Triotech got started," says Frederic. "We sold about 100 units through that distributor." In 2001, with their second product ready for launching, they hired their own sales representatives. They now have some 30 employees in Quebec and sales offices in Los Angeles and Texas.

The products Triotech Amusement develops and manufactures include video games, arcade machines, and multi-seat 3D theatres. The business is known for its technologically-advanced motion system and the sleek design of its products. Trademark products include Mad Wave Motion Theater, a two-seat coin-operated ride simulator; Wasteland Racer 2071, a driving simulator; and the XD Theater, a multi-seat motion-simulated thrill ride with 3D films. Known internationally, Triotech sells its products to amusement parks, entertainment centres, and arcade operators in the United States, England, Mexico, Russia, India, Australia, and Saudi Arabia. "Nothing beats watching people playing one of our games or enjoying one of our thrill rides," says Ernest. "Seeing their reactions makes it all worthwhile."

Frederic, David, and Ernest combine their complementary skills to run Triotech. Ernest, a video game developer since he was 12, heads the R&D unit in Montreal where he and his team develop software for new products. Frederic, president of the company, designs the actual machines that house the games and theatres and is responsible for sales and marketing strategy from Lavaltrie, outside of Montreal. David uses his technical skills in overseeing the day-to-day operations of manufacturing the units and designing the technology behind the hardware. Triotech has assembled a team of passionate people who care as much about the company as they do. "If there is anything that we're proud of it's our team," says Frederic.

As the company has grown, the three partners have faced the challenges of managing a larger organization and learning to delegate tasks. Frederic says the secret to handling growth is seeking out information, learning from others, and building a solid network of contacts. "There is no equivalent for our company in Canada," says Frederic, "and we operate in a sector that is virtually unknown in Quebec. But we've shown great growth potential; we're young and we've only touched the tip of what the possibilities are." "Since the beginning, we have dreamed of success," says Frederic. "But it's surprising how fast the business has grown. Dreams don't always come true, but for us this one has."

Performing Tasks

Trouble occurs when appropriate levels of responsibility and authority are not clearly spelled out in the working relationships between managers and subordinates. Here, the issues become delegation and accountability. **Delegation** begins when a manager assigns a task to a subordinate. **Accountability** falls to the subordinate, who must then complete the task. If the subordinate does not perform the assigned task properly and promptly, he or she may be reprimanded or punished, possibly even dismissed.

delegation Assignment of a task, a responsibility, or authority by a manager to a subordinate.

accountability Liability of subordinates for accomplishing tasks assigned by managers.

Fear of Delegating

Unfortunately, many managers have trouble delegating tasks to others. When this happens, subordinates may not be able to complete a task because their manager has not delegated sufficient authority to them. Such employees face a dilemma: They cannot do what the boss demands, but that boss will probably still hold them accountable. Effective managers surround themselves with a team of strong subordinates, and then delegate sufficient authority to those subordinates to get the job done. There are four things to keep in mind when delegating:

- Decide on the nature of the work to be done.
- Match the job with the skills of subordinates.
- Make sure the person chosen understands the objectives he or she is supposed to achieve.
- Make sure subordinates have the time and training necessary to do the task.

Experts pinpoint certain indicators that managers (particularly those in small businesses) are having trouble delegating effectively:

- the feeling that employees can never do anything as well as they can
- the fear that something will go wrong if someone else takes over a job
- the lack of time for long-range planning because they are bogged down in day-to-day operations
- the sense of being in the dark about industry trends and competitive products because of the time they devote to day-to-day operations

To overcome these tendencies, small business owners must admit that they can never go back to running all aspects of the business and that they can, in fact, prosper—with the help of their employees—if they learn to let go. But this problem isn't confined just to small businesses. Some managers in big companies also don't delegate as much or as well as they should. There are several reasons for this problem:

- the fear that subordinates don't really know how to do the job
- the fear that a subordinate might "show the manager up" in front of others by doing a superb job
- the desire to keep as much control as possible over how things are done
- a simple lack of ability as to how to effectively delegate to others

The remedies in these instances are a bit different. First, managers should recognize that they cannot do everything themselves. Second, if subordinates cannot do a job, they should be trained so that they can assume more responsibility in the future. Third, managers should recognize that if a subordinate performs well, it reflects favourably on that employee's manager. Finally, a manager who simply does not know how to delegate might need specialized training in how to divide up and assign tasks to others.

Distributing Authority

Delegation involves a specific relationship between managers and subordinates. Most businesses must also make decisions about general patterns of authority throughout the company. This pattern may be largely *centralized* or *decentralized* (or, usually, somewhere in between).

Centralized Organizations

In a **centralized organization**, top management retains the right to make most decisions, and top management must approve most lower-level decisions before they can be implemented.[6] McDonald's practises centralization as a way to maintain standardization. All restaurants must follow precise steps in buying products and making and packaging burgers and other

centralized organization Top managers retain most decision-making rights for themselves.

menu items. Most advertising is handled at the corporate level, and a regional manager must approve any local advertising. Restaurants even have to follow prescribed schedules for facilities' maintenance and upgrades like floor polishing and parking lot cleaning.[7]

Decentralized Organizations

decentralized organization Lower- and middle-level managers are allowed to make significant decisions.

As a company gets larger, more decisions must be made, and there is usually a move to a more decentralized pattern. In a **decentralized organization**, much of the decision-making authority is delegated to levels of management at various points below the top level. The purpose of decentralization is to make a company more responsive to its environment by breaking the company into more manageable units, and giving those units more autonomy. Reducing top-heavy bureaucracies is also a common goal of decentralization.

Determining the Optimum Level of Decentralization. Deciding just how centralized or decentralized a company should be is something of an art. Jack Welch, the former CEO of General Electric and a long-time proponent of decentralized management, says, "If you don't let managers make their own decisions, you're never going to be anything more than a one-person business." The logic of giving manager's more decision making autonomy is also behind the decentralizing strategy of cereal maker Kellogg Co. Top managers at Kellogg realized that to keep pace with today's eat-on-the-run lifestyles, lower-level managers had to have more autonomy to make decisions so they could rush new products to market.[8]

The idea of autonomy for managers sounds pretty reasonable, but decentralization can also cause difficulties for companies, as the story of Home Depot illustrates. Home Depot was founded in the early 1980s by Bernie Marcus and Arthur Blank. They encouraged store managers to think for themselves and to do what was best for their particular store. Authority was decentralized. Marcus and Blank said that they hired people who were actually more suited for self-employment or for running their own business. Time passed, and Marcus and Blank left the company. A new CEO—Robert Nardelli—came in and moved the company toward a much more centralized structure by emphasizing operating efficiencies, expense controls, and head office directives to store managers. He felt that operations were too loosely controlled under the founders. Nardelli loved the entrepreneurial spirit, but said that it had to be compliant more often.[9]

The advantages and disadvantages of decentralization can clearly be seen in the long history of General Motors. In the 1920s, GM's legendary president, Alfred Sloan, introduced a decentralized structure that gave each car division considerable autonomy to produce cars that would attract whatever market segment the division was pursuing. This decentralized structure continued in use as the company expanded from the United States into international markets. It worked so well that GM became the largest automobile manufacturer in the world. Although the company was large, in many parts of the world it operated more like a small regional company because its executives were given a great deal of autonomy over issues like car design. This helped GM offer cars that appealed to people in local markets.

But all this autonomy resulted in widely differing car designs that were very expensive to produce. As GM costs soared, and as competition from cost-conscious Japanese car makers became ferocious, GM's sales and overall profitability plummeted. Something had to be done. So GM *re*centralized and head office took away much of the autonomy that managers in various international divisions had. Now, GM requires its worldwide units to work much more closely together to design cars that can be sold (with modest variations) worldwide. This will reduce GM's cost per car.

The new, more centralized structure, means that engineers in various regions have less authority than they used to have when they are designing cars and the parts that will be used in those cars. A "Global Council" in Detroit now makes key decisions about how much will be spent on new car development. And the council can say "no" to proposed new car designs. For example, when GM engineers at its Daewoo joint venture with South Korea wanted to develop a sport utility vehicle especially suited for the South Korean market, the request was denied.

Another example: When the Saab 9-3 was being developed, GM asked its subsidiary to work from the same "Epsilon" architecture as the Opel Vectra (which was made in Germany) and the Chevrolet Malibu (which was made in the United States). This would allow GM to build any Epsilon vehicle at any of their production facilities around the world. But Saab's engineers changed some things like the electrical system and the engine cradle, and that meant that the Saab 9-3 couldn't easily be built at other production facilities. After that fiasco, GM transferred most of Saab's engineers to its European technical development centre, and Saab no longer has an independent engineering organization.[10]

Tall and Flat Organizations

Related to the concept of centralized or decentralized authority is the concept of tall or flat organizational structures. With relatively fewer layers of management, decentralized firms tend to have a **flat organizational structure** such as the one shown in Figure 7.4. In contrast, companies with centralized authority systems typically require multiple layers of management and thus have a **tall organizational structure**. The Canadian Forces is an example of such an organization. Because information, whether upward or downward bound, must pass through so many organizational layers, tall structures are prone to delays in information flow.

flat organizational structure An organization with relatively few layers of management.

tall organizational structure An organization with many layers of management

As organizations grow in size, it is both normal and necessary that they become at least somewhat taller. For instance, a small firm with only an owner-manager and a few employees is likely to have two layers—the owner-manager and the employees who report to that person. But as the firm grows, more layers will be needed. Born Information Services, for instance, is a small consulting firm created and run by Rick Born. At first, all employees reported to him. But when his firm grew to more than 20 people, he knew he needed help in supervising and coordinating projects. As a result, he added a layer of management consisting of what he called "staff managers" to serve as project coordinators. This move freed him up to seek new business clients.[11] Like other managers, however, Born must ensure that he has only the number of layers his firm needs. Too few layers can create chaos and inefficiency, while too many layers can create rigidity and bureaucracy.

Span of Control

As you can see from Figure 7.4, the distribution of authority in an organization also affects the number of people who work for any individual manager. In a flat organizational structure, the number of people managed by one supervisor—the manager's **span of control**—is usually wide. In tall organizations, span of control tends to be relatively narrow. Span of control, however, depends on many factors. Employees' abilities and the supervisor's managerial skills help determine whether span of control is wide or narrow, as do the similarity and simplicity of those tasks performed under the manager's supervision and the extent to which they are interrelated.[12]

span of control The number of people managed by one manager.

If lower level managers are given more decision-making authority, their supervisors will have less work to do because some of the decisions they previously made will be transferred to their subordinates. By the same token, these managers may then be able to oversee and coordinate the work of more subordinates, resulting in an increased span of control. At McDonald's, the creation of regional offices freed up time for the CEO. In turn, reorganization allowed him to then create four new executive positions, one to oversee international expansion and the others to work with new restaurant partners.

Similarly, when several employees perform either the same simple task or a group of interrelated tasks, a wide span of control is possible and often desirable. For instance, because all the jobs are routine, one supervisor may well control an entire assembly line. Moreover, each task depends on another. If one station stops, everyone stops. Having one supervisor ensures that all stations receive equal attention and function equally well.

In contrast, when jobs are more diversified or prone to change, a narrow span of control is preferable. At Case Corp., farm tractors are made to

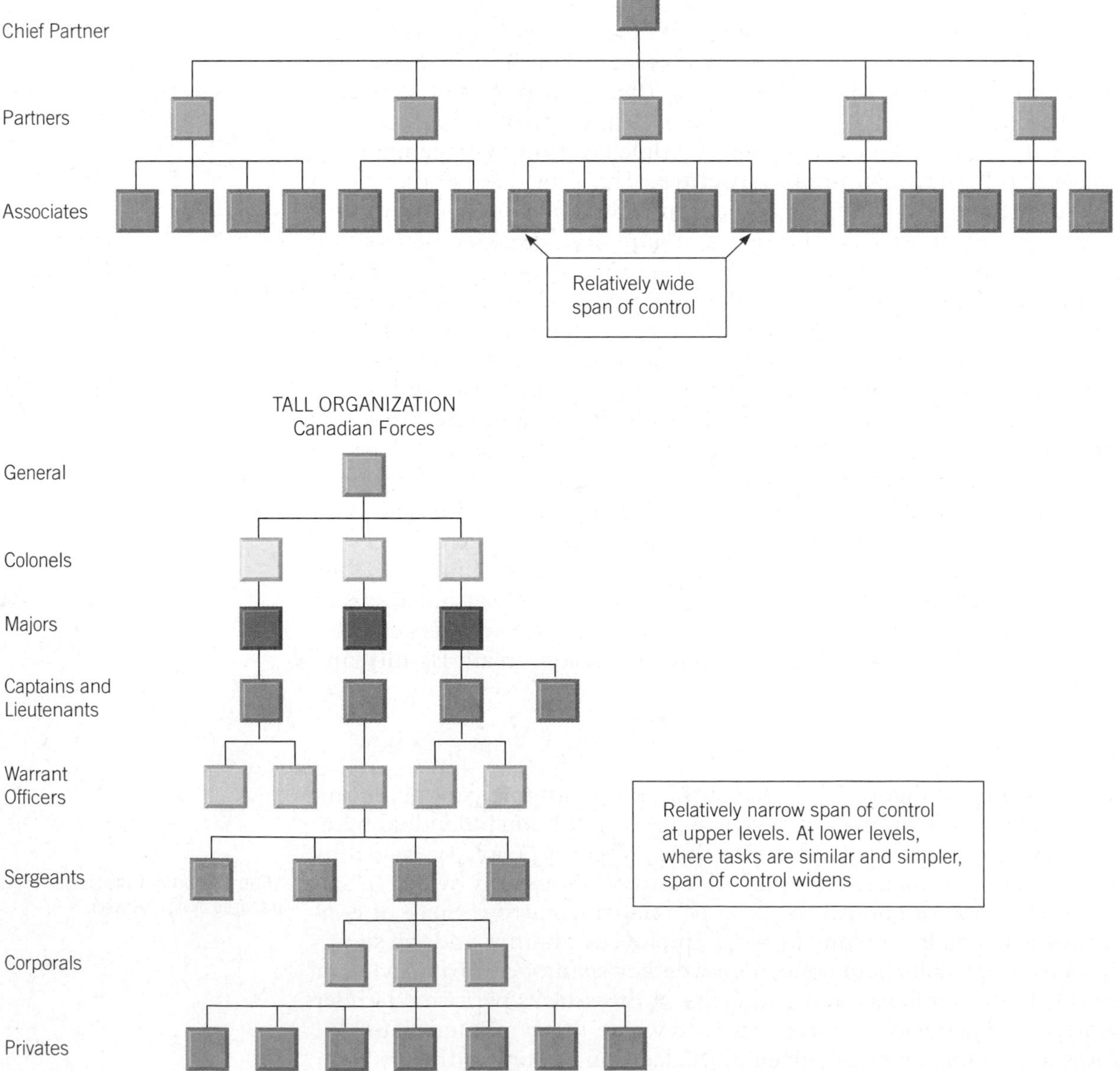

Figure 7.4 Organizational structure and span of control.

order in five to six weeks. Farmers can select from among a wide array of options, including engines, tires, power trains, and even a CD player. A wide assortment of machines and processes is used to construct each tractor. Although workers are highly skilled operators of their assigned machines, each machine is different. In this kind of set-up, the complexities of each machine and the advanced skills needed by each operator mean that one supervisor can oversee only a small number of employees.[13]

Downsizing refers to the planned reduction in the scope of an organization's activity. It usually means cutting substantial numbers of managers and workers, and reducing the number and variety of products the company produces. Downsizing may eliminate entire layers of management (creating a "flatter" corporate structure), and the remaining managers end up with larger spans of control.

downsizing The planned reduction in the scope of an organization's activity.

Three Forms of Authority

In an organization, it must be clear who will have authority over whom. As individuals are delegated responsibility and authority in a firm, a complex web of interactions develops. These interactions may take one of three forms of authority: *line, staff,* or *committee and team*. In reality, like departmentalization, all three forms may be found in a given company, especially a large one.

Line Authority

Line authority is authority that flows up and down the chain of command (refer back to Figure 7.2 on p. 208). Most companies rely heavily on **line departments**—departments directly linked to the production and sales of specific products. For example, Clark Equipment Corp. has a division that produces forklifts and small earthmovers. In this division, line departments include purchasing, materials handling, fabrication, painting, and assembly (all of which are directly linked to production) along with sales and distribution (both of which are directly linked to sales).

line authority An organizational structure in which authority flows in a direct chain of command from the top of the company to the bottom.

line department A department directly linked to the production and sales of a specific product.

Each line department is essential to an organization's success. Line employees are the "doers" and producers in a company. If any line department fails to complete its task, the company cannot sell and deliver finished goods. Thus, the authority delegated to line departments is important. A bad decision by the manager in one department can hold up production for an entire plant. For example, say that the painting department manager at Clark Equipment changes a paint application on a batch of forklifts, which then show signs of peeling paint. The batch will have to be repainted (and perhaps partially reassembled) before the machines can be shipped.

Staff Authority

Most companies also rely on **staff authority**, which is based on special expertise and usually involves counselling and advising line managers. Common **staff members** include specialists in areas such as law, accounting, and human resource management. A corporate attorney, for example, may be asked to advise the marketing department as it prepares a new contract with the firm's advertising agency. Legal staff, however, do not actually make decisions that affect how the marketing department does its job. Staff members, therefore, aid line departments in making decisions but do not have the authority to make final decisions.

staff authority Authority that is based on expertise and that usually involves advising line managers.

staff members Advisers and counsellors who aid line departments in making decisions but do not have the authority to make final decisions.

Suppose, for example, that the fabrication department at Clark Equipment has an employee with a drinking problem. The manager of the department could consult a human resource staff expert for advice on handling the situation. The staff expert might suggest that the worker stay on the job but enter a counselling program. But if the line manager decides that the job is too dangerous to be handled by a person whose judgment is often impaired by alcohol, that decision will most likely prevail.

Typically, the separation between line authority and staff responsibility is clearly delineated. As Figure 7.5 shows, this separation is usually shown in organization charts by solid lines (line authority) and dotted lines (staff responsibility). It may help to understand this separation by remembering that while staff members generally provide services to management, line managers are directly involved in producing the firm's products.

Committee and Team Authority

committee and team authority Authority granted to committees or work teams involved in a firm's daily operations.

Recently, more and more organizations have started to use **committee and team authority**—authority granted to committees or work teams that play central roles in the firm's daily operations. A committee, for example, may consist of top managers from several major areas. If the work of the committee is especially important, and if the committee will be working together for an extended time, the organization may even grant it special authority as a decision-making body that goes beyond the individual authority possessed by each of its members.

At the operating level, many firms today are also using *work teams*—groups of operating employees empowered to plan and organize their own work and to perform that work with a minimum of supervision. As with permanent committees, the organization will usually find it beneficial to grant special authority to work teams so that they may function more effectively.[14]

BASIC ORGANIZATIONAL STRUCTURES

4 Explain the differences between *functional, divisional, project,* and *international organizational structures,* and describe the most popular new forms of organizational design.

A glance at the organization charts of many organizations reveals what appears to be an infinite variety of structures. However, closer examination shows that it is possible to identify four basic forms: functional, divisional, project, and international. These structures are described below.

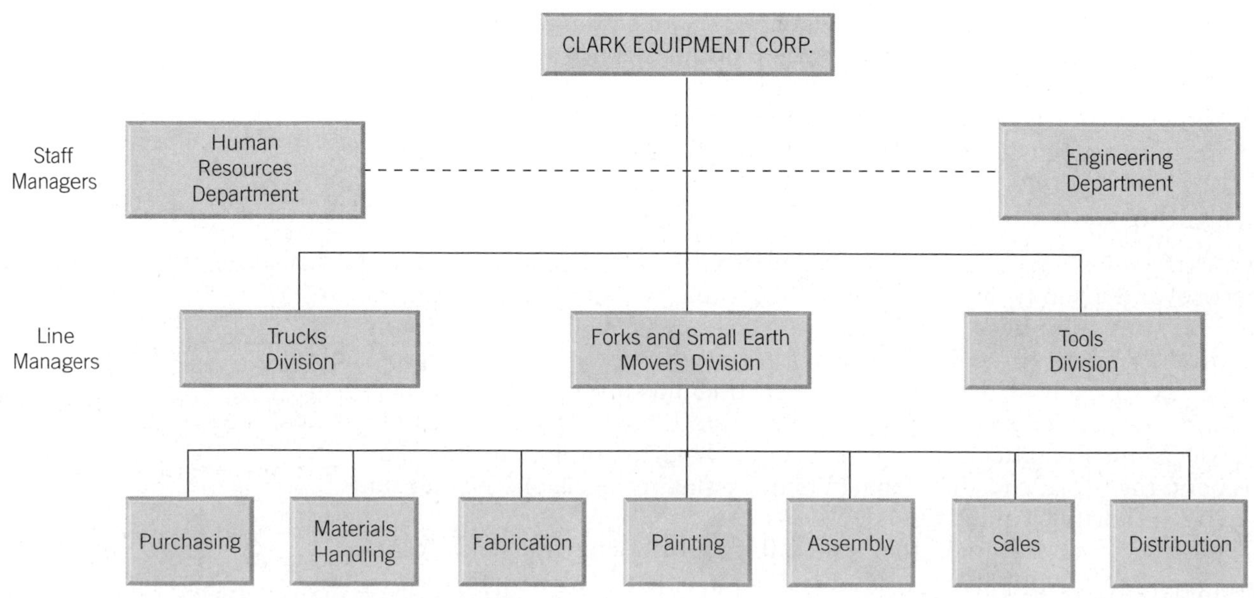

Figure 7.5 Line and staff organization: Clark Equipment Corp.

The Functional Structure

The **functional structure** is the oldest and most commonly used. In the functional organization, the various units in the organization are formed based on the functions that must be carried out to reach organizational goals. The functional structure makes use of departmentalization by function. An example of a functional structure is shown in Figure 7.2 (see p. 208). The advantages and disadvantages of the functional structure are summarized in Table 7.1.

Business firms are increasingly using work teams and allowing groups of employees to plan and organize their own work with a minimum of supervision. This contributes to employee empowerment.

The Divisional Structure

The functional structure's disadvantages can make it inappropriate for some companies. Many companies have found that the **divisional structure**—which divides the organization into several divisions, each of which operates as a semi-autonomous unit and profit centre—is more suited to their needs. Divisions in organizations can be based on products, customers, or geography. In 2002, for example, Bell Canada created three divisions based on which customers were being served: consumers, small- and medium-sized businesses, and large corporations. This new structure replaces the former divisional structure that was geographically based.[15]

functional structure Various units are included in a group based on functions that need to be performed for the organization to reach its goals.

divisional structure Divides the organization into divisions, each of which operates as a semi-autonomous unit

H.J. Heinz, one of the world's largest food-processing companies, is divisionalized along seven product lines: food service (selling small packaged products such as mustard and relish to restaurants); infant foods; condiments (Heinz ketchup, steak sauce, and tomato sauce); Star-Kist tuna; pet foods; frozen foods; and miscellaneous products, including both new lines being test-marketed and soups, beans, and pasta products. Because of its divisional structure, Heinz can evaluate the performance of each division independently. Until recently, for example, Heinz also had a division for its Weight Watchers business. But because this business was performing poorly, the company sold the Weight Watchers classroom program and folded its line of frozen foods into its existing frozen-foods division.[16]

Table 7.1 Advantages and Disadvantages of a Functional Structure

Advantages	Disadvantages
1. It focusses attention on the key activities that must be performed.	1. Conflicts may arise among the functional areas.
2. Expertise develops within each function.	2. No single function is responsible for overall organizational performance.
3. Employees have clearly defined career paths.	3. Employees in each functional area have a narrow view of the organization.
4. The structure is simple and easy to understand.	4. Decision making is slowed because functional areas must get approval from top management for a variety of decisions.
5. It eliminates duplication of activities.	5. Coordinating highly specialized functions may be difficult.

Because divisions are relatively autonomous, a firm can take such action with minimal disruption to its remaining business operations.

Like Heinz, other divisionalized companies are free to buy, sell, create, and disband divisions without disrupting the rest of their operations. Divisions can maintain healthy competition among themselves by sponsoring separate advertising campaigns, fostering different corporate identities, and so forth. They can also share certain corporate-level resources (such as market research data). Of course, if too much control is delegated to divisional managers, corporate managers may lose touch with daily operations. Competition between divisions has also been known to become disruptive, and efforts of one division may be duplicated by those of another.

The advantages and disadvantages of the divisional structure are summarized in Table 7.2.

Project Organization

A typical line or line-staff organization is characterized by unchanging vertical authority relationships. It has such a set-up because the organization produces a product or service in a repetitive and predictable way. Procter & Gamble, for example, produces millions of tubes of Crest toothpaste each year using standardized production methods. The company has done this for years and intends to do so indefinitely.

But some organizations find themselves faced with new product opportunities or with projects that have a definite starting and end point. These organizations often use a project structure to deal with the uncertainty encountered in new situations. **Project organization** involves forming a team of specialists from different functional areas of the organization to work on a specific project.[17] A project structure may be temporary or permanent; if it is temporary, the project team disbands once the project is completed and team members return to their regular functional area or are assigned to a new project.

project organization An organization that uses teams of specialists to complete specific projects.

Project organization is used extensively by Canadian firms, for example, in the construction of hydroelectric generating stations like those developed by Hydro-Québec on La Grande River and by Manitoba Hydro on the Nelson River. Once the generating station is complete, it becomes part of the traditional structure of the utility. Project organization is also used at Genstar Shipyards Ltd. in Vancouver. Each ship that is built is treated as a project and supervised by a project manager; the project manager for a given ship is responsible for ensuring that the ship is completed on time and within budget.[18] Project organization has also proven useful for coordinating the many elements needed to extract oil from the tar sands. Project management is also used in other kinds of tasks, including construction, military weapons, aerospace, and health-care delivery.[19]

A **matrix organization** is a variation of project structure in which the project manager and the regular line managers share authority. Ford, for example, used a matrix organization to design the Ford Thunderbird that

matrix organization A project structure in which the project manager and the regular line managers share authority until the project is concluded.

Table 7.2 Advantages and Disadvantages of a Divisional Structure

Advantages	Disadvantages
1. It accommodates change and expansion.	1. Activities may be duplicated across divisions.
2. It increases accountability.	2. A lack of communication among divisions may occur.
3. It develops expertise in the various divisions.	3. Adding diverse divisions may blur the focus of the organization.
4. It encourages training for top management.	4. Company politics may affect the allocation of resources.

All the signs at this 85 000-square-foot store in Numazu identify it as a Seiyu outlet run by Japan's fifth-largest supermarket chain. However, Wal-Mart owns 38 percent of Seiyu, and this giant store is part of Wal-Mart's effort to enter the world's second-largest retail market.

organization, the *team organization*, the *virtual organization*, and the *learning organization*.

Boundaryless Organization

The *boundaryless organization* is one in which traditional boundaries and structures are minimized or eliminated altogether. For example, General Electric's fluid organization structure, in which people, ideas, and information flow freely between businesses and business groups, approximates this concept. Similarly, as firms partner with their suppliers in more efficient ways, external boundaries disappear. Some of Wal-Mart's key suppliers are tied directly into the retailer's vaunted information system. As a result, when Wal-Mart distribution centres start running low on, say, Wrangler blue jeans, the manufacturer receives the information as soon as the retailer. Wrangler proceeds to manufacture new inventory and restock the distribution centre without Wal-Mart having to place a new order.

Team Organization

Team organization relies almost exclusively on project-type teams, with little or no underlying functional hierarchy. People "float" from project to project as dictated by their skills and the demands of those projects. At Cypress Semiconductor, units or groups that become large are simply split into smaller units. Not surprisingly, the organization is composed entirely of small units. This strategy allows each unit to change direction, explore new ideas, and try new methods without having to deal with a rigid bureaucratic superstructure. Although few large organizations have actually reached this level of adaptability, Apple Computer and Xerox are among those moving toward it.

Virtual Organization

Closely related to the team organization is the virtual organization. A *virtual organization* has little or no formal structure. Typically, it has only a handful of permanent employees, a very small staff, and a modest administrative facility. As the needs of the organization change, managers bring in temporary workers, lease facilities, and outsource basic support services to meet the demands of each unique situation. As the situation changes, the temporary workforce changes in parallel, with some people leaving the organization and others entering it. Facilities and subcontracted services also change. In other words, the virtual organization exists only in response to its own needs.

Global Research Consortium (GRC) is a virtual organization that offers research and consulting services to firms doing business in Asia. As clients request various services, GRC's staff of three permanent employees subcontracts the work to an appropriate set of several dozen independent consultants and/or researchers with whom it has relationships. At any given time, therefore, GRC may have several projects underway and 20 or 30 people working on various projects. As the projects change, so too does the composition of the organization. Figure 7.8 illustrates a hypothetical virtual organization.

Learning Organization

The so-called *learning organization* works to integrate continuous improvement with continuous employee learning and development. Specifically, a learning organization works to facilitate the lifelong learning and personal development of all of its employees while continually transforming itself to respond to changing demands and needs.

While managers might approach the concept of a learning organization from a variety of perspectives, the most frequent goals are improved quality, continuous improvement, and performance measurement. The idea is that the most consistent and logical strategy for achieving continuous improvement is constantly upgrading employee talent, skill, and knowledge. For example, if each employee in an organization learns one new thing each day and can translate that knowledge into work-related practice, continuous improvement will logically follow. Indeed, organizations that wholeheartedly embrace this approach believe that only through constant employee learning can continuous improvement really occur.

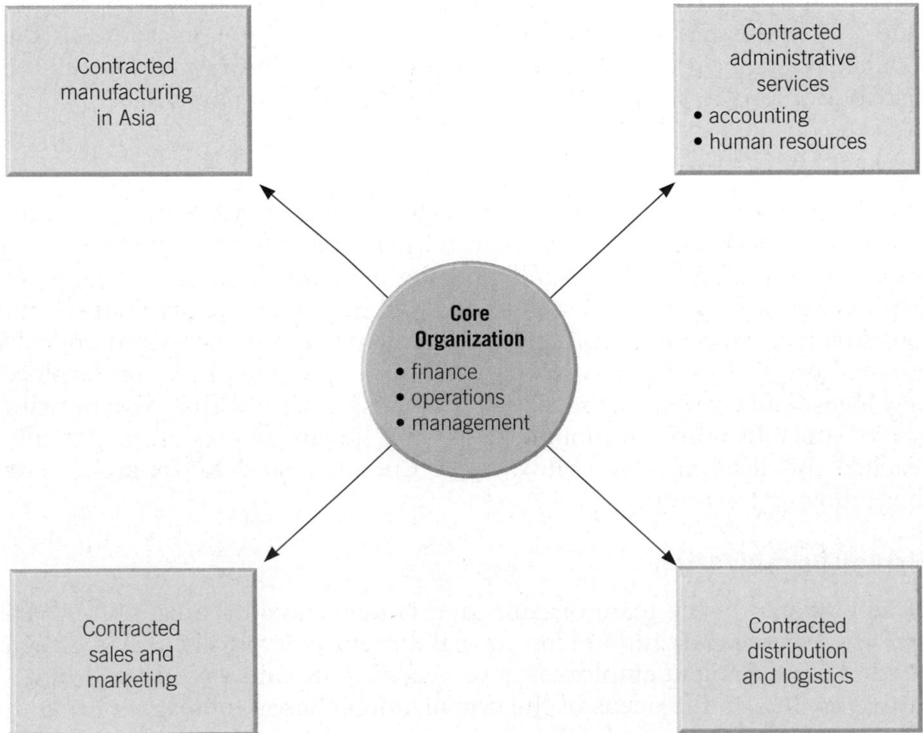

Figure 7.8 A virtual organization.

In recent years, many different organizations have implemented this approach on various levels. Shell Oil Co., for example, recently purchased an executive conference centre called the Shell Learning Center. The facility boasts state-of-the-art classrooms and instructional technology, lodging facilities, a restaurant, and recreational amenities, such as a golf course, swimming pool, and tennis courts. Line managers at the firm rotate through the centre and serve as teaching faculty. Teaching assignments last anywhere from a few days to several months. At the same time, all Shell employees routinely attend training programs, seminars, and related activities, all the while gathering the latest information they need to contribute more effectively to the firm. Recent seminar topics have included time management, balancing work and family demands, and international trade theory.

THE INFORMAL ORGANIZATION

Describe the *informal organization* and discuss *intrapreneuring*. 5

Much of our discussion so far has focussed on the organization's *formal* structure—its "official" arrangement of jobs and job relationships. In reality, however, all organizations also have another dimension—an informal organization within which people do their jobs in different ways and interact with other people in ways that do not follow formal lines of communication. The Exercising Your Ethics box at the end of the chapter presents an interesting situation that illustrates the informal organization.

Formal Versus Informal Organizational Systems

The formal organization of a business is the part that can be seen and represented in chart form. The structure of a company, however, is by no means limited to the organization chart and the formal assignment of authority. Frequently, the **informal organization**—everyday social interactions among employees that transcend formal jobs and job interrelationships—effectively alters a company's formal structure. Indeed, this level of organization is sometimes just as powerful, if not more powerful, than the formal structure.

informal organization A network of personal interactions and relationships among employees unrelated to the firm's formal authority structure.

On the negative side, the informal organization can reinforce office politics that put the interests of individuals ahead of those of the firm. Likewise, a great deal of harm can be caused by distorted or inaccurate information communicated without management input or review. For example, if the informal organization is generating false information about impending layoffs, valuable employees may act quickly (and unnecessarily) to seek other employment. Among the more important elements of the informal organization are *informal groups* and the *organizational grapevine*.

Informal Groups

Informal groups are simply groups of people who decide to interact among themselves. They may be people who work together in a formal sense or who simply get together for lunch, during breaks, or after work. They may talk about business, the boss, or non-work-related topics such as families, movies, or sports. For example, at the New York Metropolitan Opera, musicians and singers play poker during the intermissions. Most pots are in the $30 to $40 range. Luciano Pavarotti, the famed tenor, once played and lost big.

The impact of informal groups on the organization may be positive (if they work together to support the organization), negative (if they work together in ways that run counter to the organization's interests), or neutral (if what they do is unrelated to the organization).

Organizational Grapevine

grapevine An informal communications network that carries gossip and other information throughout an organization.

The **grapevine** is the informal communication network that runs through an entire organization.[23] Grapevines are found in all organizations except the very smallest, but they do not always follow the same patterns as formal channels of authority and communication, nor do they necessarily coincide with them. The internet is a worldwide grapevine. When people gather around the water cooler or on the golf course to exchange gossip and pass on information, they have names and faces. But with the internet, you may not know whom you are talking to and how reliable the person is who is providing the information.[24]

Because the grapevine typically passes information orally, messages often become distorted in the process. But most office gossip has at least some kernel of truth to it. Those passing on news may deliberately alter it, either to advance their own goals or to submarine someone else's chances. Listening to and passing on information damaging to someone's reputation can backfire, harming your credibility and making you a target for similar gossip.

In general, the more detailed the information, the less likely it is to be true. Likewise, beware the hush-hush "don't quote me on this" rumour. (Cynics claim that the better the news, the less likely it is to be true, too.) The higher the source, the greater the likelihood that the grapevine has the real story. Don't reject information from "lower" sources, however. Many an executive assistant can provide valuable insights into a corporation's plans.

Attempts to eliminate the grapevine are fruitless, but managers do have some control over it. By maintaining open channels of communication and responding vigorously to inaccurate information, they can minimize the damage the grapevine can do. In fact, the grapevine can actually be an asset. By getting to know the key people in the grapevine, for example, the manager can partially control the information they receive and use the grapevine to determine employee reactions to new ideas (e.g., a change in human resource policies or benefit packages). The manager can also receive valuable information from the grapevine and use it to improve decision making.

The grapevine is a powerful communications network in most organizations. These workers may be talking about any number of things—an upcoming deadline on an important project, tonight's football game, the stock market, rumours about an impending takeover, gossip about forthcoming promotions, or the weather.

Wise managers will tune in to the grapevine's message because it is often a corporate early warning system. Ignoring this valuable source of information can cause managers to be the last to know that they are about to get a new boss, or that they have a potentially fatal image problem. The grapevine is not infallible, however. In addition to miscommunication and attempts by some people to manipulate it for their own ends, it may carry rumours with absolutely no basis in fact. Such rumours are most common when there is a complete lack of information (apparently, human nature abhors such a vacuum and fills it). Unfortunately, baseless rumours can be very hard to kill.

Intrapreneuring

Sometimes organizations actually take steps to encourage the informal organization. They do so for a variety of reasons, two of which we have already discussed. First, most experienced managers recognize that the informal organization exists whether they want it or not. Second, many managers know how to use the informal organization to reinforce the formal organization. Perhaps more important, however, the energy of the informal organization can be harnessed to improve productivity.

Many firms, including Compaq Computer, Rubbermaid, 3M, and Xerox, are supporting a process called **intrapreneuring**—creating and maintaining the innovation and flexibility of a small-business environment within the confines of a large, bureaucratic structure. The concept is basically sound. Historically, most innovations have come from individuals in small businesses (see Chapter 4). As businesses increase in size, however, innovation and creativity tend to become casualties in the battle for higher sales and profits. In some large companies, new ideas are even discouraged, and champions of innovation have been stalled in mid-career.

intrapreneuring The process of creating and maintaining the innovation and flexibility of a small business environment within the confines of a large organization.

Compaq, which is now part of Hewlett-Packard, is an excellent example of how intrapreneuring works to counteract this trend. The firm has one major division called the New Business Group. When a manager or engineer has an idea for a new product or product application, he or she takes it to the New Business Group and "sells" it. The managers in the group are then encouraged to help the innovator develop the idea for field testing. If the product takes off and does well, it is then spun off into its own business group or division. If it doesn't do as well as hoped, it may be maintained as part of the New Business Group or phased out.

Summary of Learning Objectives

1. **Discuss the elements that influence a firm's *organizational structure*.** Every business needs structure to operate. *Organizational structure* varies according to a firm's mission, purpose, and strategy. Size, technology, and changes in environmental circumstances also influence structure. In general, while all organizations have the same basic elements, each develops the structure that contributes to the most efficient operations.

2. **Explain how *specialization* and *departmentalization* are the building blocks of organizational structure.** The building blocks of organizational structure are *job specialization* and *departmentalization*. As a firm grows, it usually has a greater need for people to perform specialized tasks (specialization). It also has a greater need to group types of work into logical units (departmentalization). Common forms of departmentalization are *customer*, *product*, *process*, *geographic*, and *functional*. Large businesses often use more than one form of departmentalization.

3. **Distinguish between *responsibility* and *authority* and explain the differences in decision making in *centralized* and *decentralized organizations*.** *Responsibility* is the duty to perform a task; *authority* is the power to make the decisions necessary to complete tasks. *Delegation* begins when a manager assigns a task to a subordinate; *accountability* means that the subordinate must complete the task. *Span of control* refers to the number of people who work for any individual manager. The more people supervised by a manager, the wider his or her span of control. Wide spans are usually desirable when employees perform simple or unrelated tasks. When jobs are diversified or prone to change, a narrower span is generally preferable.

   In a *centralized organization*, only a few individuals in top management have real decision-making authority. In a *decentralized organization*, much authority is delegated to lower-level management. Where both *line* and *line-and-staff systems* are involved, *line departments* generally have authority to make decisions while *staff departments* have a responsibility to advise. A relatively new concept, *committee and team authority*, empowers committees or work teams involved in a firm's daily operations.

4. **Explain the differences between *functional*, *divisional*, *project*, and *international organizational structures*, and describe the most popular new forms of organizational design.** In a *functional organization*, authority is usually distributed among such basic functions as marketing and finance. In a *divisional organization*, the various divisions of a larger company, which may be related or unrelated, operate in a relatively autonomous fashion. In *project organization*, in which individuals report to more than one manager, a company creates teams to address specific problems or to conduct specific projects. A company that has divisions in many countries may require an additional level of *international organization* to coordinate those operations. Four of the most popular new forms of organizational design are (a) boundaryless organizations (traditional boundaries and structures are minimized or eliminated), (b) team organizations (rely on project-type teams, with little or no functional hierarchy), (c) virtual organizations (have little formal structure and only a handful of permanent employees, a small staff, and a modest administrative facility), and (d) learning organizations (work to facilitate employees' lifelong learning and personal development while transforming the organization to meet changing demands and needs).

5. **Define the *informal organization* and discuss *intrapreneuring*.** The *informal organization* consists of the everyday social interactions among employees that transcend formal jobs and job interrelationships. To foster innovation and flexibility, some large companies encourage *intrapreneuring*—creating and maintaining the innovation and flexibility of a small business environment within the confines of a large bureaucratic structure.

KEY TERMS

accountability, 214
authority, 213
centralized organization, 215
chain of command, 208
committee and team authority, 220
customer departmentalization, 210
decentralized organization, 216
delegation, 214
departmentalization, 210
divisional structure, 221
downsizing, 219
flat organizational structure, 217
functional departmentalization, 210
functional structure, 221
geographic departmentalization, 210
grapevine, 228
informal organization, 227
international organizational structure, 223
intrapreneuring, 229
job specialization, 208
line authority, 219
line department, 219
matrix organization, 222
organization chart, 207
organizational structure, 207
process departmentalization, 211
product departmentalization, 210
profit centre, 210
project organization, 222
responsibility, 213
span of control, 217
staff authority, 219
staff members, 219
tall organizational structure, 217

QUESTIONS FOR ANALYSIS

1. Explain the significance of size as it relates to organizational structure. Describe the changes that are likely to occur as an organization grows.
2. Why do some managers have difficulties in delegating authority? Why does this problem tend to plague smaller businesses?
3. Draw up an organization chart for your college or university.
4. Describe a hypothetical organizational structure for a small printing firm. Describe changes that might be necessary as the business grows.
5. Compare and contrast the matrix and divisional approaches to organizational structure. How would you feel personally about working in a matrix organization in which you were assigned simultaneously to multiple units or groups?
6. If a company has a formal organizational structure, why is the informal organization so important?
7. Consider the organization where you currently work (or one where you have previously worked). Which of the four basic structural types was it most consistent with? What was the basis of departmentalization in the company? Why was that particular basis of departmentalization used?
8. What kinds of problems might develop in a matrix organization? *Why* would these problems develop?

APPLICATION EXERCISES

1. Interview the manager of a local service business—a fast-food restaurant. What types of tasks does this manager typically delegate? Is the appropriate authority also delegated in each case?
2. Using books, magazines, or personal interviews, identify a person who has succeeded as an intrapreneur. In what ways did the structure of the intrapreneur's company help this individual succeed? In what ways did the structure pose problems?

BUILDING YOUR BUSINESS SKILLS

Getting with the Program

Goal

To encourage students to understand the relationship between organizational structure and a company's ability to attract and keep valued employees.

The Situation

You are the founder of a small but growing high-technology company that develops new computer software. With your current workload and new contracts in the pipeline, your business is thriving except for one problem: You cannot find computer programmers for product development. Worse yet, current staff members are being lured away by other high-tech firms. After suffering a particularly discouraging personnel raid in which competitors captured three of your most valued employees, you schedule a meeting with your director of human resources to plan organizational changes designed to encourage worker loyalty. You already pay top dollar, but the continuing exodus tells you that programmers are looking for something more.

Method

Working with three or four classmates, identify some ways in which specific organizational changes might improve the working environment and encourage employee loyalty. As you analyze the following factors, ask yourself the obvious question: If I were a programmer, what organizational changes would encourage me to stay?

Level of job specialization. With many programmers describing their jobs as tedious because of the focus on detail in a narrow work area, what changes, if any, would you make in job specialization? Right now, for instance, few of your programmers have any say in product design.

Decision-making hierarchy. What decision-making authority would encourage people to stay? Is expanding employee authority likely to work better in a centralized or decentralized organization?

Team authority. Can team empowerment make a difference? Taking the point of view of the worker, describe the ideal team.

Intrapreneuring. What can your company do to encourage and reward innovation?

Follow-Up Questions

1. With the average computer programmer earning nearly $70 000 per year, and with all competitive firms paying top dollar, why might organizational issues be critical in determining employee loyalty?
2. If you were a programmer, what organizational factors would make a difference to you? Why?
3. As the company founder, how willing would you be to make major organizational changes in light of the shortage of qualified programmers?

EXERCISING YOUR ETHICS

Minding Your Own Business

The Situation

Assume that you have recently gone to work for a large high-tech company. You have discovered an interesting arrangement in which one of your co-workers is engaging. Specifically, he blocks his schedule for the hour between 11:00 a.m. and 12:00 noon each day and does not take a lunch break. During this one-hour interval, he is actually running his own real estate business.

The Dilemma

You recently asked him how he manages to pull this off. "Well," he responded, "the boss and I never talked about it, but she knows what's going on. They know they can't replace me, and I always get my work done. I don't use any company resources. So, what's the harm?" Interestingly, you also have a business opportunity that could be pursued in the same way.

Questions for Discussion

1. What are the ethical issues in this situation?
2. What do you think most people would do in this situation?
3. What would you do in this situation?

CONCLUDING CASE 7-1

Cooking Up a New Structure

A few years ago, Sara Lee CEO John H. Bryan realized that he had a problem. During the 25 years of his tenure, the firm had grown beyond its foundation in food products to encompass dozens of lines of business—everything from cake mixes to insecticide to lingerie. The new businesses were acquisitions, and the original managers controlled each one as if it were a separate company. Calculating the cost of all this duplication, Bryan reached the conclusion that the company could not afford high costs at a time when price competition was heating up.

In an effort to fix things, starting in 1997, Bryan sold or eliminated about one-quarter of the firm's 200 products. He cut redundant factories and the workforce, reduced the number of products, and standardized company-wide processes. He called his extensive restructuring program "deverticalization," and his goal was to remove Sara Lee from manufacturing while strengthening its focus and effectiveness as a marketer. In the meantime, however, he continued to acquire rival firms to sustain the company's growth. Despite Bryan's efforts, Sara Lee continued to suffer from high costs and remained unfocussed and inefficient. Said one industry analyst about Bryan's strategy: "Sometimes, the more chairs you move around, the more dust you see behind the chairs."

In 2000, C. Steven McMillan took over from Bryan at Sara Lee, and in the immortal words of Yogi Berra, "It was *déjà vu* all over again." McMillan quickly realized that Bryan's moves had had little impact on the firm's performance and that he himself would need to start making some big changes. Borrowing a page from rival Kraft Foods, he began by merging the sales forces that specialized in various brands to create smaller, customer-focussed teams. In meats alone, for instance, Sara Lee had 10 different brands, including Ball Park, Hillshire Farms, Bryan, and Jimmy Dean. "So if you're a Safeway," explained McMillan, "you've got to deal with 10 different organizations and multiple invoices." Teams reduced duplication and were more convenient for buyers—a win-win situation. National retailers like Wal-Mart responded by increasing their orders for Sara Lee products.

McMillan also centralized decision making at the firm by shutting down 50 weaker regional brands and reorganizing the firm into three broad product categories: Food and Beverage, Intimates and Underwear, and Household Products. He abolished several layers of corporate hierarchy, including many of the middle managers the firm had inherited from its acquisitions. He created category managers to oversee related lines of business, and the flattened organizational structure led to improved accountability and more centralized control over Sara Lee's far-flung operations.

McMillan also borrowed some tactics from his predecessor, divesting 15 businesses, including Coach leather goods, and laying off 10 percent of his workers. In another move that was widely questioned by industry observers, he paid $2.8 billion for breadmaker Earthgrains. The move increased Sara Lee's market share in baked goods, but many observers felt that McMillan paid too much for a small potential return.

McMillan still had a few tricks up his sleeves. One bold move was developing a chain of retail stores named Inner Self. Each store features a spa-like atmosphere in which to sell Sara Lee's Hanes, Playtex, Bali, and Wonderbra products. Susan Nedved, head of development for Inner Self, thinks that the company-owned stores provide a more realistic and comforting environment for making underwear purchases than do some specialty outlets. "There seems to be an open void for another specialty concept that complements Victoria's Secret," says Nedved. "There was a need for shopping alternatives that really cater to the aging population."

McMillan remains confident that his strategy—more centralization, coordination, and focus—will do the trick at Sara Lee. "I do believe the things we're doing will enhance the growth rate of our company," he says. But many observers are less optimistic. As for Inner Self and underwear, one analyst points out that "even if you fix that business, it's still apparel, and it's not really viewed as a high-value-added business."

Even if McMillan's strategy does manage to cut costs and increase market share, skeptics point out that there is no logic behind the idea of housing baked goods, meats, coffee, underwear, shoe polish, and household cleaners under one corporate roof. Unless McMillan can find some as-yet-undiscovered synergy among such disparate units, Sara Lee is probably headed for a breakup into several smaller, more focussed, more profitable companies.

Questions for Discussion

1. Describe the basic structural components at Sara Lee.
2. What role does specialization play at Sara Lee?
3. What kinds of authority are reflected in this case?
4. What kind of organizational structure does Sara Lee seem to have?
5. What role has the informal organization played in Sara Lee's various acquisitions and divestitures?

CONCLUDING CASE 7-2

Jersak Holdings

Vaclav Jersak was born in Prague, Czechoslovakia, in 1930. His family had long been active in the retail trade in that city. The Jersak family was very close, but the 1930s and 1940s were a time of great turbulence in central Europe. In 1938, Hitler's troops invaded Czechoslovakia and five years of war followed. After the war, Czechoslovakia came under the influence of the Soviet Union, and capitalistic ventures that had been such an integral part of the Jersak family were severely restricted. By the early 1960s, there were some hints of a return to a more capitalistic economy. To Jersak's dismay, these were snuffed out by the Soviet Union's invasion of Czechoslovakia in 1968.

The invasion was the last straw for Jersak, who had felt for some years that the environment for private business activity was very poor. At age 38, he decided to leave Czechoslovakia for a better life in Canada. He arrived in Toronto in December 1968, determined to apply his entrepreneurial talents in a more promising business environment. Jersak quickly discovered the freedom that entrepreneurs had in Canada. He started a small gas station, and over the next three years he opened several more. In 1971, he purchased a franchise of a major fast-food outlet, and by 1977 he owned four fast-food restaurants. His entrepreneurial instincts led him into a wide variety of business operations after that. From 1977 to 1991, he expanded his activity into the manufacture of auto parts, microcomputers, textiles, and office furniture. He purchased five franchises of a retail auto parts store, two automobile dealerships, and a carpet business that sells to both residential and commercial users. A mining company, a soft drink bottling plant, and a five-store chain of shoe stores are also part of Jersak Holdings Ltd.

As each new business venture was added, Jersak hired a person to manage the operating company. He also added individuals with expertise in accounting, finance, marketing, and production in his head office. Currently, Jersak Holdings Ltd. contains 17 operating companies, each headed by a manager (see Figure 7.9). Employment ranges from five to ten people in each company. In 2005, sales totalled $37 million and profits were $4.7 million.

Head office staff make most of the strategic decisions in the firm. Jersak and the other top executives have frequent informal meetings to discuss matters of importance to the firm. Discussions usually continue until a consensus is reached on a course of action. The operating managers are expected to put into practice the strategic plans that are made at head office.

Vaclav Jersak is now 76. As he looks back on the last 35+ years, he feels a great sense of satisfaction that he has accomplished so much. He has been thinking that the top management group operates smoothly because the people have worked together for many years. But he feels that areas of authority should be more clearly defined so that when changes occur in top management because of retirements, the new people will know exactly what they are responsible for.

Some of Jersak's business acquaintances are of the view that he should delegate considerably more authority to the managers of the operating companies. In effect, they recommend that he turn these operating managers into presidents of their own firms, each of them being responsible for making a profit in their particular enterprise. His acquaintances point out that giving the man-

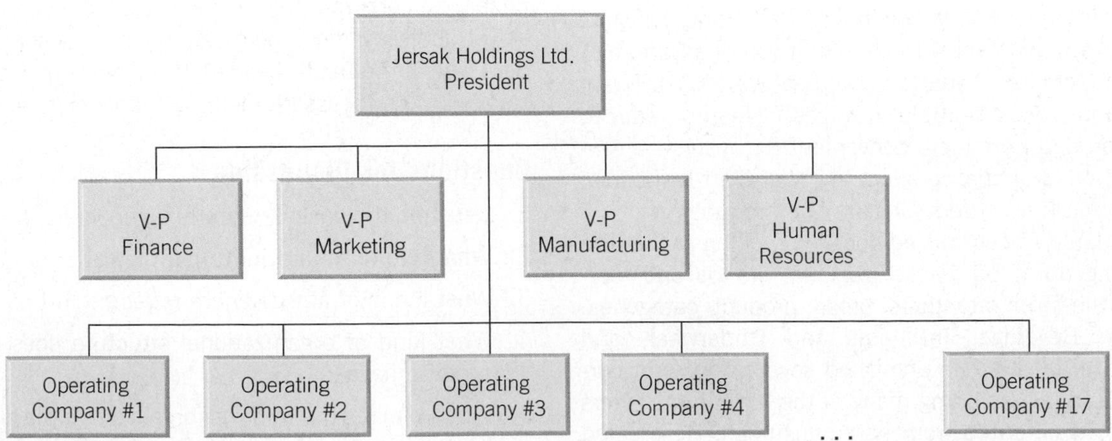

Figure 7.9 Organization of Jersak Holdings Ltd.

agers of the operating companies this level of responsibility will motivate them to achieve much more than they are now. Also, it should motivate the employees in these firms because they will have more discretion as well. Jersak sees some real benefits in this approach, but worries that the current managers of the operating companies haven't had much experience in making important decisions. He also fears that head office will lose control of the operating companies. Jersak feels that it is important for head office staff to know some of the details of each operating company. Without this knowledge, he feels that the head office staff will be unable to make good decisions regarding the operating companies.

Other friends of Jersak argue that the time has come to centralize control at head office because the firm has gotten so large and is so diverse. Only in this way, they argue, will top management be able to effectively control all the activities of Jersak Holdings Ltd.

Jersak is uncertain about what to do, but he feels he must do something to ensure that his life's work will not disappear when he retires next year.

Questions for Discussion

1. Discuss the advantages and disadvantages of centralization and decentralization as they relate to Jersak Holdings Ltd.
2. Which basic approach—centralization or decentralization—should Jersak Holdings Ltd. adopt? Defend your answer.
3. What problems are evident in the current organizational structure of Jersak Holdings Ltd.? Design a new organization chart for the company that will solve these problems.

CHAPTER 8

Managing Human Resources

After reading this chapter, you should be able to:

1. Define *human resource management*, discuss its strategic significance, and explain how managers plan for human resources.
2. Identify the issues involved in *staffing* a company, including *internal* and *external recruiting* and *selection*.
3. Discuss different ways in which organizations go about developing the capabilities of employees and managers.
4. Explain ways in which organizations evaluate employee performance.
5. Discuss the importance of *wages and salaries*, *incentives*, and *benefit programs* in attracting and keeping skilled workers.
6. Describe some of the key legal issues involved in hiring, compensating, and managing workers.
7. Discuss *workforce diversity*, the management of *knowledge workers*, and the use of *contingent and temporary workers* as important changes in the contemporary workplace.

Celebrating Workforce Diversity

The following facts about visible minorities show just how important the issue of workforce diversity has become:

- 73 percent of the people who immigrated to Canada during the 1990s were visible minorities.
- 18 percent of Canada's population was born outside Canada.
- 20 percent of Saskatchewan's population will be Aboriginal by 2015.
- In 2001, approximately 4 million Canadians were visible minorities; by 2017, that number could increase to as much as 8.5 million.
- The largest visible minority group in Canada in 2001 was the Chinese, but the South Asian population is expected to grow more quickly during the next decade.
- Visible minorities currently make up 40 percent of the population of Vancouver.
- By 2017, visible minorities will form more than 50 percent of the populations of Toronto and Vancouver.
- By 2017, 22 percent of the total Canadian population will be visible minorities.

Changes of this magnitude simply cannot be ignored, either by Canadian politicians or by Canadian business firms. Procter & Gamble Canada is one of the many Canadian businesses that are taking steps to deal with the challenges and opportunities that come with a rapidly changing population demographic.

Thirty years ago, P&G was like a lot of other Canadian companies—most of its employees were white males. But that's changing rapidly. In 2005, for example, the 800 people who are employed at P&G's Toronto headquarters organized a major social gathering to celebrate the diverse nature of the P&G workforce (employees come from 40 different countries and speak at least 30 different languages). But the event wasn't just for fun. Like other companies, P&G has learned that employees are more productive when their differences are respected in the work environment. And that translates into increased corporate success. Since the top management positions at P&G are still predominantly held by white males, the company has set a strategic goal to diversify its workforce.

P&G thinks that a diverse workforce also helps the company market its well-known brands—Pampers, Crest, Tide, Mr. Clean, etc.—to a diverse group of consumers. And the facts reported above clearly show that Canadian consumers are becoming more diverse at a dizzying pace. As consumer demographics change, it is important to get more diverse people involved in making marketing decisions. The president of P&G Canada, Tim Penner, says that a diverse workforce enriches everyone in the company because they are exposed to other cultures; also, the diversity gives employees a better understanding of P&G's customers.

There are multiple "affinity groups" at P&G, such as the Women's Leadership Council, the French Canadian Network, the Asian Professional Network, the Christian Network, and the Jewish Network. The goal of these networks is to help employees feel comfortable about participating in corporate life, and to act as resource groups for employees who want insights about how to target certain specific markets.

Western Union is another company that is focussing on diversity, and it may be further along than most companies given the nature of its business—moving money overseas to the families of new Canadians who are working here and want to help their families back in their home country. The potential customers of Western Union are not easily reached by traditional marketing methods, so the company hires people who speak the language of their target market and who know what it feels like to be an immigrant in Canada. When recruiting new employees, Western Union does not demand "Canadian experience" as many other companies do. Rather, they want employees with international experience because of the nature of the company's business. After Western Union hires these people, they seek out local business operators to act as Western Union agents for their own ethnic community.

Marketing Manager Marco Amoranto is typical of the kind of employees that are hired at Western Union. He was born in the Philippines and originally worked for Colgate Palmolive. He wanted to work in Canada but had trouble landing a job because he didn't have Canadian experience. At Western Union, he is responsible for marketing to Asian and Europeans. He recently returned from a "road show" where the company sponsored concerts featuring several top Philippine entertainers, including Freestyle, Basil Valdez, and Jaya.

The Western Union approach has yielded some interesting benefits. In one area of Toronto, for example, customers who wanted to transfer money back to the Philippines got a free loaf of Pan de Sel bread from a local Filipino baker. Thus, the results were positive for Western Union, its customers, and the baker. Western Union also brings in entertainers from its customers' home countries and then gives these customers free tickets to the concerts.

In the current, rapidly changing demographic environment, companies are discovering that they cannot be unconcerned about workforce (and customer) diversity. One company that has had some bad press recently in this area is Wal-Mart, which has been confronted with a class-action sex discrimination lawsuit, as well as a lot of negative publicity about the alleged low wages and lack of health care available to its employees. In response to these concerns, the company has hired a director of diversity.

Lee Scott, the CEO of Wal-Mart, says that Wal-Mart is a "pretty good company," but with 1.5 million employees, there are bound to be some racists and sexists among them. The company has also developed incentives to motivate top managers to reach certain diversity goals. If the goals are not met, for example, Scott could forfeit up to $600 000 of his salary. Scott says that in the past, if an employee made a racist or sexist remark, the person might just be transferred. But in today's more enlightened environment, that kind of behaviour can no longer be tolerated and the person will be terminated. With Wal-Mart opening more stores in areas where a larger proportion of customers are Hispanic and black, there will be less tolerance of unacceptable behaviour among employees. ◆

THE FOUNDATIONS OF HUMAN RESOURCE MANAGEMENT

human resource management (HRM) Set of organizational activities directed at attracting, developing, and maintaining an effective workforce.

1 Define *human resource management*, discuss its strategic significance, and explain how managers plan for human resources.

Human resource management (HRM) is the set of organizational activities directed at attracting, developing, and maintaining an effective workforce. Human resource management takes place within a complex and ever-changing environmental context and is increasingly being recognized for its strategic importance.[1]

The Strategic Importance of HRM

Human resources are critical for effective organizational functioning. HRM (or *personnel*, as it is sometimes called) was once relegated to second-class status in many organizations, but its importance has grown dramatically in the last two decades. This new importance stems from increased legal complexities, the recognition that human resources are a valuable means for improving productivity, and the awareness today of the costs associated with poor human resource management.

Indeed, managers now realize that the effectiveness of their HR function has a substantial impact on a firm's bottom-line performance. Poor human resource planning can result in spurts of hiring followed by layoffs—costly in terms of unemployment compensation payments, training expenses, and morale. Haphazard compensation systems do not attract, keep, and motivate good employees, and outmoded recruitment practices can expose the firm to expensive and embarrassing legal action. Consequently, the chief human resource executive of most large businesses is a vice-president directly accountable to the CEO, and many firms are developing strategic HR plans that are integrated with other strategic planning activities.

Human Resource Planning

The starting point in attracting qualified human resources is planning. In turn, HR planning involves *job analysis* and *forecasting* the demand for and supply of labour (see Figure 8.1).

Job Analysis

Job analysis is a systematic analysis of jobs within an organization. A job analysis is made up of two parts:

- The **job description** lists the duties of a job, its working conditions, and the tools, materials, and equipment used to perform it.
- The **job specification** lists the skills, abilities, and other credentials needed to do the job.

Job analysis information is used in many HR activities. For instance, knowing about job content and job requirements is necessary to develop appropriate selection methods and job-relevant performance appraisal systems and to set equitable compensation rates.

job analysis A detailed study of the specific duties in a particular job and the human qualities required for that job.

job description The objectives, responsibilities, and key tasks of a job; the conditions under which it will be done; its relationship to other positions; and the skills needed to perform it.

job specification The specific skills, education, and experience needed to perform a job.

Forecasting HR Demand and Supply

After managers fully understand the jobs to be performed within an organization, they can start planning for the organization's future HR needs. The manager starts by assessing trends in past HR usage, future organizational plans, and general economic trends. A good sales forecast is often the foundation,

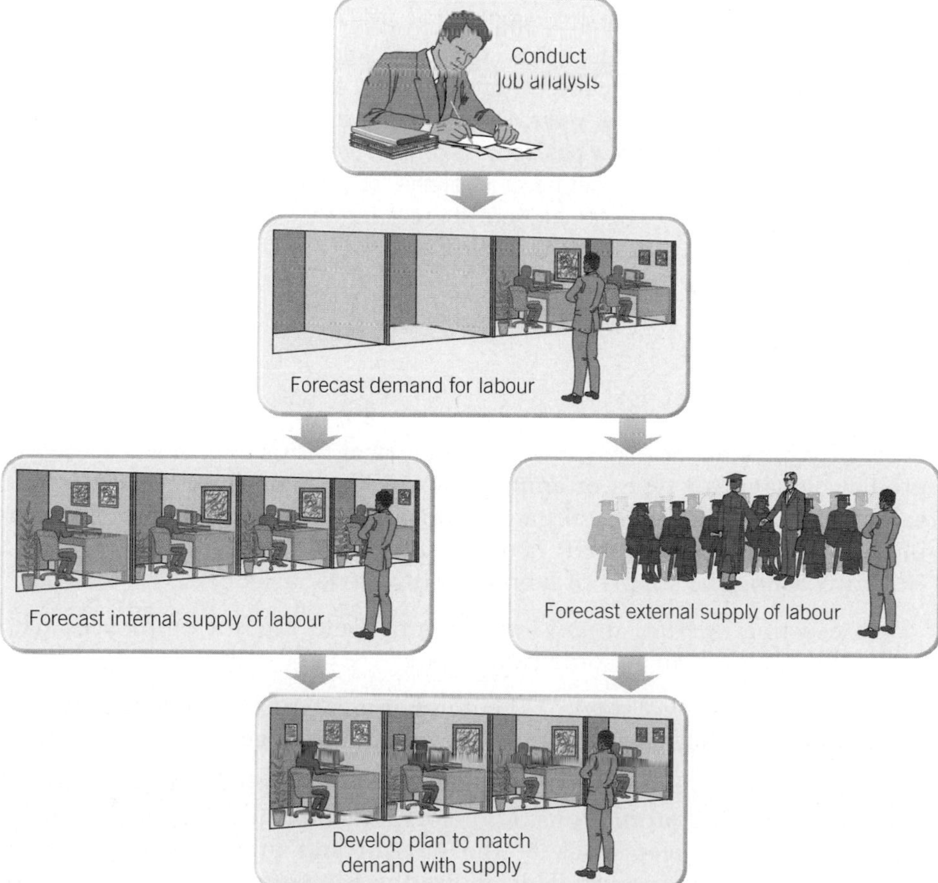

Figure 8.1 Planning for human resources.

ENTREPRENEURSHIP AND NEW VENTURES

The Guru for Fun Takes a Meeting With the V.P. of Buzz

Rather than dictating standard job titles, some new ventures and entrepreneurial firms now allow incumbents to name their own jobs. Others even let employees *create* their own jobs. Not surprisingly, some interesting twists have emerged.

It started with the internet bubble. For example, Amy Berkus, a marketing coordinator at a small dot-com, changed her job title to "marketing mechanic." "Everyone was creating new titles in Internet-speak," recalls Berkus. "We wanted titles that conveyed team spirit and a fun atmosphere.... It just fit the time." Other catchy designations included "V.P. of Buzz," "Chief People Officer," "Guru of Fun," "Gladiator," and "Chief Evangelist." Under the right circumstances, such titles encouraged creativity and got employees to think differently about their jobs. They also let everyone know that the company was hip. "It was a matter of doing away with everything that seemed to reek of the old," explains business professor Donna Hoffman. "The feeling was, 'We're going to make new rules. We need new titles.'"

But the times, of course, have changed. Executive recruiter Marc Lewis observes that "as the market has cooled, the interest in creative and unusual job titles has diminished." Smaller companies (as well as some larger ones) are now trying to create images of legitimacy, respectability, and honesty. Berkus admits that "the traditional titles [like 'customer care manager' and 'production supervisor'] lend themselves more to the image of a stable company that is driving toward profitability."

Does a return to confidence-inspiring, snooze-inducing job titles mean that companies have abandoned the effort to encourage employee creativity? By no means. Innovation is just as important during tough times as during boom times. The method, however, has changed. Today, entrepreneurial firms that want to encourage and reward creativity aren't willing to settle for window dressing. They're changing the jobs themselves.

Employers are finding, for instance, that basing positions on employee interests can be more effective than trying to fit unique individuals into predetermined job slots. Often a customized job is a reward for high performance. Steve Gluckman, a bicycle designer for REI (www.rei.com), a small supplier of outdoor gear, worked his way up from service manager to designer over 13 years. An avid cyclist, he says, "Some people sing. Some people paint. I ride my bike. Like a ballet dancer, like a gymnast, like a skateboarder, I express myself in my job." Starbucks's coffee education manager, Aileen Carrell, travels around the world educating employees about coffee. "I was hired as temporary Christmas help in 1990," explains Carrell, "and I fell madly in love with the fact that coffees came from the most amazing places, like Sulawesi." After working as a store manager for several years, Carrell herself proposed the creation of her new position. Of course, organizations will always have to define most of the jobs that have to be performed, but many are discovering that a little flexibility can lead to a lot of productivity.

especially for smaller organizations. Historical ratios can then be used to predict demand for types of employees, such as operating employees and sales representatives. Large organizations, of course, use much more complicated models to predict HR needs.

Forecasting the supply of labour involves two tasks:

- forecasting *internal supply*—the number and type of employees who will be in the firm at some future date
- forecasting *external supply*—the number and type of people who will be available for hiring from the labour market at large

The simplest approach merely adjusts present staffing levels for anticipated turnover and promotions. Large organizations use extremely sophisticated models to keep track of the present and future distributions of professionals and managers. This allows the company to spot areas where there will eventually be too many qualified professionals competing for too few promotions or, conversely, too few good people available to fill important positions.

Replacement Charts. At higher levels of the organization, managers make plans for specific people and positions. The technique most commonly used is the **replacement chart**, which lists each important managerial position, who occupies it, how long he or she will probably stay in it before moving on, and who (by name) is now qualified or soon will be qualified to move into it. This technique allows ample time to plan developmental experiences for people identified as potential successors to critical managerial jobs.

replacement chart An HR technique that lists each important managerial position, who occupies it, how long he or she will probably stay in it before moving on, and who (by name) is now qualified or soon will be qualified to move into it.

Skills Inventories. To facilitate both planning and identifying people for transfer or promotion, some organizations also have **employee information systems**, or **skills inventories**. These systems are usually computerized and contain information on each employee's education, skills, work experience, and career aspirations. Such a system can quickly locate every employee who is qualified to fill a position requiring, say, a degree in chemical engineering, three years of experience in an oil refinery, and fluency in French.

employee information systems (skills inventories) Computerized systems that contain information on each employee's education, skills, work experience, and career aspirations.

Forecasting the external supply of labour is a different problem altogether. How does a manager, for example, predict how many electrical engineers will be seeking work in Ontario or British Columbia three years from now? To get an idea of the future availability of labour, planners must rely on information from outside sources, such as government reports and figures supplied by colleges and universities on the number of students in major fields.

Matching HR Supply and Demand

After comparing future demand and internal supply, managers can make plans to manage predicted shortfalls or overstaffing. If a shortfall is predicted, new employees can be hired, present employees can be retrained and transferred into understaffed areas, individuals approaching retirement can be convinced to stay on, or labour-saving or productivity-enhancing systems can be installed.

If the organization needs to hire, the external labour-supply forecast helps managers plan how to recruit according to whether the type of person needed is readily available or scarce in the labour market. The use of temporary workers also helps managers in staffing by giving them extra flexibility. If overstaffing is expected to be a problem, the main options are transferring the extra employees, not replacing individuals who quit, encouraging early retirement, and laying people off.

STAFFING THE ORGANIZATION

Identify the issues involved in *staffing* a company, including *internal* and *external recruiting* and *selection*. **2**

Once managers have decided what positions they need to fill, they must find and hire individuals who meet the job requirements. A study by the Canadian Federation of Independent Business found that the top three characteristics employers are looking for when they hire people are a good work ethic, reliability, and willingness to stay on the job.[2] Staffing of the corporation is one of the most complex and important aspects of good human resource management. The top 10 employers by number of employees in Canada are listed in Table 8.1.

In this section, we will describe both the process of acquiring staff from outside the company (*external staffing*) and the process of promoting staff from within (*internal staffing*). Both external and internal staffing, however, start with effective recruiting.

Table 8.1 The Top 10 Employers in Canada, 2005

Company	Employees
1. George Weston Ltd.	150 000
2. Onex Corp.	138 000
3. Magna International Inc.	82 000
4. McDonald's Restaurants of Canada Ltd.	77 000
5. Wal-Mart Canada Corp.	70 000
6. Alcan Inc.	69 000
7. Metro Inc.	65 000
8. Royal Bank of Canada	60 012
9. BCE Inc.	60 001
10. Canada Post Corp.	60 000

Recruiting Human Resources

recruiting The phase in the staffing of a company in which the firm seeks to develop a pool of interested, qualified applicants for a position.

Once an organization has an idea of its future HR needs, the next phase is usually recruiting new employees. **Recruiting** is the process of attracting qualified persons to apply for the jobs that are open. Where do recruits come from? Some recruits are found internally; others come from outside the organization.

Internal Recruiting

internal recruiting Considering present employees as candidates for job openings.

Internal recruiting means considering present employees as candidates for openings. Promotion from within can help build morale and keep high-quality employees from leaving. In unionized firms, the procedures for notifying employees of internal job-change opportunities are usually spelled out in the union contract. For higher-level positions, a skills inventory system may be used to identify internal candidates or managers may be asked to recommend individuals who should be considered.

External Recruiting

external recruiting Attracting people outside the organization to apply for jobs.

External recruiting involves attracting people outside the organization to apply for jobs. External recruiting methods include advertising, campus interviews, employment agencies or executive search firms, union hiring halls, referrals by present employees, and hiring "walk-ins" or "gate-hires" (people who show up without being solicited). Of course, a manager must select the most appropriate method for each job. Private employment agencies can be a good source of clerical and technical employees, and executive search firms specialize in locating top-management talent. Newspaper ads are often used because they reach a wide audience and thus allow minorities "equal opportunity" to learn about and apply for job openings.

The old-fashioned *job fair* has survived in spite of internet career postings and the proliferation of employment agencies and headhunters. At a job fair, candidates browse through the positions available and employers can see a sample of the skills candidates have. While job postings on the internet are impersonal, at job fairs candidates and recruiters can talk to each other face-to-face. Job fairs are also cheaper than posting jobs with an employment agency or headhunter. Non-traditional recruiting methods are also used. For example, Nortel Networks recruited at a rock concert that was held near one of its manufacturing facilities. Recruiters handed out lip balm, ran a raffle, and talked about Nortel to people who were arriving to hear Counting Crows and Live.[3]

At job fairs, students and recruiters can talk face-to-face about jobs that are available. Here, recruiters talk to students about the opportunities at the company.

Internships. One method of external recruiting involves offering college and university students **internships**—short-term paid positions where students focus on a specific project. If the individual works out well, the company often hires the student full-time after they graduate. At IBM Canada's "Extreme Blue" internship program, for example, students are responsible for turning an idea into a marketable product. They also network with industry leaders and develop their professional skills.[4]

internship A short-term paid position where students focus on a specific project.

Selecting Human Resources

Once the recruiting process has attracted a pool of applicants, the next step is to select someone to hire. The intent of the selection process is to gather information from applicants that will predict their job success and then to hire the candidates likely to be most successful. Of course, the organization can only gather information about factors that are predictive of future performance. The process of determining the predictive value of information is called **validation**.

validation The process of determining the predictive value of information.

To reduce the element of uncertainty, managers use a variety of selection techniques, the most common of which are shown in Figure 8.2. Each organization develops its own mix of selection techniques and may use them in almost any order.

Application Forms

The first step in selection is usually asking the candidate to fill out an application form. An application form is an efficient method of gathering information about the applicant's previous work history, educational background, and other job-related demographic data. It should not contain questions about areas unrelated to the job, such as gender, religion, or national origin. Application-form data are generally used informally to decide whether a candidate merits further evaluation, and interviewers use application forms to familiarize themselves with candidates before interviewing them.

Tests

Tests of ability, skill, aptitude, or knowledge relevant to a particular job are usually the best predictors of job success, although tests of general intelligence or personality are occasionally useful as well. In addition to being validated,

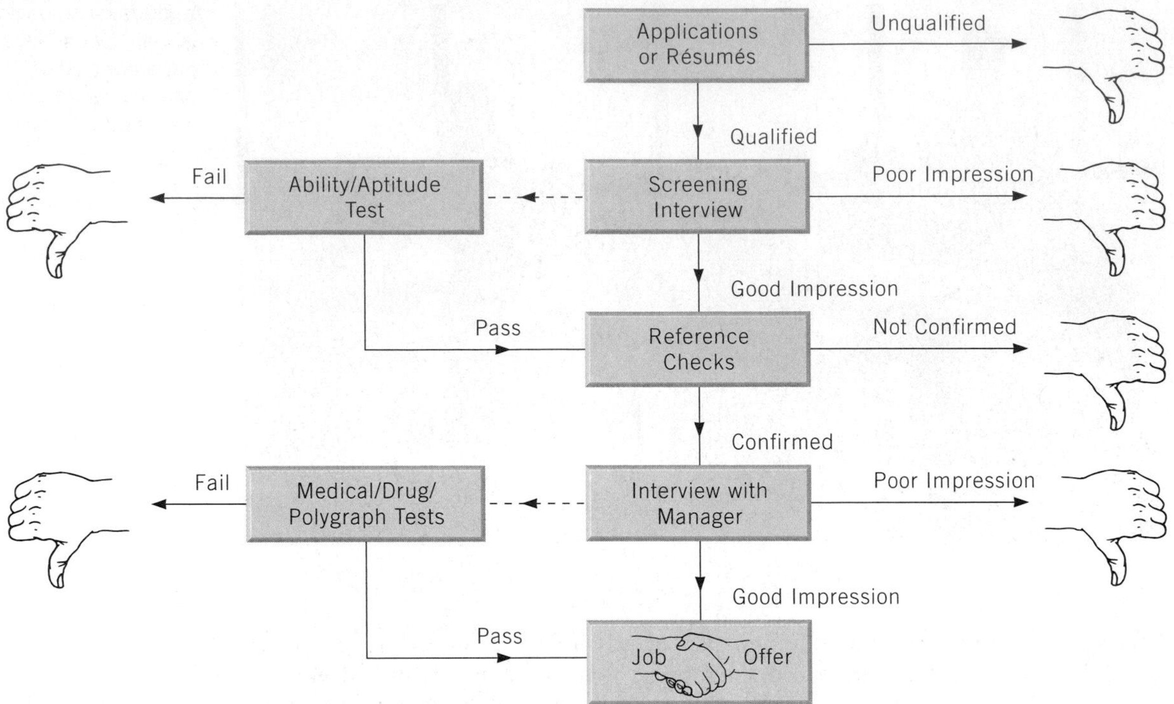

Figure 8.2 General steps in the selection process.

tests should be administered and scored consistently. All candidates should be given the same directions, allowed the same amount of time, and offered the same testing environment (e.g., temperature, lighting, distractions).

A survey conducted by Development Dimensions International found that 83 percent of hiring managers use some sort of testing as part of the hiring process. At Astral Media Inc. of Montreal, for example, job candidates are required to take a series of tests that measure verbal and numerical skills, as well as psychological traits. This testing increases the chance that Astral will hire high-performing employees who will fit in with the company's culture.[5]

assessment centre A series of exercises in which management candidates perform realistic management tasks while being observed by appraisers.

video assessment Involves showing potential hires videos of realistic work situations and asking them to choose a course of action to deal with the situation.

An **assessment centre** is a series of exercises in which candidates perform realistic management tasks under the watchful eye of expert appraisers. A typical assessment centre might be set up in a large conference room and go on for two or three days. During this time, potential managers might take selection tests, engage in management simulations, make individual presentations, and conduct group discussions. Assessors check to see how each participant reacts to stress or to criticism by colleagues. A relatively new type of test that evolved from assessment centres is **video assessment**. Here, potential hires are shown videos of realistic work situations and then asked to choose a course of action to deal with the situation. Video assessment is fast, reliable, cheap, and versatile.

Regardless of the type of test that is used, it must be job-related (that is, it must not serve as a basis for discriminating against anyone for reasons unrelated to the job) and it must be a valid predictor of performance (that is, it must provide evidence that people who score well on it are more likely to perform well in the job than are people who score poorly on it).

Interviews

The interview is a popular selection device, but it is sometimes a poor predictor of job success because biases that are inherent in the way people perceive and judge others on first meeting affect subsequent evaluations. David

An in-depth interview with a prospective employee is often part of the recruiting process, particularly for managerial jobs.

Towler, the director of creative marketing for Kitchener, Ontario-based Creative Organizational Design, says that many companies are placing more emphasis on testing and less emphasis on interviewing because job candidates are becoming very clever at interviewing and giving all the "right" answers.[6]

Interview validity can be improved by training interviewers to be aware of potential biases and by increasing the structure of the interview. In a structured interview, questions are written in advance and all interviewers follow the same question list with each candidate. Such structure introduces consistency into the interview procedure and allows the organization to validate the content of the questions. For interviewing managerial or professional candidates, a somewhat less structured approach can be used. Although question areas and information-gathering objectives are still planned in advance, specific questions vary with the candidates' backgrounds.

Interviewers can also increase interview validity by asking "curveball" questions—that is, questions that job applicants would never expect to be asked—to see how well they think on their feet. Questions such as "How would you move Mount Fuji?" or How would you sell me a glass of water?" are curveball questions. Candidate answers to seemingly off-the-wall questions like these give interviewers additional insights into a candidate's strengths and weaknesses.[7] The Business Accountability box describes further actions that interviewers can take to make interviews useful.

Other Techniques

Organizations also use other selection techniques that vary with the circumstances. A manufacturer afraid of injuries to workers on the job might require new employees to have a physical examination. This gives the company some information about whether the employees are physically fit to do the work and what (if any) pre-existing injuries they might have.

Polygraph (lie detector) tests are largely illegal now, and drug tests are also coming under fire. In 1998, for example, the Ontario Divisional Court decided that Imperial Oil Ltd.'s drug policy (which included pre-employment drug testing that made offers of work conditional on a negative result) was unlawful because Imperial Oil failed to prove that a positive drug test would indicate a failure to perform essential duties. Imperial Oil's policy also required random drug and alcohol testing, but that was also judged to be discriminatory because the company could not prove that such testing was necessary to deter alcohol or drug impairment on the job.[8]

BUSINESS ACCOUNTABILITY

Behaviour-Based Interviewing

Behaviour-based interviewing assumes that your past behaviour is a pretty good predictor of your future behaviour. Specifically, it assesses how you reacted to difficult and/or important job situations in the past, and assumes that these are a good indicator of how you will react to similar job situations in the future. The approach can be used to test for technical skills (e.g., accounting, welding, or computer programming), management skills (e.g., organizing, motivating others, or communicating), and individual skills (e.g., dependability, discipline, or the ability to work on a team).

Instead of asking a traditional interviewing question like "Do you often take the initiative?" behaviour-based interviewing asks "Tell me about a situation where you became aware of a problem. What did you do?" Asking questions like this focusses the interview much more on your *behaviour* than on what you *say* you would do if the problem arose in the future. Other typical questions that interviewers ask in behaviour-based interviewing are as follows:

- Think of a time when you were asked to analyze information and then make a specific recommendation. What kind of reasoning and thought processes did you use?
- Think of a time when you had to deal with a customer that you thought was being unreasonable. How did you deal with that person?
- Think of a time when you had to cope with a major change in your job. What did you do?
- Think of a time when you had to work with a person that was not "pulling their weight." What, if anything, did you do?

Behaviour-based interviewing requires the person who is interviewing candidates to first identify the characteristics, skills, and behaviours that are important in the job that needs to be filled. The interviewer then constructs open-ended questions that will determine if the interviewee possesses those characteristics, skills, and behaviours.

Behaviour-based interviewing is becoming more common because companies are facing increasingly competitive environments. These competitive environments have meant downsizing, which places increasing demands on the workers who remain. There is also more emphasis on working in teams. These changing work situations have motivated companies to be much more focussed in their hiring because they want workers who are more skilled and motivated than previously.

The increasing use of behaviour-based interviewing means that you are likely to be exposed to it at some point in your job search. What should you do to prepare for a behaviour-based interview? The main thing is to think about the job you are interviewing for and the skills that will be required to do it. Try to tell an interesting story (from a previous paid or volunteer position) that succinctly describes a situation you faced, the actions you took, and the outcome that resulted from your actions. If the outcome was good, the interviewer will likely be favourably impressed with your logical thinking and actions. Even if the outcome wasn't so good, you can indicate what you learned from the experience and how that experience will benefit your new employer.

The Toronto-Dominion Bank wanted to give drug tests to all new employees because it wanted to have the public's trust. However, a federal court ruled that the bank's policy was discriminatory and that it wasn't related closely enough to job performance.[9]

DEVELOPING HUMAN RESOURCES

3 Discuss different ways in which organizations go about developing the capabilities of employees and managers.

Regardless of how effective a selection system is, most employees need additional training if they are to grow and develop in their jobs. This process begins with *orientation* and then proceeds to the *assessment of training and development needs* (including the performance of a *needs analysis*) and the selection of the best *training techniques and methods*.

New Employee Orientation

An important part of an organization's training and development program is new employee orientation. **Orientation** is the process of introducing new employees to the company's policies and programs, personnel with whom they will interact, and the nature of the job so that they can more quickly become effective contributors. Poor orientation can result in disenchantment, dissatisfaction, anxiety, turnover, and other employee problems. But effective orientation can play a key role in job satisfaction, performance, and retention. An effective orientation program will help newcomers feel like part of a team, introduce them quickly to co-workers, supervisors, and other new employees, and in a variety of other ways ease the transition from outsider to insider.

orientation The initial acquainting of new employees with the company's policies and programs, personnel with whom they will interact, and the nature of the job.

Some organizations also find it appropriate to include as a part of their orientation a general overview of and introduction to the business itself. This introduction may include such things as information about the firm's history, its evolution, its successes, and perhaps even some of its failures. Organizations with strong corporate cultures are especially likely to include such information because it is a quick and efficient way to provide information about the firm's culture to new hires. This makes it easier for them to understand the culture and to know how to function within it.

Training and Development

Beyond orientation for new employees, most organizations also find it effective to continue training and development on a regular basis. In other words, employees must be continually trained and developed to enhance and otherwise improve the quality of the contributions they make to the organization.

The starting point in assessing training and development needs is conducting a *needs analysis*—determining the organization's true needs and the training programs necessary to meet them. This analysis generally focusses on two things: the organization's job-related needs and the capabilities of the current workforce. The organization's needs are determined by the nature of the work that the organization needs to be done. That is, what knowledge, skills, and abilities does the organization need to compete? What skills must its workforce possess to perform the organization's work effectively?

Depending on both the content of the program and the instructors selected to present it, a number of techniques and methods can be used for the actual delivery of information. We examine some of the more popular techniques and methods in this section.

Work-Based Programs

One major family of techniques and methods consists of various **work-based programs** that tie training and development activities directly to task performance. The most common method of work-based training is **on-the-job training**. The employee is placed in the actual work situation and is shown how to perform a task by a supervisor or an experienced employee. Much on-the-job training is informal, as when one employee shows another how to operate the photocopy machine.

work-based programs A technique that ties training and development activities directly to task performance.

on-the-job training Those development programs in which employees gain new skills while performing them at work.

Another work-based program is **vestibule training**, which is a work simulation in which the job is performed under conditions closely simulating the actual work environment. At Montreal-based CAE Inc., engineers built a simulator for the world's largest passenger jet, the Airbus A380. Pilots use the simulator to learn how to fly the new jet without ever leaving the ground.[10]

vestibule training A work simulation in which the job is performed under conditions closely simulating the actual work environment.

systematic job rotations and transfers A technique in which an employee is systematically rotated or transferred from one job to another.

Another method of work-based training program is **systematic job rotations and transfers**. This method is most likely to be used for lower level managers or for operating employees being groomed for promotions to supervisory management positions. As the term suggests, the employee is systematically rotated or transferred from one job to another. The employee thus learns a wider array of tasks, acquires more abilities, and develops a more comprehensive view of the work of an organization or a particular sub-unit.

Instructional-Based Programs

instructional-based programs Training workers through the use of classroom-based programs such as the lecture approach.

lecture or discussion approach An instructional-based program in which a trainer presents material in a descriptive fashion to those attending a trainee program.

A second family of techniques and methods involves **instructional-based programs**. The most commonly used of these programs is the **lecture or discussion approach**. In these situations, a trainer presents material in a descriptive fashion to those attending a trainee program. Just as a professor lectures students on a particular subject matter, an organizational trainer "lectures" trainees. Depending on the situation and the size of the training class, the instructor may opt for a pure lecture method or may include discussion with trainees. Sometimes lectures are on video or audio tapes so that various individuals in the organization can receive the same training at different times and/or at different locations.

off-the-job training Those development programs in which employees learn new skills at a location away from the normal work site.

Off-the-job training is performed at a location away from the work site. It may be at a classroom within the same facility or at a different location altogether. For example, refresher courses are offered to managers of McDonald's 1375 Canadian restaurants at the Canadian Institute of Hamburgerology; in addition, training videotapes are shown to restaurant workers.[11] Coffee College is a two-week cram course run by Second Cup Ltd., Canada's largest retailer of specialty coffee. During their stay at Coffee College, franchisees and managers learn how to hire workers, keep the books, detect employee theft, and boost Christmas sales.[12]

Another instructional-based program is computer-assisted instruction. A trainee sits at a personal computer and operates software that has been specifically developed to teach certain material. The actual training materials are stored on the computer's hard drive, a CD-ROM, or a website. One major advantage of this method is that it allows self-paced learning and immediate feedback.

Video conferencing has become an important part of the training function in organizations because significant interaction is possible between the trainer and trainees.

Team Building and Group-Based Training

Also increasingly popular in recent years are various team-building and group-based methods of training. As more and more organizations are using teams as a basis for doing their jobs, it should not be surprising that many of the same companies are developing training programs specifically designed to facilitate intragroup co-operation among team members.

One popular method involves various outdoor training exercises. Some programs, for example, involve a group going through a physical obstacle course that requires climbing, crawling, and other physical activities. Outward Bound and several other independent companies specialize in offering these kinds of programs, and their clients include such firms as General Foods, Xerox, and Burger King. Participants, of course, must see the relevance of such programs if they are to be successful. Firms don't want employees returning from team-building programs to report merely that the experience "was childlike and fun and fairly inoffensive."[13]

EVALUATING EMPLOYEE PERFORMANCE

Another important part of human resource management is **performance appraisal**—the specific and formal evaluation of an employee to determine the degree to which he or she is performing effectively. Appraisals are important because they provide a benchmark to assess the extent to which recruiting and selection processes are adequate. In other words, performance appraisals help managers assess the extent to which they are recruiting and selecting the best employees. They also contribute to effective training, development, and compensation.

performance appraisal A formal program for evaluating how well an employee is performing the job; helps managers to determine how effective they are in recruiting and selecting employees.

Explain ways in which organizations evaluate employee performance. **4**

The Performance Appraisal Process

Several questions must be answered as part of the performance appraisal process. These questions generally relate to who conducts the performance appraisal and provides feedback to the individual whose performance is being evaluated.

Conducting the Performance Appraisal

The individual's supervisor is the person most likely to conduct a performance appraisal. Supervisors usually have both the most knowledge of the job requirements and the most opportunity to observe employees performing their jobs. In addition, the supervisor is usually responsible for the performance of his or her subordinates. Thus, the supervisor is both responsible for employees' high performance and accountable for their inadequate performance.

Sources of Information. One possible source of information in the performance appraisal process is the subordinates of the individual being appraised. Subordinates are an especially important source of information when the performance of their own managers is being evaluated. Their input is perhaps most useful when the performance appraisal focusses on the manager's leadership potential. Another source of information is self-evaluation. In many professional and managerial situations, individuals occasionally may be asked to evaluate their own performance. A final source of information is customers. Restaurants such as Red Lobster, for example, place feedback forms in the envelopes in which customers receive their bills. These types of forms typically ask customers to evaluate their experience at the restaurant by asking questions about the service, the food, and the restaurant itself.

Managers must recognize that each source of information is subject to various weaknesses and shortcomings. As a result, many organizations find it effective to rely on a variety of different information sources in the conduct of appraisals. They may, for example, gather information not merely from supervisors or peers, but from both. Indeed, some organizations gather information from every source described in this section. This comprehensive approach is called **360-degree feedback**.

360-degree feedback Gathering information from a manager's subordinates, peers, and superiors when assessing the manager's performance.

Providing Performance Feedback

After the performance appraisal, the next major activity is providing feedback, coaching, and counselling. Many managers do a poor job in this area, in part because they don't understand how to do it properly and in part because they don't enjoy it. Almost by definition, performance appraisal in many organizations tends to focus on negatives. As a result, managers may have a tendency to avoid giving feedback because they know that an employee who receives negative feedback may be angry, hurt, discouraged, or argumentative. But clearly, if employees are not told about their shortcomings, they will have no concrete reason to try to improve and receive no guidance as to how to improve. It is critical, therefore, that managers follow up on appraisals by providing feedback.

Methods for Appraising Performance

Because of the nature of many jobs today, especially managerial work, most methods for appraising performance rely on judgments and ratings. A great deal of effort has therefore been expended trying to make relatively subjective evaluations as meaningful and useful as they can be. While some of the methods are based on relative rankings, others are based on ratings. In this section, we examine a few of the more popular methods, which we have categorized as either *ranking* or *rating methods*.

Ranking Methods

simple ranking method A method of performance appraisal that requires a manager to rank-order from top to bottom or from best to worst each member of a particular work group or department.

forced distribution method A method of performance appraisal that involves grouping employees into predefined frequencies of performance ratings.

The **simple ranking method** requires a manager to rank-order from top to bottom or from best to worst each member of a particular work group or department. The individual ranked first is the top performer, the individual ranked second is the second-best performer, and so forth. The basis for the ranking is generally global or overall performance. Another ranking method, the **forced distribution method**, involves grouping employees into predefined frequencies of performance ratings. Those frequencies are determined in advance and are imposed on the rater. A decision might be made, for instance, that 10 percent of the employees in a work group will be grouped as "outstanding," 20 percent as "very good," 40 percent as "average," 20 percent as "below average," and the remaining 10 percent as "poor." The forced distribution method is familiar to many students because it is the principle used by professors who grade on a so-called "bell curve" or "normal curve."

Rating Methods

graphic rating scale A statement or question about some aspect of an individual's job performance for which the rater must select the response that fits best.

One of the most popular and widely used methods is the **graphic rating scale**, which consists simply of a statement or question about some aspect of an individual's job performance. Following the statement or question is a series of answers or possible responses from which the rater must select the one that fits best. For example, one common set of responses to a graphic rating scale with five possible alternatives is *strongly agree, agree, neither agree nor disagree, disagree,* and *strongly disagree.* These responses, or "descriptors," are usually arrayed along a bar, line, or similar visual representation marked with numbers or letters corresponding to each descriptor. Figure 8.3 shows a sample graphic rating scale.

Graphic rating scales are appealing because they are relatively easy to develop. A manager simply "brainstorms" or otherwise develops a list of statements or questions that are presumably related to relevant indicators of performance. Moreover, a wide array of performance dimensions can be tapped with various rating scales on the same form. As we noted, a number or a letter accompanies each descriptor on the rating form. Most rating scales have ranges of one to five or one to seven. To develop a performance measure, the manager simply adds up the "points" for a particular employee's responses to obtain an overall index of performance.

Somewhat different is the **critical incident method**. A critical incident is simply an example of especially good or poor performance on the part of the employee. Organizations that rely on this method often require raters to recall such instances and then describe what the employee did (or did not do) that led to success or failure. This technique not only provides information for feedback but also defines performance in fairly clear, behavioural terms. In other cases, managers keep logs or diaries in which they record examples of critical incidents.

critical incident method A technique of performance appraisal in which raters recall examples of especially good or poor performance by an employee and then describe what the employee did (or did not do) that led to success or failure.

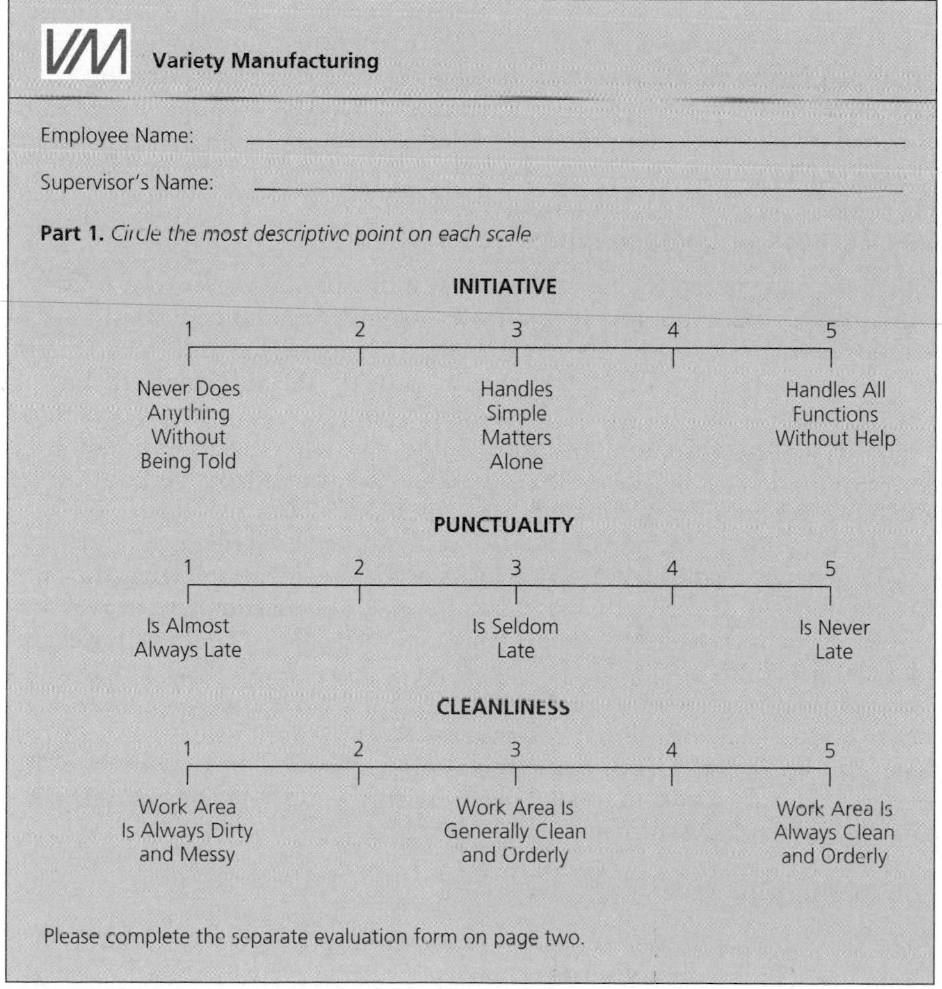

VM Variety Manufacturing

Employee Name: ______

Supervisor's Name: ______

Part 1. *Circle the most descriptive point on each scale*

INITIATIVE

1	2	3	4	5
Never Does Anything Without Being Told		Handles Simple Matters Alone		Handles All Functions Without Help

PUNCTUALITY

1	2	3	4	5
Is Almost Always Late		Is Seldom Late		Is Never Late

CLEANLINESS

1	2	3	4	5
Work Area Is Always Dirty and Messy		Work Area Is Generally Clean and Orderly		Work Area Is Always Clean and Orderly

Please complete the separate evaluation form on page two.

Figure 8.3 Performance rating scale.

PROVIDING COMPENSATION AND BENEFITS

5 Discuss the importance of *wages and salaries, incentives,* and *benefit programs* in attracting and keeping skilled workers.

Employees do not work for free—they expect to be compensated for the time, talent, and effort they devote to their jobs and to helping the organization achieve its goals. In this section, we explore basic compensation, incentives and performance-based rewards, and employee benefits and services. **Compensation** is the set of rewards that organizations provide to individuals in return for their willingness to perform various jobs and tasks within the organization. As we shall see, compensation includes a number of different elements, including base salary, incentives, bonuses, benefits, and other rewards. Compensation should never be a random decision, but rather the result of a careful and systematic strategic process.

compensation What a firm offers its employees in return for their labour.

The compensation received by CEOs can be extremely large, especially when bonuses and options are included. The most highly paid managers in the 2005 *Globe and Mail* Survey of Compensation were Hank Swartout of Precision Drilling Trust (who earned $74.8 million), Hunter Harrison of Canadian National Railway ($56.2 million), Frank Stronach of Magna International ($40.3 million), and Mike Zafirovski of Nortel Networks ($37.4 million).[14]

Determining Basic Compensation

Basic compensation means the base level of wages or salary paid to an employee. **Wages** generally refer to hourly compensation paid to operating employees. Most of the jobs that are paid on an hourly wage basis are lower-level and/or operating-level jobs. Rather than expressing compensation on an hourly basis, the organization may instead describe compensation on an annual or monthly basis. Many college and university graduates, for example, compare job offers on the basis of annual **salary**, such as $36 000 versus $38 000 a year.

wages Dollars paid based on the number of hours worked.

salary Dollars paid at regular intervals in return for doing a job, regardless of the amount of time or output involved.

Pay Surveys in Compensation

One common source of information that many organizations use to determine base compensation is **pay surveys**—surveys of compensation paid to employees by other employers in a particular geographic area, an industry, or an occupational group. Pay surveys provide the information that an organization needs to avoid an imbalance between its own pay scale and those of comparable organizations. Some pay surveys are conducted by professional associations. For example, the Canadian Federation of Business School Deans publishes an annual summary of salaries for professors teaching in business schools in Canadian universities.

pay survey A survey of compensation paid to employees by other employers in a particular geographic area, an industry, or an occupational group.

In general, a pay survey simply asks other organizations what they pay people to perform various jobs. Most organizations participate in such surveys because they will have access to the resulting data. There is, for example, a consortium of eight large electronic companies in the United States that routinely survey one another to determine what each pays new engineers and other professional employees who are hired directly out of college or university. The companies alternate the responsibility for conducting surveys from year to year, with the responsible organization sharing its results with the other members.

Job Evaluation

Another means of determining basic compensation is *job evaluation*, which should not be confused with job analysis. Recall that managers use job analysis to understand the requirements and nature of a job and its performance so that appropriate individuals can be recruited and selected. **Job evaluation** is a method for determining the relative value or worth of a job to the organization so that individuals who perform it can be appropriately compensated. In other words, it is mostly concerned with establishing internal pay equity.

job evaluation A method for determining the relative value or worth of a job to the organization so that individuals who perform it can be appropriately compensated.

Establishing a Pay Structure

A third method for determining basic compensation is establishing a *pay structure*. Compensation for different jobs is based on the organization's assessment of the relative value to the organization of each job class. Thus, there should be a logical rank ordering of compensation levels from the most valuable to the least valuable jobs throughout the organization. The organization, of course, may also find it necessary to group certain jobs together; thus, two or more jobs that are valued relatively equally will be compensated at approximately the same level. In addition, the organization decides on minimum and maximum pay ranges for each job or job class. Managers might use performance, *seniority* (a system that gives priority in promotions to employees with greater length of service), or a combination of the two to determine how much a person can be paid within the pay range for doing a particular job.

The internet allows job seekers and current employees to more easily get a sense of what their true market value is. If they can document the claim that their value is higher than what their current employer now pays or is offering, they may be in a position to demand higher salaries. One manager who met with a subordinate to discuss her raise was surprised when she produced data from five different websites to support her request for a bigger raise than he had intended to offer.

Performance-Based Compensation

Besides basic compensation, many organizations also offer performance-based rewards. The reason is obvious: When rewards are associated with higher levels of performance, employees will presumably be motivated to work harder in order to reap those awards.

Merit Pay Plans

Merit pay refers to pay awarded to employees according to the relative value of their contributions. Employees who make greater contributions receive higher pay than those who make lesser contributions. **Merit pay plans**, then, are compensation plans that base at least some meaningful portion of compensation on merit. The most general form of a merit pay plan is the raise—an annual salary increase granted to an employee because of his or her relative merit. In such plans, merit is usually determined or defined according to individual performance and overall contribution to the organization.

merit pay Pay awarded to employees according to the relative value of their contributions.

merit pay plans Compensation plans that formally base at least some meaningful portion of compensation on merit.

Skill- and Knowledge-Based Pay Systems. Although these systems are usually not strictly viewed as merit systems, it is worth noting how **skill-based pay** or **knowledge-based pay** systems focus employee attention on different areas but still rely on similar motivational processes. Instead of rewarding employees for increased performance, such systems reward them for the acquisition of more skills or knowledge. Skill-based pay systems reward employees for the acquisition of job-related skills. Knowledge-based pay systems reward employees for learning, because presumably, as they acquire more and more skills and knowledge, employees become more valuable to the organization.

skill-based pay Pay awarded to employees not for any specific level of performance, but for the acquisition of job-related skills.

knowledge-based pay Pay awarded to employees for learning.

Incentive Compensation Systems

Incentive compensation systems are among the oldest forms of performance-based rewards. Indeed, some companies were using individual piece-rate incentive plans over 100 years ago. Under a **piece-rate incentive plan**, the organization pays an employee a certain amount of money for every unit produced. An employee might, for example, be paid $1 for every 12 units of a product successfully completed. But such simplistic systems fail to account for such factors as minimum wage levels and rely on two questionable assumptions: (1) that performance is totally under an individual's control, and (2) that the individual employee does a single task continuously during the course of his or her work time. Today, therefore, incentive compensation systems tend to be much more sophisticated.

piece-rate incentive plan A compensation system in which an organization pays an employee a certain amount of money for every unit produced.

Incentive Pay Plans. Generally speaking, **individual incentive plans** reward individual performance on a real-time basis. That is, rather than increasing a person's base salary at the end of the year, an employer gives an individual a salary increase or some other financial reward for outstanding performance immediately or shortly after the performance occurred. For example, many baseball players have clauses in their contracts that pay them bonuses for hitting more than .300 over a season.

individual incentive plans A compensation system in which an employer gives an individual a salary increase or some other financial reward for outstanding performance immediately or shortly after the performance occurred.

Individual incentive systems are most common where performance can be assessed objectively (for example, by the number of units of output) rather than subjectively by a superior. Perhaps the most common form of individual incentive is the **sales commission** paid to people engaged in sales work. Salespeople "on commission" are paid based on the number of units they sell or the dollar value of sales they generate for the company.

sales commission Paying salespeople based on the number of units they sell or the dollar value of sales they generate for the company.

Other Forms of Incentives. Occasionally organizations use other forms of incentives. For example, a non-monetary incentive, such as additional time off or a special perk, might be useful. At some companies, recognition is given to employees in the form of special points that are awarded on the recommendation of a supervisor. Recipients can convert their points into money or they can use them to buy merchandise or trips from a special online catalogue.[15]

Individual incentive plans have been a big part of professional sports for many years. Some players receive multi-million dollar annual compensation for outstanding individual performance.

Team and Group Incentive Systems

The merit compensation and incentive compensation systems described in the preceding sections deal primarily with reward plans for individuals. There are also performance-based reward programs for teams and groups. Given today's increasing trend toward team- and group-based methods of work, such programs are growing in importance.

Gain Sharing. Many organizations use **gain-sharing programs**, which are designed to share with employees the cost savings from productivity improvements. Palliser Furniture Ltd., for example, introduced a gain-sharing plan that rewards employees for increasing production. Any profit resulting from production above a certain level is split 50-50 between the company and the employees.[16] The underlying assumption is that employees and the employer have the same goals and should therefore share in incremental economic gains. In general, organizations start by measuring team- or group-level productivity. The team or work group itself is then charged with lowering costs and otherwise improving productivity through any measures that members develop and their manager approves. Any resulting cost savings or productivity gains are then quantified and translated into dollar values. According to a predetermined formula, these dollar savings are then allocated to both employer and employees.

gain-sharing program An incentive program in which employees receive a bonus if the firm's costs are reduced because of greater worker efficiency and/or productivity.

Performance Increases. Some companies use incentives at the team or group level. Just like individual incentives, some team or group incentives tie rewards directly to performance increases. Like individual incentives, team or group incentives are also paid as they are earned rather than added to base salaries.

Profit Sharing. Other team- or group-level incentives go beyond the contributions of a specific work group. These are generally organization wide incentives. One long-standing type of incentive program is called a **profit-sharing plan**. At the end of the year, some portion of the company's profits is paid into a profit-sharing pool that is then distributed to all employees. In 2000, Dofasco's profit-sharing plan gave each worker $7906 beyond his or her regular pay. Dofasco annually contributes 14 percent of its pre-tax profits to the profit-sharing plan.[17] Ipsco Steel of Regina introduced a profit-sharing plan that gives all workers an identical year-end bonus. In one recent year, over $9 million was distributed to employees.[18]

profit-sharing plan An incentive program in which employees receive a bonus depending on the firm's profits.

Benefits

In addition to financial compensation, most organizations provide employees with an array of other indirect compensation in the form of benefits. **Benefits** generally refer to various rewards, incentives, and other things of value that an organization gives employees in addition to wages, salaries, and other forms of direct financial compensation. Because these benefits have tangible value, they represent a meaningful form of compensation even though they are not generally expressed in financial terms.

benefits What a firm offers its workers other than wages and salaries in return for their labour.

Canada's universal health care system is a real advantage to doing business in Canada because business firms do not have to pay to provide this coverage. Rather, its cost is supported largely from general tax revenues. A study of the cost of employee benefits as a percentage of wages and salaries in nine industrialized countries found that Canada's percentage (25 percent) was the lowest, and Germany's was the highest (70 percent). The other seven countries (United States, United Kingdom, Japan, the Netherlands, Austria, Italy, France) were somewhere between these two extremes.[19]

Mandated Protection Plans

protection plan A plan that protects employees when their income is threatened or reduced by illness, disability, death, unemployment, or retirement.

employment insurance A protection plan that provides a basic subsistence payment to employees who are between jobs.

Protection plans protect employees when their income is threatened or reduced by illness, disability, death, unemployment, or retirement. A number of these plans are required by law, but others are optional. One mandated benefit is **employment insurance**, which provides a basic subsistence payment to employees who are between jobs. It is intended for people who have stopped working for one organization but who are assumed to be actively seeking employment with another. Both employers and employees pay premiums to an employment insurance fund.

Also mandated are Canada Pension Plan payments. The original purpose of this program was to provide some limited income to retired individuals to supplement personal savings, private pensions, part-time work, and so forth. It is funded through employee and employer taxes that are withheld from payroll.

workers' compensation Mandated insurance that covers individuals who suffer a job-related illness or accident.

Workers' compensation is mandated insurance that covers individuals who suffer a job-related illness or accident. Employers bear the cost of workers' compensation insurance. The exact premium is related to each employer's past experience with job-related accidents and illnesses. For example, a steel company might pay $20 per $100 of wages, while an accounting firm might pay only 10 cents per $100 of wages.

Optional Protection Plans

Another major category of employee benefits consists of various optional protection plans. Health insurance has become the most important type of coverage, and has expanded in recent years to include vision care, mental health services, dental care, and prescription drugs. Employee prescription drug plan costs are doubling about every five years, and companies are increasingly concerned about their ability to offer this kind of coverage.[20]

Pension liabilities are also a problem. A 2005 study by the Certified General Accountants of Canada found that the shortfall in pension funding at Canada's largest corporate defined benefit plans was $29 billion. A shortfall means that the assets in the pension plan are not sufficient to meet future pension promises.[21] In 2005, 72 percent of all federally regulated pension plans had a shortfall, compared to only 53 percent at the end of 2004.[22] Employers also face mounting liabilities for *benefits* for retired workers. A study of 71 of Canada's largest companies showed that their liabilities for retiree benefits (not pensions) amounted to $16 billion. In one recent year at Suncor Energy Inc., for example, the company's benefits liability was $98 million (almost as much as its pension liability of $99 million).[23]

Paid Time Off

Paid vacations are usually for periods of one, two, or more weeks during which an employee can take time off from work and continue to be paid. Most organizations vary the amount of paid vacation with an individual's seniority, but some companies are reducing the time required to qualify for paid vacations. At Carlson Wagonlit Travel Canada, employees get four weeks of paid vacation after working at the company for just five years. Formerly, 10 years of service was required.[24]

Another common paid time off plan is *sick leave*. This benefit is provided when an individual is sick or otherwise physically unable to perform his or her job. Most organizations allow an individual to accumulate sick time according to a schedule, such as one sick day per month. Sometimes an organization will allow an employee to take off a small number of days simply for "personal business." This benefit is usually called *personal leave*. Occasions might include funerals, religious observances, weddings, birthdays, or simply personal holidays. The Catholic Children's Aid Society, for example, provides its child protection workers with time off when they need it because the workers face high-stress situations.[25]

Some companies go even further and offer their employees paid or unpaid sabbaticals. They do so to help workers rejuvenate themselves and increase their enthusiasm for their job. At Bertelsmann AG, for example, full-time employees who have 20 years of service get a 5-week, full pay sabbatical, while employees who have 10 years get 4 weeks. Employees at Procter & Gamble are eligible for a 12-week unpaid sabbatical after they have worked for the company for 1 year.[26]

Other Types of Benefits

In addition to protection plans and paid time off, many organizations offer a growing number of other benefit programs. **Wellness programs**, for example, concentrate on preventing illness in employees rather than simply paying their expenses when they become sick. In some organizations, these programs are simple and involve little more than organized jogging or walking during lunch breaks. More elaborate programs include smoking cessation, blood pressure and cholesterol screening, and stress management. Some organizations maintain full-fledged health clubs on-site and provide counselling and programs for fitness and weight loss.

wellness program A program that concentrates on preventing illness in employees rather than simply paying their expenses when they become sick.

Childcare benefits are also becoming extremely popular. In fact, any organization that wants to be considered "family friendly" must have some type of childcare benefits, and being a "family-friendly" company is increasingly becoming a competitive advantage. These plans might include scheduling help, referrals to various types of services, or reimbursement accounts for childcare expenses. In many cases, they actually include company-paid daycare. Eldercare is also going to become increasingly common as the population ages and workers care for their elderly parents. Over 300 Canadian companies sponsor childcare centres at the work site. The childcare centre run by Husky Injection Molding Systems in Bolton, Ontario provides on-site haircuts, music lessons, and a pajama party on Valentine's Day so parents can spend time together. If an employee has to work late, the staff will feed the employee's child at no cost.[27]

Cafeteria-Style Benefit Plans

Most benefit programs are designed for all employees in an organization. Although the exact benefits may vary according to the employee's level in the organization, within those levels plans are generally "one size fits all." In contrast, **cafeteria-style benefit plans** allow employees to choose the benefits they really want. Under these plans, the organization typically establishes a budget, indicating how much it is willing to spend, per employee, on benefits. Employees are then presented with a list of possible benefits and the cost of each. They are free to put the benefits together in any combination they wish. Employees at Toyota's Cambridge, Ontario, plant are given the opportunity once each year to restructure their benefit packages. For example, they can give more weight to dental coverage if they have young children, or to life insurance or disability coverage, depending on their circumstances.[28]

cafeteria-style benefit plans A flexible approach to providing benefits in which employees are allocated a certain sum to cover benefits and can "spend" this allocation on the specific benefits they prefer.

THE LEGAL CONTEXT OF HRM

As much or more than any area of business, HRM is heavily influenced by federal law, provincial law, and judicial review. In this section, we summarize some of the most important and far-reaching areas of HR regulation. These include *equal employment opportunity, comparable worth, sexual harassment, employee safety and health,* and *retirement*.

6 Describe some of the key legal issues involved in hiring, compensating, and managing workers.

Equal Employment Opportunity

equal employment opportunity regulations Regulations to protect people from unfair or inappropriate discrimination in the workplace.

The basic goal of all **equal employment opportunity regulations** is to protect people from unfair or inappropriate discrimination in the workplace. Let's begin by noting that discrimination in itself is not illegal. Whenever one person is given a pay raise and another is not, or when one person is hired and another is not, the organization has made a decision to distinguish one person from another. As long as the basis for this discrimination is purely job-related (made, for instance, on the basis of performance or qualifications) and is applied objectively and consistently, the action is legal and appropriate. Problems arise when distinctions among people are not job-related. In such cases, the resulting discrimination is illegal.

Anti-Discrimination Laws

Canadian Human Rights Act Ensures that any individual who wishes to obtain a job has an equal opportunity to apply for it.

When recruiting, firms must be careful not to violate anti-discrimination laws. The key federal anti-discrimination legislation is the **Canadian Human Rights Act** of 1977. The goal of this act is to ensure that any individual who wishes to obtain a job has an equal opportunity to compete for it. The act applies to all federal agencies, federal Crown corporations, any employee of the federal government, and business firms that do business interprovincially. Thus, it applies to such firms as the Bank of Montreal, Air Canada, Telecom Canada, Canadian National Railways, and many other public and private sector organizations that operate across Canada. Even with such wide application, the act affects only about 10 percent of Canadian workers; the rest are covered under provincial human rights acts.

The Canadian Human Rights Act prohibits a wide variety of practices in recruiting, selecting, promoting, and dismissing personnel. The act specifically prohibits discrimination on the basis of age, race and colour, national and ethnic origin, physical handicap, religion, gender, marital status, or prison record (if pardoned). Some exceptions to these blanket prohibitions are permitted. Discrimination cannot be charged if a blind person is refused a position as a train engineer, bus driver, or crane operator. Likewise, a firm cannot be charged with discrimination if it does not hire a deaf person as a telephone operator or as an audio engineer.

bona fide occupational requirement When an employer may choose one applicant over another based on overriding characteristics of the job.

These situations are clear-cut, but many others are not. For example, is it discriminatory to refuse women employment in a job that routinely requires carrying objects with a mass of more than 50 kilograms? Difficulties in determining whether discrimination has occurred are sometimes dealt with by using the concept of **bona fide occupational requirement**. An employer may choose one person over another based on overriding characteristics of the job in question. If a fitness centre wants to hire only women to supervise its women's locker room and sauna, it can do so without being discriminatory because it established a bona fide occupational requirement.

The Canadian Human Rights Commission carries out enforcement of the federal act. The commission can either respond to complaints from individuals who believe they have been discriminated against, or launch an investigation on its own if it has reason to believe that discrimination has occurred. During an investigation, data are gathered about the alleged discriminatory behaviour and, if the claim of discrimination is substantiated, the offending organization or individual may be ordered to compensate the victim.

Each province has also enacted human rights legislation to regulate organizations and businesses operating in that province. These provincial regulations are similar in spirit to the federal legislation, with many minor variations from province to province. All provinces prohibit discrimination on the basis of race, national or ethnic origin, colour, religion, sex, and marital status, but some do not address such issues as physical handicaps, criminal record, or age. Provincial human rights commissions enforce provincial legislation.

The **Employment Equity Act** of 1986 addresses the issue of discrimination in employment by designating four groups as employment disadvantaged—women, visible minorities, Aboriginal people, and people with disabilities. Companies covered by the act are required to publish statistics on their employment of people in these four groups.

Employment Equity Act Federal legislation that designates four groups as employment disadvantaged—women, visible minorities, Aboriginal people, and people with disabilities.

The Bank of Montreal recently became the first company outside the United States to win a prestigious award for promoting women's careers. The Bank of Montreal has introduced initiatives such as flexible working hours, a mentoring program, a national career information network, and a gender awareness workshop series.[29]

Companies are increasingly making provisions for disabled employees. At Rogers Cablevision, a division of Rogers Communications Inc., a large workplace area was completely redesigned to accommodate workers who were either visually disabled or in wheelchairs. Special equipment was also installed—a large-print computer for workers with partial sight, and a device that allows blind workers to read printed materials.[30]

Comparable Worth

In spite of recent advances, the average woman still earns only about three-quarters of what the average man earns. (The average *single* woman, however, earns 99 percent of what the average man earns.[31]) The average woman also spends a lower proportion of her potential years of work actually working. For example, for men aged 55–64, the proportion of potential years of work spent actually working is 92.3 percent; for women of that age, the ratio is only 64.2 percent.[32]

Various research studies show that compared to men, the average woman has less actual labour market experience, is less likely to work full time, and is more likely to leave the labour force for long periods of time. These factors very likely cause companies to differentiate between men and women in terms of salaries.

Comparable worth is a legal concept that addresses paying equal wages for jobs that are of comparable value to the employer. This might mean comparing dissimilar jobs, such as those of nurses and mechanics or secretaries and electricians. Proponents of comparable worth say that all the jobs in a company must be evaluated and then rated in terms of basic dimensions such as the level of skill they require. All jobs could then be compared based on a common index. People in different jobs that rate the same on this index would be paid the same. Experts hope that this will help to reduce the gap between men's and women's pay.

comparable worth A legal idea that aims to pay equal wages for work of equal value.

In a long-standing comparable worth dispute, the Supreme Court of Canada ruled in 2006 that flight attendants at Air Canada—who have been trying for years to achieve pay equity with male-dominated groups of employees—could compare their pay with the pay of ground crews and pilots because all these employees work for the same company. In spite of this ruling, the president of the Air Canada Canadian Union of Public Employees was concerned that it might take many years before the flight attendants actually saw a wage increase.[33]

Critics of comparable worth object on the grounds that it ignores the supply and demand aspects of labour. They say, for example, that legislation forcing a company to pay people more than the open market price for their labour (which may happen in jobs where there is a surplus of workers) is another example of unreasonable government interference in business activities. They also say that implementing comparable worth will cost business firms too much money. A study prepared for the Ontario Ministry of Labour estimated that it would cost approximately $10 billion for the public and private sectors in Ontario to establish equitable payment for jobs of equal value. Yet the cost defence cannot be easily used. In 2005, the Canadian Human Rights Tribunal ruled that a wage gap between male and female clerical workers at Canada Post was the result of systemic sex discrimination. It ordered the company to pay a total of $150 million in back pay to 6000 female clerical workers.[34] In an earlier case, the tribunal ruled that the federal government must pay a total of more than $3 billion to thousands of civil servants because it discriminated against workers in female-dominated job classifications. About 85 percent of these workers were women.

There is one very interesting fact in this debate about comparable worth: Male earning power has been declining for decades. Young males who are now entering the labour market, regardless of their education, will likely earn dramatically less than their predecessors did. Young, female university graduates, on the other hand, have recently earned more than their predecessors.[35]

Sexual Harassment

sexual harassment Requests for sexual favours, unwelcome sexual advances, or verbal or physical conduct of a sexual nature that creates an intimidating or hostile environment for a given employee.

Within the job context, **sexual harassment** refers to requests for sexual favours, unwelcome sexual advances, or verbal or physical conduct of a sexual nature that creates an intimidating or hostile environment for a given employee. The Canadian Human Rights Act takes precedence over any policies that a company might have developed on its own to deal with sexual harassment problems.

quid pro quo harassment Form of sexual harassment in which sexual favours are requested in return for job-related benefits.

hostile work environment Form of sexual harassment deriving from off-colour jokes, lewd comments, and so forth.

Quid pro quo harassment is the most blatant form of sexual harassment. It occurs when the harasser offers to exchange something of value for sexual favours. A male supervisor, for example, might tell or suggest to a female subordinate that he will recommend her for promotion or give her a raise in exchange for sexual favours. The creation of a **hostile work environment** is a subtler form of sexual harassment. A group of male employees who continually make off-colour jokes and lewd comments and perhaps decorate the work environment with questionable photographs may create a hostile work environment for a female colleague. Regardless of the pattern, the same bottom-line rules apply: Sexual harassment is illegal, and the organization is responsible for controlling it.

Verbal comments by prominent managers are also problematic. For example, when Neil French, a legendary advertising executive and the creative director of WPP Group PLC, gave a speech in Toronto in 2005, he was asked why there were so few women who were creative advertising directors. He replied that women focus too much on their family duties and this usually prevents them from succeeding in management. His comments caused quite a stir, and French soon resigned from his position. It is interesting to note that the Toronto office of Ogilvy & Mather (a subsidiary of WPP) is headed by two creative directors, both of whom are women.[36]

If a manager is found guilty of sexual harassment, the company is also liable because the manager is an agent of the company. In fact, even if one employee makes another employee feel uncomfortable, the instigator may be guilty of sexual harassment. To deal effectively with the potential for sexual harassment, managers should

- develop clear and enforceable policies dealing with sexual harassment
- inform all employees about the existence of these policies
- train employees to recognize and refrain from sexual harassment

- take complaints about sexual harassment seriously
- establish a procedure for dealing with harassment complaints
- take action against those who are involved in sexual harassment

Employee Safety and Health

Employee safety and health programs help to reduce absenteeism and turnover, raise productivity, and boost morale by making jobs safer and more healthful. Government regulations about employee safety are becoming stricter. Ontario, which loses more than seven million working days yearly because of on-the-job injuries, has passed amendments to the Ontario Occupational Health and Safety Act. Officers and directors of companies are held personally responsible for workplace health and safety and are punishable by jail terms and fines for permitting unsafe working conditions.[37]

Some industrial work—logging, construction, fishing, and mining—can put workers at risk of injury in obvious ways. But other types of work—such as typing or lifting—can also cause painful injuries. **Repetitive strain injuries (RSIs)** occur when workers perform the same functions over and over again. These injuries disable more than 200 000 Canadians each year and account for nearly half of all work-related time loss claims.

repetitive strain injuries (RSIs) Injuries that occur when workers perform the same functions over and over again.

In Canada, each province has developed its own workplace health and safety regulations. The purpose of these laws is to ensure that employees do not have to work in dangerous conditions. These laws are the direct result of undesirable conditions that existed in many Canadian businesses at the close of the nineteenth century. While much improvement is evident, Canada still has some problems with workplace health and safety. In one study of six Western industrialized nations, Canada had the worst safety record in mining and construction and the second-worst record in manufacturing and railways.

The Ontario Occupational Health and Safety Act illustrates current legislation in Canada. It requires all employers to ensure that equipment and safety devices are used properly. Employers must also show workers the proper way to operate machinery. At the job site, supervisors are charged with the responsibility of ensuring that workers use equipment properly. The act also requires workers to behave appropriately on the job. Employees have the right to refuse to work on a job if they believe it is unsafe; a legal procedure exists for resolving any disputes in this area.

In most provinces, the Ministry of Labour appoints inspectors to enforce health and safety regulations. If the inspector finds a sufficient hazard, he or she has the authority to clear the workplace. Inspectors can usually arrive at a firm unannounced to conduct an inspection.

Retirement

Until the 1990s, Canadian courts generally upheld 65 as the mandatory retirement age, but most Canadian provinces have now abolished mandatory retirement. Even though mandatory retirement is now out of favour, workers are actually retiring earlier than they used to. In the late 1970s, the average retirement age in Canada was 65, but by 2003 it had dropped to 62.3 years.[38] A Statistics Canada study showed that "boomer" couples are unlikely to retire at the same time. Often women stay in the work force longer than their husbands.[39] Some managers fear that the abolition of mandatory retirement will result in less productive employees remaining at work after age 65, but research shows that the employees who stay on the job past 65 are usually the most productive ones.

NEW CHALLENGES IN THE CHANGING WORKPLACE

7 Discuss *workforce diversity*, the management of *knowledge workers*, and the use of *contingent and temporary workers* as important changes in the contemporary workplace.

As we have seen throughout this chapter, HR managers face several ongoing challenges in their efforts to keep their organizations staffed with effective workers. To complicate matters, new challenges arise as the economic and social environments of business change. We conclude this chapter with a discussion of several of the most important HRM issues facing business today: *managing workforce diversity, managing knowledge workers,* and *managing contingent and temporary workers*.

Managing Workforce Diversity

workforce diversity The range of workers' attitudes, values, beliefs, and behaviours that differ by gender, race, age, ethnicity, physical ability, and other relevant characteristics.

As we saw in the opening case, one extremely important set of human resource challenges centres on **workforce diversity**—the range of workers' attitudes, values, beliefs, and behaviours that differ by gender, race, age, ethnicity, physical ability, and other relevant characteristics. In the past, organizations tended to work toward homogenizing their workforces, getting everyone to think and behave in similar ways. Partly as a result of affirmative action efforts, however, many organizations are now creating more diverse workforces by embracing more women, ethnic minorities, and foreign-born employees than ever before.

Organizations are increasingly recognizing that diversity can be a competitive advantage. For example, by hiring the best people available from every group rather than hiring from just one or a few groups, a firm can develop a higher-quality workforce. Similarly, a diverse workforce can bring a wider array of information to bear on problems and can provide insights on marketing products to a wider range of consumers. Says the head of workforce diversity at IBM: "We think it is important for our customers to look inside and see people like them. If they can't...the prospect of them becoming or staying our customers declines."

Managing Knowledge Workers

Traditionally, employees added value to organizations because of what they did or because of their experience. In the "information age," however, many employees add value because of what they know.[40]

The Nature of Knowledge Work

knowledge workers Workers who are experts in specific fields like computer technology and engineering, and who add value because of what they know, rather than how long they have worked or the job they do.

These employees are usually called **knowledge workers**, and the skill with which they are managed is a major factor in determining which firms will be successful in the future. Knowledge workers, including computer scientists, engineers, and physical scientists, provide special challenges for the HR manager. They tend to work for high-tech firms and are usually experts in some abstract knowledge base. They often prefer to work independently and tend to identify more strongly with their professions than with any organization—even to the extent of defining performance in terms recognized by other members of their professions.

As the importance of information-driven jobs grows, the need for knowledge workers continues to grow as well. But these employees require extensive and highly specialized training, and not every organization is willing to make the human capital investments necessary to take advantage of these jobs. In fact, even after knowledge workers are on the job, training updates are critical to prevent their skills from becoming obsolete. It has been suggested, for example, that the "half-life" of a technical education in engineering is about three years. The failure to update such skills will not only result in the loss of competitive advantage but also increase the likeli-

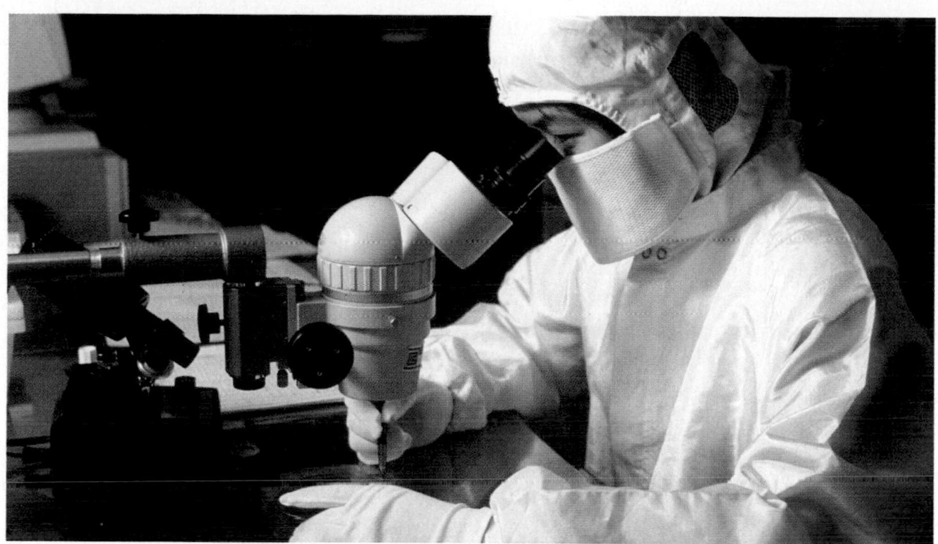

This worker has the extensive training and highly specialized skills that are needed in this high-tech manufacturing process. Management of such knowledge workers is increasingly important for business success.

hood that the knowledge worker will move to another firm that is more committed to updating his or her knowledge.

Knowledge Worker Management and Labour Markets

In recent years, the demand for knowledge workers has been growing at a dramatic rate. As a result, organizations that need these workers must introduce regular market adjustments (upward) to pay them enough to keep them. This is especially critical in areas in which demand is growing, as even entry-level salaries for these employees are skyrocketing. Once an employee accepts a job with a firm, the employer faces yet another dilemma. Once hired, workers are subject to the company's internal labour market, which is not likely to be growing as quickly as the external market for knowledge workers as a whole. Consequently, the longer an employee remains with a firm, the further behind the market his or her pay falls—unless, of course, it is regularly adjusted upward.

Not surprisingly, the growing demand for these workers has inspired some fairly extreme measures for attracting them in the first place.[41] High starting salaries and sign-on bonuses are common. British Petroleum Exploration was recently paying starting petroleum engineers with undersea platform-drilling knowledge—not experience, just knowledge—salaries in the six figures, plus sign-on bonuses of over U.S.$50 000 and immediate profit sharing. Even with these incentives, HR managers complain that they cannot retain specialists because young engineers soon leave to accept sign-on bonuses from competitors. Laments one HR executive: "We wind up six months after we hire an engineer having to fight off offers for that same engineer for more money."[42]

Managing Contingent and Temporary Workers

A final contemporary HR issue involves the use of contingent and/or temporary workers. Indeed, recent years have seen an explosion in the use of such workers by organizations.

Trends in Contingent and Temporary Employment

A **contingent worker** is a person who works for an organization on something other than a permanent or full-time basis. Categories of contingent workers include independent contractors (freelancers), on-call workers, temporary employees (usually hired through outside agencies), and contract

contingent worker A person who works for an organization on something other than a permanent or full-time basis.

and leased employees. Another category is part-time workers. The financial services giant Citigroup, for example, makes extensive use of part-time sales agents to pursue new clients.

Managing Contingent and Temporary Workers

Given the widespread use of contingent and temporary workers, HR managers must understand how to use such employees most effectively. That is, they need to understand how to manage contingent and temporary workers. One key is careful planning. Even though one of the presumed benefits of using contingent workers is flexibility, it still is important to integrate such workers in a coordinated fashion. Rather than having to call in workers sporadically and with no prior notice, organizations try to bring in specified numbers of workers for well-defined periods of time. The ability to do so comes from careful planning.

A second key is understanding contingent workers and acknowledging both their advantages and their disadvantages. That is, the organization must recognize what it can and cannot achieve by using contingent and temporary workers. Expecting too much from contingent workers, for example, is a mistake that managers should avoid.

Third, managers must carefully assess the real cost of using contingent workers. Many firms adopt this course of action to save labour costs. The organization should be able to document precisely its labour-cost savings. How much would it be paying people in wages and benefits if they were on permanent staff? How does this cost compare with the amount spent on contingent workers? This difference, however, could be misleading. Contingent workers might be less effective performers than permanent and full-time employees. Comparing employees on a direct-cost basis, therefore, is not necessarily valid. Organizations must learn to adjust the direct differences in labour costs to account for differences in productivity and performance.

Finally, managers must fully understand their own strategies and decide in advance how they intend to manage temporary workers, specifically focussing on how to integrate them into the organization. On a very simplistic level, for example, an organization with a large contingent workforce must make some decisions about the treatment of contingent workers relative to the treatment of permanent, full-time workers. Should contingent workers be invited to the company holiday party? Should they have the same access to such employee benefits as counselling services and childcare? Managers must understand that they need to develop a strategy for integrating contingent workers according to some sound logic and then follow that strategy consistently over time.[43]

This young woman is one of 1500 temporary workers at Sola Optical. Sola keeps at least 100 temps working at all times, because it gives human resource managers both scheduling flexibility and the opportunity to try potential permanent employees.

Summary of Learning Objectives

1. **Define *human resource management*, discuss its strategic significance, and explain how managers plan for human resources.** *Human resource management*, or *HRM*, is the set of organizational activities directed at attracting, developing, and maintaining an effective workforce. HRM plays a key strategic role in organizational performance. Planning for human resource needs entails several steps. Conducting a *job analysis* enables managers to create detailed, accurate job descriptions and specifications. After analysis is complete, managers must forecast demand and supply for both the numbers and types of workers they will need. Then they consider steps to match supply with demand.
2. **Identify the issues involved in *staffing* a company, including *internal* and *external recruiting* and *selection*.** *Recruiting* is the process of attracting qualified persons to apply for jobs that an organization has open. *Internal recruiting* involves considering present employees for new jobs. This approach helps build morale and rewards an organization's best employees. *External recruiting* means attracting people from outside the organization to apply for openings. When organizations are actually selecting people for jobs, they generally use such selection techniques as *application forms, tests, interviews*, and other techniques. Regardless of what selection techniques are used, they must be valid predictors of an individual's expected performance in the job.
3. **Discuss different ways in which organizations go about developing the capabilities of employees and managers.** If a company is to get the most out of its workers, it must develop both those workers and their skills. Nearly all employees undergo some initial *orientation* process that introduces them to the company and to their new jobs. Many employees are given the opportunity to acquire new skills through various *work-based* and/or *instructional-based programs*.
4. **Explain ways in which organizations evaluate employee performance.** *Performance appraisals* help managers decide who needs training and who should be promoted. Appraisals also tell employees how well they are meeting expectations. Although a variety of alternatives are available for appraising performance, employee supervisors are most commonly used. No matter who does the evaluation, however, feedback to the employee is very important. Managers can select from a variety of ranking and rating methods for use in performance appraisal.
5. **Discuss the importance of *wages and salaries, incentives*, and *benefit programs* in attracting and keeping skilled workers.** *Wages and salaries, incentives*, and *benefit packages* may all be parts of a company's compensation program. By paying its workers as well as or better than competitors, a business can attract and keep qualified personnel. *Incentive programs* can also motivate people to work more productively. *Indirect compensation* also plays a major role in effective and well-designed compensation systems.
6. **Describe some of the key legal issues involved in hiring, compensating, and managing workers.** In hiring, compensating, and managing workers, managers must obey a variety of federal and provincial laws. *Equal employment opportunity* and *equal pay* laws forbid discrimination other than action based on legitimate job requirements. The concept of *comparable worth* states that equal wages should be paid for jobs that are of comparable value to the employer. Firms are also required to provide employees with safe working environments, as set down by the guidelines of provincial occupational health and safety acts. *Sexual harassment* is another key contemporary legal issue in business.
7. **Discuss *workforce diversity*, the management of *knowledge workers*, and the use of *contingent and temporary workers* as important changes in the contemporary workplace.** *Workforce diversity* refers to the range of workers' attitudes, values, beliefs, and behaviours that differ by gender, race, ethnicity, age, physical ability, and other relevant characteristics. Many firms think that having a diverse workforce creates a competitive advantage, so they have set a goal to have a workforce that reflects the growing diversity of the population as it enters the labour pool.

   Many firms today also face challenges in managing *knowledge workers*. The recent boom in high-tech companies has led to rapidly increasing salaries and high turnover among the workers who are best prepared to work in those companies. *Contingent workers* are temporary and part-time employees hired to supplement an organization's permanent workforce. Their numbers have grown significantly since the early 1980s and are expected to rise further. The practice of hiring contingent workers is gaining in popularity because it gives managers more flexibility and because temps are usually not covered by employers' benefit programs.

KEY TERMS

360-degree feedback, 250
assessment centre, 244
benefits, 255
bona fide occupational requirement, 258
cafeteria-style benefit plans, 257
Canadian Human Rights Act, 258
comparable worth, 259
compensation, 252
contingent worker, 263
critical incident method, 251
employee information systems (skills inventories), 241
Employment Equity Act, 259
employment insurance, 256
equal employment opportunity regulations, 258
external recruiting, 242
forced distribution method, 250
gain-sharing program, 255
graphic rating scale, 250
hostile work environment, 260
human resource management (HRM), 238
individual incentive plans, 254
instructional-based programs, 248
internal recruiting, 242
internship, 243
job analysis, 239
job description, 239
job evaluation, 253
job specification, 239
knowledge workers, 262
knowledge-based pay, 253
lecture or discussion approach, 248
merit pay, 253
merit pay plans, 253
off-the-job training, 248
on-the-job training, 247
orientation, 247
pay survey, 252
performance appraisal, 249
piece-rate incentive plan, 254
profit-sharing plan, 255
protection plan, 256
quid pro quo harassment, 260
recruiting, 242
repetitive strain injuries (RSIs), 261
replacement chart, 241
salary, 252
sales commission, 254
sexual harassment, 260
simple ranking method, 250
skill-based pay, 253
systematic job rotations and transfers, 248
validation, 243
vestibule training, 247
video assessment, 244
wages, 252
wellness program, 257
work-based programs, 247
workers' compensation, 256
workforce diversity, 262

QUESTIONS FOR ANALYSIS

1. Why is a good employee–job match important? Who benefits more, the organization or the employee? Explain.
2. Why is the formal training of workers so important to most employers? Why don't employers simply let people learn about their jobs as they perform them?
3. What are your views on drug testing in the workplace? What would you do if your employer asked you to submit to a drug test?
4. Have you or anyone you know ever suffered discrimination in a hiring decision? Did you or the person you know do anything about it?
5. What training do you think you are most likely to need when you finish school and start your career?
6. What benefits do you consider most and least important in attracting workers? In keeping workers? In motivating workers to perform their jobs well?
7. Select a job currently held by you or a friend. Draw up a job description and job specification for this position.
8. How much will benefit considerations (as opposed to salary) affect your choice of an employer after graduation?

APPLICATION EXERCISES

1. Interview an HR manager at a local company. Focus on a position for which the firm is currently recruiting applicants and identify the steps in the selection process.
2. Obtain a copy of an employment application. Examine it carefully and determine how useful it might be in making a hiring decision.

BUILDING YOUR BUSINESS SKILLS

Getting Online for a Job

Goal

To introduce students to career-search resources available on the internet.

The Situation

If companies are on one side of the external staffing process, people looking for work are on the other. Companies need qualified candidates to fill job openings and candidates need jobs that are right for them. The challenge, of course, is to make successful matches. Increasingly, this matchmaking is being conducted on the internet. Companies are posting jobs in cyberspace, and job seekers are posting résumés in response. The number of job postings has grown dramatically in recent years. On a typical Sunday, you might find as many as 50 000 postings on the Monster Board, a leading job site. With so many companies looking for qualified candidates online, it makes good business sense to learn how to use the system.

Assignment

Using internet career resources means locating job databases and preparing and posting a résumé. (You will therefore need access to the internet to complete this exercise.)

Step 1

Team up with three classmates to investigate and analyze specific job databases. In each case, write a short report describing the database (which you and other group members may use during an actual job search). Summarize the site and its features as well as its advantages, disadvantages, and costs. Start with the following sites and add others you may find on your own:

The Monster Board, www.monster.com

Careerbuilder.com, www.careerbuilder.ca

College Grad Job Hunter, www.collegegrad.com

Step 2

Investigate the job opportunities listed on the home pages of various companies. Consider trying the following companies:

Air Canada, www.aircanada.com

Dofasco, www.dofasco.ca

Royal Bank, www.royalbank.com

IBM, www.ibm.com/ca/

Wal-Mart, www.walmartstores.com

McDonald's, www.mcdonalds.com

Bombardier, www.bombardier.com

Write a summary of the specific career-related information you find on each site.

Step 3

Working with group members, research strategies for composing effective cyber résumés. The following websites provide some helpful information on formats and personal and job-related information that should be included in your résumé. They also offer hints on the art of creating a scannable résumé:

Workopolis, www.workopolis.com

Career Magazine, www.careermag.com

Two books by Joyce Lain Kennedy, *Electronic Job Search Revolution* and *Electronic Résumé Revolution*, also contain valuable information.

Step 4

Working as a group, create an effective electronic résumé for a fictitious college or university graduate looking for a first job. Pay attention to format, language, style, and the effective communication of background and goals.

Step 5

Working as a group, learn how to post your résumé online. (Do not submit the résumé you created for this exercise, which is, after all, fictitious.) The databases provided will guide you in this process.

Follow-Up Questions

1. Why is it necessary to learn how to conduct an electronic job search? Do you think it will be more or less necessary in the years ahead?
2. Why do you think more computer-related jobs than non-technical jobs are posted online? Do you think this situation will change?
3. Why is it a waste of time to stylize your résumé with different fonts, point sizes, and centred headings?
4. What is the advantage of emailing your résumé directly to a company rather than applying for the same job through an online databank?

EXERCISING YOUR ETHICS

Taking Advantage of Contingent Workers

The Situation

You are a store manager in a large retail organization. Your job is full-time, and you receive good benefits from the company. However, many people in your store (cashiers, shelf-stockers, greeters, etc.) work only part-time for the company. You know that many of them want to work full-time but the company does not allow it. One of the reasons is that part-time workers are not eligible for benefits and this reduces the company's human resource expenses. Top management has emphasized on several occasions that it is imperative that costs be controlled so your store can remain competitive, and reducing human resource costs is one obvious way to do that.

The Dilemma

You have become increasingly concerned that the human resource management policies of your organization leave something to be desired. In the past few months, several workers have expressed their deep concerns to you that they are having extreme financial difficulty because they are not given enough hours of work each week. You know these workers, and they are hard-working, reliable people. You have great sympathy for them, particularly the ones who have families. You also know, however, that competition from competitors like Wal-Mart is intense, and that keeping costs low is absolutely imperative if your firm hopes to compete. You know that if the prices you charge are not competitive, customers will shop elsewhere. If that happens, there won't be any jobs for anybody, full-time or otherwise.

Questions for Discussion

1. What are the ethical issues in this situation?
2. What do you think most managers would do in this situation?
3. What would you do? Defend your answer.

CONCLUDING CASE 8-1

Las Vegas Gambles Online

Imagine this assignment: Your boss tells you that you are responsible for hiring almost 10 000 new workers. But that's the easy part. You have to have them all prepared to start working on the same day, their job skills have to be impeccable, and there can be no mistakes. Oh, and just to make it interesting, you are not allowed to use a single sheet of paper! Sound impossible? Well, that's just what a team of Las Vegas executives was asked to do.

In the few short years since it opened, Bellagio hotel and casino in Las Vegas has become one of the gambling mecca's most popular destinations. But before it opened, and behind the scenes, Bellagio also gave human resource (HR) managers new insights into how to staff a new organization. The task facing the resort's HR executives was daunting. They had to hire 9600 workers in 24 weeks and have everyone trained and on the payroll when the first customer walked through the door. The firm's HR team not only pulled this feat off without a hitch, it did it without using a single sheet of paper!

With the precision of a full-scale military operation, the Bellagio team designed and implemented one of the most sophisticated HR selection systems ever devised. To apply for a position, applicants called and requested an appointment. They were then scheduled in batches to arrive at the resort's hiring centre, where they filled out an application at a computer terminal. One hundred terminals were kept busy 12 hours a day, 6 days a week. As applications were submitted, employees at the checkout desk conducted unobtrusive assessments of the applicants' communication skills and overall demeanour, eliminating about 20 percent of the applicants.

Next came 27 000 interviews. For example, a hiring manager could sit at a PC and call up the highest-rated desk clerk candidates. The database system would rank order the candidates according to predetermined criteria. The manager could then call in, say, three applicants for each open position for face-to-face interviews. An interview consisted of a set of structured questions. During an interview, the manager would discreetly evaluate the responses to each question on a hidden keypad. These data were then fed back into the database.

If a manager wanted to hire a particular applicant, he or she could pull up a software screen and check "Conduct background check." A team of investigators would then verify employment, military, and education history; for some jobs, a drug test was mandatory. About 8 percent of applicants were rejected at this stage because of falsified information on their applications.

If a manager was ready to offer a job to a particular individual, another screen was used to check "Yes." When this happened, the applicant was invited to a job-offer meeting, which is when people were actually offered jobs. If they accepted, they then completed various required documents—again, in electronic form—for benefits and income tax purposes. They were also scheduled for relevant training sessions. And when the big day came and the Bellagio officially opened its doors, 9600 new employees were in place and ready to work.

The massive hiring job at Bellagio staggers the imagination. But in reality, many firms must routinely plan to hire large numbers of people in a coordinated fashion. Las Vegas itself reflects a microcosm of this task with each massive new casino that is opened. The Mandalay Bay, the Venetian, and similar mega-resorts have had to do the same thing as Bellagio. In other outposts, Disney must hire thousands of new employees to staff each new theme park it opens, Toyota must hire thousands of workers for each new factory it builds, and Royal Caribbean must hire thousands of service staff for each new cruise ship it launches.

Wal-Mart is in the midst of a hiring explosion that may eventually make these examples truly passé. It has announced a goal of hiring one million new people over the next five years. About 800 000 of these will be to fill newly created jobs, while the other 200 000 will be replacements for retirees and other employees forecasted to leave the firm. That's like hiring the entire city of Mississauga, Ontario.

So what does the giant retailer plan to do? For one thing, it may need to up its pay grades a bit and offer more benefits. For another, it plans to step up its university recruiting for potential new store managers. And it hopes to entice the spouses, children, and other relatives of its current employees to join its ranks. If Wal-Mart is successful, it may end up revolutionizing not only the retailing industry but the human resource management function as well.

Questions for Discussion

1. What are the unique challenges of hiring massive numbers of people?
2. Identify at least five factors that might disrupt a firm's massive hiring plans.
3. Compare and contrast the challenges faced by Bellagio and Wal-Mart.
4. What other employment situations might be able to use Bellagio's model?
5. Suppose a firm had to reduce its staff by several thousand workers in a short period of time. What might it learn from Bellagio?

CONCLUDING CASE 8-2

Galt Contracting

Galt Contracting is a small B.C.-based company that plants trees for lumber companies like Canfor, Gorman Brothers, and Riverside. In the spring of each year, Donald Galt, the owner-manager of Galt Contracting, bids on tree-planting contracts that will be available during the upcoming summer. He visits the block of land that is up for bid and looks it over with a lumber company representative. He then develops a bid and submits it to the lumber company. If he is awarded the job, Galt's profit is determined by the amount of the lumber company contract minus the amount he pays his workers.

The Business of Tree Planting

Once Galt knows that he has gotten a contract, he hires tree planters to do the actual tree planting. Galt usually hires university students who are looking for good-paying summer jobs. The work is hard, but tree planters can make very good money because they are paid on a piece-rate system, that is, they are paid a certain amount of money for each tree that they plant. The amount usually varies between 16 and 32 cents per tree, depending on the terrain and the kind of tree that is being planted. The more difficult the terrain is, the higher the piece rate that planters receive.

A tree planter may plant as few as 1000 trees or as many as 2500 each day, depending on the terrain and the planter's skill. On an average day, a reasonably experienced planter can put 1300 seedlings in the ground. Planters don't have a set lunch break, but eat on the run. They usually leave their lunch boxes at the main cache, and eat about halfway through the day on one of their return trips to the cache to pick up more seedlings.

Each planter is assigned a "piece" to plant for the day, usually an area equal in size to a football field, but not necessarily symmetrical. The limits of each planter's area are marked with flags by the planters as they begin planting in the morning. Planters leave the main cache and begin planting trees in a straight line. As they plant, they "flag a line" which indicates the boundaries of their piece. This involves staking out strips of brightly coloured tape close to the line of trees. This line helps each planter determine where their piece begins and ends. Planting is then done in a back-and-forth pattern within each piece as planters work back toward the main cache as their bag gradually empties. They monitor the number trees left in their planting bags so they can end up near the main cache when they run out of trees.

Trees must be planted in different concentrations on different pieces, and a certain jargon has arisen to describe this activity. For example, if spacing is "2.9," this means that trees must be planted 2.9 metres apart; if spacing is "3.1," this means that trees must be planted 3.1 metres apart. Planters prefer "2.9" days over "3.1" days because they don't have to cover as much ground and can therefore plant more trees and make more money.

Quality Control

A checker—who works for the lumber company—inspects the work of the planters to ensure that they are planting properly. Checkers use a cord to inscribe a circle on a randomly chosen part of a piece. On "2.9" days, the checker will ensure that 7 trees are contained in the circle within the cord. The checker also determines whether the trees are planted properly. Trees must not have any air pockets around the roots, there must be no "j-rooted" (crooked) roots, and trees must be planted on the south (sunny) side of any obstacles on the piece. Trees must also be planted close to obstacles so that they are not trampled by the cattle that sometimes graze in the area. If a planter consistently plants too many or too few trees on a piece, the checker can demand that the piece be replanted. This happens infrequently, but when it does, the planter's pay is sharply reduced.

Galt sometimes checks workers himself, especially if he has reason to believe that they are doing a sloppy job. The biggest problem he has encountered is workers who plant large numbers of trees, but do so very poorly. Planters know that if Galt is following them around for any significant period of time, that he is suspicious about the quality of their planting. Planters are very hard on each other in terms of quality. They become very upset if one of their group tries to make more money by planting large numbers of trees by cutting corners. Planters put pressure on each other to do a good job because the reputation of the whole group suffers if one or two planters do poor quality work. As well, planters resent those among them who make more money simply by planting large numbers of trees in a poor quality way. A planter who is known to do a sloppy job or who is forced to replant an area might, for example, be nicknamed "j-root."

Planters don't know when the checker will come by. If a planter "gets in good" with a checker, the checker may go easy when checking the planter's work. The checkers are themselves checked by other lumber company employees to ensure that they are doing reasonable quality control work. In turn, the lumber company is checked by the provincial government to see that trees are planted properly.

The Problem

Galt has been paying planters on a piece-rate basis for many years, but recently he has become very concerned about it because too many trees are improperly planted and die soon after planting. Galt thinks this is happening because planters are focussing on quantity at the expense of quality (they are so motivated by the money they can earn if they plant a lot of trees that they are doing sloppy work). At the end of last year's planting season, Galt was told in no uncertain terms by one lumber company that if he did not improve the quality of his tree planting, he would not get any more jobs.

The problem is significant enough that Galt has been thinking about dropping the piece-rate system and moving toward a "flat rate" system which would give planters a fixed amount of pay for each day's work. Galt thinks that this would cause planters to take more time and care when planting each tree since they would not have to worry about how much money they were going to make for the day. In the past, Galt has occasionally paid workers on a flat rate, particularly when the terrain was uneven. But this system is not problem-free either. For example, Galt gets the impression that when he pays on a flat-rate basis that planters don't work as hard, and they take more breaks. Galt also knows that planters *like* the piece rate system because they can make good money. The piece-rate system generates friendly competition among planters to see who can be the most productive. Those who plant the most trees have higher status among their peers, and they also earn more money. Overall, Galt thinks that this friendly competition increases the number of trees that are planted.

When the piece rate system is used, there is not much socializing among workers on the site, except when they are bagging up at the main cache at various times throughout the day. Socializing is generally seen as counterproductive because workers who stand around and talk aren't planting trees, and this reduces their pay.

As Galt considered all these facts, he wondered what he should do regarding the payment system he uses for planters.

▶▶▶

Questions for Discussion

1. What are the advantages and disadvantages of paying tree planters on a piece-rate system? On a flat-rate system?
2. Review the motivation theories in Chapter 10. What does each of those theories say (or imply) about Galt's idea of dropping the piece-rate system and paying planters a flat rate for each day of work?
3. Devise a payment system for tree planters that minimizes negative consequences. Describe the impact of your proposal on each of the following factors:
   - the motivation levels of the planters
   - the activities of the quality control checkers
   - the level of quality needed in tree planting
   - the needs of the lumber companies
   - Donald Galt's need to run a profitable company
4. What should Donald Galt do?

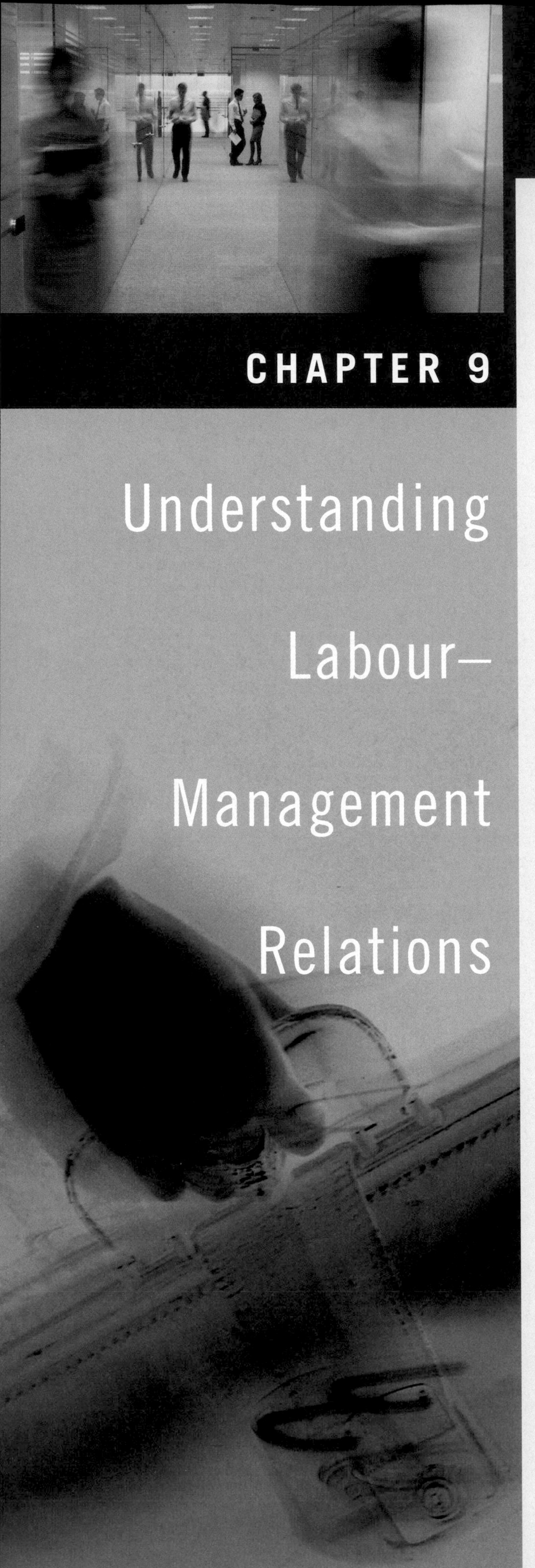

CHAPTER 9

Understanding Labour–Management Relations

After reading this chapter, you should be able to:

1. Explain why workers organize into *labour unions*.
2. Trace the evolution of unions and discuss *trends in unionism* in Canada.
3. Describe *the major laws governing labour–management relations*.
4. Describe the union *certification* and *decertification processes*.
5. Identify the steps in the *collective bargaining process*.

What Happened to Hockey Night in Canada?

Hockey is Canada's national game. It is a source of national pride, and millions of Canadians avidly follow their favourite team on television and by attending games. In mid-2004, however, storm clouds were brewing over the game, and there was a very real possibility that the 2004–05 hockey season would not take place because the NHL owners and the union representing the hockey players—the National Hockey League Players Association (NHLPA)—could not come to terms regarding a collective agreement. The main issue in the dispute was money. Specifically, the owners' claimed that players' salaries were too high in relation to league revenues, and that the owners could not make any money by running a hockey team. The owners were demanding that the players agree to sharply lower salaries, and that each team put a "cap" on its total salary bill.

Not surprisingly, the players initially rejected this idea. In spite of the fact that many of them were making multi-million dollar salaries, like all workers, they weren't interested in a salary cut. But sometimes, you have to accept things you don't like, and the players gradually learned that NHL owners were deadly serious about the salary cap idea. In fact, the owners were so serious that they were willing to sacrifice the entire 2004–05 hockey season to make their point about the need to cut salaries. By late summer of 2004, many people were convinced that at least part of the season would be cancelled. In September 2004, the owners made good on their threat and "locked out" their players, meaning that they could not play hockey until they had signed a collective agreement with the owners.

The lockout did not cause either the players or the owners to come to an agreement. Instead, negotiations dragged on and on, and many hockey games were cancelled. In December 2004, the players offered to cut their salaries by 24 percent, but the owners rejected that proposal saying it didn't go far enough. More negotiations followed, but to no avail.

By the halfway point of the 2004–05 season, over 350 players were playing for European teams. As well, increasing numbers of players were indicating that they were no longer willing to sit on the sidelines. They wanted to play, and they were willing to take a salary cut to do so.

In February 2005, the NHLPA proposed a modified salary cap idea, one that did not tie salaries to league revenues. The owners immediately rejected that idea as well because it did not give them "cost certainty." The owners' refusal to accept any variation of their salary cap idea was in sharp contrast to a previous round of negotiations a decade earlier when owners gave up trying to get the union to agree to a salary cap.

On February 9, 2005, league commissioner Gary Bettman announced that the 2004–05 season would be cancelled if the league and its players' union did not begin drawing up a new collective agreement within a few days. Nobody really believed that was very likely to happen, and in fact, the following week the season was officially cancelled. It was the first time in history that a major sport had cancelled its entire season.

In March 2005, the members of the players' executive committee finally agreed to negotiate a salary cap that was linked to league revenues. Perhaps they had finally accepted the grim reality that the owners were simply not going to sign a collective agreement unless they got a salary system that tied salaries to league revenues. In early April, when negotiations with owners resumed, the NHLPA informed the owners of their willingness to negotiate a salary cap on the owners' terms. From that point on, the heated rhetoric that had characterized the negotiations during the previous six months toned down, and the negotiators began making progress toward an agreement.

The two sides finally agreed that there would be a team-by-team salary floor and cap based on a percentage of each team's revenues. This gave the owners the "cost-certainty" that they were demanding.

The executive director of the NHLPA, Bob Goodenow, was not in favour of the salary cap. During meetings with players in 2003 and 2004, he regularly warned them that they would have to sit out at least two seasons if they hoped to avoid the kind of salary cap the owners wanted to impose. But in the end, he went along with the idea because the players' executive committee said that was the way the players felt they had to go. After that, Goodenow was much less visible in the negotiations. Whether Goodenow helped or hindered negotiations will be debated for many years.

The lockout obviously caused problems for owners, players, and fans, but it also was very disruptive for businesspeople whose livelihood depended on hockey games being played. Julie Charest, for example, was laid off from her job at a factory that makes hockey pucks and souvenirs for the NHL. There are thousands of other workers across Canada who were also affected, including those who worked at hockey arenas, and those who were directly or indirectly affected by the strike. Statistics Canada said that an unanticipated loss of 5700 jobs in January 2005 may have been related to the hockey strike.

The hockey strike was a major sports and business event in Canada. While some people might view the dispute as economically disruptive and totally unnecessary, in a democratic society the give-and-take that goes on as management and labour try to reach an agreement is part of the Canadian business scene. ◆

WHY DO WORKERS UNIONIZE?

1 Explain why workers organize into *labour unions.*

labour union A group of individuals who work together to achieve shared job-related goals.

labour relations The process of dealing with employees who are represented by a union.

Over 2000 years ago, the Greek poet Homer wrote, "There is a strength in the union even of very sorry men." There were no labour unions in Homer's time, but his comment is a particularly effective expression of the rationale for unions. A **labour union** is a group of individuals working together to achieve shared job-related goals, such as higher pay, shorter working hours, more job security, greater benefits, or better working conditions.[1] **Labour relations** describes the process of dealing with employees who are represented by a union. The opening case describes some of the complexities in labour relations at the NHL.

Labour unions grew in popularity in Canada in the nineteenth and early twentieth centuries. The labour movement was born with the Industrial Revolution, which also gave birth to a factory-based production system that carried with it enormous economic benefits. Job specialization and mass production allowed businesses to create ever-greater quantities of goods at ever-lower costs.

But there was also a dark side to this era. Workers became more dependent on their factory jobs. Eager for greater profits, some owners treated their workers like other raw materials: as resources to be deployed with little or no regard for the individual worker's well-being. Many businesses forced employees to work long hours; 60-hour weeks were common, and some workers were routinely forced to work 12 to 16 hours per day. With no minimum-wage laws or other controls, pay was also minimal and safety standards were virtually nonexistent. Workers enjoyed no job security and received few benefits. Many companies, especially textile mills, employed large numbers of children at poverty wages. If people complained, nothing prevented employers from firing and replacing them at will.

collective bargaining The process through which union leaders and management personnel negotiate common terms and conditions of employment for those workers represented by the union.

Unions appeared and ultimately prospered because they constituted a solution to the worker's most serious problem: They forced management to listen to the complaints of all their workers rather than to just the few who were brave (or foolish) enough to speak out. The power of unions, then, comes from collective action. **Collective bargaining** is the process by which union leaders and managers negotiate common terms and conditions of employment for the workers represented by unions. Although collective bargaining does not often occur in small businesses, many mid-size and larger businesses must engage in the process, which we will discuss in more detail later in this chapter.

THE DEVELOPMENT OF CANADIAN LABOUR UNIONS

Trace the evolution of unions and discuss *trends in unionism* in Canada. 2

The earliest evidence of labour unions in Canada comes from the maritime provinces early in the nineteenth century. Generally, these unions were composed of individuals with a specific craft (e.g., printers, shoemakers, barrel makers). Most of these unions were small and had only limited success. However, they laid the foundation for the rapid increase in union activity that occurred during the late nineteenth and early twentieth centuries.

A succession of labour organizations sprang up and just as quickly faded away during the years 1840–70. In 1873, the first national labour organization was formed—the Canadian Labour Union. By 1886, the Knights of Labour (a U.S.-based union) had over 10 000 members in Canada. The Canadian labour movement began to mature with the formation of the Trades and Labour Congress (TLC) in 1886. The TLC's purpose was to unite all labour organizations and to work for the passage of laws that would ensure the well-being of the working class.

The growth of labour unions began in earnest early in the twentieth century as the concept of organized labour gradually came to be accepted. Various disputes arose that resulted in numerous splits in labour's ranks. For example, there was concern that U.S.-based unions would have a detrimental effect on Canadian unions. The Canadian Federation of Labour was formed in 1908 to promote national (Canadian) unions over U.S. unions. These and other disputes (such as how communists in the movement should be handled) often led to the creation of rival union organizations that competed for membership. By 1956, these disputes had been largely resolved, and the two largest congresses of affiliated unions—the Trades and Labour Congress and the Canadian Congress of Labour—merged to form the Canadian Labour Congress. This amalgamation brought approximately 80 percent of all unionized workers into one organization. Table 9.1 highlights some of the important events in Canadian labour history.

Table 9.1 Some Important Dates in Canadian Labour History

Year	Event
1827	First union formed: boot and shoemakers in Quebec City
1873	Canadian Labour Union formed; objective was to unite unions across Canada
1879	First coal miners union in North America formed in Nova Scotia
1902	Formation of the National Trades and Labour Congress (became the Canadian Federation of Labour [CFL] in 1908); purpose was to promote national unions instead of international ones
1919	Winnipeg General Strike
1921	Confédération des Travailleurs Catholiques du Canada (CTCC) organized by the Roman Catholic clergy in Quebec; goal was to keep French-Canadian workers from being unduly influenced by English-speaking and American trade unions
1927	All-Canadian Congress of Labour (ACCL) formed; objective was to achieve independence of the Canadian labour movement from foreign control
1939	TLC expels industrial unions; Canadian Congress of Industrial Organization (CIO) Committee formed
1940	ACCL and the Canadian CIO Committee unite to form the Canadian Congress of Labour (CCL)
1956	TLC and CCL merge to form the Canadian Labour Congress (CLC)
1981	International building trades unions suspended from CLC
1982	Founding convention of Canadian Federation of Labour (CFL)
1985	Formation of United Auto Workers of Canada; formerly part of international UAW
1989	Merger of Canadian Union of Postal Workers (CUPW) and Letter Carriers Union of Canada
1994	Major league baseball players strike; no World Series played
1997	Strike of primary and secondary school teachers in Ontario
1999	Quebec nurses strike
2004–05	NHL players locked out; entire season lost

The Canadian Labour Congress (CLC), which was formed in 1956, brought the majority of unionized workers in Canada into one organization.

UNIONISM TODAY

While understanding the historical context of labour unions is important, so too is appreciating the role of unionism today, especially trends in union membership, union–management relations, and bargaining perspectives.

Trends in Union Membership

During the last 40 years, unions have experienced difficulties in attracting new members. As a result, although 4.3 million workers belonged to unions in 2005, union membership *as a proportion of the total workforce,* has stagnated, and only a minority of Canadian workers belong to unions. As shown in Figure 9.1, union membership as a proportion of the non-agricultural workforce has ranged from 23.2 percent in 1965 to 30.5 percent in 2005. Thus, less than one-third of the non-agricultural Canadian labour force is unionized.

Women are now a more important part of the union movement than in earlier years. In 1967, women accounted for less than 20 percent of union membership in Canada, but now they represent about half of all union workers. Unionized women are highly concentrated in the public sector, which provides jobs for only 19 percent of the workforce but accounts for 43 percent of all union members.[2]

The highest rates of unionization are found in Newfoundland (37.7 percent) and Quebec (37.5 percent). The lowest rates are found in Alberta (23.0 percent) and New Brunswick (26.4 percent). The public sector is quite heavily unionized (72.7 percent), but the private sector is not (18.1 percent).[3] In some occupations—for example, teaching and nursing—over 80 percent of workers are unionized. In other occupations—for example, management and food and beverage workers—less than 10 percent of the workers belong to unions.[4] The union movement is more successful in Canada than it is in the United States, where only 13 percent of the workforce is unionized.

Over the years, unions have experienced ups and downs in terms of their success at becoming certified at new locations. Many years ago, unions routinely won certification votes. But in recent years, they have encountered increasing opposition from management of companies that are trying to survive in a fiercely competitive global environment. Two factors help explain the difficulties that unions have faced in recent years.

Composition of the Workforce

Traditionally, union members have been predominantly white males in blue-collar jobs. But today's workforce is increasingly composed of women and ethnic minorities. Because these groups have much weaker traditions of union affiliation, their members are less likely to join unions when they enter the workforce. In a related trend, the workforce is increasingly employed in the service sector, which traditionally has been less heavily unionized.

Anti-Unionization Activities

A second reason for declining union membership is more aggressive anti-unionization activity on the part of employers. Federal and provincial labour legislation restricts what management of a company can do to keep out a union, but companies are free to pursue certain strategies to minimize unionization, such as creating a more employee-friendly work environment. For example, Japanese manufacturers who have set up shop in North America have avoided unionization efforts by the United Auto Workers (UAW) by providing job security, higher wages, and a work environment in which employees are allowed to participate and be actively involved in plant management. The Toyota plant in Cambridge, Ontario, is just one example.

Trends in Union–Management Relations

The gradual decline in unionization in Canada has been accompanied by some significant trends in union–management relations. In some sectors of the economy, perhaps most notably in the automobile and steel industries, labour unions remain quite strong. In these areas, unions have large mem-

Figure 9.1 Union members as a proportion of the non-agricultural workforce.

berships and considerable power in negotiating with management. The CAW, for example, is still a strong union.

In most sectors, however, unions are clearly in a weakened position. As a result, many have taken much more conciliatory stances in their relations with management. This situation contrasts sharply with the more adversarial relationship that once dominated labour relations in this country. Increasingly, for instance, unions recognize that they don't have as much power as they once held and that it is in their own best interests, as well as in the best interests of the workers they represent, to work with instead of against management. Ironically, then, union–management relations in many ways are better today than they have been in years. Admittedly, the improvement is attributable in large part to the weakened power of unions. Even so, most experts agree that improved union–management relations have benefited both sides. The Entrepreneurship and New Ventures box describes an interesting development in labour-management co-operation.

Trends in Bargaining Perspectives

Given the trends described in the two previous sections, we should not be surprised to find changes in bargaining perspectives as well. In the past, for example, most union–management bargaining situations were character-

ENTREPRENEURSHIP AND NEW VENTURES

Benchmarking Labour Relations

For Arcelor, exercising leadership is second nature. In terms of financial performance, it is considered the number one steelmaker in the world[1], with consolidated revenue of 32.6 billion euros in 2005—an increase of 8.1 percent over 2004. It also leads the various markets it serves: automotive, construction, household appliances and packaging.

But financial performance is not the only area the company seeks to excel in. It also aims to be a benchmark for labour relations and social responsibility. Toward this end, Arcelor set a precedent in 2005 when it co-signed an agreement on corporate social responsibility with both the International Metalworkers' Federation (IMF) and the European Metalworkers' Federation (EMF). In doing so it became the first company in the steel sector to participate in an international framework agreement.

Highlights of the agreement include:

- respect for the International Labour Organization's (ILO) Conventions on freedom of association, collective bargaining, non-discrimination, and no forced or child labour
- commitments on providing health and safety and life-long training for workers

Says Arcelor's CEO, Guy Dollé: "This agreement is an expression and a confirmation of our principles of responsibility and of our commitment to the respect and fair treatment of each and every member of our staff. As a global company we apply the same high ethical and social standards wherever we operate. We are convinced that this commitment will help us to grow internationally in a sustainable way."

While Peter Scherrer, the EMF representative at the the signing ceremony in Luxembourg, expressed the hope that other companies in the steel industry would adopt similar high standards in corporate social responsibility, Rob Johnston (IMF Director for Steel), representing the IMF, had this to say: "This agreement not only gives recognition to the vital importance of Arcelor's workforce, but also sets out in clear terms how the company will respect its workers worldwide. We look forward to working with Arcelor to implement this agreement, the first of its kind in the steel sector."

But actions speak louder than words. What progress has Arcelor made with respect to the terms of this agreement? If Arcelor's results in terms of health and safety are any indication, the company may be well poised to uphold its trendsetting reputation. For example, from 2004 to 2005 the occupational accident rate went from 3.7 to 2.4 (as measured by accidents with work interruption per million of hours worked). In fact, since the company's founding in 2002, the accident frequency rate has been divided by four. These are impressive results for any company, but moreso for one that only came into being in 2002. However, whether this momentum can be sustained in light of the recent merger between Arcelor and Mittal Steel remains to be seen.

[1] Arcelor: a strong commitment to value creation. *Canada NewsWire* February 27, 2006, 1.

ized by union demands for dramatic increases in wages and salaries. A secondary issue was usually increased benefits for members. Now, however, unions often bargain for different benefits, such as job security. Of particular interest in this area is the trend toward relocating jobs to take advantage of lower labour costs in other countries. Unions, of course, want to restrict job movement, whereas companies want to save money by moving facilities—and jobs—to other countries.

As a result of organizational downsizing and a decade of low inflation in Canada, many unions today find themselves able to achieve only modest wage increases for their members. A common goal of union strategy is therefore to preserve what has already been won. Unions have also tried to place greater emphasis on improved job security, but with limited success. A trend that has become especially important in recent years is toward improved pension programs for employees.

The Future of Unions

Despite declining membership and loss of power, labour unions remain a significant factor in Canadian business. The labour organizations in the Canadian Labour Congress and independent major unions such as the International Brotherhood of Teamsters and the Canadian Union of Public Employees can disrupt the economy by refusing to work. The votes of their members are still sought by politicians at all levels. In addition, the concessions they have won for their members—better pay, shorter working hours, and safer working conditions—now cover many non-unionized workers as well.

The big question is this: Will unions be able to cope with the many challenges that are currently facing them, or will their power continue to dwindle? The challenges facing unions are many, including

- the decline of the so-called "smokestack industries," where union power has traditionally been very strong
- employment growth in service industries, where union power has traditionally not been strong
- deregulation, which has led to mergers and layoffs and to the emergence of new, non-unionized companies
- free trade and the globalization of business, which has raised the very real possibility of many jobs being moved to areas of the world with lower labour costs
- technological change, which allows telecommuting and increases the difficulty of organizing workers

Unions are increasingly aware that they must co-operate with employers if both companies and unions are to survive and prosper. The goal is to create effective partnerships in which managers and workers share the same goals: profitability, growth, and effectiveness, with equitable rewards for everyone. Some experts think that a new wave of unionism may be about to sweep across Canada. This movement may be fuelled by young people (including college and university graduates) who fear they will be stuck in low-wage jobs and who hope unions can help them avoid that fate.

THE LEGAL ENVIRONMENT FOR UNIONS IN CANADA

Political and legal barriers to collective bargaining existed until well into the twentieth century. Courts held that some unions were conspirators in restraint of trade. Employers viewed their employees' efforts to unionize as

3 Describe the *major laws governing labour–management relations.*

attempts to deprive the employers of their private property. The employment contract, employers contended, was between the individual worker and the employer—not between the employer and employees as a group. The balance of bargaining power was very much in favour of the employer.

The employer–employee relationship became much less direct as firms grew in size. Managers were themselves employees. Hired managers dealt with other employees. Communication among owners, managers, and workers became more formalized. Big business had more power than workers. Because of mounting public concern, laws were passed to place the worker on a more even footing with the employer.

In 1900, government concern about labour disputes resulted in the passage of the Conciliation Act. The act was designed to help settle labour disputes through voluntary conciliation and was a first step in creating an environment more favourable to labour. A more comprehensive law, the 1907 **Industrial Disputes Investigation Act**, provided for compulsory investigation of labour disputes by a government-appointed board before a strike was allowed. However, this act was later found to violate a fundamental provision of the BNA Act (see below).

Industrial Disputes Investigation Act (1907) Provided for compulsory investigation of labour disputes by a government-appointed board before a strike was allowed.

The current environment for labour did not come into being until 1943 when **Privy Council Order 1003** was issued. This order recognized the right of employees to bargain collectively, prohibited unfair labour practices on the part of management, established a labour board to certify bargaining authority, and prohibited strikes and lockouts except in the course of negotiating collective agreements. Approximately 45 years of dealings among labour, management, and government were required before the labour movement achieved its fundamental goal of the right to bargain collectively.

Privy Council Order 1003 (1943) Recognized the right of employees to bargain collectively.

The **Constitution Act** (originally the BNA Act), passed in 1867, has also affected labour legislation. This act allocated certain activities to the federal government (e.g., labour legislation for companies operating interprovincially) and others to individual provinces (labour relations regulations in general). Thus, labour legislation emanates from both the federal and provincial governments but is basically a provincial matter. That is why certain groups of similar employees might be allowed to go on strike in one province but not in another.

Constitution Act (1867) Divided authority over labour regulations between the federal and provincial governments.

Federal Legislation—the Canada Labour Code

The **Canada Labour Code** is a comprehensive piece of legislation that applies to the labour practices of firms operating under the legislative authority of parliament. The code is composed of four major sections.

Canada Labour Code Legislation that applies to the labour practices of firms operating under the legislative authority of parliament.

Fair Employment Practices

This section prohibits an employer from either refusing employment on the basis of a person's race or religion or using an employment agency that discriminates against people on the basis of their race or religion. These prohibitions apply to trade unions as well, but not to non-profit, charitable, and philanthropic organizations. Any individual who believes that a violation has occurred may make a complaint in writing to Labour Canada. The allegation will then be investigated and if necessary, an Industrial Inquiry Commission will be appointed to make a recommendation in the case. (Since 1982, fair employment practices have been covered by the Canadian Human Rights Act; they are also covered by the Canadian Charter of Rights and Freedoms.)

Standard Hours, Wages, Vacations, and Holidays

This section covers non-managerial workers and deals with a wide variety of mechanical issues such as standard hours of work (8-hour days and 40-hour weeks), maximum hours of work per week (48), overtime pay (at least one and a half times the regular pay), minimum wages, equal wages for men and women doing the same jobs, vacations, general holidays, and maternity leave. The specific provisions are changed frequently to take into account changes in the economic and social structure of Canada, but their basic goal is to ensure consistent treatment of employees in these areas.

In 2005, a sweeping review of the Canada Labour Code was announced by the federal Minister of Labour. One of the issues that the review will focus on is whether managers and supervisors should also be protected by labour code restrictions on the number hours they work each week, and whether they should receive overtime pay. The issue came to the forefront after the Manitoba Labour Board ruled that Sharon Michalowski, a manager at Nygard International, was entitled to overtime pay, even though she was a manager and had signed a contract stipulating that she would work whatever hours were required to earn her annual salary of $42 000.[5]

Safety of Employees

This section requires that every person running a federal work project do so in a way that will not endanger the health or safety of any employee. It also requires that safety procedures and techniques be implemented to reduce the risk of employment injury. This section requires employees to exercise care to ensure their own safety; however, even if it can be shown that the employee did not exercise proper care, compensation must still be paid. This section also makes provisions for a safety officer whose overall duty is to ensure that the provisions of the code are being fulfilled. The safety officer has the right to enter any federal project "at any reasonable time."

Canada Industrial Relations Regulations

The final major section of the Canada Labour Code deals with all matters related to collective bargaining. It is subdivided into seven divisions:

- Division I—gives employees the right to join a trade union and gives employers the right to join an employers association.
- Division II—establishes the Canada Labour Relations Board whose role is to make decisions on a number of important issues (e.g., certification of trade unions).
- Division III—stipulates the procedures required to acquire or terminate bargaining rights.
- Division IV—establishes the rules and regulations that must be adhered to during bargaining; also presents guidelines for the content and interpretation of collective agreements.
- Division V—states the requirement that the Minister of Labour must appoint a conciliation officer if the parties in the dispute cannot reach a collective agreement.
- Division VI—stipulates the conditions under which strikes and lockouts are permitted.
- Division VII—is a general conclusion that states methods that might be used to promote industrial peace.

Provincial Labour Legislation

Each province has enacted legislation to deal with the personnel practices covered in the Canada Labour Code. These laws vary across provinces and are frequently revised; however, their basic approach and substance is the same as in the Canada Labour Code. Certain provinces may exceed the minimum code requirements on some issues (e.g., minimum wage). Each province also has a labour relations act. To give an indication of what these acts cover, the Ontario Labour Relations Act is briefly described below.

The Ontario Labour Relations Act

The Ontario Labour Relations Act is a comprehensive document dealing with the conduct of labour relations in that province. Some illustrative provisions of the Ontario law are noted below.

- A trade union may apply at any time to the Ontario Labour Relations Board (OLRB) for certification as the sole bargaining agent for employees in a company.
- The OLRB has the right to call for a certification vote. If more than 50 percent of those voting are in favour of the trade union, the board certifies the union as the bargaining agent.
- Following certification, the union gives the employer written notification of its desire to bargain, with the goal being the signing of a collective agreement. The parties are required to begin bargaining within 15 days of the written notice.
- On request by either party, the Minister of Labour appoints a conciliation officer to confer with the parties and to help achieve a collective agreement. On joint request, the Minister of Labour can appoint a mediator.
- The parties may jointly agree to submit unresolved differences to voluntary binding arbitration. The decision of the arbitrator is final.
- Employers are required to deduct union dues from the union members and remit these dues directly to the union.
- Every agreement must include a mechanism for settling grievances—differences between the parties arising from interpretation, application, or administration of the collective agreement.
- If a person objects to belonging to a labour union because of religious beliefs, he or she is allowed to make a contribution equal to the amount of the union dues to a charitable organization.
- If a trade union is not able to negotiate a collective agreement with management within one year of being certified, any of the employees in the union can apply to the OLRB for decertification of the union.
- No employer can interfere with the formation of a union. The employer is, however, free to express an opinion about the matter.
- No employer shall refuse to employ an individual because he or she is a member of a trade union.

The basic provisions of the Ontario Labour Relations Act are found in one form or another in the labour relations acts of all provinces, but the details and procedures vary from province to province. It is obvious that administering labour relations activity is complex and time-consuming. Company management, the union, and the government all expend much time and energy in an attempt to ensure reasonable relations between management and labour.

UNION ORGANIZING STRATEGY

A union might try to organize workers when a firm is trying to break into a new geographical area, when some workers in a firm are members and it wants to cover other workers, or when it is attempting to outdo a rival union. In some cases, a union might try to organize workers for purposes other than helping a group of employees to help themselves.

Management often becomes aware of a union organizing effort through gossip from the company grapevine. In 1999, management at Honda of Canada's Alliston, Ontario, plant and at Toyota Canada's Cambridge, Ontario, plant learned that the CAW had launched organizing drives at their plants. The CAW distributed leaflets at plant gates and contacted groups of workers inside the plant as part of its organizing drive.[6]

The Business Accountability box describes the conflict between a union that wants to organize retail workers and a company that doesn't want unionized workers.

BUSINESS ACCOUNTABILITY

The Fight for Certification Goes on at Wal-Mart

For the last decade or so, the United Food and Commercial Workers (UFCW) union has been working very hard to unionize workers in Wal-Mart stores at several locations across Canada. The fight has been bitter at times, and the eventual outcome is not yet clear. A skirmish that took place in 2004 is typical of the fight. Shortly after the UFCW succeeded in getting certified as the bargaining agent for workers at a Wal-Mart store in the Jonquiere district of Saguenay, Quebec, Wal-Mart closed the store, saying that it was unprofitable. Workers at the Jonquiere store were not able to negotiate a first contract before the store was closed. The union filed a class-action suit against Wal-Mart, claiming that the sole reason for closing the store was to break the union. The company denied that charge, and noted that it had also closed other, non-unionized stores in other locations because they weren't profitable.

The incident typifies what has been going on in the intense battle between the UFCW and Wal-Mart. The union is committed to organizing Wal-Mart's employees, while Wal-Mart's management tenaciously fights every UFCW attempt. Each side has had victories and defeats. In 2003, for example, the Labour Relations Board of British Columbia found Wal-Mart guilty of unfair labour practices, namely, that it undermined a union organizing drive at the Wal-Mart store in Quesnel, British Columbia. As part of their decision, the board required Wal-Mart management to schedule an employee meeting and read aloud the board's decision to employees.

Until the mid-1990s, Wal-Mart had never had a union in any of its stores in the United States, Canada, Puerto Rico, Argentina, Brazil, or Mexico. It had been able to resist unions partly by promoting its family-like culture. The company argued that forcing employees to work under a collective agreement would reduce their motivation and damage the company's successful formula for keeping customers happy.

In 1996, management first began hearing rumours that the Canadian Auto Workers union was approaching employees at the Windsor, Ontario, store about joining a union. During the organizing drive, there was much squabbling among employees, and when the certification vote was held, the workers voted 151–43 against joining the union. In spite of this, the Ontario Labour Relations Board (OLRB) certified the union as the employees' bargaining agent on the grounds that the company had intimidated employees during the membership drive. A first collective agreement was approved, but then 80 employees signed a petition claiming that they did not vote in favour of the contract. A few months later, a majority of the workers at the store filed an application with the OLRB to have the union decertified. In April 2000, the union was officially decertified.

During 2003 and 2004, the UFCW made efforts to organize Wal-Mart stores in Saskatchewan, British Columbia, and Manitoba. In early 2005, the UFCW succeeded in getting employees unionized in a Wal-Mart store in Saint-Hyacinthe, Quebec. But Wal-Mart also won a victory in Saskatchewan when it successfully challenged the constitutionality of that province's labour law that restricts employer-employee communication during an organizing drive. Wal-Mart says that workers should hear the whole story before deciding whether or not to join a union. The fight goes on.

When management discovers that an organizing drive is underway, it may try to counteract it. However, management must know what it can legally do to discourage the union. In Quebec, McDonald's has been the target of union organizing drives at several of its restaurants. In 1998, the McDonald's restaurant in St. Hubert closed when it appeared that the teamsters union might be successful in getting certified as the bargaining agent for the employees. Critics immediately called for a government investigation into the possibility of unfair labour practices on the part of the company.[7]

CERTIFYING A UNION: AN EXAMPLE

4 Describe the union *certification* and *decertification processes.*

bargaining unit Individuals grouped together for purposes of collective bargaining.

certification vote A vote supervised by a government representative to determine whether a union will be certified.

decertification The process by which employees terminate their union's right to represent them.

Suppose that a union is trying to organize employees of a Manitoba company. If it can show that at least 50 percent of the employees are members of the union, it can apply to the Manitoba Labour Board (MLB) for certification as the bargaining agent for the employees. A problem may arise regarding the right of different types of workers to join or not join the union. For example, supervisors may or may not be included in a bargaining unit along with non-management workers. The **bargaining unit** includes those individuals deemed appropriate by the province. The MLB has final authority in determining the appropriateness of the bargaining unit. Professional and non-professional employees are generally not included in the same bargaining unit unless a majority of the professional employees wish to be included. Once the MLB has determined that the unit is appropriate, it may order a **certification vote**. If a majority of those voting are in favour of the union, it is certified as the sole bargaining agent for the unit.

The same law that grants employees the right to unionize also allows them to decertify. **Decertification** is the process by which employees legally terminate their union's right to represent them. A labour dispute over job security and safety that arose at Goldcorp Inc.'s gold mine near Red Lake, Ontario, led to a strike involving 100 workers. The strike was settled when workers agreed to decertify their union in return for severance pay that was four times the rate mandated by Ontario law.[8] In 2005, the Manitoba Labour Board decertified Local 832 of the United Food and Commercial Workers for workers at the Hampton Inn & Suites in Winnipeg. The workers said they weren't getting value for the dues they were paying to the union.[9]

Types of Unions

craft unions Unions organized by crafts or trades; usually composed of skilled workers.

The two basic types of union are craft and industrial unions. **Craft unions** are organized by crafts or trades—plumbers, barbers, airline pilots, etc. Craft unions restrict membership to workers with specific skills. In many

An employee from Wal-Mart in Chicoutimi stands outside the store after it became the first Wal-Mart in Canada to become unionized. The Quebec Labour Relations Board gave the United Food and Commercial Workers Union the nod to represent the 180 workers.

cases, members of craft unions work for several different employers during the course of a year. For example, many construction workers are hired by their employers at union hiring halls. When the particular job for which they are hired is finished, these workers return to the hall to be hired by another employer.

Craft unions have a lot of power over the supply of skilled workers because they have apprenticeship programs. A person who wants to become a member of a plumbers' union, for example, must go through a training program. He or she starts out as an apprentice. After the training, the apprentice is qualified as a journeyman plumber.

Industrial unions are organized according to industries, for example, steel, auto, and clothing. Industrial unions include semiskilled and unskilled workers. They were originally started because industrial workers were not eligible to join craft unions. Industrial union members typically work for a particular employer for a much longer period of time than do craft union members. An industrial union has a lot of say regarding pay and human resource practices within unionized firms.

industrial unions Unions organized by industry; usually composed of semiskilled and unskilled workers.

The **local union** (or local) is the basic unit of union organization. A local of a craft union is made up of artisans in the same craft in a relatively small geographical area. A local of an industrial union is made up of workers in a given industry or plant in a relatively small geographical area. Thus, plumbers in a local labour market may be members of the local plumbers' union. Truck drivers and warehouse workers in that same area may be members of a teamsters' local.

local union The basic unit of union organization.

The functions of locals vary, depending not only on governance arrangements but also on bargaining patterns in particular industries. Some local unions bargain directly with management regarding wages, hours, and other terms and conditions of employment. Many local unions are also active in disciplining members for violations of contract standards and in pressing management to consider worker complaints.

A **national union** has members across Canada. These members belong to locals affiliated with the national union. There are many national unions in Canada, including the Canadian Union of Public Employees, the National Railway Union, and the Canadian Airline Pilots Union. About two-thirds of unionized Canadian workers belong to national unions.

national union A union with members across Canada.

An **international union** is a union with members in more than one country. One example is the United Steelworkers of America, made up of locals in the United States and Canada. About 30 percent of unionized workers in Canada belong to international unions.

international union A union with members in more than one country.

An **independent local union** is one that is not formally affiliated with any labour organization. It conducts negotiations with management at a local level, and the collective agreement is binding at that location only. The University of Manitoba Faculty Association is an independent local union. Less than 5 percent of unionized workers in Canada belong to independent local unions. Table 9.2 lists the 10 largest unions in Canada.

independent local union One not formally affiliated with any labour organization.

Union Security

The growing security consciousness of Canadian workers is reflected in union goals. The seniority provision in most contracts spells out the workers' rights when layoffs, transfers, and promotions occur. Employees are ranked by length of service. Those with longer service receive better treatment. Much conflict exists regarding seniority. For example, women and members of minority groups typically have less seniority and are the first to be laid off and the last to move up to higher jobs. These workers tend to oppose the tradition of seniority.

Table 9.2 The Top 10 Unions in Canada, 2005

Union	Membership
1. Canadian Union of Public Employees	540 000
2. National Union of Public and General Employees	337 000
3. United Steelworkers of America	280 000
4. Canadian Auto Workers	265 000
5. United Food and Commercial Workers	230 000
6. Public Service Alliance of Canada	156 000
7. Communications, Energy, and Paperworkers Union of Canada	150 000
8. International Brotherhood of Teamsters	125 000
9. Fédération de la santé et des services sociaux	110 000
10. Laborers International Union of North America	85 000

union security The maintenance of a union's membership so that it can continue to meet the criteria for certification.

Union security refers to the means of ensuring the union's continued existence and the maintenance of its membership so that it can continue to meet the criteria for certification. There is always a danger—particularly in bad economic times—that the membership may drop below the required absolute majority. The union may then lose its certification.

closed shop An employer can hire only union members.

The greatest union security is found in the **closed shop**, where an employer can hire only union members. For example, a plumbing or electrical contractor who hires workers through a union hiring hall can hire only union members.

union shop An employer can hire non-unionized workers, but they must join the union within a certain period.

In a **union shop**, an employer may hire non-union workers even if the employer's current employees are unionized. New workers, however, must join the union within a stipulated period of time (usually 30 days).

agency shop All employees for whom the union bargains must pay dues, but they are not required to join the union.

In an **agency shop**, all employees for whom the union bargains must pay dues, but they need not join the union. This compromise between the union shop and the open shop is called the Rand formula after the judge who proposed it. In the Quebec Labour Code, the Rand formula applies to all unions certified under this code.

open shop An employer may hire union or non-union workers.

In an **open shop**, an employer may hire union and/or non-union labour. Employees need not join or pay dues to a union in an open shop.

COLLECTIVE BARGAINING

5 Identify the steps in the *collective bargaining process.*

Too often, people associate collective bargaining with the signing of a contract between a union and a company or industry. In fact, collective bargaining is an ongoing process involving not only the drafting but also the administering of the terms of a labour contract.

Reaching Agreement on the Contract's Terms

The collective bargaining process begins with the recognition of the union as the exclusive negotiator for its members. The bargaining cycle begins when union leaders meet with management representatives to agree on a new contract. By law, both parties must sit down at the bargaining table and negotiate "in good faith." When each side has presented its demands, sessions focus on identifying the *bargaining zone*. This process is shown in Figure 9.2. For example, although an employer may initially offer no pay raise, it may expect to grant a raise of up to 6 percent. Likewise, the union may initially *demand* a 10 percent pay raise while *expecting* to accept a raise as low as 4 percent. The bargaining zone, then, is a raise between 4 and 6 percent. Ideally, some compromise is reached between these levels and the new agreement is submitted for a ratification vote by union membership.

Sometimes, this process goes quite smoothly. At other times, however, the two sides cannot—or will not—agree. The speed and ease with which such an impasse is resolved depend in part on the nature of the contract issues, the willingness of each side to use certain tactics, and the prospects for mediation or arbitration.

Contract Issues

The labour contract itself can address an array of different issues. Most of these issues concern demands that unions make on behalf of their members. In this section we will survey the categories of issues that are typically most important to union negotiators: *compensation, benefits,* and *job security*. Although few issues covered in a labour contract are company sponsored, we will also describe the kinds of management rights that are negotiated in most bargaining agreements.

First, note that bargaining items generally fall into two categories:

- *Mandatory items* are matters over which both parties must negotiate if either wants to. This category includes wages, working hours, and benefits.
- *Permissive items* may be negotiated if both parties agree. For example, a union demand for veto power over the promotion of managerial personnel would be a permissive bargaining item.

Neither party may bring illegal items to the table. For example, a management demand for a non-strike clause would be an illegal item.

Compensation

The most common issue is compensation. One aspect of compensation is current wages. Obviously, unions generally want their employees to earn higher wages and try to convince management to raise hourly wages for all

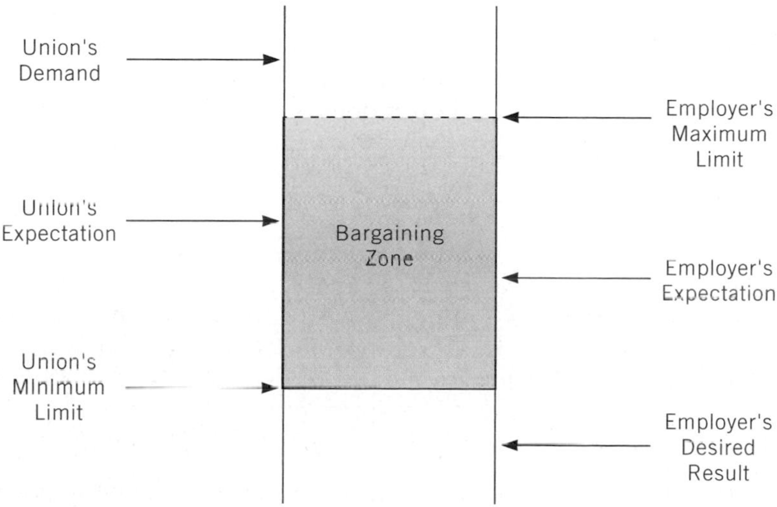

Figure 9.2 The bargaining zone.

Representatives of labour and management negotiate in an attempt to reach an agreement on a labour contract. Here, members of the Canadian Auto Workers and managers representing Ford Canada are negotiating the terms of a collective agreement.

or some employees. Of equal concern to unions is future compensation: wage rates to be paid during subsequent years of the contract. One common tool for securing wage increases is a **cost-of-living adjustment (COLA)**. Most COLA clauses tie future raises to the *consumer price index (CPI)*, a government statistic that reflects changes in consumer purchasing power. The premise is that as the CPI increases by a specified amount during a given period of time, wages will automatically increase.

cost-of-living adjustment (COLA) A contract clause specifying that wages will increase automatically with the rate of inflation.

Wage reopener clauses may also be included. Such a clause allows wage rates to be renegotiated at preset times during the life of the contract. For example, a union might be uncomfortable with a long-term contract based solely on COLA wage increases. A long-term agreement might be more acceptable, however, if management agrees to renegotiate wages every two years.

wage reopener clause A contract clause that allows wage rates to be renegotiated at preset times during the life of the contract.

Benefits

Employee benefits are also an important component of most labour contracts. Unions typically want employers to pay all or most of the costs of various kinds of insurance for employees. Other benefits commonly addressed during negotiations include retirement benefits, working conditions, and the cost of supplementary health care (prescription drugs, eyecare, dental care, etc.). The health-care issue is becomingly increasingly contentious during negotiations because the cost of health care is rapidly increasing. General Motors, for example, spends more on health-care benefits for its 1.1 million workers than it does on steel. And insurance premiums for drug plans are doubling every five years.[10]

Job Security

Job security is an increasingly important agenda item in bargaining sessions today. In some cases, demands for job security entail the promise that a company will not move to another location. In others, the contract may dictate that if the workforce is reduced, seniority will be used to determine which employees lose their jobs.

Other Union Issues

Other possible issues might include such things as working hours, overtime policies, rest period arrangements, differential pay plans for shift employees, the use of temporary workers, grievance procedures, and allowable union activities (dues collection, union bulletin boards, and so forth).

Management Rights

Management wants as much control as possible over hiring policies, work assignments, and so forth. Unions, meanwhile, often try to limit management rights by specifying hiring, assignment, and other policies. At one DaimlerChrysler plant, for example, the contract stipulates that three workers are needed to change fuses in robots: a machinist to open the robot, an electrician to change the fuse, and a supervisor to oversee the process. As in this example, contracts often bar workers in one job category from performing work that falls within the domain of another. Unions try to secure jobs by defining as many different categories as possible (the DaimlerChrysler plant has over 100). Of course, management resists this practice, which limits flexibility and makes it difficult to reassign workers.

When Bargaining Fails

An **impasse** occurs when, after a series of bargaining sessions, management and labour fail to agree on a new contract or a contract to replace an agreement that is about to expire. Although it is generally agreed that both parties suffer when an impasse is reached and action is taken, each side can employ several tactics to support its cause until the impasse is resolved.

impasse When, after a series of bargaining sessions, management and labour fail to agree on a new contract or a contract to replace an agreement that is about to expire.

Union Tactics

Unions can take a variety of actions when their demands are not met. Chief among these are *strikes*, *picketing*, *boycotts*, and *work slowdowns*.

The Strike. A **strike** occurs when employees temporarily walk off the job and refuse to work. In 2005, TELUS workers were on strike for four months because they could not reach agreement on a new collective agreement with the company. One of the key issues in dispute was the extent to which the company's would be allowed to contract out non-core jobs. The union was concerned that the company wanted to contract out a large variety of jobs. The disputing parties finally reached a settlement.[11]

strike A tactic of labour unions in which members temporarily walk off the job and refuse to work to win concessions from management.

A study of the strike records in 17 countries during the period 1981–2003 showed that Spain had the highest number of days lost to strikes per thousand employees (418), followed by Italy (315), and then Canada (310). Germany lost only 17 days. The two most strike-prone sectors in Canada were mining/energy and transport/communication.[12]

Strikes triggered by impasses over mandatory bargaining items are called *economic strikes*, even if they occur over non-economic issues such as working hours. Most strikes in Canada are economic strikes. The strike by TELUS workers in 2005, NHL players in 2004–05, and Inco workers in 2003 were over largely over economic issues.

During a strike, workers are not paid and the business is usually unable to produce its normal range of products and services. During this time, the union may try to convince the general public that the company is being unfair. When Canada Safeway workers went on strike in Alberta in 1997, they were very successful at convincing the general public not to shop at Safeway. So many people refused to cross the union's picket lines that sales at some Safeway stores fell by as much as 70 percent.[13]

After a strike is over, employees may exhibit low morale, anger, increased absenteeism, and decreased productivity. In these situations, care must be taken to improve communications between management and

Pilots who belong to the Air Canada Pilots Association walk the picket line during a strike.

workers.[14] If a strike goes on for a long time, it can create very negative outcomes for both the company and its workers. In 2000, production workers at the Versatile tractor plant in Winnipeg went on strike. After many months with no settlement in sight, the union offered to go back to work, but management then locked the workers out. The union then filed an unfair labour practices claim against the company, saying that management never intended to re-start production at the Winnipeg plant because it was planning to move operations to North Dakota. Eventually, the Manitoba Labour Relations Board fined Versatile $6 million for bargaining in bad faith. The union finally agreed to a deal that paid the workers for the entire period they were on strike, but the deal also involved closing the plant and all the workers lost their jobs.[15]

Strikes may occur in response to an employer's unfair labour practices. A firm that refuses to recognize a duly certified union may find itself with a striking workforce and having to explain its refusal to the provincial labour relations board. Such strikes are rare, however.

Not all strikes are legal. The Ontario primary and secondary school teachers strike in 1997 against the province of Ontario was illegal because the teachers had not gone through the necessary steps prior to going out on strike. The teachers voluntarily returned to work after striking for only two weeks. Nurses in Quebec and Saskatchewan also carried out illegal strikes in 1999. **Sympathy strikes** (also called **secondary strikes**), where one union strikes in sympathy with strikes initiated by another labour organization, may violate the sympathetic union's contract. **Wildcat strikes**—those that are not authorized by the union that occur during the life of a contract—deprive strikers of their status as employees and thus of the protection of labour laws.

sympathy strikes (secondary strikes) A strike where one union strikes in sympathy with strikes initiated by another labour organization.

wildcat strikes Strikes that are not authorized by the union that occur during the life of a contract.

Unions are more reluctant to use the strike weapon than they used to be. There are several reasons for this: More and more workers are in profit-sharing plans and therefore receive a portion of company profits, workers' own shares of the company's stock and their personal payoffs are tied to the success of the company, union membership continues to decline, strikes are bad publicity and hurt union efforts to recruit new union members, and technology and globalization mean that companies can easily displace highly paid but low-skilled workers.[16]

Picketing. As part of or instead of a strike, unions faced with an impasse may picket their employer. **Picketing** involves having workers march at the entrance to the company with signs explaining their reasons for striking. During the labour dispute between the Telecommunications Workers Union (TWU) and TELUS Corp., for example, union workers picketed the company. TELUS responded by getting an injunction to prevent picketers from blocking access to the company.[17]

picketing A tactic of labour unions in which members march at the entrance to the company with signs explaining their reasons for striking.

Boycotts. A **boycott** occurs when union members agree not to buy the product of the firm that employs them. Workers may also urge other consumers to shun their firm's product.

boycott A tactic of labour unions in disputes with management in which members refuse to buy the products of the company and encourage other consumers to do the same.

Work Slowdowns. In a **work slowdown**, workers perform their jobs at a much slower pace than normal. A variation is the "sickout," during which large numbers of workers call in sick.

work slowdown Instead of striking, workers perform their jobs at a much slower pace than normal.

Management Tactics

Management can also respond forcefully to an impasse. These tactics include *lockouts, strikebreakers, plant closures, contracting out, forming employers' associations,* and *decertification.*

Lockouts. **Lockouts** occur when employers physically deny employees access to the workplace. In 2005, the CBC locked its employees out for eight weeks when union and management could not agree on the terms of a new collective agreement. As we saw in the opening case, the 2004–05 NHL hockey season also began with a lockout. The lockout is illegal if it is used as an offensive weapon to give the firm an economic advantage in the bargaining process (for example, if sales are poor and management wants to avoid a buildup of inventory).

lockout A tactic of management in which the firm physically denies employees access to the workplace to pressure workers to agree to the company's latest contract offer.

Strikebreakers. Firms faced with a strike can hire temporary or permanent replacements (**strikebreakers**) to replace the striking employees. When players in the National Football League went out on strike during the 1987 season, the team owners hired free agents and went right on playing. In 1992, National Hockey League owners planned to use minor league hockey players if they could not reach an agreement with striking NHL players.

strikebreaker An individual hired by a firm to replace a worker on strike; a tactic of management in disputes with labour unions.

Plant Closures. In extreme cases, management may simply close down a plant if they cannot reach agreement with the union. In 1997, Maple Leaf closed its Edmonton hog processing plant when the workers went on strike. This cost 850 workers their jobs. A less obvious tactic is to simply not build manufacturing plants in Canada and thereby avoid the possibility of union problems. Ipsco Steel of Regina, for example, is not expanding its operations in Canada because it feels that Canada's labour laws are too restrictive. The company is constructing new steel mills in U.S. states where workers can opt out of a union.[18]

Contracting Out. Some firms contract out work as a way to blunt their unions' effects. Instead of doing all the assembly work they used to do themselves, many firms now *contract out* work to non-union contractors. This lessens the impact the unions can have because it results in fewer union workers.

Employers' Associations. **Employers' associations** are groups of companies that get together to plan strategies and exchange information about how to manage their relations with unions. They are especially important

employers' association A group of companies that get together to plan strategies and exchange information about how to manage their relations with unions.

in industries that have many small firms and one large union that represents all workers. Member firms sometimes contribute to a strike insurance fund. Such a fund could be used to help members whose workers have struck. They are similar in purpose to the strike funds built up by unions.

Mediation and Arbitration

mediation A method of settling a contract dispute in which a neutral third party is asked to hear arguments from both the union and management and offer a suggested resolution.

voluntary arbitration A method of settling a contract dispute in which the union and management ask a neutral third party to hear their arguments and issue a binding resolution.

compulsory arbitration A method of settling a contract dispute in which the union and management are forced to explain their positions to a neutral third party who issues a binding resolution.

Rather than using weapons on one another, labour and management can agree to call in a third party to help resolve the dispute. In **mediation**, the neutral third party (a mediator) can only advise—not impose—a settlement on the parties. In **voluntary arbitration**, the neutral third party (an arbitrator) dictates a settlement between two sides that have agreed to submit to outside judgment.

In some cases, arbitration is legally required to settle bargaining disputes. Such **compulsory arbitration** is used to settle disputes between government and public employees such as firefighters and police officers.

Administering a Labour Agreement

Once a labour agreement has been reached, its details are written down in the form of a contract that is legally enforceable in the courts. Labour contracts almost always have precise agreements as to how the agreement will be enforced. In some cases, of course, enforcement is quite clear. If the two sides agree that the company will increase wages by 2 percent per year over the next three years according to a prescribed schedule, then there is little opportunity for disagreement because wage increases can be mathematically calculated and union members will see its effects in their paycheques. However, other provisions may be much more prone to misinterpretation and different perceptions.

Suppose, for example, that a labour contract specifies the process for allocating overtime assignments. Such strategies are often complex, and the employer may have to take into account a variety of factors, such as seniority, previous overtime allocations, the hours or days in which the overtime work is needed, and so forth. Now suppose that a factory supervisor is trying to follow the labour contract and offers overtime to a certain employee. This employee, however, indicates that before he or she can accept the overtime, it may be necessary to check with the individual's spouse or partner about other obligations and commitments. The supervisor may feel the pressure of a deadline and instead award the overtime opportunity to someone else. If the first employee objects to this course of action, he or she may file a complaint with the union.

shop steward A regular employee who acts as a liaison between union members and supervisors.

When such differences of opinion arise, the union member takes the complaint to the **shop steward** (a regular employee who acts as a liaison between union members and supervisors). The shop steward may advise the employee that the supervisor handled things properly, but there are other appeal mechanisms, and the employee, even if refuted by the shop steward, still has channels for appeal.

Of course, if the shop steward agrees with the employee, prescribed methods for pursuing the complaint are followed. The prescribed methods might include talking with the supervisor to hear the other side of the story and then providing for lines of appeal further up the hierarchy of both the union and the company. In some cases, mediation or arbitration may be tried, as may other efforts to resolve the dispute. The overtime, for example, may be reassigned to the employee to whom it was first offered. Or the overtime may remain with the second employee while the first employee is also paid.

grievance A complaint on the part of a union member that management is violating the terms of the contract in some way.

A **grievance** is a complaint by a worker that a manager is violating the contract. Figure 9.3 traces a typical grievance procedure. The union generally promises not to strike over disputes about contract interpretation. In return, unions get the right to file grievances in a formal procedure that culminates in binding arbitration. Most grievance arbitrations take place over disputes regarding the discipline or discharge of employees, but safety issues are a cause for arbitration in some industries.

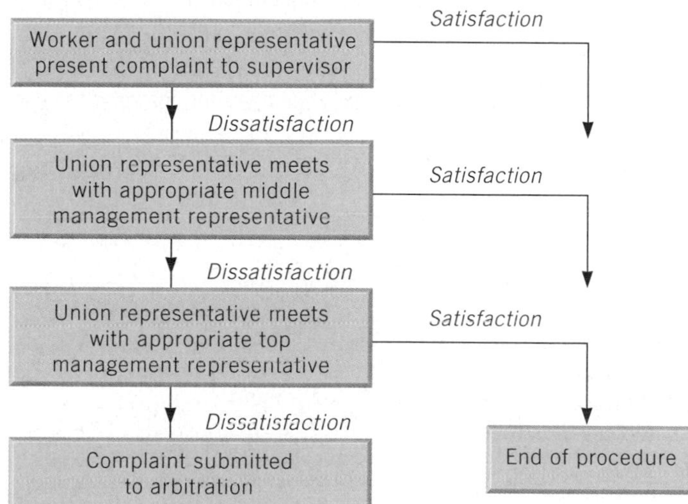

Figure 9.3 A typical grievance procedure.

Summary of Learning Objectives

1. **Explain why workers organize into *labour unions*.** The Industrial Revolution and the emergence of a factory-based production system made many workers dependent on continuing factory employment. The treatment of labour as a raw material led to such abuses as minimal pay, long workdays and workweeks, unsafe working conditions, and even child labour. Individuals had little recourse in rectifying problems. By organizing into labour unions, however, workers are able to act collectively to improve work conditions. Most importantly, acting as a group, they can engage in *collective bargaining* for higher wages, greater benefits, or better working conditions.
2. **Trace the evolution of unions and discuss *trends in unionism* in Canada.** The first unions in Canada were formed in the early nineteenth century in the maritime provinces. Many labour organizations sprang up and then faded away during the nineteenth century. In the twentieth century, unions began to develop in earnest. In 1943, Privy Council Order 1003 gave unions the right to bargain collectively with employers.

   Since the mid-1970s, labour unions in Canada have experienced increasing difficulties in attracting new members. While millions of workers still belong to labour unions, union membership as a percentage of the total workforce has been stagnant for many years. Unions recognize that they do not have as much power as they once held and that it is in their own best interests, as well as the best interests of the workers they represent, to work with management instead of against it. Bargaining perspectives have also altered in recent years.
3. **Describe the *major laws governing labour–management relations*.** Privy Council Order 1003 gave unions the right to collectively bargain in Canada. The Constitution Act of 1867 allows the federal government to pass labour legislation (such as the Canada Labour Code) for companies that operate interprovincially, and allows the provincial governments to pass legislation (such as the Ontario Labour Relations Act) for companies that operate in only one province.
4. **Describe the union *certification* and *decertification processes*.** If a union can show that a certain percentage (usually 50 percent) of employees of a company are members of the union, it can apply to a provincial labour relations board for certification as the sole bargaining agent

for the employees. A certification vote is then held. If a majority of the employees is in favour of the union, it is certified. To decertify a union, employees must vote to do so.

5. **Identify the steps in the *collective bargaining process*.** Once certified, the union engages in collective bargaining with the organization. The initial step in collective bargaining is reaching agreement on a *labour contract*. Contract demands usually involve wages, job security, or management rights.

Both labour and management have several tactics that can be used against the other if negotiations break down. Unions may attempt a *strike* or a *boycott* of the firm or may engage in a *work slowdown*. Companies may hire replacement workers (*strikebreakers*) or *lock out* all workers. In extreme cases, mediation or arbitration may be used to settle disputes. Once a contract has been agreed on, union and management representatives continue to interact to settle worker *grievances* and interpret the contract.

KEY TERMS

QUESTIONS FOR ANALYSIS

1. Why do workers in some companies unionize while workers in other companies do not?
2. Why did it take so many years for the union movement to mature in Canada?
3. The proportion of the Canadian workforce that is unionized has been nearly constant for more than 15 years. Why hasn't the proportion increased or decreased?
4. Workers at the Canadian plants of Ford, General Motors, and DaimlerChrysler are represented by the Canadian Auto Workers. Why are automobile workers at Toyota's Cambridge, Ontario, plant—who are doing exactly the same kind of work—not unionized?
5. Suppose that you are a manager in a non-unionized company. You have just heard a rumour that some of your workers are discussing forming a union. What would you do? Be specific.
6. What are the implications for management of a closed shop, a union shop, and an agency shop?
7. What impact will trends like globalization, intense global competition, and consumer interest in low prices have on the future viability of unions?

APPLICATION EXERCISES

1. *Many years ago, workers were treated very badly by management compared to the way they are treated now. Since unions exist largely to protect workers from unreasonable behaviour by management, the need for unions has disappeared.* Do you agree or disagree with this statement? Explain your position.
2. Interview the managers of two local companies, one unionized and one non-unionized. Compare the wage and salary levels, benefits, and working conditions of workers at the two firms.
3. With your instructor playing the role of management and a student playing the role of a union organizer, role play the processes involved in trying to form a union.

BUILDING YOUR BUSINESS SKILLS

A Little Collective Bargaining

Goal

To encourage students to understand why some companies unionize and others do not.

The Situation

You've been working for the same non-union company for five years. Although there are problems in the company, you like your job and have confidence in your ability to get ahead. Recently, you've heard rumblings that a large group of workers want to call for a union election. You're not sure how you feel about this because none of your friends or family members are union members.

Assignment

Step 1

Come together with three other "co-workers" who have the same questions as you do. Each person should target four companies to learn their union status. Avoid small businesses; choose large corporations such as Canadian National Railways, General Motors, and Wal-Mart. As you investigate, answer the following questions:

- Is the company unionized?
- Is every worker in the company unionized or only selected groups of workers? Describe the groups.
- If a company is unionized, what is the union's history in that company?
- If a company is unionized, what are the main labour–management issues?
- If a company is unionized, how would you describe the current status of labour–management relations? For example, is it cordial or strained?
- If a company is not unionized, what factors are responsible for its non-union status?

To learn the answers to these questions, contact the company, read corporate annual reports, search the company's website, contact union representatives, or do research on a computerized database.

Step 2

Go to the website of CUPE (www.cupe.ca) to learn more about the current status of the union movement. Then, with your co-workers, write a short report about the advantages of union membership.

Step 3

Research the disadvantages of unionization. A key issue to address is whether unions make it harder for companies to compete in the global marketplace.

Follow-Up Questions

1. Based on everything you have learned, are you sympathetic to the union movement? Would you want to be a union member?
2. Are the union members you spoke with satisfied or dissatisfied with their union's efforts to achieve better working conditions, higher wages, and improved benefits?
3. What is the union's role when layoffs occur?
4. Based on what you have learned, do you think the union movement in Canada will stagnate or thrive in the years ahead?

EXERCISING YOUR ETHICS

Operating Tactically

The Situation

Assume that you work as a manager for a medium-size non-union company that is facing a serious union organizing campaign. Your boss, who is determined to keep the union out, has just given you a list of things to do to thwart the efforts of the organizers. For example, he has suggested each of the following tactics:

- Whenever you learn about a scheduled union meeting, you should schedule a "worker appreciation" event at the same time. He wants you to offer free pizza and barbecue and to give cash prizes (that winners have to be present to receive).
- He wants you to look at the most recent performance evaluations of the key union organizers and to terminate the one with the lowest overall evaluation.
- He wants you to make an announcement that the firm is seriously considering such new benefits as on-site childcare, flexible work schedules, telecommuting options, and exercise facilities. Although you know that the firm is indeed looking

▶▶▶

into these benefits, you also know that, ultimately, your boss will provide far less lavish benefits than he wants you to imply.

The Dilemma

When you questioned the ethics—and even the legality—of these tactics, your boss responded by saying, "Look, all's fair in love and war, and this is war." He went on to explain that he was seriously concerned that a union victory might actually shut down the company's domestic operations altogether, forcing it to move all of its production capacities to lower-cost foreign plants. He concluded by saying that he was really looking out for the employees, even if he had to play hardball to help them. You easily see through his hypocrisy, but you also realize that there is some potential truth in his warning: If the union wins, jobs may actually be lost.

Questions for Discussion

1. What are the ethical issues in this situation?
2. What are the basic arguments for and against extreme measures to fight unionization efforts?
3. What do you think most managers would do in this situation? What would you do?

CONCLUDING CASE 9-1

The Long Road Back at Air Canada

On January 19, 2005, unionized ground crews at Air Canada were involved in a wildcat (unauthorized) strike over allegations that some employees were punching out the time cards of their co-workers. The strike grounded or delayed more than 60 flights. The strike was just the latest example of the long history of poor labour relations at Air Canada, and illustrates the tense relations that still exist between labour and management.

The labour difficulties at Air Canada are not surprising, given the financial problems that have beset the company during the past five years. In 2003, Air Canada was losing money at the rate of $5 million each *day*. Clearly, something had to be done, and it had to be done quickly. Since it was assumed that the demand for air travel was not likely to increase, the reduction of costs was seen as crucial. To achieve this reduction, Air Canada did three things. First, it reduced capacity by suspending service between various cities. But this was not nearly enough to achieve the cost reductions needed, so Air Canada also took a second action: laying off large numbers of people. Not surprisingly, the unions fiercely objected. Third, Air Canada reduced employee benefits and increased the number of required work hours. Flight attendants, for example, had their vacation entitlements and other allowances decreased, and saw the number of hours they were required to work each month increased from 75 to 82.

In April 2003, Justice James Farley of the Ontario Superior Court declared Air Canada insolvent and placed it under the protection of the Companies Creditors Arrangement Act (CCAA). By doing this, he shielded Air Canada (for a specified time) from actions by creditors as the company tried to work out a survival plan. Air Canada CEO Robert Milton blamed the unions for the mess the company found itself in, and claimed the unions did not take seriously his warnings that major reductions in labour costs were necessary for Air Canada to survive. Milton also said that everyone recognized that the world of commercial air travel had changed, but that union leadership had not been able to comprehend it. Union leaders complained that Milton had "put a gun to their heads" by telling them to surrender their contract rights or the company would be put in bankruptcy protection.

After Justice Farley's initial ruling, Air Canada and the unions resumed negotiations in an attempt to reach some sort of agreement. By the end of May 2003, deals had been reached with several unions that reduced labour costs by over $58 million annually. There were no reductions in wages or pensions, but 200 jobs were cut. The agreements increased productivity by 60 percent. Agreements were also reached with the machinists, baggage handlers, and ticket agents, but they involved 6000 job cuts. The unions agreed to these severe cuts because they recognized that the alternative was the unemployment line for everyone. By 2004, Air Canada had wrung a total of $1 billion in concessions from union workers.

The Air Canada case is important for labour unions because it raises the possibility that a company can renegotiate collective agreements while it is in bankruptcy protection. Other companies that are having financial difficulties may try to do the same thing. In the United States, a judge can cancel a labour contract, but not in Canada. In 2003, Justice Pierre Dalphond of the Quebec Court of Appeals ruled that a collective agreement at Jeffrey Mine Inc. could not be set aside. That decision was one reason why Air Canada filed its bankruptcy motion in Ontario, even though Air Canada is based in Quebec.

Air Canada emerged from the protection of bankruptcy in September 2004, but it still faces significant challenges like competition from low-fare airlines like WestJet, high fuel costs, and a $1.25 billion pension shortfall that will have to be made up over the next 10 years. But it has attracted new investors and lenders, partially as a result of its tough stance with its labour unions. In 2005, president and CEO Montie Brewer sent an email to employees reminding them that both management and labour had to keep in mind that keeping customers happy is a top priority. One month earlier, Chairman Robert Milton told employees that Air Canada's most recent load factor (the proportion of available seats filled) was at a record high, and that the tough changes that were instituted had caused that good outcome to happen.

Questions for Discussion

1. At Air Canada, workers reluctantly agreed to job cuts in various areas that allowed Air Canada to reduce its labour costs. Will workers in Canada now be less likely to join unions because they fear the union will not be able to protect their jobs if times get tough at a company?
2. Should a company be able to cancel a collective agreement with its labour union if the company gets into such financial difficulties that it cannot pay its workers? Explain your reasoning.
3. What proportion of the blame for Air Canada's difficulties rests with the top management of Air Canada, and what proportion rests with the company's unions? Defend your answer.
4. Air Canada has had a difficult relationship with its unions in the past. What can management and labour do to increase the chance that the two groups will work together more smoothly in the future? Describe both general and specific actions that might be taken.

CONCLUDING CASE 9-2

Hard Times for Labour Unions

Consumers benefit from lower prices when companies engage in intense price competition with each other. But intense price competition also puts pressure on company managers to reduce costs. And that often means reducing *labour* costs. When that move is made, companies with unionized work forces often face major dilemmas.

The situation at the Navistar truck plant in Chatham, Ontario, is illustrative of the problems that are facing both management and unions in an era of intense cost-cutting by companies. In July 2004, the Canadian Auto Workers (CAW) agreed to freeze wages at the plant until 2009 in return for a commitment from the company to keep the plant open and save nearly 1000 jobs that pay an average of about $26 per hour. CAW president Buzz Hargrove said that unions can't simply refuse to budge when the company presents them with the alternatives of shutdown or liquidation. A sense of "resigned pragmatism" seems to be creeping into the labour movement.

The situation in the automobile industry in general is of great concern to the United Auto Workers (UAW) and the CAW. The rapidly declining financial fortunes of Ford and General Motors spell potentially significant trouble for unionized workers at those companies. If unions don't give back many of the benefits they have won for their workers over the last few decades, the companies may not survive. If that happened, all jobs at those companies would obviously be lost. In 2005, the unions agreed to a deal that would reduce GM's health care costs by $3 billion. More cuts are likely in the future as GM and Ford try to cope with intense competition from lower-cost, non-unionized automakers like Toyota and Honda.

The current problems are quite a departure from some promising developments that occurred just a few years ago. In 1999, for example, the management negotiating team for General Motors of Canada walked into the Royal York Hotel's Tudor Room and received a standing ovation from the CAW workers who were assembled there. The GM managers then applauded the workers. Buzz Hargrove said that the atmosphere during negotiations was positive. It seemed possible that the development at GM Canada represented a real change in the traditionally adversarial relationship between unions and management

But reality has a way of complicating things. Just a few short years later, both union and company leaders in many industries are being forced to respond to new competitive realities. Labour leaders have to make sure they really understand the financial situation of a company before they can bargain intelligently. Otherwise, they run the risk to being "taken in" by management claims that labour will have to make big concessions because the company is in financial distress. For their part, managers must carefully assess their cost structure (including labour costs) to determine what strategies are required to keep the company financially viable.

Recent corporate scandals where top managers were given generous payouts have made many union leaders and their members very suspicious of claims of financial distress by management. Even when there is a legitimate financial difficulty, employees often blame managers for the mess. The Air Canada case clearly illustrates these tensions. While union members are relieved that the company has emerged from bankruptcy, many are angry at the significant pay reductions they have had to accept.

Coping with the tough negotiating positions taken by management is just one of the problems facing unions. Another is the decline in union membership, especially in the auto industry. During the past decade, CAW membership at DaimlerChrysler Canada, Ford Motor Co. of Canada, and General Motors of Canada Ltd. has declined because each company has experienced a sharp drop in their market share. Each company has closed an assembly plant in Canada. In 1996, the CAW represented 54 000 workers in the three companies, but by 2004, the number was only 39 000. These changes are not restricted to Canada. In the United States, there has been a steady decline in union membership over the last few decades, and now less than 8 percent of the private sector workforce is unionized. That is less than half the percentage that was unionized just 20 years ago.

Most workers (regardless of the industry where they work) are concerned about job security, low wages, poor health care coverage, and less generous pensions. Given these concerns, workers should be more interested in unions as a way of protecting their interests. But there are several reasons for declining worker interest in unions. First, many workers see unions as ineffective "dinosaurs" that are too rigid to cope with the rapid changes that have been occurring in recent years. Second, it is obvious that unions cannot prevent management from laying off large numbers of unionized workers if management decides it is necessary. Third, many white-collar workers aren't interested in unions because they see them as relevant for only blue-collar jobs. Fourth, increasing numbers of workers don't want to be identified with a union because they feel it will hurt their chance for promotion into management. Finally, many companies have been successful in using "labour advisers" to help them fend off union attempts to organize their workers. For example, Sullivan & Associates, a labour relations consulting firm in the United States, has been successful in defeating the formation of a union in 215 out of 218 cases.

One approach that unions have taken in response to the declining number of union members is to try to organize workers at more manufacturing plants. The CAW, for example, has renewed its efforts to unionize workers at the Toyota plant at Cambridge, Ontario, and the Honda of Canada plant at Alliston, Ontario. The CAW has been trying to organize these workers for many years, but they have not been able to convince even 50 percent of the workers at either plant to sign union cards. Each of these plants employs about 4000 workers so a successful union drive would have a very positive impact on the CAW.

Hargrove says that the union movement is not in crisis, but others disagree. One auto industry analyst noted that employment at each of the non-unionized Toyota and Honda plants has increased from about 1500 to over 4000 at the same time that it has decreased at unionized auto plants in Canada. The current union strategy during bargaining is to use the threat of a strike to lever increased Canadian investment out of the Big Three automakers. In this way, they hope to protect as many jobs as possible.

The problems that unions are having are not restricted to Canada. Consider these recent developments in Europe:

- At Siemens AG, unions agreed to allow the company to extend hours and cut benefits for 4000 employees while not raising wages. This occurred after the company threatened to move 2000 jobs from Germany to Hungary.
- Workers at a French subsidiary of Robert Bosch GmbH agreed to longer working hours with no increase in pay on the condition that their plant, not one in the Czech Republic, would get a new assembly line.
- Workers at DaimlerChrysler AG agreed to a similar deal after the company threatened to move 6000 jobs from Germany to South Africa.

Actions like these do not facilitate trust and co-operation between labour and management. While management has always had the right to lay off unionized workers, the magnitude of such layoffs has increased dramatically in the last decade. What will this do to the relationship between labour and management? Will negotiations become more hostile as labour unions try to protect their members? Or will negotiations become more focussed on ways that labour and management can work together to meet threats from outside the company?

Questions for Discussion

1. Can labour and management really work together, or are their basic goals so fundamentally opposed that it is impossible? Defend your answer.

2. Why are companies like Toyota and Honda so opposed to having unionized members? Why have workers at those companies not been willing to join a union?
3. Is there anything that labour unions can do to protect their members in the new, intensely competitive global environment?
4. "*Unions are going to have less and less power in the future because the increasingly global nature of competition will force all companies to reduce costs. Management will simply lay off large numbers of union workers to achieve cost-cutting goals, and this will mean fewer and fewer union workers.*" Do you agree or disagree with this claim? Support your position with both qualitative and quantitative arguments.

CHAPTER 10

Motivating and Leading Employees

After reading this chapter, you should be able to:

1. Describe the nature and importance of *psychological contracts* in the workplace.
2. Discuss the importance of *job satisfaction* and *employee morale* and summarize their roles in human relations in the workplace.
3. Identify and summarize the most important *theories of employee motivation.*
4. Describe some of the *strategies* used by organizations to improve job satisfaction and employee motivation.
5. Discuss different *managerial styles of leadership* and their impact on human relations in the workplace.

Keeping Employees Satisfied and Motivated

Managers would like to have employees who are satisfied and motivated to work hard. These attitudes typically cause positive employee behaviour, like persisting even in the face of difficulties, being interested in continuous learning and improvement, and being on the lookout for ways to improve quality and productivity. Behaviours like these, in turn, lead to positive outcomes for the company like higher customer satisfaction, greater profits, higher quality, and lower employee turnover.

Because employee motivation and satisfaction are so important, many employee satisfaction surveys are conducted each year. Some companies organize their own in-house surveys, while others hire independent research firms to do the work. These surveys, which ask employees to give their views about a wide range of issues, provide managers with some interesting insights into how Canadian workers feel about their jobs.

One independent research firm, Sirota Survey Intelligence, measured employee satisfaction at 237 different companies during the period 1994–2003. They found that only 14 percent of these companies had workforces that could be classified as "enthusiastic." One interesting conclusion was that the level of enthusiasm of the workforce made a difference in the company's stock prices. When the stock prices of 28 companies with enthusiastic workforces were compared to the average for publicly traded companies, it was found that they outperformed the average by more than two-and-a-half times. (Companies with *un*enthusiastic workforces lagged far behind the average stock prices.) Companies with enthusiastic workforces also had fewer customer complaints, lower employee turnover, and higher quality in their products.

Various other surveys have also been conducted on issues that relate closely to employee enthusiasm and motivation. A Watson Wyatt Canada survey of more than 3000 Canadian employees revealed the following:

- 46 percent would consider changing jobs if a comparable job became available.
- Only 40 percent of employees believe they have real opportunities for advancement with their current employer.
- Only 27 percent of employees see any connection between their job performance and their pay.

Yet another survey, this one conducted by the Gallup Organization, studied the attitudes of 7200 workers in Canada, the United States, and Great Britain. On most measures of job satisfaction, Canadian workplaces rank behind those of the United States. For example, only 47 percent of Canadian workers were completely satisfied with their boss, while 60 percent of American workers were. Only 29 percent of Canadian workers were completely satisfied with their opportunities for promotion, while 40 percent of Americans were. And 37 percent of Canadian workers were completely satisfied with the recognition they received, while 48 percent of Americans were. Canadian workers were also less satisfied than U.S. workers on several other issues, including the flexibility of their work hours, workplace safety, relationships with co-workers, and the amount of vacation time they received (even though they usually received more than Americans).

The Gallup survey also asked workers about their religious beliefs and found that 90 percent of Americans said they believe in God, but only 71 percent of Canadians do. Industrial psychologist Guy Beaudin thinks this statistic might explain why Canadian workers are less satisfied than American workers. He speculates that since faith is more important in the lives of Americans, they do not rely as much on their work for fulfillment as Canadians do. Canadians may have higher expectations about work as they attempt to give their life a sense of meaning, and this may explain why Canadian workers are less satisfied than American workers. Of course, other factors may explain the difference. For example, Canadian workers are less satisfied with their bosses than American workers are, and this may negatively influence the overall job satisfaction of Canadian workers.

Most employees start work with considerable enthusiasm, but they often lose it. Why? Much of the blame is laid at the feet of managers whose attitudes and behaviours depress employee enthusiasm. These include failing to express appreciation to employees for a job well done, assuming that employees are lazy and irresponsible, treating employees as disposable objects, failing to build trust with workers, and quickly laying people off when the business gets in trouble. Managerial assumptions about employee satisfaction with pay can be particularly problematic. For example, many managers assume that workers will never be satisfied with their pay. But research by Sirota Survey Intelligence showed that only 23 percent of workers rate their pay as "poor" or "very poor," and 40 percent rate it as "good" or "very good."

One of the simplest ways for managers to motivate workers is to praise them. Yet this occurs far less often than it should. A 2005 *Globe and Mail* web poll showed that 27 percent of the 2331 respondents had *never* received a compliment from their boss. Another 10 percent had not received a compliment in the last year, and 18 percent had not received a compliment in the last month. This result is disturbing, since another survey showed that 89 percent of employees rate recognition of their work as "very important" or "extremely important."

Bad management practices are not the only factor in reducing employee motivation to do their job well. Stress and mental disability (particularly depression) also play a large part. Warren Shepell, a company that provides employee assistance programs, found that 51 percent of the 41 000 people who sought assistance under one of its plans cited high stress as a cause. A Watson Wyatt Staying at Work survey of 100 large Canadian companies found that 56 of them identified rapidly increasing employee mental health disability claims as their top concern (these claims usually include stress as a component).

A report by the Business and Economic Roundtable on Mental Health (BERMH) concluded that employee stress is costing Canadian industry about $60 billion each year, and more than half of that is in lost productivity. The top sources of stress for employees were identified as too much (or too little) work to do, lack of two-way communication up and down the hierarchy, being unappreciated, inconsistent performance review processes, career uncertainty, unclear company policies, and office politics. In 2005, BERMH announced two initiatives to identify the causes of stress and depression among workers. One study will survey more than 100 000 Canadian employees to determine the benefits of early treatment of depression. Another will be a 10-year study of mental health in the workplace. ◆

PSYCHOLOGICAL CONTRACTS IN ORGANIZATIONS

1 Describe the nature and importance of *psychological contracts* in the workplace.

psychological contract The set of expectations held by an employee concerning what he or she will contribute to an organization (contributions) and what the organization will provide the employee (inducements) in return.

Whenever we buy a car or sell a house, both buyer and seller sign a contract that specifies the terms of the agreement—who pays what to whom, when it's paid, and so forth. In some ways, a psychological contract resembles a legal contract. On the whole, however, it's less formal and less rigidly defined. A **psychological contract** is the set of expectations held by an employee concerning what he or she will contribute to an organization (referred to as *contributions*) and what the organization will provide the employee (referred to as *inducements*) in return.

If either party perceives an inequity in the contract, that party may seek a change. The employee, for example, might ask for a pay raise, promotion, or a bigger office. He or she might put forth less effort or look for a better job elsewhere. The organization can also initiate change by training workers to improve their skills, transferring them to new jobs, or terminating them.

human relations Interactions between employers and employees and their attitudes toward one another.

All organizations face the basic challenge of managing psychological contracts. They want value from their employees, and they must give employees the right inducements. Valuable but underpaid employees may perform below their capabilities or leave for better jobs. Conversely, overpaying employees who contribute little incurs unnecessary costs. The foundation of good **human relations**—the interactions between employers and employees and their attitudes toward one another—is a satisfied and motivated workforce.[1]

The massive wave of downsizing and cutbacks that have swept the Canadian economy during the past 10 years has complicated the process of managing psychological contracts. Many organizations, for example, used to offer at least reasonable assurances of job permanence as a fundamental inducement to employees. Now, however, because job permanence is less likely, alternative inducements—such as lavish benefits packages—may be needed instead.

If psychological contracts are created, maintained, and managed effectively, the result is likely to be workers who are satisfied and motivated. On the other hand, poorly managed psychological contracts may result in dissatisfied, unmotivated workers. Although most people have a general idea of what "job satisfaction" is, both job satisfaction and high morale can be elusive in the workplace. Because they are critical to an organization's success, we now turn our attention to discussing their importance.

THE IMPORTANCE OF JOB SATISFACTION AND MORALE

2 Discuss the importance of *job satisfaction* and *employee morale* and summarize their roles in human relations in the workplace.

Broadly speaking, **job satisfaction** is the degree of enjoyment that people derive from performing their jobs. If people enjoy their work, they are relatively satisfied; if they do not enjoy their work, they are relatively dissatisfied. In turn, satisfied employees are likely to have high **morale**—the overall attitude that employees have toward their workplace. Morale reflects the degree to which they perceive that their needs are being met by their jobs. It is determined by a variety of factors, including job satisfaction and satisfaction with such things as pay, benefits, co-workers, and promotion opportunities.[2]

job satisfaction The pleasure and feeling of accomplishment employees derive from performing their jobs well.

morale The generally positive or negative mental attitude of employees toward their work and workplace.

Why Businesses Need Satisfied Employees

When workers are enthusiastic and happy with their jobs, the organization benefits in many ways. Because they are committed to their work and the organization, satisfied workers are more likely to work hard and try to make useful contributions to the organization. They will also have fewer grievances and are less likely to engage in negative behaviours (e.g., complaining, deliberately slowing their work pace, etc.). Satisfied workers are also more likely to come to work every day and are more likely to remain with the organization. So, by ensuring that employees are satisfied, management gains a more efficient and smooth-running company.

Just as the rewards of high worker satisfaction and morale are great, so are the costs of job dissatisfaction and poor morale. Dissatisfied workers, for example, are far more likely to be absent due to minor illnesses, personal reasons, or a general disinclination to go to work. Low morale may also result in high **turnover**—the percentage of an organization's workforce that leaves and must be replaced. Some turnover is a natural and healthy way to weed out low-performing workers in any organization. But high levels of turnover have many negative consequences, including numerous vacancies, disruption in production, decreased productivity, and high retraining costs.

turnover The percentage of an organization's workforce that leaves and must be replaced.

In 2005, the average turnover rate in Canada was 8 percent, up from 6.6 percent in 2004. The turnover rate varied across industries, with retail trade having the highest rate (20.4 percent), followed by services (16.9 percent). The lowest turnover rates were in natural resources (4.1 percent) and communications/telecommunications (4.3 percent). A Conference Board of Canada survey of 347 companies found that 67 percent of them had trouble retaining employees; only 43 percent reported such difficulties in 2004.[3]

ENTREPRENEURSHIP AND NEW VENTURES

Beyond the Limelight

When an Air France jet skidded off a runway at Toronto's Pearson International Airport in August 2005, most of the attention was on the safety of the 309 passengers and how the myriad fire and ambulance personnel on the scene were handling the near-disaster. But if you'd looked closely through the flames and smoke pouring from the plane's tail, you might have seen 50 security guards from ASP Inc. moving with impressive speed to secure the perimeter. Yet, what could have been a defining public moment for the Burlington, Ontario–based company went unreported in the media.

But then publicity wouldn't have fit a firm and a CEO, Dean Lovric, who are downright bashful when it comes to self-promotion—even after growing revenue by 5902 percent over five years to $7.9 million in 2005. ASP doesn't even have a sales department, and only recently booked newspaper ads to recruit the staff it needs to sustain its growth. This challenge is made even more acute by ASP's fussiness about who it picks as employees and customers. "We're not necessarily looking to expand to some phenomenal size," says Lovric. "We're looking to keep a close-knit clientele and give our clients much more personalized service."

Still, ASP does aim to go national one day. Among its brand-name clients are General Electric and Honeywell, the Greater Toronto Airport Authority, and airlines Skyservice and Air India. A customer who wished to remain anonymous praises ASP as a "higher-end security company" that's happy to accede to special requests, such as dressing its guards in suits for a facility opening.

How has a 360-employee firm grown so fast when it's up against scores of players in a sector employing 215 000 in Canada? In part by bending over backwards to satisfy clients, such as swallowing the bill if an emergency leads to overtime. In the security trade, says Lovric, it all comes down to speedy response. ASP delivers this through advanced scheduling software and a staff willing to work overtime and to respond quickly if they are off-duty. To encourage loyalty, ASP offers rewards such as movie passes, dinners, annual barbecues, and above-average pay.

Then there are the extras money can't buy. "Once I was on the way to the airport, and found out a supervisor needed additional funds to close his mortgage or he would lose his house," recalls Lovric. "I turned my car around and cleared the funds for him." That's the kind of gesture employees remember. Now ASP just needs a few more good people so it can take on a few more customers.

MOTIVATION IN THE WORKPLACE

3 Identify and summarize the most important *theories of employee motivation.*

motivation The set of forces that causes people to behave in certain ways.

Although job satisfaction and morale are important, employee motivation is even more critical to a firm's success. Motivation is one part of the managerial function of directing. Broadly defined, **motivation** is the set of forces that causes people to behave in certain ways. For example, while one worker may be motivated to work hard to produce as much as possible, another may be motivated to do just enough to get by. Managers must understand these differences in behaviour and the reasons for them.

Over the years, many theories have been proposed to address the issues of motivation. In this section, we will focus on three major approaches to motivation in the workplace that reflect a chronology of thinking in the area: *classical theory and scientific management, behaviour theory,* and *contemporary motivation theories*.

Classical Theory and Scientific Management

classical theory of motivation A theory of motivation that presumes that workers are motivated almost solely by money.

According to the so-called **classical theory of motivation**, workers are motivated almost solely by money. In his book *The Principles of Scientific Management* (1911), industrial engineer Frederick Taylor proposed a way for both companies and workers to benefit from this widely accepted view of life in the workplace.[4] If workers are motivated by money, Taylor reasoned, then paying them more would prompt them to produce more. Meanwhile, the firm that analyzed jobs and found better ways to perform them would be able to produce goods more cheaply, make higher profits, and thus pay—and motivate—workers better than its competitors.

The ideas of Frederick Taylor, the founder of scientific management, had a profound impact on the way manufacturing activities were carried out in the early twentieth century. His basic ideas are still used today.

Taylor's approach is known as *scientific management*. His ideas captured the imagination of many managers in the early twentieth century. Soon, plants across Canada and the United States were hiring experts to perform *time-and-motion studies*. Industrial-engineering techniques were applied to each facet of a job to determine how to perform it most efficiently. These studies were the first "scientific" attempts to break down jobs into easily repeated components and to devise more efficient tools and machines for performing them.

Behaviour Theory: The Hawthorne Studies

One of the first challenges to the classical theory of human relations management came about by accident. In 1925, a group of Harvard researchers began a study at the Hawthorne Works of Western Electric. Their intent was to examine the relationship between changes in the physical environment and worker output, with an eye to increasing productivity.

The results of the experiment at first confused, then amazed, the scientists. Increasing lighting levels improved productivity, but so did lowering lighting levels. And against all expectations, raising the pay of workers failed to increase their productivity. Gradually they pieced together the puzzle. The explanation for the lighting phenomenon lay in workers' response to attention. In essence, they determined that almost any action on the part of management that made workers believe they were receiving special

The Hawthorne studies were an important step in developing an appreciation for the human factor at work. These women worked under different lighting conditions as researchers monitored their productivity. The researchers were amazed to find that productivity increased regardless of whether lighting levels increased or decreased.

attention caused worker productivity to rise. This result, known as the **Hawthorne effect**, had a major influence on human relations management, convincing many businesses that paying attention to employees is indeed good for business.

Hawthorne effect The tendency for workers' productivity to increase when they feel they are receiving special attention from management.

Contemporary Motivation Theories

Following the Hawthorne studies, managers and researchers alike focussed more attention on the importance of good human relations in motivating employee performance. Stressing the factors that cause, focus, and sustain workers' behaviour, most motivation theorists are concerned with the ways in which management thinks about and treats employees. The major motivation theories include the *human-resources model, the hierarchy of needs model, two-factory theory, expectancy theory, equity theory,* and *goal-setting theory*.

The Human-Resources Model: Theories X and Y

In an important study, behavioural scientist Douglas McGregor concluded that managers had radically different beliefs about how best to use the human resources at a firm's disposal. He classified these beliefs into sets of assumptions that he labelled "Theory X" and "Theory Y."[5] The basic differences between these two theories are highlighted in Table 10.1.

Theory X A management approach based on the belief that people must be forced to be productive because they are naturally lazy, irresponsible, and uncooperative.

Theory Y A management approach based on the belief that people want to be productive because they are naturally energetic, responsible, and co-operative.

Managers who subscribe to **Theory X** tend to believe that people are naturally lazy and uncooperative and must therefore be either punished or rewarded to be made productive. Managers who incline to **Theory Y** tend to believe that people are naturally energetic, growth-oriented, self-motivated, and interested in being productive.

McGregor generally favoured Theory Y beliefs. Thus he argued that Theory Y managers are more likely to have satisfied, motivated employees. Of course, Theory X and Y distinctions are somewhat simplistic and offer little concrete basis for action. Their value lies primarily in their ability to highlight and analyze the behaviour of managers in light of their attitudes toward employees.

Maslow's Hierarchy of Needs Model

hierarchy of human needs model Theory of motivation describing five levels of human needs and arguing that basic needs must be fulfilled before people work to satisfy higher-level needs.

Psychologist Abraham Maslow's **hierarchy of human needs model** proposed that people have a number of different needs that they attempt to satisfy in their work. He classified these needs into five basic types and suggested that they are arranged in the hierarchy of importance shown in Figure 10.1. According to Maslow, needs are hierarchical because lower-level needs must be met before a person will try to satisfy those on a higher level.[6]

Table 10.1 Beliefs About People at Work

Theory X and Theory Y convey very different assumptions about people at work.

Theory X	Theory Y
1. People are lazy.	1. People are energetic.
2. People lack ambition and dislike responsibility.	2. People are ambitious and seek responsibility.
3. People are self-centred.	3. People can be selfless.
4. People resist change.	4. People want to contribute to business growth and change.
5. People are gullible and not very bright.	5. People are intelligent.

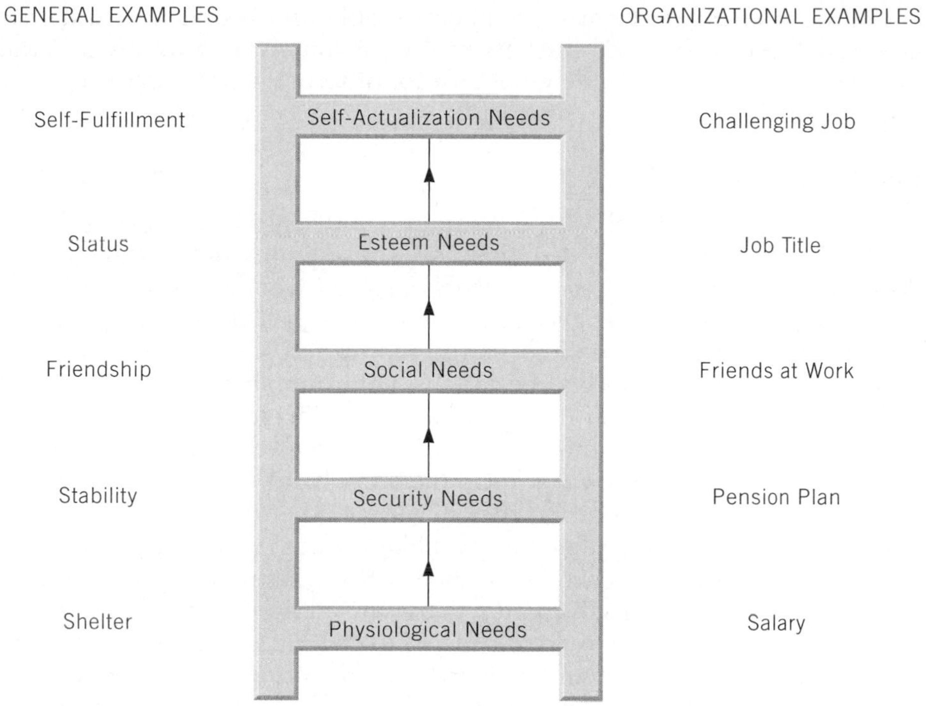

GENERAL EXAMPLES		ORGANIZATIONAL EXAMPLES
Self-Fulfillment	Self-Actualization Needs	Challenging Job
Status	Esteem Needs	Job Title
Friendship	Social Needs	Friends at Work
Stability	Security Needs	Pension Plan
Shelter	Physiological Needs	Salary

Figure 10.1 Maslow's hierarchy of human needs provides a useful categorization of the different needs people have.

- *Physiological needs* are necessary for survival; they include food, water, shelter, and sleep. Businesses address these needs by providing both comfortable working environments and salaries sufficient to buy food and shelter.
- *Security needs* include the needs for stability and protection from the unknown. Many employers thus offer pension plans and job security.
- *Social needs* include the needs for friendship and companionship. Making friends at work can help to satisfy social needs, as can the feeling that you "belong" in a company.
- *Esteem needs* include the need for status and recognition as well as the need for self-respect. Respected job titles and large offices are among the things that businesses can provide to address these needs.
- Finally, *self-actualization needs* are needs for self-fulfillment. They include the needs to grow and develop one's capabilities and to achieve new and meaningful goals. Challenging job assignments can help satisfy these needs.

According to Maslow, once one set of needs has been satisfied, it ceases to motivate behaviour. This is the sense in which the hierarchical nature of lower- and higher-level needs affects employee motivation and satisfaction. For example, if you feel secure in your job, a new pension plan will probably be less important to you than the chance to make new friends and join an informal network among your co-workers. If, however, a lower-level need suddenly becomes unfulfilled, most people immediately refocus on that lower level. Suppose, for example, that you are seeking to meet your esteem needs by working as a divisional manager at a major company. If you learn that your division—and consequently your job—may be eliminated, you might very well find the promise of job security at a new firm as motivating as a promotion once would have been at your old company.

Maslow's theory recognizes that because different people have different needs, different things motivate them. Unfortunately, research has found that the hierarchy varies widely, not only for different people but also across different cultures.

Two-Factor Theory

two-factor theory A theory of human relations developed by Frederick Herzberg that identifies factors that must be present for employees to be satisfied with their jobs and factors that, if increased, lead employees to work harder.

After studying a group of accountants and engineers, psychologist Frederick Herzberg concluded that job satisfaction and dissatisfaction depend on two factors: *hygiene factors*, such as working conditions, and *motivating factors*, such as recognition for a job well done.[7] According to **two-factor theory**, hygiene factors affect motivation and satisfaction only if they are *absent* or *fail* to meet expectations. For example, workers will be dissatisfied if they believe that they have poor working conditions. If working conditions are improved, however, they will not necessarily become *satisfied*; they will simply be *not dissatisfied*. On the other hand, if workers receive no recognition for successful work, they may be neither dissatisfied nor satisfied. If recognition is provided, they will likely become more satisfied.

Figure 10.2 illustrates two-factor theory. Note that motivating factors lie along a continuum from satisfaction to no satisfaction. Hygiene factors, on the other hand, are likely to produce feelings that lie on a continuum from dissatisfaction to no dissatisfaction. While motivating factors are directly related to the work that employees actually perform, hygiene factors refer to the environment in which they perform it.

This theory thus suggests that managers should follow a two-step approach to enhancing motivation. First, they must ensure that hygiene factors—working conditions, clearly stated policies—are acceptable. This practice will result in an absence of dissatisfaction. Then they must offer motivating factors—recognition, added responsibility—to improve satisfaction and motivation.

Research suggests that two-factor theory works in some professional settings, but it is not as effective in clerical and manufacturing settings. (Herzberg's research was limited to professionals—accountants and engineers—only.) In addition, one person's hygiene factor may be another per-

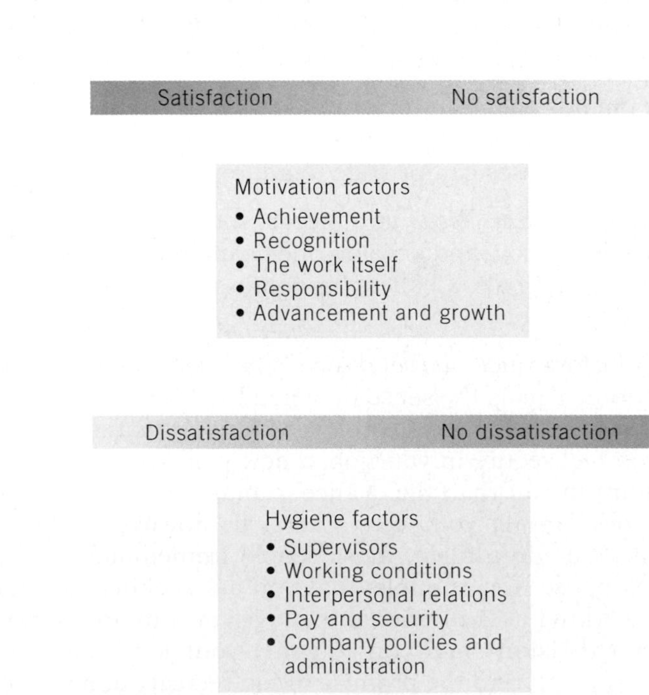

Figure 10.2 According to two-factor theory, job satisfaction depends on two factors.

son's motivating factor. For example, if money represents nothing more than pay for time worked, it may be a hygiene factor for one person. For another person, however, money may be a motivating factor because it represents recognition and achievement.

Expectancy Theory

expectancy theory The theory that people are motivated to work toward rewards that they want and that they believe they have a reasonable chance of obtaining.

Expectancy theory suggests that people are motivated to work toward rewards that they want and that they believe they have a reasonable chance—or expectancy—of obtaining.[8] A reward that seems out of reach, for example, is not likely to be motivating even if it is intrinsically positive.

Figure 10.3 illustrates expectancy theory in terms of issues that are likely to be considered by an individual employee. Consider the case of an assistant department manager who learns that her firm needs to replace a retiring division manager two levels above her in the organization. Even though she wants the job, she does not apply because she doubts that she will be selected. In this case, she raises the *performance–reward issue*: for some reason, she believes that her performance will not get her the position. Note that she may think that her performance merits the new job but that performance alone will not be enough; perhaps she expects the reward to go to someone with more seniority.

Assume that our employee also learns that the firm is looking for a production manager on a later shift. She thinks that she could get this job, but does not apply because she does not want to change shifts. In this instance, she raises the *rewards–personal goals issue*. Finally, she learns of an opening one level higher—department manager—in her own division. She may well apply for this job because she both wants it and thinks that she has a good chance of getting it. In this case, her consideration of all the issues has led to an expectancy that she can reach a given goal.

Expectancy theory helps explain why some people do not work as hard as they can when their salaries are based purely on seniority. Paying employees the same whether they work very hard or just hard enough to get by removes the financial incentive for them to work harder. In other words, they ask themselves, "If I work harder, will I get a pay raise?" and conclude that the answer is no. Similarly, if hard work will result in one or more *undesirable* outcomes—say, a transfer to another location or a promotion to a job that requires unpleasant travel—employees will not be motivated to work hard.

Equity Theory

equity theory The theory that people compare (1) what they contribute to their job with what they get in return, and (2) their input/output ratio with that of other employees.

Equity theory focusses on social comparisons—people evaluating their treatment by the organization relative to the treatment of others. This approach says that people begin by analyzing *inputs* (what they contribute to their jobs in terms of time, effort, education, experience, and so forth) relative to *outputs* (what they receive in return in terms of salary, benefits,

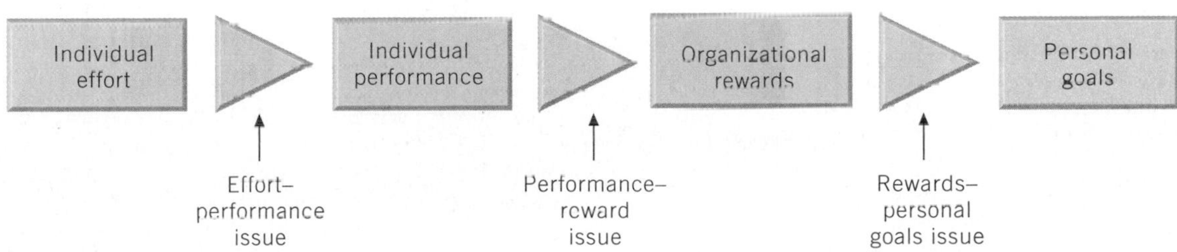

Figure 10.3 Expectancy theory model.

recognition, security, etc.). The result is a ratio of contribution to return. Then they compare their own ratios with those of other employees: They ask whether their ratios are *equal to, greater than,* or *less than* those of the people with whom they are comparing themselves. Depending on the outcome of their assessments, they experience feelings of equity or inequity. Figure 10.4 illustrates the three possible results of such an assessment.

For example, suppose that a new graduate gets a starting job at a large manufacturing firm. His starting salary is $25 000 per year, he gets a compact company car, and he shares an office with another new employee. If he later learns that another new employee has received the same salary, car, and office arrangement, he will feel equitably treated. If the other newcomer, however, has received $30 000, a full-size company car, and a private office, he may experience feelings of inequity.

Note, however, that the two ratios do not have to be the *same*—they need be only *fair*. Let's assume, for instance, that our new employee has a bachelor's degree and two years of work experience. Perhaps he learns subsequently that the other new employee has an advanced degree and 10 years of work experience. After first feeling inequity, our new employee may now conclude that his comparison person is actually contributing more to the organization. The other employee is equitably entitled, therefore, to receive more in return.

When people feel that they are being inequitably treated, they may do various things to restore fairness. For example, they may ask for raises, reduce their effort, work shorter hours, or just complain to their bosses. They may also rationalize their situation ("management succumbed to pressure to promote a woman"), find different people with whom to compare themselves, or leave their jobs altogether.

Good examples of equity theory at work can be found in professional sports. Each year, for example, rookies are signed to lucrative contracts. No sooner is the ink dry than veteran players start grumbling about raises or revised contracts.

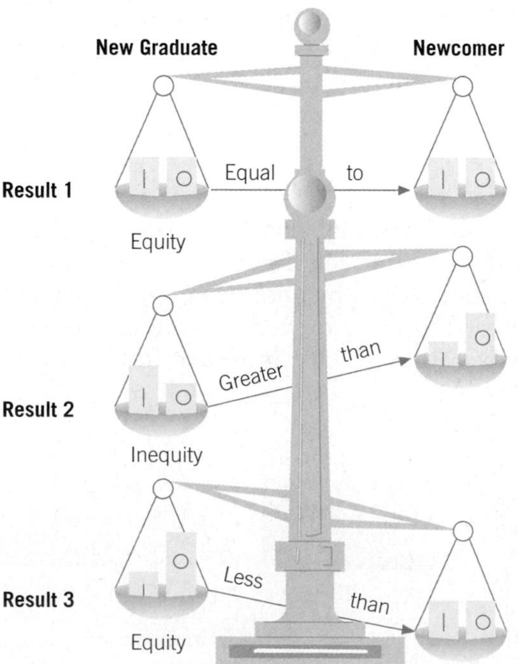

Figure 10.4 Equity theory: possible assessments.

Goal-Setting Theory

Goal-setting theory describes the kinds of goals that better motivate employees. In general, effective goals tend to have two basic characteristics. First, they are moderately difficult: While a goal that is too easy does little to enhance effort and motivation, a goal that is too difficult also fails to motivate people. Second, they are specific. A goal of "do your best," for instance, does not motivate people nearly as much as a goal such as "increase profits by 10 percent." The specificity and clarity of this goal serve to focus attention and energy on exactly what needs to be done.[9]

goal-setting theory The theory that people perform better when they set specific, quantified, time-framed goals.

An important aspect of goal setting is the employee's participation in the goal-setting process. When people help select the goals they are to work toward, they tend to accept them more readily and are more committed to achieving them. On the other hand, when goals are merely assigned to people with little or no input on their part, they are less likely to adopt them.

STRATEGIES FOR ENHANCING JOB SATISFACTION AND MORALE

Describe some of the *strategies* used by organizations to improve job satisfaction and employee motivation. 4

Deciding what motivates workers and provides job satisfaction is only part of the manager's battle. The other part is to apply that knowledge. Experts have suggested—and many companies have instituted—a wide range of programs designed to make jobs more interesting and rewarding and the work environment more pleasant. In this section, we will consider five of the most common types of programs: *reinforcement/behaviour modification theory, management by objectives, participative management, team management, job enrichment and job redesign,* and *modified work schedules*.

Reinforcement/Behaviour Modification Theory

Many companies try to control, and even alter or modify, workers' behaviour through systematic rewards and punishments for specific behaviours. In other words, they first try to define the specific behaviours they want their employees to exhibit (working hard, being courteous to customers, stressing quality) and the specific behaviours they want to eliminate (wasting

Research has shown that goals that are specific, measurable, and moderately difficult to achieve result in high performance for employees.

time, being rude to customers, ignoring quality). Then they try to shape employee behaviour by linking reinforcement with desired behaviours and punishment with undesired behaviours.

reinforcement Controlling and modifying employee behaviour through the use of systematic rewards and punishments for specific behaviours.

Reinforcement is used, for example, when a company pays *piecework* rewards—when workers are paid for each piece or product completed. In reinforcement strategies, rewards refer to all the positive things people receive for working (pay, praise, promotions, job security, and so forth). When rewards are tied directly to performance, they serve as *positive reinforcement*. For example, paying large cash bonuses to salespeople who exceed quotas prompts them to work even harder during the next selling period. Agricultural implements manufacturer John Deere uses a reward system based on positive reinforcement. The firm gives pay increases when its workers complete college or university courses and demonstrate mastery of new job skills. Workers at Maple Leaf Sports & Entertainment receive "good job" cards when they do outstanding work. These cards can be redeemed for prizes.[10]

Punishment is designed to change behaviour by presenting people with unpleasant consequences if they fail to change in desirable ways. Employees who are repeatedly late for work, for example, may be suspended or have their pay docked. When the National Hockey League or Major League Baseball fines or suspends players found guilty of substance abuse, the organization is seeking to change players' behaviour.

Extensive rewards work best when people are learning new behaviours, new skills, or new jobs. As workers become more adept, rewards can be used less frequently. Because such actions contribute to positive employer–employee relationships, managers generally prefer giving rewards and placing positive value on performance. Conversely, most managers dislike punishing employees, partly because workers may respond with anger, resentment, hostility, or even retaliation. To reduce this risk, many managers couple punishment with rewards for good behaviour.

Management by Objectives

management by objectives (MBO) A system of collaborative goal setting that extends from the top of an organization to its bottom.

Management by objectives (MBO) is a system of collaborative goal-setting that extends from the top of an organization to its bottom. As a technique for managing the planning process, MBO is concerned mainly with helping man-

Financial analysts don't like Costco as much as they do Wal-Mart, mostly because Costco doesn't work as hard to keep costs down (Costco pays its workers about 50 percent more than Wal-Mart pays its workers). It is interesting to note that Costco's 68 000 workers generated sales of $34 billion, while the 102 000 employees at Sam's Club (the Wal-Mart unit that competes directly with Costco) generated only $35 billion.

agers implement and carry out their plans. As you can see in Figure 10.5, MBO involves managers and subordinates in setting goals and evaluating progress. Once the program is set up, the first step is establishing overall organizational goals. It is also these goals that will ultimately be evaluated to determine the success of the program. At the same time, however, collaborative activity—communicating, meeting, counselling, and so forth—is the key to MBO. Therefore, in addition to acting as a planning tool, MBO can serve as a program for improving satisfaction and motivation. (Note, too, that MBO represents an effort to apply throughout an entire organization the goal-setting theory of motivation that we discussed earlier.)

According to many experts, motivational impact is the biggest advantage of MBO. When employees sit down with managers to set goals, they learn more about company-wide objectives, feel that they are an important part of a team, and see how they can improve company-wide performance by achieving their own goals. If an MBO system is used properly, employees should leave meetings not only with an understanding of the value of their contributions, but also with fair rewards for their performances. They should also accept and be committed to the moderately difficult and specific goals they have helped set for themselves.

Investors Group Financial Services has used MBO for many years to motivate its sales force in selling financial services. The MBO process begins when the vice-president of sales develops general goals for the entire sales force. This sets the stage for Planning Week, which is held annually in 73 regional centres across Canada. Sales reps review their financial accomplishments and think through their personal and financial goals for the coming year. During Planning Week, sales reps meet with their division managers and reach a consensus about the specific goals the sales reps will pursue during the next year. Each division manager then forwards the proposed objectives for his or her division to the appropriate regional manager. This process continues all the way up to the vice-president of sales, who gives final approval to the overall sales objectives of the company for the coming year.[11]

Participative Management

participative management A method of increasing employees' job satisfaction by giving them a voice in how they do their jobs and how the company is managed.

In **participative management**, employees are given a voice in how they do their jobs and in how the company is managed—they become motivated to

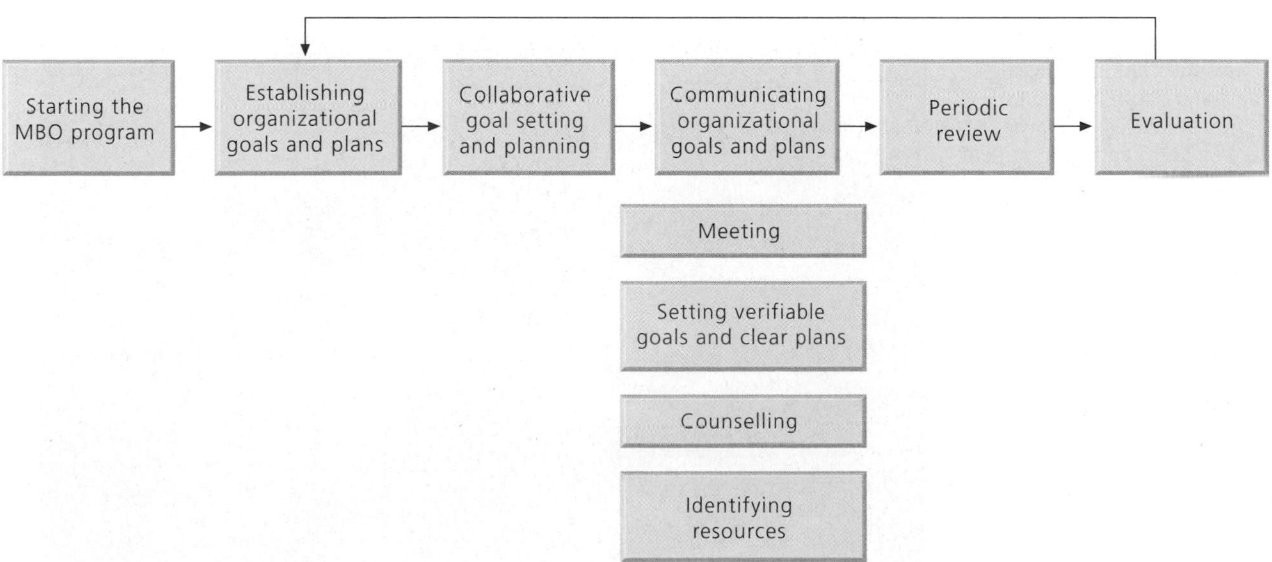

Figure 10.5 Management by objectives.

take greater responsibility for their own performance. Participation generally makes employees feel more committed to organizational goals because they have helped to shape them.

Participative management has become more popular in recent years in Canada. At CP Express and Transport, for example, truck drivers were allowed to decide how to spend $8 million on new equipment.[12] At Toronto's Delta Chelsea Hotel, employees noticed that in the summer months there were fewer business guests and more vacationers' children in the hotel. As a result of employee suggestions, the hotel installed a waterslide, appointed a "kids' concierge," and set up a game room for teens to better serve this market segment.[13]

There are advantages to participation. A survey at B.C. Telecom showed that people with a supportive boss missed less work, were less tense, felt more secure, and were more confident about their ability to get ahead in the company. Supervisors who received negative ratings usually were inflexible, supervised their workers too closely, and didn't communicate useful information to them.[14]

Managers must accept the fact that participation is not desired by all employees. Some will be frustrated by responsibilities they are not equipped to handle. Participative programs may actually result in dissatisfied employees if workers see the invitation to participate as more symbolic than substantive. A good approach is to invite participation only to the extent that employees want to have input, and only if participation will have real value for an organization.

empowerment Motivating and energizing employees to create high-quality products and to provide "bend-over-backwards" service to customers so that the company is more competitive.

Empowerment means motivating and energizing employees to create high-quality products and to provide "bend-over-backwards" service to customers so that the company is more competitive. Participation and empowerment can be used in large firms or small firms, and with managers and operating employees. For example, managers at General Electric who once needed higher-level approval for any expenditure over $5000 now have the autonomy to make their own expense decisions up to as much as $50 000. At WestJet, front-line staff have the right to issue travel credits to customers they feel have not been treated properly. WestJet thinks that the goodwill generated by the practice will increase repeat business.[15] As with participation, managers should not make the assumption that all employees will be interested in being empowered, as the Business Accountability box shows.

Participative management gets employees involved in analyzing problems and suggesting solutions. This increases employee satisfaction with, and commitment to, decisions that are made.

BUSINESS ACCOUNTABILITY

Encouraging Employees to Share Ideas

The empowerment movement involves tapping into workers' knowledge about the job, encouraging them to be self-motivated and to make suggestions for improvements, and giving them more authority and responsibility so that they feel they are a real part of the company's success. The South Bend, Indiana, manufacturing plant of the Eaton Corporation illustrates empowerment in practice. The traditional factory hierarchy is avoided, and everyone wears the same blue uniforms. There are no time clocks, and workers report their hours on an honour basis. Production statistics for each work team are posted where everyone can see them. Each work team is responsible for keeping its own members productive and motivated. Empowerment has meant more authority and more responsibility for workers.

Many workers respond favourably to empowerment opportunities, but others do not. Empowerment can be a tricky process, particularly in an era when layoffs are common and employees may not trust management. The empowerment process typically requires workers to share their job knowledge with other workers or with management, but some workers fear that such sharing will allow others to take credit for their hard-earned knowledge, or that sharing their knowledge will weaken their position in the company. So, managers who assume that all workers want to be empowered may be in for a rude shock.

One employee who cut metal shafts for industrial pumps at Blackmer/Dover Resources Inc. in Grand Rapids, Michigan, had a reputation for being both fast and accurate in his work. He refused to share his knowledge with management (or his fellow workers) because he feared that management would use the knowledge to speed up the workflow and that he would then have to work faster. He is not alone. Many workers have developed extra-fast ways of doing their work, but are reluctant to share those ideas with management. Since managers are always under pressure to improve productivity, the refusal of these workers to share information is frustrating.

One long-time employee at a small Canadian manufacturing plant taught a younger replacement worker how to run a complicated machine. Shortly thereafter, the older worker became ill and was off work for several weeks. When he returned, he found that the younger worker had essentially taken over his job. The older worker had this to say: "To pass on your experience or your knowledge to others, or to pass on to your fellow workers your secrets, how you assemble it faster, better, or more efficiently for the company, be careful; tomorrow you might have lost your job."

Robin Miller, the executive director of the Winnipeg-based Centre for Education and Work, says that there is a lot of "informal learning" that goes on in companies, but it is not generally recognized or rewarded in Canadian workplaces. If informal learning is not rewarded, we should not be surprised if employees do not share with management the efficient short-cuts they have discovered that allow them to work faster.

The main reason workers conceal knowledge seems to be related to job security. Workers fear that if they share their knowledge, management will use that knowledge to increase output. The increased output will mean that management can get by with fewer workers, so some people will lose their jobs.

In some companies, workers don't share their knowledge because they have become convinced that management doesn't think they have anything to contribute. At the Blackmer/Dover plant, for example, a new plant manager was trying to resolve some production problems that had developed under his predecessor. He asked for worker participation so that he could understand what was wrong in the plant and how things might be improved. Workers were surprised they were being asked for their ideas, because previous management had not solicited worker input. But in this case the workers agreed to help, and the story eventually had a happy ending.

Team Management

At one level, employees may be given decision-making responsibility for certain narrow activities, such as when to take lunch breaks or how to divide assignments with co-workers. On a broader level, employees are also being consulted on such decisions as production scheduling, work procedures and schedules, and the hiring of new employees.

Like participation and empowerment, teams are not for everyone. Levi Strauss, for example, encountered major problems when it tried to use teams. Individual workers previously performed repetitive, highly specialized tasks, such as sewing zippers into jeans, and were paid according to the number of jobs they completed each day. In an attempt to boost productivity, company management reorganized everyone into teams of 10 to 35 workers and assigned tasks to the entire group. Each team member's pay was determined by the team's level of productivity. In practice, however, faster workers became resentful of slower workers because they reduced the group's total output. Slower workers, meanwhile, resented the pressure put on them by faster-working co-workers. As a result, motivation, satisfaction, and morale all dropped, and Levi's eventually abandoned the teamwork plan altogether.[16]

By and large, however, participation and empowerment in general, and team management in particular, continue to be widely used to enhance employee motivation and company performance. Although teams are often less effective in traditional and rigidly structured bureaucratic organizations, they do help smaller, more flexible organizations make decisions more quickly and effectively, enhance company-wide communication, and encourage organizational members to feel more like a part of an organization. In turn, these attitudes usually lead to higher levels of both employee motivation and job satisfaction.[17]

Job Enrichment and Job Redesign

While MBO programs and participative management can work in a variety of settings, *job enrichment* and *job redesign* programs are generally used to increase satisfaction in jobs significantly lacking in motivating factors.[18]

Job Enrichment Programs

job enrichment A method of increasing employees' job satisfaction by extending or adding motivating factors such as responsibility or growth.

Job enrichment is designed to add one or more motivating factors to job activities. At Continental Airlines, for example, flight attendants now have more control over their own scheduling. The jobs of flight service managers were also enriched when they were given more responsibility and authority for assigning tasks to the flight crew.

Job Redesign Programs

job redesign A method of increasing employees' job satisfaction by improving the worker–job fit through combining tasks, creating natural work groups, and/or establishing client relationships.

Job redesign acknowledges that different people want different things from their jobs. By restructuring work to achieve a more satisfactory fit between workers and their jobs, **job redesign** can motivate individuals with strong needs for career growth or achievement. Job redesign is usually implemented in one of three ways: through *combining tasks, forming natural work groups,* or *establishing client relationships*.

Combining Tasks. The job of combining tasks involves enlarging jobs and increasing their variety to make employees feel that their work is more meaningful. In turn, employees become more motivated. For example, the job done by a programmer who maintains computer systems might be redesigned to include some system design and system development work. While developing additional skills, then, the programmer also becomes involved in the overall system package.

Forming Natural Work Groups. People who do different jobs on the same projects are candidates for natural work groups. These groups are formed to help employees see the place and importance of their jobs in the total structure of the firm. They are valuable to management because the people working on a project are usually the most knowledgeable about it, and thus the most capable problem solvers. To see how natural workgroups affect motivation, consider a group where each employee does a small part of the job of assembling radios. One person attaches red wires, while another attaches control knobs. The jobs could be redesigned to allow the group to decide who does what and in what order. The workers can exchange jobs and plan their work schedules. Now they all see themselves as part of a team that assembles radios.

Establishing Client Relationships. Establishing client relationships means allowing employees to interact with customers. This approach increases job variety. It gives workers both a greater sense of control and more feedback about performance than they get when their jobs are not highly interactive.

For example, software writers at Microsoft watch test users work with programs and discuss problems with them directly rather than receive feedback from third-party researchers. In Fargo, North Dakota, Great Plains Software has employee turnover of less than 7 percent, compared with an industry average of 15 to 20 percent. The company recruits and rewards in large part according to candidates' customer service skills and their experience with customer needs and complaints.

Modified Work Schedules

As another way of increasing job satisfaction, many companies are trying out different approaches to working hours and the workweek. Several types of modified work schedules have been tried, including *flextime, the compressed workweek, telecommuting,* and *workshare programs.*

Flextime

Some modifications involve adjusting a standard daily work schedule. **Flextime** allows people to pick their working hours. Figure 10.6 illustrates how a flextime system might be arranged and how different people might use it. The office is open from 6 a.m. until 7 p.m. Each employee works for eight hours each day. Core time is 9 a.m. until 11 a.m. and 1 p.m. until 3 p.m. Joe, being an early riser, comes in at 6 a.m., takes an hour lunch between 11 a.m. and noon, and finishes his day by 3 p.m. Sue, on the other hand, prefers a later day. She comes in at 9 a.m., takes a long lunch from 11 a.m. to 1 p.m., and then works until 7 p.m. Pat works a more traditional day from 8 a.m. until 5 p.m.

flextime A method of increasing employees' job satisfaction by allowing them some choice in the hours they work.

A survey of 206 companies conducted by Mercer Human Resource Consulting found that 60 percent of Canadian companies offer some form of flextime option to their employees.[19] Flextime programs give employees more freedom in their professional and personal lives. Such programs allow workers to plan around the work schedules of spouses and the school schedules of young children, for example. The increased feeling of freedom and control over their work life also reduces individuals' levels of stress.

Companies can also benefit from flextime programs. In large urban areas, flextime programs reduce traffic congestion that contributes to lost work time. Companies benefit from the higher levels of commitment and job satisfaction among workers in such programs.

The Compressed Workweek

In the **compressed workweek**, employees work fewer days per week, but more hours on the days they do work. The most popular compressed workweek is 4 days, 10 hours per day, but some companies have also experimented

compressed workweek Employees work fewer days per week, but more hours on the days they do work.

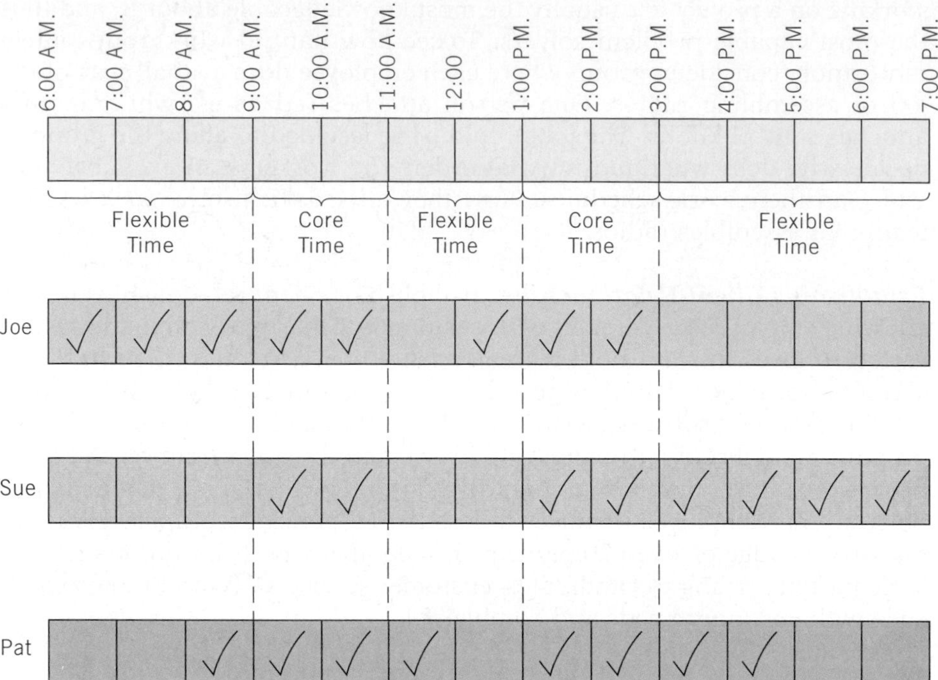

Figure 10.6 Flextime schedules include core time, when everyone must be at work, and flexible time, during which employees can set their own working hours.

with 3 days, 12 hours per day. The "weekend worker" program at 3M Canada in London, Ontario, offers workers 12-hour shifts on Saturdays and Sundays only, and pays them the same wage as if they had worked normal hours Monday through Friday. There is a long waiting list to transfer to weekend work.[20]

Tellers at the Bank of Montreal in Oakville Place work long days (up to 14 hours), but enjoy a short workweek. Some tellers work 7 a.m. to 9 p.m. Thursdays and Fridays, and 7:30 a.m. to 5:30 p.m. Saturdays. Others work Mondays to Wednesdays for 14 hours each day. Employees like the system because it allows them to do personal errands during the day on the weekdays they do not have to be at work.[21]

Telecommuting

telecommuting Allowing employees to do all or some of their work away from the office.

A third variation in work design is **telecommuting**, which allows people to do some or all of their work away from their office. The availability of networked computers, fax machines, cellular telephones, and overnight delivery services makes it possible for many independent professionals to work at home or while travelling. Statistics Canada estimates that 1.3 million Canadians were telecommuting in 2001.[22] As an extreme example, David Longstaff, a software developer, "commutes" from Waterloo, Ontario, to Leeds, England, each day to provide support for computer programs he has written for the company.[23]

While employees like telecommuting because it saves them time and money, the federal government is concerned that holes may be developing in the health and safety net because employers may not extend workplace health and safety coverage to telecommuters who work at home. That is not the only problem with telecommuting. Workers often report feeling isolated and lonely. To avoid this problem, B.C. Tel and Bentall Development Inc. jointly developed a satellite telecommuting office in Langley, British Columbia. It allows workers who used to commute to Burnaby or

The advent of computers and fax machines has made telecommuting an increasingly popular job strategy. Many people in Canada telecommute.

Vancouver to reduce their travel time considerably and still be able to interact with other workers.[24]

But telecommuting may not be for everyone. Would-be telecommuters must ask themselves several important questions: Can I meet deadlines even when I'm not being closely supervised? What will it be like to be away from the social context of the office five days a week? Can I renegotiate family rules, so my spouse doesn't come home expecting to see dinner on the table just because I've been home all day?

Another obstacle to establishing a telecommuting program is convincing management that it will be beneficial for everyone involved. Telecommuters may have to fight the perception—from both bosses and co-workers—that if they are not being supervised, they are not working. Managers are often very suspicious about telecommuting, asking "How can I tell if someone is working when I can't see them?"

Workshare Programs

A fourth type of modified work schedule, **worksharing** (also called **job sharing**), benefits both employee and employer. This approach allows two people to share one full-time job. For example, Kim Sarjeant and Loraine Champion, who are staff lawyers at NOVA Corp. in Calgary, share a position advising the human resources department. Sarjeant works Mondays through Wednesdays, and Champion works Wednesdays through Fridays.[25] A Statistics Canada survey showed that 8 percent of all part-time workers in Canada share a job with someone. People who share jobs are more likely to be women, to be university educated, and to have professional occupations such as teaching and nursing. In addition, job sharers earned more than regular part-time workers.[26]

worksharing (job sharing) A method of increasing employee job satisfaction by allowing two people to share one job.

Short-run worksharing programs can help ease experienced workers into retirement while training their replacements. Worksharing can also allow students in university co-op programs to combine academic learning with practical experience.

Long-run worksharing programs have proven a good solution for people who want only part-time work. For example, five people might decide to share one reservationist's job at Air Canada with each working one day a week. Each person earns some money, remains in the job market, and enjoys limited travel benefits.

MANAGERIAL STYLES AND LEADERSHIP

5 Discuss different *managerial styles of leadership* and their impact on human relations in the workplace.

leadership The process of motivating others to work to meet specific objectives.

In trying to enhance morale, job satisfaction, and motivation, managers can use many different styles of leadership. **Leadership** is the process of motivating others to work to meet specific objectives. Leading is also one of the key aspects of a manager's job and an important component of the directing function.

Richard Peddie, CEO of Maple Leaf Sports & Entertainment, uses a hands-on management style that includes meeting with new employees and emphasizing how important they are to the team. Peddie says it is important to understand how employees at the bottom of the corporate ladder feel about the company and how they fit in. He also knows that it is important to find out what season ticket holders and corporate sponsors are thinking.[27]

Andrall (Andy) Pearson, former chairman and new director of Yum! Brands Inc. (formerly Tricon Global Restaurants)—the parent company of Pizza Hut, Taco Bell, and KFC (Kentucky Fried Chicken)—has evolved from feared dictator to beloved guru. First, let's look at the old Andy: Pearson sums up the first 50 years of his career, saying, "I proved that I was smart by finding fault with other people's ideas." He began at the strategic consulting firm McKinsey & Co., rising to the position of senior director in charge of the firm's marketing practice. During his 14-year stint as president and COO of PepsiCo, he was known for being abrasive, numbers-oriented, and hard to please. His favourite phrase was "So what?" *Fortune* named him one of the top-10 toughest bosses in 1980, in part because he often drove employees to tears or to quitting if they failed to meet his expectations. In fact, he helped people out the door—his policy was to fire the lowest-performing 10 to 20 percent of all his employees each year.

As a tenured professor at the Harvard Business School, he contributed articles to the prestigious *Harvard Business Review* with titles such as "Tough-Minded Ways to Get Innovative." He was invited to join Tricon by CEO David Novak, who saw that Pearson's no-nonsense style would complement his people-oriented approach. When he first came to Tricon, "he was brutal," according to Aylwin Lewis, Tricon's COO. "One time he told us, 'A room full of monkeys could do better than this!'"

Now, the new Andy: Employees still weep, but now it's with gratitude for praise from Pearson. Managers who are mentored by Pearson tell him that the experience is life-changing, and Pearson says, "I get letters that would just bring tears to your eyes." Pearson is greeted with loud cheers when he tells a crowd, "My experience at Tricon represents the capstone of my career." At the beginning, Novak told Pearson, "We can learn from each other," and when Pearson arrived at headquarters, hundreds of employees were cheering and a band was playing. "All the time I was at Pepsi, nothing remotely like this had ever happened. It was overwhelming," says Pearson. "I knew something was going on that was fundamentally very powerful. If we could learn how to harness that spirit with something systematic, then we would have something unique."

Pearson has softened and transformed. When he says, "If I could only unleash the power of everybody in the organization, instead of just a few people...we'd be a much better company," he seems to truly care about employees. And his thinking about leadership has matured: "Great leaders find a balance between getting results and how they get them. A lot of people make the mistake of thinking that getting results is all there is to a job....Your real job is to get results and to do it in a way that makes your organization a great place to work."[28]

Each year a "most respected corporate leader" study is sponsored by KPMG and conducted by Ipsos-Reid. In 2005, 250 Canadian CEOs were asked to list the corporate leaders they most respected (other than themselves). Gwyn Morgan, the CEO of EnCana Corp. of Calgary topped the list. Other CEOs that ranked highly were Dominic d'Alessandro (CEO of Manulife Financial Corp.), Gordon Nixon (CEO of Royal Bank of Canada), and Clive Beddoe (CEO of WestJet Airlines).[29]

Managerial Styles

Early theories of leadership tried to identify specific traits associated with strong leaders. For example, physical appearance, intelligence, and public speaking skills were once thought to be "leadership traits." Indeed, it was once believed that taller people made better leaders than shorter people. The trait approach, however, proved to be a poor predictor of leadership potential. Ultimately, attention shifted from managers' traits to their behaviours, or **managerial styles**—patterns of behaviour that a manager exhibits in dealing with subordinates. Managerial styles run the gamut from autocratic to democratic to free rein. These three major styles involve very different kinds of responses to human relations problems. Any given style or combination of styles may prove appropriate, depending on the situation.

managerial styles Patterns of behaviour that a manager exhibits in dealing with subordinates.

- Managers who adopt an **autocratic style** generally issue orders and expect them to be obeyed without question. The military commander prefers and usually needs the autocratic style on the battlefield. Because no one else is consulted, the autocratic style allows for rapid decision making. It therefore may be useful in situations that test a firm's effectiveness as a time-based competitor. The autocratic style is also used in business firms. A former Bank of Nova Scotia CEO (Peter Godsoe) was often characterized as being an autocratic manager.[30]

autocratic style A managerial style in which managers generally issue orders and expect them to be obeyed without question.

- Managers who adopt a **democratic style** generally request input from subordinates before making decisions but retain final decision-making power. For example, the manager of a technical group may ask other group members to interview and offer opinions about job applicants. The manager, however, will ultimately make the hiring decision. The current CEO of the Bank of Nova Scotia—Rick Waugh—says that he is going to adopt a different style than his predecessor. He plans to discuss issues with his subordinates rather than simply expecting them to obey orders.[31]

democratic style A managerial style in which managers generally request input from subordinates before making decisions but retain final decision-making power.

- Managers who adopt a **free-rein style** typically serve as advisers to subordinates who are allowed to make decisions. The chairperson of a volunteer committee to raise funds for a new library may find a free rein style most effective.

free-rein style A managerial style in which managers typically serve as advisers to subordinates who are allowed to make decisions.

The relative effectiveness of any leadership style depends to a considerable degree on the desire of subordinates to share input or exercise creativity. Whereas autocratic managers frustrate some people, others prefer them because they do not want to participate in making decisions. The democratic approach, meanwhile, can be disconcerting both to people who want decision-making responsibility and to those who do not. A free-rein style lends itself to employee creativity, and thus to creative solutions to pressing problems. This style also appeals to employees who prefer to plan their own work. Not all subordinates, however, have the necessary background or skills to make creative decisions. Others are not sufficiently self-motivated to work without supervision.

"I like to think of myself as a nice guy. Naturally, sometimes you have to step on a few faces."

Canadian Versus American Management Styles

The management style of Canadian managers might look a lot like that of Americans, but there are several notable differences. Most fundamentally, Canadian managers are more subtle and subdued than are American managers. Canadian managers also seem more committed to their companies, less willing to mindlessly follow the latest management fad, and more open to different cultures because of the multicultural nature of Canada. All these characteristics may be advantageous for Canadian companies that will increasingly be competing in global markets.[32]

Manitoba-born Don McCaw is the CEO of William M. Mercer Inc. in the United States. Mercer is a leading human resource consulting firm, with 5000 employees and 130 offices around the world. McCaw previously had been the CEO of Mercer's Canadian operation. He is described as loyal, pleasant, and able to collaborate with others. He built a strong team in Canada because of his management style, and the U.S. operation wanted him to do the same thing there. The collaborative skills of Canadian managers are legendary in the eyes of many U.S. managers.[33]

Many other Canadian-born managers have achieved significant success in companies that operate outside of Canada. These include Henry McKinnell (former CEO and current chairman of the board of directors of Pfizer, the world's largest pharmaceutical company), Steven McArthur (former president of online travel company Expedia), Clara Furse (CEO of the London Stock Exchange), Simon Cooper (CEO of Ritz-Carlton Hotel), and Dominic Barton (Chairman of McKinsey & Company's Asia Region), to name just a few.[34]

The Contingency Approach to Leadership

Because each managerial style has both strengths and weaknesses, most managers vary their responses to different situations. Flexibility, however, has not always characterized managerial style or responsiveness. For most of the twentieth century, in fact, managers tended to believe that all problems yielded to preconceived, pre-tested solutions. If raising pay reduced turnover in one plant, for example, it followed that the same tactic would work equally well in another.

contingency approach An approach to managerial style holding that the appropriate behaviour in any situation is dependent (contingent) on the elements unique to that situation.

More recently, however, managers have begun to adopt a **contingency approach** to managerial style. They have started to view appropriate managerial behaviour in any situation as dependent, or contingent, on the elements unique to that situation. This change in outlook has resulted largely from an increasing appreciation of the complexity of managerial problems and solutions. For example, pay raises may reduce turnover when workers have been badly underpaid. The contingency approach, however, recognizes that raises will have little effect when workers feel adequately paid but ill treated by management. This approach also recommends that training managers in human relations skills may be crucial to solving the latter problem.[35]

The contingency approach also acknowledges that people in different cultures behave differently and expect different things from their managers. A certain managerial style, therefore, is more likely to be successful in some countries than in others. Japanese workers, for example, generally expect managers to be highly participative and to allow them input in decision making. In contrast, many South American workers actually balk at participation and want take-charge leaders. The basic idea, then, is that managers will be more effective when they adapt their styles to the contingencies of the situations they face.[36]

Motivation and Leadership in the Twenty-First Century

Motivation and leadership remain critically important areas of organizational behaviour. As times change, however, so do the ways in which managers motivate and lead their employees.

Changing Patterns of Motivation

From the motivational side, today's employees want rewards that are often quite different from those valued by earlier generations. Money, for example, is no longer the prime motivator for most people. In addition, because businesses today cannot offer the degree of job security that many workers want, motivating employees to strive toward higher levels of performance requires skilful attention from managers.

One survey asked workers to identify the things they most wanted at work. Among the things noted were flexible working hours (67 percent), casual dress (56 percent), unlimited internet access (51 percent), opportunities to telecommute (43 percent), nap time (28 percent), massages (25 percent), daycare (24 percent), espresso machines (23 percent), and the opportunity to bring pets to work (11 percent).[37] In another study focussing on fathers, many men also said they wanted more flexible working hours in order to spend more time with their families.[38] Managers, then, must recognize that today's workers have a complex set of needs and must be motivated in increasingly complicated ways.

Canadian businesses are starting to respond to these employee preferences. A Conference Board of Canada survey of 312 companies showed the following:

- Flexible working hours are offered by 75 percent.
- Leave for family-related reasons are provided by 74 percent.
- Childcare assistance or programs are offered by 54 percent.
- Telecommuting is offered by 49 percent.
- Eldercare is offered by 48 percent.
- Unpaid sabbaticals are provided by 43 percent.[39]

As we saw in Chapter 8, the diversity inherent in today's workforce also makes motivating behaviour more complex. The reasons why people work reflect more varying goals than ever before, and the varying lifestyles of diverse workers mean that managers must first pay closer attention to what their employees expect to receive for their efforts and then try to link rewards with job performance.

Changing Patterns of Leadership

Leadership, too, is taking different directions as we head into the twenty-first century. For one thing, today's leaders are finding it necessary to change their own behaviour. As organizations become flatter and workers become more empowered, managers naturally find it less acceptable to use the autocratic approach to leadership. Instead, many are becoming more democratic—functioning more as "coaches" than as "bosses." Just as an athletic coach teaches athletes how to play and then steps back to let them take the field, many leaders now try to provide workers with the skills and resources to perform at their best before backing off to let them do their work with less supervision.

Diversity, too, is affecting leadership processes. In earlier times, most leaders were white males who were somewhat older than the people they supervised—people who were themselves relatively similar to one another. But as organizations become more and more diverse, leaders are also becoming increasingly diverse. They are also increasingly likely to be younger than some of the people they are leading. Leaders, therefore, must have greater sensitivity to the values, needs, and motives of a diverse group of people as they examine their own behaviour in relation to other people.

Finally, leaders must also adopt a "network" mentality rather than a "hierarchical" one. When people worked in the same place at the same time, the organizational hierarchy had a clear vertical chain of command and lines of communication. But now people work in different places and at different times. New forms of organization design may call for a person to be the leader on one project and a team member on another. Thus, people need to become comfortable with leadership based more on expertise than on organizational position and with interaction patterns that are not tied to specific places or times. The leader of tomorrow, then, will need a different set of skills and a different point of view than did the leader of yesterday.

Summary of Learning Objectives

1. **Describe the nature and importance of *psychological contracts* in the workplace.** A *psychological contract* is the set of expectations held by an employee concerning what he or she will contribute to an organization (referred to as *contributions*) and what the organization will provide in return to the employee (referred to as *inducements*). Until the last decade or so, businesses generally offered their employees high levels of job security and employees were very loyal to their employers. More recently, however, new psychological contracts have been created in many sectors. Now, organizations offer less security but more benefits. In turn, employees are often willing to work longer hours but also more willing to leave an employer for a better opportunity elsewhere.

2. **Discuss the importance of *job satisfaction* and *employee morale* and summarize their roles in human relations in the workplace.** Good *human relations*—the interactions between employers and employees and their attitudes toward one another—are important to business because they lead to high levels of *job satisfaction* (the degree of enjoyment that workers derive from their jobs) and *morale* (workers' overall attitudes toward their work and workplace). Satisfied employees generally exhibit lower levels of absenteeism and turnover. They also have fewer grievances and engage in fewer negative behaviours.

3. **Identify and summarize the most important *theories of employee motivation*.** Views of employee motivation have changed dramatically over the years. The *classical*

theory holds that people are motivated solely by money. *Scientific management* tried to analyze jobs and increase production by finding better ways to perform tasks. The *Hawthorne studies* were the first to demonstrate the importance of making workers feel that their needs were being considered. The *human-resources model* identifies two kinds of managers—*Theory X managers*, who believe that people are inherently uncooperative and must be constantly punished or rewarded, and *Theory Y managers*, who believe that people are naturally responsible and self-motivated to be productive.

Maslow's *hierarchy of human needs model* proposes that people have several different needs (ranging from physiological to self-actualization), which they attempt to satisfy in their work. People must fulfill lower-level needs before seeking to fulfill higher-level needs. *Two-factor theory* suggests that if basic hygiene factors are not met, workers will be dissatisfied. Only by increasing more complex motivating factors can companies increase employees' performance.

Expectancy theory holds that people will work hard if they believe that their efforts will lead to desired rewards. *Equity theory* says that motivation depends on the way employees evaluate their treatment by an organization relative to its treatment of other workers.

4. **Describe some of the *strategies* used by organizations to improve job satisfaction and employee motivation.** Managers can use several strategies to increase employee satisfaction and motivation. The principle of *reinforcement*, or *behaviour modification theory*, holds that rewards and punishment can control behaviour. *Rewards*, for example, are positive reinforcement when they are tied directly to desired or improved performance. *Punishment* (using unpleasant consequences to change undesirable behaviour) is generally less effective.

   Management by objectives (a system of collaborative goal setting) and *participative management* (techniques for giving employees a voice in management decisions) can improve human relations by making an employee feel like part of a team. *Job enrichment*, *job redesign*, and *modified work schedules* (including *workshare programs*, *flextime*, *compressed workweeks*, and *telecommuting*) can enhance job satisfaction by adding motivating factors to jobs in which they are normally lacking.

5. **Discuss different *managerial styles of leadership* and their impact on human relations in the workplace.** Effective *leadership*—the process of motivating others to meet specific objectives—is an important determinant of employee satisfaction and motivation. Generally speaking, managers practise one of three basic managerial styles. *Autocratic managers* generally issue orders that they expect to be obeyed. *Democratic managers* generally seek subordinates' input into decisions. *Free-rein managers* are more likely to advise than to make decisions. The *contingency approach* to leadership views appropriate managerial behaviour in any situation as dependent on the elements of that situation. Managers thus need to assess situations carefully, especially to determine the desire of subordinates to share input or exercise creativity. They must also be aware of the changing nature of both motivation and leadership as we head into the twenty-first century.

KEY TERMS

autocratic style, 321
classical theory of motivation, 304
compressed workweek, 317
contingency approach, 322
democratic style, 321
empowerment, 314
equity theory, 309
expectancy theory, 309
flextime, 317
free-rein style, 321
goal-setting theory, 311
Hawthorne effect, 306
hierarchy of human needs model, 306
human relations, 302
job enrichment, 316
job redesign, 316
job satisfaction, 303
leadership, 320
management by objectives (MBO), 312
managerial styles, 321
morale, 303
motivation, 304
participative management, 313
psychological contract, 302
reinforcement, 312
telecommuting, 318
Theory X, 306
Theory Y, 306
turnover, 303
two-factor theory, 308
worksharing (job sharing), 319

QUESTIONS FOR ANALYSIS

1. Describe the psychological contract you currently have or have had in the past with an employer. If you have never worked, describe the psychological contract that you have with the instructor in this class.
2. Do you think that most people are relatively satisfied or dissatisfied with their work? Explain your reasoning.
3. Compare and contrast the needs-based theories of Maslow and Herzberg with expectancy theory and equity theory.
4. How can participative management programs enhance employee satisfaction and motivation? Why do some employees not want to get involved in participative management?
5. Some evidence suggests that recent college graduates show high levels of job satisfaction. Levels then drop dramatically as they reach their late twenties, only to increase gradually once they get older. What might account for this pattern?
6. As a manager, under what sort of circumstances might you apply each of the theories of motivation discussed in this chapter? Which would be easiest to use? Which would be hardest? Why?
7. Suppose you realize one day that you are dissatisfied with your job. Short of quitting, what might you do to improve your situation?
8. List two Canadian and two U.S. managers who you think would also qualify as great leaders.

APPLICATION EXERCISES

1. At the library, research the manager or owner of a company in the early twentieth century and the manager or owner of a company today. Compare and contrast the two in terms of their times, leadership styles, and views on employee motivation.
2. Interview the manager of a local manufacturing company. Identify as many different strategies for enhancing job satisfaction at that company as you can.

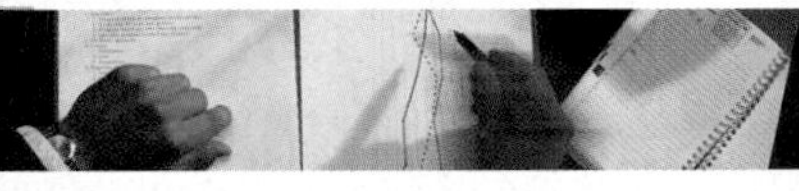

BUILDING YOUR BUSINESS SKILLS

Too Much of a Good Thing

Goal

To encourage students to apply different motivational theories to a workplace problem involving poor productivity.

The Situation

Consider a small company that makes its employees feel as if they were members of a large family. Unfortunately, this company is going broke because too few members are working hard enough to make money for it. They are happy, comfortable, complacent—and lazy. With sales dropping, the company brings in management consultants to analyze the situation and make recommendations. The outsiders quickly identify a motivational problem affecting the sales force: sales reps are paid a handsome salary and receive automatic year-end bonuses regardless of performance. They are also treated to bagels every Friday and regular group birthday lunches that cost as much as $200 each. Employees feel satisfied, but have little incentive to work very hard. Eager to return to profitability, the company's owners wait to hear your recommendations.

Assignment

Step 1

In groups of four, step into the role of management consultants. Start by analyzing your client's workforce motivation problems from the following perspectives (the questions focus on key motivational issues):

Job satisfaction and morale. As part of a long-standing family-owned business, employees are happy and loyal, in part because they are treated so well. Can high morale have a downside? How can it breed stagnation, and what can managers do to prevent stagnation from taking hold?

Theory X versus Theory Y. Although the behaviour of these workers seems to make a case for Theory X, why is it difficult to draw this conclusion about a company that focusses more on satisfaction than on sales and profits?

Two-factor theory. Analyze the various ways in which improving such motivational factors as recognition, added responsibility, advancement, and growth might reduce the importance of hygiene factors, including pay and security.

Expectancy theory. Analyze the effect on productivity of redesigning the company's sales force compensation structure: namely, by paying lower base salaries while offering greater earnings potential through a sales-based incentive system. How would linking performance with increased pay that is achievable through hard work motivate employees? How would the threat of job loss motivate greater effort?

Step 2

Write a short report based on your analysis, and make recommendations to the company's owners. The goal of your report is to change the working environment in ways that will motivate greater effort and generate greater productivity.

Follow-Up Questions

1. What is your group's most important recommendation? Why do you think it is likely to succeed?
2. Changing the corporate culture to make it less paternalistic may reduce employees' sense of belonging to a family. If you were an employee, would you consider a greater focus on profits to be an improvement or a problem? How would it affect your motivation and productivity?
3. What steps would you take to improve the attitude and productivity of long-time employees who resist change?

EXERCISING YOUR ETHICS

Practising Controlled Behaviour

The Situation

As we noted in the text, some companies try to control—and even alter workers' behaviour through systematic rewards and punishments for specific behaviours. Then they try to shape employee behaviour by linking reinforcement to desired behaviours and punishment to undesired behaviours.

The Dilemma

Assume that you are the new human resources manager in a medium-size organization. Your boss has just ordered you to implement a behaviour-modification program by creating an intricate network of rewards and punishments to be linked to specific desired and undesired behaviours. You, however, are uncomfortable with this approach. You regard behaviour-modification policies to be too much like experiments on laboratory rats. Instead, you would prefer to use rewards in a way that is consistent with expectancy theory—that is, by letting employees know in advance how they can most effectively reach the rewards they most want. You have tried to change your boss's mind, but to no avail. She says to proceed with behaviour modification with no further discussion.

Questions for Discussion

1. What are the ethical issues in this case?
2. What do you think most managers would do in this situation?
3. What would you do?

CONCLUDING CASE 10-1

Bringing the Bounty Back to P&G

As the 1990s drew to a close, consumer products powerhouse Procter & Gamble (P&G) found itself in an unfamiliar rut. Fuelled by such megabrands as Tide, Crest, Charmin, Downy, Pampers, Folgers, Bounty, and Pringles, the 1980s had been a decade of phenomenal growth, but in the 1990s—for the first time ever—P&G failed to meet its goal of doubling sales growth each decade. Part of the problem was clear—turnover at the top. P&G had gone through three different CEOs during the 1990s, each with his own unique personality and individual view of how the firm should be run.

The last of the three, Durk Jager, was appointed in 1998. Jager was an avid reorganizer who moved no fewer than 110 000 workers into new jobs. His strategy also called for focussing attention on new products rather than best-sellers. Unfortunately, the innovations that he championed, such as Olay cosmetics, often bombed. He also liked the idea of putting American brand names on P&G's global products, but shoppers in Germany and Hong Kong didn't recognize such brands as "Pantene" and "Dawn," and overseas sales plummeted. Jager tried to acquire drugmakers Warner-Lambert and American Home Products but dropped the idea under pressure from investors who thought the prices too high.

Under Jager's leadership, P&G missed earnings targets and lost $70 billion in market value. To make matters worse, his aggressive personality didn't endear Jager to P&G employees. Insiders reported that morale was falling daily, and many senior managers felt as if they no longer knew what they were supposed to be doing. "I was lost," said one vice-president. "It was like no one knew how to get anything done anymore." Jager was fired in mid-2000, after only 17 months on the job.

The announcement of his replacement, 25-year P&G veteran Alan Lafley, was met with yawns and a $4 per share drop in share price. According to conventional wisdom, Durk Jager had saddled the company with so many problems that only a dynamic, strong-willed successor stood a chance of turning things around. And by most accounts, that wasn't Alan Lafley, whose low-key style and bespectacled appearance caused one industry analyst to comment that "If there were 15 people sitting around the conference table, it wouldn't be obvious that he was the CEO." *Fortune* magazine dubbed him "the un-CEO."

But to the surprise of many—and the shock of some—the quiet and unassuming Lafley has succeeded in turning around the stumbling manufacturer when other, more flamboyant leaders might well have failed. In some ways, he's even made it seem easy, demonstrating the virtues of back-to-basics strategy and honest, straightforward leadership. Lafley has also succeeded in restoring a sense of pride in the company and its products and has lifted employee morale in dramatic style.

From day one as CEO, Alan Lafley knew that P&G could do a better job of selling its proven winners. One of his first acts was to allocate more resources to the managers of the company's top 10 brands. "The trick," he recalls, "was to find the few things that were really going to sell, and sell as many of them as you could.... The essence of our strategy," he adds, "is incredibly simple, but I believe the simplicity is its power.... It's Sesame Street–simple, but it works." For example, hair-care managers reinvented the way they marketed Pantene, the company's top-selling hair-care brand. Rather than position products by hair type (for oily hair or fine hair), new campaigns focussed on the looks that customers wanted—say, more curls or more volume. Sales went up by 8 percent.

Instead of insisting that new products be developed internally, Lafley also started acquiring small, idea-driven firms. He announced that 50 percent of the company's product innovations should come through such acquisitions. If the strategy proves successful, Lafley explains, "We would double the productivity of our current investment in R&D." Lafley also demands more marketability in new products, reminding researchers, "Innovation is in the consumer's eyes.... It isn't a great innovation until [the customer] loves it and purchases it."

Lafley is shaking up P&G's staid culture in other ways, too. "I have made a lot of symbolic, very physical changes," he says, "so people understand we are in the business of change." At the company's headquarters, product managers have moved out of executive suites to work more closely with employees. Wood panelling and oil paintings are coming down so that top managers can work as teams in modern, open spaces. The penthouse floor is now a learning centre, where top executives conduct lessons and share knowledge with the workforce. "I really believe knowledge is power," says Lafley, "and translating knowledge into action in the marketplace is one of the things that distinguishes leadership."

Not surprisingly, communication between managers, workers, board members, and even competitors has opened up. "You can tell him bad news or things you'd be afraid to tell other bosses," says one vice-president of Lafley. The CEO rewards managers for financial results, but is harsh on poor performers—half of the top team is new.

With a series of small changes, Alan Lafley has had a powerful impact on P&G's performance. Since he took over, earnings regularly beat expectations, and stock price has risen 70 percent. Profits are up 49 percent over last year. As for Lafley himself, he continues to emphasize the basics. "Nearly 2 billion times a day," he reminds his employees, "P&G products are put to the test when consumers use [them].... When we get this right...then we begin to earn the trust on which great brands are built."

Questions for Discussion

1. Discuss the role of psychological contracts at Procter & Gamble.
2. How important are job satisfaction and morale to a large firm such as P&G?
3. Show how various theories of motivation apply to P&G.
4. What does this case illustrate about the nature of leadership?
5. Compare and contrast the leadership approaches used by Durk Jager and Alan Lafley.

CONCLUDING CASE 10-2

The Importance of Perks

The perquisites (or "perks") that companies may offer to employees include things like unlimited sick days, on-site childcare, flexible work schedules, free beverages, concierge services, laundry pickup and delivery, and on-site pet care. The extent of these perks varies widely across companies, and is to some extent dependent on the state of the economy at any given time. During the economic boom times of the 1990s, for example, workers had the advantage in the employment equation. An acute shortage of knowledge and other skilled workers meant that the labour market was a seller's market. Top university and college graduates had multiple offers, and skilled technical workers could take their pick of jobs.

As the economy slowed in 2001, the advantage shifted to employers. Companies realized that they had to cut costs, and many of them turned to their labour forces to achieve the cuts. One approach was to reduce employee perks or eliminate them altogether. Bonuses, sick leave, and vacation time were also squeezed, and some firms asked workers to accept pay cuts. Many firms reduced or stopped hiring, and the hardest hit companies announced mass layoffs. The immediate repercussions of such actions included low morale, reduced productivity, or worse. And the effects may be long-lasting. Says one executive whose company instituted pay cuts, "People are lying low, but when the economy improves, they'll be out of here." In general, firms that took such actions may find that they've tarnished their reputations as employers and find it more difficult to attract workers when they need them again.

A study by Hewitt Associates showed that companies that are recognized on lists such as "The 100 Best Companies to Work For" have almost twice the number of job applications and half the annual turnover as non-ranked companies. And a study by the Gallup Organization showed that there was a strong correlation between employee satisfaction and company profitability.

The improvement in the economy during 2004–06 meant that perks were once more being considered as a way of attracting and retaining employees. Emphasizing a richer mix of employee perks makes it necessary for managers to adopt the view that employees can be trusted to do what is beneficial for the company and don't have to be watched all the time to ensure they're doing the right things. Companies are doing a variety of things to increase employee satisfaction levels and to make employees' work experiences more positive. For example:

- Labatt Brewing Co. Ltd. employs a full-time fitness coordinator who schedules nutritionists and massage therapists for employees. She organizes fundraising runs, bike rides, and yoga classes, and conducts fitness classes in the company's on-site gym, which is open every day from 6 a.m. to 10 p.m.
- Kraft Ltd. also offers on-site fitness facilities as well as flexible working arrangements, an on-site dry cleaner, noon-hour seminars on diverse topics like landscaping, and a store that provides frozen meals for employees who don't have time to buy groceries.
- Trimark Investment Management Inc. wanted to make sure it kept valued employees who liked being close to big-city amenities when the company moved from downtown Toronto to the suburbs. So it built the Energy Zone, an on-site facility that offers aerobics, self-defence, and yoga classes. It also includes

a weight room, massage room, pool tables, a big-screen TV, and an internet café. The Energy Zone gives employees some diversions from work, but it also acts as a place where they can meet and interact with people from other departments. Trimark also has a Recovery Room for employees who feel under the weather while at work.

A study done for *Report on Business Magazine* found that many of the traditional things that managers have assumed are important to employees—for example, fair pay, financial incentives such as share ownership plans, and the opportunity for further training and education—are, in fact, important. However, employees also want to work for a company where the culture values people, where their opinions count, and where their judgment is trusted. Surveys also show that it is important for today's employees to be able to balance work and life activities. Employers are increasingly willing to accommodate these wishes because employee commitment and retention rise when a company recognizes that employees have a life outside work. If a company does nothing to help employees balance work and life concerns, and if it simply assumes that people are going to be totally devoted to the company, the bottom line is negatively affected because of the stress employees will experience.

A Canada @Work™ study done by Aon Consulting found that when employers recognize employee needs outside the workplace, the company's employees are more likely to stay with the company, and are more likely to recommend the company as a good place to work. Overall, companies need to have a "people-first" attitude about their employees, and perks play a significant role in this. Flexible work arrangements such as job sharing, flextime, compressed workweeks, and work-at-home opportunities are examples of "people-first" attitudes. Consider the case of Nicole Black, who returned to her job at the Royal Bank three months after having her first child. She quickly found that she didn't have as much time with her new baby as she wanted. As a result, the bank arranged for a compressed workweek so she could work four days per week. When she became pregnant a second time, she reduced her work hours even further and started job sharing with another employee. She now works only on Mondays and Tuesdays.

But what about companies that are struggling financially? The good news is that there are still effective incentives. The most powerful, and least expensive, perk can be time off. Experts suggest, for example, that up to 20 percent of workers would be willing to work fewer hours for lower pay. Siemens, a German electronics firm, is offering workers a year-long "time-out," with reduced pay and a guaranteed job when they return. "It's a possibility for us not to lose good workers despite bad times," says Siemens' spokesperson Axel Heim. Firms are also finding that technology workers and professionals, who need to stay on the leading edge of their fields, want more training and increased job responsibilities. Many people, warns Patti Wilson, founder of a high-tech career-management firm, "will jump jobs to learn more or stay if they feel that they're being challenged."

Questions for Discussion

1. What is the difference between job satisfaction and morale? How do employee perks affect each of these concepts?
2. What do the various motivation factors discussed in this chapter say about the impact on employee satisfaction and motivation of things such as job sharing, compressed workweek, and flextime?
3. What are the various managerial styles that managers can use? What do the employee perks mentioned above imply about the most effective managerial style?
4. What strategies are available to managers to enhance employee job satisfaction?
5. Are there any potential problems with a company implementing the perks mentioned above? If so, what are they?
6. What other incentives might a company be able to offer its best workers to retain them?

PLANNING FOR YOUR CAREER

What Can You Manage?

Many people studying business have a general aspiration to be a "manager." Most of them, however, aren't entirely sure just what they want to manage. Remember from Chapter 6 that managers are responsible for dealing with various kinds of resources. Moreover, there are several different areas of management. This exercise will give you some more insights into the kinds of activities that managers in different areas actually perform.

Assignment

Start by reviewing the discussion in Chapter 6 of the different areas of management. Next, review Chapter 5 in *Beginning Your Career Search*, 3rd ed., by James S. O'Rourke IV, to learn more about researching companies that you might want to work for. Finally, make a list of up to 10 different large companies in which you have some general interest.

To complete this exercise, do the following:

1. Research each company on your list to find out what kinds of management positions it currently has available. One way is to access the "careers" option on a company website.
2. Try to find two or three examples representing each of the various areas of management identified in Chapter 6.
3. Reflect on the various jobs that you've researched and then rank them in terms of the extent to which they seem potentially appealing to you.
4. See if you can identify any common themes among those jobs toward the top of your list. How about those jobs on the bottom and in the middle of your list?
5. If there are common themes, what might they suggest regarding your career interests? Do they suggest ways in which you might better prepare yourself for a future career?
6. If there appear to be *no* common themes, what might this fact suggest about your current career interests? In this case, what can you do to better prepare yourself for a future career?

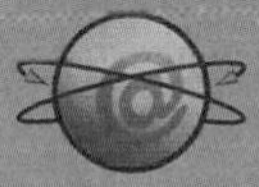

Visit the Companion Website at **www.pearsoned.ca/griffin** to view the CBC video segments that accompany the following cases.

CBC VIDEO CASE II-1

God in the Workplace

Bruce Smith used to play in the CFL. Now he is a "chaplain on call" who counsels managers in the heart of Toronto's financial district (for free). He is decidedly Christian in his views, and presents Jesus as an alternative for people who are having problems. His approach is to present this as an option. He thinks there is as much of a hunger for religion in Canada as there is in the United States, since he talks to business people every day who want to talk about Christian values. But, says Smith, Canadians are not as open about religion as Americans are. Smith feels that Canadian companies need certain basic values and convictions to function well. Smith is one of only a few people doing corporate chaplaincy in Canada, and he wants to find more chaplains so he can expand his service.

In Canada, Jesus hasn't made it into business plans like He has in the United States, but some Canadian companies are making money by satisfying the demand for religiously-themed movies. Cloud 10 is a movie making company started by Peter and Paul Lalonde from North Bay, Ontario. They have married entertainment with the Christian end of the world by making Christian films about the apocalypse (using B-actors from Hollywood). These films have been seen by millions of moviegoers, and have made Cloud 10 the most profitable independent film studio in North America.

Christian-themed entertainment is not limited to movies. Toronto-based Harlequin, which is well-known for its racy novels, now has a Steeple Hill Division which churns out Christian romance novels. Its target market is the 30 million women in the United States who want romance novels that contain no swearing, drinking, or sex. The division has achieved double digit growth in its line of Christian books; the biggest hit is the Whitney Chronicles. Editors at Harlequin say the Christian market is easy to target. More generally, Christian entrepreneurs are finding that these are boom times, and that barriers between business, religion, and the workplace are disappearing.

In the United States, religion has always been a big part of life and now it's becoming a big part of business. More Americans than ever call themselves Christians, and more and more of them are taking their faith into the workplace. This means that there is a growing demand for products related to Jesus, and in activities that connect Christianity with commerce. Consider the case of Liz Golden, the owner of a struggling embroidery business. It's not every day that you pray with your banker, but that's what Liz did when she talked to Chuck Ripka about getting a loan from the Riverview Community Bank in Otsego, Minnesota. Riverview is the first Christian bank in the United States, and Ripka says it is doing very well. He says that God promised him that if he would do the things God called him to do, that God would take care of the bottom line. Once a week during lunch Chuck networks with other Christian businesspeople. They consider Jesus their business partner, and they pray for the courage to spread their brand of faith to customers, co-workers, and employees. Ripka realizes that his bank's openly Christian focus probably turns some people off, but he points out that neither the employees nor the customers have to be Christians. But the staff who are Christians pray for the business on a daily basis.

In Dallas, Texas, corporate chaplain Gil Strickland wants to convince others that chaplains in the workplace will boost the bottom line. He served as a U.S. Army chaplain for 37 years, taking care of the emotional needs of soldiers. He says you have to reach out and love and encourage people in the Army, and he thought it would be a good idea to do that in corporate America as well. His company, Marketplace Chaplains, hires out Christian chaplains to business firms. He has 1600 people on the payroll. Marketplace Chaplains brings in $7 million a year in revenue, but Strickland says the business is not about the money; the real satisfaction comes from helping people.

It is left up to employees if they want to avail themselves of the services provided by the chaplain. The chaplains offer more than just a pat on the back. For example, when a long-distance driver is on the road, someone will check that his wife is O.K. Or, if one of his children gets sick, a chaplain from the company will visit at the hospital. At one electrical wire company where Marketplace Chaplains operates, turnover has been reduced by 40 percent since the arrival of the chaplain.

Questions for Discussion

1. What is motivation? What are the factors that motivate people at work? Can a Christian emphasis in the workplace motivate those who are interested?
2. How is job satisfaction different from morale? What is the likely effect on job satisfaction of introducing religion and/or spirituality in the workplace for those who are interested?
3. What are the advantages and disadvantages of bringing religion and spirituality into the workplace?

Source: "The Business of God: Let There Be Profits," *Venture*, March 27, 2005.

CBC VIDEO CASE II-2

The Big Switcheroo

Vancouver City Savings Credit Union (Van City for short) is Canada's biggest credit union. With 41 branches, 2000 employees, and $9 billion in assets, it is hard to miss the Van City signs around Vancouver.

Dave Mowat is the CEO of the company, and he is a powerful man. Lisa Paille, who is a front-line worker in a suburban Van City branch, doesn't have any of Mowat's responsibilities, and she isn't so powerful. A company-wide contest picks Lisa Paille as the person who will switch jobs with Mowat. Here is the story of what happened when these two people switched jobs. Who will get the bigger reality check?

On her first day as CEO, Paille finds that her day is booked solid. Her first duty is conducting the head office manager's meeting. As Lisa conducts the meeting, she really feels that she has been put on the spot. She isn't doing well, and she keeps nervously looking at her notes as she speaks. Afterwards, her vice-presidents line up to meet with her, but by the time the finance vice-president shows up, she is running 30 minutes behind schedule. She is already looking weary and it's not even 1 p.m. Lisa doesn't have time to contact her family during the day, and when she arrives home, it is past her kids' bedtime.

Mowat isn't having an easy time of it on his first day, either. His first job is as a teller. He discovers that he is breaking dress rules by not wearing a tie (this violates the dress code which states that business attire is required). He is also experiencing front-line stress at the branch. The people who are waiting in line are impatient, and Mowat gets flustered trying to deal with them. He doesn't work fast enough. He doesn't get to go home until his money balances. He comes close (just 10 cents out). His day ends early, and he gets to eat dinner with his family while it is still daylight. That doesn't often happen when he stays late at work to attend to CEO duties.

On day 2, it's more of the same for Paille. It is difficult keeping the top executives in line, running meetings, and doing everything on time, but she is doing a little better today, and she actually finishes one meeting ahead of schedule. But later she gets behind schedule again. Lunch is sent in to save time, but Paille doesn't feel comfortable eating in front of the other managers. As she deals with her work backlog, she is learning that there is never an early end to a CEOs day. She heads to a company hockey game to boost morale, and talks on the phone during the game trying to reduce her work backlog.

On his second day, Mowat is answering the phones at the call centre. He has to act quickly and move on to other calls. But he spends about twice as long on each call as he is supposed to spend. He also discovers the stress of having his supervisor monitor his calls. Later in the day, he hustles business at Save-On Foods, a partner of Van City. His job is to sign up new customers.

On day 3, Lisa arrives at 8:45 a.m. and her day is again filled with appearances, ending with another speech to a group of managers. She also gladhands at the Vancouver Board of Trade (the Van City CEO is a member of the board). She is beginning to understand the importance of networking. She also speaks at an employee's anniversary party and presents him with a gift.

On his third day, Mowat starts at 6 a.m. in the Van City mail room. He delivers mail to all the offices, including the CEOs (where he observes that Paille is not yet in her office). He also does some information technology work by changing backup tapes. He finds that the process is complicated, and comments on how important the person doing that work is. Mowat does maintenance duties in the afternoon.

At the end of the three days, Lisa leaves the executive suite and returns to the front lines. Mowat puts down his tools and resumes his CEO duties. They both report on what they learned from their job switch. Paille says she enjoyed the experience, but she is glad it is over because she had to wear a lot of different hats. She has a new appreciation for how hectic and complex the work of a top manager is. Mowat feels that he did pretty well during the switch, but his productivity was judged as too low. He says he is impressed at how well the company's systems work.

Questions for Discussion

1. Briefly describe the four functions of management. Give several examples from the case of how the four functions of management are evident at Van City. Using the four functions of management as a basis, show how the jobs of Lisa Paille and Dave Mowat are different.
2. How are technical skills, human relations skills, and conceptual skills different? Explain the relative importance of each of these skills for a CEO like Dave Mowat and for a front-line worker like Lisa Paille. Give examples from the case to demonstrate the use of these skills.
3. Briefly summarize what Henry Mintzberg discovered about the work of CEOs. Was Lisa Paille's experience as the CEO consistent with what Mintzberg found? Give examples of how Lisa Paille performed some of the roles that Mintzberg identified.
4. What kind of insights do you think Mowat and Paille gained as a result of their switching jobs? To what extent will these insights make each of them more effective in their jobs? Defend your answer.

Source: "The Big Switcheroo," *Venture*, January 16, 2005.

PART THREE

Managing Operations and Information

To be effective, Canadian business firms must produce high-quality goods and services. They must also have good information on which to base business decisions. The opening cases in the chapters in this section show how business firms do this.

Part Three, Managing Operations and Information, provides an overview of four aspects of business that are important to a firm's survival: the efficient production of goods and services, increasing productivity and quality, managing information systems, and understanding principles of accounting.

- We begin in **Chapter 11, Producing Goods and Services**, by examining how firms manage the production of goods and services, and how they control both the cost and the quality of their output.
- Then, in **Chapter 12, Increasing Productivity and Quality**, we consider the various approaches companies take to improve the productivity and the quality of their output, and thus their competitive position.
- Next, in **Chapter 13, Managing Information Systems and Communication Technology**, we describe the concept of management information systems, and how modern electronic technologies have revolutionized the work of managers. Included in this discussion is an analysis of the key elements of the information system, the concept of databases and application programs, and the importance of telecommunications and networks in the effective management of information.
- Finally, in **Chapter 14, Understanding Accounting Issues**, we examine the role of accountants in gathering, assembling, and presenting financial information about a firm. We also look at the tools accountants use and the statements they prepare to report a firm's financial standing.

CHAPTER 11

Producing Goods and Services

After reading this chapter, you should be able to:

1 Explain the meaning of the terms *production* and *operations*.

2 Describe the four kinds of *utility* provided by production and explain the two classifications of *operations processes*.

3 Identify the characteristics that distinguish *service operations* from *goods production* and explain the main differences in the *service focus*.

4 Describe the factors involved in *operations planning*.

5 Explain some factors in *operations scheduling* and describe some activities involved in *operations control*, including *materials management* and the use of certain *operations control tools*.

Toyota: The New Number 1?

If you ask people what company comes to mind when they think of automobile manufacturing on a grand scale, most would say General Motors (GM). And, in fact, for the last 60 years, GM has been the world's largest automobile manufacturer. But a momentous event is going to occur in the automobile business in the next year or two: Toyota Motor Corp. is going to surpass GM as the world's large maker of automobiles. In 2005, Toyota was the No. 2 automaker in the world and closing fast on GM. Its market share rose in every region where it competed, and it produced 11 percent more vehicles in 2006 than it did in 2005. If Toyota's growth strategy stays on track, it will pass GM before too long. As part of its plan, Toyota announced that it would build its seventh manufacturing plant in Canada near Woodstock, Ontario. The new plant—which will produce the RAV4 sport utility vehicle—will mean $600 million to the economy of Ontario. By the end of 2006, Toyota had fifteen North American manufacturing plants which made two million vehicles each year and employed 38 000 people.

GM has fallen on hard times as it tries to cope with declining consumer interest in its products and sky-high benefits costs for its unionized workers. In sharp contrast, Toyota's fortunes continue to soar, partly because consumer interest in its products is high, and partly because it has a non-unionized workforce where wages are lower than those paid by GM and Ford. But there is another (and perhaps more important) reason for Toyota's success. It is called "the Toyota way," and it includes an emphasis on quality, on continuous improvement, and on regularly questioning the company's own assumptions about the markets it serves. Toyota's emphasis on *kaizen*, or continuous improvement, is evident in the 2005 Sienna minivan. Before building the Sienna, Toyota's chief engineer drove 80 000 kilometres around North America to learn what worked in a minivan and what customers wanted. The result was a larger, more powerful minivan than the Sienna's predecessors. Toyota's experience with the Sienna demonstrates its ability to learn what customers want.

Toyota's competitors have known for years that Toyota has something special in its production system. That's why executives from Ford, Chrysler, and GM take plant tours of Toyota manufacturing facilities: They are trying to figure out how Toyota is able to make cars so efficiently. Toyota doesn't charge its competitors for these tours, and it doesn't keep anything secret from them. This seems odd; would Coke let Pepsi see its secret formula? But Toyota doesn't seem worried that competitors will see its operations up close, because it knows that those competitors have been trying (unsuccessfully) for years to match its productivity.

The Toyota Production System (TPS) is a total system of managing and thinking about people, technology, and production processes. Mercedes-Benz may have sophisticated engineering, Honda great engine technology, and Chrysler great styling, but Toyota has the most efficient production system. The Big 3 domestic automobile manufacturers have all adopted parts of TPS, but none of them has been able to match the efficiency produced by the total TPS. The system looks simple enough: maximize flow, eliminate waste, and respect people. But the implementation requires huge amounts of effort and insight.

TPS is not restricted to just the production line. It also works in important areas like new product development. With TPS, Toyota can develop a new car model in 18 months, a much shorter time than is typical in the industry.

A key aspect of TPS is consistent, smooth production. In many manufacturing plants, workers work hard during the first few hours on the job to meet their quota, and then relax later in the day. This leads to uneven production. At Toyota, overproduction at any time is considered bad practice. Workflows are designed to move from process to process with no ups or downs. Another example: In the typical automobile plant, visitors will see stacks of half-finished parts and idle workers standing along assembly lines that are temporarily shut down for one reason or another. But at Toyota plants, workers are constantly in motion and almost look like dancers in a choreographed production.

TPS requires that experienced managers work with a highly motivated and well-trained workforce. TPS also involves dependence on outside suppliers who must run their own operations completely in sync with Toyota's. Because Toyota produces just 30 percent of the parts it needs, suppliers are an integral part of Toyota's production system and often have an ownership stake in the company. If a supplier has problems, Toyota helps it to improve. Two Toyota engineers once spent seven months at a supplier improving its operations so it could meet Toyota's standards. All this took place while the supplier was under contract to a Toyota competitor.

Toyota is famous for pioneering the just-in-time parts delivery system. Suppliers deliver parts up to eight times daily to Toyota factories, allowing the company to maintain inventory levels that are only one-quarter those at GM. Toyota's suppliers are also physically much closer to Toyota production plants than GM's suppliers are to its plants—an average of 100 kilometres for Toyota versus 700 kilometres for GM. In recent years, Toyota has refined the basic JIT system even further. In 2004, Toyota engineers introduced a new assembly process that involves delivering parts to the assembly line as the vehicle is being made. With this innovation, vehicle assembly is simplified and the need for parts shelves is eliminated.

One might think that with all this good news, Toyota has no problems. But in the automobile business every company has problems with its global competitors. Like other manufacturers, Toyota is keenly interested in the rapidly growing Chinese market. But since Toyota is a Japanese company, and since there is still resentment toward Japan because of its actions against China in the Second World War, Toyota may have a tougher time in the Chinese market than its competitors. And so far, GM is doing much better in China than Toyota is. Toyota will also have to compete with lower-cost Chinese competitors and an increasingly powerful Hyundai Motor Co. But to continue to grow Toyota must do well in foreign markets because it already holds such a large share of the car market in Japan.

Another problem is that Toyota has not been able to completely export TPS to its manufacturing facilities outside Japan. Its North American plants, for example, still require substantially more time to build a car than its Japanese plants do. These difficulties have arisen because of a lack of middle managers with TPS experience, and because so much time has to be spent bringing suppliers up to Toyota's standards. ◆

Everywhere you go today, you encounter business activities that provide goods and services to their customers. You wake up in the morning, for example, to the sound of your favourite radio station. You stop at the corner newsstand for a newspaper on your way to the bus stop, where you catch the bus to work or school. Your instructors, the bus driver, the clerk at the 7-Eleven store, and the morning radio announcer are all examples of people who work in **service operations**. They provide you with tangible and intangible service products, such as entertainment, transportation, education, and food preparation. Firms that make tangible products—radios, newspapers, buses, and textbooks—are engaged in **goods production**.

service operations Production activities that yield tangible and intangible service products.

goods production Production activities that yield tangible products.

WHAT DOES "PRODUCTION" MEAN TODAY?

1 Explain the meaning of the terms *production* and *operations*.

Although the term *production* has historically referred to the making of physical goods like automobiles, toothpaste, televisions, toys, and so forth, the concept as we now use it also means services. Many of the things that we need or want, from health care to fast food, are produced by service operations. As a rule, service-sector managers focus less on equipment and technology than on the human element in operations. Why? Because success or failure may depend on provider-customer contact. Employees who deal directly with customers affect customer feelings about the service, and as we will see, a key difference between production and service operations is the customer's involvement in the latter.

Today, however, customers are increasingly involved in all kinds of production because electronic communications are key components in winning and keeping customers in a huge range of competitive industries. Orders are placed faster, schedules are accelerated, and delivery times are shrinking. Internet buyers can be linked to the production floor itself, where their orders for products ranging from cellphones to automobiles are launched and filled in real time. B2B customers also expect real-time response and online delivery.

This new plant just outside of Bangalore, India, supplies transmission systems to Toyota plants all over the world. Making auto parts is a rapidly growing business in India, and there are nearly 400 parts makers in the Bangalore area alone. Exports in the industry have skyrocketed by 38 percent in one year, to $800 million. That's only about one-tenth of what the country's software industry brings in, but the auto parts industry surge has resulted from the same factors: low labour costs and a very large, technically competent workforce.

The Growth of Global Operations

Many countries have recently joined the global competition that has reshaped production into a faster-paced, more complex business activity. Although the factory remains the centrepiece for manufacturing, it bears little resemblance to its counterpart of a decade ago. The smoke, grease, and danger have been replaced in many companies by glistening high-tech machines, computers, and "clean rooms" that are contaminant-free and climate controlled.

Production operations have also become much more environmentally friendly. Interface Inc., a Belleville, Ontario, carpet manufacturer, used to produce 500 000 litres of dirty waste water every month. They solved that problem by eliminating a printing process that used a lot of water—and saved $15 000 a month as an added benefit. They also reduced carpet remnant waste from 474 tonnes per year to 39 tonnes by making some design changes in the product. Several other innovations, such as using smaller motors, reduced the company's utility bills by 70 percent. The plant became so efficient that it now exports 60 percent of its production to the U.S.[1]

Instead of needing to maintain continuous mass production, firms today face constant change. New technologies allow machines to run more cleanly, quickly, and safely, and to operate on a global scale. In a modern factory with online manufacturing, machines can log on to the internet, adjust their own settings, and make minor decisions without human help. They can communicate with other machines in the company (via an intranet) and with other companies' machines (via the internet). So-called "smart" equipment stores performance data that become available at desktops around the world, where designers can click on machine data, simulate machine action, and evaluate performance before machines themselves ever swing into action. With the internet, producers of both services and goods are integrating their production activities with those of far-off suppliers and customers.

CREATING VALUE THROUGH PRODUCTION

2 Describe the four kinds of *utility* provided by production and explain the two classifications of *operations processes*.

To understand the production processes of a firm, you need to understand the importance of products—both goods and services. Products provide businesses with both economic results (profits, wages, goods purchased from other companies) and non-economic results (new technology, innovations,

utility The power of a product to satisfy a human want; something of value.

time utility That quality of a product satisfying a human want because of the time at which it is made available.

place utility That quality of a product satisfying a human want because of where it is made available.

ownership (possession) utility That quality of a product satisfying a human want during its consumption or use.

form utility That quality of a product satisfying a human want because of its form; requires raw materials to be transformed into a finished product.

operations (production) management The systematic direction and control of the processes that transform resources into finished goods.

production managers Managers responsible for ensuring that operations processes create value and provide benefits.

pollution). And they provide consumers with what economists call **utility**—the power of a product to satisfy a human want.

Four basic kinds of utility would not be possible without production. By making a product available at a time when consumers want it, production creates **time utility**, as when a company turns out ornaments in time for Christmas. By making a product available in a place convenient for consumers, production creates **place utility**, as when a local department store creates a "Trim-A-Tree" section. By making a product that consumers can take pleasure in owning, production creates **ownership (possession) utility**, as when you take a box of ornaments home and decorate your tree. But above all, production makes products available in the first place. By turning raw materials into finished goods, production creates **form utility**, as when an ornament maker combines glass, plastic, and other materials to create tree decorations.

Because the term *production* has historically been associated with manufacturing, it has been replaced in recent years by *operations*, a term that reflects both services and goods production. **Operations** (or **production**) **management** is the systematic direction and control of the processes that transform resources into finished goods and services. Thus production managers are ultimately responsible for creating utility for customers.

As Figure 11.1 shows, **production managers** must bring raw materials, equipment, and labour together under a production plan that effectively uses all the resources available in the production facility. As demand for a good increases, they must schedule and control work to produce the amount required. Meanwhile, they must control costs, quality levels, inventory, and plant and equipment.

Not all production managers work in factories. Farmers are also production managers. They create form utility by converting soil, seeds, sweat, gas, and other inputs into beef cattle, tobacco, heat, milk, cash, and other outputs. As production managers, farmers have the option of employing many workers to plant and harvest their crops. Or they may decide to use automated machinery or some combination of workers and machinery. These decisions affect farmers' costs, the buildings and equipment they own, and the quality and quantity of goods they produce. Table 11.1 shows examples of different types of production management.

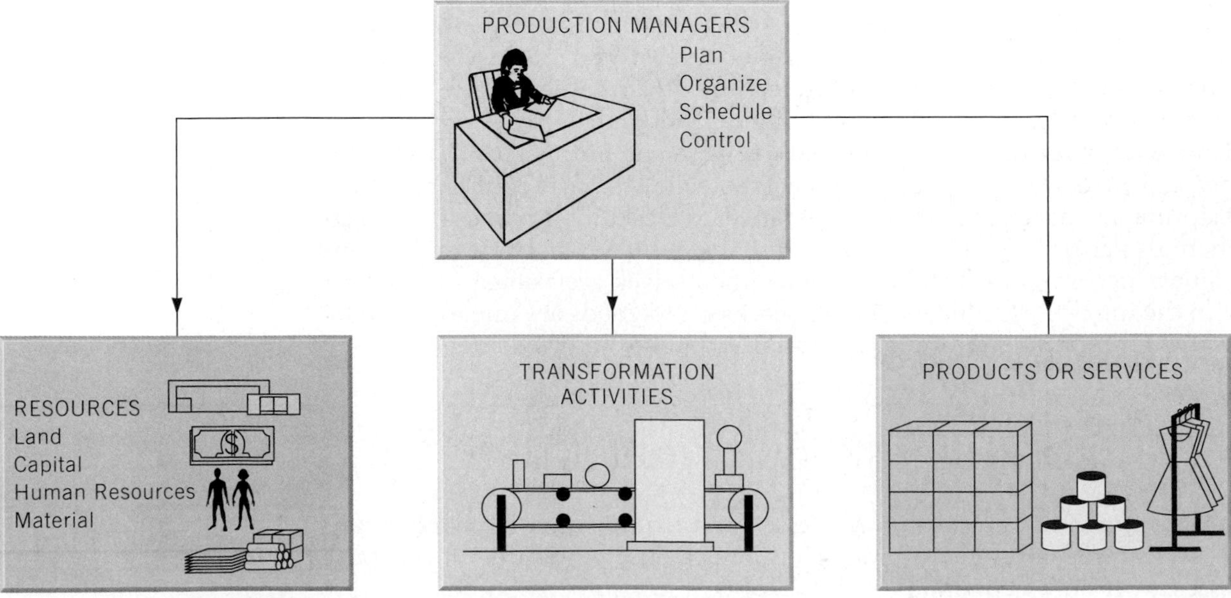

Figure 11.1 The transformation system.

Table 11.1 Inputs, Transformation, and Outputs in Production Systems

Production System	Inputs	Transformation	Outputs
Farm	Land, tractors and equipment, labour, buildings, fertilizer, farmer's management skills	Cultivation of plants and livestock	Food products, profit for owner, jobs for farmer's family
Jewellery store	Fashion-conscious customers, merchandise, sales clerks, showroom, fixtures, and equipment	Exchange of merchandise between buyer and seller	Satisfied jewellery customers
Tire producer	Rubber and chemical compounds, blending equipment, tire moulds, factory, and human skills	Chemical reactions of raw materials	Tires for autos, airplanes, trucks, trailers, and other vehicles
Furniture manufacturer	Woodworking equipment fabrics, wood, nails and screws, factory, woodworking skills	Fabrication and assembly of materials	Furniture for homes and offices

Operations Processes

An **operations process** is a set of methods and technologies used in the production of a good or a service. We classify various types of production according to differences in their operations processes. In other words, we can describe goods according to the kind of *transformation technology* they require, or according to whether their operations process combines resources or breaks them into component parts. We can describe services according to the extent of *customer contact* required.

operations process A set of methods and technologies used in the production of a good or a service.

Goods-Producing Processes

All goods-manufacturing processes can be classified in two different ways: by the *type of transformation technology* that transforms raw materials into finished goods and by the *analytic or synthetic nature of the transformation process*.

Types of Transformation Technology. Manufacturers use the following types of transformation processes to turn raw materials into finished goods:

- In *chemical processes*, raw materials are chemically altered. Such techniques are common in the aluminum, steel, fertilizer, petroleum, and paint industries.
- *Fabrication processes* mechanically alter the basic shape or form of a product. Fabrication occurs in the metal forming, woodworking, and textile industries.
- *Assembly processes* put together various components. These techniques are common in the electronics, appliance, and automotive industries.
- In *transport processes*, goods acquire place utility by being moved from one location to another. For example, trucks routinely move bicycles from manufacturing plants to consumers through warehouses and discount stores.
- *Clerical processes* transform information. Combining data on employee absences and machine breakdowns into a productivity report is a clerical process. So is compiling inventory reports at a retail outlet.

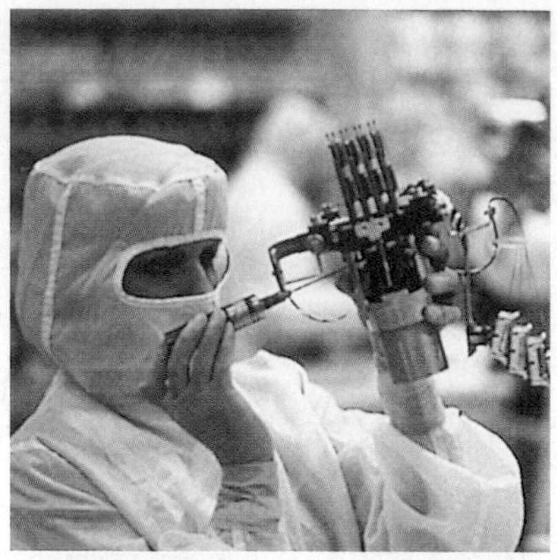

As these photos show, various industries use different transformation techniques: (from left, top) chemical, fabrication, and assembly; (bottom) transport and clerical.

analytic process Any production process in which resources are broken down.

synthetic process Any production process in which resources are combined.

Analytic Versus Synthetic Processes. A second way of classifying production processes is by the way in which resources are converted into finished goods. An **analytic process** breaks down the basic resources into components. For example, Alcan manufactures aluminum by extracting it from an ore called bauxite. The reverse approach, a **synthetic process**, combines a number of raw materials to produce a finished product such as fertilizer or paint.

Service-Producing Processes

One way of classifying services is to ask whether a given service can be provided without the customer being part of the production system. In answering this question, services are classified according to the extent of *customer contact*.

high-contact system A system in which the service cannot be provided without the customer being physically in the system (e.g., transit systems).

High-Contact Processes. Think for a moment about the service provided by your local public transit system. When you purchase transportation, you must board a bus or train, so public transit is a **high-contact system**. For this reason, transit managers must worry about the cleanliness of the trains and buses and the appearance of the stations. This is usually not the case in low-contact systems. Large industrial concerns that ship coal in freight trains, for example, are generally not concerned with the appearance inside those trains.

low-contact system A system in which the service can be provided without the customer being physically in the system (e.g., lawn care services).

Low-Contact Processes. Consider the cheque-processing operations at your bank. Workers sort the cheques that have been cashed that day and dispatch them to the banks on which they were drawn. This operation is a **low-contact system** because customers are not in contact with the bank while the service is performed. They receive the service—their funds are transferred to cover their cheques—without ever setting foot in the cheque-processing centre. Gas and electric utilities, auto repair shops, and lawn care services are also low-contact systems.

Differences Between Service and Manufacturing Operations

Identify the characteristics that distinguish *service operations* from *goods production* and explain the main differences in the *service focus.* 3

Service and manufacturing operations both transform raw materials into finished products. In service production, however, the raw materials, or inputs, are not glass or steel. Rather, they are people who choose among sellers because they have either unsatisfied needs or possessions for which they require some form of care or alteration. In service operations, then, "finished products" or "outputs" are people with needs met and possessions serviced. There are several key areas where service operations differ from production operations.

Focus on Performance

One very obvious difference exists between service and manufacturing operations: Whereas goods are produced, services are performed. Therefore, customer-oriented performance is a key factor in measuring the effectiveness of a service company. Wal-Mart, for example, sells to millions of people from California to China to Canada to Argentina. Its superstar status stems from an obsession with speedy product delivery that it measures not in days or even in hours, but in minutes and seconds. Wal-Mart's keen customer focus emphasizes avoiding unnecessary inventories, getting fast responses from suppliers, streamlining transaction processes, and knowing accurately the sales and restocking requirements for keeping the right merchandise moving from warehouses to store shelves. To implement this strategy, Wal-Mart has made technology—namely, its vaunted computer and telecommunications system—a core competency.[2]

In many ways, the focus of service operations is more complex than that of goods production. First, service operations feature a unique link between production and consumption—between process and outcome. Second, services are more intangible and more customized and less storable than most products. Finally, quality considerations must be defined, and managed, differently in the service sector than in manufacturing operations.

The hair styling service being provided to this customer illustrates the three key features of services operations: intangibility (customer pleasure or satisfaction with the service), customization (the service each person gets is customized for them), and unstorability (the service cannot be produced ahead of time).

Focus on Process and Outcome

As we saw earlier, manufacturing operations focus on the outcome of the production process. The products offered by most service operations, however, are actually combinations of goods and services. Services, therefore, must focus on both the transformation process and its outcome—both on making a pizza and on delivering it to the buyer. Service operations thus require different skills from manufacturing operations. For example, local gas company employees may need the interpersonal skills necessary to calm and reassure frightened customers who have reported gas leaks. The job, therefore, can mean more than just repairing defective pipes. Factory workers who install gas pipes while assembling mobile homes are far less likely to need such skills.

Focus on Service Characteristics

Service companies' transactions always reflect the fact that service products are characterized by three key qualities: *intangibility*, *customization*, and *unstorability*.

Intangibility. Often services cannot be touched, tasted, smelled, or seen. An important value, therefore, is the *intangible* value that the customer experiences in the form of pleasure, satisfaction, or a feeling of safety. For example,

ENTREPRENEURSHIP AND NEW VENTURES

The Silencers

In just eight years, Scott MacDonald, 30, and his father have seen their business grow from a two-person operation into a 29-person team of experts that attracts clients locally and from the United States. Noise Solutions Inc., an innovative company in the emerging sector of noise control, aims to facilitate a peaceful coexistence between industries and residents.

Founded in 1997, Noise Solutions helps large-scale industries suppress noise pollution created by their activities. The Calgary-based enterprise thrives by providing turnkey solutions, mainly for companies in the energy and mining sectors. Noise Solutions clients include notable organizations like United Space Alliance/NASA and Canadian Natural Resources. Responding to the needs of residents living near industrial sites and to help industries comply with Alberta Energy and Utilities Board guidelines, the company assesses industrial noise sources, then selects and installs appropriate sound-reducing mufflers and silencers.

"I'm particularly proud of the team that we've put together," says Scott. "They have the ability to meet any sort of challenges head-on whether it be of a technical nature, an accounting challenge, or solving a problem in the field."

"A huge part of our growth is attributable to the fact that we go beyond what our clients' needs are and improve the end result for them," explains Scott. "In fact, in the first five years, word of mouth from satisfied customers was responsible for our entire growth. They see and understand that we tend to go the extra mile for them."

Scott, a believer in continuous education, has created a work environment that focusses on learning. To attract customers from further afield, he taught himself website design and built the Noise Solutions website, which helped spark interest from industrial users in the United States. "We continuously try to keep ourselves up to date with new products, programs, and developmental concepts and we work to educate the industry," says Scott. "We try to look far enough into the future to anticipate challenges and ensure that nothing can stop us or get in our way."

when you hire an attorney to resolve a problem, you purchase not only the intangible quality of legal expertise but also the equally intangible reassurance that help is at hand. Although all services have some degree of intangibility, some provide tangible elements as well. Your attorney, for example, can draw up the living will that you want to keep in your safe deposit box.

Customization. When you visit a physician, you expect to be examined for your symptoms. Likewise, when you purchase insurance, have your pet groomed, or have your hair cut, you expect these services to be designed for your needs. Typically, therefore, services are *customized*.

Unstorability. Services such as rubbish collection, transportation, childcare, and house cleaning cannot be produced ahead of time and then stored. If a service is not used when it is available, it is usually wasted. Services, then, are typically characterized by a high degree of *unstorability*.

Focus on the Customer-Service Link

Because they transform customers or their possessions, service operations often acknowledge the customer as part of the operations process itself. For example, to purchase a haircut you must usually go to the barbershop or beauty salon. As physical participants in the operations process, service consumers have a unique ability to affect that process. In other words, as the customer, you expect the salon to be conveniently located, to be open for business at convenient times, to offer needed services at reasonable prices, and to extend prompt service. Accordingly, the manager adopts hours of operation, available services, and an appropriate number of employees to meet the requirements of the customer.

Ecommerce: The "Virtual Presence" of the Customer. The growth of ecommerce has introduced a "virtual presence," as opposed to a physical presence, of customers in the service system. Consumers interact electronically, in real time, with sellers, collecting information about product features, delivery availability, and after-sales service. They have around-the-clock access to information via automated call centres, and those who want human interaction can talk with live respondents or enter chat rooms. Many companies have invited "the virtual customer" into their service systems by building customer-communications relationships. The online travel agency Expedia.ca responds to your personalized profile with a welcome email letter, presents you with a tailor-made webpage the next time you sign on, offers chat rooms in which you can compare notes with other customers, and notifies you of upcoming special travel opportunities.

Internet technology also enables firms to build relationships with industrial customers. Electronic Data Systems (EDS), for example, helps client firms develop networks among their many desktop computers. In managing more than 700 000 desktops for clients throughout the world, EDS has created a special service called Renascence® that links clients, suppliers, and employees in a private 500 000-computer electronic marketplace. Some 2000 software products can be viewed, purchased, tracked, and delivered if you are a member of the network.[3]

Focus on Service Quality Considerations

Consumers use different criteria to judge services and goods. Service managers must understand that quality of work and quality of service are not necessarily synonymous. For example, although your car may have been flawlessly repaired, you might feel dissatisfied with the service if you were forced to pick it up a day later than promised.

OPERATIONS PLANNING

Describe the factors involved in *operations planning.* 4

Now that we've contrasted goods and services we can return to a more general consideration of production that encompasses both goods and services. Like all good managers, we start with planning. Managers from many departments contribute to the firm's decisions about operations management. As Figure 11.2 shows, however, no matter how many decision makers are involved, the process can be described as a series of logical steps. The success of any firm depends on the final result of this logical sequence of decisions.

The business plan and forecasts developed by top managers guide operations planning. The business plan outlines goals and objectives, including the specific goods and services that the firm will offer. Managers also develop a long-range production plan through **forecasts** of future demand for both new and existing products. Covering a two- to five-year period, the production plan specifies the number of plants or service facilities and the amount of labour, equipment, transportation, and storage that will be needed to meet demand. It also specifies how resources will be obtained.

forecast Estimates of future demand for both new and existing products.

In the following section, we survey the main elements of operations planning, discussing the planning activities that fall into one of five categories: *capacity, location, layout, quality,* and *methods planning.*

Capacity Planning

The amount of a product that a company can produce under normal working conditions is its **capacity**. The capacity of a goods or service firm depends on how many people it employs and the number and size of its facilities. Long-range planning must take into account both current and future capacity.

capacity The amount of a good that a firm can produce under normal working conditions.

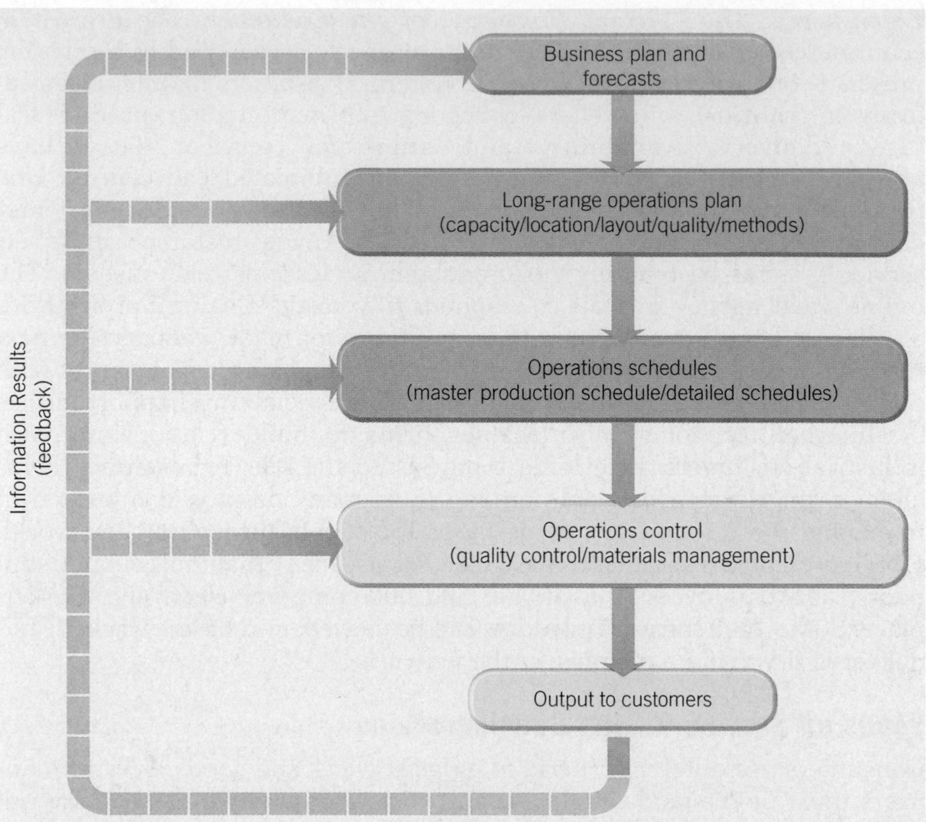

Figure 11.2 Operations planning and control.

Capacity Planning for Producing Goods

Capacity planning for goods means ensuring that a manufacturing firm's capacity slightly exceeds the normal demand for its product. To see why this policy is best, consider the alternatives. If capacity is too small to meet demand, the company must turn away customers—a situation that not only cuts into profits but also alienates both customers and salespeople. If capacity greatly exceeds demand, the firm is wasting money by maintaining a plant that is too large, by keeping excess machinery online, or by employing too many workers.

The stakes are high in the company's capacity decisions. While expanding fast enough to meet future demand and to protect market share from competitors, it must also weigh the increased costs of expanding. One reason that Intel Corp. enjoys more than 70 percent market share in the worldwide semiconductor business is the $11 billion it invested in capacity expansion in the 1990s. Will demand for semiconductors continue to grow even further? With so much invested thus far, Intel must decide whether the risks of additional capacity are worth the potential gains.[4]

Capacity Planning for Producing Services

In low-contact processes, maintaining inventory allows managers to set capacity at the level of *average demand*. For example, a catalogue sales warehouse may hire enough order fillers to handle 1000 orders per day. When daily orders exceed this average demand, some orders are placed in inventory—set aside in a "to-be-done" file—to be processed on a day when fewer than 1000 orders are received.

In high-contact processes, managers must plan capacity to meet *peak demand*. A supermarket, for instance, has far more cash registers than it needs on an average day; but on a Saturday morning or during the three days before Thanksgiving, all registers will be running at full speed.

Location Planning

Because the location of a factory, office, or store affects its production costs and flexibility, sound location planning is crucial. Depending on the site of its facility, a company may be capable of producing a low-cost product or may find itself at an extreme cost disadvantage relative to its competitors.

Location Planning for Producing Goods

In goods-producing operations, location decisions are influenced by proximity to raw materials and markets, availability of labour, energy and transportation costs, local and provincial regulations and taxes, and community living conditions. Slovakia, for example, is fast becoming the "Detroit" of Europe. With an existing Volkswagen plant producing 850 000 cars a year, two more giant carmakers—Peugeot Citroën (French) and Hyundai Motor Company (Korea)—will be opening new plants by 2006. Skilled workers, a good work ethic, and wages below those of the surrounding countries aren't the only reasons. Located in Central Europe, Slovakia has a good railroad system and nearby access to the Danube River, meaning economical transportation for incoming materials and outgoing cars once the plants are in operation.[5]

Some location decisions are now being simplified by the rise of industrial parks. Created by cities interested in attracting new industry, these planned sites come with necessary zoning, land, shipping facilities, utilities, and waste disposal outlets already in place. Such sites offer flexibility, often allowing firms to open new facilities before competitors can get started in the same area. The ready-made site also provides faster construction startups because it entails no lead time in preparing the chosen site.

Location Planning for Producing Services

In planning low-contact services, companies have some options. Services can be located near resource supplies, labour, customers, or transportation outlets. For example, the typical Wal-Mart distribution centre is located near the hundreds of Wal-Mart stores it supplies, not near the companies that supply the distribution centre. Distribution managers regard Wal-Mart stores as their customers. To better serve them, distribution centres are located so that truckloads of merchandise flow quickly to the stores.

On the other hand, high-contact services are more restricted. They must locate near the customers who are a part of the system. Accordingly, fast-food restaurants such as Taco Bell, McDonald's, and Burger King have begun moving into non-traditional locations with high traffic—dormitories, hospital cafeterias, museums, and shopping malls.

Layout Planning

Once a site has been selected, managers must decide on plant layout. Layout of machinery, equipment, and supplies determines whether a company can respond quickly and efficiently to customer requests for more and different products or finds itself unable to match competitors' production speed or convenience of service.

Layout Planning for Producing Goods

In facilities that produce goods, layout must be planned for three different types of space:

- *Productive facilities*: workstations and equipment for transforming raw materials, for example
- *Non-productive facilities*: storage and maintenance areas
- *Support facilities*: offices, restrooms, parking lots, cafeterias, and so forth

In this section, we focus on productive facilities. Alternatives for layout planning include *process*, *cellular*, and *product layouts*.

process layout A way of organizing production activities such that equipment and people are grouped together according to their function.

Process Layouts. In a **process layout**, which is well suited to job shops specializing in custom work, equipment and people are grouped according to function. In a woodworking shop, for example, machines cut the wood in an area devoted to sawing, sanding occurs in a dedicated area, and jobs that need painting are taken to a dust-free area where all the painting equipment is located. The various tasks are each performed in specialized locations.

The job shop produces many one-of-a-kind products, and each product, as you can see in Figure 11.3(a), requires different kinds of work. Whereas Product X needs only three production steps prior to packaging, Product Y needs four. When there is a large variety of products, there will be many flow paths through the shop and potentially much congestion. Machine shops, custom bakeries, and dry cleaning shops often feature process layouts.

cellular layout Used to produce goods when families of products can follow similar flow paths.

Cellular Layouts. Another workplace arrangement for some applications is called the **cellular layout**, which is used when a family of products (a group of similar products) follows a fixed flow path. A clothing manufacturer, for example, may establish a cell, or designated area, dedicated to making a family of pockets—for example, pockets for shirts, coats, blouses, trousers, and slacks. Although each type of pocket is unique in shape, size, and style, all go through the same production steps. Within the cell, therefore, various types of equipment (for cutting, trimming, and sewing) are arranged close together in the appropriate sequence. All pockets pass stage by stage through the cell from beginning to end, in a nearly continuous flow.

In plants that produce a variety of products, there may be one or two high-volume products that justify separate manufacturing cells. Figure 11.3(b) shows two production cells, one each for Products X and Y, while all other smaller-volume products are produced elsewhere in the plant.

Cellular layouts have several advantages. Because similar products require less machine adjustment, equipment set-up time in the cell is reduced, as compared with set-up times in process layouts. Because flow distances are usually shorter, there is less material handling and transit time. Finally, inventories of goods in progress are lower and paperwork is simpler because material flows are more orderly. A disadvantage of cells is the duplication of equipment. Note, for example, in Figure 11.3(b) that two saws are needed (one in each cell) as well as two paint areas, but only one of each is needed in the process layout (see Figure 11.3(a)).

product layout A way of organizing production activities such that equipment and people are set up to produce only one type of good.

assembly line A type of product layout in which a partially finished product moves through a plant on a conveyor belt or other equipment.

Product Layouts. In a **product layout**, equipment and people are set up to produce one type of product in a fixed sequence of steps and are arranged according to its production requirements. Product layouts are efficient for producing large volumes of product quickly and often use **assembly lines**. A partially finished product moves step by step through the plant on conveyor belts or other equipment, often in a straight line, until the product is completed. Figure 11.3(c), for example, shows the sequence

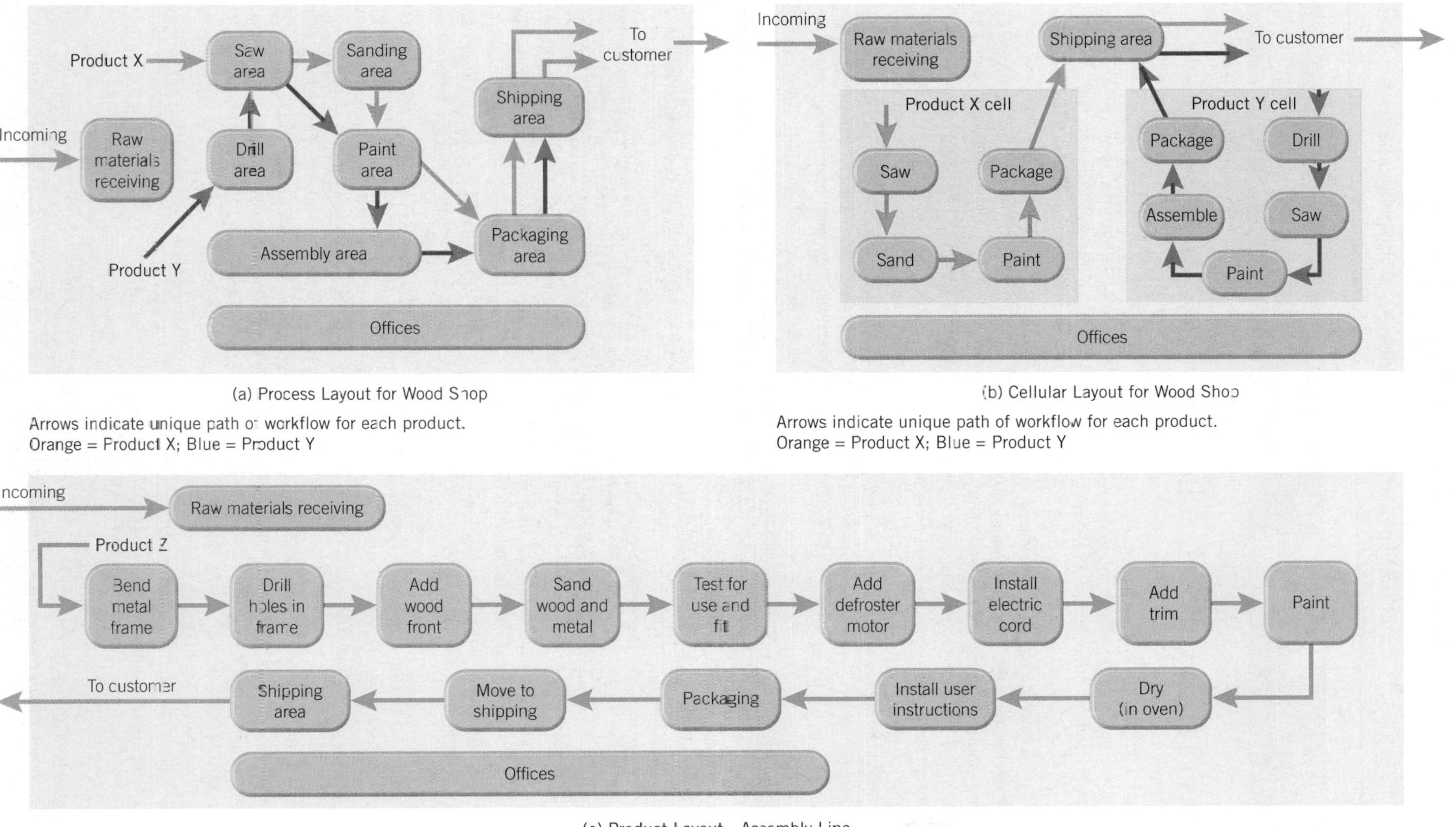

Figure 11.3 Layouts for producing goods.

of production steps performed identically, from start to finish, on all units of Product Z as they move through the line. Automobile, food processing, and television assembly plants use product layouts.

BUSINESS ACCOUNTABILITY

The Automated Factory: Just a Dream?

For many years, production managers have dreamed of the automated factory, a place where industrial robots and computer-assisted machines would tirelessly crank out products without any human involvement in the process. When industrial robots were developed in the 1970s, many people thought that they would quickly be adopted and would revolutionize the workplace. But progress was slowed because robots were high-priced. And the initial purchase price was just part of the problem. Exhaustive studies also had to be performed by company personnel to determine the precise task that could be accomplished by a robot. Workers had to be trained to operate and work with robots, and computer scientists were needed to program and reprogram the robots. It was also discovered that robots simply weren't good enough to keep making high-quality parts for hours on end without any human attention. So the dream of the automated factory faded for a while.

As the years passed, however, the dream slowly moved closer to reality. The increased reliability of industrial robots and computerized machines, and the intensification of international competition have motivated more and more companies to look at automation to increase their productivity. The use of industrial robots—often called "lights-out manufacturing" because there is no need to light the factory where the work is done—is now making steady progress in industry.

A 1999 report by a United Nations economic commission found that orders for industrial robots soared 60 percent over one year earlier. The increase points to a continuing drive toward automation of manufacturing facilities. The UN report says that we have seen only the first phase of industrial robots, and that they will increasingly be used in manufacturing and other industries. A sharp drop in the price of robots is one of the reasons for their increased adoption. The price of robots at the end of the 1990s was as much as 40 percent less than it was at the beginning of the decade. This drop in prices, coupled with increasing human labour costs, has induced more and more companies to consider the purchase of an industrial robot.

It is not difficult to find examples of the use of industrial robots:

- At Honda Canada's minivan plant in Alliston, Ontario, a giant robot with huge arms grasps an automobile chassis and welds the floor, roof, and sides in one motion.
- Canadian National Railways runs a fully computerized robotic paint shop for railroad cars in Winnipeg, Manitoba.
- At the Ford Motor plant in Oakville, Ontario, more and more robots are being used to facilitate flexible manufacturing; under the new flexible manufacturing system robots do the work in about one-third the space that was formerly required under the old production system.
- Submersible robots are replacing divers in offshore oil and gas operations, and they toil for hours in areas of nuclear power plants where humans once worked in very short relays to minimize their exposure to radiation.

While progress is evident, two factors are still inhibiting rapid movement toward automation. First, consumers demand higher-quality products. To meet these demands, machines must be increasingly sophisticated. Higher levels of investment are required to improve the capability of robots even further. But the uncertain state of the world economy in the first few years of the twenty-first century means that companies are reluctant to invest in robotic technology, particularly if it isn't certain what benefits they will gain. Companies are also concerned that workers would raise a fuss because it is obvious that the installation of robots means fewer jobs.

Second, human beings are superior to robots in a great many ways, especially in tasks requiring sensory input and adaptation. For example, the most sophisticated robots can recognize about 20 slightly different shapes as airplanes, but humans can identify thousands of slightly different shapes as planes. As one researcher notes, the human eye has about 100 million vision cells and four layers of neurons, all capable of doing about 10 billion calculations a second. In other words, it would take 100 000 supercomputers to imitate the visual calculations of a one-eyed human being.

What does the future hold? The use of robots will continue to increase in Canadian industry. But the truly automated factory still seems a long way off.

Product layouts are efficient because the work skill is built into the equipment; simplified work tasks can then use unskilled labour. However, product layouts tend to be inflexible because, traditionally, they have required heavy investment in specialized equipment that is hard to rearrange for new applications. In addition, workers are subject to boredom, and when someone is absent or overworked, those farther down the line cannot help out.

Other Developments in Layout Flexibility. In addition to variations on product layouts, there have been experiments in ways to make standard production lines more flexible. Some firms have adopted **U-shaped production lines**. Rather than stretching out in a straight line, machines are placed in a narrow U shape, with workers working from within the U. Because machines are close together, one worker in slow periods can complete all the tasks needed to make a product by moving from one side of the U to the other. In busier times, workers can be added until there is one per machine.

U-shaped production line Production layout in which machines are placed in a narrow U shape rather than a straight line.

Another development is the **flexible manufacturing system (FMS)**. Using computer-controlled instructions, one factory can make a wide variety of products. By integrating sales information with factory production activities, a manufacturer can adapt both mechanical and human resources to meet changes in customer demand. The goal of FMS is to help produce sufficient numbers of products that are in high demand, while avoiding overproduction of products that are not in as high demand.

flexible manufacturing system (FMS) A production system that allows a single factory to produce small batches of different goods on the same production line.

In the automobile business, for example, mass production used to mean turning out large numbers of identical cars to achieve high levels of efficiency. But with consumers now demanding so many different models of cars, manufacturers makers have adopted an FMS strategy. This means that they can build several different models of cars using the same basic "platform" (the underbody of the car). Nissan, Toyota, and Honda make the majority of their cars using FMS, and North American car makers are now rapidly adopting the strategy.[6] The Oakville, Ontario, Ford plant is the first flexible assembly plant in Canada. It had been making minivans on a single platform, but will now make several models on a single platform.[7]

Because many companies find large FMS operations to be too complex and prone to breakdowns, some have experimented with so-called **soft manufacturing**—reducing huge FMS operations to smaller, more manageable groups of machines. Automation is less likely to fail when relegated to jobs it does best, while human workers perform those assembly-line jobs that require dexterity and decision making. Both are supported by networks of computers programmed to assist in all sorts of tasks.

soft manufacturing Reducing huge FMS operations to smaller, more manageable groups of machines.

The very latest development is the disposable and movable factory. Because FMS is so expensive, some developing countries with lots of labour but little capital are buying up still-modern equipment from industrialized countries and then using it to produce new and untested products in their own country. For example, the Chinese want to buy the Campo Largo factory in Brazil that was built by BMW in 1998. They will dismantle the machinery and equipment and ship it to Chongqing, China, where it will be used to produce an all-Chinese car by 2008. This approach to manufacturing requires only one-third of the cost that is incurred in FMS systems that have been adopted in more industrialized countries.[8]

Layout Planning for Producing Services

Service firms use some of the same layouts as goods-producing firms. In a low-contact system, for instance, the facility should be arranged to enhance the production of the service. A mail-processing facility at UPS or Federal Express, therefore, looks very much like a product layout in a factory:

Machines and people are arranged in the order in which they are used in the mass processing of mail. In contrast, FedEx Kinko's copy centres use process layouts for different custom jobs: specific functions such as photocopying, computing, binding, photography, and laminating are performed in specialized areas of the store.

High-contact systems should be arranged to meet customer needs and expectations. For example, Piccadilly Cafeterias focusses both layout and services on the groups that constitute its primary market: families and elderly people. As you can see in Figure 11.4, families enter to find an array of highchairs and rolling baby beds that make it convenient to wheel children through the lineup. Servers willingly carry trays for elderly people and for those pushing strollers. Note, too, that customers must pass by the entire serving line before making selections. Not only does this layout help them make up their minds; it also tempts them to select more.

Quality Planning

In planning production systems and facilities, managers must keep in mind the firm's quality goals.[9] Thus any complete production plan includes systems for ensuring that goods are produced to meet the firm's quality standards. The issue of quality is discussed in detail in Chapter 12.

Methods Planning

In designing operations systems, managers must clearly identify every production step and the specific methods for performing them. They can then work to reduce waste, inefficiency, and poor performance by examining procedures on a step-by-step basis—an approach sometimes called *methods improvement*.

Methods Improvement in Goods

Improvement of production for goods begins when a manager documents the current method. A detailed description, often using a diagram called the *process flow chart*, is usually helpful for organizing and recording all information. The process flow chart identifies the sequence of production activities, movements of materials, and work performed at each stage as the product flows through production. The flow can then be analyzed to identify wasteful activities, sources of delay in production flows, and other inefficiencies. The final step is implementing improvements.

Mercury Marine, for example, used methods improvement to streamline the production of stern-drive units for powerboats. Examination of the

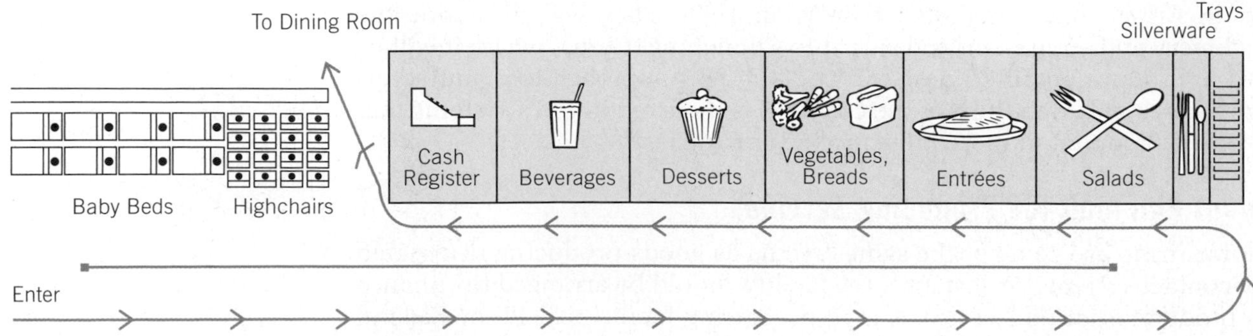

Figure 11.4 Layout of a typical Piccadilly cafeteria.

Employees at the Toyota manufacturing plant in Cambridge, Ontario, discuss a production problem. At this plant, employees are responsible not only for making automobiles, but also for monitoring quality control and for maintaining a clean work area.

process flow from raw materials to assembly (the final production step) revealed numerous instances of waste and inefficiency. Each product passed through 122 steps, travelled nearly 7 kilometres in the factory, and was handled by 106 people. Analysis revealed that only 27 steps actually added value to the product (for example, drilling, painting). Work methods were revised to eliminate non-productive activities. Mercury ultimately identified potential savings in labour, inventory, paperwork, and space requirements. Because production lead time was also reduced, customer orders were filled more quickly.

Methods Improvement in Services

In a low-contact process, managers can use methods improvements to speed services ranging from mowing lawns to filling prescriptions and

For its new XJ sedan, Jaguar wanted to use an aluminum unibody construction because it's lighter and more efficient than a steel-built body. For the same reasons, aluminum conveys a sense of high-tech design, and the company thought it was a better fit with Jaguar's elegant high-end image. But the usual method of constructing car bodies from steel—spot welding—weakens aluminum. So, at its factory in Castle Bromwich in the United Kingdom, engineers built an assembly line of 88 robots equipped with tools to drive more than 3000 rivets into each unit.

drawing up legal documents. Dell Computer, for example, sells its computers online and over the phone, mostly to medium and large companies. Methods analysis eliminates unnecessary steps so that orders can be processed quickly for production and delivery. Dell's emphasis on efficient selling by means of electronic technology speeds its response time to provide customers with a specific value—extremely fast delivery service.

service flow analysis An analysis that shows the process flows that are necessary to provide a service to customers; it allows managers to determine which processes are necessary.

Service Flow Analysis. By showing the flow of processes that make up a given service, **service flow analysis** helps managers decide whether all those processes are necessary. Moreover, because each process is a potential contributor to good or bad service, analysis also helps identify and isolate potential problems (known as fail points). In Figure 11.5, for instance, the manager of a photo-finishing shop has determined that the standard execution time for developing a roll of film is 48.5 minutes. She has also found that the "develop film" stage is the one most likely to delay service because it is the most complex. Thus, she has marked it as a potential fail point, as a reminder to give special attention to this stage of operations.

Designing to Control Employee Discretion in Services. Thus far, we have stressed the importance of the human factor in service activities—that is, the direct contact of server and customer. In some cases, however, the purpose of service design is to limit the range of activities of both employees and customers. By careful planning—and sometimes even by automating to control human discretion—managers can make services more customer-oriented because they can ensure product consistency.

McDonald's, for example, has done an outstanding job of designing the fast-food business as a mass-production system. By automating processes that would otherwise rely on judgment, McDonald's has been able to provide consistent service from a staff with little specialized training. At a central supply house, for instance, hamburger patties are automatically measured and packed. Specially designed scoops measure the same amount of french fries and other items into standard-sized containers. In addition, all drawers, shelves, and bins are designed to hold the ingredients for McDonald's standard product mixes only.

Design for Customer Contact in Services. In a high-contact service, the demands on system designs are somewhat different. Here, managers must develop procedures that clearly spell out the ways in which workers interact with customers. These procedures must cover such activities as exchanging information or money, delivering and receiving materials, and even making physical contact. The next time you visit your dentist's office,

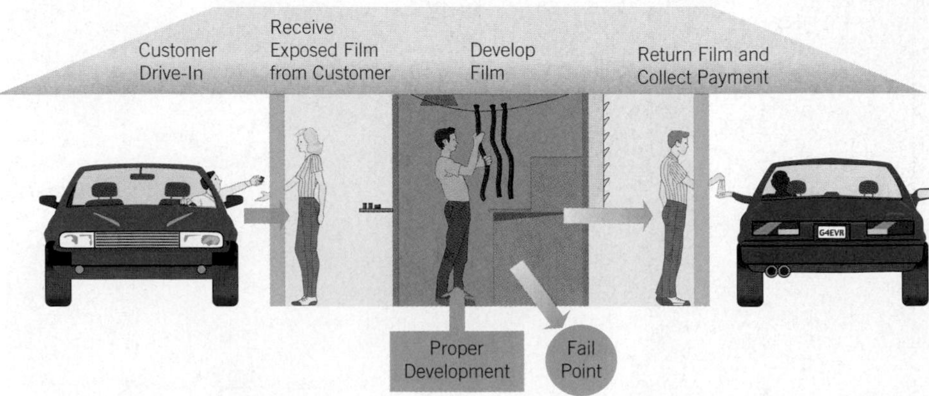

Figure 11.5 Service flow analysis.

for instance, notice the way dental hygienists scrub up and wear disposable gloves. They also scrub after patient contact, even if they intend to work on equipment or do paperwork, and they rescrub before working on the next patient. The high-contact system in a dental office consists of very strict procedures designed to avoid contact that can transmit disease.

OPERATIONS SCHEDULING

Once plans identify needed resources and how they will be used to reach a firm's goals, managers must develop timetables for acquiring resources for production. This aspect of operations is called *scheduling*.

5 Explain some factors in *operations scheduling* and describe some activities involved in *operations control*, including *materials management* and the use of certain *operations control tools*.

Scheduling Goods Operations

Scheduling of goods production occurs on different levels within the firm. First, a top-level or **master production schedule** shows which products will be produced, when production will occur, and what resources will be used during specified time periods.

master production schedule
Schedule showing which products will be produced, when production will take place, and what resources will be used.

Consider the case of Logan Aluminum Inc. Logan produces coils of aluminum that its main customers, Atlantic Richfield and Alcan Aluminum, use to produce aluminum cans. Logan's master schedule extends out to 60 weeks and shows how many coils will be made during each week. For various types of coils, the master schedule specifies how many of each will be produced. "We need this planning and scheduling system," says material manager Candy McKenzie, "to determine how much of what product we can produce each and every month."

This information, however, is not complete. For example, manufacturing personnel must also know the location of all coils on the plant floor and their various stages of production. Start and stop times must be assigned, and employees must be given scheduled work assignments. Short-term detailed schedules fill in these blanks on a daily basis. These schedules use incoming customer orders and information about current machine conditions to update the sizes and variety of coils to make each day. A classic dilemma in production scheduling is described in the Exercising Your Ethics box at the end of the chapter.

Scheduling Service Operations

Service scheduling may involve both work and workers. In a low-contact service, work scheduling may be based either on desired completion dates or on the time of order arrivals. For example, several cars may be scheduled for repairs at a local garage. Thus, if your car is not scheduled for work until 3:30 p.m., it may sit idle for several hours even if it was the first to be dropped off. In such businesses, reservations and appointments systems can help smooth ups and downs in demand.

In contrast, if a hospital emergency room is overloaded, patients cannot be asked to make appointments and come back later. As we have seen, in high-contact services, the customer is part of the system and must be accommodated. Thus, precise scheduling of services may not be possible in high-contact systems.

In scheduling workers, managers must also consider efficiency and costs. McDonald's, for example, guarantees workers that they will be scheduled for at least four hours at a time. To accomplish this goal without having workers be idle, McDonald's uses overlapping shifts—the ending hours for some employees overlap the beginning hours for others. The overlap provides maximum coverage during peak periods. McDonald's also trains employees to put off minor tasks, such as refilling napkin dispensers, until slow periods.

A 24-hour-a-day service operation, such as a hospital, can be an even greater scheduling challenge. Nurses, for example, must be on duty around the clock, seven days a week. Few nurses, however, want to work on weekends or during the early hours of the morning. Similarly, although enough nurses must be scheduled to meet emergencies, most hospitals are on tight budgets and cannot afford to have too many on-duty nurses. Thus, incentives are often used to entice nurses to work at times they might not otherwise choose. For example, would you choose to work 12 hours per day, 7 days a week? Probably not, but what if you were entitled to have every other week off in exchange for working such a schedule? A number of hospitals use just such a plan to attract nurses.

Tools for Scheduling

Special projects, such as plant renovations or relocations, often require close coordination and precise timing. In these cases, special tools, such as *Gantt* and *PERT charts*, facilitate scheduling.

Gantt chart Production schedule diagramming the steps in a project and specifying the time required for each.

Gantt Charts. A **Gantt chart** diagrams steps to be performed and specifies the time required to complete each step. The manager lists all activities needed to complete the work, estimates the time required for each step, and checks the progress of the project against the chart. If it's ahead of schedule, some workers may be shifted to another project. If it's behind schedule, workers may be added or completion delayed.[10]

Figure 11.6 shows a Gantt chart for the renovation of a college classroom. It shows progress to date and schedules for the remaining work. The current date is 5/11. Note that workers are about one-half week behind in removing old floor tiles and reworking tables and chairs.

PERT chart Production schedule specifying the sequence and critical path for performing the steps in a project.

PERT Charts. PERT—short for *Program Evaluation and Review Technique*—is useful for customized projects in which numerous activities must be coordinated. Like Gantt charts, **PERT charts** break down large projects

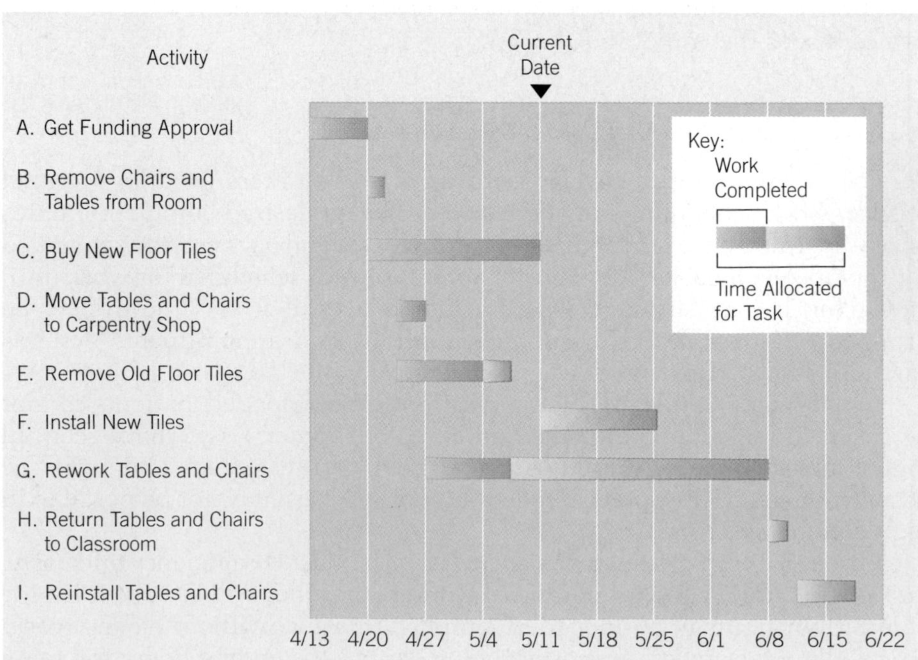

Figure 11.6 Gantt chart.

into steps and specify the time required to perform each one. Unlike Gantt charts, however, PERT not only shows the necessary sequence of activities but identifies the critical path for meeting project goals.[11]

Figure 11.7 shows a PERT chart for the classroom renovation that we visited above. The critical path consists of activities A, B, D, G, H, and I. It's critical because any delay in completing any activity will cause workers to miss the completion deadline (nine and one-half weeks after start-up). No activity along the critical path can be started until all preceding activities are done. Chairs and tables can't be returned to the classroom (H) until after they've been reworked (G) and after new tiles are installed (F). The chart also identifies activities that will cause delays unless special action is taken at the right time. By reassigning workers and equipment, managers can speed up potentially late activities and keep on schedule.

OPERATIONS CONTROL

Once long-range plans have been put into action and schedules have been drawn up, **operations control** requires production managers to monitor production performance by comparing results with detailed plans and schedules. If schedules or quality standards are not met, these managers must take corrective action. **Follow-up**—checking to ensure that production decisions are being implemented—is an essential and ongoing facet of operations control.

operations control Managers monitor production performance by comparing results with plans and schedules.

follow-up Checking to ensure that production decisions are being implemented.

Operations control features *materials management* and *production process control*. Both activities ensure that schedules are met and that production goals are fulfilled, both in quantity and in quality. In this section, we consider the nature of materials management and look at some important methods of process control.

Materials Management

Both goods-producing and service companies use materials. For many manufacturing firms, material costs account for 50 to 75 percent of total product costs. For goods whose production uses little labour, such as petroleum refining, this percentage is even higher. Thus, companies have good reasons to emphasize materials management.

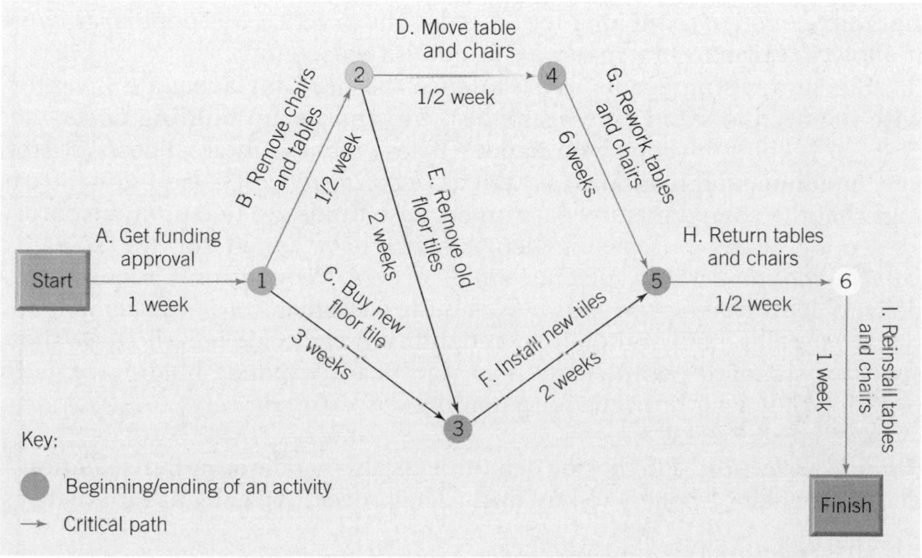

Figure 11.7 PERT chart.

materials management Planning, organizing, and controlling the flow of materials from purchase through distribution of finished goods.

standardization Using standard and uniform components in the production process.

The process of **materials management** not only controls but also plans and organizes the flow of materials (also called *logistics*). Even before production starts, materials management focusses on product design by emphasizing materials **standardization**—the use of standard and uniform components rather than new or different components. Law firms, for example, maintain standardized forms and data files for estate wills, living wills, trust agreements, and various contracts that can be adjusted easily to meet your individual needs. In manufacturing, Ford's engine plant in Romeo, Michigan, uses common parts for several different kinds of engines rather than unique parts for each. Once components were standardized, the total number of different parts was reduced by 25 percent. Standardization also simplifies paperwork, reduces storage requirements, and eliminates unnecessary material flows.

Once the product has been designed, materials managers purchase the necessary materials and monitor the production process through the distribution of finished goods. There are four major areas in materials management:

transportation The means of transporting resources to the company and finished goods to buyers.

warehousing The storage of both incoming materials for production and finished goods for physical distribution to customers.

inventory control In materials management, receiving, storing, handling, and counting of all raw materials, partly finished goods, and finished goods.

purchasing The acquisition of all the raw materials and services that a company needs to produce its products.

- **Transportation** includes the means of transporting resources to the company and finished goods to buyers.
- **Warehousing** is the storage of both incoming materials for production and finished goods for physical distribution to customers.
- **Inventory control** includes the receiving, storing, handling, and counting of all raw materials, partly finished goods, and finished goods. It ensures that enough materials inventories are available to meet production schedules.
- **Purchasing** is the acquisition of all the raw materials and services that a company needs to produce its products; most large firms have purchasing departments to buy proper materials in the amounts needed. Because purchasing is responsible for managing large transactions to acquire material resources, we will explain its activities in more detail.

Purchasing Processes

Purchasing is the acquisition of all the raw materials and services needed to make products and to conduct daily operations. Most companies have purchasing departments to buy, at reasonable prices and at the right time, proper materials in required amounts. For many years, purchasing departments practised *forward buying*. They routinely bought quantities of materials large enough to fill long-term needs. The practice was popular because it allowed a firm to buy materials at quantity discounts.

holding costs Costs of keeping extra supplies or inventory on hand.

But purchasing agents must balance the need for adequate inventory with the need to avoid excess supplies, which drive up **holding costs**—the costs of keeping inventory on hand.[12] These include the real costs of storage, handling, and insurance as well as *opportunity costs*—additional earnings that the company must pass up because funds are tied up in inventory.

lead times In purchasing control, the gap between the customer's placement of an order and the seller's shipment of merchandise.

Today, many purchasing departments have opted for the so-called *hand-to-mouth pattern*—placing small orders frequently. It requires fast delivery **lead times**—the gaps between the customer's order placement and the seller's shipment and delivery reliability. A radio maker who uses thousands of standard components may significantly reduce holding costs by ordering only what it needs for a coming day or week.

supplier selection Finding and determining suppliers to buy from.

Supplier Selection. Purchasing departments also handle **supplier selection**—deciding which suppliers to buy from. The process typically has four stages:

1. Investigating possible suppliers

2. Evaluating and isolating the best candidates
3. Negotiating terms of service with a final choice
4. Maintaining a positive buyer-seller relationship

Maintaining multiple supplier relationships is expensive. It takes time to survey, contact, and evaluate potential suppliers and build good relationships. In addition, fewer suppliers mean stronger, mutually dependent purchaser-supplier relationships. Today, therefore, most purchasers try to reduce their number of suppliers. In the first year of a supplier-reduction program, one 3M factory trimmed its supplier list from 2800 to 600—and then reduced it to 300 the following year. Dana Corp., one of the world's largest suppliers of automobile components, is dropping half of its 86 000 suppliers.[13]

Tools for Operations Process Control

Numerous tools assist managers in controlling operations. Chief among these are *worker training, just-in-time production systems, material requirements planning*, and *quality control*.

Worker Training

Customer satisfaction is closely linked to the employees who provide the service. Human relations skills are vital in anyone who has contact with the public. More and more human resource experts now realize that in businesses such as airlines, employment agencies, and hotels, employees without training in relationship skills can lose customers to better-prepared competitors. The Walt Disney Co. does an excellent job of remembering that no matter what their jobs, service employees are links to the public. For example, Disney World has a team of sweepers constantly at work picking up bits of trash as soon as they fall to the ground. When visitors have questions about directions or time, they often ask one of the sweepers. Because their responses affect visitors' overall impressions of Disney World, sweepers are trained to respond in appropriate ways. Their work is evaluated and rewarded based on strict performance appraisal standards.[14]

Just-in-Time Production Systems

To minimize manufacturing inventory costs, many companies use **just-in-time (JIT) production systems**. JIT brings together all the needed materials and parts at the precise moment they are required for each production stage, not before. All resources are continuously flowing, from their arrival as raw materials to subassembly, final completion, and shipment of finished products. JIT reduces to practically nothing the number of goods in process (that is, goods not yet finished) and saves money by replacing stop-and-go production with smooth movement. Once smooth movements become the norm, disruptions become more visible and thus are resolved more quickly. Finding and eliminating disruptions by continuous improvement of production is a major objective of JIT. Here are just two examples:

just-in-time (JIT) production system A method of inventory control in which materials are acquired and put into production just as they are needed.

- Mount Sinai Hospital uses JIT. Individual suppliers no longer go to Mount Sinai to deliver the items they have sold to the hospital. Rather, all suppliers deliver their products to Livingston Healthcare Services Inc. Livingston stores these items and fills Mount Sinai's order once each day; therefore, Mount Sinai no longer keeps any inventory. Once the goods are delivered, they are sent directly to the various departments in the hospital; the former centralized storeroom at the hospital no longer exists. In the first year using the new system, the hospital saved about $200 000.[15]

- At Toyota's Cambridge, Ontario, plant, delivery trucks constantly pull in to unload tires, batteries, steering wheels, seats, and many other items needed in the JIT production system.[16] And when General Motors of Canada's Oshawa assembly plant needs seats for cars, it sends the order electronically to a local supplier. The supplier has four hours to make the seats and ship them to the plant. The supplier loads the truck in reverse order so that the last seat loaded is the first one that will be used on the assembly line. The supplier knows, for example, that the plant will be making a certain number of one model and then a certain number of another model of car.[17]

JIT can cause some unexpected problems. As more and more companies adopt the philosophy that they will carry only minimal inventories, the ordering of supplies has become much more last-minute and frantic. By definition, this makes supply systems more volatile, and it has been one of the reasons why economic indicators like capital goods orders have been swinging so wildly. This, in turn, makes it hard to know what shape the overall economy is in. The more uncertainty there is about the economy, the less investor enthusiasm there is.[18]

Material Requirements Planning

material requirements planning (MRP) A method of inventory control in which a computerized bill of materials is used to estimate production needs so that resources are acquired and put into production only as needed.

bill of materials Production control tool that specifies the necessary ingredients of a product, the order in which they should be combined, and how many of each are needed to make one batch.

Like JIT, **material requirements planning (MRP)** seeks to deliver the right amount of materials at the right place and the right time for goods production. MRP uses a **bill of materials** that is basically a recipe for the finished product. It specifies the necessary ingredients (raw materials and components), the order in which they should be combined, and the quantity of each ingredient needed to make one batch of the product (say, 2000 finished telephones). The recipe is fed into a computer that controls inventory and schedules each stage of production. The result is fewer early arrivals, less frequent stock shortages, and lower storage costs. MRP is most popular among companies whose products require complicated assembly and fabrication activities, such as automobile manufacturers, appliance makers, and furniture companies.

manufacturing resource planning (MRP II) An advanced version of MRP that ties together all parts of the organization into the company's production activities.

Manufacturing resource planning (MRP II) is an advanced version of MRP that ties all parts of the organization into the company's production activities. For example, MRP inventory and production schedules are translated into cost requirements for the financial management department and into personnel requirements for the human resources department; information about available capacity for new orders goes to the marketing department.

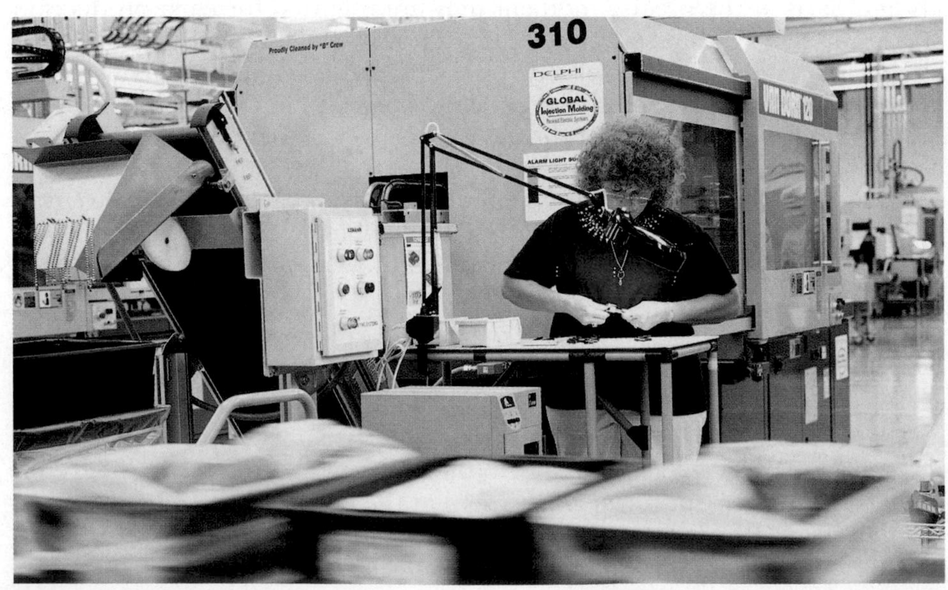

This Delphi Automotive Systems plant makes plastic housings for electrical connectors in cars and telecom equipment. Quality checkers are important members of the production team. Delphi's defect rate is only 14 parts per million. The company has spent millions of dollars on new production equipment, computers, software, and an emanufacturing network that is so efficient that the plant superintendent can work at home from his own PC.

Quality Control

Another operation control tool is **quality control**—the management of the production process to manufacture goods or supply services that meet specific quality standards. United Parcel Service Inc. (UPS), for instance, delivers 13 million packages every day, and all of them are promised to arrive on strict delivery schedules, mostly for business clients. Quality control is essential because delivery reliability—namely, avoiding late deliveries—is critical for customer satisfaction. UPS tracks the locations, time schedules, and on-time performance for some 500 aircraft and 150 000 vehicles as they carry packages through the delivery system. Our discussion of quality control continues in Chapter 12.

quality control The management of the production process so as to manufacture goods or supply services that meet specific quality standards.

Summary of Learning Objectives

1. **Explain the meaning of the terms *production* and *operations*.** *Service operations* provide intangible and tangible service products, such as entertainment, transportation, education, and food preparation. Firms that make tangible products—radios, newspapers, buses, and textbooks—are engaged in *goods production*. Because the term *production* is associated just with manufacturing, we now use *operations* to refer to both service and goods production. *Operations (or production) management* is the systematic direction and control of the processes that transform resources into finished services and goods that create value for and provide benefits to customers. In overseeing production, inventory, and quality control, *operations (or production) managers* are responsible for ensuring that operations processes create value and provide benefits.
2. **Describe the four kinds of *utility* provided by production and explain the two classifications of *operations processes*.** Products provide businesses with economic results: profits, wages, and goods purchased from other companies. They also provide consumers with utility—the ability of a product to satisfy a human want. There are four kinds of production-based utility: (1) *Time utility*: Production makes products available when consumers want them. (2) *Place utility*: Production makes products available where they are convenient for consumers. (3) *Ownership (or possession) utility*: Production makes products available for consumers to own and use. (4) *Form utility*: By turning raw materials into finished goods, production makes products available in the first place. An *operations process* is a set of methods and technologies used in the production of a good or a service. There are two types of operations processes for goods: (1) An *analytic process* breaks down resources into components. (2) A *synthetic process* combines raw materials to produce a finished product. Services are classified according to the *extent of customer contact*: (1) *High-contact processes* and (2) *low-contact processes*: To receive the service in a high-contact system, the customer must be a part of the system. In a low-contact system, customers are not in contact with the provider while the service is performed.
3. **Identify the characteristics that distinguish *service operations* from *goods production* and explain the main differences in the *service focus*.** Both service and manufacturing operations transform raw materials into finished products. In service production, the raw materials are people who have either unsatisfied needs or possessions needing some form of care or alteration. "Finished products" are, thus, people with needs met and possessions serviced. The focus of service operations differs from that of goods production in five ways: (1) *Focus on performance:* Because goods are produced and services performed, customer-oriented performance is crucial to a service company. (2) *Focus on process and outcome:* Because most service products are combinations of goods and services, services focus on both the transformation process and its outcome. (3) *Focus on service characteristics:* Service transactions reflect the three key qualities of service products: (i) *Intangibility:* Because services usually can't be touched, tasted, smelled, or seen, they provide intangible value experienced as pleasure, satisfaction, or a feeling of safety. (ii) *Customization:* Each customer expects a service to be designed (customized) for his or her specific needs. (iii) *Unstorability:* Because many services can't be produced ahead of time and then stored, they have a high degree of unstorability. (4) *Focus on the customer-service link:* Because service operations often acknowledge the customer as part of the process, consumers can directly affect that process. (5) *Focus on service quality considerations:* Service providers know that quality of work and quality of service are not necessarily the same thing (a properly repaired car is one thing, but getting it back when you need it is another).

4. **Describe the factors involved in *operations planning*.** The operations-management process is as a series of logical steps. Whereas the business plan outlines goals and objectives, managers also develop long-range production plans through *forecasts* of future demand for both new and existing products. Operations planning then focusses on five major categories: (1) *Capacity planning:* The amount of a product that a company can produce under normal working conditions is its capacity. The capacity of a goods or service firm depends on how many people it employs and the number and size of its facilities. (2) *Location planning:* In location planning, managers in goods-producing operations consider such factors as proximity to raw materials and markets; availability of labour; energy and transportation costs; regulations and taxes; and community living conditions. (3) *Layout planning:* Layout of machinery, equipment, and supplies determines how quickly a company can respond to customer demand for more and different products. In a *process layout*, which is well suited to job shops specializing in custom work, equipment and people are grouped according to function. *Cellular layouts* take groups of similar products through fixed flow paths. Equipment set-up is easier, flow distances are shorter, and material handling and transit time are reduced. In a *product layout*, equipment and people are set up to produce one type of product in a fixed sequence. (4) *Quality planning:* Products must meet standards of quality. Such standards may include reasonable price and consistent performance. (5) *Methods planning:* When managers reduce waste and inefficiency by identifying every production stage and the specific methods for performing it, they are practising *methods improvement*. A *process flow chart* can identify the sequence of production activities, movements of materials, and work performed at each stage. The flow can then be analyzed to identify wasteful activities, sources of delay, and other inefficiencies. *Service flow analysis* helps managers decide which processes in a service are necessary. It also helps isolate potential problems known as *fail points*.

5. **Explain some factors in *operations scheduling* and describe some activities involved in *operations control*, including *materials management* and the use of certain *operations control tools*.** A *master production schedule* shows which products will be produced, when production will take place, and what resources will be used during specified periods. For scheduling special projects, two tools—*Gantt charts* and *PERT charts*—assist managers in maintaining close coordination and timing. *Operations control* requires managers to monitor performance by comparing results with detailed plans and schedules. If schedules or quality standards are not met, managers take corrective action. *Follow-up*—checking to ensure that decisions are being implemented—is an essential facet of operations control. There are four areas in materials management: (1) *Transportation* includes the means of transporting resources to the company and finished goods to buyers. (2) Warehousing is the storage of incoming materials and finished goods for distribution to customers. (3) *Inventory control* includes the receiving, storing, handling, and counting of all raw materials, partly finished goods, and finished goods. It ensures that enough materials inventories are available to meet production schedules. (4) *Purchasing* is the acquisition of all the raw materials and services that a company needs for production.

KEY TERMS

QUESTIONS FOR ANALYSIS

1. What are the major differences between goods-production operations and service operations?
2. What are the major differences between high-contact and low-contact service systems?
3. What are the resources and finished products in the following services?
   - real estate firm
   - childcare facility
   - bank
   - city water and electric department
   - hotel
4. Analyze the location of a local firm where you do business (perhaps a restaurant, a supermarket, or a manufacturing firm). What problems do you see with this location? What recommendations would you make to management?
5. Pick three products (not services) that you regularly use. Then do some research to determine which of the basic production processes are used to produce these products (chemical, fabrication, assembly, transport, or clerical processes). To what extent are multiple processes used in the production of the product?
6. Develop a service flow analysis for some service that you use frequently, such as buying lunch at a cafeteria, having your hair cut, or riding a bus. Identify areas of potential quality or productivity failures in the process.
7. Pick three services (not products) that you regularly use. Explain what customization, unstorability, and intangibility mean for each of the services. How do these factors influence the way the service is delivered to customers?

APPLICATION EXERCISES

1. Find two examples of a synthetic production process and two examples of an analytic production process. Explain why you categorized them as you did.
2. Interview the manager of a local service business, such as a laundry or dry-cleaning shop. Identify the major decisions involved in planning its service operations. Prepare a class report suggesting areas for improvement.
3. Select a high-contact industry. Write an advertisement seeking workers for a company in this industry. Draw up a plan for motivating workers to produce high-quality services.

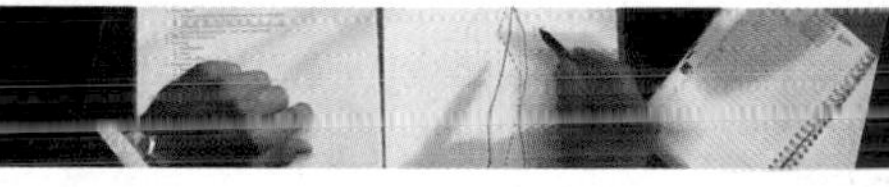

BUILDING YOUR BUSINESS SKILLS

The One-on-One Entrepreneur

Goal

To encourage students to apply the concept of customization to an entrepreneurial idea.

The Situation

You are an entrepreneur who wants to start your own service business. You are intrigued with the idea of creating some kind of customized one-on-one service that would appeal to baby boomers, who traditionally have been pampered, and working women, who have little time to get things done.

Assignment

Step 1

Get together with three or four other students to brainstorm ideas for services that would appeal to harried working people. Here are just a few:

- A concierge service in office buildings that would handle such personal and business services as arranging children's birthday parties and booking guest speakers for business luncheons.
- A personal-image consultation service aimed at helping clients improve appearance, etiquette, and presentation style.
- A mobile pet-care network through which vets and groomers make house calls.

Step 2

Choose one of these ideas or one that your team thinks of. Then write a memo explaining why you think your idea will succeed. Research may be necessary as you target any of the following:

- a specific demographic group or groups (Who are your customers, and why would they buy your service?)
- the features that make your service attractive to this group
- the social factors in your local community that would contribute to success

Follow-Up Questions

1. Why is the customization of and easy access to personal services so desirable in the twenty-first century?

▶▶▶

2. As services are personalized, do you think quality will become more or less important? Why?
3. Why does the trend toward personalized, one-on-one service present unique opportunities for entrepreneurs?
4. In a personal one-on-one business, how important are the human relations skills of those delivering the service? Can you make an argument that they are more important than the service itself?

EXERCISING YOUR ETHICS

Promises, Promises

The Situation

Unfortunately, false promises are not uncommon when managers feel pressure to pump up profits. Many operations managers no doubt recall times when excited marketing managers asked for unrealistic commitments from production to get a new customer contract. This exercise will introduce you to some ethical considerations pertaining to such promises and commitments.

The Dilemma

You are the operations manager for a factory that makes replacement car mufflers and tailpipes. Your plant produces these items for all makes and models and sells them throughout Canada to muffler-repair shops that install them on used vehicles. After several years of modest but steady growth, your company has recently suffered a downturn and must shut down 5 percent of the factory's production capacity. Two supervisors and 70 production workers have been laid off. All of the company's stakeholders—employees, managers, the union, suppliers, and owners—are concerned about prospects for the immediate future.

After returning from lunch, you receive a phone call from the general manager of one of the nation's top three muffler-repair chains. He says the following: "I suppose you know that we're about to sign a contract under which your firm will supply us with replacement parts in large volumes, beginning two months from now. Your sales manager has assured me that you can reliably meet my needs, and I just want to confirm that promise with you before I sign the contract."

This is the first you've heard about this contract. While your potential customer is talking, you realize that meeting his needs will involve a 20 percent increase in your current production capacity. Two months, however, isn't enough time to add more equipment, acquire tools, hire and train workers, and contract for supplies. In fact, an increase this large might even require a bigger building (which would, of course, take considerably more than two months to arrange). On the other hand, you also know how much your firm needs the business. Your thoughts are interrupted when the caller says, "So what's your production situation insofar as meeting our needs?" The caller waits in silence while you gather your thoughts.

Questions for Discussion

1. What are the underlying ethical issues in this situation?
2. From an ethical standpoint, what is an appropriate response to the customer's question? What steps should you take in responding to it? Explain.
3. What would you say on the phone at this time to this customer?

CONCLUDING CASE 11-1

How to Keep a Project Afloat

For football fans, the Pasadena Tournament of Roses Parade is a major New Year's event. With elegant floral floats, spirited marching bands, colourful costuming, and high-stepping equestrian units, it's one of the world's premier entertainment events for more than a million streetside onlookers and a TV audience of 400 million in more than a hundred countries. Hidden beneath the glamour, however, is a complicated maze of behind-the-scenes project-management activity. The year-long planning is coordinated as expertly as the parade itself, and includes arrangements for logistics (housing, parking, seating, food vending, toilet facilities), TV programming, moving a million visitors in and out of Pasadena on parade day, receiving applications and selecting participants, building floats, and after-parade cleanup. Without project management, the parade couldn't keep its lofty position among the world's best.

The challenges in just one activity—building a float—involve seemingly endless details. Consider, for example, the City of Burbank's 2004 float entry, "Moosic, Moosic,

Moosic." First, its designers focussed on the concept that music has always been part of herd tending, so it tied into the Tournament of Roses theme: *Music, Music, Music.* The float's drawings feature a bronco-riding balladeer perched atop a steep mesa keeping his eye on the herd while filling the valley with Gene Autry's "Back in the Saddle Again," while cows munch and chew, as prairie dogs keep a watchful eye on a nearby dog. Its finished dimensions were 25 feet high, 18 feet wide, and a hefty 48 feet long. First, however, the year's activities had to be coordinated, from final drawings and instructions to ordering flower blossoms and paste to training volunteer workers to final construction.

Activities are scheduled in phases so that preliminary steps are completed before follow-on activities are attempted. They had to be completed neither too early (lest completed work fall apart or deteriorate from sitting too long) nor too late (causing slowdowns or lateness in project completion). For six months, volunteers—many from outside the community—worked on building the float's frame, then shaping the cartoon-like cowboy, horse, dog, cows, and prairie dogs. Then they rushed frantically into last minute painting and gluing of the finishing seeds, barks, and grasses. Various skill levels ranging from novice to expert were used for developing scale drawings and for construction, metal bending, welding, hydraulics, flower cutting, electrical work, painting, gluing, dry material preparation, and merchandising.

The construction site—a warehouse building in the Burbank Water and Power Department yard—had to be large enough, initially, to accommodate a relatively few activities, workstations, and trainers, as well as materials, tools, and supplies. More capacity was needed, however, with the passage of time: The volunteer supervisors' workload grew when as many as 800 newcomers a day showed up in late December to apply last-minute finishing touches, accompanied by surging inflows of supplies and materials. Every inch of the float was covered with flowers—brought in from as far away as Venezuela, Colombia, and Trinidad—or other natural materials such as seeds, fruit rinds, and leaves. All of this had to be accomplished within the $125 000 budget and under close supervision so the float would be structurally safe, beautifully decorated, and finished on time. Although the pace got hectic, the all-volunteer project was a source of pride for the community.

Preparation for each year's Rose Parade float begins right after New Year's Day, as soon as the parade theme has been announced. The Burbank Tournament of Roses Association solicits ideas and drawings from the general public in a design contest. From the 72 drawings submitted for 2004, the Burbank Association's board of directors selected six designs and presented them to the general membership for the final choice. This one activity involved six time-phased steps:

1. *January 2*: Design contest entry form and post rules on association website.
2. *January 28*: Deadline for receiving design submissions (drawings).
3. *January 31*: Board meets to review submissions and narrow down to top six.
4. *February 5*: Full membership of association meets to rank the six drawings.
5. *February 11*: Drawings taken to Pasadena for theme draft among all float builders (lottery determines the order that drawings are approved if floats are too similar).
6. *February 12*: Board meets to announce winning design. Work can start.

Additional activities are triggered once the design is approved. By March, final drawings and plans are under examination by the construction and decoration committees. Actual physical construction of the float begins in May. Decoration materials are ordered in July and the ensuing months. Orders for live flowers are placed with various growers in September and October. Actual decoration of the float begins December 26 and continues until December 31. On New Year's Eve, a contingent of City of Burbank motorcycle police escort the float, via surface streets, to Pasadena. The project ends in the second week of January with float deconstruction.

Throughout the year, major activities consist of sub steps that are coordinated with other major activities. Consider, for example, planning for the flowers and vegetation that elaborately decorate the entire float. The cowpoke and cartoon cow heads are sculpted from foam before flowers are added. The three cows are then covered in white cushion poms with spots made of 2500 Terra Cotta roses. The cows stand on plateaus while munching on landscaping made of native grasses, sunflowers, kangaroo paws, gerbera daisies, and stargazer lilies. The towering sides of the butte are formed of red lentil, safflower, annatto seed, yellow peas, millet, purple statice, and over 15 000 various roses (Gipsy Curiosa, Tequila, Orange Unique, Blue Curiosa, and Corvette). The bronco-riding, guitar-playing cowboy atop the butte is clad in silverleaf hat, marigold bandana, and statice blue jeans, on a horse of butterscotch strawflower with a white pampas grass mane and tail. All these materials have to be purchased and received on time and in good condition, then mounted securely on the frame covering two main engines, one for driving the float and one for running the animation and sound system.

Among the 49 floats for 2004, Burbank's is one of only six "self-built" floats (other floats are contracted out to professional float-building companies). It is designed, constructed, and decorated entirely by volunteers including scout groups, high school clubs, community service groups, and Burbank residents and visitors, some as young as five years old. So skilfully was it completed that Burbank's entry was an award winner, receiving the Queen's Trophy for most effective use and display of roses in concept, design, and presentation.

Questions for Discussion

1. What other activities, in addition to building floats for the Tournament of Roses Parade, might benefit from project management methods? Explain your reasoning.
2. Suppose you are responsible for planning the City of Burbank's float for next year's Tournament of Roses Parade. You are concerned about the number of purchased items and suppliers scattered around the globe. What are some of the major project-planning problems posed by the suppliers' geographic dispersion?
3. Consider the diversity of human skills needed at various stages throughout Burbank's preparations for the Tournament of Roses Parade. What are the various required skills and what problems do they present for planning the project?
4. Suppose you are involved in planning for accommodating the million streetside onlookers in Pasadena next New Year's Day. What are the main activities that should be considered in your project planning efforts? Which of those activities must be started early in the project and which can be delayed until later?
5. How might PERT charts be used for scheduling major activities for the Tournament of Roses Parade? In what ways can PERT be of assistance to project managers in such projects?

CONCLUDING CASE 11-2

A Losing Game?

The year 2005 was not a good one for automobile manufacturing in Ontario.

In March, General Motors (GM) announced that it was dropping plans for making the Zeta rear-wheel-drive platform (the underpinning of a car) at one of its Oshawa, Ontario, plants. GM made the decision as part of its overall effort to slash costs and increase the company's ability to compete in world markets.

Then more bad news came in November 2005, when GM announced that it would close 10 manufacturing plants in North America (with one plant to close in Ontario, and two others to be downsized). It also announced plans to eliminate 30 000 jobs by the end of 2008. The cuts would cause GM's production capacity to drop 30 percent below what it was in 2002. This announcement was devastating, since GM generates $16 billion in business for 400 different auto parts companies in Ontario, and GM contracts provide about 50 000 jobs in the Canadian auto parts industry. About 12 000 of those jobs could disappear because of GM's downsizing. There is also a broader ripple effect. The chief economist for the Canadian Manufacturers & Exporters estimates that each assembly line job in automobile manufacturing creates nine other jobs.

Decisions that GM is making about reductions in other areas of North America will also negatively affect Ontario. For example, GM's plan to close a plant in Oklahoma that makes SUVs will hurt Kitchener-based Budd Canada Inc. because it makes the frames for the SUVs. Another U.S. plant that makes those SUVs will be reduced in scope, and Budd also supplies that plant with frames. To make matters worse, Budd was not sure it could retain its contract to make frames for GM because its cost was 22 percent higher than GM was willing to pay. So, Budd convinced its workers to approve changes in work rules that would save the company $40 million and allow it to reduce the price of the frames it makes.

GM's recent decision was simply the latest in a long line of announcements that automobile manufacturers have made in recent years that are causing great concern among Canadian workers, politicians, and business people. In 2002, the General Motors manufacturing plant in Boisebriand, Quebec, closed after 37 years of producing various GM cars, most recently "muscle" cars like the Camaro and Firebird. The closing occurred even though the plant was rated as one of the most efficient in North America. This was the only remaining light vehicle assembly plant in Canada outside Ontario. GM closed the plant because demand for the cars produced there was not sufficient to keep the plant open. Other auto plants in Canada that closed in 2003 were the DaimlerChrysler van plant in Windsor, Ontario, and Navistar's heavy truck assembly plant in Chatham. More than 4000 high-paying jobs were lost.

Where did the production go? It went to several southern U.S. states because carmakers like Nissan, Mercedes, Honda, and Hyundai are building new plants there. These companies have been increasing market share at the expense of the so-called "Big Three" (GM, Ford, and DaimlerChrysler). General Motors, for example, had about 50 percent of the North American market in 1970, but is now down to about a 25 percent share.

Why are these non–Big Three carmakers moving to the southern United States? There are two key reasons. First, automakers want to reduce their overall costs. Since wage rates are a big consideration in overall costs, automakers have been looking for places where wages are lower. One of the places they have found is the southern United States. Almost all of these states also happen to have "right-to-work" laws. This means that no worker can be forced to join a union or pay union dues.

Second, the auto companies are receiving large financial incentives to move to the southern United States. For example, South Carolina shelled out $135 million in incentives to attract BMW, Mississippi gave incentives of $295 million to Nissan, and Alabama gave $253 million to Mercedes to locate there. These incentives include free land, infrastructure improvements, income tax deferrals, and money for training workers. Canadian unions and Canadian automobile executives say that Canadian provinces are being left behind because they won't give the kinds of incentives that are necessary to attract carmakers. Buzz Hargrove, the Canadian Auto Workers president, is upset that DaimlerChrysler decided to cancel plans for a new assembly plant in Windsor, which would have created 2500 jobs. He blamed the federal and Ontario governments for failing to provide monetary incentives that would have convinced DaimlerChrysler to build the new plant in Canada. In February 2003, the province of Ontario did set aside $625 million to help win investments in the province from DaimlerChrysler and Ford.

Late in 2005, the federal government announced that it would give hundreds of millions of dollars in new incentives to automobile companies if they would locate in Canada. After many years of largely resisting the provision of incentives, the government may now see them as a necessary evil. Even so, in early 2006 a Conservative minority government was elected, replacing the Liberals as the governing party. What effect this will have on the incentives strategy is unclear.

The movement of manufacturing to the southern United States isn't the only move south that is evident. Automakers have also set up assembly plants in South Africa, Brazil, and Thailand. The cars produced in these plants will supply markets in Japan, Europe, and North America. Until now, automakers thought that cars produced in these areas would not be well received by consumers in industrialized countries, but that is changing. BMW, for example, has poured hundreds of millions of dollars into its South African production facility. It says the cost of land, electricity, and labour is much lower there than in industrialized countries. A survey by J.D. Power & Associates found that the quality of cars produced at BMW's South African plant beat the quality of their cars produced in Germany and the United States.

Honda has begun making cars in Thailand and will ship them to its home market in Japan. Honda is also planning to build a new plant in China that will export much of its output. GM also builds a car in Thailand for export to Europe. Ford has built a plant in northeastern Brazil that will export mini-sport utility vehicles to the United States. All of these new plants have the latest technology and quality control systems. So far, the number of cars exported from these new plants is only a small proportion of total world car production, but that will increase steadily during the next decade.

Because the wages paid to workers in these overseas locations can be as little as one-tenth that paid to North American workers, the automakers have a strong incentive to move their operations. The low wages more than make up for the cost of shipping parts to these plants and then shipping the finished cars back to North America, Japan, or Europe.

Unions in North America and Europe are increasingly concerned that this trend will mean fewer high-paying jobs for their members. Buzz Hargrove is angry that Ford is planning to import the Fusion from Brazil when it is also planning to close a pickup truck plant in Canada. Ford says the numbers are so small that they won't reduce the number of union jobs. But Ford also notes that its plant in Brazil is its lowest-cost plant, and its quality is high; that could mean much higher production and export of vehicles in the future. Ford also noted that it will produce two new SUVs at a plant in Oakville, Ontario, beginning in 2006. These vehicles were originally scheduled to be produced in Atlanta, Georgia.

Questions for Discussion

1. Explain in your own words how trends in the worldwide automobile market are causing employment problems in automobile manufacturing in Ontario and Quebec. Can anything be done to reverse the trend? If not, explain why not. If something can be done, explain what that might be.
2. Explain how problems at companies like GM have impacted the operations of parts suppliers in Canada.
3. What do the problems in the automobile business (for both manufacturers and parts suppliers) imply for other parts of the economy that are not directly related to the automobile business? Explain.
4. Southern U.S. states like Alabama have given hundreds of millions of dollars in incentives to companies that agree to set up manufacturing plants there. Should the provinces of Ontario and Quebec be more active in giving the same type of incentives to maintain employment in automobile manufacturing in Canada? Defend your answer.

CHAPTER 12

Increasing Productivity and Quality

After reading this chapter, you should be able to:

1. Describe the connection between *productivity* and *quality*.
2. Understand the importance of increasing productivity.
3. Identify the activities involved in *total quality management* and describe six tools that companies can use to achieve it.
4. Identify three trends in productivity and quality management, including *supply chain management*.
5. Explain how a supply chain strategy differs from traditional strategies for coordinating operations among firms.
6. Discuss four strategies that companies use to improve productivity and quality.

Meeting the Productivity Challenge

During the past few years, considerable publicity has been given to the economic revolution that is taking place in China. With wage rates that are far below those in Canada, China has become a formidable competitor because it is such a low-cost producer of goods. The most obvious way to cope with this competitive threat is to reduce the number of hours of labour that are required to make a product, and thereby reduce the product's cost. This is another way of saying that Canadian companies must increase labour productivity.

Growth rates in labour productivity (GDP per hour worked) vary across countries, and Canada has not fared well in recent years. In 2004, for example, Canadian labour productivity did not increase at all, while many other countries increased their labour productivity by 1.5–2.5 percent.

The productivity news is not all bad. In some industries—primary metals, wood products, construction, transport equipment, paper, and chemicals—Canadian productivity actually exceeds that of the United States. But in many other industries—including computers and electronics, fabricated metal products, textiles, furniture, retail trade, financial services, and electrical equipment—Canadian productivity lags far behind the United States.

Consider the case of the automobile industry. In 2005, Harbour Consulting ranked GM Canada's Oshawa no. 1 plant at the top of its list of most productive plants in North America. The plant, which makes Chevrolet Impalas and Monte Carlos, takes 15.85 hours to produce one car. The second most productive plant is a Nissan plant in Tennessee, which takes 15 minutes longer. Oshawa no. 2 plant was in fourth place at 17.47 hours.

But car manufacturing is a worldwide phenomenon, and car makers in Japan are even more efficient (productive) than North American car makers. In a worldwide comparison, using another benchmark, Nissan led the way, earning $1603 on the average vehicle, followed by Toyota ($1488), and Honda ($1250). Ford earned $620 and Chrysler just $186. GM *lost* $2311 on each vehicle it sold because of declining demand from consumers and high pension and health care costs.

But how can labour productivity be increased? As we saw in the Opening Case in Chapter 2, a variety of approaches have been suggested, including changes in tax policies that would encourage manufacturers to invest in more productive equipment. Consider the issue of capital cost allowance (CCA). In the United States, manufacturers are allowed to write off equipment much faster than in Canada. This means that U.S. companies pay less tax than Canadian companies. In Canada, Standen's Ltd. is a clear example of the disincentive that tax policy can create. The company, which produces truck springs, was considering buying an automotive springs plant in Wallaceburg, Ontario, but eventually decided it wouldn't make the purchase because the after-tax cost of the investment was too high. If Canadian tax laws allowed greater deductions for investment in machinery, the purchase would have been feasible.

But these suggestions are not without controversy. The Canadian Labour Congress, for example, accepts the importance of productivity and the need to increase it, but says there are good and bad ways to do that. A "bad" way, in their view, is to cut jobs, while a "good" way is to invest in innovation and employee training. The Information Technology Association of Canada says that U.S. companies in the information and communications technology sector spend more than twice as much per worker than Canadian companies do.

There is also debate about the role that managers play in this problem. Some people argue that Canadian managers are not expending enough energy or do not have enough imagination, and that is why Canadian productivity is lagging. But Jack Mintz, the head of the C.D. Howe Institute, says that Canadian managers are very good and are simply responding to their environment—in this case, the tax environment. Specifically, he notes that Canadian managers invest outside Canada because of lower tax rates on capital investment in other countries. He says that a comparison of 36 industrialized countries shows that Canada has the second-highest marginal tax rate on capital investment.

Of particular importance to Canadian businesses is the productivity comparison with their U.S. counterparts. While productivity comparisons with the much larger U.S. economy may seem unfair, Canada's immense trade with the United States makes such comparisons important. Output per hour in Canadian manufacturing was about 14 percent below the United States for the period 1977–94. Since 1994, the situation has actually worsened—output per hour in Canada was 29 percent lower than the United States in 2000 and 32 percent lower in 2001. Put another way, labour productivity growth was 3.8 *percentage points* higher in the United States than in Canada during the period 1994–2000.

To catch up to the United States, Canada will have to exceed the rate of productivity growth in the United States each year by about one percentage point for the next 15 years. One percentage point might not sound like much, but it would require Canadian industry to achieve an annual productivity growth rate of over 3 percent. That rate of productivity growth has been achieved only twice in Canada in the last 25 years.

When making productivity comparisons, we must be careful that we consider certain factors which may give one country an inherent advantage over another. For example, Canadian oil and gas producers are less productive than their U.S. counterparts. This is so partly because Canadian companies are spending large amounts of money developing expensive offshore and non-conventional oil sands deposits, while U.S. oil and gas producers continue to extract energy from wells that use technology that was developed long ago. Another example: Canadian retailers are less productive than U.S. retailers, partly because Wal-Mart has forced its U.S. competitors to cut costs to survive. This cost cutting does raise productivity and benefits *consumers*, but *employees* often suffer. One study showed that Wal-Mart workers earned 31 percent less than the average wage paid by large retailers, and that less than half of Wal-Mart's workers had health insurance.

A delicate balancing act is required to achieve higher productivity while not reducing worker well-being. Companies need to foster a competitive climate (which drives productivity growth) and at the same time promote social, environmental, and employee welfare. ◆

It is no secret that productivity and quality are watchwords in today's business. Companies are not only measuring productivity and insisting on improvements, but also insisting on quality so they can bring to market products that satisfy customers, improve sales, and boost profits. By focussing on the learning objectives of this chapter, you will better understand the increasingly important concepts of productivity and quality.

THE PRODUCTIVITY–QUALITY CONNECTION

1 Describe the connection between *productivity* and *quality*.

productivity A measure of efficiency that compares how much is produced with the resources used to produce it.

quality A product's fitness for use in terms of offering the features that consumers want.

Productivity is a measure of economic performance. It measures how much is produced relative to the resources used to produce it. The more we are able to produce the right things while using fewer resources, the more productivity grows and everyone—the economy, businesses, and workers—benefits.

Productivity considers both the amounts and the quality of what is produced. By using resources more efficiently, the quantity of output will be greater. But unless the resulting goods and services are of satisfactory quality (the "right things"), consumers will not want them. **Quality**, then, means fitness for use—offering features that consumers want.

Responding to the Productivity Challenge

As the opening case clearly shows, productivity has both international and domestic ramifications. Obviously, when one country is more productive than another, it will accumulate more wealth. Similarly, a nation whose productivity fails to increase as rapidly as that of competitor nations will see its standard of living fall.

It is important to understand the true meaning of *productivity* and to devise ways to measure it. Since *quality* must be defined in terms of value to the customer, companies must design their marketing efforts to cultivate a more customer-oriented focus. As quality-improvement practices are implemented, more and more firms will receive payoffs from these efforts. Four factors interact in this process: *customers*, *quality*, *productivity*, and *profits*.

Workers at this call centre in Bangalore, India, operated by ICICI OneSource, field calls from the customers of multinational firms headquartered in the United States and Europe. Global broadband makes this business model possible, so many of these jobs (30 000 in Canada) are outsourced to Indian service suppliers because workers get paid only a fraction of what Canadian workers would get. Even at that, they earn eight times as much as the average Indian earns per year ($450).

Measuring Productivity

How do we know how productive a country is? Most countries use **labour productivity** to measure their level of productivity:

labour productivity Partial productivity ratio calculated by dividing gross domestic product by total number of workers.

$$\text{labor productivity of a country} = \frac{\text{gross domestic product}}{\text{total number of workers}}$$

This equation reflects the general idea of productivity. It compares a country's total annual output of goods and services with the resources used to produce that output. The focus on labour, rather than on other resources (such as capital or energy), is preferred because most countries keep accurate records on employment and hours worked.

A 2005 Statistics Canada report showed that foreign-controlled manufacturing plants in Canada accounted for two-thirds of the growth in labour productivity during the period 1980–99. But the study emphasized that it wasn't the fact that the plants were foreign-controlled that led to higher productivity; rather, it was the extent to which the companies had an international orientation. In other words, Canadian producers that had foreign units were just as productive as foreign-owned plants. It seems that firms that compete internationally have more incentive to be more productive.[1]

Productivity Among Global Competitors

A study by the Organisation for Economic Co-operation and Development (OECD) reported on productivity levels in 23 participating countries. Figure 12.1 compares productivity among several OECD countries. As you can see, output per hour worked in Belgium is about 28 percent higher than the average for OECD members. At 31 percent below average, output in New Zealand is lowest among the nations listed in Figure 12.1.

A 2006 study by the U.S. Bureau of Labour Statistics showed that during 2003–04, Canada's output per hour increased by 2.9 percent. That was far less than the productivity growth in Korea (12.1 percent), Sweden (9.8 percent), and the United States (5.2 percent). The study also showed that over the longer-term (1979–2004), annual increases in Canadian productivity (2.6 percent) were less than annual productivity increases in other

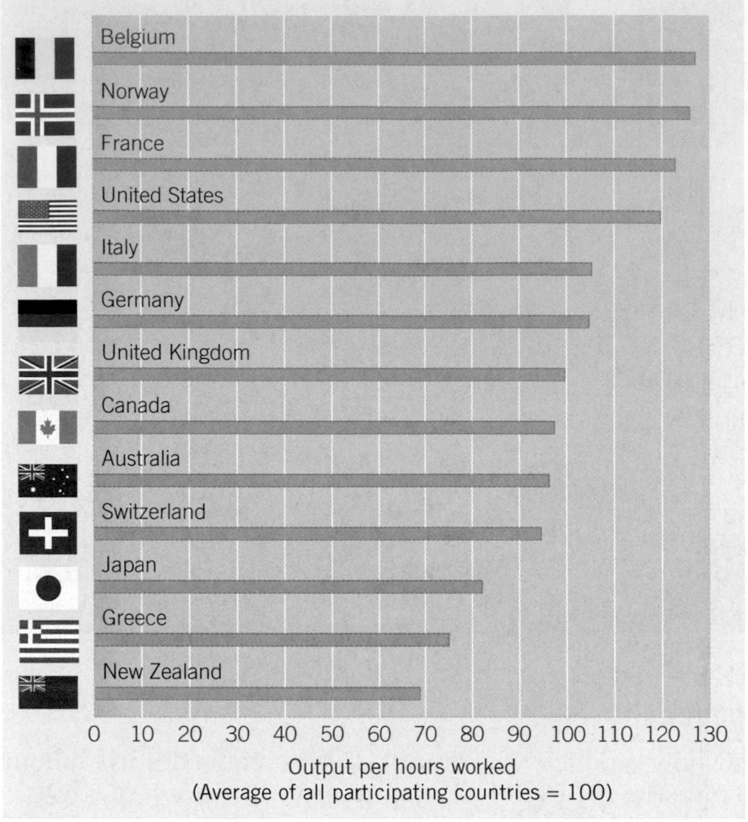

Figure 12.1 International productivity comparisons.

countries such as the United States (4.1 percent), Sweden (4.7 percent), and Taiwan (5.7 percent).[2]

Why such differences from nation to nation? The answer lies in many factors: technologies, human skills, economic policies, natural resources—and even in traditions. Consider, for example, just one industrial sector—food production. In Japan, the food-production industry employs more workers than the automotive, computer, consumer electronics, and machine-tool industries combined. It is a fragmented, highly protected industry—and, compared with U.S. food production, it is extremely inefficient. The average U.S. worker produces 3.5 times as much food as his or her Japanese counterpart. Overall, data show that in the time it takes a U.S. worker to produce \$100 worth of goods, Japanese workers produce about \$68 worth. Belgian workers, on the other hand, produce \$107 worth.[3]

According to Michael Porter, a Harvard University expert on international competitiveness, Canada's competitiveness is a concern because we have been living off our rich diet of natural resources. In Porter's view, Canada will have to start emphasizing innovation and develop a more sophisticated mix of products if it hopes to be successful in international markets. Porter criticizes Canadian business, government, and labour for failing to abandon outdated ways of thinking regarding productivity and innovation.[4]

Domestic Productivity

Nations must be concerned about domestic productivity regardless of their global standing. A country that improves its ability to make something out of its existing resources can increase the wealth of all its inhabitants. Conversely, a decline in productivity shrinks a nation's total wealth. When that happens, an increase in one person's wealth comes only at the expense of others with whom he or she shares an economic system.

For example, additional wealth from higher productivity can be shared among workers (as higher wages), investors (as higher profits), and customers (as stable prices). When productivity drops, however, wages can be increased only by reducing profits (penalizing investors) or by increasing prices (penalizing customers). It is understandable, then, that investors, suppliers, managers, and workers are all concerned about the productivity of specific industries and companies.

Manufacturing Versus Service Productivity

Manufacturing productivity is higher than service productivity. For many years, it was widely believed that the service sector suffered from "Baumol's disease," named after economist William Baumol who argued that since the service sector focussed more on hands-on activity that machines couldn't replace, it would be more difficult to increase productivity in services. Baumol, noted, for example, that it would always require four musicians to play a Mozart quartet. But the Opera company of Brooklyn is challenging Baumol's basic assumption. It now puts on the opera *The Marriage of Figaro* without the usual full orchestra. Instead, it uses just 12 musicians and a technician who oversees a computer program that plays all the other musical parts. The orchestra's productivity has increased sharply because it does not have to pay for the usual complement of musicians.[5]

Productivity gains are starting to appear among a wide array of service providers such as airlines, pet stores, package delivery companies, providers of financial services, and retail establishments. Many of these organizations have increased their productivity by becoming more like factories, and they use modern information technology to eliminate inefficiencies. Automated check-in kiosks in airports are a good example. Two-thirds of Northwest's passengers now check in using the kiosks.

Industry Productivity

Understand the importance of increasing productivity. 2

In addition to differences between the manufacturing and service sectors, industries within these sectors differ vastly in terms of productivity. Agriculture is more productive in Canada than in many other nations because we use more sophisticated technology and superior natural resources. Technological advances have also given the computer industry a productivity edge in many areas. Steel manufacturing, which experienced significant problems in the 1970s and 1980s, has improved recently. For example, in the early 1980s, about 10 hours of labour were required to produce a tonne of steel. Now, only about four hours of labour are needed. One reason for the improvement is a new technology called continuous casting. Today, machines can turn molten metal into slabs that can be processed while still red-hot. It is no longer necessary to cool the steel, strip off the moulding, and then reheat it for processing. This new process has meant immense savings in both labour and energy.[6]

In an effort to increase productivity, Canfor Corp. developed a system called Genus, which it is using to manage its forestry operations. Genus, a computerized database containing geographic information and other essential data about Canfor's vast lumber and pulp operations in British Columbia and Alberta, will be used as a strategic planning tool to determine how the company should adjust its logging plans to reflect both market demand and logging regulations laid down by the Forest Practices Code of British Columbia Act.[7]

The productivity of specific industries concerns many people for different reasons. Labour unions need to take it into account in negotiating contracts, since highly productive industries can give raises more easily than can less productive industries. Investors and suppliers consider industry

On the left, workers assemble a truck the old way, manually lowering and bolting frames onto axles. On the right, the process is highly automated (and safer), with robotic grippers to flip and align the bulky frames.

productivity when making loans, buying securities, and planning their own future production.

Company Productivity

High productivity gives a company a competitive edge because its costs are lower. As a result, it can offer its product at a lower price (and gain more customers), or it can make a greater profit on each item sold. Increased productivity also allows companies to pay workers higher wages without raising prices.

The productivity of individual companies is also important to investors, workers, and managers. Comparing the productivity of several companies in the same industry helps investors in buying and selling stocks. Employee profit-sharing plans are often based on the company's productivity improvements each year. And managers use information about productivity trends to plan for new products, factories, and funds to stay competitive in the years ahead.

TOTAL QUALITY MANAGEMENT

It is no longer enough for businesses to simply measure productivity in terms of the numbers of items produced. They must also take quality into account. In the decades after the Second World War, business consultant W. Edwards Deming tried to persuade firms in North America that they needed to improve quality at least as much as quantity. He wasn't very successful, but his arguments won over the Japanese. Through years of meticulous hard work, Japan's manufacturers have changed "Made in Japan" from a synonym for cheap, shoddy merchandise into a hallmark of reliability. More recently, North American firms have been doing much better in the quality area. In 2006, for example, J.D. Power & Associates ranked GM's

Oshawa No. 2 plant—which produces the Buick Allure and the Pontiac Grand Prix—as highest in quality out of 80 assembly plants in North America. The Oshawa No. 2 plant has won this award several times. Another example of an attempt to convey quality and accountability to consumers is described in the Business Accountability box.

Quality advocates such as Joseph Juran and Kaoru Ishikawa introduced methods and tools for implementing quality. Juran's "Quality Trilogy"—quality planning, quality control, and quality improvement—was the first structured process for managing quality. It identifies management steps for ensuring quality. In addition to management actions, Juran, like Deming and Ishikawa, championed the idea of company-wide employee participation. These theorists also developed quality tools for day-to-day work activities because they knew that without employee participation, real quality improvement would never happen. Ishikawa, for example, developed so-called "fishbone diagrams," also known as "cause-and-effect diagrams" or "Ishikawa

BUSINESS ACCOUNTABILITY

Rating the Quality of Diamonds

How do you rate the quality of diamonds? Historically, diamond quality has been assessed by reference to 4 C's: *cut, colour, clarity,* and *carat.* But perhaps a fifth C is emerging, and that is "country of origin." Better yet, the fifth C may also stand for "Canada."

Until just a few years ago, Canada was not even a player in the international diamond business. But in 1991, a promising diamond field was located in the Northwest Territories and the race was on to exploit the possibilities. Skeptics said that even if diamonds were found in commercial quantities in Canada, the diamonds would have to be sold to DeBeers, the company that controlled the world diamond trade. But once diamond wholesalers were shown the first Canadian diamonds, they realized that the quality was as high as that from the best diamond mines in the world, and they eagerly bought them. The myth of DeBeers control soon evaporated.

The first Canadian diamond mine was opened in the Northwest Territories in 1998, and by 2003 it was already producing 6 percent of the total world's supply of rough diamonds. A second mine opened in 2003, and another is scheduled for 2006. By that time, Canada will produce 12 percent of the world's diamonds. There are also promising developments in diamond mining in Saskatchewan, where core samples drilled by Shore Gold show that high quality diamonds exist there.

In recent years, there has been much negative press about so-called "blood diamonds," that is, diamonds that were mined by armed workers in war-torn African countries like Botswana. These diamonds were then exported, and the money used to support further military campaigns. The developing Canadian diamond industry has no such image problems. Diamonds in Canada are mined under very ethical and environmentally strict conditions. And there's one added advantage: The quality of Canadian diamonds is very high. Canadian rough diamonds average $170 per carat in value, far above the $100 level at which diamonds are considered precious. The new samples from Saskatchewan are valued at about U.S.$135 per carat.

But is country of origin important enough to influence consumers when they purchase a diamond? In the minds of many consumers, the quality of certain products *is* associated with the product's country of origin. Think, for example, of Swiss watches, Italian leather, and French wines. Oren Sofer, CEO of diamond wholesaler Beny Sofer & Sons LLC, says that if you can brand water, you certainly should be able to brand diamonds. He wants consumers to eventually recognize "Canadian diamonds" as an important brand name.

This is not an impossible goal. The move is already underway to establish a high quality reputation for Canadian diamonds. Sirius Diamond Inc., a Vancouver diamond wholesaler, engraves a tiny polar bear on the Canadian diamonds it sells, and Birks & Sons Inc. engraves a maple leaf on its diamonds. The government of the Northwest Territories provides a certificate for each diamond that has come from its mines. This ensures that diamonds from other countries cannot be passed off as Canadian stones.

diagrams," that help teams of employees investigate and track down causes of quality problems in their work areas. The diagram in Figure 12.2, for instance, was designed to help an airport manager find out why his facility had so many delayed departures. Focussing on five major categories of possible causes, he then noted several potential causes of the problem in each. (It turns out that there weren't enough tow trucks to handle baggage transfers.)[8]

Managing for Quality

3 Identify the activities involved in *total quality management* and describe six tools that companies can use to achieve it.

total quality management (TQM) A concept that emphasizes that no defects are tolerable and that all employees are responsible for maintaining quality standards.

Total quality management (TQM) (sometimes called *quality assurance*) includes all the activities necessary for getting high-quality goods and services into the marketplace. It must consider all parts of the business, including customers, suppliers, and employees. TQM emphasizes that no defects are tolerable, and that employees are responsible for maintaining quality standards. At Toyota's Cambridge, Ontario, plant, for example, workers can push a button or pull a rope to stop the production line when something is not up to standard.[9]

The strategic approach to TQM begins with leadership and the desire for TQM. This approach involves getting people's attention, getting them to think in an entirely new way about what they do, and then getting them to improve both processes and products.[10]

Customer focus is the starting point. Companies must develop methods for determining what customers want, and then direct all their resources toward fulfillment of those needs to gain greater customer satisfaction. Total participation is mandatory. Unless all employees are working toward improved quality, the firm is wasting potential contributions from its human resources, and is missing a chance to become a stronger competitor in the marketplace. TQM in today's competitive markets demands unending and continuous improvement of products, after-sales services, and all of the company's internal processes, such as accounting, delivery, billing, and information flow.

Says John Kay, director of Oxford University's School of Management: "You can't run a successful company if you don't care about customers and

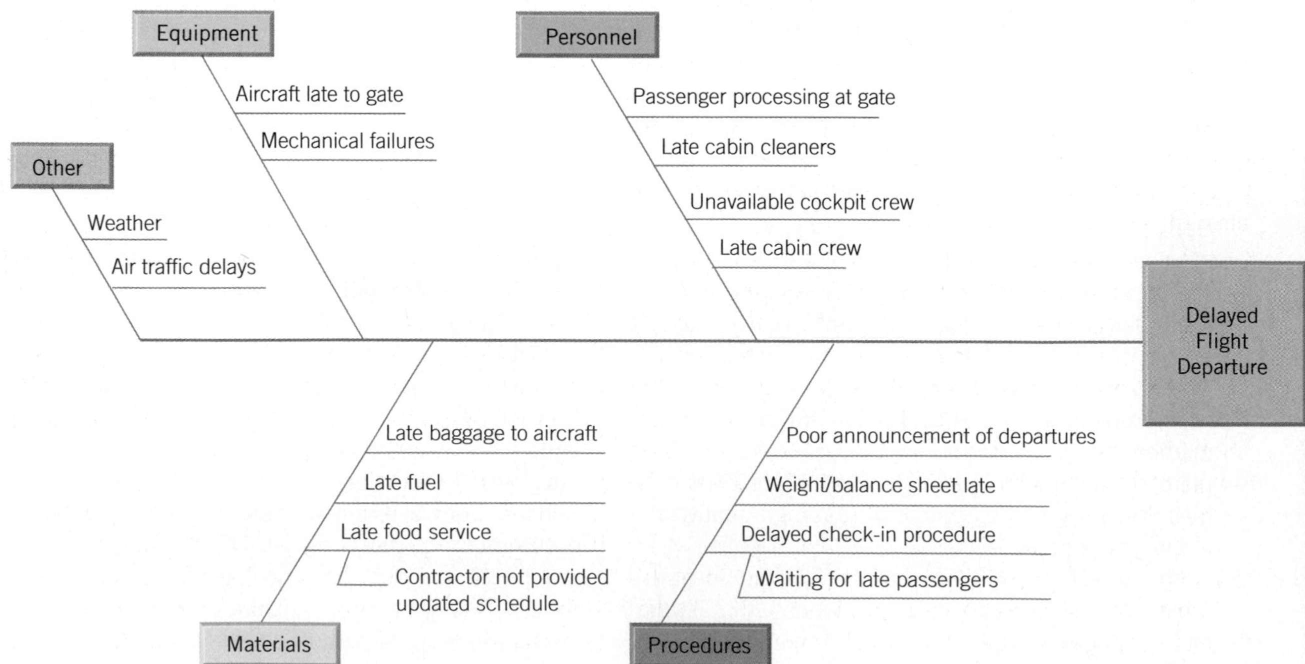

Figure 12.2 "Fishbone" or cause-and-effect diagram.

employees, or if you are systematically unpleasant to suppliers."[11] To bring the interests of all these stakeholders together, TQM involves planning, organizing, directing, and controlling.

Successful use of TQM requires a high level of commitment from all members of the organization. Consider the case of Standard Aero in Winnipeg, which is in the business of aircraft overhaul. When the company instituted TQM, the process began with the formation of a "change council" consisting of the CEO and five senior managers. This council ensured that the TQM initiative received the money, equipment, and support it needed for success. Next, a nine-person task force was formed that consisted of employees who had done the full range of jobs on one of Standard's major overhaul contracts. Its first job was to find out what the customer wanted. It did this by designing a questionnaire and visiting customer plants around the world to gather information. The task force also worked within Standard Aero to determine exactly how the company did its aircraft overhaul work. After weeks of analysis, the task force was able to significantly reduce the time required for overhaul work. For example, the number of times a certain gearbox was handled as it moved through the repair process was reduced by 84 percent.[12]

Planning for Quality

Planning for quality should begin before products are designed or redesigned. Managers need to set goals for both quality levels and quality reliability in the beginning. **Performance quality** refers to the features of a product and how well it performs. For example, Maytag gets a price premium because its washers and dryers offer a high level of performance quality. Customers perceive Maytag as having more advanced features and being more durable than other brands. (Everyone knows that the Maytag repairman is a lonely and idle person.)

performance quality The overall degree of quality; how well the features of a product meet consumers' needs and how well the product performs.

Performance quality may or may not be related to quality reliability in a product. **Quality reliability** refers to the consistency or repeatability of performance. Toyota's small cars may not equal the overall quality level or have the luxury features of Rolls Royce; consequently, Toyota's prices are much lower. But Toyotas have high quality reliability. The firm has a reputation for producing very few "lemons."

quality reliability The consistency of quality from unit to unit of a product.

Organizing for Quality

Perhaps most important to the quality concept is the belief that producing quality goods and services requires an effort from all parts of the organization. The old idea of a separate "quality control" department is no longer enough. Everyone—from the chairperson of the board to the part-time clerk-purchasers, engineers, janitors, marketers, machinists, and other personnel—must work to ensure quality. In Germany's Messerschmitt-Boelkow-Blohm aerospace company, for example, all employees are responsible for inspecting their own work. The overall goal is to reduce eventual problems to a minimum by making the product correctly from the beginning. The same principle extends to teamwork practice at Heinz Co., where teams of workers are assigned to inspect virtually every activity in the company. Heinz has realized substantial cost savings by eliminating waste and rework.

At Motorola, the concept of teamwork as a key to organizational quality has resulted in an international event called the Total Customer Satisfaction Team Competition. Teams are composed of Motorola employees and also include customers and outside suppliers. Teams are judged on their success not only in promoting productivity but also in sharing innovative ideas with people both inside and outside the company.

Although everyone in a company contributes to product quality, responsibility for specific aspects of total quality management is often assigned to specific departments and jobs. In fact, many companies have quality assurance, or quality control, departments staffed by quality experts. These people may be called in to help solve quality-related problems in any of the firm's other departments. They keep other departments informed of the latest developments in equipment and methods for maintaining quality. In addition, they monitor all quality control activities to identify areas for improvement.

Leading for Quality

Too often, firms fail to take the initiative to make quality happen. Leading for quality means that managers must inspire and motivate employees throughout the company to achieve quality goals. They need to help employees see how they affect quality and how quality affects their jobs and their company. Leaders must continually find ways to foster a quality orientation by training employees, encouraging their involvement, and tying wages to quality of work. If managers succeed, employees will ultimately accept **quality ownership**—the idea that quality belongs to each person who creates or destroys it while performing a job.

quality ownership The concept that quality belongs to each employee who creates or destroys it in producing a good or service; the idea that all workers must take responsibility for producing a quality product.

General Electric Co. embarked on a strong quality control initiative a few years ago. Top management commitment to the program was ensured by tying executive bonuses to actual implementation of the quality control program. The program involves training managers to be "Black Belts" in quality improvement. These Black Belts then spent their time in GE plants setting up quality improvement projects. Young managers were told that they wouldn't have much of a future at GE unless they became Black Belts.

Controlling for Quality

By monitoring its products and services, a company can detect mistakes and make corrections. To do so, however, managers must first establish specific quality standards and measurements. Consider the following control system for a bank's teller services. Observant supervisors periodically evaluate transactions against a checklist. Specific aspects of each teller's work—appearance, courtesy, efficiency, and so on—are recorded. The results, reviewed with employees, either confirm proper performance or indicate changes that are needed to bring performance up to standards.

In the auto industry, a key measure of quality is the number of recalls. By this standard, there's room for improvement in total quality management at General Motors, which recalled 7.5 million vehicles in the first quarter of 2004 alone. GM says that it is being proactive and dealing with potential problems to build consumer confidence.

TOOLS FOR TOTAL QUALITY MANAGEMENT

In managing for quality, many leading companies rely on assistance from proven tools. Often, ideas for improving both the product and the production process come from **competitive product analysis**. For example, Toshiba will take apart a Xerox photocopier and test each component. Test results help Toshiba's managers decide which Toshiba product features are satisfactory (in comparison to the competition), which product features need to be upgraded, or whether Toshiba's production processes need improvement.

competitive product analysis Process by which a company analyzes a competitor's products to identify desirable improvements.

There are many specific tools that can be used to achieve TQM. Here, we briefly describe the following: *value-added analysis, statistical process control, quality/cost studies, quality improvement teams, benchmarking, getting closer to the customer, ISO 9000, re-engineering,* and *adding value through supply chains*.

Value-Added Analysis

Value-added analysis refers to the evaluation of all work activities, material flows, and paperwork to determine the value that they add for customers. It often reveals wasteful or unnecessary activities that can be eliminated without jeopardizing customer service. The basic tenet is so important that Tootsie Roll Industries, the venerable candy company, employs it as a corporate principle: "We run a trim operation and continually strive to eliminate waste, minimize cost, and implement performance improvements.[13]

value-added analysis The evaluation of all work activities, material flows, and paperwork to determine the value they add for customers.

Statistical Process Control

statistical process control (SPC) Statistical analysis techniques that allow managers to analyze variations in production data and to detect when adjustments are needed to create products with high quality reliability.

process variation Any change in employees, materials, work methods, or equipment that affects output quality.

Although every company would like complete uniformity in its outputs, all firms experience unit-to-unit variations in their products. Companies can gain better control, however, by understanding the sources of variation. **Statistical process control (SPC)** methods especially process variation studies and control charts—allow managers to analyze variations in production data.

Process Variation

Variations in a firm's products may arise from the inputs in its production process. As people, materials, work methods, and equipment change, so do production outputs. While some amount of **process variation** is acceptable, too much can result in poor quality and excessive operating costs. Consider the box-filling operation for Honey Nuggets cereal. Each automated machine fills two 400-gram boxes per second. Even under proper conditions, slight variations in cereal weight from box to box are normal. Equipment and tools wear out, the cereal may be overly moist, and machinists make occasional adjustments. But how much variation is occurring? How much is acceptable?

Information about variation in a process can be obtained from a *process capability study*. Boxes are taken from the filling machines and weighed. The results are plotted, as in Figure 12.3, and compared with the

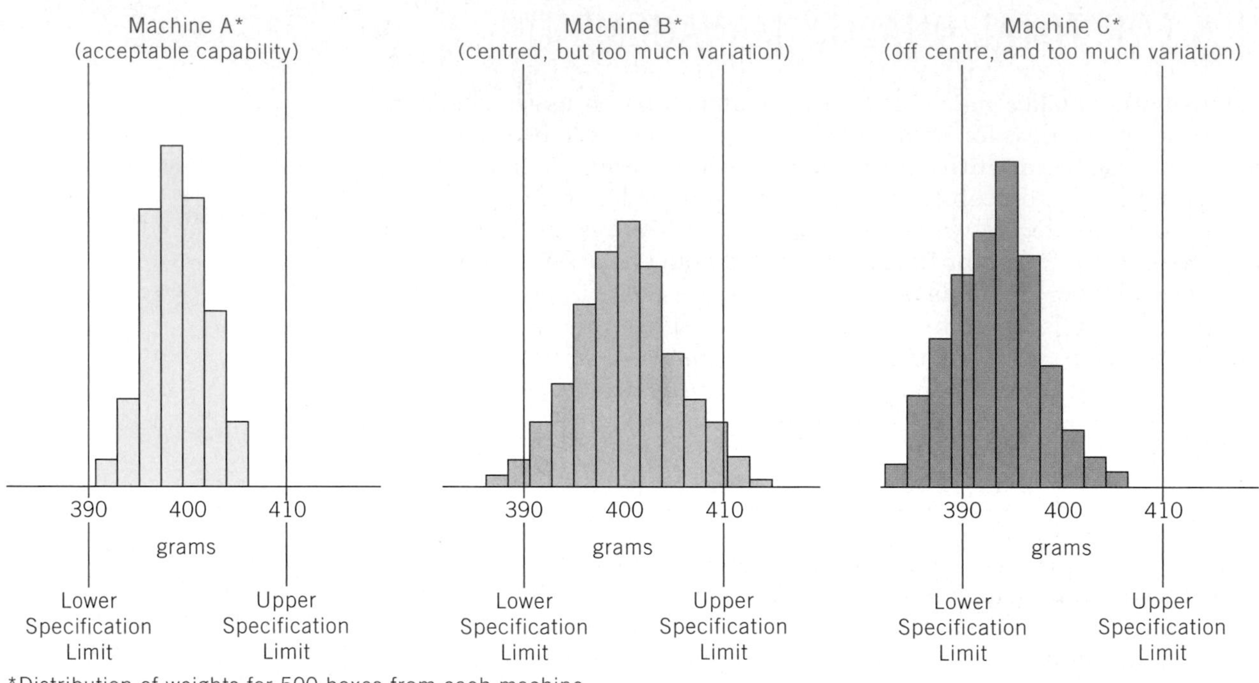

Figure 12.3 Process variation in box filling for Honey Nuggets cereal.

upper and lower specification limits (quality limits) for weight. These limits define good and bad quality for box filling. Boxes with more than 410 grams are a wasteful "giveaway." Underfilling has a cost because it is unlawful.

The chart in Figure 12.3 reveals that Machine A's output is acceptable because none of its boxes violate the quality limits. Machine A, then, is fully capable of meeting the company's quality standards. Machines B and C, however, have problems. In their present condition, they are not "capable" because they cannot reliably meet Honey Nuggets' quality standards. The company must take special—and costly—actions to sort the good from the bad boxes before releasing the cereal for shipment. Unless machines B and C are renovated, substandard production quality will plague Honey Nuggets.

Control Charts

Knowing that a process is capable of meeting quality standards is not enough. Managers must still monitor the process to prevent its drifting astray during production. To detect the beginning of bad conditions, managers can check production periodically and plot the results on a **control chart**. For example, several times a day a machine operator at Honey Nuggets might weigh several boxes of cereal together to ascertain the average weight.

control chart A statistical process control method in which results of test sampling of a product are plotted on a diagram that reveals when the process is beginning to depart from normal operating conditions.

Figure 12.4 shows the control chart for machine A, in which the first five points are randomly scattered around the centre line, indicating that the machine was operating well. However, the points for samples 5 through 8 are all above the centre line, indicating that something was causing the boxes to overfill. The last point falls outside the upper *control limit*, confirming that the process is out of control.

At this point, the machine must be shut down so that a manager and/or the operator can investigate what is causing the problem—equipment, people, materials, or work methods. Control is completed by correcting the problem and restoring the process to normal.

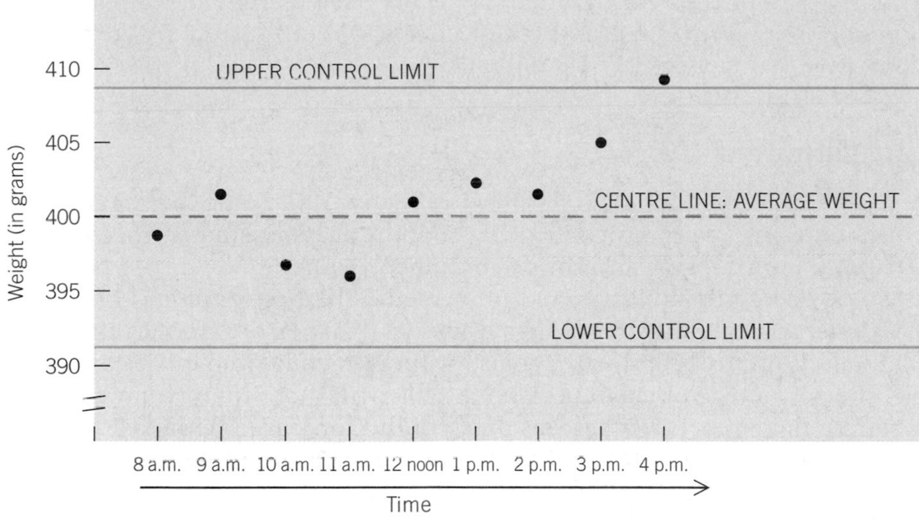

Figure 12.4 Honey Nuggets cereal process control chart for machine A.

Quality/Cost Studies

Statistical process controls help keep operations up to existing capabilities. But in today's competitive environment, firms must consistently raise quality capabilities. However, any improvement in products or production processes means additional costs, whether for new facilities, equipment, training, or other changes. Managers thus face the challenge of identifying those improvements that offer the greatest promise. **Quality/cost studies** are useful because they not only identify a firm's current costs but also reveal areas with the largest cost-savings potential.[14]

quality/cost study A method of improving product quality by assessing a firm's current quality-related costs and identifying areas with the greatest cost-saving potential.

Quality costs are associated with making, finding, repairing, or preventing defective goods and services. All of these costs should be analyzed in a quality/cost study. For example, Honey Nuggets must determine its costs for **internal failures**. These are expenses—including the costs of overfilling boxes and the costs of sorting out bad boxes—incurred during production and before bad products leave the plant. Studies indicate that many manufacturers incur very high costs for internal failures—up to 50 percent of total costs.

internal failures Expenses incurred during production and before bad products leave the plant.

Despite quality control procedures, however, some bad boxes may get out of the factory, reach the customer, and generate complaints from grocers and cereal eaters. These are **external failures** that occur outside the factory. The costs of correcting them—refunds to customers, transportation costs to return bad boxes to the factory, possible lawsuits, factory recalls—should also be tabulated in the quality/cost study.

external failures Allowing defective products to leave the factory and get into consumers' hands.

Quality Improvement Teams

Quality improvement (QI) teams are groups of employees from various work areas who meet regularly to define, analyze, and solve common production problems. Their goal is to improve both their own work methods and the products they make.[15] Many QI teams organize their own work, select leaders, and address problems in the workplace. Motorola sponsors company-wide team competitions to emphasize the value of the team approach, to recognize outstanding team performance, and to reaffirm the team's role in the company's continuous-improvement culture. Teams get higher marks for dealing with projects closely tied to Motorola's key

quality improvement (QI) team TQM tool in which groups of employees work together to improve quality.

initiatives. Over the years, competing teams have increased cellular phone production by 50 percent and cut electronic-circuit defects by 85 percent (for a one-year savings of $1.8 million).[16]

Benchmarking

benchmarking Comparing the quality of the firm's output with the quality of the output of the industry's leaders.

A powerful TQM tool that has been effective for some firms is called **benchmarking**. To improve its own products or its business procedures, a company compares its current performance against its own past performance, or one company finds and implements the best practices of others. With *internal benchmarking*, a firm tracks its own performance over time to evaluate its progress and to set goals for further improvement. As an example, the percentage of customer phone calls with more than two minutes of response time may be 15 percent this month. Compared with past months, this percentage may be high or low. In short, past performance is the benchmark for evaluating recent results.

External benchmarking begins with a critical review of competitors (or even companies in other lines of business) to determine which goods or services perform the best; these activities and products are called *best practices*. For example, Toronto Hospital gathered performance data on 26 indicators from various Canadian hospitals so that it could determine how well it was performing compared with other organizations in the health-care industry.[17] Executives from Ford, DaimlerChrysler, and General Motors frequently tour Toyota manufacturing facilities as they try to figure out how Toyota makes cars so efficiently.

Getting Closer to the Customer

As one advocate of quality improvement has put it, "Customers are an economic asset. They're not on the balance sheet, but they should be." One of the themes of this chapter has been that struggling companies have often lost sight of customers as the driving force for all business activity. Perhaps they waste resources designing products that customers do not want.

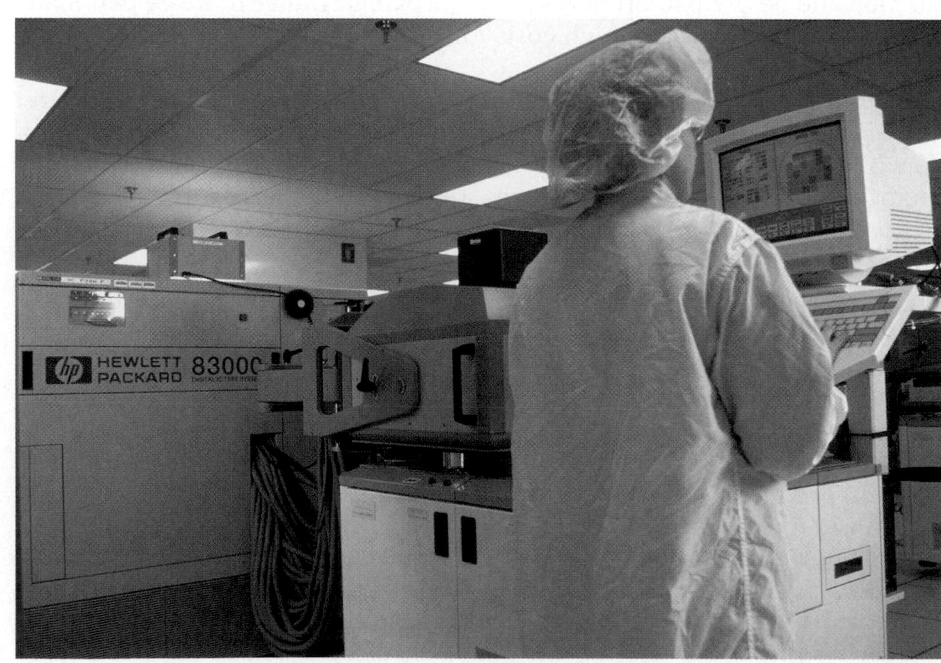

At Hewlett-Packard, testing machines use tiny probes to ensure that the electronic characteristics of every semiconductor are correct. Such systems are designed to check primarily for so-called "class defects"—problems that can affect a whole range of products on the assembly line. One bad wafer at the end of the line can represent a waste of $10 000 in costs, and its commercial value is zero.

Sometimes they ignore customer reactions to existing products or fail to keep up with changing consumer tastes. By contrast, the most successful businesses keep close to their customers and know what they want in the products they consume.

Some years ago at Greyhound Lines of Canada, the marketing and operations vice-president wanted to drive home the point to managers that clean restrooms were important to customers. He warned regional managers that he would visit bus depots on one-hour's notice to see if the restrooms were clean enough to eat dinner in. Within weeks, photos of regional managers having dinner in spotless restrooms began pouring in to the vice-president's office.[18]

Caterpillar Financial Services won the 2003 Malcolm Baldrige National Quality Award for high ratings by its customers, including dealers and buyers of Caterpillar equipment. Construction companies buying and financing equipment from Cat Financial are better satisfied, as Cat has moved its services increasingly online. Customers, who buy equipment costing anywhere from $30 000 to $2 million, now have 24-hour-a-day access to information on how much they owe and they can make payments around the clock, too. In the past, any of the 60 000 customers had to phone a Cat representative who was often unavailable, resulting in customer delays and wasted time on unsuccessful calls. Praise for the improved online system, and announcement of the quality award, is testimony to Cat Financial's dedication in knowing what customers want, and then providing it.[19]

Identify three trends in productivity and quality management, including *supply chain management*. 4

ISO 9000:2000 and ISO 14000

After the terrorist attacks in the United States in 2001, the U.S. Transportation Security Administration embarked on a mission to prevent terrorist attacks on U.S transportation systems. A unit known as AAR-500 was given responsibility for bolstering security at American airports. AAR-500 recognized a major quality problem: the need to train and certify individual employees to perform specific tasks in a revamped screening system. To train 28 000 new airport security personnel, AAR-500 turned to international quality standards that had been applied successfully in private service businesses. To instill public confidence in the new screening system, AAR-500 also adopted the principle of independent third-party certification of the system.[20]

Both the training and certification systems were based on the world-class standards of **ISO 9000**—a certification program attesting to the fact that a factory, a laboratory, or an office has met the rigorous quality management requirements set by the International Organization for Standardization. ISO 9000 (pronounced *ICE-o nine thousand*) originated in Europe to standardize materials received from suppliers in such high-technology industries as electronics, chemicals, and aviation. Today, more than 140 countries have adopted ISO 9000 as a national standard. More than 400 000 certificates have been issued in 160 countries.[21]

ISO 9000 Program certifying that a factory, laboratory, or office has met the quality management standards of the International Organization for Standardization.

The latest version, *ISO 9000:2000*, indicates that it was revised in 2000. Revised standards allow firms to show that they follow documented procedures for testing products, training workers, keeping records, and fixing defects. To become certified, companies must document the procedures followed by workers during every stage of production. The purpose is to ensure that a manufacturer's product is exactly the same today as it was yesterday and as it will be tomorrow. Ideally, standardized processes would ensure that goods are produced at the same level of quality even if all employees were replaced by a new set of workers.

ISO 14000 Certification program attesting to the fact that a factory, laboratory, or office has improved environmental performance.

The **ISO 14000** program certifies improvements in *environmental* performance. Extending the ISO approach into the arena of environmental protection and hazardous waste management, ISO 14000 requires a firm to develop an *environmental management system (EMS)*: a plan documenting how the company has acted to improve its performance in using resources (such as raw materials) and in managing pollution. A company must not only identify hazardous wastes that it expects to create, but it must also stipulate plans for treatment and disposal. ISO 14000 covers practices in environmental labelling—the use of such terms as *energy efficient* and *recyclable*—and assesses the total environmental impact of the firm's products, not just from manufacturing, but also from use and disposal.

Process Re-engineering

Every business consists of *processes*—activities that it performs regularly and routinely in conducting business. Examples abound: receiving and storing materials from suppliers, billing patients for medical treatment, filing insurance claims for auto accidents, inspecting property for termites, opening chequing accounts for new customers, filling customer orders from internet sales. Any business process can add value and customer satisfaction by performing processes well. By the same token, any business can disappoint customers and irritate business partners by managing them poorly.

business process re-engineering Redesigning of business processes to improve performance, quality, and productivity.

Business process re-engineering focusses on improving both the productivity and quality of business processes—rethinking each step of an organization's operations by starting from scratch. *Re-engineering* is the fundamental rethinking and radical redesign of business processes to achieve dramatic improvements in measures of performance, such as cost, quality, service, and speed.[22] The calling-services company GTE, for example, found that its over-the-phone service was not user-friendly for customers wanting to correct service or billing problems. To provide fast, accurate one-stop service, GTE re-engineered the whole service process by improving equipment, retraining employees, and connecting software to formerly inaccessible corporate databases.

The Re-engineering Process

Figure 12.5 shows the six steps involved in the re-engineering process. It starts with a statement of the benefits envisioned for customers and the company and then flows logically through the next five steps:

1. Identify the business activity that will be changed.
2. Evaluate information and human resources to see if they can meet the requirements for change.
3. Diagnose the current process to identify its strengths and weaknesses.
4. Create the new process design.
5. Implement the new design.

As you can see, re-engineering is a broad undertaking that requires know-how in technical matters, depends on leadership and management skills, and calls upon knowledge about customer needs and how well they are being met by the company and its competition. The bottom line in every re-engineering process is adopting a company-wide, customer-first philosophy. Redesign is guided by a desire to improve operations so that goods and services are produced at the lowest possible cost and at the highest value for the customer.

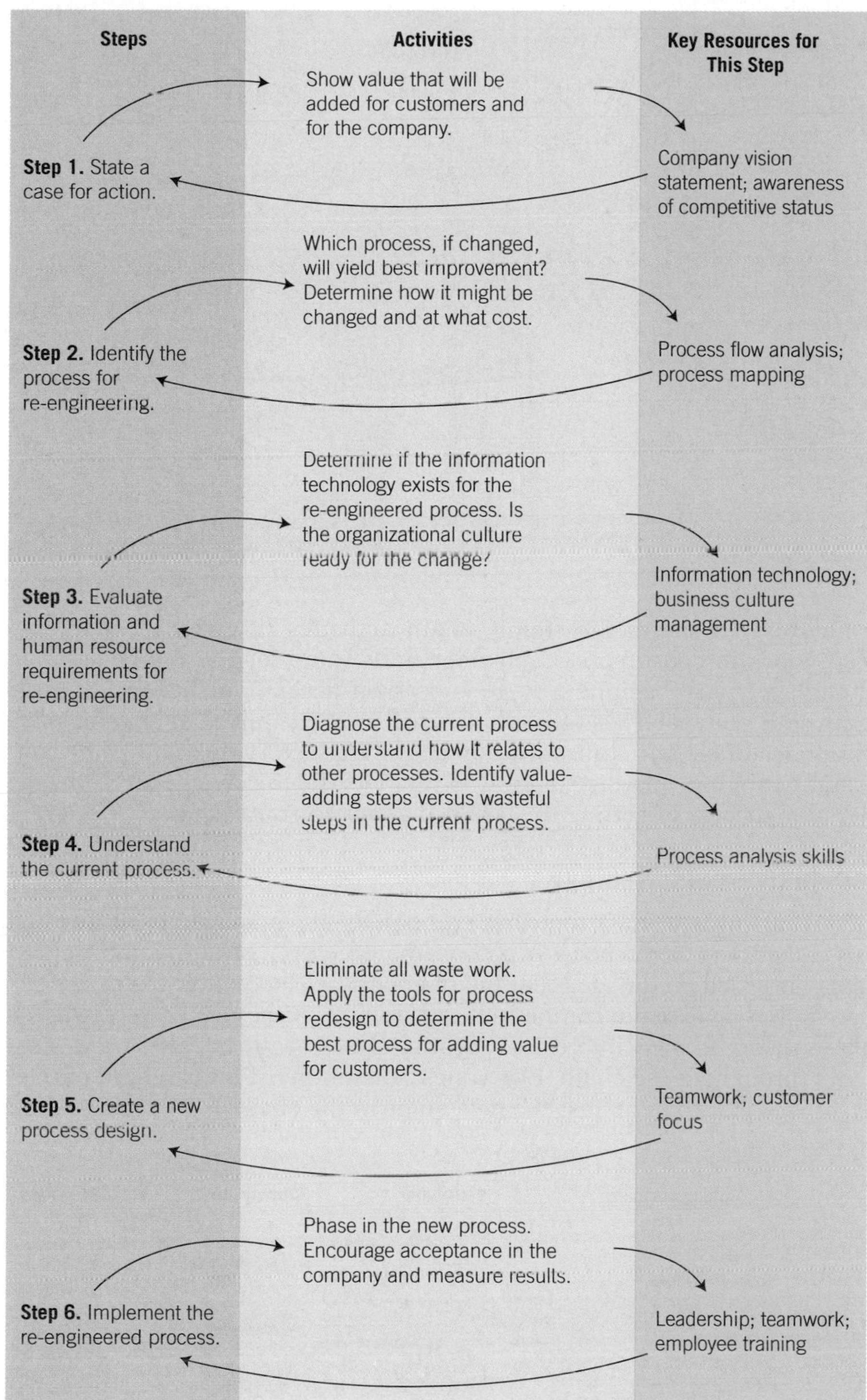

Figure 12.5 Re-engineering process.

Adding Value Through Supply Chains

Explain how a supply chain strategy differs from traditional strategies for coordinating operations among firms. 5

Managers sometimes forget that a company belongs to a network of firms that must coordinate their activities. The term *supply chain* refers to the group of companies and stream of activities that work together to create a product. A **supply chain** for any product is the flow of information, materials, and services that starts with raw-materials suppliers and continues through other stages in the operations process until the product reaches the end customer.[23]

supply chain Flow of information, materials, and services that starts with raw materials suppliers and continues through other stages in the operations process until the product reaches the end customer.

Seagate Technology, a maker of computer hard drives, used to build everything itself—disks, motors for spinning disks, and tracking mechanisms for reading and writing on disks. But it needed factories in Malaysia, Ireland, and the United States, each with its own supplies of inventory. Seagate wasn't flexible enough to respond to changes required by customers until it teamed up with a consulting firm called DesignShop and figured out how to reorganize itself. Now, company-wide operations are run by a computer-based planning system, the supplier list has been slashed, and even important components are being outsourced.

Figure 12.6 shows the supply chain activities involved in supplying baked goods to consumers. Each stage adds value for the final customer. Although a typical beginning stage is product design, our bakery example begins with raw materials (grain harvested from the farm). It also includes additional storage and transportation activities, factory operations for baking and wrapping, and distribution to retailers. Each stage depends on the others for success in getting fresh-baked goods to consumers.

The Supply Chain Strategy

Traditional strategies assume that companies are managed as individual firms rather than as members of a coordinated supply system. Supply chain strategy is based on the idea that members of the chain, working as a coordinated unit, will gain competitive advantage. Although each company looks out for its own interests, it works closely with suppliers and customers throughout the chain. Everyone focusses on the entire chain of relationships rather than on just the next stage in the chain.[24]

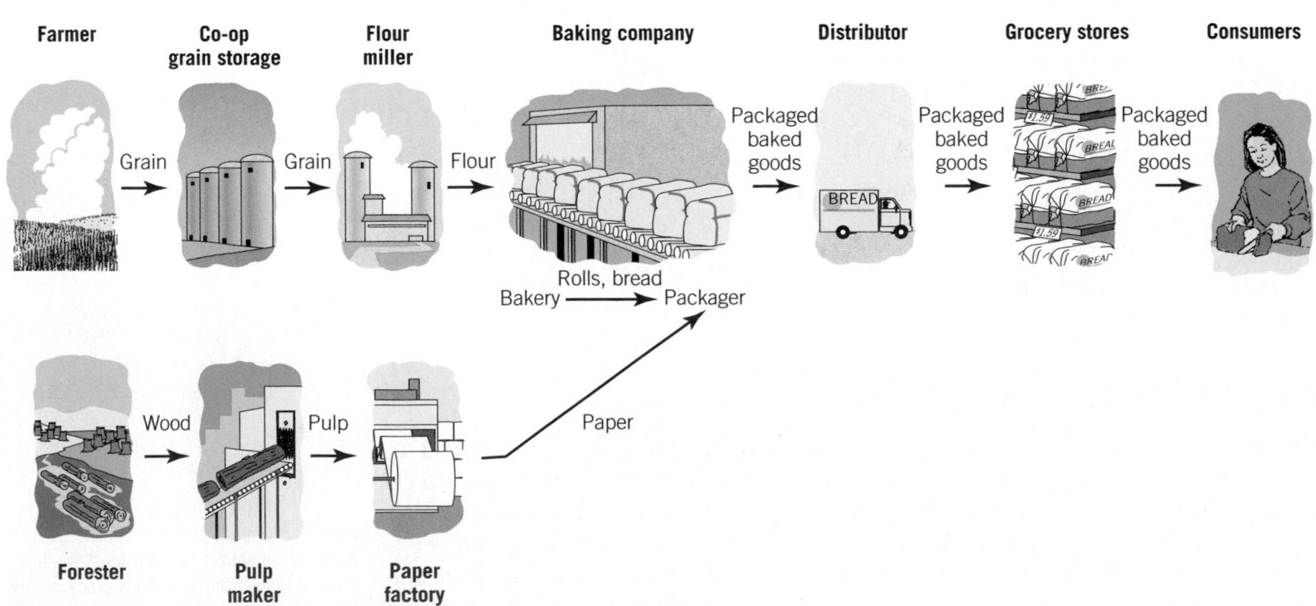

Figure 12.6 Supply chain for baked goods.

A traditionally managed bakery, for example, would focus simply on getting production inputs from flour millers and paper suppliers and supplying baked goods to distributors. Unfortunately, this approach limits the chain's performance and doesn't allow for possible improvements when activities are more carefully coordinated. Supply chain management can improve performance and, as a result, provide higher quality at lower prices.

Supply Chain Management

Supply chain management (SCM) looks at the chain as a whole to improve the overall flow through a system composed of companies working together. Because customers ultimately get better value, SCM gains competitive advantage for each supply-chain member.[25] Dell Computer's supply chain, for example, improves performance by allowing people to share information. Dell shares long-term production plans and up-to-the-minute sales data with suppliers via the internet. The process starts when customer orders are automatically translated into updated production schedules on the factory floor. These schedules are used not only by operations managers at Dell but also by such parts suppliers as Sony, which adjust their own production and shipping activities to better meet Dell's production needs. In turn, parts suppliers' updated schedules are transmitted to their materials suppliers, and so on. As Dell's requirements

supply chain management (SCM) Principle of looking at the chain as a whole to improve the overall flow through the system.

ENTREPRENEURSHIP AND NEW VENTURES

Ship Shape

Twice a year, Vanguard Global Services Inc. conducts a formal review of each of its customers' logistics processes in a search for greater efficiencies. And chances are the review will save clients time or money. "We're in a dynamic environment," says Richard Court, CEO of the cross-border logistics firm based in Mississauga, Ont. "Our capabilities and resources change, our customers' needs change, and the marketplace changes." For example, by harnessing economies of scale created by one client's fast-growing shipment volume, Vanguard was able to offer a $300 000 price reduction. While some might say Vanguard left money on the table, Court says, "The customer was thrilled."

Such initiative has won Vanguard the hearts and wallets of such customers as Sony, Hitachi, and Psion Teklogix, helping Vanguard's sales climb from $212 894 in 2000 to $12.5 million in 2005—an increase of 5774 percent in the face of trade-stifling events such as the September 11 terrorist attacks and the rise of the Canadian dollar.

Court and his two partners, Mark Bates and Edward Ayranto—who together have more than 50 years in the shipping business—launched Vanguard in 1999 to provide customized cross-border transportation services. Their focus is high-volume shippers in the automotive and electronics sectors. And their timing has been perfect: As trade between Canada and the United States gets more complicated, companies are becoming more likely to outsource shipping. Those same companies can hardly ignore Vanguard's promise of customized service for 10 percent to 50 percent less than its rivals charge.

Such savings result partly from Vanguard's preference for long-term relationships with clients. It gives Vanguard the option of performing a complex analysis of a customer's supply chain, which leads to a formal report that explains how the movement of goods can be streamlined and that quantifies the benefits.

Court says learning the ins and outs of a customer's operation typically takes three months to a year, but the effort seems to be worth it. Vanguard recently applied its magic to a handheld electronics manufacturer that had no control over shipping costs or when parts would arrive, due to its dependence on a multitude of suppliers that controlled their own shipping. Vanguard cut the firm's transportation costs by 30 percent by assuming responsibility for all shipments, leveraging economies of scale, and even providing pre-printed labels and waybills to the suppliers.

Not content to rest on its laurels, Vanguard is accelerating growth. The firm recently moved from a 40 000-sq.-ft. warehouse to a state-of-the-art 65 000-sq.-ft. facility, and is investing in warehousing systems and technology that will improve the visibility and control of shipments. "We are expanding our capabilities and increasing our capacity," says Court. "It's all part of moving to provide the whole product for our customer."

Before too long, you will be able to pick up an item from a Wal-Mart shelf and scan it automatically on to your debit card, skipping the checkout line altogether. The same technology—called radio frequency identification (RFID)—will signal the Wal-Mart storeroom to restock the item you bought.

change, suppliers synchronize their schedules to produce the right materials and parts efficiently.

Because the smooth flow of accurate information along the chain reduces unwanted inventories, avoids delays, and cuts supply times, materials move faster to business customers and individual consumers. For both, the efficiency of SCM means faster deliveries and lower costs than customers could get if each member acted only according to its own operations requirements.

Re-engineering Supply Chains for Better Results

By lowering costs, speeding up service, or coordinating flows of information and materials, process improvements and re-engineering often improve supply chains. Consider, for example, the supply chain for transistor radios. For a long time, Li & Fung, the largest export trading company in Hong Kong, imported radio components made in both the United States and Asia. After supplying these components to a Hong Kong assembly factory, Li & Fung shipped finished radios to U.S. and European distributors. Gradually, however, rising wage rates in Hong Kong became a threat to Li & Fung. Increases in assembly costs would cut into its profits and market share. The company thus re-engineered its supply chain. First, it added a new stage. It created little kits—plastic bags filled with all the components needed to make a radio. Second, one supply-chain link was replaced. The kits were shipped to a new assembler in southern China instead of to the old Hong Kong factory. Finally, another stage was added. After the Chinese supplier had completed the labour-intensive, low-wage assembly process, finished radios were shipped back to Hong Kong for final inspection and testing by Li & Fung before being shipped to customers. The result: lower prices and increased business for companies throughout the chain.

PRODUCTIVITY AND QUALITY AS COMPETITIVE TOOLS

6 Discuss four strategies that companies used to improve productivity and quality.

A company's ability to compete by improving productivity and quality depends on participation by all parts of the firm. And total firm involvement stems from having company-wide strategies that we consider in this section: the company's willingness to invest in innovation, its long-run perspective on its goals, its concern for the quality of work life, and the improving of its service operations.

Invest in Innovation and Technology

Many firms that have continued to invest in innovative technology have enjoyed rising productivity and rising incomes. For example, while Steinway & Sons' piano factory is just as concerned as ever about maintaining the highest quality in its products, it's using newer technology to help the woodworkers do their jobs more efficiently and precisely. "It still takes us a year to craft one of these things," says Steinway president Bruce Stevens, "but technology is assisting us in making more precise parts that our people can assemble. It's helping us create a better instrument."[26]

Adopt a Long-Run Perspective

Instead of emphasizing short-run results, many quality-oriented firms are committed to a long-run perspective for **continuous improvement**—the ongoing commitment to improving products and processes, step by step, in pursuit of ever-increasing customer satisfaction. Motorola is a good example. In 1996, its Six Sigma program set a target of 3.4 defects per million parts. By 2003, the company's production-monitoring software—Manufacturing Intellitrak—had helped to reduce errors in some applications to two defects per *billion* parts.[27]

continuous improvement The ongoing commitment to improve products and processes, step by step, in pursuit of ever-increasing customer satisfaction.

The Six Sigma program, which is used by many other companies besides Motorola, continuously captures, measures, and eliminates defects in every company-wide process, from financial transactions and accounting practices, to R&D and production processes, to marketing and human resources activities. The earliest adopters of Six Sigma in Canada have been full-service brokerages such as Royal LePage Commercial who have international clients.[28]

Emphasize Quality of Work Life

The products and services of businesses represent such a large part of total national output that the well-being and participation of their workers is central to improving national productivity. How can firms make their employees' jobs more challenging and interesting? Many companies are enhancing workers' physical and mental health through recreational facilities, counselling services, and other programs. In addition, more and more firms have started programs to empower and train employees.

Employee Empowerment

Many firms are replacing the work environments of yesterday, based on the principle of management-directed mass production, with worker-oriented environments that foster loyalty, teamwork, and commitment. Trident Precision Manufacturing has a program for full employee involvement. Over 95 percent of employee recommendations for process improvements have been accepted since the program started. As a result, employee turnover has fallen from 41 percent to less than 5 percent. Sales per employee have more than doubled.

As we saw in Chapter 10, firms using this approach have found success in the concept of *employee empowerment*—the principle that all employees are valuable contributors to a business and should be entrusted with certain decisions regarding their work. The Hampton Inns motel chain, for example, initiated a program of refunds to customers who were dissatisfied with their stays for any reason. Managers were pleased, and the refund policy created far more additional business than it cost. A surprise bonus was the increased morale when employees—everyone from front-desk personnel to maids—were empowered to grant refunds. With greater participation and job satisfaction, employee turnover was reduced to less than one-half its previous level. Such confidence in employee involvement contrasts sharply with the traditional belief that managers are the primary source of decision making and problem solving.

Employee Training

Employee involvement is effective when it is implemented with preparation and intelligence. *Training* is a key method of preparing employees for productivity-improvement programs. In fact, a recent American Management Association survey found a direct relationship between training and greater productivity profitability: Firms that increased training activities were 66 percent more likely to report improved productivity and three times more likely to report increased profits. Moreover, after training, waste diminishes and quality increases. Finally, team training not only teaches employees to work in groups, but it also acquaints them more fully with the company's markets and operations.[29]

Improve the Service Sector

As important as employee attitudes are to goods production, they are even more crucial to service production, since employees often *are* the service. The service sector has grown rapidly, but this growth has often come at a cost of high inefficiency. Many newly created service jobs have not been streamlined. Some companies operate effectively, but many others are very inefficient, dragging down overall productivity. As new companies enter these markets, however, the increased need to compete should eventually force service producers to operate more productively.

Quality begins with listening to customers to determine what services they want. Companies in the temporary-services industry, for example, have long emphasized the needs of clients for clerical and light-industrial employees. More recently, however, temp services have realized the need for highly skilled, specialized temps such as nurses, accountants, and scientists.

In trying to offer more satisfactory services, many providers have discovered five criteria that customers use to judge service quality:[30]

- *Reliability*: Perform the service as promised, both accurately and on time.
- *Responsiveness*: Be willing to help customers promptly.
- *Assurance*: Maintain knowledgeable and courteous employees who will earn the trust and confidence of customers.
- *Empathy*: Provide caring, individualized attention to customers.
- *Tangibles*: Maintain a pleasing appearance of personnel, materials, and facilities.

Summary of Learning Objectives

1. **Describe the connection between *productivity* and *quality*.** *Productivity* is a measure of economic performance; it compares how much is produced with the resources used to produce it. *Quality* is a product's fitness for use. However, an emphasis solely on productivity or solely on quality is not enough. Profitable competition in today's business world demands high levels of both productivity and quality.

2. **Understand the importance of increasing productivity.** It is important that Canadian business firms increase their rate of productivity growth so that they can be competitive in world markets. As Canadian business firms increase productivity, they will be able to produce a greater quantity of goods without using more resources.

3. **Identify the activities involved in *total quality management*, and describe six tools that companies can use to achieve it.** *Total quality management (TQM)* (sometimes called *quality assurance*) includes all the activities necessary for getting high-quality goods and services into the marketplace. The strategic approach to TQM begins with customer focus. It includes methods for determining what customers want and then directing all the company's resources toward satisfying those wants and needs. Total participation is mandatory, and TQM is more than part-time. It demands continuous improvement of products, services, and improvement in all of the company's internal processes, such as accounting, delivery, billing, and information flows. Six tools that are used to achieve TQM include (1) *Value-added analysis* (the evaluation of all work activities, material flows, and paperwork to determine the value that they add for customers); (2) *statistical process control (SPC)* (methods by which employees can gather data and analyze variations in production activities to determine when adjustments are needed); (3) *quality/cost studies* (identify a firm's current costs but also reveal areas with the largest cost savings potential); (4) *quality improvement (QI) teams* (groups of employees from various work areas who meet regularly to define, analyze, and solve common production problems); (5) *benchmarking* (improving business products or procedures by comparing them to either the firm's own past performance or the best practices of others); and (6) *getting closer to the customer* (know what customers want in the products they consume).

4. **Identify three trends in productivity and quality management, including *supply chain management*.** (1) *ISO 9000* is a certification program attesting to the fact that a factory, a laboratory, or an office has met the rigorous quality-management requirements set by the International Organization for Standardization. It allows firms to show that they follow documented procedures for testing products, training workers, keeping records, and fixing product defects. *ISO 14000* certifies improvements in *environmental* performance. (2) *Business process re-engineering* focusses on improving both the productivity and quality of business processes—rethinking each step of an organization's operations by starting from scratch. *Re-engineering* is the fundamental rethinking and redesign of processes to achieve dramatic improvements in measures of performance. (3) The *supply chain* refers to the group of companies and stream of activities that operate together to create a product. Traditional strategies assume that companies are managed as individual firms rather than as members of a coordinated supply chain. *Supply chain management (SCM)* looks at the chain as a whole to improve the overall flow through a system composed of companies working together. Because customers ultimately get better value, SCM gives chain members a competitive advantage.

5. **Explain how a supply chain strategy differs from traditional strategies for coordinating operations among firms.** The supply chain strategy is based on the idea that members of the supply chain can gain competitive advantage by working together as a coordinated system of units. For example, sharing information allows companies to reduce inventories, improve quality, and speed delivery of products to consumers. In contrast, traditional strategies assume that companies are managed as individual firms, with each one acting in its own interest.

6. **Discuss four strategies that companies use to improve productivity and quality.** (1) *Invest in innovation and technology*: Many firms that have continued to invest in innovative technology have enjoyed rising productivity and rising incomes. Increasingly, investments in the internet and information technology are rising, with new applications in every major industry. (2) *Adopt a long-run perspective*: Many quality-oriented firms are committed to long-term efforts at continuous improvement: the ongoing commitment to improving products and processes, step by step, in pursuit of ever-increasing customer satisfaction. (3) *Emphasize quality of work life*: Business products and services represent such a large part of total national output that the well-being and participation of workers is crucial to improving national productivity. (4) *Improve the service sector*: As important as employee attitude is to goods production, it is even more crucial to service production, where employees often are the service. In trying to offer more satisfactory services, many companies have discovered five criteria that customers use to judge service quality: *reliability*, *responsiveness*, *assurance*, *empathy*, and *tangibles*.

KEY TERMS

benchmarking, 382
business process re-engineering, 384
competitive product analysis, 379
continuous improvement, 389
control chart, 380
external failures, 381
internal failures, 381
ISO 14000, 384
ISO 9000, 383
labour productivity, 371
performance quality, 377
process variation, 379
productivity, 370
quality, 370
quality improvement (QI) team, 381
quality ownership, 378
quality reliability, 377
quality/cost study, 381
statistical process control (SPC), 379
supply chain, 385
supply chain management (SCM), 387
total quality management (TQM), 376
value-added analysis, 379

QUESTIONS FOR ANALYSIS

1. What is the relationship between productivity and quality?
2. High productivity in the service sector has historically been difficult to achieve. Why was this so? What might be changing in this area that will cause service productivity to increase during the next decade?
3. Explain how inputs and outputs relate to each other in the basic equation for measuring labour productivity.
4. What are the costs and benefits for a company that is in the process of deciding to pursue quality and productivity as competitive tools?
5. Explain how the functions of management (planning, organizing, leading, and controlling) relate to one another in the pursuit of quality.
6. How might benchmarking be used to increase productivity in the service sector?
7. Why is employee empowerment essential to the success of quality improvement teams?

APPLICATION EXERCISES

1. Interview a production manager in a local firm and determine which of the tools for total quality management the company is currently using. Also determine why the company has chosen not to use some of the tools.
2. Using a local company as an example, show how you would conduct a quality/cost study. Identify the cost categories and give some examples of the costs in each category. Which categories do you expect to have the highest and lowest costs? Why?
3. Select a company of interest to you and consider the suggestions for competing that are detailed in this chapter. Which of these suggestions apply to this company? What additional suggestions would you make to help this company improve its overall quality and productivity?

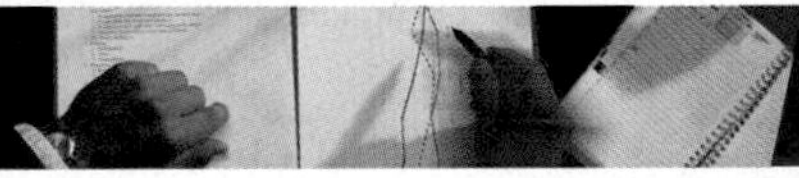

BUILDING YOUR BUSINESS SKILLS

Making Your Benchmark in the Business World

Goal

To encourage students to understand ways in which benchmarking can improve quality and productivity.

The Situation

As the director of maintenance for a regional airline, you are disturbed to learn that the cost of maintaining your 100-plane fleet is skyrocketing. A major factor is repair time; when maintenance or repairs are required, work often proceeds slowly. As a result, additional aircraft must be pressed into service to meet the schedule. To address the problem, you decide to use a powerful total quality management tool called *benchmarking*: You will approach your problem by studying ways in which other companies have successfully managed similar problems. Your goal is to apply the best practices to your own maintenance and repair operation.

Assignment

Step 1

Working with three or four other students, choose your benchmarking target from among the following choices:

▶▶▶

- the maintenance and repair operations of a competing airline
- the pit crew operations of an Indianapolis 500 race car team
- the maintenance and repair operations of a nationwide trucking company

  Write a memo explaining the reasons for your choice.

Step 2

Write a list of benchmarking questions that will help you learn the best practices of your targeted company. Your goal is to ask questions that will help you improve your own operation. These questions will be asked during on-site visits.

Step 3

As part of a benchmarking project, you will be dealing with your counterparts in other companies. You have a responsibility to prepare for these encounters, and you must remember that what you learn during the exchange process is privileged information. Given these requirements, describe the steps that you would take before your first on-site visit, and outline your benchmarking code of ethics.

Follow-Up Questions

1. Why is benchmarking an important method for improving quality?
2. Why did you make your benchmarking choice? Explain why the company you selected holds more promise than other companies in helping you solve your internal maintenance problems.
3. What kind of information would help you improve the efficiency of your operations? Are you interested in management information, technical information, or both?
4. In an age of heightened competition, why do you think companies are willing to benchmark with each other?

EXERCISING YOUR ETHICS

Calculating the Cost of Conscience

The Situation

Product quality and cost affect every firm's reputation and profitability as well as the satisfaction of customers. This exercise will expose you to some ethical considerations that pertain to certain cost and service decisions that must be made by operations managers.

The Dilemma

As director of quality for a major appliance manufacturer, Ruth was reporting to the executive committee on the results of a recent program for correcting problems with a newly redesigned rotary compressor that the company had recently begun putting in its refrigerators. After receiving several customer complaints, the quality lab and the engineering department had determined that some of the new compressor units ran more loudly than expected. Some remedial action was needed. One option was simply waiting until customers complained and responding to each complaint if and when it occurred. Ruth, however, had decided that this approach was inconsistent with the company's policy of offering the highest quality in the industry. Deciding that the firm's reputation called for a proactive, "pro-quality" approach, Ruth had initiated a program for contacting all customers who had purchased refrigerators containing the new compressor.

Unfortunately, her "quality-and-customers-first" policy was expensive. Local service representatives had to phone every customer in each area of the country, make appointments for home visits, and replace original compressors with a newer model. But because replacement time was only one-half hour, customers were hardly inconvenienced, and food stayed refrigerated without interruption. Customer response to the replacement program was overwhelmingly favourable.

Near the end of Ruth's report, an executive vice-president was overheard to comment, "Ruth's program has cost this company $400 million in service expenses." Two weeks later, Ruth was fired.

Questions for Discussion

1. What are the underlying ethical issues in this situation?
2. What are the respective roles of profits, obligations to customers, and employee considerations for the firm in this situation?
3. Suppose you were an employee who realized that your company was selling defective appliances. Suppose that the cost of correction might put the firm out of business. What would you do?

CONCLUDING CASE 12-1

Keeping Track of German Engineering

For auto enthusiasts, the first faint signs of criticism seemed an anomaly, a false blip on the radar screen, rather than the beginning of the full-scale trend that was to follow. Results of a secret European poll on car quality were leaked to the press in 2002, and Mercedes—for decades the pride of German engineering—was not at the top of the list. The poll, conducted by Europe's auto makers, showed Mercedes quality and customer satisfaction slipping since 1999 to levels even below Opel, the German-made General Motors brand with a not-so-good image in the European market. A more recent German study of durability during the first three years of ownership rated six Toyota models and five other cars ahead of the MLK, the highest-rated Mercedes model. And contrary to expectations, the quality rankings for Mercedes were nose-diving in North America as well: A 2001 J.D. Power & Associates study of vehicle dependability found Mercedes tumbling to eleventh place from sixth place the year before, leaving it alongside Jaguar, Lincoln, and Cadillac.

"Being Mercedes, quality is absolutely the highest priority," said company spokeswoman Donna Boland. "It's what our brand is based on. We will use every resource at our disposal to bring those numbers up," she added at the time. But the J.D. Power numbers indicated that a challenging climb lay ahead for this industry icon. The survey of some 156 000 car owners reported that five-year-old Mercedes cars had grown to 296 problems per 100 vehicles, versus 285 for other luxury brands. When questioned about specific problem areas, drivers gave Mercedes the biggest markdown of all premium brands for quality of "transmission" and "features/controls." J.D. Power then downgraded the overall quality of Mercedes from "good" to "fair" in 2002. "It's becoming more evident that Mercedes-built quality isn't as bulletproof as it used to be," said Al Bedwell, research manager at J.D. Power in Oxford, England.

Oddly enough, the quality downslide started when Mercedes decided to shift away from its traditional orientation of "making what the engineers want" and, instead, began focussing more on "making what consumers want." Executives insisted that engineers design cars to meet a certain price point. The idea was to increase sales with a broader range of cars, especially with smaller and less expensive models such as the A-Class. For most firms such a decision makes sense, but the long-standing reputation for engineering and precision workmanship had been a unique competitive asset in the industry for Mercedes.

Although the new consumer strategy worked—worldwide sales and profits increased—quality ratings have taken a beating. By 2003, the quality reputation suffered further with problems in advanced electronic features, and a J.D. Power survey showed customer satisfaction only slightly above the industry average and below Chrysler. Meanwhile, as sales of its upscale models began to slump, a new study announced that Mercedes had lost its first-place ranking as the car model retaining the greatest percentage of its value over time. According to *Automotive Lease Guide*, the 2004 models retained 52 percent of their value after a three-year lease, down from 54.5 percent a year earlier. Rival BMW moved into first place, followed by Honda, Lexus, Toyota, and Acura, then Mercedes. Even so, *Automotive Lease Guide* President Raj Sundaram points out that the Mercedes brand still has a strong resale: "This residual [value] that Mercedes has, a lot of other brands would love to have it." Still, that's not consolation enough for the folks at Mercedes. In one of the few times executives have publicly commented on the quality issue, DaimlerChrysler Chief Executive Jurgen Schrempp admitted the company's concern about Mercedes quality.

Customers willingly pay a premium price—up to $126 000 for a CL600 sedan—because Mercedes cars are engineered to higher standards, are in the forefront with advanced technology features, and are assembled with greater care than other cars. At least that has been the belief of luxury car-lovers—until recently. Owners and company executives alike have watched in disbelief as the Mercedes quality ranking among car brands sold in the United States tumbled from number one in 1993 to number three in 1999 to twenty-sixth place in 2003 (based on problems reported after three years). The brand's dignified top-of-the-line reputation in past years is contradicted today by angry comments—about leaky roofs, faulty electronics, non-inflating air bags, and other failed expectations—posted publicly on websites such as troublebenz.com and lemonmb.com.

The quality downslide is having its effects on profitability, too. Mercedes sold fewer cars in Europe and Japan in 2002 than in 2001, and sales were off another 2 percent in 2003. Although U.S sales were up more than 3 percent for 2003, rival BMW's sales surpassed Mercedes, and market research revealed the number of drivers wanting a Lexus is growing twice as fast as those wanting a Mercedes. In contrast to a decade or more ago, when Mercedes was one of few genuinely fine products for luxury car fans, today's drivers are not so kind to any one brand. "The market is less and less forgiving," says Garel Rhys, director of the Center for Automotive Industry Research at the University of Cardiff in Wales. "People don't have to wait for Mercedes to sort itself out. They're going to buy a BMW or Lexus."

Mercedes is taking drastic steps to keep customers happy and restore confidence in the company's once-pristine reputation. To remedy one recent problem, nearly 2000 owners were offered new E-class cars—at no charge—with factory-installed navigation systems to replace cars with failed navigation systems that had been installed after purchase. In a more strategic outreach for customer satisfaction, Mercedes executives are urging U.S. dealers to invest $500 million for expanded service facilities to handle complaints, including training for 1000 new service technicians. Meanwhile, back at Mercedes headquarters in Stuttgart, Germany, CEO Jurgen Hubbert is reorganizing the company's electronics engineering to prevent premature introduction of the latest technology in its high-end cars. In their haste to catch up with Asian car makers, over-eager engineers sometimes push for new gadgets, such as navigation, phone, radio, satellite, and computer diagnostics without first testing them as a unified system to ensure they work together reliably.

Radical redesign is high on the agenda for the M-class sport-utility vehicle, the Mercedes product receiving, perhaps, more customer complaints than any other since its introduction in 1998. With malfunctions on nearly every part of the car, dealers have been unable to keep pace with its service requirements. The 2005 model was completely re-engineered with a car-like unibody frame instead of the original truck-like body-on-frame structure. Similarly, the smallest Mercedes model—the A-Class, with a short wheel base and high roof—needed expensive re-engineering for the suspension system after the car failed a safety test conducted by a Swedish car magazine. These recent failures have revealed a recurring Mercedes problem: The company is unable to design a car right the first time, and that causes customer complaints, lower quality, expensive repairs, and a tarnished image. But it also points to an area that, if improved, could lead to the company's revival as the industry's quality leader.

Questions for Discussion

1. How would you define "quality" and how is quality measured in this industry? Are some measurements more useful than others? Explain.
2. Think about Mercedes products, the company, and its customers. What are the basic causes that led to declining quality?
3. Consider the costs that Mercedes has incurred from declining quality. What are the kinds (categories) of costs resulting from poor quality? Give examples from the case illustrating each category in your list. Which category do you suppose is most costly? Explain.
4. What further steps or actions (in addition to those listed in the case) would you recommend for restoring the quality reputation of Mercedes? What priority ordering would you assign for those steps?
5. In hindsight, what actions could have been taken at Mercedes to maintain its top quality position and prevent deterioration of quality? For each action you identify, explain how it would have prevented the company's quality downfall.

CONCLUDING CASE 12-2

Supply Chain Management at Loblaw

Loblaw Companies Limited is Canada's biggest seller of groceries, and its Real Canadian Superstores—which sell both groceries and general merchandise—are a prominent feature on the Canadian retail scene. Because price-conscious consumers are always looking for the best prices, and because Wal-Mart announced that it was poised to open its own superstores, Loblaw decided that it must improve its supply chain system to compete.

In 2005, Loblaw had come to the conclusion that it was taking too long for its products to get from its warehouses to its retail grocery stores. To fight off Wal-Mart, and to better serve customers, Loblaw embarked on a $62 million restructuring project, which involved improving its supply chain network, reorganizing grocery merchandising, procurement, and operations groups, updating its information technology systems, consolidating work formerly done in regional offices into its new Ontario head office building, reducing the number of warehouses from 32 to 26, consolidating operations in state-of-the-art facilities, and cutting 1400 jobs.

If Loblaw cannot effectively sell both groceries and general merchandise, it will be at a disadvantage compared to Wal-Mart. Loblaw must compete with Wal-Mart's legendary supply chain management system (described in the Opening Case in Chapter 13). To do so, it must develop its own system for keeping in-demand products on its shelves. Such a system will also allow Loblaw to lower its prices and compete with Wal-Mart. Loblaw has hired a supply chain expert from Wal-Mart to spearhead the resolution of its distribution problems.

Loblaw is wise to not underestimate the Wal-Mart threat. In the United States, Wal-Mart went from a zero share in groceries to become that country's largest grocer in less than a decade. If Wal-Mart has that kind of success in Canada, it will obviously have a detrimental effect on Canadian retailers like Loblaw and Sobeys.

Problems developed as system implementation began, and Loblaw president John Lederer admitted to financial analysts that the company had moved too fast in trying to implement too many different changes. For example, the company experienced problems as it tried to move 2000 administrative employees to the company's new headquarters in Brampton, Ontario. When about 75 general merchandise product buyers decided to quit the company rather than move, this turnover made it difficult to maintain continuity with suppliers. These missteps not only cost the company millions, they set back its plans for implementation by at least a year.

As well, too many distribution facilities were closed before the newer, high-tech ones were ready to cope with increased volume. One supplier shipped merchandise to the Calgary warehouse, but the shipment was refused. Many weeks passed before the shipment was finally accepted and the supplier was paid. These distribution problems forced the company to pull back on marketing its general merchandise offerings. Since it is well known in the retail business that customers get very unhappy when advertised items are not on the shelf, it made little sense to spend money on marketing if the company couldn't guarantee product availability.

Loblaw also incurred some other not-so-obvious costs because of distribution problems. For example, it had to mark down many toys because they were received too late for the Christmas season. Loblaw discovered that it isn't only groceries that are perishable.

Further problems arose in Loblaw's retail stores, where shelves were sometimes empty. Because customers don't know all the products that the superstores carry, there are often noticeably fewer people in the non-grocery sections. In 2005, Loblaw's store productivity declined 2.4 percent.

Not all of Loblaw's problems are logistical. In an attempt to compete with Wal-Mart—which is well-known for its anti-union stance (see the Business Accountability box in Chapter 9)—Loblaw is trying to reduce labour costs by getting the union to agree to wage cuts. Its employees are represented by the United Food and Commercial Workers union.

The news is not all bad for Loblaw. Even though it missed financial analysts' estimates for three straight quarters, and even though the price of the company's shares has dropped, it appears that analysts are willing to give Loblaw a break because they realize that even strong retailers occasionally encounter problems. The general consensus is that Loblaw is making the right moves to strengthen their long-term competitive position. This is particularly important given Wal-Mart's plans in Canada.

Questions for Discussion

1. What is a supply chain? Why is efficiency in its supply chain so crucial to Loblaw?
2. What is supply chain management? How is it relevant for Loblaw?
3. What is the relationship between supply chain management, productivity, and quality?

CHAPTER 13

Managing Information Systems and Communication Technology

After reading this chapter, you should be able to:

1. Explain why businesses must manage *information* and show how computer systems and communication technologies have revolutionized *information management*.
2. Identify and briefly describe three elements of *data communication networks*—the internet, the World Wide Web, and intranets.
3. Describe five *new options for organizational design* that have emerged from the rapid growth of information technologies.
4. Discuss different information-systems *application programs* that are available for users at various organizational levels.
5. Identify and briefly describe the *main elements of an information system*.
6. Briefly describe the content and role of a *database* and the purpose of *database software* for information systems.

We hear it all the time: "Information is power." And that's true. But it's also true that information is critical for business success, especially in the rapidly changing globalized economy that has emerged during the past decade or so. To survive in this "new world," managers need accurate information about not only the internal workings of their business, but also about how their business is connecting with the external environment. It is especially important that businesses connect with their customers. Some of the recent developments in inventory management, retailing, and forestry that are helping companies connect with their customers are described below.

INVENTORY MANAGEMENT

It could be the biggest new thing in inventory management since the invention of the bar code 30 years ago. It's called Radio Frequency Identification (RFID), and it allows information encoded on small tags to be transmitted by radio signal to scanners and computer networks. The tags can be "read" even when they are out of sight and on the move.

RFID is expected to eventually replace the bar code, and will allow public- and private-sector organizations to accurately keep track of people and products in real time. It will, for example, allow companies to speed up the rate at which products get to the store shelf so that in-demand products are available when customers want them. This is important because retail studies suggest that a store typically loses 4 percent of its potential sales because of out-of-stock items. The RFID tags can also give customers information they may be interested in. For example, RFID tags are used on Japanese Kobe beef. Customers can scan the tag at the retail store and find out exactly which farm the beef came from, what it was fed, and if it was treated with antibiotics.

Two Canadian companies are providing RFID products to interested businesses. Samsys Technologies Inc. of Richmond Hill, Ontario, has focussed on developing "readers" for supply chain management applications. It has already delivered an automatic tracking system to the U.S. Army Joint Munitions Command, and its readers are being used in a pilot program at Pacific Cycle LLC, the largest bicycle manufacturer in the United States. The second company is Sirit Inc. of Mississauga, Ontario, which focusses on selling transponders for vehicles using highway tolls.

RETAILING

With sales of nearly $300 billion annually, Wal-Mart has taken the retail world by storm and is the world's largest company. How has Wal-Mart accomplished this feat? First and foremost is Wal-Mart's policy of everyday low prices. But there is another important reason: product availability. Wal-Mart is a master at providing products that are virtually always in stock. Its customers are therefore confident that they can find what they want at Wal-Mart.

But exactly *how* has Wal-Mart been able to ensure product availability? The answer is a space-age information system that keeps track of every single item sold in every Wal-Mart store around the world. The system puts into practice founder Sam Walton's belief that to be successful in retailing, you have to keep an eye on what is selling at each retail store, and why it is selling.

The information system works like this. When a customer in a Wal-Mart store buys a certain item, its Uniform Product Code (UPC) is scanned. The information is first beamed to Wal-Mart's own satellite, and then to Wal-Mart's Computer Data Processing Center in Bentonville, Arkansas. All sales are recorded and put into the database that allows Wal-Mart to track the shopping and spending patterns of its customers. In each retail store, Wal-Mart employees can get the same information by reading the UPC bar code with their Telxon wireless device.

Next, orders are sent to suppliers when restocking of an item is needed. These suppliers respond by shipping the required products to the appropriate Wal-Mart distribution centre. Supplier trucks pull up on one side of the building to unload, and Wal-Mart trucks load up on the other side. Each Wal-Mart store that the distribution centre serves has its own loading door. Once loaded, the trucks race off to the local Wal-Mart to deliver the goods to re-supply the shelves.

Wal-Mart's information system not only keeps the shelves of Wal-Mart stores stocked, it also helps to cut costs because products are not sent to individual stores until they are actually needed. It is really just-in-time retailing. The information system also provides an added benefit: It allows Wal-Mart's suppliers to better plan their production schedules because they know almost instantaneously what is going on at the retail level.

Wal-Mart is adopting the RFID system because it wants to have accurate information about the location of its vast amount of inventory. In 2005, 137 of its largest suppliers tagged pallets of products. Nearly two-thirds of items are currently tagged, and the number is growing. The data are shared with Wal-Mart's suppliers and allow them to see where their products are going. Wal-Mart thinks the RFID system will help reduce product returns and recalls.

The RFID idea sounds like a good thing. But consumer and privacy advocates have raised concerns about the RFID technology because they fear that embedded chips will lead to a "Big Brother" situation where companies will be tempted to misuse the detailed information they have about consumers. This is not idle speculation. Benetton Group was going to implant RFID chips in the clothes it sells, but dropped the idea when consumers said they didn't like the fact that the company could track them after they left the store. Ontario's privacy commissioner says that RFID makers and users will have to adopt privacy safeguards if they want to avoid a consumer backlash.

FORESTRY

Something even more sophisticated than RFID technology is being contemplated by forestry companies. Canfor Corp. has a vision of the future that includes sensors attached to trees that would indicate whether the tree is ready to be harvested and how it should be cut up. These sensors (called *motes*) would provide information on the tree's growth rate and size, the soil conditions, the amount of light the tree is receiving, and other things that influence tree growth. This information would then be transmitted to a central computer. With this system of information gathering, timber companies would know exactly how much lumber inventory they have while their trees are still in the ground.

John Tolkamp, Canfor's general manager for information technology, foresees the day when a customer puts in an order and the tree that is needed to make the lumber for that customer is harvested within a few minutes. He says it will be "the Dell model of forestry." He also speculates that in the future, a house builder could give Canfor an electronic copy of the house's specifications, and then Canfor could send the builder a pre-cut house that's ready to put together. It would be a "build-by-the-numbers" system, a more sophisticated version of the old "paint-by-the-numbers" product. The technology already exists to do these things, but the cost of implementing it is prohibitive at the moment (imagine the cost of attaching sensors to millions of trees). ◆

INFORMATION MANAGEMENT: AN OVERVIEW

1 Explain why businesses must manage *information* and show how computer systems and communication technologies have revolutionized *information management*.

As the opening case shows, today's businesses rely on information management in ways that we could not foresee as recently as a decade ago. Managers now turn to digital technology as an integral part of organizational resources and as a means of conducting everyday business. Every major firm's business activities—designing services, ensuring product delivery and cash flow, evaluating personnel, creating advertising—is linked to information systems. Thus the management of information systems is a core business activity that can no longer be delegated to technical personnel.

Most businesses regard their information as a private resource—an asset that they plan, develop, and protect. It is not surprising, then, that companies have **information managers**, just as they have production, marketing, and finance managers. **Information management** is an internal operation that arranges the firm's information resources to support business performance and outcomes.

information manager The manager responsible for the activities needed to generate, analyze, and disseminate information that a company needs to make good decisions.

information management An internal operation that arranges the firm's information resources to support business performance and outcomes.

To find the information they need to make critical decisions, managers must often sift through a virtual avalanche of reports, memos, magazines, and phone calls. Thus the question that faces so many businesses today is how to get useful information to the right people at the right time. In this section, we will explore the ways in which companies manage information with computers and related information technologies.

Data Versus Information

Although business people often complain that they receive too much information, they usually mean that they get too much **data**—raw facts and figures. **Information** is usefully interpreted data (see Figure 13.1).

data Raw facts and figures.

information A meaningful, useful interpretation of data.

Consider the following data:

- Fifty million tubes of toothpaste were sold last year.
- The birth rate is rising slowly.
- Forty-four million tubes of toothpaste were sold the year before last.
- Advertising for toothpaste increased 23 percent last year.
- A major dentists' group recently came out in favour of brushing three times a day.

If all these data can be put together in a meaningful way, they may produce information about what sells toothpaste and whether manufacturers should build new plants. The challenge for businesses is to turn a flood of data into information and to manage that information to their best advantage.

Information Systems

One response to this challenge has been the growth of the **information system (IS)**—a system for transforming raw data into information and transmitting it for use in decision making. IS managers must first determine what information is needed. Then they must gather the data and apply the technology to convert data into information. They must also control the flow of information so that it goes only to those people who need it.[1]

information system (IS) An organized method of transforming data into information that can be used for decision making.

Supplied information varies according to such factors as the functional areas in which people work (say, accounting or marketing) and their management levels. At all levels, informational quality depends on an organization's

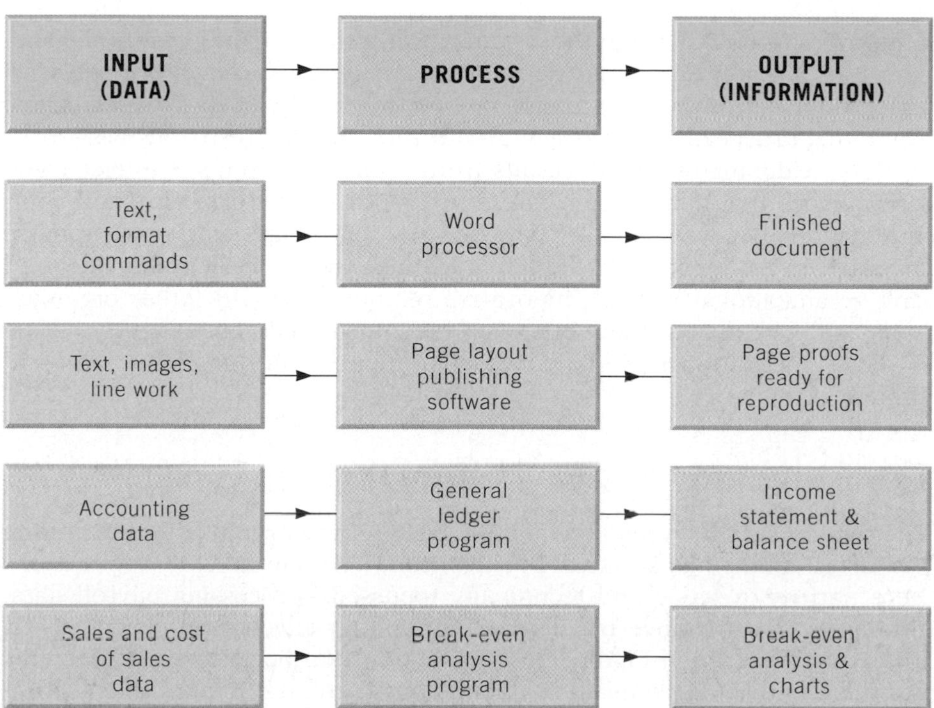

Figure 13.1 From data to information and knowledge.

Information systems are becoming increasingly important as managers try to cope with the flood of data they are confronted with each day.

technological resources and on the people who manage them. In the following section, we discuss the evolution of information-processing technology and then describe the information requirements of today's organization.

NEW BUSINESS TECHNOLOGIES IN THE INFORMATION AGE

Employees at every level in the organization, ranging from operational specialists to the top executive, use information systems to improve performance. Information systems assist in scheduling day-to-day vehicle trips, evaluating prospective employees, and formulating the firm's business strategy. The widening role of IS results from rapid developments in electronic technologies that allow faster and broader flows of information and communications. As we shall see, however, the networked enterprise is more than a firm equipped with the latest technology. Technology has inspired new organizational designs, innovative relationships with other organizations, and new management processes for improved competitiveness.

The top 10 information technology companies in Canada are listed in Table 13.1.

The Expanding Scope of Information Systems

The relationship between information systems and organizations is among the fastest-changing aspects of business today. At one time, IS applications were narrow in scope and technically focussed—processing payroll data, simulating new engineering designs, compiling advertising expenditures. But as you can see in Figure 13.2, managers soon began using IS systems not merely to solve technical problems, but to analyze management problems, especially for control purposes—applying quality-control standards to

Table 13.1 The Top 10 Information Technology Companies in Canada, 2005

Company	Annual Revenues (in billions of $)
1. CGI Group Inc.	$3.6
2. Microsoft Canada Co.	1.2
3. Cognos Inc.	1.0
4. MacDonald, Dettwiler and Associates Ltd.	0.8
5. Creo Inc.	0.8
6. Accenture Inc.	0.6
7. Geac Computer Corporation Ltd.	0.5
8. EDS Canada Inc.	0.5
9. Open Text Corp.	0.5
10. Oracle Corp. Canada Inc.	0.3

production, comparing costs against budgeted amounts, keeping records on employee absences and turnover.

Today, information systems are also crucial in planning. Managers routinely use IS to decide on a firm's products and markets for the next 5 to 10 years. The same database that helps marketing analyze demographics for millions of customers is also used for such higher-level applications as financial planning, managing materials flows, and setting up electronic funds transfers with suppliers and customers.

Another basic change in organizations is an increased interdependence between a company's business strategy and its IS. Today, the choice of a business strategy—say, to be the low-cost provider or the most flexible provider or the high-quality provider—requires an information system that can support that strategy. To effectively support a strategy, the system's software, hardware, and other components must be integrated (see Figure 13.3).

Electronic Business and Communications Technologies

The pressures to maintain better communications and information systems are increasing as competition intensifies and as organizations expand into global and ebusiness operations. Firms like Ralston Purina Co., for instance, need instantaneous communications among managers in those countries in which they either sell products or buy raw materials, including Canada,

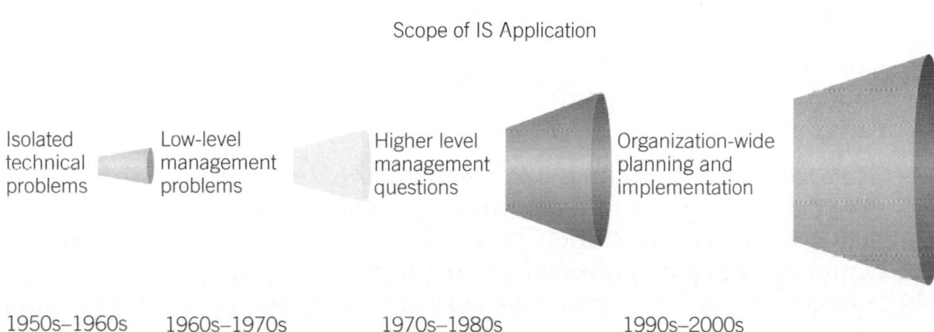

Figure 13.2 Evolution of IS scope.

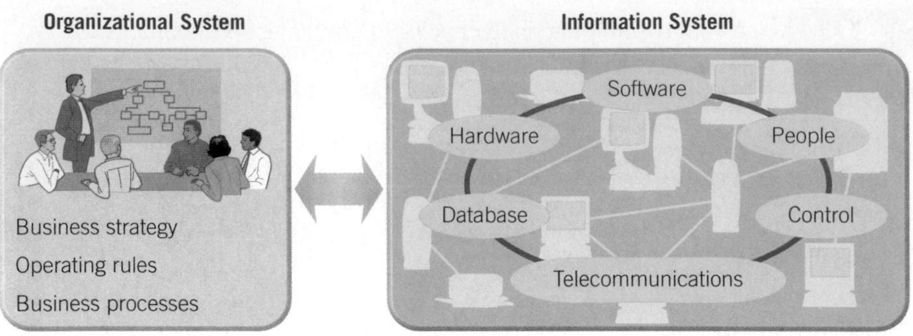

Figure 13.3 Aligning business strategy and the IS.

China, Colombia, Brazil, and the United States. New electronic information technologies and more advanced data communication networks are meeting the needs of such companies.

Electronic Information Technologies

electronic information technologies (EIT) IS applications based on telecommunications technologies.

Electronic information technologies (EIT) are IS applications based on telecommunications technologies. EITs use networks of appliances or devices (such as cellphones and computers) to communicate information by electronic means. EITs enhance the performance and productivity of general business activities by performing two functions:

1. Providing coordination and communication within the firm
2. Speeding up transactions with other firms

Six of the most widely used innovations in today's digital business systems are as follows:

fax machine A machine that can quickly transmit a copy of documents or graphics over telephone lines.

- The **fax machine** (short for *facsimile machine*) can transmit and receive digitized images of text documents, drawings, and photographs over telephone lines in a matter of seconds, thus permitting written communication over long distances. Fax machines are popular with both large and small firms because of speed and low cost.

voice mail A computer-based system for receiving and delivering incoming telephone calls.

- **Voice mail** refers to a computer-based system for receiving and delivering incoming telephone calls. Incoming calls are never missed because a voice responds to the caller, invites a message, and stores it for later retrieval. A company with voice mail networks each employee's phone for receiving, storing, and forwarding calls.

electronic mail (email) system Electronic transmission of letters, reports, and other information between computers.

- An **electronic mail** (or **email**) **system** electronically transmits letters, reports, and other information between computers, whether in the same building or in another country. It is also used for voice transmission and for sending graphics and videos from one computer to another. Email thus substitutes for the flood of paper and telephone calls that threatens to engulf many offices.

electronic conferencing Allows people to communicate simultaneously from different locations via telephone, video, or email group software.

- **Electronic conferencing** is becoming increasingly popular because it eliminates travel and thus saves money. It is also increasingly accessible and speeds up information flows. Teleconferencing allows people to communicate simultaneously from various locations via email group software or via telephone. One form of electronic conferencing, *data conferencing*, allows people in remote locations to work simultaneously on the same document. Working as a team, they can modify part of a database, revise a marketing plan, or draft a press release. Another form of electronic conferencing, *videoconferencing*, allows participants to see one another on a video screen while the teleconference is in progress.

- Collaborative work by teams and other groups is facilitated by **groupware**—software that connects members of the group for email distribution, electronic meetings, message storing, appointments and schedules, and group writing. Linked by groupware, members can work together on their own desktop computers even if they are remotely located. Groupware is especially useful when members work together regularly and rely on intensive information sharing. Groupware products include Lotus Development Corp.'s Lotus Notes, Netscape Communicator, and Microsoft's Office 2000 software suite, which uses web technology.

groupware A system that allows two or more individuals to communicate electronically between desktop PCs.

- Information from outside a company can be linked to its electronic network, and the information can be made available at every workstation. Commercial *digital information services* provide online information for both special-purpose and general topics. Lexis, for example, is specifically a source for legal-research information. In contrast, America Online offers a variety of business information as well as general-interest information.

More and more companies are turning to videoconferencing as a means of holding meetings among people located in distant places. The technology allows people to analyze each other's body language in addition to what they are saying. This helps create richer communication.

Data Communication Networks

2 Identify and briefly describe three elements of *data communication networks*—the internet, the World Wide Web, and intranets.

data communication networks Global networks that permit users to send electronic messages quickly and economically.

internet A gigantic network of networks that serves millions of computers, offers information on business, science, and government, and provides communication flows among more than 170 000 separate networks around the world.

Data communication networks carry streams of digital data (electronic messages, documents, and other forms of video and sound) back and forth quickly and economically on telecommunication systems. The most prominent network, the internet, and its companion system, the World Wide Web, have emerged as powerful communication technologies. Let's look a little more closely at each of these networks.

The Internet. The **internet**—the largest public data communications network—is a gigantic network of networks that serves millions of computers, offers information on business, science, and government, and provides communication flows among more than 170 000 separate networks around the world. Originally commissioned by the U.S. military as a communication tool for use during war, the internet allows personal computers in virtually any location to be linked together. The internet has gained in popularity because it is an efficient tool for information retrieval that makes available an immense wealth of academic, technical, and business information. Because it can transmit information quickly and at low cost—lower than long-distance phone service, postal delivery, and overnight delivery—the internet has also become the most important email system in the world. For thousands of businesses, therefore, the internet has joined—and is even replacing—the telephone, fax machine, and express mail as a standard means of communication.

internet service provider (ISP) A commercial firm that maintains a permanent connection to the internet and sells temporary connections to subscribers.

Although individuals cannot connect directly to the internet, for small monthly usage fees they can subscribe to the internet via an **internet service provider (ISP)**, such as Prodigy, America Online, or Earthlink. An ISP is a commercial firm that maintains a permanent connection to the internet and sells temporary connections to subscribers.[2] Nearly one billion internet users are active in more than 180 countries. The most intensive internet usage is in Malaysia, where 30 percent of the country's population is online.

World Wide Web A system with universally accepted standards for storing, retrieving, formatting, and displaying information on the internet.

The World Wide Web. Thanks to the **World Wide Web** (or simply "the web"), the internet is easy to use and allows users around the world to communicate electronically with little effort. The World Wide Web is a system with universally accepted standards for storing, retrieving, formatting, and displaying information.[3] It provides the "common language" that enables us to "surf" the internet and makes the internet available to a general audience, rather than merely to technical users such as computer programmers. To access a website, for example, the user must specify the *Uniform Resource Locator (URL)* that points to the resource's unique address on the web. For example, Air Canada's URL is *www.aircanada.ca*—a designation that specifies the storage location of Air Canada's web pages.

Each website opens with a *home page*—a screen display that welcomes the visitor with a greeting that may include graphics, sound, and visual enhancements introducing the user to the site. Additional *pages* provide details on the sponsor's products and explain how to contact help in using the site. Often, sites furnish URLs for related websites that the user can link to by simply pointing and clicking. The person responsible for maintaining an organization's website is usually called a *webmaster*. Large websites use dedicated workstations—large computers—known as **web servers** that are customized for managing, maintaining, and supporting websites.

web servers Dedicated workstations—large computers—that are customized for managing, maintaining, and supporting websites.

With hundreds of thousands of new webpages appearing each day, cyberspace is now serving up billions of pages of publicly accessible information. Sorting through this maze would be frustrating and inefficient without access to a web **browser**—software that enables the user to access information on the web. A browser runs on the user's PC and supports the graphics and linking

browser Software that enables a user to access information on the web.

ENTREPRENEURSHIP AND NEW VENTURES

When to Put Your Incubator on Life Support

Is Bill Gross a new-venture visionary or just a scoundrel? Once touted as an internet superstar, Gross is often credited with popularizing the concept of the incubator when, in 1996, he founded Idealab (www.idealab.com), a Pasadena-based firm for generating new companies from scratch. Gross's master plan for mass-producing start-ups sounds simple enough: Find good ideas, turn them into internet companies, recruit executives to run them, and raise start-up capital. In return for these services, Idealab takes an ownership stake in the new firms.

As CEO, Gross himself is a serial entrepreneur whose endless stream of start-up ideas forms the basis of Idealab's current portfolio, which includes more than 15 companies, including CarsDirect.com, Cooking.com, Overature, Evolution Robotics, and a host of legacy companies—CitySearch, eToys, GoTo.com, HomesDirect, Tickets.com, and PETsMART.com—that are no longer part of the Idealab network.

Gross, testifies business journalist Joseph Nocera, is "the most amazing entrepreneur I've met in 20 years covering business." Unfortunately, adds Nocera, he's also "a stupendously poor manager." Nocera isn't alone in having observed Gross's unorthodox, sometimes nonsensical business style: According to some, he always seems to have more ideas than he knows what to do with. Others say that he knows far more about starting a business than running one. Still others find him a captivating talker who has a habit of shifting from topic to topic but who is willing to try things—sometimes seemingly loony ideas—that others wouldn't dream of touching.

In any case, Gross emerged as a hero in the heyday of the internet, and his impact on the incubator industry has been profound: Since 1996, hosts of wannabe imitators have converged on Pasedena to observe Idealab in operation and copy its business model. Between 1996 and 2001, Gross's success inspired dozens of new incubator firms, including eCompanies, CMGI Inc., Internet Capital Group, and DivineInterVentures.

At the height of the tech boom, investors were enthusiastic, too: Idealab attracted $35 million in 1996, $70 million in 1997, $170 million in 1999, and a whopping $1 billion more in 2000. Dell Computer ventured $100 million, as did T. Rowe Price and the Japanese wireless company Hikari Tsushin. Five ex-Microsoft executives contributed $2.5 to $5 million each, while Travelers Insurance invested $15 million. When Hollywood talent agents, excited about Idealab's entertainment site (Z.com), insisted that they be allowed to invest, the William Morris Agency's $1.9 million was quickly overshadowed by United Talent Agency's $2.5 million. Other Hollywood notables pitched in various sums ranging from $100 000 to $4.2 million each.

But then the ebusiness bubble burst and many of Idealab's start-ups were on the fast track to failure. In early 2002, Gross's reputation took another hit when he was charged with squandering $800 million of investors' money in just eight months. Angry investors say he used their money to buy controlling interest in losing propositions such as cosmetics etailer Eve.com (not to mention Z.com itself).

Some accuse Gross and Idealab president Marcia Goodstein with mismanagement of the company's funds. So bad are so many of Idealab's current companies that investors are pressuring Gross to liquidate Idealab; most are willing to accept 35 cents on the dollar. (Gross has made a counteroffer of 10 cents on the dollar.) A group that includes Dell Computer and T. Rowe Price has filed suit to liquidate and distribute the $500 million remaining in Idealab's account. The litigation is still pending. Responds Teresa Bridwell, Idealab vice president of corporate communications: "Our belief is that there is much unrealized value in Idealab today that we would like to mature and return [funds] to all investors." Bridwell adds that the internet market went sour for everyone and that Idealab isn't the only business incubator on life support. New ventures, she suggests, are risky, and perhaps the faint of heart should consider investments other than internet incubators.

capabilities needed to navigate the web. Popular browsers include Netscape, Mozilla Firefox, and Microsoft Internet Explorer.

The web browser offers additional tools—website directories and search engines—for navigating the web. Among the most successful cyberspace enterprises are companies such as Yahoo! that maintain free-to-use **directories** of web content. When Yahoo! is notified about new websites, it classifies them in its directory. The user enters one or two key words (for

directories Features that help people find the content they want on the web. The user types in key words and the directory retrieves a list of websites with titles containing those words.

example, "compact disc"), and the directory responds by retrieving a list of websites with titles containing those words.

search engine Software for searching webpages that does not pre-classify them into a directory.

In contrast to a directory, a **search engine** will search cyberspace's millions of webpages without pre-classifying them into a directory. It searches for webpages that contain the same words as the user's search terms. Then it displays addresses for those that come closest to matching, those that are the next closest, and so on. A search engine, such as AltaVista or Lycos, may respond to millions of inquiries each day. It is thus no surprise that both directories and search engines are packed with paid ads.

intranet A company's private network that is accessible only to employees via entry through electronic firewalls.

firewall Hardware and software security systems that ensure that internal computer systems are not accessible to outsiders.

Intranets. The success of the internet has led some companies to extend its technology internally, so that employees can browse internal websites containing information. These private networks, or **intranets**, are accessible only to employees via entry through electronic firewalls. **Firewalls** are hardware and software security systems that ensure that internal computer systems are not accessible to outsiders.[4] Compaq Computer Corp.'s intranet allows employees to shuffle their retirement savings among various investment funds. Ford Motor Co.'s intranet connects 120 000 workstations in Asia, Europe, and the United States to thousands of Ford websites containing private information on Ford activities in production, engineering, distribution, and marketing. Sharing such information has helped reduce the lead time for getting new models into production from 36 to 24 months. The savings to Ford, of course, will be billions of dollars in inventory and fixed costs.[5]

extranet A network that allows outsiders limited access to a firm's internal information system.

Extranets. Sometimes firms allow outsiders access to their intranets. These so-called **extranets** allow outsiders limited access to a firm's internal information system. The most common application allows buyers to enter the seller's system to see which products are available for sale and delivery, thus providing product-availability information quickly to outside buyers. Industrial suppliers, too, are often linked to their customers' intranets so that they can see planned production schedules and ready supplies as needed for customers' upcoming operations.

Larry Page (left) and Sergey Brin started the search engine Google when both were graduate students in the mid-1990s. They originally called their program "BackRub" because it was good at analyzing the "back links" from one website to another. Raising money primarily from Silicon Valley venture capitalists, they incorporated Google in 1998. When the 6-year-old company went public in 2004, its founders, each of whom held 38 million shares, cleared $3 billion apiece.

New Options for Organizational Design: The Networked Enterprise

Describe five *new options for organizational design* that have emerged from the rapid growth of information technologies. 3

The rapid growth of information technologies has changed the very structure of business organizations. We begin this section with a discussion of changes wrought by technology in the workforce and organizational structures of many organizations. We then examine ways in which electronic networks are contributing to greater flexibility in dealing with customers. After discussing the growing importance of collaboration in the workplace, we look at the ways in which information networks can help make the workplace independent of a company's physical location. Finally, we describe new management processes inspired by the availability of electronic networks.

Leaner Organizations

Information networks are leading to leaner companies with fewer employees and simpler organizational structures. Because today's networked firm can maintain information linkages among both employees and customers, more work can be accomplished with fewer people. As a bank customer, for example, you can dial into a 24-hour information system and find out your current balance from a digital voice. You no longer need bank tellers or phone operators. In the industrial sector, assembly workers at an IBM plant used to receive instructions from supervisors or special staff. Now instructions are delivered electronically to their workstations.

Widespread reductions in middle-management positions and the shrinkage of layers in organizational structure are possible because information networks now provide direct communications between the top managers and workers at lower levels. Electronic information networks are replacing the operating managers who formerly communicated company policies, procedures, or work instructions to lower-level employees.

More Flexible Operations

Electronic networks allow businesses to offer customers greater variety and faster delivery cycles. Products such as cellular phones, PCs, and audio systems can be custom-ordered, too, with your choice of features and options and next-day delivery. The principle is called **mass-customization**: Although companies produce in large volumes, each unit features the unique variations and options that the customer prefers. As you can see in Figure 13.4, flexible production and fast delivery depend on an integrated network to coordinate all the transactions, activities, and process flows necessary to make quick adjustments in the production process. The ability to organize and store massive volumes of information is crucial, as are the electronic linkages among customers, manufacturers, materials suppliers, and shippers.

mass-customization Producing large volumes of products or services, but giving customers the choice of features and options they want.

Increased Collaboration

Collaboration, not only among internal units but with outside firms as well, is on the rise because networked systems make it cheaper and easier to contact everyone, whether other employees or outside organizations. Aided by intranets, more companies are learning that complex problems can be solved better by means of collaboration, either in formal teams or through spontaneous interaction. In the new networked organization, decisions that were once the domain of individuals are now shared as both people and departments have become more interdependent. The design of new products, for example, was once an engineering responsibility. Now, in contrast,

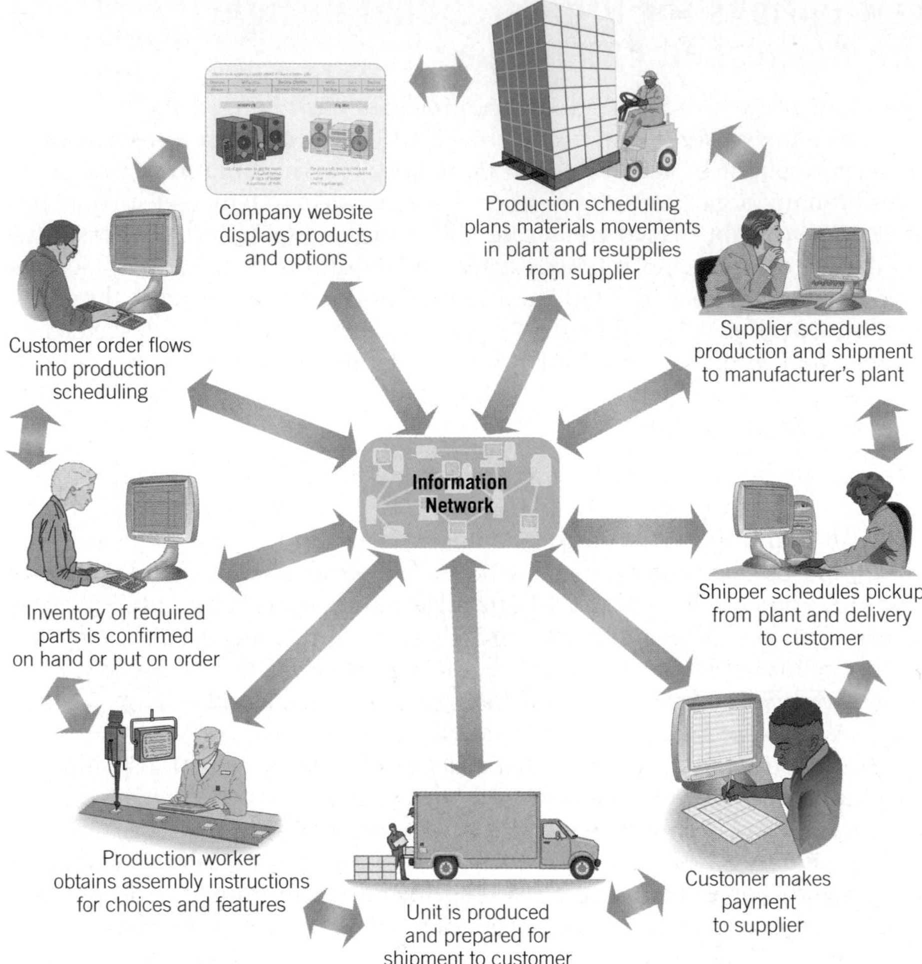

Figure 13.4 Networking for mass-customization.

it can be a shared responsibility because so much information is accessible for evaluation from various perspectives. Marketing, finance, production, engineering, and purchasing can share their different stores of information and determine a best overall design.

Networking and the Virtual Company. Networked systems can also improve collaboration between organizations through the so-called *virtual company*. This can be a temporary team assembled by a single organization, but a virtual company can also be created by several allied firms.[6] Each contributes different skills and resources that collectively result in a competitive business that wouldn't be feasible for any one of them working alone. A company with marketing and promotional skills, for example, may team up with firms with expertise in warehousing and distribution, engineering, and production. Networking lets collaborators exchange ideas, plan strategy, share customer information, and otherwise coordinate efforts, even if their respective facilities are far apart.

Greater Independence of Company and Workplace

Geographic separation of the workplace from the company headquarters is more common than ever because of networked organizations. Employees no longer work only at the office or the factory, nor are all of a company's operations performed at one location. The sales manager for an advertising agency may visit the company office in Toronto once every two weeks, preferring instead to work over the firm's electronic network from her home office in Montreal. A medical researcher for the Calgary Clinic may work at a home office networked into the clinic's system.

A company's activities may also be geographically scattered but highly coordinated, thanks to a networked system. Many ebusinesses, for example, do not conduct any activities at one centralized location. When you order products from an internet storefront—say, a chair, a sofa, a table, and two lamps—the chair may come from a co-operating warehouse in Windsor and the lamps from a manufacturer in Toronto, while the sofa and table may be direct-shipped from two manufacturers in North Carolina. All of these activities are launched instantaneously by the customer's order and coordinated through the network, just as if all of them were being processed at one location.

Improved Management Processes

Networked systems have changed the very nature of the management process. The activities, methods, and procedures of today's manager differ significantly from those that were common just a few years ago. Once, for example, upper-level managers did not concern themselves with all the detailed information that filtered upward in the workplace. Why? Because it was expensive to gather and slow in coming and quickly became out of date. Workplace management was delegated to middle and first-line managers.

With networked systems, however, instantaneous information is accessible in a convenient and usable format. Consequently, more and more upper managers use it routinely for planning, leading, directing, and controlling operations. Today, a top manager can find out the current status of any customer order, inspect productivity statistics for each workstation, and analyze the delivery performance of any driver and vehicle. More importantly, managers can better coordinate company-wide performance. They can identify departments that are working well together and those that are creating bottlenecks.

Enterprise Resource Planning. One type of networked system is **enterprise resource planning (ERP)**—a large information system for integrating the activities of all of a company's units.[7] It is supported by one large database through which everyone shares the same information when any transaction occurs. The biggest supplier of commercial ERP packages is Germany's SAP AG, followed by Oracle. Hershey Foods uses the SAP system. It identifies the status of any order and traces its progress from order entry through customer delivery and receipt of payment. Progress and delays at intermediate stages—materials ordering, inventory availability, production scheduling, packaging, warehousing, distribution—can be checked continuously to determine which operations should be more closely coordinated with others to improve overall performance.

enterprise resource planning (ERP) Large information systems for integrating all the activities of a company's business units.

TYPES OF INFORMATION SYSTEMS

In a sense, the phrase *information system* may be a misnomer. It suggests that there is one system when, in fact, a firm's employees will have different interests, job responsibilities, and decision-making requirements. One information system cannot accommodate such a variety of information requirements. Instead, "the information system" is a complex of several

4 Discuss different information-systems *application programs* that are available for users at various organizational levels.

information systems that share information while serving different levels of the organization, different departments, or different operations.

User Groups and System Requirements

knowledge workers Employees whose jobs involve the use of information and knowledge as the raw materials of their work.

Four user groups, each with different system requirements, are identified in Figure 13.5, which also indicates the kinds of systems best suited to each user level. Among users we include **knowledge workers**—employees whose jobs involve the use of information and knowledge as the raw materials of their work. Knowledge workers are specialists, usually professionally trained and certified—engineers, scientists, information technology specialists, psychologists—who rely on information technology to design new products or create new business processes.

Managers at Different Levels

Because they work on different kinds of problems, top managers, middle managers, knowledge workers, and first-line managers have different information needs. First-line (or operational) managers, for example, need information to oversee the day-to-day details of their departments or projects. Knowledge workers need special information for conducting technical projects. Meanwhile, middle managers need summaries and analyses for setting intermediate and long-range goals for the departments or projects under their supervision. Finally, top management analyzes broader trends in the economy, the business environment, and overall company performance to conduct long-range planning for the entire organization.

Consider the various information needs of a flooring manufacturer. Sales managers (first-level managers) supervise salespeople, assign territories to the sales force, and handle customer service and delivery problems.

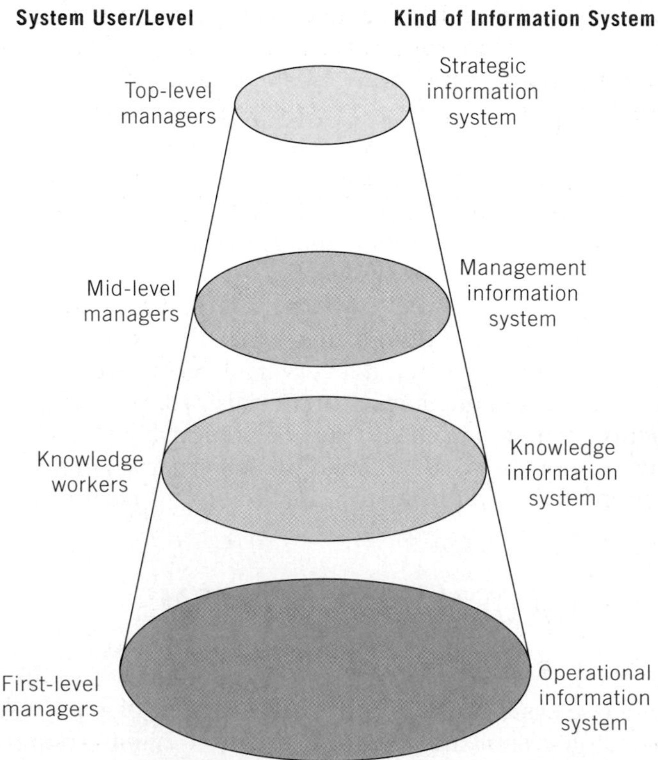

Figure 13.5 Matching users and systems.

They need current information on the sales and delivery of products: lists of incoming customer orders and daily delivery schedules to customers in their territories. Regional managers (middle managers) set sales quotas for each sales manager, prepare budgets, and plan staffing needs for the upcoming year. They need information on monthly sales by product and region. Knowledge workers developing new flooring materials need information on the chemical properties of adhesives and compression strengths for floor structures. Finally, top managers need both external and internal information. Internally, they use sales data summarized by product, customer type, and geographic region, along with comparisons to previous years. Equally important is external information on consumer behaviour patterns, the competition's performance, and economic forecasts.

Functional Areas and Business Processes

Each business *function*—marketing, human resources, accounting, production, and finance—has its own information needs. In addition, in businesses organized according to business processes, process groups need special information. Each user group and department is represented by an IS. Now add to these systems the four systems needed by the four levels of users that we just discussed: The total number of systems and applications increases significantly.

Each cell on the left side of Figure 13.6 represents a potential IS associated with a given functional group. Top-level finance managers, for instance, plan long-range spending for facilities and equipment, and they determine sources of capital. The arrows on the right side of Figure 13.6 show that a business-process group will include users, both managers and employees, drawn from all organizational levels. The supply chain management group, for instance, may need to cut the number of suppliers. The IS supporting this project would contain information cutting across different functions and management levels. The group will need information on and expertise in marketing, warehousing and distribution, production, communications technology, purchasing, and finance. It will also need input on operational, technical, and managerial issues—say, technical requirements for new suppliers and future financial requirements.

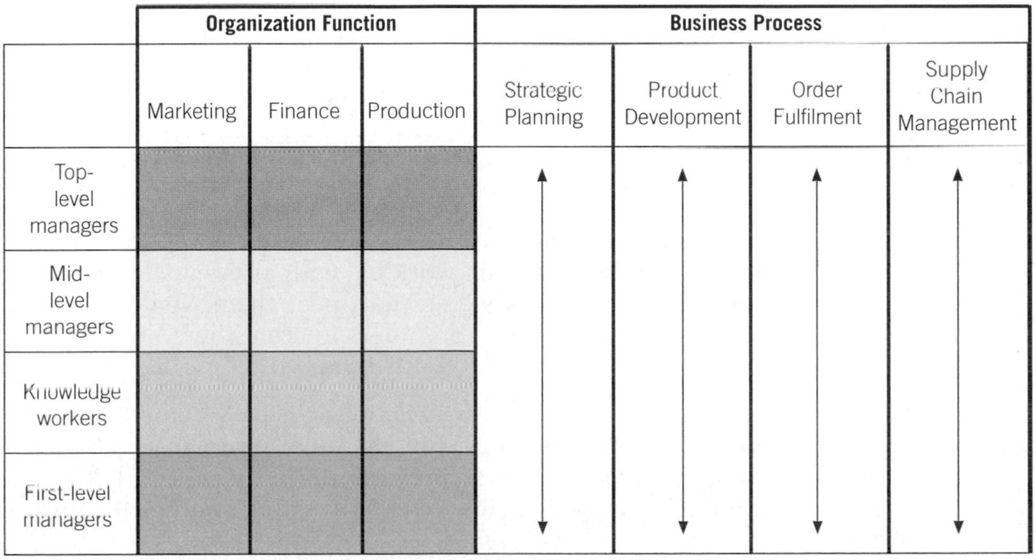

	Organization Function			Business Process			
	Marketing	Finance	Production	Strategic Planning	Product Development	Order Fulfilment	Supply Chain Management
Top-level managers				↕	↕	↕	↕
Mid-level managers							
Knowledge workers							
First-level managers							

Figure 13.6 Matching user levels with functional areas and business processes.

Major Systems by Level

In this section, we discuss different kinds of systems that provide applications at some organizational levels but not at others. For any routine, repetitive, highly structured decision, a specialized application will suffice. System requirements for knowledge workers, however, will probably vary because knowledge workers often face a variety of specialized problems. Applications of information systems for middle or top-level management decisions must also be flexible, though for different reasons. In particular, they will use a broader range of information collected from both external and internal sources.

Transaction Processing Systems

transaction processing systems (TPS) Applications of information processing for basic day-to-day business transactions.

Transaction processing systems (TPS) are applications of information processing for basic day-to-day business transactions. Customer order-taking by online retailers, approval of claims at insurance companies, receiving and confirming reservations by airlines, payroll processing and bill payment at almost every company—all are routine business processes. Typically, the TPS for first-level (operational) activities is well defined, with predetermined data requirements, and follows the same steps to complete all transactions in the system.

A diagram representing the TPS for a customer-billing process is shown in Figure 13.7. The process begins when finished products for a customer's order are packed and ready for shipment. Using data stored in the company's master files, billing staffers match the customer's identification number (from the billing master file) with code numbers for products (from the products master file). The system instantly tallies the payment amount due (including the bill of the current shipment plus any past-due payments), creates the billing document (invoice), and provides status reports to first-level managers and other system users with online access. Information from the billing and products master files flows electronically to the accounting system for updating accounts receivables and inventory accounts.

Systems for Knowledge Workers and Office Applications

Systems for knowledge workers and office applications support the activities of both knowledge workers and employees in clerical positions. They provide assistance for data processing and other office activities, including the creation of communications documents. Like other departments, the IS department includes both knowledge workers and data workers.

IS Knowledge Workers. IS knowledge workers include both systems analysts (and designers) and application (or systems) programmers:

- *Systems analysts and designers* deal with the entire computer system. They represent the IS group in working with users to learn users' requirements and to design systems that meet them. Generally, they decide on the types and sizes of computers and on how to set up links among computers to form a network of users.
- *Programmers* write the software instructions that tell computers what to do. Application programmers, for example, write instructions to address particular problems. Systems programmers ensure that a system can handle the requests made by various application programs.

system operations personnel People who run a company's computer equipment.

Operations Personnel (Data Workers). People who run the company's computer equipment are called **system operations personnel**. They ensure that the right programs are run in the correct sequence and monitor

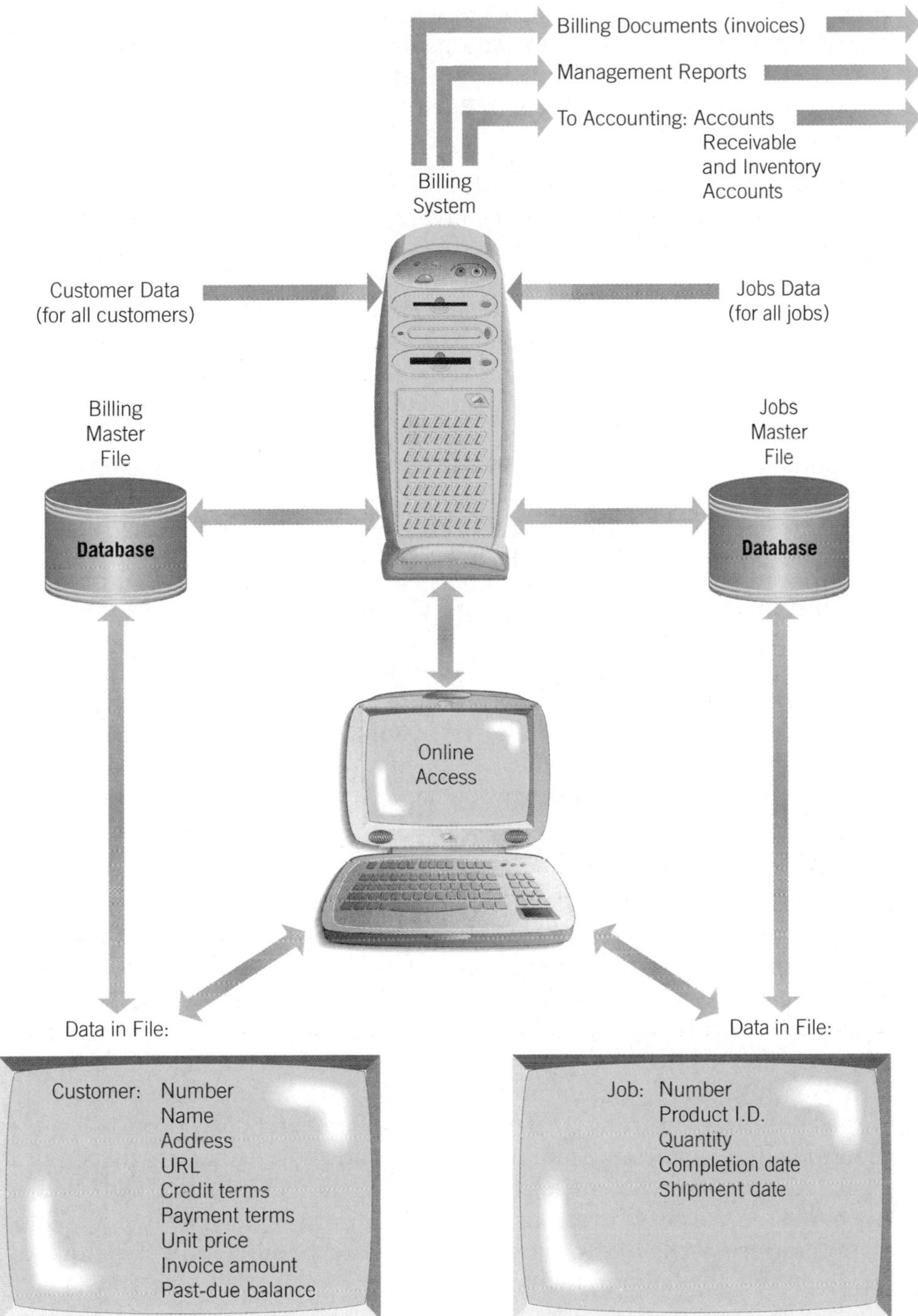

Figure 13.7 Flow diagram for customer-billing TPS.

equipment to ensure that it is operating properly. Many organizations also have personnel for entering data into the system for processing.

Knowledge-Level and Office Systems

New support systems—word processing, document imaging, desktop publishing, computer-aided design, simulation modelling—have increased the productivity of both office and knowledge workers. We will discuss word processing—systems for formatting, editing, and storing documents—later in this chapter. Desktop publishing, also discussed later, combines graphics and word-processing text to publish professional-quality print and web documents. Document imaging systems can scan paper documents and images, convert them into digital form for storage on disks, retrieve them, and transmit them electronically to workstations throughout the network.

World-class firms are using system applications for knowledge workers to reduce product-design times, reduce production-cycle times, and make faster deliveries to customers.

computer-aided design (CAD) Computer analysis and graphics programs that are used to create new products.

- **Computer-aided design (CAD)** assists in designing products by simulating the real product and displaying it in three-dimensional graphics. Immersion's MicroScribe-3D software, for example, uses a pen-like tool to scan the surface of any three-dimensional object, such as a football helmet, and electronically transforms it into a 3D graphic. The helmet designer can then try different shapes and surfaces in the computer and analyze the new designs on a video monitor.[8] Products ranging from cellphones to auto parts are created using CAD because it creates faster designs at lower cost than manual modelling methods. The older method—making handcrafted prototypes (trial models) from wood, plastic, or clay—is replaced with *rapid prototyping (RP)*: the CAD system electronically transfers instructions to a computer-controlled machine that then automatically builds the prototype.[9]

computer-aided manufacturing (CAM) Computer systems used to design and control all the equipment and tools for producing goods.

- **Computer-aided manufacturing (CAM)** is used to design the manufacturing equipment, facilities, and plant layouts for better product flows and productivity. *Computer operations control* refers to any system for managing the day-to-day production activities for either goods or service production. Hospitals, for instance, use computer-based scheduling for preparing patients' meals, just as manufacturers do for making cars, clocks, and paper products.

Management Information Systems

management information systems (MIS) Systems that support an organization's managers by providing daily reports, schedules, plans, and budgets.

Management information systems (MIS) support an organization's managers by providing daily reports, schedules, plans, and budgets. Each manager's information activities vary according to his or her functional area (say, accounting or marketing) and management level. Whereas mid-level managers focus mostly on internal activities and information, higher-level managers are also engaged in external activities. Middle managers, the largest MIS user group, need networked information to plan such upcoming activities as personnel training, materials movements, and cash flows. They also need to know the current status of the jobs and projects being carried out in their departments: What stage is it at now? When will it be finished? Is there an opening so the next job can be started? Many of a firm's management information systems—cash flow, sales, production scheduling, and shipping—are indispensable for helping managers find answers to such questions.

Decision Support Systems (DSS)

decision support system (DSS) Computer systems used to help managers consider alternatives when making decisions on complicated problems.

Middle- and top-level managers receive decision-making assistance from a **decision support system (DSS)**—an interactive system that locates and presents information needed to support the decision-making process. Whereas some DSSs are devoted to specific problems, others serve more general purposes, allowing managers to analyze different types of problems. Thus a firm that often faces decisions on plant capacity, for example, may have a *Capacity DSS* in which the manager inputs data on anticipated levels of sales, working capital, and customer-delivery requirements. Then the system's built-in transaction processors manipulate the data and make recommendations on the best levels of plant capacity for each future time period.

Executive Support Systems

An **executive support system (ESS)** is a quick-reference, easy-access application of information systems specially designed for upper-level managers. ESSs are designed to assist with executive-level decisions and problems, ranging from "What lines of business should we be in five years from now?" to "Based on forecasted developments in electronic technologies, to what extent should our firm be globalized in five years? In 10 years?" An ESS also uses a wide range of both internal information and external sources, such as industry reports, global economic forecasts, and reports on competitors.

As late as the 1980s, computers hadn't had much impact on industrial automation, largely because there were no good software programs for computer-operated manufacturing. Myron Zimmerman recognized a need, and he founded VenturCom, which develops programs for controlling industrial production equipment like this metal cutting machine.

Artificial Intelligence and Expert Systems

Artificial intelligence (AI) is the construction of computer systems to imitate human behaviour—in other words, systems that perform physical tasks, use thought processes, and learn. In developing AI systems, business specialists, modellers, and information-technology experts try to design computer-based systems capable of reasoning so that computers, instead of people, can perform certain activities. A credit-evaluation system may decide which loan applicants are creditworthy and which are too risky, and it may then compose acceptance and rejection letters accordingly.[10]

Robotics—the combination of computers with industrial robots—is a category of AI. With certain "reasoning" capabilities, robots can "learn" repetitive tasks such as painting, assembling components, and inserting screws. They also avoid repeating mistakes by "remembering" the causes of past mistakes and, when those causes reappear, adjusting or stopping until adjustments are made.

There are also AI systems that possess sensory capabilities, such as lasers that "see," "hear," and "feel." In addition, as machines become more sophisticated in processing natural languages, humans can give instructions and ask questions merely by speaking to a computer. AND Corporation, based in Toronto, Ontario, has developed a software program—called HNeT—that can learn to recognize faces. This may seem like a simple thing, but millions of dollars had been spent on this problem without success until AND Corporation developed the software. The system can be used to improve airport security and to track terrorists.[11]

executive support system (ESS) A quick-reference, easy-access application of information systems specially designed for upper-level managers.

artificial intelligence (AI) The construction and/or programming of computers to imitate human thought processes.

robotics The use of computer-controlled machines that perform production tasks.

Expert Systems. A special form of AI program, the **expert system**, is designed to imitate the thought processes of human experts in a particular field.[12] Expert systems incorporate the rules that an expert applies to specific types of problems, such as the judgments a physician makes when diagnosing illnesses. In effect, expert systems supply everyday users with "instant expertise."

Nortel Networks uses an expert system called Engineering Change Manager, which simplifies and speeds up product design changes by suggesting redesigns to meet product requirements. Campbell Soup developed an expert system to mimic complex decision processes and save the expert knowledge that was going to be lost when a long-time expert soup maker announced his intention to retire.[13]

expert system A form of artificial intelligence in which a program draws on the rules an expert in a given field has laid out to arrive at a solution for a problem.

Robotics is a category of artificial intelligence. Robots can "learn" repetitive tasks and "remember" the causes of past mistakes.

ELEMENTS OF THE INFORMATION SYSTEM

5 Identify and briefly describe the *main elements of an information system.*

We now know that an *information system* is a group of interconnected devices at several different locations that can exchange information. We also know that *networking*—connecting these devices—allows otherwise decentralized computers to exchange data quickly and easily. Obviously, a key component of the information system is its **computer network**—all of the computer and information technology devices that, working together, drive the flow of digital information throughout the system.

computer network A form of computer system architecture in which computers at different locations can function independently but are also interconnected and able to exchange information with one another.

The computer is a powerful machine, but it is only one part of the information system. Every system has six components: (1) hardware, (2) software, (3) control, (4) database, (5) people, and (6) telecommunications. We will describe each of the first four components in detail. We have already described the fifth element, the people at various levels who use and prepare the system. We will reserve our discussion of telecommunications for the next section. Remember that all six of these components must be present and properly coordinated for a networked information system to function effectively.

Hardware

Figure 13.8 shows the various systems and components that make up IS **hardware**—the physical components of a computer system. The functioning of a computer's hardware is not as complicated as it looks. To get a bird's-eye view of how the system works, suppose that you are a very simple piece of data (say, the number 3).

hardware The physical components of a computer system.

- To get into the computer, data must be entered by an **input device**. Optical scanners, voice pickups, CD drives, and computer mice are all input devices, but let's assume that you are entered by a friend using the most common input device, a keyboard. When your friend presses the number 3 on the keyboard, an electronic signal is sent to the computer's **central processing unit (CPU)**, where the actual processing of data takes place.

input device Hardware that gets data into the computer in a form the computer can understand.

central processing unit (CPU) Hardware in which the actual transforming of data into information takes place; contains the primary storage unit, the control unit, and the arithmetic logic unit.

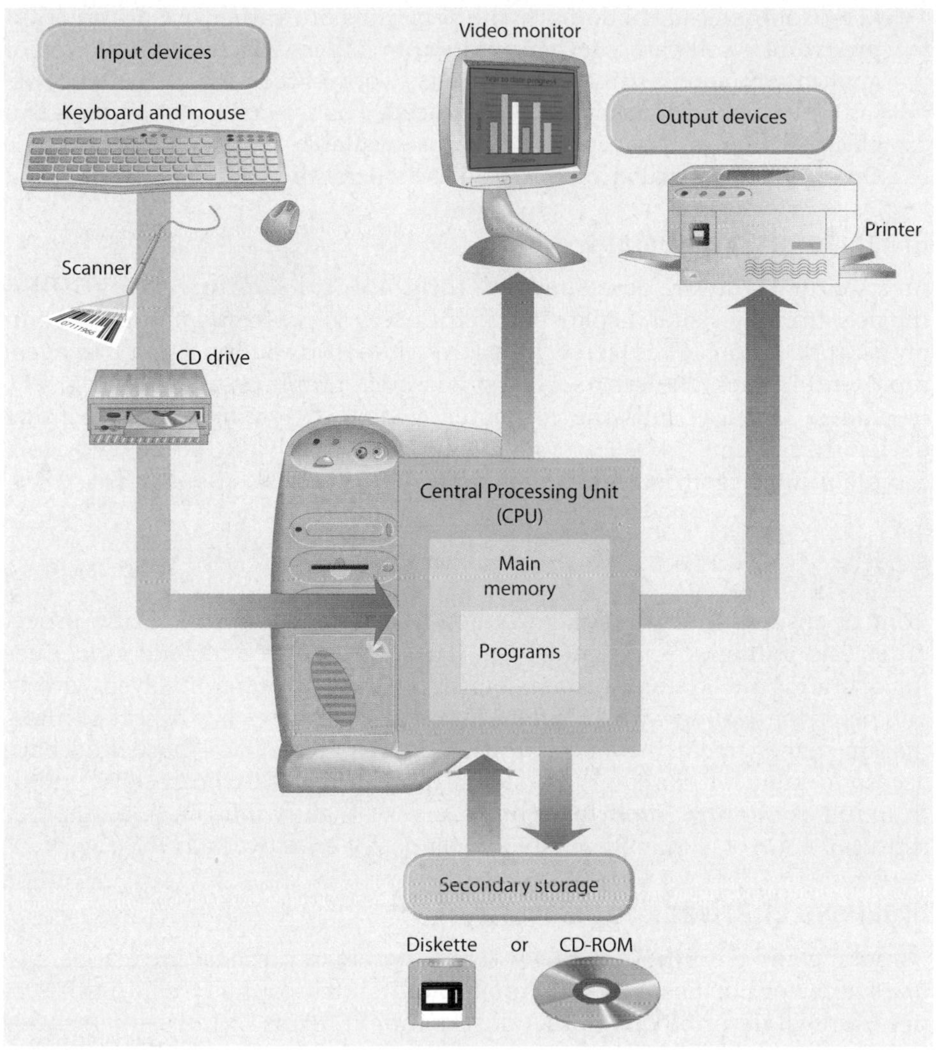

Figure 13.8 Hardware components of an IS.

- You are now inside the CPU in a form that the computer can understand. What happens now? As a piece of data, you must go first to **main memory**—the part of the computer's CPU that stores those programs that it needs to operate.

main memory The part of a computer's CPU that stores those programs that it needs to operate.

- Now the CPU searches through its memory for instructions—**programs**—on what to do with you. Using the appropriate instructions, it then performs the calculations (addition, subtraction, multiplication, and division) and comparisons as directed by the program. Then, the CPU sends the results to one or more **output devices**: a video monitor, a printer, or a speaker.

program Any sequence of instructions to a computer.

output device That part of a computer's hardware that presents results to users; common forms include printers and video monitors.

Software

Although hardware is a vital component, it needs programs—**software**—to function. There are two types of software programs:

software Programs that instruct the computer in what to do and how to do it.

- **System programs** tell the computer what resources to use and how. For example, an operating system program tells the computer how and when to transfer data from secondary to primary storage and return information to the user.

system program A program that tells a computer what resources to use and how to use them.

application program A program that actually processes data according to a particular user's specific needs.

- Most computer users do not write programs but rather use **application programs**—software packages written by others. Each different type of application (such as financial analysis, word processing, or web browsing) uses a program that meets that need. Thus, a computer system usually has many application programs available, such as Lotus 1-2-3, Quicken, and WordPerfect. We review some of these later in this chapter.

Graphical User Interface

graphical user interface (GUI) The user-friendly display that helps users select from among the many possible applications of the computer.

icons Small images on a computer screen that represent various applications.

An important software development is the **graphical user interface (GUI)**—the user-friendly visual display that helps users select from among the computer applications. The screen displays numerous **icons** (small images) representing such choices as word processing, graphics, fax, printing, CD, or games. The user tells the computer what to do by moving a pointing device (usually an arrow) around the screen to activate the desired icon. Simple printed instructions explain activated features.

Control

Control ensures that the system is operating according to specific procedures and within specific guidelines. These procedures include guidelines for operating the system, responsibilities of the personnel involved with it, and plans for dealing with system failure. For example, a key aspect of information management is controlling two groups of people—those who have access to input or change the system's data and those who receive output from it. For example, most firms limit access to salary information. Another aspect of control is management surveillance of employees as they work.

Problems of Privacy and Security

"Breaking and entering" no longer refers merely to physical intrusions into one's home or business. Today, it applies to IS intrusions as well. In this section, we will describe one of the most common forms of intrusion: *privacy invasion*. We will also discuss some of the methods that companies use to provide *security* for their information systems.[14]

Privacy Invasion. With information systems, privacy invasion occurs when intruders (hackers) gain unauthorized access, either to steal information, money, or property or to tamper with data. You have probably read or heard about computer enthusiasts who have gained access to school systems to change grades.

At Equifax Canada, computer hackers breached its system and gained access to personal information on hundreds of Canadians.[15] In the United States, a computer hacker is on trial for allegedly stealing more than one billion records from Acxiom, a data-selling company. The company admitted that the stolen data could include information about millions of people. It also admitted that it didn't even know its system had been hacked into until it was contacted by investigators in the case. Another company, CardSystems Solutions, said hackers may have obtained information on 200 000 credit card holders.[16]

Computer experts are becoming increasingly concerned that the large number of hacker attacks in recent years is causing people to question the security of the internet. If people have security concerns, they will be less likely to use the electronic medium, and this will have a negative effect on thousands of businesses that sell over the internet. Law enforcement agencies around the world are trying to catch hackers, but the criminals often stay one step ahead.

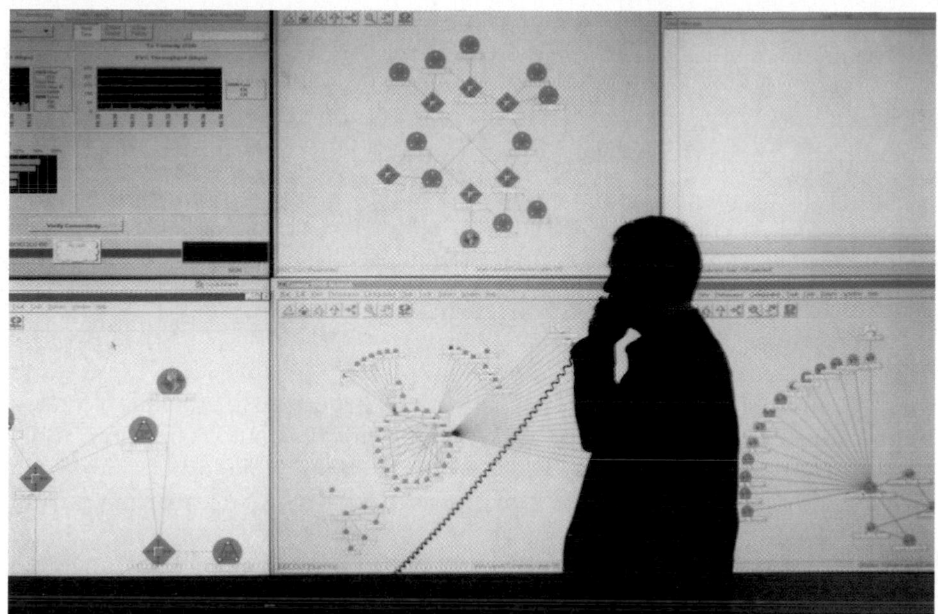

At Acxiom, computer systems track consumer data provided by nearly every credit-card issuer, bank, and insurance company in North America. The company is currently improving its computer-security models, but many people who worry about the potential for abuse point out that Acxiom itself has been successfully "hacked" more than once in the past couple of years.

Security. As we have seen, security measures for protection against intrusion are a constant challenge. To gain entry into most systems, IS users have protected passwords that guard against unauthorized access, but many firms rely on additional protective software for safeguards. To protect against intrusions by unauthorized outsiders, companies use security devices, called electronic *firewalls*, in their systems. Firewalls allow employees access to both the internet and the company's internal computer network while barring entry by outsiders. Since its system was hacked into, Acxiom has beefed up its password protocols and its encryption, and has also conducted many security audits.

Security for electronic communications is an additional concern. Electronic transmissions can be intercepted, altered, and read by intruders. To prevent unauthorized access, many firms rely on **encryption**—the use of a secret numerical code to scramble the characters in the message, so that the message is not understandable during transmission. Only personnel with the deciphering codes can read them. Protection for preserving data files and databases is not foolproof and typically involves making backup copies to be stored outside the computer system, usually in a safe. Thus, damaged system files can be replaced by backup.

encryption The use of a secret numerical code to scramble characters in a message, so that the message is not understandable during transmission.

The most important security factor is the people in the system. At most firms, personnel are trained in the responsibilities of computer use and warned of the penalties for violating system security. For example, each time a computer boots up, a notice displays the warning that software and data are protected and spells out penalties for unauthorized use.

Montreal-based La Senza Corp. understands how important people are to computer security. It blocks its staff from accessing instant message services and email sites such as Hotmail because these may compromise the company's network security. Sometimes staff become frustrated with these restrictions because they do not appreciate the importance of network security.[17]

Databases and Application Programs

Briefly describe the content and role of a *database* and the purpose of *database software* for information systems. 6

All computer processing is the processing of data. It is carried out by programs—instructions that tell the system to perform specified functions. In this section we begin by briefly describing the nature of computer data and databases. We then discuss a few of the specialized applications programs designed for business use.

Data and Databases

Computers convert data into information by organizing them in some meaningful manner. Within a computer system, chunks of data—numbers, words, and sentences—are stored in a series of related collections called fields, records, and files. Taken together, all of these data files constitute a **database**—a centralized, organized collection of related data.

database A centralized, organized collection of related data.

Application Programs

Most computer users don't write programs. Programs are available for a huge range of business-related tasks. Some address such common, long-standing needs as accounting and inventory control, while others have been developed for an endless variety of specialized needs. Most business programs fall into one of four categories: *word processing*, *spreadsheets*, *database management*, and *graphics*. Of all PC software applications, 70 percent are designed for the first three types of programs.[18]

word-processing programs Application programs that allow the computer to act as a sophisticated typewriter to store, edit, and print letters and numbers.

Word Processing. Popular **word-processing programs**, such as Microsoft Word for Windows and Lotus's Word Pro, allow computer users to store, edit, display, and print documents. Sentences and paragraphs can be added or deleted without retyping or restructuring an entire document, and mistakes are easily corrected.

electronic spreadsheets Application programs that allow the user to enter categories of data and determine the effect of changes in one category (e.g., sales) on other categories (e.g., profits).

Spreadsheets. **Electronic spreadsheets** spread data across and down the page in rows and columns. Users enter data, including formulas, at row and column intersections, and the computer automatically performs the necessary calculations. Payroll records, sales projections, and a host of other financial reports can be prepared in this manner.

Spreadsheets are good planning tools because they let managers see how making a change in one item affects related items. For example, you can insert operating-cost percentages, tax rates, or sales revenues into the spreadsheet. The computer will automatically recalculate all the other figures and determine net profit. Popular spreadsheet packages include Lotus 1-2-3, Quattro Pro, and Microsoft Excel for Windows.[19]

database management programs Application programs that keep track of and manipulate the relevant data of a business.

Database Management. Another popular type of personal-productivity software is a **database management program**. Such programs as Microsoft Access for Windows and Borland's InterBase are popular for desktop applications. Oracle9i is a popular database for internet computing. These systems can create, store, sort, and search through data and integrate a single piece into several different files.

Figure 13.9 shows how a database management program might be used at a company called Artists' Frame Service. In this case, the program is integrating the file for customer orders with the company's inventory file. When sales to Jones and Smith are entered into the customer orders file, the database system automatically adjusts the frame inventory file; the quantities of materials B5 and A3 are reduced because those materials were used to make the frames for Jones and Smith.

computer graphics programs Application programs that convert numerical and character data into pictorial forms.

Graphics. **Computer graphics programs** convert numeric and character data into pictorial information, such as charts and graphs. They make computerized information easier to use and understand in two ways. First, graphs and charts summarize data and allow managers to detect problems, opportunities, and relationships more easily. Second, graphics contribute to clearer and more persuasive reports and presentations.

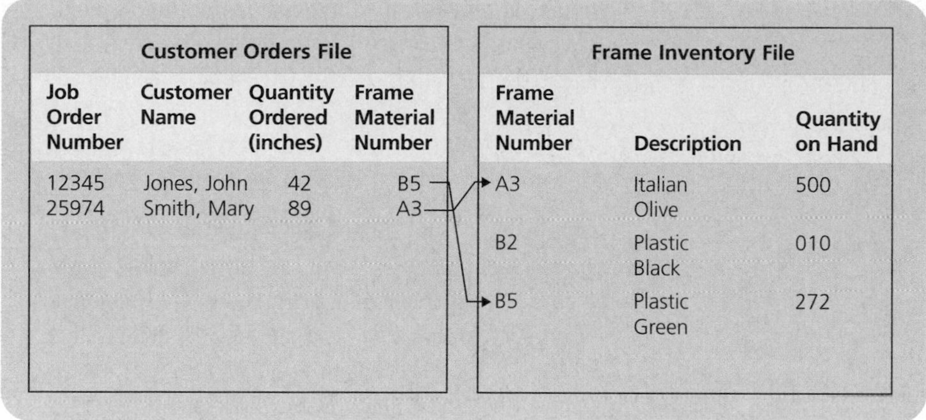

Customer Orders File

Job Order Number	Customer Name	Quantity Ordered (inches)	Frame Material Number
12345	Jones, John	42	B5
25974	Smith, Mary	89	A3

Frame Inventory File

Frame Material Number	Description	Quantity on Hand
A3	Italian Olive	500
B2	Plastic Black	010
B5	Plastic Green	272

Figure 13.9 Artists' Frame Service.

Two of the most common graphics displays are the pie chart and the bar graph. As Figure 13.10 shows, both types of graphics can convey different kinds of information—in this case, the types of materials that should be ordered by a framing shop like Artists' Frame Service. Both types of graphs are more likely to help a manager make decisions than the raw numbers on which they are based.

Presentation graphics software, such as CorelDRAW, Microsoft PowerPoint for Windows, and Microsoft Visio 2002, lets users assemble graphics for visual displays, slides, video, and even sound splices for professional presentations. By varying colours and size, and using pictures and charts with three-dimensional effects and shading, animation, and sound users can make more interesting presentations.

presentation graphics software Application programs that offer choices for assembling graphics for visual displays, slides, video, and even sound splices for professional presentations.

Computer graphics capabilities go beyond data presentation. They also include stand-alone programs for artists, designers, and special effects engineers. Everything from simple drawings to motion picture special effects are now created by computer graphics software. The sinking ship in *Titanic*, the aliens in *Men in Black II*, and the dog in *Scooby-Doo* were all created with computer graphics.

Some software allows firms to publish sales brochures, in-house magazines, and annual reports. The latest **desktop publishing** packages for the PC combine word processing and graphics to produce typeset-quality text with stimulating visual effects. They also eliminate printing costs for

desktop publishing Combines word processing and graphics capability in producing typeset-quality text from personal computers.

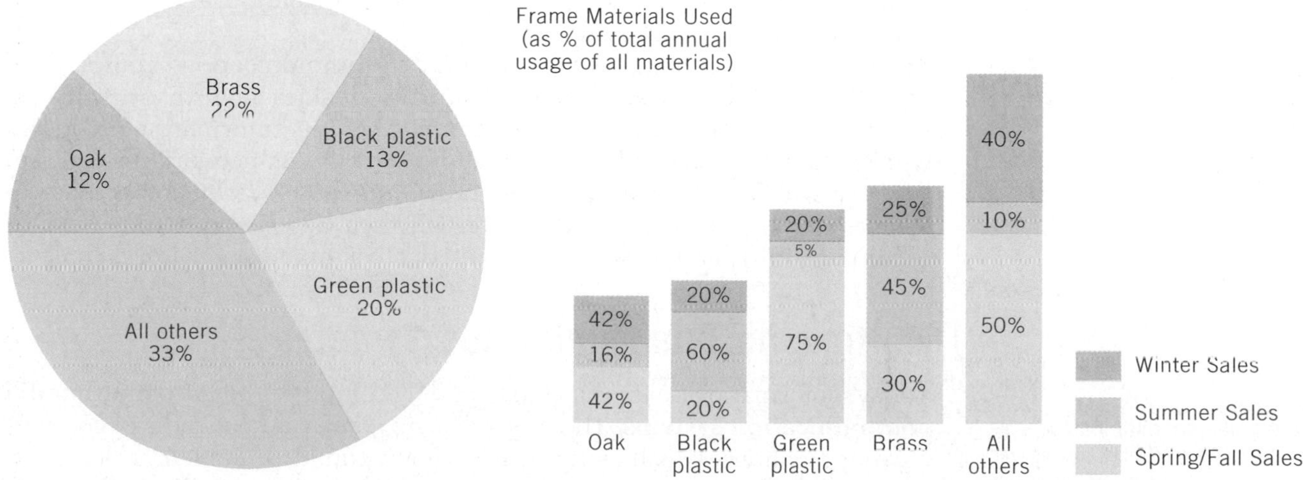

Figure 13.10 Both the pie chart and the bar graph show that four frame materials are the most used, but the bar graph also shows that brass and oak are most popular in winter.

The realism of the space creatures and alien environments in Star Wars is due to special effects created with computer graphics.

reports and proposals. QuarkXPress, which can manipulate text, tables of numbers, graphics, and full-colour photographs, is used by ad agencies such as J. Walter Thompson because its computer-generated designs offer greater control over colour and format. Other packages include Microsoft Publisher and Adobe Systems PageMaker.

software piracy The unauthorized use of software such as word processing and spreadsheets.

Software piracy—the unauthorized use of software such as word processing and spreadsheets—is a worldwide problem. The Canadian Alliance Against Software Theft (CAAST) estimates that 33 percent of software that is installed on computers in Canada is pirated. The piracy rate in countries like Vietnam and China is over 90 percent. CAAST estimates that software piracy has resulted in sales losses of $41 billion worldwide for companies that sell software.[20]

TELECOMMUNICATIONS AND NETWORKS

Although communications systems are constantly evolving (see the Business Accountability box), some of the fundamental elements are well established: computers, communications devices, and networking. The most powerful vehicle for using these elements to their full potential is the marriage of computers and communication technologies. Thanks to lower-cost, higher-capacity networks, the joining of computers, communication, and mass media is changing the nature of information and the ways in which business is conducted.

A *network* is a means of organizing telecommunications components into an effective system. When a company decides how to organize its equipment and facilities, it also determines how its information resources will be shared, controlled, and applied for users in its network. In this section, we will first discuss *multimedia communication technologies* and the devices found in today's systems. We will then describe different ways of organizing information resources into effective systems.

Multimedia Communication Systems

multimedia communication systems Connected networks of communication appliances such as faxes, televisions, sound equipment, cellphones, printers, and photocopiers that may also be linked by satellite with other remote networks.

Today's information systems include not only computers but also **multimedia communication systems**. These systems are connected networks of communication appliances such as faxes, televisions, sound equipment, cellphones, printers, and photocopiers that may also be linked by satellite with other remote networks. Not surprisingly, the integration of these elements is changing the ways in which we live our lives and manage our businesses.

BUSINESS ACCOUNTABILITY

Sharing the Wealth

Janus Friis and Niklas Zennstrom are the Baltic programmers who invented Kazaa—the most downloaded file-sharing program in the world—which provides a free market for videos, music, and porn. With lawyers tracking them, these elusive internet pirates move quietly into London, then secretly to a favourite hangout—the NoKu bar—in Tallinn (Estonia's capital) for a moment of relaxation, and further to Sweden under cover of darkness for secret strategy meetings. "They've resulted in significant damage to the record industry," says Matt Oppenheim, head legal officer for the Recording Industry Association of America (RIAA). While Oppenheim—the chief Kazaa hunter—doggedly tries to serve them legal papers, Friis and Zennstrom have launched an even grander startup, called Skype, that's going to revolutionize telephoning.

Skype—Zennstrom's unique version of what the industry calls "Voice Over Internet Protocol" (VOIP)—is software that provides nearly costless PC-to-PC telephoning. Once it's downloaded onto your computer, a window pops up so you can search the directory for other registered users. Crystal-clear calls are possible so long as both parties have microphones and are hooked up on the internet. In a recent six-month period more than 6 million users in 170 countries downloaded Skype. Zennstrom hopes for and—frighteningly for competitors—is likely to get another 25 million downloads very soon. Why? The download is free and Skype's cost to add a new user is just one-tenth of a cent, compared to $400 to add a new customer at Vonage—the biggest independent VOIP service provider in the United States. Skype's cost advantage stems from tricks Friis and Zennstrom learned while experimenting with Kazaa. It uses peer-to-peer technology in which digital files are stored on subscribers' computers rather than storing millions of files on the company's central computer, allowing Skype to grow without adding much infrastructure.

What impact, then, is in store for the telecom industry? "I knew it was over when I downloaded Skype," says Michael Powell, chairman of the U.S. Federal Communications Commission. "When the inventors of Kazaa are distributing for free a little program that you can use to talk to anybody else, and the quality is fantastic, and it's free—it's over. The world will change now inevitably." Once millions of callers get used to the idea of free phone calling, it will be a hard habit to reverse. So, Friis and Zennstrom's business plan has a global reach with a system capable of handling 6 billion customers. "We're building the next great communications platform," says Skype's product manager Andreas Sjolund.

But with no geographic or political boundaries, who is accountable for how the system is used, its growth, control over competition, and regulation of the technology? In the absence of uniform international regulations, does accountability reside with the technology's users, or the service providers? For answers, we'll have to wait because accountability issues aren't keeping pace with Skype's catch-us-if-you-can, fast-paced technology.

A good example is the modern grocery store. The checkout scanner reads the bar code on the product you buy. Data are then transmitted to the store's inventory-control system, which updates the number of available units. If inventory falls below a given level, more product is ordered electronically. Meanwhile, the correct price is added to your bill and checkout coupons are printed automatically according to the specific product you bought. Your debit card transfers funds, sales reports are generated for the store's management, and all the while, satellite transmissions are dispatching a truck to begin loading replacement supplies for the store.

Communication Devices

Today's technology lets people conduct business across large distances and from places where communications were once unavailable. *Global positioning systems (GPSs)*, for example, use satellite transmissions to track the geographic locations of targets, such as boats or even people. When you're linked to a GPS network, your firm can know your whereabouts at all times. *Personal digital assistants (PDAs)* are tiny hand-held computers with wireless telecommunications capabilities. Many can access the internet, even receiving and sending email messages from the most primitive locations. *Paging systems* and *cellular telephones* connect us instantly with distant networks.

Communication Channels

Communication channels, including wired and wireless transmission, are the media that make all these transmissions possible.[21] Most of us use communication channels when we use wired telephone systems, but today most telephone transmissions are data, not conversations. Fax data account for 90 percent of all telephone signals between the United States and Japan.

Meanwhile, microwave systems transmit wireless radio signals between transmission stations. Satellite communications have also gained popularity with the growth in demand for wireless transmission. Accessible through satellite networks built by McCaw, Hughes, Motorola, AT&T, and Loral, the net is available in remote areas where underground cable isn't feasible.

Broadband Channels. Today's broadband channels, also called ADSL connections, are replacing traditional transmission lines that, until recently, have been the mainstay for connections between computers. In contrast with traditional lines (wires), broadband channels can carry multiple signals—voice, data, audio, visual—simultaneously, rather than carrying just one kind of signal at a time. The result is faster download speed and internet access for multimedia communications.

System Architecture

There are several ways to organize the components in computer and communications networks. One way to classify networks is according to *geographic scope*. Another is according to the *pattern of connections* among the system's devices.

Local and Wide Area Networks

Networked systems classified according to geographic scope may be either local or wide area networks. Computers may be linked province-wide or even nationwide through telephone lines, microwave, or satellite communications, as in a **wide area network (WAN)**. Firms can lease lines from communications vendors or maintain private WANs. Wal-Mart, for example, depends heavily on a private satellite network that links more than 2000 retail stores to its Bentonville, Arkansas, headquarters.

wide area network (WAN) A system to link computers across the country through telephone wires or satellites.

Internal networks covering limited distances may link all of a firm's nearby computers, as in a **local area network (LAN)**. Computers within a building, for example, can be linked by cabling (fibre optic, coaxial, or twisted wire) or by wireless technology. Internally networked computers share processing duties, software, storage areas, and data. On the Home Shopping Network, hundreds of operators seated at monitors in a large room are united by a LAN to enter call-in orders from customers. This arrangement allows the use of a single computer system with one database and software system.

local area network (LAN) A system to link computers in one building or in a small geographical area by cabling or wireless technology.

Wireless Networks. Wireless technologies use airborne electronic signals for linking network appliances. In addition to mobile phones, wireless technology extends to laptops, hand-held computers, and applications in cars (including internet access and music players, map terminals, and game machines). Businesses benefit by avoiding webs of wires crisscrossing facilities. Ford, for example, uses an innovative industrial information system—WhereNet—for tracking inventory by means of identification tags that transmit radio waves. Antennas mounted on the factory ceiling receive transmissions and send information to a central computer that locates tags in the plant. The system saves time and money by coordinating the delivery of hundreds of parts to assembly lines.[22]

Client–Server Systems. An obvious advantage of networks is the sharing of resources—thus avoiding costly and unnecessary duplication. In a **client–server network**, **clients** are the users of services. They are the points of entry, usually laptop computers, workstations, or desktop computers. The **server** provides the services shared by network users. The powerful minicomputer at the network hub, for example, which is larger and more sophisticated than your PC or *microcomputer*, may be the server for the surrounding client PCs in an office network.

client–server network A network composed of both clients (users) and servers that allows the clients to access various services without costly and unnecessary duplication.

client A point of entry in a client–server network.

server A computer that provides the services shared by network users.

More specifically, the server may act as a file server, a print server, and a fax server. As a *file server*, the minicomputer has a large-capacity disk for storing the programs and data shared by all the PCs in the network. It contains customer files plus the database, word-processing, graphics, and spreadsheet programs that may be used by clients. As a *print server*, the minicomputer controls the printer, stores printing requests from client PCs, and routes jobs to the printer as it becomes available. As the *fax server*, the minicomputer receives, sends, and otherwise controls the system's fax activities. Only one disk drive, one printer, and one fax, therefore, are needed for an entire system of users. Internet computing uses the client–server arrangement.

Summary of Learning Objectives

1. **Explain why businesses must manage *information* and show how computer systems and communication technologies have revolutionized *information management*.** Because businesses are faced with an overwhelming amount of *data* and *information* about customers, competitors, and their own operations, the ability to manage this input can mean the difference between success and failure. The management of its information system is a core activity because all of a firm's business activities are linked to it. New digital technologies have taken an integral place among an organization's resources for conducting everyday business.

2. **Identify and briefly describe three elements of *data communication networks*—the internet, the World Wide Web, and intranets.** *Data communication networks*, both public and private, carry streams of digital data (electronic messages) back and forth quickly and economically via *telecommunication systems*. The largest public communications network, the *internet*, is a gigantic network of networks linking millions of computers and offering information on business around the world. The internet is the most important email system in the world. Individuals can subscribe to the internet via an *internet service provider (ISP)*. The *World Wide Web* is a system with universally accepted standards for storing, formatting, retrieving, and displaying information. It provides the common language that enables users around the world to "surf" the internet using a common format. *Intranets* are private networks that any company can develop to extend internet technology internally—that is, for transmitting information throughout the firm. Intranets are accessible only to employees, with access to outsiders prevented by hardware and software security systems called *firewalls*.

3. **Describe five *new options for organizational design* that have emerged from the rapid growth of information technologies.** Information networks are leading to *leaner* organizations—businesses with fewer employees and simpler organizational structures—because networked firms can maintain electronic, rather than human, information links among employees and customers. Operations are *more flexible* because electronic networks allow businesses to offer greater product variety and faster delivery cycles. Aided by intranets and the internet, *greater collaboration* is possible, both among internal units and with outside firms. *Geographic separation* of the workplace and company headquarters is more common because electronic links are replacing the need for physical proximity between the company and its workstations. *Improved management processes* are feasible because managers have rapid access to more information about the current status of company activities and easier access to electronic tools for planning and decision making.

4. **Discuss different information-systems *application programs* that are available for users at various organizational levels.** *Transaction processing systems (TPS)* are applications for basic day-to-day business transactions. They are useful for routine transactions, such as taking reservations and meeting payrolls, that follow predetermined steps. Systems for knowledge workers and office applications include *personal productivity tools* such as word processing, document imaging, desktop publishing, computer-aided design (CAD), and simulation modelling. *Management information systems (MIS)* support an organization's managers by providing daily reports, schedules, plans, and budgets. Middle managers, the largest MIS user group, need networked information to plan upcoming activities and track current activities. *Decision support systems (DSSs)* are interactive applications that assist the decision-making processes of middle and top-level managers. *Executive support systems (ESSs)* are quick-reference, easy-access programs to assist upper-level managers. *Artificial intelligence (AI)* and *expert systems* are designed to imitate human behaviour and provide computer-based assistance in performing certain business activities.

5. **Identify and briefly describe the *main elements of an information system*.** *Hardware* is the physical devices and components, including the computer, in the *information system (IS)*. It consists of an input device (such as a keyboard), a central processing unit (CPU), a main memory, disks for data storage, and output devices (such as video monitors and printers). *Software* includes the computer's operating system, application programs (such as word processing, spreadsheets, and web browsers), and a graphical user interface (GUI) that helps users select among the computer's many possible applications. *Control* is important to ensure not only that the system operates correctly but also that data and information are transmitted through secure channels to people who really need them. Control is aided by the use of electronic security measures, such as firewalls, that bar entry to the system by unauthorized outsiders. The *database* is the organized collection of all the data files in the system. *People* are also part of the information system. IS *knowledge workers* include systems analysts who design the systems and programmers who write software instructions that tell computers what to do. System users, too, are integral to the system. *Telecommunications* components include multimedia technology that incorporates sound, animation, video, and photography along with ordinary graphics and text. Electronic discussion groups, videoconferencing, and other forms of interactive dialogue are possible with communication devices (such as global positioning systems and personal digital assistants) and communication channels (such as satellite communications).

6. **Briefly describe the content and role of a *database* and the purpose of *database software* for information systems.** The *database* is a centralized, organized collection of related data, in digital form, within a computer system. The database is the storehouse of all the system data that are classified into fields, records, and files having numerical storage locations. The purpose of the database and *database software* is to make the data accessible on demand for system users. *Database management programs* are software applications that enable data to be conveniently stored, retrieved, sorted, and searched. This software allows system users to integrate a single piece of data into several different files within the system so that useful information is created.

KEY TERMS

application program, 420
artificial intelligence (AI), 417
browser, 406
central processing unit (CPU), 418
client, 427
client–server network, 427
computer graphics programs, 422
computer network, 418
computer-aided design (CAD), 416
computer-aided manufacturing (CAM), 416
data, 401
data communication networks, 406
database, 422
database management programs, 422
decision support system (DSS), 416
desktop publishing, 423
directories, 407
electronic conferencing, 404
electronic information technologies (EIT), 404
electronic mail (email) system, 404
electronic spreadsheets, 422
encryption, 421
enterprise resource planning (ERP), 411
executive support system (ESS), 417
expert system, 417
extranet, 408
fax machine, 404
firewall, 408
graphical user interface (GUI), 420
groupware, 405
hardware, 418

icons, 420
information, 401
information management, 400
information manager, 400
information system (IS), 401
input device, 418
internet, 406
internet service provider (ISP), 406
intranet, 408
knowledge workers, 412
local area network (LAN), 426
main memory, 419
management information systems (MIS), 416
mass-customization, 409
multimedia communication systems, 424
output device, 419
presentation graphics software, 423
program, 419
robotics, 417
search engine, 408
server, 427
software, 419
software piracy, 424
system operations personnel, 414
system program, 419
transaction processing systems (TPS), 414
voice mail, 404
web servers, 406
wide area network (WAN), 426
word-processing programs, 422
World Wide Web, 406

QUESTIONS FOR ANALYSIS

1. Why must a business manage information as a resource?
2. How can an electronic conferencing system increase productivity and efficiency?
3. Why do the four levels of user groups in an organization need different kinds of information from the IS?
4. In what ways are local area networks (LANs) different from or similar to wide area networks (WANs)?
5. Give two examples (other than those in this chapter) for each of the major types of business application programs.
6. Describe three or four activities in which you regularly engage that might be made easier by multimedia technology.
7. Give three examples (other than those in this chapter) of how a company can become leaner by adopting a networked IS.

APPLICATION EXERCISES

1. Visit a company and interview an individual who is knowledgeable about the firm's management information system. Determine what problems and opportunities exist because of the system.
2. Describe the IS at your school. Identify its components and architecture. What features either promote or inhibit collaboration?
3. Visit a small business in your community to investigate the ways it's using communication technologies and the ways it plans to use them in the future. Prepare a report for class presentation.

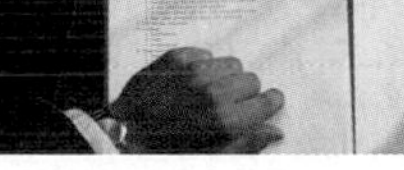

BUILDING YOUR BUSINESS SKILLS

The Art and Science of Point-and-Click Research

Goal

To introduce students to World Wide Web search sites.

Background

In a recent survey of nearly 2000 web users, two-thirds said they used the web to obtain work-related information. With an estimated 320 million pages of information on the web, the challenge for business users is fairly obvious: how to find what they're looking for.

Assignment

You'll need a computer and access to the World Wide Web to complete this exercise.

Step 1

Get together with three classmates and decide on a business-related research topic. Choose a topic that interests you—for example, "Business Implications of the Most Recent Census," "Labour Disputes in Professional Sports," or "Marketing Music Lessons and Instruments to Parents of Young Children."

▶▶▶

Step 2

Search the following sites for information on your topic (dividing them among group members to speed the process):

Alta Vista www.altavista.com
Ask.com www.ask.com
Dogpile www.dogpile.com
Excite www.excite.com
Google www.google.ca
Hotbot www.hotbot.com
Go go.com
Lycos www.lycos.com
Metacrawler www.metacrawler.com
Northern Light www.northernlight.com
Yahoo! www.yahoo.com

Take notes as you search so that you can explain your findings to other group members.

Step 3

Working as a group, answer the following questions about your collective search:

1. Which sites were the easiest to use?
2. Which sites offered the most helpful results? What specific factors made these sites better than the others?
3. Which sites offered the least helpful results? What were the problems?
4. Why is it important to learn the special code words or symbols, called operators, that target a search? (Operators are words like AND, OR, and NOT that narrow search queries. For example, using AND in a search tells the system that all words must appear in the results-for example, American AND Management AND Association.)

Follow-Up Questions

1. Research the differences between search engines and search directories. Then place the sites listed in Step 2 in the proper category. Did you find search engines or directories more helpful in this exercise?
2. Why is it important to learn how to use the search-site "Help" function?
3. Based on your personal career goals, how do you think that mastering web-research techniques might help you in the future?
4. How has the web changed the nature of business research?

EXERCISING YOUR ETHICS

Supplying the Right Answers

The Situation

Networked systems facilitate information sharing among companies and often involve sensitive customer data. This exercise asks you to consider ethical issues that might arise when firms are developing information technologies for use in networked systems.

The Dilemma

Home Sweet Home-e (HSH-e) was an ebusiness start-up that sold virtually everything in home furnishings—from linens and towels to cleaning supplies and furniture. From home computers, HSH-e members could shop in virtual storefronts, chat online with other shoppers, talk live with virtual store clerks, and pay electronically at a one-stop website. In reality, HSH-e was a virtual store: a network of numerous suppliers located around the country, each specializing in a particular line of goods. The network was connected by a centrally controlled information technology that HSH-e developed, owned, and operated. Once a customer's order was placed, suppliers instantaneously received information on what to ship, where to ship it, and how much to charge.

HSH-e chose only suppliers who guaranteed fast, reliable deliveries and promised to supply HSH-e exclusively. The linen supplier, for example, could not supply products to other home-furnishings ebusinesses. In return, the supplier was guaranteed all HSH-e orders for linen products. As HSH-e grew, suppliers stood to gain more business and prosper in an expanding etail industry. As it turns out, some prospective suppliers refused to join the network and others in the network were discontinued by HSH-e for failing to expand fast enough to keep up with demand.

Questions for Discussion

1. For a potential HSH-e supplier of a specialized product line, what are the ethical issues in this situation?
2. Consider past suppliers who have been discontinued or have withdrawn from the HSH-e network. Do they face any ethical issues involving HSH-e customers? Involving HSH-e operations? Involving other HSH-e suppliers?
3. Suppose you work at HSH-e and discover a non-network supplier that is more attractive than one of the company's existing suppliers. What ethical considerations do you face in deciding whether or not to replace an existing supplier?

CONCLUDING CASE 13-1

The Point of Cashing In

Who would expect a 120-year-old company to lead a high-tech revolution for the emerging self-service economy? When John H. Patterson founded the National Cash Register Company in 1884, he had little notion of the power of electricity, let alone the potential of employee-less digital technologies for linking buyers with sellers. Yet, this sometimes oddball and paternalistic guru spearheaded development of the mechanical cash register that was a high-tech marvel of its day. In doing so, Patterson set the tone for the company's innovative culture that persists even today. NCR, the world's largest maker of automated teller machines (ATMs), is now headed by Mark Hurd, a cyber-age visionary with aspirations of becoming the leading developer of equipment—hi-tech point-of-sale (POS) machines—for the soon-to-be self-service economy.

NCR's vision for its biggest-selling POS—the ATM—goes far beyond the cash-dispensing machines we think of today. Take cheque clearing and cash depositing, for example. Instead of inserting an envelope of cheques and waiting three days for them to clear, you insert the endorsed cheque into the ATM, where it's scanned and deposited to an account immediately. The deposit receipt will include an image of the cheque. Similarly, when the customer inserts a stack of bills, the ATM will count them and credit them immediately to the account, instead of waiting to unbundle and count the bills the next day. Both cheque clearing and bill counting are among the bank's most labour-intensive activities, so banks stand to reduce labour costs and human errors.

Looking beyond banking, Hurd expects new POS applications from a complete changeover to self-service in every kind of retailing that currently involves buyer-seller interaction. His idea is to get customers to do more themselves—and like it, just as they do for everyday tasks such as self-dialing long distance phone calls (versus operator assistance, which was dominant in an earlier age), self-service/payment at the gas pump (instead of paying inside), and message writing (typing, filing, and sending your own correspondence on a PC, rather than a secretary doing it). "There will be a continual drive to get consumers to do more of the work—and enjoy it—at places where we shop," says Hurd.

Retailers, banks, and other labour-intense service companies haven't taken advantage of POS devices and, moreover, their customer data contain a wealth of potential information that lies fallow. If companies fully utilized customer data, it would allow shoppers to buy via self-service, with nearly instant access to recommended products based on personal buying patterns. Digital assistance in everything from browsing available products to scanning, weighing, and paying in less time would eliminate the need for costly clerks and cashiers. This futuristic view of a technology-based, self-service economy is not just an illusion—for NCR, it's the core of the company's business strategy.

Dundee, Scotland, is the site of NCR's research centre for ATMs of the future. Visitors get a smiling welcome from Timmy—NCR's cheery young greeter—followed by demonstrations of the latest ATM technology. Speaking in any language, she shows visitors the newest developments: solar-power machines, anti-theft protection that stains money with ink if the machine is violated, radio-frequency identification for loading money electronically into a cellphone, and machines that can accept stacks of cheques and cash without envelopes. The most imaginative innovation, perhaps, is Timmy herself. She's an avatar—a computer-generated character driven by NCR's text-to-speech software—that you'll be seeing soon on the screen of your favourite ATM. This digital sales clerk strokes her hair as she greets customers by name, offers special promotions based on the customer's profile from NCR's data-mining software, then explains how to use various features on the new machine. NCR hopes she'll be the digital jack-of-all-trades that provides everything you need in a self-service mode that reduces expensive human labour costs. "I can be whatever and whoever you want me to be," says Timmy.

CEO Mark Hurd believes his company is uniquely positioned for endless new POS applications beyond ATMs, because there's more to such equipment than just the POS server that meets the customer's eye. Behind the scenes, sophisticated software is prowling through gigantic data warehouses, combing mounds of consumer data for clues about buying patterns and trends for the future. NCR has it all, with its lineup of automated checkout systems and digital salesclerks linked with data warehousing software. The automated checkout system, for example, is already in use at Home Depot. NCR's powerful data warehousing/mining software—the company's biggest source of revenue—is used by the U.S. Air Force to track planes, parts, and pilots, while data-driven giants SBC Communications and Wal-Mart use it for logistics and customer support. By linking those technologies to digital salesclerks-such as "Timmy"—POS applications can revolutionize retailing. Yet, Hurd believes, most companies are unaware of what NCR's technologies can enable them to do, especially in lowering costs and customizing services for individuals. Transactions that rely on employees for interfacing with customers—hotel check-ins, patient check-ins at the doctor's office, student academic advising, airport check-ins, and retail shopping to name a few—are ripe for changeover to self-service.

In today's digital world, it's hard to believe that commonplace tools like the cash register and the sales receipt—both NCR inventions—revolutionized retailing more than a century ago. In like fashion, Mark Hurd wants today's retailers to get the most from NCR's POS technologies: The supermarket shopper enters a loyalty card number into a small electronic cart recorder—much like a purse-size portable kiosk—that accompanies the cart and tracks the shopper's location, aisle-by-aisle, using infrared beacons from the ceiling. In each section of the store, data-mining software reviews the shopper's history to create special offers, customized to the individual's preferences, gives directions for finding specific items, and reminds them of items they might have forgotten. The shopping trip ends with self-service checkouts where customers don't have to empty their cart. All this is happening now, with consumers doing more of the work while creating mounds of new information. NCR, says Hurd, will "help companies ingest and dispatch that data very quickly."

Questions for Discussion

1. Do you think Mark Hurd might be too optimistic about the rise of self-service in the near future? Identify some technology and economic forces that will determine the rise or decline of self-service.
2. What industries, in addition to those mentioned in the case, are good prospects for adopting NCR's POS technologies? For at least three such industries, identify reasons why you believe they are good prospects.
3. From past experiences as a shopper, what weaknesses, if any, can you think of in NCR's POS technologies? What is your assessment of the seriousness of those weaknesses?
4. Suppose you were designing a "digital salesclerk." What are the operational features that you consider most important for customer satisfaction? Explain.
5. Do you see any potential ethical issues in the use of NCR's POS technologies? Explain.

CONCLUDING CASE 13-2

Internet Wars

There is an international drug war going on. No, not the one against heroin and cocaine. This drug war pits manufacturers of cigarettes and prescription drugs against internet companies that sell these products at cut-rate prices. Here's the story, first for cigarettes, and then for prescription drugs.

Cigarettes

During the last few years, many companies have begun selling cigarettes on the internet. Italian brothers Gianpaolo and Carlo Messina, who operate Yesmoke.ch in a duty-free customs location in Balerna, near the Italian border, are typical. They buy name-brand cigarettes like Camels and Marlboros from duty-free airport retailers for less than $1 a pack, then ship them to customers (mostly in the United States) who have placed orders on their internet site. Although it is illegal for U.S. citizens to buy cigarettes without paying taxes, anyone with a credit card can buy these cigarettes. Customers get their cigarettes at far below normal retail costs because the Messinas don't pay any cigarette taxes to U.S. jurisdictions and can therefore charge much lower prices than retailers do.

In an attempt to stop Yesmoke's activities, Philip Morris filed a lawsuit against the company, charging unfair business practices and patent infringement. Yesmoke ignored the suit and a judge ruled against Yesmoke in a default judgment. But Yesmoke says it is not breaking Swiss law by simply exporting cigarettes, and since it does not operate in the United States, it is not bound by U.S. law. An interesting twist to the story is Yesmoke's claim that Philip Morris is actually selling cigarettes to Yesmoke from one of its factories in the Philippines that produces too much for the local market there. Yesmoke claims it buys the excess cigarettes at a deep discount. Philip Morris denies that it is selling cigarettes to Yesmoke, but the European Union recently charged Philip Morris with complicity in smuggling by intentionally overproducing cigarettes at some of its European factories. As part of a larger anti-smuggling agreement with the EU, Philip Morris agreed to pay $1.25 billion (over 12 years), and the charges were dropped.

In 2004, New York City also filed a lawsuit against Yesmoke, saying that the company owed the city $17 million in back taxes on sales to residents of New York. Whether the city will ever be able to collect those back taxes is doubtful. U.S. states are very concerned that internet sales of cigarettes will prevent them from collecting millions of dollars in cigarette taxes, money which they badly need. Traditional retailers are also concerned, since internet retailers will cut into their business.

Prescription Drugs

For many years, Americans who live in border cities have been coming to Canada to purchase prescription drugs because these drugs are cheaper in Canada. When only a relatively small number of Americans came across the border to buy drugs, not much of a fuss was made. But the internet has suddenly made it possible for Americans living anywhere in the United States to purchase Canadian drugs without even coming to Canada. Instead, they can simply go online and order the drugs (they must provide a U.S. doctor's prescription).

In 2003, the U.S. House of Representatives approved a bill that allowed Americans to import drugs from 25 different nations (including Canada). This gave a big boost to Canadian internet pharmacies. All this demand for Canadian drugs has created a group of Canadian entrepreneurs who want to satisfy it (and, of course, make a profit doing so). Both the big drug companies and the Canadian Pharmacists Association (CPhA) oppose internet pharmacies. Depending on who you talk to, their reasons are either selfish (they fear loss of profit) or because they are concerned about the health and safety of others.

The big drug companies say that there are several problems with respect to internet pharmacies:

- The safety of drugs is compromised when they are sold over the internet because the internet pharmacist doesn't know if the patient is taking other drugs that might interfere with the patient's prescription request.
- The internet system can't easily verify that the person wanting the prescription filled hasn't already had it filled from some other internet pharmacy as well.
- The internet system can't verify whether the prescription is authentic.
- When drugs are shipped, they can be exposed to various hazards that might reduce their effectiveness.

The internet pharmacies respond to these claims with several counter-arguments:

- The drug companies won't sell to Canadian-based internet pharmacies because the drug companies will make lower profit margins than if they sold to U.S. pharmacies.
- Internet pharmacies are providing patients with more affordable prescription drugs; without these drugs, the quality of life of these patients would be much lower.
- Traditional pharmacists oppose internet pharmacies simply because they are resisting new ways of doing things.

Most of the big drug companies now refuse to sell any of their products to internet pharmacies, and the Canadian Competition Bureau concluded that no laws were violated by this decision. When the drug companies refused to ship their products to internet pharmacies or to the wholesalers who were supplying them, it was assumed that internet pharmacies would have great trouble getting supplies of prescription drugs. But they have continued to get access to drugs and sell those drugs to people in the United States.

How do they do it? By being very entrepreneurial and establishing elaborate supply networks, that's how. More specifically, internet pharmacies are getting their supplies from hundreds of traditional neighbourhood Canadian pharmacies. But since the big drug companies carefully examine orders from pharmacies looking for suspicious "spikes" in demand, the internet pharmacies are very careful about ordering only small amounts from traditional pharmacies. They also pay these traditional pharmacies a "commission" to supply them. These commissions range from 5 to 15 percent.

Late in 2004, Health Minister Ujjal Dosanjh announced that the government was considering shutting down internet pharmacies to protect both the pricing regime and the supply of prescription drugs for Canadians. If the internet pharmacies were shut down, it would cause the loss of thousands of jobs that were created in the industry. In June 2005, however, Dosanjh backed off from his earlier threats and instead announced that legislation would be introduced to protect Canada's drug supply by allowing the government to shut down bulk exports of prescription medicines from internet pharmacies. The legislation would allow Canadian internet pharmacies to continue to fill prescriptions from individuals in the United States. The internet pharmacies breathed a sigh of relief upon hearing this announcement, because it was a much less threatening decision than the one that Dosanjh had been considering in late 2004.

Questions for Discussion

1. Explain how the internet has facilitated the growth of companies selling cigarettes and prescription drugs.
2. Should internet cigarette sellers and internet pharmacies be allowed to operate? What regulations, if any, should the Canadian government put on these companies?
3. Would you buy cigarettes from an internet seller? Would you buy prescription drugs from an internet pharmacy? Why or why not?
4. Critique each of the arguments that are being made by the drug companies and the Canadian Pharmacists Association. Then do the same for each of the arguments being made by the internet pharmacies. On balance, which arguments do you think are the most compelling? Explain.
5. Develop arguments for and against selling cigarettes on the internet.

CHAPTER 14

Understanding Accounting Issues

After reading this chapter, you should be able to:

1. Explain the role of accountants and distinguish between the kinds of work done by *public* and *private accountants*.
2. Explain how the *accounting equation* and *double-entry accounting* are used in record keeping.
3. Describe the three basic *financial statements* and show how they reflect the activity and financial condition of a business.
4. Explain the key standards and principles for reporting financial statements.
5. Show how computing key *financial ratios* can help in analyzing the financial strengths of a business.
6. Explain some of the special issues that arise in *international accounting*.

Do We Need to Audit the Auditors?

The large amount of negative publicity that has been given to firms like Enron and WorldCom during the last few years makes for very interesting reading, but it is also making accountants very nervous. More and more investors are asking questions like, "How much confidence can I really have when I read an auditor's statement that a company's practices adhere to generally accepted accounting principles?" or "How can a company go bankrupt shortly after having their books audited by an independent auditor?" In 2002, NFO WorldGroup, a market research firm, gave outside auditors a "D" grade for their overall performance.

The case of Livent Inc., a live theatre company that formerly had theatres in Vancouver, Toronto, and New York, illustrates the problems the auditing profession is facing. Livent went bankrupt in the late 1990s amid charges of questionable accounting practices, and two of its executives—Garth Drabinsky and Myron Gottlieb—are now on trial for allegedly defrauding investors and creditors out of $500 million. Investors lost 95 percent of their investment after Livent disclosed accounting irregularities in 1998.

In 2000, the Institute of Chartered Accountants of Ontario (ICAO) took disciplinary action against Livent's senior vice president of finance, who was a Chartered Accountant. He was fined $25 000 and expelled from the ICAO after admitting that he had filed false financial statements and fraudulently manipulated Livent's books. After that, the ICAO began investigating the role of Deloitte & Touche, the accounting firm that was Livent's auditors, and in 2004, the ICAO laid charges of professional misconduct against four partners at Deloitte & Touche. (A few years earlier, in a U.S. court, a judge concluded that Deloitte had not participated in the fraud.) Deloitte is also facing several other lawsuits, including one resulting from the collapse of the Italian dairy firm Parmalat. In that case, investors are suing Parmalat executives and two partners in Deloitte's Italian branch for allegedly conspiring to hide nearly $17 billion of debt.

At a disciplinary hearing in April 2004, Deloitte's lawyer argued that the ICAO charges were "rubbish," and that the allegations were simply differences of opinion regarding the application of generally accepted accounting principles. He pointed out that Livent managers had admitted lying to Deloitte auditors to prevent them from finding out about Livent's real financial condition. The lawyer indicated that his clients were angry that they had been charged, and criticized the long delay in bringing the ICAO charges forward. He also filed an application with the Ontario Superior Court to drop the charges and prevent the ICAO from pursuing the case further.

William Parrett, the CEO of Deloitte, says that there is an "expectation gap" between what the investing public expects and what external auditors can possibly deliver. While auditors simply certify the accuracy of a company's financial statements (based on information provided by the company), investors want auditors to certify that a company is actually financially healthy. Parrett also says that it is not reasonable to hold auditing firms accountable for the illegal and secretive behaviour of corporate executives. Parrett does agree that auditing firms will have to improve the rigour of their audits, and he said that Deloitte has been working hard to overcome any existing deficiencies. The company has appointed an ethics officer in each of its national companies, has added more resources to audit teams, and rechecks initial audit results.

Parrett's explanation sounds pretty reasonable, but people still want to know how cases like Livent, Parmalat, and Enron happen even after the companies' financial statements have been audited by an independent accounting firm. One answer is that auditors are sometimes tempted to "look the other way" when they encounter questionable practices. But *why* would accounting firms not point out questionable accounting practices when they find them? One reason is that many accounting firms have historically also done management consulting for the firms they are auditing. The fees generated from this management consulting can be very lucrative, and often exceed the auditing fees the accounting firm receives. Accountants are human beings, so we should not be surprised if they worry that their clients will be upset if auditors question certain accounting practices. And if clients get upset enough, they may not give the accounting firm any more management consulting contracts. The obvious solution to this problem is to prohibit accounting firms from doing both auditing and management consulting for a given client. In 2002, the Canadian Imperial Bank of Commerce announced that it would no longer allow its auditors to do any management consulting for CIBC.

One very specific Canadian response so far is the establishment of a new Canadian Public Accountability Board (CPAB), which will oversee supervision, inspection, and discipline of Canada's largest accounting firms. The accounting firms will have to get CPAB clearance before their clients' financial statements are accepted. In short, the auditors are going to be audited.

We should not conclude from all of this that doom and gloom reigns in the auditing business. In fact, things are looking up, partly because the Sarbanes-Oxley Act was passed in 2002 by the U.S. Congress. Section 404 of the Act requires U.S.-listed companies to analyze their reporting controls and to make any improvements that are necessary. At each year-end, auditors must certify these controls. Many people in the accounting field believe that Canadian legislators will soon introduce similar legislation. And guess what? That will affect over 4000 Canadian corporations, which in turn will create a substantial increase in demand for the services of auditors. Canadian public accounting firms have already begun recruiting more staff. The increased demand for accountants who are knowledgeable about Sarbanes-Oxley is particularly evident in places like Calgary, the home of many Canadian companies that are listed on U.S. stock exchanges. ◆

WHAT IS ACCOUNTING AND WHO USES IT?

accounting A comprehensive system for collecting, analyzing, and communicating financial information.

bookkeeping Recording accounting transactions.

Accounting is a comprehensive information system for collecting, analyzing, and communicating financial information. As such, it is a system for measuring business performance and translating those measures into information for management decisions. **Bookkeeping** is just one phase of accounting—the recording of accounting transactions. Clearly, accounting is much more comprehensive than bookkeeping because accounting involves more than just the recording of information.

Accounting also uses performance measures to prepare performance reports for owners, the public, and regulatory agencies. To meet these objectives, accountants keep records of such transactions as taxes paid, income received, and expenses incurred, and they analyze the effects of these transactions on particular business activities. By sorting, analyzing, and recording thousands of transactions, accountants can determine how well a business is being managed and how financially strong it is. As the opening case shows, the accounting system can produce distorted results that, in turn, can create huge problems for both owners and managers.

accounting information system (AIS) An organized procedure for identifying, measuring, recording, and retaining financial information so that it can be used in accounting statements and management reports.

Because businesses engage in many thousands of transactions, ensuring consistent, dependable financial information is mandatory. This is the job of the **accounting information system (AIS)**: an organized procedure for identifying, measuring, recording, and retaining financial information so that it can be used in accounting statements and management reports. The system includes all the people, reports, computers, procedures, and resources for compiling financial transactions.[1]

There are numerous users of accounting information:

- *Business managers* use accounting information to set goals, develop plans, set budgets, and evaluate future prospects.
- *Employees and unions* use accounting information to get paid and to plan for and receive such benefits as health care, insurance, vacation time, and retirement pay.
- *Investors and creditors* use accounting information to estimate returns to stockholders, to determine a company's growth prospects, and to decide if the company is a good credit risk before investing or lending.
- *Taxing authorities* use accounting information to plan for tax inflows, to determine the tax liabilities of individuals and businesses, and to ensure that correct amounts are paid in a timely fashion.

- *Government regulatory agencies* rely on accounting information to fulfill their duties; the provincial securities commissions, for example, require firms to file financial disclosures so that potential investors have valid information about a company's financial status.

WHO ARE ACCOUNTANTS AND WHAT DO THEY DO?

At the head of the AIS is the **controller**, who manages all the firm's accounting activities. As chief accounting officer, the controller ensures that the accounting system provides the reports and statements needed for planning, controlling, and decision-making activities. This broad range of activities requires different types of accounting specialists. In this section, we will begin by distinguishing between the two main fields of accounting, *financial* and *managerial*. Then we will discuss the different functions and activities of the three professional accounting groups in Canada.

1 Explain the role of accountants and distinguish between the kinds of work done by *public* and *private accountants*.

controller The individual who manages all the firm's accounting activities.

Financial and Managerial Accounting

In any company, two fields of accounting—financial and managerial—can be distinguished by the different users they serve. As we have just seen, it is both convenient and accurate to classify users of accounting information as users outside the company and users inside the company. This same distinction allows us to categorize accounting systems as either *financial* or *managerial*.

Financial Accounting

A firm's **financial accounting system** is concerned with external users of information—consumer groups, unions, shareholders, and government agencies. It prepares and publishes income statements and balance sheets at regular intervals. All of these documents focus on the activities of *the company as a whole*, rather than on individual departments or divisions.

financial accounting system The process whereby interested groups are kept informed about the financial condition of a firm.

In reporting data, financial accountants must conform to standard reporting formats and procedures imposed by both the accounting profession and government regulatory agencies. This requirement helps ensure that users can clearly compare information, whether from many different companies or from the same company at different times. The information in such reports is mostly *historical*: That is, it summarizes financial transactions that have occurred during past accounting periods.

Managerial Accounting

In contrast, **managerial** (or **management**) **accounting** serves internal users. Managers at all levels need information to make decisions for their departments, to monitor current projects, and to plan for future activities. Other employees, too, need accounting information. Engineers, for instance, want to know costs for materials and production so they can make product or operations improvements. To set performance goals, salespeople need data on past sales by geographic region. Purchasing agents use information on materials costs to negotiate terms with suppliers.

managerial (management) accounting Internal procedures that alert managers to problems and aid them in planning and decision making.

Reports to these users serve *the company's individual units*, whether departments, projects, plants, or divisions. Internal reports may be designed in any form that will assist internal users in planning, decision making, and controlling. Furthermore, as *projections* and *forecasts* of both financial data and business activities, internal reports are an extremely important part of the management accounting system: They are forward-looking rather than historical in nature.

Professional Accountants

Users of financial statements want to be confident that the accountants who have prepared them have a high level of expertise and credibility. Three professional accounting organizations have developed in Canada to certify accounting expertise.

Chartered Accountants

chartered accountant (CA) An individual who has met certain experience and education requirements and has passed a licensing examination; acts as an outside accountant for other firms.

The Canadian Institute of Chartered Accountants (CICA) grants the **chartered accountant (CA)** designation. To achieve this designation, a person must earn a university degree, then complete an educational program and pass a national exam. About half of all CAs work in CA firms that offer accounting services to the public; the other half work in government or industry. CA firms typically provide audit, tax, and management services (see Table 14.1 for a list of the 10 largest CA firms in Canada). CAs focus on external financial reporting, that is, certifying for various interested parties (shareholders, lenders, Canada Customs and Revenue Agency, etc.) that the financial records of a company accurately reflect the true financial condition of the firm. In 2006, there were about 70 000 CAs in Canada.[2]

Certified General Accountants

certified general accountant (CGA) An individual who has completed an education program and passed a national exam; works in private industry or a CGA firm.

The Certified General Accountants Association of Canada grants the **certified general accountant (CGA)** designation. To become a CGA, a person must complete an education program and pass a national exam. To be eligible, a person must have an accounting job with a company. Formerly, CGAs were not allowed to audit the financial statements of publicly held companies, but this is rapidly changing, and now CGAs can audit corporate financial statements in most provinces. Most CGAs work in private companies, but there are a few CGA firms. Some CGAs also work in CA firms. CGAs also focus on external financial reporting, and emphasize the use of the computer as a management accounting tool. From time to time, CGA-Canada

Table 14.1 The Top 10 Accounting Firms in Canada, 2005

Company	Annual Revenues (in millions of $)
1. Deloitte & Touche LLP	$1151
2. KPMG LLP	885
3. PricewaterhouseCoopers LLP	876
4. Ernst & Young LLP	788
5. Grant Thornton Canada	361
6. BDO Dunwoody LLP	260
7. Meyers Norris Penny LLP	143
8. Collins Barrow National Cooperative Inc.	109
9. RSM Richter LLP	95
10. HLB/Schwartz Levitsky Feldman LLP	37

BUSINESS ACCOUNTABILITY

The Pension Crisis

Traditional pension plans are typically defined benefit plans, that is, the company promises to pay a certain defined amount of money to employees when they retire. But a CGA-Canada report showed that the total deficit of the country's largest pension plans at the end of 2004 was $26 billion. If the indexation of pension benefits is taken into account, the number soars to $190 billion. In terms of proportions, 59 percent of traditional pension plans were experiencing pension shortfalls; this number jumps to 96 percent if the indexation of benefits is taken into account.

There are also problems in funding retiree *benefits* (not pensions). A study of 71 of Canada's largest companies showed that their liabilities for retiree *benefits* amounted to $16 billion. In one recent year at Suncor Energy Inc., for example, the company's benefits liability was $98 million (almost as much as its pension liability of $99 million). With baby boomers living longer, and with large numbers of them heading into retirement, the situation for both retiree pensions and retiree benefits is likely to get worse before it gets better.

The problems in pension plans have been caused by a variety of factors, but two factors stand out. First, there have been lower than anticipated returns on investments held by the pension plans. In the 1990s, returns on pension plan investments averaged 11 percent. This rate of return was higher than the 7.5 percent that had been predicted. But during the period 2001–03, the average rate of return for pension plan investments was just 3.1 percent. This was far below the 7 percent that had been assumed. This situation was made even worse because companies began to invest more heavily in equities as a result of their positive experience in the stock market boom of the 1990s. In 1990, 64 percent of pension assets were invested in fixed-income securities and only 36 percent in the more risky equities. By 2004, however, 56 percent of pension assets were invested in equities and only 37 percent in fixed-income securities.

Second, because pension plan investments had achieved such high returns during the 1990s, many companies took pension plan contribution "holidays" and did not contribute anything to the plans they were sponsoring. When the lower investment returns of the twenty-first century started showing up, pension surpluses quickly became pension deficits. In retrospect, companies should not have taken contribution holidays.

The crisis in defined benefit pension plans has caused employers to examine alternative ways to deal with pensions. The simplest solution is to drop defined *benefit* pension plans and instead offer employees defined *contribution* pension plans. When the latter is used, the company's liability is known, but the value of the pension plan when a person retires is unknown (its value is determined solely by the rate of return that the investments in the plan have achieved). Defined contribution plans obviously reduce the uncertainty for the company, but create more uncertainty for retirees.

Companies are, in fact, shifting to defined contribution pension plans. In the United States, for example, there were 112 000 defined benefit plans in 1985, but now there are only about 29 000. The move away from defined benefit plans is also occurring in Canada, although at a slower rate. But that is likely to change, since Canadian legislation requires the company to bear the full financial burden of pension deficits. The current crisis in defined benefit plans means that over the next five years, $15 billion extra dollars will have to be put into those plans to make up for past investment losses. Companies therefore have an incentive to move away from defined benefit plans and toward defined contribution plans, because with the latter they at least know what their contribution requirements are.

Canadian accounting rules may also need to be re-examined. Under current rules, companies can delay recognizing changes in the value of their pension plans. Using a practice called "smoothing," companies can spread the reporting of changes over several years. When stock markets were booming, no one scrutinized pension plans much because their value was going up. But when stock markets started dropping in 2000, large liabilities began building up (but companies kept that information off their balance sheets). National Bank Financial studied 79 Canadian companies—representing 80 percent of the capitalization of the S&P/TSX—and found that their off–balance sheet pension deficits totalled $21 billion.

Canadian and international accounting regulators are working on changes to accounting rules that will bring more realism to pension reporting. The most obvious change involves ending the practice of smoothing and reporting pension fund returns as they actually take place. This means that income from the pension fund would be reported as investment income and the costs of running the pension fund would be reported as expenses. Regulators recognize that a change like this will increase the volatility in the earnings that corporations report, but they point out that investors will be able to more clearly see what is happening (good or bad) in a company's pension fund.

commissions reports on important issues such as pensions (see the Business Accountability box). In 2006, there were about 41 000 CGAs in Canada.[3]

Certified Management Accountants

certified management accountant (CMA) An individual who has completed a university degree, passed a national examination, and completed a strategic leadership program; works in industry and focusses on internal management accounting.

The Society of Management Accountants of Canada grants the **certified management accountant (CMA)** designation. To achieve the designation, a person must a have university degree, pass a two-part national entrance examination, and complete a strategic leadership program while gaining practical experience in a management accounting environment. CMAs work in organizations of all sizes, and focus on applying best management practices in all the operations of a business. CMAs bring a strong market-focus to strategic management and resource deployment, synthesizing and analyzing financial and non-financial information to help organizations maintain a competitive advantage. CMAs emphasize the role of accountants in the planning and overall strategy of the firm in which they work. In 2006, there were about 37 000 CMAs in Canada.[4]

Accounting Services

CAs and CGAs usually perform several accounting services for their clients. The most common of these are auditing, tax services, and management services.

Auditing

audit An accountant's examination of a company's financial records to determine if it used proper procedures to prepare its financial reports.

In an **audit**, the accountant examines a company's AIS to determine whether the company's financial reports fairly present its financial operations. Companies normally must provide audited financial reports when applying for loans or when selling stock. The audit will determine if the firm has controls to prevent errors or fraud from going undetected. Auditors also examine receipts such as shipping documents, cancelled cheques, payroll records, and cash receipts records. In some cases, an auditor may physically check inventories, equipment, or other assets, even if it means descending 200 metres underground in a lead mine.

A financial report is an integral component of the financial accounting system.

Detecting fraud is not the primary purpose of audits, but in recent years there has been much publicity about the alleged failure of auditors to detect fraud. Therefore, when audits are being conducted, sometimes **forensic accountants** are used to track down hidden funds in business firms. Because white-collar crime is on the increase, the number of forensic accountants has increased in recent years. Forensic accountants were used to examine Swiss bank accounts for assets deposited by victims of Nazi persecution during the Second World War.[5] Al Rosen, who writes articles about accounting practices, is a well-known Canadian forensic accountant.

forensic accountant An accountant who tracks down hidden funds in business firms, usually as part of a criminal investigation.

One of the auditor's responsibilities is to ensure that the client's accounting system adheres to **generally accepted accounting principles (GAAP)**—the body of theory and procedure developed and monitored by the CICA. At the end of an audit, the auditor will certify whether the client's financial reports comply with GAAP. Recently, some non-profit organizations such as churches and universities have said that they felt pressured by their auditors to use GAAP. They argue, however, that GAAP principles are designed for profit-seeking business firms, not non-profit organizations. Non-profits should be judged on how well they meet their goals—for example, helping people—rather than on a financial criterion like profit.[6]

generally accepted accounting principles (GAAP) Standard rules and methods used by accountants in preparing financial reports.

Tax Services

Tax services include helping clients not only with preparing their tax returns but also in their tax planning. Tax laws are complex. A CA's advice can help a business structure (or restructure) its operations and investments and save millions of dollars in taxes. To serve their clients best, of course, accountants must stay abreast of changes in tax laws—no simple matter.

Management Consulting Services

Management consulting services range from personal financial planning to the planning of corporate mergers. Other services include plant layout and design, marketing studies, production scheduling, computer feasibility studies, and design and implementation of accounting systems. Some accounting firms even assist in executive recruitment. Small wonder that the staffs of accounting firms may include engineers, architects, mathematicians, and even psychologists.

management consulting services Specialized accounting services to help managers resolve a variety of problems in finance, production scheduling, and other areas.

Private Accountants

To ensure the fairness of their reports, CAs and CGAs must be independent of the firms they audit. They are employees of accounting firms and provide services for many clients. But businesses also hire their own **private accountants** as salaried employees to deal with the company's day-to-day accounting needs.

private accountant An accountant hired as a salaried employee to deal with a company's day-to-day accounting needs.

Private accountants perform a variety of accounting jobs. An internal auditor at Petro-Canada, for example, might fly to the Hibernia site to confirm the accuracy of oil-flow meters on the offshore drilling platform. But a supervisor responsible for $200 million in monthly accounts payable to vendors and employees may travel no further than the executive suite. The nature of the accounting job thus depends on the specific business and the activities needed to make that business a success. Large businesses employ specialized accountants in such areas as budgets, financial planning, internal auditing, payroll, and taxation. Each accounting area has its own challenges and excitement. In small businesses, a single individual may handle all accounting tasks.

TOOLS OF THE ACCOUNTING TRADE

2 Explain how the *accounting equation* and *double-entry accounting* are used in record keeping.

All accountants, whether public or private, rely on record keeping. Private accountants use journals and ledgers to enter and keep track of business transactions for their company. Underlying these records are the two key concepts of accounting: the *accounting equation* and *double-entry bookkeeping.*

The Accounting Equation

At various points in the year, accountants use the following equation to balance the data pertaining to financial transactions:

Assets = Liabilities + Owners' equity

To understand the importance of this equation, we must first understand the terms *assets, liabilities,* and *owners' equity.*[7]

Assets and Liabilities

asset Anything of economic value owned by a firm or individual.

liability Any debt owed by a firm or individual to others.

An **asset** is any economic resource that is expected to benefit a firm or an individual who owns it. Assets include land, buildings, equipment, inventory, and payments due the company (accounts receivable). A **liability** is a debt that the firm owes to an outside party.

Owners' Equity

owners' equity Any positive difference between a firm's assets and its liabilities; what would remain for a firm's owners if the company were liquidated, all its assets were sold, and all its debts were paid.

You may have heard of the equity that a homeowner has in a house—that is, the amount of money that could be made by selling the house and paying off the mortgage. Similarly, **owners' equity** is the amount of money that owners would receive if they sold all of a company's assets and paid all of its liabilities. We can rewrite the accounting equation to highlight this definition:

Assets – Liabilities = Owners' equity

If a company's assets exceed its liabilities, owners' equity is *positive*; if the company goes out of business, the owners will receive some cash (a gain) after selling assets and paying off liabilities. If liabilities outweigh assets, owners' equity is *negative*; assets are insufficient to pay off all debts. If the company goes out of business, the owners will get no cash and some

The inventory at this car dealership is part of the company's assets. The cars constitute an economic resource because the firm will benefit financially as it sells them. When they are sold, at the end of the company's accounting period, the dealership will convert the cost of the cars as expenses and show them as costs of goods sold.

creditors won't be paid. Owners' equity is meaningful for both investors and lenders. Before lending money to owners, for example, lenders want to know the amount of owners' equity in a business. Owners' equity consists of two sources of capital:

1. The amount that the owners originally invested
2. Profits earned by and reinvested in the company

When a company operates profitably, its assets increase faster than its liabilities. Owners' equity, therefore, will increase if profits are retained in the business instead of paid out as dividends to stockholders. Owners' equity also increases if owners invest more of their own money to increase assets. However, owners' equity can shrink if the company operates at a loss or if owners withdraw assets.

Double-Entry Accounting

If your business buys inventory with cash, you decrease your cash and increase your inventory. Similarly, if you buy supplies on credit, you increase your supplies and increase your accounts payable. If you invest more money in your business, you increase the company's cash and increase your owners' equity. In other words, *every transaction affects two accounts.* Accountants thus use a **double-entry accounting system** to record the dual effects of transactions.[8] This practice ensures that the accounting equation always balances.

double-entry accounting system A bookkeeping system, developed in the fifteenth century and still in use, that requires every transaction to be entered in two ways—how it affects assets and how it affects liabilities and owners' equity so that the accounting equation is always in balance.

FINANCIAL STATEMENTS

Describe the three basic *financial statements* and show how they reflect the activity and financial condition of a business. 3

As we noted earlier, the job of accounting is to summarize the results of a firm's transactions and to issue reports to help managers make informed decisions. Among the most important reports are **financial statements**, which fall into three broad categories—*balance sheets, income statements,* and *statements of cash flows.*[9] In this section, we will discuss these three types of financial statements, as well as the function of the budget as an internal financial statement. We'll conclude by explaining the most important reporting practices and the standards that guide accountants in drawing up financial statements.

financial statement Any of several types of broad reports regarding a company's financial status; most often used in reference to balance sheets, income statements, and/or statements of cash flows.

Balance Sheets

Balance sheets supply detailed information about the accounting equation factors: assets, liabilities, and owners' equity. Because they also show a firm's financial condition at one point in time, balance sheets are sometimes called *statements of financial position.* Figure 14.1 shows the balance sheet for Perfect Posters.

balance sheet A type of financial statement that summarizes a firm's financial position on a particular date in terms of its assets, liabilities, and owners' equity.

Assets

As we have seen, an asset is any economic resource that a company owns and from which it can expect to derive some future benefit. From an accounting standpoint, most companies have three types of assets: *current, fixed,* and *intangible.*

Current Assets. **Current assets** include cash and assets that can be converted into cash within a year. They are normally listed in order of **liquidity**—the ease with which they can be converted into cash. Business

current assets Cash and other assets that can be converted into cash within a year.

liquidity The ease and speed with which an asset can be converted to cash; cash is said to be perfectly liquid.

❑❑❑❑❑❑❑❑❑❑ **Perfect Posters, Inc.**
555 Riverview, Toronto, Ontario

Perfect Posters, Inc.
Balance Sheet
As of December 31, 2006

Assets			
Current Assets:			
Cash		$7,050	
Marketable securities. . . .		2,300	
Accounts receivable.	$26,210		
Less: Allowance of. . . . . doubtful accounts.	(650)	25,560	
Merchandise inventory.		21,250	
Prepaid expenses		1,050	
Total current assets			**$57,210**
Fixed Assets:			
Land		18,000	
Building	65,000		
Less: Accumulated depreciation	(22,500)	42,500	
Equipment	72,195		
Less: Accumulated depreciation	(24,815)	47,380	
Total fixed assets. . .			**107,880**
Intangible Assets:			
Patents	7,100		
Trademarks	900		
Total intangible assets			**8,000**
Total assets			**$173,090**

Liabilities and Owners' Equity			
Current liabilities:			
Accounts payable.	$16,315		
Wages payable.	3,700		
Taxes payable.	1,920		
Total current liabilities			**$21,935**
Long-term liabilities:			
Notes payable, 8% due 2009	10,000		
Bonds payable, 9% due 2011	30,000		
Total long-term liabilities			**40,000**
Total liabilities			**$61,935**
Owners' Equity			
Common stock, $5 par		40,000	
Additional paid-in capital		15,000	
Retained earnings		56,155	
Total owners' equity			**111,155**
Total liabilities and owners' equity . . .			**$173,090**

Figure 14.1 Perfect Posters' balance sheet shows clearly that the firm's total assets equal its total liabilities and owners' equity.

debts, for example, can usually be satisfied only through payments of cash. A company that needs but cannot generate cash (in other words, a company that is not liquid) may thus be forced to sell assets at sacrifice prices or even go out of business.

By definition, cash is completely liquid. *Marketable securities* purchased as short-term investments are slightly less liquid but can be sold quickly if necessary. Marketable securities include stocks or bonds of other companies, government securities, and money market certificates. There are three other important non-liquid assets held by many companies: *accounts receivable*, *merchandise inventory*, and *prepaid expenses*.

accounts receivable Amounts due to the firm from customers who have purchased goods or services on credit; a form of current asset.

Accounts receivable are amounts due from customers who have purchased goods on credit. Most businesses expect to receive payment within 30 days of a sale. In our hypothetical example, the entry labelled *Less: Allowance of doubtful accounts* in Figure 14.1 indicates $650 in receivables that Perfect Posters does not expect to collect. Total accounts receivable assets are decreased accordingly.

merchandise inventory The cost of merchandise that has been acquired for sale to customers but is still on hand.

Following accounts receivable on the Perfect Posters balance sheet is **merchandise inventory**—the cost of merchandise that has been acquired for sale to customers and is still on hand. Accounting for the value of inventories on the balance sheet is difficult because inventories are flowing in and out throughout the year. Therefore, assumptions must be made about which ones were sold and which ones remain in storage.

prepaid expense Includes supplies on hand and rent paid for the period to come.

Prepaid expenses include supplies on hand and rent paid for the period to come. They are assets because they have been paid for and are available to the company. In all, Perfect Posters' current assets as of December 31, 2006, totalled $57 210.

Fixed Assets. **Fixed assets** (for example, land, buildings, and equipment) have long-term use or value. But as buildings and equipment wear out or become obsolete, their value decreases. To reflect decreasing value, accountants use **depreciation** to spread the cost of an asset over the years of its useful life. Depreciation means calculating an asset's useful life in years, dividing its worth by that many years, and subtracting the resulting amount each year. Each year, therefore, the asset's remaining value decreases on the books. In Figure 14.1, Perfect Posters shows fixed assets of $107 880 after depreciation.

fixed assets Assets that have long-term use or value to the firm such as land, buildings, and machinery.

depreciation Distributing the cost of a major asset over the years in which it produces revenues; calculated by each year subtracting the asset's original value divided by the number of years in its productive life.

Intangible Assets. Although their worth is hard to set, intangible assets have monetary value. **Intangible assets** usually include the cost of obtaining rights or privileges such as patents, trademarks, copyrights, and franchise fees. **Goodwill** is the amount paid for an existing business beyond the value of its other assets. Perfect Posters has no goodwill assets; however, it does own trademarks and patents for specialized storage equipment. These are intangible assets worth $8000. Larger companies, of course, have intangible assets that are worth much more.

intangible assets Non-physical assets such as patents, trademarks, copyrights, and franchise fees that have economic value but whose precise value is difficult to calculate.

goodwill The amount paid for an existing business beyond the value of its other assets.

Liabilities

Like assets, liabilities are often separated into different categories. **Current liabilities** are debts that must be paid within one year. These include **accounts payable**—unpaid bills to suppliers for materials as well as wages and taxes that must be paid in the coming year. Perfect Posters has current liabilities of $21 935.

Long-term liabilities are debts that are not due for at least one year. These normally represent borrowed funds on which the company must pay interest. Perfect Posters' long-term liabilities are $40 000.

current liabilities Any debts owed by the firm that must be paid within one year.

accounts payable Amounts due from the firm to its suppliers for goods and/or services purchased on credit; a form of current liability.

long-term liabilities Any debts owed by the firm that are not due for at least one year.

Owners' Equity

The final section of the balance sheet in Figure 14.1 shows owners' equity broken down into *common stock, paid-in capital,* and *retained earnings.* When Perfect Posters was formed, the declared legal value of its common stock was $5 per share. By law, this $40 000 ($5 × 8000 shares) cannot be distributed as dividends. **Paid-in capital** is additional money invested in the firm by its owners. Perfect Posters has $15 000 in paid-in capital.

Retained earnings are net profits minus dividend payments to stockholders. Retained earnings accumulate when profits, which could have been distributed to stockholders, are kept instead for use by the company. At the close of 2006, Perfect Posters had retained earnings of $56 155.

paid-in capital Any additional money invested in the firm by the owners.

retained earnings A company's net profits less any dividend payments to shareholders.

Income Statements

The **income statement** is sometimes called a **profit-and-loss statement**, because its description of revenues and expenses results in a figure showing the firm's annual profit or loss. In other words,

Revenues – Expenses = Profit (or loss)

Popularly known as "the bottom line," profit or loss is probably the most important figure in any business enterprise. Figure 14.2 shows the 2006 income statement for Perfect Posters, whose bottom line that year was $12 585. The income statement is divided into three major categories: *revenues, cost of goods sold,* and *operating expenses.*

income (profit-and-loss) statement A type of financial statement that describes a firm's revenues and expenses and indicates whether the firm has earned a profit or suffered a loss during a given period.

Perfect Posters, Inc.
555 Riverview, Toronto, Ontario

Perfect Posters, Inc.
Income Statement
Year ended December 31, 2006

Revenues (gross sales)..........			**$256,425**
Costs of goods sold:			
Merchandise inventory,			
January 1, 2006	$22,380		
Merchandise purchases			
during year................	103,635		
Goods available for sale........		$126,015	
Less: Merchandise inventory,			
December 31, 2006		21,250	
Cost of goods sold			104,765
Gross profit			**151,660**
Operating expenses:			
Selling and repackaging expenses:			
Salaries and wages........	49,750		
Advertising................	6,380		
Depreciation—warehouse and . .			
repackaging equipment......	3,350		
Total selling and repackaging			
expenses..................		59,480	
Administrative expenses:			
Salaries and wages...........	55,100		
Supplies....................	4,150		
Utilities	3,800		
Depreciation—office equipment .	3,420		
Interest expense	2,900		
Miscellaneous expenses...........	1,835		
Total administration expenses......		71,205	
Total operating expenses......			**130,685**
Operating income (income before taxes)...			20,975
Income taxes....................			8,390
Net income.....................			**$12,585**

Figure 14.2 Perfect Posters' income statement. The final entry on the income statement, the bottom line, reports the firm's profit or loss.

Revenues

revenues Any monies received by a firm as a result of selling a good or service or from other sources such as interest, rent, and licensing fees.

When a law firm receives $250 for preparing a will or when a supermarket collects $65 from a customer buying groceries, both are receiving **revenues**—the funds that flow into a business from the sale of goods or services. In 2006, Perfect Posters reported revenues of $256 425 from the sale of art prints and other posters.

Cost of Goods Sold

cost of goods sold Any expenses directly involved in producing or selling a good or service during a given time period.

In Perfect Posters' income statement, the **cost of goods sold** category shows the costs of obtaining materials to make the products sold during the year. Perfect Posters began 2006 with posters valued at $22 380. Over the year, it spent $103 635 to purchase posters. During 2006, then, the company had $126 015 worth of merchandise available to sell. By the end of the year, it had sold all but $21 250 of those posters, which remained as merchandise inventory. The cost of obtaining the goods sold by the firm was thus $104 765.

gross profit (gross margin) A firm's revenues (gross sales) less its cost of goods sold.

Gross Profit (or Gross Margin). To calculate **gross profit** (or **gross margin**), subtract cost of goods sold from revenues obtained from goods sold. Perfect Posters' gross profit in 2006 was $151 660 ($256 425 – $104 765). Expressed as a percentage of sales, gross profit is 59.1 percent ($151 660 ÷ $256 425).

Gross profit percentages vary widely across industries. In retailing, Home Depot reports 30 percent. In manufacturing, Harley-Davidson reports 34 percent; and in pharmaceuticals, Wyeth reports 75 percent. For companies with low gross margins, product costs are a big expense. If a company has a high gross margin, it probably has low cost-of-goods-sold but high selling and administrative expenses.

Operating Expenses

In addition to costs directly related to acquiring goods, every company has general expenses ranging from erasers to the president's salary. Like cost of goods sold, **operating expenses** are resources that must flow out of a company for it to earn revenues. As you can see in Figure 14.2, Perfect Posters had operating expenses of $130 685 in 2006. This figure consists of $59 480 in selling and repackaging expenses and $71 205 in administrative expenses.

operating expenses Costs incurred by a firm other than those included in cost of goods sold.

Selling expenses result from activities related to selling the firm's goods or services. These may include salaries for the sales force, delivery costs, and advertising expenses. General and administrative expenses, such as management salaries, insurance expenses, and maintenance costs, are expenses related to the general management of the company.

Operating Income and Net Income. Sometimes managers must determine **operating income**, which compares the gross profit from business operations against operating expenses. This calculation for Perfect Posters ($151 660 – $130 685) reveals an operating income, or income before taxes, of $20 975. Subtracting income taxes from operating income ($20 975 – $8390) reveals **net income** (also called **net profit** or **net earnings**). In 2006, Perfect Posters' net income was $12 585.

operating income Compares the gross profit from business operations against operating expenses.

net income (net profit or net earnings) A firm's gross profit less its operating expenses and income taxes.

Statement of Cash Flows

Some companies prepare only balance sheets and income statements. However, many firms also report a **statement of cash flows**. This statement describes a company's yearly cash receipts and cash payments. It shows the effects on cash of three business activities:

statement of cash flows A financial statement that describes a firm's generation and use of cash during a given period.

- *Cash flows from operations.* This part of the statement is concerned with the firm's main operating activities: the cash transactions involved in buying and selling goods and services. It reveals how much of the year's profits result from the firm's main line of business (for example, Jaguar's sales of automobiles) rather than from secondary activities (for example, licensing fees a clothing firm paid to Jaguar for using the Jaguar logo on shirts).

At the end of its accounting period, this pharmaceuticals company will subtract the cost of making the goods that it sold from the revenues received from sales. The difference will be its gross profit (or gross margin). Cost of goods sold does not include the firm's operating expenses, including such selling expenses as advertising and sales commissions. In part, gross margins in the pharmaceuticals industry are high because they do not account for high selling expenses.

- *Cash flows from investing.* This section reports net cash used in or provided by investing. It includes cash receipts and payments from buying and selling stocks, bonds, property, equipment, and other productive assets.
- *Cash flows from financing.* The final section reports net cash from all financing activities. It includes cash inflows from borrowing or issuing stock as well as outflows for payment of dividends and repayment of borrowed money.

The overall change in cash from these three sources provides information to lenders and investors. When creditors and stockholders know how firms obtained and used their funds during the course of a year, it is easier for them to interpret the year-to-year changes in the firm's balance sheet and income statement. The importance of cash flow is noted in the Entrepreneurship and New Ventures box.

The Budget: An Internal Financial Statement

budget A detailed financial plan for estimated receipts and expenditures for a period of time in the future, usually one year.

For planning, controlling, and decision making, the most important internal financial statement is the **budget**—a detailed statement of estimated receipts and expenditures for a period of time in the future. Although that period is usually one year, some companies also prepare budgets for three- or five-year periods, especially when considering major capital expenditures.

Budgets are also useful for keeping track of weekly or monthly performance. Procter & Gamble, for example, evaluates all of its business units monthly by comparing actual financial results with monthly budgeted amounts. Discrepancies in "actual versus budget" totals signal potential problems and initiate action to get financial performance back on track.

Although the accounting staff coordinates the budget process, it requires input from many people in the company regarding proposed activities, needed resources, and input sources.[10] Figure 14.3, for example, is a sample sales budget. In preparing such a budget, the accounting department must obtain from the sales group both its projections for units to be sold and expected expenses for each quarter of the coming year. Accountants then draw up the final budget, and throughout the year, the accounting department compares the budget with actual expenditures and revenues.

This concession stand at Rogers Centre is operated by the Toronto Blue Jays. It sells products manufactured mostly by members of the Sporting Goods Manufacturers Association (SGMA), which makes apparel, footwear, and equipment. Much of this merchandise is licensed from Major League Baseball Properties Inc., which distributes licensing revenues to the sport's 30 franchises. MLB Teams (who own logos and uniform designs) and MLB Properties treat sales of licensed products as cash flows from operations.

ENTREPRENEURSHIP AND NEW VENTURES

How Can You Account for a Good Beer?

Denison's, lamented in an article in the Canadian trade journal *World of Beer,* "has closed, and with it has gone our sole opportunity to enjoy Canada's finest Bavarian-style wheat beer and some of the best lagers in the land." The failure of Denison's Brewing Co., a favourite among brewpub aficionados in Toronto, Ontario, issued a stark warning to all local brewers: Even a great-tasting beer will go sour if you can't produce and sell it profitably.

The lesson of Denison's rise and fall has been studied seriously at Black Oak Brewing Co., where founders Ken Woods and John Gagliardi may be the perfect pair to survive in Canada's highly competitive beer market. Although each brings different skills to the joint venture, they share a vision: to make—and sell—the highest-quality beer possible. Gagliardi, certified as a brewmaster by the world-renowned Siebel Institute in 1993, is the quality-control expert whose responsibilities include ensuring the consistency and character of every batch of Black Oak. He admits that as a businessman, he is "first and foremost" a beer lover, and he continues to refresh the company's brand mix by releasing seasonal brews, such as Oktoberfest and Christmas Nutcracker—a practice that permits him to conduct brewing experiments without too much risk. "We're bent on making the highest-quality beer possible," says Gagliardi. "It's got to have the right taste and the perfect clarity and quality. We won't settle for anything less than the best, because we know our customers are going to be expecting a high-quality beer."

Woods, meanwhile, is a Certified Management Accountant (CMA) and a member of the Society of Management Accountants of Canada, but he shares his partner's enthusiastic interest in beer and brewing. For 10 years, he devoted his evenings to developing both his bartending skills and his business contacts, while both would-be entrepreneurs refined their concepts of beers and brewery operations. Since opening Black Oak in 1999, they've managed to develop award-winning beers such as Black Oak Nut Brown Ale, Pale Ale, and Premium Lager, which *The Bar Towel,* a website for Toronto beer lovers, calls "fine, flavourful brews."

Just as importantly, they've also managed to cultivate successful business operations. Woods's accounting background enables him to set up and monitor management and financial procedures, such as the cost controls that made it possible for the company to buy a vintage 1940s labelling machine. "It doesn't matter that it's old," explains Woods. "It's a great piece of equipment and we got it at the right price." Woods and Gagliardi also take care to buy high-quality raw materials at the right price. That's why toasted wheat comes from the nearby town of Fergus while malt is imported from western Canada.

Accounting expertise is especially important because the company's cash flows are affected by the terms of payment negotiated with suppliers and by its procedures for collecting sales revenues. Working in finance and purchasing departments while earning his CMA credentials, Woods learned a lot about payables and receivables. He also produced staff expense reports and tax documents and set up standards for keeping operating costs under control. Finally, his management-accountant training has been especially useful in dealing with the numerous guidelines and rafts of government forms that characterize Ontario's highly regulated beer industry. Being a CMA, says Woods, "is really helpful because it firms up everything you need to know in the marketplace."

Reporting Standards and Practices

4 Explain the key standards and principles for reporting financial statements.

Accountants follow numerous standard reporting practices and principles when they prepare external reports, including financial statements. The common language dictated by standard practices is designed to give external users confidence in the accuracy and meaning of the information in any financial statement. Spelled out in great detail in GAAP, these principles cover a wide range of issues, such as when to recognize revenues from operations, the so-called "matching" of revenues and expenses, and full public disclosure of financial information to the public. Without agreed-upon practices in these and many other accounting categories, users of financial statements would be unable to compare financial information from different companies and thus misunderstand—or be led to misconstrue—a given company's true financial status.

Perfect Posters, Inc.
555 Riverview, Toronto, Ontario

Perfect Posters, Inc.
Sales Budget
First Quarter, 2007

	January	**February**	**March**	**Quarter**
Budgeted sales (units)	7,500	6,000	6,500	20,000
Budgeted selling price per unit	$3.50	$3.50	$3.50	$3.50
Budgeted sales revenue	**$26,250**	**$21,000**	**$22,750**	**$70,000**
Expected cash receipts:				
From December sales	$26,210[a]			$26,210
From January sales	$17,500[b]	$8,750		26,250
From February sales		14,000	$7,000	21,000
From March sales			15,200	15,200
Total cash receipts:	**$43,710**	**$22,750**	**$22,200**	**$88,660**

[a] This cash from December sales represents a collection of the Account Receivable appearing on the December 31, 2006, Balance Sheet.
[b] The company estimates that two-thirds of each month's sales revenues will result in cash receipts during the same month. The remaining one-third is collected during the following month.

Figure 14.3 Perfect Posters, Inc. sales budget, First Quarter, 2007.

Revenue Recognition

As we noted earlier, revenues are funds that flow into a business as a result of its operating activities during the accounting period. *Revenue recognition* is the formal recording and reporting of revenues in the financial statements. Although any firm earns revenues continuously as it makes sales, earnings are not reported until the earnings cycle is completed. This cycle is complete under two conditions:

1. The sale is complete and the product has been delivered
2. The sale price to the customer has been collected or is collectable (accounts receivable)

The completion of the earning cycle, then, determines the timing for revenue recognition in the firm's financial statements. Revenues are recorded for the accounting period in which sales are completed and collectable (or collected). This practice assures the reader that the statement gives a fair comparison of what was gained for the resources that were given up.

Matching

Net income is calculated by subtracting expenses from revenues. The *matching principle* states that expenses will be matched with revenues to determine net income for an accounting period.[11] Why is this principle important? It permits the user of the statement to see how much net gain resulted from the assets that had to be given up to generate revenues during the period covered in the statement. Consequently, when we match revenue recognition with expense recognition, we get net income for the period.

Consider the hypothetical case of Little Red Wagon Co. Let's see what happens when the books are kept in two different ways:

1. Correct Method: Revenue recognition is matched with expense recognition to determine net income when the earnings cycle is *completed*.

2. Incorrect Method: Revenue recognition occurs *before* the earnings cycle is completed.

Suppose that 500 red wagons are produced and delivered to customers at a sales price of $20 each during 2005. In 2006, 600 red wagons are produced and delivered. In part (A) of Table 14.2, the correct matching method has been used: Revenues are recorded for the accounting period in which sales are completed and collectable from customers, as are the expenses of producing and delivering them. The revenues from sales are matched against the expenses of completing them. By using the matching principle, we see clearly how much better off the company is at the end of each accounting period as a result of that period's operations: It earned $2000 net income for 2005 and $3000 for 2006.

In part (B) of Table 14.2, revenue recognition and the matching principle have been violated. Certain activities of the two accounting periods are disguised and mixed together rather than separated for each period. The result is a distorted performance report that incorrectly shows that 2005 was a better year than 2006. Here's what Little Red Wagon's accountants did wrong: The sales department sold 200 red wagons (with revenues of $4000) to a customer late in 2005. Those *revenues* are included in the $14 000 for 2005. But because the 200 wagons were produced and delivered to the customer in 2006, the *expenses* are recorded, as in (A), for 2006. The result is a distorted picture of operations. It looks as if expenses for 2006 are out of line for such a low sales level, and it looks as if expenses (as compared with revenues) were kept under better control during 2005.

The firm's accountants violated the matching principle by ignoring *the period during which the earnings cycle was completed.* Although $4000 in sales of wagons occurred in 2005, the earnings cycle for those wagons was not completed until they were produced and delivered, which occurred in 2006. Accordingly, both the revenues and expenses for those 200 wagons should have been reported in the same period—namely, in 2006, as was reported in part (A). There, we can see clearly what was gained and what was lost on activities that were completed *in an accounting period.* By requiring this practice, the matching principle provides consistency in reporting and avoids financial distortions.

Full Disclosure

Full disclosure means that financial statements should include not just numbers, but also interpretations and explanations by management so that external users can better understand information contained in the statements.

Table 14.2 Revenue Recognition and the Matching Principle

(A) The correct method reveals each accounting period's activities and results

	Year ended December 31, 2005	Year ended December 31, 2006
Revenues	$10,000	$12,000
Expenses	8,000	9,000
Net income	2,000	3,000

(B) The incorrect method disguises each accounting period's activities and results

	Year ended December 31, 2005	Year ended December 31, 2006
Revenues	$14,000	$8,000
Expenses	8,000	9,000
Net income	6,000	(1,000)

Because they know more about inside events than outsiders, management prepares additional useful information that explains certain events or transactions or discloses the circumstances underlying certain financial results.

ANALYZING FINANCIAL STATEMENTS

5 Explain how computing key *financial ratios* can help in analyzing the financial strengths of a business.

Financial statements present a great deal of information, but what does it all mean? How, for example, can statements help investors decide what stock to buy or help managers decide whether to extend credit? Statements provide data, which in turn can be applied to various ratios (comparative numbers). These ratios can then be used to analyze the financial health of one or more companies. They can also be used to check a firm's progress by comparing current and past statements.

Ratios are normally grouped into three major classifications:

solvency ratios Ratios that estimate the financial risk that is evident in a company.

profitability ratios Measures of a firm's overall financial performance in terms of its likely profits; used by investors to assess their probable returns.

activity ratios Measures of how efficiently a firm uses its resources; used by investors to assess their probable returns.

- **Solvency ratios**, both short-term and long-term, estimate risk.
- **Profitability ratios** measure potential earnings.
- **Activity ratios** reflect management's use of assets.

Depending on the decisions to be made, a user may apply none, some, or all the ratios in a particular classification.

Short-Term Solvency Ratios

liquidity ratios Measures of a firm's ability to meet its immediate debts; used to analyze the risks of investing in the firm.

In the short run, a company's survival depends on its ability to pay its immediate debts. Such payments require cash. Short-term solvency ratios measure a company's relative liquidity and thus its ability to pay immediate debts. The higher a firm's **liquidity ratios**, then, the lower the risk involved for investors.

Current Ratio

current ratio A form of liquidity ratio calculated as current assets divided by current liabilities.

The current ratio has been called the "banker's ratio" because it focusses on a firm's creditworthiness. The **current ratio** measures a company's ability to meet current obligations out of current assets. It thus reflects a firm's ability to generate cash to meet obligations through the normal, orderly process of selling inventories and collecting accounts receivable. It is calculated by dividing current assets by current liabilities.

As a rule, a current ratio is satisfactory if it is 2:1 or higher—that is, if current assets are more than double current liabilities. A smaller ratio may indicate that a company will have difficulty paying its bills. Note, however, that a larger ratio may imply that assets are not being used productively and should be invested elsewhere.

How does Perfect Posters measure up? Look again at the balance sheet in Figure 14.1 (see page 444). Judging from its current assets and current liabilities at the end of 2006, we see that

$$\frac{\text{Current assets}}{\text{Current liabilities}} = \frac{\$57\ 210}{\$21\ 935} = 2.61$$

How does Perfect Posters' ratio compare with those of other companies? It's lower than O'Reilly Automotive's ratio (2.94) and higher than those of Gillette (1.56), Cisco Systems (2.14), and Starwood Hotels & Resorts Worldwide (0.23). Although Perfect Posters may be holding too much uninvested cash, it looks like a good credit risk.

working capital The difference between a firm's current assets and current liabilities.

Working Capital. A related measure is **working capital**—the difference between the firm's current assets and its current liabilities. Working capital indicates the firm's ability to pay off short-term debts (liabilities) that it owes to outsiders. At the end of 2006, Perfect Posters' working capital was $35 275 ($57 210 – $21 935). Because current liabilities must be paid off within one year, current assets are more than enough to meet current obligations.

Long-Term Solvency Ratios

To survive in the long run, a company must be able to meet both its short-term (current) debts and its long-term liabilities. These latter debts usually involve interest payments. A firm that cannot meet them is in danger of collapse or takeover—a risk that makes creditors and investors quite cautious.

Debt-to-Owners'-Equity Ratio

To measure the risk that a company may encounter this problem, analysts use long-term solvency ratios called **debt ratios**. The most commonly used debt ratio is the **debt-to-owners'-equity ratio** (or debt-to-equity ratio), which describes the extent to which a firm is financed through borrowed money. It is calculated by dividing **debt**—total liabilities—by owners' equity. Companies with debt-to-equity ratios above 1.0 are probably relying too much on debt. Such firms may find themselves owing so much that they lack the income needed to meet interest payments or to repay borrowed money.

debt ratios Measures of a firm's ability to meet its long-term debts; used to analyze the risks of investing in the firm.

debt-to-owners'-equity ratio A form of debt ratio calculated as total liabilities divided by owners' equity.

debt A company's total liabilities.

In the case of Perfect Posters, we can see from the balance sheet in Figure 14.1 that the debt-to-equity ratio calculates as follows:

$$\frac{\text{Debt}}{\text{Owners' equity}} = \frac{\$61\ 935}{111\ 155} = \$0.56$$

Leverage. Note that a fairly high debt-to-equity ratio may sometimes be not only acceptable but desirable. Borrowing funds provides **leverage**—the ability to make otherwise unaffordable purchases. In leveraged buyouts (LBOs), firms have willingly taken on huge debt to buy out other companies. When the purchased company allows the buying company to earn profits above the cost of the borrowed funds, leveraging makes sound financial sense, even if it raises the buyer's debt-to-equity ratio. Unfortunately, many buyouts have led to financial trouble when actual profits fell short of anticipated levels or when rising rates increased interest payments on the debt acquired by the buyer.

leverage Using borrowed funds to make purchases, thus increasing the user's purchasing power, potential rate of return, and risk of loss.

Profitability Ratios

Although it is important to know that a company is solvent in both the long term and the short term, safety or risk alone is not an adequate basis for investment decisions. Investors also want some measure of the returns they can expect. *Return on equity* and *earnings per share* are two commonly used profitability ratios.

Return on Equity

Owners are interested in the net income earned by a business for each dollar invested. **Return on equity** measures this performance by dividing net income (recorded in the income statement, Figure 14.2) by total owners' equity (recorded in the balance sheet, Figure 14.1).[12] For Perfect Posters, the return on equity ratio in 2006 can be calculated as follows:

return on equity A form of profitability ratio calculated as net income divided by total owners' equity.

$$\frac{\text{Net income}}{\text{Total owners' equity}} = \frac{\$12\ 585}{\$111\ 155} = 11.3\%$$

Is this figure good or bad? There is no set answer. If Perfect Posters' ratio for 2006 is higher than in previous years, owners and investors should be encouraged. But if 11.3 percent is lower than the ratios of other companies in the same industry, they should be concerned.

Earnings per Share

earnings per share A form of profitability ratio calculated as net income divided by the number of common shares outstanding.

Defined as net income divided by the number of shares of common stock outstanding, **earnings per share** determines the size of the dividend a company can pay to its shareholders. Investors use this ratio to decide whether to buy or sell a company's stock. As the ratio gets higher, the stock value increases, because investors know that the firm can better afford to pay dividends. Naturally, stock will lose market value if the latest financial statements report a decline in earnings per share. For Perfect Posters, we can use the net income total from the income statement in Figure 14.2 to calculate earnings per share as follows:

$$\frac{\text{Net income}}{\text{Number of common shares outstanding}} = \frac{\$12\,585}{8000} = \$1.57 \text{ per share}$$

As a baseline for comparison, note that Kraft Food's recent earnings were $2.01 per share, while ConocoPhillips earned $10.21.

Activity Ratios

The efficiency with which a firm uses resources is linked to profitability. As a potential investor, then, you want to know which company gets more mileage from its resources. Activity ratios measure this efficiency. For example, suppose that two firms use the same amount of resources or assets. If Firm A generates greater profits or sales, it is more efficient and thus has a better activity ratio.

Inventory Turnover Ratio

inventory turnover ratio An activity ratio that measures the average number of times inventory is sold and restocked during the year.

Certain specific measures can be used to explain how one firm earns greater profits than another. One of the most important measures is the **inventory turnover ratio**, which calculates the average number of times that inventory is sold and restocked during the year—that is, how quickly inventory is produced and sold.[13] First, a company needs to know its average inventory: the typical amount of inventory on hand during the year. Average inventory can be calculated by adding end-of-year inventory to beginning-of-year inventory and dividing by two. The company can then calculate the inventory turnover ratio, which is expressed as the cost of goods sold divided by average inventory:

$$\frac{\text{Cost of goods sold}}{\text{Average inventory}} = \frac{\text{Cost of goods sold}}{(\text{Beginning inventory} + \text{Ending inventory}) \div 2}$$

High inventory turnover ratio means efficient operations. Because a smaller amount of investment is tied up in inventory, the company's funds can be put to work elsewhere to earn greater returns. However, inventory turnover must be compared with both prior years and industry averages. An inventory turnover rate of 5, for example, might be excellent for an auto supply store, but it would be disastrous for a supermarket, where a rate of about 15 is common. Rates can also vary within a company that markets a variety of products. To calculate Perfect Posters' inventory turnover ratio for 2006, we take the merchandise inventory figures for the income statement in Figure 14.2. The ratio can be expressed as follows:

$$\frac{\$104\,765}{(\$22\,380 + \$21\,250) \div 2} = 4.8 \text{ times}$$

The inventory turnover ratio measures the average number of times that a store sells and restocks its inventory in one year. The higher the ratio, the more products that get sold and the more revenue that comes in. Supermarkets must have a higher turnover ratio than, say, auto supply or toy stores. In almost all retail stores, products with the highest ratios get the shelf spaces that generate the most customer traffic and sales.

In other words, new merchandise replaces old merchandise every 76 days (365 days divided by 4.8). The 4.8 ratio is below the average of 7.0 for comparable wholesaling operations, indicating that the business is slightly inefficient.

INTERNATIONAL ACCOUNTING

Explain some of the special issues that arise in *international accounting.* 6

As we saw in Chapter 5, many companies, such as McCain Foods, Sabian Cymbals, and Electrovert Ltd., receive large portions of their operating revenues from foreign sales. Canadian companies also purchase components from foreign countries. Retailers such as the Bay and Sears buy merchandise from other countries for sale in Canada. In addition, more and more companies own subsidiaries in foreign countries. With all this international activity, there is obviously a need to keep track of foreign transactions. One of the most basic accounting needs is translating the values of the currencies of different countries.

Foreign Currency Exchange

A unique consideration in international accounting is the value of currencies and their exchange rates. As we saw in Chapter 5, the value of any country's currency is subject to occasional change. Political and economic conditions, for instance, affect the stability of a nation's currency and its value relative to the currencies of other countries.

As it's traded around the world, market forces determine a currency's value—what buyers are willing to pay for it. The resulting values are called **foreign currency exchange rates**. When a currency becomes unstable—that is, when its value changes frequently—it is regarded as a *weak currency*. The value of the Brazilian real, for example, fluctuated between 0.416 and 0.957—a variation of 130 percent in U.S. dollars—during the period from 1997 to 2002. On the other hand, a *strong currency* historically rises or holds steady in comparison to other currencies.

foreign currency exchange rate What buyers are willing to pay for a given currency.

As changes in exchange rates occur, they must be considered by accountants when recording international transactions. They will affect, perhaps

"It's up to you now, Miller. The only thing that can save us is an accounting breakthrough."

profoundly, the amount that a firm pays for foreign purchases and the amount it gains from sales to foreign buyers.

International Transactions

International purchases, credit sales, and accounting for foreign subsidiaries all involve transactions affected by exchange rates. When a Canadian company imports Bordeaux wine from the French company Pierre Bourgeois, the Canadian company's accountant must be sure that the company's books reflect its true costs. The amount owed to Pierre Bourgeois changes daily along with the exchange rate between euros and Canadian dollars. Thus, the accountant must identify the actual rate *on the day that payment in euros is made* so that the correct Canadian-dollar cost of the purchase is recorded.

International Accounting Standards

Professional accounting groups from about 80 countries are members of the International Accounting Standards Board (IASB), which is trying to eliminate national differences in financial reporting procedures.[14] Bankers, investors, and managers want procedures that are comparable from country to country and applicable to all firms regardless of home nation. Standardization is occurring in some areas but is far from universal. IASB financial statements include an income statement, balance sheet, and statement of cash flows similar to those issued by Canadian and U.S. accountants. International standards, however, do not require a uniform format, and variety abounds.

Summary of Learning Objectives

1. **Explain the role of accountants and distinguish between the kinds of work done by *public* and *private accountants.*** *Accounting* is a comprehensive system for collecting, analyzing, and communicating financial information. It measures business performance and translates the results into information for management decisions. It also prepares performance reports for owners, the public, and regulatory agencies. To meet these objectives, accountants keep records of income, expenses, and taxes, and they analyze the effects of these transactions on particular business activities. *Bookkeeping* (just one phase of accounting) is the recording of transactions. Ensuring consistent, dependable financial information is the job of the *accounting information system (AIS)*—an organized procedure for identifying, measuring, recording, and retaining financial information so that it can be used in accounting statements and management reports. Users of such information include (1) business managers, (2) employees and unions, (3) investors and creditors, (4) taxing authorities, and (5) government regulatory agencies.

   There are two main fields in accounting: (1) A *financial accounting system* deals with external information users (consumer groups, unions, stockholders, and government agencies). It regularly prepares income statements, balance sheets, and other financial reports published for shareholders and the public. (2) *Managerial (or management) accounting* serves internal users, such as managers at all levels.

2. **Explain how the *accounting equation* and *double-entry accounting* are used in record keeping.** Accountants use the *accounting equation* to balance the data pertaining to financial transactions:

   Assets = Liabilities + Owners' equity

   (1) An *asset* is any economic resource that is expected to benefit its owner (such as buildings, equipment, inventory, and payments due the company). (2) A *liability* is a debt that the firm owes to an outside party. (3) *Owners' equity* is the amount of money that owners would receive if they sold all of a company's assets and paid all of its liabilities.

   Because every transaction affects two accounts, accountants use a *double-entry accounting system* to record the dual effects. Because the double-entry system requires at least two bookkeeping entries for each transaction, it keeps the accounting equation in balance.

3. **Describe the three basic *financial statements* and show how they reflect the activity and financial condition of a business.** Accounting summarizes the results of a firm's transactions and issues reports to help managers make informed decisions. The class of reports known as *financial statements* are divided into three categories—balance sheets, income statements, and statements of cash flows. *Balance sheets* (sometimes called *statements of financial position*) supply detailed information about the accounting-equation factors: assets, liabilities, and owners' equity. The *income statement* (sometimes called a profit-and-loss statement) describes revenues and expenses to show a firm's annual profit or loss. The *statement of cash flow* reports cash receipts and payments from operating, investing, and financing activities.

4. **Explain the key standards and principles for reporting financial statements.** Accountants follow standard reporting practices and principles when they prepare financial statements. Otherwise, users wouldn't be able to compare information from different companies, and they might misunderstand—or be led to misconstrue a company's true financial status. The following are three of the most important standard reporting practices and principles: (1) *Revenue recognition* is the formal recording and reporting of revenues in the financial statements. All firms earn revenues continuously as they make sales, but earnings are not reported until the earnings cycle is completed; (2) The *matching principle* states that expenses will be matched with revenues to determine net income. It permits users to see how much net gain resulted from the assets that had to be given up to generate revenues; (3) Because they have inside knowledge, management prepares additional information that explains certain events or transactions or discloses the circumstances behind certain results. *Full disclosure* means that financial statements include management interpretations and explanations to help external users understand information contained in statements.

5. **Show how computing key *financial ratios* can help in analyzing the financial strengths of a business.** Financial statements provide data that can be applied to *ratios* (comparative numbers). Ratios can then be used to analyze the financial health of one or more companies. They can also be used to check a firm's progress by comparing current with past statements. Ratios are grouped into three major classifications:

(1) *Solvency ratios* estimate risk. *Short-term solvency ratios* measure relative liquidity and thus a company's ability to pay immediate debts. The higher a firm's liquidity ratios, the lower the risk for investors. The most common liquidity ratio is the current ratio, which measures ability to meet current obligations out of current assets. It thus reflects a firm's ability to generate cash to meet obligations through the normal process of selling inventories and collecting accounts receivable. Working capital is the difference between current assets and current liabilities. It indicates ability to pay off short-term debts (liabilities) owed to outsiders. *Long-term solvency ratios* measure ability to meet long-term liabilities consisting of interest payments. Debt ratios are long-term solvency ratios. The most common debt ratio is the debt-to-owners' equity ratio (or debt-to-equity ratio), which describes the extent to which a firm is financed through borrowed money. A fairly high debt-to-equity ratio may sometimes be desirable because borrowing funds provides leverage—the ability to make otherwise unaffordable purchases.

(2) *Profitability ratios* measure potential earnings. Return on equity measures income earned for each dollar invested. Earnings per share determines the size of the dividend that a company can pay shareholders. Investors use it when deciding whether to buy or sell a company's stock. As it gets higher, stock value increases, because investors know that the firm can better afford to pay dividends.

(3) *Activity ratios* reflect management's use of assets by measuring the efficiency with which a firm uses its resources. The inventory turnover ratio measures the average number of times that inventory is sold and restocked annually—that is, how quickly it is produced and sold. A high inventory turnover ratio means efficient operations: Because a smaller amount of investment is tied up in inventory, the firm's funds can be put to work elsewhere to earn greater returns.

6. **Explain some of the special issues that arise in *international accounting*.** Accounting for foreign transactions involves special procedures, such as translating the values of different countries' currencies and accounting for the effects of exchange rates. Moreover, currencies are subject to change: As they're traded each day around the world, their values are determined by market forces—what buyers are willing to pay for them. The resulting values are *foreign currency exchange rates*, which can be fairly volatile. When a currency becomes unstable—when its value changes frequently—it is called a weak currency. The value of a strong currency historically rises or holds steady in comparison with the U.S. dollar.

International purchases, sales on credit, and accounting for foreign subsidiaries all involve transactions affected by exchange rates. When a Canadian company imports a French product, its accountant must be sure that its books reflect its true costs. The amount owed to the French seller changes daily along with the exchange rate between euros and dollars. The Canadian accountant must therefore identify the actual rate on the day that payment in euros is made so that the correct Canadian-dollar cost of the product is recorded.

With accounting groups from about 80 countries, the International Accounting Standards Board (IASB) is trying to eliminate national differences in financial reporting. Bankers, investors, and managers want financial reporting that is comparable from country to country and across all firms regardless of home nation. Standardization governs some areas but is far from universal.

KEY TERMS

accounting, 436
accounting information system (AIS), 436
accounts payable, 445
accounts receivable, 444
activity ratios, 452
asset, 442
audit, 440
balance sheet, 443
bookkeeping, 436
budget, 447
certified general accountant (CGA), 438
certified management accountant (CMA), 440
chartered accountant (CA), 438
controller, 437
cost of goods sold, 446
current assets, 443
current liabilities, 445
current ratio, 452
debt, 453
debt ratios, 453
debt-to-owners'-equity ratio, 453
depreciation, 445
double-entry accounting system, 443

QUESTIONS FOR ANALYSIS

1. Balance sheets and income statements are supposed to be objective assessments of the financial condition of a company. But the accounting scandals of the last few years show that certain pressures may be put on accountants as they audit a company's financial statements. Describe these pressures. To what extent do these pressures make the audit more subjective?
2. If you were planning to invest in a company, which of the three types of financial statements would you want most to see? Why?
3. A business hires a professional accountant like a CA or CGA to assess the financial condition of the company. Why would the business also employ a private accountant?
4. How does the double-entry system reduce the chances of mistakes or fraud in accounting?
5. Explain how financial ratios allow managers to monitor their own efficiency and effectiveness.
6. Suppose that Inflatables Inc., makers of air mattresses for swimming pools, has the following transactions in one week:
   - sale of three deluxe mattresses to Al Wett (paid cash—$75) on 7/16
   - received cheque from Ima Flote in payment for mattresses bought on credit ($90) on 7/13
   - received new shipment of 200 mattresses from Airheads Mfg. (total cost $2000) on 7/17

   Construct a journal for Inflatables Inc.
7. Dasar Company reports the following data in its September 30, 2006, financial statements:

   Gross sales $225 000

   Current assets 40 000

   Long-term assets 100 000

   Current liabilities 16 000

   Long-term liabilities 44 000

   Owners' equity 80 000

   Net income 7 200

   a. Compute the current ratio.

   b. Compute the debt-to-equity ratio.

   c. Compute the return on sales.

   d. Compute the return on owners' equity.

APPLICATION EXERCISES

1. Interview an accountant at a local manufacturing firm. Trace the process by which budgets are developed in that company. How does the firm use budgets? How does budgeting help its managers plan business activities? How does budgeting help them control business activities? Give examples.
2. Interview the manager of a local retail or wholesale business about taking inventory. What is the firm's primary purpose in taking inventory? How often is it done?
3. Interview the manager of a local business and ask about the role of ethics in the company's accounting practices. Is ethics in accounting an important issue to the manager? What steps are taken to ensure ethical practices internally?

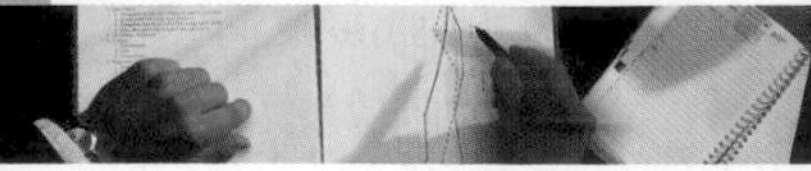

BUILDING YOUR BUSINESS SKILLS

Putting the Buzz in Billing

Goal

To encourage students to think about the advantages and disadvantages of using an electronic system for handling accounts receivable and accounts payable.

Assignment

Step 1

Study Figure 14.4. The outside cycle depicts the seven steps involved in issuing paper bills to customers, payment of these bills by customers, and handling by banks of debits and credits for the two accounts. The inside cycle shows the same bill issuance and payment process handled electronically.

Step 2

As the chief financial officer of a provincial hydroelectric utility, you are analyzing the feasibility of switching from a paper to an electronic system of billing and bill payment. You decide to discuss the ramifications of the choice with three business associates (choose three classmates to take on these roles). Your discussion

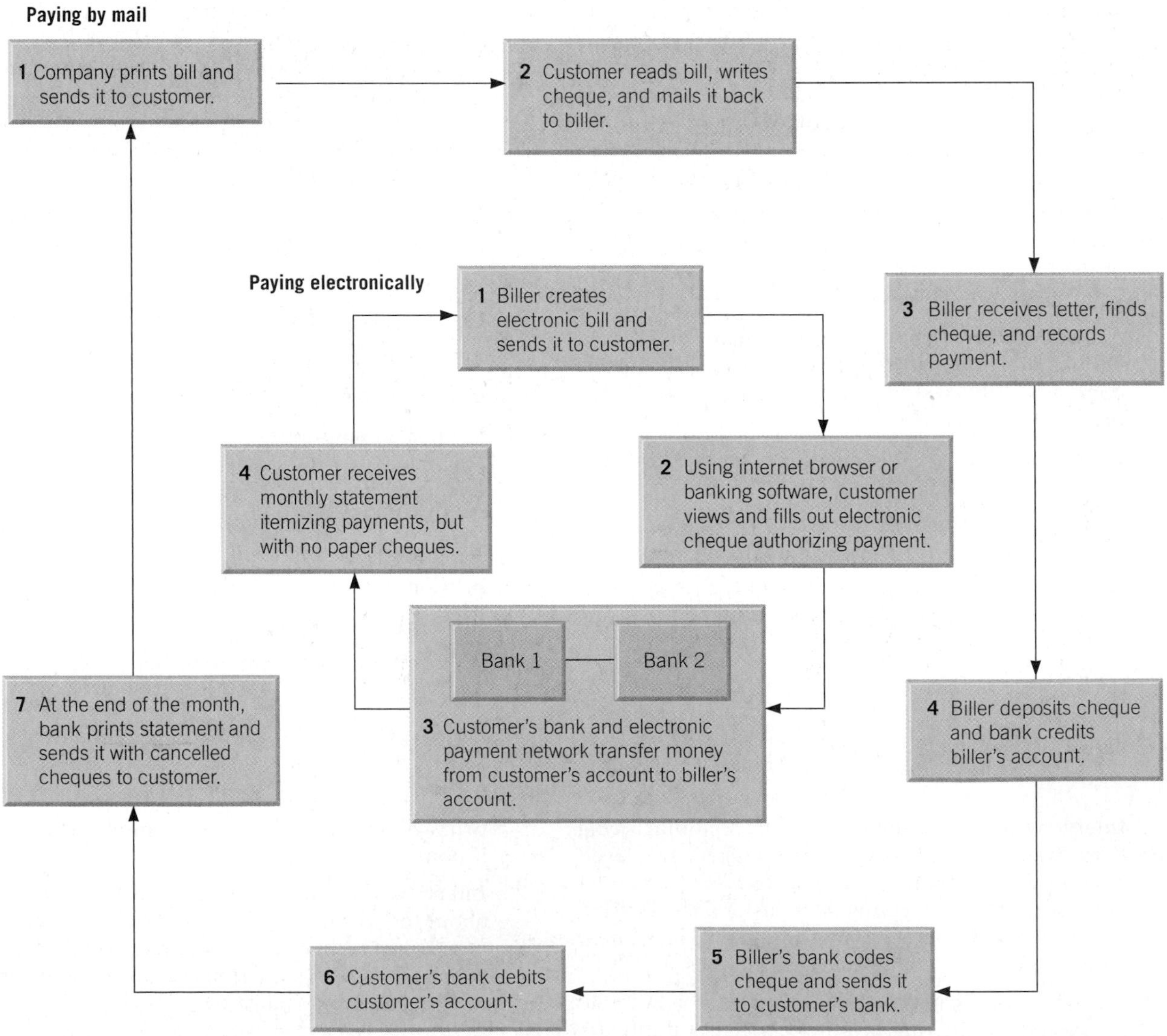

Paying by mail

1 Company prints bill and sends it to customer.

2 Customer reads bill, writes cheque, and mails it back to biller.

3 Biller receives letter, finds cheque, and records payment.

4 Biller deposits cheque and bank credits biller's account.

5 Biller's bank codes cheque and sends it to customer's bank.

6 Customer's bank debits customer's account.

7 At the end of the month, bank prints statement and sends it with cancelled cheques to customer.

Paying electronically

1 Biller creates electronic bill and sends it to customer.

2 Using internet browser or banking software, customer views and fills out electronic cheque authorizing payment.

Bank 1 — Bank 2

3 Customer's bank and electronic payment network transfer money from customer's account to biller's account.

4 Customer receives monthly statement itemizing payments, but with no paper cheques.

Figure 14.4 Managing operations and information.

requires that you research electronic payment systems now being developed. Specifically, using online and library research, you must find out as much as you can about the electronic bill-paying systems being developed by Visa International, Intuit, IBM, and the Checkfree Corp. After you have researched this information, brainstorm the advantages and disadvantages of using an electronic bill-paying system in your company.

Follow-Up Questions

1. What cost savings are inherent in the electronic system for both your company and its customers? In your answer, consider such costs as handling, postage, and paper.
2. What consequences would your decision to adopt an electronic system have on others with whom you do business, including manufacturers of cheque-sorting equipment, Canada Post, and banks?
3. Switching to an electronic bill-paying system would require a large capital expenditure for new computers and computer software. How could analyzing the company's income statement help you justify this expenditure?
4. How are consumers likely to respond to paying bills electronically? Are you likely to get a different response from individuals than you get from business customers?

EXERCISING YOUR ETHICS

Confidentially Yours

The Situation

Accountants are often entrusted with private, sensitive information that should be used confidentially. In this exercise, you're encouraged to think about ethical considerations that might arise when an accountant's career choices come up against a professional obligation to maintain confidentiality.

The Dilemma

Assume that you're the head accountant in a large electronics firm. Your responsibilities include preparing income statements and balance sheets for financial reporting to stockholders. In addition, you regularly prepare confidential budgets for internal use by managers responsible for planning departmental activities, including future investments in new assets. You've also worked with auditors and supplied sensitive information to consultants from a CA firm that assesses financial problems and suggests solutions.

Now let's suppose that you're approached by another company—one of the electronics industry's most successful firms—and offered a higher-level position. If you accept, your new job will include developing financial plans and serving on the strategic planning committee. Thus, you'd be involved not only in developing strategy but also in evaluating the competition. You'll undoubtedly be called upon to use your knowledge of your previous firm's competitive strengths and weaknesses. You realize that your insider knowledge could be useful in your new job.

Questions for Discussion

1. What are the roles of financial accounting, managerial accounting, and accounting services in this scenario?
2. What are the chief ethical issues in this situation?
3. As the central figure in this scenario, how would you handle this situation?

CONCLUDING CASE 14-1

What Numbers Can Be Crunched Offshore?

Planning on an accounting career for job security? If so, you might want to take a second look at what's happening with *business process outsourcing (BPO).* Worldwide finance and accounting outsourcing exceeded $38 billion in 2004, up from $12 billion just five years earlier. BPO is the use of third parties to perform services (not manufacturing) that a company would otherwise do internally. Universities and hospitals, for example, outsource cafeteria operations to food service firms, retailers outsource human resources (HR) activities to HR firms, and manufacturing companies outsource shipping and delivery activities to UPS, FedEx, and other delivery specialists that do the job better, at lower cost.

The outsourcer's basic philosophy is that businesses do best when they focus on their core activities, rather than getting sidetracked into non-core activities that, for many firms, includes accounting. Offshore outsourcing *(offshoring)*—using third parties in other countries—is expected to grow rapidly, with the biggest growth expected in back-office professional services that have low customer contact and require little customization—basic accounting services, radiology analysis (for example, x-rays, CT scans, MRIs), computer software and information technology development, and engineering (for example, product design, testing, and analysis). Standardized processes are easily exported for service abroad, thanks to the internet's global reach. Accounting's basic number-crunching activities—payroll, accounts receivable, accounts payable, cash accounting, inventory valuation—are easily outsourced because the same accounting rules apply to all customers.

Not surprisingly, accounts payable, followed by accounts receivable, are the accounting functions most companies choose to outsource. These high-volume transactional activities are more likely to be outsourced than payroll and taxes, and far more likely to be outsourced than internal auditing, budgeting, and financial statement preparation. Some major companies, however, among them British Petroleum (BP), Delta Airlines, International Paper, and Nortel, are established outsourcers for various parts of their accounting. Accenture, the leading outsourcing provider with more than $3 billion in contract value, handles BP's processing for accounts payable, accounts receivable, cash and banking, and value-added-tax accounting. Safeway Stores in the United Kingdom uses outsourcing of accounting for accounts payable, stock accounting, cash accounts, payroll, and parts of its financial accounting.

In addition to cost savings, better reporting quality—more accurate, with improved delivery and increased speed of reporting—is a significant benefit from outsourcing because providers focus on specialized accounting activities using professional specialists for continuous improvement. As Peter Smith, a partner in the PricewaterhouseCoopers Business Process Outsourcing division, notes, "There's a different feeling when you're providing the service externally, as opposed to internally. There's a greater expectation from the client. They really do expect a much better service." On the downside, however, outsourcing increases the risk of data security. Placing private information in faraway hands, especially in the absence of clear-cut legislation on data privacy and security (as in India), increases chances of violating the client's trust in accounting integrity.

Beyond the basics, however, companies are beginning to outsource more intricate accounting activities, too, including stock and margin accounting, financial accounting, management accounting, real estate accounting, tax compliance, and even internal auditing. For these more customized processes, one of the outside company's employees may be co-located to the outsourcer's facility because good interaction with the client and thorough understanding of its business practices are needed. Data for these more customized accounting activities are transmitted for offshore processing, then results are transmitted back to the outsourcer.

While process-driven, high-volume transaction work is ripe for outsourcing, other accountancy work that depends on domestic-based knowledge is less susceptible. Some financial accounting activities, for example, rely on interpretation of corporate governance, and much of taxation requires in-depth knowledge of domestic tax policy and the regulatory environment. Philip Middleton, financial services partner at Ernst & Young, believes that the deciding factor on outsourcing is the depth of the accountant–client relationship. "If you look around our business and ask what kinds of tasks might go to Bangalore, for example, the answer is probably not a great deal. A lot of what we do requires proximity to clients—close client relationships," he says. But with fast-developing technologies, especially in multimedia communications systems and collaborative groupware, digital proximity might overcome physical remoteness and provide enough depth in the accountant–client relationship to allow even further outsourcing in accounting.

With its abundance of well-educated and highly skilled employees, India has become the back office of the world. In medical services, for example, x-ray images are digitally transmitted to India where skilled radiologists evaluate them, then transmit results back to North American client

▶▶▶

hospitals. Accounting skills, too, are plentiful, with average salaries just one-fifth of those in Western countries and, as a former British Colony, India has a widespread English-speaking culture. With over a third of its college graduates speaking more than two languages fluently, and many speaking as many as six, India is well positioned as an international outsourcing provider. Its Chartered Accountant designation for assuring professionalism is similar in rigor and esteem to the U.S. CPA certification. It comes as no surprise, then, that Deloitte & Touche forecasts that by 2008, India's financial and accounting services will be boosted by some one million new back-office jobs and technology-related positions, moved there by the world's top 100 financial companies.

While India holds the premier position today in offshore work, other countries—Australia, Ireland, Malaysia, the Philippines, and South Africa—are gearing up for the battle of accounting outsourcing destinations, with low-cost and high-technology expertise as primary weapons. Among the strongest contenders, if it can overcome a non–English-speaking tradition, is China, with its one billion population, rapid economic growth, low-cost labour, and serious investment in technical education. Its stated goal is to become the world's top outsourcing destination for accounting.

Questions for Discussion

1. What factors do you think are most important to consider in deciding which parts of a firm's accounting system, if any, are appropriate for outsourcing?
2. Suppose the accounting firm that prepares your income tax return outsources the work to a third-party tax-service provider. Do you think the accounting firm should get your permission before outsourcing the work? Why or why not?
3. Suppose you are hoping for an accounting career. To what extent does the trend toward offshore outsourcing threaten your career prospects? In what ways does it provide new opportunities?
4. What steps might a firm take to ensure that its private information is safeguarded by its offshore accounting provider?
5. What ethical issues, if any, are involved in a decision about outsourcing a firm's accounting activities? Explain.

CONCLUDING CASE 14-2

Continuing Concerns in the Accounting Profession

The corporate accounting and insider trading scandals of a few years ago have caused users of financial data to be increasingly concerned that the balance sheets and income statements of corporations may not be exactly what they seem. Those concerns prompted a Canadian Senate Banking Committee to analyze ways to restore investor confidence in financial data. The committee made several recommendations, including forcing CEOs to vouch for the truthfulness of their financial statements, passing new legislation governing the conflicts of interest faced by investment analysts, and requiring companies to have only independent directors on their audit committees.

Most of the really dramatic cases of corporate fraud have occurred in the United States, but Canada has the dubious distinction of having one of its own in the limelight. Canadian-born Bernard Ebbers had risen from Alberta milkman and nightclub bouncer to become CEO of WorldCom, one of the largest companies in the United States. It was alleged that Ebbers conspired with subordinates to "cook the books" when a business downturn occurred. These actions wiped out $100 billion of the company's market value, cost 17 000 people their jobs, and wiped out the life savings of investors. Scott Sullivan, one of Ebbers' subordinates, pled guilty and testified that Ebbers had ordered him to cook the books to hit earnings targets. In 2005, Ebbers was found guilty on nine charges of securities fraud and filing false documents. He was sentenced to 25 years in prison for his role in the collapse of WorldCom Inc.

In addition to outright accounting fraud, concerns have been expressed about the difficulty investors have in understanding what accounting statements really mean. In recent years, two issues in this area have received attention: overstating sales revenue and understating pension liabilities. The problem of overstating sales revenue is discussed below (see the Business Accountability box on p. 439 for a discussion of the pension liability issue).

Overstating Sales Revenue

Many companies are tempted to use "creative accounting" to inflate sales revenue, and this yields a distorted picture of how much product or service a company is actually selling. This is done so that the company will not disappoint the expectations of the stock market and then see their stock price drop. There are different ways that sales revenue can be overstated. For example, some software makers sell a lot of product at the end of a quarter and then count all those sales as revenue without taking into account the future costs the firm will incur to support the software or to provide the free upgrades they promised. Or, a company that acts as a sales agent for an airline might include the ticket price, plus the commission it earns, as revenue. When the airline firm is paid, the cost goes on the expense line. This approach vastly overstates revenue (but not profit). The company should have included only its sales commissions as revenue.

High-tech firms in particular are seen as too liberal in recording revenues on their financial statements. Because of this, the Ontario Securities Commission is shifting its emphasis from examining prospectuses to analyzing the way companies report income. It has set up a continuous disclosure team to review the financial reports of corporations in a systematic manner. To get a better understanding of the revenue problem, the OSC is also asking companies how they account for revenue from things like service contracts, and whether they benchmark their accounting practices against those used by other firms in their industry.

Other Concerns

A variety of other concerns have also been raised during recent years, including the following:

- There is sometimes a "chummy" relationship between auditors and their clients; this makes it more difficult for auditors to be completely objective.
- There is considerable "elasticity" in the application of generally accepted accounting principles; thus, companies have a lot of leeway in their accounting practices.
- If a person from an accounting firm takes a management position with a firm that is a client, future audits may be too "cozy" and fail to be objective.
- Self-regulation by the accounting industry doesn't work.
- There has been much fruitless debate in accounting firms about how to deal with stock options that are given to executives (if these are shown as expenses, they depress corporation earnings and lower the stock price).
- The accounting profession has moved away from establishing broad accounting principles and instead spent much of its time drafting detailed rules; even if these detailed rules are followed, the financial statements that are produced can present a distorted picture of a company's financial condition.

What should be done to resolve these problems? A few of the more commonly heard solutions are as follows:

- Auditors should clarify their language so that readers of financial statements will have a better idea of how a company is doing before they invest in it.
- Auditors should give more consideration to the users of financial statements, perhaps emphasizing different data for different user groups.
- Auditors should be charged with detecting fraud and reporting when they find it.
- Firms should be required to change their auditors on a regular basis (for example, once every five years). to prevent "chummy" relationships from developing.
- Auditors should not be allowed to take jobs with former clients until after a specified time period has passed (say, three to five years).
- A truly independent monitoring group should be formed that would assess the extent to which companies are meeting standards in their financial reporting.
- Stock options should be shown as expenses.
- When earnings forecasts are made, there must be a clear statement of how the forecasted numbers were arrived at.
- Companies should be required to show how much they paid for auditing services, and how much they paid for management consulting from the same auditor.
- Auditors should be required to rank a company's accounting practices in terms of how "aggressive" they are, rather than just saying the books are okay or not okay.

Questions for Discussion

1. Who are the various users of accounting information? How will each of these users be influenced if sales revenues are overstated and pension liabilities are understated?
2. What are the three basic financial statements that accountants generate for business firms? What does each one show? How will overstating sales revenue and understating pension liabilities affect each of these statements?
3. Read the sections in the chapter on revenue recognition and matching. How is the material in those sections helpful in dealing with the "overstating of sales revenue" problem noted in the case?
4. Consider the following statement: "*Since sales revenues and pension returns are measured in dollars, and since dollars are easy to quantify, it should be very clear what sales revenues and investment income a firm had in a given period. It is therefore unnecessary to have policies about how sales revenues and pension returns should be reported.*" Do you agree or disagree? Explain.

PLANNING FOR YOUR CAREER

Presenting Yourself Online

We've seen that information and communication technology are valuable resources for increasing any firm's competitiveness, as discussed in Chapters 13 and 14. As you prepare for your career, you'll find that information and technology resources are also helpful for presenting yourself online to prospective employers. This exercise gives you the opportunity to look more closely at various online career information resources, including announcements of job vacancies, methods for job hunting, and hiring.

Assignment

Recall from Chapter 13 that geographic separation of the workplace from the company headquarters is more common than ever because of networked organizations. Similarly, job seekers, as well as businesses searching for employees, rely more and more on digital contact between applicants and employers, rather than face-to-face and land-mail communication. While the traditional method of sending out printed résumés is still effective, the online possibilities are too big to ignore. Your objective in this exercise is to evaluate online sources for career information and to explore ways you can use online technology for job hunting.

To complete this exercise, do the following:

1. Examine activities for online career planning that are presented in "Marketing Yourself Online" in Chapter 6 of *Beginning Your Career Search*, 3rd ed., by James S. O'Rourke IV.
2. Explore one of the internet's general-career sites, such as www.job.com, as discussed by O'Rourke. Identify three (or more) of the site's career-planning services that would be more difficult to obtain using offline sources.
3. Consider O'Rourke's suggestions for online job searches that might apply to a career field that interests you. Search in three ways for jobs in your career field: Use an online newspaper source, a general-career website, and any of the internet's general-purpose search engines. Which source provides the most useful information?
4. Using any means you choose, identify a potential employer for the career field that interests you. Explore that organization's career opportunities by visiting its website. Do its employment listings contain information that might help you adapt your résumé for a better match with opportunities at that organization?
5. Compare two methods for entering the job market: sending out printed résumés versus online postings. List the résumé-design skills for each method that are most important for job-search success. Explain differences in the skills requirements for the two methods.
6. O'Rourke cautions job seekers against using free web-hosting services that flash ads alongside your résumé. Explain the reasons for this warning.

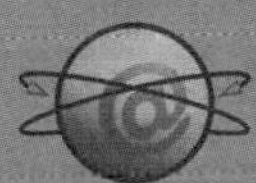

Visit the Companion Website at www.pearsoned.ca/griffin to view the CBC video segments that accompany the following cases.

CBC CBC VIDEO CASE III-1

Handmaster

Dr. Terry Zachary is a chiropractor turned entrepreneur who has developed a product that is designed to strengthen all the muscles in the human hand. The product looks pretty simple (a polyurethane sponge ball and a plastic cord), but as Terry was looking into how to produce it, he discovered that if he had it manufactured in China he could cut the production cost by 50 percent compared to what it would cost to produce in Canada.

So, Zachary decided he had to make a trip to China to look at potential manufacturers. He wants to have different companies produce the ball and the cord to reduce the chance that his product will be counterfeited and copied. His plan was to visit eight potential manufacturers in five different Chinese cities so that he could determine who might be best to work with. His first visit is to a company called Changzhou Yuming. Zachary meets with the managers and shows them a sample of the cord that he might want them to produce. He tells them that the quality must be high. Zachary tours their production facilities and is impressed by what he sees. The Yuming managers are very aggressive in assuring him that they can do the work he wants. They clearly want him as a customer, but Zachary finds that communicating through an interpreter is difficult and frustrating.

His next meeting is with managers from Erison, the company that Zachary thinks might be able to make the foam ball for his product. He tells the Erison managers that he wants three different densities for the ball (firm, medium, soft), and that the density must be just right. Later, Zachary takes a bus to the Lelpro factory in Wuxi; that company makes various items including basketballs. Eventually, Zachary decides that Lelpro will make the foam ball for his product. He then heads home.

Six weeks later, Zachary is back in China to see how things are progressing. This is make-or-break time for him. His company has orders for the Handmaster, but he has had problems getting the Chinese manufacturing companies up to speed. At Yuming, the company that is making the cord, Zachary sees the machine that will make the cord. A test run is underway, and the Yuming production managers say they are getting close to what Zachary wants. Communication is still difficult, and Zachary feels that it is hard to pin down exact dates for when the product will be ready. He is also frustrated because there seems to be a difference between what is being promised and what is actually being delivered. Still, progress is being made, and Zachary feels that his manufacturer is actually getting close to what he wants.

Zachary then goes to check on the production of the foam ball at Lelpro. He checks the all-important density and finds it is good. He thinks that Lelpro is a pretty good company to deal with, but he is taking a chance that they can actually deliver the product in 20 days as required. He didn't put a penalty clause in the contract if they don't deliver on time, but thinks perhaps he should have.

Back at Yuming, there are still problems. Zachary wants to see a final product, but is having trouble conveying that to the Yuming managers. They say they are getting close. Zachary forcefully tells the interpreter to find out the exact time a crucial mould is supposed to arrive at the factory. He also continually asks the interpreter what the Chinese managers are saying. All of this is frustrating, but Zachary can do nothing but wait. Finally, just in time, he gets the final version of the cord for the product. All of the manufacturing jobs that Zachary's product will create will stay in China, but product packaging will be done in Canada.

In the end, Zachary is impressed with way that the Yuming managers worked through the problems that developed. He says a cordial goodbye to the people at Yuming and returns to Canada.

Questions for Discussion

1. What are the different kinds of utility? What kind of utility is being generated by these Chinese manufacturers?
2. What are the five types of transformation technology that are available? Which one is being used by the manufacturers in this situation?
3. What is the difference between analytic and synthetic processes? Which process is being used here?
4. What kind of layout is likely used in the manufacture of the Handmaster product?
5. Which of the total quality management techniques might be useful in the production of the Handmaster product?

Source: "Handmaster: Made in China," *Venture*, March 14, 2004.

CBC CBC VIDEO CASE III-2

African Accountants

In Canada's business jungle, all tracks lead to Bay Street, where lions of modern industry reign. Accountants keep Bay Street's books, but the heat is on to keep better books. Accountants don't like people who bring in shoeboxes full of receipts and then ask the accountant to organize them. Instead, accountants want the material organized before they try to do any calculations. But all this organizing costs money, and small- and mid-sized businesses don't usually have the money to pay for it.

For George Wall, of Wall & Associates, finding enough casual workers to do data organization and entry was a big challenge. He had to pay them up to $20 an hour, and that service was way too pricey for many of his clients. But what if Wall could find workers who would do this work for one-tenth the hourly wage he had to pay people in Toronto? He found the solution by adopting global outsourcing. It works like this: When that shoebox arrives, each piece of paper is first fed into a high-speed scanner and then stored on a server. While Bay Street sleeps, the material is sent to Kampala, Uganda, over the internet, where the data are keyed in by African accountants who are paid only about $1 a day.

In a freshly painted office in Kampala, a dozen computers have just been taken out of their boxes, and a dozen workers have just been hired. Their boss is 20-something Abu Luaga, a Ugandan with a commerce degree who has the contract to do accounting work for Wall & Associates. He teaches the new hires what to do. His start-up funds came from his family, and he got involved with Wall & Associates through his connections with a Canadian business consultant.

There is much competition from other developing countries to get this kind of business. But his workers are keen, and they're already trained as bookkeepers. They're eager to see what the developed world has to offer, but many have never had a computer before and need training so that they can recognize various financial documents and learn Canadian accounting jargon. They're also being trained to think the way Canadian businesses do. As well, Luaga reminds them about deadlines and privacy. Because these workers are dealing with sensitive information, no cellphones are allowed in the office and the copying or saving of files or images is prohibited.

What are the implications of all this information flowing from the first world to the third world and back again? It may be just the kind of miracle Uganda needs. The telecommunications industry has been a bright spot in the Ugandan economy, but Ugandans still make only about $1 a day. The country still relies on money earned by exporting coffee, and the government is dependent on foreign donors for part of its budget. Officials admit that the technical skills of workers aren't as good as those of people in some Asian countries, but this system allows educated Ugandans to work in their home country.

Luaga's workers say the work has already changed their career prospects. But not all Canadian clients have jumped at the chance to zip their documents to Africa. George Wall is convinced they will eventually be comfortable with the idea, and Luaga is banking on it. He's leasing bigger and better office space because he thinks that a new office and clients in Canada will impress other potential clients in Africa.

Questions for Discussion

1. What is the difference between financial and managerial accounting? Is the work that the African accountants are doing financial or managerial accounting? Explain.
2. Why might Canadian clients be reluctant to have Wall & Associates send their data to Africa for organizing? What can George Wall do to respond to their concerns?
3. Suppose that you read a newspaper editorial condemning the practice of sending documents to Africa on the grounds that this was yet another example of exporting Canadian jobs overseas to low-wage countries. How would you respond?

Source: "African Accountants," *Venture*, February 16, 2003.

PART FOUR

Managing Marketing

What is the first thing you think of when you hear the names Coffee Crisp, Post-It, Crest, and Eno? If you grew up in Canada, you probably didn't hesitate at all before picturing candy, little slips of paper with one sticky edge, toothpaste, and something to calm your stomach. Your rapid association of company names and the goods or services they provide is a tribute to the effectiveness of the marketing managers of the firms that produce these goods. These and many other names have become household words because companies have developed the right products to meet customers' needs, have priced those products appropriately, have made prospective customers aware of the products' existence and qualities, and have made the products readily available.

Part Four, Managing Marketing, provides an overview of the many elements of marketing, including developing, pricing, promoting, and distributing various types of goods and services.

- We begin in **Chapter 15, Understanding Marketing Processes and Consumer Behaviour**, by examining the ways in which companies distinguish their products, determine customer needs, and otherwise address consumer buying preferences.
- Then, in **Chapter 16, Developing and Promoting Goods and Services**, we explore the development of different types of products, the effect of brand names and packaging, how promotion strategies help a firm meet its objectives, and the advantages and disadvantages of several promotional tools.
- Finally, in **Chapter 17, Pricing and Distributing Goods and Services**, we look at the strategies firms use to price their products. We also consider the various outlets business firms use to distribute their products, and we discuss the problems of storing goods and transporting them to distributors.

CHAPTER 15

Understanding Marketing Processes and Consumer Behaviour

After reading this chapter, you should be able to:

1. Explain the concept of *marketing* and describe the five forces that constitute the *external marketing environment*.
2. Explain the purpose of a *marketing plan* and identify the four components of the *marketing mix*.
3. Explain *market segmentation* and show how it is used in *target marketing*.
4. Explain the purpose and value of *marketing research*.
5. Describe the key factors that influence the *consumer buying process*.
6. Discuss the three categories of *organizational markets* and explain how *organizational buying behaviour* differs from consumer buying behaviour.
7. Describe the *international* and *small business marketing mixes*.

Marketers Pay Attention to the Older Folks

For many years, marketers directed their attention to consumers in the 18–35 age bracket because it was assumed that if they could get younger consumers to like their products, these consumers would continue to be loyal to it as they grew older. But this assumption has been called into question by marketing research data showing that customers are quite willing to switch brands if given the incentive to do so. Companies are also realizing that older consumers simply have a lot more money to spend than younger consumers do. For example, the net worth of people aged 65–69 is about 15 times the net worth of people aged 34 and younger.

Another factor is demographics: By 2010, about one-third of the population will be over 50 years of age. Between 2003 and 2016, the number of Canadians aged 55–64 will increase by 51 percent, and the number over 65 will increase by 41 percent. The number of Canadians aged 18–24 will increase by only 5 percent during that same period.

Is it possible for a company to attract older customers while still making younger ones think their products are cool? Sony thinks so. Its advertisement showing a grandmother taking underwater pictures of sharks scored well with younger viewers who liked the adventure aspect of the advertisement. Sony calls customers in the 50–64 age bracket "zoomers" to reflect the fact that they have more active lifestyles than their parents did. Here are several other examples of marketing to older people:

- Ford Motor Co. is introducing the Ford Five Hundred, a sedan (which older drivers like) that has some of the features of an SUV (it also has a roomy trunk for golf bags).
- Procter & Gamble has identified about 30 different products (including Puffs and Downey fabric softener) that can be marketed to people over 50; it has targeted older women with two new products (Rejuvenating Effects toothpaste and Olay Anti-Aging Cream), and has also developed Actonel, an osteoporosis drug, which is likely to do well in Japan, Italy, and France because of the aging populations there.
- Motorola introduced a new phone that should be of interest to older consumers because its zoom function allows the user to increase the font size so that it's more readable; the phone also has speakers that can be connected to a hearing aid.
- Vodafone introduced a new phone that shows a clear message that the batteries need recharging rather than a tiny icon that is hard for older folks to see.
- In Japan, Meiji Dairies Corp. started making a yogurt brand for people over 40.
- Walt Disney World developed a program aimed at people over 50 called "Magical Gatherings" that allows customers to use a website to plan trips with golf buddies or old schoolmates.
- Anheuser-Busch attracted older drinkers away from wine and other less-filling beverages by introducing a low-carb Michelob beer and calling it "Michelob Ultra"; it was introduced in three Florida retirement communities.
- Francine Tremblay launched *Le Bel Age*, a French-language magazine for "mature" Canadians; she also produced *Good Times*, an English-language magazine aimed at the same age group.

Of course, companies are not giving all their attention to older people. Rather, they are using demographics (studying characteristics of the population such as age, income, ethnic background, etc.) to determine how to best market to their customers. The age distribution of a country's population is important and it has a big impact on the marketing strategies of companies that are trying to sell everything from diapers to arthritis medicine. For example, the strategy of focussing on the youth market still looks pretty good in places like Brazil, Mexico, and Vietnam (because a large proportion of their population is young), but not so good in countries like Japan, Germany, and France (where a large proportion of the population is old).

In North America, the importance of demographics in marketing can be seen in a variety of situations. Consider the following:

- Ford Motor of Canada gives graduates a $750 rebate on their first-time purchase of a car.
- In 2003, the *Toronto Star* started a youth-oriented newspaper aimed at kids 9 to 14; this offering complements the existing *Starship* feature, which is aimed at kids 6 to 12 and the *boom!* feature (aimed at teenagers).
- Mattel Inc., the maker of the Barbie doll, formerly targeted girls aged 2 to 8 for this product, but 7- and 8-year-old girls are now less and less interested in Barbie dolls and see them as something that "little kids" play with.
- Major League Baseball Enterprises tracks demographic trends to set marketing goals for its $6 billion-a-year business; 20 years ago, the typical fan was a child, but today's average fan is about 37 years old. ◆

WHAT IS MARKETING?

1 Explain the concept of *marketing* and describe the five forces that constitute the *external marketing environment.*

What do you think of when you hear the word "marketing"? If you are like most people, you probably think of advertising for something like detergent or soft drinks. But marketing is more than just advertising. **Marketing** is the "the process of planning and executing the conception, pricing, promotion, and distribution of ideas, goods, and services to create exchanges that satisfy individual and organizational goals."[1]

marketing Planning and executing the development, pricing, promotion, and distribution of ideas, goods, and services to create exchanges that satisfy both buyers' and sellers' objectives.

Because we are all consumers and because we all buy goods and services, we are influenced by the marketing activities of companies that want us to buy their products. But as consumers, we are in fact *the* essential ingredients in the marketing process. Every day, we express *needs* for such essentials as food, clothing, and shelter and *wants* for such nonessentials as entertainment and leisure activities. Our needs and wants are the forces that drive marketing.

marketing concept The idea that the whole firm is directed toward serving present and potential customers at a profit.

The **marketing concept** means that the whole firm is coordinated to achieve one goal—to serve its present and potential customers and to do so at a profit. This concept means that a firm must get to know what customers really want and follow closely the changes in tastes that occur. The various departments of the firm—marketing, production, finance, and human resources—must operate as a system, well coordinated and unified in the pursuit of a common goal—customer satisfaction.

We begin our study of marketing by looking at how marketing focusses on providing value and utility for consumers. We then explore the marketing environment and the development of marketing strategy. Finally, we focus on the four activities that comprise the marketing mix: *developing, pricing, promoting,* and *placing products*.

Providing Value and Satisfaction

What attracts buyers to one product instead of another? While our desires for the many goods and services available to us may be unbounded, limited financial resources force most of us to be selective. Accordingly, consumers buy products that offer the best value when it comes to meeting their needs and wants.

Value and Benefits

value Relative comparison of a product's benefits versus its costs.

Value compares a product's benefits with its costs. The benefits of a *high-value* product are much greater than its costs. *Benefits* include not only the functions of the product, but also the emotional satisfactions associated with owning, experiencing, or possessing it. Every product has costs, including sales price, the expenditure of the buyer's time, and the emotional costs of making a purchase decision. The satisfied buyer perceives the benefits derived from the purchase to be greater than its costs. Thus the simple but important ratio for value:

$$\text{Value} = \frac{\text{Benefits}}{\text{Costs}}$$

Marketing strategies focus on increasing value for customers. Marketing resources are deployed to add value to products to satisfy customers' needs and wants. Satisfying customers may mean developing an entirely new product that performs better (provides greater benefits) than existing products. Or it may mean keeping a store open extra hours during a busy season (adding the benefit of greater shopping convenience). Some companies simply offer price reductions (the benefit of lower cost). Customers may also gain benefits from an informational promotion that explains how a product can be used in new ways.

Value and Utility

To understand how marketing creates value for customers, we need to know the kind of benefits that buyers get from a firm's goods or services. Products provide consumers with **utility**—the ability of a product to satisfy a human want or need. Marketing strives to provide four kinds of utility:

utility Ability of a product to satisfy a human want or need.

- When a company turns out ornaments in time for Christmas, it creates *time utility*: It makes products available when consumers want them.
- When a department store opens its annual Christmas department, it creates *place utility*: It makes products available where customers can conveniently purchase them.
- When the store sells ornaments, it provides *ownership utility* by conveniently transferring ownership from store to customer.
- By making products available in the first place—by turning raw mate rials into finished ornaments—the ornament maker creates *form utility*.

Marketing plays a role in all four areas—determining the timing, place, terms of sale, and product features that provide utility and add value for customers. Marketers, therefore, must begin with an understanding of customers' wants and needs. Their methods for creating utility are described in this and the following two chapters.

Goods, Services, and Ideas

The marketing of tangible goods is obvious in everyday life. You walk into a department store and are given a free scented paper strip as an initial product sample of a new perfume. A pharmaceutical company proclaims the virtues of its new cold medicine. Your local auto dealer offers to sell you an automobile with no interest charges for four years. These products—the perfume, the cold medicine, and the car—are all **consumer goods**: products that you, the consumer, buy for personal use. Firms that sell products to consumers for personal consumption are engaged in *consumer marketing*.

consumer goods Products purchased by individuals for their personal use.

Marketing is also important for **industrial goods**, which are products used by companies to produce other products. Surgical instruments and earthmovers are industrial goods, as are such components and raw materials as integrated circuits, steel, and unformed plastic. Firms that sell products to other manufacturers are engaged in *industrial marketing*.

industrial goods Products purchased by companies to use directly or indirectly to produce other products.

Marketing is also relevant for **services**—intangible products such as time, expertise, or some activity that you can purchase. *Service marketing* has become a major growth area in Canada. Insurance companies, airlines,

services Intangible products, such as time, expertise, or an activity that can be purchased.

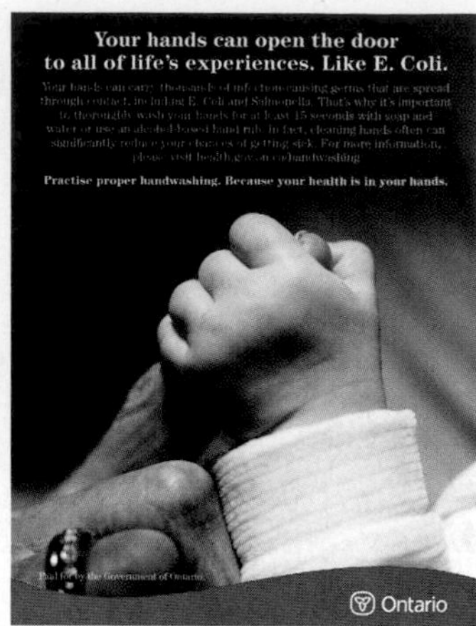

Each of these advertisements provides information about a specific product, service, or idea. The soy milk, for example, is a tangible consumer product. The advertisement for the fitness club promotes a service that can be enjoyed. The public service ad promotes the idea of healthy behaviour.

investment counsellors, health clinics, and accountants all engage in service marketing, both to individuals and to other companies.

Finally, marketers also promote *ideas*. Television ads, for example, can remind us that teaching is an honourable profession and that teachers are "heroes." Other ads stress the importance of driving only when sober and the advantages of not smoking.

BUSINESS ACCOUNTABILITY

When Smoke Gets in Your Eyes

In Canada, government restriction on the advertising of cigarettes has a long history. Television advertising of cigarettes has been prohibited since 1971, and various other restrictions (including some rather dramatic label requirements) have come into force since then. Recently, for example, new legislation came into effect designed to discourage tobacco companies from sponsoring sports and cultural events so that they could get their brands prominently displayed to consumers. At a charity dinner in Toronto 2004, for example, the Rothmans Benson & Hedges table simply said "anonymous" in spite of the fact that the company had paid thousands of dollars to sponsor the table. Tobacco companies are still allowed to advertise in magazines and newspapers, but the rules are so restrictive they generally don't try anymore. Yves-Thomas Dorval, a spokesman for Imperial Tobacco Canada Ltd., says that since "promotion" is essentially prohibited by law, tobacco companies are focussing on the three other "Ps" of marketing (price, place, and product).

Clashes between stop-smoking groups and tobacco companies are common, particularly when tobacco companies appear to be ignoring the spirit of the restrictions that have been placed on them. For example, as part of the TD Canada Downtown Jazz Festival, Imperial Tobacco set up an outdoor smoking lounge in Toronto's Nathan Phillips Square. The lounge was criticized by the Ontario Free-Tobacco Network, which called on the mayor of Toronto to stop Imperial from using "scantily-clad girls" to promote cigarettes on city property.

All of these situations are interesting, but an important question remains: Who is accountable for the negative effects of tobacco use? Government agencies in both Canada and the United States (Health Canada and the American Public Health Association, respectively) seem to take the position that it is the companies who sell cigarettes that bear most of the responsibility. Not surprisingly, cigarette companies argue that because tobacco use is an individual behaviour choice for which potential health risks are well known, accountability falls to the consumer instead of the producer of the product. How accountable should tobacco firms be?

Coalitions of health advocacy groups—including the World Health Organization—and other grassroots public health organizations—are insisting that corporate accountability be formally acknowledged. In the United States, the $39 billion in settlement revenues that was given to states during a recent five-year period is cited as tangible recognition of the industry's accountability, but only for after-affects. Not far enough, insist the health advocates, arguing that the more than 400 000 tobacco-related deaths each year in North America are preventable: Companies should also be accountable for effective preventive measures that are absent now and are likely to remain so until more regulation is imposed on them. Tobacco firms, in response, point to several recent court rulings in the United States that denied more than $50 billion in claims brought by HMOs and insurance companies for reimbursement of tobacco-related health expenses. They point to these cases as supportive of the industry's argument that it is not accountable.

While the issue of accountability simmers, marketing finds itself on both sides of the controversy. Advertising expenditures by Canadian and U.S. tobacco's companies have soared to more than $11 billion each year. Health advocates cite "predatory marketing practices" as the industry advertises in youth magazines and develops advertising campaigns targeted at Hispanic, Asian, and other population groups that as yet may not be fully aware of health risks from smoking. Young adults with low incomes and lower education levels are representative of the target-market demographics of smoking. Consider the following statistics:

- The rate of smoking among people who did not complete high school is three times the rate for those with an undergraduate university degree.
- Smoking among pregnant women is 15 times greater for those who did not graduate from high school than it is for those with a university education.
- About one-third of people living below the poverty line are smokers, compared with only one-quarter of those above the poverty line.
- Low-wage workers smoke more than those with high wages.

Health advocates say that tobacco companies have increasingly paid retailers to display tobacco advertising, have used "buy one, get one free" promotions, and have set up promotional racks and giveaways that make cigarettes easier to buy for these targeted smokers.

Marketing by health advocacy groups has embraced "idea-and-information" messages to promote the stop-smoking idea and to appeal for more corporate accountability. The American Legacy Foundation's award-winning TV "truth" campaign debunks the idea that smoking is glamorous, and features information about the social costs and health consequences of tobacco. A report by the U.S. National Cancer Institute publicized the idea that "light" cigarettes don't reduce health risks and often simply lead to brand switching rather than quitting. Community-based and grassroots efforts include counter-marketing campaigns to educate higher risk groups—targeted by the tobacco industry—about tobacco's harmful effects. Media ads and promotional materials targeted at legislators and regulators are appealing for more regulation and explicit acknowledgement of industry's accountability for reducing the ill effects from tobacco. Meanwhile, both sides know that each day brings with it hundreds of new smokers, quitters, and tobacco-related deaths.

Relationship Marketing

Although marketing often focusses on single transactions for products, services, or ideas, marketers also take a longer-term perspective. Thus, **relationship marketing** emphasizes lasting relationships with customers and suppliers. Stronger relationships—including stronger economic and social ties—can result in greater long-term satisfaction and customer loyalty.[2]

relationship marketing A type of marketing that emphasizes lasting relationships with customers and suppliers.

Banks, for example, offer *economic* incentives to encourage longer-lasting relationships. Customers who purchase more of the bank's products (for example, chequing accounts, savings accounts, and loans) accumulate credits toward free or reduced-price services, such as free traveller's cheques. As another example, motorcycle manufacturer Harley-Davidson offers social incentives through the Harley Owners Group (H.O.G.). H.O.G. gives motorcyclists the opportunity to bond with other riders and to develop long-term friendships.

The Marketing Environment

external environment Outside factors that influence marketing programs by posing opportunities or threats.

Marketing plans, decisions, and strategies are not determined unilaterally by any business—not even by marketers as experienced and influential as Coca-Cola and Procter & Gamble. Rather, they are strongly influenced by powerful outside forces. As you can see in Figure 15.1, any marketing program must recognize the outside factors that comprise a company's **external environment**. In this section, we will describe five of these environmental factors: *the political/legal, social/cultural, technological, economic*, and *competitive environments*.

Political and Legal Environment

Political activities, both foreign and domestic, have profound effects on business (refer back to Chapter 1 for a discussion of how government influences business). Legislation on the use of cellphones in cars and pollution legislation can determine the destinies of entire industries. Marketing managers therefore try to maintain favourable political/legal environments in several ways. For example, to gain public support for their products and activities, marketing uses advertising campaigns for public awareness on issues of local, regional, or national importance. They also lobby and contribute to political candidates (although there are legal restrictions on how much they can contribute). Such activities sometimes result in favourable laws and regulations and may even open new international business opportunities.

Social and Cultural Environment

More people are working at home, more women are entering the workforce, the number of single-parent families is increasing, food preferences and physical activities reflect the growing concern for healthful lifestyles, and the growing recognition of cultural diversity continues. These and other issues reflect the values, beliefs, and ideas that form the fabric of Canadian society today. Obviously, these broad attitudes toward issues have direct effects on business. Today, for example, as we continue to insist on a

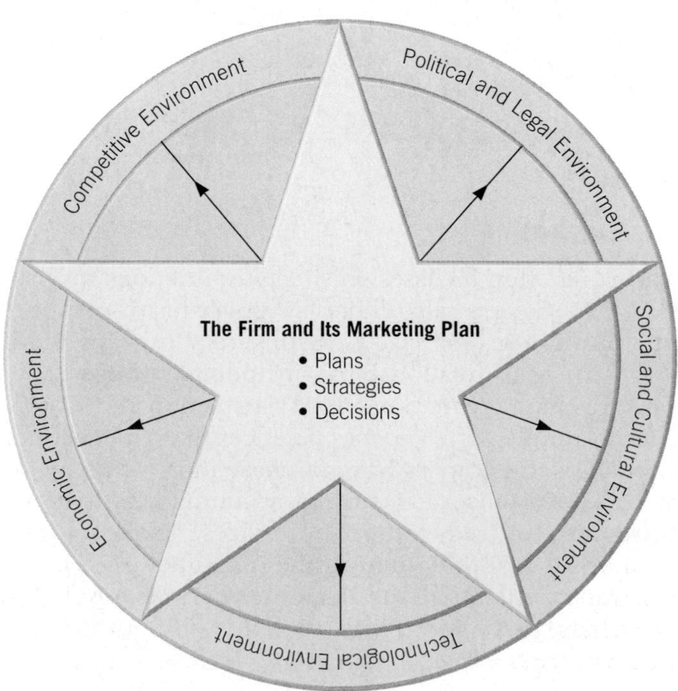

Figure 15.1 The external marketing environment.

"greener" Canada, we have seen the demise of freon in air conditioners and increased reliance on recycling materials in the goods that we consume.

Changing social values force companies to develop and promote new products for both individual consumers and industrial customers. For example, although most of us value privacy, web surfers are discovering that a loss of privacy is often a price for the convenience of internet shopping. Dot-com sites regularly collect personal information that they use for marketing purposes and which they often sell to other firms. Responding to the growing demand for better privacy protection, firms like iNetPrivacy offer such products as Anonymity 4 Proxy software, which allows you to surf the Net anonymously.

Technological Environment

New technologies affect marketing in several ways. Obviously, they create new goods (say, the satellite dish) and services (home television shopping). New products make some existing products obsolete (for example, compact discs are replacing audiotapes), and many of them change our values and lifestyles. In turn, they often stimulate new goods and services not directly related to the new technology itself. Cellular phones, for example, not only facilitate business communication, but also free up time for recreation and leisure.

Consider the phenomenon of DNA "fingerprinting." The O.J. Simpson trial (United States), the Guy Paul Morin case (Canada), and the television show *CSI: Crime Scene Investigation* have made just about everyone aware of its availability to law-enforcement officials. Bear in mind, however, that it is also the focal point of a new industry—one that involves biological science and laboratory analysis and instrumentation as well as criminology. DNA fingerprinting, then, is a product. Along with its technical developments, therefore, it involves marketing decisions—such as pricing and promotion. This has been the case with literally thousands of technological breakthroughs in such fields as genetics, electronics, aeronautics, medicine, information sciences, communications systems, transportation, the internet (which we discussed in Chapter 13), and emarketing (which we discuss in Chapter 17).

In 2006, gas prices exceeded $1 per litre in most locations in Canada. The price of a barrel of crude oil—more than $70—was the highest ever recorded. The jump in prices reflects a variety of circumstances in the global economic environment, including fears of terrorism in the Middle East and increased demand for oil in China and India.

Economic Environment

Economic conditions determine spending patterns by consumers, businesses, and governments. Thus they influence every marketer's plans for product offerings, pricing, and promotional strategies. Among the more significant economic variables, marketers are concerned with inflation, interest rates, recession, and recovery. In other words, they must monitor the general business cycle, which typically features a pattern of transition from periods of prosperity to recession to recovery (return to prosperity). Not surprisingly, consumer spending increases as "consumer confidence" in economic conditions grows during periods of prosperity. Conversely it decreases during low-growth periods, when unemployment rises and purchasing power declines.

Traditionally, analysis of economic conditions focussed on the national economy and the government's policies for controlling or moderating it.

Increasingly, however, as nations form more and more economic connections, the "global economy" is becoming more prominent in the thinking of marketers everywhere.[3] At U.S.-based Wal-Mart, for example, more than 18 percent of all sales revenue comes from the retailer's international division. Although international sales were up 17 percent for 2004, sales in some Latin American countries stalled. Why? Because economic conditions in such markets as Argentina and Brazil differ significantly from those in Mexico, which, in turn, differ from those in China, South Korea, and Germany.

Competitive Environment

In a competitive environment, marketers must convince buyers that they should purchase their products rather than those of some other seller. In a broad sense, because both consumers and commercial buyers have limited resources to spend, every dollar spent to buy one product is no longer available for other purchases. Each marketing program, therefore, seeks to make its product the most attractive; theoretically, a failed program loses the buyer's dollar forever (or at least until it is time for the next purchase decision).

By studying the competition, marketers determine how best to position their own products for three specific types of competition:

substitute product A product that is dissimilar from those of competitors but that can fulfill the same need.

- **Substitute products** are dissimilar from those of competitors but can fulfill the same need. For example, your cholesterol level may be controlled with either a physical-fitness program or a drug regimen; the fitness program and the drugs compete as substitute products.

brand competition Competitive marketing that appeals to consumer perceptions of similar products.

- **Brand competition** occurs between similar products, such as the auditing services provided by large accounting firms like Ernst & Young and KPMG Peat Marwick. The competition is based on buyers' perceptions of the benefits of products offered by particular companies.

international competition Competitive marketing of domestic against foreign products.

- **International competition** matches the products of domestic marketers against those of foreign competitors—say, a flight on Swissair versus Air Canada. The intensity of international competition has been heightened by the formation of alliances such as the European Union and NAFTA.

2 Explain the purpose of a *marketing plan* and identify the four components of the *marketing mix.*

Strategy: The Marketing Mix

marketing managers Managers responsible for planning and implementing all the marketing-mix activities that result in the transfer of goods or services to customers.

marketing plan A detailed strategy for gearing the marketing mix to meet consumer needs and wants.

marketing mix The combination of product, price, place, and promotion strategies used in marketing a product.

As a business activity, marketing requires management. Although many individuals also contribute to the marketing of a product, a company's **marketing managers** are typically responsible for planning and implementing all the marketing-mix activities that result in the transfer of goods or services to its customers. These activities culminate in the **marketing plan**: a detailed and focussed strategy for gearing marketing activities to meet consumer needs and wants. Marketing, therefore, begins when a company identifies a consumer need and develops a product to meet it.

In planning and implementing strategies, marketing managers develop the four basic components (often called the "Four Ps") of the **marketing mix** (see Figure 15.2). In this section, we briefly describe each of those components: *product, price, place,* and *promotion.*

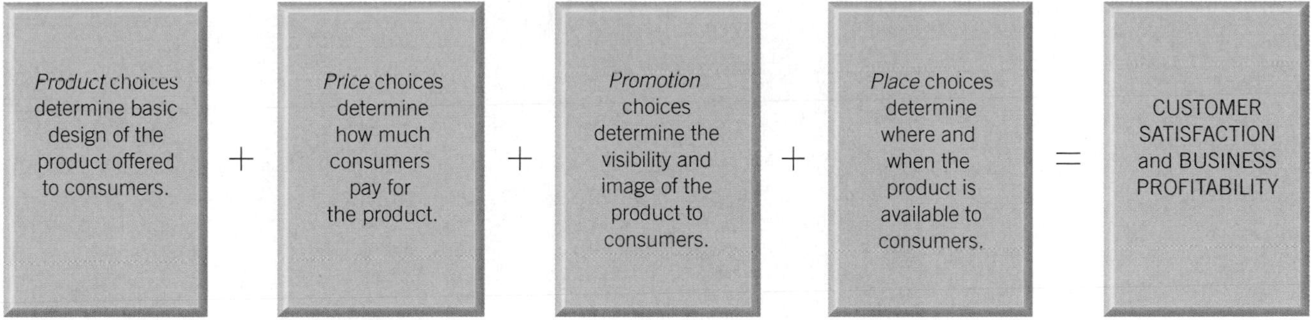

Figure 15.2 Choosing the marketing mix for a business.

Product

Marketing begins with a **product**—a good, a service, or an idea designed to fill a consumer need or want. Conceiving and developing new products is a constant challenge for marketers, who must always consider the factor of change—changing technology, changing consumer wants and needs, and changing economic conditions. Meeting consumer needs, then, often means changing existing products to keep pace with emerging markets and competitors. *Mass-customization*, which was explained in Chapter 13, allows marketers to provide products that satisfy very specific needs of consumers.

product A good, service, or idea that satisfies buyers' needs and demands.

Producers often promote particular features of products to distinguish them in the marketplace. **Product differentiation** is the creation of a feature or image that makes a product differ enough from existing products to attract consumers. For example, Volvo automobiles provide newer, better safety features to set them apart from competitors. Customers of E*Trade™, the online investment service, gain value from after-hours trading not offered by conventional investment-service firms.

product differentiation The creation of a product or product image that differs enough from existing products to attract consumers.

Price

Price refers not only to the actual amount of money that consumers must pay for a product or service, but also to the total value of things that consumers are willing to give up in return for being able to have the benefits of the product or service. For example, if a person wants to own a Chrysler 300M, that person may have to take money out of a savings account to pay for the car. The value of the interest that would have been earned on the savings account is part of the value that the customer gives up to own the car. From the seller's perspective, determining the best **price** at which to sell a product is often a balancing act. On the one hand, prices must support a variety of costs—operating, administrative, research, and marketing costs. On the other hand, prices can't be so high that consumers turn to competitors products. Successful pricing means finding a profitable middle ground between these two requirements.

price That part of the marketing mix concerned with choosing the appropriate price for a product to meet the firm's profit objectives and buyers' purchasing objectives.

Both low- and high-price strategies can be effective in different situations. Low prices, for example, generally lead to larger sales volumes. High prices usually limit market size but increase profits per unit. High prices may also attract customers by implying that a product is of high quality. We discuss pricing in more detail in Chapter 17.

Jann Wenner started *Rolling Stone* magazine in 1967, and it's been the cash cow of Wenner Media ever since. In 1985, Wenner bought *Us* magazine and set out to compete with *People*, perhaps the most successful magazine ever published. Wenner's latest strategy calls for greater differentiation between the two products. *People* is news driven, reporting on ordinary people as well as celebrities, and Wenner intends to punch up *Us* with more coverage of celebrity sex and glitter. So far, he hasn't been successful. *People* reaches 3.7 million readers, *Us* about 900 000.

Place (Distribution)

distribution That part of the marketing mix concerned with getting products from the producer to the buyer, including physical transportation and choice of sales outlets.

In the marketing mix, *place* refers to **distribution**. Placing a product in the proper outlet—say, a retail store—requires decisions about several activities, all of which are concerned with getting the product from the producer to the consumer. Decisions about warehousing and inventory control are distribution decisions, as are decisions about transportation options.

Firms must also make decisions about the *channels* through which they distribute products. Many manufacturers, for instance, sell goods to other companies that, in turn, distribute them to retailers. Others sell directly to major retailers such as Sears, Wal-Mart, or Safeway. Still others sell directly to final consumers. We explain distribution decisions further in Chapter 17.

Promotion

promotion Techniques for communicating information about products.

The most highly visible component of the marketing mix is **promotion**, which refers to techniques for communicating information about products. The most important promotional tools include advertising, personal selling,

By providing both distribution and advertising for Grand & Toy, this truck plays a dual role in the company's marketing.

sales promotions, and public relations. We describe promotional activities more fully in Chapter 16.

Product, price, place, and promotion focus on the seller's perspective. From the buyer's perspective, each of the 4 Ps provides a certain benefit. In effect, the seller's 4 Ps are a mirror image of the buyer's 4 Cs: customer solution (product), customer cost (price), customer convenience (place), and customer communication (promotion).[4]

TARGET MARKETING AND MARKET SEGMENTATION

Explain *market segmentation* and show how it is used in *target marketing*. 3

Marketing managers long ago recognized that they cannot be "all things to all people." People have different tastes, different interests, different goals, different lifestyles, and so on. The marketing concept's recognition of consumers' various needs and wants led marketing managers to think in terms of target marketing. **Target markets** are groups of people with similar wants and needs.

target market Any group of people who have similar wants and needs and may be expected to show interest in the same product(s).

market segmentation Dividing a market into categories according to traits customers have in common.

Target marketing clearly requires **market segmentation**, dividing a market into categories of customer types or "segments." For example, Mr. Big-and-Tall sells to men who are taller and heavier than average. Certain special interest magazines are oriented toward people with specific interests (see Table 15.1). Once they have identified market segments, companies may adopt a variety of product strategies. Some firms decide to provide a range of products to the market in an attempt to market their products to more than one segment. For example, General Motors of Canada offers compact cars, vans, trucks, luxury cars, and sports cars with various features and prices. Its strategy is to provide an automobile for nearly every segment of the market.

In contrast, some businesses restrict production to one market segment. Rolls Royce understands that only a relatively small number of people are willing to pay $310 000 for exclusive touring limousines. Rolls, therefore,

Table 15.1 Magazines with Specific Target Audiences

Accounting	**Fishing/Hunting**
CAmagazine	*Canadian Fly Fisher*
CGA Magazine	*Outdoor Canada*
CMA Management	*B.C. Outdoors Sport Fishing*
Agriculture	**Automotive**
Agro-Nouvelles	*Aftermarket Canada*
Meat & Poultry Magazine	*Bodyshop*
Country Life in B.C.	*World of Wheels*
Sports	**Boating**
Cycle Canada	*Boating Business*
Chalk and Cue	*Canadian Boating*
Athletics Canada	*Porthole Magazine*
Gardening	**Music**
Canadian Gardening	*CHART Magazine*
The Gardener for the Prairies	*CODA Magazine*
Gardening Life	*Opus*

makes no attempt to cover the entire range of possible products; instead, it markets only to a very small segment of the total automobile buyers market.

Table 15.2 shows how a marketer of home-electronic equipment might segment the radio market. Note that segmentation is a strategy for analyzing consumers, not products. The analysis in Table 15.2, for example, identifies consumer-users—joggers, commuters, and travellers. Only *indirectly*, then, does it focus on the uses of the product itself. In marketing, the process of fixing, adapting, and communicating the nature of the product itself is called *positioning*.

Identifying Market Segments

By definition, the members of a market segment must share some common traits or behaviours that will affect their purchasing decisions. In identifying market segments, researchers look at *geographic*, *demographic*, *psychographic*, and *product-use variables*.

Geographic Variables

geographic variables Geographical units that may be considered in a segmentation strategy.

In some cases, where people live affects their buying decisions. The heavy rainfall in British Columbia prompts its inhabitants to purchase more umbrellas than does Arizona's desert. Urban residents have less demand for pickup trucks than do their rural counterparts. Sailboats sell better along both coasts than they do in the prairie provinces. **Geographic variables** are the geographical units, from countries to neighbourhoods, that may be considered in a segmentation strategy.

These patterns affect marketing decisions about what products to offer, at what price to sell them, how to promote them, and how to distribute them. For example, consider the marketing of down parkas in rural Saskatchewan. Demand will be high, price competition may be limited, local newspaper advertising may be very effective, and the best location may be one easily reached from several small towns.

Although the marketability of some products is geographically sensitive, others enjoy nearly universal acceptance. Coke, for example, gets more than 70 percent of its sales from markets outside the United States. It is the market leader in Great Britain, China, Germany, Japan, Brazil, and Spain. By

Table 15.2 Possible Segmentation of the Radio Market

Segmentation	Product/Target Market
Age	Inexpensive, unbreakable, portable models for young children
	Inexpensive equipment—possibly portable—for teens
	Moderate-to-expensive equipment for adults
Consumer attitude	Sophisticated components for audio buffs
	All-in-one units in furniture cabinets for those concerned with room appearance
Product use	Miniature models for joggers and commuters
	"Boom box" portables for taking outdoors
	Car stereo systems for travelling
	Components and all-in-one units for home use
Location	Battery-powered models for use where electricity is unavailable
	AC current for North American users
	DC current for other users

contrast, Pepsi earns 78 percent of its income from the United States. Coke's chief competitor in most countries is not Pepsi, but some local soft drink.

Demographic Variables

Demographic variables describe populations by identifying characteristics such as age, income, gender, ethnic background, marital status, race, religion, and social class. These are objective criteria that cannot be altered. Marketers must work with or around them. Table 15.3 lists some demographic market segments. Depending on the marketer's purpose, a segment can be a single classification (*aged 20–34*) or a combination of categories (*aged 20–34, married with children, earning $25 000–$34 999*). Foreign competitors, for example, are gaining market share in auto sales by appealing to young buyers (*under age 30*) with limited incomes (*under $30 000*). While companies such as Hyundai, Kia, and Daewoo are winning entry-level customers with high-quality and generous warranties, Volkswagen targets under-35 buyers with its entertainment-styled VW Jetta.[5]

demographic variables Characteristics of populations that may be considered in developing a segmentation strategy.

Another important demographic variable is ethnic diversity. Canada's great ethnic diversity requires companies to pay close attention to ethnicity as a segmentation variable. For example, Rogers Communication Inc.'s television advertising campaign for its Bollywood Oye! video-on-demand service is designed to promote its business to South Asian communities in Canada. Rogers currently has 32 multicultural channels and wants to be a leader in customizing services to suit specific ethnic groups. Visible minorities in Canada control $76 billion in annual buying power, and to be effective in multicultural marketing, companies must really understand the underlying values that ethnic minority customers hold.[6]

Psychographic Variables

Members of a market can also be segmented according to such **psychographic variables** as lifestyle, opinions, interests, and attitudes. One company that is using psychographic variables to revive its brand is Burberry, whose plaid-lined gabardine raincoats have been a symbol of

psychographic variables Psychological traits that a group has in common, including motives, attitudes, activities, interests, and opinions.

Table 15.3 Demographic Market Segmentation

Age	Under 5; 5–11; 12–19; 20–34; 35–49; 50–64; 65+
Education	Grade school or less; some high school; graduated high school; some college or university; college diploma or university degree; advanced degree
Family life cycle	Young single; young married without children; young married with children; older married with children under 18; older married without children under 18; older single; other
Family size	1, 2–3, 4–5, 6+
Income	Under $9000; $9000–$14 999; $15 000–$25 000; over $25 000
Nationality	Including but not limited to African, Asian, British, Eastern European, French, German, Irish, Italian, Latin American, Middle Eastern, and Scandinavian
Race	Including but not limited to Inuit, Asian, black, and white
Religion	Including but not limited to Buddhist, Catholic, Hindu, Jewish, Muslim, and Protestant
Sex	Male, female
Language	Including but not limited to English, French, Inuktitut, Italian, Ukrainian, and German

British tradition since 1856. After a recent downturn in sales, Burberry is repositioning itself as a global luxury brand, like Gucci and Louis Vuitton. The strategy calls for luring top-of-the-line, fashion-conscious customers. Burberry pictures today's luxury-product shopper as a world traveller who identifies with prestige fashion brands and monitors social and fashion trends in *Harper's Bazaar*.[7]

Psychographics are particularly important to marketers because, unlike demographics and geographics, they can sometimes be changed by marketing efforts. For example, many companies have succeeded in changing at least some consumers' opinions by running ads highlighting products that have been improved directly in response to consumer desires. Many companies in Poland have succeeded in overcoming consumer resistance to buying on credit by promoting the safety and desirability of using credit rather than depending solely on cash for family purchases. One product of such changing attitudes is a booming economy and the emergence of a growing and robust middle class. The increasing number of Polish households that own televisions, appliances, automobiles, and houses is fuelling the status of Poland's middle class as the most stable in the former Soviet bloc.[8]

Product-Use Variables

product-use variables Consumer characteristics based on the use of a product, benefits expected from it, reasons for purchasing it, and loyalty to it.

The term **product-use variables** refers to the ways in which consumers use a product, the benefits they expect from it, their reasons for purchasing it, and their loyalty to it.[9] A women's shoemaker might identify three segments—wearers of athletic, casual, and dress shoes. Each segment is looking for different benefits in a shoe. A woman buying an athletic shoe may not care about its appearance but may care a great deal about arch support and traction in the sole. A woman buying a casual shoe will want it to look good and feel comfortable. A woman buying a dress shoe may require a specific colour or style and may even accept some discomfort. Consumers who always buy one brand are classified as *hard-core loyalists*, whereas *switchers* buy various brands.

Whatever basis is used for segmenting a market, care must be taken to position the product correctly. A product's position refers to the important attributes that consumers use to assess the product. For example, a low-

Although Nike leads the $15.5 billion athletic footwear industry, it still has a serious problem: Women's footwear accounts for about one-third of industry sales but generates only about one-fifth of Nike's. Nike is going after this demographic segment with a marketing campaign that focuses on differences between the way men and women think about sports and the way they shop for clothing. According to Nike marketers, for example, women are more interested in image trends and active lifestyles than in athletic competition and sports celebrities.

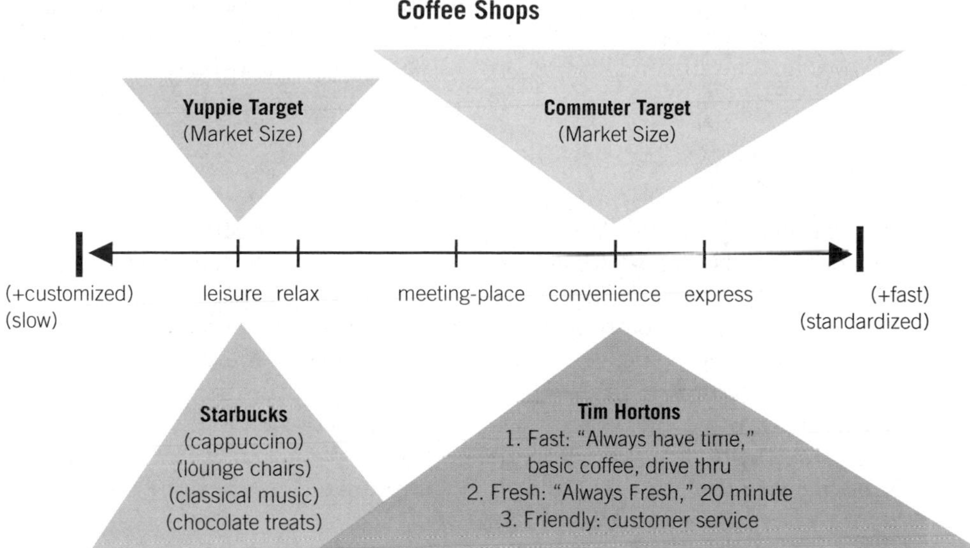

Figure 15.3 Product positioning.

priced car like a Ford Focus tends to be positioned on the basis of *economy*, while a Porsche is positioned in terms of *high performance*. In Figure 15.3, the product positioning chart shows that Tim Hortons emphasizes a standardized product and provides fast service to people in a hurry, while Starbucks provides more customized products in more leisurely surroundings.

Market Segmentation: A Caution

Segmentation must be done carefully. A group of people may share an age category, income level, or some other segmentation variable, but their spending habits may be quite different. Look at your friends in school. You may all be approximately the same age, but you have different needs and wants. Some of you may wear cashmere sweaters while others wear sweatshirts. The same holds true for income. University professors and truck drivers frequently earn about the same level of income. However, their spending patterns, tastes, and wants are generally quite different.

In Canada, the two dominant cultures—English and French—have historically shown significant differences in consumer attitudes and behaviour. Researchers have found, for example, that compared with English Canadians, French Canadians are more involved with home and family, attend ballet more often, travel less, eat more chocolate, and are less interested in convenience food. But this does not necessarily mean that companies must have different product offerings for Quebec. When Headspace Marketing Inc. asked 1000 Quebecers to rate how well 12 different retail brands had adapted to the needs and expectations of Quebecers, they found that the top three brands were Tim Hortons, Canadian Tire, and Bureau en gros (in that order). Interestingly, Tim Hortons ranked much higher than Starbucks (which ranked last) in spite of the fact that Tim Hortons did very little to adapt its product line to the Quebec market and Starbucks did a lot. What Tim Hortons did do well was get involved with community charities and activities that brought it closer to local residents. The company also used two Quebec actors in their ad campaigns. This apparently made the Tim Hortons brand "resonate" better with Quebecers. The situation is similar for second-ranked Canadian Tire. The chain sells pretty much the same product line in Quebec as in the rest of Canada, but it also got involved in local charities and used Quebec singer Jici Lauzon as a spokesperson.[10]

MARKET RESEARCH

4 Explain the purpose and value of *marketing research.*

market research The systematic study of what buyers need and how best to meet those needs.

Market research, which is the study of what buyers need and how best to meet those needs, can address any element in the marketing mix. Business firms spend millions of dollars each year as they try to figure out their customers' habits and preferences. Market research can greatly improve the accuracy and effectiveness of market segmentation.[11] Failure to do market research can lead to significant problems. For example, in 2004 the CEO of Coca-Cola admitted that the company had missed the change in consumer tastes away from carbonated drinks and toward healthier, non-carbonated drinks. PepsiCo Inc., on the other hand, capitalized on these trends with its Propel Fitness Water and Gatorade.[12]

The place of marketing research in the overall marketing process is shown in Figure 15.4. Ultimately, its role is to increase the firm's competitiveness by understanding the relationship among the firm's customers, its marketing variables, and its marketing decisions. Marketing researchers use a variety of methods to obtain, interpret, and use information about customers. They determine the kinds of information that are needed for decisions on marketing strategy, goal setting, and target-market selection. In doing so, they may conduct studies on how customers will respond to proposed changes in the current marketing mix. One researcher, for example, might study consumer response to an experimental paint formula (new

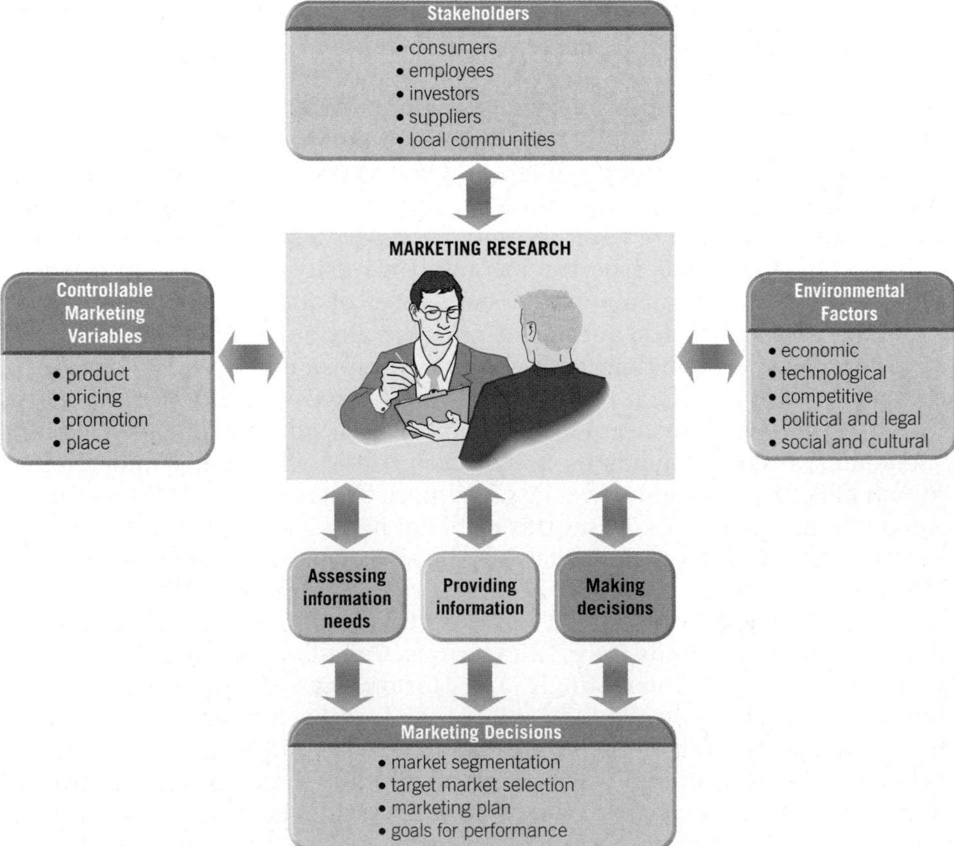

Figure 15.4 Market research and the marketing process.

product). Another might explore the response to a price reduction (new price) on calculators. A third might check response to a proposed advertising campaign (new promotion). Marketers can also try to learn whether customers are more likely to purchase a given product in a specialty shop or on the internet (new place).

Most companies will benefit from market research, but they need not do the research themselves. O-Pee-Chee Co. Ltd. of London, Ontario (the bubble gum and candy manufacturer) does no market research and no product testing, yet it continues to be successful in a market where products change at a dizzying pace. By signing a licensing agreement with two U.S. giants, O-Pee-Chee simply looks at what's hot in the United States and then starts manufacturing those lines in Canada.[13]

The Research Process

Market research can occur at almost any point in a product's existence. Most commonly, however, it is used when a new or altered product is being considered. These are the five steps in performing market research:[14]

1. *Study the current situation.* What is the need and what is being done to meet it at this point?
2. *Select a research method.* In choosing a method, marketers must bear in mind the effectiveness and costs of different methods.
3. *Collect data.* **Secondary data** is information already available as a result of previous research by the firm or other agencies. For example, Statistics Canada publishes a great deal of data that is useful for business firms. Using secondary data can save time, effort, and money. But in some cases secondary data are unavailable or inadequate, so **primary data**—new research by the firm or its agents—must be obtained. Hostess Frito Lay, the maker of Doritos, spent a year studying how to best reach its target market—teenagers. The researchers hung around shopping malls, schools, and fast-food outlets to watch the teens.[15]
4. *Analyze the data.* Data are not useful until they have been organized into information.
5. *Prepare a report.* This report should include a summary of the study's methodology and findings. It should also identify alternative solutions (where appropriate) and make recommendations for the appropriate course of action.

secondary data Information already available to market researchers as a result of previous research by the firm or other agencies.

primary data Information developed through new research by the firm or its agents.

Research Methods

The four basic types of methods used by market researchers are *observation*, *surveys*, *focus groups*, and *experimentation*.

Observation

Probably the oldest form of market research is simple **observation** of what is happening. It is also a popular research method because it is relatively low in cost, often drawing on data that must be collected for some other reason, such as reordering. In earlier times, when a store owner notices that customers were buying red children's wagons, not green ones, the owner reordered more red wagons, the manufacturer's records showed high sales of red wagons, and the marketing department concluded that customers wanted red wagons. But observation is now much more sophisticated. For example, electronic scanners in supermarkets allow marketers to "observe" consumers' preferences rapidly and with tremendous accuracy.

observation A market research technique involving viewing or otherwise monitoring consumer buying patterns.

"I'd get out of children and into older people."

Another example: Procter & Gamble sent video crews into about 80 households in the United Kingdom, Germany, and China to capture people's daily routines and how they use products. By analyzing the tapes, P&G hoped to get insights into consumer behaviour. The company can use this information to develop new products to satisfy needs that consumers didn't even know they had.[16]

Using video equipment to observe consumer behaviour is called *video mining*. It is being adopted by many stores in North America who use hidden cameras to determine the percentage of shoppers that buy and the percentage that only browse. They do this by comparing the number of people taped with the number of transactions the store records. Some consumer organizations are raising privacy concerns, since shoppers are unaware that they are being taped.[17]

Surveys

survey A market research technique based on questioning a representative sample of consumers about purchasing attitudes and practices.

Sometimes marketers need to ask questions about new marketing ideas or about how well the firm is doing its marketing tasks. One way to get answers is by conducting a **survey**. When United Parcel Service (UPS) surveyed customers to find out how it could improve service, it found that clients wanted more interaction with drivers because they can offer practical advice on shipping. UPS thus added extra drivers, freeing up some time for drivers to get out of their trucks and spend time with customers.[18]

Because no firm can afford to survey everyone, marketers must be careful to get a representative group of respondents when they do surveys. They must also construct the survey questions so that they get honest answers that address the specific issue being researched. Surveys can be expensive to carry out and may vary widely in their accuracy.

In the past, surveys have been mailed to individuals for their completion, but online surveys are now gaining in popularity because the company gets immediate results, and because the process is a less intrusive way of gathering data. At Hudson's Bay Co., customers can use online surveys to tell the company how happy or unhappy they are about the service they received at any of the Bay's department stores. The company can then make any changes that are needed to keep customers happy. The Bay used to hire mystery shoppers to find out how well it was serving the public, but that program ended when the online survey system was adopted.[19]

Focus Groups

Many firms also use **focus groups**, where 6 to 15 people are brought together to talk about a product or service. A moderator leads the group's discussion, and employees from the sponsoring company may observe the proceedings from behind a one-way mirror. The people in the focus group are not usually told which company is sponsoring the research. The comments of people in the focus group are taped, and then researchers go through the data looking for common themes.

focus group A market research technique involving a small group of people brought together and allowed to discuss selected issues in depth.

When Procter & Gamble was developing a new air freshener, it asked people in focus groups to describe their "desired scent experience." They discovered that people get used to a scent after about half an hour and no longer notice it. P&G used this information to develop a "scent player" called Febreze Scentstories that gives off five different scents every 30 minutes.[20] Focus groups at farm implement manufacturer John Deere have suggested many improvements in farm tractors, including different ways to change the oil filter and making the steps to the tractor cab wider.[21]

Experimentation

The last major form of market research, experimentation, also tries to get answers to questions that surveys cannot address. As in science, **experimentation** in market research attempts to compare the responses of the same or similar individuals under different circumstances. For example, a firm trying to decide whether to include walnuts in a new candy bar probably would not learn much by asking people what they thought of the idea. But if it made some bars with nuts and some without and then asked people to try both, the responses could be very helpful.[22]

experimentation A market research technique in which the reactions of similar people are compared under different circumstances.

Data Warehousing and Data Mining

Almost everything you do leaves a trail of information about you. Your preferences in movie rentals, television viewing, internet sites, and groceries; the destinations of your phone calls, your credit-card charges, your financial status; personal information about age, gender, marital status, and even health—these are just some of the items in a huge cache of data that are stored about each of us. The collection, storage, and retrieval of such data in electronic files is called **data warehousing**. For marketing researchers, the data warehouse is a gold mine of clues about consumer behaviour.[23]

data warehousing Process of collecting, storing, and retrieving data in electronic form.

As they watch a sitcom with six commercial breaks, these women are participating in a marketing research experiment. The researchers think that their results will be more accurate than questionnaire and focus-group responses because they're getting them straight from the subjects' brains. A spike in a subject's left prefrontal cortex means that she probably likes a product or an ad. A spike in the right prefrontal cortex is bad news for the advertiser. Using machines designed to detect brain tumours, researchers can even tell which part of an ad makes a dent in the subject's long-term memory.

data mining Application of electronic technologies for searching, sifting, and reorganizing data to collect marketing information and target products in the marketplace.

The Uses of Data Mining. After collecting information, marketers use **data mining**—the application of electronic technologies for searching, sifting, and reorganizing pools of data—to uncover useful marketing information and to plan for new products that will appeal to target segments in the marketplace.[24] Using data mining, for example, the insurance company Farmers Group discovered that a sports car is not an exceptionally high insurance risk if it's not the only family car. The company thus issued more liberal policies on Corvettes and Porsches and so generated more revenue without significantly increasing payout claims. Among retailers, Wal-Mart has long been a data-mining pioneer, maintaining perhaps the world's largest privately held data warehouse. Data include demographics, markdowns, returns, inventory, and other data for forecasting sales and the effects of marketing promotions.[25]

UNDERSTANDING CONSUMER BEHAVIOUR

Market research in its many forms can be of great help to marketing managers in understanding how the common traits of a market segment affect consumers' purchasing decisions. Why do people buy DVDs? What desire are they fulfilling? Is there a psychological or sociological explanation for why consumers purchase one product and not another? These questions and many others are addressed in the area of marketing known as **consumer behaviour**, which focusses on the decision process by which customers come to purchase and consume a product or service.

consumer behaviour The study of the process by which customers come to purchase and consume a product or service.

Influences on Consumer Behaviour

To understand consumer behaviour, marketers draw heavily on the fields of psychology and sociology. The result is a focus on four major influences on consumer behaviour: psychological, personal, social, and cultural. By identifying the four influences that are most active, marketers try to explain consumer choices and predict future purchasing behaviour:

- *Psychological influences* include an individual's motivations, perceptions, ability to learn, and attitudes.
- *Personal influences* include lifestyle, personality, economic status, and life-cycle stage.
- *Social influences* include family, opinion leaders (people whose opinions are sought by others), and reference groups such as friends, co-workers, and professional associates.
- *Cultural influences* include culture (the "way of living" that distinguishes one large group from another), subculture (smaller groups, such as ethnic groups, with shared values), and social class (the cultural ranking of groups according to criteria such as background, occupation, and income).

Although these factors can have a strong impact on a consumer's choices, their effect on actual purchases is sometimes weak or negligible. Some consumers, for example, regularly purchase certain products because they are satisfied with their performance. Such people (for example, users of Craftsman tools) are less subject to influence and stick with preferred brand names. On the other hand, the clothes you wear and the food you eat often reflect social and psychological influences on your consuming behaviour.

The Consumer Buying Process

Describe the key factors that influence the *consumer buying process.* 5

Researchers who have studied consumer behaviour have constructed models that help marketing managers understand how consumers come to purchase products. Figure 15.5 presents one such model. At the heart of this and similar models is an awareness of the psychosocial influences that lead to consumption. Ultimately, marketing managers use this information to develop marketing plans.

Problem/Need Recognition

The buying process begins when a consumer becomes aware of a problem or need. After strenuous exercise, you may recognize that you are thirsty and need refreshment. After the birth of twins, you may find your one-bedroom apartment too small for comfort. After standing in the rain to buy movie tickets, you may decide to buy an umbrella. Need recognition also occurs when you have a chance to change your purchasing habits. For example, the income from your first job after graduation will allow you to purchase items that were too expensive when you were a student. You may also discover a need for professional clothing, apartment furnishings, and cars. Visa and the Bay recognize this shift and market their credit cards to graduates.

Information Seeking

Having recognized a need, consumers seek information. This search is not always extensive. If you are thirsty, you may ask where the pop machine is, but that may be the extent of your information search. Other times you simply rely on your memory for information. Before making major purchases, most people seek information from personal sources, marketing sources, public sources, and experience. For example, if you move to a new town, you will want to find out who is the best local dentist, physician, hair stylist, butcher, or pizza maker. To get this information, you may check with personal sources such as acquaintances, co workers, and relatives. Before buying an exercise bike, you may go to the library and read the latest *Consumer Reports*—a public source of consumer ratings—on such equipment.

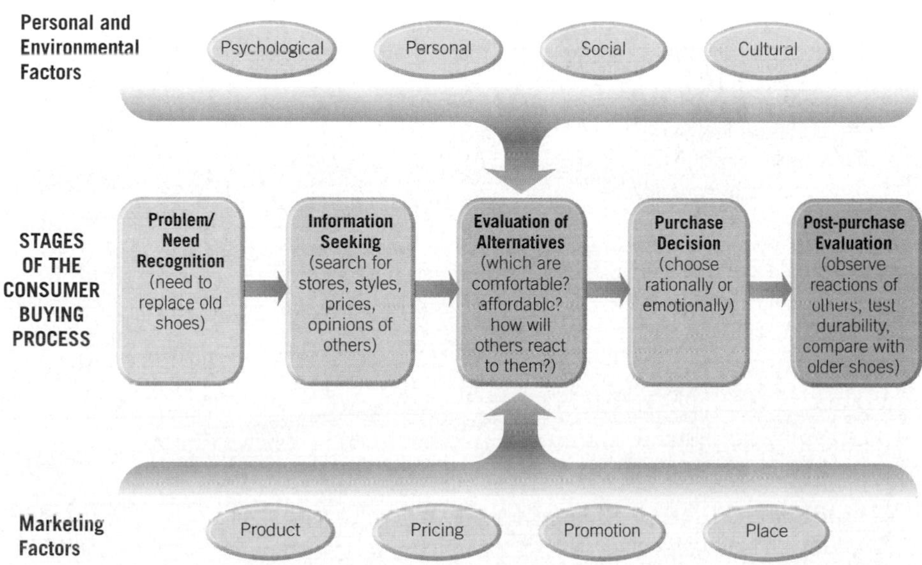

Figure 15.5 Consumer buying process.

You may also ask market sources such as the salesclerk or rely on direct experience. For example, you might test ride the bike to learn more before you buy. The internet has become an important source of information; one-third of consumers rely on the internet to gather information.[26]

Evaluation of Alternatives

If you are in the market for a set of golf clubs, you probably have some idea of who produces clubs and how they differ. You may have accumulated some of this knowledge during the information-seeking stage and combined it with what you knew before. Based on product attributes such as colour, taste, price, prestige, quality, and service record, you will decide which product best meets your needs.

Purchase Decisions

rational motives Those reasons for purchasing a product that involve a logical evaluation of product attributes such as cost, quality, and usefulness.

emotional motives Those reasons for purchasing a product that involve non-objective factors.

Ultimately, you make a purchase decision. You may decide to defer the purchase until a later time or you may decide to buy now. "Buy" decisions are based on rational and emotional motives. **Rational motives** involve a logical evaluation of a product's cost, quality, and usefulness. **Emotional motives** include fear, sociability, imitation of others, and aesthetics. You might buy mouthwash to avoid ostracism, or you might buy the same brand of jeans as your friends. Emotional motives can lead to irrational purchase decisions.

Post-Purchase Evaluations

Marketing does not stop with the sale of a product or service, but includes the process of consumption. What happens *after* the sale is therefore very important. Marketers know that consumers do not want to go through a complex decision process for every purchase, and that they often choose a product they have used and liked in the past. Therefore marketers are very motivated to keep consumers happy so they will make repeat purchases of the product. Unfortunately for marketers, when consumers are not satisfied with a purchase they typically complain to friends rather than to the company. This negative word-of-mouth advertising can be very harmful to a company. In more extreme cases, unhappy consumers may file a lawsuit or publicly criticize the product and the company.

What information is this shopper looking for to decide on his purchase? Marketers would like to know how and why consumers buy the products they buy. A better understanding of the customer buying process allows sellers to tailor their products to meet customer needs.

ORGANIZATIONAL MARKETING AND BUYING BEHAVIOUR

Discuss the three categories of *organizational markets* and explain how *organizational buying behaviour* differs from consumer buying behaviour. 6

Buying behaviour is observable daily in the consumer market, where marketing activities, including buying–selling transactions, are visible to the public. Equally important, however, but far less visible, are *organizational* (or *commercial*) *markets*—organizations that buy goods and services to be used in creating and delivering consumer products. Marketing to these buyers involves different kinds of organizational markets and buying behaviours that are quite different from those found in consumer markets.

Organizational Markets

Organizational or commercial markets fall into three categories: *industrial*, *reseller*, and *government/institutional markets*.

Industrial Market

The **industrial market** includes businesses that buy goods falling into one of two categories: goods to be converted into other products and goods that are used up during production. This market includes farmers, manufacturers, and some retailers. For example, Seth Thomas purchases electronics, metal components, and glass to make clocks for the consumer market. The company also buys office supplies, tools, and factory equipment—items never seen by clock buyers—to be used during production.

industrial market Businesses that buy goods to be converted into other products that will be sold to ultimate consumers.

Reseller Market

Before products reach consumers, they pass through a **reseller market** consisting of intermediaries, including wholesalers and retailers, who buy the finished goods and resell them (wholesalers and retailers are discussed in Chapter 17). Retailers like department stores, drugstores, and supermarkets buy clothing, appliances, foods, medicines, and other merchandise for resale to the consumer market. Retailers also buy such services as maintenance, housekeeping, and communications.

reseller market Intermediaries like wholesalers and retailers who buy finished products and resell them.

Government and Institutional Market

Federal, provincial, and municipal governments purchase millions of dollars worth of computer equipment, buildings, paper clips, and other items. The **institutional market** consists of non-governmental organizations, such as hospitals, churches, museums, and charitable organizations, which also comprise a substantial market for goods and services. Like organizations in other commercial markets, these institutions use supplies and equipment, as well as legal, accounting, and transportation services.

institutional market Non-government organizations such as hospitals, churches, and schools.

Organizational Buying Behaviour

In some respects, industrial buying behaviour bears little resemblance to consumer buying practices. Differences include the buyers' purchasing skills and an emphasis on buyer–seller relationships.

Differences in Buyers

Unlike most consumers, organizational buyers are professional, specialized, and expert (or at least well informed).

- As *professionals*, organizational buyers are trained in methods for negotiating purchase terms. Once buyer–seller agreements have been reached, they also arrange for formal contracts.
- As a rule, industrial buyers are company *specialists* in a line of items. As one of several buyers for a large bakery, for example, you may specialize in food ingredients. Another buyer may specialize in baking equipment (industrial ovens and mixers), while a third may buy office equipment and supplies.
- Industrial buyers are often *experts* about the products they buy. On a regular basis, organizational buyers study competing products and alternative suppliers by attending trade shows, by reading trade magazines, and by conducting technical discussions with sellers' representatives.

Differences in the Buyer–Seller Relationship

Consumer–seller relationships are often impersonal, short-lived, one-time interactions. In contrast, industrial situations often involve frequent and enduring buyer–seller relationships. The development of a long-term relationship provides each party with access to the technical strengths of the other as well as the security of knowing what future business to expect. Thus, a buyer and a supplier may form a design team to create products of benefit to both. Accordingly, industrial sellers emphasize personal selling by trained representatives who understand the needs of each customer.

THE INTERNATIONAL MARKETING MIX

7 Describe the *international* and *small business marketing mixes.*

Marketing products internationally means mounting a strategy to support global business operations. Obviously, this is no easy task since foreign customers may differ from domestic buyers in language, customs, business practices, and consumer behaviour. When companies decide to go global, marketers must consider how each element of the marketing mix might be affected.

International Products

Some products (for example, Budweiser, Coca-Cola, and Marlboros) can be sold in many different countries with virtually no changes, but often only a redesigned (or completely different) product will meet the needs of foreign buyers. To sell the Macintosh in Japan, for example, Apple Computer had to develop a Japanese-language operating system.

Mattel, the maker of Barbie dolls, is just one company that has learned some interesting lessons about the international market. When it conducted focus groups with kids in dozens of countries, it found that worldwide demand existed for many of the same products. Mattel discovered, in essence, that children have similar tastes no matter where they live. Mattel's experience with its famous Barbie doll is illustrative. The dolls sold in Japan, for example, had always had black hair and Asian features, not the blonde, blue-eyed appearance of Barbie dolls sold in North America. This seemed to make intuitive sense, but now Mattel is finding that the original Barbie doll is selling just as well in Asia as in North America.

Mattel's experience is not unique. Various other companies that sell products to international consumers have found the same phenomenon:

- The Harry Potter book series already had a global following when the first Harry Potter movie was released.

- Harlequin Enterprises, which sells millions of romance novels in many different countries, uses the same book covers around the world. The pictures of Caucasians on the book covers do not seem to deter customers in other countries from buying Harlequin romance novels.
- Sports is another universal language. Basketball stars like Michael Jordan and Shaquille O'Neal have high name recognition overseas. In a poll of Chinese students in rural Shaanxi province, Michael Jordan tied with former Chinese premier Zhou En-lai for the title "World's Greatest Man."

But there are still important differences between countries, and these cannot be ignored. For example, German children aren't attracted to action toys the way Canadian and U.S. children are. There are also differences even within basic product lines. U.S. kids, for example, want NASCAR toy cars, while European children want Formula One models.

ENTREPRENEURSHIP AND NEW VENTURES

When in Rome

When Art Aylesworth first tried to sell solar-powered LED lights for bus stops in Britain's capital, he was stymied. Oh, they might speak English in London, but the strategy he used to sell lights to the North American marine industry didn't translate to both a new country and sector.

Five years later, Aylesworth's Carmanah Technologies Corp. targets nine industries in 115 countries. Exports, which yield 92 percent of sales, powered five-year revenue growth of 1246 percent, with Carmanah now ranked number one in the world in sales of solar-powered LED lights. Its new winning strategy? Customizing sales and marketing to each industry and country.

That may sound daunting, but, like it or not, the rules of play are set by prospective clients. "You have to be a chameleon in the way you present your products and do business," says Aylesworth, Carmanah's CEO. "Figure out how they do things and join in."

Shape-shifting is hard and complicated work, but Aylesworth says it's worth it: "Had we stuck with the [original] strategy, the business would have grown about fivefold in five years. By adapting the way we have, it has grown about 35 times as big."

Rather than offer a single website, Carmanah has 11, tailored to various industries and subsectors (e.g., railwaylights.com and solarairportlights.com), with more in the works. Customers want to know you understand their world, says Aylesworth, and a customized site yields opportunities more easily and affordably than a sales rep. Carmanah has also added new sales channels to suit client preferences. It used to sell only through distributors, but now also uses its own salespeople, contracted sales agents, and strategic partnerships.

Geographically, it tailors its technology to each market as regulations or local practices require. But, Aylesworth says, Carmanah's main export challenge has been learning foreign cultures and business processes, which takes time and no small amount of trial and error. Deals in Europe and Asia, for example, require far more patience and relationship-building than in Canada. Indeed, Carmanah's five-year, $16-million deal with London's transit authority was four years in the making.

Carmanah crafts a strategy for each prospect by first asking a series of questions: which products they want and use, how and why they use them, how they buy or replace technology (including regulatory and approval procedures), who they partner with, and which sales channels they prefer. It's crucial to find the right "lead investigator" to gather such market feedback. The first senior manager Carmanah sent to the Middle East failed to earn the trust of locals, even after many trips and meetings. Aylesworth now stresses the importance of hiring a business-development manager who's hard to deter, astute, and "tough-natured but nice when they need to be."

Shape-shifting isn't cheap, either. Carmanah invested $5 million over five years to develop new products and markets. Still, the approach doesn't require vast resources: Carmanah had just 12 staff when it adopted this strategy.

What you do need, advises Aylesworth, is enough money to invest for the long haul. You should also hone your communication skills and hire people with relevant geographical or industry expertise to shorten the learning curve. Above all, weigh your decision to enter a market carefully so you don't misjudge your resources, opportunity, or desire. "If you ever walk away," warns Aylesworth, "you won't get back in easily."

International Pricing

When pricing for international markets, marketers must handle all the considerations of domestic pricing while also considering the higher costs of transporting and selling products abroad. Some products cost more overseas than in Canada because of the added costs of delivery. Due to the higher costs of buildings, rent, equipment, and imported meat, a McDonald's Big Mac that sells for $2.99 in Canada has a price tag of over $10 in Japan. In contrast, products like jet airplanes are priced the same worldwide because delivery costs are incidental; the huge development and production costs are the major considerations regardless of customer location.

International Promotion

Some standard Canadian promotional techniques do not always succeed in other countries. In fact, many Europeans believe that a product must be inherently shoddy if a company does any hard-sell advertising. International marketers must also be aware that cultural differences can cause negative reactions to products that are advertised improperly. Some Europeans, for example, are offended by television commercials that show weapons or violence. Advertising practices are regulated accordingly. Consequently, Dutch commercials for toys do not feature the guns and combat scenes that are commonplace on Saturday morning television in North America. Meanwhile, liquor and cigarette commercials that are banned from Canadian and U.S. television are thriving in many Asian and European markets.

Symbolism, too, is a sometimes-surprising consideration. In France, for instance, yellow flowers suggest infidelity. In Mexico, they are signs of death—an association made in Brazil by the colour purple. Clearly, product promotions must be carefully matched to the customs and cultural values of each country.

International Distribution

In some industries, delays in starting new distribution networks can be costly. Therefore, companies with existing distribution systems often enjoy

Feathercraft is a small British Columbia manufacturer that has been successful selling kayaks in the Japanese market.

an advantage over new businesses. Several companies have gained advantages in time-based competition by buying existing businesses. Procter & Gamble, for example, saved three years of start-up time by buying Revlon's Max Factor and Betrix cosmetics, both of which are well established in foreign markets. P&G can thus immediately use these companies' distribution and marketing networks for selling its own brands in the United Kingdom, Germany, and Japan.

Other companies contract with foreign firms or individuals to distribute and sell their products abroad. Foreign agents may perform personal selling and advertising, provide information about local markets, or serve as exporters' representatives. But having to manage interactions with foreign personnel complicates a marketing manager's responsibilities. In addition, packaging practices in Canada must sometimes be adapted to withstand the rigours of transport to foreign ports and storage under conditions that differ radically from domestic conditions.

SMALL BUSINESS AND THE MARKETING MIX

As we noted in Chapter 4, far more small businesses fail than succeed. Yet many of today's largest firms were yesterday's small businesses. McDonald's began with one restaurant, a concept, and one individual (Ray Kroc) who had tremendous foresight. Behind the success of many small firms lies a skilful application of the marketing concept and careful consideration of each element in the marketing mix.

Small-Business Products

Some new products—and firms—are doomed at the start simply because few consumers want or need what they have to offer. Too often, enthusiastic entrepreneurs introduce products that they and their friends like, but they fail to estimate realistic market potential. Other small businesses offer new products before they have clear pictures of their target segments and how to reach them. They try to be everything to everyone, and they end up serving no one well. In contrast, sound product planning has paid off for many small firms. "Keep it simple" is a familiar key to success—that is, fulfill a specific need and do it efficiently.

Small-Business Pricing

Haphazard pricing that is often little more than guesswork can sink even a firm with a good product. Most often, small-business pricing errors result from a failure to project operating expenses accurately. Owners of failing businesses have often been heard to utter statements like "I didn't realize how much it costs to run the business!" and "If I price the product high enough to cover my expenses, no one will buy it!" But when small businesses set prices by carefully assessing costs, many earn very satisfactory profits—sometimes enough to expand or diversify.

Small-Business Promotion

Successful small businesses plan for promotional expenses as part of start-up costs. Some hold down costs by taking advantage of less expensive promotional methods. Local newspapers, for example, are sources of publicity when they publish articles about new or unique businesses. Other small businesses have succeeded by identifying themselves and their products with associated groups, organizations, and events. Thus a custom-crafts gallery might join with a local art league and local artists to organize public showings of their combined products.

Small-Business Distribution

Problems in arranging distribution can make or break small businesses. Perhaps the most critical aspect of distribution is facility location, especially for new service businesses. The ability of many small businesses—retailers, veterinary clinics, and gourmet coffee shops—to attract and retain customers depends partly on the choice of location.

In distribution, as in other aspects of the marketing mix, however, smaller companies may have advantages over larger competitors, even in highly complex industries. They may be quicker, for example, in applying service technologies. Everex Systems Inc. sells personal computers to wholesalers and dealers through a system the company calls "Zero Response Time." Phone orders are reviewed every two hours so that the factory can adjust assembly to match demand.

Summary of Learning Objectives

1. **Explain the concept of *marketing* and describe the five forces that constitute the *external marketing environment*.** Marketing is "the process of planning and executing the conception, pricing, promotion, and distribution of ideas, goods, and services to create exchanges that satisfy individual and organizational goals." Products provide consumers with *utility*—the ability of a product to satisfy a human want or need. Marketing can be used to promote consumer and industrial goods and services, as well as ideas. The *external environment* consists of the outside forces that influence marketing strategy and decision making. The *political/legal environment* includes laws and regulations, both domestic and foreign, that may define or constrain business activities. The *social and cultural environment* is the context within which people's values, beliefs, and ideas affect marketing decisions. The *technological environment* includes the technological developments that affect existing and new products. The *economic environment* consists of the conditions, such as inflation, recession, and interest rates, that influence both consumer and organizational spending patterns. Finally, the *competitive environment* is the environment in which marketers must persuade buyers to purchase their products rather than their competitors'.

2. **Explain the purpose of a *marketing plan* and identify the four components of the *marketing mix*.** *Marketing managers* plan and implement all the marketing activities that result in the transfer of products to customers. These activities culminate in the *marketing plan*—a detailed strategy for focussing the effort to meet consumer needs and wants. Marketing managers rely on the "Four Ps" of marketing, or the *marketing mix*. (1) *Product*: Marketing begins with a product, a good, a service, or an idea designed to fill a consumer need or want. *Product differentiation* is the creation of a feature or image that makes a product differ from competitors. (2) *Pricing*: Pricing is the strategy of selecting the most appropriate price at which to sell a product. (3) *Place* (*Distribution*): All distribution activities are concerned with getting a product from the producer to the consumer. (4) *Promotion*: Promotion refers to techniques for communicating information about products and includes advertising.

3. **Explain *market segmentation* and show how it is used in *target marketing*.** Marketers think in terms of *target markets*—groups of people who have similar wants and needs and who can be expected to show interest in the same products. Target marketing requires *market segmentation*—dividing a market into customer types or "segments." Four of the most important influences are: (1) *geographic variables* (the geographical units that may be considered in developing a segmentation strategy); (2) *demographic variables* (describe populations by identifying such traits as age, income, gender, ethnic background, marital status, race, religion, and social class); (3) *psychographic*

variables (such as lifestyles, interests, and attitudes); and (4) *product-use variables* (the ways in which consumers use a product, the benefits they expect from it, their reasons for purchasing it, and their loyalty to it).

4. **Explain the purpose and value of *marketing research*.** *Market research* is the study of what buyers need and of the best ways to meet those needs. This process involves a study of the current situation, the selection of a research method, the collection of data, the analysis of data, and the preparation of a report that may include recommendations for action. The four most common research methods are *observation, surveys, focus groups,* and *experimentation.*

5. **Describe the key factors that influence the *consumer buying process*.** *Consumer behaviour* is the study of the process by which customers decide to purchase products. The result is a focus on four major influences on consumer behaviour: (1) *Psychological influences* include motivations, perceptions, ability to learn, and attitudes. (2) *Personal influences* include lifestyle, personality, and economic status. (3) *Social influences* include family, opinion leaders, and such reference groups as friends, co-workers, and professional associates. (4) *Cultural influences* include culture, subculture, and social class. By identifying which influences are most active in certain circumstances, marketers try to explain consumer choices and predict future purchasing behaviour.

6. **Discuss the three categories of *organizational markets* and explain how *organizational buying behaviour* differs from consumer buying behaviour.** *Organizational* (or *commercial*) *markets,* in which organizations buy goods and services to be used in creating and delivering consumer products, fall into three categories. (1) The *industrial market* consists of businesses that buy goods to be converted into other products or goods that are used during production. (2) Before products reach consumers, they pass through a *reseller market* consisting of intermediaries that buy finished goods and resell them. (3) *Government and institutional market*: Federal, provincial, and local governments buy durable and nondurable products. The institutional market consists of non-governmental buyers such as hospitals, churches, museums, and charities. Organizational buying behaviour differs from consumer buyer behaviour in two major ways: (1) *Differences in buyers*: Organizational buyers are professionals trained in arranging buyer–seller relationships and negotiating purchase terms. They are usually specialists in a line of items and are often experts about the products they are buying. (2) *Differences in the buyer–seller relationship*: Whereas consumer–seller relationships are often fleeting, one-time interactions, industrial situations often involve frequent, enduring buyer–seller relationships.

7. **Describe the *international* and *small business marketing mixes*.** When they decide to go global, marketers must reconsider each element of the marketing mix. (1) *International products*: Whereas some products can be sold abroad with virtually no changes, sometimes only a redesigned product will meet the needs of foreign buyers. (2) *International pricing*: When pricing for international markets, marketers must consider the higher costs of transporting and selling products abroad. (3) *International distribution*: In some industries, companies have gained advantages by buying businesses already established in foreign markets. (4) *International promotion*: Occasionally, a good ad campaign can be transported to another country virtually intact. Quite often, however, standard Canadian promotional tactics do not succeed in other countries.

   Behind the success of many small firms lies an understanding of each element in the marketing mix. (1) *Small-business products*: Understanding of what customers need and want has paid off for many small firms. (2) *Small-business pricing*: Haphazard pricing can sink even a firm with a good product. Small-business pricing errors usually result from failure to project operating expenses accurately. But when small businesses set prices by carefully assessing costs, many earn satisfactory profits. (3) *Small-business distribution*: Perhaps the most critical aspect of distribution is facility location: The ability of many small businesses to attract and retain customers depends partly on the choice of location. (4) *Small-business promotion*: Successful small businesses plan for promotional expenses as part of start-up costs. Some take advantage of less expensive promotional methods.

KEY TERMS

brand competition, 478
consumer behaviour, 490
consumer goods, 473
data mining, 490
data warehousing, 489
demographic variables, 483
distribution, 480
emotional motives, 492
experimentation, 489
external environment, 476
focus group, 489
geographic variables, 482
industrial goods, 473
industrial market, 493
institutional market, 493
international competition, 478
market research, 486
market segmentation, 481
marketing, 472
marketing concept, 472
marketing managers, 478
marketing mix, 478
marketing plan, 478
observation, 487
price, 479
primary data, 487
product, 478
product differentiation, 479
product-use variables, 484
promotion, 480
psychographic variables, 483
rational motives, 492
relationship marketing, 475
reseller market, 493
secondary data, 487
services, 473
substitute product, 478
survey, 488
target market, 481
utility, 473
value, 472

QUESTIONS FOR ANALYSIS

1. Why and how is market segmentation used in target marketing?
2. Select an everyday product (books, CDs, skateboards, dog food, or shoes, for example). Show how different versions of your product are aimed toward different market segments. Explain how the marketing mix differs for each segment.
3. Select another product and describe the consumer buying process that likely occurs before it is purchased.
4. Explain the key differences between consumer buying behaviour and organizational buying behaviour.
5. What is the value to consumers of things like loyalty cards and discount cards? Why would companies offer consumers such cards?
6. Why has the in-store use of hidden cameras become so popular? Is this "video mining" ethical? If not, how could it be made more acceptable?
7. If you were starting your own small business, what are the key marketing pitfalls you would try to avoid?
8. Select a product or service that you regularly use. Explain the relative importance of each of the four elements in the marketing mix (product, price, promotion, and place). Then select another product and determine the extent to which the relative emphasis changes. If it changed, why did it change?

APPLICATION EXERCISES

1. Interview the marketing manager of a local business. Identify the degree to which this person's job is focussed on each element in the marketing mix.
2. Select a product made by a foreign company and sold in Canada. What is the product's target market? What is the basis on which the target market is segmented? Do you think that this basis is appropriate? How might another approach, if any, be beneficial? Why?

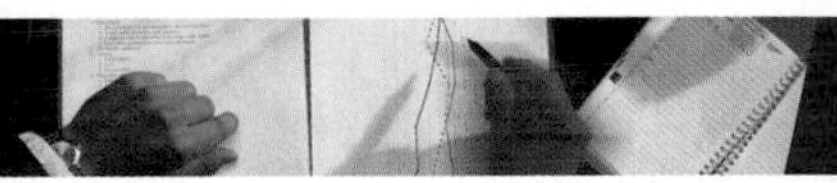

BUILDING YOUR BUSINESS SKILLS

Dealing in Segments and Variables

Goal

To encourage students to analyze the ways in which various market segmentation variables affect business success.

The Situation

You and four partners are thinking of purchasing a heating and air conditioning (H/AC) dealership that specializes in residential applications priced between $2000 and $40 000. You are now in the process of deciding where that dealership should be. You are considering four locations: Miami, Florida; Toronto, Ontario; Vancouver, B.C.; and Dallas, Texas.

Assignment

Step 1

Working with four classmates (your partnership group), do library research to learn how H/AC makers market their residential products. Check for articles in *The Globe and Mail*, *Canadian Business*, *The Wall Street Journal*, and other business publications.

Step 2

Continue your research. This time, focus on the specific marketing variables that define each prospective location. Check Statistics Canada data at your library and on the internet and contact local chambers of commerce (by phone and via the internet) to learn about the following factors for each location:

- geography
- demography (especially age, income, gender, family status, and social class)
- psychographic variables (lifestyles, interests, and attitudes)

Step 3

Meet with group members to analyze which location holds the greatest promise as a dealership site. Base your decision on your analysis of market segment variables and their effects on H/AC sales.

Follow-Up Questions

1. Which location did you choose? Describe the market segmentation factors that influenced your decision.
2. Identify the two most important variables you believe will have the greatest impact on the dealership's success. Why are these factors so important?
3. Which factors were least important in your decision? Why?
4. When equipment manufacturers advertise residential H/AC products, they often show them in different climate situations (in winter, summer, or high-humidity conditions). Which market segments are these ads targeting? Describe these segments in terms of demographic and psychographic characteristics.

EXERCISING YOUR ETHICS

Driving a Legitimate Bargain

The Situation

This exercise illustrates how ethical issues can become entwined with personal selling activities, product pricing, and customer relations.

The Dilemma

In buying his first-ever new car, Matt visited showrooms and websites for every make of SUV. After weeks of reading and test-driving, he settled on a well-known Japanese-made vehicle with a manufacturer's suggested retail price of $34 500 for the 2006 model. The price included accessories and options that Matt considered essential. Because he planned to own the car for at least five years, he was willing to wait for just the right package rather than accept a lesser-equipped car already on the lot. Negotiations with Gary, the sales representative, continued for two weeks. Finally, a sales contract was signed for $32 600, with delivery due no more than two or three months later if the vehicle had to be special-ordered from the factory, earlier if Gary found the exact car when he searched other dealers around the country. On April 30, to close the deal, Matt had to write a cheque for $1000.

Matt received a call on June 14 from Angela, Gary's sales manager: "We cannot get your car before

October," she reported, "so it will have to be a 2007 model. You will have to pay the 2007 price." Matt replied that the agreement called for a stated price and delivery deadline for 2006, pointing out that money had exchanged hands for the contract. When asked what the 2007 price would be, Angela responded that it had not yet been announced. Angrily, Matt replied that he would be foolish to agree now on some unknown future price. Moreover, he didn't like the way the dealership was treating him. He told Angela to send back to him everything he had signed; the deal was off.

Questions for Discussion

1. Given the factors involved in the consumer buying process, how would you characterize the particular ethical issues in this situation?
2. From an ethical standpoint, what are the obligations of the sales rep and the sales manager regarding the pricing of the product in this situation?
3. If you were responsible for maintaining good customer relations at the dealership, how would you handle this matter?

CONCLUDING CASE 15-1

Dell-ivering on Consumer Electronics

There's a good reason why competitors don't match Dell's success in selling computers. From the outset, Michael Dell's vision recognized a market with different kinds of potential users—the business sector, non-business organizations such as schools and other institutions, as well as the growing segment of PC users in homes—each with different needs and resources. Choosing to focus more on the business and institutional segments, Dell envisioned an unheard-of combination of service features for PC customers: high-quality products, lowest cost, ease in ordering and receiving products, live interaction with expert technical assistance for building a PC "the way you like it," super-fast deliveries, and after-the-sale communications to ensure product performance and keep users informed about upgrades to enhance their PCs.

The market response has been overwhelming, resulting in Dell's dominant position as industry leader. Dell's unique vision for integrating all stages of marketing—development of the product and related services, pricing it, selling to consumers directly via telephone or the internet, delivering directly to customers from efficient manufacturing plants, and promotional messages for product awareness and use—are unmatched by competitors that are struggling to copy Dell's way of doing business.

As if that were not enough to cause headaches in the PC industry, Dell recently launched itself into the broader consumer electronics market for even greater revenue growth. Today's giant electronics retailers, such as Circuit City and Best Buy, may soon be looking over their shoulders if Dell's customer-friendly business model is successfully carried over into flat-panel TVs, DVD recorders, MP3 players, and digital cameras. Plans even call for opening an online music-downloading store on the same popular website where PC users buy other Dell products. The potential range of products is enormous because music, movies, photos, and other entertainment are increasingly digital and, thus, are becoming compatible extensions of PCs. Commenting on the company's new thrust, Chairman Michael Dell states, "The whole new ballgame is these worlds [computing and consumer electronics] converging, and that's a world we're comfortable in."

But will they necessarily succeed? Some experts think the crossover into consumer products could be a problem because, unlike Gateway and Hewlett-Packard's focus on the consumer segment, Dell's primary PC focus has been on business and institutional markets. A classic example of a failed crossover is IBM's ill-fated attempt in the 1980s to woo consumers with its downsized PC Jr. computer. With hugely successful sales and technical support for business customers, IBM never understood the consumer market, and Big Blue's efforts proved a mismatch that ended with the withdrawal of the PC Jr. from the marketplace in the late 1990s. But Dell CEO Kevin Rollins says such risks are largely offset by Dell's brand familiarity in both business and consumer markets.

Price is equally important to consumers, says industry analyst Peter Kastner. "Dell's no-middleman model almost guarantees a value-based price," and that means more intense price-for-performance competition than exists now in consumer electronics. The bottom line for consumers will be lower prices while other firms in the industry try to imitate Dell's low-price–high-value business model.

For masses of electronics lovers, Dell's entry comes as welcome news. Consumers will see prices fall as competition drives down profit margins and prices. Retailers and etailers, in contrast, will experience what might be called "reverse sticker shock." Sellers currently enjoying net profit margins of 25 to 40 percent on consumer electronics may have to survive on the modest 10 percent margin to which PC sellers are accustomed. That leaves lots of room for Dell to push electronics prices down, gain large volume sales, and reap high total profits while competing firms in the industry try to imitate its low-price, high-value business model.

Dell's promotional efforts, at first, are aimed at building brand familiarity by dramatically increasing daily interaction with consumers. Electronics lovers from Canada, Japan, the United States, and Brazil who are accustomed to brands such as Sony and Samsung may be surprised to see the Dell name on TVs, pocket PCs, MP3 players, and the Digital Jukebox, among its upcoming line of products. Winning this massive customer base is essential for high-volume sales, and Dell plans to attract them to its new Dell.com website with Music Store, an online music-downloading service that will include the major labels and performers. Unlike Apple's iTunes service, which is available only to users of Apple products, Dell's downloading version is open to the public, not just to Dell PC users. It has the additional advantage of working with Microsoft Windows and, promises CEO Kevin Rollins, at prices below competitors'.

The new Dell.com is reportedly designed to appeal to consumers to set it apart from Dell's business products. Its main screen will provide easy ways to find not only electronics equipment but also music, radio stations, photos, and other media, all of which capitalize on the logical linkages between home computers and consumer electronics. More and more consumers in the "digital home" are running DVDs, video clips, games, and photos through their computers. So Dell plans to sell related media products the same way it sells other PC peripherals such as printers.

Because consumer buying habits don't change overnight, no one at Dell expects to dominate the electronics market the way it does in PCs, where it leads with an 18-percent market share and 29-percent growth rate (more than twice the growth rate of its nearest competitor, Hewlett-Packard). Before buying an expensive flat-screen TV, for example, most consumers want to see the quality of its picture firsthand rather than buying through catalogues or a website. As Forrester Research analyst Jed Kolko notes, "With video products it's harder to demonstrate value online." Consumers hold similar reservations about the sound quality of audio products as well. So, only with the passage of time can Dell establish relationships with consumers by informing them, convincing them to switch over from an already-crowded list of competing sellers—including newcomers such as Apex Digital, which is already underpricing more established brands—and by demonstrating superior product value in the Dell brand. Both industry experts and electronics consumers will soon witness Dell's bottom-line results in this new venture.

Questions for Discussion

1. What social and technological factors have influenced the growth of the consumer electronics market?
2. What demographics would you use to define the flat-screen TV target market? How about the target market for home PCs?
3. Identify the main factors favouring success for Dell's crossover into consumer electronics. What prominent factors suggest major problems or even failure for this crossover attempt?
4. Applying the textbook's definition for product value to Dell's plans, what are the "benefits" in Dell's consumer electronics offerings? What are the "costs"?
5. Applying the textbook's definition for product value to electronics retailers such as Best Buy or Circuit City, what are the "benefits" and "costs"? How well or poorly does Dell's product value ratio stack up against its competitors' ratios?

CONCLUDING CASE 15-2

Television Viewership: How Do You Measure It?

Business firms spend a lot of money each year on marketing research trying to figure out customers' habits and preferences. Advertisers, for example, want to know what television programs consumers are watching so they can effectively direct their advertisements. If it can be demonstrated that some TV shows are more popular than others, advertisers are willing to pay more to have their ads appear on those programs.

Not surprisingly, when there is a need for information like this, one or more companies will agree to provide it (for a price, of course). Nielsen Media Research is the best-known company providing such information. It gets its revenues by selling its viewer data to advertising agencies and television companies. Nielsen has reported on the TV viewing habits of Canadians and Americans for many years. Until recently, the system involved having selected viewers write down the channel number they were watching and who was watching TV each quarter hour of the day. But this system was cumbersome, and consumers often made errors when they were filling out the forms. The system gradually began to break down as technology changed. For example, when remote controls became popular, so did channel surfing, but channel surfing is virtually impossible to reflect in a diary. The introduction of digital video recorders (DVRs) and the delivery of shows via cellphone, computer, and iPod is quickly making Nielsen's old system obsolete. One consultant says it is ridiculous to expect people to accurately write down what they view in this new, high-tech environment.

Nielsen initially responded to criticisms by attaching electronic meters to household TVs. The meter determined what channel was being watched and who was watching, but viewers still had to punch in a pre-assigned number on their remote control whenever they started to watch. These meters likely improved the accuracy of in-home viewing data, but they did not address the growing problem of measuring viewing habits of people when they were not at home but who were still watching TV. For example, measuring the viewing habits of students who live away from home at university is not easy. *The O.C.*—a drama about teen life in Orange County, California—is very popular with students attending U.S. universities, but almost none of these viewers are counted in Nielsen ratings because Nielsen's system doesn't capture the viewing habits of university students. Not only that, it continues to count these students as if they are living at home and watching no TV at all. Nielsen also doesn't monitor viewing in offices, bars, hotels, prisons, and many other out-of-home venues.

Dissatisfaction with Nielsen is also evident at cable companies, who argue that Nielsen's system doesn't accurately capture the large number of people who watch cable TV. Differences can be substantial with different measuring systems. For example, in a side-by-side analysis in New York City, an episode of *The Simpsons* on the Fox Network showed a 27 percent decline when the new electronic meters were used, but new shows on Comedy Central cable saw gains of 225 percent using the same electronic measurement.

In Montreal and Quebec City, consumers are being paid a few dollars a month to carry a pager-sized device that records each advertisement they see or hear and every store or restaurant they go into. BBM Canada is using something called the Personal Portable Meter (PPM) to determine television ratings. These devices, which listen for cues that broadcasters have embedded in their broadcasts, enable BBM to assess television viewing outside people's homes. They reduce the errors that were evident in the old hard-wired systems where people had to press buttons to indicate who was watching what. The new system will eventually allow advertisers to correlate the advertisements people hear with the products they buy. They can therefore determine how effective their advertisements are. Early tests of the PPM show recorded audiences about 15 percent higher than traditional methods. Nielsen is studying the PPM technology, but says it needs much more work. It likes the idea that the PPM measures out-of-home viewership and that it measures audio very well.

Nielsen is still getting a lot of criticism and not much sympathy. Nielsen's system was developed in a long-ago time when families gathered around the sole TV in the house to watch a program. But times have changed. While Dad is watching a sporting event in the den, junior is watching MTV in the basement, and Mom is channel surfing in the bedroom. In 2006, Nielsen announced that it would introduce technology that would allow it to capture DVR viewing on a daily basis. It will also begin measuring video-on-demand and testing ways of measuring viewing on the internet and on hand-held devices such as iPod's and cellphones. If these new measuring systems show significantly differing viewing patterns than historical data, it will likely result in advertisers shifting their money around accordingly. It could also result in increased advertising rates for some programs and decreased rates for others.

▶▶▶

But even if these improvements are made, some critics will not be happy. The vice-president at one advertising space-buying company, for example, says that the only thing that is important to measure is "live" viewing. That's because people who are watching a DVR program are probably not even watching the ads. Not surprisingly, TV companies disagree with that assessment. They argue that ad rates should be determined by the total viewership an ad gets.

Questions for Discussion

1. What are the various methods that are available to market researchers as they gather data about customers? Which method does Nielsen use?
2. The viewership data that Nielsen's develops is important in determining how much advertisers pay to place their ads on TV. What are the advantages and disadvantages of the system? Are there alternative systems that might work better? Explain.
3. The argument has been made that counting DVR viewing isn't useful because people either don't watch program advertisements when using a DVR, or that advertisements simply don't have the same urgency even if they are watched. Do you agree or disagree with this argument? Give reasons. Whatever your position, how does uncertainty over issues like this influence the value of marketing research data? What could be done to improve the data?
4. Suppose that you are buying advertising space on TV. Would you be more likely to accept Nielsen data for, say, sports programs than you would for dramas? Explain. What kind of biases might you have and why?

CHAPTER 16

Developing and Promoting Goods and Services

After reading this chapter, you should be able to:

1. Explain the definition of a product as a *value package*.
2. Describe the *new product development process* and trace the stages of the *product life cycle*.
3. Explain the importance of *branding*, *packaging*, and *labelling*.
4. Identify the important objectives of *promotion* and discuss the considerations in selecting a *promotional mix*.
5. Discuss the most important *advertising strategies* and describe the key *advertising media*.
6. Outline the tasks involved in *personal selling* and list the steps in the *personal selling process*.
7. Describe the various types of *sales promotions*, and distinguish between *publicity* and *public relations*.
8. Describe the development of *international promotion strategies*.

The Fuel Cell: Still a Long, Rough Road Ahead

At the 2004 annual meeting of Vancouver-based Ballard Power Systems Inc., shareholders listened to CEO Dennis Campbell explain what progress was being made on a radical new product—the hydrogen fuel cell, which combines hydrogen (one of earth's most common elements) with oxygen to produce electricity. The only exhaust is warm water. The electricity generated by the fuel cell can be used to power anything that runs on electricity, including cars. The fuel cell greatly interests car makers because they have been trying for years to develop a new engine to replace the internal combustion engine that has powered automobiles for over a century.

All of this sounds very promising, but Ballard shareholders were not happy with what they heard because their company has been developing the fuel cell for over a decade and progress has been very slow. Back in the mid-1990s, Ballard had generated great excitement when it first announced that it was going to develop a fuel cell that would solve the world's energy problems and save the environment at the same time. Initially, enthusiasm for the hydrogen fuel cell was high. DaimlerChrysler invested $450 million in Ballard, and Ford Motor Co. put in another $600 million to pursue the development of fuel cells. A DaimlerChrysler executive even said a few years ago that the company expected to sell 100 000 cars powered by fuel cells by 2004. Ballard sold prototypes to several automobile companies for testing, the Chicago Transit Authority put three fuel cell–powered buses into service, and the B.C. government purchased three buses.

But significant problems have arisen for Ballard as it has tried to make the fuel cell commercially viable. Sales revenues haven't kept up with development costs, and the revolution, which was always just around the corner, has stayed tantalizingly in the future. In 2003, Ballard estimated that it wouldn't become profitable until 2007. Reality has hit the company hard. From a high of $210 per share in 2000, Ballard stock now sells for less than $10. What's worse, skepticism about the commercial viability of the fuel cell is steadily increasing. It is clear that fuel-cell powered cars are not going to be on sale anytime soon, and some skeptics wonder if they ever will be.

Why has the fuel cell not lived up to its earlier promise? Consider the following list of daunting problems facing the development of fuel cells:

- Hydrogen must first be extracted from substances that contain it (e.g., natural gas), but stripping the hydrogen from natural gas creates carbon dioxide, which is precisely what the standard internal combustion car engines emit.
- Safety is an issue (when the word "hydrogen" is mentioned, many people immediately think of the spectacular explosion and fire that destroyed the hydrogen-powered Hindenburg dirigible in 1937).
- If insufficient numbers of hydrogen-dispensing gas stations are built, consumer demand will never be high enough to encourage mass production of cars that are powered by fuel cells; it is going to be a long time before there will be enough such stations.
- The hydrogen fuel cell is likely to be very expensive because the most environmentally sound way to make hydrogen—extracting it from water using electricity made from solar or wind power—is costly and requires large areas of land covered in solar panels that produce the required electricity.
- Other costs associated with the product are also high; for example, it currently costs about $4500 per kilowatt to produce the fuel "stacks" in the hydrogen fuel cell, but experts estimate that this cost needs to be reduced to about $45 per kilowatt in order to be commercially viable.
- Hybrid cars like the Toyota Prius and the Honda Civic have been very successful and are providing strong competition for the hydrogen fuel cell.
- Improvements are being made in the internal combustion engine, and this reduces the incentive to develop the hydrogen fuel cell.
- There are now at least 50 different companies in competition with Ballard to build a successful fuel cell.

If there are so many problems, why has so much time and money been invested in the development of hydrogen fuel cells? The answer is both environmental (less air pollution) and political (less reliance on foreign oil). This new product may be commercially viable in 20 or 30 years, but there are still many developmental problems to be overcome. General Motors and Ford, which formerly invested large amounts of money in fuel cell research, now seem to be more interested in developing hybrid cars.

But maybe the hydrogen fuel cell will eventually become common in automobiles. Keep in mind what critics said when internal combustion-powered automobiles were introduced a hundred years ago: "They'll never become popular because there would have to be gas stations all over the place." Well, that's exactly what happened. ◆

In Chapter 15, we introduced the four components of the marketing mix: product, price, promotion, and place (distribution). In this chapter, we look in more detail at products and how they are priced. New product development—like that at Ballard Power Systems Inc.—is a critically important activity for companies because all products—including once-popular TV shows like *Seinfeld*, *Everybody Loves Raymond*, *Friends*, and *Frasier*—eventually reach the end of their life cycles and expire.

We begin this chapter by looking at the products that have been developed by Oracle Corp., IBM, and Microsoft Corp. These companies are all major players in database-software products—computer programs that other companies use for storing and manipulating massive volumes of internal data. While all are successful, surveys show that they rely on quite different strategies. Oracle is the hands-down winner in terms of product innovation, specializing in cutting-edge features that substantially improve performance. Microsoft products rate lower in both reliability and performance, but they are priced below Oracle software and cost less to operate. IBM gets high marks for satisfaction with technical and customer support. So whose product is best? Says one industry analyst, "It's hard to say who is the technological leader in this market, since it depends on what you value and how you want it delivered."[1]

In making their strategic decisions, Oracle, IBM, and Microsoft face a basic fact of business: It is virtually impossible to focus on just one element of the marketing mix (for example, product design) without having to deal with the other marketing variables (price, promotion, and distribution). It is important that you keep this fact in mind as you read Chapters 16 and 17.

WHAT IS A PRODUCT?

1 Explain the definition of a product as a *value package*.

In developing the marketing mix for any products—whether ideas, goods, or services—marketers must consider what consumers really buy when they purchase products. Only then can they plan their strategies effectively. We will begin this section where product strategy begins—with an understanding of product *features* and *benefits*. Next, we will describe the major *classifications of products*, both consumer and industrial. Finally, we will discuss the most important component in the offerings of any business—its *product mix*.

The Value Package

features The qualities, both tangible and intangible, that a company builds into its products.

Whether it is a physical good, a service, or some combination of the two, customers get value from the various benefits, features, and even intangible rewards associated with a product. Product **features** are the qualities, tangible and intangible, that a company builds into its products, such as a 12-horsepower motor on a lawn mower. But to attract buyers, features also must provide *benefits*: The mower must produce an attractive lawn. The owner's pleasure in knowing that the mower is nearby when needed is an intangible reward.

Today's consumer regards a product as a bundle of attributes which, taken together, marketers call the **value package**. Increasingly, buyers expect to receive products with greater *value*—with more benefits at reasonable costs. For example, the possible attributes in a personal computer value package are things like easy access to understandable pre-purchase information, choices of colour, attractive software packages, fast ordering via the internet, assurance of speedy delivery, and internet chat room capability. Although the computer includes physical *features*—like processing devices and other hardware—most items in the value package are services or intangibles that, collectively, add value by providing *benefits* that increase the customer's satisfaction.

value package Product marketed as a bundle of value-adding attributes, including reasonable cost.

Keep in mind that products are much more than just *visible* features and benefits. In buying a product, consumers are also buying an image and a reputation. The marketers of Swatch Chrono watch, for example, are well aware that brand name, packaging, labelling, and after-the-purchase service are also indispensable parts of their product. Advertisements remind consumers that they don't just get "real" features like shock and water resistance, quartz precision, and Swiss manufacture; they also get Swatch's commitment that its products will be young and trendy, active and sporty, and stylistically cool and clean.

Look carefully at the ad in Figure 16.1 for SAS Institute (www.sas.com), a major designer of statistical software. In this ad SAS does not emphasize the technical features of its products, nor even the criteria that companies use in selecting software—efficiency, compatibility, support. Rather, the ad focusses on the customer-oriented benefits that a buyer of SAS software can expect from using the firm's products: "Only SAS provides you with a complete view of your customers." These benefits are being marketed as part of a complete value package.

Today, more and more firms compete on the basis of enhanced value packages. They find that the addition of a simple new service often pleases customers far beyond the cost of providing it. Just making the purchase transaction more convenient, for example, adds value by sparing customers long waits and cumbersome paperwork.[2]

convenience goods/services Relatively inexpensive consumer goods or services that are bought and used rapidly and regularly, causing consumers to spend little time looking for them or comparing their prices.

shopping goods/services Moderately expensive consumer goods or services that are purchased infrequently, causing consumers to spend some time comparing their prices.

Figure 16.1 SAS ad.

Classifying Goods and Services

One way to classify a product is according to expected buyers. Buyers fall into two groups: buyers of *consumer* products and buyers of *industrial* products. As we saw in Chapter 15, the consumer and industrial buying processes differ significantly. Not surprisingly, then, marketing products to consumers is vastly different from marketing them to other companies.

Classifying Consumer Products

Consumer products are commonly divided into three categories that reflect buyers' behaviour: convenience, shopping, and specialty products.

- **Convenience goods** (such as milk and newspapers) and **convenience services** (such as those offered by fast-food restaurants) are consumed rapidly and regularly. They are relatively inexpensive and are purchased frequently and with little expenditure of time and effort.
- **Shopping goods** (such as stereos and tires) and **shopping services** (such as insurance) are more expensive and are purchased less frequently than convenience

goods and services. Consumers often compare brands, sometimes in different stores. They may also evaluate alternatives in terms of style, performance, colour, price, and other criteria.

specialty goods/services Very expensive consumer goods or services that are purchased rarely, causing consumers to spend a great deal of time locating the exact item desired.

- **Specialty goods** (such as wedding gowns) and **specialty services** (such as catering for wedding receptions) are extremely important and expensive purchases. Consumers usually decide on precisely what they want and will accept no substitutes. They will often go from store to store, sometimes spending a great deal of money and time to get a specific product.

Classifying Industrial Products

Depending on how much they cost and how they will be used, industrial products can be divided into two categories:

expense items Relatively inexpensive industrial goods that are consumed rapidly and regularly.

- **Expense items** are any materials and services that are consumed within a year by firms producing other goods or supplying services. The most obvious expense items are industrial goods used directly in the production process, for example, bulk loads of tea processed into tea bags.

capital items Expensive, long-lasting industrial goods that are used in producing other goods or services and have a long life.

- **Capital items** are permanent—that is, expensive and long lasting—goods and services. All these items have expected lives of more than a year—typically up to several years. Expensive buildings (offices, factories), fixed equipment (water towers, baking ovens), and accessory equipment (computers, airplanes) are capital goods. Capital services are those for which long-term commitments are made. These may include purchases for employee food services, building and equipment maintenance, or legal services. Because capital items are expensive and purchased infrequently, they often involve decisions by high-level managers.

The Product Mix

product mix The group of products a company has available for sale.

The group of products a company has available for sale, be it consumer or industrial, is known as the firm's **product mix**. Black & Decker, for example, makes toasters, vacuum cleaners, electric drills, and a variety of other appliances and tools. 3M makes everything from Post-it Notes to laser optics.

Product Lines

product line A group of similar products intended for a similar group of buyers who will use them in a similar fashion.

A group of products that are closely related because they function in a similar manner or are sold to the same customer group who will use them in similar ways is a **product line**. Many companies begin with a single product, such as simple iced tea. Over time, they find that the initial product fails to suit every consumer shopping for the product type. To meet market demand, they introduce similar products—such as flavoured teas—designed to reach more tea drinkers. As another example, ServiceMaster was among the first successful home services that offered mothproofing and carpet cleaning. Subsequently, the company expanded into other closely related services for homeowners—lawn care (TruGreen, ChemLawn), pest control (Terminix), and cleaning (Merry Maids).

Companies may extend their horizons and identify opportunities outside existing product lines. The result—*multiple* (or *diversified*) *product lines*—is evident at firms such as ServiceMaster. After years of serving residential customers, ServiceMaster has added business and industry services (landscaping and janitorial), education services (management of schools and institutions, including physical facilities and financial and personnel resources), and health-care services (management of support services—plant operations, asset management, laundry/linen supply—for long-term care facilities). Multiple product lines allow a company to grow rapidly and can help to offset the consequences of slow sales in any one product line.

DEVELOPING NEW PRODUCTS

To expand or diversify product lines—indeed, just to survive—firms must develop and successfully introduce streams of new products. Faced with competition and shifting consumer preferences, no firm can count on a single successful product to carry it forever. Even basic products that have been widely purchased for decades require nearly constant renewal. Consider one of Canada's most popular brands—Levi's. Its riveted denim styles were once market leaders, but the company failed to keep pace with changing tastes, fell behind new products from competitors, and lost market share among 14- to 19-year-old males. In 1999, one industry analyst reported that Levi's "hasn't had a successful new product in years." More recently, in recognizing fashion trends among female consumers, the company got back on track with the Superlow line of jeans that emphasizes femininity. And in 2003, on the 130th anniversary of the company's invention of jeans, Levi's introduced the new Signature brand of casual clothing. The brand has become very popular, and Levi's has opened Signature stores in several countries.

The Time Frame of New Product Development

Describe the *new product development process* and trace the stages of the *product life cycle*. 2

Companies often face multi-year time horizons and high risks when developing new products. In 1989, discussions about the possibility of manufacturing a new long-range executive jet began at Bombardier Inc. of Montreal. Over the next few years, the company spent millions of dollars developing the product, which finally became available in 1998. But there is a lot of uncertainty in new product development. In 2005, Bombardier announced that it would build a new line of passenger jets, but in 2006 it announced that it was shelving the project.[3]

As we saw in the Opening Case, the hydrogen fuel cell has taken much longer to develop than expected. High-definition television (HDTV)—which gives much-improved picture quality—is another example of a new product that has been slower to develop than expected. The technology of HDTV clearly works, but this promising new product suffers from a classic "chicken-and-egg" problem. *Broadcasters* haven't offered a lot of high-definition programs because to do so requires special transmitters and cameras. *Manufacturers* of HDTVs have been holding back because they don't know whether broadcasters are going to produce high-definition programs for consumers to watch. *Consumers* were slow to buy HDTV sets because they are expensive, so they waited to see how many programs would be broadcast in HDTV format. During 2004 and 2005, sales of HDTVs finally started to increase rapidly. There were about three million HDTVs in Canadian homes at the end of 2006. But many Canadians seem to be confused about HDTV. An Ipsos-Reid survey conducted in 2005 revealed that over half of the people who purchased a high-definition television didn't have the set-top box that is required to actually receive programs in high-definition.[4] The Entrepreneurship and New Ventures box provides another example of new product development.

Product Mortality Rates

It takes about 50 new product ideas to generate one product that finally reaches the market. Even then, only a few of these survivors become *successful* products. Many seemingly great *ideas* have failed as *products*.

ENTREPRENEURSHIP AND NEW VENTURES

The Patriotic Entrepreneur

Serious discussions about biotechnology seldom touch on Malaysia. That situation, however, may soon change as Malaysia takes its first steps toward what officials hope will be world-class status in the biotech sector. The Malaysian vision calls for developing not one dominant product but rather families or streams of biologically based products to compete on world markets.

Unfortunately, Malaysians are starting from scratch: Malaysia, critics scoff, doesn't have the science community necessary to compete with Europe and the United States in attracting the needed investment. In fact, experts question whether Malaysia can even compete with regional neighbours such as Singapore, which has similar ambitions and more money to lure talent from abroad. Malaysia's response to seemingly insurmountable odds is simple: Bring in Kim Tan, regarded by many as the world's top biochemistry entrepreneur.

Tan has already built three major biotech companies, with facilities in Canada, China, Britain, and the United States, while amassing a personal fortune estimated at $500 million. He has decided to collaborate with the Malaysian government to set up the country's first biotech venture fund—dubbed Springhill Biotech Ventures. As founding father of the country's biotech industry, Tan will manage Malaysia's planned life-sciences activities from its new biotech hub—called Biovalley—near the capital of Kuala Lumpur. The plan calls for Springhill to invest in new technologies from abroad that are almost ready to hit the market and that hold promise for future Biovalley research. The fund will also form joint ventures with companies that agree to locate facilities and conduct research in Malaysia.

Just how valuable is Tan's participation? Born in Malaysia and educated in Britain in the 1970s, Tan is an ideal role model for biotech entrepreneurs. "We really need more people like him to jump-start this industry," says Gurinder Shahi, a Singapore-based biotech consultant. "He's a good example of people that were part of the brain drain that now are returning and combining science and business skills that pay off." Tan's patents have already led to new drugs for treatment of cancer and chronic illnesses, and his research in genetic engineering has developed hormones for treating diabetes and arthritis.

In addition to his contributions of money and scientific knowledge to Biovalley, Tan also brings biotech-management and business skills. In 1986, he sold his first company, a diagnostics firm, using the proceeds to form KS Biomedics to commercialize his ideas for growing cancer-fighting antibodies in sheep. More recently, he formed TranXenoGen for genetic engineering in chickens to produce eggs containing therapeutic proteins for use in drugs. Yet another company—Genemedix—mass-produces low-cost generic drugs for reducing the fatal side effects of chemotherapy.

Tan has no illusions about the monumental task ahead: Biovalley starts with an inexperienced scientific base, few patents, and little venture capital. So, after all his success, why is Tan risking yet another start-up project? "Nationalism," he says. "I could make far more money and it's easier over there [in Britain]. The main reason: I'm a Malaysian. One has a responsibility to [his] country." Significantly, the country did not recruit Tan for the job; rather, it was Tan who took the initiative: "I took it to them. I've been waiting to see what the government was going to do [about building the sector]. They are committed. So I decided, right, let's do something."

Indeed, creating a successful new product has become increasingly difficult—even for the most experienced marketers. Why? The number of new products hitting the market each year has increased dramatically, and thousands of new household, grocery, and drugstore items are introduced annually. But at any given time, the average supermarket carries a total of only 20 000 to 25 000 different items. Because of lack of space and customer demand, about 9 out of 10 new products will fail. Those with the best chances are innovative and deliver unique benefits.

Speed to Market

speed to market Strategy of introducing new products to respond quickly to customer and/or market changes.

The more rapidly a product moves from the laboratory to the marketplace, the more likely it is to survive. By introducing new products ahead of competitors, companies establish market leadership. They become entrenched in the market before being challenged by newer competitors. How important is **speed to market**—that is, a firm's success in responding to customer demand or market changes? A product that is only three months late to market (three months behind the leader) loses 12 percent of its lifetime profit potential. At six months, it will lose 33 percent.[5]

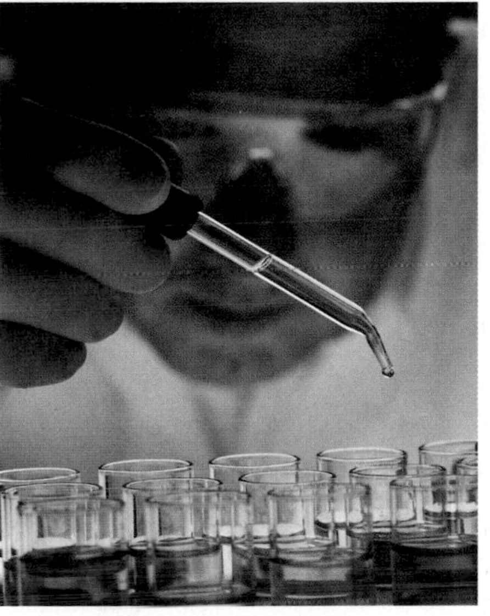

Pharmaceutical companies spend large amounts of money on research and development, yet bring relatively few products to market.

The Seven-Step Development Process

To increase their chances of developing a successful new product, many firms adopt some variation on a basic seven-step process (see Figure 16.2).

1. *Product ideas*. Product development begins with a search for ideas for new products. Product ideas can come from consumers, the sales force, research and development people, or engineering personnel. The key is to actively seek out ideas and to reward those whose ideas become successful products.
2. *Screening*. This second stage is an attempt to eliminate all product ideas that do not mesh with the firm's abilities, expertise, or objectives. Representatives from marketing, engineering, and production must have input at this stage.
3. *Concept testing*. Once ideas have been culled, companies use market research to solicit consumers' input. In this way, firms can identify benefits that the product must provide as well as an appropriate price level for the product.
4. *Business analysis*. This stage involves developing an early comparison of costs versus benefits for the proposed product. Preliminary sales projections are compared with cost projections from finance and production. The aim is not to determine precisely how much money the product will make but to see whether the product can meet minimum profitability goals.
5. *Prototype development*. At this stage, product ideas begin to take shape. Using input from the concept-testing phase, engineering and/or research and development produce a preliminary version of the product. Prototypes can be extremely expensive, often requiring extensive hand crafting, tooling, and development of components, but this phase can help identify potential production problems.

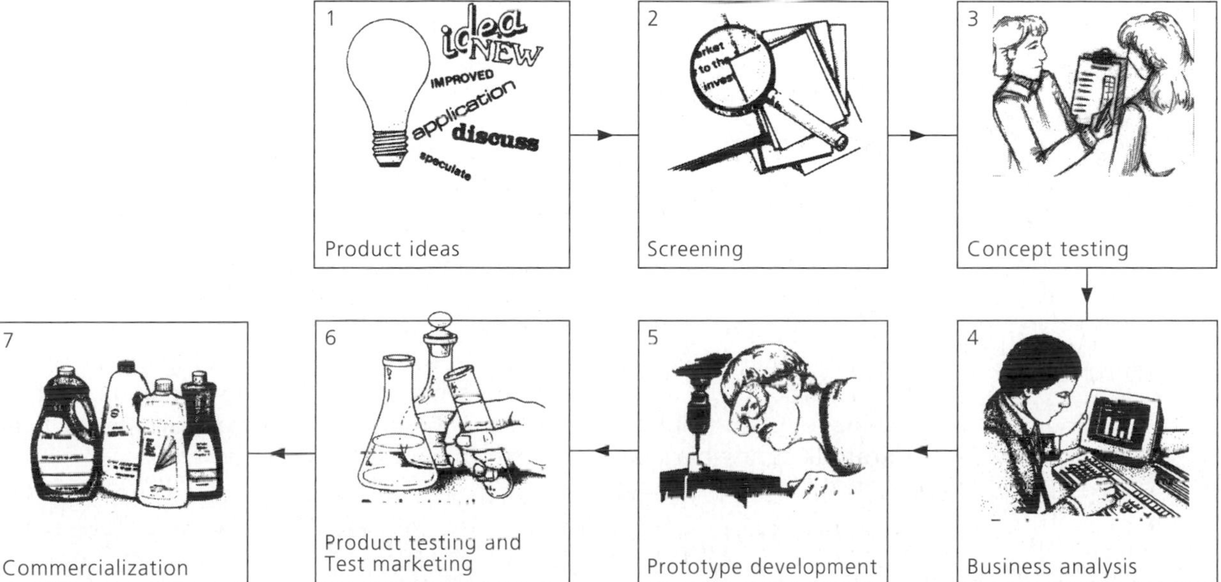

Figure 16.2 The new product development process.

6. *Product testing and test marketing*. Using what it learned from the prototype, the company begins limited production of the item. The product is then tested internally to see if it meets performance requirements. If it does, it is made available for sale in limited areas. This stage is very costly, since promotional campaigns and distribution channels must be established for test markets. But test marketing gives a company its first information on how consumers will respond to a product under real market conditions.
7. *Commercialization*. If test-marketing results are positive, the company will begin full-scale production and marketing of the product. Gradual commercialization, with the firm providing the product to more and more areas over time, prevents undue strain on the firm's initial production capabilities. But extensive delays in commercialization may give competitors a chance to bring out their own version.

Variations in the Process for Services

The development of services (both for consumers and industrial buyers) involves many of the same stages as goods development. Basically, Steps 2, 3, 4, 6, and 7 are the same. There are, however, some important differences in Steps 1 and 5:

service package Identification of the tangible and intangible features that define the service.

1. *Service ideas*. The search for service ideas includes a task called defining the **service package**, which involves identification of the tangible and intangible features that define the service (see Chapter 11) and stating service specifications. For example, a firm that wants to offer year-end cleaning services to office buildings might commit itself to the following specifications: "The building interior will be cleaned by midnight, January 5, including floor polishing of all aisles, carpets swept free of all dust and debris, polished washbowls and lavatory equipment, with no interruption or interference to customer."

service process design Selecting the process, identifying worker requirements, and determining facilities requirements so that the service can be effectively provided.

5. *Service process design*. Instead of prototype development, services require a **service process design**. This step involves selecting the process, identifying worker requirements, and determining facilities requirements so that the service can be provided as promised in the service specifications. *Process selection* identifies each step in the service, including the sequence and the timing. *Worker requirements* specify employee behaviours, skills, capabilities, and interactions with customers during the service encounter. *Facilities requirements* designate all of the equipment that supports delivery of the service.

THE PRODUCT LIFE CYCLE

product life cycle (PLC) The concept that the profit-producing life of any product goes through a cycle of introduction, growth, maturity (levelling off), and decline.

Products that reach the commercialization stage begin a new series of stages known as the product life cycle. **Product life cycle (PLC)** is the concept that products have a limited profit-producing life for a company. This life may be a matter of months, years, or decades, depending on the ability of the product to attract customers over time. Strong products such as Kellogg's Corn Flakes, Coca-Cola, Ivory soap, Argo cornstarch, and Caramilk candy bars have had extremely long productive lives.

Stages in the Product Life Cycle

The life cycle for both goods and services is a natural process in which products are born, grow in stature, mature, and finally decline and die.[6]

Look at the two graphics in Figure 16.3. In Figure 16.3(a), the four phases of the PLC are applied to several products with which you are familiar.

1. *Introduction*. The introduction stage begins when the product reaches the marketplace. During this stage, marketers focus on making potential consumers aware of the product and its benefits. Because of extensive promotional and development costs, profits are nonexistent.
2. *Growth*. If the new product attracts and satisfies enough consumers, sales begin to climb rapidly. During this stage, the product begins to show a profit. Other firms in the industry move rapidly to introduce their own versions.
3. *Maturity*. Sales growth begins to slow. Although the product earns its highest profit level early in this stage, increased competition eventually leads to price cutting and lower profits. Toward the end of the stage, sales start to fall.
4. *Decline*. During this final stage, sales and profits continue to fall. New products in the introduction stage take away sales. Companies remove or reduce promotional support (ads and salespeople) but may let the product linger to provide some profits.

Figure 16.3(b) plots the relationship of the PLC to a product's typical sales, costs, and profits. Although the early stages of the PLC often show negative cash flows, successful products usually recover those losses and, in fact, continue to generate profits until the decline stage. For most products, profitable life spans are short—thus, the importance placed by so many firms on the constant replenishment of product lines. In the pension indus-

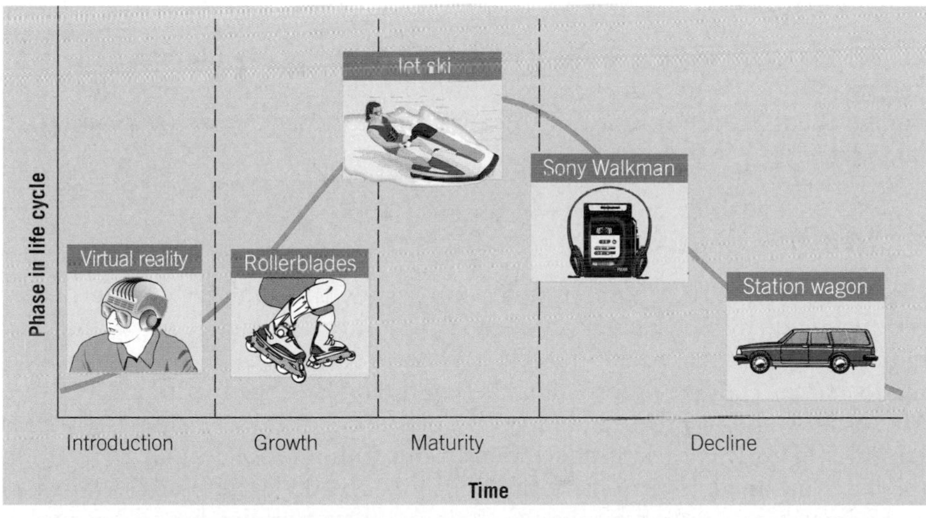

(a)

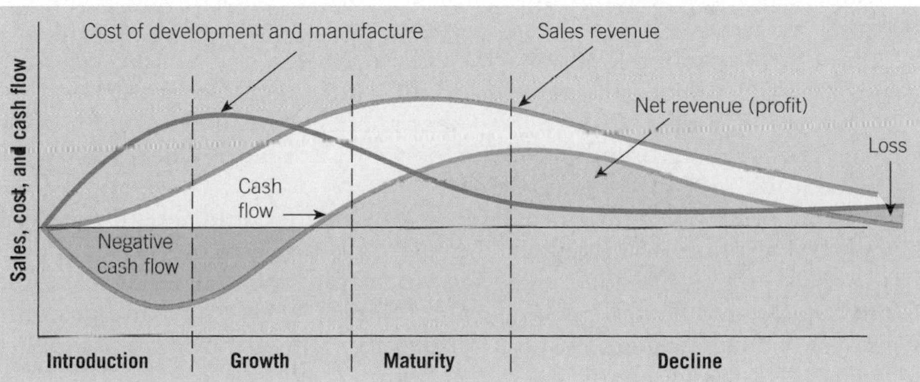

(b)

Figure 16.3 The product life cycle: stages, sales, cost, and profit.

try, for example, "defined benefit" programs are approaching the end of their life cycle, while "defined contribution" plans are in the growth stage. In 2003 sales of digital cameras surpassed film cameras for the first time, and Kodak announced stoppage of film camera production, after decades as the market leader.

Extending Product Life: An Alternative to New Products

Companies try to keep products in the maturity stage as long as they can. Sales of TV sets, for example, have been revitalized by such feature changes as colour, portability, miniaturization, and stereo capability. In fact, companies can extend product life through a number of creative means. Foreign markets, for example, offer three possibilities for lengthening product life cycles:

product extension Existing, unmodified product that is marketed globally.

product adaptation Product modified to have greater appeal in foreign markets.

reintroduction Process of reviving for new markets products that are obsolete in older ones.

1. In **product extension**, an existing product is marketed globally instead of just domestically. Coca-Cola and Levi's 501 jeans are prime examples of international product extensions.
2. With **product adaptation**, the product is modified for greater appeal in different countries. In Germany, a McDonald's meal includes beer, and in Japan Ford puts the steering wheel on the right side. Because it involves product changes, this approach is usually more costly than product extension.
3. **Reintroduction** means reviving, for new markets, products that are becoming obsolete in older ones. NCR, for instance, has reintroduced manually operated cash registers in Latin America.

IDENTIFYING PRODUCTS

3 Discuss the importance of *branding*, *packaging*, and *labelling*.

As we noted earlier, developing a product's features is only part of a marketer's job. Marketers must also identify products so that consumers recognize them. Three important tools for this task are *branding, packaging*, and *labelling*.

Branding Products

branding Process of using symbols to communicate the qualities of a product made by a particular producer.

Branding is the use of symbols to communicate the qualities of a particular product made by a particular producer. Brands are designed to signal uniform quality: Customers who try and like a product can return to it by remembering its name. The three most valuable brand names in the world in 2006 were Microsoft, General Electric, and Coca-Cola (see Table 16.1). Chinese brands have not historically been ranked highly, but China Mobile ranked fourth on the list. No Canadian firm has a brand in the top 100 list of brands.[7]

Sometimes companies change the name of a popular brand because it is "tired," or because of legal requirements. For example, when Circuit City acquired 874 Canadian RadioShack stores in 2004, a court ruling required that it drop the RadioShack name. Circuit City decided to rename the stores "The Source by Circuit City." Scott Paper changed the name of Cottonelle, Canada's best-selling brand of toilet paper, to "Cashmere" when a licensing agreement with Kimberly-Clark expired.[8]

Just as products can be branded, so can entire countries. In the 2005 Anholt-GMI Nation Brands Index, Canada ranked as one of the best places in the world to live. Canada ranked second overall, ahead of Britain and the United States, and behind only Australia.[9] Simon Anholt, a co-author of the survey, says that Canada's positive nation brand should increase its ability to sell goods to other countries.

Table 16.1 The World's Top 10 Brands

Brand	Value (in billions of $)
1. Microsoft	$62.0
2. General Electric	55.8
3. Coca-Cola	41.4
4. China Mobile	39.1
5. Marlboro	38.5
6. Wal-Mart	37.5
7. Google	37.4
8. IBM	36.0
9. Citibank	31.0
10. Toyota	30.2

Adding Value Through Brand Equity

Many companies that once measured assets in terms of cash, buildings, equipment, and inventories now realize that a strong brand is an equally important asset. Widely known and admired brands are valuable because of their power to attract customers. Those with higher **brand equity** generate greater brand awareness and loyalty on the part of consumers and larger market shares than competing brands (and are perceived to have greater quality). In the 2005 survey of Canadian brand equity, the top three companies were the Royal Bank of Canada (whose brand equity was valued at $4.5 billion), Loblaw ($3.3 billion), and Bell Canada ($3.1 billion).[10] The Irving family of New Brunswick recently embarked on a plan to increase the brand equity of Royale, a once-popular brand of tissue. The goal is to make Royale a major brand in Canada.[11]

brand equity Degree of consumers' loyalty to and awareness of a brand and its resultant market share.

Because a brand adds value to a product, marketers manage brand names to increase that value. A 2005 survey by the research firm Strategic Counsel revealed that Canada's best-managed brand names were Tim Hortons, President's Choice, Loblaws, Cirque du Soleil, and Canadian Tire (first through fifth, respectively). The worst-managed brand names were Jetsgo (now bankrupt), Air Canada, Bell/Bell Mobility, and Rogers Wireless.[12]

Ebusiness and International Branding

The expensive and fierce struggle for brand recognition is very evident in the branding battles among dot-com firms. Collectively, the top internet brands—Google, America Online, Yahoo!, and Amazon.com—spend billions a year. Even with 210 million visitors each month, Yahoo! still faces formidable competitors in AOL Time Warner and Microsoft. The mounting costs of brand identity mean that many would-be ebusinesses will fail.[13]

It takes a long time to establish national or global brand recognition.[14] After years of work, Cisco Systems Inc., the network-equipment manufacturer, finally reached new heights in branding for business-to-business, or B2B, ecommerce. The company's "Cisco Internet Generation" promotional campaign stressed reliability and innovation, and in analyzing the campaign, Cisco found that its brand awareness had increased by 80 percent (boosting it past rivals Lucent Technologies and Nortel Networks). The campaign also lifted Cisco's reputation as an internet expert above that of Microsoft, IBM, and Lucent.[15]

Firms that sell products internationally must consider how product names will translate in various languages. In Spanish, for example, the name of Chevrolet's now-defunct Nova simply became *no va*—"it does not go." Not surprisingly, sales were poor in South America. Similarly, Rolls-Royce was once going to name a new touring car "Silver Mist," but changed the name to "Silver Shadow" when it discovered that "mist" is German for "manure."[16]

Types of Brand Names

Virtually every product has a brand name of some form. However, different types of brand names tell the alert consumer something about the product's origin.

national brands Products distributed by and carrying a name associated with the manufacturer.

National Brands. Brand name products that are produced and distributed by the manufacturer are called **national brands**. These brands, such as Scotch tape, are often widely recognized by consumers because of large national advertising campaigns. The costs of developing a positive image for a national brand are high, so some companies use their national brand on several related products. Procter & Gamble now markets Ivory Shampoo, capitalizing on the widely recognized name of its soaps.

licensed brands Selling the right to use a brand name, a celebrity's name, or some other well-known identification mark to another company to use on a product.

Licensed Brands. More and more nationally recognized companies and personalities have sold other companies the right to place their names on products, which are **licensed brands**. Licensing has become big business. The logo *"2004 Olympic Games—Athens"* generated millions in revenues for the International Olympic Committee, which licenses its name on license plates, clothing, tableware, coins, and countless other merchandise items. Harley-Davidson's famous logo—emblazoned on boots, eyewear, gloves, purses, lighters, and watches—brings the motorcycle maker more than $210 million annually. Along with brands such as Coors and Ferrari, licensing for character-based brands—Punisher, Spider-Man, and Pokeman—are equally lucrative. Franklin the Turtle, the subject of 26 books and an animated television series produced by Nelvana, is a Canadian product that is also popular in the United States. Nelvana and U.S.-based Sears Roebuck & Co. signed a licensing agreement allowing Sears to set up Franklin boutiques at its stores. These boutiques market Franklin clothing and accessories that are available exclusively at Sears.[17] Marketers exploit brands because of their public appeal—the image and status that consumers hope to gain by associating with them. The free advertising that comes with some licensing, such as T-shirts and other clothing, is an added bonus.

SpongeBob macaroni and cheese is Kraft Foods' top-selling licensed pasta product, and SpongeBob Band-Aids now outsell Scooby Doo bandages. There are SpongeBob dolls and bowling balls, and the brand also appears on toothpaste and underwear. SpongeBob belongs to Nickelodeon Enterprises, a children's TV programmer that's been the highest-rated basic cable network since 1995. Product licensing is worth about $2.5 billion to Nickelodeon each year.

Private Brands. When a wholesaler or retailer develops a brand and has the manufacturer place that brand name on the product, the resulting product name is a **private brand**. One of the best-known purveyors of private brands is Sears, with its Craftsman tools and Kenmore appliances. But it's not alone. J. Sainsbury PLC, the largest supermarket chain in Britain, introduced its own private brand of cola in a can that looks strikingly like the one used by Coke. The product is made by Cott Corp. of Toronto, which also makes the "American Choice" label for Wal-Mart.

private brands Products promoted by and carrying a name associated with the retailer or wholesaler, not the manufacturer.

Loblaw Cos. Ltd., owned by George Weston, has created a line of upscale products under the private brand "President's Choice." Clever advertising, fancy labels, and exotic product names differentiate the line and draw consumer attention to items such as peanut butter and cookies. Shoppers Drug Mart produces a line of products under the "Life" label. It hopes to make the Life label as prestigious as the President's Choice label.[18] E.D. Smith, a maker of jams and pie fillings makes private label items for retailers like Wal-Mart and Pizza Pizza Ltd.[19] Private brands usually yield more profit than national brands because of reduced marketing costs. And customers like these brands because they are lower-priced than national brands.

Brand Loyalty

Companies that spend the large amount of money it takes to develop a brand are looking for one thing from consumers: **brand loyalty**. That is, they want to develop customers who, when they need a particular item, will go back to the same brand and buy the company's products. Brand loyalty can have a major impact on a company's profits. In the beer industry, for example, each market share point is worth about $25 million in profit. This is why companies like Labatt and Molson have such fierce competitive battles for market share.[20]

brand loyalty Customers' recognition of, preference for, and insistence on buying a product with a certain brand name.

Brand loyalty exists at three levels. *brand awareness* (customers recognize the brand name), *brand preference* (consumers have a favourable attitude toward the product), and *brand insistence* (consumers demand the product and are willing to go out of their way to get it). Brand insistence implies a lot of consumer trust in a brand, but a survey sponsored by *Reader's Digest Canada* found that Canadians have less trust in brands than they did 20 years ago. However, some well-known brands like Becel Margarine, Robin Hood flour, Wal-Mart, and Black & Decker are still viewed positively.[21]

Trademarks, Patents, and Copyrights. Because brand development is very expensive, a company does not want another company using its name and confusing consumers into buying a substitute product. Many companies apply to the Canadian government and receive a **trademark**, the exclusive legal right to use a brand name. Trademarks are granted for 15 years and may be renewed for further periods of 15 years, but only if the company continues to protect its brand name.

trademark The exclusive legal right to use a brand name.

Just what can be trademarked is not always clear, however. If the company allows the name to lapse into common usage, the courts may take away protection. Common usage occurs when the company fails to use the ® symbol for its brand. It also occurs if the company fails to correct those who do not acknowledge the brand as a trademark. Windsurfer (a popular brand of sailboards by WSI Inc.) lost its trademark. Like the trampoline, yo-yo, and thermos, the brand name has become the common term for the product and can now be used by any sailboard company. But companies owning brands like Xerox, Coke, Jello, and Scotch tape have successfully defended their brand names.

Companies want to be sure that both product brands and new product ideas are protected. A **patent** protects an invention or idea for a period of 20 years. The cost is $1000 to $1500; it takes from nine months to three years

patent Protects an invention or idea for a period of 20 years.

to secure a patent from the Canadian Patent Office.[22] Patents can be very valuable. In 2006, Toronto-based Research In Motion (RIM), maker of the immensely popular BlackBerry device, agreed to pay $612.5 million to NTP Inc., a U.S. firm that claimed RIM was infringing on some patents it held.[23] Two months later, RIM was sued by another U.S. company claiming that RIM had also infringed on its patents.[24]

copyright Exclusive ownership rights granted to creators for the tangible expression of an idea.

Copyrights give exclusive ownership rights to the creators of books, articles, designs, illustrations, photos, films, and music. Computer programs and even semiconductor chips are also protected. In Canada, the copyright process is relatively simply, requiring only the use of the copyright symbol © and the date. Copyrights extend to creators for their entire lives and to their estates for 50 years thereafter in Canada (70 years in the United States). Copyrights apply to the tangible expressions of an idea, not to the idea itself. For example, the idea of cloning dinosaurs from fossil DNA cannot be copyrighted, but Michael Crichton, the author of *Jurassic Park,* has copyright for his novel because it is the tangible result of the basic idea.

Packaging Products

packaging The physical container in which a product is sold, including the label.

With a few exceptions, including fresh fruits and vegetables, structural steel, and some other industrial products, almost all products need some form of **packaging** so they can be transported to the market. Packaging serves as an in-store advertisement that makes the product attractive, clearly displays the brand, identifies product features and benefits, and reduces the risk of damage, breakage, or spoilage. It is the marketer's last chance to say "buy it" to the consumer

Companies are paying close attention to consumer concerns about packaging. Beyond concerns about product tampering, packaging must be tight enough to withstand shipping, but not so tight that it frustrates consumers when they try to open the package. For example, Nestlé—which spends more than $6 billion annually on packaging—spent nine months coming up with a new easier-opening lid and an easier-to-grip container for its new Country Creamery Ice Cream. In general, companies have found that packaging costs can be as high as 15 percent of the total cost to make a product, and features like zip-lock tops can add 20 percent to the price that is charged.[25]

Labelling Products

label That part of a product's packaging that identifies the product's name and contents and sometimes its benefits.

Every product has a **label** on its package. Like packaging, labelling can help market the product. First, it *identifies* the product or the brand, as do the names "Campbell" on a can or "Chiquita" on a banana. Labels also *promote* products by getting consumers' attention; attractive colours and graphics provide visual cues to products that otherwise might be overlooked on the shelf. Finally, the label *describes* the product: It provides information about nutritional content, directions for use, proper disposal, and safety.

Consumer Packaging and Labelling Act A federal law that provides comprehensive rules for packaging and labelling of consumer products.

The federal government regulates the information on package labels. The **Consumer Packaging and Labelling Act** has two main purposes: the first is to provide a comprehensive set of rules for packaging and labelling of consumer products, and the second is to ensure that the manufacturer provides full and factual information on labels. All pre-packaged products must state in French and English the quantity enclosed in metric units, as well as the name and description of the product.

Sellers are very sensitive to what is on the label of the products they sell. For example, the Maple Leaf is on all beer that Labatt Brewing Co. Ltd. sells in Canada—except in Quebec. There, the label has a stylized sheaf of wheat instead of the Maple Leaf. Interestingly, the Maple Leaf is much more prominent on Labatt's beer sold in the United States.[26] Many companies have different labels for their products in Quebec, partly because "Canadian" symbols may not resonate well with Quebec sovereigntists.

PROMOTING PRODUCTS AND SERVICES

Identify the important objectives of *promotion* and discuss the considerations in selecting a *promotional mix.* 4

As we noted in Chapter 15, **promotion** is any technique designed to sell a product. It is part of the *communication mix*: the total message a company sends to consumers about its product. Promotional techniques, especially advertising, must communicate the uses, features, and benefits of products. Sales promotions also include various programs that add value beyond the benefits inherent in the product. For example, it is nice to get a high-quality product at a reasonable price but even better when the seller offers a rebate or a bonus pack with "20 percent more *free*."

promotion Any technique designed to sell a product.

In this section, we will look at the different objectives of and approaches to promotion. We will show when and why companies use particular strategies and tools and then describe the special promotional problems faced by both international and small businesses. First, however, we will explain the two general values to be gained from any promotional activity, regardless of the particular strategy or tools involved: *communicating information* and *creating satisfying exchanges*.

Information and Exchange Values

In free-market systems, a business uses promotional methods to communicate information about itself and its products to consumers and industrial buyers. The purpose, of course, is to influence purchase decisions. From an information standpoint, promotions seek to accomplish four things with potential customers:

- make them aware of products
- make them knowledgeable about products
- persuade them to like products
- persuade them to purchase products

The buyer gains from the exchange (a more attractive product), as does the seller (sales and profits). Successful promotions provide communication about the product and create exchanges that satisfy both the customer's and the organization's objectives. However, because promotions are expensive, choosing the best promotional mix becomes critical. The promotional program, then, whether at the introduction stage (promoting for new product awareness) or the maturity stage (promoting brand benefits and customer loyalty), can determine the success or failure of any business or product.

Promotional Objectives

The ultimate objective of any promotion is to increase sales. However, marketers also use promotion to *communicate information*, *position products*, *add value*, and *control sales volume*.[27]

Communicating Information

Consumers cannot buy a product unless they have been informed about it. Information can advise customers about the availability of a product, educate them on the latest technological advances, or announce the candidacy of someone running for a government office. Information may be communicated in writing (newspapers and magazines), verbally (in person or over the telephone), or visually (television, a matchbook cover, or a billboard). Today, the communication of information regarding a company's products or services is so important that marketers try to place it wherever consumers may be. If you are an average consumer, you come in contact with approximately 1500 bits of promotional communication per day.

Positioning Products

product positioning The establishment of an easily identifiable image of a product in the minds of consumers.

As we saw in Chapter 15, **product positioning** establishes an easily identifiable image of a product in the minds of consumers. For example, by selling only in department stores, Estée Lauder products are positioned as more upscale than cosmetics sold in drugstores. With product positioning, the company is trying to appeal to a specific segment of the market rather than to the market as a whole.

Adding Value

Today's value-conscious customers gain benefits when the promotional mix is shifted so that it communicates value—added benefits in its products. Burger King, for instance, shifted its promotional mix by cutting back on advertising dollars and using those funds for customer discounts. Receiving the same food at a lower price is "value-added" for Burger King's customers.

Controlling Sales Volume

Many companies, such as Hallmark Cards, experience seasonal sales patterns. By increasing promotional activities in slow periods, these firms can achieve more stable sales volume throughout the year. They can thus keep production and distribution systems running evenly. Promotions can even turn slow seasons into peak sales periods. For example, greeting card companies and florists together have done much to create Grandparents' Day. The result has been increased consumer demand for cards and flowers in the middle of what was once a slow season for both industries.

Promotional Strategies

push strategy A promotional strategy in which a company aggressively pushes its product through wholesalers and retailers, which persuade customers to buy it.

pull strategy A promotional strategy in which a company appeals directly to customers, who demand the product from retailers, which demand the product from wholesalers.

Once a firm's promotional objectives are clear, it must develop a promotional strategy to achieve these objectives. Promotional strategies may be of the push or pull variety. A company with a **push strategy** will aggressively "push" its product through wholesalers and retailers, who persuade customers to buy it. In contrast, a company with a **pull strategy** appeals directly to customers, who demand the product from retailers, who in turn demand the product from wholesalers. Advertising "pulls" while personal selling "pushes." In rare cases, a company may purposely do very little promotion of its products. For example, Langlitz Leathers makes leather jackets that cost as much as $800. They are worn by rebels like Hell's Angels, rockers like Bruce Springsteen, and actors like Sylvester Stallone. Even though the company does virtually no advertising, customers who want a Langlitz have to wait seven months to get one after they place their order.[28]

Makers of industrial products most often use a push strategy, and makers of consumer products most often use a pull strategy. Many large firms use a combination of the two strategies. For example, General Foods uses advertising to create consumer demand (pull) for its cereals. It also pushes wholesalers and retailers to stock these products.

The Promotional Mix

As we noted in Chapter 15, there are four types of promotional tools: *advertising, personal selling, sales promotions,* and *publicity and public relations*. The best combination of these tools—the best **promotional mix**—depends on many factors. The most important is the target audience.

promotional mix That portion of marketing concerned with choosing the best combination of advertising, personal selling, sales promotions, and publicity and public relations to sell a product.

The Target Audience: Promotion and the Buyer Decision Process

In establishing a promotional mix, marketers match promotional tools with the five stages in the buyer decision process:

1. Buyers must first recognize the need to make a purchase. At this stage, marketers must make sure that buyers are aware of their products. Advertising and publicity, which can reach many people quickly, are important.
2. Buyers also want to learn more about available products. Advertising and personal selling are important because both can be used to educate consumers.
3. Buyers compare competing products. Personal selling can be vital. Sales representatives can demonstrate product quality and performance in comparison with competitors' products.
4. Buyers choose products and purchase them. Sales promotion is effective because it can give consumers an incentive to buy. Personal selling can help by bringing products to convenient purchase locations.
5. Buyers evaluate products after purchase. Advertising, or even personal selling, is sometimes used to remind consumers that they made wise purchases.[29]

Figure 16.4 summarizes the effective promotional tools for each stage of the consumer buying process, and Figure 16.5 shows different combinations of products, promotional tools, and target consumers.

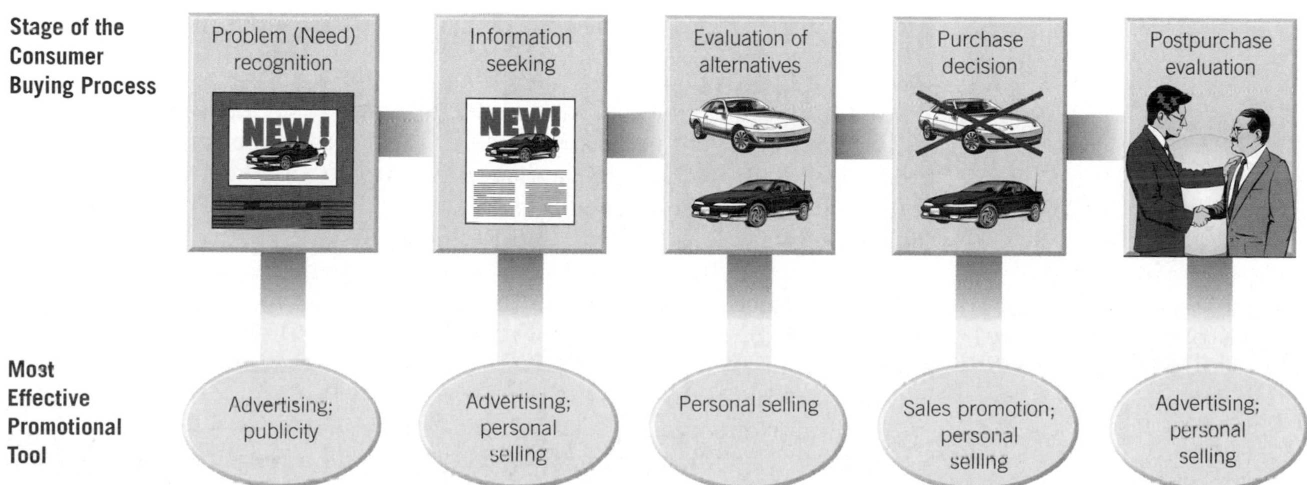

Figure 16.4 The consumer buying process and the promotional mix.

Goods Promotion: House (real estate)
Tool: Personal selling
Consumer: House buyer

Service Promotion:
Weight-loss program
Tool: Sales promotion (coupon)
Consumer: Overweight person

Organizational Promotion: Scouts Canada
Tool: Publicity
Consumer: Young men and women

Event Promotion: Rock concert
Tool: Advertising
Consumer: Cheering fan

Person or Idea Promotion:
Candidate for prime minister
Tool: Publicity/advertising/personal sales
Consumer: Voter

Figure 16.5 Each promotional tool should be properly matched with the product being promoted and the target consumer.

ADVERTISING PROMOTIONS

5 Discuss the most important *advertising strategies* and describe the key *advertising media.*

advertising Promotional tool consisting of paid, non-personal communication used by an identified sponsor to inform an audience about a product.

What candy bar is "one of life's sweet mysteries"? What soap is "99 and 44/100% pure"? What is the store where "the lowest price is the law"? What product is "only available in Canada, Pity"? If you are like most Canadians, you can answer these questions because of **advertising**. (The answers are Caramilk, Ivory Soap, Zellers, and Red Rose Tea, respectively.) Consumers remember brand names more easily if the company has a catchy advertising slogan. Buckley's Mixture, a well-known product in Canada, is trying to crack the U.S. market. In one advertisement on U.S. television, the announcer intones "Buckley's Mixture, the famous Canadian cough remedy, is now available here. It tastes awful, and it works."[30]

As important and high profile as advertising is, it has limits. Both Eaton's and Canadian Airlines were enthusiastic advertisers, but it didn't keep them in business. Advertising might convince customers to try a company's product or service, but it is the customer's experience with the product or service that determines whether they will make repeat purchases.

Advertising Strategies

Advertising strategies depend on which stage of the product life cycle the product is in. During the introduction stage, **informative advertising** can help develop an awareness of the company and its product among buyers and can establish a primary demand for the product. For example, before a new textbook is published, instructors receive direct-mail advertisements notifying them of the book's contents and availability. During the growth stage, **persuasive advertising** can influence a larger number of consumers to buy the company's products. During the maturity stage, **comparative advertising**—which involves comparing the sponsoring company's brand name with a competitor's brand name in such a way that the competitor's brand looks inferior—is often used. For example, Procter & Gamble aired advertisements claiming that its Bounty brand had more absorbency than Scott Paper's competing product. Scott retaliated by producing an advertisement that said that Scott Clean Ultra was 60 percent more absorbent than P&G's Bounty.[31] During the latter part of the maturity stage and all of the decline stage, **reminder advertising** keeps the product's name in front of the consumer.

informative advertising An advertising strategy, appropriate to the introduction stage of the product life cycle, in which the goal is to make potential customers aware that a product exists.

persuasive advertising An advertising strategy, appropriate to the growth stage of the product life cycle, in which the goal is to influence the customer to buy the firm's product rather than the similar product of a competitor.

comparative advertising An advertising strategy, appropriate to the maturity stage of the product life cycle, in which the goal is to influence the customer to switch from a competitor's similar product to the firm's product by directly comparing the two products.

reminder advertising An advertising strategy, appropriate to the latter part of the maturity stage of the product life cycle, in which the goal is to keep the product's name in the minds of customers.

Advertising Media

Consumers tend to ignore the bulk of advertising messages that bombard them. Marketers must therefore find out who their customers are, which media they pay attention to, what messages appeal to them, and how to get their attention. Thus, marketers use several different **advertising media**—specific communication devices for carrying a seller's message to potential customers. For example, IBM uses television ads to keep its name fresh in the minds of consumers, newspaper and magazine ads to educate them about product features, and trade publications to introduce new software. Often marketers turn to a multimedia company so that the seller's message is the same across the different advertising media. The top 10 multimedia companies in Canada are listed in Table 16.2.

advertising medium The specific communication device—television, radio, newspapers, direct mail, magazines, billboards—used to carry a firm's advertising message to potential customers.

An advertiser selects media with a number of factors in mind. The marketer must first ask: Which medium will reach the people I want to reach? If a firm is selling hog breeding equipment, it might choose a business magazine read mostly by hog farmers. If it is selling silverware, it might choose a magazine for brides. If it is selling toothpaste, the choice might be a general audience television program or a general audience magazine such as

Table 16.2 The Top 10 Multimedia Companies in Canada, 2005

Company	Annual Revenues (in billions of $)
1. CanWest Global Communications Corp.	$3.0
2. Shaw Communications Inc.	2.2
3. Rogers Cable Inc.	2.0
4. Bell Globemedia Inc.	1.5
5. Rogers Media Inc.	1.0
6. Alliance Atlantis Communications Inc.	1.0
7. Vidéotron Ltée	1.0
8. Bell ExpressVu LP	0.9
9. Corus Entertainment Inc.	0.6
10. Cogeco Inc.	0.6

Reader's Digest (or *Sélection du Reader's Digest*, for exposure to a similar audience of francophones).

Newspapers

Newspapers are a widely used advertising medium, but in recent years the volume of classified ads placed in newspapers has declined as advertisers have shifted their emphasis to the internet. The *Toronto Star* has tried to counter this trend by giving a free internet posting to anyone who buys a classified ad in the newspaper.[32] Newspapers offer excellent coverage, since each local market has at least one daily newspaper, and many people read the paper every day. This medium offers flexible, rapid coverage, since ads can change from day to day. It also offers believable coverage, since ads are presented side by side with news. However, newspapers are generally thrown out after one day, often do not print in colour, and have poor reproduction quality. Moreover, newspapers do not usually allow advertisers to target their audience well.

Television

Television allows advertisers to combine sight, sound, and motion, thus appealing to almost all of the viewer's senses. Information on viewer demographics for a particular program allows advertisers to promote to their target audiences. One disadvantage of television is that too many commercials cause viewers to confuse products. In addition, viewers who record programs on VCRs or DVRs (digital video recorders) often fast-forward past the ads of TV shows they have recorded. The brevity of TV ads also makes television a poor medium in which to educate viewers about complex products. Television is the most expensive medium in which to advertise. A 30-second commercial during the NFL Super Bowl cost U.S.$2.4 million for the 2005 game.[33] Ads during prime-time evening hours are lower, but still expensive, at upwards of U.S.$190 000 for a 30-second commercial.

Direct Mail

direct mail Printed advertisements, such as flyers, mailed directly to consumers' homes or places of business.

Direct mail involves flyers or other types of printed advertisements mailed directly to consumers' homes or places of business. Direct mail allows the company to select its audience and personalize its message. Although many people discard "junk mail," targeted recipients with stronger-than-average interest are more likely to buy. Direct mail involves the largest advance costs of any advertising technique, but it appears to have the highest cost effectiveness. Particularly effective have been "fax attacks," in which advertisers send their "mail" messages electronically via fax machines and get higher response rates than they would if they used Canada Post.

Radio

A tremendous number of people listen to the radio each day, and radio ads are inexpensive. In addition, since most radio is programmed locally, this medium gives advertisers a high degree of customer selectivity. For example, radio stations are segmented into listening categories such as rock and roll, country and western, jazz, talk shows, news, and religious programming. Like television, however, radio ads are very short. And radio permits only an audio presentation. People tend to use the radio as "background" while they are doing other things, and this means they may pay little attention to advertisements.

Magazines

The many different magazines on the market provide a high level of consumer selectivity. The person who reads *Popular Photography* is more likely to be interested in the latest specialized lenses from Canon than is a

Gourmet magazine subscriber. Magazine advertising allows for excellent reproduction of photographs and artwork that not only grab buyers' attention but also may convince them of the product's value. And magazines allow advertisers plenty of space for detailed product information. Magazines have a long life and tend to be passed from person to person, thus doubling and tripling the number of exposures.

Outdoor Advertising

Outdoor advertising—billboards, signs, and advertisements on buses, taxis, and subways—is relatively inexpensive, faces little competition for customers' attention, and is subject to high repeat exposure. Because roadside billboards are prohibited on some major Ontario arteries, a company called Moving Impressions Inc. introduced "rolling billboards"—advertisements attached to the sides of large freight trucks. The truck companies get a piece of the action.[34] Many billboards now feature animation and changing images, and today's billboard messages are cheaper because they can be digitally printed in color in large quantities. On the downside, outdoor ads can present only limited information, and sellers have little control over who sees their advertisements.

Word of Mouth

Consumers form very strong opinions about products as a result of conversations with friends and acquaintances. Marketers have known about the power of word of mouth for many years. When consumers start talking about a new product or idea, the information can build momentum and spread like wildfire. If **word of mouth** (also called *buzz marketing*) says that a product is good, higher product sales are likely. Nike spent very little money advertising its Presto line of stretchy sneakers, but kids and teens spread the word to each other about the shoes and the fashion statement they could make by having them.[35]

word of mouth Opinions about the value of products passed among consumers in informal discussions.

The Internet

Ecommerce refers to buying and selling processes that make use of electronic technology, while **internet marketing** refers to the promotional efforts of companies to sell their products and services to consumers over

ecommerce Buying and selling processes that make use of electronic technology.

internet marketing The promotional efforts of companies to sell their products and services to consumers over the internet.

Speed and creativity have given billboards like these a new prominence in the world of advertising media. Instead of relying on highly skilled human artists, outdoor ad sellers can now commission digital creations that not only turn heads but also cost less than most other media. Whereas it used to take a month to launch a billboard-based campaign, it now takes just days.

the internet.[36] The internet is the most recent advertising medium to arise, and thousands of well known and lesser-known firms have placed ads there. Online ad sales were valued at $519 million in 2005, up 43 percent from 2004. Craigslist.org offers free local classified advertising on 204 websites around the world. Eleven cities in Canada had Craigslist sites in 2006.[37]

Internet advertising offers advantages for both buyers and sellers. For buyers, advantages include *convenience* (websites can be accessed 24 hours a day, and there is no need to fight traffic at shopping malls), *privacy* (no face-to-face high-pressure sales tactics are possible), *selection* (the products and services that are available are almost unlimited), *useful information* (about competing products and services), and *control* (consumers can "build" custom products for themselves).

For sellers, advantages include *reach* (access to consumers around the world), *direct distribution* (eliminating intermediaries), *reduced expenses* (which would normally be incurred when owning "bricks-and-morter" outlets), *relationship building* (with customers on interactive websites), *flexibility* (sellers can quickly change prices or the terms of sale based on market developments), and *feedback* (sellers can measure the success of messages by counting how many people see each ad and track the number of click-throughs to their own website.[38]

While internet marketing has some obvious advantages for both buyers and sellers, it also has weaknesses, including *profitability problems* (many internet marketers are unprofitable and the failure rate is high), *information overload* (consumers may not know what to do with all the information available to them), and *limited markets* (consumers who use the web are typically more highly educated).

In addition to these weaknesses, internet marketers must also cope with consumer concerns about two security-related issues. First, an Angus Reid/*Globe and Mail* poll of 1500 Canadians found that their main concern about internet marketing was security. People who had made at least one purchase on the internet were *more* likely to list security as their top concern than were those who had never purchased anything on the internet. In particular, people were concerned that their credit card number might end up in the wrong hands, and that their privacy would be invaded if they purchased on the internet.[39]

Second, consumers object to "spyware" software, which monitors websites they visit and observes their shopping habits. This software is often implanted on their personal computers as they wander the web. It then generates "pop-up" advertisements that are targeted to that particular consumer. Because people are often unaware that such spyware is on their computer, the technique has generated a lot of anger among consumers. Consumers can, however, get free anti-spyware software that removes spyware from their computer. Spyware is also a concern for companies that sell from their own websites because the pop-ups are designed to divert web surfers from the products offered by the website.[40] If it going to reach its full potential, internet marketing is going to have to improve its image.

Virtual Advertising

An even newer method of advertising, called *virtual advertising*, uses digital implants of brands or products onto live or taped programming, giving the illusion that the product is part of the show. With this technique, an advertiser's product can appear as part of the television show—when viewers are paying more attention—instead of during commercial breaks. In a televised basketball game, for example, the digital image of a brand—for example, the round face of a Rolex watch or an Acura hubcap—can be electronically enlarged and superimposed on centre court without physically changing the playing floor. For videotaped movies, digital images can be inserted easily. A Kmart shopping bag can be digitally added to the table in a kitchen scene, or a Philips Flat TV can be superimposed on the wall for display during a dramatic scene in the den.[41]

Other Advertising Channels

A combination of many additional media, including catalogues, sidewalk handouts, *Yellow Pages*, skywriting, telephone calls, special events, and door-to-door communications, make up the remaining advertisements to which Canadians are exposed. The combination of media through which a company chooses to advertise its products is called its **media mix**. Although different industries use different mixes, most depend on multiple media to advertise their products and services.

media mix The combination of media through which a company chooses to advertise its products.

Types of Advertising

Regardless of the media used, advertisements fall into one of several categories. **Brand advertising** promotes a specific brand, such as the Canon Rebel digital camera, Air Canada, or Nike Air Jordan basketball shoes. A variation on brand advertising, **product advertising** promotes a general type of product or service such as dental services and milk. The "Got Milk?" advertisements are an example of product advertising. **Advocacy advertising** promotes a particular candidate or viewpoint, as in ads for political candidates at election time and anti-drug commercials. **Institutional advertising** promotes a firm's long-term image rather than a specific product.

In consumer markets, local stores usually sponsor **retail advertising** to encourage consumers to visit the store and buy its products and services. Larger retailers, such as Kmart and the Bay, use retail advertising both locally and nationally. Often retail advertising is actually **co-operative advertising**, with the cost of the advertising shared by the retailer and the manufacturer.

In industrial markets, to communicate with companies that distribute its products, some firms use **trade advertising** publications. For example, a firm that makes plumbing fixtures might advertise in *Hardware Retailer* to persuade large hardware stores to carry its products. And to reach the

brand advertising Advertising that promotes a specific brand-name product.

product advertising A variation on brand advertising that promotes a general type of product or service.

advocacy advertising Advertising that promotes a particular viewpoint or candidate.

institutional advertising Advertising that promotes a firm's long-term image, not a specific product.

retail advertising Advertising by retailers designed to reach end-users of a consumer product.

co-operative advertising Advertising in which a manufacturer together with a retailer or a wholesaler advertise to reach customers.

trade advertising Advertising by manufacturers designed to reach potential wholesalers and retailers.

Once the master of mass marketing (especially the 30-second TV spot), Coca Cola has bowed to audience fragmentation and the advent of devices like TiVo, which allow people to skip TV ads altogether. Coke has begun experimenting with alternative approaches to promotion, focussing on events and activities that can be integrated into the daily routines of targeted consumers. In Europe, the company posts interactive websites built around music, and in the United States it has installed Coke Red Lounges in a few select malls, offering teenagers exclusive piped-in music, movies, and videos.

industrial advertising Advertising by manufacturers designed to reach other manufacturers' professional purchasing agents and managers of firms buying raw materials or components.

professional purchasing agent and managers at firms buying raw materials or components, companies use **industrial advertising**.

Preparing the Campaign with an Advertising Agency

advertising campaign The arrangement of ads in selected media to reach target audiences.

An **advertising campaign** is the arrangement of ads in selected media to reach target audiences. It includes several activities that, taken together, constitute a program for meeting a marketing objective, such as introducing a new product or changing a company's image in the public mind. A campaign typically includes six steps:

1. Identifying the target audience
2. Establishing the advertising budget
3. Defining the objectives of the advertising messages
4. Creating the advertising messages
5. Selecting the appropriate media
6. Evaluating advertising effectiveness

advertising agency A firm that specializes in creating and placing advertisements in the media for clients.

Advertising agencies—independent companies that provide some or all of their clients' advertising needs—help in the development of advertising campaigns by providing specialized services. The agency works together with the client company to determine the campaign's central message, create detailed message content, identify advertising media, and negotiate media purchases.[42] The Business Accountability box provides further information about the relationship between advertising agencies and the companies they do work for.

The advantage offered by agencies is expertise in developing advertising themes, message content, and artwork, as well as in coordinating advertising production and advising on relevant legal matters. As payment for its services, the agency usually receives a percentage, traditionally 15 percent of the media purchase cost. For example, if an agency purchases a $1 million television commitment for a client's campaign, it would receive $150 000 for its services.

The globalization of business has affected advertising agencies, both in Canada and elsewhere. Increasingly, large U.S. companies are using one sin-

MUSIC UP AND UNDER THROUGHOUT
BROOKS V/O: I learned from...

my father and my grandfather.

don't think about trying to buy

but concentrate on buying the best.

You work hard for your money.

You've got to put it where you know it's gonna do the best.

That have held their quality.

But for my money,

I would go out and buy a Stihl chainsaw.

A company hires an advertising agency to identify the target audience for its product and to ensure that the whole range of its advertising is aimed at that market. The agency is also responsible for planning the campaign and selecting the appropriate media. In this campaign for Stihl Power Tools, the Howard, Merrell & Partners advertising agency uses television as the best medium for putting the product in the most effective context. That context, in turn, is determined by the agency's understanding of the product and the crucial message that the company wants to get across. For Stihl, the message is the importance of buying the best possible equipment.

BUSINESS ACCOUNTABILITY

Who's Accountable for Results?

New frontiers in ad accountability are changing relationships among advertisers, ad agencies, and media outlets. Many companies, instead of conducting their own advertising programs, outsource to advertising agencies for media planning and strategy. Consider just one example, Masterfoods, a division of Mars Inc., and its ad account of U.S.$325 million with Starcom MediaVest Group, which is responsible for media buying and planning for Masterfoods brands such as Snickers, Uncle Ben's, and Whiskas. Extend this to thousands of companies, and the stakes become enormous in this mega-billion-dollar industry. But are clients getting results from ad agencies? That question reflects a new movement toward closer scrutiny of ad agencies by marketers who, themselves, are accountable for demonstrating bottom-line results in return for their firms' huge ad expenditures.

Under growing accountability for media effectiveness, clients are asking agencies more probing questions about ad programs and media buys: How are the media plans developed, who buys the current mix of media, and how well have they performed? Up to now, marketing managers at client firms have had little grounding in the technical details of media, so they're not at ease with practices that seem routine to advertising agency managers. "Generally, marketing executives don't come in with that kind of training and oftentimes they're intimidated by some of the terms and the more technical areas of media. For many of them it is a black box," explains Allan Linderman, president of the Linderman Media Group. To overcome this deficiency, two kinds of help are on the way: (1) Schools to teach media are being conducted by Association of National Advertisers along with the Center for Marketing Excellence, and (2) third-party intermediaries—ad agency auditors—are helping clients evaluate value received from ad campaigns and agencies.

Faced with growing accountability to perform, ad agencies are, in turn, imposing more accountability from media outlets. Local and national TV may no longer rely solely on Nielsen ratings as evidence for ad effectiveness; more convincing proof of performance would show how much they contribute to advertiser's sales. Newsprint, magazines, radio, and other media will be asked for more convincing evidence of effectiveness. While reliable proof-of-performance measures don't currently exist, research is underway to develop them. Media research is testing new models to measure the effects of media on consumer attention, persuasion and consumer thinking, and responsiveness in buying behaviour. Reliable measurements will allow agencies' media planners to compare bottom-line results from alternative media expenditures—newsprint, radio, magazines, local TV, national TV—and to pinpoint the best combination of media buys for the agency's client. They will also be evidence of success or failure in accountability-for-performance by media, agencies, and clients alike.

gle agency (often headquartered somewhere other than Canada). The Association of Quebec Advertising Agencies says that big U.S. companies often bypass Montreal-based advertising agencies when they are developing advertising campaigns for Quebec. The group says that it is pointless to try to simply translate into French a campaign that is developed by a New York or Toronto agency for the rest of Canada. As an example of the right way to do it, consider advertisements for Pepsi. In the rest of English-speaking North America, big name singers and movie stars were used to promote the product, but in Quebec, successful commercials featured popular local comedian Claude Meunier to make Pepsi the number one soft drink in the province.[43]

PERSONAL SELLING

6 Outline the tasks involved in *personal selling* and list the steps in the *personal selling process.*

Virtually everyone has done some personal selling. Perhaps as a child you had a lemonade stand or sold candy for the drama club. Or you may have gone on a job interview, selling your abilities as an employee to the interviewer's company. In personal selling, a salesperson communicates one-to-one with a potential customer to identify the customer's need and match that need with the seller's product.

personal selling Promotional tool in which a salesperson communicates one-on-one with potential customers.

Personal selling—the oldest form of selling—provides the personal link between seller and buyer. It adds to a firm's credibility because it provides buyers with someone to interact with and to answer their questions. Because it involves personal interaction, personal selling requires a level of trust between the buyer and the seller. When a buyer feels cheated by the seller, that trust has been broken and a negative attitude toward salespeople in general can develop.

Personal selling is the most expensive form of promotion per contact because presentations are generally made to one or two individuals at a time. Personal selling expenses include salespeople's compensation and their overhead, usually travel, food, and lodging. The average cost of an industrial sales call has been estimated at nearly $300.[44]

Costs have prompted many companies to turn to *telemarketing*: using telephone solicitations to conduct the personal selling process. Telemarketing is useful in handling any stage of this process and in arranging appointments for salespeople. For example, it cuts the cost of personal sales visits to industrial customers, each of whom requires about four visits to complete a sale. Such savings are stimulating the growth of telemarketing, which places billions of phone calls each year and is responsible for billions of dollars of sales in North America. It averages more than a $7 return for every dollar invested.[45]

Sales Force Management

sales force management Setting goals at top levels of an organization; setting practical objectives for salespeople; organizing a sales force to meet those objectives; implementing and evaluating the success of a sales plan.

Sales force management means setting goals at top levels of the organization, setting practical objectives for salespeople, organizing a sales force that can meet those objectives, and implementing and evaluating the success of the overall sales plan. Obviously, then, sales management is an important factor in meeting the marketing objectives of any large company. In this section, we first describe the basic types of *personal selling situations*. Then we discuss the *personal selling tasks* for which managers set objectives and the *personal selling process* whose success managers judge.

Personal Selling Situations

Managers of both telemarketers and traditional salespeople must consider the ways in which personal sales activities are affected by the differences between consumer and industrial products:

retail selling Selling a consumer product for the buyer's own personal or household use.

industrial selling Selling products to other businesses, either for manufacturing other products or for resale.

- **Retail selling** is selling a consumer product for the buyer's personal or household use.
- **Industrial selling** is selling products to other businesses, either for the purpose of manufacturing other products or for resale.

Levi's, for instance, sells jeans to the retail clothing chain Gap Inc. (industrial selling). In turn, consumers purchase Levi's jeans at one of The Gap's stores (retail selling). Each of these situations has distinct characteristics. In retail selling, the buyer usually comes to the seller, but in industrial selling, the salesperson comes to the buyer.

Personal Selling Tasks

Improving sales efficiency requires marketers to consider salespeople's tasks. Three basic tasks are generally associated with selling: *order processing*, *creative selling*, and *missionary selling*. Sales jobs usually require salespeople to perform all three tasks to some degree, depending on the product and the company.

Order Processing. At selling's most basic level, **order processing**, a salesperson receives an order and oversees the handling and delivery of that order. Route salespeople are often order processors. They call on regular customers to check the customer's supply of bread, milk, snack foods, or soft drinks. Then, with the customer's consent, they determine the size of the reorder, fill the order from their trucks, and stack the customer's shelves.

order processing In personal sales, the receiving and follow-through on handling and delivery of an order by a salesperson.

Creative Selling. When the benefits of a product are not clear, **creative selling** may persuade buyers. Most industrial products involve creative selling because the buyer has not used the product before or may not be familiar with the features and uses of a specific brand. Personal selling is also crucial for high-priced consumer products, such as homes, where buyers comparison shop. Any new product can benefit from creative selling that differentiates it from other products. Finally, creative selling can help to create a need.

creative selling In personal sales, the use of techniques designed to persuade a customer to buy a product when the benefits of the product are not readily apparent or the item is very expensive.

Missionary Selling. A company may also use **missionary selling** to promote itself and its products. Drug company representatives promote their companies' drugs to doctors who, in turn, prescribe them to their patients. The sale is actually made at the drugstore. In this case, the goal of missionary selling is to promote the company's long-term image rather than to make a quick sale.

missionary selling In personal sales, the indirect promotion of a product by offering technical assistance and/or promoting the company's image.

The Personal Selling Process

Although all three sales tasks are important to an organization using personal selling, perhaps the most complicated is creative selling. It is the creative salesperson who is responsible for most of the steps in the personal selling process described here.

Prospecting and Qualifying. To sell, a salesperson must first have a potential customer or *prospect*. **Prospecting** is the process of identifying potential customers. Salespeople find prospects through past company records, customers, friends, relatives, company personnel, and business associates. Prospects must then be **qualified** to determine whether they have the authority to buy and the ability to pay.

prospecting In personal sales, the process of identifying potential customers.

qualifying In personal sales, the process of determining whether potential customers have the authority to buy and the ability to pay for a product.

Approaching. The *approach* refers to the first few minutes that a salesperson has contact with a qualified prospect. The success of later stages depends on the prospect's first impression of the salesperson, since this impression affects the salesperson's credibility. Salespeople need to present a neat, professional appearance and to greet prospects in a strong, confident manner.

Presenting and Demonstrating. Next, the salesperson must *present* the promotional message to the prospect. A presentation is a full explanation of the product, its features, and its uses. It links the product's benefits to the prospect's needs. A presentation may or may not include a demonstration of the product. But it is wise to demonstrate a product whenever possible, since most people have trouble visualizing what they have been told.

Handling Objections. No matter what the product, prospects will have some *objections*. At the very least, prospects will object to a product's price, hoping to get a discount. Objections show the salesperson that the buyer is interested in the presentation and which parts of the presentation the buyer is unsure of or has a problem with. They tell the salesperson what customers feel is important and, essentially, how to sell to them.

closing In personal sales, the process of asking the customer to buy the product.

Closing. The most critical part of the selling process is the **closing**, in which the salesperson asks the prospective customer to buy the product. Successful salespeople recognize the signs that a customer is ready to buy. For example, prospects who start to figure out monthly payments for the product are clearly indicating that they are ready to buy. The salesperson should then attempt to close the sale. Salespeople can ask directly for the sale or they can indirectly imply a close. Questions such as "Could you take delivery Tuesday?" and "Why don't we start you off with an initial order of 10 cases?" are implied closes. Such indirect closes place the burden of rejecting the sale on the prospect, who will often find it hard to say no.

Following Up. The sales process does not end with the close of the sale. Most companies want customers to come back again. Sales *follow-up* activities include fast processing of the customer's order and on-time delivery. Training in the proper care and use of the product and speedy service if repairs are needed may also be part of the follow-up.

SALES PROMOTIONS

7 Describe the various types of *sales promotions,* and distinguish between *publicity* and *public relations.*

sales promotion Short-term promotional activities designed to stimulate consumer buying or co-operation from distributors and other members of the trade.

Sales promotions are short-term promotional activities designed to stimulate consumer buying or co-operation from distributors, sales agents, or other members of the trade. For example, soap may be bound into packages of four with the promotion, "Buy three and get one free." Sales promotions are important because they enhance product recognition and increase the likelihood that buyers will try products. To be successful, sales promotions must be convenient and accessible when the decision to purchase occurs.

Types of Sales Promotions

The best known sales promotions are coupons, point-of-purchase displays, purchasing incentives (such as free samples, trading stamps, and premiums), trade shows, and contests and sweepstakes.

Tom Giorgio sells tools and other industrial supplies for W.W. Grainger Inc. After 9/11, the business of his best clients started to slump, so Giorgio made some changes in his selling strategies. He used to spend 80 percent of his time with 20 percent of his customers—the ones who bought big-ticket items, such as hydraulic coolers and belt-driven generators. Now, his presentations feature more modest products from the Grainger catalogue, such as light fixtures and janitorial supplies, and he calls more often on the prospects that are likely to buy them.

- Certificates entitling the bearer to stated savings off a product's regular price are **coupons**. Coupons may be used to encourage customers to try new products, to attract customers away from competitors, or to induce current customers to buy more of a product. They appear in newspapers and magazines and are often sent through direct mail.

coupon A method of sales promotion featuring a certificate that entitles the bearer to stated savings off a product's regular price.

- To grab customers' attention as they walk through a store, some companies use **point-of-purchase (POP) displays**. Displays located at the end of the aisles or near the checkout in supermarkets are POP displays. POP displays often coincide with a sale on the item(s) being displayed. They make it easier for customers to find a product and easier for manufacturers to eliminate competitors from consideration. The cost of shelf and display space, however, is becoming more and more expensive.

point-of-purchase (POP) display A method of sales promotion in which a product display is so located in a retail store as to encourage consumers to buy the product.

- Free samples and premiums are *purchasing incentives*. *Free samples* allow customers to try a product for a few days without any risk. They may be given out at local retail outlets or sent by manufacturers to consumers via direct mail. **Premiums** are free or reduced-price items, such as pens, pencils, calendars, and coffee mugs, given to consumers in return for buying a specified product. For example, Molson Canadian includes a free T-shirt with certain packages of its beer.[46] Premiums may not work as well as originally hoped, since customers may switch to a competitor's brand just to get the premiums that company is offering and then return to their customary brand.

premium A method of sales promotion in which some item is offered free or at a bargain price to customers in return for buying a specified product.

- Periodically, industries sponsor **trade shows** for their members and customers. Trade shows allow companies to rent booths to display and demonstrate their products to customers who have a special interest in the products or who are ready to buy. Trade shows are relatively inexpensive and are very effective, since the buyer comes to the seller already interested in a given type of product. International trade shows are becoming more important.

trade shows A method of sales promotion in which members of a particular industry gather for displays and product demonstrations designed to sell products to customers.

- Customers, distributors, and sales representatives may all be persuaded to increase sales of a product through the use of *contests and sweepstakes*. For example, distributors and sales agents may win a trip to Hawaii for selling the most pillows in the month of February, or customers may win $1 million in a magazine sweepstake.

Best Buy, a 1900-store chain once known for consumer electronics and appliances, has added software and entertainment to its inventory and is now a major retailer of CDs and DVDs. To promote its entertainment products, Best Buy uses promotional tie-ins, such as deals to become the exclusive retailer of U2's latest DVD. In return, Best Buy spent $10 million to put U2 in newspaper circulars and on the sides of buses. Meanwhile, CEO Richard Schultze (right) pursues his strategy of putting electronics and entertainment under one roof.

PUBLICITY AND PUBLIC RELATIONS

publicity Information about a company that is made available to consumers by the news media; not controlled by the company, but it does not cost the company any money.

Much to the delight of marketing managers with tight budgets, **publicity** is free. Moreover, because it is presented in a news format, consumers see publicity as objective and highly believable. However, marketers often have little control over publicity, and that can have a very negative effect on the company. In 2003, for example, the New Delhi-based Center for Science and Environment published a report claiming that pesticide residues in Coke and Pepsi were 30 times the acceptable limits in Europe. The two companies jointly called a press conference to deny the allegations. In spite of that, sales of Coke and Pepsi dropped 30–40 percent in the weeks following publication of the report.[47]

public relations Public-service announcements by the company designed to enhance the company's image.

In contrast to publicity, **public relations** is company-influenced activity that attempts to establish a sense of goodwill between the company and its customers through public-service announcements that enhance the company's image. For example, a bank may announce that senior citizens' groups can have free use of a meeting room for their social activities. Corporate sponsorships of athletic events also help promote a company's image. In spite of doping and bribery scandals at the Olympic Games, big-name sponsors such as McDonald's, Coca-Cola, and UPS have continued to sponsor Olympic athletes.

INTERNATIONAL PROMOTION STRATEGIES

8 Describe the development of *international promotion strategies.*

As we saw in Chapter 5, recent decades have witnessed a profound shift from "home-country" marketing to "multi-country" marketing and now to "global" marketing. Nowhere is this rapidly growing global orientation more evident than in marketing promotions, especially advertising.

Emergence of the Global Perspective

global perspective Company's approach to directing its marketing toward worldwide rather than local or regional markets.

Every company that markets products in several countries faces a basic choice: use a *decentralized approach*, maintaining separate marketing management for each country, or adopt a *global perspective*, directing a coordinated marketing program at one worldwide audience. Thus, the **global perspective** is a philosophy that directs marketing toward a worldwide rather than toward local or regional markets.

The Movement Toward Global Advertising

A truly global perspective means designing products for multinational appeal—that is, genuinely global products.[48] A few brands, such as Coca-Cola, McDonald's, Mercedes Benz, Rolex, and Xerox, enjoy global recognition and have become truly global brands. Not surprisingly, globalization is affecting the promotional activities of such firms. In effect, they have already posed the question, "Is it possible to develop global advertising?"

Certainly, one universal advertising program would be more efficient and cost-effective than developing different programs for each of many countries. For several reasons, however, global advertising is not feasible for many companies. Four factors make global advertising a challenging proposition:

- *Product variations.* Even if a product has universal appeal, some variations, or slightly different products, are usually preferred in different cultures. In the magazine business, Hearst Corp. has expanded to 33 editions of *Cosmopolitan* magazine, including one for Central America; English and Spanish editions for the United States; and local editions for Italy, Turkey, Russia, Hong Kong, and Japan. *Reader's Digest* has 48 editions in 19 languages.

- *Language differences.* Compared with those in other languages, ads in English require less print space and airtime because English is a more efficient and precise language than most others. Moreover, translations are often inexact and confusing: When Coke first went to China, the direct translation of "Coca-Cola" came out "Bite the wax tadpole." Advertising agencies have set up worldwide agency networks that can coordinate a campaign's central theme while allowing regional variations.
- *Cultural receptiveness.* There is a lot of difference across nations regarding the mass advertising of sensitive products (such as birth control or personal hygiene products), not to mention those for which advertising may be legally restricted (alcohol, cigarettes). A Canadian in Paris may be surprised to see nudity in billboard ads and even more surprised to find that France is the only country in the European Union (EU) that bans advertising or selling wine on the internet. In the EU and through much of Asia, comparative advertising is considered distasteful or even illegal.
- *Image differences.* Any company's image can vary from nation to nation, regardless of any advertising appeals for universal recognition. American Express, IBM, and Nestlé have better images in the United States than in the United Kingdom, where Heinz, Coca-Cola, and Ford have better images.

Universal Messages and Regional Advertising Skills

Although universal advertising themes are cost-effective and promote brand awareness, major companies have found that without a local or national identity, universal ads don't cause consumers to buy. Coca-Cola's "think global, act local" strategy and Nestlé's approach to small-scale local advertising call for ads tailored to different areas. Such ads are designed to toy with variations on a universal theme while appealing to local emotions, ideas, and values.

PROMOTIONAL PRACTICES IN SMALL BUSINESS

From our discussion so far, you might think that only large companies can afford to promote their goods and services. Although small businesses generally have fewer resources, cost-effective promotions can improve sales and enable small firms to compete with much larger firms.

Small-Business Advertising

Has any other development in modern history provided more advertising opportunities than the internet? Cheaper access to computing equipment, to online services, and to website expertise puts cyberspace within the grasp of nearly every firm. Still, owners must decide which audiences to target and what messages to send. And even though the web can instantaneously reach distant customers, other methods depend on the market that the small business is trying to reach: local, national, or international.

Non-prime-time ads on local or cable TV have good impact at costs within the reach of many small firms. More often, however, they use newspaper, radio, and, increasingly, direct mail to reach local markets. For year-round advertising, the *Yellow Pages* are popular for both industrial and consumer products. However, many small businesses, especially those selling to consumer markets, rely more on seasonal advertising.

Many businesses have grown by using direct mail, particularly catalogues. By purchasing mailing lists from other companies, small firms can cut costs with targeted mailings. The ability to target an audience also makes specialized magazines attractive to small businesses. When it comes to international markets, television, radio, and newspapers are too expensive for small businesses. Most small firms find direct mail and carefully targeted magazine ads the most effective tools.

The Role of Personal Selling in Small Business

As with advertising, small-business personal-selling strategies depend on intended markets. Some small firms maintain sales forces, especially in local markets, where clients can be quickly visited. But most small companies cannot afford to establish international offices (though some entrepreneurs, such as Art de Fehr of Winnipeg-based Palliser Furniture, do visit prospective customers in other countries). For most small businesses, even sending sales representatives overseas is too expensive. Others contract with *sales agencies*—companies that act on behalf of several clients. Because the costs of a national sales force are high, small companies prefer sales agencies and such methods as telemarketing. By combining telemarketing with catalogues or other print media, small businesses can sometimes compete with larger companies on a national scale. Syncsort Inc. combined a telemarketing staff with eight national sales reps to become the number-one developer of computer software for sorting data into convenient formats. Number two is IBM.

Small-Business Promotions

Small companies use the same sales promotion incentives as larger companies. Large firms tend to rely on coupons, POP displays, and sales contests, but because these tools are expensive and difficult to manage, small firms prefer premiums and special sales.[49] An automobile dealership, for example, might offer you a fishing reel if you come in to road-test a new four-wheel-drive vehicle. Service companies ranging from martial arts centres to dry cleaners frequently feature special sale prices.

Summary of Learning Objectives

1. **Explain the definition of a product as a *value package*.** A *product* is a good, service, or idea that is marketed to fill consumer needs and wants. A successful product is a *value package* that provides the right features and offers the right benefits. *Features* are the qualities, tangible and intangible, that a company builds into its products.

   Consumer products are divided into three categories that reflect buyer behaviour: (1) *Convenience goods* and *convenience services* are inexpensive and purchased often and with little expenditure of time and effort. (2) *Shopping goods* and *shopping services* are more expensive; consumers often compare brands and evaluate alternatives. (3) *Specialty goods* and *specialty services* are important and expensive purchases; consumers usually decide on precisely what they want and accept no substitutes.

   Industrial products can be divided into two categories: (1) *Expense items* are goods and services consumed within a year by firms producing other goods or services. (2) *Capital items* are permanent (expensive and long-lasting) goods and services. Capital services are those for which long-term commitments are made.

   The group of products that a company makes available for sale, whether consumer, industrial, or both, is its *product mix*. A group of similar products intended for similar but not identical buyers who will use them in similar ways is a *product line*. When companies expand beyond existing product lines, the result is multiple (or diversified) product lines, which allow a company to grow rapidly and can help to offset the consequences of slow sales in any one product line.

2. **Describe the new *product development process* and trace the stages of the *product life cycle*.** To expand or diversify product lines, firms must develop and introduce new products. *Speed to market* is often key to a product's survival. To increase their chances of developing successful new products, many firms adopt some version of a basic seven-step process: (1) *Product ideas*: searching for ideas for new products. (2) *Screening*: eliminating all product ideas that do not mesh with the firm's abilities or objectives. (3) *Concept testing*: using market research to get consumers' input about product benefits and prices. (4) *Business analysis*: comparing manufacturing costs and benefits to see whether a product meets minimum profitability goals. (5) *Prototype development*: producing a preliminary version of a product. (6) *Product testing and test marketing*: going into limited production, testing the product to see if it meets performance requirements, and, if so, selling it on a limited basis. (7) *Commercialization*: beginning full-scale production and marketing.

   In the development of services, there are two important differences in the seven-step model (in Steps 1 and 5): (1) *Service ideas*: The search for service ideas means defining the service package: identifying the tangible and intangible features that characterize the service and stating service specifications. (5) *Service process design*: Instead of prototype development, services require a three-part service process design. Process selection identifies each step in the service, including the sequence and the timing, as well as worker requirements and facility requirements.

   The *product life cycle (PLC)* is a series of four stages or phases characterizing a product's profit-producing life: (1) *Introduction*: Marketers focus on making potential consumers aware of the product and its benefits. (2) *Growth*: Sales begin to climb and the product begins to show a profit. (3) *Maturity*: Although the product earns its highest profit level, increased competition eventually leads to price cutting and lower profits; sales start to fall. (4) *Decline*: Sales and profits are further lost to new products in the introduction stage.

   Foreign markets offer three approaches to longer life cycles: (1) In *product extension*, an existing product is marketed globally instead of just domestically. (2) With *product adaptation*, the basic product is modified to give it greater appeal in different countries. (3) *Reintroduction* means reviving for new markets products that are becoming obsolete in older ones.

3. **Explain the importance of *branding, packaging*, and *labelling*.** *Branding* is a process of using symbols to communicate the qualities of a particular product made by a particular producer. There are three types of brand names: (1) national brands, (2) licensed brands, and (3) private brand (or private label).

   With a few exceptions, a product needs some form of *packaging*—a physical container in which it is sold, advertised, or protected. A package makes the product attractive, displays the brand name, and identifies features and benefits. It also reduces the risk of damage, breakage, or spoilage, and it lessens the likelihood of theft. Every product has a *label* on its package that identifies its name, manufacturer, and contents; like packaging, labelling can help market a product.

4. **Identify the important objectives of *promotion* and discuss the considerations in selecting a *promotional mix*.** *Promotion* is any technique designed to sell a product. It is part of the *communication mix*: the total message any company sends to consumers about its products. Promotional techniques must communicate the uses, features, and benefits of products. There are two general values to be gained from any promotional activity: (1) *communicating information*, and (2) *creating satisfying exchanges.*

   Besides the ultimate objective of increasing sales, marketers may use promotion to accomplish any of the following four goals: (1) *communicating information*, (2) *positioning products*, (3) *adding value*, and (4) *controlling sales volume*.

   Once its larger marketing objectives are clear, a firm must develop a *promotional strategy* to achieve them. Two strategies are available: (1) A *pull strategy* appeals directly to consumers who will demand the product from retailers who, in turn, will demand it from wholesalers. (2) A *push strategy* aggressively markets a product to wholesalers and retailers who then persuade consumers to buy it. Many large firms use a combination of pull and push strategies.

   There are four types of *promotional tools*: advertising, personal selling, sales promotions, and publicity and public relations. The best combination of these tools—the best *promotional mix*—depends on several factors, the most important of which is the target audience and buyer decision process: Marketers try to match promotional tools with stages in the buyer decision process.

5. **Discuss the most important *advertising strategies* and describe the key *advertising media*.** Advertising is paid, non-personal communication used by an identified sponsor to inform an audience about a product. The advertising strategies used for a product most often depend on the stage of the product life cycle the product is in. As products become established and competition increases, advertisers may choose one of three strategies: (1) *persuasive*

advertising, (2) *comparative advertising*, and (3) *reminder advertising*.

Marketers use several different advertising media-specific communication devices for carrying a seller's message to potential customers: (1) *television*, (2) *newspapers*, (3) *direct mail*, (4) *radio*, (5) *magazines*, (6) *outdoor advertising*, (7) *internet advertising*, and (8) *virtual advertising*.

Other advertising channels include catalogues, sidewalk handouts, *Yellow Pages*, skywriting, telephone calls, special events, and door-to-door communication. The combination of media through which a company advertises is its media mix. Different industries use different mixes, and most depend on a variety of media rather than on just one to reach target audiences.

An *advertising campaign* is the arrangement of ads in selected media to reach target audiences. *Advertising agencies*—independent companies that provide some or all of a client's advertising needs—provide specialized services to help develop campaigns.

6. **Outline the tasks involved in *personal selling* and list the steps in the *personal selling process*.** In *personal selling*, a salesperson communicates one-on-one with potential customers to identify their needs and align them with a seller's products. It adds to a firm's credibility because it allows buyers to interact with and ask questions of the seller. Unfortunately, expenses are high, and high costs have turned many companies to *telemarketing*—the use of telephone solicitations to conduct the personal selling process.

   Sales force management means setting goals at the top levels of the organization, setting practical objectives for salespeople, organizing a sales force that can meet those objectives, and implementing and evaluating the success of the overall plan. Managers of both telemarketers and traditional salespeople must always consider the ways in which personal sales are affected by the differences between consumer and industrial products: (1) *Retail selling* promotes a consumer product for the buyer's own personal or household use. (2) *Industrial selling* promotes products to other businesses, either for the purpose of manufacturing other products or for resale.

   There are three basic tasks in personal selling: (1) *order processing*, (2) *creative selling*, and (3) *missionary selling*.

   The creative salesperson goes through most of the following six steps in the personal selling process. (1) *Prospecting and qualifying*: Prospecting identifies potential customers, who are then qualified to determine whether they have the authority to buy and ability to pay. (2) *Approaching*: The first few minutes of a contact with a qualified prospect make up the approach. (3) *Presenting and demonstrating*: After the approach, the salesperson makes a presentation. (4) *Handling objections*: Objections pinpoint the parts of the presentation with which the buyer has a problem and which the salesperson must overcome. (5) *Closing*: In the closing, the salesperson asks the prospective customer to buy the product. (6) *Following up*: To cement lasting relationships with buyers, sellers supply additional after-sale services.

7. **Describe the various types of *sales promotions*, and distinguish between *publicity* and *public relations*.** *Sales promotions* are short-term promotional activities designed to stimulate consumer buying or co-operation from members of the trade. The following are the best-known forms of promotions: (1) Certificates entitling bearers to savings off regular prices are *coupons*. (2) To grab customers' attention as they move through stores, companies use *point-of-purchase (POP) displays*. (3) *Free samples* are purchasing incentives that allow customers to try products without risk. (4) *Premiums* are gifts to consumers in return for buying certain products. (5) Industries sponsor *trade shows*, at which companies rent booths to display and demonstrate products to customers with a special interest in them. (6) Customers, distributors, and sales reps may all be persuaded to increase sales by means of *contests*.

   Publicity is a promotional tool in which information about a company or product is created and transmitted by general mass media. It is free, and because it is presented in a news format, consumers often see it as objective and credible. However, marketers often have little control over it, and it can be as easily detrimental as beneficial. *Public relations* is company-influenced publicity that seeks to build good relations with the public and to deal with unfavourable events.

8. **Describe the development of *international promotion strategies*.** Recent decades have witnessed a profound shift from home country marketing to global marketing. Every company that markets its products in several countries faces a basic choice: use a *decentralized approach*, with separate marketing management for each country or adopt a *global perspective*, directing marketing toward a worldwide rather than a local or regional market. There are four factors that determine whether global advertising is feasible: *product variations*, *language differences*, *cultural receptiveness*, and *image differences*. In recognizing national differences, many global marketers try to build on a universal advertising theme that nevertheless allows for variations. In doing so, they rely on help from different advertising agencies in various geographic regions.

KEY TERMS

advertising, 524
advertising agency, 530
advertising campaign, 530
advertising medium, 525
advocacy advertising, 529
brand advertising, 529
brand equity, 517
brand loyalty, 519
branding, 516
capital items, 510
closing, 534
comparative advertising, 525
Consumer Packaging and Labelling Act, 520
convenience goods/services, 509
co-operative advertising, 529
copyright, 520
coupon, 535
creative selling, 533
direct mail, 526
ecommerce, 527
expense items, 510
features, 508
global perspective, 536
industrial advertising, 530
industrial selling, 532
informative advertising, 525
institutional advertising, 529
internet marketing, 527
label, 520
licensed brands, 518
media mix, 529
missionary selling, 533
national brands, 518
order processing, 533
packaging, 520
patent, 519
personal selling, 532
persuasive advertising, 525
point-of-purchase (POP) display, 535
premium, 535
private brands, 519
product adaptation, 516
product advertising, 529
product extension, 516
product life cycle (PLC), 514
product line, 510
product mix, 510
product positioning, 522
promotion, 521
promotional mix, 523
prospecting, 533
public relations, 536
publicity, 536
pull strategy, 522
push strategy, 522
qualifying, 533
reintroduction, 516
reminder advertising, 525
retail advertising, 529
retail selling, 532
sales force management, 532
sales promotion, 534
service package, 514
service process design, 514
shopping goods/services, 509
specialty goods/services, 510
speed to market, 512
trade advertising, 529
trade shows, 535
trademark, 519
value package, 509
word of mouth, 527

QUESTIONS FOR ANALYSIS

1. What impact do the different levels of brand loyalty (recognition, preference, insistence) have on the consumer buying process that was described in Chapter 15?
2. Why would a business use a push strategy rather than a pull strategy?
3. Analyze several advertisements that use comparative advertising. Do these advertisements leave you with a positive or negative image of the company? Also, analyze differences in the comparative advertisements that are shown on U.S. and Canadian networks. Do these differences affect your opinion of the advertiser?
4. How would you expect the branding, packaging, and labelling of convenience, shopping, and specialty goods to differ? Why? Give examples to illustrate your answers.
5. Choose two advertising campaigns that have recently been conducted by business firms in your area. Choose one that you think is effective and one that you think is ineffective. What differences in the campaigns make one better than the other?
6. Select a good or service that you have purchased recently. Try to retrace the relevant steps in the buyer decision process as you experienced it. Which steps were most important to you? Which steps were least important?
7. Find examples of publicity about some business, either a local firm or a national firm. Did the publicity have, or is it likely to have, positive or negative consequences for the business? Why?

APPLICATION EXERCISES

1. Interview the manager of a local manufacturing firm. Identify the company's different products according to their positions in the product life cycle.
2. Select a product that is sold nationally. Identify as many media used in its promotion as you can. Which medium is used most often? On the whole, do you think the campaign is effective? What criteria did you use to make your judgment about effectiveness?
3. Interview the owner of a local small business. Identify the company's promotional objectives and strategies, and the elements in its promotional mix. What, if any, changes would you suggest? Why?
4. Check out your college or university's website and determine how effective it is as a tool for promoting your school.

BUILDING YOUR BUSINESS SKILLS

Greeting Start-Up Decisions

Goal

To encourage students to analyze the potential usefulness of two promotional methods—personal selling and direct mail—for a start-up greeting card company.

The Situation

You are the marketing adviser for a local start-up company that makes and sells specialty greeting cards in a city of 400 000. Last year's sales totalled 14 000 cards, including personalized holiday cards, birthday cards, and special-events cards for individuals. Although revenues increased last year, you see a way of further boosting sales by expanding into card shops, grocery stores, and gift shops. You see two alternatives for entering these outlets:

1. Use direct mail to reach more individual customers for specialty cards
2. Use personal selling to gain display space in retail stores

Your challenge is to convince the owner of the start-up company which alternative is the more financially sound decision.

Assignment

Step 1

Get together with four or five classmates to research the two kinds of product segments: *personalized cards* and *retail store cards*. Find out which of the two kinds of marketing promotions will be more effective for each of the two segments. What will be the reaction to each method from customers, retailers, and card company owners?

Step 2

Draft a proposal to the company owner. Leaving budget and production details to other staffers, list as many reasons as possible for adopting direct mail. Then list as many reasons as possible for adopting personal selling. Defend each reason. Consider the following reasons in your argument:

- *Competitive environment:* Analyze the impact of other card suppliers that offer personalized cards and cards for sale in retail stores.
- *Expectations of target markets:* Who buys personalized cards, and who buys ready-made cards from retail stores?
- *Overall cost of the promotional effort:* Which method—direct mail or personal selling—will be more costly?
- *Marketing effectiveness:* Which promotional method will result in greater consumer response?

Follow-Up Questions

1. Why do you think some buyers want personalized cards? Why do some consumers want ready-made cards from retail stores?
2. Today's computer operating systems provide easy access to software for designing and making cards on home PCs. How does the availability of this product affect your recommendation?
3. What was your most convincing argument for using direct mail? For using personal selling?
4. Can a start-up company compete in retail stores against industry giants such as Hallmark?

EXERCISING YOUR ETHICS

Cleaning Up in Sales

The Situation

Selling a product—whether a good or a service—requires the salesperson to believe in it, to be confident of his or her own sales skills, and to keep commitments made to clients. Because so many people and resources are involved in making and delivering a product, numerous uncertainties and problems arise that can raise ethical issues. This exercise encourages you to examine some of the ethical issues that can surface in the personal selling process for industrial products.

The Dilemma

Along with 16 other newly hired graduates, Ethel Skilsel has just completed the sales training program for a new line of high-tech machinery that ABC Technologies manufactures for industrial cleaners. As an aspiring salesperson, Ethel is eager to get on the road and meet potential clients, all of whom are professional buyers for companies—such as laundries and dry cleaners, carpet cleaners, and military cleaners—that use ABC products or those of ABC's competitors. Ethel is especially enthusiastic about several facts that she learned during training: ABC's equipment is the most technically advanced in the industry, carries a 10-year performance guarantee, and is safe—both functionally and environmentally.

The first month was difficult but successful: In visits to seven firms, Ethel successfully closed three sales, earning handsome commissions (her pay is based on sales results) as well as praise from her sales manager. Moreover, after listening to her presentations, two more potential buyers had given verbal commitments and were about to sign for much bigger orders than any Ethel had closed to date. But as she was catching her flight to close those sales, Ethel received two calls—one from a client and one from a competitor. The client was just getting started with ABC equipment and was having some trouble: Employees stationed nearby were getting sick when the equipment was running. The competitor told Ethel that he thought ABC's new technology was environmentally unsafe because of noxious emissions.

Questions for Discussion

1. As a sales professional, does Ethel have any ethical obligations to ABC Technologies?
2. From an ethical standpoint, what should Ethel say to the two client firms she is scheduled to visit? What would you say to those clients?
3. Are there any ethical issues involved when an employee of one company calls a competitor's employee, as in this case of an ABC competitor calling Ethel? Explain.

CONCLUDING CASE 16-1

Advertising: Not What It Used to Be

A long time ago (in the 1960s and 1970s), advertising was simple. Sellers of products paid for radio, TV, and newspaper advertisements to get the attention of prospective customers. Consumers basically put up with advertisements because they knew that advertisers were providing the content in return for their advertisements being shown. But consumers have never liked most advertisements, and when they are given an opportunity to avoid them, they'll take it. And that opportunity has increasingly been provided as consumers are given the tools to help them avoid advertisements.

In TV, the problem (from the advertisers perspective) is caused by VCRs and digital video recorders like TiVo. While primarily designed to allow consumers to tape TV shows when they had other commitments, consumers quickly discovered that they could fast forward through those annoying advertisements. This obviously defeated the purpose for which TV advertisements were produced. It is estimated that by 2010, almost half of all television programming will be watched this way, and that consumers will fast forward through 80 percent of the advertisements they might have otherwise seen.

In radio, the development of satellite radio poses another threat to advertisers. Earth-based radio stations beam their signal to orbiting satellites, which in turn beam the signal to a satellite radio company such as Sirius Satellite or XM Satellite. These companies then make the signal available to consumers who pay a monthly fee for the service. In 2005, the CRTC approved licences for Canadian companies to start providing ad-free satellite radio service. In addition to allowing listeners to avoid advertisements, satellite radio may threaten the competitive position of existing AM radio stations because the satellite radio companies are required to have only 10 percent Canadian content, while existing AM radio stations are required to have 35 percent Canadian content. Consumer interest in satellite radio has to date been much higher in the United States than in Canada; there were about eight million subscribers in the United States at the end of 2005, and the number is rapidly growing.

Advertisers are not sitting idly by as these trends unfold. Instead, they are using several new tactics to reach consumers. These include *stealth advertising*, *product placement*, *cellphone advertising*, and *interactive television advertising*.

Stealth Advertising

As the name implies, stealth advertising is designed to advertise a company's product without consumers knowing that they are the target of an actual advertisement. (For a description of stealth advertising, see p. 88 in Chapter 3).

Product Placement

In the area of television advertising, one of the newer tactics is something called "product placement," which involves using brand name products as part of the actual storyline of TV shows. For example, Home Depot has been able to embed its brand name into shows like *Trading Spaces*, *Survivor*, and *The Apprentice*. On one episode of *The Apprentice*, teams had to run a workshop inside a Home Depot store. The winning team developed a workshop to build a storage chest, and after that episode, Home Depot stores ran their own workshops on how to build the chests.

Many other companies are using product placement, including Bell Canada (on CBC's *Making the Cut*), Coke (on *American Idol*), and Buick (on *Desperate Housewives*).

Product placement is not limited to TV advertising; it can also be found in movies, novels, video games, pop songs, music videos, and Broadway plays. It is also rapidly increasing in importance. A PQ Media survey showed that from 2003 to 2004, product placement increased by 46 percent. The increased importance of product placement has influenced how companies spend their promotion dollars. In 2005, Procter & Gamble cut the amount of money it spent on traditional TV advertising and shifted some of that money into product placement. P&G's global marketing officer, Jim Stengel, says that companies must "embrace the consumer's point of view about TV and create advertising consumers choose to watch."

Product placement must be done carefully because it is a complex type of advertising. Pat Wilkinson, director of Marketing for Home Depot Canada, says that for every dollar the company spends on branded entertainment, it must spend an additional $3–$5 to make it deliver further results. And Michael Beckerman, the chief marketing officer for the Bank of Montreal, says that product placements must be "natural." He says that if a person is watching, say, *Desperate Housewives* and the characters started talking about BMO mutual funds, viewers would see it as a blatant advertisement, and it would not likely be effective.

The Canadian Radio-television and Telecommunications Commission (CRTC) is looking into product placement advertising because Canadian broadcasters cannot have more than 12 minutes of advertising per hour of programming. If there are more than 12 minutes of advertising, the show is classified as an infomercial, and is no longer considered Canadian content (and is not eligible for government funding incentives). For example, when Global TV's *Rona Dream Home* contained too much time featuring the sponsor, it was ruled non-Canadian content.

Cellphone Advertising

Capitalizing on new technology and the popularity of cellphones, Maiden Group PLC and Filter UK Ltd. have developed a system where transmitters detect cellphones that are equipped with Bluetooth, a short-range wireless technology, and then the transmitters beam out text messages to these cellphones. For example, passengers in the first-class lounge who were waiting to board a Virgin Atlantic Airways flight at London's Heathrow airport were asked if they would like to watch a video-clip about a new SUV on their phone. The transmitters are also installed in billboards in train stations in the United Kingdom. In one test, the transmitters discovered 87 000 Bluetooth-equipped phones at the railway station; of those, 13 000 people agreed to view the advertisement when asked. Cellphone advertising is important to advertisers because people are spending less time watching TV or reading newspapers.

Interactive Television Advertising

Another possibility for advertisers is something called interactive television advertising. It allows viewers of advertisements to opt for more information about products if they are interested. Consider this example: Sony Corp. produced a TV advertisement for the action movie "XXX: State of the Union" that included an icon that appeared on TV screens. The icon invited viewers to press a button on their remote to learn more about the movie. If they pushed the button, they got access to a 30-minute program that included 10 minutes of the actual movie as well as interviews with the stars. A unit of DaimlerChrysler has also developed an interactive ad that lets viewers go to a special screen where they can customize a car. And Mercedes ran an interactive ad in 2005 that generated 15 000 requests for more information. This far exceeded the advertiser's expectations.

The idea of giving consumers an opportunity to interact with advertisers is also evident on the internet. Procter & Gamble developed an online contest for its Crest Whitening Expressions brand where internet users voted for their favourite potential new flavour. Crest promised to make a product based on the winning flavour. Over 785 000 votes were recorded over a three-month period. To promote its Malibu Maxx vehicle, General Motors of Canada ran an online search for the Canadian couple with the greatest height difference. Contestants logged on to *LongandShort.gmcanada.com* and completed a survey.

Questions for Discussion

1. Consumers are taking advantage of ways to avoid seeing advertisements, but companies are also developing new techniques to increase the visibility of their products. What do you think will be the eventual outcome in this "contest"? Give examples to demonstrate your reasoning.
2. Will the emphasis on each of the four Ps of marketing (product, price, promotion, and place) change in importance as consumers get more opportunities to avoid viewing advertisements? Why or why not?
3. To what extent will the changes that are occurring in advertising affect the new product development process in companies?
4. Does the value of brand names increase or decrease when consumers are able to take advantage of ways to avoid seeing advertisements?

CONCLUDING CASE 16-2

The Nostalgia Merchant

Reuben Harley was 17 years old in 1991 when he bought his first throwback—a replica of an old sports jersey. Then, an Oprah Winfrey TV show about "following your dreams" inspired him to pursue selling, not just buying, vintage jerseys. Why did Reuben Harley think that throwbacks would catch on? Call it instinct, street smarts, observing the reactions of others, or whatever you will, he trusted his personal tastes. While making a living doing odd jobs, he saved enough money to buy classic jerseys of legendary players such as Julius Irving, Nolan Ryan, and Jackie Robinson. Harley soon decided that there were profit opportunities in old sports jerseys, and he eventually teamed up with Peter Capolino, the owner of Mitchell & Ness Nostalgia Company (M&N). Harley first offered to help Capolino sell 1950s baseball jerseys to inner-city youths. In just two years' time they changed M&N into the best-known marketer of clothing for urban teen African Americans.

The potential market as seen by Harley was worlds apart from Capolino's vision for M&N. Harley envisioned an urban, largely African-American youth segment that idolizes basketball players with baggy shorts and brightly coloured jerseys with striking patterns in double-knits and mesh. Capolino, in contrast, was aiming for middle-aged collectors of sports items, mostly from its retro-baseball line with body hugging gray flannels. At an age in life when established businesspeople might take a safer path, Capolino made a gutsy call in deciding to go along with Harley. "It's an all-sport thing, but guys identify with basketball players more than anybody," says Harley. Now basketball, instead of baseball, accounts for the largest share of M&N's business.

Harley started by focussing on celebrities—rappers and pro athletes—who could afford the $250 to $470 price tag for these intricately stitched designs with authentic team colours. He began meeting them by going uninvited to their parties in New York and Philadelphia nightclubs, soon becoming a trusted acquaintance with his charming and unassuming personality. When shown samples of M&N's jerseys, hip-hop great Sean (P. Diddy) Combs immediately bought them, as did rapper Fabulous, whose album *Street Dreams* contains a track named "Throwback," dedicated to M&N. Building on these initial successes, Harley—now M&N's new marketing director—targeted major music and sporting events, along with the celebrity consumers performing at them. During the NBA All-Star weekend, for example, Rap star Eve wore an oversized Michael Jordon Chicago Bulls Jersey. Indiana Pacers basketball star Jermaine O'Neal, who owns 150 throwbacks, says, "Acquiring the hottest model is a competitive sport among teammates." The jerseys are so popular you'll find entertainment stars wearing them most any day in action movies and on MTV.

Because it holds exclusive licences from the NFL, Major League Baseball, the National Basketball Association, and the National Hockey League, M&N can reproduce authentic jerseys that have been out of circulation for at least five years. The fabric, the stitching, and the lettering are all accurate duplicates of the originals the players wore years ago. Therein, according to Reuben, lies the staying power of M&N's throwbacks: "This isn't a fad. These uniforms are the history of sports. Styles come and go, but you can't change the '79 Magic Johnson jersey." That's why they captured an enthusiastic audience, even at such hefty prices as $325 for a 1979 Willie Stargell Pirates, $450 for the 1963 Lance Alworth Chargers, $300 for the 1983–84 Sidney Moncrief Bucks, and $250 for the 1966–67 Dave Bing Pistons.

Today, Harley is vice president of marketing with a lofty salary, lots of size XXXXL jerseys, and duties that include everything from hitting the road as travelling salesman to serving as M&N's public face to clothes designers. With many of his clients, the conversations aren't just about the latest in jerseys but also personal matters and plain talk. And he takes time to be there to help. Backstage when P. Diddy hosted ABC's American Music Awards, Reuben took charge of the star's costume changes during commercial breaks, with 11 different jerseys worn throughout the performance, including a '73 George McGinnis Pacers and a '74 Hank Aaron Braves. "Shaq called the next day; he wanted every piece that Puff wore," says Harley. The success in his personal approach to marketing is aided by encouragement from the clients he serves. In his album *Street Dreams*, Fabulous yells out a message to the duo at M&N: "Rube, tell Pete to keep it comin'."

Questions for Discussion

1. Which promotional tools are most prominent in Harley's marketing strategy for M&N's products?
2. In what ways do you believe M&N's earlier promotional strategy differs from its current promotional strategy?
3. What kinds of advertising promotions, if any, are being used for the M&N marketing strategy? Would you advise using a different mix of advertising?
4. What kind of promotional mix(es) would you recommend as most effective for reaching M&N's target market(s)?
5. Why is personal selling so effective for M&N? What factors have led to its effectiveness?
6. Assume that M&N is thinking about expanding into Canada. What do you think are the most important factors it should consider?

CHAPTER 17

Pricing and Distributing Goods and Services

After reading this chapter, you should be able to:

1. Identify the various *pricing objectives* that govern pricing decisions and describe the price-setting tools used in making these decisions.
2. Discuss *pricing strategies* and tactics for existing and new products.
3. Explain the distribution mix, the different *channels of distribution*, and different *distribution strategies*.
4. Explain the differences between *merchant wholesalers* and *agents/brokers*, and describe the activities of e-intermediaries.
5. Identify the different types of *retailing* and *retail stores*.
6. Define *physical distribution* and describe the major activities in *warehousing* operations.
7. Compare the five basic forms of *transportation* and explain how distribution can be used as a marketing strategy.

The Importance of Price

There has always been a tension between sellers of goods and the customers who buy them. The seller naturally wants to get the highest price possible, and the buyer, just as naturally, wants to get the lowest price possible. In the last few years, the tension between buyers and sellers over price has reached a new intensity in several different areas, including retailing, online auctions, beer, automobiles, and cigarettes.

THE RETAILING INDUSTRY

The most obvious example of consumer pressure for low prices is the success of Wal-Mart. But there are many other examples of how consumers have become obsessed with paying the least amount possible for goods and services. Consider the recent success of so-called dollar stores—retailers that offer ultra-cheap prices on a limited selection of goods. These include stores like The Silver Dollar, Dollarama, and Buck or Two. Sales revenues for this type of retail outlet have doubled in the last five years, and the number of stores has tripled. While dollar stores originally targeted low income shoppers, they now are appealing to buyers at all income levels, and they are gaining the attention of companies that once ignored them. Procter & Gamble, for example, created a special version of Dawn dish soap that sells for $1, and Kraft Foods sells boxes of macaroni and cheese in dollar stores. All of this activity is driven by consumers who demand low prices. As one customer said, "Why should I pay $4 for a greeting card when I can get one at a dollar store for $1?"

THE ONLINE AUCTION INDUSTRY

In 2005, eBay announced that it was increasing the fees it charges those who sell their goods online. For goods advertised at $25 or less, eBay formerly charged 5.25 percent of the closing price. That rate has now increased to 8 percent of the closing price. When eBay announced this increase, thousands of users threatened to stop using eBay's service. Trisha Dixon is typical. She had been selling scrapbooks, children's clothes, and health products on eBay for six years to make a little extra money. But when eBay announced its price increases, Dixon estimated that her monthly eBay bill would increase from $750 to $1500. Like Dixon, many eBay sellers operate small businesses from their homes, and they say they cannot afford to pay higher monthly fees and still make their business work. But eBay is popular with many different kinds of sellers, and its dollar volume of goods sold continues to rapidly increase, so these complaints may not have much effect on eBay's business. Small business owners who are unhappy with the price increases may have no alternative but to go to some less well-known online auction service like iOffer.com or Wagglepop.com to sell their goods.

THE BEER INDUSTRY

Price wars have long been common in the Canadian beer market, but in recent years competition from wineries, liquor manufacturers, discount beers, and imported beers has made it difficult to raise prices. In 2004, when Sleeman Breweries Ltd., Canada's third-largest brewer, tried to increase the price of its beer to $42 a case, it quickly found that consumers wouldn't accept the increase because they had cheaper alternatives. Shortly thereafter, it dropped the price to $36 per case. Sleeman and the two largest brewers—Molson and Labatt—have found the discount brewers hard to ignore. For example, Hamilton-based Lakeport Brewing Corp. began selling its Honey Lager brew for $1 a bottle in 2003. Since then, its share of the Ontario at-home market has risen from 1.8 percent to nearly 10 percent. Waterloo-based Brick Brewing Co. more than doubled its volume by pricing significantly lower than either Molson Canadian or Labatt Blue. The title of an article that appeared in the *Globe and Mail* nicely summed up the price dilemma facing beer makers. It read: "In Hamilton, they like beer cold... and cheap." Discount beer is taking market share away from long-time industry leaders like Labatt and Molson.

THE AUTOMOBILE INDUSTRY

While the absolute price that a company charges for its products is important, it's not the only issue causing tension between buyers and sellers. The pricing *system* can also raise the ire of consumers. It used to be the case when you purchased a new car that you got involved in much haggling with the salesperson over the price you would pay. Some consumers liked the give-and-take, but most of them didn't. So, in 2000, Toyota introduced what seemed like a consumer-friendly idea: a "no-haggle" policy (one-price) policy. But in 2004 Toyota announced that it was terminating the program. It is not exactly clear why Toyota decided to drop the idea (it may have been that their dealers had become less aggressive in the marketplace, or because lawsuits challenging the legality of the program were filed against the company in Quebec and British Columbia, or because the Competition Bureau had looked into allegations that the pricing system amounted to price fixing). One study by CarCost Canada found that buyers who purchased a Toyota Sequoia under the one-price system in British Columbia paid an average of $63 171, while buyers in Ontario (where the one-price policy was not in effect) paid only $57 881. Evidence like this does not make consumers happy.

THE CIGARETTE INDUSTRY

For many years, the North American cigarette market has been an oligopoly that is dominated by a few very large tobacco companies like Imperial Tobacco, R.J. Reynolds, Philip Morris, Brown & Williamson, and Lorillard Tobacco. The pricing strategy that has historically been used by these companies is to increase prices to maintain (or increase) profits. This strategy worked for decades because customers were very loyal to their favourite brand. But the cigarette business has become much more difficult for the major cigarette companies in the last few years—they must put explicit warnings on their products indicating that cigarettes are dangerous, cigarettes are highly taxed by the government, and class action lawsuits have resulted in some billion-dollar judgments against the major companies. To make matters worse, some new cigarette manufacturing companies have started up and are pricing their cigarettes as much as 50 percent lower than the majors. The majors are responding with incentives like 2-for-1 deals, but that has reduced their profits by 50 percent or more. The major cigarette companies are likely to have less control over the market than they used to, and they are going to have much more difficulty simply raising prices in the future.

Companies are well aware that raising prices can cause customers to be unhappy, so they may try to raise prices without *appearing* to have done so. Consider these examples:

- Kimberly-Clark Corp. cut the price of its diapers, but cut the quantity in the package even more (this was, in effect, a 5 percent price increase).
- General Motors started charging extra for antilock brakes instead of including them at no charge as it used to do (this also constituted a price increase).
- Goodyear Tire & Rubber Co. tire distributors had routinely been given big discounts on the tires they purchased. But the company discovered that the discounts were so deep that the distributors were ordering large quantities of tires and selling them outside their normal business area. This reduced the sales of smaller distributors in other areas that Goodyear also sold tires to, and had the overall effect of reducing the price of Goodyear tires in the marketplace. In 2003, Goodyear reduced the discounts it had been giving to its biggest distributors, and found that revenue per tire went up. ◆

In this chapter, we continue with our analysis of the four Ps of marketing by looking at first at "price" and then at "place" (channels of distribution). As the Opening Case shows, the price element of the marketing mix has become intensely competitive during the last few years. It is an important element of the marketing mix because it influences both consumer demand for a product and company profitability. Consumers want products that satisfy their needs, and they want them to be available in the right places, but they also look aggressively for the lowest prices possible.

1 Identify the various *pricing objectives* that govern pricing decisions and describe the price-setting tools used in making these decisions.

PRICING OBJECTIVES AND TOOLS

pricing Deciding what the company will receive in exchange for its product.

In **pricing**, managers decide what the company will receive in exchange for its products. In this section, we first discuss the objectives that influence a firm's pricing decisions. Then we describe the major tools that companies use to meet those objectives.

Pricing to Meet Business Objectives

Companies often price products to maximize profits, but they also hope to attain other **pricing objectives** when selling their products. Some firms want to dominate the market or secure high market share. Pricing decisions are also influenced by the need to survive in the marketplace, by social and ethical concerns, and even by corporate image.

pricing objectives Goals that producers hope to attain in pricing products for sale.

Profit-Maximizing Objectives

Pricing to maximize profits is tricky. If prices are set too low, the company will probably sell many units of its product, but it may miss the opportunity to make additional profit on each unit—and may in fact lose money on each exchange. Conversely, if prices are set too high, the company will make a large profit on each item but will sell fewer units, resulting in excess inventory and a need to reduce production operations. Again, the firm loses money. To avoid these problems, companies try to set prices to sell the number of units that will generate the highest possible total profits.

Companies often try out new pricing systems as they try to increase profits. Coca-Cola tested a vending machine that automatically raised the price of a Coke as the temperature climbed; it also tried setting prices at different vending machines at different levels, depending on how many customers used the machine.[1] In professional baseball, the New York Mets charged fans twice as much for tickets when they were playing their cross-town rivals the New York Yankees, and when home run king Barry Bonds played with the visiting San Francisco Giants. The Ottawa Senators increased prices 20 percent for games against the Toronto Maple Leafs and the champion Detroit Red Wings.[2]

In calculating profits, managers weigh receipts against costs for materials and labour to create the product. But they also consider the capital resources (plant and equipment) that the company must tie up to generate that level of profit. The costs of marketing (such as maintaining a large sales staff) can also be substantial. Concern over the efficient use of these resources has led many firms to set prices so as to achieve a targeted level of return on sales or capital investment.[3]

"O.K., who *can* put a price on love? Jim?"

Pricing for Ebusiness Objectives. Marketers pricing for sales on the internet must consider different kinds of costs and different forms of consumer awareness than those pricing products to be sold conventionally. Many ebusinesses are lowering both costs and prices because of the internet's unique marketing capabilities. Because the web, for example, typically provides a more direct link between producer and ultimate consumer, buyers avoid the costs entailed by wholesalers and retailers.

Another factor in lower internet prices is the ease of comparison shopping. Obviously, point-and-click shopping is much more efficient than driving from store to store in search of the best price. In addition, both consumers and businesses can force lower prices by joining together in the interest of greater purchasing power. Numerous small businesses, for instance, are joining forces on the internet to negotiate lower prices for employee health care.

Market Share Objectives

market share A company's percentage of the total market sales for a specific product.

In the long run, a business must make a profit to survive. Nevertheless, many companies initially set low prices for new products. They are willing to accept minimal profits—even losses—to get buyers to try products. In other words, they use pricing to establish **market share**: a company's percentage of the total market sales for a specific product. Even with established products, market share may outweigh profits as a pricing objective. For a product like Philadelphia Brand Cream Cheese, dominating a market means that consumers are more likely to buy it because they are familiar with a well-known, highly visible product.

Other Pricing Objectives

In some instances, neither profit maximizing nor market share is the best objective. During difficult economic times, for instance, loss containment and survival may become a company's main objectives. In 2003, Universal cut the price it charged for CDs by one-third as a response to consumer complaints about high CD prices, and competition from illegal downloading services.[4]

Price-Setting Tools

Whatever a company's objectives, managers must measure the potential impact before deciding on final prices. Two basic tools are often used for this purpose: *cost-oriented pricing* and *break-even analysis*. As a rule, these tools are combined to identify prices that will allow the company to reach its objectives.

Cost-Oriented Pricing

Cost-oriented pricing considers the firm's desire to make a profit and takes into account the need to cover production costs. A music store manager, for instance, would price CDs by calculating the cost of making them available to shoppers. Included in this figure would be store rent, employee wages, utilities, product displays, insurance, and, of course, the cost of buying CDs from the manufacturer.

Let's assume that the cost from the manufacturer is $8 per CD. If the store sells CDs for this price, it will not make any profit. Nor will it make a profit if it sells CDs for $8.50 each or even for $10 or $11. The manager must account for product and other costs and set a figure for profit. Together, these figures constitute markup. In this case, a reasonable markup of $7 over costs would result in a $15 selling price. Markup is usually stated as a percentage of selling price. Markup percentage is thus calculated as follows:

$$\text{Markup percentage} = \frac{\text{Markup}}{\text{Sales price}}$$

In the case of our CD retailer, the markup percentage is 46.7:

$$\text{Markup percentage} = \frac{\$7}{\$15} = 46.7\%$$

In other words, out of every dollar taken in, 46.7 cents will be gross profit for the store. From this profit the store must still pay rent, utilities, insurance, and all other costs. Markup can also be expressed as a percentage of cost: The $7 markup is 87.5 percent of the $8 cost of a CD ($7 ÷ $8).

In some industries, cost-oriented pricing doesn't seem to work. When you go to a first-run movie theatre, for example, you pay the same price for each film you see. But it may cost as little as $2 million or as much as $200 million to make a film. Shouldn't the admission price be based on how much the film cost to make? After all, you pay a lot more for a Lincoln Continental than you do for a Ford because the Lincoln costs more to make. Shouldn't the same pricing system apply to Hollywood? Apparently not. Market-based pricing is at work here (i.e., consumers are simply not willing to pay more than a certain amount to see a movie).

Break-even Analysis: Cost-Volume-Profit Relationships

Using cost-oriented pricing, a firm will cover its **variable costs**—costs that change with the number of goods or services produced or sold. It will also make some money toward paying its **fixed costs**—costs that are unaffected by the number of goods or services produced or sold. But how many units must the company sell before all of its fixed costs are covered and it begins to make a profit? To determine this figure, it needs a **break-even analysis**.[5]

To continue our music store example, suppose again that the variable cost for each CD (in this case, the cost of buying the CD from the producer)

variable costs Those costs that change with the number of goods or services produced or sold.

fixed costs Those costs unaffected by the number of goods or services produced or sold.

break-even analysis An assessment of how many units must be sold at a given price before the company begins to make a profit.

Some homeowners have the opportunity to take out fixed-price fuel oil contracts to lock in the heating oil prices they'll pay during the winter. In some years, it's a good bet. If a homeowner locks in at $1.15 per gallon and prices go up to $1.80 per gallon, the homeowner obviously benefits. But if prices decline to $0.85 per gallon, the homeowner loses. "It's like buying insurance," says one analyst. "When you buy a fixed-price deal, you're saying you want the peace of mind."

is \$8. This means that the store's annual variable costs depend on how many CDs are sold—the number of CDs sold multiplied by \$8 cost per CD. Say that fixed costs for keeping the store open for one year are \$100 000. These costs are unaffected by the number of CDs sold; costs for lighting, rent, insurance, and salaries are steady however many CDs the store sells. Therefore, how many CDs must be sold to cover both fixed and variable costs and to start to generate some profit? The answer is the **break-even point**, which is 14 286 CDs. We arrive at this number through the following equation:

break-even point The number of units that must be sold at a given price before the company covers all of its variable and fixed costs.

$$\text{Break-even point (in units)} = \frac{\text{Total fixed costs}}{\text{Price} - \text{Variable cost}}$$

$$= \frac{\$100\ 000}{\$15 - \$8} = 14\ 286 \text{ CDs}$$

Figure 17.1 shows the break-even point graphically. If the store sells fewer than 14 286 CDs, it loses money for the year. If sales exceed 14 286 CDs, profits grow by \$7 for each CD sold. If the store sells exactly 14 286 CDs, it will cover all of its costs but will earn zero profit. Zero profitability at the break-even point can also be seen by using the following profit equation:

$$\text{Profit} = \text{total revenue} - (\text{total fixed costs} + \text{total variable costs})$$

$$= (14\ 286 \text{ CDs} \times \$15) - (\$100\ 000 \text{ fixed costs} + [14\ 286 \text{ CDs} \times \$8 \text{ variable costs}]$$

$$\$0 = (214\ 290) - (\$100\ 000 + 114\ 288) \text{ (rounded to the nearest whole CD)}$$

The music store owner would certainly like to hit the break-even quantity as early as possible so that profits will start rolling in. Why not charge \$20 per CD and reach the break-even point earlier? The answer lies in the downward-sloping demand curve we discussed in Chapter 1. At a price of \$20 per CD, sales at the store would drop. In setting a price, the manager must consider how much CD buyers will pay and what the store's local competitors charge.

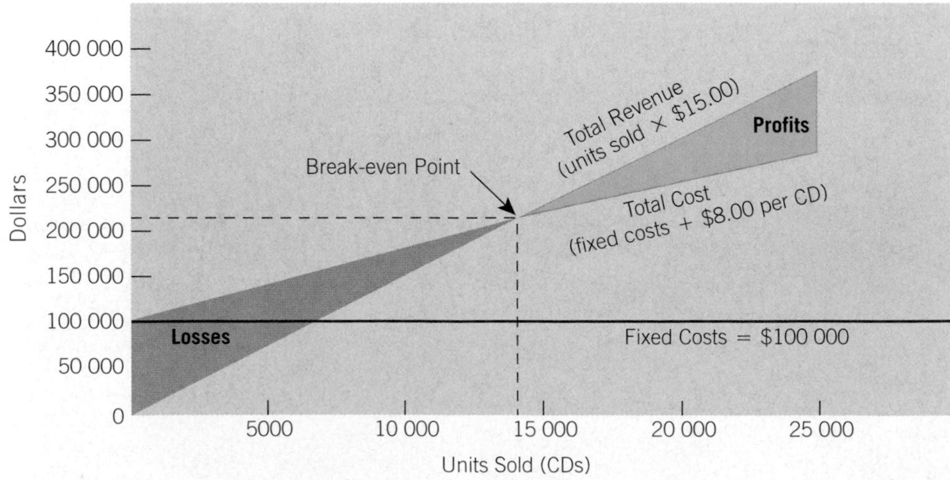

Figure 17.1 Break-even analysis.

PRICING STRATEGIES AND TACTICS

Discuss *pricing strategies* and tactics for existing and new products. 2

The pricing tools discussed in the previous section provide a valuable guide for managers trying to set prices on specific goods. But they do not provide general direction for managers trying to decide on a pricing philosophy for their company. In this section, we discuss *pricing strategy*—that is, pricing as a planning activity that affects the marketing mix. We then describe some basic *pricing tactics*—ways in which managers implement a firm's pricing strategies.

Pricing Strategies

Let's begin this section by asking two questions. First: Can a manager really identify a single "best" price for a product? The answer is: probably not. For example, a study of prices for popular non-aspirin pain relievers (such as Tylenol and Advil) found variations of 100 percent.[6] In this market, in other words, some products sold for *twice* the price of other products with similar properties. Such differences may reflect some differences in product costs, but the issue is more complex than that. Such wide price differences reflect differing brand images that attract different types of customers. In turn, these images reflect vastly different pricing philosophies and strategies.

Our second question is this: Just how important is pricing as an element in the marketing mix? As we have already seen, it is a mistake to try to isolate any element in the marketing mix from the others. Nevertheless, because pricing has a direct and visible impact on revenues, it is extremely important to overall marketing plans. It is also critical in the minds of most consumers. The Business Accountability box illustrates the importance of pricing as an important element in the marketing mix.

Pricing Existing Products

A firm can sets prices for its products *above* prevailing market prices for similar products, *below* the prevailing price, or *at* the prevailing price. Companies pricing above the market play on customers' beliefs that higher price means higher quality. Curtis Mathes, a maker of televisions, VCRs, and stereos, promotes itself as the most expensive television set, "but worth it." Companies such as Godiva chocolates and Rolls-Royce have also succeeded with this pricing philosophy. In contrast, both Budget and Dollar car rental companies promote themselves as low-priced alternatives to Hertz and Avis. Pricing below the prevailing market price can succeed if the firm can offer a product of acceptable quality while keeping costs below those of higher-priced options.

In some industries, a dominant firm establishes product prices and other companies follow along. This is called **price leadership**. (Don't confuse this approach with *price fixing*, the illegal process of producers agreeing among themselves what prices will be charged.) Price leadership is often evident in products such as structural steel, gasoline, and many processed foods because these products differ little in quality from one firm to another. Companies compete through advertising campaigns, personal selling, and service, not price.

price leadership The dominant firm in the industry establishes product prices and other companies follow suit.

Pricing New Products

Companies introducing new products into the market have to consider two contrasting pricing policy options: coming in with either a very high price or a very low one. **Price skimming**—setting an initially high price to

price-skimming strategy The decision to price a new product as high as possible to earn the maximum profit on each unit sold.

BUSINESS ACCOUNTABILITY

Pricing in the Airline Industry: The Sky Is No Longer the Limit

For the last 40 years, major airlines like Air Canada and United Airlines dominated the industry. Their business model involved providing many frills such as in-flight meals, movies, special business class seats with more legroom, and a fare structure that featured relatively low-priced "restricted" tickets (that included a penalty if customers wanted to change their schedule at the last minute) and high-priced "unrestricted" tickets (which allowed last minute changes with no penalty). They also used a "hub-and-spoke" systems that funnelled travellers in from various regional areas to major centres. From there they transferred to other, longer-haul destinations that were more lucrative for the airlines. This was an expensive system, because the airlines had to lease many airport gates to accommodate all the transferring passengers.

In the 1990s, several airlines (including Southwest Airlines in the United States and WestJet in Canada) introduced a far different business model which involved abandoning the hub-and-spoke system, selling all tickets at bargain prices (many of them on the internet), offering good customer service (but no meals), flying mostly short-haul trips between carefully chosen markets, using newer planes (which require far less maintenance), and using non-union workers. This new business model caught on so quickly that within a few years the major airlines were in big financial trouble. Several of them (including Air Canada, United Airlines, US Airways, Delta, and Northwest Airlines) declared bankruptcy and were forced to do a major overhaul of the way they did business. This included laying off thousands of employees. In essence, discount airlines like WestJet, Southwest, JetBlue, and others were clearly doing a better job of giving customers what they wanted, namely low-priced air travel. The discount airlines essentially "Wal-Marted" the airline business.

Just a few years ago, the pricing system used by the major airlines meant that a business traveller flying from Toronto to Vancouver might pay five to ten times what a leisure traveller in the next seat was paying. This is very much less likely now because of the impact of the discount airlines. A study by Sabre Holdings Corp. revealed that in 2001, 15 percent of the passengers on a New York to Los Angeles flight paid over $2000 for a round-trip ticket; in 2004, only 3 percent paid that much. In 2001, only 28 percent of passengers paid between $200 and $400; in 2004, 55 percent paid that amount.

It is now widely recognized that the major airlines have a major problem: Their costs exceed their revenues, and they can't cut costs or raise fares enough to make a profit. In terms of *cost-cutting*, the airlines' unionized workers naturally resist wage and benefit cuts. The battle between Air Canada and its union as the company tried to emerge from bankruptcy is just one example of this problem (see Concluding Case 9-1 for more details). One study showed that major airlines spend U.S.$4.53 on labour costs per seat for each mile flown, while the discount airlines, with their non-unionized workforces, spend only U.S.$2.42. In terms of *raising fares*, competition is so fierce that this is generally not possible. Airline tickets have increased in price only 4 percent over the last decade, while prices of other products and services have increased by 27 percent.

In the 1980s, airlines developed so-called "yield-management systems" which were designed to get the most revenue out of each flight. The system was built on many complex assumptions about which travellers would be willing to pay which amounts for seats. But with the advent of discount airlines, the assumptions underlying the yield management systems are no longer accurate. Pricing assumptions are now much simpler: Everyone (both business and leisure travellers) wants low-priced seats. That fact, coupled with the oversupply of airline seats and the ability of customers to do price comparisons on the internet before buying a ticket, has driven down the prices that airlines can charge.

The move to low fares for all flyers is now putting pressure on all airlines, including the discounters. Initially, Southwest Airlines was the most successful of the discount airlines. Its emphasis on reliability and customer service, combined with a dedication to cost control and a corporate culture that attracts only the best employees, allowed Southwest to remain virtually unchallenged. Then along came Blue—JetBlue. Since its founding in 1999, it has become one of the most profitable start-up carriers in the United States, and it has done so in large part by applying many of the ideas introduced by Southwest.

CEO David Neeleman's creativity as a manager and marketer is a major factor in JetBlue's success. He originally worked at Southwest, but after he was fired, he decided to form a rival airline that would beat his former employer at its own game. He copied elements of Southwest's discount strategy, such as point-to-point scheduling, reliance on a single type of aircraft, and use of non-union employees. Then he added some extras of his own: reserved seats, upscale snacks, leather chairs, and seat-back televisions with 24 channels of DirecTV. Relying on his extensive industry experience (including a stint at WestJet), Neeleman focussed most of his energy on a few key factors that he felt would make or break his company. By hiring younger workers and giving them stock options in lieu of high wages, JetBlue kept labour expenses down to 25 percent of revenues (compared to Southwest's 33 percent and Delta's 44 percent). JetBlue fills planes to capacity, gets more flying hours out of each aircraft, and saves on maintenance costs because its fleet is brand new. Even the luxurious leather seats are cost-effective because they're easier to clean. Neeleman regards on-time arrival as a critical element in customer service, and his pager (which he wears to bed) beeps whenever a JetBlue flight touches down more than one minute late.

Neeleman's dedication to monitoring JetBlue's performance is matched by his passion for feedback. He jumps on a plane once a week or so, and not just to ride: He loads baggage and serves drinks. Along the way, he smiles politely when passengers tell him how well he's doing, but he prefers to hear their complaints. No concern is too small or too large, whether a desire for better biscotti or a request for more flights to a certain destination. Neeleman gives employees the authority to make immediate customer-service decisions. "Employees at other airlines," he explains, "get so caught up in procedure—rules, rules, rules—that they often forget there is a paying customer there." JetBlue passengers get discount coupons and free accommodations if their flight is diverted, compensation that rival airlines don't always provide.

cover costs and generate a profit—may generate a large profit on each item sold. The revenue is often needed to cover development and introduction costs. Skimming works only if marketers can convince consumers that a product is truly different from those already on the market. Today's expensive high-definition television (HDTV) is an example. Like HDTVs, microwave ovens, calculators, video games, and video cameras were all introduced at high skimming prices. In contrast, **penetration pricing**—setting an initially low price to establish a new product in the market—seeks to create consumer interest and stimulate trial purchases.

penetration-pricing strategy The decision to price a new product very low to sell the most units possible and to build customer loyalty.

Whatever price strategy a company is using, it must be communicated to buyers. Wal-Mart consistently communicates a low price strategy to consumers, but some other retailers do not. Zellers, for example, tried to compete with Wal-Mart by adopting an "everyday low prices" (EDLP) policy a few years ago, but in 2005 abandoned it and returned to its former practice of promotional markdowns on some products to attract customers to its stores.[7]

Fixed Versus Dynamic Pricing for Ebusiness

The electronic marketplace has introduced a highly variable pricing system as an alternative to more conventional—and more stable—pricing structures for both consumer and B2B products. *Dynamic pricing* works because information flow on the web notifies millions of buyers of instantaneous changes in product availability. To attract sales that might be lost under traditional fixed-price structures, sellers can alter prices privately, on a one-to-one, customer-to-customer basis.[8]

At present, fixed pricing is still the most common option for cybershoppers. Etail giant Amazon.com has maintained the practice as the pricing strategy for its 16 million retail items. That situation, however, is beginning to change as dynamic-price challengers, such as eBay (the online, person-to-person auction website) and Priceline.com (the online clearinghouse for person-to-business price negotiation), grow in popularity.

Roy Cooper scours the markets of Quito, Ecuador, for tapestries, baskets, and religious relics. He pays $10 to $15 for selected items and then posts them on eBay, where they usually sell at substantial markups. His online enterprise nets Cooper about $1300 a month ($2500 in November and December). His Ecuadorean suppliers, whose average income is $1460 per year, seem happy with their share. In a country where only 2.7 percent of the population has ever been online, very few people have heard of dynamic pricing.

Pricing Tactics

Regardless of its pricing strategy, a company may adopt one or more *pricing tactics*, such as *price lining* or *psychological pricing*. Managers must also decide whether to use *discounting* tactics.

Price Lining

price lining The practice of offering all items in certain categories at a limited number of predetermined price points.

Companies selling multiple items in a product category often use **price lining**—offering all items in certain categories at a limited number of prices. Three or four *price points* are set at which a particular product will be sold. If price points for men's suits are $175, $250, and $400, all men's suits will be priced at one of these three levels. The store's buyers, therefore, must select suits that can be purchased and sold profitably at one of these three prices.

Psychological Pricing

psychological pricing The practice of setting prices to take advantage of the nonlogical reactions of consumers to certain types of prices.

odd-even psychological pricing A form of psychological pricing in which prices are not stated in even dollar amounts.

Psychological pricing takes advantage of the fact that customers are not completely rational when making buying decisions. One type of psychological pricing, **odd-even pricing**, is based on the theory that customers prefer prices that are not stated in even dollar amounts. Thus customers regard prices of $1000, $100, $50, and $10 as significantly higher than $999.95, $99.95, $49.95, and $9.95, respectively.

Discounting

discount Any price reduction offered by the seller to persuade customers to purchase a product.

cash discount A form of discount in which customers paying cash, rather than buying on credit, pay lower prices.

seasonal discount A form of discount in which lower prices are offered to customers making a purchase at a time of year when sales are traditionally slow.

trade discount A discount given to firms involved in a product's distribution.

quantity discount A form of discount in which customers buying large amounts of a product pay lower prices.

The price that is eventually set for a product is not always the price at which all items are sold. Many times a company has to offer a price reduction—a **discount**—to stimulate sales. In recent years, **cash discounts** have become popular. Stores may also offer **seasonal discounts** to stimulate the sales of products during times of the year when most customers do not normally buy the product. **Trade discounts** are available only to those companies or individuals involved in a product's distribution. Thus, wholesalers, retailers, and interior designers pay less for fabric than the typical consumer does. **Quantity discounts** involve lower prices for purchases in large quantities. Discounts for cases of motor oil or soft drinks at retail stores are examples of quantity discounts.

If the manufacturer says a product should retail for $349, why does every retailer sell it for, say, $229? Such discrepancies between a manufacturer's suggested retail price and the actual retail price are the norm in the electronics industry, and consumers have come to expect discounted prices. "You can't have a discount until there's a price to discount it from," explains an editor at *Consumer Reports*, but the practice raises an interesting question: If no one charges suggested retail prices, is anyone really getting a discount?

International Pricing

When Procter & Gamble reviewed its prospects for marketing products in new overseas markets, it encountered an unsettling fact: Because it typically priced products to cover hefty R&D costs, profitably priced items were out of reach for too many foreign consumers. The solution was, in effect, to reverse the process. Now P&G conducts research to find out what foreign buyers can afford and then develops products that they can buy. P&G penetrates markets with lower-priced items and encourages customers to trade up as they become able to afford higher-quality products.

As P&G's experience shows, pricing products for other countries is complicated because additional factors are involved. Income and spending trends must be analyzed. In addition, the number of intermediaries varies from country to country, as does their effect on a product's cost. Exchange rates change daily, there may be shipping costs, import tariffs must be considered (Chapter 5), and different types of pricing agreements may be permitted. Sometimes companies try to increase their foreign market share by pricing products below cost, causing the product to be priced lower in a foreign market than in its home market. As we saw in Chapter 5, this is called *dumping*, and it is illegal.

THE DISTRIBUTION MIX

Explain the distribution mix, the different *channels of distribution*, and different *distribution strategies.* 3

We have already seen that a company needs an appropriate *product mix*. But the success of any product also depends in part on its **distribution mix**—the combination of distribution channels a firm selects to get a product to end-users. In this section, we will consider some of the many factors that enter into decisions about the distribution mix. We will first explain the need for *intermediaries*, then discuss the basic *distribution strategies*, then consider some special issues in channel relationships—namely, conflict and leadership.

distribution mix The combination of distribution channels a firm selects to get a product to end-users.

Intermediaries and Distribution Channels

intermediary Any individual or firm other than the producer who participates in a product's distribution.

Once called *middlemen*, **intermediaries** are the individuals and firms who help distribute a producer's goods. They are generally classified as

wholesalers Intermediaries who sell products to other businesses, which in turn resell them to the end-users.

retailers Intermediaries who sell products to end-users.

wholesalers or retailers. **Wholesalers** sell products to other businesses, which resell them to final consumers. **Retailers** sell products directly to consumers. While some firms rely on independent intermediaries, others employ their own distribution networks and sales forces.

Distribution of Consumer Products

distribution channel The path a product follows from the producer to the end-user.

A **distribution channel** is the path that a product follows from producer to end-user. Figure 17.2 shows how eight primary distribution channels can be identified according to the kinds of channel members involved in getting products to buyers. Note that all channels must begin with a producer and end with a consumer or an industrial user. Channels 1 through 4 are most often used for the distribution of consumer goods and services.

direct channel A distribution channel in which the product travels from the producer to the consumer without passing through any intermediary.

Channel 1: Direct Distribution of Consumer Products. In a **direct channel**, the product travels from the producer to the consumer without intermediaries. Using their own sales forces, companies such as Avon, Fuller Brush, and Tupperware use this channel. The direct channel is also prominent on the internet. The Gateway 2000 internet storefront, for example, handles annual sales of billions of dollars in computers and related products for home and workplace. Likewise, you can purchase airline reservations (and thousands of other products and services) directly from internet sites.

Channel 2: Retail Distribution of Consumer Products. In Channel 2, producers distribute products through retailers. Goodyear, for example, maintains its own system of retail outlets. Levi's has its own outlets but also produces jeans for other retailers such as Gap Inc. Many retailers also offer internet sales.

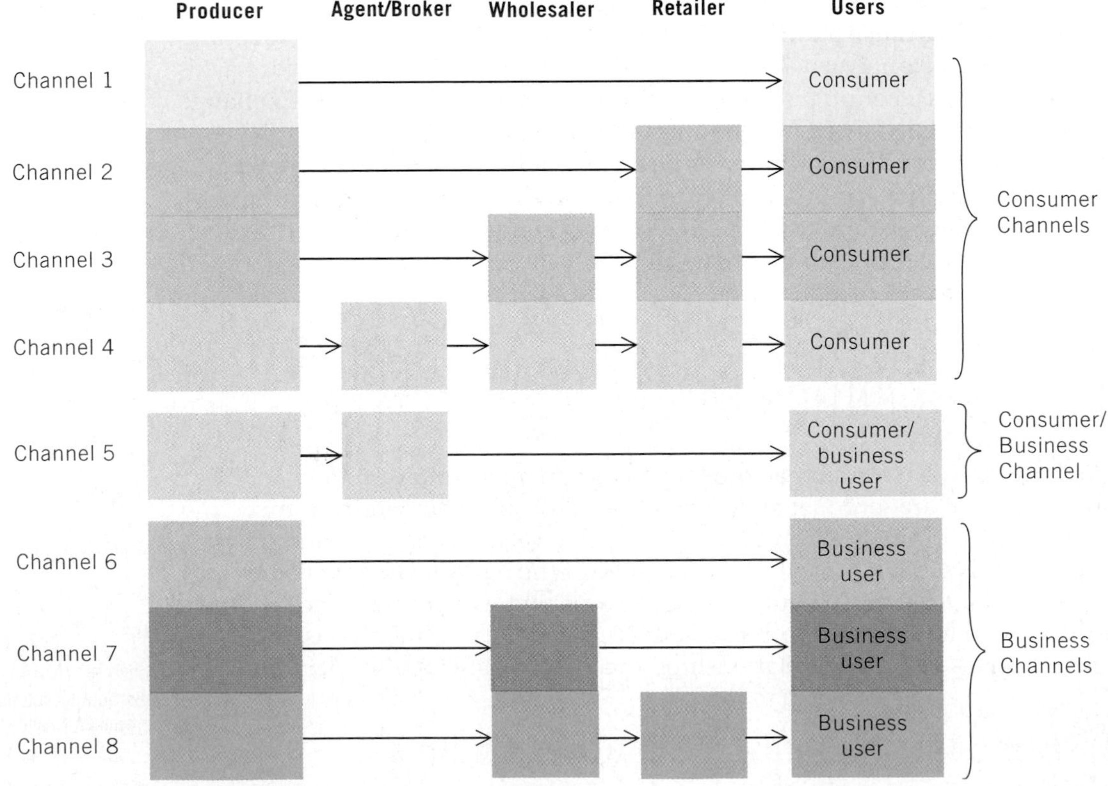

Figure 17.2 Channels of distribution: How the product travels from producer to consumer or user.

Channel 3: Wholesale Distribution of Consumer Products. Once the most widely used method of non-direct distribution, Channel 2 requires a large amount of floor space, both for storing merchandise and for displaying it in stores. Faced with the rising cost of store space, many retailers found that they could not afford both retail and storage space. Thus, wholesalers entered the distribution network to perform the storage function. The combination convenience store/gas station is an example of Channel 3. With approximately 90 percent of the space used to display merchandise, only 10 percent is left for storage and office facilities. Wholesalers store merchandise and restock it frequently.

Wholesalers are prominent in ecommerce because internet stores give customers access to information and product displays 24 hours a day. Buyers can also place orders electronically and confirm delivery almost instantaneously. In the diamond industry, retail companies can access wholesalers such as Diasqua Group, visually examine diamonds, place orders, and receive delivery dates, all over the internet.

Channel 4: Distribution Through Sales Agents or Brokers. Channel 4 uses **sales agents**, or **brokers**, who represent producers and sell to wholesalers, retailers, or both. They receive commissions based on the prices of the goods they sell. Lafferty and Co. Food Brokers Inc. represents several prominent food manufacturers—Pillsbury, Old El Paso, and Sunkist—in the Midwestern United States. To relieve manufacturers of sales activities, Lafferty arranges sales of their products to other companies, allowing manufacturers to do what they do best—process food products—rather than divert resources to sales and distribution.

sales agent (or broker) An independent business person who represents a business and receives a commission in return, but never takes legal possession of the product.

Agents generally deal in the related product lines of a few producers and work on a long-term basis. Travel agents, for example, represent airlines, car-rental companies, and hotels. In contrast, brokers match sellers and buyers as needed. The real estate industry relies on brokers to match buyers and sellers of property.

The Pros and Cons of Non-Direct Distribution

Each link in the distribution chain makes a profit by charging a markup or commission. Thus, non-direct distribution means higher prices. The more members in the channel—the more intermediaries—the higher the final price. Calculated as a percentage of cost, *markups* are applied each time a

When the dot-com bubble burst in 2000–01, most online grocery services dried up. In August 2001, however, one of them—Peapod—was salvaged by the Dutch grocery giant Royal Ahold. It now operates Peapod according to a strategy that's much more cautious than that of the original and now defunct cyberspace grocers, who invested large sums of money in vast, high-tech warehouses. Like other bricks-and-mortar chains who've ventured online, Ahold fills online orders out of existing stores and enters only a few markets at a time.

"On the one hand, eliminating the middleman would result in lower costs, increased sales, and greater consumer satisfaction; on the other hand, we're the middleman."

product is sold. They may range from 10 to 40 percent for manufacturers, from 2 to 25 percent for wholesalers, and from 5 to 100 percent for retailers. *E-intermediaries*—wholesalers and agents who use internet channels—also charge markups. In general, markup levels depend on competitive conditions and practices in a particular industry.

Creating Added Value. Intermediaries provide *added value* by saving consumers both time and money. Moreover, the value accumulates with each link in the supply chain. Intermediaries provide time-saving information and make the right quantities of products available where and when you need them. Figure 17.3 illustrates the problem of making chili without benefit of a common intermediary—the supermarket. As a consumer/buyer, you would obviously spend a lot more time, money, and energy if you tried to gather all the ingredients from one retailer at a time.

Even if intermediaries are eliminated, the costs associated with their functions are not. Intermediaries exist because they do necessary jobs in cost-efficient ways. For example, in this do-it-yourself era, more and more people are trying to save money by opting to sell their homes without using the services of a real estate agent. Since the agent's fee is normally between 5 and 6 percent of the purchase price of the house, the savings can be substantial. But the seller has to do all the work that brokers would normally do to earn their fee. Intermediaries are even appearing in places where most people might think they aren't needed. A Canadian company called Imagine This Sold Ltd. began operating in 2004. For a percentage of the selling price, it provides expertise to people who are trying to sell items on eBay. This company exists because trading has become so competitive on eBay that more expertise is needed to succeed than a lot of people thought.[9]

Channel 5: Distribution by Agents to Consumers and Businesses. Channel 5 differs from previous channels in two ways: (1) An agent functions as the sole intermediary, and (2) the agent distributes to both con-

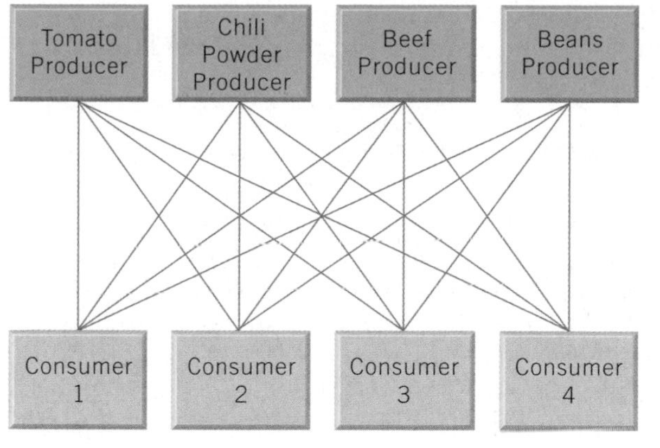

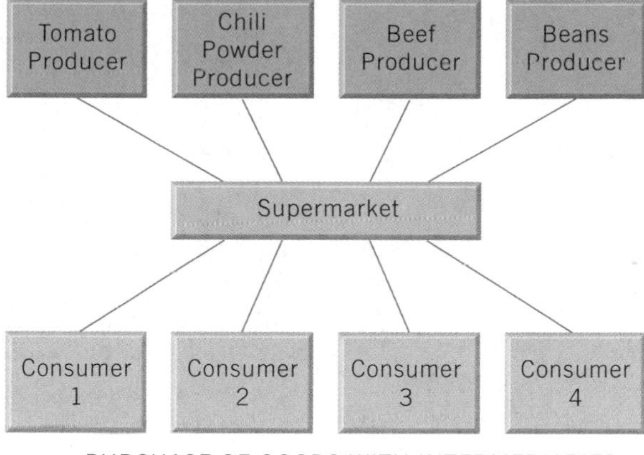

Figure 17.3 Advantages of intermediaries.

sumers and business customers. Consider Vancouver-based Uniglobe Travel International, a travel agent representing airlines, car-rental companies, and hotels. Uniglobe books flight reservations and arranges complete recreational-travel services for consumers. The firm also services companies whose employees need lodging and transportation for business travel.

Ecommerce works well in this channel because it directly informs more people about products. At Uniglobe, for instance, a new online subsidiary combines a high-tech website with an old-fashioned human touch in a specialty market—booking cruises. Customers can scan for destinations, cruise lines, restaurants, and cabin locations for any of 70 ships. Using Uniglobe's online chat function, travellers can simply open a window to speak in real time with one of 75 cruise specialists. The strategy has paid off: Uniglobe.com leads the market in online cruise bookings.[10]

industrial (business) distribution The network of channel members involved in the flow of manufactured goods to industrial customers.

sales offices Offices maintained by sellers of industrial goods to provide points of contact with their customers.

ArvinMeritor makes auto and truck parts for buyers like DaimlerChrysler, Volvo, and International Truck. Unfortunately, it's not the most lucrative business in the world. To get a multi-year contract with a major automaker, the supplier has to agree to annual price reductions, cutting prices by 2 to 5 percent each year, and profits can be as little as 2 percent on $8 billion in sales. To stay afloat, ArvinMeritor has spent years developing lean manufacturing and continuous improvement programs. This central parts "supermarket" allows every department in the factory to access parts without having to pull them from storage.

Distribution of Business Products

Industrial channels are important because every company is also a customer that buys other companies' products. The Kellogg Co., for example, buys grain to make breakfast cereals, and Imperial Tobacco buys tobacco to make cigarettes. **Industrial (business) distribution** is the network of channel members involved in the flow of manufactured goods to business customers. Unlike consumer products, business products are traditionally distributed through Channels 6, 7, and 8 (refer back to Figure 17.2).

Channel 6: Direct Distribution of Business Products. Most business goods are sold directly by the manufacturer to the industrial buyer. Lawless Container Corp., for instance, produces packaging containers for direct sale to Fisher-Price (toys), Dirt Devil (vacuum cleaners), and Mr. Coffee (coffeemakers). Many manufacturers maintain **sales offices** as contact points with customers and headquarters for salespeople. Ecommerce technologies have popularized Channel 6. Dell Computer Corp., a pioneer in direct internet sales, now gets about two thirds of its sales from other businesses, governments, and schools.[11]

Channel 7: Wholesale Distribution of Industrial Products. Channel 7 mostly handles accessory equipment (computers, fax machines, and other office equipment) and supplies (floppy disks, pencils, copier paper). Manufacturers produce these items in large quantities, but companies buy them in small quantities. For example, few companies order truckloads of paper clips, so intermediaries help end-users by breaking down large quantities into smaller sales units.

Channel 8: Wholesale Distribution to Business Retailers. In the office-products industry, Channel 7 is being displaced by a channel that looks very much like Channel 3 for consumer products: Instead of buying office supplies from wholesalers (Channel 7), many businesses are now shopping at office discount stores such as Staples, Office Depot, and Office Max. Before selling to large companies, these warehouse-like superstores originally targeted retail consumers and small businesses that bought supplies at retail stores (and at retail prices). Today, however, small-business buyers shop at discount stores designed for industrial users, selecting from 7000 items at prices 20 to 75 percent lower than retail.

Distribution Strategies

A distribution network can make the difference between success and failure for a company because the choice of distribution strategy determines the amount of market exposure the product gets and the cost of that exposure. The appropriate strategy depends on the product class. The goal is to make a product accessible in just enough locations to satisfy customers' needs. Milk can be purchased at many retail outlets (high exposure), but there may be only one distributor for a very expensive product in a given city.

intensive distribution A distribution strategy in which a product is distributed in nearly every possible outlet, using many channels and channel members.

Three strategies—*intensive*, *exclusive*, and *selective distribution*—provide different degrees of market coverage. **Intensive distribution** means distributing a product through as many channels and channel members (using both wholesalers and retailers) as possible. For example, as Figure 17.4 shows, Caramilk bars flood the market through all suitable outlets. Intensive distribution is normally used for low-cost consumer goods such as candy and magazines.

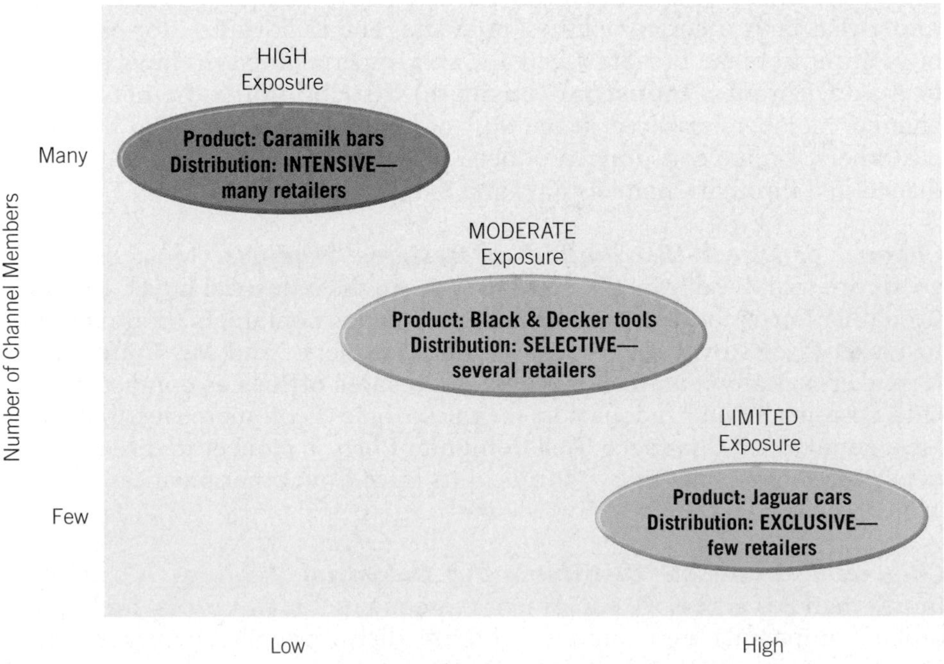

Figure 17.4 Amounts of market exposure from the three kinds of distribution.

In contrast, **exclusive distribution** occurs when a manufacturer grants the exclusive right to distribute or sell a product to one wholesaler or retailer in a given geographic area. Exclusive distribution agreements are most common for high-cost, prestige products. For example, only a single dealer servicing a large metropolitan area sells Jaguar or Rolls-Royce automobiles.

exclusive distribution A distribution strategy in which a product's distribution is limited to only one wholesaler or retailer in a given geographic area.

Selective distribution falls between intensive and exclusive distribution. A company that uses this strategy carefully selects only wholesalers and retailers who will give special attention to the product in terms of sales efforts, display position, etc. Selective distribution policies have been applied to virtually every type of consumer product. It is usually embraced by companies like Black & Decker, whose product lines do not require intense market exposure to increase sales.

selective distribution A distribution strategy that falls between intensive and exclusive distribution, calling for the use of a limited number of outlets for a product.

Para Paints uses an interesting selective distribution policy. It keeps its high-end paint products out of the "big-box" stores such as Canadian Tire and Home Depot. Doing so has increased Para's margins (because big-box stores demand steep discounts), and has also increased sales by 15 to 20 percent because the independent stores that sell Para paint have remained loyal to Para.[12]

Channel Conflict and Channel Leadership

Channel conflict occurs when members of the channel disagree over the roles they should play or the rewards they should receive. John Deere, for example, would object if its dealers began distributing Russian and Japanese tractors. Similarly, when a manufacturer-owned factory outlet store discounts the company's apparel or housewares, it runs the risk of alienating the manufacturer's retail accounts. Channel conflict may also arise if one member has more power than others or is viewed as receiving preferential treatment. Such conflicts defeat the purpose of the system by disrupting the flow of goods to their destinations.

channel conflict Conflict arising when the members of a distribution channel disagree over the roles they should play or the rewards they should receive.

Conflicts are resolved when members' efforts are better coordinated. A key factor in coordinating the activities of independent organizations is channel leadership. Usually, one channel member—the **channel captain**—can determine the roles and rewards of other members. Often, the channel captain is a manufacturer, particularly if the manufacturer's product is in high demand. In some industries, an influential wholesaler or a large retailer such as Wal-Mart may emerge as the channel captain because of its large sales volumes.

channel captain The channel member that is the most powerful in determining the roles and rewards of organizations involved in a given channel of distribution.

To overcome problems posed by channel conflict and issues of channel leadership, the **vertical marketing system (VMS)** has emerged. In a VMS, separate businesses join to form a unified distribution channel, with one member coordinating the activities of the whole channel. There are three main types of VMS arrangements. In a *corporate* VMS, all stages in the channel are under single ownership. The Limited, for example, owns both the production facilities that manufacture its apparel and the retail stores that sell it. In a *contractual* VMS, channel members sign contracts agreeing to specific duties and rewards. The Independent Grocers' Alliance (IGA), for example, consists of independent retail grocers joined with a wholesaler who contractually leads—but does not own—the VMS. Most franchises are contractual VMSs. In an *administered* VMS, channel members are less formally coordinated than in a corporate or contractual VMS. Instead, one or more of the members emerge as leader(s) and maintain control as a result of power and influence. Although the administered VMS is more fragile than the corporate and contractual forms, it is more unified than channels relying on independent members.

vertical marketing system (VMS) A system in which there is a high degree of coordination among all the units in the distribution channel so that a product moves efficiently from manufacturer to consumer.

WHOLESALING

4 Explain the differences between *merchant wholesalers* and *agents/brokers*, and describe the activities of e-intermediaries.

Now that you know something about distribution channels, we can consider the broader role played by intermediaries. Wholesalers provide a variety of functions for their customers, who are buying products for resale to consumers or to businesses. In addition to storing products and providing an assortment of products for their customers, wholesalers offer delivery, credit, and information about products. The specific services that wholesalers offer depend on the type of intermediary involved: *merchant wholesaler, agent/broker,* or *e-intermediary*.

Merchant Wholesalers

merchant wholesaler An independent wholesaler that buys and takes legal possession of goods before selling them to customers.

full-service merchant wholesaler A merchant wholesaler that provides storage and delivery in addition to wholesaling services.

limited-function merchant wholesaler An independent wholesaler that provides only wholesaling—not warehousing or transportation—services.

drop shipper A type of wholesaler that does not carry inventory or handle the product.

rack jobber A full-function merchant wholesaler specializing in non-food merchandise that sets up and maintains display racks of some products in retail stores.

Most wholesalers are independent operators who derive their income from sales of goods produced by a variety of manufacturers. All **merchant wholesalers** take title to merchandise. That is, merchant wholesalers buy and own the goods they resell to other businesses. They usually provide storage and a means of delivery.

A **full-service merchant wholesaler** provides credit, marketing, and merchandising services. Approximately 80 percent of all merchant wholesalers are full-service wholesalers. **Limited-function merchant wholesalers** provide only a few services, sometimes merely storage. Their customers are normally small operations that pay cash and pick up their own goods. One such wholesaler, the **drop shipper**, does not even carry inventory or handle the product. Drop shippers receive orders from customers, negotiate with producers to supply goods, take title to them, and arrange for shipment to customers. The drop shipper bears the risks of the transaction until the customer takes title to the goods.

Other limited-function wholesalers, known as **rack jobbers**, market consumer goods—mostly non-food items—directly to retail stores.[13] Procter & Gamble, for example, uses rack jobbers to distribute products like Pampers diapers. After marking prices, setting up display racks, and displaying diapers in one store, the rack jobber moves on to another outlet to check inventories and shelve products.

Agents and Brokers

Agents and brokers, including internet e-agents, serve as sales forces for various manufacturers. They are independent representatives of many companies' products. They work on commissions, usually about 4 to 5 percent of net sales. Unlike merchant wholesalers, they do not take title to—that is, they do not own—the merchandise they sell. Rather, they serve as the sales and merchandising arms of manufacturers that do not have their own sales forces.

The value of agents and brokers lies primarily in their knowledge of markets and their merchandising expertise. They also provide a wide range of services, including shelf and display merchandising and advertising layout. Finally, they maintain product saleability by removing open, torn, or dirty packages, arranging products neatly, and generally keeping them attractively displayed. Many supermarket products are handled through brokers.

The Advent of the E-Intermediary

e-intermediaries Internet-based distribution-channel members that collect information about sellers and present it in convenient form to consumers and/or help deliver internet products to consumers.

E-intermediaries are internet-based distribution-channel members that perform one or both of the following functions: (1) They collect information about sellers and present it in convenient form to consumers, or (2) they help deliver internet products to consumers. Internet intermediaries such as chapters.indigo.ca and Amazon.com account for sales to millions of consumers who otherwise might walk into traditional retail outlets instead of shopping online. There are several types of e-intermediaries.

Syndicated selling occurs when one website offers another a commission for referring customers. Expedia.com—a popular travel-services website—illustrates how this idea works. Expedia has given Dollar Rent A Car a special banner on its webpage. When Expedia customers click on the banner for a car rental, they are transferred from the Expedia site to the Dollar site. Dollar pays Expedia a fee for each booking that comes through this channel.[14]

syndicated selling Occurs when a website offers other websites a commission for referring customers.

Shopping agents (or **e-agents**) help internet consumers by gathering and sorting information. Although they don't take possession of products, they know which websites and stores to visit, give accurate comparison prices, identify product features, and help consumers complete transactions by presenting information in a usable format—all in a matter of seconds. PriceScan is a well-known shopping agent for computer products.

shopping agent (e-agent) A type of intermediary that helps internet consumers by gathering and sorting information they need to make purchases.

Ecommerce intermediaries called *business-to-business (B2B) brokers* have also emerged for business customers. The pricing process between B2B buyers and sellers of commodities can be outsourced, for example, to an internet company like FreeMarkets Inc. (which recently merged with Ariba). As a pricing broker, FreeMarkets links any large-volume buyer with potential suppliers that bid to become the supplier for the industrial customer. Client companies (the commodity buyers), such as Quaker Oats or Emerson Electric, pay FreeMarkets a fixed annual subscription fee and receive networking into FreeMarkets' auction headquarters, where real-time bids come in from suppliers at remote locations. The website (www.freemarkets.com) provides up-to-date information until the bidding ends with the low-price supplier. In conducting the pricing transactions electronically, FreeMarkets doesn't take possession of any products. Rather, it brings together timely information and links businesses to one another.[15]

RETAILING

If you are like most Canadians, you buy nearly all the goods and services you consume from retailers. Most retailers are small operations, often consisting of just the owners and part-time help. But there are a few very large retailers, and these account for billions of dollars of sales each year in Canada (see Table 17.1).

Identify the different types of *retailing* and *retail stores*. **5**

Types of Retail Outlets

Retail operations in Canada vary as widely by type as they do by size. They can be classified in various ways: by pricing strategies, location, range of services, or range of product lines. Choosing the right types of retail outlets is a crucial aspect of every seller's distribution strategy. In this section, we describe retail stores by using two classifications: *product line retailers* and *bargain retailers*.

Product Line Retailers

Retailers that feature broad product lines include **department stores**, which are organized into specialized departments such as shoes, furniture, women's clothing, and so forth. Stores are usually large and handle a wide range of goods. In addition, they usually offer a variety of services, such as generous return policies, credit plans, and delivery. Similarly, **supermarkets**

department stores Large retail stores that offer a wide variety of high-quality items divided into specialized departments.

supermarkets Large retail stores that offer a variety of food and food-related items divided into specialized departments.

Table 17.1 The Top 10 Retailers in Canada, 2005

Company	Annual Revenues (in billions of $)
1. Wal-Mart Canada Corp.	$13.5
2. Costco Wholesale Canada Ltd.	8.1
3. Canadian Tire Corp. Ltd.	7.7
4. Hudson's Bay Co.	6.9
5. Sears Canada Inc.	6.2
6. Home Depot Canada	5.5
7. Home Hardware Stores Ltd.	4.2
8. Best Buy Canada Ltd.	3.5
9. Liquor Control Board of Ontario	3.5
10. Direct Energy Marketing Ltd.	3.3

are divided into departments of related products: food products, household products, and so forth. The emphasis is on low prices, self-service, and wide selection.

specialty stores Small retail stores that carry one line of related products.

In contrast, **specialty stores** are small stores that carry one line of related products. They serve specific market segments with full product lines in narrow product fields and often feature knowledgeable sales personnel. Sunglass Hut International, for instance, has 1600 outlets in Canada, the United States, Europe, and Australia that carry a deep selection of competitively priced sunglasses. Retailers who carry an extremely deep selection of goods in a relatively narrow product line and hire technical experts to give customers advice are called **category killers**. Home Depot and Staples are examples of category killers.

category killers Retailers who carry a deep selection of goods in a narrow product line.

Bargain Retailers

bargain retailers Retail outlets that emphasize low prices as a means of attracting consumers.

discount houses Bargain retail stores that offer major items such as televisions and large appliances at discount prices.

Bargain retailers carry wide ranges of products and come in many forms. The first **discount houses** sold large numbers of items (such as televisions and other appliances) at substantial price reductions to certain customers. As name-brand items became more common, they offered better product assortments while still transacting cash-only sales in low-rent facilities. As they became firmly entrenched, they began moving to better locations, improving decor, and selling better-quality merchandise at higher prices. They also began offering a few department store services, such as credit plans and non-cash sales. Wal-Mart and Zellers are bargain retailers.

catalogue showroom A bargain retail store in which customers place orders for items described in a catalogue and pick up those items from an on-premises warehouse.

factory outlets Bargain retail stores that are owned by the manufacturers whose products they sell.

warehouse club (wholesale club) Huge, membership-only, combined retail-wholesale operations that sell brand-name merchandise.

convenience stores Retail stores that offer high accessibility, extended hours, and fast service on selected items.

Catalogue showrooms use mail catalogues to attract customers into showrooms to view display samples, place orders, and wait briefly while clerks retrieve orders from attached warehouses. **Factory outlets** are manufacturer-owned stores that avoid wholesalers and retailers by selling merchandise directly from factory to consumer. The **warehouse club** (or **wholesale club**) offers large discounts on a wide range of brand-name merchandise to customers who pay annual membership fees. Neighbourhood food retailers such as 7-Eleven and Circle K stores are **convenience store** chains, which offer ease of purchase: They stress easily accessible locations, extended store hours, and speedy service. They differ from most bargain retailers in that they do not feature low prices. Like bargain retailers, they control prices by keeping in-store service to a minimum.

Non-store and Electronic Retailing

Not all goods and services are sold in stores. In fact, some of the nation's largest retailers sell all or most of their products without bricks-and-mortar stores.

Non-store Retailing

Certain types of consumer goods—soft drinks, candy, and cigarettes—lend themselves to distribution in vending machines. However, vending machine sales still represent only a small proportion of all retail sales.

Non-store retailing also includes **direct-response retailing**, in which firms contact customers directly to inform them about products and to receive sales orders. The oldest form of retailing, **direct selling**, is still used by companies that sell door-to-door or through home-selling parties. Most of us have talked with salespeople from World Book, Avon, or Fuller Brush as they make door-to-door sales calls. Avon Products has more than 4 million sales reps in 100 different countries.[16]

direct-response retailing A type of retailing in which firms make direct contact with customers both to inform them about products and to receive sales orders.

direct selling Form of non-store retailing typified by door-to-door sales.

The Fuller Brush Company was started in 1906 by Arthur Fuller, a self-described "country bumpkin" from Nova Scotia. The company used to be well known in door-to-door selling, but sweeping changes in North American society—women leaving the home to work, mass retailing, and the globalization of business—caused the company to fall on hard times. Two of its most famous salesmen were the Reverend Billy Graham and disc jockey Dick Clark. The company has continued to be successful in Mexico and Argentina, where direct selling still works well.

Mail order (**catalogue marketing**), such as that practised by Eddie Bauer, is a form of direct-response retailing. So is **telemarketing**—the use of the telephone to sell directly. Telemarketing is growing rapidly in Canada and Great Britain but is facing a downturn with the recent national do-not-call registry in the United States. After topping $700 billion annually, U.S. sales fell to $500 billion in 2004, and some are predicting a near-collapse as more households object to intrusive phone calls.[17] Another kind of non-store retailing is described in the Entrepreneurship and New Ventures box.

mail order (catalogue marketing) A form of non-store retailing in which customers place orders for merchandise shown in catalogues and receive their orders via mail.

telemarketing Use of the telephone to sell directly to consumers.

Electronic Retailing

Electronic retailing (also called *etailing*) allows consumers to shop from home using the internet. Sears Canada, one of the most popular etailers in Canada, offers more than 10 000 items for sale on its website.[18] Etailing is made possible by communications networks that let sellers post product information on consumers' PCs. And so-called "etailing" sales are expected to increase sharply during the next few years as people shop online with their personal computers.

electronic retailing Non-store retailing in which information about the seller's products and services is provided over the internet, allowing consumers to receive the information and purchase the products in the home.

Internet-Based Stores. Use of the internet to interact with customers—to inform, sell to, and distribute to them—is growing rapidly. For example, Ice.com, a Montreal-based company, sells mid- and low-priced jewellery over the internet. Almost all of the company's customers are in the United States. The company is profitable because margins on jewellery are higher than they are for books or electronics. Jewellery fits well in the ecommerce environment because it is high in value but small in size. This makes it easy to ship products to customers. Most of the items that Ice.com sells cost between $50 and $750. More than two-thirds of the Ice.com shoppers are female.[19]

In Canada, just over half of the people with access to the internet have made an online purchase. In 2005, Canadian consumers spent $4.6 billion while shopping online, and this is expected to increase to over $8 billion by

ENTREPRENEURSHIP AND NEW VENTURES

There Must Be a Better Way to Distribute Confusion, Demand, and Dysfunction

Bolivian Marcelo Claure started his distribution career selling cellphones out of the trunk of his car when he was just 23. Today his Brightstar Corp. is a dominant distributor in Latin America, with 700 employees working at 21 facilities in 16 countries and annual revenues topping $1.2 billion. This constant-talking empire builder thinks big and plays for high stakes, meets rival distributors head on, and is always looking for new opportunities and an innovative advantage for future business growth.

As an entrepreneur, Marcelo sees opportunities where others perceive only obstacles. After deciding to go into global distribution, for example, he and three friends chose Latin America as the ideal starting place because, as Marcelo says, it has three perfect characteristics for would-be entrepreneurs—*confusion, demand,* and *dysfunction. Confusion* stems from the region's many countries with various currencies, trade restrictions, dissimilar government regulations, import tariffs, and volatile economic conditions. This mix of problems poses a headache for foreign manufacturers who would willingly pay a middleman to handle the confusion. *Demand* is on the rise with the region's rapidly growing population and their fondness for phones. *Dysfunction* stems from the limited availability of telephone landlines—only 17 percent of the Latin American people have access—so affordable satellite service can capture the untapped phone market. They eagerly set up for business where other companies wouldn't.

Brightstar's operations started by distributing lacklustre Ericsson cellphones that for years held only a tiny share of market in the region. Phone companies complained about the phone's ugly appearance and high price, which Brightstar couldn't control. All Brightstar controlled was shipping, so newcomer Marcelo took a different tack, saying, "What if we make Ericsson the easiest brand to do business with?" He promised irresistible shipping, with direct delivery to phone carriers—Brightstar handled all the complications of importing the phones and getting them through customs—no minimum order, longer than 30 days to pay, and immediate delivery. Ericsson's market share doubled within a year. "After a while," says Marcelo, "the carriers got dependent on us. They knew that if they needed a phone tomorrow, they could get one from Brightstar."

Marcelo is quick to notice what competitors are doing wrong, then he capitalizes on it. An example is Brightstar's first encounter with Motorola, using a manoeuvre that didn't endear them to the giant cellphone manufacturer. After discovering that Motorola was selling phones cheaper to Bell Canada than in the United States, Marcelo talked Bell Canada into buying extra phones that were, in turn, sold to Brightstar, who resold them at bargain prices to U.S. retailers. While undercutting Motorola's U.S. prices, Brightstar made millions of sales for weeks and, says Marcelo, "We managed to make Motorola miserable." After further thought, however, Motorola came to Marcelo's way of thinking: By using Brightstar's strength in distributing, Motorola is freed up for what it does best—making phones. Having learned that lesson, Motorola signed Brightstar as its main Latin America distributor after Ericsson's contract with Brightstar expired in 2000. By 2003, Motorola's market share had jumped from 16 percent to 33 percent, tying it for leadership with Nokia, whose share fell from 60 percent during the same period. When asked how it all happens, the answer is simple: "The secret was," Marcelo says, "that I changed the rules of distribution."

2008.[20] As large as this number is, it still represents only about 1 percent of total operating revenues for private businesses in Canada. Ecommerce is still in its infancy, and there is a lot of room for growth. Using the internet to do comparison shopping is also increasing rapidly. Internet sites like Ask.com, Google.ca, and Yahoo!.ca allow consumers to compare prices and products before making a purchase.

ecatalogues Non-store retailing that uses the internet to display products and services for both retail shoppers and business customers.

Electronic Catalogues. **Ecatalogues** use the internet to display products for both retail and business customers. By sending electronic versions (instead of traditional mail catalogues), firms give millions of users instant access to pages of product information. The seller avoids mail-distribution and printing costs, and once an online catalogue is in place, there is little cost in maintaining and accessing it. Recognizing these advantages, about 85 percent of all cataloguers are now on the internet, with sales via websites accounting for 10 percent of all catalogue sales. The top 10 consumer ecatalogues include JCPenney (number 1), Fingerhut (number 3), L.L. Bean (number 7), and Victoria's Secret (number 8). Top B2B ecatalogues include Dell Computer (number 1) and Office Depot (number 5).[21]

Electronic Storefronts and Cybermalls. Today, a seller's website is an **electronic storefront** (or *virtual storefront*) from which consumers collect information about products and buying opportunities, place orders, and pay for purchases. Producers of large product lines, such as Dell Computer, dedicate storefronts to their own product lines. Other sites are category sellers whose storefronts feature products from many manufacturers.

electronic storefront A seller's website in which consumers collect information about products and buying opportunities, place sales orders, and pay for their purchases.

Search engines like Yahoo! serve as **cybermalls**—collections of virtual storefronts representing diverse products. After entering a cybermall, shoppers can navigate by choosing from a list of stores (for example, Eddie Bauer), product listings (Pokémon or MP3 players), or departments (apparel or bath/beauty). When your virtual shopping cart is full, you check out and pay your bill. The value-added properties of cybermalls are obvious: speed, convenience, 24-hour access, and, most important, efficient searching that avoids the "click-'til-you-drop" syndrome—the endless wandering through cyberspace experienced by early internet users.[22]

cybermalls Collections of virtual storefronts representing diverse products.

From Door-to-Door to Esales? Not surprisingly, cyberspace is encroaching on door-to-door distribution. Amway is famous for a **multilevel marketing** channel in which self-employed distributors get commissions for recruiting new customers and new Amway reps. Now Amway is expanding this system to the internet with a spinoff called Quixstar. With help from Quixstar, you can start your own at-home internet business. You will be paid for directing new customers to the Quixstar site and for encouraging others to become Quixstar reps. The internet's huge at-home sales potential is also luring other famous door-to-door names—Tupperware, Avon, and Mary Kay. Such firms are racing to board the internet train even though they are courting potential channel conflict. Thousands of loyal door-to-door sales reps stand to lose customers to their own companies' internet outlets.[23]

multilevel marketing A system in which a salesperson earns a commission on their own sales and on the sales of any other salespeople they recruit.

Interactive and Video Marketing. Today, both retail and B2B customers interact with multimedia websites using voice, graphics, animation, film clips, and access to live human advice. One good example of **interactive marketing** is LivePerson, a leading provider of real-time sales and customer service for over 450 websites. When customers log on to the sites of e-Loan, Playboy, or IgoGolf—all of which are LivePerson clients—they enter a live chat room where a service operator initiates a secure one on one text chat. Questions and answers go back and forth to help customers with answers to specific questions that must be answered before they decide on a product. Another form of interaction is the so-called *banner ad* that changes as the user's mouse moves about the page, revealing new drop-down, check, and search boxes.[24]

interactive marketing Selling products and services by allowing customers to interact with multimedia websites using voice, graphics, animation, film clips, and access to live human advice.

Video marketing, a long-established form of interactive marketing, lets viewers shop at home using their TV. Most cable systems offer video marketing through home-shopping channels that display and demonstrate products and allow viewers to phone in or email orders. One network, QVC, operates in the United Kingdom, Germany, Mexico, and South America and has also launched QVC.com as an interactive website.

video marketing Selling to consumers by showing products on television that consumers can buy by telephone or mail.

Veteran QVC host Bob Bowersox is getting ready to offer bedding made by a company called Northern Lights, which distributes regularly through the TV home shopping channel. Northern Lights, which sells sheets, pillows, and other bedding products, markets through such electronic retailing outlets as eBay and Shopping.com as well as QVC.

PHYSICAL DISTRIBUTION

6 Define *physical distribution* and describe the major activities in *warehousing* operations.

Physical distribution refers to the activities needed to move products efficiently from manufacturer to consumer. The goals of physical distribution are to keep customers satisfied, to make goods available when and where consumers want them, and to keep costs low. Thus physical distribution includes *warehousing* and *transportation operations*, as well as *distribution for ecustomers*.

physical distribution Those activities needed to move a product from the manufacturer to the end consumer.

warehousing That part of the distribution process concerned with storing goods.

Warehousing Operations

Storing, or **warehousing**, is a major part of distribution management. In selecting a strategy, managers must keep in mind both the different characteristics and costs of warehousing operations.

Types of Warehouses

There are two basic types of warehouses: *private* and *public*. Facilities can be further divided according to use as *storage warehouses* or *distribution centres*.

private warehouse A warehouse owned and used by just one company.

public warehouse An independently owned and operated warehouse that stores the goods of many firms.

Public and Private Warehouses. **Private warehouses** are owned by a single manufacturer, wholesaler, or retailer. Most are run by large firms that deal in mass quantities and need regular storage. **Public warehouses** are independently owned and operated. Because companies rent only the space they need, they are popular with firms needing storage only during peak periods. Manufacturers who need multiple storage locations to get products to multiple markets also use them.

storage warehouse A warehouse used to provide storage of goods for extended periods of time.

distribution centre A warehouse used to provide storage of goods for only short periods before they are shipped to retail stores.

Storage Warehouses and Distribution Centres. **Storage warehouses** provide storage for extended periods. Producers of seasonal items, such as agricultural crops, use this type of warehouse. **Distribution centres** provide short-term storage of products whose demand is both constant and high. Retail chains, wholesalers, and manufacturers who need to break down large quantities of merchandise into the smaller quantities that stores or customers demand use them. Distribution centres are common in the grocery and food industry. Kellogg's, for example, stores virtually no products at its plants. Instead, it ships cereals from factories to regional distribution centres.

Warehousing Costs

Typical warehouse costs include such obvious expenses as storage-space rental or mortgage payments (usually computed on a square-foot basis), insurance, and wages. They also include the costs of *inventory control* and *materials handling*.

Inventory Control. **Inventory control** means more than keeping track of what is on hand at any time. It often involves the tricky balancing act of ensuring that although an adequate supply of a product is in stock at all times, excessive supplies are avoided.

inventory control The part of warehouse operations that keeps track of what is on hand and ensures adequate supplies of products in stock at all times.

Materials Handling. Most warehouse personnel are involved in **materials handling**—the transportation, arrangement, and orderly retrieval of inventoried goods. Holding down materials-handling costs means developing a strategy that takes into account product placement within the warehouse. Other considerations include packaging decisions (whether to store products as individual units, in multiple packages, or in sealed containers).

materials handling The transportation and arrangement of goods within a warehouse and orderly retrieval of goods from inventory.

The strategy known as **unitization** calls for standardizing the weight and form of materials. A GE warehouse in Kentucky, for instance, receives apartment-size refrigerators from Europe in containers of 56 refrigerators each. Dealing with the huge containers rather than individual boxes not only makes handling easier but also reduces theft and damage. It also optimizes shipping space and makes restocking easier.

unitization Standardizing the weight and form of materials.

Transportation Operations

7 Compare the five basic forms of *transportation* and explain how distribution can be used as a marketing strategy.

The major transportation modes are rail, water, truck, air, and pipelines. In the early part of the twentieth century, railroads dominated the Canadian transportation system, but by the 1970s, truck and air transportation had become important as well. Using operating revenue as the basis for comparisons, the most important modes of transportation in Canada are now trucks, air, and rail.

Cost is a major factor when a company chooses a transportation method. But cost is not the only consideration. A company must also consider the nature of its products, the distance the product must travel, timeliness, and customers' needs and wants. A company shipping orchids or other perishable goods will probably use air transport, while a company shipping sand or coal will use rail or water transport.

Transportation Modes

The major transportation modes are trucks, railroads, planes, water carriers, and pipelines. Differences in cost are most directly related to delivery speed.

Trucks. The advantages of trucks include flexibility, fast service, and dependability. All sections of Canada except the far north can be reached by truck. Trucks are a particularly good choice for short-distance distribution and more expensive products. Large furniture and appliance retailers in major cities, for example, use trucks to shuttle merchandise between their stores and to make deliveries to customers. Trucks can, however, be delayed by bad weather. They also are limited in the volume they can carry in a single load.

Planes. Air is the fastest available transportation mode, and in Canada's far north, it may be the *only* available transportation. Other advantages include greatly reduced costs in packing, handling, unpacking, and final preparations necessary for sale to the consumer. Also, eliminating the need to store certain commodities can reduce inventory-carrying costs. Fresh fish, for example, can be flown to restaurants each day, avoiding the risk of spoilage that comes with packaging and storing. However, air freight is the most expensive form of transportation.

Railroads. Railroads have been the backbone of our transportation system since the late 1800s. Until the 1960s, when trucking firms lowered their rates and attracted many customers, railroads were fairly profitable. They are now used primarily to transport heavy, bulky items such as cars, steel, and coal.

Water Carriers. Of all the transportation modes, transportation by water is the least expensive. Unfortunately, it is also the slowest way to ship. Boats and barges are mainly used for extremely heavy, bulky materials and products (like sand, gravel, oil, and steel) for which transit times are unimportant. Manufacturers are beginning to use water carriers more often because many ships are now specially constructed to load and store large standardized containers. The St. Lawrence Seaway is a vital link in Canada's water transportation system. Water transportation is also important in Canada's far north, where barges deliver commodities such as fuel oil to various isolated hamlets along the western edge of Hudson's Bay during the summer months. Northern Transportation Company Ltd. moves freight on the Athabasca River because of demand created by the oilsands projects in Northern Alberta.[25]

Pipelines. Like water transportation, pipelines are slow in terms of overall delivery time. They are also completely inflexible, but they do provide a constant flow of the product and are unaffected by weather conditions. Traditionally, this delivery system has transported liquids and gases. Lack of adaptability to other products and limited routes make pipelines a relatively unimportant transportation method for most industries.

Changes in Transportation Operations

For many years, transport companies specialized in one mode or another. With deregulation, however, this pattern has changed. New developments in cost-efficiency and competitiveness include *intermodal transportation*, *containerization*, and *order fulfillment through ecommerce channels*.

intermodal transportation The combined use of different modes of transportation.

Intermodal Transportation. The combined use of different modes of transportation—**intermodal transportation**—has come into widespread use. For example, shipping by a combination of truck and rail (piggyback), water and rail ("fishyback"), or air and rail ("birdyback") has improved flexibility and reduced costs.

containerization The use of standardized heavy-duty containers in which many items are sealed at the point of shipment and opened only at the final destination.

Containerization. To make intermodal transport more efficient, **containerization** uses standardized heavy-duty containers into which many items are sealed at point of shipment and opened at their final destination. Containers may be stowed on ships for ocean transit, transferred to trucks, loaded onto railcars, and delivered to final destinations by other trucks. Unloaded containers are then returned for future use.

order fulfillment All activities involved in completing a sales transaction, beginning with making the sale and ending with on-time delivery to the customer.

Order Fulfillment Through Ecommerce Channels. New ecommerce companies often focus on sales, only to discover that delays in after-sale distribution cause customer dissatisfaction. Any delay in physical distribution is a breakdown in fulfillment. **Order fulfillment** begins when the sale is made: It involves getting the product to each customer in good condition and on time. But the volume of a firm's transactions can be huge and fulfillment performance—in terms of timing, content, and terms of payment—has been disappointing for many ebusinesses.

A container train crosses the Salmon River bridge in New Brunswick.

To improve on-time deliveries, many businesses, such as Amazon.com, maintain distribution centres and ship from their own warehouses. Other etailers, however, entrust order-filling to distribution specialists such as the giant UPS e-logistics and the much smaller Atomic Box. Atomic Box clients range from manufacturers to dot-coms that prefer to concentrate on selling while outsourcing logistics and storage activities. The company maintains 325 000 square feet of warehousing through which it annually delivers products worth more than $200 million. It handles the flow of goods and information in both B2B and business-to-consumer transactions.

Both Atomic Box and UPS e-logistics process customer orders, ship goods, provide information about product availability, inform customers about the real-time status of orders, and handle returns. To perform these tasks, the client's computer system must be integrated with that of the distribution specialist. In deciding whether to build their own distribution centres or to use third-party distributors, clients must consider fixed costs as well as the need for shipping expertise. Because the capital investment required for a one-million-square-foot distribution centre is $60 to $80 million, only high-volume companies can afford it. The alternative is paying a third-party distributor about 10 percent of each sale to fulfill orders.[26]

Companies Specializing in Transportation

The major modes of transportation are available from one or more of four types of transporting companies: *common carriers, freight forwarders, contract carriers,* and *private carriers*.

Common carriers transport merchandise for any shipper—manufacturers, wholesalers, retailers, and even individual consumers. They maintain regular schedules and charge competitive prices. The best examples of common carriers are truck lines and railroads.

common carriers Transportation companies that transport goods for any firm or individual wishing to make a shipment

In 1897, the Crow's Nest Pass Agreement established the rate that railways could charge for hauling grain. This agreement was essentially a freight subsidy that helped prairie farmers pay some of their transportation costs to distant ports. But in 1995, the Liberal government abolished the Crow subsidy. Freight rates increased for prairie farmers, which caused them to reduce their emphasis on growing wheat and increase their emphasis on raising livestock.[27] Since the Crow rate was eliminated, livestock production and agricultural processing have increased on the prairies.

freight forwarders Common carriers that lease bulk space from other carriers and resell that space to firms making small shipments.

Not all transportation companies own their own vehicles. A **freight forwarder** is a common carrier that leases bulk space from other carriers, such as railroads or airlines. It then resells parts of that space to smaller shippers. Once it has enough contracts to fill the bulk space, the freight forwarder picks up whatever merchandise is to be shipped. It then transports the goods to the bulk carrier, which makes delivery to an agreed-on destination and handles billing and any inquiries concerning the shipment.

contract carriers Independent transporters who contract to serve as transporters for industrial customers only.

Some transportation companies will transport products for any firm for a contracted amount and time period. These **contract carriers** are usually self-employed operators who own the vehicle that transports the products. When they have delivered a contracted load to its destination, they generally try to locate another contract shipment (often with a different manufacturer) for the return trip.

private carriers Transportation systems owned by the shipper.

A few manufacturers and retailers maintain their own transportation systems (usually a fleet of trucks) to carry their own products. The use of such **private carriers** is generally limited to very large manufacturers such as Kraft Foods and Canada Safeway.

Distribution as a Marketing Strategy

Distribution is an increasingly important way of competing for sales. Instead of just offering advantages in product features and quality, price, and promotion, many firms have turned to distribution as a cornerstone of their business strategies. This approach means assessing and improving the entire stream of activities—wholesaling, warehousing, and transportation—involved in getting products to customers.

The Use of Hubs

hub Central distribution outlet that controls all or most of a firm's distribution activities.

One approach to streamlining is the use of **hubs**—central distribution outlets that control all or most of a firm's distribution activities. Two contrasting strategies have emerged from this approach: *supply-side and "pre-staging" hubs* on the one hand and *distribution-side hubs* on the other.

Supply-Side and "Pre-Staging" Hubs. *Supply-side hubs* are located at the same site where production activities take place. They make sense when large shipments flow regularly to a single industrial user, such as an automobile manufacturer. But these incoming shipments can create a lot of congestion, so some firms use *pre-staging hubs*, which are located near the factory. For example, Saturn maintains a pre-staging hub—managed by Ryder System—where all incoming material is organized to ensure that Saturn's production schedule at the factory is not disrupted. At the hub, long-haul tractors are disconnected from trailers and sent on return trips to any of 339 suppliers in 39 states. Responding to Saturn's up-to-the-minute needs, hub headquarters arranges transport for pre-sorted and pre-inspected materials to the factory by loading them onto specially designed tractors.

The chief job of the hub, then, is to coordinate the customer's materials needs with supply-chain transportation. If the hub is successful, factory inventories are virtually eliminated, storage-space requirements reduced, and long-haul trucks kept moving instead of queued up at the unloading dock. By outsourcing distribution activities to its hub, Saturn can focus on what it does best: manufacturing. Meanwhile, Ryder, the nation's largest logistics-management firm, is paid for its specialty: handling transportation flows.

Distribution-Side Hubs. Whereas supply-side hubs are located near industrial customers, *distribution-side hubs* may be located much farther away, especially if customers are geographically dispersed. National Semiconductor, one of the world's largest chip makers, is an example. Finished silicon microchips are produced in plants around the world and shipped to customers such as IBM, Toshiba, Siemens, Ford, and Compaq, which also run factories around the globe. Chips originally sat waiting at one location after another—on factory floors, at customs, in distributors' facilities, and in customers' warehouses. Typically, they travelled 20 000 different routes on as many as 12 airlines and spent time in 10 warehouses before reaching customers. National has streamlined the system by shutting down six warehouses and now airfreights chips worldwide from a single centre in Singapore. Every activity—storage, sorting, and shipping—is run by Federal Express. As a result, distribution costs have fallen, delivery times have been reduced by half, and sales have increased.

Summary of Learning Objectives

1. **Identify the various *pricing Objectives* that govern pricing decisions and describe the price-setting tools used in making these decisions.** In *pricing*, managers decide what the company will get in exchange for its products. *Pricing Objectives* refer to the goals that producers hope to attain as a result of pricing decisions. These objectives can be divided into two major categories: (1) pricing to maximize profits (pricing to sell the number of units that will generate the highest possible total profits), and (2) market share objectives (ensuring continuous sales by maintaining a strong percentage of the total sales for a specific product type). Sometimes, neither profit maximizing nor market share is the best objective. During difficult economic times, loss containment and survival may be the main objectives.

   Managers must measure the potential impact before deciding on final prices. For this purpose, they use two basic tools (which are often combined): (1) *cost-oriented pricing* (managers price products by calculating the cost of making them available to shoppers, including rent, wages, and manufacturer's cost), and (2) *break-even analysis* (using cost-oriented pricing, a firm will cover its variable costs and will also make some money to pay fixed costs). Break-even analysis assesses total costs versus revenues for various sales volumes. It shows, at any particular sales price, the financial result—the amount of loss or profit—for each possible sales volume.

2. **Discuss *pricing strategies* and tactics for existing and new products.** Pricing strategy is important because pricing has a direct impact on revenues and is very flexible. There are three options for pricing existing products: (1) *Pricing above the market* takes advantage of the common assumption that higher price means higher quality. (2) *Pricing below the market* works if a firm can offer a product of acceptable quality while keeping costs below those of higher priced competitors. (3) *Pricing at or near market prices* is often another option.

   Companies pricing new products must often choose between two pricing policy options: (1) *Price skimming*—setting an initially high price to cover costs and generate a profit—may allow a firm to earn a large profit on each item sold; marketers must convince consumers that a product is truly different from existing products. (2) *Penetration pricing*—setting an initially low price to establish a new product in the market—seeks to generate consumer interest and stimulate trial purchase.

   Regardless of its pricing strategy, a company may adopt various pricing tactics. (1) Companies selling multiple items in a product category often use *price lining*, offering all items in certain categories at a limited number of prices. (2) *Psychological pricing* takes advantage of the fact that customers are not completely rational when making buying decisions. *Odd-even pricing* is based on the theory that customers prefer prices not stated in even-dollar amounts. (3) Often a seller must offer *price reductions*—discounts—to stimulate sales.

3. **Explain the distribution mix, the different *channels of distribution*, and different *distribution strategies*.** In selecting a distribution mix, a firm may use all or any of eight distribution channels. The first four are aimed at getting products to consumers, the fifth is for consumers or business customers, and the last three are aimed at getting products to business customers. Channel 1 involves direct sales to consumers. Channel 2 includes a *retailer*. Channel 3 involves both a retailer and a *wholesaler*, and Channel 4 includes an *agent* or *broker* who enters the system before the wholesaler and retailer. Channel 5 includes only an agent between the producer and the customer. Channel 6, which is used extensively for ecommerce, involves a direct sale to an industrial

user. Channel 7, which is used infrequently, entails selling to business users through wholesalers. Channel 8 includes retail superstores that get products from producers or wholesalers (or both) for re-selling to business customers. *Distribution strategies* include intensive, exclusive, and selective distribution, which differ in the number of products and channel members involved and in the amount of service performed in the channel.

4. **Explain the differences between *merchant wholesalers* and *agents/brokers*, and describe the activities of e-intermediaries.** Services offered by wholesalers to buyers of products for resale depend on the type of intermediary involved: (1) *Merchant wholesalers* buy products from manufacturers and sell them to other businesses, usually providing storage and delivery. A *full-service merchant wholesaler* also provides credit, marketing, and merchandising. *Limited-function merchant wholesalers* provide only a few services, sometimes merely storage. (2) *Agents and brokers* are independent representatives of many companies and work on commissions. They serve as sales and merchandising arms of producers that don't have sales forces.

   E-intermediaries are internet-based channel members who perform one or both of two functions: (1) They collect information about sellers and present it to consumers; (2) they help deliver internet products. There are three types of e-intermediaries: (1) *Syndicated selling* occurs when a website offers other websites a commission for referring customers. (2) *Shopping agents* (or *e-agents*) help internet consumers by gathering and sorting information (such as comparison prices and product features) for making purchases. (3) *Business-to-business brokers* are ecommerce intermediaries for business customers. They may provide up-to-date market information and price and product data.

5. **Identify the different types of *retailing* and *retail stores*.** Retail operations fall under two classifications: (1) *Product line retailers* feature broad product lines. Types of stores include department stores and supermarkets, which are divided into departments of related products. Small specialty stores serve clearly defined market segments by offering full product lines in narrow product fields. (2) *Bargain retailers* carry wide ranges of products and come in many forms, such as discount houses, catalogue showrooms, factory outlets, the warehouse club (or wholesale club), and convenience stores.

   Important forms of *non-store retailing* include direct-response retailing, in which firms make direct contact with customers to inform them about products and take sales orders. *Mail order* (or *catalogue marketing*) is a form of direct-response retailing, as is *telemarketing*—using the telephone to sell directly to consumers. *Direct selling* is still used by companies that sell door-to-door or through home-selling parties.

   Electronic retailing uses communications networks that allow sellers to connect to consumers' computers. Sellers provide members with internet access to product displays. Buyers can examine detailed descriptions, compare brands, send for free information, or purchase by credit card. *Ecatalogues* use the internet to display products for both retail and business customers. Today, a seller's website is an electronic storefront in which consumers collect information about products, place orders, and pay for purchases. Search engines such as Yahoo! serve as *cybermalls*: collections of virtual storefronts representing diverse products and offering such added value as speed, convenience, and efficient searching.

   Cyberspace is encroaching on door-to-door distribution channels. In a *multilevel marketing channel*, self-employed distributors get commissions for recruiting new customers and reps. Both retail and B2B customers participate in *interactive marketing*: They interact with multimedia websites featuring voice, graphics, animation, film clips, and access to live human advice. The so-called banner ad, for example, changes as the user's mouse moves about the page. *Video marketing* lets viewers shop at home from television screens.

6. **Define *physical distribution* and describe the major activities in *warehousing* operations.** *Physical distribution* refers to the activities needed to move products from manufacturer to consumer. These activities make goods available when and where consumers want them, keep costs low, and provide customer services. They include *warehousing*, or the storage of goods. There are two types of warehouses: *Private warehouses* are owned and used by a single manufacturer, wholesaler, or retailer. *Public warehouses* are independently owned and operated and permit companies to rent only the space they need. Facilities can be further divided according to their uses: *Storage warehouses* provide storage for extended periods. *Distribution centres* store products whose market demand is constant and high. Retail chains, wholesalers, and manufacturers use them to break down large quantities of merchandise into the smaller quantities that stores or customers demand.

   Typical warehouse operations include two important costs: In addition to keeping track of what is on hand at any time, *inventory control* involves the balancing act of ensuring that although an adequate supply of a product is in stock at all times, excessive supplies are avoided. *Materials handling* refers to the transportation, arrangement, and orderly retrieval of inventoried goods.

7. **Compare the five basic forms of *transportation* and explain how distribution can be used as a marketing strategy.** The highest cost faced by many companies is the cost of physically moving a product. But firms must consider other factors: the nature of the product, the distance it must travel, the speed with which it must be received, and customer wants and needs. There are five different modes of transportation. (1) *Trucks*: The advantages of trucks include flexibility, fast service, and dependability. (2) *Railroads*: Railroads are now used primarily to transport heavy, bulky items such as cars and steel. Railroad services now include faster delivery and piggyback service, in which truck trailers are placed on railcars. (3) *Planes*: Air is the fastest available mode of transportation and also boasts lower costs in handling and packing and unpacking. However, air freight is the most expensive form of transportation. (4) *Water carriers*: Transportation by water is the least expensive and the slowest. (5) *Pipelines*: Used to transport liquids and gases, pipelines are slow and inflexible but do provide a constant flow of products and are unaffected by weather.

   Important developments in cost-efficiency and competitiveness include *intermodal transportation*—combining different modes of transportation. *Containerization* uses standardized heavy-duty containers in which goods are sealed at point of shipment and opened at the final destinations. To improve *order fulfillment*—all activities involved in sales transactions—many ebusinesses maintain distribution centres and ship their own products from warehouses near major shipping hubs. Others entrust order filling to distribution specialists.

   Many firms regard distribution as a cornerstone of business strategy. One approach to streamlining distribution is the use of *hubs*. Two contrasting strategies have emerged from this approach: (1) *Supply-side hubs* make the most sense when large shipments flow regularly to a single industrial user. To clear congestion, some firms operate *pre-staging hubs* at which all incoming supplies are managed to meet production schedules. (2) Whereas supply-side hubs are located near industrial customers, *distribution-side hubs* may be located much farther away, especially if customers are geographically dispersed. From these facilities, finished products, which may be produced in plants throughout the world, can be shipped to customer locations around the globe.

KEY TERMS

QUESTIONS FOR ANALYSIS

1. How do cost-oriented pricing and break-even analysis help managers measure the potential impact of prices?
2. From the manufacturer's point of view, what are the advantages and disadvantages of using intermediaries to distribute products? From the end-user's point of view?
3. In what key ways do the four channels used only for consumer products differ from the channels used only for industrial products?
4. Explain how the activities of e-agents (internet shopping agents) or brokers differ from those of traditional agents/brokers.
5. Suppose that a small publisher selling to book distributors has fixed operating costs of $600 000 each year and variable costs of $3 per book. How many books must the firm sell to break even if the selling price is $6? If the company expects to sell 50 000 books next year and decides on a 40 percent markup, what will the selling price be?
6. Novelties Ltd. produces miniature Canadian flag decals. The fixed costs for their latest project are $5000. The variable costs are $0.70/flag, and the company should be able to sell them for $2 apiece. How many flags must Novelties Ltd. sell to break even? How many flags must the company sell to make a profit of $2000? If the maximum number of flags the company can sell is 5000, should it get involved in this project?
7. Consider the various kinds of non-store retailing. Give examples of two products that typify the kinds of products sold to at-home shoppers through each form of non-store retailing. Are different products best suited to each form of non-store retailing? Explain.
8. A retailer buys a product from a manufacturer for $25 and sells it for $45. What is the markup percentage? Explain what the term "markup percentage" means.
9. Suppose that your company produces industrial products for other firms. How would you go about determining the prices of your products? Describe the method you would use to arrive at a pricing decision.
10. Give three examples (other than those provided in the chapter) of products that use intensive distribution. Do the same for products that use exclusive distribution and selective distribution. For which category was it easiest to find examples? Why?
11. If you could own a firm that transports products, would you prefer to operate an intermodal transportation business or one that specializes in a single mode of transportation (say, truck or air)? Explain your choice.

APPLICATION EXERCISES

1. Select a product with which you are familiar and analyze various possible pricing objectives for it. What information would you want to have if you were to adopt a profit-maximizing objective? A market share objective? An image objective?
2. Interview the manager of a local manufacturing firm. Identify the firm's distribution strategy and the channels of distribution that it uses. Where applicable, describe the types of wholesalers or retail stores used to distribute the firm's products.
3. Choose any consumer item at your local supermarket and trace the chain of physical distribution activities that brought it to the store shelf.

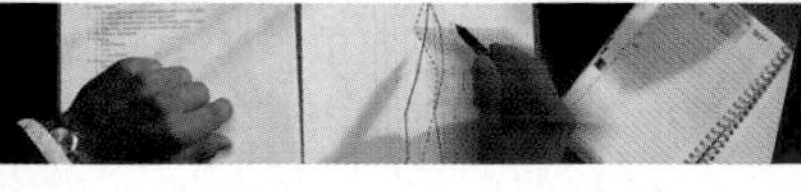

BUILDING YOUR BUSINESS SKILLS

Are You Sold on the Net?

Goal

To encourage students to consider the value of online retailing as an element in a company's distribution system.

The Situation

As the distribution manager of a privately owned clothing manufacturer specializing in camping gear and outdoor clothing, you are convinced that your product line is perfect for online distribution. However, the owner of the company is reluctant to expand distribution from a successful network of retail stores and a catalogue operation. Your challenge is to convince the boss that retailing via the internet can boost sales.

Assignment

Step 1

Join together with four or five classmates to research the advantages and disadvantages of an online distri-

▶▶▶

bution system for your company. Among the factors to consider are the following:

- The likelihood that target consumers are internet shoppers. Young, affluent consumers who are comfortable with the web generally purchase camping gear.
- The industry trend to online distribution. Are similar companies doing it? Have they been successful?
- The opportunity to expand inventory without increasing the cost of retail space or catalogue production and mailing charges.
- The opportunity to have a store that never closes.
- The lack of trust many people have about doing business on the web. Many consumers are reluctant to provide credit card data over the web.
- The difficulty that electronic shoppers have in finding a website when they do not know the store's name.
- The frustration and waiting time involved in web searches.
- The certainty that the site will not reach consumers who do not use computers or who are uncomfortable with the web.

Step 2

Based on your findings, write a persuasive memo to the company's owner stating your position about expanding to an online distribution system. Include information that will counter expected objections.

Follow-Up Questions

1. What place does online distribution have in the distribution network of this company?
2. In your view, is online distribution the wave of the future? Is it likely to increase in importance as a distribution system for apparel companies? Why or why not?

EXERCISING YOUR ETHICS

The Chain of Responsibility

The Situation

Because several stages are involved when distribution chains move products from supply sources to end consumers, the process offers ample opportunity for ethical issues to arise. This exercise encourages you to examine some of the ethical issues that can emerge during transactions among suppliers and customers.

The Dilemma

A customer bought an expensive wedding gift at a local store and asked that it be shipped to the bride in another province. Several weeks after the wedding, the customer contacted the bride because she had sent no word confirming the arrival of the gift. In fact, it hadn't arrived. Charging that the merchandise had not been delivered, the customer requested a refund. The store manager uncovered the following facts:

- A well-known national delivery firm handles all shipments from the store.
- The delivery firm verified that the package had been delivered to the designated address two days after the sale.
- Normally, the delivery firm does not obtain recipient signatures; deliveries are made to the address of record, regardless of the name on the package.

The gift giver argued that even though the package had been delivered to the right address, it had not been delivered to the named recipient. It turns out that, unbeknownst to the gift giver, the bride had moved. It stood to reason, then, that the gift was in the hands of the new occupant of the bride's former address. The manager informed the gift giver that the store had fulfilled its obligation. The cause of the problem, she explained, was the incorrect address given by the customer. She refused to refund the customer's money and suggested that the customer might want to recover the gift by contacting the stranger who received it at the bride's old address.

Questions for Discussion

1. What are the responsibilities of each party—the customer, the store, the delivery firm—in this situation?
2. From an ethical standpoint, in what ways is the store manager's action right? In what ways is it wrong?
3. If you were appointed to settle this matter, what actions would you take?

CONCLUDING CASE 17-1

This Distribution Net's for You

For many years, two Canadian beer brands—Molson Canadian and Labatt's Blue—have been locked in an intense battle for market share dominance in the Canadian market. But now there is a new brand that just may be the top selling beer in Canada. That beer is Budweiser, which is brewed by Labatt as part of an agreement with Anheuser-Busch (AB) of St. Louis, Missouri. Those familiar with the beer industry estimate that Molson has about 11 percent of the Canadian market, and Labatt has about 20 percent (11 percent from Budweiser and about 9 percent from Blue). The talk in the industry is that Molson Canadian is a brand in crisis because of competition from various sources, including American beers, cheap discount beers, chic micro-breweries, and trend imports.

This development may come as an unpleasant surprise to Canadians, but if you ask beer connoisseurs to name the world's largest-selling brand, they'll all likely say Budweiser. The secret to AB's market leadership is a combination of factors: good-tasting products, four generations of brand development and recognition, and a superior distribution system that has become a formidable competitive weapon. AB's state-of-the-art distribution system is a cornerstone in Budweiser's marketing strategy.

BudNet, AB's nationwide data network, is a space-age information technology that's integrated into AB's long-established distribution channel. The information technology and the distribution network, working together, are part and parcel of a strategy for moving product to more consumers. While sales reps from AB's 700 beer distributors continue with traditional services—convincing retailers to put more Bud products on the shelf, order taking, rearranging displays, restocking shelves, and installing promotional materials and displays—they also gather real-time data that AB uses for product promotions and sales strategies.

Here's how they do it. First, the several thousand sales reps and drivers for AB wholesalers are the eyes and ears of the system. When reps visit customer stores they bring book-size hand-held PCs and scanners for gathering retail sales data. Commenting on using the PC in a customer's store, sales rep Derek Gurden says, "First I'll scroll through and check accounts receivable, make sure everything's current. Then it'll show me an inventory screen with a four-week history. I get past sales, package placements—facts and numbers on how much of the sales they did when they had a display in a certain location." But information doesn't stop with just AB products: Gurden walks through the store noting what competitors are doing—product displays, shelf space, packaging—inputting what he sees in painstaking detail. "Honestly? I think I know more about these guys' businesses than they do. At least in the beer section," says Gurden.

Connecting their PCs to a cellphone, the reps transmit marketing data along with new sales orders to the warehouse where the distributor compiles the data, then transmits it daily to AB corporate headquarters where marketing specialists analyze it to see what beer lovers are buying. They know how much the consumer pays, time of sales, whether it's in bottles or cans, cold or warm, and the kind of store, all correlated with recent sales promotions for each sale. The accumulated data are stored in a digital "data warehouse" for fast retrieval and scientific analysis of consumer behaviour. Using the detailed analysis possible with *data mining*, computers comb through possible matchups between different sales promotions and consumer buying patterns, along with competitors' marketing actions, so brand managers can design marketing promotions to suit the ethnic makeup of various markets. The resulting new promotional plans are entered into BudNet, where distributors log on daily to get the latest recommendations for store displays and stock rotations. The results—AB's steadily increasing market share—seem to confirm what August Busch IV, president for domestic operations, told a recent gathering of distributors: "Brewers and wholesalers with a clear data-driven focus will have a distinct competitive advantage."

In 2004, AB reached its highest domestic market share ever in the United States: 50.1 percent—more than 2-1/2 times the volume of Miller Brewing Company, the second-largest U.S. brewer. And, as noted earlier, AB is doing very well in Canada as well. This lofty market position in both countries stems from BudNet's technology, with up-to-the-minute information on consumer buying patterns and competitors' distribution and sales activities. It replaces slow moving weekly or monthly written reports that once flowed from retailer to wholesaler to brewer, a practice that still exists at some of AB's competitors. By providing current field intelligence to its marketing specialists, wholesaler reps are essential in AB's "Seamless Selling" program, a strategy for removing barriers between brewer, wholesalers, and retailers.

Seamless Selling energizes the entire supply chain for fast reaction in moving million of barrels of brew annually in the right varieties of customer-ready packages from brewer to consumer. Using product managers' overnight analysis of what products consumers will buy in different kinds of stores—convenience stores, supermarkets, spirits shops, restaurants—and in various geographic regions and neighbourhoods, AB's distribution network responds with next-day deliveries.

BudNet's evolution is no accident: In 1997, chairman August Busch III announced AB's commitment to industry leadership in mining customers' buying patterns, with a technology investment costing $100 million. Since then, comments Joe Patti, vice president for retail planning, "Wholesaler and store-level data have become the lifeblood of our organization."

The introduction of hand-held PCs provides greater efficiencies at the distributor level, too, for day-to-day scheduling of deliveries to retail stores. Before PCs, sales orders were accumulated from store-to-store throughout the day and delivered at day's end from sales reps to the warehouse. Sorting through large batches of orders presented a huge surge in evening workload and warehouse congestion, causing excessive time to pick products from storage, load them into delivery trucks, maintain accurate warehouse records, and have trucks loaded for delivery starting early the next morning. Even worse, when sales reps were late getting back at day's end, the evening's warehousing activities were delayed, causing costly overtime to load trucks for morning deliveries. With hand-held PCs, congestion has all but vanished: Sales reps communicate in real time with the warehouse, so sales orders flow in throughout the day. In addition to savings on costly overtime, it reduces administrative time in the warehouse and, even more importantly, gives sales reps more time with customers. The resulting increase in distributors' sales improves AB's chances for even greater gains in market share.

Questions for Discussion

1. In what ways has BudNet changed the wholesaler rep's job, as compared to pre-BudNet days?
2. Among the eight channels of distribution described in the text, which channel is used for distributing Anheuser-Busch products? Do you think another channel might be better?
3. Considering the roles and activities of each member in the distribution channel, which channel member is the channel captain? Explain your reasoning.
4. What are the warehousing activities performed by AB wholesalers? What are their transportation activities?
5. In what specific ways does BudNet remove barriers between brewer, wholesalers, and retailers so that the supply chain is more effective than before?

CONCLUDING CASE 17-2

A New Distribution Channel: Downloading Music from the Internet

An important new channel of distribution developed during the last decade: the internet. To the delight of consumers, and the dismay of music and movie industry people, this new channel of distribution allowed consumers to download—for free—a wide variety of music and movies. All of this was made possible by something called file-sharing. As often happens, new technology made this revolution possible. How it will all end is anybody's guess, but here is the story as it has unfolded so far.

For many years, music was distributed through record stores. Consumers visited the stores, looked over their merchandise, and then decided what to buy. Then came internet stores, many of them offering discount prices. You could go to a site like www.cdhitlist.com, which offers thousands of titles among CDs, cassettes, and VHS/DVD movies, search the lists, place orders electronically or over the phone, and then receive your music or movie by mail.

Then came an online music service called Napster. You first went to the website to obtain Napster software, which you could download (for free) onto your computer. The software found albums that you had stored (in MP3 format) on your hard disk and published that information on Napster's website, along with similar lists from millions of other users. Then you could start trading with anyone else who was live on the internet at the same time. It is easy to see why Napster was so popular: It was accessible 24 hours per day, you didn't have to leave your home to shop, and it was free.

Not surprisingly, recording industry executives were not impressed with this new channel of distribution. They argued that file-sharing denied music artists the royalties they were due. If consumers didn't pay for an album, how could the costs of production be recovered? And if the market price of an album was essentially zero, record stores could not hope to stay in business.

The threat from Napster was seen as so great that a recording industry trade organization, the Recording Industry Association of America (RIAA), decided to prosecute. Napster proclaimed its innocence, arguing that it did nothing more than supply software. It neither took possession of albums nor did it buy or sell them. The trading of albums occurred solely among individuals on the open market. The courts didn't buy this argument, and Napster was shut down for copyright infringement. To the recording industry's dismay, the victory was short-lived, as other file-sharing services like Morpheus, KaZaA, and Grokster popped up.

As part of their overall strategy to combat illegal downloading, the recording industry launched two online music services—MusicNet and Pressplay. If you use MusicNet, you pay $9.95 a month and get 100 downloads (but you can't copy them and the deal expires at the end of the month). If you use Pressplay, you get 100 downloads for $24.95 per month (and the right to burn 20 tracks to a CD). Other similar services are offered by iTunes (the industry leader), Microsoft, Yahoo!, and a rejuvenated Napster. To date, consumer demand for these services is much weaker than the demand for free downloading. A study by NPD Group Inc. revealed that in 2004, 243 million songs were downloaded through services such as Grokster, while only 26 million songs were purchased from online stores. But things may be changing. During 2004, several companies announced plans to provide online music for a fee.

The recording industry also filed lawsuits against Grokster and StreamCast Networks (the makers of Morpheus). The defendants initially succeeded in getting a ruling from a U.S. appeals court that what they were doing was not illegal, but in 2005, the U.S. Supreme Court ruled that the entertainment industry could sue companies like Grokster and Morpheus. A few months later, Grokster agreed to shut down and pay $50 million to settle piracy complaints by the music industry. Grokster then announced plans to launch a legal service called 3G, which will require customers to pay a fee to get access to songs that can be downloaded.

Will this court ruling stop the illegal downloading of music and movies that has become so popular in recent years? Not likely. Unlike pioneer Napster (which had a central server that could be shut down), Grokster and Morpheus software is in the hands of millions of consumers who can still engage in illegal downloading. And more file-sharing software is becoming available all the time. Another problem for the entertainment industry is overseas programmers who offer new software to consumers. They are beyond the reach of the law in North America. A survey by Forrester Research found that 80 percent of consumers who were surveyed said they were not going to stop free downloading.

Companies should never underestimate how clever consumers can be when they are highly motivated to get something (like music for free). Consider what has happened with Apple's iTunes software. There is an option on the software called "share my music," which allows users to make their library of songs available to any other computer running iTunes. The software allows people to *listen* to other peoples' collection of music, but not to *copy* it. Or so Apple thought when it developed the software. Now, some clever programmers have figured out a way to get around the restriction and they are using iTunes software to facilitate illegal downloading.

Where will this fascinating story end? Will the aggressive action by record companies alienate their customers and make them even more determined to get their music for free? Will customers be willing to start paying for the right to download, especially if they might be arrested if they don't? Can the record industry succeed in its attempts to stop file-sharing? Time will tell.

Questions for Discussion

1. Consider the traditional channels of distribution for music albums. Which channel elements are most affected by the presence of services like Grokster, KaZaA, and Morpheus? Explain how those elements are affected.
2. Why is the music industry so concerned about internet distribution? Are there any opportunities for the recording industry in internet distribution?
3. Develop arguments opposing the legality of services offered by Grokster and Morpheus. Then take the reverse position and develop an argument in favour of these services.
4. What types of ethical or social responsibility issues does file-sharing raise?
5. What other products, besides music albums, are the most likely candidates for distribution on the internet, now and in the future?

PLANNING FOR YOUR CAREER

Selling Yourself

We've seen how marketing managers apply the principles discussed in Chapters 15–17 to sell products to target markets. As you prepare for your career, you're searching for useful skills and tools to help sell yourself to prospective employers. This exercise gives you an opportunity to look more closely at basic marketing principles as potential career-building tools.

Assignment

Recall from Chapters 15 and 16 that, as a customer, you buy a product because you like what it can do for you—because it has the right features and benefits to satisfy your needs. Try thinking of yourself as a product—a business professional—and visualize potential employers as customers in the market for business professionals. Your objective in this exercise is to evaluate the product–customer match and use your findings to improve your career portfolio, as discussed in *Beginning Your Career Search*, 3rd ed., by James S. O'Rourke IV.

To complete this exercise, do the following:

1. Make a list of product *features* (tangible and intangible) that you possess (or intend to possess by the time you graduate) as a business professional.
2. Make a list of product *benefits* that your features provide (or will provide) for potential employers.
3. Identify an industry or organization(s) that you are considering for your career. This is your target market. List key *characteristics* of the customers in this target market. What are some specific needs that they expect employees to satisfy?
4. Compare your features and benefits lists in questions 1 and 2 with your target-market needs list in question 3. Are your features and benefits well matched with your target market's needs? Do you detect any gaps that might indicate a mismatch?
5. What changes in your career plans might improve the match between you and your target customers?
6. Reconsider your findings in the context of *Beginning Your Career Search*, 3rd ed. In particular, which of your career portfolio documents might benefit from the results of this exercise? Try to make two or more specific improvements to your portfolio.

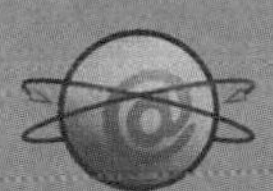

Visit the Companion Website at **www.pearsoned.ca/griffin** to view the CBC video segments that accompany the following cases.

CBC VIDEO CASE IV-1

Buying into Sexy

Girls in the 8–12 years old age group (often called "tweens") are increasingly the target of advertisements that use sex to sell products. Companies are bombarding kids with sexy images to try to get them to buy their products. They are also using an "age compression" strategy—which involves pushing adult products on younger and younger kids. Chains like Miss Teen and LaSenza sell questionable products to tween girls. Advertisers say there is a demand for these products, but critics argue that advertisers have created the demand.

Kids may not get all the innuendo in the advertisements, but they have reached the conclusion that sexy is cool. Tweens see hundreds of sexual images each day, and this seems to be causing them to move out of childhood more quickly than children in earlier generations did. In short, tweens don't want to be kids, even though that's what they are.

Parents are put in a very tough spot when they are confronted with a daughter who wants to go to school wearing a suggestive outfit. Consider 12-year-old Amanda, who says she wants to look sexy. Where did she get these ideas? The answer is that young girls are bombarded with sexy images every day from pop stars, from magazines like *Tween*, from the internet, and from television. Entire chains are devoted to tween shoppers, and they sell racy clothing, makeup, and lingerie. This is a multi-billion dollar industry.

When tween girls are asked *why* they buy sexy clothes, they give several reasons. They say, for example, that they like the attention they get when they wear such clothes. It's also a reaction against their parents, who don't like them wearing such clothes. Peer pressure is also important; if girls don't wear sexy clothes, they fear they won't be popular and will become isolated from their friends.

Parents are very concerned about the trend to sexy clothes among tween girls. Amanda's mother, for example, prefers that Amanda wear a baggy T-shirt and jeans, but she also wants her daughter to be popular, and wearing "cool" clothes is seen to facilitate popularity. Amanda's dad is uncomfortable with the clothes she wears. The parents of another girl, Alexia, are also concerned. Alexia's mother was raised in a strict Italian home where sexy clothing was forbidden. But, she says she wants her daughter to "fit in," so she usually doesn't say no to Alexia's clothes. Her father says he feels powerless because Alexia sees so many sexy images and then she imitates what she sees. Alexia is very unhappy when her parents don't agree with her choice of clothes.

Where do girls learn about sexy fashions? One place is dolls, where Bratz has replaced Barbie. Bratz books give tips on being a flirt and how to attract boys. One critic says this is "Cosmopolitan for 6-year olds." Young girls are encouraged to be very conscious about their looks, but child psychologists say this is not age-appropriate. Parents are often too busy to have an effect. Couple that with the increasing money that kids have and their access to the media promoting sex, and you have a potent mixture.

Pop stars like Ashley Simpson also convey mixed messages to tween girls. Her posters, for example, show both teddy bears and high heels. Tweens are also big consumers of music videos, which have much sexual content. MuchMusic says it doesn't show sexual images during prime time viewing hours, but one analysis of MuchMusic videos shown in the late afternoon and early evening clearly showed a great deal of explicit sexual content. The target audience of MuchMusic (18–24 year-olds) are obviously not tweens, but that doesn't stop tweens from watching MuchMusic.

What do boys think of all this? When a Candie's shoe advertisement was shown to boys, they said the model was "hot." Boys seem to be consuming a "bimbo" image of women. Even skateboarding games have sexy images. The storyline of one Tony Hawk skateboarding game, for example, involves a strip club and scantily clad women. Hawk says that the game contains these images because teenage boys like girls.

Critics of sexualized content worry that it teaches boys to devalue women and to lose respect for them. The images that are being sent to tween girls are apparently received quite differently by the girls than they are by the boys.

Questions for Discussion

1. There are several different variables that marketers use to segment markets. Which variable(s) is (are) being used in marketing that is directed at tween girls?
2. What is a brand? How do brand names fit into the issues described in the case?
3. Do advertisers merely respond to what consumers want, or do advertisers actually create wants in consumers for certain products? Defend your answer.
4. Consider the following statement: "*Advertisers are using their expertise to convince tween girls to buy products that sexualize their image and are inappropriate for their age group. By doing this, advertisers are robbing tween girls of the innocence of childhood, and at the same time are demeaning the value of women in the eyes of men.*" Do you agree or disagree? Defend your answer.

Source: "Buying into Sexy," *CBC Marketplace*, January 5, 2004.

CBC VIDEO CASE IV-2

Avery's Brand Man

Venture found a business on the brink of bankruptcy and a marketing expert who thought he could revive the brand. The business was a B.C. vineyard and winery run by David and Liz Avery. Their vineyard produced a very fine wine, but for some reason sales were very poor. Six years of work and 8 acres of heartache had put the Avery's $1 million in debt. They decided they needed a new image, a new name, and a new label for their wine, so they called on Joseph Beauregard (Bernie) to help them out.

Bernie is an expert on names and branding. He dreams up new names and new looks for products and services: things as diverse as chocolates, beer, and garbage trucks. But he wants to make wine brands his specialty. He has already successfully re-branded two wines, and he needs a third success to seal his reputation. It's a good thing that Bernie loves a challenge, because the Avery wine challenge is big one. After he chooses a new name for the Avery's wine (Lotusland), he is in for a couple of surprises. His clients are less than enthusiastic about the new name, and he has to schmooze famous people and tell them about the Avery label.

Because his wine has been selling poorly, David Avery is not on good terms with his bank, and he badly needs to make some changes. But the co-operation between Bernie and the Averys leaves a lot to be desired. There is a crisis getting labels designed, approved, and printed because the Averys at various times refuse to communicate with Bernie. In frustration, Bernie sends them an email indicating that their refusal to communicate is preventing him from doing an effective job of re-branding their wine. David responds that he is preoccupied with winemaking, and that he can't deal with several different projects at once. He says he can only wear the winemaker's hat at certain times of the year. Finally, these coordination problems are solved and the bottles get labelled.

Bernie aggressively touts the new Lotusland brand to a multitude of retail outlets. His reputation is on the line. In the end, he is able to get 30 different restaurants signed on to sell Lotusland wine. David and Liz are happy.

Eighteen months later, Bernie's branding business is booming, and he is branding wines all over British Columbia. He has come up with provocative names like "Dirty Laundry," and bottles with wild looks like Star Galaxy. And that's not all. His success has been noticed in other countries. Brand man Bernie has been hired by a winery from the state of Washington, and someone in New Zealand is also interested in his work. Bernie is busy pursuing his dream of transforming the world of wine.

As for the Averys, their new Lotusland wine is doing very well, and their world has been changed forever thanks to Bernie. David says their business is "awesome," and the bank is finally happy because the increased sales mean increased cash flow to pay the winery's bills. The company should be out of debt soon. David is so positive about these developments that he wants to start another organic vineyard in partnership with a land developer. David won't own the land the vineyard will be on, but the vineyard and the winery will be the centerpiece of a subdivision of luxurious homes.

But Bernie is doubtful about working with David again because of the frustrations he experienced the first time around. For his part, David says he would love to work with Bernie again and would like to have his expertise on this new project, but David thinks that maybe he (David) is too hard to work with.

Questions for Discussion

1. What is branding? How does branding add value to a product like Lotusland wine?
2. Describe the different kinds of brands that Canadian consumers see. In which brand category does Lotusland wine fit?
3. What are the different levels of brand loyalty? What level of brand loyalty does Lotusland wine likely have at the moment?
4. What are the key differences between advertising and personal selling? What kind of promotion did Bernie do for the Averys? What kind of promotion is called for in the future?

Source: "Avery Wine's Brandman," *Venture*, March 27, 2005.

PART FIVE

Managing Financial Issues

Management of the financial transactions of a business firm is absolutely critical to its survival. Whether it involves raising money to start a new firm, assessing the riskiness of the firm's investments, managing the firm's cash, or monitoring the firm's activities in securities markets, financial management is a key business activity.

Part Five, Managing Financial Issues, provides an overview of business finance, including how firms raise and manage money, how they define and manage risk, and how they use Canadian and international securities markets to meet their financial needs.

- We begin in **Chapter 18, Understanding Money and Banking**, by exploring the nature of money, its creation through the banking system, and the role of the Bank of Canada in the nation's financial system. We also describe other important financial services organizations.
- Next, in **Chapter 19, Understanding Securities and Investments**, we consider the markets in which firms raise long-term funds by examining how these markets operate and how they are regulated.
- Finally, in **Chapter 20, Financial Decisions and Risk Management**, we look at three reasons businesses need funds and how financial managers raise both long- and short-term funds. We also examine the kinds of risks businesses encounter and the ways in which they deal with such risks.

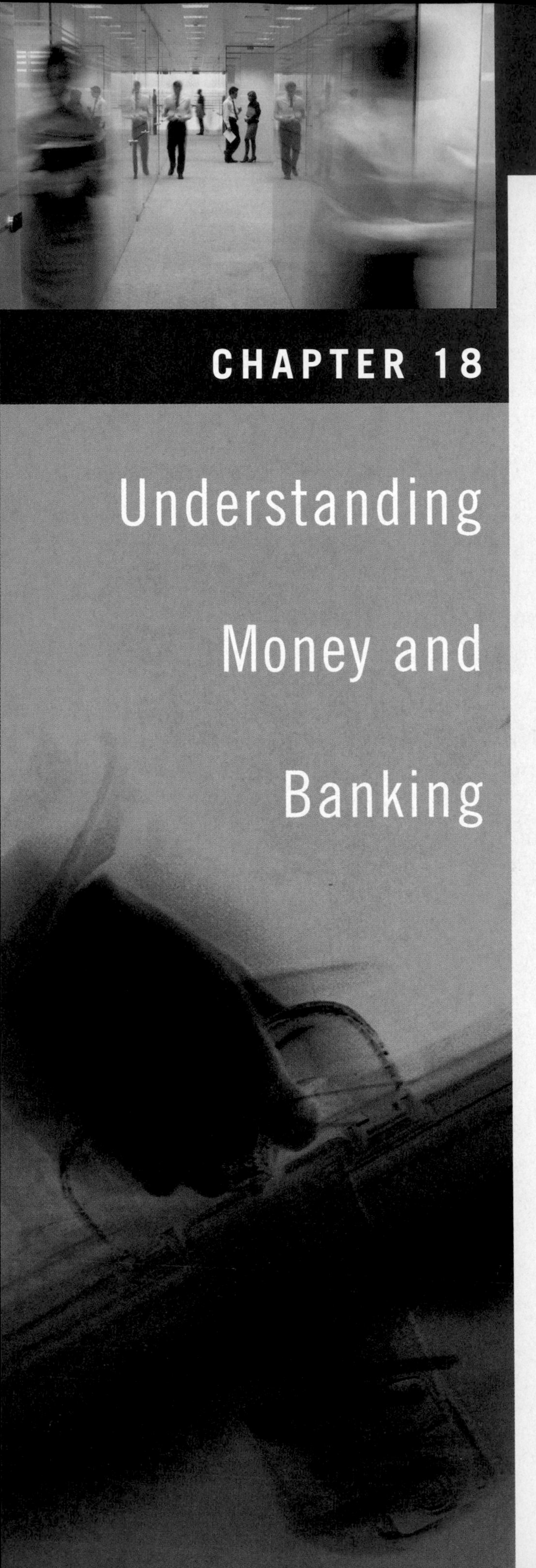

CHAPTER 18

Understanding Money and Banking

After reading this chapter, you should be able to:

1. Define *money* and identify the different forms it takes in the nation's money supply.
2. Describe the different kinds of *financial institutions* that make up the Canadian financial system and explain the services they offer.
3. Explain how banks create money and identify the means by which they are regulated.
4. Identify ways in which the banking industry is changing.
5. Explain the functions of the *Bank of Canada* and describe the tools it uses to control the money supply.
6. Understand the key concepts and activities in *international banking and finance*.

Who Could Have Imagined This?

On May 2, 2006, David Watt, an economist at BMO Nesbitt Burns, predicted that the Canadian dollar would reach U.S.$0.95 by the spring of 2007. The chief economist at the National Bank of Canada went even further and predicted that the Canadian dollar would be on par with the U.S. dollar by the fall of 2007. These were dramatic predictions, given that the Canadian dollar was worth only 62 cents as recently as 2003. What is happening to the Canadian dollar, and why is it happening?

First, a bit of history. Back in the 1960s, the Canadian dollar was worth slightly more than the U.S. dollar, but by 1976, the two currencies were equal in value. After that, the Canadian dollar began a long slide downward as prices of commodities like oil weakened and as government deficits rose. By 2003, the Canadian dollar was valued at just U.S.$0.62, and it looked the dollar might drop even further.

But then several factors conspired to drive the Canadian dollar sharply upward. For one thing, the U.S. dollar started declining in value, partly because of the huge budget deficits that the United States was incurring as a result of its military activities in Iraq and Afghanistan. In this same period, Canada had budget surpluses. Another factor was interest rates. Economists concluded that the U.S. Federal Reserve was not going to increase U.S. interest rates further, but that the Bank of Canada was not yet finished increasing Canadian interest rates. This would make Canada a more attractive place to invest money, and this would put upward pressure on the loonie. Yet another factor was the high demand for oil, partly caused by the rapid growth of the economies of China and India. This increased demand developed at the same time that Canada's massive tar sands oil development was finally starting to produce significant amounts of oil. As the tar sands output increases in the future, Canada will become a truly significant player on the world oil scene, and this will put further upward pressure on the Canadian dollar.

Canadians have lived for many years with a dollar that is worth less than the U.S. dollar, so many Canadians feel good about the newfound strength of the Canadian dollar. But there are both winners and losers when the Canadian dollar rises in value.

WINNERS

The following groups are better off when the Canadian dollar increases in value:

- *Canadian consumers* (giant retailers like Wal-Mart can cut prices because they also benefit when the value of the Canadian dollar increases)
- *Canadian professional sports teams* (they pay their players in U.S. funds, so when the Canadian dollar goes up, it costs them less money; an NHL team with a U.S.$30 million payroll, for example, would have had to pay $46.78 million in 2002 when the Canadian dollar was worth just 62 cents, but in 2006, the team would have had to pay only $33.02 million because the Canadian dollar was worth 90 cents).
- *Canadians travelling to the United States* (the Canadian dollar is worth more, so it costs less to travel in the United States)
- *Canadian firms with U.S. dollar debt* (their debt declines as the value of the Canadian dollar increases)

The increase in the value of the Canadian dollar is having a direct, positive effect on Canadian consumers by putting downward pressure on the price of products that consumers buy. For example, the price of California strawberries dropped from $4 a pound early in 2006 to just over $2 a pound by mid-2006. Price reductions were also evident for many other products.

LOSERS

The following groups are worse off when the Canadian dollar increases in value:

- *The domestic Canadian tourism industry* (a high Canadian dollar discourages foreign visitors and encourages Canadians to travel abroad)
- *Canadian farmers* who export grain (for every one-cent rise in the Canadian dollar, there is a $2 dollar per tonne loss in revenue)
- *Canadian manufacturers who export to the United States* (Canadian products cost more in the United States when the Canadian dollar rises)

- *Canadian railroads* (they take in much of their revenue in U.S. dollars, so when the Canadian dollar increases in value, they get less money than they did when the Canadian dollar was low)
- *Canadian film production* (the cost of Canadian film production rises for U.S. companies, so they are less likely to come to Canada)
- *Canadians who invest in U.S. stocks* (if the increase in the value of the Canadian dollar exceeds the increase in the value of U.S. stocks, Canadian investors' mutual funds will be worth less than when the Canadian dollar was low)
- *Canadians who keep U.S. dollars savings accounts* (the value of the U.S. dollar has declined relative to the Canadian dollar)

The rise in the value of the Canadian dollar has caused great consternation in Canada's manufacturing sector. As the dollar approached U.S.$0.90 in the spring of 2006, more and more doomsday predictions were being made. For example, Rob McBain, co-chair of the Canadian Manufacturers and Exporters, said that even a 90-cent dollar was having a devastating effect on Canada's manufacturing sector. He said that manufacturers need the Canadian dollar to be in the high 70s or low 80s. When the dollar is higher than that, Canadian goods are not as competitive in export markets, *and* Canadian retailers are more likely to buy foreign-made products. He fears that Canadian manufacturers will have no alternative but to go out of business or move their operations out of Canada. If that happens, thousands of jobs will be lost.

Many manufacturers want the federal government to help them cope with the rapid rise of the loonie. The most commonly heard suggestion is to allow companies to increase the pace at which they write off capital investments which are designed to increase productivity. This equipment is needed to allow them to compete more effectively. ◆

WHAT IS MONEY?

1 Define *money* and identify the different forms it takes in the nation's money supply.

When someone asks you how much money you have, what do you say? Do you count the bills and coins in your pockets? Do you mention the funds in your chequing and savings accounts? What about stocks, bonds, or your car? Taken together, the value of everything you own is your personal *wealth*. Not all of it, however, is *money*. In this section, we will consider what money is and what it does. As the opening case shows, the value of money can fluctuate, and this can have a big effect on a country and the people living in it.

The Characteristics of Money

Under the Celts some 2500 years ago, ancient Ireland had a simple agrarian economy. Instead of using coins, the cow was the unit of exchange. Modern money usually takes the form of stamped metal or printed paper—Canadian dollars, U.S. dollars, British pounds, Japanese yen—that is issued by governments. But over the centuries, items as diverse as stone wheels, salt, wool, livestock, shells, and spices have been used as money. As early as 1100 BCE, the Chinese were using metal money that represented the objects they were exchanging (for example, bronze spades and knives). Coins probably came into use sometime around 600 BCE and paper money around 1200 CE. Just about any object can serve as **money** if it is portable, divisible, durable, and stable. To understand why these qualities are important, imagine using as money something valuable that lacks these features—a 35-kilogram salmon, for example.

money Any object generally accepted by people as payment for goods and services.

- *Portability*. If you wanted to use the salmon to buy goods and services, you would have to lug a 35-kilogram fish from shop to shop. Modern currency, by contrast, is lightweight and easy to handle.
- *Divisibility*. Suppose you wanted to buy a hat, a book, and some milk from three different stores—all using the salmon as money. How would

you divide the fish? First, out comes a cleaver at each store. Then, you would have to determine whether a kilogram of its head is worth as much as a kilogram from its middle. Modern currency is easily divisible into smaller parts with fixed values for each unit. In Canada, for example, a dollar can be exchanged for 4 quarters, 10 dimes, 20 nickels, 100 pennies, or any combination of these coins. It is easy to match units of money with the value of all goods.

- *Durability*. Fish seriously fail the durability test. Each day, whether or not you "spend" it, the salmon will be losing value (and gaining scents). Modern currency, on the other hand, does not spoil, it does not die, and, if it wears out, it can be replaced with new coins and paper money.
- *Stability*. If salmon were in short supply, you might be able to make quite a deal for yourself. But in the middle of a salmon run, the market would be flooded with fish. Since sellers would have many opportunities to exchange their wares for salmon, they would soon have enough fish and refuse to trade for salmon. While the value of the paper money we use today has fluctuated over the years, it is considerably more stable than salmon.

The Functions of Money

Imagine a successful fisherman who needs a new sail for his boat. In a *barter economy*—one in which goods are exchanged directly for one another—he would have to find someone who not only needs fish but who is willing to exchange a sail for it. If no sailmaker wants fish, the fisherman must find someone else—say, a shoemaker—who wants fish and will trade for it. Then the fisherman must hope that the sailmaker will trade for his new shoes. In a *money economy*, the fisherman would sell his catch, receive money, and exchange the money for such goods as a new sail. The barter economy is quite inefficient, but it is still used in various places around the world. It is active in Russia, where major problems have arisen as the country tries to move toward a market-based system and away from the command economy that existed under communism. In the late 1990s, barter accounted for more than half of the business transactions in Russia.[1]

Money serves three functions:

- *Medium of exchange*. Like the fisherman "trading" money for a new sail, we use money as a way of buying and selling things. Without money, we would be bogged down in a system of barter.

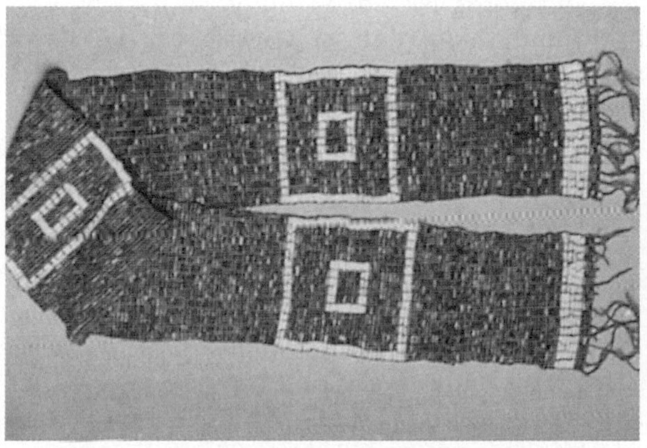

Throughout the ages, people have used many monetary devices. Two interesting ones that were in common circulation are the Iroquois wampum belt (early nineteenth century from eastern North America), and this ancient Greek coin (circa 375 BCE).

In the modern world, we've become used to highly structured monetary systems. But in some places, centuries-old systems still survive. In Quetta, Pakistan, for example, traders like Mohammad Essa transfer funds through handshakes and code words. The system is called *hawala*, which means "trust" in Arabic. The worldwide *hawala* system, though illegal in most countries, moves billions of dollars past regulators annually and is alleged to be the system of choice for terrorists because it leaves no paper trail.

- *Store of value.* Pity the fisherman who catches a fish on Monday and wants to buy a few bars of candy on, say, the following Saturday. By then, the fish would have spoiled and be of no value. In the form of currency, however, money can be used for future purchases and therefore "stores" value.
- *Unit of account.* Money lets us measure the relative values of goods and services. It acts as a unit of account because all products can be valued and accounted for in terms of money. For example, the concepts of "$1000-worth of clothes" or "$500 in labour costs" have universal meaning because everyone deals with money every day.

The Spendable Money Supply: M-1

For money to serve as a medium of exchange, a store of value, or a unit of account, buyers and sellers must agree on its value. The value of money, in turn, depends in part on its supply, that is, how much money is in circulation. When the money supply is high, the value of money drops. When the money supply is low, the value of money increases.

Unfortunately, it is not easy to measure the supply of money, nor is there complete agreement on exactly how it should be measured. The "narrow" definition of the money supply is called M-1. **M-1** counts only the most liquid forms of money: currency and demand deposits (chequing accounts) in banks. As of February 2006, M1 totalled $190.8 billion.[2]

M-1 Only the most liquid forms of money (currency and demand deposits).

currency Paper money and coins issued by the government.

Currency is paper money and coins issued by the government. It is widely used to pay small bills. Canadian currency states clearly: "This note is legal tender." Legal tender is money the law requires a creditor to accept in payment of a debt. Counterfeiting of paper currency has been a problem for many years. It is now a worldwide problem, partly because new technologies like scanners and colour copiers allow counterfeiters to make real-looking bills rather easily. In 2004, 55 000 counterfeit Canadian bills (worth $13 million) were discovered. Most of these were $20 bills.[3]

A survey conducted by SES Canada Research Inc. found that 18 percent of Canadians have received a counterfeit bill, and 39 percent felt that it was likely that they would receive a counterfeit bill at some point.[4] In an attempt to reduce counterfeiting, the Bank of Canada has issued new $20 and $5 bills with more sophisticated security features.[5] Further information about counterfeiting is provided in Video Case V-1 on p. 685.

The majority of Canadian households have chequing accounts against which millions of cheques are written each year. A **cheque** is an order instructing the bank to pay a given sum to a specified person or firm. Although not all sellers accept cheques in payment for goods and services, many do. Cheques enable buyers to make large purchases without having to carry large amounts of cash. Sellers gain a measure of safety because the cheques they receive are valuable only to them and can later be exchanged for cash. Money in chequing accounts, known as **demand deposits**, is counted in M-1 because such funds may be withdrawn at any time without notice.

cheque An order instructing the bank to pay a given sum to a specified person or firm.

demand deposit Money in chequing accounts; counted as M-1 because such funds may be withdrawn at any time without notice.

M-1 Plus the Convertible Money Supply: M-2

M-2 includes everything in M-1 plus items that cannot be spent directly but that are easily converted to spendable forms: *time deposits, money market mutual funds*, and *savings deposits*. M-2 accounts for nearly all of the nation's money supply. It thus measures the store of monetary value that is available for financial transactions. As this overall level of money increases, more is available for consumer purchases and business investment. When the supply is tightened, less money is available; financial transactions, spending, and business activity thus slow down. As of February 2006, M-2 totalled $670.4 billion.[6]

M-2 Everything in M-1 plus savings deposits, time deposits, and money market mutual funds.

Unlike demand deposits, **time deposits** require prior notice of withdrawal and cannot be transferred by cheque. On the other hand, time deposits pay higher interest rates. The supply of money in time deposits—such as *certificates of deposit (CDs)* and *savings certificates*—grew rapidly in the 1970s and 1980s as interest rates rose to 15 percent. But when interest rates dropped in the late 1990s, consumers began putting more of their money in mutual funds.

time deposit A deposit that requires prior notice to make a withdrawal; cannot be transferred to others by cheque.

Money market mutual funds are operated by investment companies that bring together pools of assets from many investors. The fund buys a collection of short-term, low-risk, financial securities. Ownership of and profits (or losses) from the sale of these securities are shared among the fund's investors. These funds attracted many investors in the 1980s and 1990s because of high payoffs. But the sharp decline in the stock market in 2001–2002 meant reduced consumer interest in mutual funds.

money market mutual funds Funds operated by investment companies that bring together pools of assets from many investors.

The hub of operations at Amazon.com is this 840 000 square-foot warehouse, where workers can ship as many as 11 000 boxes an hour. The key to the efficiency of the facility is technology all orders are processed electronically. The most important technology of all may be the credit card. If you had nothing but cash, you'd find it hard to shop on the internet, and internet retailers who depend on credit card transactions (like Amazon, Dell, and eBay) couldn't exist in a cash-only world.

Credit Cards: Plastic Money?

Although not included in M-1 or M-2, credit—especially credit cards—has become a major factor in the purchase of consumer goods in Canada. The use of MasterCard, Visa, American Express, Discover, and credit cards issued by individual businesses has become so widespread that many people refer to credit cards as "plastic money." Nevertheless, credit cards do not qualify as money. Rather, they are a *money substitute*; they serve as a temporary medium of exchange but are not a store of value.

Credit cards are big business for two reasons. First, they are quite convenient. Second, credit cards are extremely profitable for issuing companies. Profits derive from two sources:

1. Some cards charge annual fees to holders. All charge interest on unpaid balances. Depending on the issuer, cardholders pay interest rates ranging from 11 to 20 percent.
2. Merchants who accept credit cards pay fees to card issuers. Depending on the merchant's agreement with the issuer, 2 to 5 percent of total credit-sales dollars goes to card issuers.

THE CANADIAN FINANCIAL SYSTEM

2 Describe the different kinds of *financial institutions* that make up the Canadian financial system and explain the services they offer.

Many forms of money, especially demand deposits and time deposits, depend on the existence of financial institutions to provide a broad spectrum of services to both individuals and businesses. Just how important are reliable financial institutions to both businesses and individuals? Try asking financial consumers in a country in which banking can be an adventure.

In Russia, for example, there is very little regulation of banks, and no way to distinguish qualified from unscrupulous bankers in the thousands of different financial institutions, large and small, that exist. Businesses need stable financial institutions to underwrite modernization and expansion, and individuals need them to handle currency. The Moscow City Bank has no deposit insurance, and only recently added a customer service desk, loan officers, and a cash machine. Imagine, then, just before these new steps toward modernization, the disappointment of Vladimir Shcherbakov, who needed to withdraw U.S.$500 from his account to buy a car but was turned away by a sign announcing that no withdrawals would be allowed for 10 days. "I'm resigned to losing my money," sighed Shcherbakov. "But if I do get it back, I'll change my rubles into dollars and hold on to it myself."

In the sections that follow, we describe the major types of financial institutions, explain how they work, and survey some of the special services they offer. We also explain their role as creators of money and discuss the regulation of the Canadian banking system.

Financial Institutions

The main function of financial institutions is to ease the flow of money from sectors with surpluses to those with deficits. They do this by issuing claims against themselves and using the proceeds to buy the assets of—and thus invest in—other organizations. A bank, for instance, can issue financial claims against itself by making available funds for chequing and savings accounts. In turn, its assets will be mostly loans invested in individuals and businesses and perhaps in government securities.

There are a variety of financial intermediaries in Canada. They vary in size, in importance, in the types of sources they appeal to, in the form of the claim they give to sources of funds, in the users they supply credit to, and in the type of claim they make against the users of funds.

For many years, the financial community in Canada was divided rather clearly into four distinct legal areas. Often called the "four financial pillars," they were: (1) chartered banks; (2) alternate banks, such as trust companies and *caisses populaires* or credit unions; (3) life insurance companies and other specialized lending and saving intermediaries, such as factors, finance companies, venture capital firms, mutual funds, and pension funds; and (4) investment dealers. We will discuss the role of these four financial divisions in a moment, but it is important to understand that so many changes have taken place in the financial services industry that the differences across the four divisions are now very blurred.

The crumbling of the four financial pillars began in 1980 when several changes were made to the Bank Act. The process accelerated when additional changes were made in 1987 and 1992. Canadian banks, for example, are now permitted to own securities dealers (in 1996, Royal Bank purchased investment dealer Richardson Greenshields); they are also permitted to sell commercial paper and to own insurance companies (although they are not allowed to sell insurance in their own bank branches). Banks have also established subsidiaries to sell mutual funds.

The changes to the Bank Act have also allowed subsidiaries of U.S. banks to set up business in Canada, and over 40 of them have done so. In 1997, legislation was changed again to allow branches of U.S. banks to conduct business in Canada.

Trust companies have declined in importance during the last few years, and many trust companies have been bought by banks or insurance companies. The largest trust company—Canada Trust—merged with the Toronto-Dominion Bank and is now called TD Canada Trust. Insurance companies are facing increased challenges since banks can now sell insurance. The mutual fund business is booming and has created many new jobs during the last decade. All of these significant changes must be kept in mind as we now turn to a discussion of the four financial pillars of the Canadian economy.

FINANCIAL PILLAR #1—CHARTERED BANKS

A **chartered bank** is a privately owned, profit-seeking firm that serves individuals, non-business organizations, and businesses as a financial intermediary. Chartered banks offer chequing and savings accounts, make loans, and provide many other services to their customers. They are the main source of short-term loans for business firms.

chartered bank A privately owned, profit-seeking firm that serves individuals, non-business organizations, and businesses as a financial intermediary.

Chartered banks are the largest and most important financial institutions in Canada. In March 2006, Canadian chartered banks had assets totalling $1.3 trillion.[7] They offer a unique service. Their liability instruments (the claims against their assets) are generally accepted by the public and by business as money or as legal tender. Initially, these liability instruments took the form of bank notes issued by individual banks. The Bank Act amendments of 1944 removed the right to issue bank notes.

Canada has a branch banking system. Unlike the United States, where there are hundreds of banks, each with a few branches, in Canada there are only a few banks, each with hundreds of branches. The largest chartered banks in Canada are shown in Table 18.1.

The 1980 Bank Act requires Schedule A banks to be Canadian-owned and have no more than 10 percent of voting shares controlled by a single interest. It also permits Schedule B banks, which may be domestically owned banks that do not meet the 10 percent limit or may be foreign controlled. Schedule B

Table 18.1 The Top 10 Banks in Canada, 2005

Company	Annual Revenues (in billions of $)
1. Royal Bank of Canada	$29.4
2. Canadian Imperial Bank of Commerce	18.7
3. The Toronto-Dominion Bank	18.6
4. The Bank of Nova Scotia	18.3
5. Bank of Montreal	15.2
6. National Bank of Canada	5.3
7. HSBC Bank Canada	2.4
8. Laurentian Bank of Canada	0.9
9. Amex Bank of Canada	0.8
10. Alberta Treasury Branches	0.8

banks are initially limited to one main office and one branch. Since the passing of the act, several foreign banks have set up Schedule B subsidiaries. The act limits foreign-controlled banks to deposits that do not exceed 8 percent of the total domestic assets of all banks in Canada.

The five largest Schedule A banks account for about 90 percent of total bank assets. Some of them also have branches in other countries. There are thousands of branch bank offices in Canada, about one for every 3300 people.

Services Offered by Banks

The banking business today is a highly competitive industry. No longer is it enough for banks to accept deposits and make loans. Most, for example, now offer bank-issued credit cards and safe-deposit boxes. In addition, many offer pension, trust, international, and financial advice, and electronic money transfer.

Pension Services

Most banks help customers establish savings plans for retirement. Banks serve as financial intermediaries by receiving funds and investing them as directed by customers. They also provide customers with information on investment possibilities.

Trust Services

trust services The management of funds left "in the bank's trust."

Many banks offer **trust services**—the management of funds left "in the bank's trust." In return for a fee, the trust department will perform such tasks as making your monthly bill payments and managing your investment portfolio. Trust departments also manage the estates of deceased persons.

International Services

The three main international services offered by banks are *currency exchange*, *letters of credit*, and *banker's acceptances*. Suppose, for example, that a Canadian company wants to buy a product from a French supplier. For a fee, it can use one or more of three services offered by its bank:

1. It can exchange Canadian dollars for euros at a Canadian bank and then pay the French supplier in euros.
2. It can pay its bank to issue a **letter of credit**—a promise by the bank to pay the French firm a certain amount if specified conditions are met.
3. It can pay its bank to draw up a **banker's acceptance**, which promises that the bank will pay some specified amount at a future date.

letter of credit A promise by a bank to pay money to a business firm if certain conditions are met.

banker's acceptance A promise that the bank will pay a specified amount of money at a future date.

A banker's acceptance requires payment by a particular date; letters of credit are payable only after certain conditions are met. The French supplier, for example, may not be paid until shipping documents prove that the merchandise has been shipped from France.

Financial Advice

Many banks, both large and small, help their customers manage their money. Depending on the customer's situation, the bank may recommend different investment opportunities. The recommended mix might include guaranteed investment certificates, mutual funds, stocks, and bonds. Today, bank advertisements often stress the role of banks as financial advisers.

Automated Teller Machines

Electronic automated teller machines (ATMs) allow customers to withdraw money and make deposits 24 hours a day, seven days a week. They also allow transfers of funds between accounts and provide information on account status. Some banks offer cards that can be used in affiliated nationwide systems. Machines are now located at bank buildings, grocery stores, airports, shopping malls, and other locations around the world. Among the world's nearly one million ATMs, 32 percent are located in Asia, 31 percent are located in North America, 25 percent in Western Europe, and 8 percent in Latin America. Many banks now offer international ATM services. Citicorp, for example, installed Shanghai's first 24-hour ATM and is the first foreign bank to receive approval from the People's Bank of China to issue local currency through ATMs. The Exercising Your Ethics box at the end of the chapter provides an interesting dilemma with regard to ATMs.

"And, hey, don't kill yourself trying to pay it back. You know our motto—'What the hell, it's only money.'"

Figure 18.1 summarizes the services that chartered banks offer. Banks are chartered by the federal government and are closely regulated when they provide these services.

Bank Deposits

Chartered banks provide a financial intermediary service by accepting deposits and making loans with this money. Banks make various types of loans to businesses. When applying for a business loan, it is wise for the manager to remember that the banker is interested in making money for the bank through the loan. The banker is also interested in how the loan will be repaid and how it will be secured. A brief written statement accompanied by a cash-flow analysis is a useful approach when applying for a loan.

chequable deposit A chequing account.

One type of deposit a customer can make in a bank is a chequable, or demand, deposit. A **chequable deposit** is a chequing account. Customers who deposit coins, paper currency, or other cheques in their chequing accounts can write cheques against the balance in their accounts. Their banks must honour these cheques immediately; this is why chequing accounts are also called demand deposits.

term deposit Money that remains with the bank for a period of time with interest paid to the depositor.

The other type of deposit a customer can make in a chartered bank is a term deposit. A **term deposit** is one that remains with the bank for a period of time. Interest is paid to depositors for the use of their funds. There are two types of term deposits. The most popular is the regular passbook savings account. Although banks can require notice before withdrawals can be made, they seldom do. These accounts are intended primarily for small individual savers and non-profit organizations.

Another type of term deposit is the guaranteed investment certificate. This deposit is made for a specified period of time ranging from 28 days to several years. These certificates are available to all savers. The interest rate paid on a guaranteed investment certificate is higher than that paid on a regular savings account, but many GICs cannot be cashed in before their maturity dates, so they are less flexible than a savings account.

Bank Loans

Banks are the major source of short-term loans for business. Although banks make long-term loans to some firms, they prefer to specialize in providing short-term funds to finance inventories and accounts receivable.

Figure 18.1 Examples of services by many chartered banks and trust companies.

Devout Muslims can't pay or receive interest, a fact that complicates banking operations. Because money has to work to earn a return, institutions like the Shamil Bank in Bahrain invest deposits directly in such ventures as real estate and then pay back profit shares rather than interest. Buying a car is possible through a complex arrangement in which the bank takes temporary ownership and then sells the car to the individual at a profit. Mortgage arrangements are similar but even more complicated.

A *secured* loan is backed by collateral such as accounts receivable or a life insurance policy. If the borrower cannot repay the loan, the bank sells the collateral. An *unsecured* loan is backed only by the borrower's promise to repay it. Only the most creditworthy borrowers can get unsecured loans.

Borrowers pay interest on their loans. Large firms with excellent credit records pay the prime rate of interest. The **prime rate of interest** is the lowest rate charged to borrowers. This rate changes constantly owing to changes in the demand for and supply of loanable funds as well as to policies of the Bank of Canada. The so-called "Big Six" Canadian banks (Royal Bank, CIBC, Bank of Montreal, Bank of Nova Scotia, TD Canada Trust, and National Bank of Canada) typically act in concert with respect to the prime rate.

prime rate of interest The lowest rate charged to borrowers.

Banks as Creators of Money

Explain how banks create money and identify the means by which they are regulated.  3

In the course of their activities, banks provide a special service to the economy—they create money. This is not to say that they mint bills and coins. Rather, by taking in deposits and making loans, they expand the money supply. We will first look at how this expansion process works, assuming that banks have a **reserve requirement**, that is, that they must keep a portion of their chequable deposits in vault cash or as deposits with the Bank of Canada. (This is simply an assumption, since the reserve requirement was dropped in 1991.)

reserve requirement The requirement (until 1991) that banks keep a portion of their chequable deposits in vault cash or as deposits with the Bank of Canada.

Suppose that you saved $100, took it to a bank, and opened a chequing account. Let's assume that there is a reserve requirement, and that it is 10 percent. Your bank must therefore keep $10 of your $100 deposit in reserve, so it has only $90 to lend. Now suppose that a person named Jennifer Leclerc borrows $90 from your bank. She now has $90 added to her chequing account. Assume that she writes a cheque for $90 payable to Canadian Tire. Canadian Tire's bank ends up with a $90 deposit, and that bank is also required to keep $9 in reserve. It therefore has $81 to lend out to someone else. This process of deposit expansion is shown in abbreviated form in Figure 18.2. As you can see, your original deposit of $100 increases the total supply of money.

Deposit	Money Held in Reserve by Bank	Money to Lend	Total Supply
$100.00	$10.00	$90.00	**$190.00**
90.00	9.00	81.00	**271.00**
81.00	8.10	72.90	**343.90**
72.90	7.29	65.61	**409.51**
65.61	6.56	59.05	**468.56**

Figure 18.2 How the chartered banking system creates money.

What happens if there is no reserve requirement? At the extreme, it means that banks could (theoretically) create infinite amounts of money because they don't have to keep any in reserve. But banks will not do this because it is risky. So, in practice, the dropping of the reserve requirement simply means that banks will be able to create more money than they did when there was a reserve requirement.

Other Changes in Banking

4 Identify ways in which the banking industry is changing.

Fundamental changes in addition to those already described are taking place in banking. These include deregulation, changing consumer demands, the impact of electronic technologies, and changes in international banking.

Deregulation

Deregulation has caused banks to shift away from their historical role as intermediaries between depositors and borrowers. Canada's banks are diversifying to provide a wider array of financial products to their clients. Training bankers to be effective in this environment is necessary. For example, over 100 executives at TD Canada Trust attended a Harvard University course that taught them to think like investment bankers. The Bank of Montreal conducted a similar course for over 400 executives.

In the last few years, large companies have reduced their use of bank loans. To compensate for this loss, banks are setting up money market operations. For example, until deregulation, only securities firms were allowed to sell commercial paper, but banks expect to dominate in this area before too long. (Commercial paper is usually issued by blue-chip companies that pay a fee to investment dealers or banks to sell the security. See Chapter 20 for more information about commercial paper.) Banks have been allowed to sell commercial paper since June 1987, when deregulation opened up this possibility. The Bank of Montreal and the Toronto-Dominion Bank have been the most active in this market. In Canada, about 200 companies have a credit rating good enough for commercial paper. Banks want to use commercial paper more because they do not have to keep capital reserves on hand for commercial paper as they do for acceptances.

Changing Consumer Demands

Consumers are no longer content to simply keep money in a bank when they can get more for it elsewhere. They are increasingly turning to non-traditional, electronic banks like ING Direct and President's Choice

Financial that have very few tellers or branches. As well, retailers like Sears and Canadian Tire are opening their own branches.[8] Traditional banks are responding by selling a growing array of corporate and government securities through their branches. All of this activity is transforming the profit base of banks. In the past, they made most of their money from the spread between interest rates paid to depositors and the rates charged on loans. Investment banking, on the other hand, is fee-based. Banks are making a larger proportion of their profits from fees, and this is blurring the traditional boundary between banks and securities firms.

Electronic Funds Transfer

Chartered banks and other financial institutions now use electronic funds transfer to provide many basic financial services. **Electronic funds transfer** combines computer and communication technology to transfer funds or information into, from, with, and among financial institutions. ATM's are the most popular form of electronic funds transfer. Some banks offer TV banking, in which customers use television sets and terminals—or home computers—to make transactions. Five major Canadian banks allow you to send money from your bank account to anyone with an email address. The age of electronic money has arrived. Digital money is replacing cash in stores, taxicabs, subway systems, and vending machines.

electronic funds transfer A financial service that combines computer and communication technology to transfer funds or information into, from, with, and among financial institutions.

Debit Cards. One of the electronic offerings from the financial industry that has gained popularity is the debit card. Unlike credit cards, **debit cards** allow only the transfer of money between accounts. They do not increase the funds at an individual's disposal. They can, however, be used to make retail purchases. In stores with **point-of-sale (POS) terminals**, customers insert cards that transmit to terminals information relevant to their purchases. The terminal relays the information directly to the bank's computer system. The bank automatically transfers funds from the customer's account to the store's account.

debit card A plastic card that, immediately on use, reduces the balance in the user's bank account and transfers it to the store's account.

point-of-sale (POS) terminals Electronic device that allows customers to pay for retail purchases with debit cards.

Smart Cards. The so-called **smart card** is a credit card-size plastic card with an embedded computer chip that can be programmed with "electronic money." Also known as electronic purses or stored-value cards, smart cards have existed for more than a decade. Phone callers and shoppers in Europe and Asia are the most avid users, holding the majority of the nearly two billion cards in circulation in 2001. Although small by European standards, card usage in North America more than doubled since 2000, reaching 85 million cards in 2003. They are most popular in gas pump payments, followed by prepaid phone service, ATM's, self-operated checkouts, and automated banking services.[9]

smart card A credit card-sized plastic card with an embedded computer chip that can be programmed with "electronic money."

Why are smart cards increasing in popularity today? For one thing, the cost of producing them has fallen dramatically, from as much as $10 to as little as $1. Convenience is equally important, notes Donald J. Gleason, president of Smart Card Enterprise, a division of Electronic Payment Services. "What consumers want," Gleason contends, "is convenience, and if you look at cash, it's really quite inconvenient."

Smart cards can be loaded with money at ATM machines or with special telephone hookups, even at home. After using your card to purchase an item, you can then check an electronic display to see how much money your card has left. Analysts predict that in the near future, smart cards will function as much more than electronic purses. For example, travel industry experts predict that people will soon book travel plans at home on personal computers and then transfer their reservations onto their smart cards. The cards will then serve as airline tickets and boarding passes. As an added benefit, they will allow travellers to avoid waiting in lines at car rental agencies and hotel front desks.

ecash Money that moves among consumers and businesses via digital electronic transmissions.

Ecash. A new, revolutionary world of electronic money has begun to emerge with the rapid growth of the internet. Electronic money, known as **ecash**, is money that moves along multiple channels of consumers and businesses via digital electronic transmissions. Ecash moves outside of the established network of banks, cheques, and paper currency. Companies as varied as new start-up Mondex and giant Citicorp are developing their own forms of electronic money that allow consumers and businesses to spend money more conveniently, quickly, and cheaply than they can through the banking system. In fact, some observers predict that within a few years, as much as 20 percent of all household expenditures will take place on the internet.

How does ecash work? Traditional currency is used to buy electronic funds, which are downloaded over phone lines into a PC or a portable "electronic wallet" that can store and transmit ecash. Ecash is purchased from any company that issues (sells) it. When shopping online—for example, to purchase jewellery—a shopper sends digital money to the merchant instead of using traditional cash, cheques, or credit cards. Businesses can purchase supplies and services electronically from any merchant that accepts ecash. It flows from the buyer's into the seller's ecash funds, which are instantaneously updated and stored on a microchip. One system, operated by CyberCash, tallies all ecash transactions in the customer's account and, at the end of the day, converts the ecash balance back into dollars in the customer's conventional banking account.

Although ecash transactions are cheaper than handling cheques and the paper records involved with conventional money, some potential problems can arise. Hackers, for example, may break into ecash systems and drain them instantaneously. Moreover, if the issuer's computer system crashes, it is conceivable that money "banked" in memory may be lost forever. Finally, regulation and control of ecash systems remain largely nonexistent, with virtually none of the protection that covers government-controlled money systems.

Pay-by-Phone. This system lets you telephone your financial institution and instruct it, by pushing the proper buttons on your phone, to pay certain bills or to transfer funds between accounts.

Direct Deposit. This allows you to authorize in advance specific and regular deposits and withdrawals. You can arrange to have paycheques and social assistance cheques automatically deposited and recurring expenses, such as insurance premiums and utility bills, automatically paid.

Changes in International Banking

Another change concerns international banking. Because U.S. and other foreign banks are now allowed to do business in Canada, Canada's banks are going to experience increased competition. They are responding to this threat with a variety of tactics, including attempts to merge with one another so they can afford the millions of dollars in technology investment that will be needed to remain competitive. In 1998, for example, the Canadian Imperial Bank of Commerce and the Toronto-Dominion Bank tried to merge, as did the Royal Bank and the Bank of Montreal. But both mergers were blocked by the federal government because it feared the mergers would reduce competition and harm consumers. But, as we saw earlier, the government did allow Canada Trust and Toronto-Dominion Bank to merge. Banks are also trying other things to be more competitive, like co-operating to spread their fixed costs. Syncor Services, for example, is a joint venture between three of the "Big Six" banks that provides cheque-clearing services across Canada.[10]

ENTREPRENEURSHIP AND NEW VENTURES

Check It Out!

In the fall of 2005, Calgary-based CHEQ-IT Ltd. announced that six new clients had joined the fold. Arcan Resources Ltd., Dual Energy Ltd., Focus Energy Trust, Grizzly Resources Ltd., Thunder Energy Trust, and Yoho Resources have all implemented the CHEQ-IT system to process their vendor payments in recent months.

CHEQ-IT Ltd. has come a long way since its founding in 1992, when its focus was on being a supplier of cheque printing software and hardware. At that time its niche was in the oil and gas sector. Now, CHEQ-IT's client base includes companies in financial services, transportation, consulting, and other business sectors. Companies as diverse as Grimshaw Trucking and AMEC Engineering Consultants depend on CHEQ-IT products.

Currently considered a leading-edge provider of electronic funds transfer capability, CHEQ-IT Ltd. develops, sells, and supports payment processing for electronic funds transfer (EFT), electronic data interchange (EDI), cheque printing software systems, and related supplies. The systems, currently in use by companies across Canada, work with a variety of corporate accounting systems and provide a robust, secure, and efficient means to process payments at a low cost. The CHEQ-IT system, with its security encryption, is one of the most secure and efficient methods of making payments and preventing fraudulent acts. For CHEQ-IT, in addition to the immediate income from the system sales, the ongoing maintenance and transaction fees from these installations contribute to their increasing recurring revenue base.

The rationale cited for selecting the CHEQ-IT system was that it was the most compatible with clients' existing accounting applications. Additionally, most of these clients received a recommendation from their accounting system provider P2 Energy Solutions, with whom CHEQ-IT has a close and ongoing relationship. Follow-up comments from new clients indicated that the implementation of the CHEQ-IT system was virtually seamless, facilitating payment processing shortly after installation.

The Bank of Canada

Explain the functions of the *Bank of Canada* and describe the tools it uses to control the money supply. 5

The **Bank of Canada**, formed in 1935, is Canada's central bank. It has a crucial role to play in managing the Canadian economy and in regulating certain aspects of chartered bank operations. The Bank of Canada is managed by a board of governors composed of a governor, a deputy governor, and 12 directors appointed from different regions of Canada. The directors, with cabinet approval, appoint the governor and deputy governor. The deputy minister of finance is also a non-voting member of the board. Between meetings of the board, normally held eight times per year, an executive committee acts for the board. This committee is composed of the governor, the deputy governor, two directors, and the deputy minister of finance. The executive committee meets at least once a week. The Business Accountability box provides additional information on the Bank of Canada.

Bank of Canada Canada's central bank; formed in 1935.

Operation of the Bank of Canada

The Bank of Canada plays an important role in managing the money supply in Canada. (See Figure 18.3.) If the Bank of Canada wants to increase the money supply, it can buy government securities. The people selling these bonds deposit the proceeds in their banks. These deposits increase banks' reserves and their willingness to make loans. The Bank of Canada can also lower the bank rate; this action will cause increased demand for loans from businesses and households because these customers borrow more money when interest rates drop.

If the Bank of Canada wants to decrease the money supply, it can sell government securities. People spend money to buy bonds, and these withdrawals bring down banks' reserves and reduce their ability to make loans. The Bank of Canada can also raise the bank rate; this action will cause

BUSINESS ACCOUNTABILITY

Fixing the System on a National Scale

Bankers and economists recently did a follow-up evaluation of the Bank of Canada's fixed-date system, launched in December 2000, for announcing its key policy interest rate—the overnight rate that individual banks pay to borrow from one another. The overnight rate is among the bank's strongest tools for influencing short-term interest rates that, in turn, affect mortgage rates, prime rates charged by chartered banks, and other asset prices in Canada's financial markets. Under the old system, the bank's monetary policy decisions could be made on any business day, without warning, and were governed largely by tactical considerations. That's quite different from today's announcements on eight pre-specified or "fixed" dates each year.

The changeover to fixed dates was launched with four objectives in mind, including one that involves the bank's accountability. First, policymakers wanted to reduce uncertainty in Canada's financial markets by eliminating investors' guesswork about when rate changes would be announced. Knowing that the bank would make changes only on specific dates would allow financial institutions to plan ahead without fear of unexpected rate changes. A second objective was to overcome an unfavourable public perception that Canada was taking its cues for monetary policies from those of the U.S. Federal Reserve. The new system would provide greater focus on Canada's economic context rather than its relationship to U.S. conditions. Another objective was to increase the public's awareness of the forward-looking nature of monetary policy, requiring 18 to 24 months to have its full impact on the economy instead of thinking only of its short-term results. The final objective concerns the bank's accountability to the public. In addition to making monetary policy understandable by explaining clearly to Canadians the how's and why's of its decisions, the bank has an obligation to let citizens know how well it's doing its job and report its progress in meeting the objectives.

Follow-up evaluations on the first objective indicate a reduction of economic uncertainties resulting from reduced volatility of interest rates under the fixed-date system. For the second objective—greater focus on Canada's economic context—media coverage has shifted more onto Canadian economic issues as separate from U.S. conditions. Writing in the *Globe and Mail* on monetary policy two years into the fixed-date system, for example, Bruce Little commented, "Our economy has followed a different path than that of the United States....[W]hat happens in the U.S. affects Canada, but Canada's economy is not a clone of the U.S. economy." Shifting of the public's perspective from short- to medium-term still poses a significant challenge because the public tends to be impatient about looking beyond a week or month for monetary policy to take affect.

Regarding accountability, the fixed-date system has helped in several ways. Among the banks, investors, and financial institutions, regularity of communications has brought a convergence of expectations on the overall direction of monetary policy. It has improved the predictability of Bank of Canada decisions by eliminating surprises in terms of timing and enables financial institutions to better anticipate the general direction of interest rates. Finally, fixed-announcement dates have given Canadians a regular opportunity to hear the bank's recent views about the economy and its current thinking about monetary policy. The net effect is a more stable economic environment, an obligation for which the bank is accountable to the Canadian public.

decreased demand for loans from businesses and households because these customers borrow less money when interest rates rise.

Member Bank Borrowing from the Bank of Canada

bank rate (rediscount rate) The rate at which chartered banks can borrow from the Bank of Canada.

The Bank of Canada is the lender of last resort for chartered banks. The rate at which chartered banks can borrow from the Bank of Canada is called the **bank rate**, or **rediscount rate**. It serves as the basis for establishing the chartered banks' prime interest rates. By raising the bank rate, the Bank of Canada depresses the demand for money; by lowering it, the demand for money increases. In practice, chartered banks seldom have to borrow from the Bank of Canada. However, the bank rate is an important instrument of monetary policy as a determinant of interest rates.

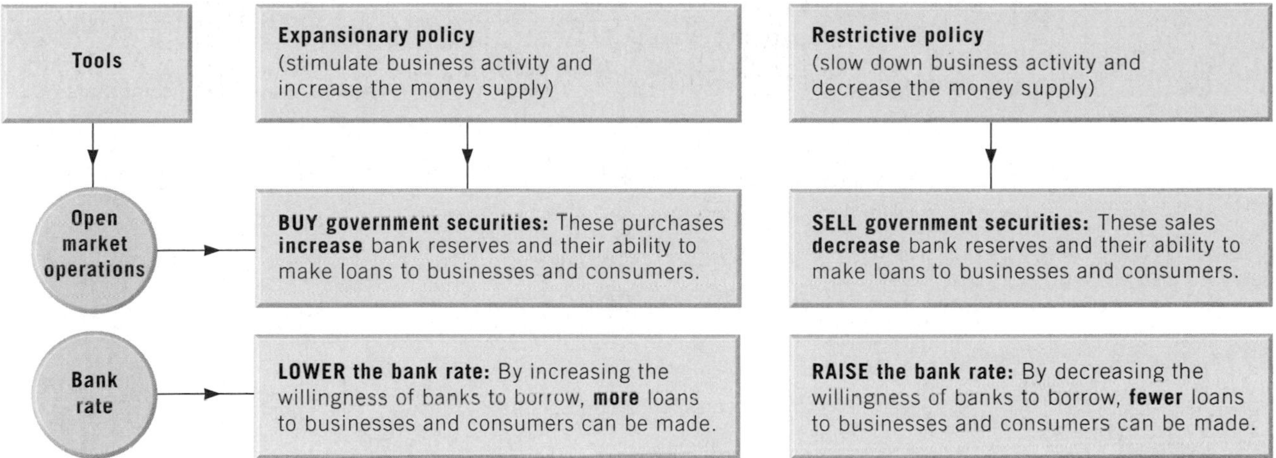

Figure 18.3 Bank of Canada monetary policy actions.

FINANCIAL PILLAR #2—ALTERNATE BANKS

Trust Companies

Another financial intermediary that serves individuals and businesses is the alternate, or near, bank: the trust company. A **trust company** safeguards property—funds and estates—entrusted to it; it may also serve as trustee, transfer agent, and registrar for corporations and provide other services.

trust company Safeguards funds and estates entrusted to it; may also serve as trustee, transfer agent, and registrar for corporations.

A corporation selling bonds to many investors appoints a trustee, usually a trust company, to protect the bondholders' interests. A trust company can also serve as a transfer agent and registrar for corporations. A transfer agent records changes in ownership of a corporation's shares of stock. A registrar certifies to the investing public that stock issues are correctly stated and comply with the corporate charter. Other services include preparing and issuing dividend cheques to shareholders and serving as trustee for employee profit-sharing funds. Trust companies also accept deposits and pay interest on them.

Credit Unions/Caisses Populaires

Credit unions (called *caisses populaires* in Quebec) are also alternate banks. They are important to business because they lend money to consumers to buy durable goods such as cars and furniture. They also lend money to businesses. **Credit unions** and *caisses populaires* are co-operative savings and lending associations formed by a group with common interests. Members (owners) can add to their savings accounts by authorizing deductions from their paycheques or by making direct deposits. They can borrow short-term, long-term, or mortgage funds from the credit union. Credit unions also invest substantial amounts of money in corporate and government securities. The largest credit unions in Canada are listed in Table 18.2.

credit union Co-operative savings and lending association formed by a group with common interests.

FINANCIAL PILLAR #3—SPECIALIZED LENDING AND SAVINGS INTERMEDIARIES

Life Insurance Companies

An important source of funds for individuals, non-business organizations, and businesses is the life insurance company. A **life insurance company**

life insurance company A mutual or stock company that shares risk with its policyholders for payment of premiums.

Table 18.2 The Top 10 Credit Unions in Canada, 2005

Company	Annual Revenues (in millions of $)
1. Mouvement des caisses Desjardins	$9071
2. Vancouver City Savings Credit Union	592
3. Caisse centrale Desjardins	523
4. Coast Capital Savings Credit Union	423
5. Credit Union Central of Saskatchewan	286
6. Concentra Financial Services Association	195
7. Meridian Credit Union Ltd.	181
8. Credit Union Central of British Columbia	171
9. Envision Credit Union	151
10. Capital City Savings and Credit Union Ltd.	144

shares risk with its policyholders in return for payment of a premium. It lends some of the money it collects from premiums to borrowers. Life insurance companies are substantial investors in real estate mortgages and in corporate and government bonds. Next to chartered banks, they are the largest financial intermediaries in Canada. We discuss insurance companies in more detail in Chapter 20.

Factoring Companies

factoring company Buys accounts receivable from a firm for less than their face value, and then collects the face value of the receivables.

An important source of short-term funds for many firms is factoring companies. A **factoring company** (or factor) buys accounts receivable (amounts due from credit customers) from a firm. It pays less than the face value of the accounts but collects the face value of the accounts. The difference, minus the cost of doing business, is the factor's profit.

A firm that sells its accounts receivable to a factor without recourse shifts the risk of credit loss to the factor. If an account turns out to be uncollectible, the factor suffers the loss. However, a factor is a specialist in credit and collection activities. Using a factor may enable a business firm to expand sales beyond what would be practical without the factor. The firm trades accounts receivable for cash. The factor then notifies the firm's customers to make their overdue payments to the factor.

Financial Corporations

sales finance company Specializes in financing instalment purchases made by individuals or firms.

There are two types of financial corporations: sales finance companies and consumer finance companies. A **sales finance company** specializes in financing instalment purchases made by individuals and firms. When you buy durable goods from a retailer on an instalment plan with a sales finance company, the loan is made directly to you. The item itself serves as security for the loan. Sales finance companies enable many firms to sell on credit, even though the firms could not afford to finance credit sales on their own. General Motors Acceptance Corporation (GMAC) is a sales finance company. It is a captive company because it exists to finance instalment contracts resulting from sales made by General Motors. Industrial Acceptance Corporation is a large Canadian sales finance company. Sales finance companies also finance instalment sales to business firms.

consumer finance company Makes personal loans to consumers.

A **consumer finance company** makes personal loans to consumers. Often the borrower pledges no security (collateral) for the loan. For larger loans, collateral may be required, such as a car or furniture.

Venture Capital or Development Firms

A **venture capital firm** provides funds for new or expanding firms thought to have significant potential. A venture capital firm wants a situation where a company in which it has invested becomes very successful and experiences substantial increases in its stock price. Venture capital firms may provide either equity or debt funds to businesses, but they typically buy shares in companies they are interested in. They may demand an ownership stake of 50 percent or more before they will buy into a company. Because financing new, untested businesses is so risky, venture capital firms want to earn a higher-than-normal return on their investment. They may insist that they be given at least one seat on the board of directors so they can observe first-hand how their investment is faring.

venture capital firm Provides funds for new or expanding firms thought to have significant potential.

Venture capital firms obtain their funds from initial capital subscriptions, from loans from other financial intermediaries, and from retained earnings. The amount of venture capital that is raised varies according to economic conditions. For example, during May 2005, Canadian companies raised $434 million through venture capital firms. That was up sharply from earlier months and indicated continuing improvement in the Canadian economy.[11] In recent years, U.S.-based venture capital firms have become a significant presence in the Canadian market, and are pushing aside smaller Canadian venture capital firms.

Pension Funds

A **pension fund** accumulates money that will be paid out to plan subscribers at some time in the future. The money collected is invested in corporate stocks and bonds, government bonds, or mortgages until it is to be paid out.

pension fund Accumulates money that will be paid out to plan subscribers in the future.

FINANCIAL PILLAR #4—INVESTMENT DEALERS

Investment dealers (called stockbrokers or underwriters) perform two important financial functions. First, they are the primary distributors of new stock and bond issues (underwriting). In 2004, Canadian corporations raised $44.2 billion in equity funds and $56.3 billion in debt funds. CIBC World Markets Inc. was the largest equity (stock) underwriter, selling $10.7 billion.[12] RBC Dominion Securities was the largest debt seller, with $11.4 billion in bond sales.[13] Second, investment dealers facilitate secondary trading of stocks and bonds, both on stock exchanges and on over-the-counter stock and bond markets (the brokerage function). These two functions are discussed in more detail in Chapter 19.

OTHER SOURCES OF FUNDS

In Canada, a number of different government suppliers of funds are important to business. In general, they supply funds to new and/or growing companies. However, established firms can also use some of them.

The Business Development Bank of Canada (BDC) makes term loans, primarily to smaller firms judged to have growth potential but unable to secure funds at reasonable terms from traditional sources. It provides proportionally more equity financing and more management counselling services. A variety of provincial industrial development corporations also provide funds to developing business firms in the hope that they will provide jobs in the province. A number of federal and provincial programs are specifically designed to provide loans to agricultural operators. Most of these are long-term loans for land purchase.

The federal government's Export Development Corporation finances and insures export sales for Canadian companies. The Canada Mortgage and Housing Corporation (CMHC) is involved in providing and guaranteeing mortgages. The CMHC is particularly important to the construction industry.

In addition to these activities, governments are involved in providing grants to business operations. For example, the federal government, through the Department of Regional Industrial Expansion (DRIE), gives grants for certain types of business expansion in designated areas of the country. Other federal government grants are available for activities such as new product development.

INTERNATIONAL BANKING AND FINANCE

6 Understand the key concepts and activities in *international banking and finance.*

Along with international banking networks, electronic technologies now permit nearly instantaneous financial transactions around the globe. The economic importance of international finance is evident from both the presence of foreign banks in the Canadian market and the sizes of certain banks around the world. In addition, each nation tries to influence its currency exchange rates for economic advantage in international trade. The subsequent country-to-country transactions result in an *international payments process* that moves money between buyers and sellers on different continents.

Exchange Rates and International Trade

As we saw in Chapter 5, a country's currency exchange rate affects its ability to buy and sell on the global market. The value of a given currency (say, the Canadian dollar) reflects the overall supply and demand for Canadian dollars both at home and abroad. This value changes with economic conditions. Around the world, therefore, firms will watch those trends, and decisions about doing business in Canada will be affected by more or less favourable exchange rates. At one point in 2006, for example, the Canadian dollar was valued at U.S.$0.90. This was up sharply from its 2002 value of $0.63, but lower than its value in the 1960s, when the U.S. and Canadian dollars were about equal. With the Canadian dollar now trading for less than the U.S. dollar, American companies have become more interested in buying Canadian companies.

The Law of One Price

How do firms determine when exchange rates are favourable? When a country's currency becomes overvalued, its exchange rate is higher than warranted by its economic conditions. Its high costs make it less competitive. Because its products are too expensive to make and buy, fewer are purchased by other countries. The likely result is a trade deficit (see Chapter 5). In contrast, an undervalued currency means low costs and low prices. It attracts purchases by other countries, usually leading to a trade surplus.

law of one price The principle that identical products should sell for the same price in all countries.

How do we know whether a currency is overvalued or undervalued? One method involves a simple concept called the **law of one price**—the principle that identical products should sell for the same price in all countries. In other words, if the different prices of a Rolex watch in different countries were converted into a common currency, the price should be the same everywhere.

But what if prices are not equal? In theory, the pursuit of profits should equalize them. Sellers in high-priced countries will have to reduce prices if they are to compete successfully and make profits. As prices adjust, so should the exchange rates between different currencies until the Rolex can be purchased for the same price everywhere.

A simple example that illustrates over- and undervalued currencies is the Big Mac Currency index, which is published annually in the British magazine the *Economist*. The identical product here is always a McDonald's Big Mac, which is made locally in many countries. Table 18.3 lists selected countries and Big Mac prices in terms of U.S. dollars (based on recent exchange rates). As you can see, the Canadian dollar is undervalued by 4 percent. The Icelandic kronur is the most overvalued currency (against the U.S. dollar), and the Chinese yuan is the most undervalued currency. In theory, this means that you could buy Big Macs in China (using yuan) and resell them in Iceland (for kronur) at a handsome profit. If you did that, the demand for burgers would increase in China, driving up the price toward the higher prices in the other countries. In other words, the law of one price would set in.

Government Influence on Exchange Rates

What happens when a currency becomes overvalued or undervalued? A nation's economic authorities may take action to correct its balance-of-payments conditions. Typically, they will devalue or revalue the nation's currency. The purpose of *devaluing* is to cause a decrease in the home country's exchange value. It will then be less expensive for other countries to buy the home country's products. As more of its products are purchased, the home country's payment deficit goes down. The purpose of *revaluation*, of course, is the reverse: to increase the exchange value and reduce the home country's payment surplus.

In 2001, for instance, the exchange rate was 1.0 Argentine peso per U.S. dollar throughout the year. Then, in January 2002, the Argentine government devalued the peso to 1.4 pesos per dollar. By July 2002, the rate had gone to 3.57 on the world market, meaning that each peso was worth just $0.28. Argentine officials sought the more favourable exchange rate to encourage other countries to buy more Argentine products, thereby reducing Argentina's payments deficit.

The International Payments Process

Now we know why a nation tries to control its balance of payments and what, at least in part, it can do about an unfavourable balance. Exactly how are payments made? Transactions among buyers and sellers in different countries are simplified through the services provided by their banks. For example, payments from buyers flow through a local bank that converts them from the local currency into the foreign currency of the seller. Likewise, the local bank receives and converts incoming money from the banks of foreign buyers. The payments process is shown in Figure 18.4.[14]

Step 1. A Canadian olive importer withdraws $1000 from its chequing account to buy olives from a Greek exporter. The local Canadian bank converts those dollars into Greek drachmas at the current exchange rate (230 drachmas per dollar).

Step 2. The Canadian bank sends the cheque for 230 000 drachmas (230 × 1000) to the exporter in Greece.

Steps 3 and 4. The exporter sends olives to its Canadian customer and deposits the cheque in its local Greek bank. While the exporter now has drachmas that can be spent in Greece, the importer has olives to sell in Canada.

At the same time, a separate transaction is being made between a Canadian machine exporter and a Greek olive oil producer. This time, the importer/exporter roles are reversed between the two countries: The Greek firm needs to import a $1000 olive oil press from Canada.

Table 18.3 Big Mac Currency Index

Country	Big Mac Prices: In Local Currency	Big Mac Prices: In Dollars	Implied PPP* of the Dollar	Actual Dollar Exchange Rate Jan 31st	Under (–)/Over (+) Valuation Against the Dollar, %
United States†	$3.22	3.22			
Argentina	Peso 8.25	2.65	2.56	3.11	–18
Australia	A$3.45	2.67	1.07	1.29	–17
Brazil	Real 6.4	3.01	1.99	2.13	–6
Britain	£1.99	3.90	1.62‡	1.96‡	+21
Canada	C$3.63	3.08	1.13	1.18	–4
Chile	Peso 1,670	3.07	519	544	–5
China	Yuan 11.0	1.41	3.42	7.77	–56
Colombia	Peso 6,900	3.06	2,143	2,254	–5
Costa Rica	Colones 1,130	2.18	351	519	–32
Czech Republic	Koruna 52.1	2.41	16.2	21.6	–25
Denmark	DKr27.75	4.84	8.62	5.74	+50
Egypt	Pound 9.09	1.60	2.82	5.70	–50
Estonia	Kroon 30	2.49	9.32	12.0	–23
Euro area§	€2.94	3.82	1.10**	1.30**	+19
Hong Kong	HK$12.0	1.54	3.73	7.81	–52
Hungary	Forint 590	3.00	183	197	–7
Iceland	Kronur509	7.44	158	68.4	+131
Indonesia	Rupiah 15,900	1.75	4,938	9,100	–46
Japan	¥280	2.31	87.0	121	–28
Latvia	Lats 1.35	2.52	0.42	0.54	–22
Lithuania	Litas 6.50	2.45	2.02	2.66	–24
Malaysia	Ringgit 5.50	1.57	1.71	3.50	–51
Mexico	Peso 29.0	2.66	9.01	10.9	–17
New Zealand	NZ$4.60	3.16	1.43	1.45	–2
Norway	Kroner 41.5	6.63	12.9	6.26	+106
Pakistan	Rupee 140	2.31	43.5	60.7	–28
Paraguay	Guarani 10,000	1.90	3,106	5,250	–41
Peru	New Sol 9.50	2.97	2.95	3.20	–8
Philippines	Peso 85.0	1.74	26.4	48.9	–46
Poland	Zloty 6.90	2.29	2.14	3.01	–29
Russia	Rouble 49.0	1.85	15.2	26.5	–43
Saudi Arabia	Riyal 9.00	2.40	2.80	3.75	–25
Singapore	S$3.60	2.34	1.12	1.54	–27
Slovakia	Crown 57.98	2.13	18.0	27.2	–34
South Africa	Rand 15.5	2.14	4.81	7.25	–34
South Korea	Won 2,900	3.08	901	942	–4
Sri Lanka	Rupee 190	1.75	59.0	109	–46
Sweden	SKr32.0	4.59	9.94	6.97	+43
Switzerland	SFr6.30	5.05	1.96	1.25	+57
Taiwan	NT$75.0	2.28	23.3	32.9	–29
Thailand	Baht 62.0	1.78	19.3	34.7	–45
Turkey	Lire 4.55	3.22	1.41	1.41	nil
UAE	Dirhams 10.0	2.72	3.11	3.67	–15
Ukraine	Hryvnia 9.00	1.71	2.80	5.27	–47
Uruguay	Peso 55.0	2.17	17.1	25.3	–33
Venezuela	Bolivar 6,800	1.58	2,112	4,307	–51

Sources: McDonald's; *The Economist*

*Purchasing-power parity: local price divided by price in United States; †Average of New York, Atlanta, Chicago and SanFrancisco; ‡Dollars per pound; §Weighted average of prices in euro area; **Dollars per euro

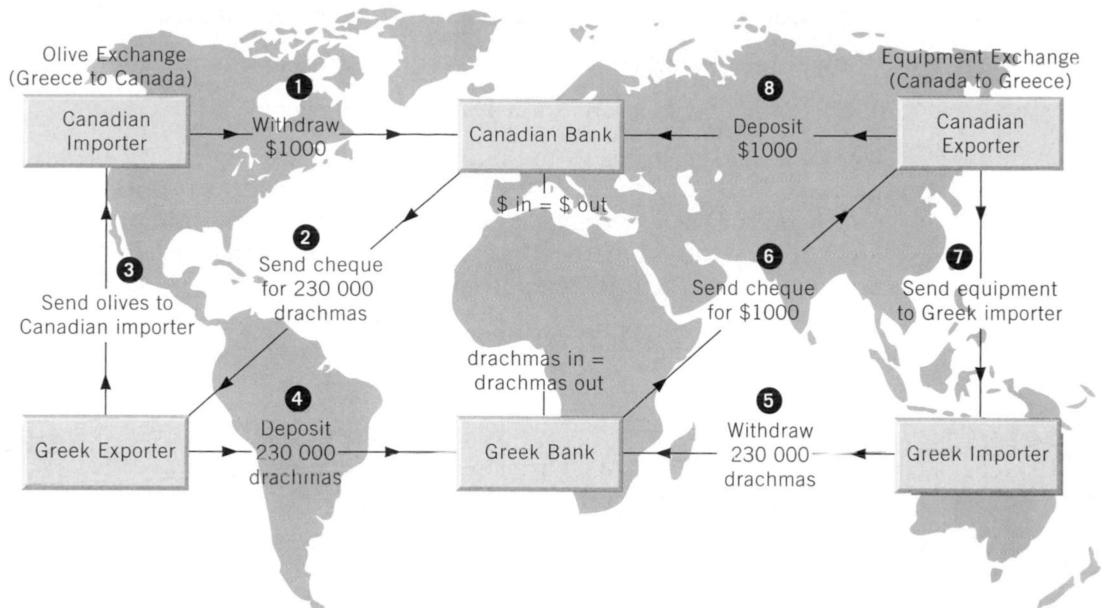

Figure 18.4 The international payments process.

Steps 5 and 6. Drachmas (230 000) withdrawn from a local Greek bank account are converted into $1000 Canadian and sent via cheque to the Canadian exporter.

Steps 7 and 8. The olive oil press is sent to the Greek importer, and the importer's cheque is deposited in the Canadian exporter's local bank account.

In this example, trade between the two countries is *in balance*: Money inflows and outflows are equal for both countries. When such a balance occurs, *money does not actually have to flow between the two countries*. Within each bank, the dollars spent by local importers offset the dollars received by local exporters. In effect, therefore, the dollars have simply flowed from Canadian importers to Canadian exporters. Likewise, the drachmas have moved from Greek exporters to Greek importers.

The International Bank Structure

There is no worldwide banking system that is comparable, in terms of policy making and regulatory power, to the system of any single industrialized nation. Rather, worldwide banking stability relies on a loose structure of agreements among individual countries or groups of countries.

The World Bank and the IMF

Two United Nations agencies, the World Bank and the International Monetary Fund (IMF), help to finance international trade. Unlike true banks, the **World Bank** (technically the International Bank for Reconstruction and Development) actually provides only a very limited scope of services. For instance, it funds national improvements by making loans to build roads, schools, power plants, and hospitals. The resulting improvements eventually enable borrowing countries to increase productive capacity and international trade.

World Bank A United Nations agency that provides a limited scope of financial services, such as funding national improvements in undeveloped countries.

The **International Monetary Fund** is a group of some 150 nations that have combined their resources for the following purposes:

International Monetary Fund (IMF) A United Nations agency consisting of about 150 nations who have combined resources to promote stable exchange rates, provide temporary short-term loans, and serve other purposes.

- to promote the stability of exchange rates

- to provide temporary, short-term loans to member countries
- to encourage members to co-operate on international monetary issues
- to encourage development of a system for international payments

The IMF makes loans to nations suffering from temporary negative trade balances. By making it possible for these countries to continue buying products from other countries, the IMF facilitates international trade. However, some nations have declined IMF funds rather than accept the economic changes that the IMF demands. For example, some developing countries reject the IMF's requirement that they cut back social programs and spending to bring inflation under control.

Summary of Learning Objectives

1. **Define *money* and identify the different forms it takes in the nation's money supply.** Any item that is portable, divisible, durable, and stable satisfies the four basic characteristics of *money*. Money also serves three functions: It is a medium of exchange, a store of value, and a unit of account. The nation's money supply is often determined by two measures: *M-1* includes liquid (or spendable) forms of money—currency (bills and coins), demand deposits, and other "chequable" deposits (such as chequing accounts and ATM withdrawals). *M-2* includes M-1 plus items that cannot be directly spent but which can be easily converted to spendable forms: time deposits, money market funds, and savings deposits. Credit must also be considered as a factor in the money supply.
2. **Describe the different kinds of *financial institutions* that make up the Canadian financial system and explain the services they offer.** The financial intermediaries that form the "four financial pillars" in Canada are chartered banks, alternate banks, specialized lending and savings intermediaries, and investment dealers. The chartered banks, which are at the heart of our financial system, are the most important source of short-term funds for business firms. The chartered banking system creates money in the form of expanding demand deposits. The four kinds of financial institutions offer services like financial advice and brokerage services, electronic funds transfer, pension and trust services, and lending of money.
3. **Explain how banks create money and identify the means by which they are regulated.** By taking in deposits and making loans, banks create money, or more accurately, they expand the money supply. The Bank of Canada controls the overall supply of money.
4. **Identify ways in which the banking industry is changing.** The clear divisions between the activities of the "four financial pillars" are becoming less obvious. For example, deregulation has allowed banks to begin selling commercial paper. Other financial intermediaries are also beginning to get involved in new financial activities. For example, life insurance companies are starting to take over trust companies so they can get a foothold in the trust business. *Electronic technologies* offer a variety of new financial conveniences to customers. *Debit cards* are plastic cards that permit users to transfer money between bank accounts. *Smart cards* are credit card-sized plastic cards with an embedded computer chip that can be loaded with "electronic money" at ATMs or over special telephone hookups. *Ecash* is money that can be moved among consumers and businesses via digital electronic transmissions.
5. **Explain the functions of the *Bank of Canada* and describe the tools it uses to control the money supply.** The Bank of Canada manages the Canadian economy, controls the money supply, and regulates certain aspects of chartered banking operations. If the Bank of Canada wants to increase the money supply, it can buy government securities or lower the bank rate. If it wants to decrease the money supply, it can sell government securities or increase the bank rate.
6. **Understand the key concepts and activities in *international banking and finance*.** Electronic technologies now permit speedy global financial transactions to support the growing importance of international finance. Country-to-country transactions are conducted according to an *international payment process* that moves money among buyers and sellers in different nations. Each nation tries to influence its currency exchange rates to gain advantage in international trade. For example, if its currency is overvalued, a higher exchange rate usually results in a trade deficit. Conversely, undervalued currencies can attract buyers and create trade surpluses. Governments may act to influence exchange rates by *devaluing* or *revaluing* their national currencies (that is, by decreasing or increasing them). Devalued currencies make it less expensive for other countries to buy the home country's products.

KEY TERMS

Bank of Canada, 603
bank rate (rediscount rate), 604
banker's acceptance, 597
chartered bank, 595
chequable deposit, 598
cheque, 593
consumer finance company, 606
credit union, 605
currency, 592
debit card, 601
demand deposit, 593
ecash, 602
electronic funds transfer, 601
factoring company, 606
International Monetary Fund (IMF), 611
law of one price, 608
letter of credit, 597
life insurance company, 606
M-1, 592
M-2, 593
money, 590
money market mutual funds, 593
pension fund, 607
point-of-sale (POS) terminals, 601
prime rate of interest, 599
reserve requirement, 599
sales finance company, 606
smart card, 601
term deposit, 598
time deposit, 593
trust company, 605
trust services, 596
venture capital firm, 607
World Bank, 611

QUESTIONS FOR ANALYSIS

1. What kinds of changes in banking are shifting banks away from their historical role?
2. Do we really need all the different types of financial institutions we have in Canada? Could we make do with just chartered banks? Why or why not?
3. Should credit cards be counted in the money supply? Why or why not? Support your view by using the definition of *money*.
4. Should chartered banks be regulated or should market forces be allowed to set the money supply? Defend your answer.
5. If the Bank of Canada wants to increase the money supply, what options does it have? Explain how each of these options work to increase the money supply.
6. Explain the difference between factoring companies and financial corporations.
7. What is the logic behind the "law of one price" concept? Give an example using Switzerland and China.

APPLICATION EXERCISES

1. Start with a $1000 deposit and assume a reserve requirement of 15 percent. Now trace the amount of money created by the banking system after five lending cycles.
2. Interview several consumers to determine which banking services and products they use (debit cards, ATMs, smart cards, etc.). If interviewees are using these services, determine the reasons. If they are not, find out why not.
3. Interview the manager of a local chartered bank. Identify the ways in which the Bank of Canada helps the bank and the ways in which it limits the bank.

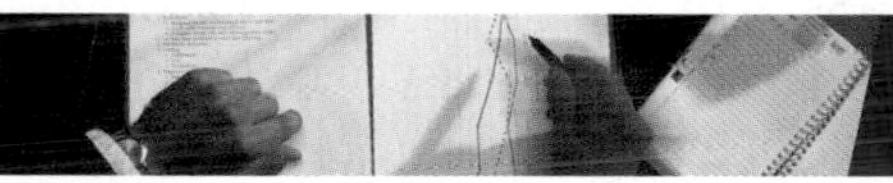

BUILDING YOUR BUSINESS SKILLS

The Risks and Rewards of Credit Cards

Goal

To help students evaluate the risks and rewards associated with excessive credit card use.

The Situation

Suppose that you've been out of school for a year and are now working in your first job. Your annual $30 000 salary is enough to support your apartment, car, and the basic necessities of life, but the luxuries are still out of reach. You pay cash for everything until one day you get a pre-approved credit card solicitation in the mail, which offers you a $1500 line of credit. You decide to take the offer and begin charging purchases. Within a year, five other credit card companies have contacted you, and you accumulate a total credit card debt of $12 000.

Assignment

Step 1

Working with three or four classmates, evaluate the advantages and dangers inherent in this situation, both to the consumer and to credit card issuers. To

▶▶▶

address this issue, research the current percentage of credit card delinquencies and rate of personal bankruptcies. Find out, for example, how these rates compare with those in previous years. In addition, research the profitability of the credit card business.

Step 2

Evaluate the different methods that credit card companies use to attract new customers. Specifically, look at the following practices:

- sending unsolicited, pre-approved credit card applications to consumers with questionable and even poor credit
- offering large credit lines to consumers who pay only monthly minimums
- lowering interest rates on accounts as a way of encouraging revolving payments
- charging penalties on accounts that are paid in full at the end of every billing cycle (research the GE Rewards MasterCard)
- sending cardholders catalogues of discounted gifts that can be purchased with their charge cards
- linking credit card use to a program of rewards—say, frequent flyer miles linked to amounts charged

Step 3

Compile your findings in the form of a set of guidelines designed for consumers receiving unsolicited credit card offers. Your guidelines should analyze the advantages and disadvantages of excessive credit card use.

Follow-Up Questions

1. If you were the person in our hypothetical example, how would you handle your credit situation?
2. Why do you think credit card companies continue to offer cards to people who are financially overextended?
3. What criteria can you suggest to evaluate different credit card offers?
4. How do you know when you have enough credit?

EXERCISING YOUR ETHICS

Telling the Ethical from the Strictly Legal

The Situation

When upgrading services for convenience to customers, chartered banks are concerned about setting prices that cover all costs so that, ultimately, they make a profit. This exercise challenges you to evaluate one banking service—ATM transactions—to determine if there are also ethical issues that should be considered in a bank's pricing decisions.

The Dilemma

Assume that a bank has more than 300 ATMs serving the nearly 400 000 chequing and savings accounts of its customers. Customers are not charged a fee for their 30 million ATM transactions each year, so long as they use their bank's ATMs. For issuing cash to non-customers, however, the bank charges a $2 ATM fee. The bank's officers are re-examining their policies on ATM surcharges because of public protests.

In considering its current policies, the bank's vice-president for community relations is concerned about more than mere legalities. She wants to ensure that her company is "being a good citizen and doing the right thing." Any decision on ATM fees will ultimately affect the bank's customers, its image in the community and industry, and its profitability for its owners.

Questions for Discussion

1. From the standpoint of a chartered bank, can you find any economic justification for ATM access fees?
2. Based on the scenario described for our bank, do you find any ethical issues in this situation? Or do you find the main issues legal and economic rather than ethical?
3. As an officer for this bank, how would you handle this situation?

CONCLUDING CASE 18-1

The Struggle to Finance Cod Aquaculture

During the heyday of cod fishing in the 1980s, commercial fishing operators from Newfoundland harvested more than 220 000 tonnes of cod each year. But by 1992, cod stocks had declined sharply, and the federal fisheries minister drastically reduced the number of fish that could be harvested. Thousands of people involved in fish catching and fish processing lost their jobs, and the industry has never recovered.

In 1997, after it had become clear that the wild cod fishery would not be viable for many years, the federal government suggested that Newfoundland become a pioneer in cod aquaculture, or fish farming. The idea seemed sound, particularly when it was learned that cod could double in size in 60 days if fed regularly. By 1999, 18 cod aquaculture operations had started. But the project encountered a series of problems that kept the promise of cod aquaculture from being fulfilled. Newfoundland did produce 227 tonnes of cod in 2002, but big problems developed in the industry in 2003. For one thing, the market price of cod declined sharply and that led to much lower sales revenue. But the biggest factor was the industry's inventory problem—fish farmers couldn't get young cod (called fry) because financial and other problems had forced two large hatcheries out of business. By 2006, there was not a single cod farm in operation in Newfoundland. What happened?

One answer is the high cost of feed, which constitutes about 80 percent of total expenses in cod farming. This feed, of course, must be purchased up front. Most Newfoundland fish farmers were able to get credit from the companies they purchased their feed from. These feed companies were essentially acting as bankers for the cod farmers. But there were only three major feed companies in Atlantic Canada, and fish farmers found they were paying interest rates of more than 25 percent on their loans. The cod farmers couldn't get lower-cost bank loans because Canadian banks would not loan them any money. The banks were not interested in making loans to cod farmers because it is a risky business and the time frame for getting revenue from sales is long (it takes three years to raise cod fry to a size where they can be sold to consumers). Some *foreign* banks—in Iceland and Norway—have funded other, more traditional seafood industries in Canada, but none appeared interested in fish farming.

There are several factors that make cod farming (and salmon farming) a risky business. First, factors like bad weather and fish diseases can wipe out a whole year's work in short order. Second, if a cod farming operation does go bankrupt, there are very few assets which can be sold to help investors recoup their money. Third, the high Canadian dollar means that Canadian seafood products that are exported to the United States (where most of Canada's seafood is sold) have become more expensive for consumers, and this has reduced demand.

The federal government of Canada did not make any moves to bail out the cod farming business, but Newfoundland tried to provide alternative financing that was not dependent on feed companies extending credit to cod farmers. The province developed a provincial loan guarantee program that guarantees 80 percent of any debt owed if a fish farming company needs to be liquidated. But the program requires that at least one bank participate, and so far only one company has gotten bank approval.

Most people seem to agree that the Newfoundland cod farming industry can move forward only if there is a local hatchery to provide cod fry to the fish farmers. There is a cod farming research facility in Pool's Cove. It has been supported by a $12.4 million grant provided by several different organizations, including the provincial and federal governments, the Canadian Foundation for Innovation, and the Atlantic Innovation Fund. But there are no cod farming operations.

The difficulties in Newfoundland are a bit perplexing, since cod farming has been demonstrated to work elsewhere. Cod cages are in the water in the Bay of Fundy, and the cod grown there were featured on the menus of some high-end restaurants in the northeastern United States in late 2005. In Scotland, Johnson Seafarms has raised more than $48 million to pursue organic cod farming. Investors became interested after they were informed that 20 percent of their initial investment would be tax free; also, if they hold their stock for at least three years, they won't have to pay any capital gains tax. Norway has had even more success in cod farming. In 2006, it produced 40 000 tonnes of cod. By 2010, the Norwegian industry is expected to be producing 225 000 tonnes of cod.

In 2006, the Newfoundland Minister of Fisheries and Aquaculture, announced that $33 450 worth of funding had been approved to help the Newfoundland Aquaculture Industry Association (NAIA) develop a business plan for a demonstration cod farm. The funding will help the NAIA identify what will be required to develop commercial cod farming operations. The Minister acknowledged that cod farming is still in the development stage in Newfoundland, but thought that it was a promising industry that would benefit rural communities.

▶▶▶

There are plenty of obstacles that must be cleared before cod farming is commercially viable. And now a new one has arisen: environmental concerns. As fish farming becomes more common, and as fish farms get larger, the waste dropped by the fish is becoming a problem. In 2006, there were 96 salmon fish farming sites in New Brunswick, and each of these sites had between 200 000 and 300 000 fish. Waste from these fish collects on the sea floor, and studies have shown that the sea floor under fish cages is not normal. Oxygen levels are low, and a layer of sludge up to 20 centimetres deep exists. The water simply can't neutralize the large amount of waste that is concentrated in a relatively small area, so other marine life is harmed. These problems are particularly evident in Passamaquoddy Bay, where there are many salmon farms. Introducing cod into the Bay of Fundy will cause the same thing to happen there. It doesn't matter which fish species is involved. It is the technology of fish farming that causes the problem.

The dilemma is that wild stocks of most fish species are declining because of overfishing. Consumer demand for fish is high, so aquaculture is a tempting solution. Experts say that ocean stocks are going to keep declining, so aquaculture may be the thing of the future. If the experimental cod farms can show a profit, a new era will dawn. But large investments are needed to secure the future of aquaculture.

Questions for Discussion

1. Why did feed companies charge such high interest rates to cod farmers?
2. Why were banks not interested in providing loans to cod farmers?
3. Read the material in Chapter 20 on sources of funds for businesses. Which source were cod farmers using? Why were they using that source? What other sources of funding might be possible for this type of business?
4. Do you think that the latest provincial government financing will move the cod farming industry toward real commercial success? Defend your answer.

CONCLUDING CASE 18-2

Going with the Currency

Euros, pesos, dollars, and yen—money comes in all sizes and stripes, and almost everyone seems to want more of it. When it comes to choosing one currency over others, the best choice changes from day to day and depends on how you plan to use it. A currency's value reflects global supply and demand—what traders are willing to pay—for one currency relative to others. At any one time, then, some currencies are "strong"—selling at a higher price and thus worth more—while others are "weak." Most people would prefer a "strong" currency, right? Well, not so fast. Using money for international activities is one of those "good news–bad news" situations.

Consider the euro, up 20 percent against the U.S. dollar in 2003 and again in 2004. If you were a citizen in one of the 12 euro-area countries—say, France—you chose wisely if you delayed that U.S. vacation until 2004. Each euro in 2004 paid for $1.26 of the trip, but it would have covered only $1.06 the year before. That's the good news: The stronger euro means more purchasing power against the weaker dollar. It's bad news, though, for French innkeepers because Americans go elsewhere to avoid expensive European travel—it takes $1.26 for one euro of vacation cost, up from $1.06 just a year earlier.

The stronger euro is proving to be a stumbling block for Europe's economic recovery, especially for industries that export to non-euro countries with weaker currencies. Prices had to be increased, for example, on German-made Mercedes and BMW auto exports to the United States to cover euro-based manufacturing costs, causing weaker demand and sales. Louis Vuitton Moët Hennessy, a French luxury goods firm, had a 9 percent rise in profits for 2003 that would have been 20 percent if the euro had remained at its 2002 level. STMicroelectronics, Europe's largest computer chip maker, reported lower profits because of the stronger euro. For 2003, Europe's exports overall fell 3 percent; one industry expert estimates that European firms lost 8 to 10 percent in revenue growth due to weakness of the U.S. dollar.

While the weaker dollar has hurt many European firms, others have gained by increasing their foreign investments. When DaimlerChrysler, for example, produces Mercedes M-class autos in Alabama, it pays in weaker dollars for manufacturing them, exports cars to Europe, and sells in euros for windfall profits. Tire and auto-parts maker Continental AG is building facilities in countries with weaker currencies—a plant in Mexico, a low-cost research-and-development centre in Romania, a factory in Brazil—to hedge against a stronger euro. Aside from foreign investments, increased purchasing power, too, is a plus. Airbus saved millions by buying $4 billion in aircraft parts, priced in weaker dollars, from U.S. companies in 2003. By the end of 2003, the euro-zone's import prices, overall, had fallen by 12 percent from the peak levels three years earlier.

"We are seriously worried about the negative consequences of the super-strong euro on...Europe," says a member of Morgan Stanley's European economic team. Euro-zone companies are less competitive against global counterparts and Europe's economic recovery is slower than expected. Even so, the European Central Bank (ECB) refuses to weaken the euro by cutting interest rates. In contrast, the U.S. Federal Reserve's rapid rate slashing during 2003 and 2004 is credited with weakening the U.S. dollar and stimulating the current economic recovery there. As pressures mount, some observers expect ECB will soon concede. "We expect growth in the euro zone to remain sluggish, and therefore we think a rate cut by the ECB would act as insurance against the downside risk," says Olivier Garnier, a research manager at Société Générale Asset Management in Paris.

In managing the money supply and interest rates, the U.S. Federal Reserve System strongly influences the dollar's strength against other currencies. The European Central Bank (ECB) has the same role in the 12-nation euro zone, the world's second-largest economic system. While both systems have struggled for economic recovery, their central banks adopted dissimilar monetary policies in the years since 2000, with contrasting results.

Consider the U.S. economy's recent rapid growth, with a 45-year low federal funds rate—the interest rate governing overnight interbank loans—at 1 percent, high productivity, moderate unemployment, a weak dollar, low inflation, and strong economic recovery. Europe's monetary position, in contrast, clings to a policy of higher interest rates—standing at 2 percent compared with 1 percent in the United States—and a strengthening euro has risen by some 50 percent against the dollar since its low in mid-2001.

The economic results are disappointing. Exports, for example, remain less competitive while imports to European markets are more competitive. In a growing global economy, Europe's exports fell 3 percent in 2003. Overall economic growth in the region is lower than in either Canada or the United States. The region's unemployment is nearly 9 percent, productivity gains are modest, and inflation stands at 1.6 percent—well below the ECB's preferred 2 percent target. German profits are off 74 percent, French profits are down 67 percent, and Italian profits are off 25 percent. In short, the still-fragile economic recovery is sluggish.

The interest rate is a key policy variable in accounting for differences in U.S. and euro-zone results. The raising of interest rates tends to increase an economic system's currency value, while lowering the rate has the opposite effect. The prevailing rates for the United States and the euro zone are expected to change soon—but in opposite directions. U.S. rates started to rise in 2005, while the ECB recognizes the need for lower rates to stimulate the European recovery. Thus, the interest-rate differential—1 percent versus 2 percent—will lessen and possibly even disappear. We can then expect a strengthening of the dollar against the euro and a reversal of positions, somewhat, between the two economic systems.

Meanwhile, anxious U.S. tourists can rest easy because European travel vendors are offering attractive rate-cutting deals to overcome the dollar's weak buying power. Some are allowing travellers to book trips at year-ago exchange rates, which means savings over the current exchange rate. One company offered Americans a 1:1 exchange rate at its Italian properties, so the 465-euro room would cost the U.S. traveller $465 (465 euros was worth $570 at the time). Once you arrive, though, be prepared to pay dearly for food, souvenirs, and entertainment (unless the euro weakens against the dollar).

Questions for Discussion

1. In late 2000, the euro stood at U.S.$0.82, whereas it reached a peak of nearly U.S.$1.30 in early 2004. What does this change mean to a U.S. importer of euro-zone products? What does it mean to an exporter of U.S. goods to the euro zone?
2. Under what economic conditions might you expect the Federal Reserve in the United States to raise interest rates? To lower them? Explain.
3. Consider the policy position taken by the European Central Bank. Why do you suppose it held to a 2 percent target inflation rate and a 2 percent interest rate for the European community's post-recession recovery?
4. Why do you think the U.S. Federal Reserve might reverse recent trends by raising the interest rate governing overnight interbank loans from the recent 45-year low? How might a rate increase affect inflation, if at all?
5. Suppose you are a businessperson planning to build a new facility in either the United States or the euro zone. How might your choice of where and when to build be influenced by monetary policies of the European Central Bank and the U.S. Federal Reserve?

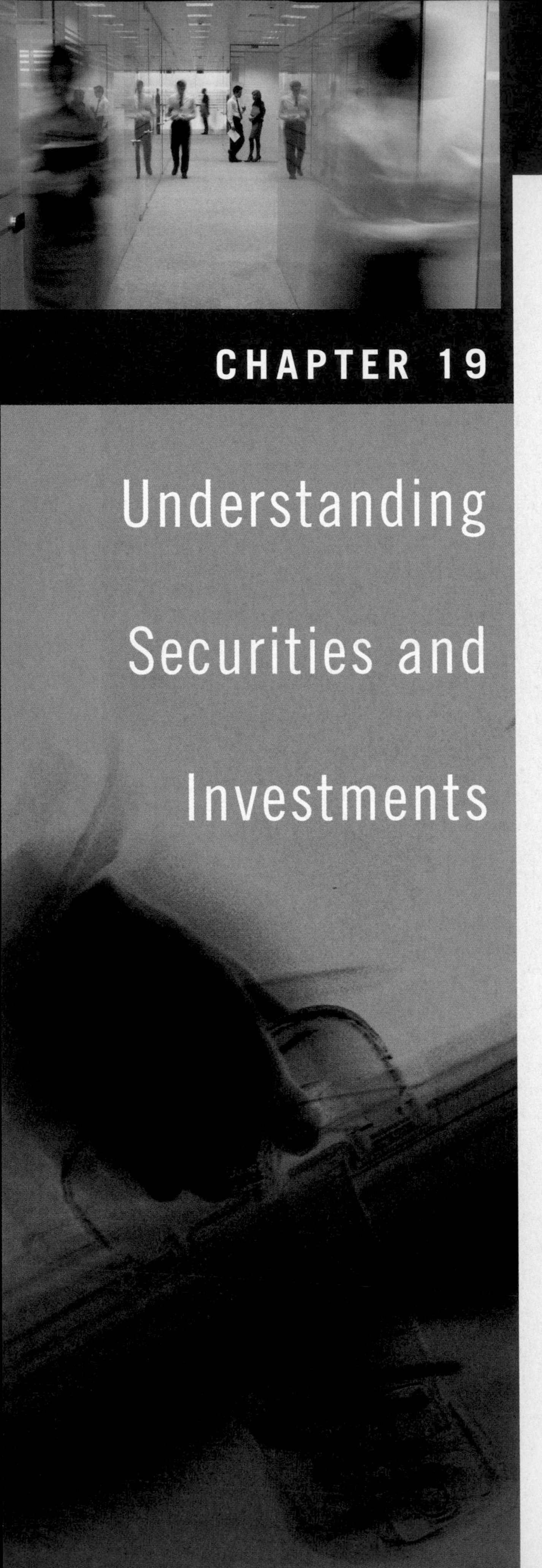

CHAPTER 19

Understanding Securities and Investments

After reading this chapter, you should be able to:

1. Explain the difference between *primary* and *secondary securities markets*.
2. Discuss the value of *common stock* and *preferred stock* to shareholders and describe the secondary market for each type of security.
3. Distinguish among various types of *bonds* in terms of their issuers, safety, and retirement.
4. Describe the investment opportunities offered by *mutual funds* and *commodities*.
5. Explain the process by which securities are bought and sold.
6. Explain how securities markets are regulated.

To some people, the stock market is a place where you can increase your assets over time if you invest in conservative stocks and have patience. Other people have a more speculative bent, and invest in companies that are more risky ventures. In either case, the financial fortunes of these people are determined by the market. But some people don't want to be at the mercy of the market, so they try to manipulate the market to their advantage. Over the last 50 years, many individuals have attempted to do this. A brief summary of their escapades is presented below, beginning with the most recent cases.

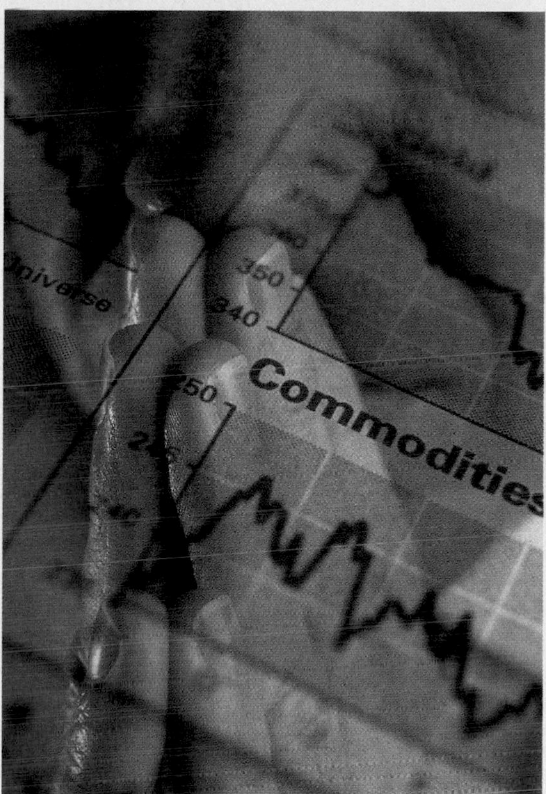

ANDREW RANKIN

An investment banking star with RBC Dominion Securities, Rankin was charged with insider trading and "tipping" his friend Daniel Duic about several big corporate deals that were about to take place. Using the information provided by Rankin, Duic made over $4 million in profit by buying and selling the stocks of these companies at opportune times. When this was discovered, Duic made a deal with the Ontario Securities Commission to testify against his friend Rankin. In September 2005, Rankin was convicted of "tipping" and was sentenced to six months in jail. It was the first time an executive had been jailed for "tipping."

MICHAEL HOLODAY

He once had it all—the big house, cars, and all the other toys that rich people have. But he was a ruthless scammer and a con man with no conscience. While working for a brokerage firm, he skimmed the cash from the accounts of ordinary folks who came to him for advice. When investors received notices from the brokerage firm that showed their account was dropping in value, they became concerned and called Holoday. He said the company statements were in error and produced fake statements showing that investors were making money. Finally, one investor blew the whistle and the game was over.

VISA GOLD EXPLORATION

This company hunts for treasure found in sunken ships off the coast of Cuba. Officials at the Toronto-Dominion Bank alerted government regulators to suspicious trading patterns in the company's stock in November 2000. The alleged manipulation involved "wash trading," which occurs when the people who want to manipulate the price of a stock use several different brokerage accounts to establish an artificial price for a stock. This makes it look like there is a lot of interest in the stock by the general public, and that may cause its price to go up. Those individuals who already own the stock benefit because of the increased price. In reality, very few buyers were involved in purchasing the stock of Visa Gold Exploration. The price of Visa Gold's stock declined from $1.15 per share in November 2000 to 5 cents a share by the end of 2001. Trading in the stock was suspended in 2002.

GLEN HARPER

In July 2000, an Ontario court found Glen Harper, the president of Golden Rule Resources Ltd., guilty of insider trading. He had sold $4 million worth of shares in his company after he found out that its supposedly huge gold find in Ghana was in doubt. When Harper sold his shares, the price of Golden Rule's stock was trading at about $13 per share. After the bad news became public, the stock fell to 10 cents a share. Harper was sentenced to one year in prison and fined nearly $4 million.

G. SCOTT PATERSON

The CEO of Yorkton Securities, Paterson (and several other executives) bought stock in various companies for pennies a share, then converted them to high tech companies. They then began promoting these stocks to clients. When these companies were taken public, the Yorkton executives made large profits because the stock price had risen a great deal. In 2001, the Ontario Securities Commission (OSC) concluded that Paterson consistently put his own interests ahead of those of Yorkton's clients. Yorkton Securities was fined $1.25 million for violating Toronto Stock Exchange rules. Paterson agreed that some of his actions were contrary to the public interest, but he denied that he had broken any specific securities rules. He was fined $1 million, banned from trading for six months, and fired from his job.

RT CAPITAL MANAGEMENT

In 2000, several employees at RT Capital Management Inc., the investment arm of the Royal Bank of Canada, were charged with illegal trading in an attempt to manipulate stock prices. The OSC and the Toronto Stock Exchange (TSX) concluded that the stock prices of many different Canadian companies were being manipulated using a practice called "juicing" or "high-closing." The practice works like this: Just before the stock exchange closes, a trader buys enough shares of a given stock so that the price of that stock rises above the price of the previous trade. This makes it look as if the stock has upward momentum. The motivation to "high-close" a stock can be strong for money managers, because they are under intense pressure to increase the value of their portfolios so they can demonstrate high performance and attract more clients. The temptation is particularly strong at year-end because money managers' annual bonuses are tied to their performance. RT Capital admitted that it had manipulated the closing price of 26 stocks over 8 days in late 1998 and early 1999. The employees who were involved included a senior vice-president and two traders, all of whom were suspended, and the company was fined $3 million.

DAVID WALSH

David Walsh started a small gold mining company in Calgary that he called Bre-X. After claiming that the company had found a major gold deposit in Indonesia, the price of the stock rose from 27 cents a share to nearly $300 dollars a share. Unfortunately, the core samples had been tampered with, and it was later discovered that there was no gold at all at the site. The shares of Bre-X quickly became worthless and investors lost millions. To date, no one has been prosecuted in this scam. At about the same time, two other gold exploration companies—Timbuktu Gold Corp. and Delgratia Mining Corp.—also revealed that their core samples had been tampered with.

VIOLA MACMILLAN

One of the first successful women in business in the twentieth century, Macmillan found gold in Ontario and lead in British Columbia in the 1920s and 1930s. After hearing about a mineral strike in northern Ontario, she bought property close by. Investors bought shares in her company, hoping that there would be valuable minerals on her property as well. She sold off her own shares knowing her claim might be worthless. She was charged with fraud, but found not guilty. She was, however, found guilty of manipulating stock prices in another company she owned. She went to jail for two months, but years later was given the Order of Canada. ◆

SECURITIES MARKETS

1 Explain the difference between *primary* and *secondary securities markets.*

Stocks and bonds are known as **securities** because they represent *secured,* or *asset-based,* claims on the part of investors. In other words, holders of stocks and bonds have a stake in the business that issued them. As we saw in Chapter 4, stockholders have claims on some of a corporation's assets (and a say in how the company is run) because each share of stock represents part ownership. In contrast, *bonds* represent strictly financial claims for money owed to holders by a company. Companies sell bonds to raise long-term funds. The markets in which stocks and bonds are sold are called *securities markets*.

securities Stocks and bonds (which represent a secured-asset-based claim on the part of investors) that can be bought and sold.

Primary and Secondary Markets for Securities

primary securities market The sale and purchase of newly issued stocks and bonds by firms or governments.

Primary securities markets handle the buying and selling of new stocks and bonds by firms or governments. New securities are sometimes sold to one buyer or a small group of buyers. These so-called *private placements* allow the businesses that use them to keep their plans confidential.

Investment Banking

Most new stocks and some bonds are sold to the wider public market. To bring a new security to market, the issuing corporation must obtain approval from a provincial securities commission. It also needs the services of an **investment banker**. Investment bankers serve as financial specialists in issuing new securities. Such well-known firms as RBC Dominion Securities and TD Securities provide three types of investment banking services:

investment banker Any financial institution engaged in purchasing and reselling new stocks and bonds.

1. They advise the company on the timing and financial terms for the new issue.
2. By *underwriting* (buying) the new securities, investment bankers bear some of the risk of issuing the new security.
3. They create the distribution network that moves the new securities through groups of other banks and brokers into the hands of individual investors.

New securities represent only a small portion of securities traded, however. The market for existing stocks and bonds, the **secondary securities market**, is handled by organizations such as the Toronto Stock Exchange. We will consider the activities of these markets later in this chapter.

secondary securities market The sale and purchase of previously issued stocks and bonds.

STOCKS

Each year, financial managers, along with millions of individual investors, buy and sell the stocks of thousands of companies. This widespread ownership has become possible because of the availability of different types of stocks and because markets have been established for conveniently buying and selling them. In this section, we will focus on the value of *common* and *preferred stock* as securities. We will also describe the *stock exchanges* where they are bought and sold.

Discuss the value of *common stock* and *preferred stock* to shareholders and describe the secondary market for each type of security. 2

Common Stock

Individuals and other companies buy a firm's common stock in the hope that the stock will increase in value, affording them a capital gain, and/or will provide dividend income. But what is the value of a common stock? Stock values are expressed in three different ways: as *par value*, as *market value*, and as *book value*.

Par Value

The face value of a share of stock, its **par value**, is set by the issuing company's board of directors. Each company must preserve the par value money in its retained earnings, and it cannot be distributed as dividends.

par value The arbitrary value of a stock set by the issuing company's board of directors and stated on stock certificates; used by accountants but of little significance to investors.

Market Value

A stock's real value is its **market value**—the current price of a share on the stock market. Market value reflects buyers' willingness to invest in a company. The market price of a stock can be influenced by both objective factors (e.g., a company's profits) and by subjective factors. Subjective factors include *rumours* (unverified information such as a claim that a company has made a big gold strike), *investor relations* (playing up the positive

market value The current price of one share of a stock in the secondary securities market; the real value of a stock.

aspects of a company's financial condition to financial analysts and financial institutions), and *stockbroker recommendations* (a recommendation to buy a stock may increase demand for the stock and cause its price to increase, while a recommendation to sell can decrease demand and cause the price to fall). None of these actions are illegal, but others, like the ones described in the opening case, are.

Book Value

book value Value of a common stock expressed as total owners' equity divided by the number of shares of stock.

Recall from Chapter 14 our definition of *owners' equity*—the sum of a company's common stock par value, retained earnings, and additional paid-in capital. The **book value** of common stock represents owners' equity divided by the number of shares. Book value is used as a comparison indicator because, for successful companies, the market value is usually greater than its book value. Thus, when market price falls to near book value, some investors buy the stock on the principle that it is underpriced and will increase in the future.

Investment Traits of Common Stock

Common stocks are among the riskiest of all securities. Uncertainties about the stock market itself, for instance, can quickly change a given stock's value. Furthermore, when companies have unprofitable years, they often cannot pay dividends. Shareholder income—and perhaps share price—may both drop. At the same time, however, common stocks offer high growth potential. Naturally the prospects for growth in various industries change from time to time, but the blue-chip stocks of well-established, financially sound firms such as IBM and Imperial Oil have historically provided investors with steady income through consistent dividend payouts.

What Is a Blue-Chip Stock?

Because the very nature of the stock market is continuously changing, the future performance of any stock is often unpredictable. With the proliferation of internet and start-up dot-coms, experts realize that many of the old rules for judging the market prospects of stocks are changing. Conventional methods don't seem to apply to the surprising surges in "new economy" stock prices. Old performance yardsticks—a company's history of dividend payouts, steady growth in earnings per share, and a low price-earnings ratio (current stock price divided by annual earnings per share)—do not seem to measure the value of new economy stocks. In some cases, market prices are soaring for start-ups that have yet to earn a profit.

blue-chip stocks Stocks of well-established, financially sound firms.

While some of the newcomers—America Online, Amazon, eBay, Yahoo!—are regarded by many on Wall Street as Internet Blue Chips, their financial performance is quite different from that of traditional **blue-chip stocks**, which are well-established, financially sound firms.[1] Let's compare Yahoo! and Wal-Mart. If you had invested $10 000 in Wal-Mart stock in July 1997, the market value of this blue chip would have increased to more than $35 000 by 2002 (see Figure 19.1). The same investment in Yahoo! would have also grown to about $140 000. At peak value during the five-year period, however, the Yahoo! investment surged to nearly $600 000 versus Wal-Mart's nearly $40 000.

Could this huge difference be predicted from indicators traditionally used by market experts? Hardly. The initial public offering (IPO) of Yahoo! stock in 1996 was priced at $13 per share. It quickly jumped to $43, then settled down to close the day at $33 even though the company had not yet turned a profit. Subsequently, because Yahoo! was the leading internet portal brand name, investors were betting that it would become a profitable business in the future—a bet that many traditionalists would view as extremely risky.

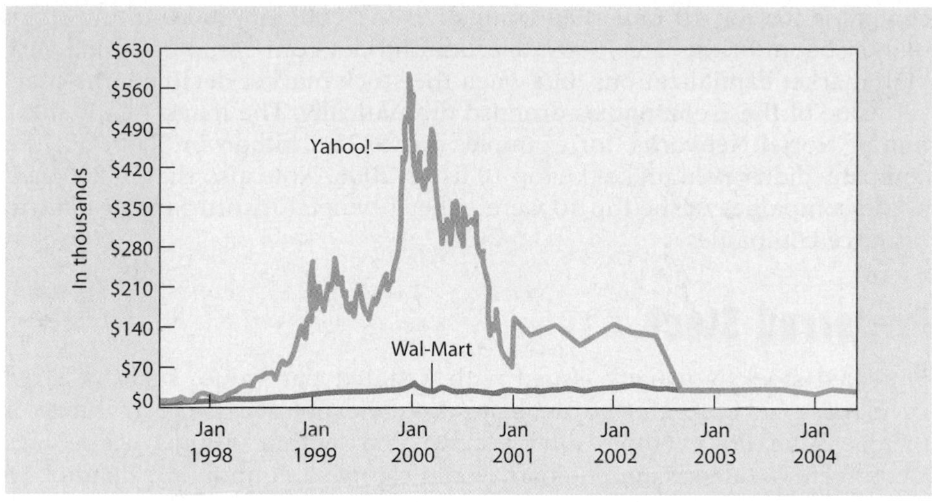

Figure 19.1 Market value growth: Wal-Mart versus Yahoo!

Consider the fact that Wal-Mart's book value is more than double that of Yahoo!. Even more glaring is the fact that entering 2002, Yahoo! has had zero or negative earnings per share for the last six years, whereas Wal-Mart's net earnings have grown steadily during the previous 10 years. The comparison is similar for dividends: Whereas Wal-Mart has a steady history of payouts to stockholders, Yahoo! has never paid a cash dividend. Overall, then, the traditional performance yardsticks favour Wal-Mart heavily. Nevertheless, investors are betting the future on Yahoo!. In July 2000, the original $10 000 investment had accumulated in three years to a market value more than 10 times that of the same investment in Wal-Mart.[2]

The drastic change in the price of Yahoo! was illustrative of the sharp drop that occurred in high-tech stocks as 2000 drew to a close. Two Calgary-based high-tech stocks—Cell-Loc and Wi-Lan—also dropped dramatically during 2000. By December 2000, Cell-Loc had dropped 84 percent from its March high, and Wi-Lan had dropped 88 percent.

Market Capitalization. The market value of a company's stock is known as its **market capitalization**. It is computed by multiplying the number of a company's outstanding shares times the value of each share. Table 19.1

market capitalization The dollar value (market value) of stocks listed on a stock exchange.

Yahoo! Japan is just one of dozens of net-related companies in the portfolio of Japan's Softbank Corp., which is riding the crest of an 83 percent surge in profits from online retail transactions. Softbank has sunk its profits in Yahoo! BB, a high-speed consumer broadband service that's already attracted 4.3 million users at $20–$30 per month. To strengthen its hold on broadband service in Japan, Softbank also delved into the "old economy," buying up the country's third largest fixed line provider, Japan Telecom.

compares the top 10 Canadian companies in 2000 and 2006. In the stock market boom of the late 1990s, telecom and dot-com companies had very high market capitalizations, but when the stock market declined, the market value of these companies dropped dramatically. The market capitalization of Nortel Networks, for example, was $221.9 billion in 2000, but the company didn't even make the top 10 list in 2006. Note also that in 2006, *all* of the companies in the top 10 were either financial institutions or natural resource companies.

Preferred Stock

Preferred stock is usually issued with a stated par value, such as $100. Dividends paid on preferred stock are usually expressed as a percentage of the par value. For example, if a preferred stock with a $100 par value pays a 6 percent dividend, shareholders would receive an annual dividend of $6 on each share.

Some preferred stock is *callable*. The issuing firm can require the preferred shareholders to surrender their shares in exchange for a cash payment. The amount of this cash payment, known as the *call price*, is specified in the agreement between the preferred shareholders and the firm.

Investment Traits of Preferred Stock

cumulative preferred stock Preferred stock on which dividends not paid in the past must first be paid up before the firm may pay dividends to common shareholders.

Because of its preference on dividends, preferred stock's income is less risky than the common stock of the same company. Moreover, most preferred stock is cumulative. With **cumulative preferred stock**, any dividend payments the firm misses must be paid later, as soon as the firm is able. Typically, the firm cannot pay any dividends to its common shareholders until it has made up all late payments to preferred shareholders. If a firm with preferred stock having a $100 par value and paying a 6 percent dividend fails to pay that dividend for two years, it must make up the arrears of $12 per share before it can pay dividends to common shareholders.

Even the income from cumulative preferred stock is not as certain as the corporate bonds of the same company. The company cannot pay dividends if it does not make a profit. The purchase price of the preferred stock can also fluctuate, leading to a capital gain or loss for the shareholder. And the growth potential of preferred stock is limited due to its fixed dividend.

Table 19.1 The Top 10 Canadian Companies, 2000 and 2006 (as Measured by Market Capitalization)

Company	Market Capitalization (in billions of $)	
	2000	2006
1. Royal Bank of Canada	$18.8	$61.3
2. Manulife Financial Corp.	—	57.5
3. The Bank of Nova Scotia	13.7	47.1
4. The Toronto-Dominion Bank	22.7	46.8
5. EnCana Corp.	—	40.0
6. Suncor Energy Inc.	—	38.9
7. Imperial Oil Ltd.	11.6	36.4
8. Bank of Montreal	11.7	34.6
9. Canadian Natural Resources Ltd.	—	33.3
10. Shell Canada Ltd.	—	31.5

Stock Exchanges

Most of the secondary market for stocks is handled by organized stock exchanges. In addition to stock markets, a so-called "dealer," or the over-the-counter market, handles the exchange of some stocks. A **stock exchange** is an organization of individuals formed to provide an institutional setting in which stock can be bought and sold. The exchange enforces certain rules to govern its members' trading activities. Most exchanges are non-profit corporations established to serve their members.

stock exchange A voluntary organization of individuals formed to provide an institutional setting where members can buy and sell stock for themselves and their clients in accordance with the exchange's rules.

To become a member, an individual must purchase one of a limited number of memberships—called "seats"—on the exchange. Only members (or their representatives) are allowed to trade on the exchange. In this sense, because all orders to buy or sell must flow through members, they have a legal monopoly. Memberships can be bought and sold like other assets.

The Trading Floor

Each exchange regulates the places and times at which trading may occur. Trading is allowed only at an actual physical location called the *trading floor*. The floor is equipped with a vast array of electronic communications equipment for conveying buy and sell orders or confirming completed trades. A variety of news services furnish important up-to-the-minute information about world events as well as business developments. Any change in these factors, then, may be swiftly reflected in share prices.

On April 23, 1997, the Toronto Stock Exchange trading floor closed after 145 years of operation. Buy and sell orders are now placed through computers. At its heyday in the 1980s, over 400 traders worked on the floor.[3]

Brokers

Some of the people working on the trading floor are employed by the exchange; others trade stocks for themselves. A large number of those working on the trading floor are brokers. A **broker** receives buy and sell orders from those who are not members of the exchange and executes the orders. In return, the broker earns a commission from the order placer.

broker An individual licensed to buy and sell securities for customers in the secondary market; may also provide other financial services.

Discount Brokers. Like many products, brokerage assistance can be purchased at either discount or at full-service prices. Buying 200 shares of a $20 stock in 2004 cost the investor $10.99 at Ameritrade, $9.99 to $12.99 at E*Trade, $9.95 to $19.95 at Charles Schwab, and up to $100 at a full-service brokerage firm. Price differences are obvious even among the discount brokers—Ameritrade, E*Trade, and Schwab—but the highest discount price is well below the price of the full-service broker.[4]

Discount brokers offer well-informed individual investors a fast, low-cost way to participate in the market. Discount brokerage services are low cost because sales personnel receive fees or salaries, not commissions. Unlike many full-service brokers, they do not offer investment advice or person-to-person sales consultations. They do, however, offer automated online services, such as stock research, industry analysis, and screening for specific types of stocks.

Online Trading. The popularity of online trading stems from convenient access to the internet, fast no-nonsense transactions, and the opportunity for self-directed investors to manage their own portfolios while paying low fees for trading. Only 14 percent of all equity trades were executed online in 1998, but the number was growing rapidly until the market decline started in 2000. It remains to be seen what will happen to online trading. One thing that has happened: The competition among brokers has driven commission fees sharply downward.[5]

Full-Service Brokers. Despite the growth in online investing, there remains an important market for full-service brokerages, both for new, uninformed investors and for experienced investors who don't have time to keep up with all the latest developments. When you deal with busy people who want to invest successfully, says Joseph Grano of UBS Financial Services, "you can't do it through a telephone response system. In a world that's growing more and more complicated, the advice and counsel of a broker will be more important, not less important."

With full lines of financial services, firms such as Merrill Lynch can offer clients consulting advice in personal financial planning, estate planning, and tax strategies, along with a wider range of investment products. IPOs of stock, for example, are generally not available to the public through online retail brokers. Rather, a full-service broker, who is also the investment banker that sells the IPO shares, can sell IPO shares to its clients. Financial advisers also do more than deliver information. They offer interpretations of and suggestions on investments that clients might overlook when trying to sift through an avalanche of online financial data. The Business Accountability box provides information on the financial advisers who help investors.

BUSINESS ACCOUNTABILITY

Accountability Goes Professional

Investment recommendations by financial advisers offer clients possibilities of both losses and gains. As professionals, advisers should be, but sometimes haven't been, trustworthy stewards of clients' private information. That's why the financial industry, as early as 1947, began establishing societies that later merged to become the Association for Investment Management and Research (AIMR). Today, its members include more than 60 000 investment practitioners—securities analysts, portfolio managers, financial strategists—and educators in more than 100 countries. AIMR serves three broad areas for which members are accountable—continuing education, conduct and ethics, and standards of practice—to maintain high standards of professionalism in their field.

The association's flagship activity is the Chartered Financial Analyst (CFA) program. Regarded as the industry's premier certification, the CFA designation has been earned by more than 55 000 investment professionals, from among some 480 000 CFA examtakers, since 1963. Commenting on the value of the CFA designation, Charles Ruifrok Jr., CFA and portfolio management associate at Bank of America, says, "Since becoming a CFA charter holder, I have become a resource to others I work with and a mentor to younger associates. The charter has expanded my visibility in my firm. Clients have taken notice, too." Industry giants such as Citigroup, Prudential Financial, Morgan Stanley, and Deutsche Bank encourage and compete for CFA professionals in banking, investments, mutual funds, insurance, and consulting.

Earning a charter involves a progression of postgraduate tests and three years of professional experience. The program's three levels of study each require 250 hours of preparation and an examination covering a broad-based "Body of Knowledge" for the investment community. Level 1 includes tools and concepts for determining the value of investments, portfolio management, and AIMR's code of ethics and professional conduct. Level 2 applies the tools from Level I in analyzing investments and applies the code of ethics and conduct in practical situations. Level 3 explores the portfolio management process, including ethics and conduct, in thorough detail. After meeting these requirements and signing a professional conduct statement, the AIMR member has the right to use the CFA designation.

While the testing hurdle is a one-time requirement, professional accountability is a never-ending obligation. Every year, members must disclose any customer complaints or disciplinary procedures about their professional conduct. The public, too, may file complaints against an AIMR member for unethical behaviour, misconduct, or incompetence. Officials review each disclosure or complaint and conduct inquiries that could lead to disciplinary actions. Punishments range from letters of caution to public censure, and even removal from membership or revocation of the CFA charter. Continuous accountability is a cornerstone for maintaining ethical and professional standards.

The Toronto Stock Exchange is one of several in Canada where shares of stock in Canadian companies are bought and sold.

Canadian Stock Exchanges

There are two major Canadian stock exchanges. The *Toronto Stock Exchange (TSX)* is the largest stock exchange in Canada. It is made up of about 100 individual members who hold seats. The securities of most major corporations are listed here. A company must pay a fee before it can list its security on the exchange. Formerly, there were also stock exchanges in Calgary, Vancouver, and Montreal, but in 1999 an agreement was reached that (1) created the new Canadian Venture Exchange (CDNX) from the Vancouver and Alberta stock markets, (2) shifted all derivative trading to the Montreal stock exchange, and (3) consolidated all senior equity trading at the TSE.[6] The CDNX now focusses on junior companies.

Foreign Stock Exchanges

Many foreign countries also have active stock exchanges. In fact, several foreign stock exchanges—most notably those in the United States and England—trade far more shares each day than the TSX does.

The New York Stock Exchange. For many people, "the stock market" means the *New York Stock Exchange (NYSE)*. Founded in 1792 and located at the corner of Wall and Broad Streets in New York City, the largest of all U.S. exchanges is the model for exchanges worldwide. An average of 1.4 billion shares valued at U.S.$38 billion change hands each day. About 59 percent of all shares traded on U.S. exchanges are traded here. Only firms meeting certain minimum requirements—earning power, total value of outstanding stock, and number of shareholders—are eligible for listing on the NYSE.[7]

The American Stock Exchange. The second-largest floor-based U.S. exchange, the *American Stock Exchange (AMEX)*, is also located in New York City. It accounts for about 2 percent of all shares traded on U.S. exchanges and, like the NYSE, has minimum requirements for listings. They are, however, less stringent. The minimum number of publicly held shares, for example, is 500 000 versus 1.1 million for the NYSE.

Regional Stock Exchanges. Regional stock exchanges were established long before the advent of modern communications. They were organized to serve investors in places other than New York. The largest regional

In 2004, the Tehran Stock Exchange rewarded Iranian investors with gains of 130 percent. Oil revenues still dominate the economy (and foreign companies are barred from owning Iranian oil rights), but other industries, such as automobiles and information technology, have emerged. Although government agencies and religious organizations still control 50 percent of all economic activity, IPOs of newly privatized automakers, shipping companies, and banks have attracted more and more budding capitalists to the stock market floor.

exchanges are the Chicago (formerly the Midwest) Stock Exchange and the Pacific Stock Exchange in Los Angeles and San Francisco. Other exchanges are located in Philadelphia, Boston, Cincinnati, and Spokane, Washington. Many corporations list their stocks both regionally and on either the NYSE or the AMEX.

Other Foreign Stock Exchanges. As recently as 1980, the U.S. market accounted for more than half the value of the world market in traded stocks. Indeed, as late as 1975, the equity of IBM alone was greater than the national market equities of all but four countries. Market activities, however, have shifted as the value of shares listed on foreign exchanges continues to grow. The annual dollar value of trades on exchanges in London, Tokyo, and other cities is in the trillions. In fact, the London exchange exceeds even the NYSE in number of stocks listed. In market value, however, transactions on U.S. exchanges remain larger than those on exchanges in other countries. Relatively new exchanges are also flourishing in cities from Shanghai to Warsaw.

over-the-counter (OTC) market Organization of securities dealers formed to trade stock outside the formal institutional setting of the organized stock exchanges.

The Over-the-Counter Market. The **over-the-counter (OTC) market** is so called because its original traders were somewhat like retailers. They kept supplies of shares on hand and, as opportunities arose, sold them over the office counter to interested buyers. Even today, the OTC market has no trading floor. Rather, it consists of many people in different locations who hold an inventory of securities that are not listed on any of the major exchanges. The over-the-counter market consists of independent dealers who own the securities that they buy and sell at their own risk. Although OTC activities are of interest from a historical perspective, trading volume is small in comparison with other markets.[8]

National Association of Securities Dealers Automated Quotation (NASDAQ) A stock market implemented by NASD that operates by broadcasting trading information on an intranet to more than 350 000 terminals worldwide.

NASDAQ and NASD. In the 1960s, a study by the U.S.-based Securities and Exchange Commission recommended automation of the OTC, calling for a new system to be implemented by the National Association of Securities Dealers Inc. (NASD). The resulting automated OTC system, launched in 1971, is known as the **National Association of Securities Dealers Automated Quotation**—or **NASDAQ**—system, the world's first electronic stock market.[9] In 2001, NASD became a separate organization from the NASDAQ system so that NASD could focus solely on securities regulation.

With more than 5000 member firms, NASD is the largest private-sector securities-regulation organization in the world. Every broker/dealer in the

United States who conducts securities business with the public is required by law to be a member of the NASD.[10] NASD includes dealers (not just brokers) who must pass qualification exams and meet certain standards for financial soundness. The privilege of trading in the market is granted by federal regulators and by NASD.

Meanwhile, the NASDAQ telecommunications system operates the NASDAQ Stock Market by broadcasting trading information on an intranet to over 350 000 terminals worldwide. Whereas orders at the NYSE are paired on the trading floor, NASDAQ orders are paired and executed on a computer network. Currently, NASDAQ is working with officials in an increasing number of countries who want to replace the trading floors of traditional exchanges with electronic networks like NASDAQ.

NASDAQ trades the stocks of about 4000 companies. Newer firms are often listed here when their stocks first become available in the secondary market. Current listings include Starbucks and such well-known technology stocks as Intel, Dell Computer, Oracle Technology, and Microsoft.

Compared with other markets, the NASDAQ has enjoyed a remarkable level of activity. By 1998, so many shares were being traded on NASDAQ that its share of market surpassed that of the NYSE. In early 2001, NASDAQ set a record volume of over three billion shares traded in one day. Its 2003 average daily volume of 1.69 billion shares traded was the industry leader, and it is the leading U.S. market for non-U.S. listings, with a total of about 400 non-U.S. companies. Figure 19.2 shows the steady growth in the dollar volume of NASDAQ trades, which continued to capture market share through 1999. Since then, however, while the NASDAQ traded more shares than the NYSE, the dot-com downfall led to lower per-share prices, especially for technology and small-company stocks, such that the NASDAQ's annual dollar volume fell below the NYSE's.

Steps Toward a Global Stock Market. With its electronic telecommunication system, NASDAQ possesses an infrastructure that could eventually lead to a truly global stock market—one that would allow buyers and sellers to interact from any point in the world. Currently, NASDAQ provides equal access to both the market and market information via simultaneous

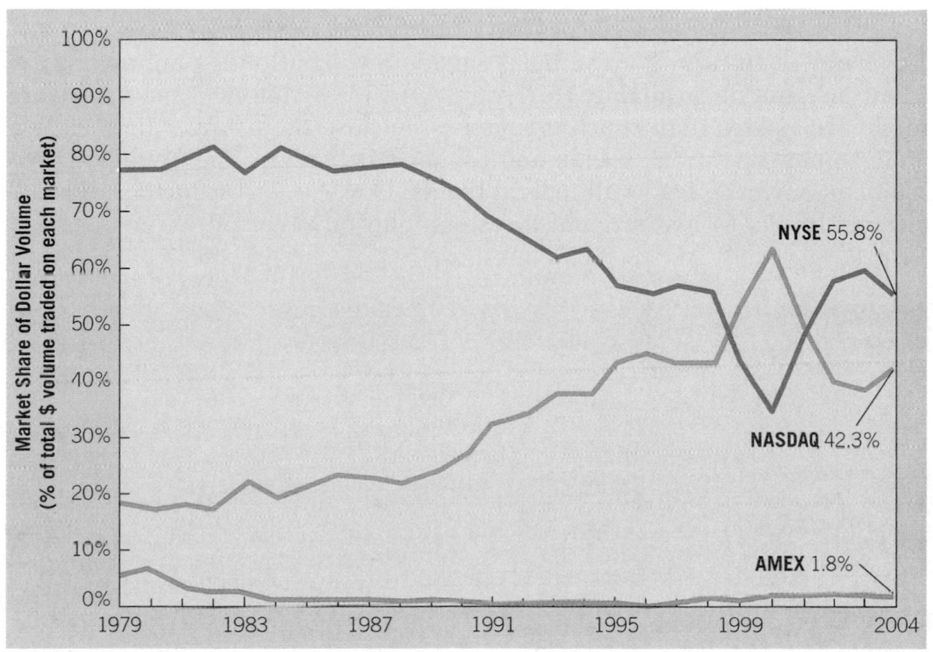

Figure 19.2 The U.S. stock markets: Comparative dollar volume of trades.

broadcasts of quotes from more than 1000 participating firms. NASDAQ communication networks enter customer orders and then display new quotes reflecting those orders. NASDAQ also undertook certain initiatives such as the NASDAQ Japan Market and the NASDAQ Canada market, and also opened offices in China, India, and Australia. But in 2003, NASDAQ decided to withdraw from international expansion and, instead, return to its core focus in the United States. Although international initiatives are promising, these early setbacks have demonstrated that it will take several years to resolve differences in market regulation and trading practices that currently separate various countries.

BONDS

3 Distinguish among various types of *bonds* in terms of their issuers, safety, and retirement.

bond A written promise that the borrower will pay the lender, at a stated future date, the principal plus a stated rate of interest.

A **bond** is an IOU—a written promise that the borrower will pay the lender, at some stated future date, a sum of money (the principal) and a stated rate of interest. Bondholders have a claim on a corporation's assets and earnings that comes before the claims of common and preferred shareholders. Bonds differ from one another in terms of maturity, tax status, and level of risk versus potential yield (the interest rate). Potential investors must take these factors into consideration to evaluate which particular bond to buy.

To help bond investors make assessments, several services rate the quality of bonds from different issuers. Table 19.2 shows ratings by two principal rating services: Moody's and Standard & Poor's (which acquired the former Canadian Bond Rating Service). The rating measures the bond's default risk—the chance that one or more promised payments will be deferred or missed altogether.

Although all corporations issue common stock, not all issue bonds. Shareholders provide equity (ownership) capital, while bondholders are lenders (although they are also considered "investors" as far as the securities market is concerned). Stock certificates represent ownership, while bond certificates represent indebtedness. Federal, provincial, and city governments as well as non-profit organizations also issue bonds.

Government Bonds

government bond Bond issued by the federal government.

Government bonds—for example, Canada Savings Bonds—are among the safest investments available. However, securities with longer maturities are somewhat riskier than short-term issues because their longer lives expose them to more political, social, and economic changes. The Canadian government, however, backs all federal bonds. Government securities are sold in large blocks to institutional investors who buy them to ensure desired

Table 19.2 Bond Ratings

	High Grade	Medium Grade (Investment Grade)	Speculative	Poor Grade
Moody's	Aaa Aa	A Baa	Ba B	Caa to C
Standard & Poor's	AAA AA	A BBB	BB B	CCC to D

levels of safety in portfolios. As their needs change, they may buy or sell government securities to other investors.

Provincial and local governments also issue bonds (called **municipal bonds**) to finance school and transportation systems and a variety of other projects. Banks invest in bonds nearing maturity because they are relatively safe, liquid investments. Pension funds, insurance companies, and private citizens also make longer-term investments in municipal bonds.

municipal bonds Bonds issued by provincial or local government.

Corporate Bonds

Corporate bonds are a major source of long-term financing for Canadian corporations. They have traditionally been issued with maturities ranging from 20 to 30 years, but in the past few years, 10-year maturities have come into wider use. As with government bonds, longer-term corporate bonds are somewhat riskier than shorter-term bonds. Bond ratings of new and proposed corporate issues are published to keep investors informed of the latest risk evaluations on many bonds. Negative ratings do not preclude a bond's success, but they do raise the interest rate that issuers must offer. Corporate bonds may be categorized in one of two ways: (1) according to methods of interest payment, and (2) according to whether they are *secured* or *unsecured*.

corporate bond Bond issued by a company as a source of long-term funding.

registered bond The names of holders are registered with the company.

bearer (coupon) bond Require bondholders to clip coupons from certificates and send them to the issuer to receive interest payments.

secured bonds Bonds issued by borrowers who pledge assets as collateral in the event of nonpayment.

debentures Unsecured bonds.

Interest Payment: Registered and Bearer Bonds

Registered bonds register the names of holders with the company, which simply mails out cheques to the bondholders. Certificates are of value only to registered holders. **Bearer** (or **coupon**) **bonds** require bondholders to clip coupons from certificates and send them to the issuer to receive payment. Coupons can be redeemed by anyone, regardless of ownership.

Secured Bonds

With **secured bonds**, borrowers can reduce the risk of their bonds by pledging assets to bondholders in the event of default. First mortgages, other mortgages, or other specific assets can back secured bonds. If the corporation does not pay interest when it is due, the firm's assets can be sold and the proceeds used to pay the bondholders.

Unsecured Bonds

Unsecured bonds are called **debentures**. No specific property is pledged as security for these bonds. Holders of unsecured bonds generally have claims against property not otherwise pledged in the company's other bonds. Accordingly,

Private corporations are not the only organizations that issue bonds. The government of Canada issues Canada Savings Bonds to finance its debt.

debentures have inferior claims on the corporation's assets. Financially strong corporations often use debentures.

The Retirement of Bonds

Maturity dates on bonds of all kinds may be very long. Of course, all bonds must be paid off, or retired, at some point. With regard to maturity dates, there are three types of bonds: *callable*, *serial*, and *convertible*.

Callable Bonds

callable bond A bond that may be paid off by the issuer before the maturity date.

The issuer of **callable bonds** may call them in and pay them off at a price stipulated in the indenture, or contract, before the maturity date. Usually the issuer cannot call the bond for a certain period of time after issue, often within the first five years. Issuers usually call in existing bonds when prevailing interest rates are lower than the rate being paid on the bond. The issuer must still pay a *call price* to call in the bond. The call price usually gives a premium to the bondholder. The premium is merely the difference between the face value and call price. For example, a bond that bears a $100 face value might be callable by the firm for $108.67 any time during the first year after issue. The call price (and therefore the premium) decreases annually as bonds approach maturity.

Sinking Funds

sinking fund provision A clause in the bond indenture (contract) that requires the issuing company to put enough money into a special bank account each year to cover the retirement of the bond issue on schedule.

Callable bonds are often retired by the use of **sinking fund provisions**. The issuing company is required to put a certain amount of money into a special bank account annually. At the end of a certain number of years, the money (including interest) will be sufficient to redeem the bonds. Failure to meet the sinking fund provision places the issue in default. Obviously, such bonds are generally regarded as safer investments than many other bonds.

Serial and Convertible Bonds

serial bond A bond issue in which redemption dates are staggered so that a firm pays off portions of the issue at different predetermined dates.

convertible bond Any bond that offers bondholders the option of accepting common stock instead of cash in repayment.

Some corporations issue serial or convertible bonds. With a **serial bond**, the firm retires portions of the bond issue in a series of different preset dates. For example, a company with a $100 million issue maturing in 20 years may retire $5 million each year. Serial bonds are most popular among local and state governments.

Corporations can issue **convertible bonds**. These bonds can be converted into the common stock of the issuing company. At the option of the holder, payment is made in stock instead of in cash. When holders are given such flexibility and because of the potential benefits of converting bonds into stock, firms can offer lower interest rates when the bonds are issued. However, because holders cannot be forced to accept stock instead of cash, conversion works only when the bond buyer also regards the issuing corporation as a good investment.

Suppose that in 1999, Canadian Arctic Explorations sold a $100 million issue of 4.5 percent convertible bonds. The bonds were issued in $1000 denominations; they mature in 2009. At any time before maturity, each debenture of $1000 is convertible into 19.125 shares of the company's common stock. Between October 1999 and March 2006, the stock price ranged from a low of $28 to a high of $67. In that time, then, 19.125 common shares had a market value ranging from $535 to $1281. The bondholder could have exchanged the $1000 bond in return for stock to be kept or sold at a possible profit (or loss).

Secondary Markets for Bonds

Nearly all secondary trading in bonds occurs in the OTC market rather than on organized exchanges. Thus, precise statistics about annual trading volumes are not recorded. As with stocks, however, market values and prices change daily. The direction of bond prices and interest rates move in opposite directions. As interest rates move up, bond prices tend to go down. The prices of riskier bonds fluctuate more widely than those of higher grade bonds.

OTHER INVESTMENTS

Although stocks and bonds are very important, they are not the only marketable securities for businesses. Financial managers are also concerned with investment opportunities in *mutual funds*, *hedge funds*, *commodities*, and *options*. In striking the right balance for risk among investment alternatives, financial managers use *diversification* and *asset allocation*.

Describe the investment opportunities offered by *mutual funds* and *commodities*. 4

Mutual Funds

Companies called **mutual funds** pool investments from individuals and other firms to purchase a portfolio of stocks, bonds, and short-term securities. Investors are part owners of this portfolio. For example, if you invest $1000 in a mutual fund that has a portfolio worth $100 000, you own 1 percent of the portfolio. Mutual funds usually have portfolios worth many millions of dollars. Investors in **no-load funds** are not charged a sales commission when they buy into or sell out of the mutual fund. **Load funds** levy a charge of between 2 and 8 percent of the invested funds.

mutual fund Any company that pools the resources of many investors and uses those funds to purchase various types of financial securities, depending on the fund's financial goals.

no-load fund A mutual fund in which investors are not charged a sales commission when they buy into or sell out of the fund.

load fund A mutual fund in which investors are charged a sales commission when they buy into or sell out of the fund.

Mutual funds vary by the investment goals they stress. Some stress safety. The portfolios of these mutual funds include treasury bills and other safe issues that offer immediate income (liquidity). Other funds seek higher returns and are willing to sacrifice some safety. Long-term municipal bond mutual funds, corporate bond mutual funds, and income mutual funds (which invest in common stocks with good dividend-paying records) all fall into this category.

Still other funds stress growth. Examples include balanced mutual funds, which hold a mixture of bonds, preferred stocks, and common stocks. Growth mutual funds stress common stocks of established firms. Aggressive growth mutual funds seek maximum capital appreciation. To get it, these funds sacrifice current income and safety. They invest in stocks of new companies, troubled companies, and other high-risk securities.

Mutual funds that stress socially responsible investing are called **ethical funds**. They avoid investing in companies that make products like cigarettes or weapons, and instead focus on investing in companies that produce safe and useful products and do good in terms of employee relations, environmental practices, and human rights policies. Clean Environment Equity, Summa Investors, and Ethical Growth are examples of ethical funds. In spite of the many corporate scandals in recent years, ethical funds have not attracted as much interest in Canada as they have in the United States and Europe. They have also not performed as well as other mutual funds.[11]

ethical funds Mutual funds that stress socially responsible investing.

Mutual funds give small investors access to professional financial management. Their managers have up-to-date information about market conditions and the best large-scale investment opportunities. But there are no guarantees of good returns, and in the difficult market conditions that prevailed in 2001–03, many people pulled their money out of mutual funds. Table 19.3 lists the top 10 mutual funds in Canada.

Table 19.3 The Top 10 Mutual Fund Companies in Canada, 2006

Company	Assets (in billions of $)
1. IGM Financial Inc.	$96.3
2. RBC Asset Management Inc.	61.5
3. C.I. Investments	53.1
4. CIBC Asset Management Inc.	45.9
5. TD Asset Management Inc.	45.2
6. AIM Trimark Investments	45.1
7. Fidelity Investments Canada Inc.	35.4
8. BMO Investments Inc.	26.2
9. AGF Management Ltd.	23.5
10. Franklin Templeton Investments Corp.	23.3

Hedge Funds

hedge funds Private pools of money that try to give investors a positive return regardless of stock market performance.

Hedge funds are private pools of money that try to give investors a positive return regardless of stock market performance. Hedge funds often engage in risky practices like *short-selling* (essentially betting that a company's stock price will go down) and *leveraging* (borrowing money against principal). Historically, interest in hedge funds has been limited to wealthy people (called "accredited investors") who are assumed to be very knowledgeable about financial matters and are able to weigh the risks of investing. But recently, hedge funds have begun marketing their products to the average investor with something called "principal-protected notes." These guarantee that investors will get their original investment back at a certain time, but they do not guarantee that any additional returns will be forthcoming.

The number of hedge funds has increased rapidly in recent years—from less than 2000 in 1993 to over 6000 in 2005—and the majority of money invested in hedge funds is now in the form of principal-protected notes.[12] Hedge funds are not as closely regulated as mutual funds, and are not required to report management fees. But these management fees can be higher than those charged by mutual funds, so there is increasing concern that investors will be shortchanged. As a result, there are now calls for increased regulation of hedge funds.[13]

Commodities

futures contract Agreement to purchase specified amounts of a commodity (or stock) at a given price on a set future date.

commodities market Market in which futures contracts are traded.

Individuals and businesses can buy and sell commodities as investments. *Commodities* are products ranging from coffee beans and hogs to propane and platinum. **Futures contracts**—agreements to purchase specified amounts of commodities at given prices on set dates—can be bought and sold in the **commodities market**. These contracts are available not only for commodities but also for stocks. Because selling prices reflect traders' *estimates* of future events and values, futures prices are quite volatile, and trading is risky.

Let's look at an example. On November 1, 2003, the price of gold on the open market was $387 per ounce. Futures contracts for June 2004 gold were selling for $385 per ounce. This price reflected investors' judgment that gold prices would be slightly lower the following June. Now suppose that you purchased a 100-ounce gold futures contract in November for $38 500 ($385 × 100). If in January 2004 the June gold futures sold for $418 (which they really did), you could sell your contract for $41 800. Your profit after the two months would be $3300.

ENTREPRENEURSHIP AND NEW VENTURES

Marching to a Different Drum

It's a beautiful thing when your business model delivers hypergrowth while your rivals refuse to copy it. Partners Chris Enright and Glenn Butt have ridden that beautiful thing all the way to five-year growth of 6230 percent.

At the core of its model is flat-fee pricing that sees FundTrade give the independent financial advisers who are its clients every cent of the commissions they earn selling and servicing mutual funds. Rather than follow industry practice by taking a share of those commissions, FundTrade charges each of its 236 clients $15 000 a year to provide compliance, trade, and back-office services. Enright, the firm's managing director, says that's a bargain for big producers, who could easily pay royalties of $70 000 a year to a traditional mutual fund dealer. It also eliminates this conflict of interest: Dealers are supposed to ensure compliance with regulations against any trades not in the best interests of an adviser's customer—at the cost of reducing their own commission revenue.

So, why is FundTrade almost alone in this model? "If you're a publicly traded company, you don't want to cap the upside of your revenue," says Enright. "We don't have to report to shareholders who are requesting more and more return on equity and shareholder value." He and Butt are content with a profitable, self-sustaining firm that continues to add clients—16 so far this year.

FundTrade's flat fees yield predictable revenue, and save sales training and other educational costs because the advisers most attracted to flat fees are big producers who don't need much assistance. Still, this isn't a low-service model. Butt, the company's chief compliance officer, and Enright personally monitor most of their advisers' operations biannually, twice as often as regulations require. And both of them coach clients on compliance, passing along tips about new regulations in the works garnered through their senior roles in industry bodies.

Although FundTrade's only marketing is word of mouth, its revenue has grown explosively, from $518 300 in 2000 to $32.8 million in 2005. (That includes commissions collected from fund companies and turned over to advisers.) While the partners had long planned to max out at 300 clients, the number they figure they can oversee personally, they've just invested six figures in a higher-capacity back-office system. As the regulatory environment grows more complex and costs rise, says Enright, "we may need to be bigger." It seems a lot more growth is still to come from their beautiful business model.

Margins

Usually, buyers of futures contracts need not put up the full purchase amount. Rather, the buyer posts a smaller amount—the **margin**—that may be as little as $3000 for contracts up to $100 000. Let us look again at our gold futures example. If you had posted a $3000 margin for your June gold contract, you would have earned a $3300 profit on that investment of $3000 in only two months.

margin The percentage of the total sales price that a buyer must put up to place an order for stock or a futures contract.

However, you also took a big risk involving two big *ifs*: If you had held onto your contract until June *and* if gold had dropped, say to $340, you would have lost $4500 ($38 500 – $34 000). If you had posted a $3000 margin to buy the contract, you would have lost all of that margin and would owe an additional $1500. As it turns out, June gold prices increased to $394, so your investment of $38 500 would have gained $900 in June. In fact, however, between 75 and 90 percent of all small-time investors lose money in the futures market. For one thing, the action is fast and furious, with small investors trying to keep up with professionals ensconced in seats on the major exchanges. Although the profit potential is exciting, experts recommend that most novices retreat to safer stock markets. Of course, as one veteran financial planner puts it, commodities are tempting. "After trading commodities," he reports, "trading stocks is like watching the grass grow."

Stock Options

stock option The purchased right to buy or sell a stock.

call option The purchased right to buy a particular stock at a certain price until a specified date.

put option The purchased right to sell a particular stock at a certain price until a specified date.

A **stock option** is the right to buy or sell a stock. A **call option** gives its owner the right to buy a particular stock at a certain price, with that right lasting until a particular date. A **put option** gives its owner the right to sell a particular stock at a specified price, with that right lasting until a particular date. These options are traded on several stock exchanges.

Suppose that you thought the price of Alcan (which sold for $49.10 per share on August 15, 2000) was going to go up. You might buy a call option giving you the right to buy 100 shares of Alcan any time in the next two months at a so-called strike price of $65. If the stock rose to $75 before October, you would exercise your call option. Your profit would be $10 per share ($75 – $65) less the price you paid to buy the option. However, if the stock price fell instead of rising, you would not exercise your call option because Alcan would be available on the open market for less than $65 per share. (Your stock option would be "under water," that is, it would be worthless.) You would lose whatever you paid for the option.

In contrast, if you thought the price of Alcan would fall below $49.10 sometime during the two months after August 15, 2000, you might buy a put option. Assume that this option gave you the right to sell 100 shares for $54.10 per share any time before October 2000. If the stock price fell to $44.10, your profit would be $10 per share ($54.10 – $44.10), less whatever you paid for the option. Assume that the price of a put option was $3.00 per share at that time. If the stock price increased, you would not exercise your option to sell, and you would lose what you paid for the put option. The daily prices of put and call options are listed in the financial press.

In recent years, there has been much publicity about stock options that are given to executives. Concluding Case 19-2 examines this issue in detail.

Making Choices for Diversification, Asset Allocation, and Risk Reduction

Investors seldom take an extreme approach—total risk or total risk avoidance—in selecting their investments. Extreme positions attract extreme results, and most investors have a preference toward either risk or risk avoidance, but they are not totally immersed at either end of the risk spectrum. Instead, they select a mixture, or *portfolio*, of investments—some riskier and some more conservative—that, collectively, provides the level of

Traders deal in futures contracts—agreements to buy or sell commodities for certain prices at a future time. This day (May 18, 2004) was an interesting one. The assassination of an Iraqi leader rekindled concerns about supplies of crude oil, so the price went up to (at that time) a record of $41.55 per barrel. Since that time, other uncertainties on the world scene have caused the price of oil to rise above $70 per barrel.

risk and financial stability at which they are comfortable. They do this in two ways: through *diversification* and *asset allocation*.

Diversification

diversification Purchase of several different kinds of investments rather than just one.

Diversification means buying several different kinds of investments rather than just one. Diversification as applied to common stocks means, for example, that you invest in stocks of several different companies, such as Inco, IBM, Cisco Systems, and Bombardier, rather than put all your money into just one of them. The risk of loss is reduced by spreading the total investment across more stocks because, while any one stock may tumble, there is less chance that all of them will fall, especially if the companies are from different industries. Even more diversification is gained when funds are spread across more kinds of investment alternatives—stocks, bonds, mutual funds, real estate, and so on. Among the tragedies resulting from the scandals at Enron and WorldCom are the lifelong employees who did not diversify their retirement investments and, instead, had all their retirement funds invested in their firm's stock. This was an extremely risky position, as they sorrowfully learned. When their firm's stock took a free-fall to near zero, their retirement funds disappeared. The Exercising Your Ethics box at the end of the chapter presents a decision-making dilemma that illustrates the idea of risk.

Asset Allocation

asset allocation The relative amount of funds invested in (or allocated to) each of several investment alternatives.

Asset allocation is the proportion—the relative amounts—of funds invested in (or allocated to) each of the investment alternatives. You may decide for example, to allocate $20 000 to common stocks, $10 000 to a money market mutual fund, and $10 000 to a Canada Savings Bond. Ten years later, you may decide on a less risky asset allocation of $10 000, $15 000, and $15 000 in the same investment categories, respectively. As your investment objectives change (in this example from moderate risk to lower risk for capital preservation), your asset allocation must be changed accordingly.

BUYING AND SELLING SECURITIES

Explain the process by which securities are bought and sold. 5

The process of buying and selling stocks, bonds, and other financial instruments is complex. To start, you need to find out about possible investments and match them to your investment objectives. Then you must decide whether you want to use a broker to buy and sell stocks, or whether you want to do it yourself.

Using Financial Information Services

Have you ever looked at the financial section of your daily newspaper and found yourself wondering what all those tables and numbers mean? If you cannot read stock and bond quotations, you probably should not invest in these issues. Fortunately, this skill is easily mastered.

Stock Quotations

Figure 19.3 shows the type of information newspapers provide about daily market transactions of individual stocks. The corporation's name (for example, Inco) is shown along with the number of shares sold, the high and low prices of the stock for that trading day, the closing price of the stock, and the change from the closing price on the previous day.

- *Stock*
  Inco (Name of Company)
- *Volume*
  18 640 (total number of shares traded on this date [in 100's]).
- *High and Low*
  During the trading day, the highest price was $58.82 and the lowest price was $57.01.
- *Close*
  At the close of trading on this date, the last price paid per share was $58.05.
- *Net Change*
  Difference between today's closing price and the previous day's closing price. Price increased by 84 cents per share.

Company	Volume	High	Low	Close	Change
Four Seasons	663	67.49	65.27	66.15	−1.13
Goldcorp	35 233	31.99	30.65	31.15	+0.83
GW Life	54	25.80	25.57	25.80	−0.22
Hudson Bay	32 376	15.06	15.00	15.04	−0.02
Inco	**18 640**	**58.82**	**57.01**	**58.05**	**+0.84**
Ipsco	4341	106.40	104.09	105.75	−0.25
Jean Cou	6918	14.56	14.31	14.31	−0.06
Kinross	72 321	13.68	12.92	13.10	+0.27

Figure 19.3 How to read a daily stock quotation.

Bond Quotations

Bond prices also change from day to day. These changes form the *coupon rate*, which provides information for firms about the cost of borrowing funds. Prices of domestic corporation bonds, Canadian government bonds, and foreign bonds are reported separately. Bond prices are expressed in terms of 100, even though most have a face value of $1000. Thus, a quote of 85 means that the bond's price is 85 percent of its face value, or $850.

A corporation bond selling at 155 1/4 would cost a buyer $1552.50 ($1000 face value × 1.5525), plus commission. The interest rate on bonds is also quoted as a percentage of par, or face, value. Thus "6 1/2s" pay 6.5 percent of par value per year. Typically, interest is paid semi-annually at half of the stated interest or coupon rate.

The market value (selling price) of a bond at any given time depends on its stated interest rate, the "going rate" of interest in the market, and its redemption or maturity date. A bond with a higher stated interest rate than the going rate on similar quality bonds will probably sell at a premium above its face value—its selling price will be above its redemption price. A bond with a lower stated interest rate than the going rate on similar quality bonds will probably sell at a discount—its selling price will be below its redemption price. How much the premium or discount is depends largely on how far in the future the maturity date is. The maturity date is shown after the interest rate. Figure 19.4 shows the type of information daily newspapers provide about bond transactions.

Bond Yield. Suppose you bought a $1000 par-value bond in 1983 for $650. Its stated interest rate is 6 percent, and its maturity or redemption date was 2003. You therefore received $60 per year in interest. Based on your actual investment of $650, your yield is 9.2 percent. If you held it to maturity, you got $1000 for a bond that originally cost you only $650. This extra $350 increased your true, or effective, yield.

- *BC Tel*
  Company name is British Columbia Telephone.
- *Coupon*
  The annual rate of interest at face value is 9.65 percent.
- *Maturity*
  The maturity date is April 8, 2022.
- *Price*
  On this date, $138.48 was the price of the last transaction.
- *Yield*
  The yield is computed by dividing the annual interest paid by the current market price.

Issuer	Coupon	Maturity	Price	Yield
		GOVERNMENT OF CANADA		
Canada	3.00	June 1, 07	99.85	4.08
Canada	6.00	June 1, 08	103.83	4.08
Canada	5.00	June 1, 14	103.71	4.45
Canada	8.00	June 1, 27	145.92	4.58
		PROVINCIALS		
BC	6.00	June 9, 08	103.61	4.20
Hy Que	6.50	Feb. 15, 11	108.55	4.50
Man	7.75	Dec. 22, 25	135.19	4.93
		CORPORATE		
BC Tel	**9.65**	**Apr 8, 22**	**138.49**	**6.48**
Loblaw	6.65	Nov. 8, 27	107.91	5.99
Royal Bank	4.18	June 1, 09	99.04	4.51
Suncor	6.10	Aug 7, 07	100.95	5.96

Figure 19.4 How to read a bond quotation.

Mutual Funds Quotations

Selling prices for mutual funds are reported daily or weekly in most newspapers. Additional investor information is also available in the financial press. Figure 19.5 shows a partial listing of T. Rowe Price funds from *Barron's: Mutual Funds*, a prominent weekly financial newspaper. Three funds are listed in the figure—Balanced, Science and Technology, and Short-Term Bond—but the published list would include all of Price's more than 90 different funds.

The fund's net asset value (NAV), the current market value of one share, is, perhaps, the key term for understanding the quotations. The fund managers calculate NAV at day's end by taking the fund's net assets—securities it owns, plus cash and any accumulated earnings, minus liabilities—and

1	2	3	4	5	6	7	8
52 Week		Fund	Close	Wk's	% Return		
High	Low	Name	NAV	Chg	1-Wk	YTD	3-Yrs
		Price Funds:					
19.04	16.51	Balanced *n*	18.37	−0.01	−0.1	+0.4	+7.8
20.00	15.03	SciTec *n*	18.29	−0.21	−1.1	−2.7	−33.4
4.90	4.75	Sht-Bd *n*	4.75	−0.01	0.2	0.3	+13.5

Figure 19.5 How to read a mutual fund quotation.

dividing the remainder by the number of shares outstanding. Let's focus on the first fund listed, the Balanced fund:

- Column 1 shows the fund's highest *net asset value* (NAV)—$19.04—during the past 52 weeks.
- Column 2 contains the 52-week low NAV, $16.51.
- Column 3 lists the company name (Price Funds) at the top and the individual fund names beneath the company name. The "*n*" code indicates no front-end or back-end sales charge (a *no-load fund*).
- Column 4 lists the NAV—$18.37—at the close of the most recent week.
- Column 5 shows the *net asset value change*—the dollar gain or loss based on the previous week's NAV. The Balanced fund closed $0.01 lower this week than in the previous week.
- The next three columns report *each fund's recent and longer-term performance*. These numbers reflect the percentage change in NAV. These three columns show the return of the fund (percentage return) for the most recent past week (column 6), current year-to-date (column 7), and the last 3 years (column 8).

Market Indexes

market index A measure of the market value of stocks; provides a summary of price trends in a specific industry or of the stock market as a whole.

bull market A period of rising stock prices; a period in which investors act on a belief that stock prices will rise.

bear market A period of falling stock prices; a period in which investors act on a belief that stock prices will fall.

Dow Jones Industrial Average (DJIA) Market index based on the prices of 30 of the largest firms listed on the NYSE and NASDAQ.

Although they do not indicate how specific securities are performing, **market indexes** provide a useful summary of trends in specific industries and the stock market as a whole. Market indexes reveal bull and bear market trends. **Bull markets** are periods of upward-moving stock prices. The years 1981–90, 1993–99, and 2004–06 featured strong bull markets. Periods of falling stock prices are called **bear markets**. The years 1972–74, 1991–92, and 2000–02 were bear markets. During the last period, financial failures closed many dot-com firms, and the terrorist attacks on the U.S. occurred.

The Dow Jones Industrial Average. The most widely cited market index is the **Dow Jones Industrial Average (DJIA)**. The Dow measures the performance of U.S. financial markets by focussing on 30 blue-chip companies as reflectors of the economic health. The Dow is the average of the stock prices for these 30 large firms. By tradition, the Dow is an indicator of blue-chip stock price movements. Because of the small number of firms it considers, however, it is a limited gauge of the overall stock market. The Dow increased sharply during the late 1990s and reached 11 000 early in 2000. But then it dropped to below 8000 in 2002. By early 2007, it had risen again to be more than 12 000.

Over the decades, the firms included in the Dow have been changed to reflect the changing composition of U.S. companies and industries. In 2004, for example, three companies were added: American International Group, Pfizer, and Verizon. They replaced AT&T, Eastman Kodak, and International Paper. These changes better reflect today's information-based economy and the increasing prominence of financial services and pharmaceuticals.

Standard & Poor's Composite Index (S&P 500) Market index based on the performance of 400 industrial firms, 40 utilities, 40 financial institutions, and 20 transportation companies.

The S&P 500. Because it considers very few firms, the Dow is a limited gauge of the overall U.S. stock market. **Standard & Poor's Composite Index (S&P 500)** is a broader report. It consists of 500 stocks, including 400 industrial firms, 40 utilities, 40 financial institutions, and 20 transportation companies. Because the index average is weighted according to market capitalization of each stock, the more highly valued companies exercise a greater influence on the index.

The S&P/TSX Average. The **S&P/TSX index** is an average computed from 225 different large Canadian stocks from various industry groups.[14] The index (formerly called the TSE 300) has been very volatile during the last few years. It moved sharply upwards during the bull market of the late 1990s, and topped 11 000 in the summer of 2000. It then dropped to 6500 by the end of 2000. By early 2007, the S&P/TSX index had risen to above 13 000.

S&P/TSX index An average computed from 225 different large Canadian stocks from various industry groups.

The NASDAQ Composite. Because it considers more stocks, some Wall Street observers regard the **NASDAQ Composite Index** as the most important of all market indexes. Unlike the Dow and the S&P 500, all NASDAQ-listed companies, not just a selected few, are included in the index, for a total of over 4000 firms (both domestic and foreign)—more than most other indexes. The popularity of the NASDAQ index goes hand in hand with investors' growing interest in technology and small-company stocks. The NASDAQ index has been even more volatile than the Dow. In early 2000, it reached 5000, but by 2001 had dropped to just 1300. By 2006, it had increased to 2400.

NASDAQ Composite Index Value-weighted market index that includes all NASDAQ-listed companies, both domestic and foreign.

Buying and Selling Stocks

Based on your own investigations and/or recommendations from your broker, you can place many types of orders. A **market order** authorizes the broker to buy or sell a certain stock at the prevailing market price. A **limit buy order** authorizes the broker to purchase a stock if its price is less than or equal to a given limit. For example, a limit buy order at $80 per share means that the broker is to buy it if and only if the stock price is $80 or less. A **limit sell order** authorizes the sale of a stock when its price is equal to or greater than a given limit. For example, a limit sell order at $80 per share means that the broker is to sell it if and only if the stock price is $80 or more. A **stop order** instructs the broker to sell a stock if its price falls to a certain level. For example, a stop order of $80 on a particular stock means that the broker is to sell it if and only if its price falls to $80 or below.

market order An order to a broker to buy or sell a certain security at the current market price.

limit buy order An order to a broker to buy a certain security only if its price is less than or equal to a given limit.

limit sell order An order to a broker to sell a certain security only if its price is equal to or greater than a given limit.

stop order An order to a broker to sell a certain security if its price falls to a certain level or below.

You can also place orders of different sizes. A **round lot** order, requests 100 shares or some multiple thereof. Fractions of a round lot are called **odd lots**. Trading odd lots is usually more expensive than trading round lots, because an intermediary called an odd-lot broker is often involved, which increases brokerage fees.

round lot The purchase or sale of stock in units of 100 shares.

odd lots The purchase or sale of stock in units other than 100 shares.

The business of buying and selling stocks is changing rapidly. Formerly, a person had to have a broker to buy and sell stocks. However, major changes have occurred in this industry in the last few years. More and more individuals are buying and selling stocks on the internet, and traditional brokers are worried that before long customers will avoid using their services altogether. To make matters worse for brokers, it will soon be possible for Canadians to purchase shares of stock directly from the companies that issue them instead of having to go through a broker or the internet. The fees that customers will have to pay for these direct purchases will be even lower than the fees currently charged by discount brokers. Thus, customers will be able to "cut out the middleman."[15]

Financing Securities Purchases

When you place a buy order of any kind, you must tell your broker how you will pay for the purchase. You might maintain a cash account with your broker. Then, as stocks are bought and sold, proceeds are added into the account and the broker withdraws commissions and costs of purchases. In addition, as with almost every good in today's economy, you can buy shares on credit.

Margin Trading

As with futures contracts, you can buy stocks on margin—putting down only a portion of the stock's price. You borrow the rest from your broker, who, in turn, borrows from the banks at a special rate and secures the loans with stock.

Margin trading offers several advantages. Suppose you purchased $100 000 worth of stock in WestJet. Let's also say that you paid $50 000 of your own money and borrowed the other $50 000 from your broker at 10 percent interest. Valued at its market price, your stock serves as your collateral. If shares have risen in value to $115 000 after one year, you can sell them and pay your broker $55 000 ($50 000 principal plus $5000 interest). You will have $60 000 left over. Your original investment of $50 000 will have earned a 20 percent profit of $10 000. If you had paid the entire price out of your own pocket, you would have earned only a 15 percent return.

Although investors often recognize possible profits to be made in margin trading, they sometimes fail to consider that losses, too, can be amplified. The rising use of margin credit by investors had become a growing concern during the recent bull market. Investors who seemed focussed on the upside benefits were confident that the market trend would continue upward, and they were less sensitive to the downside risks of margin trading. Especially at online brokerages, inexperienced traders were borrowing at an alarming rate, and some were using the borrowed funds for risky and speculative day trading. So-called *day traders* visited websites online to buy and sell a stock in the same day (so-called *intraday trades*), seeking quick in-and-out fractional gains on large volumes (many shares) of each stock. While some day traders were successful, most ended up financial losers. With more investors buying on debt, more of them were headed for a serious accelerated crash.

Short Sales

short sale A short sale occurs when a person borrows stock from a stockbroker and then sells the stock.

In addition to money, brokerages also lend securities to buyers. A **short sale** begins when you borrow a security from your broker and sell it (one of the few times it is legal to sell what you do not own). At a given time in the future, you must restore an equal number of shares of that issue to the brokerage, along with a fee.

For example, suppose that in June you believe the price of Alcan stock will soon fall. You order your broker to sell short 100 shares at the market price of $38 per share. Your broker will make the sale and credit $3800 to

If you're a day trader, are volatile markets good or bad? When the market's volatile there are often wider spreads between bid prices (what traders pay for a share of stock) and ask prices (what they charge for it). The difference isn't necessarily large, but if you can make a number of quick hits during the day, you can make a dime here and a dollar there. That strategy appeals to traders at large firms, but also to individual traders working on their own.

your account. If Alcan's price falls to $32 per share in July, you can buy 100 shares for $3200 and give them to your broker, leaving you with a $600 profit (before commissions). The risk is that Alcan's price will not fall but will hold steady or rise, leaving you with a loss.

SECURITIES REGULATION

The buying and selling of securities is regulated in both Canada and the United States. We describe the regulatory environment in the two countries below. There are both similarities and differences in the way the two countries regulate securities.

Explain how securities markets are regulated. 6

U.S. Securities Regulation

In addition to regulation by government agencies, both the NASD and the NYSE exercise self-regulation to maintain the public trust and to ensure professionalism in the financial industry. A visible example is the NYSE's actions in establishing so-called *circuit breakers*—trading rules for reducing excessive market volatility and promoting investor confidence—that suspend trading for a preset length of time. For example, if the DJIA drops more than 1050 points before 2 p.m., trading is halted for an hour. The interruption provides a "cooling off" period that slows trading activity, gives investors time to reconsider their trading positions, and allows computer programs to be revised or shut down.[16] Bigger drops lead to longer "cooling off" periods.

One oft-cited cause of sudden market fluctuations is **program trading**—the portfolio trading strategy involving the sale or purchase of a group of stocks valued at $1 million or more, often triggered by computerized trading programs that can be launched without human supervision or control. It works in the following way. As market values change and economic events transpire during the course of a day, computer programs are busy recalculating the future values of stocks. Once a calculated value reaches a critical point, the program automatically signals a buy or sell order. Because electronic trading could cause the market to spiral out of control, it has contributed to the establishment of circuit breakers.

program trading Large purchase or sale of a group of stocks, often triggered by computerized trading programs that can be launched without human supervision or control.

The Securities and Exchange Commission (SEC)

To protect the investing public and to maintain smoothly functioning markets, the SEC oversees many phases of the process through which securities are issued. The SEC regulates the public offering of new securities by requiring that all companies file prospectuses before proposed offerings commence. To protect investors from fraudulent issues, a **prospectus** contains pertinent information about both the offered security and the issuing company. False statements are subject to criminal penalties.

prospectus A detailed registration statement about a new stock filed with a provincial securities exchange; must include any data helpful to a potential buyer.

Insider Trading. The SEC also enforces laws against **insider trading**—the use of special knowledge about a firm for profit or gain. In June 2002, for example, the SEC filed suit in federal court in New York against Samuel Waksal, the former CEO of ImClone Systems, Inc., on charges of using insider information to gain illegal profits. The suit charged that Waksal received disappointing news in late December 2001 that the U.S. Food and Drug Administration (FDA) would soon reject ImClone's application to market its cancer treatment drug, Erbitux. The next day, before the FDA was scheduled to notify ImClone of its rejection, Waksal's family members sold more than $9 million in ImClone stock. For two days, Waksal himself

insider trading The use of special knowledge about a firm to make a profit on the stock market.

tried to sell his shares, which were worth nearly $5 million, but two brokerage firms refused to execute the orders. The following day, after the stock market had closed, ImClone publicly announced the FDA decision. The next trading day, ImClone's stock price dropped 16 percent—from $55.25 to $46.46. Family members had avoided millions in losses by illegally using the insider information.

While Waksal pleaded guilty to committing securities fraud, the infamous scandal led to the trial of Martha Stewart, the home décor entrepreneur and friend of Waksal, who sold 3900 shares at $58 each the day *before* ImClone made its public announcement. Stewart commented, "In placing my trade I had no improper information." By mid-2002, ImClone's stock had plummeted to $8 per share. In an ironic turnaround for the company, Erbitux was given FDA approval in February 2004, and by mid-2004, ImClone's stock rocketed to a four-year high of $83 per share.[17]

Canadian Securities Regulations

Canada, unlike the United States, does not have comprehensive federal securities legislation or a federal regulatory body. Government regulation is primarily provincial and emphasizes self-regulation through the various provincial securities exchanges. A 2003 report by a government-appointed committee that studied Canada's system of securities regulation concluded that it is in dire need of reform. The committee noted that Canada is the only country in the industrialized world with a patchwork of provincial regulations. It recommended a single regulator for Canada. The main complaints the committee noted were lack of meaningful enforcement of securities laws, and unnecessary costs and time delays that make Canada's capital markets uncompetitive internationally.

Ontario is generally regarded as having the most progressive securities legislation in Canada. The Ontario Securities Act contains disclosure provisions for new and existing issues, prevention of fraud, regulation of the Toronto Stock Exchange, and takeover bids. It also prohibits insider trading. The Toronto Stock Exchange provides an example of self-regulation by the industry. The TSX has regulations concerning listing and delisting of securities, disclosure requirements, and issuing of prospectuses for new securities.

blue-sky laws Laws regulating how corporations must back up securities.

In 1912, the Manitoba government pioneered in Canada laws applying mainly to the sale of new securities. Under these **blue-sky laws**, corporations issuing securities must back them up with something more than the "blue sky." Similar laws were passed in other provinces. Provincial laws also generally require that stockbrokers be licensed and securities be registered before they can be sold. In each province, issuers of proposed new securities must file a prospectus with the provincial securities exchange. The prospectus must be made available to prospective investors.

When the United States and Canadian stock markets declined during 2000–01, there was a public outcry for more regulation of securities. Both countries are in the process of developing much tougher legislation in the hope of restoring public trust in the stock market.

Summary of Learning Objectives

1. **Explain the difference between *primary* and *secondary securities markets*.** *Primary securities markets* involve the buying and selling of new securities, either in public offerings or through *private placements* (sales to single buyers or small groups of buyers). *Investment bankers* specialize in trading securities in primary markets. *Secondary securities markets* involve the trading of existing stocks and bonds through such familiar bodies as the New York Stock Exchange and Toronto Stock Exchange.

2. **Discuss the value of *common stock* and *preferred stock* to shareholders and describe the secondary market for each type of security.** *Common stock* affords investors the prospect of capital gains, dividend income, or both. Common stock values are expressed in three ways: as *par value* (the face value of a share when it is issued), *market value* (the current market price of a share), and *book value* (the value of shareholders' equity compared with that of other stocks). Market value is the most important value to investors. *Preferred stock* is less risky than common stock; for example, cumulative preferred stock entitles holders to receive missed dividends when the company is financially capable of paying. It also offers the prospect of steadier income than common stock. Shareholders of preferred stock must be paid dividends before shareholders of common stock.

   Both common and preferred stock are traded on *stock exchanges* (institutions formed to conduct the trading of existing securities) and in *over-the-counter (OTC) markets* (dealer organizations formed to trade securities outside stock exchange settings). "Members" who hold seats on exchanges act as *brokers*—agents who execute buy-and-sell orders—for non-members. Exchanges include the New York Stock Exchange, the Toronto Stock Exchange, and regional and foreign exchanges. In the OTC market, licensed traders serve functions similar to those of exchange members.

3. **Distinguish among various types of *bonds* in terms of their issuers, safety, and retirement.** The safety of bonds issued by various borrowers is rated by such services as Moody's and Standard & Poor's. *Government bonds* are the safest investment because the federal government backs them. *Municipal bonds*, which are offered by provincial and local governments to finance a variety of projects, are also usually safe. *Corporate bonds* are issued by businesses to gain long-term funding. They may be *secured* (backed by pledges of the issuer's assets) or *unsecured* (debentures) and offer varying degrees of safety. *Serial bonds* are retired as portions are redeemed at preset dates; *convertible bonds* may be retired by conversion into the issuer's common stock or by cash. Some government and corporate bonds are callable; that is, they can be paid off by the issuer prior to their maturity dates.

4. **Describe the investment opportunities offered by *mutual funds* and *commodities*.** Like stocks and bonds, *mutual funds*—companies that pool investments to purchase portfolios of financial instruments—offer investors different levels of risk and growth potential. *Load funds* require investors to pay commissions of 2 to 8 percent; *no-load funds* do not charge commissions when investors buy in or out. *Futures contracts*—agreements to buy specified amounts of commodities at given prices on preset dates—are traded in the *commodities market*. Commodities traders often buy on *margins*, percentages of total sales prices that must be put up to order futures contracts.

5. **Explain the process by which securities are bought and sold.** Investors generally use such financial information services as newspaper and online stock, bond, and OTC quotations to learn about possible investments. *Market indexes* such as the S&P/TSX index, the Dow Jones Industrial Average, Standard & Poor's Composite Index, and the NASDAQ Composite Index provide useful summaries of trends, both in specific industries and in the market as a whole. Investors can then place different types of orders. *Market orders* are orders to buy or sell at current prevailing prices. Because investors do not know exactly what prices will be when market orders are executed, they may issue *limit* or *stop orders* that are to be executed only if prices rise to or fall below specified levels. *Round lots* are purchased in multiples of 100 shares. *Odd lots* are purchased in fractions of round lots. Securities can be bought on margin or as part of *short sales*—sales in which investors sell securities that are borrowed from brokers and returned at a later date.

6. **Explain how securities markets are regulated.** To protect investors, provincial securities commissions regulate the public offering of new securities and enforce laws against such practices as *insider trading* (using special knowledge about a firm for profit or gain). Many provincial governments prosecute the sale of fraudulent securities and enforce *blue-sky laws* that require corporations to back up securities with something more than the "blue sky." As well, stockbrokers must be licensed and securities registered before they can be sold.

KEY TERMS

asset allocation, 637
bear market, 640
bearer (coupon) bond, 631
blue-chip stocks, 622
blue-sky laws, 644
bond, 630
book value, 622
broker, 625
bull market, 640
call option, 636
callable bond, 632
commodities market, 634
convertible bond, 632
corporate bond, 631
cumulative preferred stock, 624
debentures, 631
diversification, 637
Dow Jones Industrial Average (DJIA), 640
ethical funds, 633
futures contract, 634
government bond, 630
hedge funds, 634
insider trading, 643
investment banker, 621
limit buy order, 641
limit sell order, 641
load fund, 633
margin, 635
market capitalization, 623
market index, 640
market order, 641
market value, 621
municipal bonds, 631
mutual fund, 633
NASDAQ Composite Index, 641
National Association of Securities Dealers Automated Quotation (NASDAQ), 628
no-load fund, 633
odd lots, 641
over-the-counter (OTC) market, 628
par value, 621
primary securities market, 620
program trading, 643
prospectus, 643
put option, 636
registered bond, 631
round lot, 641
S&P/TSX index, 641
secondary securities market, 621
secured bonds, 631
securities, 620
serial bond, 632
short sale, 642
sinking fund provision, 632
Standard & Poor's Composite Index (S&P 500), 640
stock exchange, 625
stock option, 636
stop order, 641

QUESTIONS FOR ANALYSIS

1. Assume that the price of gold on the open market was $400 per ounce on March 31, 2003. Assume also that futures contracts for June 2004 gold were selling for $428 per ounce. This price reflected investors' judgments that gold prices would be higher the following June. Now suppose that you purchased a 100-ounce gold futures contract in October 2003 for $42 800 (428 × 100). If in December 2003 the June gold futures sold for $453, what could you sell your contract for? What would your profit be after the two months?
2. Suppose you decided to invest in common stocks as a personal investment. Which kind of broker—full-service or online discount—would you use for buying and selling stock? Why?
3. Choose a stock from the TSX and find a newspaper listing of a recent day's transactions for the stock. Explain what each element in the listing means.
4. Choose a bond from the TSX and find a newspaper listing of a recent day's transactions for the bond. Explain what each element in the listing means.
5. Which of the three measures of common stock value is most important? Why?
6. Explain how an investor might make money in a commodities trade. Then explain how an investor might lose money in a commodities trade.
7. How do the provincial securities commissions regulate securities markets? Give an example of how they are doing their job well and an example of how they failed to do their job.
8. Which type of stock or bond would be most appropriate for your investment purposes at this time? Why? Which type of mutual fund would be most appropriate for your investment purposes at this time? Why?

APPLICATION EXERCISES

1. Interview the financial manager of a local business. What are the investment goals of the organization? What mix of securities does it use? What advantages and disadvantages do you see in its portfolio?
2. Contact a broker for information about setting up a personal account for trading securities. Prepare a report on the broker's requirements for placing buy/sell orders, credit terms, cash account requirements, services available to investors, and commissions/fees schedules.

BUILDING YOUR BUSINESS SKILLS

Market Ups and Downs

Goal

To encourage students to understand the forces that cause fluctuations in stock prices.

Background

Investing in stocks requires an understanding of the various factors that affect stock prices. These factors may be intrinsic to the company itself or part of the external environment.

- Internal factors relate to the company itself, such as an announcement of poor or favourable earnings, earnings that are more or less than expected, major layoffs, labour problems, management issues, and mergers.
- External factors relate to world or national events, such as a threatened war in the Persian Gulf, the possibility of a bird flu epidemic, weather conditions that affect sales, the Bank of Canada's adjustment of interest rates, and employment figures that were higher or lower than expected. By analyzing these factors, you will often learn a lot about why a stock did well or why it did poorly. Being aware of these influences will help you anticipate future stock movements.

Assignment

Step 1

Working alone, choose a common stock that has experienced considerable price fluctuations in the past few years. Here are several examples (but there are many others): Nortel Networks, IBM, Amazon.com, and Apple Computer. Find the symbol for the stock and the exchange on which it is traded.

Step 2

At your library, find the *Daily Stock Price Record*, a publication that provides a historical picture of daily stock closings. There are separate copies for the various stock exchanges. Find your stock, and study its trading pattern.

Step 3

Find four or five days over a period of several months or even a year when there have been major price fluctuations in the stock. (A two- or three-point price change from one day to the next is considered major.) Then research what happened on that day that might have contributed to the fluctuation. The best place to begin is with the *Globe and Mail* or the *Wall Street Journal*.

Step 4

Write a short analysis that links changes in stock price to internal and external factors. As you analyze the data, be aware that it is sometimes difficult to know why a stock price fluctuates.

Step 5

Get together with three other students who studied different stocks. As a group, discuss your findings, looking for fluctuation patterns.

Follow-Up Questions

1. Do you see any similarities in the movement of the various stocks during the same period? For example, did the stocks move up or down at about the same time? If so, do you think the stocks were affected by the same factors? Explain your thinking.
2. Based on your analysis, did internal or external factors have the greater impact on stock price? Which factors had the more long-lasting effect? Which factors had the shorter effect?
3. Why do you think it is so hard to predict changes in stock price on a day-to-day basis?

EXERCISING YOUR ETHICS

Are You Endowed with Good Judgment?

The Situation

Every organization faces decisions about whether to make conservative or risky investments. Let's assume that you have been asked to evaluate the advantages and drawbacks of conservative versus risky investments, including all relevant ethical considerations, by Youth Dreams Charities (YDC), a local organization that assists low-income families in gaining access to educational opportunities. YDC is a non-profit firm that employs a full-time professional manager to run daily operations. Overall governance and policy making reside with a board of directors—10 part-time community-

▶▶▶

minded volunteers who are entrusted with carrying out YDC's mission.

For the current year, 23 students receive tuition totalling $92 000 paid by YDC. Tuition comes from annual fundraising activities (a white-tie dance and a seafood carnival) and from financial returns from YDC's $2.1 million endowment. The endowment has been amassed from charitable donations during the past 12 years, and this year, it has yielded some $84 000 for tuitions. The board's goal is to increase the endowment to $4 million in five years to provide $200 000 in tuition annually.

The Dilemma

Based on the finance committee's suggestions, the board is considering a change in YDC's investment policies. The current, rather conservative approach invests the endowment in GICs and other low-risk instruments that have consistently yielded a 6 percent annual return. This practice has allowed the endowment to grow modestly (at about 2 percent per year). The remaining investment proceeds (4 percent) flow out for tuitions. The proposed plan would invest one-half of the endowment in conservative instruments and the other half in blue-chip stocks. Finance committee members believe that with market growth, the endowment has a good chance of reaching the $4 million goal within five years. While some board members like the prospects of faster growth, others think the proposal is too risky. What happens if, instead of increasing, the stock market collapses and the endowment shrinks? What will happen to YDC's programs then?

Questions for Discussion

1. Why might a conservative versus risky choice be different at a non-profit organization than at a for-profit organization?
2. What are the main ethical issues in this situation?
3. What action should the board take?

CONCLUDING CASE 19-1

Scandal in the Mutual Fund Industry

During the past 20 years, Canadians have invested heavily in the stock market. Some of them do their own trading, and some use the services of a broker, but most of them buy shares in mutual funds. Fund managers pool the money of many individual investors and then decide which companies they will invest in and how much they will invest. Mutual funds are touted as a good deal for individual investors who do not have the time or expertise to intelligently invest in the stock market.

This sounds pretty good, but in the last five years or so, mutual funds have received some very negative publicity because their actions are not always in the best interests of the average investor. Concerns have been raised about mutual funds in three areas: management fees, market timing, and late trading.

Management Fees

It is important to investors that mutual fund managers are efficient in their work so that management costs do not unduly reduce the returns that mutual funds earn. In 2004, the *Globe and Mail* reported the results of a study which assessed the performance of 615 mutual funds during the period 1999–2004. The study used a key measure of mutual fund performance: the *"Fee-to-Performance Value Indicator"* (which shows how much of a fund's returns are used for fees like managers' salaries and commissions). The study found that the typical mutual fund has a score of 25 on the fee-to-performance indicator, meaning that about 25 cents out of every dollar earned goes to cover management fees. But fee-to-performance scores varied a lot. The *best* funds in the study were Ferique Equity (where only 6.5 cents of every dollar earned was used for management fees), PH&N Dividend Income (7.4 cents), and Sprott Canadian Equity (7.4 cents). The *worst* funds were Investors Canadian Enterprise (where 88.9 cents of every dollar was used for management fees), Clarica Canadian Diversified (76.9 cents), and Ethical Growth (62.7 cents).

The study also found that billions of dollars have been invested by Canadians in mutual funds that are not giving them good value for their money. During the period 1999–2004, $32.7 billion was contributed to mutual funds like AGF American Growth Class and BMO International Equity Fund that actually lost money. These funds delivered no value at all to investors (and because they lost money, it is not possible to calculate a negative fee-to-performance score for these funds). But these same mutual funds collected millions of dollars in fees from investors. Canadians also invested $21 billion dollars in mutual funds where more than 50 percent of the gross revenue of the fund was used to pay management fees. These firms delivered questionable value to investors.

Ken Kivenko, a spokesman for the Small Investor Protection Association, said that most individual investors don't even realize that they are paying fees to mutual funds. He found it surprising that some mutual funds can attract billions of dollars of investment from Canadians even though their fees are uncompetitive. Mutual funds that charge high fees counter these claims by noting that they provide better service to customers than do mutual funds that charge lower fees.

Market Timing

This refers to the practice of rapid in-and-out trading in mutual fund shares to profit from near-term price changes. While it is not technically illegal, it violates a basic principle of fairness because mutual funds typically have a strategy of long-term investing and do not normally allow people to do in-and-out trading (unless they pay a penalty). If a select few traders are allowed to engage in market timing without paying the penalty, this obviously works to the detriment of small investors who are not given this deal.

In 2004, four large Canadian mutual funds were fined a total of $156 million for allowing certain traders to engage in market timing. These traders made a total of $301 million in profits by using market timing. Three brokerages that were owned by banks were also fined a total of $46.5 million. All of the money will be used to reimburse investors who were disadvantaged by market timing. Paul Moore, the vice-chairman of the Ontario Securities Commission, said that by allowing only certain people to make market timing trades, these companies reduced returns for their long-term investors and failed in their duty to protect their interests. He also said that the fines will remind mutual fund managers that they have a responsibility to be vigilant in monitoring the activities of the people who work in their firms.

Michael Watson, the OSC's enforcement director, said he was disturbed by the fact that the problem of market timing was brought to the OSC's attention by New York Attorney General Elliot Spitzer, who was prosecuting U.S. mutual funds that allowed the practice. Watson said there must have been many people in Canada who knew that market timing was going on, but no one said anything.

In the United States, charges were filed against several firms, including Putnam Investments, which is the fifth-largest mutual fund firm in the United States, with $272 billion in assets. Regulators allege that executives knew that two of the firm's managers were market timing their own funds for personal profit, told them to stop, but didn't fire them, and let them keep the profits they made from market timing. After this became known, CEO Lawrence Lasser and four managers were fired.

Late Trading

Sounds incredible, doesn't it, that someone can bet on events from the past? It turns out that's what's been going on in the $7 trillion scandal-laden mutual funds industry. Some mutual fund managers have been making transactions after the market outcomes are known. It's what you might call a "sure thing"—a great way to erase market risk and take profits that are inaccessible to honest investors.

It's called "late trading"—trading in fund shares after the market closes, but at the close-of-trade price—and it's illegal. After the 4:00 p.m. (Eastern Time) cutoff, when the day's closing price is known, preferred customers get to trade—buy or sell—at the pre-4:00 p.m. price. It's like betting after the game is over. Late trading gives an unfair information advantage over other investors because when big news breaks after the 4:00 p.m. closing—news that will almost certainly affect the next day's securities markets—late traders are nearly assured of a next-day quick profit or avoidance of a loss.

In the United States, the Securities and Exchange Commission's (SEC) enforcement director, Stephen Cutler, told a Senate hearing that about 10 percent of fund groups may have engaged in late trading and as many as one-fourth of America's largest mutual funds helped favoured clients by allowing illegal late trading. Preferential trading arrangements for big-money clients can be draining off billions of dollars from ordinary investors in mutual funds.

The SEC, the New York Attorney General's Office, and the Wisconsin Department of Financial Institutions are all looking into alleged market-timing transactions by Richard Strong, the board chairman of Strong Mutual Funds, that may have benefited him, his family, and friends. Strong Mutual Funds has policies against market timing because it hurts long-term shareholders and increases the fund's costs of operations. Under those conditions, regulators say, it's fraudulent to allow favoured people to do market timing without disclosing it to shareholders. The company confirmed that Strong invested assets in a small number of short-term, next-day transactions taking advantage of market-moving news. Strong resigned as board chairman of the $42 billion fund and said he would reimburse investors for any losses they suffered because of his trading.

What should be done to reduce the problems of marketing timing and late trading? An indignant U.S. Congress proposed possible remedies and pledged that new, stiffer SEC regulations will eventually emerge. Meanwhile, the SEC and the National Association of Securities Dealers brought actions seeking injunctions, penalties, and financial relief for investors against several more illicit brokerages and mutual funds. But fixing the problem won't be easy because each proposal seems to create new potential problems, and there's no agreement on the best course of action. For example, proposals by the Investment Company Institute to outlaw all late trading could extend the time to process a trade—what now takes one day could take three or more days. That means mutual fund insiders would know about investment movements underway by big pension funds, and have more time to use that information for self-gain. The trick is to fix the old problems without causing new ones.

Questions for Discussion

1. Why do you suppose the Ontario Securities Commission was slow in detecting the industry's market-timing abuses?
2. What remedies do you believe would be appropriate for fund managers who are found guilty of market timing and late trading? Defend your answer.
3. Suppose you are the manager of one of the equity funds for a large mutual funds firm. What steps would you take to ensure compliance with OSC regulations by your employees?
4. As a Chartered Financial Analyst (CFA) working at a mutual funds firm, what would you do if you suspected other employees of doing market timing or late trading?
5. Think of an after-hours news event that resulted in a next-day decline in the stock market. Then think of an after-hours news event that resulted in a next-day increase in the stock market. Why do you think the market would fall in one case and increase in the other?

CONCLUDING CASE 19-2

Are Stock Options a Good Idea?

At one time in the not-too-distant past, stock options were touted as a great idea because they seemed like an effective tool to motivate managers to work hard for the company. Both executives and shareholders would benefit (or so the argument went) because the price of the stock would go up. But the flaws in options were revealed in the stock market boom and bust of the last few years. Greed was one of those flaws.

Suppose you were a manager in a company and you were given 100 000 options to buy the company's shares at $20 per share (the current market price is $15). You know that if the market price rises above the option price, you will make a profit. If the market price rises to, say, $40 per share, you could exercise your options and buy 100 000 shares at $20 per share and then turn around and sell the shares for $40 per share. You would therefore make a $2 million profit (100 000 × $20). Would this be enough to motivate you to work hard to increase the market price of the company's shares? Probably. Would it be enough to cause you to do something unethical or illegal (such as recording sales revenues before they actually occurred)? Maybe!

Ironically, when options first became common in the 1980s, it was thought that they would cause managers to see the world like shareholders saw it. But the soaring stock market of the late 1990s caused a fundamental human characteristic—greed—to emerge. Managers soon started thinking: "How fast can I get my money out?" Many executives became obsessed with the price of their company's stock and took short-term actions that were designed to increase it because that's the way you make money with options. The motivation was overwhelming to do almost anything to make sure the options were valuable. In some companies, executives were paid a very low salary, but were attracted on the basis that they could make a lot of money on stock options. It is not surprising that these executives would become obsessed with the price of the company's stock.

Some managers made stunning amounts of money from stock options. At the end of 2002, the *Wall Street Journal* published a "Top 10" list of managers who made the most money from exercising stock options. Number 1 on the list was Lawrence Ellison, CEO of Oracle ($706 million), followed by Michael Eisner, CEO of Disney ($569 million), and Michael Dell, CEO of Dell Computer ($233 million). Even the number 10 person on the list (Howard Solomon, CEO of Forest Laboratories) made $147 million. The average person cannot really comprehend the magnitude of these payments.

There has been a great deal of negative publicity in the business press about stock options during the last few years. Shareholders have also complained loudly as the value of their stock tumbled during the stock market decline of 2001–02. Regular investors are not impressed when already-rich executives get richer while shareholders see their investments decline in value. Shareholders also don't like the fact that options have the effect of diluting the company's stock (because more shares are issued to honour stock options given to executives). In many companies, the price of the shares dropped shortly after top executives exercised their options. The executives made large profits, and the common shareholders watched as the value of their stock declined.

Recently, companies have begun to change the way they deal with stock options. Here are some examples:

- Royal Bank of Canada has eliminated options for members of its board of directors and reduced their availability to executives; as well, executives are now required to keep the shares they gain from exercising options.
- Nortel Networks now expenses the cost of its stock options.
- Bank of Montreal has also reduced the use of stock options and introduced performance hurdles that must be met before the options can be exercised.

Questions for Discussion

1. Summarize the arguments that say stock options are a good idea. Then summarize the arguments that say stock options are a bad idea. Which set of arguments are more compelling? Explain your answer.
2. Make suggestions for revising the system of giving stock options such that the positive aspects of stock options are retained and the negative aspects are reduced.
3. Do some research to find out what companies are doing currently to deal with the important issue of stock options. What are the strong and weak points of the current proposals?

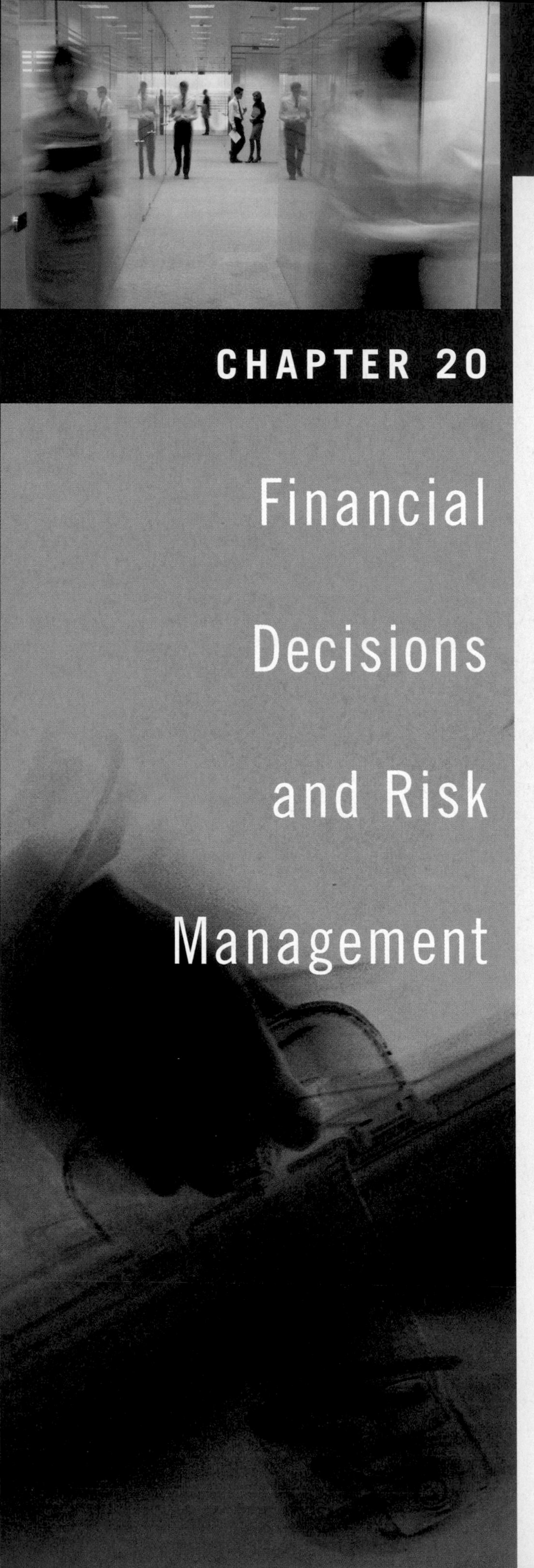

CHAPTER 20

Financial Decisions and Risk Management

After reading this chapter, you should be able to:

1. Describe the responsibilities of a *financial manager.*
2. Distinguish between *short-term (operating)* and *long-term (capital) expenditures.*
3. Identify four sources of *short-term financing* for businesses.
4. Distinguish among the various sources of *long-term financing* and explain the risks involved in each.
5. Discuss some key issues in financial management for small businesses.
6. Explain how *risk* affects business operations and identify the five steps in the *risk-management process.*
7. Explain the distinction between *insurable* and *uninsurable risks*, and distinguish among the different *types of insurance* purchased by businesses.

The Increasing Importance of Risk Management

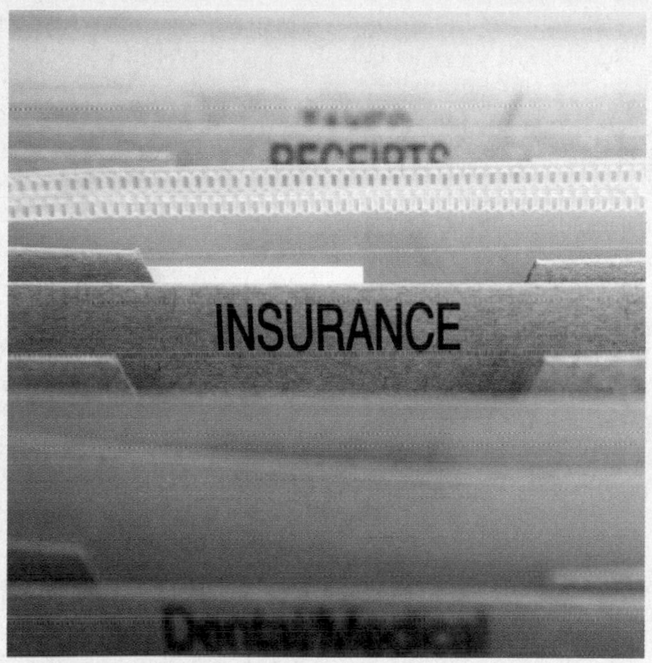

Canadian business firms face risks in many different areas. The company's computer network may be hacked into, or interest rates may change, or executive talent may be raided by another company, or a natural disaster or terrorist attack may occur, or consumers may sue the company, or all of the above may happen. How do business firms cope with these risks? There are several things that can be done, including the creation of a top-level executive position to oversee risk management, buying insurance to shield the company from various kinds of risks, and instituting control systems that will reduce the risk that inappropriate employee behaviour will cause financial harm to the company.

CREATING A TOP-LEVEL POSITION TO OVERSEE RISK MANAGEMENT

Companies usually have a chief executive officer (CEO), a chief operating officer (COO), and a chief financial officer (CFO), but not too many of them have chief risk officers (CRO). At least not yet. But the realization is growing that a business needs a high-level executive who is responsible for developing and implementing plans for dealing with risk, rather than just trying to respond to risk after something unexpected happens. In 2005, Forrester Research predicted that by 2007, 75 percent of large organizations in North America would have a CRO.

Hydro One Inc. already has a CRO, partly because the deregulation of electricity means that it needs to manage the risk of price fluctuations in the new market-based pricing system. But it's not just pricing risk that Hydro One needs to deal with. John Fraser, Hydro One's CRO, has already dealt with a major risk situation that has little to do with pricing. When Hydro One offered an early retirement package to employees, 1400 people took the offer. This was far more than the company expected, so Fraser was charged with analyzing how the loss of so many people might affect the company's ability to achieve its objectives. After a department-by-department analysis, he concluded that by hiring 125 people and paying consultants to do some other critical work, Hydro One could reduce its risks to an acceptable level.

BUYING INSURANCE

There are many different types of business insurance that are available (see pp. 675–677). Risk managers must decide what kind of insurance the company needs to carry, and whether it can afford to carry such insurance. Consider what happened to Kitchener, Ontario-based Kentain Products, which manufactures chemical tank liners. Its products have been very successful in Canada, so owner Glen Lippert thought it was a natural extension of the business to begin exporting the products to the United States. He was in for a rude shock. When his insurance company found out what he was planning, they would no longer sell him liability insurance because they felt that selling to the United States was too risky. When Lippert checked around at other insurance companies, he discovered that it would cost him $50 000 in annual premiums to get liability insurance. Since that figure exceeded the profit he expected to make in the United States, he abandoned his export plans.

It's not just companies that export that are having trouble with insurance premiums. One Waterloo, Ontario-based company that sells industrial air compressors had its premiums increased from $6500 to $40 000 in one year. A cabinet maker saw its premiums double from $10 000 to $20 000 in one year, and then to $60 000 two years later. Many small businesses can't get insurance at any price. This is a big problem because banks usually demand that a company have liability insurance before they will loan it money. A survey by the Federation of Independent Business found that most small businesses have faced increases in the 30 percent range during each of the last few years. In the survey, 83 percent of the respondents said that high insurance premiums were their single biggest cost.

The insurance industry gives a variety of reasons for the rapidly escalating insurance premiums—uncertainty in the stock market (where insurance companies have much of their money invested), low interest rates, terrorist activity, natural disasters, and liability lawsuits against companies. Put simply, insurance companies are not getting enough revenue from premium payments and their investments to pay all the claims that are arising.

So they increase premiums and refuse to cover some high-risk activities.

Some people think that the insurance business is not very interesting, what with all the mathematical calculations and actuarial tables that are required. But insurance is not only practical and important; it can also be very interesting. Consider the following situations:

- Canadian companies routinely buy liability insurance for members of their board of directors to shield them from lawsuits that allege negligence or failure to carry out their duty to shareholders. Lately, lawyers for disgruntled shareholders have started suing boards of directors for failing to protect shareholders. Some big wins for shareholders meant that insurance companies had to pay out large sums of money. After this became a trend, insurance companies started sharply raising their rates.
- Producers of the Broadway show *Titanic* paid about U.S.$400 000 for insurance to cover things such as a member of the audience being hit by a flying deck chair, or a cast member being injured during the performance. Interestingly, Chubb Corp., the company that covered the real *Titanic* (the one that sank on April 15, 1912, claiming 1523 lives), also covered the Broadway show. That real *Titanic* disaster cost the insurance company U.S.$100 000, but the Broadway show was insured for U.S.$14 million.
- In the musical *Victor/Victoria*, an insurance policy was purchased on Julie Andrews. The policy premium—U.S.$157 985—insured the producers of the show for up to $2 million if Andrews missed some performances, and up to $8.5 million if she had to leave the show. Producers routinely buy this kind of insurance because if a star is unable to perform on a given night, many patrons who have bought tickets want their money back. As it happened, Andrews missed many performances because of various illnesses, and an unusually large number of patrons requested refunds. Total losses to the producers exceeded $1 million. But when the producers tried to collect their money, the insurance companies refused to pay, arguing that Andrews had given false answers to questions about her medical history.
- Rap artists such as Snoop Doggy Dogg can earn more than U.S.$50 000 per night on a multi-city concert tour. But national tours by rap artists have been virtually nonexistent for over a decade because stabbings and gunfire were becoming all too common at these shows.
- Diamond State Insurance Company, which issued an insurance policy to the band Limp Bizkit, claimed it had no liability for damages awarded following the death of a teenage fan at a Limp Bizkit rock concert in Australia in 2001. The insurance company argued that singer Fred Durst "incited" the crowd and that led to the teenager's death when she was trampled.
- Reliance National Insurance is one of the largest underwriters of music events. It also insures many concerts by crooners and rappers. When musicians perform live, insurance costs are usually shared by the performer, the concert promoter, and the arena where the event is being held. Music companies also take out "key man" insurance on musicians.

IMPLEMENTING EFFECTIVE CONTROL SYSTEMS

There is always a risk that some employees will act in ways that are financially detrimental to the company. In recent years, several high-profile cases have demonstrated just how high the losses can be if effective risk control systems are not in place. For example, John Rusnak, a currency trader at Allfirst Financial, defrauded the company of $691 million by creating phony currency trades. Stephen Humphries, a trader at Sussex Futures Ltd. in England engaged in so much fraudulent trading activity that he destroyed the company he worked for. He lost U.S.$1.1 million in just one 90-minute period. Sussex Futures ceased operations, and 70 people lost their jobs. Nicholas Leeson, who worked for Barings PLC, a British merchant bank, bought and sold futures contracts, particularly investments known as derivatives. Over a three-week period, Leeson managed to incur trading losses of nearly $1 billion. When losses spiralled out of control, Leeson fled, and Barings had to declare bankruptcy. Leeson was eventually sentenced to six-and-a-half years in prison.

In all of these cases, there was a failure to properly manage risk. That failure led to massive financial losses, corporate bankruptcies, and the loss of many jobs. ◆

THE ROLE OF THE FINANCIAL MANAGER

Describe the responsibilities of a *financial manager.* 1

We have seen that production managers are responsible for planning and controlling the output of goods and services. We have noted that marketing managers must plan and control the development and marketing of products. Similarly, **financial managers** plan and control the acquisition and dispersal of the company's financial assets. The business activity known as **finance** (or **corporate finance**) typically involves four responsibilities:

- determining a firm's long-term investments
- obtaining funds to pay for those investments
- conducting the firm's everyday financial activities
- helping to manage the risks that the firm takes

financial managers Those managers responsible for planning and overseeing the financial resources of a firm.

finance (corporate finance) The business function involving decisions about a firm's long-term investments and obtaining the funds to pay for those investments.

Objectives of the Financial Manager

Financial managers collect funds, pay debts, establish trade credit, obtain loans, control cash balances, and plan for future financial needs. But a financial manager's overall objective is to increase a firm's value—and thus stockholders' wealth. Whereas accountants create data to reflect a firm's financial status, financial managers make decisions for improving that status. Financial managers, then, must ensure that a company's earnings exceed its costs—in other words, that it earns a profit. In sole proprietorships and partnerships, profits translate directly into increases in owners' wealth. In corporations, profits translate into an increase in the value of common stock.

Responsibilities of the Financial Manager

The various responsibilities of the financial manager in increasing a firm's wealth fall into three general categories: *cash flow management, financial control,* and *financial planning.*

Cash Flow Management

To increase a firm's value, financial managers must ensure that it always has enough funds on hand to purchase the materials and human resources that it needs to produce goods and services. At the same time, of course, there

Financial managers have the responsibility of ensuring that the financial assets of a company are used effectively. This includes investments it may have in other companies in the form of shares of stock. Regular assessment of how these investments are performing is an important responsibility of financial managers.

may be funds that are not needed immediately. These must be invested to earn more money for a firm. This activity—**cash flow management**—requires careful planning. If excess cash balances are allowed to sit idle instead of being invested, a firm loses the cash returns it could have earned.

cash flow management Managing the pattern in which cash flows into the firm in the form of revenues and out of the firm in the form of debt payments.

How important to a business is the management of its idle cash? One study has revealed that companies averaging $2 million in annual sales typically hold $40 000 in non-interest-bearing accounts. Larger companies hold even larger sums. More and more companies, however, are learning to put their idle funds to work. By locating idle cash and putting it to work, firms not only gain additional income, but also can avoid having to borrow from outside sources. The savings on interest payments can be substantial.

Financial Control

Because things never go exactly as planned, financial managers must be prepared to make adjustments for actual financial changes that occur each day. **Financial control** is the process of checking actual performance against plans to ensure that the desired financial status occurs. For example, planned revenues based on forecasts usually turn out to be higher or lower than actual revenues. Why? Simply because sales are unpredictable. Control involves monitoring revenue inflows and making appropriate financial adjustments. Excessively high revenues, for instance, may be deposited in short-term interest-bearing accounts. Or they may be used to pay off short-term debt. Otherwise earmarked resources can be saved or put to better use. In contrast, lower-than-expected revenues may necessitate short-term borrowing to meet current debt obligations.

financial control The process of checking actual performance against plans to ensure that the desired financial status is achieved.

Budgets (as we saw in Chapter 14) are often the backbone of financial control. The budget provides the "measuring stick" against which performance is evaluated. The cash flows, debts, and assets not only of the whole company but also of each department are compared at regular intervals against budgeted amounts. Discrepancies indicate the need for financial adjustments so that resources are used to the best advantage.

Financial Planning

The cornerstone of effective financial management is the development of a **financial plan**. A financial plan describes a firm's strategies for reaching some future financial position. In constructing the plan, a financial manager must ask several questions:

financial plan A description of how a business will reach some financial position it seeks for the future; includes projections for sources and uses of funds.

- What amount of funds does the company need to meet immediate plans?
- When will it need more funds?
- Where can it get the funds to meet both its short-term and its long-term needs?

To answer these questions, a financial manager must develop a clear picture of *why* a firm needs funds. Managers must also assess the relative costs and benefits of potential funding sources. In the sections that follow, we will examine the main reasons for which companies generate funds and describe the main sources of business funding, for both the short term and the long term.

2 Distinguish between *short-term (operating)* and *long term (capital)* expenditures.

WHY DO BUSINESSES NEED FUNDS?

Every company needs money to survive. Failure to make a contractually obligated payment can lead to bankruptcy and the dissolution of the firm. However, the successful financial manager must distinguish between two different kinds of financial outlays: *short-term (operating) expenditures* and *long-term (capital) expenditures*.

Short-Term (Operating) Expenditures

A firm incurs short-term expenditures regularly in its everyday business activities. To handle these expenditures, financial managers must pay attention to *accounts payable*, *accounts receivable*, and to *inventories*. We also describe the measures used by some firms in managing the funds known as *working capital*.

Accounts Payable

In Chapter 14, we defined *accounts payable* as unpaid bills owed to suppliers plus wages and taxes due within the upcoming year. For most companies, this is the largest single category of short-term debt. To plan for funding flows, financial managers want to know *in advance* the amounts of new accounts payable as well as when they must be repaid. For information about such obligations and needs—say, the quantity of supplies required by a certain department in an upcoming period—financial managers must rely on other managers. The Exercising Your Ethics box at the end of the chapter presents an interesting dilemma regarding accounts payable.

Accounts Receivable

As we also saw in Chapter 14, *accounts receivable* consist of funds due from customers who have bought on credit. A sound financial plan requires financial managers to project accurately both how much credit is advanced to buyers and when they will make payments on their accounts. For example, managers at Kraft Foods must know how many dollars' worth of cheddar cheese Safeway supermarkets will order each month; they must also know Safeway's payment schedule. Because accounts receivable represent an investment in products for which a firm has not yet received payment, they temporarily tie up its funds. Clearly, the seller wants to receive payment as quickly as possible.

Credit Policies. Predicting payment schedules is a function of **credit policy**—the rules governing a firm's extension of credit to customers. This policy sets standards as to which buyers are eligible for what type of credit. Typically, credit is extended to customers who have the ability to pay and who honour their obligations. Credit is denied to firms with poor payment histories.

credit policy Rules governing a firm's extension of credit to customers.

Credit policy also sets payment terms. For example, credit terms of "2/10, net 30" mean that the selling company offers a 2 percent discount if the customer pays within 10 days. The customer has 30 days to pay the regular price. Under these terms, the buyer would have to pay only $980 on a $1000 invoice on days 1 to 10, but all $1000 on days 11 to 30. The higher the discount, the more incentive buyers have to pay early. Sellers can thus adjust credit terms to influence when customers pay their bills.

Inventories

Between the time a firm buys raw materials and the time it sells finished products, it ties up funds in **inventory**—materials and goods that it will sell within the year. Failure to manage inventory can have grave financial consequences. Too little inventory of any kind can cost a firm sales. Too much inventory means tied-up funds that cannot be used elsewhere. In extreme cases, a company may have to sell excess inventory at low profits simply to raise cash.

inventory Materials and goods currently held by the company that will be sold within the year.

There are three basic types of inventories: *raw materials*, *work-in-process*, and *finished goods*. The basic supplies a firm buys to use in its production process are its **raw materials inventory**. Levi Strauss's raw materials inventory includes huge rolls of denim. **Work-in-process inventory** consists of goods partway through the production process. Cut-out but not-yet-sewn jeans are part of the work-in-process inventory at Levi's. Finally, **finished goods inventory** is items that are ready for sale. Completed blue jeans ready for shipment to dealers are finished goods inventory.

raw materials inventory That portion of a firm's inventory consisting of basic supplies used to manufacture products for sale.

work-in-process inventory That portion of a firm's inventory consisting of goods partway through the production process.

finished goods inventory That portion of a firm's inventory consisting of completed goods ready for sale.

Working Capital

As we saw in Chapter 14, working capital is the difference between a firm's current assets and current liabilities. It is a liquid asset out of which current debts can be paid. A company calculates its working capital by adding up the following:

- inventories—that is, raw materials, work-in-process, and finished goods on hand
- accounts receivable (minus accounts payable)

How much money is tied up in working capital? Large companies typically devote 20 cents of every sales dollar to working capital. What are the benefits of reducing these sums? There are two very important pluses:

1. Every dollar that is not tied up in working capital becomes a dollar of more useful cash flow.
2. Reduction of working capital raises earnings permanently.

The second advantage results from the fact that money costs money (in interest payments and the like). Reducing working capital, therefore, means saving money.

Long-Term (Capital) Expenditures

Companies need funds to cover long-term expenditures for fixed assets. As noted in Chapter 14, *fixed assets* are items that have a lasting use or value, such as land, buildings, and machinery. The Hudson Bay Oil and Gas plant in Flin Flon, Manitoba, is a fixed asset.

Long-term expenditures are usually more carefully planned than short-term outlays because they pose special problems. They differ from short-term outlays in the following ways, all of which influence the ways that long-term outlays are funded:

- Unlike inventories and other short-term assets, they are not normally sold or converted into cash.
- Their acquisition requires a very large investment.
- They represent a binding commitment of company funds that continues long into the future.

3 Identify four sources of *short-term financing* for businesses.

SOURCES OF SHORT-TERM FUNDS

Firms can call on many sources for the funds they need to finance day-to-day operations and to implement short-term plans. These sources include *trade credit*, *secured and unsecured loans*, and *factoring accounts receivable*.

Trade Credit

Accounts payable are not merely an expenditure. They are also a source of funds to the company, which has the use of both the product purchased and the price of the product until the time it pays its bill. **Trade credit**, the granting of credit by one firm to another, is effectively a short-term loan. Trade credit can take several forms.

trade credit The granting of credit by a selling firm to a buying firm.

- The most common form, **open-book credit**, is essentially a "gentlemen's agreement." Buyers receive merchandise along with invoices stating credit terms. Sellers ship products on faith that payment will be forthcoming.
- When sellers want more reassurance, they may insist that buyers sign legally binding **promissory notes** before merchandise is shipped. The agreement states when and how much money will be paid to the seller.
- The **trade draft** is attached to the merchandise shipment by the seller and states the promised date and amount of payment due. To take possession of the merchandise, the buyer must sign the draft. Once signed by the buyer, the document becomes a **trade acceptance**. Trade drafts and trade acceptances are useful forms of credit in international transactions.

open-book credit Form of trade credit in which sellers ship merchandise on faith that payment will be forthcoming.

promissory note Form of trade credit in which buyers sign promise-to-pay agreements before merchandise is shipped.

trade draft Form of trade credit in which buyers must sign statements of payment terms attached to merchandise by sellers.

trade acceptance Trade draft that has been signed by the buyer.

Secured Short-Term Loans

For most firms, bank loans are a vital source of short-term funding. Such loans almost always involve a promissory note in which the borrower promises to repay the loan plus interest. In **secured loans**, banks also require the borrower to put up **collateral**—to give the bank the right to seize certain assets if payments are not made as promised. Inventories, accounts receivable, and other assets may serve as collateral for a secured loan.

secured loan A short-term loan in which the borrower is required to put up collateral.

collateral Any asset that a lender has the right to seize if a borrower does not repay a loan.

Secured loans allow borrowers to get funds when they might not qualify for unsecured credit. Moreover, they generally carry lower interest rates than unsecured loans. Collateral may be in the form of inventories or accounts receivable, and most businesses have other types of assets that can be pledged. Some, for instance, own marketable securities, such as stocks or bonds of other companies (see Chapter 19). Many more own fixed assets, such as land, buildings, or equipment. Fixed assets, however, are generally used to secure long-term rather than short-term loans. Most short-term business borrowing is secured by inventories and accounts receivable.

Inventory Loans

When a loan is made with inventory as a collateral asset, the lender loans the borrower some portion of the stated value of the inventory. Inventory is more attractive as collateral when it provides the lender with real security for the loan amount: For example, if the inventory can be readily converted into cash, it is relatively more valuable as collateral. Other inventory—say, boxes full of expensive, partially completed lenses for eyeglasses—is of little value on the open market. Meanwhile, a thousand crates of boxed, safely stored canned tomatoes might well be convertible into cash.

Accounts Receivable as Collateral

When accounts receivable are used as collateral, the process is called **pledging accounts receivable**. In the event of nonpayment, the lender may seize the receivables—that is, funds owed the borrower by its customers. If these assets are not enough to cover the loan, the borrower must make up the difference. This option is especially important to service companies

pledging accounts receivable Using accounts receivable as collateral for a loan.

such as accounting firms and law offices. Because they do not maintain inventories, accounts receivable are their main source of collateral. Typically, lenders who will accept accounts receivable as collateral are financial institutions with credit departments capable of evaluating the quality of the receivables.

Factoring Accounts Receivable

A firm can raise funds rapidly by *factoring*: selling the firm's accounts receivable. In this process, the purchaser of the receivables, usually a financial institution, is known as the factor. The factor pays some percentage of the full amount of receivables due to the selling firm. The seller gets this money immediately.[1] For example, a factor might buy $40 000 worth of receivables for 60 percent of that sum ($24 000). The factor profits to the extent that the money it eventually collects exceeds the amount it paid. This profit depends on the quality of the receivables, the cost of collecting them, and interest rates.

Unsecured Short-Term Loans

unsecured loan A short-term loan in which the borrower is not required to put up collateral.

With an **unsecured loan**, the borrower does not have to put up collateral. In many cases, however, the bank requires the borrower to maintain a *compensating balance*: The borrower must keep a portion of the loan amount on deposit with the bank in a non-interest-bearing account.

The terms of the loan—amount, duration, interest rate, and payment schedule—are negotiated between the bank and the borrower. To receive an unsecured loan, then, a firm must ordinarily have a good banking relationship with the lender. Once an agreement is made, a promissory note will be executed and the funds transferred to the borrower. Although some unsecured loans are one-time-only arrangements, many take the form of *lines of credit*, *revolving credit agreements*, or *commercial paper*.

line of credit A standing agreement between a bank and a firm in which the bank specifies the maximum amount it will make available to the borrower for a short-term unsecured loan; the borrower can then draw on those funds, when available.

Lines of Credit

A standing agreement with a bank to lend a firm a maximum amount of funds on request is called a **line of credit**. With a line of credit, the firm knows the maximum amount it will be allowed to borrow if the bank has

As CFO of *Nylon* magazine, which focusses on fashion and pop culture for women, Larry Rosenblum is responsible for collecting the money that advertisers owe the publication. The magazine depends on that money for its cash flow. To get the money, Rosenblum typically resorts to factors—lenders who buy the legal right to collect a company's outstanding invoices (in return for up to 3 percent of the amount due). Among Canadian and U.S. business firms, factoring accounts for more than $1 trillion in credit. The bill collecting business no longer has the unsavoury reputation that it once had.

sufficient funds. The bank does not guarantee that the funds will be available when requested, however.

For example, suppose that TD Canada Trust gives Sunshine Tanning Inc. a $100 000 line of credit for the coming year. By signing promissory notes, Sunshine's borrowings can total up to $100 000 at any time. Sunshine benefits from the arrangement by knowing in advance that the bank regards the firm as creditworthy and will loan funds to it on short notice.

Revolving Credit Agreements

Revolving credit agreements are similar to bank credit cards for consumers. Under a revolving credit agreement, a lender agrees to make some amount of funds available on demand to a firm for continuing short-term loans. The lending institution guarantees that funds will be available when sought by the borrower. In return, the bank charges a *commitment fee*—a charge for holding open a line of credit for a customer even if the customer does not borrow any funds. The commitment fee is often expressed as a percentage of the loan amount, usually 0.5 to 1 percent of the committed amount.

revolving credit agreement A guaranteed line of credit for which the firm pays the bank interest on funds borrowed as well as a fee for extending the line of credit.

For example, suppose that TD Canada Trust agrees to lend Sunshine Tanning up to $100 000 under a revolving credit agreement. If Sunshine borrows $80 000, it still has access to $20 000. If it pays off $50 000 of the debt, reducing its debt to $30 000, then it has $70 000 available to it. Sunshine pays interest on the borrowed funds and also pays a fee on the unused funds in the line of credit.

Commercial Paper

Some firms can raise funds in the short run by issuing **commercial paper**. Since commercial paper is backed solely by the issuing firm's promise to pay, it is an option for only the largest and most creditworthy firms. Here's how it works. Corporations issue commercial paper with a face value. Companies that buy commercial paper pay less than that value. At the end of a specified period (usually 30 to 90 days but legally up to 270 days), the issuing company buys back the paper—*at the face value*. The difference between the price the buying company paid and the face value is the buyer's profit.

commercial paper A method of short-run fundraising in which a firm sells unsecured notes for less than the face value and then repurchases them at the face value within 270 days; buyers' profits are the difference between the original price paid and the face value.

For example, if Inco needs to borrow $10 million for 90 days it might issue commercial paper with a face value of $10.2 million. Insurance companies with $10 million excess cash will buy the paper. After 90 days, Inco would pay $10.2 million to the insurance companies.

SOURCES OF LONG-TERM FUNDS

Distinguish among the various sources of *long-term financing* and explain the risks involved in each. **4**

Firms need long-term funding to finance expenditures on fixed assets—the buildings and equipment necessary for conducting their business. They may seek long-term funds through *debt financing* (that is, from outside the firm) or through *equity financing* (by drawing on internal sources). We will discuss both options in this section, as well as a middle ground called *hybrid financing*. We will also analyze some of the options that enter into decisions about long-term financing, as well as the role of the *risk-return relationship* in attracting investors to a firm.

Debt Financing

Long-term borrowing from outside the company—**debt financing**—is a major component of most firms' long-term financial planning. The two primary sources of such funding are *long-term loans* and the sale of *corporate bonds*.

debt financing Raising money to meet long-term expenditures by borrowing from outside the company; usually takes the form of long-term loans or the sale of corporate bonds.

Long-Term Loans

Most corporations get their long-term loans from a chartered bank, usually one with which the firm has developed a long-standing relationship. Credit companies (like Household Finance Corp.), insurance companies, and pension funds also grant long-term business loans. Long-term loans are attractive to borrowers for several reasons:

- Because the number of parties involved is limited, loans can often be arranged very quickly.
- The firm need not make public disclosure of its business plans or the purpose for which it is acquiring the loan. (In contrast, the issuance of corporate bonds requires such disclosure.)
- The duration of the loan can easily be matched to the borrower's needs.
- If the firm's needs change, loans usually contain clauses making it possible to change terms.

Long-term loans also have some disadvantages. Large borrowers may have trouble finding lenders to supply enough funds. Long-term borrowers may also have restrictions placed on them as conditions of the loan. They may have to pledge long-term assets as collateral. And they may have to agree not to take on any more debt until the borrowed funds are repaid.

Interest Rates. Interest rates are negotiated between borrower and lender. Although some bank loans have fixed rates, others have floating rates tied to the prime rate that the bank charges its most creditworthy customers (see Chapter 18). A loan at 1 percent above prime, then, is payable at one percentage point higher than the prime rate. This rate may fluctuate, or float, because the prime rate itself goes up and down as market conditions change.

Corporate Bonds

Like commercial paper, a corporate bond is a contract—a promise by the issuing company or organization to pay the holder a certain amount of money on a specified date. Unlike commercial paper, however, bond issuers do not pay off quickly. In many cases, bonds may not be redeemed for 30 years from the time of issue. In addition, unlike commercial paper, most bonds

This corporate bond will be used to purchase items like machinery that are necessary for the production of goods.

pay the bondholder a stipulated sum of interest semi-annually or annually. If it fails to make a bond payment, the company is in default.

Corporate bonds are the major source of long-term debt financing for most corporations. Bonds are attractive when companies need large amounts of funds for long periods of time. The issuing company gets access to large numbers of lenders through nationwide bond markets and stock exchanges. But bonds involve expensive administrative and selling costs. They also may require very high interest payments if the issuing company has a poor credit rating.

Bond Indenture. The terms of a bond, including the amount to be paid, the interest rate, and the maturity (payoff) date, differ from company to company and from issue to issue. They are spelled out in the bond contract, or **bond indenture**. The indenture also identifies which of the firm's assets, if any, are pledged as collateral for the bonds.

bond indenture Statement of the terms of a corporate bond.

Equity Financing

Although debt financing has strong appeal in some cases, looking inside the company for long-term funding is preferable under other circumstances. In small companies, the founders may increase their personal investment in the firm. In most cases, however, **equity financing** takes the form of issuing common stock or of retaining the firm's earnings. As you will see, both options involve putting the owners' capital to work.

equity financing Raising money to meet long-term expenditures by issuing common stock or by retaining earnings.

Common Stock

When shareholders purchase common stock, they seek profits in the form of both dividends and appreciation. Overall, shareholders hope for an increase in the market value of their stock because the firm has profited and grown. By selling shares of stock, the company gets the funds it needs for buying land, buildings, and equipment.

Suppose that Sunshine Tanning's founders invested $10 000 by buying the original 500 shares of common stock (at $20 per share) in 1997. If the company used these funds to buy equipment and succeeded financially, by 2006 it might need funds for expansion. A pattern of profitable operations and regularly paid dividends might allow Sunshine to raise $50 000 by selling 500 new shares of stock for $100 per share. This additional paid-in capital would increase the total shareholders' equity to $60 000, as shown in Table 20.1.

Table 20.1 Stockholders' Equity for Sunshine Tanning

Common Stockholders' Equity, 1997	
Initial common stock (500 shares issued @ $20 per share, 1997)	$10 000
Total stockholders' equity	$10 000
Common Stockholders' Equity, 2006	
Initial common stock (500 shares issued @ $20 per share, 1997)	$10 000
Additional paid-in capital (500 shares issued @ $100 per share, 2006)	50 000
Total stockholders' equity	$60 000

The use of equity financing via common stock can be expensive because paying dividends is more expensive than paying bond interest. Why? Interest paid to bondholders is a business expense and, hence, a tax deduction for the firm. Stock dividends are not tax-deductible.

Retained Earnings

Another approach to equity financing is to use retained earnings. As we saw in Chapter 14, these earnings represent profits not paid out in dividends. Using retained earnings means that the firm will not have to borrow money and pay interest on loans or bonds. A firm that has a history of eventually reaping much higher profits by successfully reinvesting retained earnings may be attractive to some investors. But the smaller dividends that can be paid to shareholders as a result of retained earnings may decrease demand for—and thus the price of—the company's stock.

For example, if Sunshine Tanning had net earnings of $50 000 in 2006, it could pay a $50-per-share dividend on its 1000 shares of common stock. But if it plans to remodel at a cost of $30 000 and retains $30 000 of earnings to finance the project, only $20 000 is left to distribute for stock dividends ($20 per share).

Financial Burden on the Firm

If equity funding can be so expensive, why don't firms rely instead on debt capital? Because long-term loans and bonds carry fixed interest rates and represent a fixed promise to pay, regardless of economic changes. If the firm defaults on its obligations, it may lose its assets and even go into bankruptcy.

During the 2001–02 Argentine financial crisis, banks around the world suffered when borrowers (large companies and government borrowers) could not repay outstanding debt. Some borrower companies went bankrupt, defaulting on obligations to foreign investors. Faced with a struggling economy, Argentina's government could not meet payments on its $132 billion debt. Argentine President Fernando de la Rua proposed a rescue plan that would require holders of the debt to swap their bonds for ones paying lower interest, leaving lenders no choice but to take losses on their original agreements. FleetBoston Financial Corp., the Boston-based banking company, attributed much of its $386 million second-quarter losses for 2002 to investments in Argentina. Spanish banks like Santander Central Hispano and Banco Bilbao Vizcaya Argentaria have written off losses in Argentina. Credit Lyonnais and SocGen, two French banks, set aside more than 500 million francs to cover bad loans, while Lloyds of London lost more than 100 million pounds as a result of bad loans. Even as it defaults on current obligations, however, the Argentine government is seeking additional instalments of new credit from the International Monetary Fund (IMF) to help make payments on existing debt.[2]

Because of the risk of default, debt financing appeals most strongly to companies in industries that have predictable profits and cash flow patterns. For example, demand for electric power is quite steady from year to year and predictable from month to month. Thus, provincial hydroelectric utility companies enjoy steady streams of income and can carry substantial amounts of debt.

Hybrid Financing: Preferred Stock

Falling somewhere between debt and equity financing is the *preferred stock* (see Chapter 19). Preferred stock is a hybrid because it has some of the features of corporate bonds and some features of common stocks. As with bonds, payments on preferred stock are for fixed amounts, such as $6 per share per year. Unlike bonds, however, preferred stock never matures. It can be held indefinitely, like common stock. And dividends need not be paid if the company makes no profit. If dividends are paid, preferred shareholders receive them first in preference to dividends on common stock.

A major advantage of preferred stock to the issuing corporation is its flexibility. It secures funds for the firm without relinquishing control, since preferred shareholders have no voting rights. It does not require repayment of principal or the payment of dividends in lean times.

Choosing Between Debt and Equity Financing

Part of financial planning involves striking a balance between debt and equity financing to meet the firm's long-term need for funds. Because the mix of debt versus equity provides the firm's financial base, it is called the **capital structure** of the firm. Financial plans contain targets for the capital structure, such as 40 percent debt and 60 percent equity. But choosing a target is not easy. A wide range of debt-versus-equity mixes is possible.

capital structure Relative mix of a firm's debt and equity financing.

The most conservative strategy would be to use all equity financing and no debt. Under this strategy, a company has no formal obligations for financial payouts. But equity is a very expensive source of capital. The most risk-filled strategy would be to use all debt financing. While less expensive than equity funding, indebtedness increases the risk that a firm will be unable to meet its obligations and will go bankrupt. Magna International, for example, has had a high debt-to-equity ratio in the past. Industry analysts believe that increased demand for automobiles will allow the firm to make large profits and pay off much of the debt, causing its debt-to-equity ratio to fall.[3] Somewhere between the two extremes, financial planners try to find a mix that will maximize shareholders' wealth. Figure 20.1 summarizes the factors management must take into account when deciding between debt and equity financing.

Indexes of Financial Risk

To help understand and measure the amount of financial risk they face, financial managers often rely on published indexes for various investments.

If bond rating agencies like Moody's and Standard & Poor's downgrade a company's ratings to low enough levels, its bonds become junk bonds. That's what happened to The Gap after sales at virtually every store in the chain fell every single month for nearly two years. As a result, The Gap is finding it harder to raise money.

Debt financing 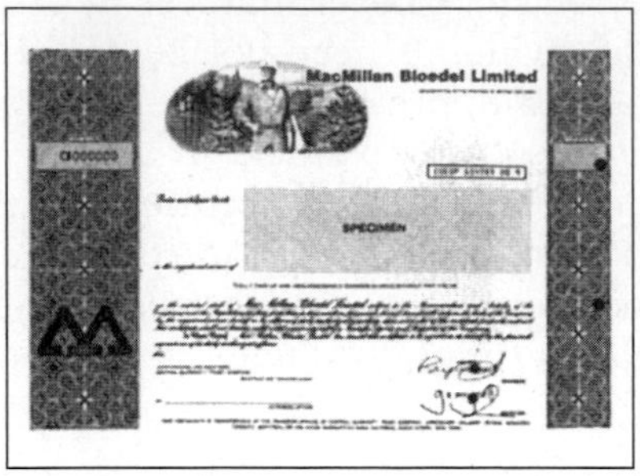	Equity financing 
When must it be repaid?	
Fixed deadline	No limit
Will it make claims on income?	
Yes, regular and fixed	Only residual claim
Will it have claims on assets?	
In liquidation, creditors come first	In liquidation, shareholders must wait until creditors are paid and preferred equity precedes common equity
Will it affect management control?	
No	May cause challenge for corporation control
How are taxes affected?	
Bond interest is deductible	Dividends are not deductible
Will it affect management flexibility?	
Yes, many constraints	No, few constraints

Figure 20.1 Comparing debt and equity financing.

Financial World, for example, publishes independent appraisals of mutual funds (see Chapter 19), using risk-reward ratings of A (very good) to E (poor) to indicate each fund's riskiness in comparison with its anticipated financial returns. An A-rated fund is judged to offer very good returns relative to the amount of risk involved. An E-rated fund carries the greatest risk with smaller returns. Similarly, Standard & Poor's publishes various indexes for numerous funds and for stocks that are available for purchase by financial managers.

By using such indexes, financial managers can determine how a particular investment compares with other opportunities in terms of its stability. A bond, for example, is considered to be investment grade if it qualifies for one of the top four ratings of either S&P or Moody's. Bonds below investment grade are called junk bonds because they have unusually high default rates. Nonetheless, junk bonds appeal to many investors because they promise uncommonly high yields.

The Risk–Return Relationship

While developing plans for raising capital, financial managers must be aware of the different motivations of individual investors. Why, for example, do some individuals and firms invest in stocks while others invest only in bonds? Investor motivations, of course, determine who is willing to buy a given company's stocks or bonds. Everyone who invests money is expressing a personal preference for safety versus risk. Investors give money to firms and, in return, anticipate receiving future cash flows.

Some cash flows are more certain than others. Investors generally expect to receive higher payments for higher uncertainty. They generally do not expect large returns for secure investments such as government-insured bonds. Each type of investment, then, has a **risk–return relationship**. Figure 20.2 shows the general risk–return relationship for various financial instruments. High-grade corporate bonds, for example, rate low in terms of risk on future returns but also low on size of expected returns. The reverse is true of junk bonds, those with a higher risk of default.

risk–return relationship Shows the amount of risk and the likely rate of return on various financial instruments.

Risk–return differences are recognized by financial planners, who try to gain access to the greatest funding at the lowest possible cost. By gauging investors' perceptions of their riskiness, a firm's managers can estimate how much it must pay to attract funds to their offerings. Over time, a company can reposition itself on the risk continuum by improving its record on dividends, interest payments, and debt repayment.

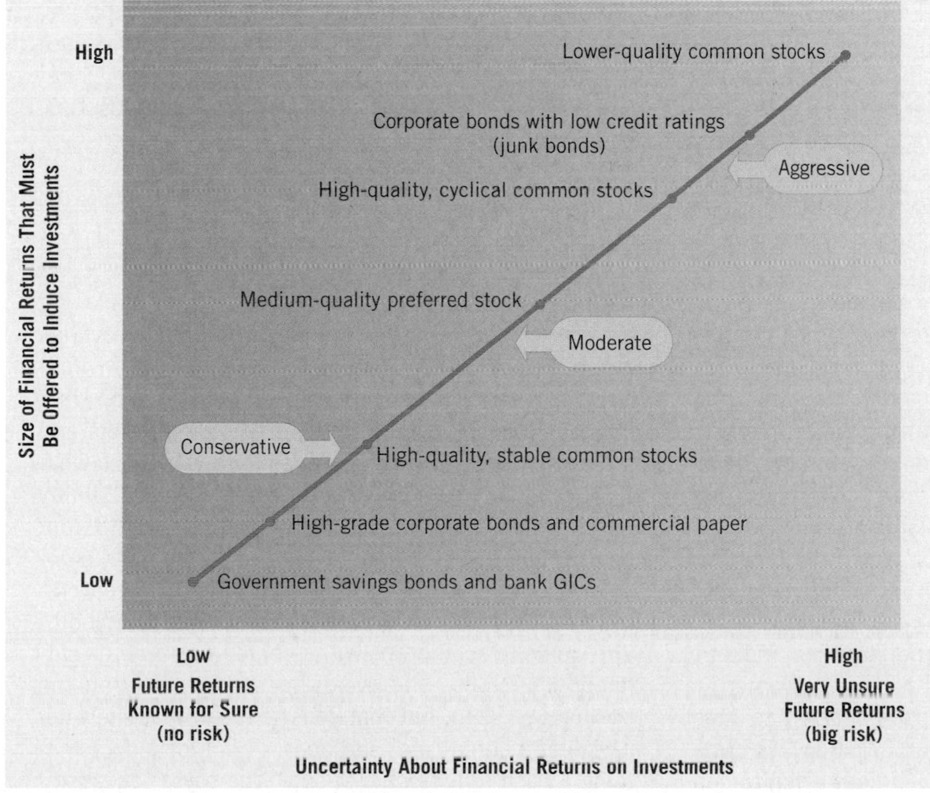

Figure 20.2 The risk–return relationship.

FINANCIAL MANAGEMENT FOR SMALL BUSINESSES

5 Discuss some key issues in financial management for small businesses.

Most new businesses have inadequate funding. An Ontario government study found that the average investment needed to start a new enterprise was about \$58 000, but that more than half of all new companies had less than \$15 000 invested.[4] Another study of nearly 3000 new companies revealed a survival rate of 84 percent for new businesses with initial investments of at least \$50 000. Those with less funding had a much lower survival rate.[5] The Entrepreneurship and New Ventures box describes help that is available for those who want to determine the risk of investing in small businesses.

Why are so many start-ups underfunded? For one thing, entrepreneurs often underestimate the value of establishing *bank credit* as a source of funds and use *trade credit* ineffectively. In addition, they often fail to con-

ENTREPRENEURSHIP AND NEW VENTURES

The Personality of a Risk Taker

Thanks to the risks entailed in setting up and growing her own business, Lucy Marcus, founder of London-based Marcus Venture Consulting, has become an expert at assessing the risk involved in starting up a new business, investing in it, and managing it. In many ways, risk is the mainstay of Marcus's business. Her clients—mostly venture capital investors—want answers to such questions as "If I invest in XYZ Venture Capital Fund, how well will it be managed? How well does it treat entrepreneurial clients? What kind of financial return can I expect?" Her clients include individuals, companies, and pension funds—investors seeking a clear picture of the risks posed by potential investment opportunities. Her assessments help them determine the right balance between prospective gains and losses.

As one of a handful of senior female executives in the private equity industry, Marcus has to gain the trust of all sorts of clients by demonstrating dependable judgment about risk. It's a business with few women in leadership roles, but Marcus says it's just a matter of time until more women get into venture capital. "Private equity is all about managing risk," she says. "An investor will be drawn to what is familiar, where there is common ground, and familiarity—be it because two people are the same sex or from the same neighbourhood—is a way of eliminating some of that risk."

To encourage women in the equities industry, Marcus set up a network called HighTech Women—a 2500-member discussion group for women to meet and mentor one another. "HighTech Women was something I had to do," she explains. "I kept going to conferences and being one of four women in a roomful of 200 CEOs. I found that I'd meet the most interesting people in the ladies' room."

Marcus's success—she was selected as a World Economic Forum Global Leader for Tomorrow in 2002—stems from diverse career-building experiences, self-developed personal practices designed to sharpen creativity, and energetic drive. A native New Yorker, Marcus attended Wellesley College and did a summer internship with U.S. Senator Edward Kennedy. Before getting a master's degree in political philosophy from the University of Cambridge, she worked in public policy for the U.S. Treasury Department and Price-Waterhouse. She later held positions in various U.S. and European technology companies before opening Marcus Venture Consulting.

As an entrepreneur advising other entrepreneurs, Marcus's outlook is also influenced by a number of personal characteristics. For professional reasons, she won't tell anyone her age: "I'm too young for some people and too old for others." She regards herself as a maverick who's too outspoken for the average corporate environment, and she thinks people should be judged on what they achieve. She admires people who do different and interesting work, who buck trends, and who know what they're talking about. She prides herself on an ability to walk in other people's shoes and appreciate different points of view. She claims to be a quick judge of character and admits that she has to work hard at networking because she doesn't make friends with everybody. She wants to spend time with people in completely different industries. She avoids focussing solely on the business she's in, but that doesn't mean that she's not passionate about what she does. "I couldn't do something I wasn't passionate about," she says, "because I couldn't put the energy into it."

sider *venture capital* as a source of funding, and they are notorious for not *planning cash-flow needs* properly.

Establishing Bank Credit and Trade Credit

Some banks have liberal credit policies and offer financial analysis, cash flow planning, and suggestions based on experiences with other local firms. Some provide loans to small businesses in bad times and work to keep them going. Some, of course, do not. Obtaining credit, therefore, begins with finding a bank that can—and will—support a small firm's financial needs. Once a *line of credit* is obtained, the small business can seek more liberal credit policies from other businesses. Sometimes, for instance, suppliers give customers longer credit periods—say, 45 or 60 days rather than 30 days. Liberal trade credit terms with their suppliers let firms increase short-term funds and avoid additional borrowing from banks.

The Business Plan as a Tool for Credit

Start-up firms without proven financial success usually must present a business plan to demonstrate that the firm is a good credit risk.[6] As we saw in Chapter 4, a business plan is a document that tells potential lenders why the money is needed, the amount, how the money will be used to improve the company, and when it will be paid back.

Photographer David Cupp, for example, needed $50 000 in funding for his new firm, Photos Online Inc., which displays and sells photos over the internet. His business plan had to be rewritten many times until it became understandable, in financial terms, to potential lenders. The plan eventually reached 35 pages and contained information on the competition as well as cash flow projections. After four failed attempts, Cupp found a fifth bank that approved a $26 000 term loan and granted a $24 000 line of credit, to be used for computers, software, and living expenses to get the business started.[7]

Venture Capital

Many newer businesses—especially those undergoing rapid growth—cannot get the funds they need through borrowing alone. They may, therefore, turn to **venture capital**—outside equity funding provided in return for part ownership of the borrowing firm. As we saw in Chapter 4, venture capital firms actively seek chances to invest in new firms with rapid growth potential. Because failure rates are high, they typically demand high returns, which are now often 20 to 30 percent.

venture capital Outside equity financing provided in return for part ownership of the borrowing firm.

Planning for Cash-Flow Requirements

Although all businesses should plan for their cash flows, it is especially important for small businesses to do so. Success or failure may hinge on anticipating times when cash will be short and when excess cash is expected.

Figure 20.3 shows possible cash inflows, cash outflows, and net cash position (inflows minus outflows), month by month, for Slippery Fish Bait Supply. In this highly seasonal business, bait stores buy heavily from Slippery during the spring and summer months. Revenues outpace expenses, leaving surplus funds that can be invested. During the fall and winter, expenses exceed revenues. Slippery must borrow funds to keep going until sales revenues pick up again in the spring. Comparing predicted cash inflows from sales with outflows for expenses shows the firm's monthly cash-flow position.

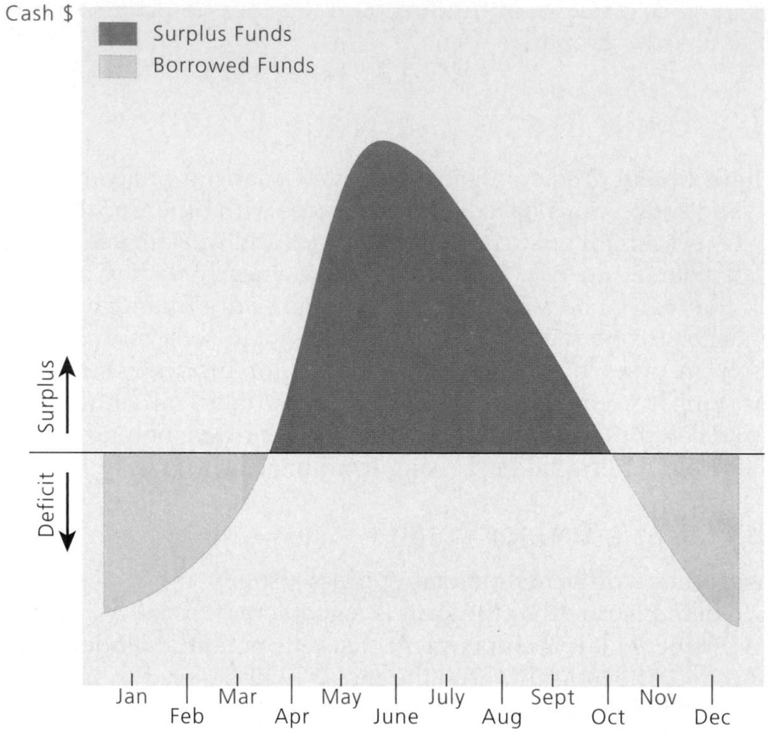

Figure 20.3 Cash flow for Slippery Fish Bait Supply Company.

By anticipating shortfalls, a financial manager can seek funds in advance and minimize their cost. By anticipating excess cash, a manager can plan to put the funds to work in short-term, interest-earning investments. The Business Accountability box describes how one entrepreneur was successful by helping other individuals organize their financial matters.

RISK MANAGEMENT

6 Explain how *risk* affects business operations and identify the five steps in the *risk-management process.*

Risk is a factor in every manager's job, and because nearly every managerial action involves risk—that is, the possibility of either desirable outcomes or negative results—risk management is essential.[8] Not surprisingly, then, firms devote considerable resources not only to recognizing potential risks but also to positioning themselves to make the most advantageous decisions.

Coping with Risk

risk Uncertainty about future events.

speculative risk An event that offers the chance for either a gain or a loss.

pure risk An event that offers no possibility of gain; it offers only the chance of a loss.

Businesses constantly face two basic types of **risk**—that is, uncertainty about future events. **Speculative risks**, such as financial investments, involve the possibility of gain or loss. **Pure risks** involve only the possibility of loss or no loss. Designing and distributing a new product, for example, is a speculative risk: The product may fail or it may succeed and earn high profits. The chance of a warehouse fire is a pure risk.

risk management Conserving a firm's (or an individual's) financial power or assets by minimizing the financial effect of accidental losses.

For a company to survive and prosper, it must manage both types of risk in a cost-effective manner. We can thus define the process of **risk management** as "conserving the firm's earning power and assets by reducing the threat of losses due to uncontrollable events."[9] The Opening Case for this chapter describes several situations where risk management activities were not properly carried out. In every company, each manager must be alert for

BUSINESS ACCOUNTABILITY

A Quicken Course in Accountability

After deciding to hold himself accountable for designing new products, Scott Cook created some unique methods to ensure he'd meet those design obligations when he founded a company back in 1983. Cook is the former CEO of Intuit, the $1.7 billion company whose well-known software tools—Quicken and QuickBooks—have changed the way we manage our financial lives.

Cook initially envisioned three core principles for product design that eventually led to superb commercial success:

First: It's the customer that's most important. Listen to the customer and design the product for customer value.

Second: Be open-minded in identifying all competing ways the customer could perform the task, not just the obvious ways.

Third: Simplify and improve the product so it provides the easiest way for the customer to complete the task to be performed.

From the beginning, Cook believed these principles would lead to superior, user-friendly, preferred products that customers would buy and use. Accordingly, customer acceptance of the products would be the ultimate measure of success or failure of product designs for which Cook was accountable.

Although the firm was selling computer software, Cook didn't restrict his vision to just software competitors. As the second design principle stipulates, Intuit's products had to perform better than any alternative way of doing the task, including competitors' software, hand calculators, and pencil-and-paper methods. Otherwise, users wouldn't prefer Intuit's products for cheque writing and the many other financial tasks they had to perform.

While the initial version of Quicken worked well, Cook's insistence on pleasing customers meant that he wasn't satisfied when it first came on the market. Seeking user-based improvements, the first design principle was applied by assigning employees in computer stores to observe consumers when they bought Quicken off the shelf. Cook's imaginative "Follow Me Home" program surprised customers when they were asked if the employee could come home with them to watch their reaction to the software. Everything about the user's experience was noted, beginning with ease or difficulty in opening the package, reading instructions, installing the software on a computer, using it, and even turning away to write with pencil and paper. Cook insisted that anything preventing ease of use, no matter how small, was Intuit's fault, not the customer's. So watching for even the tiniest display of displeasure or frustration, the employee silently observed the user's facial expressions, body language, vocal reactions, pauses, and re-reading of instructions in each stage from opening the shrink-wrapped package to using the product.

Guided by what was learned from "Follow Me Home," the third principle was invoked for simplifying and improving Quicken. As word spread about the software's success with personal finance on PCs at home, entrepreneurs started using it—making changes to suit their needs—for financial management tasks in their companies. Once again, by listening to these new customers, Intuit modified the software into a new product—QuickBooks—especially designed for business financial management. Because these companion tools—Quicken and QuickBooks—are the most popular in the industry, the firm's $1.7 billion sales revenues and market leadership are evidence that Cook fulfilled the product-design obligations for which he was accountable.

risks to the firm and their impact on profits. The risk-management process usually involves the five steps outlined in Figure 20.4.

Step 1: Identify Risks and Potential Losses

Managers analyze a firm's risks to identify potential losses. For example, a firm with a fleet of delivery trucks can expect that one of them will eventually be involved in an accident. The accident may cause bodily injury to the driver or others, may cause physical damage to the truck or other vehicles, or both.

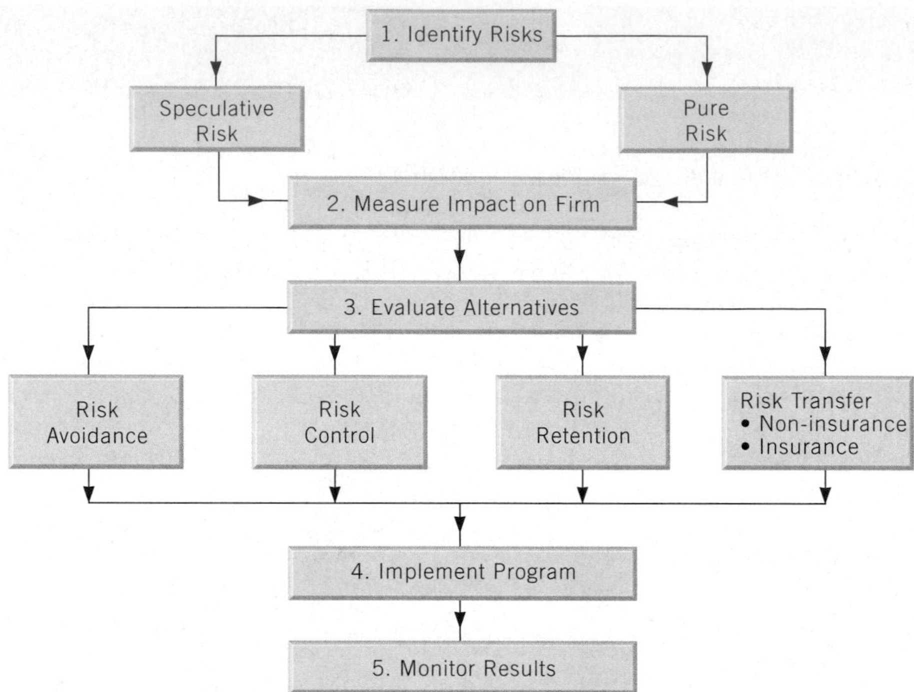

Figure 20.4 The risk-management process.

Step 2: Measure the Frequency and Severity of Losses and Their Impact

To measure the frequency and severity of losses, managers must consider both past history and current activities. How often can the firm expect the loss to occur? What is the likely size of the loss in dollars? For example, our firm with the fleet of delivery trucks may have had two accidents per year in the past. If it adds trucks, however, it may reasonably expect the frequency of accidents to increase.

Step 3: Evaluate Alternatives and Choose the Techniques that Will Best Handle the Losses

Having identified and measured potential losses, managers are in a better position to decide how to handle them. With this third step, they generally have four choices: *risk avoidance, control, retention,* or *transfer.*

risk avoidance Stopping participation in or refusing to participate in ventures that carry any risk.

Risk Avoidance. A firm opts for **risk avoidance** by declining to enter or by ceasing to participate in a risky activity. For example, the firm with the delivery trucks could avoid any risk of physical damage or bodily injury by closing down its delivery service. Similarly, a pharmaceutical maker may withdraw a new drug for fear of liability suits.

risk control Techniques to prevent, minimize, or reduce losses or the consequences of losses.

Risk Control. When avoidance is not practical or desirable, firms can practise **risk control**—say, the use of loss-prevention techniques to minimize the frequency of losses. A delivery service, for instance, can prevent losses by training its drivers in defensive-driving techniques, mapping out safe routes, and conscientiously maintaining its trucks.

Risk Retention. When losses cannot be avoided or controlled, firms must cope with the consequences. When such losses are manageable and predictable, they may decide to cover them out of company funds. The firm is thus said to "assume" or "retain" the financial consequences of the loss: hence the practice known as **risk retention**. For example, the firm with the fleet of trucks may find that vehicles suffer vandalism totalling $100 to $500 per year. Depending on its coverage, the company may find it cheaper to pay for repairs out of pocket rather than to submit claims to its insurance company.

risk retention The covering of a firm's unavoidable losses with its own funds.

Risk Transfer. When the potential for large risks cannot be avoided or controlled, managers often opt for **risk transfer**. They transfer the risk to another firm—namely, an *insurance company*. In transferring risk to an insurance company, a firm pays a sum called a *premium*. In return, the insurance company issues an *insurance policy*—a formal agreement to pay the policyholder a specified amount in the event of certain losses. In some cases, the insured party must also pay a *deductible*—an agreed-upon amount of the loss that the insured must absorb prior to reimbursement. Thus, our hypothetical company may buy insurance to protect itself against theft, physical damage to trucks, and bodily injury to drivers and others involved in an accident. Table 20.2 lists the top 10 life insurance companies in Canada.

risk transfer The transfer of risk to another individual or firm, often by contract.

Step 4: Implement the Risk-Management Program

The means of implementing risk-management decisions depends on both the technique chosen and the activity being managed. For example, risk avoidance for certain activities can be implemented by purchasing those activities from outside providers, such as hiring delivery services instead of operating delivery vehicles. Risk control might be implemented by training employees and designing new work methods and equipment for on-the-job safety. For situations in which risk retention is preferred, reserve funds can be set aside out of revenues. When risk transfer is needed, implementation means selecting an insurance company and buying the right policies.

Step 5: Monitor Results

Because risk management is an ongoing activity, follow-up is always essential. New types of risks, for example, emerge with changes in customers, facilities, employees, and products. Insurance regulations change, and new types of insurance become available. Consequently, managers must continually monitor a company's risks, re-evaluate the methods used for handling them, and revise them as necessary.

Table 20.2 The Top 10 Life Insurance Companies in Canada, 2005

Company	Annual Revenues (in billions of $)
1. Manulife Financial Corp.	$32.0
2. Great-West Lifeco Inc.	23.8
3. Sun Life Financial Inc.	21.9
4. Industrial Alliance Insurance Inc.	4.0
5. Desjardins Financial Security Life Assurance	3.0
6. SSQ Société d'assurance-vie Inc.	1.1
7. RBC Life Insurance Co.	0.9
8. Transamerica Life Canada	0.8
9. The Empire Life Insurance Co.	0.8
10. The Independent Order of Foresters	0.7

When the National Highway Traffic Safety Administration in the U.S. informed General Motors that the suspension on its Saturn Vue SUV had failed a new government rollover test, CEO Rick Wagoner decided to practise a little risk retention and recall 245 000 SUVs sold in Canada and the United States over the previous four years. GM then redesigned the vehicle's rear suspension, and dealers began making modifications at no cost to owners.

Insurance as Risk Management

To deal with some risks, both businesses and individuals may choose to purchase one or more of the products offered by insurance companies. Buyers find insurance appealing for a very basic reason: In return for a relatively small sum of money, they are protected against specific losses, some of which are potentially devastating. In this sense, buying insurance is a function of risk management. To define it as a management activity dealing with insurance, we can thus amplify our definition of *risk management* to say that it is the logical development and implementation of a plan to deal with chance losses.

With insurance, then, individuals and businesses share risks by contributing to a fund out of which those who suffer losses are paid. But why are insurance companies willing to accept these risks for other companies? Insurance companies make profits by taking in more **premiums** than they pay out to cover policyholders' losses. Quite simply, although many policyholders are paying for protection against the same type of loss, it is highly unlikely that all of them will suffer such a loss.

premiums Money paid to an insurance company by customers in return for being covered for certain types of losses should they occur.

Losses are reduced or prevented when this security specialist uses electronic surveillance (left), when valuables are stored under lock and key (top right), and when workers are reminded to wear safety gear at this construction site (bottom right).

Insurable Versus Uninsurable Risks

Explain the distinction between *insurable* and *uninsurable risks*, and distinguish among the different *types of insurance* purchased by businesses. 7

Like every business, insurance companies must avoid certain risks. Insurers thus divide potential sources of loss into *insurable* and *uninsurable risks*.[10] Obviously, they issue policies only for insurable risks. An insurable risk must generally satisfy the four criteria of *predictability*, *casualty*, *unconnectedness*, and *verifiability* described below.

Predictability. The insurer must be able to use statistical tools to forecast the likelihood of a loss. For example, an auto insurer needs information about the number of car accidents in the past year to estimate the expected number of accidents for the following year. With this knowledge, the insurer can translate expected numbers and types of accidents into expected dollar losses. The same forecast, of course, also helps insurers determine premiums charged to policyholders.

Casualty. A loss must result from an accident, not from an intentional act by the policyholder. Obviously, insurers do not have to cover damages if a policyholder deliberately sets fire to corporate headquarters. To avoid paying in cases of fraud, insurers may refuse to cover losses when they cannot determine whether policyholders' actions contributed to them.

Unconnectedness. Potential losses must be random and must occur independently of other losses. No insurer can afford to write insurance when a large percentage of those who are exposed to a particular kind of loss are likely to suffer such a loss. One insurance company, for instance, would not want all the hail coverage in Saskatchewan or all the earthquake coverage in Vancouver. By carefully choosing the risks it will insure, an insurance company can reduce its chances of a large loss or even insolvency.

Verifiability. Finally, insured losses must be verifiable as to cause, time, place, and amount. Did an employee develop emphysema because of a chemical to which she was exposed or because she smoked 40 cigarettes per day for 30 years? Did the policyholder pay the renewal premium before the fire destroyed his factory? Were the goods stolen from company offices or from the president's home? What was the insurable value of the destroyed inventory? When all these points have been verified, payment by the insurer goes more smoothly.

The Insurance Product

The types of insurance coverage they offer often distinguish insurance companies. Whereas some insurers offer only one area of coverage—life insurance, for example—others offer a broad range. In this section, we briefly describe three major categories of business insurance: *liability*, *property*, and *life*. (A more detailed description of insurance products is presented in Appendix B.)

Liability Insurance. *Liability* means responsibility for damages in case of accidental or deliberate harm to individuals or property. **Liability insurance** covers losses resulting from damage to people or property when the insured party is judged liable.

A business is liable for any injury to an employee when the injury arises from activities related to occupation. When workers are permanently or temporarily disabled by job-related accidents or disease, employers are required by law to provide **workers' compensation coverage** for medical expenses, loss of wages, and rehabilitation services.

liability insurance Covers losses resulting from damage to people or property when the insured party is judged liable.

workers' compensation coverage Compensation for medical expenses, loss of wages, and rehabilitation services for injuries arising from activities related to occupation.

There is growing concern about fraudulent claims submitted by people who buy liability insurance. One popular scam is the "staged accident." The swindler purposely (but carefully) runs into a telephone pole, and then everyone in the car claims that they are suffering from whiplash. After the accident is reported, the insurance company contacts the car occupants and sends them accident benefit packages. Sometimes people who aren't even insured are paid benefits because they use counterfeit "proof of insurance" cards.[11]

Every year in Canada, well over $1 billion is lost to insurance fraud. The insurance industry estimates that between $10 and $15 of every $100 dollars you pay in premiums goes to cover fraud losses. The Canadian Coalition Against Insurance Fraud (CCAIF) exists to curb this fraud. CCAIF members include mutual and private insurance companies, public automobile insurers, and representatives from health-care, law enforcement, and consumer advocacy groups. Part of the CCAIF's mandate is to ensure that consumers are aware of the connection between insurance fraud and higher insurance rates. Working with Crime Stoppers, the CCAIF offers a reward to tipsters who provide information leading to the discovery of fraud. Visit the CCAIF website at www.fraudcoalition.org.

property insurance Covers injuries to firms resulting from physical damage to or loss of real estate or personal property.

Property Insurance. Firms purchase **property insurance** to cover injuries resulting from physical damage to or loss of real estate or personal property. Property losses may result from fire, lightning, wind, hail, explosion, theft, vandalism, or other destructive forces such as hurricanes. In 2005, insurance companies received claims exceeding $55 billion dollars as a result of several hurricanes that hit the southern United States and flooded New Orleans. That figure is double the previous record (which was set in 2004). Canadian insurers were expected to pay out about $570 million of the 2005 total. Because seven of the most costly hurricanes in history hit the United States during 2004 and 2005, it is possible that insurers will no longer make property insurance available to individuals and businesses in hurricane-prone areas.[12]

In some cases, loss to property is minimal in comparison with loss of income. A manufacturer, for example, may have to close down for an extended time while repairs to fire damage are being completed. During that time, of course, the company is not generating income. Even so, however, certain expenses—such as taxes, insurance premiums, and salaries for key personnel—may continue. To cover such losses, a firm may buy business interruption insurance.

Catastrophic losses like those caused by fire are avoided when a business buys property insurance. The insurance company will pay the cost of the rebuilding. But interruption of the firm's normal operations will also be harmful, so many businesses buy business interruption insurance as well.

Life Insurance. Insurance can also protect a company's human assets. As part of their benefits packages, many businesses purchase **life insurance** for employees. Life insurance companies receive premiums in return for the promise to pay beneficiaries after the death of insured parties. As with other types of insurance, a portion of the premium is used to cover the insurer's own expenses.

life insurance Insurance that pays benefits to survivors of a policyholder.

Life insurance can, of course, also be purchased by individuals. For many years, Canadian life insurance companies have sold insurance policies to Canadians, but now they are rapidly expanding overseas, particularly in China and India. Sun Life Financial, for example, has formed a joint venture with Aditya Birla Group to sell life insurance and mutual funds in India. As a result of this partnership, Sun Life is already the second-largest privately owned life insurance company in India.[13] In some areas of the world, unstable and dangerous situations have motivated entrepreneurs to sell special kinds of insurance. For example, the al Ameen Insurance Co. pays out $3500 to beneficiaries of people who are killed as a result of insurgent activity in Iraq. The annual premium is about $35.[14]

Most companies buy **group life insurance**, which is underwritten for groups as a whole rather than for each individual member. The insurer's assessment of potential losses and its pricing of premiums are based on the characteristics of the entire group.

group life insurance Life insurance underwritten for a group as a whole rather than for each individual member.

Special Forms of Business Insurance

Many forms of insurance are attractive to both businesses and individuals. For example, homeowners are as concerned about insuring property from fire and theft as are businesses. Businesses, however, have some special insurable concerns. In this section, we will discuss two forms of insurance that apply to the departure or death of key employees or owners.

Key Person Insurance. Many businesses choose to protect themselves against loss of the talents and skills of key employees. For example, if a salesperson who annually rings up $2.5 million dies or takes a new job, the firm will suffer loss. It will also incur recruitment costs to find a replacement and training expenses once a replacement is hired. **Key person insurance** is designed to offset both lost income and additional expenses.[15]

key person insurance Insurance that protects a company against loss of the talents and skills of key employees.

Business Continuation Agreements. Who takes control of a business when a partner or an associate dies? Surviving partners are often faced with the possibility of having to accept an inexperienced heir as a management partner. This contingency can be handled in **business continuation agreements**, whereby owners make plans to buy the ownership interest of a deceased associate from his or her heirs. The value of the ownership interest is determined when the agreement is made. Special policies can also provide survivors with the funds needed to make the purchase.

business continuation agreement An agreement in which owners of a business make plans to buy the ownership interest of a deceased associate from his or her heirs.

Summary of Learning Objectives

1. **Describe the responsibilities of a *financial manager*.** *Finance* (or corporate finance) entails four responsibilities: (1) determining long-term investments; (2) obtaining funds to pay for those investments; (3) conducting everyday financial activities; and (4) helping to manage risks. *Financial managers* plan and control the acquisition and dispersal of financial resources. But a financial manager's overall objective is to increase a firm's value and stockholders' wealth.

   The responsibilities of the financial manager fall into three general categories: (1) *Cash flow management*: Financial managers must ensure that the company has enough funds on hand to purchase the resources that it needs to produce products. Funds not needed immediately must be invested to earn money. (2) *Financial control*: This is the process of checking actual performance against plans to ensure that desired financial results occur. (3) *Financial planning:* Financial managers develop a plan that describes how a firm will reach some future financial position.

2. **Distinguish between *short-term (operating)* and *long-term (capital)* expenditures.** *Short-term (operating) expenditures* are incurred in a firm's everyday business activities. Managers must pay special attention to three areas of financial activity: (1) *accounts payable,* (2) *accounts receivable*—predicting payment schedules is a function of *credit policy* (the rules governing a firm's extension of credit to customers), and (3) *inventories*: Between the time a firm buys raw materials and the time it sells finished products, it ties up funds in inventory—materials and goods that it will sell within the year. Too little inventory can cost sales; too much inventory means tied-up funds. *Working capital* is the difference between a firm's current assets and current liabilities. It is a liquid asset from which current debts can be paid. We calculate working capital by adding up (i) inventories (raw materials, work-in-process, and finished goods on hand) and (ii) accounts receivable (minus accounts payable).

3. **Identify four sources of *short-term financing* for businesses.** (1) *Trade credit* is really a short-term loan from one firm to another. (2) *Secured short-term loans*: Bank loans usually involve promissory notes in which the borrower promises to repay the loan plus interest. In secured loans, banks also require collateral: a legal interest in assets that can be seized if payments are not made as promised. (3) *Factoring accounts receivable*: A firm can raise funds rapidly by factoring—selling the firm's accounts receivable. (4) *Unsecured short-term loans*: With an unsecured loan, the borrower does not have to put up collateral. The bank may, however, require the borrower to maintain a *compensating balance*—a portion of the loan amount kept on deposit with the bank.

4. **Distinguish among the various sources of *long-term financing* and explain the risks involved in each.** Firms may seek long-term funds to pay for fixed assets through two channels. (1) Long-term borrowing from sources outside the company is called *debt financing.* There are two primary sources of such funding: (i) Many corporations get *long-term loans* from chartered banks. (ii) A *corporate bond* is a promise by the issuer to pay the holder a certain amount of money on a specified date. Bonds are attractive when firms need large amounts for long periods of time. (2) Looking inside the company for long-term funding is sometimes preferable to debt financing. *Equity financing* usually means issuing common stock or retaining earnings. (i) *Common stock*: Equity financing by means of common stock can be expensive because paying dividends is more expensive than paying bond interest. (ii) *Retained earnings*: Retained earnings are profits retained for the firm's use rather than paid out in dividends.

   A middle ground between debt financing and equity financing is the use of *preferred stock.* As with bonds, payments on preferred stock are fixed amounts. But like common stock, preferred stock can be held indefinitely. A key aspect of financial planning is striking a balance between debt and equity financing. A firm relies on a mix of debt and equity to raise the cash needed for capital outlays; that mix is called its *capital structure.* A range of mixes is possible, and strategies range from conservative to risky. The most conservative strategy is all-equity financing and no debt; the riskiest strategy is all-debt financing.

5. **Discuss some key issues in financial management for small businesses.** Obtaining credit begins with finding a bank that will support a small firm's financial needs. Once a line of credit is obtained, the small business can seek more liberal credit policies from other businesses. Obtaining long-term loans is more difficult for new businesses than for established companies, and start-ups pay higher interest rates than older firms. To demonstrate that it's a good credit risk, a start-up must usually present a business plan—a document explaining why the

money is needed, the amount, how it will be used to improve the company, and when it will be paid back.

Many newer businesses can't get needed funds through borrowing alone. They may turn to *venture capital*: outside equity funding provided in return for part ownership. But with high failure rates, such investors demand high returns. Planning for cash flows is especially important for small businesses. Success or failure may hinge on anticipating those times when either cash will be short or excess cash can be expected.

6. **Explain how *risk* affects business operations and identify the five steps in the *risk management process*.** Businesses face two basic types of *risk*. (1) *Speculative risks*, such as financial investments, involve the possibility of gain or loss. (2) *Pure risks* (such as the chance of a warehouse fire) involve only the possibility of loss or no loss. *Risk management* entails conserving earning power and assets by reducing the threat of losses due to uncontrollable events. The process has five steps. Step 1: Identify risks and potential losses: Analyze risks to identify potential losses. Step 2: Measure the frequency and severity of losses and their impact: To measure the frequency and severity of losses, consider past history and current activities. (How often can the firm expect a loss to occur?) Step 3: Evaluate alternatives and choose the techniques that will best handle the losses: Decide how to handle risks from among four choices: (1) A firm opts for *risk avoidance* by declining to enter or by ceasing to participate in a risky activity. (2) Firms can practise *risk control* when they use loss-prevention techniques to minimize the frequency of losses. (3) When unavoidable losses are manageable and predictable, firms may cover them out of company funds. Thus, they assume or retain the financial consequences through *risk retention*. (4) When the potential for large risks can't be avoided or controlled, firms may opt for *risk transfer*: They transfer the risk to another firm—namely, an *insurance company*. Step 4: Implement the risk-management program: The means of implementing risk-management decisions depend on both the technique chosen and the activity being managed. Step 5: Monitor results: Managers must monitor risks, re-evaluate methods for handling them, and revise them as necessary.

7. **Explain the distinction between *insurable* and *uninsurable risks*, and distinguish among the different *types of insurance* purchased by businesses.** In return for a relatively small sum of money, insurance buyers are protected against certain losses. Thus, buying *insurance* is a function of risk management, which is the implementation of a plan to deal with chance losses. Insurance companies make profits by taking in more *premiums* than they pay out to cover policyholders' losses. Insurers divide potential losses into *insurable* and *uninsurable risks*, and an insurable risk must meet four criteria: (1) *Predictability*: The insurer must be able to use statistical tools to forecast the likelihood of a loss. (2) *Casualty*: A loss must result from an accident, not from an intentional act. (3) *Unconnectedness*: Potential losses must be random and occur independently of other losses. (4) *Verifiability*: Insured losses must be verifiable as to cause, time, place, and amount.

There are three major categories of business insurance: (1) *Liability insurance*: Liability means responsibility for damages in case of accidental or deliberate harm, and liability insurance covers losses resulting from damage to people or property when the insured party is held liable. The law requires most employers to provide employees injured on the job with *workers' compensation coverage* for medical expenses, loss of wages, and rehabilitation services. (2) *Property insurance*: Firms purchase property insurance to cover injuries to themselves resulting from damage to or loss of real estate or personal property. A firm may buy *business interruption insurance* to cover expenses incurred when it is closed down and generating no income. (3) *Life insurance*: Life insurance policies promise to pay beneficiaries after the death of insured parties. Most companies buy *group life insurance*, which is underwritten for groups as a whole rather than for each individual member.

Two forms of business insurance apply to the loss of key employees or owners: (1) Many businesses protect themselves against loss of the talents and skills of key employees by buying *key person insurance*. (2) Certain contingencies are handled in *business continuation agreements*, in which owners make plans to transfer the ownership interest of a deceased associate.

KEY TERMS

bond indenture, 663
business continuation agreement, 677
capital structure, 665
cash flow management, 656
collateral, 659
commercial paper, 661
credit policy, 657
debt financing, 661
equity financing, 663
finance (corporate finance), 655
financial control, 656
financial managers, 655
financial plan, 656
finished goods inventory, 658
group life insurance, 677
inventory, 657
key person insurance, 677
liability insurance, 675
life insurance, 677
line of credit, 660
open-book credit, 659
pledging accounts receivable, 659
premiums, 674
promissory note, 659
property insurance, 676
pure risk, 670
raw materials inventory, 658
revolving credit agreement, 661
risk, 670
risk avoidance, 672
risk control, 672
risk management, 670
risk retention, 673
risk transfer, 673
risk–return relationship, 667
secured loan, 659
speculative risk, 670
trade acceptance, 659
trade credit, 659
trade draft, 659
unsecured loan, 660
venture capital, 669
workers' compensation coverage, 675
work-in-process inventory, 658

QUESTIONS FOR ANALYSIS

1. In what ways do the two sources of debt financing differ from each other? How do they differ from the two sources of equity financing?
2. Describe the relationship between investment risk and return. In what ways might the risk–return relationship affect a company's financial planning?
3. What is the basic relationship between the amount of risk associated with a project and the likelihood of gains (or losses) on the project? Explain how several financial instruments (GICs, common stocks, preferred stocks, corporate bonds) illustrate this basic relationship.
4. What factors would you take into account when deciding on the best mix of debt and equity for a company?
5. Why would a business "factor" its accounts receivable?
6. Give two examples of risks that are uninsurable. Why are they uninsurable?
7. Why is liability insurance important to business firms?
8. As a risk manager of a large firm, what risks do you think your firm faces? For a small firm? What accounts for the most important differences?

APPLICATION EXERCISES

1. Interview the owner of a small local business. Identify the types of short-term and long-term funding that this firm typically uses. Why has the company made the financial management decisions that it has?
2. Interview the owner of a small local business. Ask this person to describe the risk management process that he or she follows. What role, for example, is played by risk transfer? Why has the company made the risk-management decisions that it has?

BUILDING YOUR BUSINESS SKILLS

Understanding Risk-Management Issues

Goal

To encourage students to gain a better understanding of the major financial and risk-management issues that face large companies.

Assignment

During the last few years, all of the following companies reported financial problems relating to risk management:

Air Canada

Bombardier

EarthLink Inc.

Levi Strauss & Co.

Nortel Networks

Step 1

Working alone, research one of the companies listed above to learn more about the financial risks that were reported in the news.

Step 2

Write a short explanation of the risks and financial-management issues that were faced by the firm you researched.

Step 3

Join in teams with students who researched other companies and compare your findings.

Follow-Up Questions

1. Were there common themes in the "big stories" in financial management?
2. What have the various companies done to minimize future risks and losses?

EXERCISING YOUR ETHICS

Doing Your Duty When Payables Come Due

The Situation

Assume you work as a manager for one of the world's best-known conglomerates. As the end of the fiscal year approaches, you are attending an executive committee meeting at which the CEO, the firm's dominant leader, expresses concern that the firm's year-end cash position will be less favourable than projected. The firm has exceeded analysts' performance expectations in each of his eight years at the helm and he is determined that stockholders will never be disappointed as long as he is CEO. The purpose of the meeting is to find solutions to the cash problem and decide on a course of action.

The Dilemma

To open the meeting, the CEO announces, "We have just two weeks either to reduce expenses or to increase revenues; we need a $400 million swing to get us where market analysts predicted we'd be on cash flows for the year. Any suggestions?"

Discussion reveals that the firm has outstanding payables, amounting to hundreds of millions of dollars, owed to hundreds of firms that supply manufacturing components and operating supplies. The payables are due before year-end. According to the financial officer, "Our cash outflows for the year will be lower if we delay paying suppliers, which will help the bottom line. And, it's like getting a free loan." The procurement director is concerned, however. "Our agreements with suppliers call for faithful payments at designated times, and many of the smaller firms depend on receiving that cash to meet their obligations. Also, we've worked hard for two years at improving relationships with all suppliers, and that effort could go down the drain if we don't meet our financial commitments as promised."

As the meeting drew to a close, the CEO announced, "Keep me posted on any unexpected developments, but if nothing helpful comes up in the next few days, let's go ahead and withhold supplier payments for three weeks."

Questions for Discussion

1. What are the ethical issues in this case?
2. What are the basic arguments for and against the CEO's position on withholding payments?
3. What do you think most managers would do in this situation? What would you do?

CONCLUDING CASE 20-1

Never Stop Sweating the Small Stuff

Janie and Victor Tsao both worked in information technologies for other companies, so they understood the PC industry. While holding down full-time jobs they set up a small consulting firm—dubbed DEW International—with headquarters in their garage at home. It matched up North American technology vendors such as Northgate Computer with Taiwanese manufacturers that produced computer hardware at lower cost. Working evenings and weekends, the Tsaos decided in 1988 that Janie would quit her job and head up the consultancy, as revenues reached $500 000. Soon, the Taiwanese firms came up with new connector designs—low-cost cables and other networking devices—for linking hardware components in PC systems. The firms wanted the Tsaos to market their wares in the United States. In 1991, DEW International was renamed Linksys, Victor quit his outside job and, with a steady diet of 100-hour work weeks, the Tsaos eventually supplied components to regional retailers, national chains, catalogues, and online retailers.

Linksys's 15-year journey, from garage start-up to industry leader, was powered by the Tsaos' personal convictions about how to run a business—with calculated risks, financial frugality, meticulous attention to detail in every part of the business, and hard work. Knowing they're not inventors, they instead popularize existing technologies like the Multishare print server, a cable that connects multiple PCs to multiple printers. Their financial orientation is pretty simple, too: Watch costs, don't waste resources, spend money only for necessities, and make sure you get something of value for each expenditure. They invested only $7000 of their own money for start-up costs in Linksys. They don't pay the highest wages (Victor drew no salary until the mid-1990s). They work in no-frills facilities. In growing from a three-employee firm in 1988 to more than 200 employees now, Tsaos needed outside capital only once—a bank loan in 2001 that they paid back in less than six months. The debt-free and stockholder-free financial structure avoided financial risks that most start-ups face from providers of start-up capital. It also preserved the Tsaos' complete control over the direction, strategy, and management of the company's business.

With a clear vision for the company, the Tsaos were selective in the kinds of risks they accepted and avoided. For the Tsaos, the risk reducer for introducing the four-port router in 1999 was confidence in their company's abilities and the needs of the industry—low price and speed to market would win the day. Their intimate knowledge of the industry—knowing what users needed by watching what PC nerds were buying in retail stores, awareness of competing products, listening to manufacturers about upcoming products in the industry, and talking with industry enthusiasts about where networking was headed in homes and businesses—convinced them of the need for the new broadband connector. "Everyone knew in the late nineties of the broadband explosion," Victor says. "It wasn't really a secret."

They knew Linksys's capabilities, too: what they could provide off the shelf, or what could be redesigned in-house, and sold at a low price. Rather than relying on lengthy outside market studies, these assessments were based on confidence in their own knowledge and experience. In acting fast—they got the first sub-$300 consumer router to market first, three months ahead of competitors—Linksys captured the market. That meant jumping from a 10.8 percent share of the networking market in 1999 to 18.6 percent in 2000, while revenues leaped from $108 million to $206 million. They knew, then, that by outpacing competitors the future was even brighter.

Janie and Victor Tsao are also willing to take risks with employees. An example is offered by Glen McLaughlin, vice-president of North American sales, who says, "We'll give you enough rope to either hang yourself or be successful," an approach that requires confidence and trust in employees. Janie and Victor let McLaughlin switch the Linksys product-distribution system from using 15 regional distributors to three national distributors, even though they were skeptical that it would work. The Tsaos required daily updates but, otherwise, left McLaughlin alone to work it out, and he built a successful new distribution system.

However, the biggest risk in computer technology is not keeping ahead in new developments. The Tsaos' next big jump came with wireless connections in 2001, when Linksys launched a system of wireless routers and computer cards. Revenue jumped to $346.7 million with market share reaching 34.2 percent. Again, the Tsaos were not inventors but, instead, were quick to supply the market with low-priced, newest-technology products to meet leading-edge needs of computer users. They soon took another calculated risk by launching more wireless products—so-called Wi-Fi (wireless fidelity, networking using radio waves)—in the fall of 2002, even while the industry was still working on a new standard, 802.11g, for faster wireless. The Tsaos wanted their new 802.11g products on retail shelves before Christmas, even though they could become obsolete if the standard was changed in the coming months. Linksys launched its new products in December 2002, three months before competitors,

▶▶▶

and sold 300 000 units in the first two months. Revenue for 2002 bounced up to $430 million, and J. P. Morgan analyst Ehud Gelblum estimated revenues at $538 million for fiscal year 2004.

With more than 300 employees and 49 percent of the networking market, in 2003 the Tsaos sold Linksys to Cisco Systems for $500 million in stock. While reluctant to sell, they recognized impending risks from two formidable business issues: expansion overseas and big-company competition. The Tsaos realized they didn't have the cash or infrastructure to expand overseas, yet it was critical since 90 percent of Linksys's revenues are from the United States and Canada. Moreover, the big hitters—Microsoft, HP, Dell—were sizing up the market and one or more were sure to enter. Cisco, a giant in big-business networking, needed Linksys to fill its void in small-office and home-office (SOHO) products. The buyout has enabled Linksys products to be advertised for the first time on national television. Cisco has also added an international presence via new Linksys offices in Italy, China, Hungary, Australia, and India.

After 15 years of immersing their lives in Linksys, and agreeing to stay on for two more years with Cisco, Janie and Victor Tsao still hang their hats at the modest, two-story Irvine, California, headquarters. Victor's traditional 100-hour work weeks have eased off to a more comfortable 70 hours a week, while Janie still negotiates with retailers and is adamant about protecting market share. Linksys, meanwhile, is aiming for a 70 percent share of market. As home networking becomes more popular, the market is expected to grow to 37 million homes by 2008.

Questions for Discussion

1. Give examples of two or more speculative risks from the Linksys case. What characteristics allow your examples to be labelled as speculative risks rather than pure risks?
2. Give an example of risk avoidance exhibited by the Tsaos in this case. In what ways is your example one of risk avoidance, as distinct from risk control or risk retention?
3. The Tsaos grew Linksys from a start-up to an industry leader with no outside financing in the firm's capital structure. What steps were taken to accomplish this? What advantages resulted from no outside financing? What disadvantages?
4. How would you characterize the Tsaos' approach to financial management? Would you have taken a different approach? Explain why or why not.
5. What kinds of financial planning activities were used at Linksys? Do you think cash-flow management and financial controls were in place? Explain why or why not.

CONCLUDING CASE 20-2

Brascan Is Making Progress

When Bruce Flatt took over as CEO of Brascan Corp. in 2002, the company owned a diverse group of other companies, including Noranda Inc. (mining), Nexfor (paperboard), Brookfield Properties Corp. (real estate), Great Lakes Power Inc. (hydroelectric generation), Trilon Corp. (financial services), and two Brazilian cattle ranches. Flatt quickly announced that he was going to convert the company from a conglomerate (i.e., a company that owns a diverse group of other companies) into an asset management company that would focus on just three areas: real estate, power generation, and infrastructure.

Flatt's strategy contrasted sharply with that of his predecessor, Jack Cockwell, who is remembered as the last of a dying breed of conglomerate moguls who once ruled the Canadian business scene. Cockwell's strategy was to buy undervalued companies, even if they were very diverse. For example, in the early 1990s, he took $20 million of stock owned by Peter and Edward Bronfman and parlayed it into Canada's most powerful and controversial conglomerate—Edper Group. But when real estate prices dropped, Edper faced bankruptcy because it was unable to pay its debts. The company sold assets to stay alive and by the mid-1990s had sold nearly $5 billion in assets and had raised $6.6 billion in new financing. The company was renamed Brascan in 2000.

Flatt made his decision to move Brascan away from the conglomerate model because stock markets now like so-called "pure play" companies that are highly focussed, and because investors had essentially attached a "holding company discount" to Brascan's stock price. That occurred in spite of the fact that Brascan had regularly been profitable. By the middle of 2005, Flatt had made some progress toward his goal. Brascan bought controlling interest in an office property in London's Canary

Wharf, purchased B.C. coastal timberlands to boost its infrastructure assets, and purchased several hydroelectric generating plants in the United States and Brazil. Brascan now owns about $20 billion in assets, including 70 office towers and 120 power plants. The stock market liked what it saw, and the price of Brascan stock rose from $23 per share in September 2003 to $38 per share in July 2004.

The purchase of the B.C. timberlands included two lumber processing plants, five sawmills, and rights to harvest large tracts of crown land. Brascan will likely sell the sawmills and logging rights, perhaps for $300 million. Brascan executives point out that timberlands are a much more stable investment than lumber or paper companies, and will generate predictable cash returns. Trees also rise in value over time. Unlike mining, which is cyclical, tree harvesting is predictable. If prices decline, a company can simply let the trees keep growing until prices improve.

Other initiatives designed to change the look of Brascan have also been positive (after a few bumps in the road). At one point, it looked like China Minmetals Corp. would buy Noranda, but that deal fell through. Then, Noranda and Falconbridge Nickel merged, but that meant that Brascan was still involved in the resource industry. Finally, in 2005 Noranda was sold to Inco.

Financial analysts say Brascan is making progress, but think the company still has a ways to go. Flatt thinks the market is finally recognizing Brascan's progress, but says that some people expect too much in a short period of time. He points out that just 10 years ago 80 percent of Brascan's assets were in resource-based industries, but the figure now is less than 10 percent.

Flatt says that assets must meet a threshold return or they won't be kept. He wants to achieve a 15 percent annual growth in sustainable cash flow and a 20 percent cash return on equity. These goals may be achievable in real estate, financial services, and power generation, but not in highly cyclical businesses like mining and paperboard.

In 2005, Brascan changed its name to Brookfield Asset Management to distance itself from its conglomerate past, and to suggest its new focus.

Questions for Discussion

1. Why might a profitable company like Brascan be out of favour with investment analysts? What can a company do to regain favour?
2. What are the advantages and disadvantages of debt and equity financing? How did these advantages and disadvantages manifest themselves at Brascan?
3. Discuss the risk–return relationship as it applies to Brascan.
4. How is Bruce Flatt's view of the organization different from that of former CEO Jack Cockwell?

PLANNING FOR YOUR CAREER

The Application Letter

In Chapters 18, 19, and 20, we explained the Canadian banking system, described the activities of various financial institutions, explored markets for buying and selling securities, and examined key issues in financial and risk management. Financial organizations, of course, are all prospective employers that rely on employees to provide services for customers. This exercise gives you an opportunity not only to look into entry-level job possibilities in banking but also to sharpen a specific job-hunting and career-building tool: application-letter writing.

Assignment

Reread the material on the Bank of Canada in Chapter 18. Think of yourself as a potential employee who's looking for an entry-level job in an interesting area of activity at the Bank of Canada. Your objective in this exercise is to write an effective, job-specific application letter to the Bank of Canada using the methods described by James S. O'Rourke IV in Chapter 4, "Employment Correspondence," of *Beginning Your Career Search,* 3rd ed.

To complete this exercise, do the following:

1. Suppose you're applying for a summer internship. Start by visiting the Bank of Canada's website at (www.bank-banque-canada.ca). Click on "Careers," then on "Current Opportunities" and "Who We Hire." Does the summer internship program interest you? What types of other positions interest you? Which ones do you think you would be qualified for?
2. Using the guidelines furnished by O'Rourke, draw up an outline for your letter.
3. Write your letter using the three-paragraph structure recommended by O'Rourke. Be sure that your letter is tailored specifically for the area that you've targeted. Save this draft of your letter for later use in this exercise.

4. Compare your letter with the sample letters in Appendix A of O'Rourke. Evaluate your draft using O'Rourke's lists of suggestions for good cover letters and common mistakes to avoid. Identify those areas of your letter that need improvement.
5. Rewrite your letter by making necessary improvements. Now compare your revised draft with the original. How did the changes improve the letter? In what ways—specifically—is the revised version better? Is there any room for further improvement?
6. Suppose you're applying for a part-time job as a teller at a local bank. Write a letter applying for the position. Compare it with the letter you wrote for the internship at the Bank of Canada. In what specific ways do the letters differ, and why?

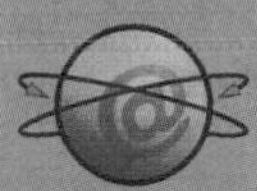

Visit the Companion Website at **www.pearsoned.ca/griffin** to view the CBC video segments that accompany the following cases.

CBC CBC VIDEO CASE V-1

The Cost of Counterfeiting

Wesley Weber is one of Canada's most famous counterfeiters. In just a few short years, he was able to print over $16 million in counterfeit $100 bills. He says that he was running a business (albeit an illegal one), and just like a regular manager, he hired employees, paid wages, worried about efficient operations, and tried to improve the quality of his product. Unfortunately, he was an example of the entrepreneurial instinct gone wrong.

Why did he do it? He says he got a real "rush" from counterfeiting, and, of course, it also allowed him to buy whatever he wanted—cars, boats, expensive televisions, trips, and so forth. Weber, who sees himself a classic computer geek, says he had a strong urge to make money when he was quite young. When he got his first computer, he put a $10 bill in the scanner to see what would happen. His father was very upset.

Computer technology facilitated his illegal activities. All he needed was a computer, a printer, and some software. He began by making counterfeit $20 bills, but he was soon caught and spent three months in jail. After he got out of jail, he and some friends started making fake $100 bills. He chose that denomination because it was more efficient to make and required smaller amounts of supplies than making $20 bills. To get the equipment he needed, he passed himself off as a legitimate businessman. He was able to get a supply of the material needed to make the shiny square on the $100 bill by posing as an employee of Ford Motor (he said he needed the material to make patches for car seats). To get the material needed to create the proper texture on the $100 bill he told an engraver he needed special metal stamps for replacement parts for a manufacturing operation. He always wore a suit and tie, and this apparently increased the legitimacy of his requests and helped him talk people into selling him what he wanted.

At first, Weber simply spent his fake cash. But then he increased the scale of his operations and began selling the $100 bills to distributors who paid $24 for each one. When Weber's fake bills started getting noticed, police alerted people to flaws in the bills. Weber responded by improving the bills and getting rid of their deficiencies. In the end, he was making very good fakes.

He was living the high life, but he became careless and greedy. The RCMP tracked him to a cottage where he was making the fake bills and put him under surveillance from a building next door. Weber says he was so engrossed in making money that he didn't see the obvious fact that the RCMP had a command headquarters next door. One July day, Weber met his "neighbours" as they burst into his cottage with guns drawn and placed him under arrest.

Weber was convicted of counterfeiting and sentenced to three years in prison. After serving his time, he was out on day parole. He became a regular at a local internet café, where he helped the owner detect fake bills. He also earned his living as a day trader. Shortly before completing his parole period, he went on an unauthorized trip and was arrested for parole violation. He will now have to pay the price (possibly 18 more months in jail).

Reflecting on his escapades, he now says that the counterfeit money brought him nothing but heartache. His girlfriend left him, his parents were devastated, and he has nothing from the proceeds of his crime (but he knows that people will think he has money buried all over the province). He thinks that perhaps $6 million of his counterfeit bills are still circulating in the Canadian economy.

Because of the activities of people like Wesley Weber, Canadian businesses are becoming more and more wary of accepting $100 or $50 bills. If a business accepts a counterfeit bill, it must eat the cost of the bill. Fears about counterfeiting are well-founded, since counterfeiting is becoming more and more common. One study found that counterfeiting is up 300 percent in the last few years. In some retail businesses (e.g., sports bars) it is relatively easy for crooks to pass bad bills because the pace of activity is so hectic. As well, patrons often leave money for their bill on the table, and by the time the staff check the bill for authenticity, the patrons are gone. Studies show that 6 out 10 retailers check the $100 bill, but only one in 10 checks lower denominations.

The Bank of Canada has responded to the counterfeiting problem by redesigning Canadian paper money to make it harder to copy. The new bills have more security features such as new holographic images, more raised printing, and images that show up only when the bill is held up to a light. The Bank of Canada has also spent $1 million on publicity about the new bills. But the bad guys are clever, and they are always improving their product.

Questions for Discussion

1. What is the meaning of the term "money supply?" What are the different measures of the money supply?
2. What is the impact of counterfeiting on the money supply?
3. How does counterfeiting harm individuals, business owners, and the Canadian economy?

Source: "Easy Money," *Venture*, September 22, 2002.

CBC VIDEO CASE V-2

Canadian Emeralds

At Regal Ridge in the Yukon, True North mining is developing an emerald mine, and millions of dollars of investment money is at stake. Publicity is very important to small mining companies, so True North has hired a TV crew to produce a promotional video showing the mine's prospects. The video shows real emeralds being dug out of the ground. But the big question is this: Are there enough emeralds to make a mine worthwhile? And what about the quality? Many of the surface emeralds have been damaged by frost, so the company is planning to dig deeper and sift through tons of rock in the hope of finding undamaged (and bigger) stones.

A lot of money is required to develop a mine, so True North's CEO—Andy Smith—needs to find new investors who are willing to put money into True North, and he needs to keep current investors happy. One big investor—Dundee Securities—is concerned about its $1 million investment. Its managers want to know when a commercial mine is likely to be built, and when retail sales of emeralds are likely to begin. Smith asks Dundee for patience. He points out that the emerald find is a unique story with potentially huge value for shareholders. After listening to Smith, Dundee Securities decides to stick with the company. But Smith knows that the underground results had better be good or investors like Dundee could cash out quickly.

Small investors are important too. Smith knows that True North needs visibility in Whitehorse, because many of True North's investors live there (and they own more than half the company's stock). As well, the emerald business means a lot to the people in Whitehorse, so Smith wants to keep investor confidence high. Don Murphy, a government geologist, says that any new mining activity is welcome in the Yukon, but he is cautious when predicting what effect True North's hoped-for mine will have on the area.

A few weeks later, the underground emeralds are being sorted at True North's headquarters. Smith can't resist taking a peek at how things are going. The news is quite promising. Some of the emeralds that have been found may retail for as much as U.S.$3000. True North has also discovered a new kind of gem at Regal Ridge that is apparently found only in Canada. It is called a true blue beryl. The value of the new blue gem is unknown, but the media attention it receives is very valuable for True North. The day after the discovery was reported on *The National*, over 1 million shares of True North were traded, and the stock jumped to $1.24 per share.

On the eve of the shareholders meeting two weeks later, the first results are in. The deeper underground the company digs, the better the quality and size of the emeralds. But the sample is small, and the company doesn't know how much the total deposit may be worth. But at least this year the company can show investors real emeralds. At its meeting last year, they didn't have any emeralds, and investors were not happy.

Just before the shareholders meeting, Andy meets with the company geologist in a strategy session. They need to figure out what message they want to give to investors. He can't hype the company too much or he will run into trouble with securities regulators. But he also can't be too negative or vague, because investors want to see some action. At the meeting, Smith reports that the emerald sector looks comparable to the diamond sector (although it is less well developed at the moment). He emphasizes that the company has found bigger stones underground in recent digging, and he tells the shareholders that True North's emerald deposit could eventually be worth billions of dollars. The company's geologist is more cautious, and simply says that that the results look interesting from an economic point of view.

The geologist then shows shareholders some real emeralds taken from the Yukon property. Investors are happy with this hard evidence that something real is happening.

Emerald fever is still alive, but until True North starts actually selling stones at the retail level, nothing is for sure. For now, shareholders seem willing to continue backing the company. But an operating mine is at least two years away, and many tasks remain to be completed: various permits are needed, more testing must be done at Regal Ridge, and there are environmental questions that must be answered.

Questions for Discussion

1. Explain the difference between par value, market value, and book value of a company's stock. Which of these values are investors of True North concerned about? Why?
2. What subjective factors influence the price of a company's stock? Which of these are relevant for this case? Explain.
3. Briefly describe the major sources of short- and long-term funds for businesses. Which of these sources would a firm like True North be most likely to use? Why?
4. What are the factors that a company must take into account when deciding between debt and equity financing? Explain which of these are relevant for True North, and the type of financing that the company would likely choose, given a consideration of these factors.

Source: "Canadian Emeralds," *Venture*, March 28, 2004.

Appendix A

BUSINESS LAW

THE ROLE OF LAW IN CANADIAN SOCIETY

law The set of rules and standards that a society agrees upon to govern the behaviour of its citizens.

Law is the set of rules and standards that a society agrees upon to govern the behaviour of its citizens. Both the British and the French influenced the development of law in Canada. In 1867, the British North America (BNA) Act created the nation of Canada. The BNA Act was "patriated" to Canada in 1982 and is known as the Constitution Act. This act divides legislative powers in Canada between the federal and provincial governments.

Sources of Law

The law in Canada has evolved and changed in response to our norms and values. Our laws have arisen from three sources: (1) customs and judicial precedents (the source of common law), (2) the actions of provincial and federal legislatures (the source of statutory law), and (3) rulings by administrative bodies (the source of administrative law).

common law The unwritten law of England, derived from precedent and legal judgments.

Common law is the unwritten law of England, derived from ancient precedents and judges' previous legal opinions. Common law is based on the principle of equity, the provision to every person of a just and fair remedy. Canadian legal customs and traditions derive from British common law. All provinces except Quebec, which uses the French Civil Code, have laws based on British common law, and court decisions are often based on precedents from common law. That is, decisions made in earlier cases that involved the same legal point will guide the court.

statutory law Written law developed by city councils, provincial legislatures, and parliament.

administrative law Rules and regulations that government agencies develop based on their interpretations of statutory law.

Statutory law is written law developed by city councils, provincial legislatures, and parliament. Most law in Canada today is statutory law.

Administrative law is the rules and regulations that government agencies and commissions develop based on their interpretations of statutory laws. For example, Consumer and Corporate Affairs Canada develops regulations on false advertising using federal legislation.

The Court System

In Canada, the judiciary branch of government has the responsibility of settling disputes among organizations or individuals by applying existing laws. Both provincial and federal courts exist to hear both criminal and civil cases. The Supreme Court of Canada is the highest court in Canada. It decides whether to hear appeals from lower courts.

BUSINESS LAW

business law Laws that specifically affect how businesses are managed.

Business firms, like all other organizations, are affected by the laws of the country. **Business law** refers to laws that specifically affect how business firms are managed. Some laws affect all businesses, regardless of size, industry, or location. For example, the Income Tax Act requires businesses to pay income tax. Other laws may have a greater impact on one industry than on others. For example, pollution regulations are of much greater concern to Inco than they are to Carlson Wagonlit Travel.

Business managers must have at least a basic understanding of eight important concepts in business law:

- contracts
- agency
- bailment
- property
- warranty
- torts
- negotiable instruments
- bankruptcy

Contracts

Agreements about transactions are common in a business's day-to-day activity. A **contract** is an agreement between two parties to act in a specified way or to perform certain acts. A contract might, for example, apply to a customer buying a product from a retail establishment or to two manufacturers agreeing to buy products or services from each other. A valid contract includes several elements:

contract An agreement between two parties to act in a specified way or to perform certain acts.

- *an agreement*—All parties must consciously agree about the contract.
- *consideration*—The parties must exchange something of value (e.g., time, products, services, money, etc.).
- *competence*—All parties to the contract must be legally able to enter into an agreement. Individuals who are below a certain age or who are legally insane, for example, cannot enter into legal agreements.
- *legal purpose*—What the parties agree to do for or with each other must be legal. An agreement between two manufacturers to fix prices is not legal.

The courts will enforce a contract if it meets the criteria described above. Most parties honour their contracts, but occasionally one party does not do what it was supposed to do. **Breach of contract** occurs when one party to an agreement fails, without legal reason, to live up to the agreement's provisions. The party who has not breached the contract has three alternatives under the law in Canada: (1) discharge, (2) sue for damages, or (3) require specific performance.

breach of contract When one party to an agreement fails, without legal reason, to live up to the agreement's provisions.

An example will demonstrate these three alternatives. Suppose that Barrington Farms Inc. agrees to deliver 100 dozen long-stemmed roses to the Blue Violet Flower Shop the week before Mother's Day. One week before the agreed-upon date, Barrington informs Blue Violet that it cannot make the delivery until after Mother's Day. Under the law, the owner of Blue Violet can choose among any of the following:

Discharge

Blue Violet can also ignore its obligations in the contract. That is, it can contract with another supplier.

Sue for Damages

Blue Violet can legally demand payment for losses caused by Barrington's failure to deliver the promised goods. Losses might include any increased price Blue Violet would have to pay for the roses or court costs incurred in the damage suit.

Require Specific Performance

If monetary damages are not sufficient to reimburse Blue Violet, the court can force Barrington's to live up to its original contract.

AGENCY

agency–principal relationship When one party (the agent) is authorized to act on behalf of another party (the principal).

In many business situations, one person acts as an agent for another person. Well-known examples include actors and athletes represented by agents who negotiate contracts for them. An **agency–principal relationship** is established when one party (the agent) is authorized to act on behalf of another party (the principal).

The agent is under the control of the principal and must act on behalf of the principal and in the principal's best interests. The principal remains liable for the acts of the agent as long as the agent is acting within the scope of authority granted by the principal. A salesperson for IBM, for example, is an agent for IBM, the principal.

Bailment

bailor–bailee relationship When a bailor, a property owner, gives possession of the property to a bailee, a custodian, but retains ownership of the property.

Many business transactions are not covered by the agency–principal relationship. For example, suppose that you take your car to a mechanic to have it repaired. Because the repair shop has temporary possession of something you own, it is responsible for your car. This is a **bailor–bailee relationship**. In a bailor–bailee relationship, the bailor (the car owner) gives possession of his or her property to the bailee (the repair shop) but retains ownership of the item. A business firm that stores inventory in a public warehouse is in a bailor–bailee relationship. The business firm is the bailor and the warehouse is the bailee. The warehouse is responsible for storing the goods safely and making them available to the manufacturer upon request.

The Law of Property

property Anything of tangible or intangible value that the owner has the right to possess and own.

real property Land and any permanent buildings attached to that land.

personal property Tangible or intangible assets other than real property.

Property includes anything of tangible or intangible value that the owner has the right to possess and use. **Real property** is land and any permanent buildings attached to that land. **Personal property** is tangible or intangible assets other than real property. Personal property includes cars, clothing, furniture, money in bank accounts, stock certificates, and copyrights.

Transferring Property

deed A document that shows ownership of real property.

lease A document that grants the use of an asset for a specified period of time in return for payment.

title A document that shows legal possession of personal property.

From time to time, businesses and individuals need to transfer property to another person or business. A **deed** is a document that shows ownership of real property. It allows the transfer of title of real property.

A **lease** grants the use of an asset for a specified period of time in return for payment. The business or individual granting the lease is the lessor and the tenant is the lessee. For example, a business (the lessee) may rent space in a mall for one year from a real estate development firm (the lessor).

A **title** shows legal possession of personal property. It allows the transfer of title of personal property. When you buy a snowmobile, for example, the former owner signs the title over to you.

Warranty

warranty A promise that the product or service will perform as the seller has promised it will.

express warranty A specific claim that a manufacturer makes about a product.

When you buy a product or service, you want some assurance that it will perform satisfactorily and meet your needs. A **warranty** is a promise that the product or service will perform as the seller has promised it will.

There are two kinds of warranties—express and implied. An **express warranty** is a specific claim that the manufacturer makes about a product. For example, a warranty that a screwdriver blade is made of case-hardened steel is an express warranty. An **implied warranty** suggests that a product will perform as the manufacturer claims it will. Suppose that you buy an outboard motor for your boat and the engine burns out in one week. Because the manufacturer implies by selling the motor that it will work for a reasonable period of time, you can return it and get your money back.

implied warranty An assumption that a product will perform as the manufacturer claims it will.

Because opinions vary on what is a "reasonable" time, most manufacturers now give limited time warranties on their products. For example, they will guarantee their products against defects in materials or manufacture for six months or one year.

Torts

A **tort** is a wrongful civil act that one party inflicts on another and that results in injury to the person, to the person's property, or to the person's good name. An **intentional tort** is a wrongful act intentionally committed. If a security guard in a department store suspects someone of shoplifting and uses excessive force to prevent him or her from leaving the store, the guard might be guilty of an intentional tort. Other examples are libel, embezzlement, and patent infringement.

tort A wrongful civil act that one party inflicts on another.

intentional tort A wrongful act intentionally committed.

Negligence is a wrongful act that inadvertently causes injury to another person. For example, if a maintenance crew in a store mops the floors without placing warning signs in the area, a customer who slips and falls might bring a negligence suit against the store.

negligence A wrongful act that inadvertently causes injury to another person.

In recent years, the most publicized area of negligence has been product liability. **Product liability** means that businesses are liable for injuries caused to product users because of negligence in design or manufacturing. **Strict product liability** means that a business is liable for injuries caused by their products even if there is no evidence of negligence in the design or manufacture of the product.

product liability The liability of businesses for injuries caused to product users because of negligence in design or manufacture.

strict product liability The liability of businesses for injuries caused by their products even if no evidence of negligence in the product's design or manufacture exists.

Negotiable Instruments

Negotiable instruments are types of commercial paper that can be transferred among individuals and business firms. Cheques, bank drafts, and certificates of deposit are examples of negotiable instruments.

negotiable instrument Types of commercial paper that can be transferred among individuals and business firms.

The Bills of Exchange Act specifies that a negotiable instrument must

- be written
- be signed by the person who puts it into circulation (the maker or drawer)
- contain an unconditional promise to pay a certain amount of money
- be payable on demand
- be payable to a specific person (or to the bearer of the instrument)

Negotiable instruments are transferred from one party to another through an endorsement. An **endorsement** means signing your name to a negotiable instrument; this makes it transferable to another person or organization. If you sign only your name on the back of a cheque, you are making a *blank* endorsement. If you state that the instrument is being transferred to a specific person, you are making a *special* endorsement. A *qualified* endorsement limits your liability if the instrument is not backed up by sufficient funds. For example, if you get a cheque from a friend and want to use it to buy a new stereo, you can write "without recourse" above your name. If your friend's cheque bounces, you have no liability. A *restrictive* endorsement limits the negotiability of the instrument. For example, if you write "for deposit only" on the back of a cheque and it is later stolen, no one else can cash it.

endorsement Signing your name to a negotiable instrument, making it transferable to another person or organization.

Bankruptcy

bankruptcy Permission granted by the courts to individuals and organizations not to pay some or all of their debts.

At one time, individuals who could not pay their debts were jailed. Today, however, both organizations and individuals can seek relief by filing for **bankruptcy**, which is the court-granted permission to not pay some or all of their debts.

Thousands of individuals and businesses file for bankruptcy each year. They do so for various reasons, including cash flow problems, reduced demand for their products, or some other problem that makes it difficult or impossible for them to resolve their financial problems. In recent years, large businesses like Eaton's, Olympia & York, and Enron have sought the protection of bankruptcy laws. Three main factors account for the increase in bankruptcy filings:

1. The increased availability of credit
2. The "fresh-start" provisions in current bankruptcy laws
3. The growing acceptance of bankruptcy as a financial tactic

insolvent person (or company) One who cannot pay current obligations to creditors as they come due, or whose debts exceed their assets.

bankrupt person (or company) One who has either made a voluntary application to start bankruptcy proceedings (voluntary bankruptcy) or has been forced by creditors into bankruptcy (involuntary bankruptcy) by a process referred to as a receiving order.

In Canada, jurisdiction over bankruptcy is provided by the Bankruptcy and Insolvency Act. An **insolvent person (or company)** is defined as one who cannot pay current obligations to creditors as they come due, or whose debts exceed their assets. A **bankrupt person (or company)** is one who has either made a voluntary application to start bankruptcy proceedings (voluntary bankruptcy) or has been forced by creditors into bankruptcy (involuntary bankruptcy) by a process referred to as a *receiving order*. A person who is insolvent may or may not be bankrupt, and a person who is bankrupt may or may not be insolvent, as there are other bases for bankruptcy under the act. Another procedure under the act is referred to as a *proposal*, which can delay or avoid liquidation by providing the debtor with time to reorganize affairs and/or propose a payment schedule to creditors.

On a practical basis, business bankruptcy under the act may be resolved or avoided by one of three methods:

- Under a *liquidation plan*, the business ceases to exist. Its assets are sold and the proceeds are used to pay creditors.
- Under a *repayment plan*, the bankrupt company works out a new payment schedule to meet its obligations. The time frame is usually extended, and payments are collected and distributed by a court-appointed trustee.
- *Reorganization* is the most complex form of business bankruptcy. The company must explain the sources of its financial difficulties and propose a new plan for remaining in business. Reorganization may include a new slate of managers and a new financial strategy. A judge may also reduce the firm's debts to ensure its survival. Although creditors naturally dislike debt reduction, they may agree to the proposal, since getting, say, 50 percent of what you are owed is better than getting nothing at all.

MANAGING YOUR PERSONAL FINANCES

Appendix B

For many people, the goal of financial success isn't *being* wealthy: It's the things that they can *do* with wealth. That's why chapter one in so many financial success stories deals with a hard reality: Like it or not, dealing with personal finances is a life-long job. As a rule, it involves a life-altering choice between two options:

- committing to the rational management of your personal finances—controlling them as a way of life and helping them grow
- letting the financial chips fall where they may and hoping for the best (which seldom happens)

Not surprisingly, option 1 results in greater personal satisfaction and financial stability. Ignoring your finances, on the other hand, invites frustration, disappointment, and, quite often, acute financial distress.

TAKING YOUR FINANCES PERSONALLY

In Chapter 20, we explored some basic financial-management activities, including the role of financial managers in cash flow management, financial planning and control, and debt and equity financing. We discussed the activities of financial managers—clarifying financial goals, determining short-term and long-term funding needs, and managing risk. Many of the principles of organizational finance pertain to personal finance as well. Recall, for example, the principle of reducing organizational financial risk by diversifying investments. When Enron collapsed, many employees lost their entire savings because their retirement portfolios consisted of just one security—Enron common stock—instead of a broader selection of investments.

In managing your own finances and pursuing your own personal financial goals, you must consider the activities that we'll revisit in the following sections: cash management, financial planning and control, investment alternatives, and risk management. We start by describing a key factor in success: the personal financial plan. Then we'll detail the steps in the planning process and relate them to some core concepts and crucial decisions in personal financial management.

BUILDING YOUR FINANCIAL PLAN

Financial planning is the process of looking at your current financial condition, identifying your goals, and anticipating your requirements for meeting those goals. Once you've determined the assets you need to meet your goals, you'll then identify the best sources and uses of those assets for eventually reaching your goals. But remember: Because your goals and financial position will change as you enter different life stages, your plan should always make room for revision. Figure B.1 summarizes a step-by-step approach to personal financial planning.

Knowing Your Net Worth

Begin by assessing your current financial position. Your personal net worth is the value of all your assets minus all your liabilities or debts. Bear in

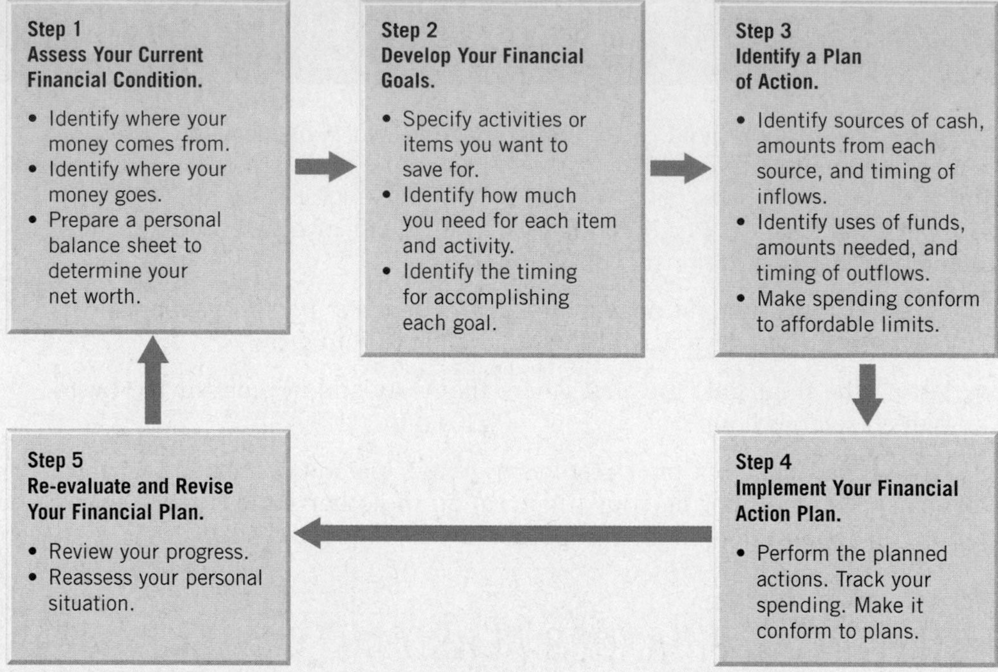

Figure B.1

mind that personal net worth doesn't refer to the resources that you plan to manage in the future (as in a budget): It's a measure of *your wealth at the present time.* The worksheet in Figure B.2 provides some sample calculations for developing your own personal "balance sheet." Because assets and liabilities change over time, updating your balance sheet not only allows you to monitor changes but also provides more accurate information for realistic budgeting and planning.

Using Your Net Worth to Set and Evaluate Goals

Your personal balance sheet lets you review your *current* overall financial condition. Once you know where you presently stand, you can move on to Step 2 in financial planning: setting specific goals for the future by calculating *changes in net worth.* The worksheet in Figure B.3 allows for goal setting in three time frames: *immediate* (within one year), *intermediate* (within five years), and *long term* (over more than five years). This kind of planning should encourage you to set measurable goals and completion times when calculating your future financial needs. It also lets you set priorities for rationing your resources if, at some point, you don't have the wherewithal to pursue all of your goals.

Because subsequent planning steps—beginning with Step 3 (identifying a plan of action) and including implementation—will affect assets and liabilities, your balance sheet will change over time. That's why it needs periodic updating to reflect your current net worth, to monitor your progress, and to help you start a new planning cycle.

The Time Value of Money

The time value of money is perhaps the single most important concept in personal finance. It's especially relevant for setting financial goals and evaluating investments. The concept of *time value* recognizes the basic fact that, while it's invested, money grows by earning interest or yielding some other form of return. Thus, whenever you make everyday purchases, you're giv-

Assets: What You Own		Example Numbers	Your Numbers
LIQUID ASSETS			
1. Cash	$	300	______
2. Savings	+	3700	______
3. Chequing	+	1200	______
INVESTMENTS:			
4. RRSPs	+	12 400	______
5. Securities	+	500	______
6. Retirement Plan	+	—	______
7. Real Estate (other than primary residence)	+	—	______
HOUSEHOLD:			
8. Cars (market value)	+	18 000	______
9. House (market value)	+	84 000	______
10. Furniture	+	3400	______
11. Personal Property	+	6600	______
12. Other assets		—	______
13. Total Assets (add lines 1–12)		**= $130 100**	______
Liabilities (Debt): What You Owe			
CURRENT LIABILITIES:			
14. Credit card balance	$	1300	______
15. Unpaid bills due	+	1800	______
16. Alimony and child support	+	—	______
LONG-TERM LIABILITIES:			
17. Home mortgage	+	72 500	______
18. Home equity loan	+	—	______
19. Car loan	+	4100	______
20. Student loan	+	3600	______
21. Other liabilities	+	2400	______
22. Total Liabilities (add lines 14–21)		**= $85 700**	______
Net Worth			
23. Total Assets (line 13)	$	130 100	______
24. Less: Total Debt (line 22)	+	85 700	______
25. Results: Net Worth		**= $44 400**	______

Figure B.2

ing up interest that you could have earned with the same money if you'd invested it instead. From a financial standpoint, "idle" or uninvested money—money that could be put to work earning more money—is a wasted resource.

Why Money Grows

The value of time stems from the principle of compound growth—the compounding of interest paid over given time periods. With each additional time period, interest payments accumulate and earn even more interest, thus multiplying the earning capacity of the investment. Let's say, for example, that you invest $1 today at 10 percent annual interest. As you can see from Table B.1, you'll have $1.10 at the end of one year (your $1 original investment plus $0.10 in interest). If you reinvest your whole $1.10, you'll earn interest on both your first year's interest and your original investment. During year 2, therefore, your savings will grow to $1.21 (your $1.10 reinvestment plus $0.11 in interest). Obviously, each year's interest will be

Name the Goal	Financial requirement (amount) for this goal	Time frame for accomplishing goal	Importance (1 = highest, 5 = lowest)
Immediate Goals:			
Live in a better apartment	______	______	______
Obtain adequate life, disability, liability, property insurance	______	______	______
Establish an emergency cash fund	______	______	______
Pay off credit card debt	______	______	______
Other	______	______	______
Intermediate Goals:			
Save for wedding	______	______	______
Save to buy new car	______	______	______
Establish regular savings program (5% of gross income)	______	______	______
Save for college for self	______	______	______
Pay off major outstanding debt	______	______	______
Make a major purchase	______	______	______
Save for home remodeling	______	______	______
Save for down payment on a home	______	______	______
Other	______	______	______
Long-Term Goals:			
Pay off home mortgage	______	______	______
Save for college for children	______	______	______
Save for vacation home	______	______	______
Increase personal net worth to $__ in __ years.	______	______	______
Achieve retirement nest egg of $__ in __ years.	______	______	______
Accumulate fund for travel in retirement	______	______	______
Save for long-term care needs	______	______	______
Other	______	______	______

Figure B.3

Table B.1 Calculating Compound Growth

Year	Beginning Amount	+	Annual Interest Earned	=	Ending Amount
1	$1.000	+	$0.100 [0.10 × $1.000 = $0.10]	=	$1.100
2	1.100	+	0.110 [0.10 × $1.100 = $0.11]	=	1.210
3	1.210	+	0.121 [0.10 × $1.210 = $0.121]	=	1.331
4	1.331	+	0.133 [0.10 × $1.331 = $0.133]	=	1.464
5	1.464	+	0.146 [0.10 × $1.464 = $0.146]	=	1.610
6	1.610	+	0.161 [0.10 × $1.610 = $0.161]	=	1.771
7	1.771	+	0.177 [0.10 × $1.771 = $0.177]	=	1.948
8	1.948	+	0.195 [0.10 × $1.948 = $0.195]	=	2.143

greater than the previous year's. The interest accumulated over a single time period may seem rather modest, but when you add it up over many periods, the growth can be impressive. After about 7 1/2 years at 10 percent, your original $1 will have doubled. In other words, if you had invested $10 000, you'd have $20 000.

The Rule of 72

How long does it take to double an investment? A handy rule of thumb is called the "Rule of 72." You can find the number of years needed to double your money by dividing the annual interest rate (in percent) into 72. If, for example, you reinvest annually at 8 percent, you'll double your money in about 9 years:

$$\frac{72}{8} = 9$$

The Rule of 72 can also calculate how much interest you must get if you want to double your money in a given number of years: Simply divide 72 by the desired number of years. Thus, if you want to double your money in 10 years, you need to get 7.2 percent:

$$\frac{72}{10} = 7.2$$

Finally, the Rule of 72 highlights the downside as well as the upside of the compound-growth principle. The process means greater wealth for savers but increased indebtedness for borrowers. As we have seen, for example, an 8 percent rate doubles the principal every 9 years:

$$\frac{72}{8} = 9$$

Over a period of 36 years, the amount doubles four times:

$$\frac{36}{9} = 4$$

At 4 percent, by contrast, it doubles only twice over 36 years. Table B.2 charts the accumulation of the difference—$16 000 versus $4000—between investments (or loans) made at 8 percent versus 4 percent. The lesson for the personal-finance manager is clear: When investing (or saving), seek higher interest rates because money doubles more frequently; when borrowing, seek lower interest rates because indebtedness grows more slowly.

Table B.2 The Power of Doubling

Initial Investment (or Initial Unpaid Debt) = $1000

Number of Times Doubled	Value after Doubling
1	$2000
2	$4000
3	$8000
4	$16 000

Making Better Use of Your Time Value

Most people want to save for the future, either for things they need (down payments on a house, university or college tuition, retirement nest eggs) or for nonessentials (luxury items and recreation). Needless to say, the sooner you get started, the greater your financial power will be. You will have taken advantage of the time value of money for a longer period of time.

Consider the following illustration. Co-workers Ellen and Barbara are both planning to retire in 25 years. Let's assume that they are planning for a 10 percent annual return on investment (stock markets in North America have averaged about 10 percent over the past 75 years, with higher returns in some years and lower returns in others). Their savings strategies, however, are different. Whereas Barbara begins saving immediately, Ellen plans to start later but invest larger sums. Barbara will invest $2000 annually for each of the next five years (years 1–5), for a total investment of $10 000. She'll let interest accumulate through year 25. Ellen, meanwhile, wants to live a little larger by spending rather than saving for the next 10 years. Then, for years 11–20, she'll start saving $2000 annually, for a total investment of $20 000. She, too, will allow annual returns to accumulate until year 25, when both she and Barbara retire. Will Ellen have a larger retirement fund in year 25 because she's ultimately contributing twice as much as Barbara?

Not by a long shot. Barbara's retirement wealth will be much larger—$90 358 versus Ellen's $56 468—even though she invested only half as much ($10 000 versus $20 000). We explain the disparity by crunching all the numbers in Figure B.4. As you can see, Barbara's advantage lies in timing

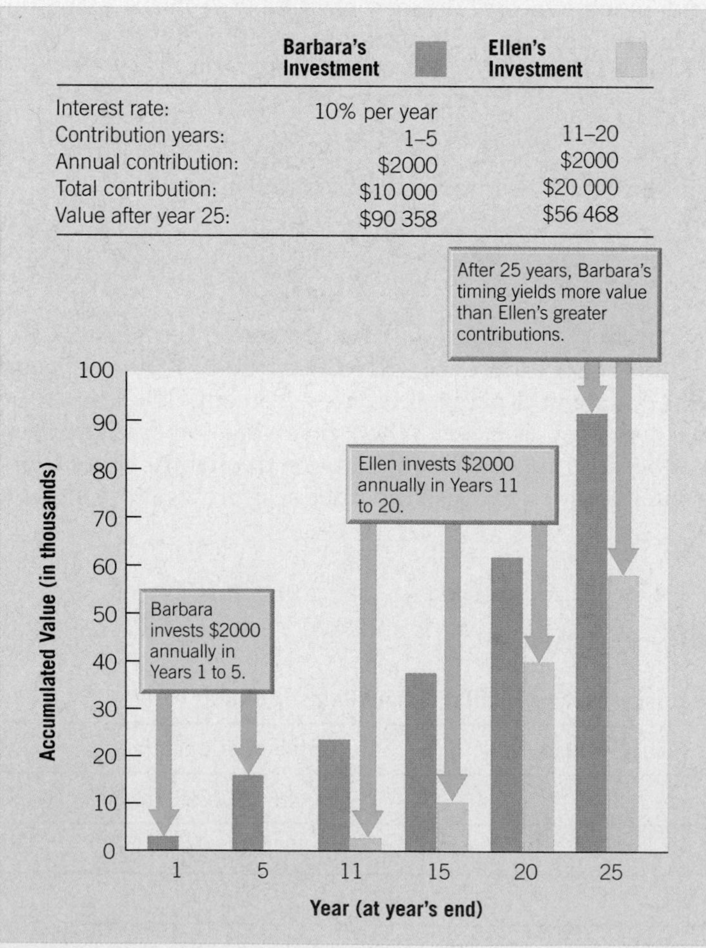

Figure B.4

—namely, the length of her savings program. Her money is invested longer—over a period of 21 to 25 years—with interest compounding over that range of time. Ellen's earnings are compounded over a shorter period—6 to 15 years. Granted, Ellen may have had more fun in years 1 to 5, but Barbara's retirement prospects look brighter.

Time Value as a Financial-Planning Tool

How much must you set aside today to accumulate enough money for something you want tomorrow? By its very nature, financial planning takes into account not only future needs (retirement, vacations, a wedding, major purchases) but also sources of funds for meeting those needs. Timing, however, is important. The timing of financial transactions will determine whether your plan works or doesn't work the way you intend. Start by considering the time value of money at the outset of your planning cycle. In this respect, various time-based tables for financial calculations are quite useful.[1] Table B.3, for example, shows how much a $1 investment will grow over different lengths of time and at different interest rates. Let's see how we can use this tool for financial planning.

Having recently inherited $50 000, Jason wants to invest for his old age. Specifically, he wants to accumulate a $200 000 nest egg by the time he reaches 55 (30 years from now). He also wants to spend some of the money while he's young enough to enjoy it, but he doesn't know how much he'll have left to spend after he's determined the amount needed to meet his retirement goal.

To help Jason with his planning, we first need to focus on our 30-year investment; thus $n = 30$ in Table B.3. As you can see, the accumulated value of that investment depends on the annual interest rate. At 4 percent, for instance, the growth factor is 3.243. Over 30 years, therefore, $1 invested now will grow to $3.243. Our question, then, is this: If $1 invested now yields $3.243, how many dollars must we invest now to accumulate $200 000 in 30 years? The answer is fairly simple. If $1 provides $3.243 in 30 years, and if we want to accumulate $200 000, we divide $200 000 by $3.243 to determine Jason needs to invest $61 671 to reach his retirement goal.

Jason's worksheet, which is shown in Table B.4, reveals trial calculations made with three different interest rates—conservative, moderate, optimistic—available from alternative investments. As you can see, a 4 percent return on investment won't provide the desired $200,000. If he gets only 4 percent, Jason would have to invest $61 671; but, as we know, he has only $50 000. As a matter of fact, if he invested the entire $50 000 at 4 percent, he'd end up with just $162 150 ($50 000 × $3.243 = $162 150), which is well below his $200 000 goal.

Thus Jason has two choices: find a higher-paying investment or, if he's willing to settle for 4 percent, reduce the amount of his desired nest egg. To make his decision, Jason can use the trial data contained in Table B.4. Projecting an investment at 8 percent, he needs to allocate only about $20 000 to start his nest egg and still have more than $30 000 for other uses. If he considers the 8 percent investment too risky, he may opt for the safer 6 percent return; in that case, he'd still have $15 175 left ($50 000 – $34 825).

CONSERVING MONEY BY CONTROLLING IT

Several steps in the financial planning process call for conserving money by paying attention to where it goes—by keeping spending within affordable limits and understanding on what you're spending your money.[2] As too many people have found out the hard way, a major pitfall in any financial

Table B.3 Timetable for Growing $1

n	1%	2%	3%	4%	5%	6%	7%	8%	9%	10%
1	1.010	1.020	1.030	1.040	1.050	1.060	1.070	1.080	1.090	1.100
2	1.020	1.040	1.061	1.082	1.102	1.124	1.145	1.166	1.188	1.210
3	1.030	1.061	1.093	1.125	1.158	1.191	1.225	1.260	1.295	1.331
4	1.041	1.082	1.126	1.170	1.216	1.262	1.311	1.360	1.412	1.464
5	1.051	1.104	1.159	1.217	1.276	1.338	1.403	1.469	1.539	1.611
6	1.062	1.126	1.194	1.265	1.340	1.419	1.501	1.587	1.677	1.772
7	1.072	1.149	1.230	1.316	1.407	1.504	1.606	1.714	1.828	1.949
8	1.083	1.172	1.267	1.369	1.477	1.594	1.718	1.851	1.993	2.144
9	1.094	1.195	1.305	1.423	1.551	1.689	1.838	1.999	2.172	2.358
10	1.105	1.219	1.344	1.480	1.629	1.791	1.967	2.159	2.367	2.594
11	1.116	1.243	1.384	1.539	1.710	1.898	2.105	2.332	2.580	2.853
12	1.127	1.268	1.426	1.601	1.796	2.012	2.252	2.518	2.813	3.138
13	1.138	1.294	1.469	1.665	1.886	2.133	2.410	2.720	3.066	3.452
14	1.149	1.319	1.513	1.732	1.980	2.261	2.579	2.937	3.342	3.797
15	1.161	1.346	1.558	1.801	2.079	2.397	2.759	3.172	3.642	4.177
16	1.173	1.373	1.605	1.873	2.183	2.540	2.952	3.426	3.970	4.595
17	1.184	1.400	1.653	1.948	2.292	2.693	3.159	3.700	4.328	5.054
18	1.196	1.428	1.702	2.026	2.407	2.854	3.380	3.996	4.717	5.560
19	1.208	1.457	1.753	2.107	2.527	3.026	3.616	4.316	5.142	6.116
20	1.220	1.486	1.806	2.191	2.653	3.207	3.870	4.661	5.604	6.727
21	1.232	1.516	1.860	2.279	2.786	3.399	4.140	5.034	6.109	7.400
22	1.245	1.546	1.916	2.370	2.925	3.603	4.430	5.436	6.658	8.140
23	1.257	1.577	1.974	2.465	3.071	3.820	4.740	5.871	7.258	8.954
24	1.270	1.608	2.033	2.563	3.225	4.049	5.072	6.341	7.911	9.850
25	1.282	1.641	2.094	2.666	3.386	4.292	5.427	6.848	8.623	10.834
30	1.348	1.811	2.427	3.243	4.322	5.743	7.612	10.062	13.267	17.449
40	1.489	2.208	3.262	4.801	7.040	10.285	14.974	21.724	31.408	45.258
50	1.645	2.691	4.384	7.106	11.467	18.419	29.456	46.900	74.354	117.386

continued

Table B.3 *continued*

n	11%	12%	13%	14%	15%	16%	17%	18%	19%	20%
1	1.110	1.120	1.130	1.140	1.150	1.160	1.170	1.180	1.190	1.200
2	1.232	1.254	1.277	1.300	1.322	1.346	1.369	1.392	1.416	1.440
3	1.368	1.405	1.443	1.482	1.521	1.561	1.602	1.643	1.685	1.728
4	1.518	1.574	1.630	1.689	1.749	1.811	1.874	1.939	2.005	2.074
5	1.685	1.762	1.842	1.925	2.011	2.100	2.192	2.288	2.386	2.488
6	1.870	1.974	2.082	2.195	2.313	2.436	2.565	2.700	2.840	2.988
7	2.076	2.211	2.353	2.502	2.660	2.826	3.001	3.185	3.379	3.583
8	2.305	2.476	2.658	2.853	3.059	3.278	3.511	3.759	4.021	4.300
9	2.558	2.773	3.004	3.252	3.518	3.803	4.108	4.435	4.785	5.160
10	2.839	3.106	3.395	3.707	4.046	4.411	4.807	5.234	5.695	6.192
11	3.152	3.479	3.836	4.226	4.652	5.117	5.624	6.176	6.777	7.430
12	3.498	3.896	4.334	4.818	5.350	5.936	6.580	7.288	8.064	8.916
13	3.883	4.363	4.898	5.492	6.153	6.886	7.699	8.599	9.596	10.699
14	4.310	4.887	5.535	6.261	7.076	7.987	9.007	10.147	11.420	12.839
15	4.785	5.474	6.254	7.138	8.137	9.265	10.539	11.974	13.589	15.407
16	5.311	6.130	7.067	8.137	9.358	10.748	12.330	14.129	16.171	18.488
17	5.895	6.866	7.986	9.276	10.761	12.468	14.426	16.672	19.244	22.186
18	6.543	7.690	9.024	10.575	12.375	14.462	15.879	19.673	22.900	26.623
19	7.263	8.613	10.197	12.055	14.232	16.776	19.748	23.214	27.251	31.948
20	8.062	9.646	11.523	13.743	16.366	19.461	23.105	27.393	32.429	38.337
21	8.949	10.804	13.021	15.667	18.821	22.574	27.033	32.323	38.591	46.005
22	9.933	12.100	14.713	17.861	21.644	26.186	31.629	38.141	45.923	55.205
23	11.026	13.552	16.626	20.361	24.891	30.376	37.005	45.007	54.648	66.247
24	12.239	15.178	18.788	23.212	28.625	35.236	43.296	53.108	65.031	79.496
25	13.585	17.000	21.230	26.461	32.918	40.874	50.656	62.667	77.387	95.395
30	22.892	29.960	39.115	50.949	66.210	85.849	111.061	143.367	184.672	237.373
40	64.999	93.049	132.776	188.876	267.856	378.715	533.846	750.353	1051.642	1469.740
50	184.559	288.996	450.711	700.197	1083.619	1670.669	2566.080	3927.189	5988.730	9100.191

n = Number of time periods
% = Various interest rates

Table B.4 Nest Egg Worksheet

	Investment Returns (annual rate)			Your numbers
	Conservative 4%	Moderate 6%	Optimistic 8%	%
Ending amount after 30 years:	$200 000	$200 000	$200 000	____
Growth factor (from table):	3.243	5.743	10.062	____
Amount* to invest now (end amount/ growth factor):	$61 671**	$34 825	$19 877	____
	($200 000/3.243)	($200 000/5.743)	($200 000/10.062)	

*Rounded to nearest whole dollar.
**This amount is greater than the available $50 000.

plan is the temptation to spend too much, especially when credit is so easy to get. Consumers often lose track of how much they spend, and, to make matters worse, some don't consider the costly finance charges associated with easy credit. Because many credit-card issuers target university and college students and recent graduates with tempting offers appealing to the desire for financial independence, we'll use the following section to explain the financial costs entailed by credit cards. Keep in mind, however, that the same lessons apply equally to home-equity loans, consumer finance agreements, and other sources of credit.

Credit Cards: Keys to Consumer Satisfaction or Fiscal Handcuffs?

Although some credit cards don't charge annual fees, all of them charge interest on unpaid (outstanding) balances. Because credit-card debt is one of the most expensive sources of funds, you need to understand the costs before you start charging instead of being surprised when you open the bill. For one thing, many card users don't realize how much interest they're paying or how long it will take them to pay off their bills.

Table B.5 reprints a page from California's "Minimum Payment Credit Card Calculation." Using the table as a guide, let's consider the following situation. Suppose you owe $5000 for credit-card purchases and your card company requires a minimum monthly payment of 5 percent of the unpaid balance. The interest rate is 18 percent APR (annual percentage rate) on the outstanding balance. (By the way, these aren't too high: Some rates are well above 20 percent.)

Thus, Table B.5 reflects an account with $5000 outstanding balance at the end of last month. This is the amount on which your interest of 18 percent APR is charged. Remember, too, that your card company requires a minimum monthly payment (minimum payment due—or MPD) of 5 percent (of the current balance). Let's assume that you pay only the monthly minimum and ask ourselves two questions:

1. How many months will it take to pay off the $5000?
2. How much interest will you have paid when you do pay it off?

In Table B.5, the column labelled "MPD 5%" reveals that at 18 percent APR it will take you 115 months to pay off $5000. That's approximately 9 1/2 years! And remember: This number assumes that your balance gradually diminishes to zero because you add no other purchases to the card. Your total payment of $7096.70 covers your $5000 debt plus interest charges. An immediate cash payoff, therefore, would avoid $2096.70 in interest payments.

Why does repayment take so long? In Table B.6, we run through some sample calculations for the first two months in your 115-month repayment process. As you can see, your minimum monthly payment decreases because your ending balance gets smaller with each monthly payment. Your $250 payment in February includes $75 in interest owed on the $5000 balance in the previous month. At 18 percent APR, interest on $5000 would be $900 for a year (0.18 × $5000), but for one month (January), it's only 1/12 of that amount—$75. You're paying the rest of your February instalment of $175 ($250 – $75) on the principal amount, thereby reducing the month-end balance to $4825. If we carry out these calculations over 115 months, we find that, when your account is paid in full, you've made "payments on principal" of $5000 and interest payments of $2096.70.

Table B.5 Paying Off Credit-Card Debt

Balance = $5000.00

	MPD 2%		MPD 3%		MPD 4%		MPD 5%		MPD 10%	
APR	**Months**	**Cost**	**Months**	**Cost**	**Months**	**Cost**	**Months**	**Cost**	**Months**	**Cost**
6%	211	$6,576.80	144	$5,965.56	111	$5,696.30	92	$5,544.58	50	$5,260.74
7%	221	$6,945.82	148	$6,164.85	114	$5,831.99	93	$5,647.25	50	$5,306.87
8%	233	$7,360.22	153	$6,378.23	116	$5,974.39	95	$5,753.83	51	$5,353.84
9%	246	$7,829.02	158	$6,607.24	119	$6,124.04	96	$5,864.56	51	$5,401.63
10%	262	$8,363.77	163	$6,853.07	122	$6,281.51	98	$5,979.70	52	$6,450.30
11%	279	$8,979.59	169	$7,119.61	125	$6,447.40	100	$6,099.50	52	$5,499.87
12%	299	$9,696.61	175	$7,407.50	128	$6,622.45	102	$6,224.26	53	$5,550.32
13%	323	$10,542.23	182	$7,720.16	131	$6,807.42	104	$6,354.29	53	$5,601.75
14%	351	$11,554.78	189	$8,060.94	134	$7,003.17	106	$6,489.94	53	$5,654.11
15%	385	$12,789.56	197	$8,433.88	138	$7,210.72	108	$6,631.59	54	$5,707.49
16%	428	$14,329.44	206	$8,843.78	142	$7,431.13	110	$6,779.63	54	$5,761.88
17%	482	$16,304.46	216	$9,296.40	146	$7,665.64	112	$6,934.49	55	$5,817.33
18%	553	$18,931.11	226	$9,798.89	150	$7,915.67	115	$7,096.70	55	$5,873.86
19%	652	$22,598.52	238	$10,359.98	155	$8,182.84	117	$7,266.77	56	$5,931.51
20%	799	$28,083.97	251	$10,990.60	160	$8,468.05	120	$7,445.32	56	$5,990.30
21%	1040	$37,198.63	266	$11,704.63	165	$8,776.09	123	$7,632.92	57	$6,050.28
22%	1518	$55,367.78	283	$12,519.87	171	$9,106.71	126	$7,830.38	58	$6,111.48
23%	2930	$109,673.97	303	$13,459.58	177	$9,463.60	129	$8,038.42	58	$6,173.93
24%	*	*	325	$14,554.76	184	$9,850.03	132	$8,257.96	59	$6,237.69
25%	*	*	352	$15,847.75	191	$10,269.86	135	$8,489.97	59	$6,302.77

Practise Paying Off Your Debt

Using the method illustrated in Table B.6, you should be able to answer the following questions about credit-card repayment (the answers appear at the end of this appendix):

1. According to the data in Table B.6, your minimum monthly payment for April would be which of the following? [select one] (a) $232.81; (b) $253.47; (c) $230.56; (d) $226.18.
2. According to the data in Table B.6, for April, the interest owed on your previous balance would be which of the following? [select one] (a) $70.43; (b) $71.94; (c) $69.84; (d) $68.32.
3. According to the data in Table B.6, for April, your ending balance owed on principal would be which of the following? [select one] (a) $4182.16; (b) $4493.16; (c) $4517.22; (d) $4334.97.

Save Your Money: Lower Interest Rates and Faster Payments

A closer look at Table B.5 confirms two principles for saving money that you can apply when borrowing from any source, not just credit cards: Look for lower interest rates and make faster repayments.

Seeking Lower Interest Rates

Because higher interest rates obviously mean more expensive money, you save money with lower interest rates (money that you can "stretch" by using it for other things). With a little research, you'll find that potential creditors charge different rates (ranging from below 10 percent to over 20 percent APR among credit-card issuers). How much can you save? Look again at Table B.5 and compare the cost of borrowing $5000 at 18 percent with the cost of borrowing it at 9 percent. If you assume the same 5 percent minimum monthly payment, how much interest does 9 percent save you over the life of the repayment? The answer is $1232.14 ($864.56 instead of $2096.70). That's a nearly 59 percent savings.

Making Faster Payments

Because money has a time value, lenders charge borrowers according to the length of time for which they borrow it. In general, longer lending periods increase the cost, while shorter periods are cheaper. Accordingly, borrowers often speed up payments to cut interest costs. Using Table B.5, for example, compare the costs of the "5% MPD" (required monthly payment of 5 percent

Table B.6 Calculating Minimum Monthly Payments

Month	Minimum Monthly Payment (5% of Previous Ending Balance)	=	Interest Owed on Previous Balance* (1/12 × 18%) Previous Balance)	+	Payment on Principal	Ending Balance Owed on Principal
January	—		—		—	$5000
February	$250 [0.05 × $5000]	=	$75 [1/12 × 0.18 × $5000]	+	$175	$4825 [5000 – 175]
March	$241.25 [0.05 × 4825]	=	$72.38 [1/12 × 0.18 × 4825]	+	$168.87	$4656.13 [4825 – 168.87]

*Monthly interest is calculated using 1/12 of annual interest rate.

on the remaining balance) with the faster "10% MPD." The faster schedule cuts the repayment period from 115 to 55 months and, at 18 percent APR, reduces interest costs by $1222.84 (7096.70 – 5873.86).

What if you combined both faster repayment and the lower interest rate (9 percent versus 18 percent)? You'd cut your total interest cost to just $450.30—a savings of $1695.07 over the amount you'd pay if you made slower repayments at the higher rate.

FINANCIAL COMMITMENTS OF HOME OWNERSHIP

Should you rent or buy the roof you need over your head? The answer to that question involves a variety of considerations, including life stage, family needs, career, financial situation, and preferred lifestyle. If you decide to buy, for example, you have to ask yourself how much house you can afford. To answer that question, you need to ask yourself a number of questions about your personal financial condition and your capacity for borrowing.

To Buy or Not to Buy: That Is the Question

Renting is attractive because you can move in without making an initial investment (or at least making a hefty down payment). That's why it's a popular choice among young adults, especially singles with limited budgets and people whose lifestyles aren't congenial to settling down in a fixed location. Flexibility, mobility, and freedom from obligations of maintenance and upkeep are important advantages. Financially speaking, however, rent payments are cash outflows that provide future financial benefits to owners instead of renters.

By the same token, first-time homebuyers cite the prospect of future financial gain as an attractive reason for buying. The financial inducements are in fact powerful, including home equity, increasing property values, and tax advantages. You can see if buying is a good idea for you by consulting a "rent-versus-buy calculator" on the Web, such as the one at www.ginniemae.gov/. By letting you try various interest rates, down payments, loan lengths, and rental costs, calculators specify the financial advantages of renting or buying under a wide range of financial circumstances.

Many younger adults with children report that they choose to buy because they want privacy, space, and the freedom to choose a neighbourhood. Finally, most home buyers say that they get satisfaction from a sense of ownership—from having their own property. Table B.7 summarizes the key considerations in deciding whether to rent or buy a place to live.

How Much House Can You Afford?

For most people, buying a home is the biggest investment they'll ever make. But even though ownership, as we've seen, bestows several benefits, many people make the regrettable mistake of buying a house that's too expensive for their pocketbooks. Don't saddle yourself with house payments that you can't afford. In addition, new homebuyers quickly discover that the typical demands of ownership—especially the demand on their time and other resources for maintaining and improving a home—tend to cut into the money left over for recreation, eating out, taking vacations, and buying new cars. You can reduce the financial pressure by calculating in advance a realistic price range—one that not only lets you buy a house but also lets you live a reasonably pleasant life once you're in it.

Most people need a loan to buy a house or a condominium. A mortgage loan is a loan that's secured by the property—the home—being purchased. Because the size of a loan depends on the cost of the property, both borrowers and lenders want to know whether the buyer can afford the house they want. How can you determine how much you can afford? One time-tested (though somewhat conservative) rule of thumb cautions the buyer to keep the price below 2 1/2 times his or her annual income. Thus, if your income is $48 000, look for a house priced below $120 000.

Any such calculation, however, will give you just a rough estimate of what you can afford. There are other considerations. What you can afford also depends on how much money you have for a down payment and how much you can borrow. Lending institutions use two guidelines for estimating a buyer's borrowing capacity: (1) the borrower's ability to meet the recurring costs of buying and owning, and (2) other long-term debt that the buyer has already incurred.

PITI

What are those recurring costs? Every month, the homeowner must pay principal, interest, taxes, and insurance—*PITI,* for short. Because all four costs are greater for more expensive homes, the buyer's monthly obligation depends on how much house he or she has bought. The size of principal and interest payments depends on the mortgage amount, the length of the mortgage loan, and the interest rate. Obviously, if you borrow a fixed amount, the larger your monthly payment, the faster you'll pay off your loan. As Table B.8 shows, monthly payments on conventional loans are lower for longer-term loans and higher for larger interest rates.

In evaluating loan applications, lenders use PITI calculations to estimate the buyer's financial capacity—his or her ability to meet monthly payments. To determine how much someone is likely to lend you, calculate 28 percent of your gross monthly income (that is, before taxes and other deductions). If your PITI costs don't exceed that figure, you'll probably get the loan. With a monthly gross income of $4000, for example, your PITI costs shouldn't exceed $1120 (28 percent of $4000). Figure B.5 gives a sample calculation, and you should be able to make step-by-step computations by plugging your own numbers into the worksheet.

Table B.7 To Buy or Not to Buy

Renting	Buying
• No down payment to get started	• Must make payments for mortgage, property taxes, and insurance
• Flexibility to leave	• Equity builds up over time
• No obligation for upkeep or improvements	• More privacy
• No groundskeeping	• Value of property may increase
• Easy cash-flow planning (a single monthly payment)	
• May provide access to recreation and social facilities	• Financial gains from selling house can be exempt from taxes
• Rental conditions may be changed by owner	• Greater control over use of property and improvements
• Timing for repairs controlled by owner	• The home can become a source of cash by refinancing with another mortgage loan or a home-equity loan

Other Long-Term Debt

In evaluating financial capacity, lenders also look at any outstanding debt that will take the borrower more than 10 months to pay off, such as car loans, child support and alimony payments, student loans, and credit-card bills. In general, they will accept long-term indebtedness (including PITI) that amounts to 36 percent of gross income. Remember: Because PITI itself can be up to 28 percent, you might be allowed as little as 8 percent in other long-term debt. With your $4000 monthly gross income, your total debt should be less than $1440 (which allows $1120 for PITI and $320 for other debt). If your total debt exceeds $1440, you may have to settle for a smaller loan than the one you calculated with the PITI method. Figure B.6 gives an example of such an alternative calculation; again, you can plug your own numbers into the worksheet.

Table B.8 Monthly Mortgage Payments on a $10 000 Loan

	Length of Loan					
Interest Rate (%)	**10 Years**	**15 Years**	**20 Years**	**25 Years**	**30 Years**	**40 Years**
5.0	$106.07	$79.08	$66.00	$58.46	$53.68	$48.22
5.5	108.53	81.71	68.79	61.41	56.79	51.58
6.0	111.02	84.39	71.64	64.43	59.96	50.22
6.5	113.55	87.11	74.56	67.52	63.21	58.55
7.0	116.11	89.88	77.53	70.68	66.53	62.14
7.5	118.71	92.71	80.56	73.00	69.93	65.81
8.0	121.33	95.57	83.65	77.19	73.38	69.53
8.5	123.99	98.48	86.79	80.53	76.90	73.31
9.0	126.68	101.43	89.98	83.92	80.47	77.14
9.5	129.40	104.43	93.22	87.37	84.09	81.01
10.0	132.16	107.47	96.51	90.88	87.76	84.91
10.5	134.94	110.54	99.84	94.42	91.48	88.86
11.0	137.76	113.66	103.22	98.02	95.24	92.83
11.5	140.60	116.82	106.65	101.65	99.03	96.83
12.0	143.48	120.02	110.11	105.33	102.86	100.85
12.5	146.38	123.26	113.62	109.04	106.73	104.89
13.0	149.32	126.53	117.16	112.79	110.62	108.95
13.5	152.27	129.83	120.74	116.56	114.54	113.03
14.0	155.27	133.17	124.35	120.38	118.49	117.11
14.5	158.29	136.55	128.00	124.22	122.46	121.21
15.0	161.33	139.96	131.68	128.08	126.44	125.32

If you want to go into more detail about your own payment capabilities, search for websites that provide mortgage calculators for testing interest rates, lengths of loans, and other personal financial information.

PROTECTING YOUR NET WORTH

With careful attention, thoughtful saving and spending, and skilful financial planning (and a little luck), you can build up your net worth over time. In addition to steps for accumulating net worth, therefore, every financial plan should consider steps for preserving it. One approach involves the risk–return relationship that we discussed in Chapter 20. Do you prefer to protect your current assets, or are you willing to risk them in return for greater growth? At various life stages, and whenever you reach a designated level of wealth, you should adjust your asset portfolio to conform to your risk and return preferences—conservative, moderate, or aggressive. Another approach is life insurance.

ASSUMPTIONS:

30-year mortgage
Closing costs (fees for property survey, credit report, title search, title insurance, attorney, interest advance, loan origination) = $5000
Funds available for closing costs and down payment = $25 000
Interest rate on mortgage = $6\frac{1}{2}$% per year
Estimated real estate taxes = $200 per month
Estimated homeowner's insurance = $20 per month

Example Numbers		Your Numbers
1. Monthly income, gross (before taxes or deductions).......	$4000	________
2. Apply PITI ratio (0.28 x amount on line 1) to determine borrower's payment capacity: 0.28 x $4000 = ...	$1120	________
3. Determine mortgage payment (principal and interest) by subtracting taxes and insurance from PITI (line 2):...	– $ 220	________
4. Result: Maximum mortgage payment (principal and interest)..	**$ 900**	________
5. Using Table B.8, find the monthly mortgage payment on a $10 000 loan at $6\frac{1}{2}$% interest for 30 years...	$63.21	________
6. Since each $10 000 loan requires a $63.21 monthly payment, how many $10 000 loans can the borrower afford with the $900 payment capacity? The answer is determined as follows: $900.00/$63.21 = 14.2382 loans of $10 000 each.		________
7. Result: Maximum allowable mortgage loan calculated as follows: 14.2382 loans (from line 6 above) x $10 000 per loan] = ...	**$142 382**	________
8. Result: Maximum house price borrower can afford using PITI (amount of house that can be bought with available funds):		
From loan..................	$142 382	________
From down payment....	$ 25 000	________
Less closing cost.......	– $ 5 000	________
....	**$162 382**	________

Figure B.5

Life Insurance

You can also think of life insurance as a tool for financial preservation. As explained in Chapter 20, a life insurance policy is a promise to pay beneficiaries after the death of an insured party. In return, of course, insurance companies collect *premiums*—payments from the insurance purchaser—during his or her lifetime.

What Does Life Insurance Do?

From a personal-finance perspective, the purpose of life insurance is to replace income upon the death of the policyholder. Accordingly, the amount of insurance you need depends on how many other people rely on your income. Insurance, for example, is crucial for the married parent who is a family's sole source of income. On the other hand, a single person with no

ASSUMPTIONS:

30-year mortgage
Closing costs = $5000
Funds available for closing costs and down payment = $25 000
Interest rate on mortgage = $6\frac{1}{2}$% per year
Estimated real estate taxes = $200 per month
Estimated homeowner's insurance = $20 per month

Example Numbers		Your Numbers
1. Monthly income, gross (before taxes or deductions)............	$4000	______
2. Apply debt ratio (0.36 x amount on line 1) to determine borrower's payment capacity: 0.36 x $4000 = ...	$1440	______
3. Less current payments on non-mortgage debts that will last more than 10 months: car loan.......................-$ 300; student loan................-$ 100; credit card debt...........-$ 100	-$ 500	
4. Less taxes and insurance for house................................	-$ 220	______
5. Result: Maximum mortgage payment (principal and interest)....................	**$ 720**	______
6. Using Table B.8, find the monthly mortgage payment payment on a $10 000 loan at $6\frac{1}{2}$% interest for 30 years....................	$63.21	______
7. Since each $10 000 loan requires a $63.21 monthly payment, how many $10 000 loans can the borrower afford with the $720 payment capacity? The answer is determined as follows: $720.00/$63.21 = 11.3906 loans of $10 000 each		______
8. Result: Maximum allowable mortgage loan [calculated as follows: 11.3906 loans (from line 7 above) x $10 000 per loan]........................	**$113 906**	______
9. Result: Maximum house price borrower can afford (amount of house that can be bought with available funds):		
From loan..................$113 906		______
From down payment...$ 25 000		______
Less closing costs.....-$ 5 000		______
....	**$133 906**	______

Figure B.6

financial dependents needs little or no insurance and will probably prefer to put money into higher-paying investments.

How Much Should I Buy?

To estimate the amount you need, begin by adding up all of the annual expenses—rent, food, clothing, transportation, schooling, debts to be paid—that you pay for the dependents who would survive you. Then multiply the total by the number of years that you want the insurance to cover your dependents. Typically, this sum will amount to several times your current annual income. Thus many policyholders, especially during the life stages of highest need—are insured for 10 to 20 times their annual salaries.

Two Basic Types of Insurance

Term insurance pays a predetermined benefit when death occurs during the stipulated term—say, 10, 20, or 30 years—covered by the policy. If the insured outlives the term, the policy loses its value and simply ceases. When it is in force, however, the insured knows that it will provide funds to beneficiaries if he or she dies. Premiums for term life insurance are significantly lower than premiums for whole life insurance.

Unlike term life, *whole-life insurance*—also known as *cash-value insurance*—remains in force as long as premiums are paid. In addition to paying a death benefit, whole life accumulates cash value over time—a form of savings. Once the insured reaches a point at which he or she no longer needs the coverage, paid-in money can be withdrawn. Whole-life savings, however, earn less interest than most alternative forms of investment.

How Much Does It Cost?

The cost of insurance, of course, depends on how much you buy. But it also depends on your life expectancy and other risk factors that insurers determine statistically. Premiums are higher for people whose life expectancies are shorter, whether because of gender, age, weight, occupation, or pre-existing health conditions.

The lower cost of term insurance is an important consideration, not just for people on limited incomes, but also for those seeking higher returns from other types of investment. A healthy, 30-year-old, non-smoking female, for example, can expect to pay about $360 a year for a $300 000 term policy and about $600 to $700 a year for a $1 million term policy. Depending on the insurer and the conditions of coverage, whole life may cost the same person up to 10 times as much as term. To get the best match between your policy and your personal situation, therefore, you should evaluate the terms and conditions of a variety of policies. You can get convenient comparisons on websites such as IntelliQuote.com (www.intelliquote.com).

Answers to "Practise Paying Off Your Debt"

1. Item (a) is the correct answer, obtained as follows:

   Minimum monthly payment
   (5% of previous ending balance):
   April $232.81 = (0.05 × $4656.13)

2. Item (c) is the correct answer, obtained as follows:

   Interest owed on previous balance
   (1/12 × 0.18 × previous balance):
   April $69.84 = (1/12 × 0.18 × $4656.13)

3. Item (b) is the correct answer, obtained as follows:

Payment on principal (monthly payment– monthly interest)	Ending balance owed on principal (previous balance– payment on principal)
April \$162.97 = (\$232.81 – \$69.84)	\$4493.16 = (\$4656.13 – \$162.97)

A Midsummer Day's Nightmare

Lindsay Sawyer and John Melnyk

DISCUSSION QUESTIONS/OBJECTIVES

1. What is the problem here? Why is it a problem?
2. To whom or to what do you have a responsibility in this situation? Why?
3. What fundamental purposes, principles, and potential consequences are relevant here? Construct consequential, principled, and purposive arguments, both for and against alternatives you consider relevant.
4. As the decision maker of this case, how would you proceed and why?

A Midsummer Day's Nightmare

I started work at a nationally known fast food restaurant when I was seventeen. I had had other jobs, but none of them was as much fun as this one. I reported for my first shift and was introduced to a new atmosphere that was unlike anything I had experienced before.

One of the first things I learned was that having fun was really encouraged. Smiles were the norm, and, in fact, expected. This friendly environment led to a lot of fast friendships with my co-workers, especially since we all went to neighbouring high schools. Our employer encouraged these ties and would organize activities for us outside of work.

We enjoyed these outings, but the best "perk" by far was the food, which was half price to employees, even outside of scheduled shifts! We could even informally extend this discount to friends once in a while, which made it an even more enviable privilege.

I loved my job and worked very hard at it. After fourteen months I got my first promotion. Six months later I was promoted again to a junior management position along with two of my co-workers.

We received very little preparation to deal with this move up to management. We were given a workbook covering topics such as food safety, employee relations, shift planning, scheduling, etc., and were supposed to get time on the job to work through it and then go to classes. But that never happened. However, we were all told immediately about the importance of management always presenting a united front. Most of our training was on the job—we were given a different colour shirt, a new nametag, and encouraged to do our best. My first shift as a manager I was left alone to supervise a busy dinner hour.

My promotions brought me into more frequent contact with Michael Roberts, area manager for the district. Michael was a scary figure to all store employees because whenever he came in he found faults. Heaven help you if your personal grooming wasn't perfect, if you didn't have your nametag on, or even if you weren't using the prescribed pattern to mop the floor!

Now that I was in a management position, Michael knew me by name, and made a point of talking to me every time he came in. I suddenly had to develop a working relationship with him and meet his high standards.

There were many benefits to this promotion though, the best of which was now, free food! The expensive items on the menu were now always available to us. We would take advantage of this whenever we could, sometimes eating three meals a day at our restaurant! We now also had the authority to reward our subordinates with free food.

Because we were a small branch, we rarely had more than one manager working at a time, which left me completely in charge during my shift. This meant that it was up to me to ensure that company standards were met and that all customers were satisfied, as well as to deal with any complaints. I also had to make sure everything was in place for the next shift; if there was something that I wasn't able to finish, I had to communicate it clearly to the manager of the next shift.

I also became privy to more knowledge about our store. I quickly learned that we had trouble making a profit because the restaurant was so small. As a result we had to be very careful about expenses, especially food wastage. We would order $5000 to $6000 of supplies every week to ten days, and try to be careful to order only what we would need. As a result sometimes we would run out of something, or several things, before the next order. I hated when that happened.

If it was just a little thing, like milk or tomatoes, we would buy some at retail to tide us over, although this was not encouraged. For more basic items, like hamburger patties and buns, I had to phone around to other outlets and "beg" to "borrow" some supplies. This was a real hassle, and irritating to the other managers too. Furthermore, we often had only two or three employees working at a time, so it was a huge inconvenience to send one to pick up supplies—that is, provided I could convince someone with a driver's licence and gas in their car to go. I once had to go myself on a busy Saturday during Christmas season to pick up eighty trays of buns. It took me three hours and my mom's SUV.

Most of the equipment in our restaurant was old and in bad repair. We couldn't get authorization to replace it, so we had to make do. When I complained, I was told to use the manuals and try to fix it myself! I had absolutely no idea how to service these temperamental machines that would often act up, especially when we were busy. I once had an ice cream machine explode goo all over me for my trouble trying to fix it.

The air conditioning didn't always work either, but the grills were by far the most troublesome. They would stop heating properly in the middle of the day and not cook the food thoroughly. I got to know several repairmen on a first-name basis; we spent many hours going over this problem together.

Nevertheless I persevered, and over the next ten months I gained valuable experience and completed all the necessary steps to be promoted again. Towards the end of this period I met with my restaurant manager several times, and she assured me that a promotion was in the works, subject to the approval of the area manager.

I was really looking forward to that... it would mean I would no longer have to wear a hat on the job!

ONE SUMMER DAY...

One summer day I came in to open the restaurant after a day off. It was 6:00 a.m. and already warm outside, even more so inside the store because the air conditioning didn't work well. I started getting the computer system up and counting the cash, and sent the open staff person, Jason, to start making the muffins and getting the tables ready for our 7:00 a.m. opening.

As I was counting the cash, Jason called to me from the back. He was young and somewhat excitable, so I didn't think anything of it as I went over to see what was the matter.

Jason gestured excitedly and directed me towards the large walk-in freezer, insisting I look inside. I went into the freezer to take a look. I didn't like going in there because it was always so cold. But not today!

The freezer was room temperature! It must have been off overnight!

> *"Oh NO!"* I thought,

as I looked in an open box of chicken and picked up a piece. It was warm and squishy; the coating crumbled off on my hand. I opened a box of hamburger patties and touched one on top. It felt mushy, and was beginning to lose its shape. I leaned over and opened a box in the middle. It was cool, and the meat in the centre of the box seemed still frozen.

My mind started racing. I ran to the phone to call my restaurant manager; I knew she was opening at another location that morning. It was about 6:30 a.m. Pat picked up the phone after several rings.

> *"Hi Pat, it's me... umm... I have a really big problem. You see... uh... "*
>
> *"Jennifer, I'm really busy! Hurry up!"* she snapped.
>
> *"I came in this morning and the freezer has been off for hours. Everything is goopy and gross and I don't know what to do. It's disgusting!"*
>
> *"WHAT! You've got to be kidding. Who the hell was working yesterday? I just don't believe this. Damn! I'm too busy to deal with this now. Call Mike."* Click—she hung up.

I looked at my watch; it was 6:35 a.m. I had to call Michael at home.

> *"Hi Michael, it's Jennifer from 82nd West... Pat told me to call you!"* I blurted out. *"Sorry about this, but I have a big problem. Our freezer has been off for several hours, the food's gross and mushy. I don't know what to do."*

There was a brief pause as Michael woke up.

> *"What? Are you joking? Why is the freezer off? Is it broken? Is it unplugged?"*
>
> *"Umm... I don't really know."*

In a panic I ran to the back room to figure out why the freezer wasn't on. The answer was at the fuse box, where I discovered the freezer circuits were in the "off" position. Quickly I reset them. I knew we had received a supply order the day before. In order to save energy in the heat of the day, the freezer was likely shut off while the order was carried in. This wouldn't have been a problem... if only someone had remembered to turn it back on.

I could tell Michael was seething, but he controlled it well.

> *"OK, as long as all the cooking temperatures are met, the food will be all right. You can still use everything there."*
>
> He went on, *"It's important that we don't cause a panic about this. Don't talk about it in the restaurant and make sure food temperatures are met. Everything will be OK. Continue your shift Jennifer." "Uh... OK... umm... "*

I hung up the phone in a daze. I couldn't quite bring myself to carry out those instructions right away. I felt confused and upset, as I stood lost in my thoughts searching for some instruction or part of my training for guidance. I knew what to do if there was a bomb threat, but nothing had prepared me for this.

I had about twenty minutes worth of food in our small freezers up front. Jason was waiting for my instructions. I looked at my watch—it was 6:45 a.m.

APPENDIX

Exhibit 1 Excerpts from the Food and Drug Act, and Food and Drug Regulations, as Administered by Health Canada

Interpretation

"Unsanitary conditions" means such conditions or circumstances as might contaminate with dirt or filth, or render injurious to health, a food, drug or cosmetic.

Food

4. No person shall sell an article of food that
   a) has in or on it any poisonous or harmful substance;
   b) is unfit for human consumption;
   c) consists in whole or in part of any filthy, putrid, disgusting, rotten, decomposed or diseased animal or vegetable substance;
   d) is adulterated; or
   e) was manufactured, prepared, preserved, packaged or stored under unsanitary conditions.

Sale of Barbecued, Roasted or Broiled Meat or Meat By-Products

B.14.072 No person shall sell meat or a meat by-product that has been barbecued, roasted or broiled and is ready for consumption unless the cooked meat or meat by-product

(a) at all times

(i) has a temperature of 40° F (4.4° C) or lower, or 140° F (60° C) or higher,

or

(ii) has been stored at an ambient temperature of 40° F (4.4° C) or lower, or 140° F (60° C) or higher

(b) carries on the principal display panel of the label a statement to the effect that the food must be stored at a temperature of 40° F (4.4° C) or lower, or 140° F (60° C) or higher.

An Evaluation of the Parking Ticket Payment Processing System in the City of Waterloo

David Hemsworth, Loralee Nicol, Jon Mesquita, Cristóbal Sánchez-Rodriguez, Bettina Bosch, and Sarah Gage

Case Study Number: 050031-W

The City of Waterloo is aware of residents' complaints about the payment options available for paying parking tickets. This, compounded with the high costs and potential inefficiencies of their current processing systems, has prompted Carol Walker to investigate possible options. This case focuses on the evaluation of their current information system and three other possible options.

DISCUSSION QUESTIONS/OBJECTIVES

QUESTIONS

1. Should Waterloo outsource the processing of parking tickets and get out of the parking ticket business entirely?
2. Which system(s) should they select, if any?
3. Should Waterloo hide the online patron ticket fee ($1.50) in the ticket costs to promote online or phone usage, or, alternately, should the city "eat" the patron online ticket fee since they will save money in administration, thus promoting use of the system? Should this cost be spread across all of the tickets or levied against only those who would use the new system? Remember, if people pay online, the lineups at the city centre will be shorter!

OBJECTIVES

1. *IT Project Selection:* Students will learn how to apply the tools and techniques that IT professionals use when assessing various project alternatives. This includes an in-depth financial analysis as well as an examination of the qualitative aspects involved in the decision.

2. *Technology:* Students will gain insights into the complexities, technology, and infrastructure of a typical city's manual parking ticket payment information system.
3. *IT Deployment:* Students will be able to identify and discuss how new technology can be implemented to increase customer satisfaction and automate the ticket payment process.

An Evaluation of the Parking Ticket Payment Processing System in the City of Waterloo

INTRODUCTION

Carol Walker sighed and shook her head as she hung up the phone. Yet another customer was complaining that they could not pay their ticket on the Web or by phone. It was only Tuesday afternoon, but already this week she had received five calls that made similar complaints, and expressed frustration with the current lack of choices available for parking ticket payment. Unfortunately, the City of Waterloo (population 100,000) had not upgraded its parking ticket system to include any of the new payment options, such as over the Internet, by phone, or at the bank. Tickets could be paid only in person at the Waterloo City Centre, or by mailing a cheque to the city. Each year the City of Waterloo issues 32,000 tickets. It was Carol's aspiration to provide more convenient methods of ticket payment, possibly through the web, telephone, kiosks, or banks.

Carol, the team leader for the Bylaw Enforcement Department, was as frustrated by this inefficient system as the ticket payers were. Under the current system, tickets were being paid very slowly and administrative costs to collect on overdue accounts were high. Carol was thinking that something had to be done to satisfy these needs as she quickly drafted an email to Jerry Filmore, the Director of Information Systems. She referred to the large number of phone calls she had received from annoyed patrons who were unimpressed with the current payment methods. In the past, Carol had spoken with Jerry regarding the possibility of enhancing the current payment system, however, the discussions never really evolved into a plan of action.

BACKGROUND

After sending an email to Jerry regarding the problem, Carol walked out of her office and towards the staff lounge. On her way there, she happened to pass the city's vision statement. It read, "The City of Waterloo is a progressive organization built on principles which anticipate and satisfy the requirements of our customers, achieved through a team of committed, highly skilled and valued people" (**www.city.waterloo.on.ca**). While reading this statement, she thought, "this sure doesn't describe the evolution of the parking ticket payment system in Waterloo."

Carol had begun researching on-line systems that had recently been implemented by nearby cities that were a similar size to Waterloo. Specifically, she had been looking at the City of Burlington's system for paying parking tickets on-line, because of its similar size and structure. Once Burlington had made the decision over what type of on-line ticket payment system was preferred, it took about six weeks to implement. It was implemented on September 3, 2002 and by November 2002, 10 percent of patrons were paying parking tickets through the Internet using a MasterCard or Visa credit card. To inform the public of this new payment option, the department posted signs at the Burlington City Centre, and a press release and article were featured in the local newspaper. The web address was printed on the back of the ticket as the first method of payment.

PARKING TICKET PAYMENT IN WATERLOO

Revenue

The City of Waterloo is expecting revenue of $500,000.00 this year (2003) from parking tickets. The city issues approximately 32,000 tickets per year, which translates to an average of $15.63 in revenue per ticket. In the past, the city has found that the number of tickets issued remain constant despite the rising ticket fines (the demand for tickets is inelastic!). The streets surrounding the city's two universities remain a hot spot to issue tickets.

Human Resources

There are currently thirteen people who are employed to service the administration of the parking ticket payment system at the City of Waterloo. Carol Walker is one of the primary workers involved in the parking ticket payment process at the City of Waterloo and supervises the system. Assisting her is Sherry Bell, the by-law administrative assistant. In addition, the city employs three tellers who process payments for the tickets that are paid on time; these tellers have direct customer contact. The department that issues tickets employs eight by-law enforcement officers, three of whom have fixed daytime routes they patrol: one daytime officer roams the city (s/he has a police radio and is in constant contact with the dispatcher) and four officers patrol at night. The approximate salaries and the percentage of time spent directly on parking-ticket-related activities, as well as the associated overhead costs, are summarized in Appendix A.

Current Information System

The City of Waterloo currently uses a system called "Autoprocess" to manage their parking ticket database and payments. When a ticket is issued, the by-law enforcement officer enters the information into a hand-held device. The information must be downloaded from the device at the end of the officer's shift, making it impossible for a customer who received a ticket in the morning to pay the same day. This adds to the frustration of patrons who find time to pay the ticket the same day, but are unable to because the ticket information is not yet recognized by the system.

Tickets can be paid by cheque, cash, or debit card in person at the city centre, or through the mail by cheque. Once the ticket payments have been processed, the tickets are stored in boxes for a period of two years.

One drawback of the current system is that it requires a lot of labour input. Tellers spend unnecessary time taking in-person payments that could be made without their involvement if there were alternative payment methods. Customers who pay in person are frequently inconvenienced due to long waits in large line-ups (at most there are only three tellers available) and in addition, the city centre is open only during normal working hours.

Ticket Aging Process

In the event that a ticket is not paid within the allotted fifteen-day period, a complicated process with many different steps is set in motion. The following is a systematic outline of the ticket aging process.

Day 1	Patron receives parking ticket.
Day 16–20	License plate number is sent to Ministry of Transportation. Patrons personal information is sent to the city the same day from the Ministry.
Day 22	Notice of impending conviction is sent to registered owner of the vehicle. Payment due date is set for Day 40.
Day 40	Parking ticket payment due date.
Day 41	City prints Certificate Requesting Conviction (on the nearest Tuesday to Day 41). Ticket fine rises by $16 ($4.75 goes to the City of Waterloo, $3.00 to Ontario Court of Justice, $8.25 to M.T.O. to get license plate ownership information).
Day 44	Certificate Requesting Conviction is sent to Waterloo. Provincial Court identifies ticket as not being contested or paid (on Friday closest to Day 44). After conviction is filed, customer receives a notice of Final Due Date. Patron has been convicted by the Courts and no longer has the ability to contest the ticket.
Day 120	Patron's license plate number is sent to the Ministry of Transportation for "plate denial" (customer cannot renew vehicle license unless fee is paid). Additional $20 added to ticket price for Ministry of Transportation fee for looking up license plate information and plate denial process (none of which goes to the City of Waterloo).

Cost Structure and Payment Details

An analysis of ticket payments is as follows:

- 25% of the tickets received are paid before the 15th day
- 25% of the tickets received are paid between the 15th day and the 40th day
- 25% of the tickets received are paid between the 40th day and 120th day
- 25% of the tickets received are not paid until the payer is subjected to a "plate denial"

The cost structure changes as the ticket aging process evolves. It begins with a standard cost to the city of $1.25 to process each ticket that is paid before the fifteenth day. These costs are in addition to the salaries paid to the teller staff mentioned earlier. If the ticket is not paid by the fifteenth day, an additional $1.25 cost is incurred to process a notice and send the notification to the registered owner of the vehicle. Ten percent of payments received after one notice arrive in an incorrect amount, and an additional notice is sent to the registered owner of the vehicle requesting that the correct payment be made. This results in an additional cost of $1.25. On Day 41, the city processes a "Certificate of Conviction" to be signed by the court, which leads to a processing and printing cost of $5. An additional $1 is incurred for delivery of this certificate to the court, while filing the signed version of this costs the City of Waterloo another $1. Out of all issued tickets, 5 percent are contested and presented in court. This costs an average $12.50 per ticket, reflecting the cost of having an officer present. For simplicity, ignore how this 5 percent is represented in the remainder of the ticket payments and just include it as an additional cost. See Appendix B for a table containing the cost structure of the ticket aging process.

DECISION CRITERIA FOR A NEW PAYMENT SYSTEM

The City of Waterloo has decision criteria that must be met in any ticket payment system they choose to implement. According to the city, the new system should:

- Be cost effective
- Increase convenience to their customers
- Reduce the average payment period
- Decrease manual labour for administrative staff
- Lower the costs incurred by the city per ticket issued
- Create possibilities for future expansion into other payment areas
- Be compatible with the current Oracle-based information system

ALTERNATIVES

The two alternatives that the City of Waterloo is considering are an online payment system and/or a phone-based system. Payment through the bank was ruled out because it causes difficulty in payment timing due to processing time delays in the bank (e.g., if payment is delayed by the bank, the ticket may "age" to the next step which would cause major complexities with the current system).

On-line Website System

The use of a website to facilitate on-line payments would increase the access to Waterloo's ticket payment system. Creating an on-line option could be implemented using the city's current website, adding a link on the home page to the new parking ticket payment system. Rather than using internal resources to develop this new system, Waterloo would contract either a company that specializes in on-line ticket payment or a programming company to design and customize a web-based system in accordance to the specific needs of the city. Both would include having a secure payment system, the required customer web interface, as well as a back-office system that would interface to current "Autoprocess" software. This integration would be required to verify and reconcile ticket information in the Autoprocess database with information being submitted by the on-line customer (e.g., current ticket payment amount, timing, name, address, etc.). In addition, a receipt/payment confirmation, which would either be printed out or e-mailed to the customer, would be necessary. Carol realized that it is often quite inefficient to build from scratch an information system rather than to use a product that already exists, has technical support and provides a wide range of features.

A favourable example for this alternative of a web-based application would be to employ the services provided by a third party such as "Paytickets.ca," rather than having it built from scratch. Paytickets.ca "is a service that allows individuals and businesses to pay their parking tickets online through an Internet portal. This is provided by a unique partnership between Royal Bank of Canada and Teranet Enterprise Inc." (**www.paytickets.ca**). To pay a ticket, a patron simply logs onto the website for the city, and clicks on the link to "Pay Parking Tickets." This then takes them to a screen where they enter the details of the ticket, including ticket number, infraction date, license plate, province of plate, and the ticket amount. Patrons must then re-enter the ticket number for validation. The system then shows an interim summary verifying information just entered. The next screen is the payment screen where the patron enters their credit card information and email address. They are then provided with a payment summary and a receipt with confirmation number.

Paytickets.ca requires a minimum contract term of five years, with a set fee of $3,000 per annum. The variable cost structure uses a progressive method. The first 5,000 tickets of the year paid on-line costs the city $1.50 per transaction; for between 5,001 and 12,000 tickets a fee of $1.25 per ticket is charged; and finally on any tickets above 12,001, a fee of $1.00 is charged to the city. There is an annual minimum fee charged of $2,000. The city will pay the greater of $2,000 or the result of the progressive payment system. See Appendix C for a table containing the fixed and variable costs of the website.

One benefit of using Paytickets.ca is its compatibility with the existing back-office system at the city. Implementing this system avoids the costs of raising the capital necessary to develop an in-house on-line payment system, and allows for a timelier implementation period. It would also decrease the workload for tellers because a percentage of people who would normally be served by tellers would now be automatically processed through the Internet.

Finally, payment within the first fifteen days is expected to rise to 30 percent of total tickets issued, an additional 30 percent by Day 40, which would further reduce costs. Between the 40th and 120th day, it is expected that 20 percent of the tickets will be paid and finally, the remaining 20 percent of the tickets will be paid when the owner is subject to a "plate denial." From the customer's perspective, it is a huge increase in convenience to be able to pay the ticket at any time during the day, instead of waiting to pay during city office hours. It is also expected that if it was implemented, 33 percent of the payments would go through the internet site, 33 percent through the mail, and the remaining 33 percent would be paid in person.

Unfortunately, one of the drawbacks to implementing the on-line system is the internal training needed to support residents that phone in for help accessing the system which might require a larger time commitment from staff. Furthermore, not all customers have access to computers or the Internet. However, for purposes of this case, assume the labour and capital expenses do not change from the current system with this or the phone-based system (described subsequently).

Phone System

Another alternative to the current payment system could be to implement a telephone-based system. A teller would be designated to answer phone calls from patrons who wish to pay their tickets over the phone. This would require an authorization procedure for credit cards. Tellers would manually input the information into the system and confirm that the credit card payment has been cleared. This would require the credit card authorization system to contact the credit company and confirm credit availability, while the patron is holding on the other line. This also has the benefit of allowing in-person payments to be accepted via credit card.

One of the benefits of implementing a phone-based payment system is the potential for a large number of patrons to utilize this method because of its ease of use and accessibility. Customers would be able to call from home or the workplace, making it easier to pay the ticket during the city centre's office hours. Additionally, a shorter implementation period and less up-front capital would be necessary since the city would use the existing Autoprocess system.

One of the negative aspects of establishing a phone-based payment system is that it would still involve a large time commitment for a teller to handle the patrons' phone calls. Patrons who elect to pay at the city centre may also be frustrated if they see a teller handling telephone calls while they wait in line. This has already been a source of customer aggravation in the past.

It is expected that use of the telephone system would increase the number of payments at each stage by the same amount as the Web-based system. It is also expected that if it was implemented, that one-third of the payments would go through the phone system, one third through the mail, and the remaining third would be paid in person.

Finally, it is expected that both of the new systems would increase the number of tickets paid earlier in the process; however, because of human nature and procrastination, it is not expected that the combination of two systems would together increase the number of ticket payments beyond the increase that would be seen if either system was individually implemented (i.e., beyond the 30 percent, 30 percent, 20 percent, and 20 percent seen at each of the four stages respectively). Since the number of tickets processed will not change, it is assumed that the amount of labour will remain constant.

Outsourcing

The City of Waterloo also has the option of outsourcing the processing and collection functions of the ticket business to a third party (see Appendix D). Although the city would still be responsible for handing out the parking tickets, they would not be required to send out notices or receive payments for the tickets. This would reduce Carol's involvement in the parking ticket area from 60 percent of her position to 30 percent. In addition, only 25 percent of one teller's position would be required to answer telephone questions. Finally, this alternative would also allow the City to retrieve the $60,000 opportunity cost of the building (i.e., potentially reduce costs associated with the leasing of equivalent space). If this option were chosen, a third party, such as MSB (**www.muniserv.com/gov_parking.html**), would charge the City $1.50 CDN per ticket, and an additional $1.25 CDN per ticket for each additional notice sent to the patron (i.e., the notice sent after 15 days if the ticket has not been paid).[1] Such companies claim that their payment collection methods and notice mailing system produce measurable savings and potentially increase the likelihood of quicker payment. Mail-in, phone-based, and online web-based payment options would be available to pay parking tickets, and ticket payment rates are expected to be similar to the phone-based and web-based projections discussed earlier.

PLANS FOR THE FUTURE

The City of Waterloo has a number of services it would like to examine in the future. First, if it decides to implement an on-line system to pay parking tickets, this investment would likely provide the experience to enable them to accommodate other city payments in the future. For example, currently patrons must pay for dog tags and facility bookings at the city office. The city wants the system to handle these payments, and in addition, eventually allow patrons to pay their taxes using the Internet. Another idea for the future is to establish kiosk units at specified locations in the city where patrons can pay their parking tickets, dog tag fees, and facility booking fees. These kiosks may be set up at the local mall or city centre. This would provide patrons who do not have access to the Internet with a means of paying city-related fees quickly and easily.

---

[1]Marjorie Fleming, Senior Vice President, MSB, Newport Beach, CA. Interviewed by Melissa Barfoot. June 26, 2003.

CONCLUSION

Carol shut Jerry's office door and sighed. "This is not going to be an easy decision," she thought to herself. She had just spent the last hour with Jerry discussing the issues of the current system and possible solutions to the problem. One of the stipulations that she and Jerry both agreed on was that whatever choice was made, it would have to be communicated effectively to the public. The solution would not be successful if customers are unaware of it. Some of the key questions that needed answering included what solution will satisfy the decision criteria set out by the city? Should they choose one or more of the available alternatives? And is it worth the costs to change the current system? These decisions must be made with careful consideration and in a timely fashion.

Appendix A Employee Salaries and Overhead Expenses

Employee	Annual Salary	# Employed	% *	Total
Carol Walker	$45,000	1	60%	$27,000
Sherry Bell	$27,000	1	60%	$16,200
Tellers	$24,000	3	25%	$18,000
Day officers	$26,000	3	100%	$78,000
Night officers	$27,000	4	100%	$108,000
Roaming officer	$27,000	1	100%	$27,000
Total				**$274,200**

* Percentage of time spent on parking tickets

Note: The City must own four cars at $20 000/yr. (depreciation and operating costs). The cost of office overhead to house the parking ticket department can be assumed to be $60 000/yr.

Appendix B Cost Structure of Ticket Aging Process

			Current system	Online
Costs	**Timing**	**Cost per Transaction**	**% of tickets incurring costs**	**% of tickets incurring costs**
Processing costs	t ≤ 15 days	$1.25	100%	100%
First notice	t > 15 days	$1.25	75%	70%
Incorrect info after first notice		$1.25	25% × 10%	30% × 10%
Certificate of conviction	t > 40	5 + 1 + 1	50%	40%
5% Contested tickets		12.5	5%	5%

FIXED AND VARIABLE COSTS

Since the on-line payment system will be used only by those paying their fees within the first forty days, a maximum of 60 percent of the total number of tickets issued will be susceptible to on-line transaction costs. Moreover, it is estimated that 33 percent of those tickets will be paid online. Therefore, (0.6 × 32 000) 0.33 = **6336** tickets will incur online transaction costs. There is a fixed fee of $3000 in addition to the progressive ticket-processing costs.

Appendix C Website Costs

Website Costs—Variable Costs for the 6336 tickets that will be processed online

Progressive ticket structure	Cost per transaction	Transaction costs	Total transaction costs
First 5,000 tickets	$1.50	5,000 × $1.50 = $7,500	$7,500 + $1,670 = $9,170
5,001 – 12,000	$1.25	(6,336–5,000) × $1.25 = $1,670	
12,001 +	$1.00	0	

Note: An annual set fee of $3,000 + the greater of $2,000 or the result of the progressive payment system (above).

Appendix D Outsourcing Costs

Quantity of tickets being outsourced	Cost per ticket (US$)	Cost per ticket for each additional notice (US$)
32,000	$1.35	$1.00

Building Guanxi Between Westport China and Nanjing ZP Chemical Company Limited (A)[1]

Neil Remington Abramson and Hemant Merchant

It was near the end of September, 2002. Howard Zhao stood at the window of his 21st floor office at the Westport China Shipping Company Limited where he worked as the brokerage department manager. The autumn sun was rising and the towers of Pudong stood dark against the light, casting shadows over the Yangtze River that flowed between Shanghai and its newest business district. Howard felt confused. Soon the leaves of autumn would be flying down, and like them his hopes of building a guanxi relationship with Pan Weidong, the logistics director of the Nanjing ZP Chemical Company (NZP), seemed destined to fall into ruin.

Ever since he had received the assignment to build guanxi with NZP from the Singapore head office of Westport Singapore Maritime Pte. Limited almost exactly a year ago, he had been actively doing his best. Now Pan had been reassigned to one of NZP's small town sub-factories and it looked as if he might have been demoted. It was said that the transfer was part of the joint venture's manager training program. It was, however, highly unusual for a Chinese Communist Party (CCP) member to be promoted by first being transferred to a lower position.

NZP was the biggest producer of liquid chemical products coming on line in central China in the near future. Once it was up and running in 2005, NZP would be exporting 150 thousand metric tons of liquid chemical to the international chemical market every year. It was critical to Westport's whole corporate strategy that it obtained NZP's export business. The Westport China office could close without it. Howard felt sure that he would be in serious trouble in Singapore if he did not figure out how to successfully deal with this unexpected situation.

WESTPORT AND THE SHIPBROKER INDUSTRY

Westport was one of Asia's largest shipbrokers. With a team of 30 experienced brokers, 60 total personnel, and offices in Singapore, China, North America

[1]Reprinted with permission from Dr. Hemant Merchant, Faculty of Business Administration, Simon Fraser University, Vancouver (Canada). Copyright held by Dr. Hemant Merchant.

and Europe, Westport provided shipping services for petroleum, chemical, vegetable oil, and dry cargo, and had arranged 1.2 million metric tons of cargo in the last year. It had long-term business relationships with about one thousand ship owners and charters.[2] Westport China had been established in 1995 with an office in Shanghai. It served as the gateway to the Chinese chemical market for the entire Westport Group global network. Specializing in China chemical products spot chartering,[3] Westport China maintained daily business contacts with approximately 200 ship owners and one hundred fifty charters. In 2000, twenty percent of the Westport Group's total tonnage had been booked by Westport China. In March, 2002, Westport China expanded by opening a Nanjing subsidiary company. According to Martin Zhu, Westport Singapore's general manager, the Westport Group's whole long-term strategy was to benefit from China's booming economy.[3]

Howard had been with Westport China since it opened. Originally from Shandong Province, Howard had been responsible for ship chartering at the Shanghai office of Sunway Chemical Company Limited, an American chemical producer. He was headhunted by Westport Singapore in 1994 because of his exceptional work performance. After a year of training in Singapore, he became the manager of Westport China's brokerage department.

Howard's responsibility was to arrange water transportation for shippers (manufacturers) through shipping companies (ship owners and charters). He would arrange contracts of affreightment (COA) with shippers. These were agreements to book cargo space on vessels at specified times and prices. Once a COA was in place, he would notify the shipping companies, issue draft letters of indemnity/bills of lading, settle various issues related to freight, demurrage and claims, and provide whatever supporting services were required for vessel operations, ship arrivals and departures. For these services, Westport China received a 2.5 percent commission of the value of the amount paid to the shipping companies. As Westport China prospered, so did Howard who had three assistant brokers working for him by 2002.

Many at the Westport Group believed that the Chinese subsidiary's success was to a large extent due to Howard's ability to build guanxi. Westport China had become one of the largest liquid chemical products shipping service providers in China and in large part the company relied on the large network of government officials, ship owners, charters, port authority managers and port agents that he had built. It was his comprehensive knowledge of ships, direct access to some of China's largest fleets, and good connections with local small and medium sized ship owners that enabled Westport China to provide first-class brokerage services.

Howard also believed that the secret of his success was his ability to build guanxi relationships. Guanxi, or personal connection, represented a reciprocal flow of transactions and benefits between two parties over the course of their relationship. While many Western managers believed that guanxi was tantamount to corruption because it involved offering and expecting gifts and favors, most Chinese believed that the essence of guanxi was trust, shared goals, and mutual benefits. Very few Chinese believed that guanxi was a corrupt practice. Mutual trust and a personal relationship were developed based on long-term reliability. As a relationship became more durable, both parties developed ganqing, or a positive emotional and personal feeling for each other. The guanxi, or gifts and favors part, was just

---

[2]Ship owners and charters would arrange their shipping schedules and routes to receive and deliver cargo arranged by brokers. Charters were companies that chartered ships from owners. Both were dependent on brokers because individual ships were unable to guarantee the comprehensive scheduling service requirements of shippers, and it was easier for shippers to arrange a schedule through a broker than deal with a host of individual ships.

[3]Arranging cargo and ship space on the spot market.

a series of symbolic or material exchanges that developed and signaled the ganqing feelings.

Guanxi was an important practice in China because the Chinese strongly preferred doing business through durable and trust-based relationships with those they regarded as insiders. The most durable relationships were with family who were always insiders. Next best were relationships with long time friends such as old school classmates. Least best were "meat and potatoes" friendships established solely for business purposes—often over lunches and dinners—with people regarded as outside the circle of true friendship. These "meat and potato relationships were secured with gifts and favors but the Chinese regarded them as producing only small and short-term obligations. To create a successful business relationship, you needed to establish durable insider friendship based on feelings of ganqing.

Howard had his own definition of guanxi based on the values he had learned growing up in Shandong Province where people were known to be especially hospitable, honest and candid with each other. Guanxi was a process for transforming an outsider into an insider. He said,

> Guanxi is an art. I heard many people say that guanxi was connection. However, I think connection touches only the surface part of guanxi. For me, it is not only connection. It is a special kind of relationship based on trust, reciprocity, common interests and mutual obligations. The basic code of Confucianism—benevolence, righteousness and fidelity—taught me how to act and deal with the relationship with others. Great attention is paid to people's morality according to the proverb, 'learn to be a good man first, then learn how to do business.'

Morality issues were crucial and Howard believed that the key was building trust over time.

> If I'm not a man worthy of trust, I do not have the ability or willingness to repay my friends' favors anymore. Guanxi building is a long-term investment of time, money and energy through social interactions such as gift-giving, voluntary favors and banquets.

Over the years Howard applied his principles to develop good guanxi with about seventy domestic ship owners and thirty-five cargo charters. He became known at Westport China as "hui zuo ren" or, a person who is good at developing guanxi. In October, 2001, it was natural for Westport China's management to appoint Howard to the task of building guanxi with NZP's logistics department in order to eventually obtain a COA for the shipment of NZP export production.

NANJING ZP CHEMICAL COMPANY

In the Chinese proverb of the fox and the tiger, the fox receives no respect in the woods because of his lack of physical size and strength. No one takes him seriously. His solution is to make friends with a strong and respectable tiger. Then, the fox can walk through the jungle with his friend and enjoy the same fearful respect accorded the tiger. For Westport China, NZP was a tiger and if it shared Westport's vision and point-of-view, Westport China would have the presence of a tiger.

NZP was a 50-50 joint venture (JV) signed in 1998 between a German multinational corporation (MNC) and a Nanjing based state-owned petrochemical company owned by China United Chemical Company Limited. Since the mid 1990s, China's chemical market had been growing at about nine percent per year, and the industry was considered one of the fastest growing in China. In 2000, total sales of petroleum and chemical products in China were US$172 billion and trade value was approximately US$ 72.2 billion. Many MNCs flocked to China hoping to set up JVs so as to be able to enter China with the help of local partners. The purpose of NZP was to build and operate a high technology and integrated petrochemical site producing LDPE, toluene, and xylene. While most product would be sold within China, about 150 thousand metric tons would be shipped to international chemical markets after full production started in 2005. In the meantime, German managers worked alongside Chinese counterparts with the expectation that by 2005, NZP would be primarily managed by local Chinese.

It was clear that NZP's chemical exports would have to be moved to market by bulk carrier ships. There was no pipeline planned and container ships were out of the question due to the liquid nature of the cargo. The only real transportation option was shipping brokerage because the product would not be available for at least two or three years and large bulk shipping companies could not commit to abandoning existing customers or build capacity for such an eventuality. The attention of many logistics service providers was attracted and all approached NZP's logistics department knowing that a service contract with NZP would guarantee a strong position in Jiangsu Province's liquid chemical transportation market. Of this multitude, only two companies had the size and international network to satisfy NZP's service and price requirements. Westport China was one and the other was SSK. Other brokerage companies looked to be interested in setting up shop in China but it took as long as five years to build a credible network of local shipping companies. Howard observed,

> The ship owners in China are not qualified enough to meet NZP's standards. Most cargoes will need to be shipped by domestic shipping companies which are mainly small or medium sized companies. It will be difficult to meet NZP's service and price requirements. NZP will be required to investigate the options. They will have to establish regular contacts with the major players to get fully prepared for full production in 2005. If they can't find a carrier at that time, they will be in trouble.

SSK Shipping Company Limited was one of the world's largest and oldest independent ship brokering companies and it was the Westport Group's greatest worldwide competitor. SSK was a London-based company with wholly owned offices in ten cities around the world including London, Jakarta, Singapore and Hong Kong. Rumor had it that SSK planned to open in Shanghai if it managed to obtain the NZP COA. Howard believed that the SSK Hong Kong office had already established contact with NZP. Brokering cargo space on ships was pretty much selling a commodity and because SSK was larger and had a more extensive worldwide network, Howard guessed that it might be able to offer slightly better service and prices than could the Westport Group. They might be especially aggressive if NZP was the key to entering Jiangsu Province. If Howard could successfully build guanxi as a basis for doing business with NZP, then the relationship would differentiate Westport's service. Howard observed,

> It's highly possible in a state-owned company that Chinese customers will pay more for reliable shipping. Also, if two parties have good guanxi, even though the shipping price is higher than somebody else, the guanxi partner will get the business.

If Westport got the COA, then it would ensure that Westport China was a long-term success and perhaps temporarily freeze SSK out of Jiangsu. If Westport didn't get the COA, then the survival of Westport China would depend on Howard's ability to keep his existing much smaller customers who might be tempted by SSK's success. Success was also personally important to Howard. Everyone at Westport thought of Howard as the master of guanxi. If he failed, he would lose face among his colleagues and maybe also with his customers.

BUILDING GUANXI AT NZP

It took Howard three long months of careful investigation to identify the one key person that he needed build guanxi with. This was Pan Weidong who was the logistics director at NZP. Pan seemed to have the authority to determine with whom NZP would sign its COA and there seemed not to be others inside or outside the NZP hierarchy that could, or would be able to direct the business elsewhere. Three months was not too long to invest in making a correct decision. Building guanxi was a long-term and time consuming investment of emotion, energy and financial resources. No quick returns were to be expected and if you picked the wrong target, there would never be the hoped for returns. Quoting a Chinese proverb, Howard said,

> 'You should use a long cord to catch a big fish.' Otherwise it is highly possible that you will be treated as a 'meat-and-potatoes' friend. Such a friendship can only be temporary. It is unreliable and shallow. They will not offer you precious support when you are in trouble.

Trying to learn more about Pan, Howard visited a friend in the Nanjing municipal government trying to access Pan's personnel file since he worked for a state-owned company. Sun Tzu had said in *The Art of War* that you needed to know both yourself and your enemy to ensure victory. The great Communist Leader Mao Zedong had said that business was war and that one had to have as much information as possible and think deeply before making every move. Howard's friend referred him to another friend in Beijing who used to work at the China United Chemical Company headquarters. Howard found out that Pan had been born in 1955 in Ningbo City, Zhejiang Province in southern China. This was important because people from north and south China often viewed guanxi differently. Howard explained,

> With North Chinese, more attention will be given to the emotional attachment of guanxi. Generally speaking, North Chinese treasure friendship very much. If you have good guanxi with them, they will give you the shirt off their back. South Chinese are more realistic and materialistic. As a result, mutual benefits or shared interests need to be emphasized. Favors should be tendered more frequently.

Pan was known to be an excellent CCP member. He had completed his executive MBA at Shanghai Fudan University. He was married to a Beijing woman, Lin, and she had refused to give up her work in Beijing when Pan had moved to Nanjing to work at NZP. As a result, Pan traveled to Beijing every two weeks to visit her. The couple had one son who was planning to take the College Entrance Examination in 2003. One frustration for Howard was that he could not determine what hobbies Pan had. He said,

> I like to collect information regarding friends' habits, hobbies and their ways of working, and adjust my methods of getting along with them accordingly. I'd like to focus on my friends' hobbies in order to arouse their interests before conducting business with them.

Howard's first chance to meet Pan occurred in February, 2002, at Pan's EMBA alumni reunion. One of Pan's classmates was the vice president of a Shanghai based state-owned shipping company. He had also been doing business with Howard for three years and the two shared a guanxi relationship. He introduced Howard to Pan. Howard commented,

> In my network, the guanxi with classmates, relatives and fellow villagers is the core. My relationship with classmates is extremely important. It's the most stable and valuable intangible asset I have. Pure and real friendship was developed between classmates because we were young and did not have conflicts of interest when we were at university. Alumni association meetings are a good way for me to expand my guanxi network.

Howard hoped that he could build a relationship with Pan based on classmate connections. This would already be one step higher than a "meat-and-potatoes" relationship. Howard and Pan exchanged business cards and Howard told Pan that he wanted to take an EMBA program and asked Pan for advice. He told Pan that he would be more than happy to go to Shanghai Fudan University if people like Pan had studied there. Pan seemed, however, uninterested in conversing with Howard and offered no advice. It was difficult to know what his real opinion was and his responses and reactions were not that positive. He only asked Howard how old he was and seemed surprised that a man of thirty would already be the manager of a department in a foreign company. Howard's impression of Pan was that he spent his time quietly watching and studying people. He said,

> It was difficult to tell if my endeavor was effective or not. Pan is composed and conservative. He is good at examining someone's words and observing their countenance. He's an excellent listener and much more cunning and conscious than I have imagined. Confucius said that a true gentleman speaks slowly but acts quickly. Pan follows this proverb strictly.

Trying to obtain more information, Howard directed Jiang, the general manager of the newly formed Westport China subsidiary in Nanjing, to organize a dinner and karaoke party for Pan's subordinates. Jiang was a retired manager from China General Agency Company's Nanjing branch. This gathering was a big success for Howard because it turned out that one of Pan's subordinates, Zhang, was also from Shandong. Intimate personal relationships can be established quickly between Shandong people if they meet outside their own hometowns. Howard bonded easily with Zhang through constant personal visits and entertainments. When Zhang's sister needed a job in Shanghai, Howard got her one with one of his guanxi contacts. When Zhang's mother had a heart attack, Howard got her into the best hospital in Shanghai and put up Zhang's father in Westport's Shanghai dormitory. Now, Howard could keep close contact with an "insider" in Pan's department at NZP and be able to obtain much more information about Pan and his predilections. Zhang told Howard that Pan spent most of his time writing a thesis called *Chemical Logistics in China* and that he had written other articles on the same subject. Howard also found out that Pan had been invited to give a thirty-minute presentation at a distribution logistics conference to be held in Shanghai in April.

Pan prepared carefully for this event. With Zhang's help, he gathered and studied all of Pan's articles. At the end of Pan's presentation, he asked several well-prepared questions. Pan was astonished by Howard's deep understanding of his subject. Pan gave detailed answers and recommended several references. He willingly agreed when Howard asked if he could come see Pan if he had any other questions. Subsequently, Howard visited Pan frequently to ask for assistance on logistics-related subjects. He prepared well-designed questions beforehand. He said,

> I called him Teacher Pan and found him much more talkative on such occasions. I seldom spoke and pretended to be a good student and listener during these meetings. On the one hand, what he said was meaningful and useful for my business. On the other hand, I was sure that Pan gained face when his study was appreciated by others.

At the end of April, Pan had a car accident. The accident was not serious but Pan was ordered by his doctor to rest at home for a week. Lin, Pan's wife, came from Beijing to take care of him. Howard decided to try to meet Lin and arrange some entertainment or sightseeing for her. He hoped that Pan would notice his friendly gesture and gain face. Howard followed the Chinese proverb that you must not only bow and scrape before the tiger. You must also seek every opportunity to ingratiate yourself with the tiger's relatives, friends, mistress or wife. Pan asked Sina Du, his general manager at the Westport Shanghai office to accompany Lin. Sina was a tough, clear-minded and determined businesswoman. She invited Lin for a two-day shopping and relaxation trip in Shanghai in early May after Pan had recovered. She invited Pan as well but he declined due to the pent up demand for his return to work.

For those two days, Howard and Sina made themselves out to be the most warm-hearted hosts in the world. They booked Lin a five-star hotel suite and rented a luxury Mercedes Benz to show her around. All lunches and dinners were served either at first class restaurants or famous bars. At the end, they offered to pay for Lin's shopping bills as well but she declined. Howard confirmed that Pan and Lin's son was studying for the 2003 College Entrance Exam and discovered that Lin was afraid that her son would not do well. After checking with Singapore, Howard offered the full support of Westport Singapore to help get Lin's son into a Singapore University. Lin said, "Howard, you are so nice! Pan should tell me beforehand that he has such a good friend like you in Shanghai." When Lin returned to Beijing, she gave gifts to Howard and Sina and invited them to visit she and her husband in Beijing.

A week later, Pan called Howard's cell to express his gratitude. Howard took it as a sign that Pan was touched by his friendship and understood the basic reciprocity principle of guanxi. "If you receive a favor, you need to repay it in the future but there is no need to repay it immediately," he said. In fact, it was a sign of greater trust and a stronger relationship when friends were willing to wait longer for a better return.

This gave Howard much hope. In a guanxi relationship, give-and-take is expected, and returns are balanced for both sides in the long term. What constitutes balance depends on the relative power and position of the two parties. Each is expected to give the best they can but the gifts of the tiger will be greater than anything the fox can offer. If the more powerful individual does not offer the greater gift, then he/she will be seen to lose face.

The favor Howard wanted from Pan was his support in coordinating the signing of a strategic COA with NZP. This COA contract would keep other competitors like SSK away. It would secure the cooperation between the shipbroker and the shipping companies for a certain period of time at a reasonable profit margin for both sides. At the very minimum, Howard hoped that Pan would promise to grant him first priority in the submission of quotations when NZP's cargo came to market. In the meantime, Howard hoped that Pan would signal his friendship by making frequent requests for market information and quotations. He said,

> At the beginning, he can only talk with me about the market, but gradually this increases intimacy with me and not with my competitors. This will be a sign that eventually the COA will come to me and not my competitors.

Now Howard wanted to give Pan "the big gift" to cement the relationship and to show his expectation of receiving a big favor. In guanxi, there were small gifts and big gifts. Small gifts represented friendship and it was not their small value that mattered but the emotional attachment that they symbolized. Small gifts, meals and drinks created a sense of obligation far exceeding their cost. Howard gave them to friends, and to the relatives and friends of those he hoped to influence, during traditional Chinese festivals, birthdays, and at weddings. Howard had given small gifts to Pan and none had ever been returned. Big gifts were intended to seal the deal and were only given to those with great influence. They were dangerous, however, because they could be interpreted as bribes and the Chinese central government had recently passed strict laws to prevent the spread of corruption. Many officials and senior managers at state-owned corporations had been jailed or even sentenced to death for taking bribes. Howard noted,

> I have been considering preparing some big gifts for Pan. However, I finally gave it up. From my point-of-view, the big gift is a double-edged sword because the line between bribery and gift-giving is really difficult to distinguish. The big gift should be used wisely according to different situations and people.

On the one hand, Pan was from the south and this suggested that he would be more pragmatic and be pleased to receive the big gift. On the other hand, his wife Lin was from Beijing where big gifts were especially dangerous. Also, Pan was an honored member of the CCP which indicated that he must cherish his political reputation and would want to stay away from even the hint of a corruption scandal. Zhang supported this view saying, "I saw Pan refuse many people's personal visits on weekends. He once threw a bag out in the corridor when one guest tried to leave it in his room." Pan concluded that it would definitely jeopardize his guanxi with Pan if he was indelicate about a big gift. "If I am not one hundred percent sure about the result, I would rather forget it," he dithered.

Howard observed that Pan would only do favors for "qualified friends". These were people who not only enjoyed a good relationship with Pan but who were also capable of fulfilling a contract and handling mutual business properly. Howard repeatedly stressed Westport's competitive advantage as one of the biggest chemical shipping brokers in China, arguing to Pan that Westport could reduce NZP's shipping costs and expand NZP's worldwide business contacts.

To help demonstrate Westport's advantages, Howard arranged for David Zhou, Westport Singapore's managing director, to accompany him to visit Pan in June. Zhou prepared a one-hour presentation about the history and key core competencies of Westport and presented it for Pan's whole department. Pan was impressed and began to contact Howard asking for more information about the domestic and international liquid chemical marketplaces, and freight market trends. He also asked Howard to submit a quotation for regular spot ship chartering. Howard was excited by Pan's positive response and worked even harder to boost guanxi with Pan hoping to "strike while the iron is hot."

TERRIBLE NEWS

At the end of September, Howard was shocked to learn that Pan was being re-assigned to one of NZP's sub-factories in a small city outside Nanjing. It was claimed that this was part of a senior manager-training program that intended to fully qualify Chinese managers to run NZP by 2005. Howard had doubts. Ever since the Cultural Revolution in the 1960s and 1970s, being sent down to the countryside was considered an extreme punishment and very few ever came back. Howard recalled his feelings,

> I was so upset and surprised. The dilemma is what will happen next. If Pan won't come back after this program, then all my previous investments of time and money will be wasted. I have to start again from the very beginning with the new manager. I need to decide whether or not to stay with Pan. If I continue the guanxi building with him, my effort will become worthless if Pan leaves the logistics department.

Trying to figure things out, Howard visited Pan in the small city and tried to find out what had happened. It seemed to Howard that Pan was reluctant to talk about what had happened to him, and he didn't seem to want to say too much about his new assignment or status. Pan said, "Now I understand that what is out of sight is out of mind," and he joked that he was a dragon who went near the shallow water and got bullied by a fish. Howard terminated the meeting quickly. He simply didn't know what to say to help pacify Pan. There was already a new German expatriate, Mr. Hans Hol, who had been appointed the manager of the NZP logistics department.

Howard wondered what he should do. He could stick with Pan and hope for the best. If Howard kept building guanxi with Pan and Pan recovered his position, then he would be very grateful for Howard's loyalty. It was a Chinese proverb that bad time builds good relationship, and that Chinese will use a crisis to test the true nature of guanxi. Howard remembered that foreign companies that had pulled out of China at the time of the Tiananmen crisis in 1989 had been unwelcome when they tried to come back later. Other companies that stayed in China had been rewarded later for their loyalty to China during a time of crisis.

Yet Pan hadn't sounded at all confident about his imminent return—all that talk about dragons bullied by little fish—and if he didn't come back within a couple of years it could be too late. Realistically, the point of guanxi was to invest your time and energy with those who could benefit you the most either now or sometime in the future. The giver always benefited equally or even more than the recipient especially when the recipient was the tiger and the giver was the fox. The world was like a pyramid of people struggling with each other. You didn't have a choice about whether you joined the struggle—that was just life. You could, however, choose where you struggled. You didn't want to fight your battle at the bottom of the pyramid in the midst of the crowd. It was easier to fight at the top. In China, conditions changed quickly and unpredictably. The government could pass a new economic manifesto and suddenly the basis of competition was completely different. The man who governed today could be in disgrace tomorrow and someone else would be in charge. It was important to remember the Taoist proverb of the staunchness of the oak and the yielding of the grass. The grass bends easily in the wind but the great oak stands unmoved. A strong wind can uproot the oak but no wind, however strong, can uproot the grass that bends flat before it. It was important to honor and maintain your values but it was also important to know which were the true standards that should govern your life and which were arbitrary standards that you upheld hoping that others would like you. Sometimes you had to have the courage to do what you must without regard for what others might think. If Howard stuck with Pan and he was not rehabilitated, then Pan might be pleased but Westport would lose the COA and Howard would lose face with his colleagues who were counting on his abilities. It was another proverb that the successful man played leapfrog. People and relationships that had no further use were cast off. You always did your best to leap to the top to gain endorsement from the established authorities and to ally yourself with the powerful and the wise. You must always leap towards an association with the tiger.

Howard wondered if he could switch his guanxi building efforts to Mr. Hol. Hol was apparently the new tiger of NZP's logistics department and represented the German half of the joint venture. He could entertain Hol by taking him sightseeing, shopping and to meals but, in his experience, Germans were less likely than Chinese to trade friendship for business. Mr. Hol probably thought that business was business and would make his decisions about the COA based on the service and the cost, and not based on whether he was friends with Howard. He said,

> I find the whole prospect of building guanxi with Mr. Hol very confusing. I don't quite know what to do because my experience is building guanxi with Chinese. Do the same things work with Germans or other foreigners?

Or, Howard could start again. It had taken him a few months to identify Pan as the person to build guanxi with and his efforts had taken about a year. He still had two or three years left. If he could find a Chinese manager higher than Mr. Hol, perhaps that manager could influence Mr. Hol to support signing a COA with Westport China. Certainly, this was the option Howard felt most confident about.

Standing in the window of his office looking down at Pudong and the Yantze River, Howard worried that just when he was ready to walk through the forest with his friend the tiger, he was being cast down to struggle again at the base of the pyramid. Pudong was the shining symbol of China's transformation of world commerce. Howard needed the COA with NZP as his shining symbol ensuring that Westport China would continue to be a part of the Chinese economic miracle. What should he do now?

Casablanca Kids

Lisa Giguere and David Rose

In October 2005, Ricki Glinert assumed the new position of Artist & Repertoire and Marketing Manager for Casablanca Kids, a private Canadian-based children's music label. The owners of Casablanca Kids believed that children's music required more attention and gave Ricki the task of increasing artist signings, overseeing product development and increasing brand recognition and marketing of the product line to increase sales. As Ricki began gathering information to develop a plan for increasing sales and profitability in the next year, she realized that her new position was going to be very challenging.

The Company

Ed Glinert and Jennifer Mitchell founded Casablanca Kids in 2001, as a division of Casablanca Media Acquisitions Inc. ("Casablanca"). Casablanca Kids produced children's music, while Casablanca's other divisions were involved in the production and distribution of a variety of music genres as well as music publishing and television production services. Casablanca Kids' products were well-produced quality entertainment of various musical styles (i.e. blues, jazz, reggae, etc.), designed for children, without being patronizing. The founders strongly believed that their company had one of the most impressive children's music catalogues in all of North America. They had titles from well-established artists, most of whom had over 20 years of experience in the industry. Notable signed artists included Sharon, Lois and Bram, Fred Penner, Jack Grunsky, Al Simmons, Norman Foote and Bob King. Casablanca Kids' releases included original CDs by established artists, compilation CDs by lesser known artists, DVDs and interactive games. According to Jennifer Mitchell, the company's products were "competitively priced at a mid-range level of approximately $9.99 to $12.99 per CD, midway between the high end products and the discount products". As a testament to the quality of the product, Casablanca Kids had won numerous consumer choice awards including Parents Choice Awards, National Parenting Publications Awards, iParenting Awards and Juno Awards. However, Mitchell acknowledged that although these awards were meaningful to consumers, they had little impact on the retailers that Casablanca Kids relied on to distribute their products. (Exhibit 1 provides biographies for Ricki Glinert, Jennifer Mitchell and Ed Glinert.)

Typical of a company with less than $1 million in sales, Casablanca Kids faced some challenges as its net income continued to decrease from declining sales and a lower profit margin as Wal-Mart continued to force retail prices down and CD manufacturing costs remained the same. (Exhibit 2 provides a breakdown of variable costs for CDs.) In 2005, over 50% of total sales volume was attributed to budget compilations (or discount CDs). Although margins on mid-range CDs were much higher, the discount CDs had a much higher potential sales volume. Casablanca was considering whether to enter the dollar store market where margins would be even lower but volumes could be much higher, perhaps several hundred thousand units per sale.

Casablanca Kids had limited financial resources for any marketing initiatives. Compounding this challenge was the need to "front-end" the marketing of children's music products (i.e., upfront marketing costs that cannot be recouped until two years after the expenses are incurred). "Front-end" marketing costs totaled approximately 10% of Casablanca Kids' mid-range CD sales. Marketing expenses were a requirement in order to promote mid-range CDs, whereas discount CDs were sold on the basis of low price with little marketing support. Dollar store CDs would receive no marketing support and would not even carry the Casablanca Kids name.

Casablanca Kids had no current television presence to assist in promoting the product line, as none of the company's signed artists currently had a regular television program. Further, Casablanca Kids was very reliant on a single act as over 50% of total Canadian sales volume was attributed to Sharon, Lois and Bram.

The Children's Music Market

While the total world market for children's music was unknown, Ricki thought there had been little sales growth during the past few years. Recently, the preschool market (children under the age of six) had been declining due to a decrease in the number of families having children. However this market was expected to experience moderate growth within five years as the Echo generation (the children of the Baby Boom generation) started having children. Casablanca Kids estimated that Canada represented about 10% of the total world market for children's music, while the US market was estimated to be as much as 45% of the total world market.

More detailed information was available about the overall music industry, compared to the limited data about the children's music market. According to figures available to Casablanca, in 2005:

- Tracking firm Nielsen SoundScan, which measured point-of-sale purchases across the United States, indicated that total album sales, including current and catalogue titles, fell 7.2 percent from 2004 to 618.9 million units, the lowest since 1996, when they were 616.6 million. After enjoying an "up" year in 2004, prompting predictions that the worst was over, sales flagged during 2005, hurt by competition from illegal downloads, rival forms of entertainment such as video games, and a lack of breakout musical acts.
- Overall music sales, which included albums, singles, music videos, and digital tracks, jumped 22.7 percent to just over a billion units in 2005. The rise was fuelled by a 194 percent increase in digital downloads.
- Sales of physical albums bought via the internet were up 11.3 percent.
- Breaking down sales by genre, every type of music took a hit in 2005 with the exception of Latin, which saw a 12.6 percent increase.

Distribution

The primary channel of distribution for Casablanca Kids' products in Canada was through two large music distributors, EMI and Universal. These two distributors accounted for approximately 75% of the total sales volume for the company. EMI and Universal sold the product directly to mass merchants including Wal-Mart, Zellers, and Best Buy; major book chains including Indigo and Chapters; major record chains such as HMV; and non-traditional outlets such as major grocery and drug chains. In terms of an overall promotion mix strategy, EMI and Universal used a push strategy, directing all marketing activities (mainly personal selling and trade promotion) toward wholesalers and retailers to encourage them to stock the product and promote it to the end consumer.

Ricki recognized that sales in the children's music industry were dominated by mass merchant accounts including Wal-Mart, Zellers, and Best Buy. She thought that in 2005 Wal-Mart accounted for 50% to 60% of total retail sales of children's music in Canada. She described non-traditional outlets such as grocery and drug chains as "problematic since these stores are not used to selling music. There is often low compliance from staff to ensure that the product is properly merchandised." Compounding this issue was the fact that Casablanca Kids did not have dedicated staff to call on retailers and maintain merchandising displays.

EMI and Universal also sold the product to wholesalers who would stock the titles for smaller retail accounts including small chain stores and privately owned independent stores who would be likely to purchase less than 10 copies of a single title in the span of a year.

Direct sales accounted for the remaining 25% of total company sales volume. This included sales to small retailers who might, for example, purchase products from the Casablanca Kids website as well as direct sales to consumers who could purchase the product directly 'off-stage' during the artists' concerts and from the online store at the Casablanca Kids website (**www.casablancakids.com**). According to Ricki, "There are no plans to expand the direct sales channel as this would require a huge financial investment." Exhibit 3 provides an illustration of the various distribution channels.

Buying Behaviour of Retailers

In the children's music industry, product was 100% returnable for a full refund. This meant that retailers could return the product to Casablanca Kids for a full refund if the product did not sell. In addition, the two primary distributors, EMI and Universal, charged a refurbishing cost to Casablanca Kids for all returned product. Ricki felt that mass merchants such as Wal-Mart were most concerned with profit per square foot and would rather carry CDs from well known adult artists that would be guaranteed to move quickly.

> If the CDs are not sold within a couple of weeks, mass merchants and non-traditional retail outlets will return the product to Casablanca Kids for a full refund. They tend to buy low priced children's music products or brands advertised nationally on television. Mass merchant buyers are not particularly knowledgeable about children's music.

Ricki believed that children's music occupied the least amount of shelf space, relative to other categories of music, in all retail stores. Further, she recognized that with the maturation of the CD format, retailers were beginning to carry far less CD inventory in general.

Buying Behaviour of Consumers

The primary purchasers of children's music were parents who tended to purchase the same music that was purchased for them as a child, prompting Ricki to describe the industry as being "evergreen". In addition, grandparents, other relatives and friends also purchased children's music as gifts. However, children's music was a low priority purchase for the vast majority of buyers. According to Ricki:

> A fundamental problem is that the majority of parents don't believe that children need to be exposed to music. With the introduction of DVD players in automobiles, parents can now choose to let children watch a DVD in the car instead of listening to music.

Buyers of children's music could be divided into four main categories. The "keep them quiet" buyer group purchased children's music to keep children occupied and quiet, particularly during long car trips. These buyers were not well informed about the quality of children's music or the developmental benefits of exposing children to music at an early age. The second group of buyers, the "developmental buffs", believed that regular exposure to music from birth was fundamental to a child's brain development. This group purchased children's music because they firmly believed that exposing children to music at an early age made them smarter. These buyers were searching for a quality music product and were willing to pay a premium to ensure that children had the proper exposure to music. The third group, "music enthusiasts", were music lovers themselves and wanted to share their love of music with children. This group was very knowledgeable about a variety of music and was willing to pay more for a quality recording. A fourth group, "gift givers" included a wide range of behaviours, depending on a number of factors such as the occasion and the relationship of the giver to the child.

Most buyers who shopped at big box stores such as Wal-Mart and Zellers tended to be looking to purchase low-end product for $2.00 to $5.00 per CD. Although big box stores did stock some mid-range product, i.e., approximately $9.99 to $12.99 per CD, the focus was on offering a wide range of low-end product to meet the needs of the target customers. Conversely, buyers who shopped at specialty children's stores such as Mastermind were prepared to spend more money. As such, children's music sold in these specialty stores tended to be high-end product in the $16.00 to $19.99 per CD range.

Children's music was generally not purchased by the person who would listen to the music, i.e., the child, so the product had to be appealing to both the buyer (parents, relatives, friends) and the user (the child). Both parents and children chose children's music based on familiarity with the performing artist. According to Ricki:

> Most parents grew up listening to Sharon, Lois and Bram. That's what is driving our high sales for this act. Parents are choosing Sharon, Lois and Bram because they know that the music is great.

Ricki felt that the target demographic for Casablanca Kids' product was getting younger, as children were growing up at a younger age, a phenomenon often called "age compression".

> With artists like Sharon, Lois and Bram, we need to focus on younger children, as kids today are growing up faster at an earlier age. Our target demographic has become children under the age of five. The industry is in a cycle of animation, meaning that the majority of children's music performers are animated characters. Children are being exposed to and love animated characters. This presents a challenge as our signed artists are not animated, but are real people. However, this trend is slowly beginning to change in our favour with the movement toward live performances.

Promotions

In terms of marketing to retail accounts, Casablanca Kids provided catalogues and 'sell sheets' that contained information about a CD that would be released in the near future. The release information contained in both the sell sheets and catalogues served as marketing tools to convince the distributors, wholesalers and retailers to carry the product. In addition, Casablanca Kids advertised in trade magazines including Canadian Music Network, Canadian Entertainment Network and Billboard Magazine.

Marketing efforts by Casablanca Kids towards end consumers were more limited. Whenever possible, public relations was used as a tool to promote new releases in the various media including print, television, radio and the website. The main exception was the budget compilation CDs, where the primary factor driving the consumer purchase decision was price. However, it was generally very difficult to interest the media in the company's news. According to Ricki:

> The media is just not that interested in children's music. Ideally, we like to get positive product reviews in the media, but this is a challenge given the media's overall lack of interest in the industry.

Giveaways had proven to be a more successful form of promotion. For example, Casablanca Kids often provided prizes for draws held at "Movies for Mommies", movie viewings restricted to mothers who brought their babies with them. Some advertising was placed in parenting magazines and on children's television and radio shows, but only a very limited amount due to the relatively high cost.

Opportunities for Growth

In 2005, Casablanca Kids introduced Jazz Baby, a CD with traditional children's songs recorded by celebrities and famous musicians including Jim Belushi, Cybill Shepherd, Megan Mullally and Taj Mahal. Short-term promotional plans for Jazz Baby included the creation of t-shirts with the Jazz Baby logo and the possibility of a live concert on television, which would result in a DVD for sale.

Casablanca Kids was attempting to increase its music DVD product line. Given the maturation of the CD format, more retail shelf space was available for music DVDs than CDs. The company was also beginning to introduce interactive music games.

Casablanca Kids planned to aggressively enter the US market in 2006. In the longer term, the company planned to expand internationally into the UK market, given the cultural similarities between the Canadian and UK markets. However, each country had its own group of notable children's music artists and it was very difficult for a children's music artist to gain international exposure. Such exposure was only obtained through the television media. The Wiggles, an Australian act, had gained international recognition with children through their own television program, which aired in many countries. The Casablanca Kids' artists were not well known in the US, making it difficult for the company to effectively penetrate the market. Recently, the company had been trying to sign more US artists in an effort to overcome this lack of awareness.

Casablanca Kids had been exploring the potential of digital music stores as another distribution channel for the product. Use of this channel would require a relationship with a digital aggregator who would then distribute the Casablanca Kids recordings to the digital music stores. According to Ricki, the digital music market was growing significantly.

Another opportunity existed in the educational market, selling music to schools, but it was not a market that Ricki found attractive:

> The educational segment is difficult to penetrate and restricted by funding guidelines. In addition, it's very hard to reach the buyers, i.e., the teachers, and building relationships with these individual buyers would take a long period of time. If we were to go after this market, the best way for us to reach the buyers directly would be to have a strong presence at relevant industry trade shows. But this presents a challenge given our limited resources.

Competitors

Casablanca Kids' largest direct competitor was Disney, who produced the best known products in the industry. In 2005, Ricki estimated that Disney's share of the worldwide children's music market was approximately 30%. Other significant competitors included:

- branded television characters, such as the Wiggles and Sesame Street
- "tween" entertainers, such as Hilary Duff, who targeted children aged 9 to 12
- budget compilation CDs consisting of collections of songs by unknown artists, selling for $1 to $2
- video/early learning games, such as Baby Einstein (a Disney product).

In addition to direct competitors, indirect competition existed in the form of other children's entertainment products such as DVDs, toys, games, and books. The total market in Canada for children's entertainment products was estimated to be at least $2 billion. Most of the sales were through large retailers such as Wal-Mart and Zellers, with a much smaller amount through specialty retailers. Typically products were not carried by the large discount retailers and the specialty retailers at the same time, with specialty retailers tending to carry newer, higher-end products. Once products ended up at the large discount retailers, where they were often heavily discounted, it was difficult for specialty retailers to continue selling them.

The Decision

Ricki wondered how she could increase the brand recognition and therefore sales of Casablanca Kids' products. The company had an established relationship with both EMI and Universal, but was that the best method of distribution? Were there other channels that might provide more support? The mass merchant retailers currently accounted for the vast majority of the company's sales, but would that continue, given their limited interest in children's music? Which consumer groups represented Casablanca's most attractive target market? She wondered how she could increase sales when it seemed like the distribution channels were not interested in carrying the products and consumers were not aware they existed. Ed and Jennifer were anxious to hear what Ricki had planned for the business so she soon needed to make some important decisions.

Exhibit 1 Biographies

Ricki Glinert, Artist & Repertoire and Marketing Manager

Ricki has over 25 years of experience in television production and has most recently focused on kids tv because she can look them directly in the eye. Ricki was the creator and producer of Treehouse TV's "Crazy Quilt", as well as the creator and producer of "100% True" for Discovery Kids. She has also written numerous television series for kids and spent 5 years at TVO producing, directing and writing in the children's department. Her credits include "Join In", "Way Up There", "World of Nature" and "Mathica's Mathsop". She has also worked on children's shows for OWL Communications and CTV. At Casablanca Television she has served as Executive In Charge of Production on the 13 part space series "Rocket Science" and produced, directed and wrote the 2 hour special on the science of wrestling, "Slam Bam". Both of these series aired on The Discovery Channel.

Jennifer Mitchell, Vice-President

Jennifer has specialized in the areas of entertainment, media and corporate law for the past 10 years, working with Edmund L. Glinert in private practice and co-founding Casablanca Media Acquisitions Inc. She has been involved in the acquisition and sale of numerous entertainment related transactions as well as film and television tax shelters. Ms. Mitchell is the Senior Vice President of Casablanca Media Acquisitions Inc. and is involved in the buying, selling, administration, and exploitation of music publishing and recording catalogues and has been overseeing the day to day operations of all areas of Casablanca since its inception.

Ed Glinert, President

Ed has specialized in the areas of entertainment, media and communications law for the past 25 years. Prior to becoming a lawyer, he founded, owned and operated Frederick Lewis Artist Placement Bureau, one of Canada's largest theatrical agencies, from 1967 through 1971. From 1977 through 1982, he was also a co-owner of National Variety Promotions ("NVP"), one of Canada's largest adult contemporary concert promoters, which presented such acts as Liza Minnelli, Frank Sinatra, Don Rickles and Steve Lawrence as well as producing the stage play, Pirates of Penzance starring Barry Bostwick and Andy Gibb at the Royal Alexandra Theatre. In 1990, he co-founded The Children's Group, owner of the hit series "Classical Kids" which has been one of the most successful series of children's records in history. In 2000, he founded Casablanca Media Acquisitions Inc., along with Jennifer Mitchell.

Exhibit 2 Variable Costs Per CD*

	Dollar Store CD	Budget CD	Mid-Range CD
Retail Price	$1.00	$5.99	$9.99
Wholesale Price	$ 0.50	$2.99	$4.99
Distribution Costs 25%	$0.12	$ .75	$1.25
Manufacturing	$0.25	$1.00	$1.30
Mechanical Licenses	$0.05	$0.32	$0.50
Master Licenses	$0.05	$0.32	$0.50
Casablanca Income	$0.03–$0.04	$0.60	$1.44

*Figures represent estimates of average costs for music companies with less than $1 million in sales. Some figures may have been disguised.

Exhibit 3 Distribution Channels

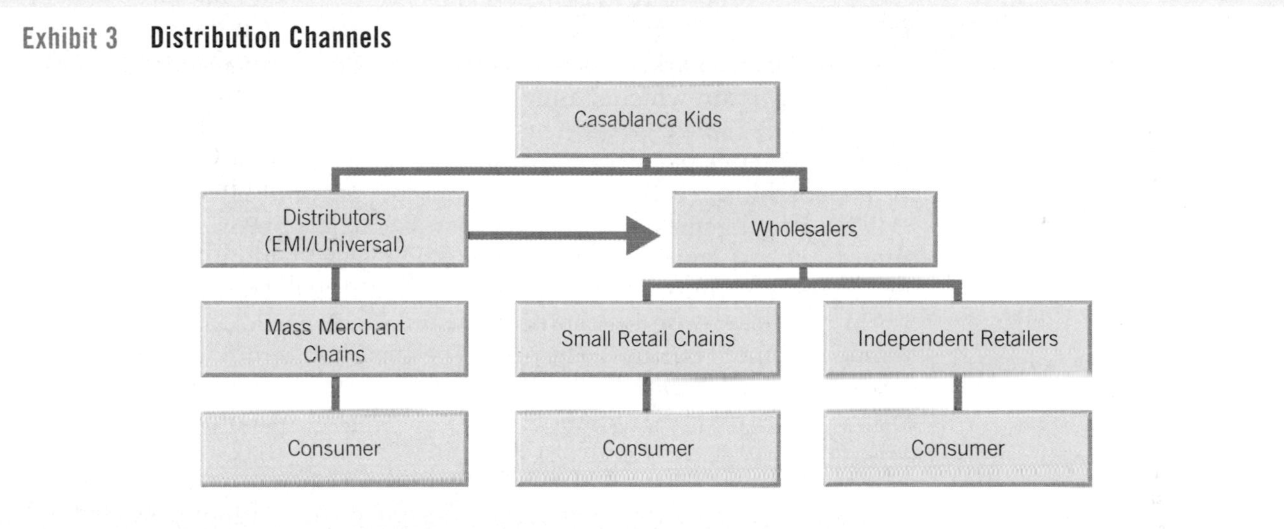

Mediaspark

Doug Lionais, Sherry Finney, and Melissa Cameron

This case was written by Doug Lionais, Sherry Finney, and Melissa Cameron of Cape Breton University, Nova Scotia, Canada. It is intended as a basis for classroom discussion and is not intended to represent either correct or incorrect handling of administration issues.

In September of 2001, Mathew Georghiou, the President and CEO of MediaSpark (**http://www.mediaspark.com**) in Sydney, Nova Scotia, finished a phone conversation with IBM Canada. IBM had just informed Georgiou that they were interested in exclusively carrying MediaSpark's new product, GoVenture Entrepreneur (**http://www.goventure.net**) in the Canadian market. Georghiou had been researching possible distribution channels for GoVenture in North America. The phone call with IBM completed Georghiou's research and he now needed to sift through the information and decide how he was going to get his product to market.

BACKGROUND

Georghiou completed a two year engineering diploma at Cape Breton University (then University College of Cape Breton), before transferring to Dalhousie University in Halifax, Nova Scotia, to complete his Electrical Engineering Degree. After Georghiou's second year at Dalhousie, IBM awarded him a sixteen month internship in Toronto, an offer which he took. In 1991, Georgiou received a national award for innovation during his internship which led IBM to guarantee him a position upon graduation.

After graduating in 1993, Georghiou immediately moved back to Toronto to work for IBM. While employed at IBM, Georghiou gained much experience in the engineering field which included programming and computer product manufacturing.

Georghiou had a vision to establish his own business and left IBM in 1994. He moved back to Sydney, Nova Scotia, and with personal savings and financing from Enterprise Cape Breton Corporation (ECBC), he established MediaSpark. The business began in the basement of his home and after only two years, he needed to expand and he relocated his offices downtown. MediaSpark focused on technology and design; the business offered a wide range of services such as multi-media production, Internet development, e-learning, technology consulting, and image and print design.

GOVENTURE ENTREPRENEUR

In 2000, MediaSpark launched GoVenture Entrepreneur, an educational software program which simulated establishing and running a small business (Exhibit 1, page C–34). This software created a practical replication of an entrepreneur's business start-up, daily management, and personal activities. Georghiou felt GoVenture Entrepreneur would be a perfect learning tool for any business education class because it provided students the opportunity to gain experience and knowledge without risk. Georghiou described GoVenture Entrepreneur as a "flight simulator for business."

In the GoVenture Entrepreneur simulation, participants establish and manage a small business start-up. The program simulates all aspects of entrepreneurial decision making, including business and personal outcomes. Performance evaluation tools included in the simulation allow the user and/or the instructor to set goals, adjust performance evaluation weightings and measure outcomes in terms of business success and personal work-life balance. MediaSpark designed the product to be as flexible as possible for teachers.

MediaSpark identified the broader market for GoVenture Entrepreneur as middle school to adult; however, the primary target was high school classes. Georghiou saw GoVenture Entrepreneur as enhancing the existing curriculum. MediaSpark positioned it for use in business, marketing, and entrepreneurship courses. Georghiou identified three general ways of using GoVenture Entrepreneurship in the classroom. First, educators could use GoVenture Entrepreneurship as an introduction to a course to demonstrate the purpose of learning the concepts in the course. Second, they could use it to end a course as a capstone module to apply the lessons of the course. Third, educators could use it throughout a course to complement ongoing lessons.

To serve the educational market, MediaSpark developed a number of support materials for GoVenture Entrepreneurship. For example, institutions that purchased software licenses received an "Experiencing Entrepreneurship" text. MediaSpark developed this book as an easy to use summary of the subject that educators could use either as a textbook or as a complement to existing textbooks. MediaSpark's educational bundle also included an instructor's manual, lesson plans focusing on different topics, and a test bank.

THE MARKET

Georghiou divided the educational publishing industry between the K–12 market and the university market. Georghiou's target market fell in the K–12 category. Georghiou felt the market in the United States was much larger than the Canadian market, with more growth in the educational software sector. There were 90 000 to 100 000 elementary and secondary schools in the United States while there were only 16 500 in Canada, and Canada's K–12 enrolment was 5.3 million students, approximately one-tenth the size of the United States. According to market studies that Georghiou had reviewed, U.S. schools spent $5.50 per student on software and the market for CD-ROMs in schools approximated US$300 million. Georghiou hoped to generate significant sales in both the Canadian and the U.S. market, but the focus was on the U.S. market because it was much larger than the Canadian market and it had greater access to funding.

MARKETING AND PRICING STRATEGY

Georghiou was concerned about how to sell and distribute the product. The education market was accustomed to purchasing texts rather than multimedia products. Whereas a catalogue description can describe a text fairly well, Georghiou felt that educators would need to experience GoVenture Entrepreneur before considering it for use in the classroom. Georghiou felt that it would be difficult to convince educators of the value of his product as either a text complement or as a text replacement without a hands-on trial. Georghiou commented, "To sell the product, people need to see it; they need to try it out for themselves." Thus, he was only interested in marketing channels which placed the product in educators' hands for a decision or at least provided an opportunity to demonstrate the product in action.

The price of GoVenture Entrepreneur varied depending on the user and country. Georghiou identified six user groups: individuals, educational K–12, educational post-secondary, home school, non-profit or government, and all others. He wanted his initial target market to be the educational K–12 and offered this segment a 50% price reduction for a limited time in an effort to break into the market. The regular price varied per package depending on the quantity purchased (Exhibit 2, page C–34). The cost of goods sold was generally 5% to 10% of the suggested retail price.

DISTRIBUTION CHANNELS

Georghiou identified two basic distribution alternatives for GoVenture Entrepreneur: direct or indirect. Indirect distribution channels would include catalogue companies, textbook publishers, or software publishers. If Georghiou was to sell directly, MediaSpark would have to handle the full advertising and distributing duties.

Educational product catalogue companies sold thousands of products to educational institutions through published or on-line catalogues. The larger publishers would send out educational catalogues to most schools in North America, though Georghiou questioned how many actually got to teachers he wished to reach. Catalogue companies would typically only list a product in exchange for an exclusive deal. Thus, Georghiou would not be able to sell GoVenture Entrepreneur in the same region through any other channel. Georghiou had researched the reseller discount for all possible distribution channels. The reseller discount was the percentage of the final price that the reselling company retained. For catalogue companies, Georghiou reported the reseller discount to be between 20% and 35%.

Georghiou's second indirect option, textbook publishers, supplied most schools with their core text books. Textbook publishers differed from catalogue companies as they employed a sales force as well as a published catalogue of products. Sales representatives would travel to schools and trade shows to present the product catalogue, and potential purchasers would have a better chance of seeing a demonstration of the product. Text publishers, however, would also require an exclusive deal to carry a product and would demand a reseller discount of 40%–60%.

Georghiou had identified two main text publishers: Glencoe McGraw-Hill and Southwestern. Georghiou knew that Glencoe was already carrying a competing product: Virtual Business (**http://www.knowledgematters.com**). Georghiou had heard that Southwestern had turned down his competitor's product, but thought it would likely want to pick up a competing product since Glencoe started carrying Virtual Business. Georghiou identified Southwestern as the leading business education provider to the K–12, higher education, and professional markets in the United States. It did not, however, distribute in Canada. Its main focus was text books; however, it had distributed some interactive software in keyboarding, marketing, management, and accounting. Glencoe also focused on text books with a small amount of software titles (like Virtual Business).

Because of the technological nature of his product, Georghiou also considered software distribution companies as a third indirect distribution channel. A software distributor could give Georghiou's product more profile when compared to being "lost in the thousands of traditional text products in a publisher's catalogue." Again, software distributors would require an exclusive deal to carry a product. Georghiou found that the software distribution market was highly fragmented. There were no companies that operated in both the Canadian and the U.S. markets. Furthermore, in the United States, there were very few national distributors; many were small companies who would carry other firms' products as well as their own. The reseller discount for software distributors was comparable to that of text publishers at 40% to 60%.

One option within the United States was to distribute through a nonprofit company called MarkED, a consortium of 40 state education departments and other organizations. As an industry-run organization, MarkED would lend credibility to the products it supported. MarkED sold products through a catalogue it distributed to its constituent organizations. However, it did not have a sales force to complement the catalogue and Georghiou could not be sure that the catalogue would reach the right teachers.

In Canada, the software distribution choices were much different. The most prominent distributor was IBM which operated a software distribution division in Canada.[1] Established in 1880, IBM was the world's largest and most recognizable information technology company. IBM Canada had its own sales force which was already distributing to schools. Since 1995, IBM invested $75 million in its Reinventing Education program which it established to break down barriers to academic achievement. IBM estimated that this program would reach 100 000 teachers and 10 million students in 10 countries by the end of 2004. IBM provided research and technical expertise, as well as equipment and cash contributions, to improve teaching and learning. The educational software currently available to the K–12 market focused on reading, language arts, mathematics, and science. In addition to this, IBM supplied many schools with the interface and internet software for their computers, as well as interactive white boards.

Georghiou felt that IBM was a good candidate because it was technology based, had brand recognition, and was already distributing to schools.

IBM also sold software in the United States but it was in the midst of changing its strategy and moving towards only carrying a very small number of products. Because it was undergoing some changes, MediaSpark saw no real opportunity to work with them.

IBM had proposed a two-year exclusive deal with MediaSpark to distribute to the K–12 educational market. Georghiou's only reservation was that he felt IBM may focus its attention on its hardware sales rather than software.

Finally, Georghiou could also consider an in-house direct distribution channel. MediaSpark currently employed only one marketing/sales person. Georghiou estimated that to effectively market GoVenture, he would have to hire 5 to 10 sales representatives and an additional 2 to 3 marketing people located in various areas throughout Canada and the United States. The majority of his sales would originate from tradeshows, events, and inside sales calls. Georghiou expected that MediaSpark would have to appear at over ten trade shows in the United States and at least two in Canada. MediaSpark's sales team would have to be responsible for inside sales calls, email campaigns, direct mail, CD demos, seminars, public speaking, and catalogue sales. Georghiou estimated that if MediaSpark did market and sell GoVenture independently, he would not be able to hire all the sales representatives he required and would have to survive with only one or two marketing/sales people. In such a situation, Georghiou himself would likely attend a number of tradeshows and make sales trips throughout the year. The advantage of selling in-house was that MediaSpark would make a much higher margin on each unit sold as there would be no reseller discount. However, tradeshows were expensive and the need to sell GoVenture Entrepreneur may distract MediaSpark from new product development.

THE DECISION

Georghiou struggled with the distribution decision. He first had to decide whether or not to go with a third party distributor and if he did, which one or ones to go with. Georghiou was most worried about the exclusivity required by distributors. In essence, if Georghiou went with a distributor, he was putting all his eggs in one basket; he had to have absolute confidence in the distributor he chose. If the distributor did not succeed in selling the product, Georghiou would have no other avenues to make a sale. Georghiou worried that his product would be one product among many in any distributor's product line and that they may put more focus on other products. The lack of technology knowledge of some of the potential distributors was another worry. As Georghiou explained, "Success depended on leveraging a distributor's brand awareness and market reach to sell more units than we can on our own."

Exhibit 1 MediaSpark GoVenture Entrepreneur Website

GoVenture Entrepreneur is a highly visual and realistic business simulation that recreates the day-to-day experiences involved in starting and running a small business.

Like a flight simulator for small business, Entrepreneur engages you in realistic situations and problems. Take your own test flights, at your own speed. Within the world of Entrepreneur, the decisions and the consequences are highly realistic. So virtual entrepreneurs rapidly gain the authentic wisdom that normally only comes from on-the-job experience.

The GoVenture Experience

- **Experience** what it is like to manage numerous business and personal tasks.
- **Make** necessary compromises to reach both business and personal success.
- **Learn** what you need to know to start a business in minutes, not months.

This simulation makes learning about being an entrepreneur fun. You can run the simulation for as long as you want. You can dive in using the Quick Start feature or take the time to go through the Personal and Business Profiles to select and start a business. You can conduct business, get advice, attend training seminars, and even close or sell your company. At any point, you may save your simulation and return to it later.

There is no penalty for failure, so if your first business doesn't succeed, try another. You can even control how fast the simulation time clock runs!

You can check your own personal financial status or your company's at any time. Review the business' financial statements and charts on recent operations. If you're doing well, you can pay yourself a bonus and buy one of those items on your wish list.

Watch out for random events—you could become injured and have to stay home for a while. Or if you forget your spouse's birthday your stress level may go up. If your stress level is too high, you may have to take some time off from the company. Can your employees run it without you?

The simulation immerses you in a life-like world of entrepreneurship and small business—a world where you still have to remember to pay your bills and get enough sleep.

It is an engaging experience, which makes learning fun, as you build an understanding of what it is like to be an entrepreneur and to meet the challenges of starting and running a small business.

The Entrepreneur CD-ROM simulation can be used in schools, in self-paced home or work study, in life-long learning programs, and in corporate training initiatives for employees or customers. Never before has it been so easy to experience the life of an entrepreneur.

Exhibit 2 MediaSpark GoVenture Entrepreneur Pricing

GOVENTURE ENTREPRENEUR PRODUCT PRICE

	1 SEAT*	5 SEAT*	30 Seat*	SITE**
GoVenture Entrepreneur Software License – Educational (USD)	$199	$349	$749	$1199
GoVenture Entrepreneur Software License - Educational (CAD)	$199	$499	NA	$1499

Software License Includes:

- License for a specified number of concurrent user(s). See Software License Descriptions below for important information.
- 1 CD-ROM for Windows (GoVenture Entrepreneur is also compatible with Macintosh). Program can be copied from CD to computer hard drives or network drive.
- User Guide.
- Performance Reports (built into the software).
- FREE Experiencing Book (text on Entrepreneurship).
- FREE Education Bundle (including instructor guide, lesson plans and test bank).
- FREE Value Option for 1 Year (includes additional customer service support).

* **SEAT License:** This license allows for many people to use the software at the same organization (or school) at one physical address location. The number of seats purchased determines how many computers may run the software concurrently (at the same time). For example, a 5-Seat License allows for the software to be run on up to 5 computers at the same time. In this example, the software may be installed on a network, or installed on more than 5 computers, but the software may not be run on more than 5 computers concurrently. Individual Seats cannot be shared amongst different organizations (or schools).

** **SITE License:** This license allows for use of the software on all your organization's (or school's) computers at one physical address location at any time. There are no limits on how many computers may run the software concurrently—as long as they are on the same site (one physical address location). A SITE License cannot be shared amongst different organizations.

NOTES, SOURCES, AND CREDITS

Reference Notes

Chapter 1

1 *Financial Post Business*, Special Edition, 2006, 64.

2. See Robert A. Collinge and Ronald M. Ayers, *Economics by Design: Principles and Issues*, 2nd ed. (Upper Saddle River, NJ: Prentice Hall, 2000), 41–42; Michael J. Mandel, "The New Economy," *Business Week* (January 31, 2000): 73–77.

3. Karl E. Case and Ray C. Fair, *Principles of Economics*, 6th ed. (Upper Saddle River, NJ: Prentice Hall, 2003), 224–225.

4. Richard I. Kirkland, Jr., "The Death of Socialism," *Fortune* (January 4, 1988): 64–72.

5. See Karl E. Case and Ray C. Fair, *Principles of Economics*, 5th ed. (Upper Saddle River, NJ: Prentice Hall, 1999), 69–74; Robert A. Collinge and Ronald M. Ayers, *Economics by Design: Principles and Issues*, 2nd ed. (Upper Saddle River, NJ: Prentice Hall, 2000), 51–52.

6. Deborah Orr, "The Post Office with a Ticker," *Forbes* (November 29, 1999): 77–78; Matthew L. Wald, "Canada's Private Control Towers," *The New York Times*, October 23, 1999, C1. See also National Center for Policy Analysis, "Privatization," www.public-policy.org/~ncpa/pd/private/privat.html, March 8, 2000.

7. Andy Hoffman, "Labatt Convicted in Quebec Discount Beer Case," *The Globe and Mail*, November 24, 2005, B10

8. Barrie McKenna, "Hyundai Gorged on Federal Funds," *The Globe and Mail*, March 25, 1994, B3.

9. See Karl E. Case and Ray C. Fair, *Principles of Economics*, 5th ed. (Upper Saddle River, NJ: Prentice Hall, 1999), 70–90; Robert A. Collinge and Ronald M. Ayers, *Economics by Design: Principles and Issues*, 2nd ed. (Upper Saddle River, NJ: Prentice Hall, 2000), 74–77.

10. Joel Millman, "Metal is so Precious that Scrap Thieves Now Tap Beer Kegs," *The Wall Street Journal*, March 14, 2006, A1, A15.

11. Wendy Stueck, "Ginseng Growers at Root of Problem," *The Globe and Mail*, May 21, 2001, B1, B3.

12. See Paul Heyne, Peter J. Boettke, and David L. Prychitko, *The Economic Way of Thinking*, 10th ed. (Upper Saddle River, NJ: Prentice Hall, 2003), 190, 358–359.

13. See Gina M. Larson, "bebe Bridges Style Gap," www.office.com/global/0,2724,509-10386_1,FF.html, July 10, 2001; Natural Fibers Information Center, "Ranking of Top U.S. Public Apparel Companies," www.utexas.edu/depts/bbr/natfiber, June 2001; "bebe.com Finishes #1," *Fashion Windows.com*, www.fashionwindows.com/beauty/2002/bebe.asp, January 14, 2002.

14. Karl E. Case and Ray C. Fair, *Principles of Economics*, 6th ed., updated (Upper Saddle River, NJ: Prentice Hall, 2003), 300–309.

15. *Hoover's Handbook of World Business 2002* (Austin, TX: Hoover's Business Press, 2002), 74–75.

16. John Partridge and Lawrence Surtees, "Rogers Faces Assault from Telcos," *The Globe and Mail*, March 28, 1994, B1–B2.

17. "Royal Mail's Reign Comes to an End," *The Globe and Mail*, January 2, 2006, B7.

18. Madelaine Drohan, "Ottawa Targets Interprovincial Barriers," *The Globe and Mail*, May 14, 1991, B5.

Chapter 2

1. See Jay B. Barney and William G. Ouchi, eds., *Organizational Economics* (San Francisco: Jossey-Bass, 1986), for a detailed analysis of linkages between economics and organizations.

2. Karl E. Case and Ray C. Fair, *Principles of Economics*, 6th ed., updated (Upper Saddle River, NJ: Prentice Hall, 2003), 432–433.

3. Karl E. Case and Ray C. Fair, *Principles of Economics*, 6th ed., updated (Upper Saddle River, NJ: Prentice Hall, 2003), 15.

4. Karl E. Case and Ray C. Fair, *Principles of Economics*, 6th ed., updated (Upper Saddle River, NJ: Prentice Hall, 2003), 15.

5. *Bank of Canada Banking and Financial Statistics*, Table H1 (April 2006), S94.

6. Barry Marquardson, "GDP Fails as a Measurement," *The Globe and Mail*, July 16, 1998, B2.

7. Richard Bloom, "Report Analyzes Income Gap with U.S.," *The Globe and Mail*, October 6, 2003, B1, B4.

8. Olivier Blanchard, *Macroeconomics*, 3rd ed. (Upper Saddle River, NJ: Prentice Hall, 2003), 24–26.

9. Jay Heizer and Barry Render, *Operations Management*, 6th Ed. (Upper Saddle River, NJ, Prentice Hall, 2001), 15–16.

10. *Bank of Canada Banking and Financial Statistics*, Table J1 (April 2006), S108.

11. Greg Hitt and Murray Hiebert, "U.S. Trade Deficit Ballooned to a Record in 2005," *The Wall Street Journal*, February 11–12, 2006, A1, A10.

12. *Bank of Canada Banking and Financial Statistics*, Table G1 (May 2006), S83.

13. This section is based on Paul Heyne, Peter J. Boettke, and David L. Prychitko, *The Economic Way of Thinking*, 10th ed. (Upper Saddle River, NJ: Prentice Hall, 2003), 491–493.

14. See Warren J. Keegan, *Global Marketing Management*, 7th ed. (Upper Saddle River, NJ: Prentice Hall, 2002), 39–42.

15. Tavia Grant, "Lard in 1913, Plasma TV Now: CPI Tracks Changes," *The Globe and Mail*, April 21, 2005, B1, B15.

16. Bruce Little, "There's Been a Huge Shift in How Consumers Spend," *The Globe and Mail*, July 5, 2004, B4.

17. Paul Heyne, Peter J. Boettke, and David L. Prychitko, *The Economic Way of Thinking*, 10th ed. (Upper Saddle River, NJ: Prentice Hall, 2003), 403–409, 503–504.

18. Statistics Canada, *Industrial Research and Development, 2005 Intentions:* 10.

19. Statistics Canada, *Industrial Research and Development, 2005 Intentions:* 10.

20. Statistics Canada, *Industrial Research and Development, 2005 Intentions:* 17.

21. Statistics Canada, *Industrial Research and Development, 2005 Intentions:* 10.

22. Statistics Canada, *Industrial Research and Development, 2005 Intentions:* 10.

23. Thomas Wheelen and J. David Hunger, *Strategic Management and Business Policy* (Upper Saddle River, NJ: Pearson, 2004), 280.

24. L. G. Franko, "Global Corporate Competition: Who's Winning, Who's Losing, and the R&D Factor as One Reason Why," *Strategic Management Journal* (September–October, 1989): 449–474.

25. Roberta S. Russell and Bernard W. Taylor III, *Operations Management*, 4th ed. (Upper Saddle River, NJ: Prentice Hall, 2003), Chapter 12.

26. Terrence Belford, "The Little Guys Are Getting with Big Boys' Program," *The Globe and Mail*, June 2, 2005, B16.

27. Brian Laghi, "U.S. Backlash Seen Growing," *The Globe and Mail*, March 27, 2003, B1, B10.

28. Sinclair Stewart, "CIBC's Solid Profit Overshadowed by Woes," *The Globe and Mail*, February 27, 2004, B1, B6.

29. KPMG, "Eleventh Annual Survey of Canada's Most Respected Corporations, 2005," www.mostrespected.ca.

30. Michael Porter. *Competitive Strategy: Techniques for Analyzing Industries and Competitors* (New York: The Free Press, 1980).

31. Judy Strauss and Raymond Frost, *E-Marketing* (Upper Saddle River, NJ: Prentice Hall, 2001), 245–246.

32. Tessa Wegert, "Advertisers Get Creative in Bid to Infect the Internet," *The Globe and Mail*, October 27, 2005, B13.

33. Lee J. Krajewski and Larry P. Ritzman, *Operations Management: Strategy and Analysis*, 6th ed. (Upper Saddle River, NJ: Prentice Hall, 2002), 3–4.

34. Lee J. Krajewski and Larry P. Ritzman, *Operations Management: Strategy and Analysis*, 6th ed. (Upper Saddle River, NJ: Prentice Hall, 2002), Chapter 3.

35. Lawrence Surtees, "Takeover Concern Prompts BCE Poison Pill Plan," *The Globe and Mail*, February 25, 2000, B5.

36. Margot Gibb-Clark, "Share Plans Can Benefit More Than Employees," *The Globe and Mail*, February 14, 2000, B6.

37. "Nunavut Diamond Find Sends Shares Soaring," *The Winnipeg Free Press*, February 4, 2003, B10.

38. "Inco, LionOre Mining Form Strategic Alliance," *The Winnipeg Free Press*, March 14, 2003, B6.

Chapter 3

1. Constance L. Hays, "Aide Was Reportedly Ordered to Warn Stewart on Stock Sales," *The New York Times*, August 6, 2002, C1, C2.

2. Thomas Donaldson and Thomas W. Dunfee, "Toward a Unified Conception of Business Ethics: An Integrative Social Contracts Theory," *Academy of Management Review* 19, no. 2 (1994): 252–284.

3. "Drug Companies Face Assault on Prices," *The Wall Street Journal*, May 11, 2000, B1, B4.

4. John Saunders, "Bitter Air Carrier Dogfight Heads to Court," *The Globe and Mail*, July 8, 2004, B3.

5. Ann Zimmerman and Anita Raghavan, "Diamond Group Widens Probe of Bribe Charges, *The Wall Street Journal*, March 8, 2006, B1-B2.

6. This section follows the logic of Gerald F. Cavanaugh, *American Business Values with International Perspectives*, 4th ed. (Upper Saddle River, NJ: Prentice Hall, 1998), Chapter 3.

7. Patricia Sellers, "Crunch Time for Coke," *Fortune* (July 19, 1999): 72–74+.

8. Mark Schwartz, "Heat's on to Get an Effective Code," *The Globe and Mail*, November 27, 1997, B2.

9. Jeffrey S. Harrison and R. Edward Freeman, "Stakeholders, Social Responsibility, and Performance: Empirical Evidence and Theoretical Perspectives," *Academy of Management Journal* 42, no. 5, 479–485. See also David P. Baron, *Business and Its Environment*, 3rd ed. (Upper Saddle River, NJ: Prentice-Hall, 2000), Chapter 17.

10. James R. Healey, "Ford to Reveal Plans for Think Brand," *USA Today*, January 10, 2000, 1B; Gwen Kinkead, "In the Future, People Like Me Will Go to Jail," *Fortune* (May 24, 1999): 190–200.

11. David P. Baron, *Business and Its Environment*, 4th ed. (Upper Saddle River, NJ: Prentice Hall, 2003), Chapter 11.

12. Jeremy Main, "Here Comes the Big New Cleanup," *Fortune* (November 21, 1988): 102–118.

13. Patrick Brethour, "Canada's Big Emitters Brace for Investment Climate Change," *The Globe and Mail*, February 19, 2005, B4.

14. Bill Curry, "Ottawa Wants Kyoto Softened," *The Globe and Mail*, May 12, 2006, A1, A7.

15. Andrew C. Revkin, "Who Cares About a Few Degrees?" *New York Times*, December 12, 1997, F4.

16. Catherine Collins, "The Race for Zero," *Canadian Business* (March 1991): 52–56.

17. Allan Robinson and Allan Freeman, "Mining's Dam Problem," *The Globe and Mail*, May 16, 1998, B1–B2.

18. "Hot Spots," *Canadian Business* (March 17, 2003): 30–31.

19. Geoffrey Scotton, "Cleanups Can Hurt, Companies Warned," *The Financial Post*, June 25, 1991, 4.

20. Marc Huber, "A Double-Edged Endorsement," *Canadian Business* (January 1990): 69–71.

21. Egle Procuta, "One Man's Garbage is Another's Gold," *The Globe and Mail*, April 11, 2006, B7.

22. Richard B. Schmitt and Robert Langreth, "American Home Products Agrees to Pay Up to $3.75 Billion in Diet-Drug Lawsuits," *WSJ Interactive Edition*, www.productslaw.com/diet21.html, July 11, 2001. See also Nancy Shute, "Pills Don't Come with a Seal of Approval," *U.S. News Online*, www.usnews.com/usnews/issue/970929/29fen.htm, July 11, 2001.

23. John Saunders, "Polar Plastic Plot Flops," *The Globe and Mail*, June 10, 1994, B1.

24. John Wilke, "Cases, Fines, Soar in Fraud Probes of Drug Pricing," *The Wall Street Journal*, June 7, 2005, A1, A10.

25. Jonathan Cheng, "False Ads: Chinese Consumers Awaken to a Western Problem," *The Wall Street Journal*, July 8, 2005, B9.

26. Shawn McCarthy, "Crackdown on New York's Canal Street," *The Globe and Mail*, August 30, 2004, B1, B11.

27. Jeff Sanford, "Knock-off Nation," *Canadian Business* (November 8–21, 2004): 67–71.

28. Gordon Fairclough, "Tobacco Firms Trace Fakes to North Korea," *The Wall Street Journal*, January 27, 2006, B1–B2.

29. Tim Barker, "Word-of-Mouth Advertising Grows in Influence, Concern," *Orlando Sentinel*, March 17, 2006, A1, A19.

30. Michael McCarthy and Lorrie Grant, "Sears Drops Benetton After Controversial Death Row Ads," *USA Today*, February 18, 2000, 2B.

31. Shona McKay, "Willing and Able," *Report on Business Magazine* (October 1991): 58–63.

32. "Why Business Is Hiring the Mentally Abled," *Canadian Business* (May 1991): 19.

33. J. Southerst, "In Pursuit of Drugs," *Canadian Transportation* (November 1989): 58–65.

34. G. Bylinsky, "How Companies Spy on Employees," *Fortune* (November 4, 1991): 131–140.

35. Greg Farrell, "Enron Law Firm Called Accounting Practices 'Creative,'" *USA Today*, January 16, 2002, 1B.

36. Jerald Greenberg and Robert A. Baron, *Behavior in Organizations: Understanding and Managing the Human Side of Work*, 7th ed. (Upper Saddle River, NJ: Prentice Hall, 2000), 374–375.

37. Rick Lyman, "A Tobacco Whistle-Blower's Life Is Transformed," *The New York Times*, October 15, 1999, A24.

38. Cora Daniels, "'It's a Living Hell,'" *Fortune* (April 15, 2002): 367–368.

39. Andy Pasztor and Peter Landers, "Toshiba to Pay $2B Settlement on Laptops," *ZD Net News* www.zdnet.com/zdnn/stories/news/0,4586,2385037,00.html, July 12, 2001.

40. Greg Farrell, "Enron Law Firm Called Accounting Practices 'Creative,'" *USA Today*, January 16, 2002, 1B.

41. Daniel Stoffman, "Good Behavior and the Bottom Line," *Canadian Business* (May 1991): 28–32.

42. Tom Kierans, "Charity Begins at Work," *Report on Business Magazine* (June 1990): 23.

43. Theresa Ebden and Dawn Walton, "Walkerton Recipient of New-Style Corporate Giving," *The Globe and Mail*, June 3, 2000, B1, B6.

44. Theresa Ebden and Dawn Walton, "Walkerton Recipient of New-Style

Corporate Giving," *The Globe and Mail*, June 3, 2000, B1, B6.

45. "Private Sector Comes to Rescue in Asia," *The Globe and Mail*, December 30, 2004, B5.

46. Paul Waldie, "Firms Mull Response to Disaster," *The Globe and Mail*, December 31, 2004, B1–B2.

47. Sandra Waddock and Neil Smith, "Corporate Responsibility Audits: Doing Well by Doing Good," *Sloan Management Review* (Winter 2000): 75–85.

48. Janet McFarland, "Are You Making Yourself Accountable?" *The Globe and Mail*, April 20, 2006, B12.

49. Alison Arnot, "The Triple Bottom Line," *CGA Magazine* (January–February 2004): 27–32.

Chapter 4

1. Statistics Canada, *Business Dynamics in Canada*, Catalogue no. 61-534-XIE (Ottawa: Minister of Industry, 2006).

2. P. D. Reynolds, S. M. Camp, W. D. Bygrave, E. Autio, and M. Hay, *Global Entrepreneurship Monitor: 2001 Executive Report*. (Kansas City, MO: Kauffman Center for Entrepreneurial Leadership, 2001); P. D. Reynolds, M. Hay, W. D. Bygrave, S. M. Camp, and E. Autio, *Global Entrepreneurship Monitor: 2000 Executive Report* (Kansas City, MO: Kauffman Center for Entrepreneurial Leadership, 2000).

3. Industry Canada, *Key Small Business Statistics* (Ottawa: Public Works and Government Services Canada, 2006), 24.

4. Industry Canada, Key Small Business Statistics, (Ottawa: Public Works and Government Services Canada, 2006), 3.

5. Monica Diochon, Teresa Menzies and Yvon Gasse, "Exploring the Relationship Between Start-up Activities and New Venture Emergence: A Longitudinal Study of Canadian Nascent Entrepreneurs," *International Journal of Management and Enterprise Development* 2, no. 3/4 (2005): 408–426.

6. Nancy M. Carter, William B. Gartner and Paul D. Reynolds, "Firm Founding," in *Handbook of Entrepreneurial Dynamics: The Process of Business Creation*, ed. W. B. Gartner, K. G. Shaver, N. M. Carter, and P. D. Reynolds (Thousand Oaks, CA: Sage, 2004), 311–323.

7. William D. Bygrave and C. W. Hofer, "Theorizing About Entrepreneurship," *Entrepreneurship Theory and Practice* 16, no. 2 (Winter 1991): 14; Donald Sexton and Nancy Bowman-Upton, *Entrepreneurship: Creativity and Growth*, (New York, NY: MacMillan Publishing Company, 1991), 7.

8. John Cooper, "A Pint of Success," *CMA Management* (December 1999/January 2000): 44–46.

9. Angela Dale, "Self-Employment and Entrepreneurship: Notes on Two Problematic Concepts," in *Deciphering the Enterprise Culture*, ed. Roger Burrows, London: Routledge, 1991), 45, 48; Holt 1992, 11.

10. Donald Sexton and Nancy Bowman-Upton, *Entrepreneurship: Creativity and Growth* (New York, NY: MacMillan Publishing Company, 1991), 11; Kao, 1991, 21.

11. Allan A. Gibb, "The Enterprise Culture and Education: Understanding Enterprise Education and Its Links with Small Business, Entrepreneurship and Wider Educational Goals," *International Small Business Journal* 11, no. 3 (1993): 13–34; Donald Sexton and Nancy Bowman-Upton, *Entrepreneurship: Creativity and Growth*, (New York, NY: MacMillan Publishing Company, 1991).

12. Terrence Belford, "Intrapreneurs Combine Big-biz Clout with Entrepreneurial Style," CanWest News (March 23). Retrieved June 25, 2006, from CBCA Current Events database. (Document ID: 1009719591).

13. Statistics Canada, Business Register, National Income and Expenditure Accounts 2005; Estimates of Population by Age and Sex for Canada, the Provinces and the Territories, June 2005.

14. Industry Canada, *Key Small Business Statistics* (Ottawa: Public Works and Government Services Canada, 2006), 10

15. Industry Canada, *Key Small Business Statistics* (Ottawa: Public Works and Government Services Canada, 2006), 10.

16. Industry Canada, *Key Small Business Statistics* (Ottawa: Public Works and Government Services Canada, 2006), 23.

17. William B. Gartner, Kelly G. Shaver, Nancy M. Carter, and Paul D. Reynolds, *Handbook of Entrepreneurial Dynamics* (Thousand Oaks, CA: Sage Publications, Inc., 2004), ix.

18. Statistics Canada, *Business Dynamics in Canada 2003* (Ottawa: Minister of Industry, March 2006), Catalogue no. 61-534-XIE, 6.

19. Richard Bloom, "Building a Future on Sweet Dreams," *The Globe and Mail*, October 21, 2004, B9.

20. Angela Barnes, "Doing It for Themselves," *The Globe and Mail*, October 19, 2005, E1–E2.

21. Virginia Galt, "Female Entrepreneurs to be Honoured Tonight," *The Globe and Mail*, November 22, 2005, B9.

22. Christine Carrington, "Women Entrepreneurs," *Journal of Small Business and Entrepreneurship* 19, no. 2 (2006): 83–94.

23. Murray McNeill, "Patience Pays Off for Native Owner," *The Winnipeg Free Press*, November 6, 2002, B3.

24. Sarah Kennedy, "Self-Styled Pioneer Aims to Alter Face of Fashion," *The Globe and Mail*, July 1, 2002, B12.

25. Geoff Kirbyson, "Market-Research Firm Lands Major Contract," *The Winnipeg Free Press*, July 19, 2004, D7.

26. Donald F. Kuratko and Richard M. Hodgetts, *Entrepreneurship: Theory, Process, Practice*, 7th ed. (Mason, OH: Thomson South-Western, 2007), 118–125; John A. Hornday, "Research About Living Entrepreneurs," in *Encyclopedia of Entrepreneurship*, ed. Calvin Kent, Donald Sexton, and Karl Vesper (Englewood Cliffs, NJ: Prentice-Hall, 1982), 26–27; Jeffry A. Timmons and Stephen Spinelli, *New Venture Creation: Entrepreneurship for the 21st Century* (Boston, MA: McGraw-Hill Irwin, 2007), 9.

27. Jeffry A. Timmons and Stephen Spinelli, *New Venture Creation: Entrepreneurship for the 21st Century*, 7th Edition (Boston, MA:McGraw-Hill Irwin, 2007), 19.

28. J. D. Kyle, R. Blais, R. Blatt, and A. J. Szonyi, "The Culture of the Entrepreneur: Fact or Fiction," *Journal of Small Business and Entrepreneurship* (1991): 3–14.

29. R. H. Brockhaus and Pam S. Horwitz, "The Psychology of the Entrepreneur," in *The Art and Science of Entrepreneurship*, ed. D. L Sexton and Raymond W. Smilor (Cambridge, MA: Ballinger Pub. Co., 1986); William B. Gartner, "What Are We Talking About When We Talk About Entrepreneurship?" *Journal of Business Venturing* 5, no. 1 (1990): 15–29; Allan A. Gibb, "The Enterprise Culture and Education: Understanding Enterprise Education and Its Links with Small Business, Entrepreneurship and Wider Educational Goals," *International Small Business Journal* 11, no. 3 (1993): 13–34; J. C. Mitchell, "Case and Situation Analysis," *Sociological Review* 31, no. 2 (1983): 187–211.

30. Donald Sexton and Nancy Bowman-Upton, *Entrepreneurship: Creativity and Growth* (New York, NY: MacMillan Publishing Company, 1991); Karl H. Vesper, *New Venture Strategies* (Englewood Cliffs, NJ: Prentice Hall, 1990); W. D. Bygrave and C. W. Hofer, "Theorizing About Entrepreneurship," *Entrepreneurship Theory and Practice* 16, no. 2 (Winter 1991): 14.

31. Walter Good, *Building a Dream*, (Toronto: McGraw Hill Ryerson, 1998), 40.

32. Wayne A. Long and W. Ed McMullan. *Developing New Ventures* (San Diego: Harcourt Brace Jovanovich, 1990), 374–375.

33. "Sally Fox: Innovation in the Field," www.vreseis.com/sally_fox_story.htm, June 27, 2006.

34. Michael E. Porter, "Know Your Place," *Inc.* 13, no. 9 (September 1992): 90–93.

35. Howard H. Stevenson, H. Irving Grousbeck, Michael J. Roberts, and Amarnath Bhide, *New Business Ventures and the Entrepreneur* (Boston: Irwin McGraw-Hill, 1999), 19.

36. Howard H. Stevenson, H. Irving Grousbeck, Michael J. Roberts, and Amarnath Bhide, *New Business Ventures and the Entrepreneur* (Boston: Irwin McGraw-Hill, 1999), 21.

37. Marc J. Dollinger, *Entrepreneurship: Strategies and Resources* (Upper Saddle River, NJ: Prentice Hall, 1999), 94–101.

38. Thomas W. Zimmerer and Norman M. Scarborough, *Essentials of Entrepreneurship and Small Business Management*, 4th ed. (Upper Saddle River, NJ: Pearson Prentice Hall), 359.

39. Michael E. Porter, "Know Your Place," *Inc.* 13, no. 9 (September 1992): 90–93.

40. Karl H. Vesper, *New Venture Mechanics* (Englewood Cliffs, NJ: Prentice Hall, 1993), 105.

41. Jeffry A. Timmons, *New Venture Creation* (Boston: Irwin McGraw-Hill, 1999), 277.

42. Lisa Stephens, "With Some Shape Shifting, This Company Has Legs," *The Globe and Mail*, October 5, 2005, B10.

43. Gordon Pitts, "An Empire Looks to the Future," *The Globe and Mail*, March 26, 2005, B4.

44. George Anders, Carol Hymowitz, Joann Lublin, and Don Clark, "All in the Family," *The Wall Street Journal*, August 1, 2005, B1, B4.

45. Ronald J. Ebert, Ricky W. Griffin, and Frederick A. Starke, *Business Essentials*, 4th Canadian ed. (Toronto: Pearson Education Canada, 2006), 63.

46. Mary Agnes Welch, "When Name Is Everything," *The Winnipeg Free Press*, May 12, 2002, B1–B2.

47. Quoted in Lowell B. Howard, *Business Law* (Woodbury, NY: Barron's Woodbury Press, 1965), 332.

48. Richard Bloom, "IPO's Surge on Mood Swing," *The Globe and Mail*, February 8, 2005, B3.

49. Richard Bloom, "Cara Shareholders Vote to Take Company Private," *The Globe and Mail*, February 25, 2005, B7; and Greg Keenan, "Magna Reverses Strategy, Plans to Take Parts Subsidiaries Private," *The Globe and Mail*, October 26, 2004, B1, B10.

50. Terry Pedwell, Income Trusts Face Tough Rules," *The Winnipeg Free Press*, November 1, 2006, B7.

51. "An Overview of Available Business Structures," www.umanitoba.ca/afs/agric_economics/MRAC/structures.html #Cooperatives, July 2, 2006.

52. Monica Diochon, Teresa Menzies, and Yvon Gasse, "Nascent Entrepreneurs' Start-up Efforts: Outcomes and Individual Influences on Sustainability," *Journal of Small Business and Entrepreneurship* (2005), 53–74.

53. Kevin Marron, "Want to Succeed? Read This," *The Globe and Mail*, October 19, 2005, E1, E5. Several excellent articles on starting and operating a small business are found in Section E, "Report on Small Business" in *The Globe and Mail*, October 19, 2005.

54. See Norman M. Scarborough and Thomas W. Zimmerer, *Effective Small Business Management: An Entrepreneurial Approach*, 7th ed. (Upper Saddle River, NJ: Prentice Hall, 2003).

Chapter 5

1. Ricky W. Griffin and Michael W. Pustay, *International Business: A Managerial Perspective*, 2nd ed. (Reading, MA: Addison-Wesley, 1999), 431–433; John J. Wild, Kenneth L. Wild, and Jerry C.Y. Han, *International Business: An Integrated Approach* (Upper Saddle River, NJ: Prentice Hall, 2000), 456–458.

2. Ricky W. Griffin and Michael W. Pustay, *International Business: A Managerial Perspective*, 2nd ed. (Reading, MA: Addison-Wesley, 1999), 44–45. See also Warren J. Keegan, *Global Marketing Management*, 6th ed. (Upper Saddle River, NJ: Prentice Hall, 1999), 42–45.

3. Trade Partners UK, "Automotive Industries Market in Mexico," www.tradepartners.gov.uk/automotive/mexico/profile/characteristics.shtml, July 10, 2001; NAFTA Works, "Mexico Auto Sector Sees $15 Billion Investment in 5 Years," www.naftaworks.org/papers/2000/automex.htm, July 10, 2001.

4. David Fairlamb and Gail Edmondson, "Work in Progress," *Business Week* (January 31, 2000): 80–81+.

5. David Fairlamb and Gail Edmondson, "Work in Progress," *Business Week* (January 31, 2000): 80–81+.

6. Edmund L. Andrews, "The Metamorphosis of Germany Inc.," *The New York Times*, March 12, 2000, section 3, 1, 12.

7. Mark Landler, "Mapping Out Silicon Valley East," *The New York Times*, April 5, 1999, C1, C10; Bruce Einhorn with Cathy Yang, "Portal Combat," *Business Week* (January 17, 2000): 96–97.

8. John Wild, Kenneth Wild, and Jerry Han, *International Business*, 2nd ed. (Upper Saddle River, NJ: Prentice Hall, 2003), 239.

9. Ricky W. Griffin and Michael W. Pustay, *International Business: A Managerial Perspective*, 2nd ed. (Reading, MA: Addison-Wesley, 1999), Chapter 3. Dominick Salvatore, *International Economics*, 6th ed. (Upper Saddle River, NJ: Prentice Hall, 1998), 27–33; Karl E. Case and Ray C. Fair, *Principles of Economics*, 5th ed. (Upper Saddle River, NJ: Prentice Hall, 1999), 813–817.

10. This section is based on Michael Porter, *The Competitive Advantage of Nations* (Boston: Harvard Business School Press, 1990), Chapters 3 and 4; Warren J. Keegan, *Global Marketing Management*, 6th ed. (Upper Saddle River, NJ: Prentice Hall, 1999), 312–321; John J. Wild, Kenneth L. Wild, and Jerry C.Y. Han, *International Business: An Integrated Approach* (Upper Saddle River, NJ: Prentice Hall, 2000), 175–178.

11. Heather Scoffield, "Canada's Slipping on the World Stage, WEF Study Shows," *The Globe and Mail*, September 27, 2006, B7.

12. Madelaine Drohan, "Dependency on U.S. Leaves Canada 'Vulnerable': WTO," *The Globe and Mail*, November 20, 1996.

13. Table J2, *Bank of Canada Banking and Financial Statistics*, April 2006, S110.

14. Karl E. Case and Ray C. Fair, *Principles of Economics*, 5th ed. (Upper Saddle River, NJ: Prentice Hall, 1999), 818–821.

15. Robyn Meredith, "Dollar Makes Canada a Land of the Spree," *The New York Times*, August 1, 1999, sec. 3, 1, 11.

16. "Exports, Eh?" *Canadian Business* (January 1997): 21.

17. "China Rising: Where We're At," *The Globe and Mail*, October 29, 2005, introduction to the "Report on Business" section.

18. Shirley Won, "Small Firms Beating a Path to the Middle Kingdom," *The Globe and Mail*, August 31, 2004, B7.

19. Ray August, *International Business Law: Text, Cases, and Readings*, 3rd ed. (Upper Saddle River, NJ: Prentice Hall, 2000), 192–197.

20. Paola Hjelt, "The Fortune Global 500," *Fortune* (July 22, 2003): 144–147.

21. Celeste Mackenzie, "Rumble in the Jungle," *Canadian Business* (February 28–March 13, 2005): 57–63.

22. Warren J. Keegan, *Global Marketing Management*, 6th ed. (Upper Saddle River, NJ: Prentice Hall, 1999), 290–292; Ricky W. Griffin and Michael W. Pustay, *International Business: A Managerial Perspective*, 2nd ed. (Reading, MA: Addison-Wesley, 1999), 427–431; John J. Wild, Kenneth L. Wild, and Jerry C.Y. Han, *International Business: An Integrated Approach* (Upper Saddle River, NJ: Prentice Hall, 2000), 454–456.

23. Ricky W. Griffin and Michael W. Pustay, *International Business: A Managerial Perspective*, 2nd ed. (Reading, MA: Addison-Wesley, 1999), 431–433; John J. Wild, Kenneth L. Wild, and Jerry C.Y. Han, *International Business: An Integrated Approach* (Upper Saddle River, NJ: Prentice Hall, 2000), 456–458.

24. Shirley Won, "Small Firms Beating a Path to the Middle Kingdom," *The Globe and Mail*, August 31, 2004, B7.

25. Shirley Won, "Small Firms Beating a Path to the Middle Kingdom," *The Globe and Mail*, August 31, 2004, B7.

26. John J. Wild, Kenneth L. Wild, and Jerry C.Y. Han, *International Business: An Integrated Approach* (Upper Saddle River, NJ: Prentice Hall, 2000), Chapter 7; Ricky W. Griffin and Michael W. Pustay, *International Business: A Managerial Perspective*, 2nd ed. (Reading, MA: Addison-Wesley, 1999), 436–439.

27. Eric Beauchesne, "Foreign Control of Economy Hits 30-Year High," *The Winnipeg Free Press*, November 19, 2005, B7.

28. Eric Beauchesne, "Foreign Control of Economy Hits 30-Year High," *The Winnipeg Free Press*, November 19, 2005, B7.

29. Shawn McCarthy, "Business Sounds Alarm on Vulnerability," *The Globe and Mail*, May 8, 2000, B1, B3.

30. Steven Chase, "Canada Slaps Duties on Chinese-made Barbecues," *The Globe and Mail*, August 28, 2004, B2.

31. Peter Kennedy, "Softwood Decision Gets Mixed Reviews," *The Globe and Mail*, December 8, 2005, B6.

32. Jennifer Ditchburn, "Canada, U.S. Pen Deal to End Lumber Dispute," *The Winnipeg Free Press*, July 2, 2006, A6.

33. Paul Veira, "Emerson Warns Lumber Leaders of 'Consequences'," *Financial Post*, August 1, 2006, FP1, FP5. Steve Merti, "Lumber Exporters Taste Sting of Softwood Deal," *The Winnipeg Free Press*, September 22, 2006, B5.

34. Scott Kilman and Roger Thurow, "In Fight Against Farm Subsidies, Even Farmers Are Joining Foes," *The Wall Street Journal*, March 14, 2006, A1, A16.

35. Roger Thurow and Geoff Winestock, "How an Addiction to Sugar Subsidies Hurts Development," *The Wall Street Journal*, September 16, 2002, A1, A10.

36. "WTO Strikes Down U.S. Cotton Subsidy Appeal," *The Globe and Mail*, March 4, 2005, B10.

37. Scott Kilman and Roger Thurow, "To Soothe Anger Over Subsidies, U.S. Cotton Tries Wooing Africa," *The Wall Street Journal*, August 5, 2005, A1, A6.

38. Simon Tuck, "Farmers to WTO: If It Ain't Broke...," *The Globe and Mail*, August 9, 2004, B1–B2.

39. Anthony DePalma, "Chiquita Sues Europeans, Citing Banana Quota Losses," *The New York Times*, January 26, 2001, C5; Brian Lavery, "Trade Feud on Bananas Not as Clear as It Looks," *The New York Times*, February 7, 2001, W1; David E. Sanger, "Miffed at Europe, U.S. Raises Tariffs for Luxury Goods," *The New York Times*, March 4, 1999, A1, A5.

40. Wendy Stueck, "Mining Firms Hit Again By Chavez Threat," *The Globe and Mail*, September 23, 2005, B4; Barrie McKenna, "A Nation of Big Riches, Bigger Risks," *The Globe and Mail*, September 24, 2005, B4.

41. Konrad Yakabuski, "Quebec Courts Margarine War," *The Globe and Mail*, October 14, 1997, B1, B4.

42. Bertrand Marotte, "Ontario Calls for Dispute Panel in Quebec Margarine Battle, " *The Globe and Mail*, March 26, 2002, B10.

43. Neville Nankivell, "Spilled Milk Over Provincial Trade," *National Post*, April 24, 2000, C9.

44. Gerry Stobo, "Cross-Border Mobility," *CGA Magazine* (May June 2005): 13–16.

45. "The 2005 Transparency International Corruption Perceptions Index," www.infoplease.com/ipa/A0781359.html.

46. Geoffrey York, "Blowout in Bangladesh," *The Globe and Mail*, April 1, 2006, B4–B5.

47. Barrie McKenna, "Aluminum Producers Whispering Dirty Word," *The Globe and Mail*, March 5, 1994, B1, B5.

48. Jalil Hamid, "Coffee Rally Reignited," *The Globe and Mail*, May 22, 1997, B9.

49. Oliver Bertin, "Coffee Cartel Moves Fast on Price," *Globe and Mail*, May 20, 2000, B3.

50. Steven Chase, "Canadian Bike Makers Fear Hit from Cheap Chinese Imports," *The Globe and Mail*, September 7, 2004, B4.

51. "New Global Trade Regulator Starts Operations Tomorrow," *The Winnipeg Free Press*, December 31, 1994, A5.

52. Helene Cooper and Bhushan Bahree, "World's Best Hope for Global Trade Topples Few Barriers," *The Wall Street Journal*, December 3, 1996, A1, A8.

53. Heather Scoffield and Greg Keenan, "Canada Told to Scrap Auto Pact," *The Globe and Mail*, October 14, 1999, A1, A2.

54. Barrie McKenna, "NAFTA Dealt Blow by WTO Ruling," *The Globe and Mail*, July 12, 2003, B1, B5.

55. Michelle MacAfee, "Trade Protest Turns Violent," *The Winnipeg Free Press*, July 29, 2003, A9.

56. "European Union Expands into 10 New Countries," *Reuters*, news release, April 30, 2004.

57. Bruce Little, "Free-Trade Pact Gets Mixed Reviews," *The Globe and Mail*, June 7, 2004, B3.

58. Andrew Purvis, "Super Exporter," *Time* (April 28, 1997): 36.

59. Peter Cook, "Free Trade Free-for-All Causes Confusion," *The Globe and Mail*, December 5, 1994, B7.

Chapter 6

1. *Hoover Handbook of American Business 2006* (Austin, TX: Hoover's Business Press, 2006).

2. Stephen P. Robbins and Mary Coulter, *Management*, 7th ed. (Upper Saddle River, NJ: Prentice Hall, 2002), 202–204; Thomas L. Wheelan and J. David Hunger, *Strategic Management and Business Policy*, 7th ed. (Upper Saddle River, NJ: Prentice Hall, 2000), 107.

3. Melanie Wells, "Red Baron," *Forbes* (July 3, 2000): 150–160; Andrew Ross Sorkin, "Taking Virgin's Brand into Internet Territory," *The New York Times*, February 14, 2000, C1, C17.

4. Brent Jang, "CanJet Plans Steady Growth, One Airplane at a Time," *The Globe and Mail*, April 11, 2005, B1–B2.

5. Michael Porter, *Competitive Strategy: Techniques for Analyzing Industries and Competitors* (New York: The Free Press, 1980).

6. Bertrand Marotte, "Gildan Takes T-shirt Making to the Cutting-Edge of Casual Apparel," *The Globe and Mail*, July 3, 2004, B3.

7. "Cruise-Ship Delays Leave Guests High and Dry," *The Wall Street Journal*, October 24, 1997, B1, B10; *Hoover's Handbook of American Business 2000* (Austin, TX: Hoover's Business Press, 2000), 1512–1513.

8. Richard Bloom, "How Parmalat Juggled the Struggle," *The Globe and Mail*, May 23, 2005, B3.

9. Richard Bloom, "McMakeover on Fast-Food Strip," *The Globe and Mail*, April 23, 2005, B4.

10. Peter Burrows, "The Hottest Property in the Valley?" *Business Week* (August 30, 1999): 69–74.

11. Alex Taylor III, "How a Top Boss Manages His Day," *Fortune* (June 19, 1989): 95–100.

12. Gordon Pitts, "Taking a Stand: How One CEO Gained Respect," *The Globe and Mail*, January 31, 2006, B8.

13. Virginia Galt, "Lousy People Skills Are Biggest Hurdle for Leaders," *The Globe and Mail*, October 15, 2005, B11.

14. Frank Rose, "Vivendi's High Wireless Act," *Wired*, www.wired.com/wired/archive/8.12/vivendi.html, July 18, 2001;

Mike Trigg, "Vivendi Grabs Houghton Mifflin," *The Motley Fool*, www.fool.com/news/2001/v010601.htm, July 18, 2001.

15. "The 2005 Rankings," *The Globe and Mail*, May 9, 2006, B8.

16. Kamal Fatehi, *International Management: A Cross-Cultural and Functional Perspective* (Upper Saddle River, NJ: Prentice Hall, 1996), 5–8, 153–164.

17. Andrew Wahl, "Culture Shock," *Canadian Business* (October 10–23, 2005): 115–116.

18. Ric Dolphin, "Magna Force," *Canadian Business* (May 1988).

19. Isadore Sharp, "Quality for All Seasons," *Canadian Business Review* (Spring 1990): 21–23.

20. Bruce McDougall, "The Thinking Man's Assembly Line," *Canadian Business* (November 1991): 40–44.

21. Peter Verburg, "Prepare for Takeoff," *Canadian Business* (December 25, 2000): 95–99.

22. Doug Nairne, "Mounties Riding the Vision Thing," *The Winnipeg Free Press*, September 16, 1996, A5.

23. Sinclair Stewart and Andrew Willis, "Hunkin is De-Risking the Place," *The Globe and Mail*, December 11, 2004, B4.

24. Gordon Pitts, "It Boiled Down to a Culture Clash," *The Globe and Mail*, June 11, 2005, B5.

Chapter 7

1. Robert L. Simison, "Ford Rolls Out New Model of Corporate Culture," *The Wall Street Journal*, January 13, 1999, B1, B4.

2. Joann Muller, "Ford: Why It's Worse Than You Think," *Business Week* (June 25, 2001): 80–84.

3. John A. Wagner and John R. Hollenbeck, *Management of Organizational Behavior* (Englewood Cliffs, NJ: Prentice Hall, 1992), 563–565.

4. Jay Diamond and Gerald Pintel, *Retailing*, 6th ed. (Upper Saddle River, NJ: Prentice Hall, 1996), 83–84.

5. Industry Report: Restaurant Industry," *U.S. Business Reporter*, July 19, 2001; Michael Arndt, "There's Life in the Old Bird Yet," *Business Week* (May 14, 2001): 77–78.

6. Michael E. Raynor and Joseph L. Bower, "Lead from the Center," *Harvard Business Review* (May 2001): 93–102.

7. Bruce Horovitz, "Restoring the Golden-Arch Shine," *USA Today*, June 16, 1999, 3B

8. Joann Muller, "Thinking Out of the Cereal Box," *Business Week* (January 15, 2001): 54–55.

9. Dan Morse, "A Hardware Chain Struggles to Adjust to a New Blueprint," *The Wall Street Journal*, January 27, 2003, A1, A4; Chad Terhune and Dan Morse, "Tweaking Home Depot," *The Wall Street Journal*, June 25, 2002, B1, B5; Debbie Howell, "The Super Growth Leaders—The Home Depot: Diversification Builds Bridge to the Future," *DSN Retailing Today* 40, no. 23 (December 10, 2001): 17–18.

10. Lee Hawkins, "Reversing 80 Years of History, GM is Reining in Global Fiefs," *The Wall Street Journal*, October 6, 2004, A1, A14.

11. Donna Fenn, "Redesign Work," *Inc.* (June 1999): 75–83.

12. Gary Yukl, *Leadership in Organizations*, 5th ed. (Upper Saddle River, NJ: Prentice Hall, 2002), 35–36.

13. "Multi-Tasking: Cost-Reduction Strategy at Case Corp.," *Machinery Systems Inc.*, www.machinerysystems.com/RavingFan/CaseCorp.html, July 20, 2001.

14. Donna Fenn, "The Buyers," *Inc.* (June 1996): 46–48+.

15. Nelson Wyatt, "Bell Canada Plan Creates 3 Divisions," *The Winnipeg Free Press*, May 8, 2003, B7.

16. Robert Berner and Kevin Helliker, "Heinz's Worry: 4,000 Products, Only One Star," *The Wall Street Journal*, September 17, 1999, B1, B4.

17. J. Galbraith, "Matrix Organization Designs: How to Combine Functional and Project Forms," *Business Horizons* (1971): 29–40; H.F. Kolodny, "Evolution to a Matrix Organization," *Academy of Management Review* 4 (1979): 543–553.

18. Interview with Tom Ward, operations manager for Genstar Shipyards.

19. Lawton R. Burns, "Matrix Management in Hospitals: Testing Theories of Matrix Structure and Development," *Administrative Science Quarterly* 34 (1989): 48–50.

20. Diane Brady, "Martha Inc.," *Business Week* (January 17, 2000): 62–66.

21. Gail Edmondson, "Danone Hits Its Stride," *Business Week* (February 1, 1999): 52–53.

22. Thomas A. Stewart, "See Jack. See Jack Run," *Fortune* (September 27, 1999): 124–127+.

23. Jerald Greenberg and Robert A. Baron, *Behavior in Organizations: Understanding and Managing the Human Side of Work*, 7th ed. (Upper Saddle River, NJ: Prentice Hall, 2000), 308–309.

24. Tyler Hamilton, "Welcome to the World Wide Grapevine," *The Globe and Mail*, May 6, 2000, B1, B6.

Chapter 8

1. See Angelo S. DeNisi and Ricky W. Griffin, *Human Resource Management* (Boston: Houghton Mifflin, 2001) for a complete overview.

2. Elizabeth Church, "Store Owners Struggle with Staffing," *The Globe and Mail*, November 25, 1996, B6.

3. Elizabeth Church, "Nortel Recruits to a Different Beat," *The Globe and Mail*, August 23, 2000, M1.

4. Virginia Galt, "Extreme Blue Is the Taj Mahal of Internships," *The Globe and Mail*, July 17, 2004, B9.

5. Wallace Immen, "Prospective Hires Put to the Test," *The Globe and Mail*, January 26, 2005, C1, C2.

6. Wallace Immen, "Prospective Hires Put to the Test," *The Globe and Mail*, January 26, 2005, C1, C2.

7. Katie Rook, "Curveball Job Questions: How Not to Strike Out," *The Globe and Mail*, September 3, 2005, B9.

8. Malcolm MacKillop, "An Employer's Guide to Drug Testing," *The Globe and Mail*, April 9, 1998, B13.

9. Margot Gibb-Clark, "Ruling Narrows Options for Drug Testing," *The Globe and Mail*, July 28, 1998, B11.

10. Mark Blanchard, "Pilots Enter Superjumbo Virtual Reality," *The Globe and Mail*, January 20, 2005, B8.

11. Charles Davies, "Strategy Session 1990," *Canadian Business* (January 1990): 50.

12. Scott Feschuk, "Phi Beta Cuppa," *The Globe and Mail*, March 6, 1993, B1, B4.

13. Abby Ellin, "Training Programs Often Miss the Point on the Job," *The New York Times*, March 29, 2000, C12.

14. "The 2005 Rankings," *The Globe and Mail*, May 9, 2006, B8.

15. Elizabeth Church, "Nortel Workers Pick Tailor-Made Perks," *The Globe and Mail*, December 8, 2000, B11.

16. David Roberts, "A Long Way from Cambodia," *The Globe and Mail*, July 5, 1994, B18.

17. Ken Kilpatrick and Dawn Walton, "What a Joy to Work for Dofasco," *The Globe and Mail*, February 23, 2000, B1, B8.

18. Peter Verburg, "The Man of Steel's Fed Up," *Canadian Business* (June 26/July 10, 1998): 69.

19. Virginia Galt, "Medicare Cut Seen Raising Labour Costs," *The Globe and Mail*, February 12, 2002, B10.

20. Virginia Galt, "Companies, Unions, Expect Little Relief," *The Globe and Mail*, September 15, 2004, B4.

21. Elizabeth Church, "Pension Funding Shortfall Increases Dramatically," *The Globe and Mail*, November 8, 2005, B5.

22. Elizabeth Church, "Pension Fund Shortfall Soars in First Half," *The Globe and Mail*, November 23, 2005, B1, B7.

23. Elizabeth Church, "Cost of Retiree Benefit Liabilities 'Sleeping Giant,'" *The Globe and Mail*, August 23, 2004, B4.

24. Virginia Galt, "Gift of Time Pays off for Savvy Employers," *The Globe and Mail*, December 28, 2004, B3.

25. Virginia Galt, "Gift of Time Pays off for Savvy Employers," *The Globe and Mail*, December 28, 2004, B3.

26. Erin White, "Sabbaticals: The Pause That Refreshes," *The Wall Street Journal*, August 2, 2005, B1, B4.

27. Elizabeth Church, "Workplace Daycare Takes Baby Steps Toward Acceptance, But Some Not Sold," *The Globe and Mail*, July 2, 2001, B1, B3.

28. Bruce McDougall, "The Thinking Man's Assembly Line," *Canadian Business* (November 1991): 40.

29. John Partridge, "B of M Lauded for Promoting Women's Careers," *The Globe and Mail*, January 7, 1994, B3.

30. Vivian Smith, "Breaking Down the Barriers," *The Globe and Mail*, November 17, 1992, B24.

31. Bob Cox, "Women Gaining on Men's Wages," *The Globe and Mail*, January 18, 1994, B4.

32. Marie Drolet, "The Male-Female Wage Gap," *Perspectives on Labour and Income*, the Online Edition (December, 2001), www.statcan.ca/english/freepub/75-001-XIE/01201/hi-fs_200112_01a.html

33. Richard Blackwell and Brent Jang, "Top Court Sides with Airline Attendants," *The Globe and Mail*, January 27, 2006, B1, B6.

34. Neco Cockburn, "Clerks to Get $150 Million in Back Pay," *The Winnipeg Free Press*, October 8, 2005, A3.

35. Bruce Little, "Male Earning Power Wanes," *The Globe and Mail*, September 18, 1997, B1, B4.

36. Keith McArthur, "Criticism of Women's Fitness for Top Jobs Causes International Stir," *The Globe and Mail*, October 21, 2005, A1, A14.

37. Ted Kennedy, "Beware of Health and Safety Law: It Could Bite You," *Canadian Business* (December 1990): 19.

38. Wallace Immen, "Post-65 Workers 'Productive and Engaged,'" *The Globe and Mail*, March 18, 2005, C1.

39. Omar El Akkad, "A Woman's Work May Never Be Done," *The Globe and Mail*, March 28, 2006, B1, B4.

40. Max Boisot, *Knowledge Assets* (Oxford: Oxford University Press, 1998).

41. Thomas Stewart, "In Search of Elusive Tech Workers," *Fortune* (February 16, 1998): 171–172.

42. Matt Richtel, "Need for Computer Experts Is Making Recruiters Frantic," *The New York Times*, December 18, 1999, C1.

43. Aaron Bernstein, "When Is a Temp Not a Temp?" *Business Week* (December 7, 1998): 90–92.

Chapter 9

1. David Lipsky and Clifford Donn, *Collective Bargaining in American Industry* (Lexington, MA: Lexington Books, 1981).

2. Susan Bourette, "Organized Labour Lures Growing Number of Youth," *The Globe and Mail*, July 4, 1997, B1, B4; Susan Bourette, "Women Make Strides in Union Movement," *The Globe and Mail*, August 29, 1997, B1–B2.

3. Statistics Canada, "Perspectives in Labour and Income," Autumn 2003, 15, 3, p. 50.

4. Statistics Canada, "Perspectives in Labour and Income," Autumn 2003, 15, 3, p. 51.

5. Virginia Galt, "Worn-Out Middle Managers May Get Protection," *The Globe and Mail*, January 3, 2005, B1, B8.

6. Greg Keenan, "CAW Targets Honda, Toyota," *The Globe and Mail*, June 15, 1999, B1, B8.

7. Sarah Binder, "McDonald's Store Closes, Union Wails," *The Globe and Mail*, February 14, 1998, B23.

8. Paul McKie, "Goldcorp Workers Accept Offer, Dismantle Union," *The Winnipeg Free Press*, April 22, 2000, A6.

9. Murray McNeill, "Hotel Workers Sever Relationship with Union," *The Winnipeg Free Press*, July 22, 2005, B14.

10. Paul Waldie, "How Health Costs Hurt the Big Three," *The Globe and Mail*, March 22, 2005, B1–B2; Virginia Galt, "Companies, Unions Expect Little Relief," *The Globe and Mail*, September 15, 2004, B4.

11. Catherine McLean, "Telus, TWU Settle Labour Conflict," *The Globe and Mail*, October 11, 2005, B1.

12. Jack Mintz, "The Perils of the Picket Line," *Canadian Business* (February 27–March 12, 2006): 15.

13. Andrew Nikiforuk, "Why Safeway Struck Out," *Canadian Business* (September 1997): 27.

14. Margot Gibb-Clark, "Wounds Left by Strike Require Healing," *The Globe and Mail*, September 30, 1991, B4.

15. Martin Cash, "Tractor Plant Workers Locked Out," *The Winnipeg Free Press*, March 28, 2001, B3; Paul McKie, "A Bitter End at Versatile," *The Winnipeg Free Press*, August 14, 2001, A1–A2.

16. Jeffrey Ball, Glenn Burkins, and Gregory White, "Why Labor Unions Have Grown Reluctant to Use the S-word," *The Wall Street Journal*, December 16, 1999, A1, A8.

17. Patrick Brethour, "Telus Gets Injunction Against Union," *The Globe and Mail*, July 25, 2005, B1, B4.

18. Peter Verburg, "The Man of Steel's Fed Up," *Canadian Business* (June 26–July 10, 1998): 68.

Chapter 10

1. Michael Stern, "Empowerment Empowers Employees," *The Globe and Mail*, December 9, 1991, B4.

2. For a detailed treatment of this entire subject area, see Gregory Moorhead and Ricky W. Griffin, *Organizational Behavior*, 6th ed. (Boston: Houghton Mifflin, 2001).

3. Virginia Galt, "Keeping Key Workers a Tougher Task," *The Globe and Mail*, October 25, 2005, B6.

4. Frederick W. Taylor, *Principles of Scientific Management* (New York: Harper and Brothers, 1911).

5. Douglas McGregor, *The Human Side of Enterprise* (New York: McGraw-Hill, 1960).

6. Abraham Maslow, "A Theory of Human Motivation," *Psychological Review* (July 1943): 370–396.

7. Frederick Herzberg, Bernard Mausner, and Barbara Bloch Snydeman, *The Motivation to Work* (New York: Wiley, 1959).

8. Victor Vroom, *Work and Motivation* (New York: Wiley, 1964); Craig Pinder, *Work Motivation* (Glenview, IL: Scott, Foresman, 1984).

9. Edwin Locke, "Toward a Theory of Task Performance and Incentives," *Organizational Behavior and Human Performance* 3 (1968): 157–189.

10. Andy Holloway, "How the Game Is Played," *Canadian Business* (April 2, 2001): 26–35.

11. Interviews with Sterling McLeod and Wayne Walker, senior vice-presidents of sales for Investors Group Financial Services.

12. Wilfred List, "On the Road to Profit," *The Globe and Mail*, July 10, 1991, B1, B3.

13. Virginia Galt, "Change Is a Good Thing When Everyone Is Involved," *The Globe and Mail*, June 25, 2005, B11.

14. Margot Gibb-Clark, "BC Telecom Managers Get an Overhaul," *The Globe and Mail*, July 23, 1994, B3;

15. Brent Jang, "High-Flying WestJet Morale Gets Put to the Test," *The Globe and Mail*, November 25, 2005, B3.

16. Gregory Moorhead and Ricky W. Griffin, *Organizational Behavior*, 6th ed. (Boston: Houghton Mifflin, 2001), Chapter 7.

17. Gregory Moorhead and Ricky W. Griffin, *Organizational Behavior*, 6th ed. (Boston: Houghton Mifflin, 2001), Chapter 7.

18. Gregory Moorhead and Ricky W. Griffin, *Organizational Behavior*, 6th ed.

(Boston: Houghton Mifflin, 2001), Chapter 7.

19. Virginia Galt, "Flex-Time Helps to Attract, Keep Best Workers," *The Winnipeg Free Press*, August 12, 2003, D7.

20. Robert White, "Changing Needs of Work and Family: A Union Response," *Canadian Business Review* (Autumn 1989): 31–33.

21. Margot Gibb-Clark, "Banks' Short Work Week Improves Service," *The Globe and Mail*, September 23, 1991, B4.

22. "Telecommuting Causing Work Condition Worries," *The Globe and Mail*, January 7, 2000, B8.

23. Margot Gibb-Clark, "What Shaped the Workplace in 1998," *The Globe and Mail*, December 29, 1998, B6.

24. Margot Gibb-Clark, "Satellite Office a Hit with Staff," *The Globe and Mail*, November 18, 1991, B4.

25. "Slaves of the New Economy," *Canadian Business* (April 1996): 86–92.

26. Dawn Walton, "Survey Focuses on Job Sharing," *The Globe and Mail*, June 10, 1997, B4.

27. Andy Holloway, "How the Game Is Played," *Canadian Business* (April 2, 2001): 26–35.

28. David Dorsey, "Andy Pearson Finds Love," *Fast Company* (August 2001): 78–86.

29. Gordon Pitts, "Taking a Stand: How One CEO Gained Respect," *The Globe and Mail*, January 31, 2006, B8.

30. Jason Kirby, "In the Vault," *Canadian Business* (March 1–14, 2004): 69.

31. Jason Kirby, "In the Vault," *Canadian Business* (March 1–14, 2004): 69.

32. Madelaine Drohan, "What Makes a Canadian Manager?" *The Globe and Mail*, February 25, 1997, B18.

33. Natalie Southworth, "Canadian Team Builders Turn U.S. Heads," *The Globe and Mail*, August 28, 2000, B8.

34. Zena Olijnyk, Mark Brown, Andy Holloway, Calvin Leung, Alex Mlynek, Erin Pooley, Jeff Sanford, Andrew Wahl, and Thomas Watson, "Canada's Global Leaders," *Canadian Business* (March 28–April 10, 2005): 37–43.

35. Gregory Moorhead and Ricky W. Griffin, *Organizational Behavior*, 6th ed. (Boston: Houghton Mifflin, 2001), Chapters 13 and 14.

36. Gregory Moorhead and Ricky W. Griffin, *Organizational Behavior*, 6th ed. (Boston: Houghton Mifflin, 2001), Chapters 13 and 14.

37. "A Better Workplace," *Time* (April 17, 2000): 87.

38. Stephanie Armour, "More Dads Tap into Family Benefits at Work," *USA Today*, June 16, 2000, 1B.

39. Employee-Friendly Workplaces Raises Issues for Unions," *The Globe and Mail*, December 27, 2000, B1, B4.

Chapter 11

1. Andrew Nikiforuk, "Pure Profit," *Canadian Business* (April 3, 2000): 70–76.

2. Eryn Brown, "America's Most Admired Companies," *Fortune* (March 1, 1999): 68, 70–73; www.walmartstores.com, April 24, 2000.

3. Judy Strauss and Raymond Frost, *Marketing on the Internet* (Upper Saddle River, NJ: Prentice Hall, 1999), 266–271.

4. Intel Corp., "Digital and Intel Complete Sale of Digital Semi-Conductor Manufacturing Operations," news release, May 18, 1998.

5. Mark Lander, "Slovakia No Longer a Laggard in Automaking," *nytimes.com*, April 13, 2004, www.nytimes.com/2004/04/13/business/worldbusiness.

6. Neal Boudette, "Chrysler Gains Edge by Giving New Flexibility to Its Factories," *The Wall Street Journal*, April 11, 2006, A1, A15.

7. Greg Keenan, "Ford's New Maxim: Flex Manufacturing," *The Globe and Mail*, May 10, 2006, B3.

8. Gordon Pitts, "Industrial Evolution," *The Globe and Mail*, May 29, 2006, B1, B4.

9. Don Marshall, "Time for Just in Time," *P&IM Review* (June 1991): 20–22. See also Gregg Stocker, "Quality Function Deployment: Listening to the Voice of the Customer," *APICS: The Performance Advantage* (September 1991): 44–48.

10. Lee J. Krajewski and Larry P. Ritzman, *Operations Management: Strategy and Analysis*, 6th ed. (Upper Saddle River, NJ: Prentice Hall, 2002), 153–154, 828–829; Robert S. Russell and Bernard W. Taylor III, *Operations Management*, 4th ed. (Upper Saddle River, NJ: Prentice Hall, 2003), 221–222, 593–595.

11. Robert S. Russell and Bernard W. Taylor III, *Operations Management*, 4th ed. (Upper Saddle River, NJ: Prentice Hall, 2003), 222–224.

12. Lee J. Krajewski and Larry P. Ritzman, *Operations Management: Strategy and Analysis*, 6th ed. (Upper Saddle River, NJ: Prentice Hall, 2002), 595.

13. Tom Murphy, "E Cyber Squeeze: The Pressure Is On," *Ward's Auto World* (December 2000): 44–47.

14. "The Disney Institute," www.disney.go.com/DisneyWorld/DisneyInstitute/ProfessionalPrograms/DisneyDifference/index.html, April 25, 2000.

15. Bruce Little, "Stock Answers," *The Globe and Mail*, June 6, 1995, B12.

16. Bruce McDougall, "The Thinking Man's Assembly Line," *Canadian Business* (November 1991): 40.

17. Alan Freeman, "Why Firms Avoid Taking Inventory," *The Globe and Mail*, December 12, 1994, B1, B4.

18. Clare Ansberry, "A New Hazard for Recovery: Last-Minute Pace of Orders," *The Wall Street Journal*, June 25, 2002, A1, A12.

Chapter 12

1. Gordon Pitts, "Message for Manufacturers: Go Big, Don't Stay at Home," *The Globe and Mail*, December 6, 2005, B1, B7.

2. United States Department of Labor, "International Comparisons of Manufacturing Productivity and Unit Labor Cost Trends, 2005," news release, September 26, 2006, www.bls.gov/news.release/prod4.nr0.htm.

3. Bart VanArk and Robert McGuckin, "International Comparisons of Labor Productivity and per Capita Income," Monthly Labor Review (Washington, DC: U.S. Department of Labor, July 1999), 33–41.

4. Harvey Enchin, "Canada Urged to Stop Living Off Fat of the Land," *The Globe and Mail*, October 25, 1991, B1, B6.

5. Jon Hilsenrath, "Behind Surging Productivity: The Service Sector Delivers," *The Wall Street Journal*, November 7, 2003, A1, A8.

6. John Sheridan, "More Steel Productivity Gains Ahead?" *Industry Week* (September 15, 1997): 86–96.

7. Peter Kennedy, "Canfor Goes High Teach to Cut Costs," *The Globe and Mail*, July 29, 2000, 3.

8. Lee J. Krajewski and Larry P. Ritzman, *Operations Management: Strategy and Analysis*, 5th ed. (Reading, MA: Addison-Wesley, 1999), 229–230.

9. Bruce McDougall, "The Thinking Man's Assembly Line," *Canadian Business* (November 1991): 40.

10. Thomas Foster Jr., *Managing Quality: An Integrative Approach* (Upper Saddle River, NJ: Prentice Hall, 2001), 22–23.

11. Joel Kurtzman, "Is Your Company Off Course? Now You Can Find Out Why," *Fortune* (February 17, 1997): 133.

12. Ted Wakefield, "No Pain, No Gain," *Canadian Business* (January 1993): 50–54.

13. Tootsie Roll Industries Inc. *Annual Report, 2003* (Chicago, 2004), 1.

14. Thomas Foster Jr., *Managing Quality: An Integrative Approach* (Upper Saddle River, NJ: Prentice Hall, 2001), 325–339.

15. Thomas Foster Jr., *Managing Quality: An Integrative Approach* (Upper Saddle River, NJ: Prentice Hall, 2001), 325–329.

16. James Evans and James Dean Jr., *Total Quality: Management, Organization, and Strategy*, 2nd ed. (Cincinnati, OH: South-Western, 2000), 230.

17. Margot Gibb-Clark, "Hospital Managers Gain Tool to Compare Notes," *The Globe and Mail*, September 9, 1996, B9

18. "Customer Service You Can Taste," *Canadian Business* (July 1991): 19–20.

19. Del Jones, "Baldrige Award Honors Record 7 Quality Winners, *USA Today*, November 26, 2003, 6B.

20. "ISO 9001 Registration Helps Improve Airport Security," *Quality Digest*, www.qualitydigest.com/currentmag/html/news.html, June 9, 2002; "A Call for Consistency in the Quality of Airline Security Screening Services," *American Society for Quality*, www.asq.org/news/interest/airportsecurity.html, December 18, 2002.

21. Roberta S. Russell and Bernard W. Taylor III, *Operations Management*, 4th ed. (Upper Saddle River, NJ: Prentice Hall, 2003), 658–662; and Thomas Foster Jr., *Managing Quality: An Integrative Approach* (Upper Saddle River, NJ: Prentice Hall, 2001), 85–86.

22. Roberta S. Russell and Bernard W. Taylor III, *Operations Management*, 4th ed. (Upper Saddle River, NJ: Prentice Hall, 2003), 137–140.

23. Sunil Chopra and Peter Meindl, *Supply Chain Management: Strategy, Planning, and Operation*, 6th ed. (Upper Saddle River, NJ: Prentice Hall, 2001), 3–6; Lee J. Krajewski and Larry P. Ritzman, *Operations Management: Strategy and Analysis*, 5th ed. (Reading, MA: Addison-Wesley, 1999), Chapter 11; Roberta S. Russell and Bernard W. Taylor III, *Operations Management*, 4th ed. (Upper Saddle River, NJ: Prentice Hall, 2003), Chapter 7; and Thomas Foster Jr., *Managing Quality: An Integrative Approach* (Upper Saddle River, NJ: Prentice Hall, 2001), Chapter 9.

24. Sunil Chopra and Peter Meindl, *Supply Chain Management: Strategy, Planning, and Operation*, 6th ed. (Upper Saddle River, NJ: Prentice Hall, 2001), Chapter 20.

25. Sunil Chopra and Peter Meindl, *Supply Chain Management: Strategy, Planning, and Operation*, 6th ed. (Upper Saddle River, NJ: Prentice Hall, 2001), 348–349.

26. Catherine Greenman, "An Old Craft Learns New Tricks," *The New York Times*, June 10, 1999, G1, G7.

27. Gillian Babicz, "Six Sigma Software Generates Improvements," *Quality* (April 2002): 28.

28. Terrence Belford, "Real Estate Heaven Is No Mistake," *The Globe and Mail*, March 22, 2005, B9.

29. Evaluate the Value of Training," *Quality* (April 2002): 48.

30. Leonard L. Berry, A. Parasuraman, and Valarie A. Zeithaml, "Improving Service Quality in America: Lessons Learned," *Academy of Management Executive* 8, no. 2 (1994): 32–45.

Chapter 13

1. Kenneth C. Laudon and Jane P. Laudon, *Management Information Systems: Managing the Digital Firm*, 7th ed. (Upper Saddle River, NJ: Prentice Hall, 2002), 7–11.

2. Kenneth C. Laudon and Jane P. Laudon, *Essentials of Management Information Systems*, 3rd ed. (Upper Saddle River, NJ: Prentice Hall, 1999), 267.

3. Kenneth C. Laudon and Jane P. Laudon, *Essentials of Management Information Systems*, 3rd ed. (Upper Saddle River, NJ: Prentice Hall, 1999), 273.

4. Mary J. Cronin, "Ford's Intranet Success," *Fortune* (March 30, 1998): 158.

5. Lee J. Krajewski and Larry P. Ritzman, *Operations Management: Strategy and Analysis*, 6th ed. (Upper Saddle River, NJ: Prentice Hall, 2002), 106.

6. Lee J. Krajewski and Larry P. Ritzman, *Operations Management: Strategy and Analysis*, 6th ed. (Upper Saddle River, NJ: Prentice Hall, 2002), 232–233.

7. Joshua Macht, "The Ultimate Head Trip," *Inc. Technology* 3 (1997): 77.

8. Gene Bylinsky, "Industry's Amazing Instant Prototypes," *Fortune* (January 12, 1998): 120(B-D).

9. Kenneth C. Laudon and Jane P. Laudon, *Essentials of Management Information Systems*, 3rd ed. (Upper Saddle River, NJ: Prentice Hall, 1999), 383–391.

10. Geoffrey Rowan, "Unique Software Thinks Like a Human," *The Globe and Mail*, December 31, 1996, B1, B4.

11. Kenneth C. Laudon and Jane P. Laudon, *Essentials of Management Information Systems*, 3rd ed. (Upper Saddle River, NJ: Prentice Hall, 1999), 383–388; E. Wainwright Martin et al., *Managing Information Technology: What Managers Need to Know*, 3rd ed. (Upper Saddle River, NJ: Prentice Hall, 1999), 225–227.

12. Emily Smith, "Turning an Expert's Skills into Computer Software," *Business Week* (October 7, 1985): 104–107.

13. Heather Green et al., "It's Time for Rules in Wonderland," *Business Week* (February 21, 2000): 82-88+; Ira Sager et al., "Cyber Crime," *Business Week* (February 21, 2000): 36-42; Ira Sager, Neil Gross, and John Carey, "Locking Out the Hackers," *Business Week* (February 28, 2000): 32–34.

14. Larry Long and Nancy Long, *Computers: Information Technology in Perspective*, 9th ed. (Upper Saddle River, NJ: Prentice Hall, 2002), 52–54.

15. Simon Avery, "Hunting Season for Computer Attackers," *The Globe and Mail*, July 6, 2005, B1, B4.

16. Ann Carrns, "Trial Highlights Vulnerability of Databases," *The Wall Street Journal*, August 3, 2005, B1, B3.

17. Mark Blancahrd, "A Day in the Life of Superhighway Cops," *The Globe and Mail*, October 7, 2004, B15.

18. Larry Long and Nancy Long, *Computers: Information Technology in Perspective*, 9th ed. (Upper Saddle River, NJ: Prentice Hall, 2002), 101–106.

19. Kenneth C. Laudon and Jane P. Laudon, *Management Information Systems: Managing the Digital Firm*, 7th ed. (Upper Saddle River, NJ: Prentice Hall, 2002), 237–244.

20. "Canada's Software Piracy Rate Decreases," *The Winnipeg Free Press*, May 24, 2006, B7.

21. Nathalie Raffray, "Portal Power," *Communications International* (August 2001), 30–35; and David Maloney, "The Newest Better Idea at Ford," *Modern Materials Handling* (June 2000), 34–39. Kenneth C. Laudon and Jane P. Laudon, *Management Information Systems: Managing the Digital Firm*, 7th ed. (Upper Saddle River, NJ: Prentice Hall, 2002), 239–244.

22. Nathalie Raffray, "Portal Power," *Communications International* (August 2001): 30–35; David Maloney, "The Newest Better Idea at Ford," *Modern Materials Handling* (June 2000): 34–39; Kenneth C. Laudon and Jane P. Laudon, *Management Information Systems: Managing the Digital Firm*, 7th ed. (Upper Saddle River, NJ: Prentice Hall, 2002), 239–244.

Chapter 14

1. Ronald Hilton, *Managerial Accounting*, 2nd ed. (New York: McGraw-Hill, 1994), 7.

2. Brian Christmas, "Buttoned Down and In Demand," *The Globe and Mail*, April 19, 2006, B13.

3. Brian Christmas, "Buttoned Down and in Demand," *The Globe and Mail*, April 19, 2006, B13.

4. Brian Christmas, "Buttoned Down and in Demand," *The Globe and Mail*, April 19, 2006, B13.

5. Elizabeth MacDonald, "Accounting Sleuths Ferret Hidden Assets," *The Wall Street Journal*, December 18, 1996, B1–B2.

6. Philip Mathias, "Non Profits Fight Move to GAAP Accounting," *The Financial Post*, March 5, 1994, 15.

7. Charles T. Horngren, Walter T. Harrison Jr., and Linda Smith Bamber, *Accounting*, 5th ed. (Upper Saddle River, NJ: Prentice Hall, 2002), 11–12, 39–41.

8. Charles T. Horngren, Walter T. Harrison Jr., and Linda Smith Bamber, *Accounting,* 5th ed. (Upper Saddle River, NJ: Prentice Hall, 2002), 41–56.

9. Charles T. Horngren, Walter T. Harrison Jr., and Linda Smith Bamber, *Accounting,* 5th ed. (Upper Saddle River, NJ: Prentice Hall, 2002), 17–20.

10. Ronald Hilton, *Managerial Accounting,* 2nd ed. (New York: McGraw-Hill, 1994), 402–403.

11. Billie Cunningham, Loren Nikolai, and John Bazley, *Accounting: Information for Business Decisions* (Fort Worth, TX: Dryden, 2000), 133–134.

12. Charles T. Horngren, Walter T. Harrison Jr., and Linda Smith Bamber, *Accounting,* 4th ed. (Upper Saddle River, NJ: Prentice Hall, 1999), 562–563; Arthur J. Keown et al., *The Foundations of Finance: The Logic and Practice of Financial Management*, 2nd ed. (Upper Saddle River, NJ: Prentice Hall, 1998), 89–95.

13. Charles T. Horngren, Walter T. Harrison Jr., and Linda Smith Bamber, *Accounting,* 4th ed. (Upper Saddle River, NJ: Prentice Hall, 1999), 201–202.

14. Frederick D. S. Choi, Carol Ann Frost, and Gary K. Meek, *International Accounting,* 4th ed. (Upper Saddle River: Prentice Hall, 2002), 267–279.

Chapter 15

1. American Marketing Association, "Marketing Services Guide," www.ama.org/about/ama/markdef.asp, August 23, 2001.

2. Philip Kotler, *Marketing Management*, 11th ed. (Upper Saddle River, NJ: Prentice Hall, 2003), 76–78.

3. Warren J. Keegan and Mark C. Green, *Global Marketing*, 3rd ed. (Upper Saddle River, NJ: Prentice Hall, 2003), 8–15.

4. Philip Kotler and Peggy Cunningham, *Marketing Management* (Toronto: Prentice-Hall, 2004), 18.

5. Chris Isadore, "Sweet Spot: Luxury SUV's are Hot," *CNN/Money*, January 7, 2004, http://cnnmoney.com.

6. Aparita Bhandari, "Ethnic Marketing—It's More Than Skin Deep," *The Globe and Mail*, September 7, 2005, B3.

7. Lauren Goldstein, "Dressing Up an Old Brand," *Fortune* (November 9, 1998): 154–156.

8. Jane Perlez, "Joy of Debts: Eastern Europe on Credit Fling," *The New York Times*, May 30, 1998, A3.

9. Philip Kotler, *Marketing Management*, 11th ed. (Upper Saddle River, NJ: Prentice Hall, 2003), 292–294.

10. Marina Strauss, "The Secret to Gaining Success in Quebec," *The Globe and Mail*, September 27, 2005, B4.

11. John Morton, "How to Spot the Really Important Prospects," *Business Marketing* (January 1990): 62–67.

12. Barrie McKenna, "Coke Plans Major Revamp to Put Fizz Back in Its Shares," *The Globe and Mail*, November 12, 2004, B1, B6.

13. Paul Sutter, "How to Succeed in Bubble Gum Without Really Trying," *Canadian Business* (January 1992): 48–50.

14. Alvin C. Burns and Ronald F. Bush, *Marketing Research*, 3rd ed. (Upper Saddle River, NJ: Prentice Hall, 2000), 70–84.

15. Marina Strauss, "First You Have to Get Their Attention," *The Globe and Mail*, July 12, 1991, B1.

16. Emily Nelson, "P&G Checks Out Real Life," *The Wall Street Journal*, May 17, 2001, B1, B4.

17. Joseph Pereira, "Spying on the Sales Floor," *The Wall Street Journal*, December 21, 2004, B1, B4.

18. Alvin C. Burns and Ronald F. Bush, *Marketing Research*, 3rd ed. (Upper Saddle River, NJ: Prentice Hall, 2000), Chapter 9.

19. Marina Strauss, "Mining Customer Feedback, Firms Go Undercover and Online," *The Globe and Mail*, May 13, 2004, B1, B25.

20. Deborah Ball, Sarah Ellison, and Janet Adamy, "Probing Shoppers' Psyche," *The Wall Street Journal*, October 28, 2004, B1, B8.

21. Oliver Bertin, "John Deere Reaps the Fruits of Its Labors," *The Globe and Mail*, September 2, 1991, B1, B3.

22. Alvin C. Burns and Ronald F. Bush, *Marketing Research*, 3rd ed. (Upper Saddle River, NJ: Prentice Hall, 2000), 140–148.

23. Kenneth C. Laudon and Jane P. Laudon, *Management Information Systems: Managing the Digital Firm*, 7th ed. (Upper Saddle River, NJ: Prentice Hall, 2002), 221–222.

24. Kenneth C. Laudon and Jane P. Laudon, *Management Information Systems: Managing the Digital Firm*, 7th ed. (Upper Saddle River, NJ: Prentice Hall, 2002), 222–224.

25. Paul S. Foote and Malini Krishnamurthi, "Forecasting Using Data Warehousing Model: Wal-Mart's Experience," *The Journal of Business Forecasting Methods & Systems* (Fall 2001): 13–17.

26. Robyn Greenspan, "The Web as a Way of Life," www.cyberatlas.com, May 21, 2002.

Chapter 16

1. Dan Verton, "Oracle Scraps Unpopular Database Pricing Model: Oracle Faces Challenges in the Marketplace," *Computerworld* (June 18, 2001): 6, 8.

2. Philip Kotler, *Marketing Management*, 11th ed. (Upper Saddle River, NJ: Prentice Hall, 2003), Chapter 3; Roger J. Best, *Market-Based Management: Strategies for Growing Customer Value and Profitability*, 2nd ed. (Upper Saddle River, NJ: Prentice Hall, 2000), 87–100.

3. Simon Tuck, "Bombardier to Gamble on New Jet," *The Globe and Mail*, March 16, 2005, A1–A2; Bertrand Marotte, "Bombardier Shelves C Series," *The Globe and Mail*, February 1, 2006, B1, B6.

4. Richard Blackwell, "High-Definition TV a Bit Fuzzy, Poll Finds," *The Globe and Mail*, May 2, 2005, B4.

5. James C. Anderson and James A. Narus, *Business Market Management: Understanding, Creating, and Delivering Value* (Upper Saddle River, NJ: Prentice Hall, 1999), 203–206.

6. Philip Kotler, *Marketing Management*, 11th ed. (Upper Saddle River, NJ: Prentice Hall, 2003), 328–339.

7. Keith McArthur, "Big Mac, Coke, Marlboro and...China Mobile?" *The Globe and Mail*, April 4, 2006, B1, B9.

8. Keith McArthur, "How to Survive an Identity Crisis," *The Globe and Mail*, November 14, 2005, B1, B11.

9. Caroline Alphonso, "A Great Place to Do Business—Just No Beacon for Culture," *The Globe and Mail*, August 2, 2005, B1, B9.

10. John Gray, "What's in a Brand?" *Canadian Business* (December 26, 2005–January 15, 2006): 73–74.

11. Gordon Pitts, "New Irving Generation Broadens Horizons," *The Globe and Mail*, January 18, 2003, B1, B4.

12. Keith McArthur, "Tim Hortons Scores Winning Goal as a Brand," *The Globe and Mail*, June 6, 2005, B3.

13. Lori Mitchell, "Branding Equals Smart E-Business," *InfoWorld*, www.InfoWorld.com/articles/tc/xml/00/12/18/001218tcbranding.xml, December 15, 2000; Robyn Greenspan, "Brand Opening," *ECommerce-Guide*, http://ecommerce.internet.com/news/insights/ectips/article/0,,6311_557131,00.html, January 10, 2001; Kris Wadia, "Top 10 Myths of E-Branding," *Business-Minds*, www.business-minds.com/article.asp?item=68, May 17, 2001.

14. Eloise Coupey, *Marketing and the Internet* (Upper Saddle River, NJ: Prentice Hall, 2001), 174–179.

15. John Frook, "Cisco Scores with Its Latest Generation of Empowering Tools," *B to B* (August 20, 2001): 20.

16. Cyndee Miller, "Little Relief Seen for New Product Failure Rate," *Marketing News* (June 21, 1993): 1; Nancy J. Kim,

"Back to the Drawing Board," *The Bergen [New Jersey] Record*, December 4, 1994, B1, B4.

17. Brian Milner, "Canada's Franklin the Turtle Heads South," *The Globe and Mail*, February 14, 2000, B1, B10.

18. Marina Strauss, "Shoppers Sees Gold in Private Labels," *The Globe and Mail*, January 3, 2005, B1–B2.

19. Richard Bloom, "Taking on the World, One Jar at a Time," *The Globe and Mail*, July 4, 2005, B3.

20. Keith McArthur, "Why Molson Is Crying in Its Beer," *The Globe and Mail*, July 10, 2004, B4.

21. Marina Strauss, "Consumers Less Trusting of Brands," *The Globe and Mail*, February 13, 2003, B3.

22. David Square, "Mouse Pad Gets Oodles of Nibbles," *The Winnipeg Free Press*, July 26, 1997, B10.

23. Paul Waldie, "How RIM's Big Deal Was Done," *The Globe and Mail*, March 6, 2006, B1, B14.

24. Simon Avery, "RIM Faces New U.S. Fight Over Patents," *The Globe and Mail*, May 2, 2006, B3.

25. Deborah Ball, "The Perils of Packaging: Nestle Aims for Easier Openings," *The Wall Street Journal*, November 17, 2005, B1, B5.

26. Keith McArthur, "Oh? Canada? Ads Beg to Differ," *The Globe and Mail*, July 1, 2004, B1, B18.

27. William Pride and O.C. Ferrell, *Marketing*, 5th ed. (Boston: Houghton Mifflin, 1987).

28. Robert Berner, "The Rolls-Royce of Leather Jackets Is Hard to Come By," *The Wall Street Journal*, November 22, 1996, A1, A10.

29. Kenneth E. Clow and Donald Baack, *Integrated Advertising, Promotion, and Marketing Communications* (Upper Saddle River, NJ: Prentice Hall, 2002), Chapter 5.

30. John Heinzl, "Buckley Wants U.S. to Swallow Its Bad Taste," *The Globe and Mail*, November 11, 1999, B1, B12.

31. Marina Strauss, "Towel War Turns to Name-Naming," *The Globe and Mail*, December 5, 1995, B1, B10.

32. Andrew Wahl, "Red All Over," *Canadian Business* (February 13–26, 2006): 53–54.

33. Allan Kreda, "Advertisers Lured by Super Bowl's Glitz, Huge Ratings," *The Globe and Mail*, December 30, 2004, B3.

34. Marina Strauss, "This Billboard Wants to Pass You By," *The Globe and Mail*, February 27, 1992, B4.

35. Erin White, "Word of Mouth Makes Nike Slip-On Sneakers Take Off," *The Globe and Mail*, June 7, 2001, B1, B4.

36. P. Kotler, G. Armstrong, and P. Cunningham, *Principles of Marketing*, 6th Canadian ed., (Toronto: Pearson, 2005), 88.

37. Andrew Wahl, "Red All Over," *Canadian Business* (February 13–26, 2006): 53–54.

38. P. Kotler, G. Armstrong, and P. Cunningham, *Principles of Marketing*, 6th Canadian ed., (Toronto: Pearson, 2005), 89–91.

39. Simon Tuck, "Security Rated Top On-Line Fear," *The Globe and Mail*, July 5, 1999, B5.

40. James Hagerty and Dennis Berman, "New Battleground in Web Privacy War: Ads that Snoop," *The Wall Street Journal*, August 27, 2003, A1, A8.

41. Stuart Elliott, "Real or Virtual? You Call It," *The New York Times*, October 1, 1999, C1, C6.

42. William Wells, John Burnett, and Sandra Moriarty, *Advertising: Principles and Practice*, 5th ed. (Upper Saddle River, NJ: Prentice Hall, 2000), 77–83.

43. Ann Gibbon, "Ad Group Tries to Demystify Quebec," *The Globe and Mail*, November 25, 1993, B6.

44. "Regulators Wary of Ads Rapping Rivals," *The Globe and Mail*, May 23, 1991, B4.

45. Ira Teinowitz and Cara B. Dipasquale, "Direct Marketers Take Issue with Proposed FTC Rules," *Advertising Age* (January 28, 2002): 3, 29; Larry Neilson, "Look Out for Telemarketing Speed Bumps," *National Underwriter* (September 17, 2001): 12–14.

46. John Heinzl, "Beer Firms Rethink Giveaways," *The Globe and Mail*, March 3, 2003, B1, B5.

47. Joanna Slater, "Coke, Pepsi Fight Product-Contamination Charges in India," *The Wall Street Journal*, August 15, 2003, B1, B5.

48. Warren J. Keegan, *Global Marketing Management*, 7th ed. (Upper Saddle River, NJ: Prentice Hall, 2002), Chapter 14.

49. Norman M. Scarborough and Thomas W. Zimmerer, *Effective Small Business Management: An Entrepreneurial Approach*, 6th ed. (Upper Saddle River, NJ: Prentice Hall, 2000), Chapter 11.

Chapter 17

1. Constance L. Hays, "Coke Tests Weather-Linked Pricing," *The Globe and Mail*, October 29, 1999, B11.

2. Stefan Fatsis, "The Barry Bonds Tax: Teams Raise Prices for Good Games," *The Wall Street Journal*, December 3, 2002, D1, D8.

3. Stephen Kindel, "Tortoise Gains on Hare," *Financial World* (February 23, 1988): 18–20.

4. Ethan Smith, "Universal Slashes CD Prices in Bid to Revive Music Industry," *The Wall Street Journal*, September 4, 2003, B1, B8.

5. Chet Zelasko, "Acesulfame-K," *Better Life Institute*, www.blionline.com/HDB/Acesulfame-K.htm, May 17, 2001.

6. Stewart A. Washburn, "Establishing Strategy and Determining Cost in the Pricing Decision," *Business Marketing* (July 1985): 64–78.

7. Marina Strauss, "Why Everyday Low Prices Failed Zellers," *The Globe and Mail*, March 22, 2005, B8.

8. Judy Strauss and Raymond Frost, *E-Marketing*, 2nd ed. (Upper Saddle River, NJ: Prentice Hall, 2001), 166–167; Eloise Coupey, *Marketing and the Internet* (Upper Saddle River, NJ: Prentice Hall, 2001), 281–283.

9. Marina Strauss, "Taking 'e' Out of E-commerce: Meet the eBay Middleman," *The Globe and Mail*, October 6, 2004, B1, B19.

10. Ahmad Diba, "An Old-Line Agency Finds an Online Niche," *Fortune* (April 3, 2000): 258.

11. Dell Annual Report: *FY2001 Year in Review*, www.dell.com, April 22, 2002.; Qiao Song, "Legend Outlines Role in China's Wireless Future," *ebn* (March 25, 2002): 3; Faith Hung, "Legend Looks to Defend Its Turf—WTO Entry Will Force China's Top PC Maker to Fend Off Unrestricted Rivals," *ebn* (December 17, 2001): 44; Neel Chowdhury, "Dell Cracks China," *Fortune* (June 21, 1999): 120–124.

12. Keith McArthur, "Para Paints' Bold Stroke," *The Globe and Mail*, October 18, 1999, M1.

13. Dale M. Lewison, *Retailing*, 5th ed. (New York: Macmillan, 1994), 454; Louis Stern and Adel I. El-Ansary, *Marketing Channels*, 4th ed. (Englewood Cliffs, NJ: Prentice Hall, 1992), 129–130.

14. *Expedia.com*, www.expedia.com, July 8, 2002.

15. Ann Bednarz, "Acquisitions Tighten Supply-Chain Market," *Network World* (February 9, 2004): 21–22.

16. Direct Selling Association, May 4, 2004, www.dsa.org.

17. American Teleservices Association, May 4, 2004, www.ataconnect.org.

18. Marina Strauss, "E-tailing in Age of Refinement," *The Globe and Mail*, August 3, 2005, B6.

19. Zena Olijnyk, "Dot-Com Wonder Boys, *Canadian Business* (April 14, 2003): 30–36.

20. Tessa Wegert, "Catalogue Shopping Is So Yesterday," *The Globe and Mail*, November 24, 2005, B13.

21. "Did You Know?" *Catalog News.com*, www.catalog-news.com, April 8, 2002; Judy Strauss and Raymond Frost,

E-Marketing, (Upper Saddle River, NJ: Prentice Hall, 2001), 140.

22. Carolyn Brackett, "Setting Up Shop in Cyberspace," *Inc.com,* www.inc.com/conducting_commerce/advice/15237.html, May 20, 2002; David Radin, "'Electronic Mall Syndrome' Gives Way to Unified Buying," *eBusiness News*, http://ebusiness.dci.com/articles/1998/05/14radin.htm, May 20, 2002; Garrett Wasny, "Free Electronic Storefronts," www.howtoconquertheworld.com/gohome111.htm, July, 2000.

23. Peter Elkind, "Shhhhh! Amway's on the Web," *Fortune* (March 6, 2000): 76.

24. "LivePerson.com™," www.liveperson.com, April 19, 2000.

25. Gordon Jaremko, "River Highway in Canada's North Open for Business," *The Winnipeg Free Press*, July 25, 2006, B10.

26. Anne T. Coughlan et al., *Marketing Channels*, 6th ed. (Upper Saddle River, NJ: Prentice Hall, 2001), 458–462.

27. Bill Redekop, "The Crow Subsidy Is History," *The Winnipeg Free Press*, February 28, 1995, 1.

Chapter 18

1. Andrew Higgins, "Lacking Money to Pay, Russian Firms Survive on Deft Barter System," *The Wall Street Journal*, August 27, 1998, A1, A6.

2. *Bank of Canada Banking and Financial Statistics*, Table E1 (April 2006), S50.

3. John Partridge, "Phony $10, $20 Bills Rampant in '04," *The Globe and Mail*, March 15, 2005, B5.

4. Dean Beeby, "Canadians Worry About Counterfeit Cash: Survey," *The Winnipeg Free Press*, June 26, 2006, B8.

5. Omar El Akkad, "Canada's $5 Bill Offers New Security Features," *The Globe and Mail*, April 5, 2006, B5.

6. *Bank of Canada Banking and Financial Statistics*, Table E1 (April 2006), S50.

7. *Bank of Canada Banking and Financial Statistics*, Table C1 (May 2006), S16.

8. Nancy Carr, "More Canadians Turning to Alternative Banks," *The Winnipeg Free Press*, July 21, 2003, B7.

9. "Statistics for Smart Cards," *ePaynews.com*, June 14, 2004, www.epaynews.com/statistics/scardstats.html.

10. Karen Horcher, "Reconstruction Zone," *CGA Magazine* (June 1997): 19.

11. Andrew Willis, "American VC Firms Trouncing Canadians at Home," *The Globe and Mail*, June 13, 2005, B1, B3.

12. Andrew Willis, "CIBC Leads Underwriting Pack for Fourth Year," *The Globe and Mail*, January 26, 2005, B7.

13. Andrew Willis, "RBC Dominion King of the Debt Dealers," *The Globe and Mail*, January 26, 2005, B7.

14. Robert J. Carbaugh, *International Economics*, 5th ed. (Cincinnati: South-Western, 1995), Chapter 11.

Chapter 19

1. Joseph Nocera, "Do You Believe? How Yahoo! Became a Blue Chip," *Fortune* (June 7, 1999): 76–81.

2. Cory Johnson, "The Internet Blue Chip," *The Industry Standard*, www.thestandard.com/article/0,1902,4088,00html, August 7, 2001; and Chris Nerney "Yahoo!: Bargain or Big Trouble?" *The Internet Stock Report*, www.internetstockreport.com/column/print/0,,530021,00.html, August 7, 2001.

3. George G. Kaufman, *The U.S. Financial System: Money, Markets, and Institutions*, 6th ed. (Englewood Cliffs, NJ: Prentice Hall, 1995), 432.

4. Louise Lee and Lauren Young, "Is Schwab's Latest Come-On Enough?" *Business Week* (June 7, 2004): 44.

5. Borzou Daragahi, "E-Finance Forecast," *Money* (March 2001): 129–133; and Joseph Kahn, "Schwab Lands Feet First on Net," *The New York Times*, February 10, 1999, C1, C5.

6. Richard Blackwell, "TSE Sees Few Gains from Realignment," *The Globe and Mail*, May 23, 2000, 12.

7. Gordon J. Alexander, William F. Sharpe, and Jeffery V. Bailey, *Fundamentals of Investments*, 3rd ed. (Upper Saddle River, NJ: Prentice Hall, 2001), 36–39.

8. Gordon J. Alexander, William F. Sharpe, and Jeffery V. Bailey, *Fundamentals of Investments*, 3rd ed. (Upper Saddle River, NJ: Prentice Hall, 2001), 44–46.

9. *NASDAQ*, www.nasdaq.com/about/timeline.stm, June 25, 2000.

10. *NASD*, www.nasd.com, June 25, 2000.

11. Keith Damsell, "Ethical Investing Proving a Hard Sell in Canada," *The Globe and Mail*, August 12, 2004, B10.

12. Rob Carrick, "Tread Carefully in the World of Hedge Funds," *The Globe and Mail*, May 27, 2006, B8.

13. Paul Waldie and Sinclair Stewart, "Hedge Funds in the Crosshairs," *The Globe and Mail*, May 30, 2005, B4; Sinclair Stewart and Paul Waldie, "The New Breed of 800-Pound Gorilla," *The Globe and Mail*, May 31, 2005, B7.

14. Richard Blackwell, "TSE 300 Shift Will Shrink Index," *The Globe and Mail*, January 31, 2002, B17.

15. Rob Carrick, "Direct Plans Cut Brokers Out," *The Globe and Mail*, August 21, 1999, B8.

16. Gordon J. Alexander, William F. Sharpe, and Jeffery V. Bailey, *Fundamentals of Investments*, 3rd ed. (Upper Saddle River, NJ: Prentice Hall, 2001), 37–38.

17. U.S. Securities and Exchange Commission, "SEC Charges Former ImClone CEO Samuel Waksal with Illegal Insider Trading," June 12, 2002, www.sec.gov/news/press; Andrew Pollack, "ImClone's Ex-Chief in Talks with U.S. on Plea Agreement," *The New York Times on the Web*, July 13, 2002, www.nytimes.com/2002/07/13/business; "Martha Scrutiny Heats Up," *CNNMoney*, June 14, 2002, www.cnnfn.com.

Chapter 20

1. David F. Scott et al., *Basic Financial Management*, 8th ed. (Upper Saddle River, NJ: Prentice Hall, 1999), 626–627.

2. "Britain's Third Biggest Bank Sees 2001 Net Profit Fall as Bad-Debt Provisions Rise," *CNNMoney*, www.cnnfn.com, February 15, 2002; "SocGen, Abbey National Set Aside Money for Bad Loans, Profits Decline," *CNNMoney*, www.cnnfn.com, February 21, 2002; and James Cox, "Argentina Pins Hope on Debt-Swap Proposal," *World Business*, www.usatoday.com, November 11, 2002.

3. John Heinzl, "Good Strategy Gone Awry, Top Retailer's Tale of Woe," *The Globe and Mail*, March 7, 1992, B1, B4.

4. The State of Small Business, 1989 Annual Report on Small Business in Ontario (Toronto: Ministry of Industry, Trade and Technology, 1990).

5. J. W. Duncan, *D&B Reports* (September–October 1991): 8.

6. Norman M. Scarborough and Thomas W. Zimmerer, *Effective Small Business Management: An Entrepreneurial Approach*, 6th ed. (Upper Saddle River, NJ: Prentice Hall, 2000), esp. 298–300.

7. Susan Hodges, "One Big Step Toward a Loan," *Nation's Business* (August 1997): 34–36.

8. Richard S. Boulton, Barry D. Libert, and Steve M. Samek, "Managing Risk in an Uncertain World," *Upside* (June 2000): 268–278.

9. Thomas Fitch, *Dictionary of Banking Terms*, 2nd ed. (Hauppauge, NY: Barron's, 1993), 531.

10. Mark S. Dorfman, *Introduction to Risk Management and Insurance*, 6th ed. (Upper Saddle River, NJ: Prentice Hall, 2000), Chapter 1.

11. Denyse O'Leary, "The Scams That Drive Up Premiums," *The Globe and Mail*, May 2, 1995, B1; Denyse O'Leary, "Insurers United Against Fraud Face Serious Obstacles," *The Globe and Mail*, May 2, 1995, B1.

12. Sinclair Stewart, "Insurers Take a Category 5 Hit in the Pocketbook," *The Globe and Mail*, October 27, 2005, B1, B26.

13. Sinclair Stewart, "Sun Life's Insurance Policy: The Great Indian Middle Class," *The Globe and Mail*, October 1, 2005, B1, B6.

14. Yochi Dreazen, "As Iraq Terror Rises, Businessmen Find Niche in Life Insurance," *The Wall Street Journal*, August 19, 2005, A1, A16.

15. Mark S. Dorfman, *Introduction to Risk Management and Insurance*, 6th ed. (Upper Saddle River, NJ: Prentice Hall, 2000), 420–421.

Appendix B

[1]See Chris Arthur J. Keown, *Personal Finance*, 3rd ed. (Upper Saddle River, NJ: Pearson Prentice Hall, 2004), 600–609.

[2]Christopher Farrell, "No Need to Hit the Panic Button," *Business Week*, July 26, 2004, 76–80.

Source Notes

Chapter 1

Canadian Megaprojects Wendy Stueck, "Vindication of Voisey's Bay," *The Globe and Mail*, September 3, 2005, B4; Dave Ebner, "CNQ Bets $25 Billion on Oil Sands," *The Globe and Mail*, November 3, 2005, B1, B6; Patrick Brethour, "Alberta's Earth-Shaking Ambitions," *The Globe and Mail*, April 4, 2005, B4, B5; Wendy Stueck, "Voisey's Bay at Last Getting Off the Ground," *The Globe and Mail*, June 17, 2004, B1, B4; Wendy Stueck, "Nickel Prices Continue to Shine" *The Globe and Mail*, October 13, 2003; Wendy Stueck, "Inco Shares Fall on Voisey's Overrun," *The Globe and Mail*, March 21, 2003, B13; Allan Robinson, "Inco, Province Inch Toward Deal on Voisey's Bay," *The Globe and Mail*, October 12, 2001, B3; James Stevenson, "Inco Grilled Despite Impressive Rebound," *The Winnipeg Free Press*, April 20, 2000, B7; "Giant Newfoundland Nickel Project May Soon Proceed," *The Winnipeg Free Press*, November 23, 1999, B8; Allan Robinson, "Inco President Willing to Compromise on Voisey's Bay," *The Globe and Mail*, April 29, 1999, B1, B4; Allan Robinson, "Inco to Halt Voisey's Bay Work," *The Globe and Mail*, July 28, 1998, B1, B6; Allan Robinson, "Inco Chairman Defends Actions," *The Globe and Mail*, April 23, 1998, B3. **Business Accountability** Andres Oppenheimer, "Latin America Is Skeptical," *The Orlando Sentinel*, February 20, 2006, A19; Bradley Martin, "Hermit Kingdom Mixes Stalin, Profits," *The Globe and Mail*, December 29, 2005, B1, B8; James Kynge, "Private Firms' Growth in China Striking: Report," *National Post*, May 11, 2000, C14; Howard French, "On the Street, Cubans Fondly Embrace Capitalism," *The New York Times*, February 3, 1994, A4. **Table 1.1** *Financial Post Business*, Special Edition, 2006, 128; Material reprinted with the express permission of "National Post Company," a CanWest Partnership. **Entrepreneurship and New Ventures** "Murad Al-Katib Quickens the Pulse of the Saskatchewan Agricultural Industry," Business Development Bank of Canada website www.bdc.ca/en/about/mediaroom/news_releases/2005/2005101811.htm; Bruce Johnstone, "Al-Katib Named Young Entrepreneur of the Year," Saskatchewan News Network, *Regina Leader-Post*, Tuesday, October 15, 2005, A8, www.saskcan.com/news.html. Material reprinted with the express permission of Regina Leader Post Group Inc., a CanWest Partnership. **Concluding Case 1-1** Barrie McKenna, "Welcome to the Age of Scarcity," *The Globe and Mail*, May 22, 2005, B15; Harris Anwar, "Are Saudi Reserves Drying Up?," *The Globe and Mail*, May 21, 2005, B19; Peter Tertzakian, "Canada: Energy Superpower?" *The Globe and Mail*, May 28, 2005, B6; Michael Lynch, "Oil Discovery Forecasts Doomed," *The Globe and Mail*, May 28, 2005, B6; John Heinzl, "Now's a Good Time to Cut Back on that Coffee Drinking Habit," *The Globe and Mail*, February 25, 2005, B10; "Price of Oil Spurts to $42.90 a Barrel," *USA Today*, July 29, 2004, 1B; "Higher and Higher—Again: Gasoline Prices Set Record," *USA Today*, May 25, 2004, 1B; Brad Foss, "Drivers Pay Price for Imported Gas," Associated Press Wire Story, May 22, 2004; Allan Sloan, "Why $2 Gas Isn't the Real Energy Problem," *Newsweek*, May 24, 2004, 40; Gregory L. White, "How Ford's Big Batch of Rare Metal Led to $1 Billion Write Off," *The Wall Street Journal*, February 6, 2002, A1, A6. **Concluding Case 1-2** Dan Lett, "Wine Stores Collect $8 Million," *The Winnipeg Free Press*, June 21, 2006, A3; Eric Reguly, "Ontario's Liquor Stores Look Good, but Where's the Profit?" *The Globe and Mail*, July 19, 2005, B2; Trevor Harrison, "Demon Rum and the Perils of Privatization," *The Winnipeg Free Press*, June 19, 2003, A13; John Cotter, "Privatized Liquor Stores a Flop, Study Suggests," *The Winnipeg Free Press*, June 6, 2003, A20; Bill Redekopp, "Private Wine Stores Cheesed with MLCC," *The Winnipeg Free Press*, July 8, 2000, A6; David Menzies, "Sour Grapes," *Canadian Business*, February 26, 1999, 28–35; Brian Hutchinson, "Cheers!," *Canadian Business*, November 1994, 23–28.

Chapter 2

Productivity and the Standard of Living Virginia Galt, "Productivity Buckling Under the Strain of Stress, CEO's Say," *The Globe and Mail*, June 9, 2005, B1, B15; John Partridge, "Several Causes Seen Possible for 'Unprecedented' Productivity Gap," *The Globe and Mail*, June 24, 2005, B6; "Canada Lags in Productivity, Investment: Study," *The Winnipeg Free Press*, October 19, 2005, B12; Gordon Pitts, "Ottawa's New, Improved Mantra: Productivity," *The Globe and Mail*, October 3, 2005, B1, B6; Simon Tuck, "Canada's Standard of Living Takes Downturn," *The Globe and Mail*, March 3, 2005, B1, B9; Jacquie McNish, "'Mediocre' Report Card Says Canada not Making the Grade," *The Globe and Mail*, October 4, 2004, B1, B10; Bruce Little, "Board Warns Productivity Must Rise," *The Globe and Mail*, October 5, 2004, B3; "Canada's Standard of Living," *National Post Business*, June 2003, 19–20; Pierre Fortin, "Differences in Annual Work Hours per Capita Between the United States and Canada," *International Productivity Monitor* (Spring 2003): 38–46; Frank Graves and Richard Jenkins, "Canadian Attitudes Towards Productivity: Balancing Standard of Living and Quality of Life," *The Review of Economic Performance and Social Progress* (2002): 243–258; Andrew Sharpe, "Why Are Americans More Productive Than Canadians?" *International Productivity Monitor* (Spring 2003): 19–37; Pierre Fortin, "Canadian Productivity: When Do We Catch Up?," *ISUMA* (Spring 2002). **Figure 2.3** 2005 data is from the *Bank of Canada Banking and Financial Statistics*, Table H8, May 2006, S-102-103 **Figure 2.4** *Bank of Canada Banking and Financial Statistics*, Table H5, May 2006, S-99. **Figure 2.5** Statistics Canada, Industrial Research and Development, 2005 *Intentions*, 13. **Entrepreneurship and New Ventures Want a MacBrioche with That MacEspresso?** Amy Tsao, "For McDonald's, the Fat's in the Fire," *Business Week*, October 15, 2003, 52 53; Julie Forster, Thinking Outside the Burger Box," *Business Week*, September 16, 2003, 66–67; Shirley Leung, "Armchairs, TVs and Espresso—Is It McDonald's?" *Wall Street Journal*, August 30, 2003, A1, A6. **Business Accountability** John Partridge, "Agency Predicts Further Outsourcing," *The Globe and Mail*, April 26, 2005, B5; Rebecca Buckman, "Outsourcing with a Twist," *The Wall Street Journal*, January 18, 2005, B1, B4; Norihiko Shirouzu, "Big Three's Outsourcing Plan: Makes Parts Suppliers Do It," *The Wall Street Journal*, June 10, 2004, A1, A6; Lee J. Krajewski and Larry Ritzman, *Operations Management: Strategy and Analysis*, 6th ed. (Upper Saddle River, NJ: Prentice Hall, 2002), 102–106; Virginia Galt, "Take Our Business, Take Our People: BMO," *The Globe and Mail*, May 19, 2003, B1, B4; Anne T. Coughlin et al., *Marketing Channels*, 6th ed. (Upper Saddle River, NJ: Prentice Hall, 2001), 168–172. **Concluding Case 2-1** Ronald Alsop, "Ranking Corporate Reputations," *The Wall Street Journal*, December 6, 2005, B1, B14; Gordon Pitts, "The RBC Dynasty Continues," *The Globe and Mail*, January 30, 2006, B1, B10. **Concluding Case 2-2** Gautam Naik, Vanessa Fuhrmans, Jonathan Karp, Joel Millman, Farnaz Fassihi, and Joanna Slater, "Global Baby Bust," *The Wall Street Journal*, January 24, 2003, B1, B4.

Chapter 3

The Price of Bad Behaviour James Bagnall, "Enron Verdict Sends CEO's Strong Message," *The Winnipeg Free*

Press, May 27, 2006, B10; Mark Maremont, "Tyco Ex-Officials Get Jail Terms, Big Fines," *The Wall Street Journal*, September 20, 2005, C1, C4; Simon Houpt and Shawn McCarthy, "Ebbers' Storied Career Ends with Record-Fraud Conviction," *The Globe and Mail*, March 16, 2005, B1, B7; Peter Brieger, "$2.4 Billion Gets CIBC Out of Class Action," *The Winnipeg Free Press*, August 3, 2005, B7; Paul Waldie and Richard Blackwell, "Several Charges Against Drabinsky Dropped," *The Globe and Mail*, September 23, 2005, B5; Karen Howlett, "Livent's Auditors Charged with Misconduct," *The Globe and Mail*, April 6, 2004, B1, B4; Barbara Shecter, "Black's $80 Million Fraud Charges," *The Winnipeg Free Press*, November 18, 2005, A1, A4; Shawn McCarthy, "The Case Against Black," *The Globe and Mail*, November 18, 2005, B1, B6; Jacquie McNish, "How the OSC Tipped the Scales on Rankin," *The Globe and Mail*, November 2, 2005, p. B13; Shirley Won, "Rankin Gets Six Months in Jail," *The Globe and Mail*, October 28, 2005, B1, B16; Elena Cherney, "Radler Pleas May Trigger Showdown," *The Globe and Mail*, September 19, 2005, p. B4; Sinclair Stewart, "RBC Pays Enron to Resolve Lawsuit," *The Globe and Mail*, July 29, 2005, B1–B2; Paul Waldie, "Black's Right-Hand Man Pleads Guilty to Fraud," *The Globe and Mail*, September 21, 2005, A1, A7; Jacquie McNish and Shirley Won, "OSC Wins Trading Case Against Andrew Rankin," *The Globe and Mail*, July 16, 2005, B1, B3; Gillian Livingston, "Scandal Hits Canada," *The Globe and Mail*, October 23, 2002, B3; David Wessel, "Why the Bad Guys of the Boardroom Emerged en Masse," *The Wall Street Journal*, June 20, 2002, A1, A6; Barrie McKenna, "Andersen Hit with Charges," *The Globe and Mail*, March 15, 2002, B1, B4. **Figure 3.1** Based on Gerald S. Cavanaugh, *American Business Values: With International Perspectives*, 4th ed. (Upper Saddle River, NJ: Prentice Hall, 1998), 71, 84. **Business Accountability** Andrew Willis, "CIBC Puts Ethics on the Line," *The Globe and Mail*, January 8, 2005, B2; Sinclair Stewart, "CIBC Sues 6 Former Employees, Alleges They Took Confidential Data, Recruited Colleagues to Upstart Genuity," *The Globe and Mail*, January 6, 2005, B1, B4; Andrew Willis, "CIBC Sues 6 Former Employees, Lawsuit Makes Both Parties Look Bad—But the Bank Gets the Worst of the Deal," *The Globe and Mail*, January 6, 2005, B1, B13. **Figure 3.2** Courtesy of Mountain Equipment Co-op, *www.mec.ca*. **Figure 3.3** David P. Baron, *Business and Its Environment*, 4th ed. (Upper Saddle River, NJ: Prentice Hall, 2003), 768. **Entrepreneurship and New Ventures** Abridged with permission from Ralph Shaw, "Peak Performance: Mountain Equipment Co-op has a better way of climbing," Alernatives Journal, Jan/Feb 2005, Vol. 31, Issue 1, p. 19–20. Annual subscriptions $35.00 <www.alternativesjournal.ca>.; **Figure 3.5** Based on Andrew C. Revkin, "Who Cares About a Few Degrees?" *The New York Times*, December 12, 1997, F1. **Concluding Case 3-1** Bill McAllister, "Alaska Still Out Front on Environmental Monitoring," *The Juneau Empire*, May 29, 2004; Marilyn Adams, "Former Carnival Exec Says He Was Fired for Helping Federal Inquiry," *USA Today*, November 8–10, 2003; Marilyn Adams, "Cruise-Ship Dumping Poisons Seas, Frustrates U.S. Enforcers," *USA Today*, November 8–10, 2003; Michael Connor, "Norwegian Cruise Line Pleads Guilty in Pollution Case," Reuters, December 7, 2002; "What Is a Dead Zone?" *Oceana Interactive* (June 10, 2004), www.oceana.org. **Concluding Case 3-2** Stephen Power and Matthew Karnitschnig, "VW's Woes Mount Amid Claims of Sex Junkets for Union Chiefs," *The Wall Street Journal*, November 17, 2005, A1, A8, A9; Gabriella Mitchener, "VW Agrees to Big Settlement with GM," *The Wall Street Journal*, January 10, 1997, A3; "Lopez Indicted for Taking from GM," *The Globe and Mail*, May 23, 2000, B9.

Chapter 4

Stepping Up Robeez Footwear Ltd. website: www.robeez.com/en-us/about/sandra.htm?PriceCat=1&Lang=EN-US; Rebecca Gardiner, "It Pays to Be Nice," *Profit* 24, no. 6 (December 2005): 23. Reprinted with permission of Robeez Footwear Ltd. and Profit Magazine. **Figure 4.1** Statistics Canada, Business Register, June 2005. **Figure 4.2a and Figure 4.2b** Statistics Canada, Business Register, June 2005. **Figure 4.3a and Figure 4.3b** Statistics Canada, Survey of Employment, Payrolls and Hours (SEPH), March 2005, and calculations by Industry Canada. **Entrepreneurship and New Ventures** © Rick Spence, "The Fastest Five," *Profit* 24, no. 3 (June 2005): 49. Retrieved May 14, 2006, from ABI/INFORM Global database. (Document ID: 856224751). Reprinted with permission; BDC website, www.bdc.ca/en/about/mediaroom/news_releases/2005/2005101808.htm, accessed June 12, 2006. **Table 4.3** *Financial Post Business*, Special Edition, 2006, 64; Material reprinted with the express permission of "National Post Company," a CanWest Partnership. *Financial Post Business*, Special Edition, 2006, p. 64. **Business Accountability** "Report on Business Corporate Governance Rankings," *The Globe and Mail*, October 17, 2005, B5; Louis Lavelle, "The Best and Worst Boards," *Business Week*, April 7, 2004; Stefani Eads, "Why Amazon's Board Is Part of the Problem," *Business Week*, April 7, 2004; "Mixing It Up," *Corporate Board Member*, November/December, 2003; Jacquie McNish, "Onex Chief Ripped for Appointing Wife," *The Globe and Mail*, May 9, 2003, B1, B7; Jennifer Reingold, "Dot.Com Boards are Flouting the Rules," *Business Week*, December 20, 2003; Janet McFarland, "How ROB Created the Rating System," *The Globe and Mail*, October 7, 2002, B6. **Concluding Case 4-1** Paul Judge, "From Country Boys to Big Cheese," *Fast Company* (December 2001): 38–40; Sue Robinson, "Saving Our Farms," BurlingtonFreePress.com, November 27, 2001. **Concluding Case 4-2** Marlene Cartash, "My Best Sale: Asked to Recall the Defining Moment of their Selling Careers, 10 Celebrated Entrepreneurs Cited Gutsy Moves that Still Fill Them with Pride," *Profit* 13, no. 4 (1995): 34–41; Bruce Erskine, "Gibson got in on ground floor," *The Halifax Herald Limited*, Wednesday, April 26, 2006, www.thechronicleherald.ca/external/bbi/index11.html, July 3, 2006. Used with permission.

Chapter 5

Canadian Exporters: Opportunities and Problems Gordon Pitts, "Manulife's Army of Agents on the March for Middle Class," *The Globe and Mail*, October 23, 2004, B4; Rick Cash, "Dealing with the Dragon," *The Globe and Mail*, October 23, 2004, B3; Stephanie Nolen, "McCain Learns Tough Cultural Lesson on South Africa," *The Globe and Mail*, October 21, 2004, B1, B19; Bertrand Marotte, "Coutu Takes on Fortress Retail, U.S.A.," *The Globe and Mail*, September 4, 2004, B5; Gordon Pitts, "Learn This Mantra: Customer Is King in China," *The Globe and Mail*, July 12, 2004, B1, B5; Gordon Pitts, "McCain Boss Picks up Pace of Global French Fry Assault," *The Globe and Mail*, June 14, 2004, B1, B12; John Heinzl, "China Feasts on Canada's Resources," *The Globe and Mail*, May 22, 2004, B6; Oliver Bertin, "Firms Face Major Hurdles en Route to U.S. Markets," *The Globe and Mail*, April 29, 2004, B16; Shirley Won, "Small Furniture Firm Pegged for Success," *The Globe and Mail*, April 10, 2004, B5; "Exports, Eh?" *Canadian Business* (January 1997): 21; Peggy Berkowitz, "You Say Potato, They Say McCain," *Canadian Business* (December 1991): 44–48. **Figure 5.3** *Bank of Canada Banking and Financial Statistics*, Table J1, May 2006, S108. **Table 5.1** *Bank of Canada Banking and Financial Statistics*, Table J3, May 2006, S111. **Entrepreneurship and New Ventures** Ron Lieber, "Give Us This Day Our Global Bread," *Fast Company* (March 2001): 164–167. **Table 5.3** *Financial Post Business*, Special Edition, 2006, 121; Material reprinted with the express permission of "National Post Company," a CanWest Partnership. *Financial Post Business*, Special Edition, 2006, 121. **Business Accountability** Clay Chandler, "Japan's Horror Show," *Fortune* (November 10, 2003): 114–118; "Quick Studies," *Business Week* (November 18, 2003): 48–49. **Concluding Case 5-1** Wal-Mart, "International Operations," "Wal-Mart International Operations," "Wal-Mart Stores Inc. at a Glance," *2002 Annual Report* (November 27, 2002), www.walmartstores.com; Amy Tsao, "Will Wal-Mart Take Over the

World?" *Business Week* (November 27, 2002): 76–79; Geri Smith, "War of the Superstores," *Business Week* (September 23, 2002): 60; "The 2002 Global 500," *Fortune* (July 8, 2002). **Concluding Case 5-2** Martin Cash, "China Wins Apparel War?" *The Winnipeg Free Press*, July 30, 2005, B8, B11; Gordon Pitts, "Peerless on a Mission: Stop China Now," *The Globe and Mail*, January 14, 2005, B8; Bertrand Marotte, "Gildan Takes T-shirt Making to the Cutting-Edge of Casual Apparel," *The Globe and Mail*, July 3, 2004, B3; Gordon Pitts, "Who Will Be the Next Huntingdon?" *The Globe and Mail*, January 8, 2005, B7.

Chapter 6

Looking for Redemption? Shawn McCarthy, "Bronfman Is Eager to Gain Redemption for His Music Gambit," *The Globe and Mail*, January 4, 2005, B4; Allen Swift, "Bronfman Jr. Wants His Toy Again," *The Winnipeg Free Press*, May 26, 2003, B7; Shawn McCarthy, "Bronfman Jumps Back into Music with Winning Bid," *The Globe and Mail*, November 25, 2003; Brian Milner, "Broken Spirits," *Report on Business Magazine* (September 2002): 26–38; Allan Swift, "Polygram Bid Heats Up," *The Winnipeg Free Press*, November 5, 1998, B12; Brian Milner, "Seagram's Top Gun Shoots for the Stars," *The Globe and Mail*, June 6, 1998, B1, B6; Brian Milner, "Seagram Snares Polygram," *The Globe and Mail*, May 22, 1998, B1, B4, Brian Milner, "The Selling of Edgar Bronfman Jr.," *The Globe and Mail*, February 15, 1999, B15. **Figure 6.1** Based on Stephen P. Robbins and Mary Coulter, *Management*, 7th ed. (Upper Saddle River, NJ: Prentice Hall, 2002), 199. **Entrepreneurship and New Ventures** © Rick Spence. Used with permission; Reprinted with permission of Pet Health Inc. **Figure 6.2** Based on Thomas L. Wheelen and J. David Hunger, *Strategic Management and Business Policy*, 7th ed. (Upper Saddle River, NJ: Prentice Hall, 2000), 13. **Business Accountability** Henry Mintzberg, *The Nature of Managerial Work* (New York: Harper and Row, 1973); Harvey Schachter, "Monday Morning Manager," *The Globe and Mail*, November 8, 2005, B2. **Concluding Case 6-1** "Coach's Driver Picks Up the Pace," *Business Week* (March 29, 2004): 98–100; Julia Boorstin, "How Coach Got Hot," *Fortune* (October 28, 2003): 131–134; Marilyn Much, "Consumer Research Is His Bag," *Investor's Business Daily*, December 16, 2003; "S&P Stock Picks and Pans: Accumulate Coach," *Business Week* (October 22, 2003). **Concluding Case 6-2** Andrew Willis, Jacquie McNish, and Grant Robertson, "How the Deal Was Done: Embarking on Project Odyssey's Stormy Water," *The Globe and Mail*, December 3, 2005, B4; Gordon Pitts, "Bell Adopts a New Party Line," *The Globe and Mail*, May 14, 2005, B4; Simon Avery, "Sabia Lays Out a New BCE: Lower Costs, More Wireless," *The Globe and Mail*, December 16, 2004, B1, B7; Dave Ebner, "BCE Cutting Costs, Staff, Focusing on Bell Canada," *The Globe and Mail*, December 19, 2002, B1, B4; Jacquie McNish and Paul Waldie, "BCE Reacquiring 20% Stake in Bell Canada," *The Globe and Mail*, June 29, 2002, B1, B4; Karen Howlett and John Saunders, "Teleglobe to Abandon Huge Internet Investment," *The Globe and Mail*, May 16, 2002, B1, B11; Ian Austen, "On the Hook," *Canadian Business* (May 13, 2002): 35–39; Bertrand Marotte, "Sabia: BCE Committed to Emergis," *The Globe and Mail*, May 8, 2002, B5; Eric Reguly, "Decision Time for BCE Boss Is Now," *The Globe and Mail*, March 22, 2002, B1–B2; Gordon Pitts, "Monty Ends 28 Years with a Clean Break," *The Globe and Mail*, April 25, 2002, B3.

Chapter 7

Frantic Films Is Getting More Organized Interviews with Jamie Brown, CEO of Frantic Films, as well as documents provided by Frantic Films. **Business Accountability** Joann Lublin, "Place vs. Product: It's Tough to Choose a Management Model," *The Wall Street Journal*, June 27, 2001, A1, A4; Richard Blackwell, "New CIBC Boss Promises Shakeup," *The Globe and Mail*, April 2, 1999, B1, B4; Rekha Bach, "Heinz's Johnson to Divest Operations, Scrap Management of Firm by Region," *The Wall Street Journal*, December, 1997, B10-B12; Jana Parker-Pope and Joann Lublin, "P&G Will Make Jager CEO Ahead of Schedule," *The Wall Street Journal*, September, 1998, B1, B8. **Entrepreneurship and New Ventures** *Profit* magazine, "The 18th Annual *Profit* 100 Ranking of Canada's Fastest Growing Companies," http://canadianbusiness.com, Tuesday, June 13, 2006; Business Development Bank of Canada *www.bdc.ca*. **Concluding Case 7-1** Sara Lee "Our Brands," www.saralee.com, July 3, 2002; Deborah Cohen, "Sara Lee Opens Alternative to Victoria's Secret," *The Wall Street Journal*, January 3, 2003, B4; Julie Forster, "Sara Lee: Changing the Recipe—Again," *Business Week* (September 10, 2001): 87–89; "Sara Lee: Looking Shapely," *Business Week* (October 21, 2002): 52.

Chapter 8

Celebrating Workforce Diversity Virginia Galt, "P&G Leverages Its Cultural Diversity," *The Globe and Mail*, April 7, 2005, B1, B18; Jill Mahoney, "Visible Majority by 2017," *The Globe and Mail*, March 23, 2005, A1, A7; Kamal Dib, "Diversity Works," *Canadian Business* (March 29, 2004): 53–54; Valerie Marchant," The New Face of Work, *Canadian Business* (March 29, 2004): 38; Ann Zimmerman, "Defending Wal-Mart," *The Wall Street Journal*, October 4, 2004, B1, B10; Virginia Galt, "Western Union Remakes 'Canadian' Image," *The Globe and Mail*, November 23, 2004, B1, B24. **Entrepreneurship and New Ventures**. **The Guru of Fun Takes a Meeting with the V.P. of Buzz** Eric Wahlgren, "Online Extra: Goodbye, 'Guru of Fun,'" *Business Week*, February 6, 2003, 74–77; Lee Clifford, "You Get Paid to Do What? *Fortune*, January 20, 2003, 106–108. **Table 8.1** *Financial Post Business*, Special Edition, 2006, 122. Material reprinted with the express permission of "National Post Company," a CanWest Partnership. **Business Accountability** Celene Adams, "Interview Style Probes Past to Predict Future," *The Globe and Mail*, April 29, 2002, B16. **Concluding Case 8-1** "While Hiring at Most Firms Chills, Wal-Mart's Heats Up," *USA Today*, August 26, 2003, 3B; "Personnel File," *Fast Company* (January 2003): 118–122; *Hoover's Handbook of American Business 2004* (Austin: Hoover's Business Press, 2005), 554–555.

Chapter 9

What Happened to Hockey Night in Canada? Tim Wharnsby, "NHL: Zero Hour Looms," *The Globe and Mail*, February 10, 2005, A1, A15; Ingrid Peritz, "A Hockey Family Loses Faith," *The Globe and Mail*, February 10, 2005, A1, A15; Pierre LeBrun, "Union's OK of Cap Was Key," *The Winnipeg Free Press*, July 14, 2005, C3; David Shoalts, "NHL Sides Agree on Salary Cap," *The Globe and Mail*, June 9, 2005, A1, A9. **Figure 9.1**. Statistics Canada, "Perspectives in Labour and Income," Autumn 2003, 15, 3, p. 50. **Entrepreneurship and New Ventures**. "Arcelor: a strong commitment to value creation." Canada NewsWire, February 27, 2006, 1; www.imfmetal.org/main/index.cfm?n=47&l=2&c=12371; http://biz.yahoo.com/iw/060216/0110163.html; www.goiam.org/content.cfm?cID=5563. **Business Accountability** Peter Rakobowchuk, "Early Closing of Unionized Wal-Mart Called Cowardly," *The Winnipeg Free Press*, April 30, 2005, C15; Marina Strauss, "Wal-Mart Faces Another Unionized Store in Quebec," *The Globe and Mail*, January 20, 2005, B4; Barrie McKenna, "Unions Starting to Make Inroads at Wal-Mart," *The Globe and Mail*, August 23, 2004, B1, B12; Aldo Santin, "Wal-Mart vs. Union Battle Now Shifts to Manitoba," *The Winnipeg Free Press*, August 5, 2004, B3; Patrick Brethour, "Wal-Mart Hails Saskatchewan Court Ruling in Union Drives," *The Globe and Mail*, July 28, 2004, B1, B20; Virginia Galt, "Wal-Mart Must Give Union Access," *The Globe and Mail*, May 13, 2003, B5; "Union Is Trying to Organize Staff at Wal-Mart," *The Winnipeg Free Press*, May 13, 2003, A7; Zena Olijnyk, "CAW Walks Away from Wal-Mart, *National Post*, April 20, 2000, C5; Susan Bourettte, "Wal-Mart Staff Want Out of Union," *The Globe and Mail*, April 23, 1999, B9; John Heinzl and Marina Strauss, "Wal-Mart's Cheer Fades," *The Globe and Mail*, February 15, 1997, B1, B4; Margot Gibb-Clark, "Why Wal-Mart Lost the Case," *The Globe and Mail*, February 14, 1997, B10. **Table 9.2**. Source: Human Resources and Social Development Canada, Union Membership in Canada—January 1, 2006. Reprinted with the permission of Her Majesty the Queen in Right of Canada 2006. www.hrsdc.gc.ca/en/lp/wid/union_membership.shtml. **Figure 9.3** Labour Canada, *Labour Organization in Canada, 1991*, xxv. Used by permission of the Minister of Supply and Services Canada. **Concluding Case 9-1** Brent Jang, "Air Canada Labour Relations Tested," *The Globe and Mail*, January 21, 2005, B4; Keith McArthur, "Cuts Take Harsh Toll on Air Canada Employees," *The Globe and Mail*, May 2, 2004, B1, B16; "Unions, Airline Give Nod to Deal," *The Winnipeg Free Press*, May 25, 2003, A6; Cassandra Szklarski, "Air Canada Reaches Tentative Deal with Machinists," *The Winnipeg Free Press*, May 28, 2003, B6, B10; "1,000 AirCan Mechanics Told to Take Summer Off," *Winnipeg Free Press*, May 16, 2003, B7; David Paddon, "Airline Charting New Territory," *The Winnipeg Free Press*, April 2, 2003, B4, B5; Keith McArthur, "Air Canada to Fight Hostile Motions," *The Globe and Mail*, April 21, 2003, B1, B8; Allan Swift, "Air Canada Unions OK Cuts," *The Winnipeg Free Press*, April 1, 2003, B1, B8; David Paddon, "Air Canada to Shed More Jobs," *The Winnipeg Free Press*, April 23, 2003, B9. **Concluding Case 9-2** Barrie McKenna, "As Big 3 Skid, UAW Braces for Inevitable World of Pain," *The Globe and Mail*, October 21, 2005, B10; Robert Matthews and Kris Maher, "Labor's PR Problem," *The Wall Street Journal*, August 15, 2005, B1, B4; Kris Maher, "Unions' New Foe: Consultants," *The Wall Street Journal*, August 15, 2005, B1, B4; Greg Keenan, "CAW Crisis? No Way, Hargrove Says," *The Globe and Mail*, December 28, 2004, B1, B5; Bruce Little, "EU's Expansion Bound to Put the Screws to Cushy Labour Rules," *The Globe and Mail*, August 4, 2004, B2; Greg Keenan, "CAW Renews Drive to Unionize Toyota," *The Globe and Mail*, July 13, 2004, B1, B4; Virginia Galt, "Their Backs Against the Wall, Unions Are Opting for Compromise," *The Globe and Mail*, July 5, 2004, B1, B9; Greg Keenan, "GM and CAW Forge an Improved Relationship," The *Globe and Mail*, October 23, 1999, B1, B14.

Chapter 10

Keeping Employees Satisfied and Motivated Wallace Immen, "The Continuing Divide Over Stress Leave," *The Globe and Mail*, June 10, 2005, C1; Jeff Buckstein, "In Praise of Praise in the Workplace," *The Globe and Mail*, June 15, 2005, C1, C5; Virginia Galt, "This Just In: Half Your Employees Ready to Jump Ship," *The Globe and Mail*, January 26, 2005, B1, B9; David Sirota, Louis Mischkind, and Michael Meltzer, "Nothing Beats an Enthusiastic Employee," *The Globe and Mail*, July 29, 2005, C1; Virginia Galt, "Business's Next Challenge: Tackling Mental Health in the Workplace," *The Globe and Mail*, April 12, 2005, B1, B20; Virginia Galt, "Canadian Take Dour View on Jobs, Bosses, Angels," *The Globe and Mail*, October 18, 2004, B1, B7; Virginia Galt, "Worker Stress Costing Economy Billions, Panel Warns," *The Globe and Mail*, July 21, 2000, B9. **Entrepreneurship and New Ventures** © Andy Holloway, "The Dream Team," *Profit* magazine (June 2006) www.canadianbusiness.com/rankings/profit100/index.jsp?pageID=article&type=top10&year=2006&content=top10&page=9&print=. **Figure 10-2** Ricky Griffin and Ronald Ebert, *Business*, 2nd ed. (Englewood Cliffs, NJ: Prentice Hall, 1996). **Business Accountability** Virginia Galt, "Ideas: Employees' Best-Kept Secrets," *The Globe and Mail*, June 18, 2005, B11; Frederick A. Starke, Bruno Dyck, and Michael Mauws, "Coping with the Sudden Loss of an Indispensable Worker," *Journal of Applied Behavioural Science* 39, no. 2 (2003): 208–229; Timothy Aeppel, "On Factory Floors, Top Workers Hide Secrets to Success," *The Wall Street Journal*, July 1, 2002, A1, A10; Timothy Aeppel, "Not All Workers Find Idea of Empowerment as Neat as It Sounds," *The Wall Street Journal*, September 8, 1997, A1, 13. **Concluding Case 10-1** A. G. Lafley, "Letter to Shareholders," Procter & Gamble, *2002 Annual Report*; "A Healthy Gamble," *Time* (September 16, 2002): 46–48; Katrina Booker, "The Un-CEO," *Fortune* (September 16, 2002): 88–96; Robert Berner, "Procter & Gamble's Renovator-in-Chief," *Business Week* (December 11, 2002): 98–100; Robert Berner, "The Best and Worst Managers: A. G. Lafley, Procter & Gamble," *Business Week* (January 13, 2003): 67. **Concluding Case 10-2** Virginia Galt, "Statscan Studies Workplace Stress," *The Globe and Mail*, June 26, 2003, B3; Anne Howland, "There's No Place Like Work," *CGA Magazine* (July–August, 2000): 21–25; David Leonhardt, "Did Pay Incentives Cut Both Ways?" *The New York Times*, April 7, 2002, BU1-3; Dean Foust and Michelle Conlin, "A Smarter Squeeze?" *Business Week* (December 31, 2001): 42–44; Rick Perera, "Siemens Offers Workers 'Time-Outs' to Save Cash," *The Industry Standard*, August 31, 2001; Tischelle George, "Bye-Bye Employee Perks," *Information Week* (October 15, 2001).

Chapter 11

Toyota: The New Number 1? Barrie McKenna, "Made in America, Toyota-Style," *The Globe and Mail*, June 10, 2006, B4; Jathon Sapsford, Norihiko Shirouzu, and Joseph White, "Toyota Maps Plan to Displace GM as Top Car Maker," *The Wall Street Journal*, November 19–20, 2005, A1, A4; Greg Keenan, "Global Domination, the Toyota Way," *The Globe and Mail*, June 18, 2005, B4; Greg Keenan, "Japan's Big Three Still Lead Race," *The Globe and Mail*, June 19, 2003, B6; Alex Taylor, "How Toyota Defies Gravity," *Fortune* (December 8, 1997): 100–108. **Entrepreneurship and New Ventures** Business Development Bank of Canada, "Scott MacDonald Brings the Sound of Silence to Alberta and Beyond," news release, October 18, 2005, www.bdc.ca/en/about/mediaroom/news_releases/2005/2005101812.htm. **Business Accountability** Greg Keenan, "Ford's New Maxim: Flex Manufacturing," *The Globe and Mail*, May 10, 2006, B3; Timothy Aeppel, "Workers Not Included," *The Wall Street Journal*, November 19, 2002, B1, B11; Martin Stinson, "Assembly Line Robots Taking Workers' Jobs: UN Report," *The Globe and Mail*, February 8, 2000, B6; Wally Dennison, "Robotics Paint System Makes Splash at CN," *The Winnipeg Free Press*, October 6, 1988, 30. **Concluding Case 11-1** Pasadena Convention and Visitors Bureau, "Pasadena Tournament of Roses Parade and Rose Bowl Game: A Grand Tradition," news release, March 29, 2004, www.pasadenacal.com; Burbank Tournament of Roses Association, "2004 Float Entry Fact Sheet," March 29, 2004, www.burbankrosefloat.com; Cindy Chang, "Finally, a Chance to Relax," *Pasadena Star-News*, January 1, 2004, www. pasadenastarnews.com, March 29, 2004; Bill Hetherman, "Overnighters in Partying Mood," *Pasadena Star-News*, January 1, 2004, www.pasadenastarnews.com, March 29, 2004; Naush Boghossian, "Float Volunteers Feel the Moosic of Rose Parade," *Los Angeles Daily News*, December 26, 2003, www.dailynews.com, January 6, 2004; personal observations of the author as a volunteer assembling the float on December 28, 2003. **Concluding Case 11-2** Simon Tuck, "Ottawa Taking Brakes Off Auto Lures," *The Globe and Mail*, November 23, 2005, B1, B4; Gordon Pitts, "GM Economic Aftershocks Set to Hit Southern Ontario," *The Globe and Mail*, November 22, 2005, B1, B11; Greg Keenan, "GM Scraps New Car Platform Intended for Oshawa Plant," *The Globe and Mail*, March 22, 2005, B1–B2; Greg Keenan, "Ford Plans SUV's for Oakville," *The Globe and Mail*, June 18, 2003, B1, B18; Oliver Bertin, "Appliance Makers in Canada: A Dying Breed," *The Globe and Mail*, March 31, 2003, B5; Greg Keenan, "Auto Sector's Best-Paid Jobs Vanishing," *The Globe and Mail*, March 29, 2003, B1, B2; Thomas Watson, "Car Trouble," *Canadian Business* (March 17, 2003): 69–71; Steve Erwin, "Auto Workers 'Angry and Frustrated,'" *The Winnipeg Free Press*, May 23, 2003, B5; Bertrand Marotte, "Quebec GM Plant

Closing the End of an Era," *The Globe and Mail*, August 24, 2002, B1, B5; Todd Zaun, Gregory White, Norihiko Shirouzu, and Scott Miller, "Auto Makers Get Even More Mileage from Third World," *The Wall Street Journal*, July 31, 2002, A1, A8; Greg Keenan, "Auto Plants Gone with the Wind," *The Globe and Mail*, June 24, 2002, B1, B4.

Chapter 12

Meeting the Productivity Challenge Gordon Pitts, "Ottawa's New, Improved Mantra: Productivity," *The Globe and Mail*, October 3, 2005, B1, B6; Greg Keenan, "GM Oshawa Cranks Out Productivity Award," *The Globe and Mail*, June 3, 2005, B1, B8; Grant Robertson, "In the Boardroom at the General Motors Oshawa Plant Is a Baseball Bat. Two Words are Carved on It: Beat Toyota," *The Globe and Mail*, September 15, 2005, B16; Gordon Pitts, "Manufacturers' Choice—Compete or Die," *The Globe and Mail*, October 5, 2005, B7; "Canada's Standard of Living," *National Post Business*, June 2003, 19–20; Jeffrey Bernstein, Richard Harris, and Andrew Sharpe, "The Widening Canada–US Manufacturing Productivity Gap," *International Productivity Monitor* (Fall 2002): 3–22; Pierre Fortin, "Differences in Annual Work Hours per Capita Between the United States and Canada," *International Productivity Monitor* (Spring 2003): 38–46; Frank Graves and Richard Jenkins, "Canadian Attitudes Towards Productivity: Balancing Standard of Living and Quality of Life," *The Review of Economic Performance and Social Progress* (2002): 243–258; Andrew Sharpe, "Why Are Americans More Productive Than Canadians?," *International Productivity Monitor* (Spring 2003): 19–37; Jason Myers, "Back to Basics: Canada's Productivity Challenge," *Canadian Manufacturers and Exporters* (April 2003): 14–18; Pierre Fortin, "Canadian Productivity: When Do We Catch Up?," *ISUMA* (Spring 2002). **Figure 12.1** Bart Van Ark and Robert McGuckin, "International Comparisons of Labor Productivity and Per Capita Income," *Monthly Labor Review* (July 1999): 33–41. **Business Accountability** Calvin Leung, "Diamonds in the Rough," *Canadian Business* (February 28–March 13, 2005): 65–67; Joel Baglole, "Political Correctness by the Carat," *The Wall Street Journal*, April 17, 2003, B1, B3; Matthew Hart, "The Ice Storm," *Canadian Business* (November 2002): 52–62. **Figure 12.2** Adapted from D. Daryl Wickoff, "New Tools for Achieving Service Quality," *The Cornell Hotel and Restaurant Administrative Quarterly* (November 1984): 89. Cornell HRA Quarterly. Used by permission. All rights reserved. **Figure 12.5** Adapted from Richard B. Chase, Nicholas J. Aquilano, and F. Robert Jacobs, *Production and Operations Management*, 8th ed. (Boston: Irwin McGraw-Hill, 1998), 771. **Entrepreneurship and New Ventures** © Camilla Cornell, "The Dream Team," *Profit* magazine (June 2006), www.canadianbusiness.com/rankings/profit100/index.jsp?pageID=article&type=top10&year=2006&content=top10&page=11&print=, June 13, 2006. **Concluding Case 12-1** Chris Isidore, "Mercedes Loses Top Resale Spot," *CNNMoney* (November 10, 2003), http://cnnmoney.printthis.clickability.com; Alex Taylor III, "Mercedes Hits a Pothole," *Fortune* (October 27, 2003): 140–146; Neal E. Boudette, "DaimlerChrysler Drops Truck Plant," *Wall Street Journal*, September 24, 2003, A11; Scott Miller and Karen Lundegaard, "An Engineering Icon Slips—Quality Ratings for Mercedes Drop in Several Surveys," *Wall Street Journal*, February 4, 2002, B1. **Concluding Case 12-2** Marina Strauss, "Loblaw's Supply Chain Reaction," *The Globe and Mail*, February 25, 2006, B4; "Canadian Retailer Loblaw's Earnings Hit Due to Delays and Challenges in Supply Chain Network Redesign Project," www.scdigest.com/assets, November 17, 2005; Blaise Robinson, "Bay Street Week Ahead—Food Fight in Canada Grocery Aisle," www.globeinvestor.com/servlet/ArticleNews/story/ROC, January 6, 2006; "Analysts Dismiss Loblaw's Woes," www.canada.com/national/nationalpost/financialpost/investing/story.html, April 28, 2006.

Chapter 13

The Information Revolution Simon Avery, "Radio Frequency Identification the New Bar Code," *The Globe and Mail*, June 30, 2004, B10; Derrick Penner, "High-Tech Devices an Important Part of Canfor's Future," *The Globe and Mail*, December 30, 2005, B10; Marina Strauss and Simon Avery, "New System Gets a Boost in Bar Code Battle," *The Globe and Mail*, April 6, 2005, B4; Kevin Lubin, "The Last Retailer in Canada?" *Canadian Business* (March 18, 2002): 31–40; Casey Mahood, "Wal-Mart Claims Another Victim," *The Globe and Mail*, February 7, 1998, B1, B5; Mark Stevenson, "The Store to End All Stores," *Canadian Business* (May 1994): 20–29. **Table 13.1** *Financial Post Business* (Special Edition, 2006): 142. Material reprinted with the express permission of "National Post Company," a CanWest Partnership. **Figure 13.3** Adapted from Kenneth C. Laudon and Jane P. Laudon, *Essentials of Management Information Systems: Managing the Digital Firm*, 5th ed. (Upper Saddle River, NJ: Prentice Hall, 2003), 16. **Entrepreneurship and New Ventures**. "They All Want a Piece of Bill Gross," *Fortune*, November 11, 2002, 139–144; Patty Enrado, "Here Comes the Lynch Mob," *Upside*, June 2002, 15; Seth Lubove, "The Final Act," *Forbes*, March 4, 2002, 44; Christopher Palmeri and Linda Himelstein, "The Bloom Is Off Idealab," *Business Week*, December 31, 2001, 10; Joseph Nocera, "Bill Gross Blew through $800 Million in 8 Months (and He's Got Nothing to Show for It). Why Is He Still Smiling?" *Fortune*, March 5, 2001, 81–83. **Figure 13.5** Kenneth C. Laudon and Jane Laudon, *Essentials of Management Information Systems*, 3rd ed. (Upper Saddle River, NJ: Prentice Hall, 1999), 39. **Figure 13.7** Adapted from Kenneth C. Laudon and Jane P. Laudon, *Essentials of Management Information Systems: Managing the Digital Firm*, 5th ed. (Upper Saddle River, NJ: Prentice Hall, 2003), 44. **Business Accountability** Daniel Roth, "Catch Us if You Can," *Fortune* (February 9, 2004): 64–74. **Concluding Case 13-1** Erick Schonfeld, "The Wizard of POS," *Business 2.0* (April 2004): 101–110; Michael Gros, *CRN* (August 25, 2003): 93; "No Tools Required for This Work Station," *Computing Canada* (November 14, 2003): 29; Gary Hilson, "Hardware Fit for a King," *Computing Canada* (February 14, 2003): 19; Larry Greenemeier, "Retailers Buy into Real-time Business," *Information Week* (January 20, 2003): 22. **Concluding Case 13-2** Paul Samyn and Leah Janzen, "Bulk-Sale Ban Hailed by Online Drug Industry," *The Winnipeg Free Press*, June 30, 2005, B15; Mia Rabson, "Feds Would Kill City Jobs to Safeguard Drug Supply," *The Winnipeg Free Press*, December 16, 2004, A1, A4; Dan Lett, "Drug Pipeline Goes Underground," *The Winnipeg Free Press*, July 18, 2004, B1; Marton Dunai, "Duty-Free Site's Cigarette Sales Draw Scrutiny," *The Wall Street Journal*, August 5, 2004, B1, B7; Leonard Zehr, "Net Pharmacies Cheer New U.S. Import Bill," *The Globe and Mail*, July 26, 2003, B1, B4; Leah Janzen, "Internet Pharmacy's Drug Search Denounced," *The Winnipeg Free Press*, July 5, 2003, A3; David Kuxhaus, "An Internet Pharmacy Primer," *The Winnipeg Free Press*, June 22, 2003, A1, A8; Carol Sanders, "Net Druggists Pen Deal," *The Winnipeg Free Press*, June 3, 2003, B1; David Kuxhaus, "U.S. Drug Agency Deals Blow to Net Pharmacy Operation," *The Winnipeg Free Press*, March 27, 2003, A3; Paul Samyn, "Competition Bureau Backs Drug Giant," *The Winnipeg Free Press*, March 22, 2003, B3.

Chapter 14

Do We Need to Audit the Auditors? Jeff Buckstein, "SOX Provision Holds Management's Feet to the Fire," *The Globe and Mail*, April 19, 2006, B13; Claire Gagne, "The Sarbanes-Oxley Act Restores Shine to Auditors' Reputation—and Fills Their Coffers," *Canadian Business* (September 27–October 10, 2004): 47–49; Karen Howlett, "Livent's Auditors Charged with Misconduct," *The Globe and Mail*, April 6, 2004, B1, B4; Karen Howlett, "Accounting Hearing Is Told Misconduct Charges Against Auditors Are 'Rubbish,'" *The Globe and Mail*, April 14, 2004, B3; Shawn McCarthy, "Investors Expect Too Much: Deloitte CEO," *The Globe and Mail*, October 17, 2005, B10; Elizabeth Church, "Accounting Overhaul Coming," *The Globe and Mail*, December 23, 2002,

B1, B6; Richard Blackwell, "Auditing Firms Get Tighter Rules," *The Globe and Mail*, July 18, 2002, B1, B4; John Partridge and Karen Howlett, "CIBC Restricts Its Auditors," *The Globe and Mail*, March 1, 2002, B1, B4; Lily Nguyen, "Accountants Primed for Change," *The Globe and Mail*, February 4, 2002, B9; Richard Blackwell, "Accountants to Issue New Rules," *The Globe and Mail*, March 28, 2002, B1, B7; John Gray, "Hide and Seek," *Canadian Business* (April 1, 2002): 28–32; Steve Liesman, Jonathan Weil, and Michael Schroeder, "Accounting Debacles Spark Calls for Change: Here's the Rundown," *The Wall Street Journal*, February 6, 2002, A1, A8; Edward Clifford, "Big Accounting Firms Face Insurance Crunch," *The Globe and Mail*, November 13, 1993, B3; Patricia Lush, "Gap Widens Between Views on Auditor's Role in Canada," *The Globe and Mail*, February 14, 1986, B3; Chris Robinson, "Auditor's Role Raises Tough Questions," *The Financial Post*, June 22, 1985. **Table 14.1** *Financial Post Business* (Special Edition, 2006): 160; Material reprinted with the express permission of "National Post Company," a CanWest Partnership. **Business Accountability** Luis Millan, "Death Knell of the Nest Egg?," *CGA Magazine* (May–June, 2006): 13–19; "Addressing the Pension Dilemma in Canada" and "The State of Defined Benefit Pension Plans in Canada," www.cga-online.org/canada/ar; Elizabeth Church, "Pension Fund Shortfall Soars in First Half," *The Globe and Mail*, November 23, 2005, B1, B7; Elizabeth Church, "Cost of Retiree Benefit Liabilities 'Sleeping Giant,'" *The Globe and Mail*, August 23, 2004, B4; Elizabeth Church, "Accounting Overhaul Coming," *The Globe and Mail*, December 23, 2002, B1, B6. **Entrepreneurship and New Ventures** "Brew Tour Update Form," *The Real Beer Page* (February 14, 2003), www.realbeer.com; "Black Oak Nut Brown Ale," *Beer Advocate.com* (February 14, 2003), www.beeradvocate.com; Stephen Beaumont, "Lament for a Brewpub—February 2003," *Stephen Beaumont's World of Beer* (February 14, 2003), www.worldofbeer.com; "Brewery Profile," *The Bar Towel* (February 14, 2003), www.bartowel.com/breweries/blackoak.phtml; John Cooper, "A Pint of Success," *CMA Management* (December 1999–January 2000): 44–46. **Concluding Case 14-1** Beth Ellyn Rosenthal, "Deloitte Study Discovers 75 Percent of Global Financial Institutions Plan to Outsource Offshore," *BPO Outsourcing Journal* (June 2003), www.bpo-outsourcing-journal.com; Lawrence M. Gill, "Questions Loom as Accountants Outsource Work Abroad," January 26, 2004, *Chicago Lawyer* (Chicago: Law Bulletin Publishing Company); "How to Evaluate an Outsourcing Provider and Watch the Bottom Line," *The CPA Journal* (June 2002): 19; Liz Loxton, "Offshoring—Offshore Accounting," *Accountancy* (February 2004): 48; Todd Furniss and Michel Janssen, "Offshore Outsourcing Part 1: The Brand of India," *OutsourcingAsia.com* (April 2003) www.outsourcing-asia.com; Todd Furniss, "China: The Next Big Wave in Offshore Outsourcing," *OutsourcingAsia.com* (June 2003) www.outsourcing-asia.com; "Outsourcing the Finance Function—Out with the Count," *Accountancy* (September 1, 2001): 32. **Concluding Case 14-2** Elizabeth Church, "Pension Funding Shortfall Increases Dramatically," *The Globe and Mail*, November 8, 2005, B5; Elizabeth Church, "Pension Fund Shortfall Soars in First Half," *The Globe and Mail*, November 23, 2005, B1, B7; Elizabeth Church, "Cost of Retiree Benefit Liabilities 'Sleeping Giant,'" *The Globe and Mail*, August 23, 2004, B4; Paul Waldie and Karen Howlett, "Reports Reveal Tight Grip of Ebbers on WorldCom," *The Globe and Mail*, June 11, 2003, B1, B7; Barrie McKenna, Karen Howlett, and Paul Waldie, "Probes Cite Ebbers in 'Fraud,'" *The Globe and Mail*, June 10, 2003, B1, B16; Elizabeth Church, "Accounting Overhaul Coming," *The Globe and Mail*, December 23, 2002, B1, B6; Richard Blackwell, "OSC Targets Tech Accounting," *The Globe and Mail*, September 26, 2000, B1, B6.

Chapter 15

Marketers Pay Attention to the Older Folks David Pringle, "In Mobile Phones, Older Users Say, More Is Less," *The Wall Street Journal*, August 15, 2005, A1, A9; John Partridge, "Leisureworld Purchase Revs Up Retirement Debate," *The Globe and Mail*, March 24, 2005, B15; Kelly Greene, "Marketing Surprise: Older Consumers Buy Stuff, Too," *The Wall Street Journal*, April 6, 2004, A1, A12; Andre Mayer, "Star's New Paper Woos Tween Readers," *The Globe and Mail*, March 12, 2003, B7; Gautam Naik, Leslie Chang, and Joanna Slater, "Leveraging the Age Gap," *The Wall Street Journal*, February 27, 2003, B1, B4; Cris Prystay and Sarah Ellison, "Time for Marketers to Grow Up?," *The Wall Street Journal*, February 27, 2003, B1, B4; Sebastian Moffett, "For Ailing Japan, Longevity Begins to Take Its Toll," *The Wall Street Journal*, February 11, 2003, A1, A12; John Heinzl, "Crayon Maker Draws in an Older Kid," *The Globe and Mail*, March 5, 1998; Shawna Steinberg, "Have Allowance, Will Transform Economy," *Canadian Business* (March 13, 1998): 59–71; Lisa Bannon, "Little Big Spenders," *The Wall Street Journal*, October 13, 1998, A1, A6; Sheryl Ubelacker, "Magazines Target Over-50 Crowd," *The Winnipeg Free Press*, April 9, 2000, B3; Allen St. John, "Baseball's Billion Dollar Question: Who's On Deck?" *American Demographics* (October, 1998): 60–62, 65–69. **Business Accountability** Keith McArthur, "A Year Later: No Medium for the Message," *The Globe and Mail*, November 1, 2004, B3; Cheryl Healton and Kathleen Nelson, "Reversal of Misfortune: Viewing Tobacco as a Social Justice Issue," *American Journal of Public Health*, February 2004, 186 *t.*; *Federal Trade Commission Cigarette Report for 2001* (June 15, 2003), www.ftc.gov/os/2003/06/cigreport.pdf. **Figure 15.3** From Kotler, *Principles of Marketing*, Sixth Canadian Edition, page 358. Copyright 2005 Pearson Education Canada. Based on material by Mark E. Smith. **Figure 15.5** Adapted from Naresh K. Malhorta, *Marketing Research: An Applied Orientation*, 3rd ed. (Upper Saddle River, NJ: Prentice Hall, 1999), 10. **Entrepreneurship and New Ventures** © Susanne Ruder, "When in Rome..." *Profit* (March 2006), www.canadianbusiness.com/entrepreneur/sales_marketing/article.jsp?content=20060210_125140_5560, June 12, 2006. Used with permission. **Concluding Case 15-1** Kevin Maney, "Dell to Dive into Consumer Electronics Market," *USA Today*, September 25, 2003, 1B–2B; David Teather, "Michael Dell Quits as Chief of His Own Company," *The Guardian*, March 5, 2004. **Concluding Case 15-2** Brooks Barnes, "New TV Ratings Will Produce Ad-Price Fight," *The Wall Street Journal*, December 22, 2005, B1, B3; Brooks Barnes, "Where're the Ratings, Dude?" *The Wall Street Journal*, March 7, 2005, B1, B6; Keith McArthur, "New TV Ratings Devices Know What You're Watching," *The Globe and Mail*, November 29, 2004, B1, B12; Keith McArthur, "Advertisers Wary of Plan to Fuse TV Ratings Systems," *The Globe and Mail*, July 13, 2004, B1, B20; Brooks Barnes, "For Nielsen, Fixing Old Ratings System Causes New Static," *The Wall Street Journal*, September 16, 2004, A1, A8; Elizabeth Jensen, "Networks Blast Nielsen, Blame Faulty Ratings for Drop in Viewership," *The Wall Street Journal*, November 22, 1996, A1, A8.

Chapter 16

The Fuel Cell: Still a Long, Rough Road Ahead Peter Kennedy, "Ballard's Celebrated Drive Hits a Bumpy Road," *The Globe and Mail*, July 17, 2004, B6; Peter Kennedy, "GM Aims to Finish First in Fuel Cell Race," *The Globe and Mail*, June 10, 2003, B5; Chris Nuttall-Smith, "Waiting for the Revolution," *Report on Business* (February, 2003): 44–54; Jeffrey Ball, "Hydrogen Fuel May Be Clean, But Getting It Here Looks Messy," *The Wall Street Journal*, March 7, 2003; Rebecca Blumenstein, "Auto Industry Reaches Surprising Consensus: It Needs New Engines," *The Wall Street Journal*, January 5, 1998, A1, A10. **Entrepreneurship and New Ventures** Cris Prystay, "Bio-Boost," *Far Eastern Economic Review* (February 6, 2003): 38; Charles Bickers, "Medicine Man Returns," *Far Eastern Economic Review* (August 23, 2001): 30–33. **Table 16.1** Keith McArthur, "Big Mac, Coke, Marlboro and...China Mobile?" *The Globe and Mail*, April 4, 2006, B1, B9. Reprinted with permission from The *Globe and Mail*. **Table 16.2** *Financial Post Business*, (Special Edition, 2006): 146; Material reprinted with the express permission of "National Post Company," a CanWest Partnership. **Business**

Accountability Joe Mandese, "The Age of Accountability," *TelevisionWeek* (February 16, 2004): 28; Joe Mandese, "Shifting Ad Accountability to Media," *TelevisionWeek* (October 6, 2003): 15; Erin White, "Media & Marketing—Advertising: Making Sure the Work Fits the Bill," *The Wall Street Journal*, February 3, 2004, B8. **Concluding Case 16-1** Keith McArthur and Grant Robetson, "CRTC Ponders Impact of Product Placement," *The Globe and Mail*, November 21, 2005, B1, B10; Grant Robertson and Richard Blackwell, "Eased Satellite Radio Rules Could 'Shock' System," *The Globe and Mail*, September 23, 2005, B7; Tessa Wegert, "On-Line Marketing Concept Gives Consumers a Say," *The Globe and Mail*, October 13, 2005, B13; Aaron Patrick, "Commercials by Cellphone," *The Wall Street Journal*, August 22, 2005, B1, B3; Frazier Moore, "You Can't Fast-Forward Past These Commercials," *The Winnipeg Free Press*, July 25, 2005, D3; Simon Tuck, "CRTC Turns Radio on Its Head with Landmark Satellite Ruling," *The Globe and Mail*, June 17, 2005, B1, B6; Eric Reguly, "Blame the Act, Not the Regulator," *The Globe and Mail*, June 16, 2005, B2; Joe Flint and Brian Steinberg, "Procter & Gamble Tweaks Its Traditional TV Ad Strategy," *The Wall Street Journal*, June 13, 2005, B6; Peter Grant, "Interactive Ads Start to Click on Cable and Satellite TV," *The Wall Street Journal*, May 26, 2005, B1, B6; Keith McArthur, "Branded Content Generates Buzz," *The Globe and Mail*, April 6, 2005, B4; Keith McArthur, "A Year Later: No Medium for the Message," *The Globe and Mail*, November 1, 2004, B3. **Concluding Case 16-2** Alexander Wolff, "Rockin' the Retros," *Sports Illustrated* (December 22, 2003): 46–54; Sean Gregory, "How Old Jerseys Got Hot," *Time* (online edition), April 7, 2003, www.time.com/time/insidebiz/article/0,9171,1101030407.

Chapter 17

The Importance of Price "Avery Wine's Brandman," *Venture*, March 27, 2005; Andy Hoffman, "Cheap Suds Give Lakeport Rivals Brand Hangover," *The Globe and Mail*, March 14, 2006, B6; Derek DeCloet, "Trouble Brewing in Beer Industry, " *The Globe and Mail*, May 7, 2005, B4; Jon Swartz, "Some eBay Sellers Are Going, Going, Gone," *USA Today*, February 2, 2005, 3B; Keith McArthur, "In Hamilton, They Like Beer Cold...and Cheap," *The Globe and Mail*, July 10, 2004, B4; Keith McArthur, "Why Molson Is Crying in Its Beer," *The Globe and Mail*, July 10, 2004, B4; Greg Keenan, "Toyota Kills No-Haggle Sales Price Strategy, " *The Globe and Mail*, June 17, 2004, B1, B25; Ann Zimmerman, "Behind the Dollar-Store Boom: A Nation of Bargain Hunters," *The Wall Street Journal*, December 13, 2004, A1, A10; Gordon Fairclough, "Four Biggest Cigarette Makers Can't Raise Prices as They Did," *The Wall Street Journal*, October 25, 2002, A1, A8; Timothy Aeppel, "After Cost Cutting, Companies Turn Toward Price Increases," *The Wall Street Journal*, September 18, 2002, A1, A12. **Business Accountability** David Wessel and Susan Carey, "Airlines Captive to Costs and Competition," *The Wall Street Journal*, September 19, 2005, B8; Evan Perez and Nicole Harris, "Despite Early Signs of Victory, Discount Airlines Get Squeezed," *The Wall Street Journal*, January 17, 2005, A1, A6; Melanie Trottman, "Equalizing Air Fares," *The Wall Street Journal*, August 17, 2004, B1, B4; Julia Boorstin, "JetBlue's IPO Takes Off," *Fortune* (April 29, 2002): 96–100; Melanie Wells, "Lord of the Skies," *Forbes* (October 14, 2002): 130–138; Paul C. Judge, "How Will Your Company Adapt?" *Fast Company* (February 2003): 105–110. **Table 17.1** *Financial Post Business* (Special Edition, 2006): 144; Material reprinted with the express permission of "National Post Company," a CanWest Partnership. **Entrepreneurship and New Ventures** Chris McDougall, "Closing the Deal," *Inc.* (March 2004): 70–84. **Concluding Case 17-1** Keith McArthur, "Why Molson Is Crying in Its Beer," *The Globe and Mail*, July 10, 2004, B4; Kevin Kelleher, "66,207,896 Bottles of Beer on the Wall," *Business 2.0* (January–February 2004): 47–49, Tim Davis, "Surfin' the Net, Bud Style," *Beverage World* (August 1995): 28; "This Budnet's for You," *Progressive Grocer*, (May 1996): 16; *2003 Annual Report* (St. Louis: Anheuser-Busch Companies Inc., 2004). **Concluding Case 17-2** Shawn McCarthy, "U.S. Court Shuts Door on Internet File-Sharing," *The Globe and Mail*, June 28, 2005, B3; "File Sharing Firm Will Shut Down," *The Winnipeg Free Press*, November 8, 2005, A11; Nick Wingfield, "Online Music's Latest Tune," *The Wall Street Journal*, August 27, 2004, B1, B2; Nick Wingfield, "New File-Swapping Software Limits Sharers to a Select Few," *The Wall Street Journal*, October 4, 2004, B1, B4; Sarah McBride, "Stop the Music!" *The Wall Street Journal*, August 23, 2004, B1; Vauhini Vara, "On Campus, iTunes Finds an Illicit Groove, *The Wall Street Journal*, August 23, 2004, B1–B2; Nick Wingfield and Sarah McBride, "Green Light for Grokster," *The Wall Street Journal*, August 20, 2004, B1, B3; Nick Wingfield, "The Day the Music Died," *The Wall Street Journal*, May 2, 2003, B8; "The End of File-Shares as We Know Them," *The Winnipeg Free Press*, July 4, 2003, A8; Ted Birdis, "Music Industry Escalates Net Fight," *The Winnipeg Free Press*, June 26, 2003, A12; Matthew Ingram, "Digital Music Industry Gets New Spin on Napster Judge's Decision," *The Globe and Mail*, February 26, 2002; Nick Wingfield, "Napster Boy, Interrupted," *The Wall Street Journal*, October 1, 2002, B1, B3; Anna Matthews and Charles Goldsmith, "Music Industry Faces New Threats on Web," *The Wall Street Journal*, February 21, 2003, B1, B4.

Chapter 18

Who Could Have Imagined This? Tim Campbell, "Hockey Plays Dollar Game," *The Winnipeg Free Press*, June 30, 2006, D8; Murray McNeill and Larry Kusch, "Manitoba's Manufacturing Sector Suffers While Buck Rises," *The Winnipeg Free Press*, May 2, 2006, B1, B6; Eric Beauchesne, "Loonie Predicted to Hit Par Next Fall," *The Winnipeg Free Press*, May 2, 2006, B1, B6; "20 Ways the Rising Loonie Is Changing Canada's Landscape," *The Globe and Mail*, July 5, 2003, B1, B4; John Saunders, "Exporters Facing Some Loonie Math," *The Globe and Mail*, May 7, 2003, B1, B4. **Table 18.1** *Financial Post Business* (Special Edition, 2006): 156; Material reprinted with the express permission of "National Post Company," a CanWest Partnership. **Entrepreneurship and New Ventures** Canada NewsWire, "Announcing CHEQ-IT Ltd. System Sales," October 13, 2005, p. 1; CHEQ-IT Ltd. home page; Reprinted with permission of Cheq-It Ltd. **Business Accountability** Nocolas Parent, Phoebe Munro, and Ron Parker, "An Evaluation of Fixed Announcement Dates," *Bank of Canada Review* (Autumn 2003): 3. **Table 18.2** *Financial Post Business* (Special Edition 2006): 156; Material reprinted with the express permission of "National Post Company," a CanWest Partnership. **Table 18.3** http://economist.com, June 9, 2005. **Concluding Case 18-1** "Newfoundland Aquaculture Industry Association Receives Funding for Cod Aquaculture Initiative,", January 30, 2006; Lindsay Royston, "Cod Walloped," *Canadian Business* (November 21–December 4, 2005): 110–114; "Newfoundland Projects Work Toward Cod Commercialization," April 2005; "Newfoundland Cod Comeback," January 16, 2004; CBC series "Land & Sea," May 21, 2006. **Concluding Case 18-2** "Business: Tested by the Mighty Euro," *The Economist* (March 20, 2004): 78; G. Thomas Sims, "Tale of Two Recoveries. EU and Tokyo Diverge," *The Wall Street Journal*, April 2, 2004, A7; Justin Lahart, "Is the Euro Too Strong?" *CNNMoney*, January 8, 2004, http://cnnmoney. com; Jamie McGeever, "Dollar May Gain More Against Euro on ECB Outlook," *The Wall Street Journal*, March 29, 2004, C5.

Chapter 19

The Urge to Manipulate the Stock Market "Scandalist," CBC *Venture* series, November 6, 2005; Richard Blackwell, "OSC Scores Trading Conviction," *The Globe and Mail*, July 22, 2000, B1–B2; "CEO Jailed for Insider Trading," *The Winnipeg Free Press*, September 19, 2000, B8; Karen Howlett, "Below The Decks of Treasure Ship Deals," *The Globe and Mail*, July 19, 2003, B1, B4; Karen Howlett, Sinclair Stewart, and Paul Waldie, "Brokers Caught Up in Police Probe," *The Globe and Mail*, June 20, 2003, B1, B20; Richard Blackwell, "Firm, Ex-CEO Pay Millions in Penalties," *The Globe and*

Mail, December 20, 2001, B1, B6; Andrew Willis, "Paterson's Words Give Ugly Spin to Debacle," *The Globe and Mail*, December 20, 2001, B1, B6; David Paddon and Hollie Shaw, "Top Heads Roll at Royal After Scandal," *The Winnipeg Free Press*, July 21, 2000, B7, B12; Karen Howlett, Janet McFarland, and Dawn Walton, "Stock Rigging Appears Widespread," *The Globe and Mail*, July 1, 2000, B1, B4; Keith McArthur, "Business Seeps Away from Royal Pensions," *The Globe and Mail*, July 1, 2000, B1, B5; Richard Blackwell and Jacquie McNish, "OSC Prepared to Deal with RT," *The Globe and Mail*, July 1, 2000, B5; Jacquie McNish, "How the High Closing High Fliers Got Caught," *The Globe and Mail*, July 3, 2000, B1, B3. **Figure 19.1** "Yahoo Inc (YHOO)/Wal-Mart Stores Inc (WMT)," *Quicken.com*, www.quicken.com/investments/charts/, July 13, 2002. **Table 19.1** *Financial Post Business* (Special Edition, 2006): 98; Material reprinted with the express permission of "National Post Company," a CanWest Partnership. **Table 19.2** *National Post* (June 2000): 168. **Table 19.3** *Financial Post Business* (Special Edition, 2006): 158; Material reprinted with the express permission of "National Post Company," a CanWest Partnership. **Entrepreneurship and New Ventures** Camilla Cornell, "The Dream Team," *Profit* (June 2006), www.canadianbusiness.com June 13, 2006. **Business Accountability** "Our True Identity Revealed: AIMR Changes Name to CFA Institute," CFA Institute (April 19, 2004), www.cfainstitute.org. **Concluding Case 19-1** Karen Howlett and John Saunders, "Fund Firms Admit Role in Market Timing Trades," *The Globe and Mail*, December 17, 2004, B1, B4; Janet McFarland and Rob Carrick, "The Fee Crunch: Not All Investors Get Value for Money," *The Globe and Mail*, June 24, 2004, B6; Christine Dugas, "Putnam Ousts CEO in Midst of Fund Probe," *USA Today*, November 3, 2003, www.usatoday.com/money; "Senators Blast SEC over Mutual Fund Trading Scandal," *USA Today*, November 3, 2003, www.usatoday.com/money; John Waggoner, Christine Dugas, and Thomas A. Fogarty, "Scandal Outrage Keeps Growing," *USA Today*, November 3, 2003, www.usatoday.com/money; "NYC Pensions Pull Assets from Putnam," *CNNMoney*, November 4, 2003, www.cnnmoney.com; "Chairman of Strong Mutual Resigns," *USA Today*, November 3, 2003, www.usatoday.com/money. **Concluding Case 19-2** Janet McFarland, "Companies Reform Stock Option Plans," *The Globe and Mail*, February 24, 2003, B1, B5; Matt Murray, "Options Frenzy: What Went Wrong?," *The Wall Street Journal*, December 17, 2002, B1, B3; David Wessel, "Why the Bad Guys of the Boardroom Emerged En Masse," *The Wall Street Journal*, June 20, 2002, A1, A6.

Chapter 20

The Increasing Importance of Risk Management Oliver Bertin, "Sector Hit Hard by Sharp Increases in Premiums," *The Globe and Mail*, April 27, 2004, B14; Oliver Bertin, "Firms Face Major Hurdles En Route to U.S. Markets," *The Globe and Mail*, April 29, 2004, B16; Harris Anwar, "Chief Risk Officer: A Valuable addition to the C-Suite," *The Globe and Mail*, June 20, 2005, B13; "Singer 'Incited' Crowd," *The Winnipeg Free Press*, August 15, 2005, D2; Leslie Scism," If Disaster Strikes This 'Titanic,' Chubb Could Lose Millions," *The Wall Street Journal*, April 9, 1997, A1, A4; Leslie Scism, "Maybe Julie Andrews Could Offer Insurers a Spoonful of Sugar," *The Wall Street Journal*, April 4, 1997, A1, A4; Patrick Reilly, "Insurers Are Downbeat on Rap Concert Tours," *The Wall Street Journal*, March 26, 1997, B1, B12. **Entrepreneurship and New Ventures** Tom Stein, "Every Step You Take, LPs Will Be Watching You," *Venture Capital Journal*, January 1, 2003, 1; Yasmine Chinwala, "US Survey Shows Gender Gap," *eFinancial News*, February 25, 2002, www.marcusventures.com/financialnews.html; Alison Maitland, "An Idea from the Ladies Room," *FT.com/Financial Times*, February 2, 2003, www.marcusventures.com/FT.html. **Business Accountability** Michael S. Hopkins, "Because He Learns, and Teaches," *Inc.* (April 2004): 119–120. **Table 20.2** *Financial Post Business* (Special Edition, 2006): 158; Material reprinted with the express permission of "National Post Company," a CanWest Partnership. **Concluding Case 20-1** Ian Mount, " Be Fast, Be Frugal, Be Right," *Inc.* (January 2004): 64–70; Winston Chai, "Linksys Finds Its Voice," *CNET News.com*, April 21, 2004, http://news.com.com; Drew Robb, "Linksys Router Named Top Wireless Product," *Datamation*, March 25, 2004, www.wi-fiplanet.com; Mark Boslet, "Cisco Pushes into New Market: the "Digital Living Room," *The Wall Street Journal*, January 21, 2004, 1. **Concluding Case 20-2** Shirley Won, "What's in a Name? Plenty, if It's Brascan," *The Globe and Mail*, September 16, 2005, B3; Shirley Won, "Brascan's Plan Pleases Analysts, but Some Preach Wait-and-See," *The Globe and Mail*, March 18, 2005, B12; Andrew Willis, "Brascan Remakes Itself, This Time with Trees," *The Globe and Mail*, February 19, 2005, B7; Andrew Willis, "How Flatt Is Reforging Brascan," *The Globe and Mail*, September 25, 2004, B6; John Partridge, "Brascan Looks to Power Plants for Added Juice in Bottom Line," *The Globe and Mail*, August 6, 2004, B9; Andrew Willis, "Investors Betting on Brascan Dismantling," *The Globe and Mail*, July 19, 2004, B1, B10.

Photo and Cartoon Credits

PART ONE

2–3 © Ron Fehling/Masterfile www.masterfile.com.

Chapter 1

5 Courtesy of Inco.; **6** © The New Yorker Collection; **12** AP Wide World Photos; **21** Dwight Eschliman; **24** © Masterfile (Royalty-Free Div.) www.masterfile.com; **28** (top) Ritz Sino/New York Times Pictures, (margin) Namas Bhojani.

Chapter 2

37 © Steve Craft/Masterfile; **44** © Louie Psihoyos/CORBIS; **47** © Bettmann/CORBIS; **52** AP Wide World Photos.

Chapter 3

71 JESSICA KOURKOUNIS/AP/CP Images; **73** KENNETH LAMBERT / AP/CP Images; **82** AFP/Getty Images; **88** Donna Terek Photography; **89** Courtesy of Construction Association of Ontario; **91** © The New Yorker Collection; **96** McDonald's Restaurant.

Chapter 4

103 Courtesy of Robeez Footwear Ltd. www.robeez.com; **106** S. Houston.

Chapter 5

139 © Robert Holmes/CORBIS; **142** Amit Barghava/CORBIS-NY; **145** Everett Collection; **155** Uriel Sinai/Getty Images; **157** Mark Gibson/Digital Vision/Getty Images; **161** Namas Bhojani.

PART TWO

172–173 © Rick Gomez/Corbis

Chapter 6

175 CP Picture Archive (Laurent Rebours); **177** EPA/Sergei Chirikov/Landov LLC; **181** Neema Frederic/Corbis/Sygma; **184** © Matthew Mcvay/CORBIS; **188** Najlah Feanny/CORBIS-NY; **190** (left) ColorBlind Images/Getty Images, (middle) © PhotoAlto/Alamy, (right) Stuart:Pearce/agefotostock/firstlight.ca; **195** Kistone Photography; **197** Courtesy of Mainframe Entertainment Inc.

Chapter 7

205 Courtesy of Frantic Films; **209** Everett Collection; **211** Dick Hemingway; **221** Adamsmith/Taxi/Getty Images; **223** GE Transportation Aircraft Engines; **225** AP Wide World Photos; **228** Bob Scott/Image Bank.

Chapter 8

237 © ImageSource; **243** Javier Larrea/ agefotostock/firstlight.ca; **245** © Creatas; **248** Harry Sieplinga/HMS Images/Getty Images; **254** KATHY WILLENS/AP/ CP Images; **263** © Chris Sattlberger/ Corbis; **264** Mark Richards; **273** FRANK GUNN /CP Images.

Chapter 9

273 FRANK GUNN /CP Images; **276** Prentice Hall Archives; **284** JEANNOT LéVESQUE/CP Images; **288** Kevin Frayer/CP Photo Archive; **290** AFP/Getty Images.

Chapter 10

301 © Masterfile (Royalty-Free Div.) www.masterfile.com; **305** (top) Corbis, (bottom) Courtesy Western Electric; **311** © Masterfile (Royalty-Free Div.) www.masterfile.com; **312** Tim Boyle/ Getty Images; **314** Loren Santow/Stone/ Getty Images; **319** Frank Gunn /CP Photo Archive; **322** © The New Yorker Collection 1997 Mark Twohy from cartoonbank.com. All rights reserved.

PART THREE

334–335 © George Steinmetz/Corbis

Chapter 11

337 © Masterfile (Royalty-Free Div.) www.masterfile.com; **339** Namas Bhojani; **342** (top two right and bottom left) Canapress Photo Service, (top left) Plus Pix/first Light, (bottom right) PhotoDisc; **343** © Masterfile (Royalty-Free Div.) www.masterfile.com; **353** (top) Toyota Motor Manufacturing Canada Inc., (bottom) Jaguar Cars Limited; **360** LTI New York.

Chapter 12

369 © J.P. MOCZULSKI/Reuters/Corbis; **371** Christopher Anderson; **374** (both) Ted Rice; **378** AP Wide World Photos; **379** Aaron Bacall from cartoonbank.com. All rights reserved.; **382** Ray Ng Photography, Inc.; **386** Dofasco Canada; **388** AP Wide World Photos.

Chapter 13

399 © kolvenbach /Alamy; **402** Bruce Ayers/Stone; **405** (both) Richard B. Levine/Frances M. Roberts; **408** AP Wide World Photos; **417** Jonathan Saunders; **421** Alec Soth Photography; **424** Photofest.

Chapter 14

435 Artifacts Images/Getty Images; **440** PhotoDisc; **442** AP Wide World Photos; **447** Contact Press Images, Inc.; **448** Kevin Frayer/CP Photo Archive; **455** Getty Images Inc.—Hulton Archive Photos; **456** © The New Yorker Collection 1997 Robert Weber from cartoonbank.com. All rights reserved.

PART FOUR

468–469 Werner Dieterich/ Photographer's Choice/Getty Images.

Chapter 15

471 © Rick Gomez/Corbis; **474** Courtesy of Nutrisoya Foods Inc., Courtesy of Publicis USA, Dallas, and Courtesy of the Ministry of Health and Long-Term Care/Philip Lee Harvey/Stone+/Getty Images; **477** JACQUES BOISSINOT/CP Images; **480** (top) New York Times Pictures, (bottom) Grand & Toy; 484 New York Times Pictures; **488** © The New Yorker Collection 1992 Bernard Schoenbaum from cartoonbank.com. All rights reserved; **489** Rachel Epstein, PhotoEdit, Inc.; **492** © Bryan F. Peterson/ CORBIS/Magmaphoto.com; **496** Feathercraft Products, Ltd.

Chapter 16

507 Ballard Power Systems, Inc.; **513** PhotoDisc; 518 Michelle V. Agins/ New York Times Pictures; **524** (bottom left) Scouting Canada, (middle right) CP Photo/Didier Debusschere, (bottom right) TOM HANSON/CP Images; **527** Contract Press Images, Inc.; **529** David Burtow/Redux Pictures; **530** Howard, Merrel & Partners, Inc.; **534** New York Times Pictures; **535** Agence France-Presse AFP.

Chapter 17

547 © Najlah Feanny/Corbis; **549** © The New Yorker Collection 1991 Jack Zeigler from cartoonbank.com. All rights reserved; **551** New York Times Pictures; **556** Guillermo Granja/Corbis/Reuters America LLC; **557** Daniel Acker/ Bloomberg News/Landov LLC; **559** Tim Boyle/Getty Images; **560** © the New Yorker Collection 1997 Robert Mankoff from cartoonbank.com. All rights reserved; **561** Steven Ahlgren; **570** QVC, Inc.; **573** Canadian National.

PART FIVE

586–587 Courtesy of TSX.

Chapter 18

589 © Corey Hochachka; **591** The Granger Collection; **592** New York Times Pictures; **593** Maduff Everton/ CORBIS-NY; **597** © The New Yorker Collection 1997 J.B. Handelsman from cartoonbank.com. All rights reserved; **598** Bob Carroll/Leucar; **599** Nikolai Ignatiev/Network Photographers, Ltd.

Chapter 19

619 Trevor Bonderud/First Light **623** Jeremy Sutton-Hibbert/Network Photographers Ltd; **627** *Toronto Star*/ D. Loek; **631** Reproduced with the permission of the Minister of Finance; **636** Bloomberg/Landov LLC; **642** Dan Krauss/New York Times Pictures.

Chapter 20

653 © Russell Underwood/Corbis; **655** © Stock Connection Blue/Alamy; **660** Naomi Harris; **662** BellSouth Advertising & Publishing; **665** Aileen Tat Photography; **674** Joe Polimeni/GM/ Bloomberg News/Landov LLC; **674** Lawrence Migdale, Ulrich Welch, Eunice Harris/Photo Researchers; **676** David Mah/CP Photo Archive.

NAME AND ORGANIZATION INDEX

D

E

S

T

U

V

SUBJECT INDEX

D

E

F

N

O

T

U

V

W

Y

Z

"AS IS" LICENSE AGREEMENT AND LIMITED WARRANTY

READ THIS LICENSE CAREFULLY BEFORE OPENING THIS PACKAGE. BY OPENING THIS PACKAGE, YOU ARE AGREEING TO THE TERMS AND CONDITIONS OF THIS LICENSE. IF YOU DO NOT AGREE, DO NOT OPEN THE PACKAGE. PROMPTLY RETURN THE UNOPENED PACKAGE AND ALL ACCOMPANYING ITEMS TO THE PLACE YOU OBTAINED THEM. THESE TERMS APPLY TO ALL LICENSED SOFTWARE ON THE DISK EXCEPT THAT THE TERMS FOR USE OF ANY SHAREWARE OR FREEWARE ON THE DISKETTES ARE AS SET FORTH IN THE ELECTRONIC LICENSE LOCATED ON THE DISK:

1. GRANT OF LICENSE and OWNERSHIP: The enclosed computer programs and any data ("Software") are licensed, not sold, to you by Pearson Canada Inc. ("We" or the "Company") in consideration of your adoption of the accompanying Company textbooks and/or other materials, and your agreement to these terms. You own only the disk(s) but we and/or our licensors own the Software itself. This license allows instructors and students enrolled in the course using the Company textbook that accompanies this Software (the "Course") to use and display the enclosed copy of the Software for academic use only, so long as you comply with the terms of this Agreement. You may make one copy for back up only. We reserve any rights not granted to you.

2. USE RESTRICTIONS: You may not sell or license copies of the Software or the Documentation to others. You may not transfer, distribute or make available the Software or the Documentation, except to instructors and students in your school who are users of the adopted Company textbook that accompanies this Software in connection with the course for which the textbook was adopted. You may not reverse engineer, disassemble, decompile, modify, adapt, translate or create derivative works based on the Software or the Documentation. You may be held legally responsible for any copying or copyright infringement that is caused by your failure to abide by the terms of these restrictions.

3. TERMINATION: This license is effective until terminated. This license will terminate automatically without notice from the Company if you fail to comply with any provisions or limitations of this license. Upon termination, you shall destroy the Documentation and all copies of the Software. All provisions of this Agreement as to limitation and disclaimer of warranties, limitation of liability, remedies or damages, and our ownership rights shall survive termination.

4. DISCLAIMER OF WARRANTY: THE COMPANY AND ITS LICENSORS MAKE NO WARRANTIES ABOUT THE SOFTWARE, WHICH IS PROVIDED "AS-IS." IF THE DISK IS DEFECTIVE IN MATERIALS OR WORKMANSHIP, YOUR ONLY REMEDY IS TO RETURN IT TO THE COMPANY WITHIN 30 DAYS FOR REPLACEMENT UNLESS THE COMPANY DETERMINES IN GOOD FAITH THAT THE DISK HAS BEEN MISUSED OR IMPROPERLY INSTALLED, REPAIRED, ALTERED OR DAMAGED. THE COMPANY DISCLAIMS ALL WARRANTIES, EXPRESS OR IMPLIED, INCLUDING WITHOUT LIMITATION, THE IMPLIED WARRANTIES OF MERCHANTABILITY AND FITNESS FOR A PARTICULAR PURPOSE. THE COMPANY DOES NOT WARRANT, GUARANTEE OR MAKE ANY REPRESENTATION REGARDING THE ACCURACY, RELIABILITY, CURRENTNESS, USE, OR RESULTS OF USE, OF THE SOFTWARE.

5. LIMITATION OF REMEDIES AND DAMAGES: IN NO EVENT, SHALL THE COMPANY OR ITS EMPLOYEES, AGENTS, LICENSORS OR CONTRACTORS BE LIABLE FOR ANY INCIDENTAL, INDIRECT, SPECIAL OR CONSEQUENTIAL DAMAGES ARISING OUT OF OR IN CONNECTION WITH THIS LICENSE OR THE SOFTWARE, INCLUDING, WITHOUT LIMITATION, LOSS OF USE, LOSS OF DATA, LOSS OF INCOME OR PROFIT, OR OTHER LOSSES SUSTAINED AS A RESULT OF INJURY TO ANY PERSON, OR LOSS OF OR DAMAGE TO PROPERTY, OR CLAIMS OF THIRD PARTIES, EVEN IF THE COMPANY OR AN AUTHORIZED REPRESENTATIVE OF THE COMPANY HAS BEEN ADVISED OF THE POSSIBILITY OF SUCH DAMAGES. SOME JURISDICTIONS DO NOT ALLOW THE LIMITATION OF DAMAGES IN CERTAIN CIRCUMSTANCES, SO THE ABOVE LIMITATIONS MAY NOT ALWAYS APPLY.

6. GENERAL: THIS AGREEMENT SHALL BE CONSTRUED AND INTERPRETED ACCORDING TO THE LAWS OF THE PROVINCE OF ONTARIO. This Agreement is the complete and exclusive statement of the agreement between you and the Company and supersedes all proposals, prior agreements, oral or written, and any other communications between you and the company or any of its representatives relating to the subject matter.

Should you have any questions concerning this agreement or if you wish to contact the Company for any reason, please contact in writing: Permissions, Pearson Education Canada, a division of Pearson Canada Inc., 26 Prince Andrew Place, Toronto, Ontario M3C 2T8.